WEST'S LAW SCHOOL ADVISORY BOARD

CURTIS J. BERGER
Professor of Law, Columbia University

JESSE H. CHOPER
Professor of Law,
University of California, Berkeley

DAVID P. CURRIE
Professor of Law, University of Chicago

YALE KAMISAR
Professor of Law, University of Michigan

MARY KAY KANE
Dean and Professor of Law, University of California,
Hastings College of the Law

WAYNE R. LaFAVE
Professor of Law, University of Illinois

ARTHUR R. MILLER
Professor of Law, Harvard University

GRANT S. NELSON
Professor of Law,
University of California, Los Angeles

JAMES J. WHITE
Professor of Law, University of Michigan

CHARLES ALAN WRIGHT
Professor of Law, University of Texas

HANDBOOK OF THE LAW OF ANTITRUST

By

LAWRENCE ANTHONY SULLIVAN

Professor of Law, University of California
School of Law, Berkeley

HORNBOOK SERIES

ST. PAUL, MINN.
WEST PUBLISHING CO.
1977

COPYRIGHT © 1977
By
WEST PUBLISHING CO.
All rights reserved

Library of Congress Catalog Card Number: 76–50220

ISBN 0–314–32432–1

Hornbook Series and the key symbol appearing on the front cover are registered trademarks of West Publishing Co. Registered in U.S. Patent and Trademark Office.

 TEXT IS PRINTED ON 10% POST CONSUMER RECYCLED PAPER

Sullivan Law of Antitrust HB
6th Reprint—1996

To Ralda

FOREWORD

There are now several excellent books of cases and materials dealing with antitrust law. There is, however, no textual treatment of the field adequate either to the needs of the modern student or to the needs of the practitioner in search of an integrated treatment of the major areas of the subject. This book is intended primarily to fill the first of those needs; it is also intended to contribute toward meeting the second of them.

My obligations are numerous. My experience with antitrust began as a practitioner. My greatest debts are to my former partners and associates at Foley, Hoag & Eliot, in Boston, primarily to Henry E. Foley, my mentor as an antitrust counselor, and Lewis H. Weinstein, my mentor at the bar. As a student and teacher of antitrust I have drawn upon and been influenced by the work of all who are cited in these pages and doubtless by others, but primarily, I think, by the books of Joe E. Bain and F. M. Scherer among the works of economists, and, among the works of lawyers, by the basic articles of Donald Turner and the course book and teaching notes of Philip Areeda and the course book of Harlan Blake and Robert Pitofsky, all of which contributed importantly to the conceptualization and analysis of antitrust issues exemplified in this text. I would also like to express thanks to my colleagues Stefan Riesenfeld, Richard Buxbaum, Robert Mnookin and Jack Owens for encouragement and counsel, to Robert Darby, Eric Behrens and Jean Hawkes for research assistance, and to Susan Pernu for unflagging work on the manuscript.

LAWRENCE A. SULLIVAN

Berkeley, Calif.
November, 1976

*

SUMMARY OF CONTENTS

	Page
FOREWORD	V

Chapter
1. Introduction — 1
2. Monopoly — 18
   - A. Monopoly Power — 19
   - B. Defining the Relevant Market — 41
   - C. Estimating a Firm's Strength — 74
   - D. Conduct Tests for Monopolization — 94
   - E. Examples of Conduct Which May Constitute Monopolization — 106
   - F. Conspiracies and Attempts to Monopolize — 132
   - G. Remedies for Monopolization — 141
3. Horizontal Restraints of Trade — 150
   - A. Cartels and Interdependent Conduct — 152
   - B. Development of the Rule of Reason and the *Per Se* Doctrine — 165
   - C. The Current Construction of Section 1 of the Sherman Act — 186
   - D. "Naked" Price Restraints — 197
   - E. Horizontal Market Division — 213
   - F. Boycotts — 229
   - G. Data Dissemination — 265
   - H. Standardization Programs — 275
   - I. Miscellaneous Joint Activities — 282
   - J. Contract, Combination and Conspiracy — 311
4. Antitrust and Oligopolistic Markets — 330
   - A. The Oligopoly Problem — 331
   - B. Planning a Public Response to Oligopoly — 344
   - C. Legal Theories for Dealing with Oligopoly — 354
   - D. Legislative Proposals — 367
5. Arrangements Between Suppliers and Customers in Restraint of Trade — 374
   - A. Resale Price Maintenance — 377
   - B. Territorial, Customer and Location Restrictions in the Distribution Process — 399
   - C. Tying Arrangements and Related Arrangements Involving the Leverage Concept — 431
   - D. Exclusive Dealing, Requirements Contracts and Related Arrangements — 471
   - E. "Reasonable" Vertical Restrictions — 495

SUMMARY OF CONTENTS

Chapter		Page
6.	Antitrust Law and Patents	501
	A. Introduction	502
	B. Single-Firm Antitrust Violations and the Patent Laws	506
	C. Patent Arrangements Constituting Contracts Combinations and Conspiracies in Restraint of Trade	525
7.	Mergers	575
	A. A Historical Perspective	576
	B. Horizontal and Market Extension Mergers	600
	C. Conglomerate Mergers	653
	D. Vertical Mergers	657
	E. Remedies	669
8.	The Price Discrimination Law	676
	A. Introduction	677
	B. Horizontal Competitive Effects	683
	C. Vertical Competitive Effects	689
	D. Brokerage and Advertising Allowances	697
	E. Affirmative Defenses	700
	F. Buyer Liability	703
9.	Coverage, Exemptions and Procedure	707
	A. Relationship to Trade or Commerce	708
	B. Exemptions	717
	C. Governmental Enforcement	751
	D. Private Enforcement	769
Appendices		797
Index		855
Table of Cases		877

TABLE OF CONTENTS

	Page
FOREWORD	V

CHAPTER 1. INTRODUCTION

Sec.
		Page
1.	Antitrust and Economics	1
2.	An Eclectic View of Antitrust and Legal Doctrine	10
3.	Basic Statutory Materials	13
4.	The Literature of Antitrust	14

CHAPTER 2. MONOPOLY

A. MONOPOLY POWER

5.	Introduction	19
6.	Market Performance, Conduct and Structure	22
7.	The Prohibition Against Monopolizing	29
8.	The Nature of Market Power	30
9.	The Nature of the Legal Inquiry About Power	33
10.	The Practical Approach of the Early Cases	35
11.	The Modern Predominance of Structural Analysis	39

B. DEFINING THE RELEVANT MARKET

12.	Introduction	41
13.	Homogeneous Products	44
14.	Technological Differences	47
15.	Differentiated Products	48
16.	Substitute Products	51
17.	Diversified Products and Product Clusters	59
18.	The Limits of Economic Theory	63
19.	Local, Regional or National Markets	67
20.	National or International Markets	70
21.	An Eclectic Approach	72

C. ESTIMATING A FIRM'S STRENGTH

22.	Market Concentration	74
23.	Entry Barriers	77
24.	Other Structural Features	79
25.	Conduct Analysis	80
26.	Performance Analysis—In General	82
27.	Profits	84

TABLE OF CONTENTS

Sec.		Page
28.	Responsiveness of Price	86
29.	Price Discrimination	88
30.	Limitations of Performance Analysis	89
31.	The Absolute Size of a Firm	90
32.	Other Non-Economic Factors	92

D. CONDUCT TESTS FOR MONOPOLIZATION

33.	Introduction	94
34.	The Deliberateness Test	94
35.	Exclusionary Conduct—The Classic Test	97
36.	The Modern Test of Exclusionary Conduct	99
37.	The *Prima Facie Approach*	101
38.	Choosing Among Conduct Tests	102
39.	Intent to Exclude as a Surrogate for Conduct	105

E. EXAMPLES OF CONDUCT WHICH MAY CONSTITUTE MONOPOLIZATION

40.	Introduction	106
41.	Horizontal Merger	106
42.	Concerted Action Resulting in Joint Monopolization	107
43.	Predatory Practices	108
44.	Conduct Increasing Entry Barriers	114
45.	Invasion of a Thin Market	115
46.	Wrongful Exercise of Lawfully Attained Monopoly Power	115
47.	Pricing Policies	116
48.	Customer Selection	125

F. CONSPIRACIES AND ATTEMPTS TO MONOPOLIZE

49.	Conspiracies to Monopolize	132
50.	Attempts to Monopolize	134
51.	Evidence of Intent	135
52.	Evidence of the Market	139

G. REMEDIES FOR MONOPOLIZATION

53.	Introduction	141
54.	The Law of Remedies	142
55.	Institutional Limitations to Effective Remedies	144
56.	Enforcement Problems of Conduct Decrees	147
57.	Criminal Sanctions	148
58.	Private Remedies	149

CHAPTER 3. HORIZONTAL RESTRAINTS OF TRADE

A. CARTELS AND INTERDEPENDENT CONDUCT

59.	Introduction	152
60.	Restraints of Trade at Common Law	155

TABLE OF CONTENTS

Sec.		Page
61.	The Nature of a Cartel	161
62.	Interdependent Conduct	163

B. DEVELOPMENT OF THE RULE OF REASON AND THE *PER SE* DOCTRINE

63.	Introduction	165
64.	The Early Cases	167
65.	The Classic Rule of Reason	171
66.	The Scope of the Rule of Reason	175
67.	The *Per Se* Doctrine	182

C. THE CURRENT CONSTRUCTION OF SECTION 1 OF THE SHERMAN ACT

68.	Rule of Reason Analysis Today	186
69.	The Place of Market Power in Rule of Reason Analysis	189
70.	Power, Purpose, and Effect in *Per Se* Analysis	192
71.	The Relationship of Purpose and Effect in Section 1 Analysis	194
72.	The Relationship of the *Per Se* Doctrine to the Rule of Reason	195

D. "NAKED" PRICE RESTRAINTS

73.	Introduction	197
74.	Purpose and Effect as Guides to Characterization	198
75.	Possible Benefits from Price Restraints	203
76.	Naked Restraints Distinguished from Arrangements to Make or Improve a Market	205
77.	Naked Price Restraints Distinguished from Restrictions Resulting from Partial Integration	206
78.	Agreements Establishing Maximum Prices	210

E. HORIZONTAL MARKET DIVISION

79.	History of the Rule—The Cases Before Topco	213
80.	The Topco Case	216
81.	The Implications of Topco—Issues of Characterization	219
82.	Market Division and Price Fixing Compared	224

F. BOYCOTTS

83.	The Characteristics of a Boycott	229
84.	History and Development of the *Per Se* Rule Against Boycotts	232
85.	The Justification for a *Per Se* Approach	238
86.	Purpose and Effect as Guides to Characterization	241
87.	Explicit Boycotts Used to Police Industry Self-Regulation	245
88.	Industry Self-Regulation by Conduct Tending to Have the Effects of a Boycott	247

TABLE OF CONTENTS

Sec.		Page
89.	Application of Boycott Doctrine to Cases of Partial Integration	253
90.	*Per Se* Doctrine and Concerted Refusals to Deal Other Than Classic Boycotts	256
91.	Exclusive Franchises Distinguished from Boycotts	260
92.	Application of Boycott Doctrine to Cases Where Political, Religious, Social or Other Non-Commercial Purposes are Involved	261

G. DATA DISSEMINATION

93.	Introduction	265
94.	Economic Effects of Disseminating Prices	266
95.	The Early Cases	268
96.	The Container Case and Structural Analysis as a Guide to Legality of Price Information Programs	270
97.	Dissemination of Non-Price Data, Commentary and Recommendations for Action	274

H. STANDARDIZATION PROGRAMS

98.	Product Standardization	275
99.	Standardization of Trade Terms Other Than Price	277
100.	Standardization of Hours, Facilities and Other Elements of Competitive Style	279

I. MISCELLANEOUS JOINT ACTIVITIES

101.	Concerted Decision Making	282
102.	Joint Negotiation with Suppliers, Customers, or Unions	285
103.	Horizontal Agreements (Other Than Boycotts) Not to Deal	289
104.	Joint Agencies for Buying or Selling	292
105.	Joint Research	298
106.	Joint Activities in Making a Market	303
107.	Joint Arrangements Concerning Advertising	307

J. CONTRACT, COMBINATION AND CONSPIRACY

108.	Introduction	311
109.	The Classic Conspiracy	311
110.	"Conscious Parallelism" as Evidence of a Classic Conspiracy	315
111.	The Strengths and Deficiencies of the Classical Concept of Contract, Combination and Conspiracy	320
112.	Performance Evidence as "Plus Factor" Evidence of Conspiracy When Conscious Parallelism Has Been Shown	321
113.	Remedies in Cases of Classic Conspiracy	323
114.	Intra-Enterprise Conspiracy	323

TABLE OF CONTENTS

CHAPTER 4. ANTITRUST AND OLIGOPOLISTIC MARKETS

A. THE OLIGOPOLY PROBLEM

Sec.		Page
115.	Introduction	331
116.	The Pervasiveness of Oligopoly	331
117.	Structure, Conduct and Performance in Oligopolistic Markets	333

B. PLANNING A PUBLIC RESPONSE TO OLIGOPOLY

118.	Avoidance of Extreme Responses	344
119.	Planning Antitrust Enforcement in Oligopolistic Industries	347
120.	Factors for Analysis in Studies of Oligopolistic Industries	351

C. LEGAL THEORIES FOR DEALING WITH OLIGOPOLY

121.	Unsettled Issues	354
122.	Challenging Non-Collusive, Interdependent Pricing as a Violation of Section 1	355
123.	Oligopolistic Structure and Poor Performance as Evidence of Classic Conspiracy	358
124.	Oligopolistic Interdependence as Joint Monopolizing in Violation of Section 2	361
125.	The Federal Trade Commission, Section 5 of the FTC Act, and Non-Collusive Interdependence	364
126.	Merger in Oligopolistic Markets	365
127.	The Relationship Between Legal Theory and Policy Perceptions Which Warrant Legal Intervention	366

D. LEGISLATIVE PROPOSALS

128.	The "Concentrated Industries" Legislation	367
129.	Other Legislative Approaches to Oligopoly	371

CHAPTER 5. ARRANGEMENTS BETWEEN SUPPLIERS AND CUSTOMERS IN RESTRAINT OF TRADE

130.	Introduction	376

A. RESALE PRICE MAINTENANCE

131.	*Per Se* Illegality of Resale Price Maintenance	377
132.	History of "Fair Trade," An Alternative to Retail Competition	378
133.	Basic Market Effects of Resale Price Maintenance	379
134.	Manufacturer Motives for Resale Price Maintenance and Their Relationship to Competitive Effect	380
135.	Justification for the *Per Se* Rule	385
136.	Price Effect on the Ultimate Consumer	387

TABLE OF CONTENTS

Sec.		Page
137.	Agency, Consignment and Related Arrangements for Controlling Resale Price	388
138.	Maximum Resale Prices	390
139.	Refusal to Deal as a Means of Restricting Resale Prices (or Imposing Other Vertical Restraints)	391
140.	The Scope of Liability in Vertical Restraint Cases	395
141.	Suggested Resale Prices and Vertical "Tampering" with the Price System	397

B. TERRITORIAL, CUSTOMER AND LOCATION RESTRICTIONS IN THE DISTRIBUTION PROCESS

142.	The Varieties of Franchise Arrangements in the Distribution of Goods and Services and the Nature of the Impulses Which Lead to Restrictive Arrangements	399
143.	Territorial and Customer Restrictions	402
144.	Characterization Issues Under the *Schwinn Rule*	406
145.	The Justification for *Per Se* Treatment of Vertical Territorial and Customer Resale Restraints	411
146.	Consignment and Related Arrangements to Achieve Territorial Separation	421
147.	Exclusive Franchise Arrangements	423
148.	Terminating One Dealer at the Request of Another	427
149.	Exclusive Franchises and the Dominant Manufacturer	429

C. TYING ARRANGEMENTS AND RELATED ARRANGEMENTS INVOLVING THE LEVERAGE CONCEPT

150.	Introduction	431
151.	Section 3 of the Clayton Act and the Threshold Test of Competitive Effect	432
152.	The Development of the Basic Rule Respecting Tying	434
153.	The Relationship between Clayton and Sherman Act Standards	440
154.	The Patent Misuse Doctrine and the Tying Concept	441
155.	The Need for Two Distinct Commodities or Services	443
156.	Purposes and Effects of Tying	445
157.	"Package" Pricing	454
158.	"Full Line" Requirements	456
159.	Block Booking of Movies and the Licensing of Libraries of Music	459
160.	Package Licensing of Patents, Grant Back Provisions and Royalties which Extend Beyond the Period of the Patent	463
161.	Promotional Techniques Used by Manufacturers with Dealers	466
162.	Devices Used by Merchants to Maintain Continuity of Relationship with Consumers	470

TABLE OF CONTENTS

D. EXCLUSIVE DEALING, REQUIREMENTS CONTRACTS AND RELATED ARRANGEMENTS

Sec.		Page
163.	Introduction	471
164.	The Development of the Law	472
165.	Competitive Effects of Requirements and Exclusive Dealing Arrangements	479
166.	Duration of the Contract Term	484
167.	Agency Arrangements and Exclusivity	486
168.	Problems of Characterization Under Section 3	487
169.	Integrating the Law Respecting Requirements Contracts with that Governing Similar Vertical Arrangements	489
170.	The Nature and Effect of Reciprocal Dealing	490
171.	Reciprocity Arrangements as *Per Se* Violations	492

E. "REASONABLE" VERTICAL RESTRICTIONS

172.	Introduction	495
173.	Restrictions to Control the Quality of Goods and Services Sold Under a Trademark License	496
174.	Requirements about "Competitive Style" in "Franchise" Arrangements Which Do Not Entail Carrying on Business Under the Name and Mark of the Franchisor	497
175.	Sales "For Professional Application" and the Like	499

CHAPTER 6. ANTITRUST LAW AND PATENTS

A. INTRODUCTION

176.	Allocating Resources Between Present Production and Research and Development	502
177.	The Major Features of the Patent System and Their Relationship to Antitrust	504

B. SINGLE–FIRM ANTITRUST VIOLATIONS AND THE PATENT LAWS

178.	The Conduct Element in Section 2 Offenses and Its Relation to Policies for the Acquisition of Patents	506
179.	Circumstances Under Which Patent Acquisitions May Constitute Exclusionary Conduct	508
180.	The Application of Section 5 of the FTC Act and Section 7 of the Clayton Act to Patent Acquisitions	517
181.	Patent Enforcement Policy as Exclusionary Conduct	520
182.	License Restrictions (and Restrictions on Assignees) as Exclusionary Conduct	524

TABLE OF CONTENTS

C. PATENT ARRANGEMENTS CONSTITUTING CONTRACTS, COMBINATIONS AND CONSPIRACIES IN RESTRAINT OF TRADE

Sec.		Page
183.	Introduction	525
184.	Licenses or Assignments Which Impose Horizontal Restrictions on Territories	528
185.	Licenses Which Restrict Prices Horizontally	541
186.	License Provisions Which Impose Horizontal Restrictions Respecting the Fields of Use Within Which the Patent Will be Practiced	554
187.	Customer Restrictions in Licenses	562
188.	Settlement of Patent Disputes	563
189.	Grant Back Provisions and Agreements Not to Contest	570
190.	Vertical Restraints and the Inherency Test	571
191.	Price, Territorial, Customer and Use Restrictions Imposed by a Patentee Upon Purchasers	572

CHAPTER 7. MERGERS

A. A HISTORICAL PERSPECTIVE

192.	Introduction	576
193.	Early Consolidation Movement and Its Relationship to Pre-Sherman Act Common Law	577
194.	Earliest Sherman Act Merger Cases and Their Effect on the Merger Movement	579
195.	The Period from 1904 to 1911	581
196.	The Rule of Reason—Basic Cases and Beyond	584
197.	Merger Provisions of Original Clayton Act	587
198.	1930 to 1950	590
199.	The 1950 Amendment to Section 7	592
200.	New Clayton Merger Law and the Coalescence of Clayton and Sherman Standards	593
201.	Impact of Current Merger Policy on Industrial Structure	597

B. HORIZONTAL AND MARKET EXTENSION MERGERS

202.	Statutory Provisions Relevant to Legality of Mergers	600
203.	Market Definition in Merger Cases	605
204.	Mergers Between Direct Competitors	613
205.	Market Extension Mergers	631
206.	Corporate Joint Ventures and Potential Competition	649

C. CONGLOMERATE MERGERS

207.	Competitive Effects and Other Social Concerns	653
208.	The Section 7 Enforcement Effort to Date	654
209.	Possible Bases for Illegality	655

TABLE OF CONTENTS

D. VERTICAL MERGERS

Sec.		Page
210.	Competitive Effects	657
211.	Substantial Foreclosures in Concentrated Markets	661
212.	Relevance of a Trend Toward Vertical Integration	664
213.	Other Bases for Illegality	666
214.	Efficiency and Other Justifications	667

E. REMEDIES

215.	Preliminary Relief	669
216.	Final Relief	672

CHAPTER 8. THE PRICE DISCRIMINATION LAW

A. INTRODUCTION

217.	Nature of the Legislation	677
218.	Scope of the Principal Statutory Concepts	679
219.	Meaning and Significance of Discrimination	681

B. HORIZONTAL COMPETITIVE EFFECTS

220.	Discrimination as an Exclusionary Practice Affecting the Seller's Level	683
221.	Discrimination Which Diverts Business from Competitors or Threatens Adverse Structural Change	684

C. VERTICAL COMPETITIVE EFFECTS

222.	Social Effects in General	689
223.	Loss of Business by Disfavored Customers as a *Prima Facie* Case	691
224.	Substantial Profit Advantage for the Favored Customer as a *Prima Facie* Case	692
225.	Rebutting a *Prima Facie* Case of Competitive Injury	693

D. BROKERAGE AND ADVERTISING ALLOWANCES

226.	The Brokerage Provision	697
227.	The Advertising Allowance Provision	699

E. AFFIRMATIVE DEFENSES

228.	Cost Justification	700
229.	Meeting Competition	702

F. BUYER LIABILITY

230.	Inducing and Receiving Price Discriminations	703
231.	Inducing and Receiving Brokerage or Advertising Allowances	705

TABLE OF CONTENTS

CHAPTER 9. COVERAGE, EXEMPTIONS AND PROCEDURE

A. RELATIONSHIP TO TRADE OR COMMERCE

Sec.		Page
232.	Introduction	708
233.	Interstate Commerce	708
234.	Foreign Commerce	714

B. EXEMPTIONS

235.	Introduction	717
236.	Agricultural Cooperatives	719
237.	The Labor Exemption	723
238.	Governmental Action and Its Solicitation	731
239.	Regulated Industries	743

C. GOVERNMENTAL ENFORCEMENT

240.	The Antitrust Division of the Department of Justice	751
241.	The Federal Trade Commission	752
242.	Antitrust Investigations	754
243.	Informal Enforcement and Prior Clearance Procedures	756
244.	Civil Actions	759
245.	Criminal Actions	768

D. PRIVATE ENFORCEMENT

246.	Introduction	769
247.	Standing, Injury and Causation	770
248.	Statute of Limitations	775
249.	Class Actions and *Parens Patriae*	777
250.	*In Pari Delicto* and Unclean Hands	783
251.	Damages	785
252.	Passing On	787
253.	Attorney's Fees	792

Appendices ____ 797

Table of Cases ____ 877

Index ____ 855

†

THE LAW
OF
ANTITRUST

Chapter 1

INTRODUCTION

Table of Sections

Sec.
1. Antitrust and Economics.
2. An Eclectic View of Antitrust and Legal Doctrine.
3. Basic Statutory Materials.
4. The Literature of Antitrust.

§ 1. Antitrust and Economics

a. Introduction

This book is about law, not economics. But antitrust differs markedly from most branches of law in that the subjects with which it deals—competition and the kinds of industrial structures which stimulate competition—are also the explicit subjects of a branch of economics, that of industrial organization. Habits of thought, techniques of analysis, and value preferences derived from economics have come increasingly to play a substantial part in the development and application of the law. Today, one interested in antitrust cannot ignore economics. The topic is addressed at the outset not only to stress its current importance, but also to put economics into perspective and to mark out both its utility and the severe limitations upon what it offers to the law, limitations which are too often ignored.

During the period, now nearly a century, since antitrust became national policy, theoretical economics relevant to competition has developed apace. Early on, economists tended to be indifferent or even hostile to antitrust. Most of them saw tariffs as the predominant cause of monopoly and regarded the issues addressed by the Sherman Act of 1890 as something less than momentous. In consequence the courts in the early cases did their own analyzing of competition without much help from economics; indeed, some concepts upon which industrial organization theorists turned serious attention only in the middle years of this century were first dealt with at least embryonically by perceptive and analytical judges trying much earlier to piece out an understanding of how competition works. In time all this changed. For the last several decades many economists have been addressing the theoretical and empirical study of competition, the antitrust law's basic concern, in sustained ways. Increasingly and with varying degrees of frustration and satisfaction courts have turned toward theoretical economics for insight and aid in the development of antitrust doctrine. This text, therefore, will introduce or reacquaint the reader with those concepts from industrial organization economics which courts in antitrust cases have used and tried to make their own. Chapter 2 is most heavily oriented in that direction, partly because it's subject matter, monopolization, draws upon economics more fully than do many antitrust topics, and partly because what the reader picks up about economic analysis in that chapter will be use later on. The interaction of antitrust with economics (and it is precisely that; that law's concerns and development affect the ways in which industrial organization economists perceive their intellectual universe, as well as the other way round) enhances interest in antitrust. Its study is not only the pursuit of an important and interesting branch of law, but also an opportunity to make acquaintance with some economic concepts, to experience their power and their limitations, and to observe the relationship between two quite differentiated institutions, a theoretical social science and judge-made law.

b. Allocative Efficiency as an Antitrust Goal

A major confusion about economics and antitrust concerns the objectives toward which the law is directed and the relationship of economics to these. There are two principle approaches to antitrust which draw upon economic analysis, the Chicago and the Harvard schools. There are differences between them which this book will take some pains to point out. But some exponents of each postulate efficient allocation of resources either as the sole or as the major goal of antitrust, and both put forward micro-economics as the mode of analysis for identifying those market structures and those types of conduct which facilitate and those which tend to inhibit the achievement of that goal. In truncated and simplified form, the argument runs like this: Assume, as in the neo-classical tradition, that all sellers want to maximize profits. Assume also, as in that tradition, that a seller's costs for the product will tend to rise as his output is increased (because the seller must pay more as he bids more and more to attract away from others the resources with which he makes the product). Assume further that the less the seller charges the more he will be able to sell (and conversely) because as the price goes up or down relative to other goods, some buyers will substitute other goods for it or it for them. Upon accepting these assumptions of economics, one must conclude that a seller will expand output until the point where (as costs go up) the sale of an additional unit will add less to revenues than to costs. Any higher output, by increasing costs more than revenue, would reduce profits; any lower output, by reducing costs less than revenues, would reduce profits. Having taken us this far, the economist can demonstrate that under monopoly output will be smaller and price will be higher than under competition. In a competitive market, competition will (in the long run and assuming other things to be stable) force the price down to the point where it equals the cost of production plus a reasonable return. In a monopolized market (assuming fully off-setting scale economies are not achieved and passed on to buyers) the price will stabilize at a point higher than this; there will be a monopoly profit. Any elementary text book will make the demonstration. For convenience, one version of it is set forth in Appendix A.

Predicated on this demonstration, the economist makes his value claim—a preference for competitive markets over monopolistic ones on the grounds of allocative efficiency. In a competitive market widgets, which cost $1.00 to make, sell for $1.00; in a monopolized market they sell for, say, $1.25. In the competitive market every buyer who is willing to pay the *cost* of a widget in order to obtain a widget will be able to do so because widgets sell at their cost. In the monopolized market, the only buyers who get widgets are those ready to pay well in excess of cost. Those who would pay amounts equal to or higher than costs, though not the full monopoly price, must substitute other products. Thus, buyers who would pay, say, $1.20 for a widget buy something else instead, say a gizmo selling for that price or a little less. If the gizmo is selling for its cost of production (as presumably it is unless the market for gizmos is also monopolized), allocative efficiency is distorted. The gizmo, which costs $1.20 to produce, is being demanded, produced and sold, in place of the widget, a product costing only $1.00 to produce, which would have satisfied the human want involved as well or better. More resources—$1.20's worth, instead of $1.00's worth—are being devoted to meeting this human want, and so are not available to meet other needs. This, neo-classical economics teaches, is the social cost of monopoly.

That demonstration has an enormous appeal to anyone interested in antitrust policy. It holds up the image of a comprehensive, rational way to predict the allocation effects of alternative ways in which markets are structured and alternative ways traders in the market may conduct themselves. But, like a mirage, the image fades upon a close approach to it. The gravest difficulty is that the standard demonstration about the allocative efficiency of a competitive market over a monopolized one is subject to stringent theoretical conditions which are never fulfilled in the real world. It has no welfare implications except as part of a general equilibrium analysis.[1] Economic theory would warrant the conclusion that consumers would in the aggregate be able to attain what they value in larger measure if a particular monopoly market were (without loss of scale economies) converted into a competitive market only if all other markets were already competitive and there were no other distortions in resource allocation due to taxes, tariffs, or externalities. Except on these assumptions, which in the real world are never fulfilled, economics provides no theoretical basis for making judgments about whether allocative efficiency, in the welfare sense, is improved, worsened, or left unchanged by action aimed at making the structure or the conduct in any given market more competitive.

What is said here derives from what the welfare economists call "second best" analysis.[2] Simply stated, if a theory indicates that prescribed consequences rationally follow when several, specified, independent conditions obtain, the theory affords no basis for assuming that something approaching the prescribed consequences will emerge when some but not all of those conditions are encountered. To paraphrase another commentator, a person stranded on a barren island who understands that there is a fertile one twenty miles distant to the west may be convinced that he can greatly improve his circumstance if he succeeds in swimming twenty miles at a 270° compass heading. But this gives him no basis for concluding that he will be better off than at present if he swims 18 miles in that direction or swims twenty miles, but at a drift of 10° off course.

Some economists, though purporting to take second best problems into account when addressing policy issues, have concluded intuitively that an antitrust policy which moves toward more competitive markets will tend generally toward improving allocative efficiency. Others have rather tended to ignore the whole problem. But it will not so easily be put aside. Allocative efficiency in the welfare economics sense is simply not a functional goal for antitrust policy and the claims sometimes heard that antitrust issues must inevitably be resolved in the fashion of the Chicago school economist at the risk of injury to consumer welfare simply will not wash. Those who ignore the second best problem commit an analytical default no less serious for being so seldom remarked upon; those who recognize the problem but assume that somehow antitrust will improve allocations are taking a generous dose of wishful thinking.[3] Second best analysis, as the name implies, sets for itself the task of working out ways to decide rationally whether and under what circumstances alloca-

1. See the discussion in F. Scherer, Industrial Market Structure and Economic Performance 8–26 (1970).

2. A basic contribution is Lipsey & Lancaster, The General Theory of Second Best, 24 Rev. of Econ. Studies 11 (1956).

3. See the discussion in Sullivan, Book Review, 75 Colum.L.Rev. 1214, 1219–22 (1975).

tions can be improved by changing some variables even though all conditions of optimality cannot be attained.[4] Theorizing has not yet reached a degree of comprehension which warrants trying to put it to use in formulating policies; and though one may plausibly contend that in working on narrow and manageable second best issues intuition can be called upon where logic has been exhausted, it hardly follows that intuition is warranted as a guide to achieving better allocation throughout the entire economy by means of a vast, but less than comprehensive, set of antitrust policies.[5]

None of this is to suggest that economic theory is useless to the antitrust analyst. Although it does not provide to the law a single, glorious goal, it distinctly has its uses. Although the concept "allocative efficiency" is usually used by economists in the broad, comparative, welfare sense implied by the discussion above, it can be used in a narrower sense. It can be taken to describe any particular productive activity in which there is a close relationship between the aggregate cost of input factors (land, labor and materials) and the market price of the output. There are social reasons to value allocative efficiency in this more limited sense. There is a sense of economic justice which suggest that profits ought to bear a reasonable relationship to costs and risks, that they ought to be no greater than necessary to call forth the investment which yields them. There are also social concerns about the relationship of high profits to inflation. Al-

---

4. See, e.g., Athanasiou, Some Notes on the Theory of Second Best, in Oxford Economic Papers 83 (1966); Mishan, Second Thoughts on Second Best in Oxford Economic Papers 205 (1962).

5. Perhaps the most interesting efforts to take into account second best problems in making micro-economic policy judgments which take efficient resource allocation as a basic goal are those found in the voluminous writings of Richard Markovits, most of which are directed toward lawyers and appear in law reviews. This analyst, without purporting to do a general equilibrium analysis, seeks in dealing with policy issues to achieve a more comprehensive equilibrium analysis than the partial analysis of conventional neo-classical theory. However, he must in the process make myriad factual assumptions for which there is little if any theoretical or empirical support. Thus, although he never makes impressionistic claims so sweeping as the assertion sometimes heard that antitrust must be leading the economy in the right direction in allocative terms, Markovits, also is, in the end, intuitive and impressionistic in crucial judgments that he makes. A fine example of his work is Markovits, Oligopolistic Pricing Suits, The Sherman Act, and Economic Welfare (Part IV), 28 Stan.L.Rev. 45 (1975). Markovits there concludes (on assumptions such as that fairly close competitors tend to have similar price-marginal cost ratios, and that distant competitors of a firm with a high price-marginal cost ratio will tend to have average price-marginal cost ratios) that the effect of a policy against certain kinds of oligopolistic pricing on some kinds of resource misallocation cannot be predicted, but that the effect of that policy will be to reduce other kinds of resource misallocation.

It is to be hoped that in the future Markovits or others will seek to test some of the important factual assumptions which he makes and which are, at best, only weakly justified by theory about how people act and which are not validated empirically. See also Markovits, A Response To Professor Posner, 28 Stan.L.Rev. 919 (1976).

locative efficiency in this narrower sense is plausible as one of the important goals of antitrust. Indeed, it was the dread of enhancement of prices, not fear of inefficient resource allocation, which provided the impetus for the Sherman Act.[6] Given the goal of inhibiting monopoly prices and profits neo-classical economic analysis becomes helpful. Theory teaches quite convincingly that in a monopoly industry prices are likely to outrun costs by a wide margin, and that in a competitive industry they are not.[7]

But even here, in respect of allocative efficiency in the narrower sense of a good relationship between prices and costs, care must be taken not to presume upon economics too much. For example, though theory is convincing that social gains could be achieved by introducing competition into a monopolized market (if this could be done without excessive transaction costs and losses of scale efficiency), theory tells nothing about whether allocative efficiency would be enhanced if a monopoly market were converted not into a competitive one, but into a market of two, three or four sellers; it tells nothing about whether price-cost relationships could be improved by reconstructing a market of, say, seven sellers, three with 60% of output, into one of, say, twelve sellers of more or less equal size; it tells nothing about whether allocative efficiency is hurt in any way by a merger say, of two firms with 6% each of a market in which there are nine or ten firms, the largest with 25% of the market; it tells little about the choice which ought to be made, if one is essential, between a more competitive market and a more efficient one.

It is not that economics does not address issues pertaining to oligopolistic industries; indeed, it does. But when it does address them it speaks no longer *ex cathedra*, but with a babble of voices. On many issues crucial to the law there are alternative (and often conflicting) theoretical positions, each intrinsically plausible; and there are no empirical studies effectively discriminating between the competing theories, nor obvious means of obtaining such studies. Conflicts about whether vertical restrictions can injure competition, about whether advertising expenditures can serve as a barrier against entry of new firms into a market and about whether a policy to reduce concentration in oligopolistic markets would yield greater gains from competition than losses from reduced efficiencies are among many examples.

In short, even about allocative efficiency in the limited sense economics speaks with assurance only with respect to the two types of markets which are least often encountered in fact, markets with many sellers and markets with one seller; it speaks with least assurance about those markets most often encountered, markets with from two or three to several sellers, not just one, nor yet a crowd.

6. See Standard Oil Co. of New Jersey v. United States, 221 U.S. 1, 31 S.Ct. 502, 55 L.Ed. 619 (1911).

7. See Appendix A.

There is yet another difficulty. The economists' theoretical positions, once accepted, are often difficult or impossible to apply to actual markets because factual indeterminancies cannot be resolved at all, or can be resolved only at excessive cost. To the law it avails nothing to conclude, say, that a particular legal intervention will yield greater allocative efficiency in a market characterized theoretically as a tight oligopoly when barriers to entry are substantial if, when it comes to the point, we possess no satisfactory techniques for determining whether a particular set of firms do constitute a "tight oligopoly" within the meaning of the theory or to determine empirically whether or not entry barriers exceed the threshold which the theoretical position makes crucial.

c. *Characteristics of Law Which Limit the Utility of Economics*

Beyond all those factors which are, in a sense, internal to economic science, is another quite distinctive factor which limits the utility of economics in the development of antitrust law, a factor which touches upon the nature of legal process. To the extent, and it is a very large one, that courts are relied upon for antitrust enforcement, antitrust must be enforced in ways amenable to judicial methods of operation. Insofar as a sensitive antitrust policy, a policy for the enhancement of competition, may be thought to entail the subtle manipulation of the varied strands of economic theory and the skilled application of techniques for gathering and evaluating myriad economic data, there is a certain disjuncture between the task of antitrust enforcement and the nature of the agency to which the task is assigned. Let me stress this point. There is a position which asserts that courts can only function effectively in areas where the applicable values are clearly and authoritatively identified and where critical factual questions are sufficiently determinate so that use of the ordinary devices for judicial inquiry, characterization, rule making and rule application will yield results which are predictable and which demonstrably turn on principles of general application. Policies capable only of less explicit articulation, factual issues less determinate, should be left to the political agencies. Even one who disputes this position must concede that it articulates an intuition deeply rooted in American judicial process, an intuition of considerable force with which all who would work with courts must come to terms. Whether they ought to or not, most judges do not want to take on the task of regulating the economy, of making decisions where norms are vague and shifting, where factual inquiry is intricate, time consuming and in the end highly indeterminate. They tend to resist the task with vigor and to redefine it in terms more acceptable to their conception of the judicial role.

To the evolution of legal process the meaning of antitrust, its foremost significance, has to do with this intensive engagement with economics. The law's accustomed ways do not take up the materials of economics easily. The law seeks out explicit norms which, it ever hopes, can be applied with assurance on the basis of discernable fact. Economics gives itself over more easily to a markedly different manner of approaching issues to be resolved, to a mode better described as policy planning than as law. Consider, if you will, other judgments made in the realm of economic policy; those rendered by the Federal Reserve Board about the level of the money supply which will best meet national needs will serve as an example. The policy determinations and the factual perceptions which effuse toward any given resolution about such matters as the rediscount rate are not only numerous, complexly interrelated, and fuzzy in configuration, but are also adopted only tentatively, experimentally; as experience accumulates and perceptions either about facts or policies are altered, changes or adjustments may be made. It seems unthinkable that these matters could be dealt with as law, that we could, for example, develop rules of general application about when the rediscount rate should go up or down, or that we could utilize adjudicatory procedures to find the relevant facts.

Yet, to the extent we ask courts to adopt modes of economic analysis in the application of the antitrust laws, we do something rather like asking the Federal Reserve Board to proceed to manage the economy in the manner of a court. This is a problem even when the particular mode of economic analysis being urged upon the court is highly generalized. Theory about monopoly, for example, is a rather general theory, and there is a good deal of consensus about it. Even here many ramifications are deep in shadow and application of theoretical learning to particular settings is an exceedingly iffy occupation. When one moves to tendentious issues, of which there are many, the difficulties multiply. And if one adopts the view that very wide economic generalizations are likely to mislead, that the better course of antitrust policy is to proceed industry by industry to develop understanding of the special dynamic of the particular industry and that strategies for legal intervention should be tailor-made for each individual industry, the distance from law as conventionally perceived and the closeness to policy planning as practiced by the executive and legislative branches are both readily remarked.[8] It is no wonder that in the antitrust area we find courts transforming economic theory and economic analysis into something else; they could not deal with it if they did not.

d. *The Utility of Economics as a Source of Analytical Techniques and the Transformation of Economics into Law*

Despite all of the difficulties stressed above, industrial organization economics has become an important source of antitrust doctrine and, even more, a well nigh essential source of analytical techniques

---

8. See Sullivan, Politics, Planning and Trade Regulations: A Glance Toward An Emerging Utopia, 16 U.C.L.A. Law Rev. 1 (1968).

useful in solving some of the problems which the law presents, even though the law comprehends a wider set of values than does the relevant economic theory. If economics cannot supply the law with prefabricated policy goals, it can provide techniques which the law may use as tools in pursuit of its own objectives. Economics has much to teach about how to identify competition or its absence or, more precisely, about how to gauge the degree to which it is present or absent in a market even though it has less to teach about why the law ought to value competition. All of these techniques are not always usable; many often press hard against the constraining limits of judicial process. But many of them, as well as the judgments one can make about their power and their costs, are relevant to and usable in the extension and application of antitrust law.

Industrial organization economics, then, is a language in which the competent antitrust lawyer must be literate. Economics plays an important part in the law; but it is only a part which it plays and in the process economics is altered and combined with other strands of policy in a seldom entirely stable fabric. The great thing is to understand the power of economics and its potential, but also its limits—to draw upon it not as one who borrows, or imposes, but as one possessing a tool; to use it selectively, both wisely and well. It is to that goal that this book seeks to contribute, particularly through the economic material introduced in Chapter 2.

Finally, it should be noted that to obtain oil for the lamp from economists is to gain no assurance of a steady flame. It is not just that at any time debate abounds on crucial issues, it is also that the orthodox solutions change over time and can be expected to continue to do so. We started by noting that a typical turn of the century economist would have supposed that monopoly was no threat except as sustained by government through tariffs or other interventions. Later, during the mid years of this century economists turned to structural analysis (which we will much attend) as a means of understanding market power. That mode of analysis, with, be assured, its own numerous and different schools, has now become the dominant orthodoxy, and is utilized increasingly by the courts. But the vanguard of economists may have begun to press beyond. Some are turning more seriously and earnestly to performance analysis, quite a different way to approach the same issues; a small band of neo-structuralists now seem to stand again where their fore-fathers stood at the turn of the century—they feel that monopoly can only be sustained by direct governmental intervention. The economics of antitrust is, perhaps, less a science than an applied art. One must understand as well as may be the industrial context in which a problem is presented. Then one must choose from the varied and sometimes competing models which may have bearing the one or more of them which presents itself as having potential for enhancing understanding.

One can behold an ebb and flow of judicial attitude in antitrust cases, an attraction toward economics as a source of policy and technique uniquely fitting for the task at hand, then again a revulsion from the unfathomable, a sense of the unfitness of judicial involvement with matters so many sided and provisional. In addition to these tides, there is a slow yet discernable movement toward a resolution, a persistent judicial impulse to fashion out of the complex materials of economics sets of principles, law-like in their simplicity and generality. The process is anything but complete. The secular movement is not implacable. It is more advanced in some areas than in others; in a few it is discernable barely or not at all; in some where it has shown itself strongly there is reaction and regression. But viewing antitrust as a single phenomenon, its most pronounced dynamic characteristic is its absorption of theoretical economic materials and its distorting simplification of these as they are transformed into generalizations capable of being applied through adjudication. Antitrust becomes, for all of this, less potent, no doubt, as economic policy; but it also becomes because of this more possible as law.

Part of the task of learning antitrust is that of identifying in each area the degree to which those lawlike generalizations have emerged, of gaining control over the emerging general propositions, of understanding not only the economics which inform them but also the other values to which they are sensitive and the points at which in their articulation as rules each of those various sources may be recognized and given sway and where they need to be moderated or even choked off. The task also involves learning to deal knowledgeably and skillfully with areas, preeminently monopoly, where the process of absorbing economic materials is well advanced, but the process of converting these into legal generalizations is ill advanced. Here, antitrust is most like policy planning of the kinds customarily assigned to political agencies; values and norms are far more tentative and analysis far more open than is characteristic in areas where it is usual to work out policy through adjudication.

§ 2. An Eclectic View of Antitrust and Legal Doctrine

So long as antitrust is implemented as law there are, then, limits to the utility of economics in its elaboration. These are due to the deficiencies of both institutions, that of economics and that of law; economics does not comprehend enough and law, without extreme transformations in its own structure, cannot adequately deal with all that economics does comprehend.

One might assert that the great deficiency of the antitrust system is that it is court and lawyer ridden, that it ought, like aspects of macro-economic policy, be in the hands of an agency not similarly constrained, such as the Federal Reserve Board. To be sure, the Federal Trade Commission which possesses an antitrust jurisdiction, is a specialized agency which could, perhaps, transcend some of the limitations of adjudicatory form; we shall, before we are done, emphasize some of the differences discernible and potential between judicial and Commission enforcement. But these differences are within a narrow range and leave untouched the larger question whether matters of industrial organization policy ought to be addressed not as law but through more explicitly political processes.

If antitrust law is, then, to remain a system of law, not a system of applied economics, it must be responsive to values other than allocative efficiency (in either of the senses explored above). And it must be open to influences other than economics. In enacting the antitrust laws Congress had in view other desiderata in addition to the one to which economics grants recognition. The courts have an obligation to attend all of these goals, not just the one which economists also sanction. Thinking and writing about the law as though rational resource allocation were the only goal can only lead to confusion.

Among the non-economic goals of antitrust, all quite tenable as policy objectives, are a preference for decentralization of economic power, reduction of the range within which private discretion may be exercised in matters materially affecting the welfare of others, enhancement of the opportunity for more people to exercise independently entrepreneurial impulses, and, most blatantly, a social preference for the small rather than the large—if you will, a nostalgia for that mythical past when social, governmental and economic organization was simpler, more comprehensible. Antitrust, indeed, is founded on a populist tradition, a tradition quite at odds with the scientific rationality that informs economic theory and that tradition, which shows itself persistently in legislative developments, makes its own legitimate claim on judicial attention and, viewed quite pragmatically, has its effects on the developing law which the lawyer cannot ignore even if the economist can or must.

Antitrust also links with other goals than that which economics singles out simply because antitrust is rooted in a common law tradition. To the extent that it is influenced by that tradition the order which it seeks to impose upon the chaos of the market place is narrower and more tentative than is the ordering pointed to by economic analysis. Economics is the most cohesive of the social sciences. It invites the assumption that markets can be caused to perform in more or less ideal ways, almost independently of the varied characteristics of individuals who are actors in any given situation, so long as identifiable structural conditions for such performance are established and maintained. But legal analysis, if it can be likened to a social science at all, is more humanistic both in its aspirations and its methodology. It is closer, surely, to history, perhaps even to literature, than it is to economics. In ideal form law presupposes few easily predictable sequences in human affairs, and aims at no form of perfection. Rather, it seeks to understand recurrent human situations in terms of motivations commonly perceived and to judge specific human actions which occur in such situations with reference to a cultural experience, with reference to a tradition. Indeed, when it is most candid, law recognizes that even this modest search for meaning and order is foredoomed; any generalization about human conduct will inevitably be too imprecise adequately to account for all of the complexities in any real life situation. In common law methodology recognition of this can be a source of growth as precedents are distinguished and doctrine refined.

To adequately deal with the complex social goals to which it relates antitrust can also utilize modes of understanding in addition to economic analysis. An historical perspective is useful, as would be a comparative one. The policy which at any time in any nation governs industrial structure and conduct can be fully understood only in its own context and as a product of the forces which shaped it. Nor can one ever look for complete cohesion and rationality. A policy as general in character and as wide in application as antitrust will show elements of instability and tendencies toward the irrational. Competing interests will seek expression through it and compromise solutions will occur which are only loosely related to doctrine. Moreover, antitrust will seldom live a life of its own. Changes and developments in ways of thinking about it will be correlated with other developments in national life, as well as with developments in the intellectual universes of economists and others who may contribute to policy development. In addition to history, sociological and perhaps psychological studies of organizational behavior might contribute usefully to antitrust analysis. Since Weber, most sociologists interested in law seem to have focused on crime and the family. It is unfortunate that the survey techniques and conceptual equipment of this discipline are not engaged more fully in studies relating to the development and expression of economic power. In all events the student of antitrust is not willy-nilly in the hands of the economists.

Does law out of its own portfolio, as it were, have something unique and timely to contribute to the ongoing development of antitrust? The strengths and limitations of economic material in analyzing antitrust issues have been suggested as has the potential for the complimentary use of other techniques of analysis. But law has another office besides analysis; it is the prior, more primitive task of synthesis, of framing workable generalizations and knitting them into a cohesive structure. In recent years, as economics has become more ascendant, much pre-existing antitrust doctrine has become dismantled or obscure. It is time, then, to seek again for greater doctrinal clarity. This is what legal scholarship now has to offer antitrust—the work of system building, of generalizing as well as analyzing, the work of doctrinal restatement. There is a need now in antitrust to discern the elements in the case law which offer potential for bringing the cases into conceptual order; there is a need to identify and express the analogies and distinctions which enhance results by putting them into ordered relation to other results, thus giving them doctrinal forms and larger meanings; there is a need to relate such doctrinal statements to the historical development of the law in a fashion which gives due emphasis to elements of constancy, transformation, and novelty; there is a need to specify the way these doctrinal concepts relate to generalizations of a wider scope or higher order, having an ethical or a policy content (whether drawn from economics or elsewhere). This book will attempt to contribute to that process also.

§ 3. Basic Statutory Materials

The basic antitrust legislation is the Sherman Antitrust Act of 1890.[1] Most substantive antitrust law derives from the analysis and application of the concepts contained in Sections 1 and 2 of that Act. The Clayton Act of 1914[2] and the Federal Trade Commission Act,[3] passed also in 1914, are important supplementary statutes which elaborate and extend some of the Sherman Act concepts and provide additional enforcement mechanisms. The texts of these statutes appear in Appendix B.

The substantive provisions of the Sherman Act are stated in brief compass but in broad, suggestive language. Section 1 declares contracts, combinations and conspiracies in restraint of trade to be unlawful. The gravamen is concerted conduct by two or more actors having the forbidden effect on interstate trade. Section 2 forbids monopolization, combinations or conspiracies to monopolize and attempts to monopolize. The Clayton Act is a longer statute which specifies offenses more precisely. Where the effect may be substantially to lessen competition or to tend to create a monopoly, Section 2 (amended by the Robinson-Patman Act in 1936) forbids certain discriminations in price and in services, Section 3 forbids certain tying arrangements, requirements contracts, and other exclusive arrangements, and Section 7 forbids certain mergers or other stock or asset acquisitions between corporations. The Federal Trade Commission Act, in addition to establishing the Commission which, along with the courts, has jurisdiction to enforce a number of antitrust pro-

---

1. Act of July 2, 1890 c. 647, 26 Stat. 209, 15 U.S.C.A. §§ 1–7 (1976), as most recently amended by Act of December 12, 1975, Public Law 94–145, CCH Trade Reg.Rep. ¶ 25,125 (1976), effective March 11, 1976. Principal statutory provisions relevant for antitrust, including the full text of the Sherman and Clayton Acts and relevant portions of the Federal Trade Commission Act are set forth in Appendix B of this book.

2. Act of October 15, 1914, c. 322, 38 Stat. 730, 15 U.S.C.A. §§ 12–27 (1976).

3. Act of September 26, 1914, c. 11, 38 Stat. 717, 15 U.S.C.A. §§ 41–44 (1976), as most recently amended by Act of December 12, 1975, Public Law 94–145, CCH Trade Reg.Rep. ¶ 25,125 (1976).

visions, declares in sweeping terms that unfair methods of competition in commerce are unlawful.

The purpose of the antitrust laws is to promote competition and to inhibit monopoly and restraints upon freedom of trade in all sectors of the economy to which these laws apply. This purpose is as plenary as is the statutory language which embodies it. Hence, the antitrust laws have not merely been open to doctrinal elaboration, they have required it; the process of adjudication, more than a means of enforcement, has been an indispensable element in the formation of the law. In applying Sherman the courts drew first upon an ample, though not highly consistent, common law background, and upon a set of vaguely perceived and ill-integrated values discernible in the social and political developments which led to the enactment of antitrust. As more elaborate factual situations or novel questions of construction were presented common law was left behind. Increasingly, courts drew upon and sought to refine and in some degree to integrate the unique legislative heritage of antitrust with the vague yet forceful populist values, as well as with perceptions more fully articulated in the debates, about the nature and functions of competition. The study of antitrust is an examination of the ongoing dynamic thus initiated.

§ 4. The Literature of Antitrust

In addition to the primary sources, the sources for the study of antitrust fall into several classes. Most useful, surely, are the case books. One of the leading books, P. Areeda *Antitrust Analysis, Problems, Text and Cases* (2d Ed. 1974) is representative of the Harvard school of antitrust analysis. While labelling allocative efficiency as a basic goal it also recognizes other antitrust goals. It places considerable stress on legal process and the need to develop rules, consistent with economic theory, which are manageable for enforcement by courts. Another leading book, M. Handler, H. Blake, R. Pitofsky and H. Goldschmid, *Cases and Materials on Trade Regulation* (1975) takes a similar approach, but is essentially more eclectic. It offers more comparative material and draws on a wide range of sources. They are in important ways similar books. Both organize the material largely in terms of categories drawn from industrial organization economics, both provide sufficient economic textual material to facilitate understanding, both set forth the cases and statutes, a number of provocative problems, and a generous provision of commentary. This book draws frequently upon the scholarship reflected in each of those works and upon the analyses of problems suggested by the teaching notes prepared by their authors. Also of considerable interest is R. Posner, *Antitrust, Cases, Economic Notes and Other Materials* (1974) a more idiosyncratic course book which pursues with some rigor, and to the exclusion of other perspectives, an economic point of view and, indeed, a very particular one, representative of the "Chicago school," a point of view which is narrower, especially in its approach to vertical issues, then either the law itself or most industrial organizations economists would countenance.[1] Another provocative course book is L. Schwartz, *Free Enterprise and Economic Organization* (4th ed. 1972) which deals with interrelated problems of antitrust and industry regulation. Oppenheim and Weston, *Federal Antitrust Laws* (3d ed. 1969), the last case book of note, is more conventionally legal in its organization and presents in addition to edited versions of leading cases and textual commentary, comprehensive citations of case law and secondary legal material on virtually every topic.

Texts and monographs relevant to antitrust subdivide into economics materials, of which there are many worth study, legal materials of which these are few which reward attention, and legislative history, of which there are a few studies of high quality. There are also two important works which straddle these categories. C. Kaysen and D. Turner, *Antitrust Policy* (1959) is a towering statement which gathered together much of the wisdom distilled from an engagement at Harvard among economists like Mason and Bain, as well as Kaysen, and lawyers like Bok and Sacks as well as Turner. It is an essentially analytical treatment of the law from the vantage point of a pragmatic structuralism. It, along with two or three articles by Turner and one by Bok which examine key issues more deeply, but from the same stance, have influenced antitrust considerably. Though the law has moved on since 1959 and though some of the policy positions have been modified, even by the authors, the Kaysen-Turner book still repays reading. In the same genre, and also worth reading are B. Massel, *Competition and Monopoly, Legal and Economic Issues* (1962) and D. Dewey, *Monopoly in Economics and Law* (1959).

Turning to more explicitly economic analysis and commentary, the leading comprehensive texts are J. Bain, *Industrial Organization* (2d ed. 1968) and F. Scherer, *Industrial Market Structure and Economic Performance* (1970). A lawyer seriously interested in antitrust will eventually own both. Bain is a major intellectual figure in the development of structural analysis and though he writes here not for the specialist, he writes with precision and authority as well as understandably. Scherer's book is, in its way, even more inviting stylistically to the non-economist lawyer. It is lucid and displays a comfortable, balanced judgment in setting forth what is known theoretically,

1. The Handler, Blake, Pitofsky & Goldschmid case book as well as the Areeda and Posner case books are discussed in Sullivan, Book Review, 75 Colum.L.Rev. 1214 (1975). This book, like all three of those books, is indebted to H. Packer, The State of Research in Antitrust Law (1963) in that all adopt Packer's basic proposal of organizing antitrust material in terms of relevant economic concepts and hue more or less closely to many of Packer's more specific organizational suggestions. While the organizational scheme of this book is most closely related to the Areeda book, its organizational conceptions are sufficiently compatible with each of the others so that this book and any one of those leading case books can conveniently be used together.

and in gauging the degree to which portions of this are validated empirically. There are other works at about the same level such as J. Blair, *Economic Concentration, Structure, Behavior and Public Policy* (1972) and W. Shepherd, *Market Power and Economic Welfare* (1970) and one useful, though more elementary statement, R. Caves, *American Industry: Structure, Conduct, Performance* (2d ed. 1967). Then too, a few of the more advanced and technical studies are approachable by the non-specialist. One of importance because of the new theoretical positions it marked out, which is reasonably accessible to the non-economist and non-quantitative reader, is J. Bain, *Barriers to New Competition* (1956).

By contrast, there are few textual treatments expressly about the law, which warrant serious attention. *The Report of the Attorney General's National Committee to Study the Antitrust Laws* (1955), which is organized in legal and statutory categories, did little to constructively criticize the law or to assist in its development, but it did serve a generation of lawyers as a simple, summary text. It is supplemented by American Bar Association, Antitrust Section, *Antitrust Developments* 1955–1968 (1968), and Antitrust Law Developments (1975), as well as by an annual issue of the ABA published Antitrust Law Journal. Another text of value is A. Neale, *The Antitrust Laws of the U.S.A.* (2d ed. 1970). M. Handler, *Twenty-Five Years of Antitrust* (1973) also bears mention; it is a collection of the annual review articles which Professor Handler turned out over the years and serves as a source book of changing perspectives on antitrust issues, as well as a documentation of the author's own changes in perspective.

An examination of the legislative history of the Sherman Act is completed with depth and style in H. Thorelli, *The Federal Antitrust Policy* (1955). This is an engaging book which enriches perspective immensely. The other classic, historic treatment is the W. Letwin, *Law and Economic Policy in America* (1965).

Industry studies (which vary greatly in orientation, technical sophistication, quality and utility) have a special claim on the interest of the antitrust lawyer. A well developed understanding of a structural issue of significant complexity requires not only a command of general theory, but a sense for the dynamic of the industry in which the problem is rooted. Industry studies, then, are not only important as ways of enriching and refining understanding of antitrust issues by seeing them in context, they are quite essential if antitrust is to be used significantly to improve conditions in an industry. If none is available before litigation begins, then the litigation process itself must yield one; otherwise, whatever the competitive ills perceived, they may be only partly understood, and the remedy fashioned to eradicate them may prove quite inadequate. There are many excellent industry studies and collections of them. Typical of these are

W. Adams, *The Structure of American Industry* (4th ed. 1971) (a collection); L. White, *The Automobile Industry Since 1945* (1971); J. Markham, *Competition in the Rayon Industry* (1952); and J. McKie (*Tin Cans and Tin Plate* (1959)). Citations to useful studies of numerous industries can be found by using the index of Professor Scherer's book, which is cited above.

There is also periodical literature, both in law and economics, some of it quite important. Leading works germane to the topics being discussed will be cited as we proceed, particularly those which are primarily legal in orientation. There is also a specialized secondary literature. The CCH Trade Regulation Reporter is the looseleaf "service" for the field which communicates current developments. BNA's Antitrust and Trade Regulation Reporter is a weekly newsletter on current developments. Also to be mentioned are *The Antitrust Bulletin,* a quarterly journal of articles on antitrust, foreign antitrust and related economics, the ABA's *Antitrust Law Journal* published six times each year, the *Antitrust Law and Economics Review,* the *Journal of Reprints for Antitrust,* and the *Journal of Law and Economics*. Topical analyses contained in BNA's reporter have been updated, integrated and published in a desk book, *Antitrust Questions and Answers* (1974).

Sullivan Law of Antitrust HB—2

Chapter 2

MONOPOLY

Table of Sections

Part	Sections
A. Monopoly Power	5–11
B. Defining the Relevant Market	12–21
C. Estimating a Firm's Strength	22–32
D. Conduct Tests for Monopolization	33–39
E. Examples of Conduct Which May Constitute Monopolization	40–48
F. Conspiracies and Attempts to Monopolize	49–52
G. Remedies for Monopolization	53–58

PART A. MONOPOLY POWER

Sec.
5. Introduction.
6. Market Performance, Conduct and Structure.
7. The Prohibition Against Monopolizing.
8. The Nature of Market Power.
9. The Nature of the Legal Inquiry About Power.
10. The Practical Approach of the Early Cases.
11. The Modern Predominance of Structural Analysis.

PART B. DEFINING THE RELEVANT MARKET

12. Introduction.
13. Homogeneous Products.
14. Technological Differences.
15. Differentiated Products.
16. Substitute Products.
17. Diversified Products and Product Clusters.
18. The Limits of Economic Theory.
19. Local, Regional or National Markets.
20. National or International Markets.
21. An Eclectic Approach.

PART C. ESTIMATING A FIRM'S STRENGTH

22. Market Concentration.
23. Entry Barriers.
24. Other Structural Features.
25. Conduct Analysis.
26. Performance Analysis—In General.
27. Profits.

Sec.
28. Responsiveness of Price.
29. Price Discrimination.
30. Limitations of Performance Analysis.
31. The Absolute Size of a Firm.
32. Other Non-Economic Factors.

PART D. CONDUCT TESTS FOR MONOPOLIZATION

33. Introduction.
34. The Deliberateness Test.
35. Exclusionary Conduct—The Classic Test.
36. The Modern Test of Exclusionary Conduct.
37. The Prima Facie Approach.
38. Choosing Among Conduct Tests.
39. Intent to Exclude as a Surrogate for Conduct.

PART E. EXAMPLES OF CONDUCT WHICH MAY CONSTITUTE MONOPOLIZATION

40. Introduction.
41. Horizontal Merger.
42. Concerted Action Resulting in Joint Monopolization.
43. Predatory Practices.
44. Conduct Increasing Entry Barriers.
45. Invasion of a Thin Market.
46. Wrongful Exercise of Lawfully Attained Power.
47. Pricing Policies.
48. Customer Selection.

PART F. CONSPIRACIES AND ATTEMPTS TO MONOPOLIZE

49. Conspiracies to Monopolize.
50. Attempts to Monopolize.
51. Evidence of Intent.
52. Evidence of the Market.

PART G. REMEDIES FOR MONOPOLIZATION

53. Introduction.
54. The Law of Remedies.
55. Institutional Limitations to Effective Remedies.
56. Enforcement Problems of Conduct Decrees.
57. Criminal Sanctions.
58. Private Remedies.

PART A. MONOPOLY POWER

§ 5. Introduction

In much of the American economy, government exercises little or no responsibility for basic decisions. Resource allocations, production and distribution methods, prices, and technological development are all managed without public participation through ownership or regulation. This predominantly private sector contrasts sharply with such functions as education, fire protection, the production of weapons systems, and provision of national security, which are subject to comprehensive social control through government ownership, government financing, and government purchases; it also contrasts with the public service or public utility sector in which, though various functions are left to private firms, government controls entry and regulates rates. In the private sector, many socially important matters are determined almost entirely through the interaction of private decisions by buyers and sellers in the market place. The public may intervene in the private market to impose minimum standards (for example, in the interest of health), to keep an industry from imposing excessive, uncompensated costs on others (for example, through restrictions on activities tending to pollute air or water), or to protect against fraud or similar conduct; however, basic decisions affecting resource allocation, efficiency, innovation and conservation are usually left to private decision-makers and regulated only by the forces of the market.

As legislative history [1] and case law [2] both disclose, the general objective of the antitrust laws is the maintenance of competition.[3] Competition per se thus becomes a goal of the legal order. Yet, competition is not a concept which defines itself; notions about the desirability of competition may shape judgments about how the law should apply, at least at its indistinct edges.

The first rationale for a pro-competition policy is the historic one. The national commitment to competition embodied in the antitrust laws had its genesis in a rough-hewn and intemperate populist conviction: all should have free access to the market place, but evil men for their own greed may choke off this access by stifling competition. Exponents of the populist tradition tend to see life in caricature; wrong and right both in institutions and individuals stand out with Dickensian clarity and can be identified by the presence or absence of certain polar characteristics. For them, institutions and individuals are large or small, rich or poor, lords of commerce or struggling, small businessmen, and much is thought to follow from such categorizations.

---

1. See generally H. Thorelli, The Federal Antitrust Policy (1955). See also Report of the Attorney General's National Committee To Study The Antitrust Laws 1–2 (1955).

2. E.g., Standard Oil Co. of N.J. v. United States, 221 U.S. 1, 58, 31 S.Ct. 502, 515, 55 L.Ed. 619, 644 (1911); Northern Pac. R.R. v. United States, 356 U.S. 1, 4, 78 S.Ct. 514, 517, 2 L.Ed.2d 545, 549 (1958); United States v. Philadelphia Nat'l. Bank, 374 U.S. 321, 338, 83 S.Ct. 1715, 1727, 10 L.Ed. 2d 915, 930 (1963).

3. E.g., United States v. Aluminum Co. of America, 148 F.2d 416 (2d Cir. 1945).

A more sophisticated rationale for a policy designed to foster competition has developed over the years since 1890, a rationale which has become an important part of the antitrust tradition. Competition, it asserts, operates to keep private markets working in ways which are socially acceptable. If functioning ideally, private markets would achieve several socially important ends. They would encourage efficient resource allocations, stimulate the use of efficient methods of production and distribution, and encourage a progressive technology and high productivity. Yet they would also encourage conservation of scarce and irreplaceable resources—they would not discount the future unduly. Withal, dynamic market elements would be contained by a basic stability; prices would not fluctuate excessively and adjustments would be made in an orderly way as new productive activities were initiated and old ones abandoned.

No market will ever function so effectively as to achieve all of these goals. Indeed, given the fact that all markets cannot be kept fully competitive there is serious doubt about the extent to which the resource allocation advantages which theoretical economics has attributed to competition can be achieved.[4] Yet, it is a plausible policy assumption that competitive markets perform tolerably well in most of the above respects, and it seems a plausible hypothesis that where competition is maintained markets will perform better than where it is not.[5]

The third set of justifications for a policy favoring competition emphasizes that competition tends toward desired social goals besides better market performance. Thus, competition tends to disperse private power; this is a value in itself in a liberal society, reducing the need for large governmental power to regulate private power. Relatedly, competition substitutes the impersonal forces of the market for individual or bureaucratic decision-making about resource allocation and related economic matters. Finally, competitive markets, by facilitating entry at the smallest efficient scale and facilitating exit by an entrepreneur who wishes to withdraw, help to maintain the widest possible degree of economic opportunity.

All of these policy considerations will be encountered and dealt with by the student of antitrust and may be of use in marking out some of the limits of the law.

---

4. F. Scherer, Industrial Market Structure and Economic Performance 22–27 (1970).

5. Id. at 25–27. Despite much in the elementary economic literature to the contrary, there is no theoretical reason to assume that maintaining competition in any given market will tend toward the goal of optimum resource allocation in the welfare sense. See §§ 1 and 2 supra. However, maintaining competition in any industry will in that industry tend toward prices which are closely related to cost, efficient methods of production and distribution, and the social and political goals of antitrust discussed in the text which follows this note.

§ 6. Market Performance, Conduct and Structure

a. Introduction

This chapter begins with the introduction of several simple economic concepts. To fully understand the case law about monopoly it is necessary to understand these concepts; to effectively analyze fact situations in terms of the law, one must be able to manipulate these concepts. An analysis of the ways markets work is informed in large measure by that branch of micro-economics called industrial organization which deals with relationships between the ways in which industries are structured, the ways firms within those industries act, and the resulting performance of the industry as a whole. This branch of economics is not value-free; it is infused with the conviction that the kinds of performance which it predicts are likely to be achieved in competitive markets are socially preferable to those which non-competitive markets will yield. Thus, its basic value orientation is consistent with the antitrust laws.

However, the economics of industrial organization does more than point toward ultimate social goals. If one takes as established by law the goal of maintaining competition, this branch of economics can be a source of concepts and analytical techniques which will be useful in discerning whether competition is present or absent and in making judgments about the kinds of industrial structures and conduct which will be consistent with the maintenance of competition. A number of concepts from this branch of economics must be grasped.

b. Market Performance

An analysis of market performance deals with questions such as whether prices are closely related to associated costs, whether prices are responsive to changes in demand and supply, whether sufficient resources are allocated to the industry, and whether technology is efficient and progressive. Performance, then, is a normative concept: it can be good, bad or something in between. If an industry is performing well, prices will tend to be just high enough to cover costs plus a reasonable return on the capital invested, considering the risk. Firms will perform efficiently; they will seek the least expensive ways of producing the range of products most desired by consumers. Prices will tend to rise or fall as consumer demand increases or decreases and sales, in addition to capital investment in the industry, will tend to expand or contract accordingly. A dynamic level of innovation will be maintained as will a level of advertising calculated to provide adequate information to consumers without excessive costs. Entry and exit from the industry will be easy and not uncommon as efficient firms prosper and less efficient ones fail.

Economic theory proposes that market performance is a function both of the structure of the market and of the conduct of firms striving, under the constraints of the market's structure, to maximize some variable relevant to their success, usually assumed to be their profits, but sometimes assumed to be their sales or some other variable.

c. *Market Conduct*

To the lawyer, market conduct (or behavior) is a relatively familiar concept. By market conduct is meant the choices the firm makes among alternative possible responses to the conditions which it faces, its tactics as it strives in the market to achieve its goals. To illustrate, picture a firm operating in an industry where demand for the product is contracting, thus putting downward pressure on prices and profits. Various responses are open to the firm. It might seek to reduce per-unit production costs by changing the ratio of factors it draws upon to produce its goods (using more machinery and less labor, or more of one raw material and less of another); it might alter its outputs, so as to make and sell more of the products in its line for which demand is holding up, and fewer of those for which demand is lagging; it might withdraw some or all of its resources from the industry by closing a plant and selling it to a firm which would use it for other purposes. How the firm acts as demand expands or contracts, as technology changes, as it encounters more or less competition—in short, how the firm responds to the stimulations of the marketplace—is called the firm's market conduct.

Until theoretical economics began to make contributions to antitrust, conduct analysis was the only analysis known to antitrust. Though courts did not use this label for their activity, they did determine whether a firm violated the antitrust laws by looking at what the firm had done and, in an effort to gain a fuller understanding of the conduct and its likely consequences, at the reasons behind the firm's actions.[1] Though alternative modes of analysis are now also relied upon, conduct analysis remains a major element in antitrust law. Some things a firm may do in an effort to achieve its market objectives are lawful, while others are not;[2] some conduct is deemed consistent with competition, other conduct is not. Motive or purpose, moreover, remains a guide in characterizing conduct.[3] A difference in emphasis is noticeable, however, between the attitude which exemplified conduct analysis during the early Sherman Act years and the attitude taken today. Formerly, conduct which was seen as stifling competition was identified as wrong without necessity for further ex-

---

1. Standard Oil Co. of N. J. v. United States, 221 U.S. 1, 31 S.Ct. 502, 55 L. Ed. 619 (1911); United States v. American Tobacco Co., 221 U.S. 106, 31 S.Ct. 632, 55 L.Ed. 663 (1911).

2. E.g., Klor's Inc. v. Broadway-Hale Stores, Inc., 359 U.S. 207, 79 S.Ct. 705, 3 L.Ed.2d 741 (1959).

3. E.g., United States v. McKesson & Robbins, Inc., 351 U.S. 305, 76 S.Ct. 937, 100 L.Ed. 1209 (1956).

planation; today, courts looking at motive and conduct may express an interest in its impact on market performance.

The way market conduct and market performance relate becomes clearer when attention is directed to the conduct of multiple firms within an industry. Consider again the hypothetical industry in which demand is contracting. The socially preferable performance would be for resources to be withdrawn from the industry and introduced into other activities in an orderly way until a better balance were established between resource allocation and consumer desires. If each firm in the declining industry gathers information, considers the alternatives open to it, perhaps probes and tests to some extent, and then makes the adjustments which afford the best solution for it, a good industry-wide adjustment—that is, good performance—should result. Low-cost producers will tend to remain in the industry, while high-cost producers, unable to operate profitably under the new demand conditions, will tend to withdraw and convert to the production of goods for which demand is strong or increasing. But suppose that, faced with declining demand, firms in the industry agree together to "hold the line" on prices, to let volume fall, and to allocate orders among themselves. Such concerted market conduct would yield a different and socially poorer performance than would independent responses by each firm. Prices would remain higher and sales would fall lower than under a competitive response, and excess capacity would tend to remain in the industry, rather than finding other employments more highly valued by consumers.

d. *Market Structure*

Thus, conduct is important to performance; but conduct is not a wholly independent variable. One of the most important insights which theoretical economics has provided to antitrust analysis is that market conduct is strongly influenced by market structure.[4] Structure is the term which describes the way the market is organized, the basic characteristics which are likely to persist over a substantial period of time. Market structure thus includes the degree of concentration—the number and size distribution of firms producing a particular product or range of products. It includes the extent to which the product of one firm is differentiated in the mind of the consumer from that of other firms and the manner in which differentiation is achieved (whether through functional differences between the products of one manufacturer and another, through stylistic differences, or merely through advertising of a brand name). Market structure also includes the extent to which the products of firms in an industry are diversified, and the variety and technological complexity of products. Further, structure includes the extent to which firms are integrated vertically—that is, the extent to which successive stages in

---

4. See generally, F. Scherer, Industrial Market Structure and Economic Performance (1970); J. Bain, Industrial Organization (1959).

the production and distribution process are performed by a single firm. It includes, too, the nature of cost conditions—whether fixed costs are relatively high and variable costs relatively low, as in the railroad and some other utility industries, or whether variable costs are relatively high and fixed costs relatively low, as in many manufacturing industries. All of these characteristics of an industry tend to be more or less permanent, and all of them tend to condition, in significant respects, the ways in which firms in the industry respond to market stimulations.

Additionally and most importantly, structure includes the character of any barriers to the entry of new firms into the industry. Such barriers may result from various causes: license requirements, concentrated ownership of scarce resources such as ore, economies of scale which cause per unit costs of a firm whose output is small relative to total industry output to be significantly higher than the per unit costs of a firm producing a substantial percentage of total industry output, and concentration of control of patents or secret technology. The higher these entry barriers, the greater the opportunity for firms in the industry to increase prices without attracting new firms into the industry.

e. Competitive Structure

The relationship between structure and conduct can be illustrated by examples. In an industry with a very large number of sellers, each relatively small, the individual firm will not assume that market prices will be affected by its own output decisions. Nor will it be obvious to such a firm that it could successfully get together with other firms to set price and allocate output. The problems of communication, management and policing of any such concerted arrangement would be substantial and the possibility of achieving a stable and profitable concerted arrangement might appear rather remote. The firm may therefore take the prevailing market price as given and vary its output and its input factors in a continual striving to achieve its market goals. In short, a multi-firm or competitive structure encourages independent, competitive conduct. Concerted action among firms in such an industry is of course conceivable and has at times occurred. Yet, there will be a tendency for each firm in such a market to act competitively. Consequently the market as a whole will tend to perform competitively.

f. Monopolistic Structure

In highly concentrated markets, by contrast, structure may stimulate quite different conduct. If there is only one firm supplying the full market demand, that firm is called a monopolist. It will recognize that it can alter market price by altering its own output. As it produces a larger and larger volume and offers it for sale, the price it can obtain will tend to decline; as it produces and offers a smaller and smaller volume, the price it can obtain will tend to increase. The firm can therefore manipulate output to affect price in an effort to maximize profit, a course not open to the firm which faces a competitive structure. In consequence, an industry dominated by a monopolist will tend to produce less, charge a higher price, and earn a larger aggregate profit than would that industry with a competitive structure. Monopoly structure virtually dictates conduct which yields socially poor performance. (See Appendix A).

g. Oligopolistic Structure

There are intermediate structures between the monopolistic and the highly competitive. Consider an industry with five or six large firms, each with a substantial share of the market, and ten or twelve small, fringe firms—the kind of industry which may be defined as a loose oligopoly. While economic theory warrants fairly confident prediction about how traders will act in monopolistic or competitive markets, the conduct which will take place (and the performance which will result) in an oligopolistic market is highly indeterminate. For this reason Chicago school economists do not use oligopoly as a structural model. They treat questions that arise in these markets as conduct questions. They ask whether firms in the industry have entered into a cartel—an agreement to fix prices, divide territories, or restrict output. On the other hand, Harvard school economists use an oligopolistic market model; though they recognize that little can with precision be inferred solely on the basis of structure, they assume that in oligopolistic markets firms may act non-competitively (somewhat as do firms in monopolistic markets) even without agreement.

At all events it is clear that just what is happening in these kinds of markets will often be difficult to discover. Pressures toward rivalry may be sufficient to generate conduct similar to that in multi-firm, competitive industry. However, firms in an oligopolistic industry will recognize that it would be in their interests to make price and output decisions concertedly, thereby achieving jointly a control over price and output similar to that which a monopolist exercises; they are not likely to see the problems of coordination as being unmanageable. If they do engage in such concerted conduct by joining together (in what is usually termed a "cartel") to set prices at a level which tends to maximize industry profits and to allocate production on an agreed basis, performance will be more like that in a monopolistic industry than in a competitive one. And if an oligopolistic structure is tight enough, something similar to concerted conduct to fix price and to divide output may occur, as Harvard school theory supposes, even without any agreement, express or implied.

Suppose, for example, there were only three firms in an industry, one with half of the market, the others with one-fourth each. Suppose that in such an industry prices were at a competitive level and that there then occurred a change in demand and supply conditions of a kind which in a competitive market would have prompted a price reduction. Each firm would be aware that if it reduced price toward the new competitive level, the other two firms would do the same; the result of any reduction would be to share the business in the same proportion but at a lower return for each. On these assumptions the three firms may each forebear to reduce prices. Thus, prices may settle at a level which under comparable conditions would be established by a monopolist. Consequently, the industry profits which the firms share will be maximized. If so, noncollusive but interdependent market responses will have resulted in prices and profits which are higher and output which is lower than under competition —just as in the case of a monopoly or of a cartel. Concentrated structure, by stimulating interdependent market conduct, will have resulted in poor market performance.

h. *Other Structural Features*

In the above discussion of the influence of structure on conduct only the extent of concentration has been assumed to vary. In actuality the matter is far less simple. Other structural elements, such as the extent of vertical integration and the kind and nature of entry barriers, will also vary from industry to industry and over time. Those structural features are also important to the kinds of conduct adopted and to the performance which results. Indeed, every structural feature will tend to influence conduct and, through conduct, performance.

The instance of entry barriers illustrates this best. Unless there are conditions which would preclude or delay entry, even an industry which appears to be concentrated may display reasonably competitive conduct and satisfactory performance. If it would be relatively easy for new firms to enter at any time, the potential competition of firms which would be attracted to enter should profits rise appreciably above competitive levels will tend to discipline the conduct of firms in the market in a manner similar to, though not so effectively, as would the actual presence of additional competitors.

Other structural features will similarly have their impact on conduct.[5] If products are technologically complex and those of each firm vary significantly from those of others, collusion or interdependent coordination will be more difficult. If fixed costs are a relatively high percentage of total costs, falling demand will have an earlier and more drastic impact on profits than if such costs are relatively low and variable costs are relatively high; this might stimulate sharp price cutting or urgent attempts at collusion when demand falls. Differences in the degree of diversification or in the structure of the re-

---

5. Scherer, supra note 4, chs. 6–7.

sale organization—the extent and type of vertical integration—may also stimulate or inhibit collusion or interdependence.

i. *Other Interactions Between Conduct and Structure*

The relation between conduct and structure can be complex in other ways. The basic assumption underlying the analysis here presented is that structure influences conduct, thereby affecting performance. But conduct may also influence structure in ways having impact on performance. For example, the manufacturer of a consumer product may adopt as a competitive strategy the use of annual product model changes and extensive advertising of each new model; this course of conduct may prompt others in the market to do the same. Once that strategy becomes widespread it may act as an entry barrier. In order to also make annual model changes new entrants might face annual retooling costs which could be managed only by quickly obtaining a very substantial share of the market. Also, a new firm might face a relative disadvantage in seeking consumer loyalty through advertising. To achieve effects comparable to those achieved by established firms, it might have to spend a higher percentage of sales revenue on advertising. Both of these consequences of the market conduct of existing firms would take on a structural quality; they would tend to persist over time and would reduce the likelihood of new entry.

j. *Performance, Conduct and Structure in the Development of Antitrust Rules*

In analyzing antitrust issues, performance, structure and conduct are all interrelated and all relevant. But in developing specific antitrust rules, conduct and structure have thus far been paramount; performance, though the ultimate social concern, fades into the background. The rationale for this is that conduct and structure are more amenable to the development of reasonably specific and enforceable legal norms than is performance. Both conduct and structure are easier to evaluate directly than is performance. Also, remedies based on conduct or structure will be easier to fashion and to enforce than would be remedies dealing directly with performance. Competitors can be told by the law not to agree on price, for example; this is an understandable conduct norm. Similarly, the law can promulgate reasonably specific rules about structure. For example, it can forbid mergers which substantially increase concentration in any market. Because of the causal interaction between structure, conduct and performance, both conduct rules and structural rules may yield better performance—the efficient use of scarce resources and decisions about what to produce which are responsive to consumer desires, the progressive use of new technology, and reasonable stability of production and employment. But businessmen cannot usefully be ordered to set reasonable prices, to be efficient, to produce what consumers want, or to be progressive; these concepts are too vague.

In fact, much of antitrust consists of conduct rules. There are also many antitrust rules which make legality turn in whole or part upon the structure of the market and antitrust frequently utilizes remedies which are aimed at fostering competitive structure and inhibiting noncompetitive structure. Rules respecting monopoly, for example, are concerned primarily with structure and remedies in monopoly cases often deal with structure.

Despite its difficulties, however, there is room for a direct analysis of performance in antitrust. Often available evidence will leave in doubt whether or not a structure is reasonably competitive, or whether or not traders in the market place are engaging in anticompetitive conduct. Examination of performance may help to resolve such doubt, for anticompetitive structure and conduct may be expected to yield poor performance, while competitive structure and conduct will not. Though bad performance is itself difficult to identify, it is possible at times to make informed judgments about some aspects of performance from available evidence. Price-cost relationships, for example, are operationally significant, as is existence of price discrimination. Also, price rigidity in the face of changes in demand is sometimes quite apparent. The potential for using performance evidence in effective ways will be explored from time to time in specific contexts later in this volume.

§ 7. The Prohibition Against Monopolizing

The general theoretical discussion above provides a backdrop for a consideration of antitrust legislation concerning monopoly.[1] Section 2 of the Sherman Act enumerates three distinct offenses; it makes it a crime to "monopolize, or attempt to monopolize, or combine or conspire * * * to monopolize" any part of interstate or foreign commerce. The first of these offenses, to "monopolize," will be discussed at length in this chapter. The other two offenses, "attempt to monopolize" and "conspiracy to monopolize," are discussed briefly at the end of the chapter.[2]

A firm has monopolized in violation of Section 2 if it has deliberately followed a course of market conduct through which it has obtained or maintained power to control price or exclude competition in some part of the trade or commerce covered by the act.[3] The offense

---

1. Useful, generally, in understanding public policy toward monopoly are J. Bain, Industrial Organization (1959); F. Scherer, Industrial Market Structure and Economic Performance (1970); D. Dewey, Monopoly in Economics and Law chs. 1, 5–8 (1964); C. Kaysen & D. Turner, Antitrust Policy ch. 2 (1959); E. Mason, Economic Concentration and the Monopoly Problem, chs. 1–2 (1957).

2. See Part F infra.

3. Standard Oil Co. of N.J. v. United States, 221 U.S. 1, 31 S.Ct. 502, 55 L. Ed. 619 (1911); United States v. American Tobacco Co., 221 U.S. 106, 31

involves two distinct elements. The first is a matter of capacity—the possession of power to control prices or exclude competition. But the mere possession of such monopoly power does not violate the act. There is also a second element to the offense, that of conduct or intent. To be in violation the firm must be shown either to have obtained its power by deliberately pursuing a course of conduct which had the effect of expanding or maintaining power,[4] or to have formed a specific intent to maintain its power by such conduct.[5] That both elements, power to control price and to exclude competitors and some element of deliberateness, must be shown has long been settled, though the law has developed and changed significantly in respect to the way power is identified, and the degree of deliberateness which must be shown.[6]

Monopoly power is but an extreme degree of single-firm market power. Even in less stark forms market power may adversely affect performance and thus be of antitrust concern. Throughout the discussion the purpose will be to elucidate and clarify existing law. Offerings from theoretical economics will be utilized, for in this area of antitrust especially, economic theory has influenced the law. There will, however, be occasion to note some of the ways in which economics can prove unsatisfying as a source of antitrust wisdom, and to see some of the responses made by those responsible for the development of antitrust law when they have turned toward the light which economic theory has held before them, only to find it grow dimmer as they approached.

After inquiry concerning how market power—and its extreme degree, monopoly power—can be identified, the conduct element of monopolizing, the need to show some degree of deliberateness, will be examined in its turn.

§ 8. The Nature of Market Power

Although the term market power is not used in the Sherman Act, to understand Section 2 it is essential to grasp this concept. Initially an approximation will do: market power is the power of a firm to affect the price which will prevail on the market in which the firm trades. Whether a seller possesses such power depends upon the reaction of buyers to price changes initiated by the seller. Buyer re-

---

S.Ct. 632, 55 L.Ed. 663 (1911); United States v. E. I. DuPont De Nemours & Co., 351 U.S. 377, 76 S.Ct. 994, 100 L.Ed. 1264 (1956); United States v. Grinnell Corp., 384 U.S. 563, 86 S.Ct. 1698, 16 L.Ed.2d 778 (1966); United States v. Aluminum Co. of America, 148 F.2d 416 (2d Cir. 1945); United States v. United Shoe Mach. Corp., 110 F.Supp. 295 (D.Mass.1953), aff'd per curiam 347 U.S. 521, 74 S.Ct. 699, 98 L.Ed. 910 (1954); Telex Corp. v. IBM Corp., 510 F.2d 894 (10th Cir. 1975); Twin City Sport-service, Inc., v. Charles O. Finley & Co., Inc., 512 F.2d 1264 (9th Cir. 1975).

4. See cases in note 3 supra.

5. United States v. Griffith, 334 U.S. 100, 68 S.Ct. 941, 92 L.Ed. 1236 (1948).

6. See cases in note 3 supra.

actions, in turn, will depend upon availability of substitutes for the seller's product. The functions involved will be clarified by further discussion.[1]

In a sense, every seller has control over his own goods; he can decide what quantities he is willing to sell and what prices he will accept. But because of the availability to buyers of substitutes, the range of options open to a seller in some markets is very limited. Consider the choices open to a farmer possessed of a silo full of wheat. Wheat of identical grade offered by large numbers of other sellers will also be available to those buyers whom the farmer could reach, and a large number of buyers will be seeking to buy wheat from the various available sources. The institutional media through which these aggregate forces of supply and demand interact constitute the market in which the farmer operates and the forces interacting on the market will result at any given time in a "going market price" for wheat. The single farmer will be able to sell all or any part of his wheat at that price. He need not sell for less even if, absent other options, he would be willing to do so. He cannot sell for more because if he asks more, buyers will turn elsewhere. His only choice is whether to take or leave the prevailing market price for all or any part of the wheat in his silo. Though he "controls" that part of interstate trade and commerce defined by his own production in the limited sense that he can decide whether or not to sell, he in fact possesses no power to affect price or quantity to any degree that could be of social concern. He totally lacks market power.

Contrast the options open to a quarryman who owns land which, due to geological fortuity, is the only known source of distinctive, ruggedly beautiful granite sought after by many who buy and pay for lavish, monumental buildings.[2] The quarryman, like the farmer, can decide what quantities he is willing to sell at what prices; but for him this control over his own product is vastly more meaningful than is that of the farmer. The unique qualities of his stone differentiate it from other products. Buyers will no doubt compare it with other granite, even with other building materials, and will compare prices and qualities of alternative products before deciding what to buy. The quarryman will therefore not be able to increase price without losing sales; if his price goes progressively higher, buyers in increasing numbers will turn to substitutes. But the quarryman can elect his course from among a range of alternatives: he can at any time chose either to sell a relatively small quantity at a relatively high price, a relatively large quantity at a low price, or some inter-

---

[1]. What follows draws upon basic price theory and industrial structure theory. Standard price theory texts include G. Stiegler, The Theory of Price (3rd ed. 1966); C. Ferguson, Microeconomic Theory (rev. ed. 1969). On industrial organization theory, see the works cited in § 3 supra.

[2]. Compare H. E. Fletcher Co. v. Rock of Ages Corp., 326 F.2d 13 (2d Cir. 1963).

mediate quantity at an intermediate price. Since a significant number of buyers regard his product as preferable to available substitutes, he will not lose all sales even if he sets his price substantially above the price currently charged by other sellers of granite.

The condition of the quarryman is distinguished from that of the wheat farmer by saying that the quarryman has market power. Any seller who can significantly increase his price, so long as he is willing to sell a smaller volume, or who can significantly increase his volume, so long as he is willing to set a lower price, has market power. Such a firm does not face a market which says to it—take the going price or sell nothing. Such a firm is also aware of its power to affect price by its own decisions about the quantities it will sell.[3]

Any discussion of market power quickly presents questions of degree. On the one hand, most sellers are insulated at least in modest degree and in the short run from their competitors. A consumer in a supermarket is not likely to replace a quart of milk and go elsewhere if he learns while waiting in the checkout line that the price he must pay is a penny higher than the price quoted in the ad of another store; a buyer of raw materials for a manufacturing firm may not alter an ongoing relationship with a supplier because of a modest price disparity he regards as temporary. At least a minute degree of market power, then, is a common, perhaps a near universal, phenomenon. On the other hand, all sellers are disciplined to some extent by the quantities offered and prices charged by other sellers, even for vastly different products. What a consumer spends to see a baseball game he cannot spend to see a ballet; and if there are even a few buyers who view the ballet and the ballgame as alternatives, demand functions for these two services are not totally independent. Indeed, some goods and services, though distinct in important respects, may be seen by many consumers as alternatives. A baseball game, as a leisure time activity, may compete for the patronage of many customers with a movie, a play, the pleasurable ambience of a local pub, a TV comedy, or the latest science fiction paperback. In a time when impulse buying seems a common phenomenon, even the suggestion that all consumer goods can be seen as being traded on an all-inclusive "consumer goods market" is not utterly farfetched.

But if the evaluation of market power is to be pursued it is necessary to confine analysis to a manageable range, to focus attention on that which is most salient. It is not whether a single buyer at the

---

3. Most discussions of market power focus on the power of sellers. Buyers can also have power. For example, if there were numerous sellers of a given product and only one buyer, the buyer could affect price by decisions about how much it would pay. It could not get all it wanted at whatever price it set, because as price went down sellers would withdraw. But it could choose whether to pay a relatively high price, and attract a relatively large supply, or to pay a relatively low price, and attract a relatively low supply. Its position, then, would be precisely analogous to that of the seller with power.

supermarket check stand will respond to a price differential on milk that is of interest; it is the extent to which the aggregate of the store's sales will be affected by a price change. Again, it is not whether an occasional customer will choose between baseball and ballet on the basis of relative prices that is of interest, but whether consumers in the aggregate substitute one for the other often enough so that price changes for the one significantly affect total sales of the other. The process of establishing the area of inquiry is usually referred to as defining the relevant market. The way in which this is done, and the manner in which the degree of power within a market is evaluated, can be best shown by discussing some of the cases dealing with monopoly power.

§ 9. The Nature of the Legal Inquiry About Power

Monopoly power has been defined as power to control price or to exclude competition. How have the courts sought to gauge the degree of a firm's market power when considering whether it is a monopolist? There is no easy or settled answer to this inquiry. Antitrust law has been developing; antitrust analysis is an emerging process. The early cases, strongly oriented toward conduct and focusing upon the ethical quality of defendants' acts, found monopoly only where significant power was manifested by its predatory exercise.[1] In recent years courts exploring issues of single firm power have drawn insight from economic theory and sought to utilize some of the analytical techniques of economists.[2] The principal device used has been a simplified structural analysis. Typically the analysis begins by defining the relevant market in which power is to be measured. It then seeks to evaluate the extent of power wielded within that market. A primary means for doing so is to measure the degree of concentration within the market—that is, the percentage of all transactions on the market which are controlled by the firm charged with monopolizing—and then to draw inferences about power from the degree of concentration.[3] Barriers to entry, another structural feature, have also been deemed relevant in reaching conclu-

---

1. Compare, e.g., United States v. American Tobacco Co., 221 U.S. 106, 31 S.Ct. 632, 55 L.Ed. 663 (1911) with United States v. United States Steel Corp., 251 U.S. 417, 40 S.Ct. 293, 64 L.Ed. 343 (1920).

2. E.g., United States v. E. I. DuPont De Nemours & Co., 351 U.S. 377, 76 S.Ct. 994, 100 L.Ed. 1264 (1956); United States v. Aluminum Co. of America, 148 F.2d 416 (2nd Cir. 1945); United States v. United Shoe Mach. Corp., 110 F.Supp. 295 (D.Mass.1953), aff'd per curiam 347 U.S. 521, 74 S.Ct. 699, 98 L.Ed. 910 (1954).

3. E.g., United States v. E. I. DuPont De Nemours & Co., 351 U.S. 377, 76 S.Ct. 994, 100 L.Ed. 1264 (1956); United States v. Aluminum Co. of America, 148 F.2d 416 (2nd Cir. 1945). Among the basic articles discussing the law's approach to monopoly are: Levi, The Antitrust Laws and Monopoly, 14 U.Chi.L.Rev. 153 (1947); Rostow, Monopoly Under the Sherman Act, 43 Ill.L.Rev. 745 (1949) and Bowman, Toward Less Monopoly, 101 U.Pa.L.Rev. 577 (1953).

sions about whether a particular level of concentration signifies monopoly power [4]; the harder it would be for new firms to enter, the greater is the significance of a given firm's present market share.

In addition to structural analysis, performance analysis (which contrasts the performance of subject firm with the performance which economic theory suggests would be achieved under monopoly conditions) has been utilized, at least in a tentative way.[5] Conduct analysis, which loomed large during the early history of Section 2, remains germane to evaluating whether a firm has monopoly power, though the frequency with which conduct analysis is relied upon for this purpose is presently small.[6]

Each of the approaches which has been used to identify monopoly power presents its own difficulties. Where (as in the early cases) courts consider primarily conduct and motive, they must apply norms with a strong moralistic flavor to problems of economic organization, problems which seem to call for less judgmental responses. Yet the resolutions which economic theory seems to offer often elude the grasp. In part, this is due to the intrinsic limits of economic theory. These show themselves less starkly in respect to monopoly than in connection with other antitrust questions; nevertheless, they are apparent. In part the difficulty is due to gaps that exist, even where theoretical knowledge is wholly satisfactory, between that knowledge and the ability to gather sufficient empirical information about any given industry to classify it confidently in theoretical terms. In part difficulty results from uncertainty over basic policy questions about how the law should deal with market power. The limits of law and of adjudication as means for regulating economic structure add to all of these problems. Lawyers and judges are not economists and trials are not scientific investigations. Antitrust, ultimately, is a system of law—a system of general norms and of techniques for applying these norms in a variety of particular settings. The search for rules which are selective enough to achieve satisfactory results, yet amenable to judicial administration, has been a groping one.

In what follows the leading cases will be discussed to illuminate the issues presented, to evaluate the responses thus far made, and to identify possible lines for future doctrinal growth. A brief review of early cases will come first; these dealt with the issue of power in a

---

4. United States v. United Shoe Mach. Corp., 110 F.Supp. 295 (D.Mass.1953), aff'd per curiam 347 U.S. 521, 74 S.Ct. 699, 98 L.Ed. 910 (1954).

5. United States v. E. I. DuPont De Nemours & Co., 351 U.S. 377, 420–23, 76 S.Ct. 994, 1020–21, 100 L.Ed. 1264, 1294–95 (dissenting opinion); United States v. United Shoe Mach. Corp., 110 F.Supp. 295 (D.Mass.1953), aff'd per curiam 347 U.S. 521, 74 S.Ct. 699, 98 L.Ed. 910 (1954).

6. An examination of conduct for the purpose of deciding whether a firm possesses monopoly power is to be distinguished from the conduct test applied once a firm has been found to possess monopoly power. The former is treated in § 25 infra, the latter in Part D infra.

practical, almost off-handed way. Then, the more recent cases will be organized for discussion around functional economic concepts.

§ 10. The Practical Approach of the Early Cases

The towering cases decided during the period of the early growth of the Sherman Act are *Standard Oil*[1] and *American Tobacco*,[2] both written by Mr. Justice White early in the second decade of this century. The story of these cases, and the judicial, political and economic battles which they brought to some sort of a culmination, is told elsewhere in more of its richness.[3] The purpose here is a limited analytical one—to stress the approach of the early cases to the issue of power.

Less than a decade earlier in an opinion which implied that any consolidation of firms which ended significant competition between the constituents would violate the act, the Court in *Northern Securities* had held unlawful a railroad merger which brought a trunk line controlled by Moran and Hill into common ownership with one controlled by Harriman.[4] The sweep of that and other earlier cases had led to lively controversy[5] which was brought to resolution, at least for a time, by the announcement of the rule of reason in *Standard Oil* and *American Tobacco*.

From the point of view of the Taft administration these cases, involving as they did a direct attack on the Rockefeller oil interests and the tobacco barons of rather infamous image politically, were fitting sequels to the earlier Roosevelt administration case against Morgan and Harriman groups.[6] In each the evidence presented by the government respecting the economic domination by the defendant group of its industry was overwhelming, and there was little serious effort by defendants to establish that they lacked substantial power.

Standard Oil reached the Supreme Court in 1911. The government charged that the individual and corporate defendants had violated Sections 1 and 2 of the Sherman Act in the course of the development of Standard Oil of Ohio and its affiliates. Standard had been

---

1. Standard Oil Co. of N.J. v. United States, 221 U.S. 1, 31 S.Ct. 502, 55 L.Ed. 619 (1911).

2. United States v. American Tobacco Co., 221 U.S. 106, 31 S.Ct. 632, 55 L.Ed. 663 (1911).

3. See, for example, W. Letwin, Law and Economic Policy in America (1965), especially ch. 7. The early cases are also more fully discussed in Chapter 7, Part A. infra. See also ch. 3, § 64 infra.

4. Northern Sec. Co. v. United States, 193 U.S. 197, 24 S.Ct. 436, 48 L.Ed. 679 (1904).

5. See Letwin, supra note 3. See also Bork, The Rule of Reason and the Per Se Concept: Price Fixing and Market Division, 74 Yale L.J. 775 (1965) and 75 Yale L.J. 373 (1966), which reviews the early cases from an analytical perspective which focuses more on judicial history and less on general social and political history than does Letwin.

6. See note 5 supra.

organized in 1870 and evidence indicated that through it the defendants had obtained preferential rail rates which were usd to force competitors to join the combine at the risk of being driven out of business. There was also some evidence of predatory price cutting to drive out competition where it was encountered or to force reluctant competitors to join the consolidation.[7] Standard by these and related methods had gained control over 90% of refined petroleum.

In *Northern Securities,* proscecuted by the Roosevelt administration which purported to be able to distinguish between good and bad trusts,[8] the Court had implied, at least, that all consolidations leading to substantial power were unlawful. In *Standard Oil,* prosecuted by the Taft administration which was uncompromisingly critical of all powerful trusts,[9] the Court took a more permissive and temperate position. In finding monopolization (and attempt to monopolize) in violation of Section 2, the Court emphasized not Standard's market position, but the methods by which it had achieved and through which it exercised the power it had gained. Because of this, the Court's concern with Standard's power is seldom stressed in discussions of the case.

But concern with power of course there was. In holding that Standard was guilty of monopolizing, Justice White's opinion notes that Standard had obtained "mastery over the oil industry" through which it was "able to fix the price of crude and refined petroleum."[10] The Court would not have found Standard guilty of monopolizing on the basis of power alone. But it seems equally true that, whatever the case is deemed to hold about conduct as a prerequisite for a violation, the Court would not have found Standard guilty of monopolizing, regardless of the excesses of its conduct, had it not succeeded in gaining power over price. It is, if you will, a holding that monopoly power must be shown if monopolization is to be proven.

But what needs now to be stressed is the basis upon which the Court concluded that Standard exercised power over price. To the antitrust analyst today, discussion of monopoly brings to mind the concepts drawn from economics which pertain to market power. The Court in 1911 was neither armed with nor encumbered by the theoretical tools which it has now been assimilating for thirty years or so. Justice White drew the inference of power not on the basis of a theoretical analysis but by the exercise of a practiced intuition. Far from seeking to identify theoretical mechanisms for explaining and

---

7. In McGee, Predatory Price Cutting: The Standard Oil (N.J.) Case, 1 J. Law & Econ. 137 (1958) the author reports on a detailed search of the Standard Oil record which failed to warrant an inference of predatory price cutting. But see D. Dewey, Monopoly in Economics and Law 180 (1959).

8. See Letwin, supra note 3.

9. Id.

10. Standard Oil Co. of N.J. v. United States, 221 U.S. 1, 33, 31 S.Ct. 502, 505, 55 L.Ed. 619, 634 (1911).

understanding how power over price is generated in a market of the kind involved in the case, the opinion does not even display in the discussion of power a striving for those middle level generalizations of the kind in which legal analysis is often so rich, and which would have helped the bar and the business community to understand the basis for the conclusion of power in this case and to identify the kinds of situations in which power might be found in others. It was enough for Justice White to know that Standard had control over 90% of the refining business. Without need for any discussion or analysis he inferred from this an absolute power to control the price of refined petroleum; on the basis of a very limited discussion and analysis he concluded that this mastery over refined petroleum gave "a substantial power over the crude product" which had to be sold to the refiners, despite the fact that the defendants had very little direct control over crude production.[11]

If this practical orientation failed to uncover elements in the situation with which a more theoretical imagination would have engaged, it also completed the task in a manner which a broad consensus of commentators over several generations has viewed as essentially sound in its particular outcome.[12] Whatever the attraction of the analytical tools which theoretical thinking can provide, the utility of an informed intuition such as that displayed by Justice White should not be disdained. The intuition of a practical observer, knowledgeable about the matters at hand, may not be satisfactory as a jurisprudence. Yet intuitions of these kinds, when shared widely enough to form a consensus, do provide an adequate basis upon which to strike out in new directions at the growth points of the law.

Legal rules are by their very nature generalizations; and generalizations by their very nature are blind to the unique elements displayed by a particular fact situation, by a specific case. The art of judging begins with those intuitions which point out the proper result. But the artful judge will not stop just there as in this instance Justice White is seen to have done. If there is an existing rule, a generalization, which satisfactorily explains the result, the judge ought to point it out and explain its applicability. If existing rules do not satisfy, if, perchance, they seem to call for a different result than intuition invites, the art of judging becomes the art of making exceptions, of identifying what it is in the particular situation which warrants declining to apply the general proposition which by its terms claims to apply. But even that is not an end to the process; to complete his task, the judge will find from his experience in testing

11. 221 U.S. at 77, 31 S.Ct. at 523, 55 L.Ed. at 652 (1911). See also United States v. Lehigh Valley R. Co., 254 U.S. 255, 269–70, 41 S.Ct. 104, 109, 65 L.Ed. 253, 265 (1920) where the Court held a combination to control the coal supply to a single, large railroad system, a "monopolization of a part of * * * trade or commerce * * *."

12. See, e.g., Letwin, supra note 3; Dewey, supra note 7, 179–82 (1959).

an old rule and finding it wanting a way of restating the matter, once again in general terms, but this time in terms which comprehend all of the elements now apparent, yet do no violence to his sense of what is right in the particular application before him or others which he can imagine.

Though the *Standard Oil* opinion fails on the issue of power to come up with a fresh generalization, with a rule, there is nevertheless in the opinion a core of wisdom to which it is profitable to return after half a century. Justice White asked few instrumental questions; his inquiry was sharply focused on whether power over price existed and was being exercised. It did not matter to him that the share of the crude market controlled by the combination was exceedingly small, since it appeared that power over crude prices was exceedingly large. Today, with elaborate theoretical tools for analyzing power, courts have developed a set of instrumental issues. They ask not the ultimate question, does the firm have power?, but a series of subsidiary ones like, what market does the firm engage in?, what is its share of that market?, are there entry barriers?, and the like. These instrumental inquiries are of true worth only in such degree as they throw light on the ultimate issue. Sometimes, however, they get in the way. They are allowed to block off appropriate responses toward which a more direct concern with power, such as that shown in *Standard Oil,* would lead.

It may be that the practical approach to power implicated in *Standard Oil* and also in *American Tobacco* could even yet be more fully and more satisfactorily developed. What kinds of facts would an informed participant in the market place look to in deciding whether a large firm had monopoly power? In part perhaps to size; in part perhaps to the firm's history, to the way it was put together; in part perhaps to its patterns of market conduct, for these may display its own perception of its position. All of these elements were entailed in *Standard Oil* and *American Tobacco*. They are factors to which courts may hereafter wish to recur, which might hereafter be used as building blocks in the construction of a generalization about power which is less dependent upon the concept and style of the economist then, as we shall see, the courts have become.

Though both opinions are suggestive, neither *Standard Oil* nor *American Tobacco* explicitly states the values which underlie the legal concern with power over price. In *Standard Oil* the Court repeatedly refers to the interest of consumers ("the general public") whose pocketbooks are adversely affected by conduct violative of the act.[13] But there is also reference to "the right of individuals" to engage freely in trade,[14] and to the purpose of the act to restrict limitations

---

13. Standard Oil Co. of N. J. v. United States, 221 U.S. 1, 50, 58, 31 S.Ct. 502, 512, 515, 55 L.Ed. 619, 641, 644 (1911).

14. Id. at 58, 31 S.Ct. at 515, 55 L.Ed. 644.

imposed upon that right which arise out of combination or monopoly.[15] In *American Tobacco* a record of predatory and malicious behavior arrested the Court's attention and the emphasis was reversed. That opinion stresses the purpose of the act to protect against market conduct "designed to injure others" by "driving competitors out of business," and erecting "barriers to the entry." [16]

The deficiencies of an intuitive approach to power, of the failure to encapsulate attitudes in a generalization against which future cases might be tested, are suggested by another of the early cases, *United States v. United States Steel Corp.*,[17] decided a decade later. The Court once again marked out conduct and purpose for particular attention, and expressly held that power to control price is a prerequisite to monopolization. But in a rather unsatisfactory opinion it declined to draw from defendant's massive holding in basic steel the inference about power which had been drawn from seemingly comparable evidence in *Standard Oil*. The Court affirmed the finding below that power over price either was never obtained or if it was obtained was never exercised and was dissipated as the strength of competitors grew.[18]

Interestingly enough, the evidence upon which the Court most heavily relied in finding that United States Steel alone could not control price was the evidence presented by the government to prove that the defendant had sought to induce others to combine with it in a price conspiracy. The *Steel* case, then, because of the softness with which the Court analyzed the question of power, does not fit comfortably into a consistent pattern with the *Oil* and *Tobacco* cases. But the *Steel* case strongly reinforces the conclusion that unilateral power over price is one of the essentials to the offense of monopolization and displays a readiness by the Court to rely on practical indicia in deciding whether power is present.

§ 11. The Modern Predominance of Structural Analysis

Modern legal analysis of monopoly issues begins with the opinion by Judge Learned Hand in United States v. Aluminum Company of America,[1] a source book of concepts pertinent to the evaluation of

---

15. Id.

16. United States v. American Tobacco Co., 221 U.S. 106, 182–83, 31 S.Ct. 632, 649, 55 L.Ed. 663, 695 (1911).

17. 251 U.S. 417, 40 S.Ct. 293, 64 L.Ed. 343 (1920).

18. Over the years United States Steel's share of the market did fall and the industry was transformed from what had the look at its inception of a monopoly into an oligopoly. See R. Posner, Antitrust Cases, Economic Notes, and Other Materials 376–79. In a sense, therefore, the Court read well what was happening in the industry. But it failed to perceive or react to indications of power in the original formation, or to be concerned about (or, at any rate, to think the act had relevance to) the oligopoly which developed.

1. 148 F.2d 416 (2d Cir. 1945).

single firm power and related issues. Judge Hand was true to the basic teaching of the early monopolization cases, but eschewed their practical, intuitive approach and attempted a more rigorous analysis which used some of the tools of theoretical economics to determine whether the defendant had power. He noted that the extent to which Alcoa dominated the aluminum industry could be computed in several ways, but recognized that if any such computation was to be a useful gauge of power, it had to include a meaningful statement about the dynamics of the market. He then proceeded with a simplified structural analysis of aluminum production. The basic mechanism of that analysis was to define the market in which it would be appropriate to evaluate Alcoa's power, and then to measure the extent of concentration and Alcoa's share within that market as a basis for judging the extent of Alcoa's power. That approach, with elaborations, has been used consistently in monopoly cases since *Alcoa* was decided.[2] What later cases have added has been attempted refinements in structural analysis. For example, a market must be delimited in geographic terms as well as in terms of product;[3] also, entry barriers should be considered as well as the degree of concentration when a judgment is made about power.[4] Other refinements entail the use of conduct and performance analysis as subsidiaries to a structural analysis in making a judgment about power.[5] The extent to which the analysis used in *Alcoa* has proved successful, the extent to which the concepts of theoretical economics are useful to the antitrust analyst, and the extent to which the law has been successful in making the accommodations which those techniques demand, are all questions to which the materials that follow invite attention.

The two step process which the Hand opinion utilizes, first defining the market and then measuring power, has been followed at least in form in most of the cases since *Alcoa*.[6] It will be utilized as an organizational principle here. This tradition, however, should not obscure the interrelationship which exists between the two parts of the process. The ultimate question being asked is whether the defendant exercises power over price and power to exclude competition.

---

2. E.g., United States v. E. I. DuPont De Nemours & Co., 351 U.S. 377, 76 S.Ct. 994, 100 L.Ed. 1264 (1956); United State v. Grinnell Corp., 384 U.S. 563, 86 S.Ct. 1698, 16 L.Ed.2d 778 (1966); Telex Corp. v. IBM Corp., 510 F.2d 894 (10th Cir. 1975); Twin City Sportservice, Inc. v. Charles O. Finley & Co., Inc., 512 F.2d 1264 (9th Cir. 1975); United States v. United Shoe Mach. Corp., 110 F.Supp. 295 (D.Mass.1953), aff'd per curiam 347 U.S. 521, 74 S.Ct. 699, 98 L.Ed. 910 (1954).

3. United States v. Grinnell Corp., 384 U.S. 563, 86 S.Ct. 1698, 16 L.Ed.2d 778 (1966). Cf. United States v. Pabst Brewing Co., 384 U.S. 546, 86 S.Ct. 1665, 16 L.Ed.2d 765 (1966).

4. United States v. United Shoe Mach. Corp., 110 F.Supp. 295 (D.Mass.1953), aff'd per curiam 347 U.S. 521, 74 S.Ct. 699, 98 L.Ed. 910 (1954).

5. See §§ 26 and 27 infra.

6. See, e.g., the cases in note 2 supra.

PART B. DEFINING THE RELEVANT MARKET

§ 12. Introduction

Market definition is not a jurisdictional prerequisite, or an issue having its own significance under the statute; it is merely an aid for determining whether power exists.[1] To define a market in product and geographic terms is to say that if prices were appreciably raised or volume appreciably curtailed for the product within a given area, while demand held constant, supply from other sources could not be expected to enter promptly enough and in large enough amounts to restore the old price or volume. If sufficient supply would promptly enter from other geographic areas, then the "defined market" is not wide enough in geographic terms; if sufficient supply would promptly enter in the form of products made by other producers which had not been included in the product market as defined, then the market would not be wide enough in defined product terms. A "relevant market," then, is the narrowest market which is wide enough so that products from adjacent areas or from other producers in the same area cannot compete on substantial parity with those included in the market.

However, economic relationships are seldom so simple that a relevant market can be defined with exactitude and confidence. There is not for any product a single, real "market" waiting to be discovered. A seller of a given product, for example corn flakes, faces various degrees of competition: other brands of corn flakes are certainly competitive products and in the same market; other dry cereals, say corn puffs, or wheat flakes, are no doubt competitive in substantial degree; less competitive, but still significant perhaps, are cooked cereals; and not to be ignored entirely are other products which might be served instead of cereal—bacon, eggs, toast, danish pastries, etc. Realistically, no single definition of a product market is likely to be decisive, in the sense that all sellers within it directly limit the power of the seller whose power is the subject of inquiry and all sellers outside of it affect the subject seller so little that they can be ignored. A firm making corn flakes may be able to increase price not at all because other corn flake makers would respond. But if it is the sole or the dominant corn flake maker it may be able to lift prices slightly, but not very much, without substantial losses to other cold cereal makers. If it is the sole or dominant cold cereal maker, its power may be much greater; it may have a wide price discretion before significant diversion of sales to hot cereals or other products begins. But even if it is the only cereal maker in the country its power is not

---

1. F. Scherer, Industrial Market Structure & Economic Performance 52–57 (1970).

unlimited; there are other foods besides cereal to which buyers at some point will turn.²

Similarly, in geographic markets there are tendencies, rather than absolutes. Other firms within a 50 mile radius may be directly competitive. It may be possible to ignore those 100 miles away in reference to a 1% price increase, but not in reference to a 3% increase.³

Another dimension about which unexpressed assumptions are often made is time. It is seldom critical in the process of defining the market geographically. If a seller in Minneapolis raises his price a seller in St. Paul may be able to respond immediately. The response of a seller in Chicago may be delayed; but if it would ship goods to Minneapolis within a week in response to that increase, that response would surely be sufficiently prompt to significantly limit the power of the first seller. But time delays may be crucial in defining a product market. Competition among alternative products which is almost non-existent in the short run may appear intense in the long run. Steel, aluminum, magnesium and copper may be directly competitive in only a limited number of uses in the short run, but if we assume a long enough reaction time there are relatively few uses of any of these metals for which another of them could not substitute. For example, if an increase in the price of steel relative to other metals is big enough and persists long enough, steel buyers will alter their operations to allow substitution of other metals. This fact no doubt limits the power of steel producers to some not insignificant degree.

To define a market is to take a step toward gauging market power; to evaluate a seller's strength within a market as defined is to complete the inquiry—to determine whether the defendant firm sufficiently controls the supply within the market so that it can at its election raise prices within a substantial range.⁴ Though the law's need is for norms sufficiently specific for courts to apply, it cannot be too forcefully emphasized that there are no absolutes in the analysis. Power is always a matter of degree, and market definition always is a matter of judgment. One way to proceed would be to consider two or three alternative market definitions when making a judgment about a firm's power.⁵ If we are considering the power of K Co., a corn flake maker, competing sellers within the narrowest market

---

2. Turner, Antitrust Policy and the Cellophane Case, 70 Harv.L.Rev. 281 (1956).

3. See, Elzinga & Hogarty, The Problem of Geographic Market Delineation in Antimerger Suits, 18 Antitrust Bull. 45, 52–59 (1973).

4. Adelman, Economic Aspects of the Bethlehem Opinion, 45 U.Va.L.Rev. 684, 688 (1959).

5. The deficiencies of conventional market share analysis, which assumes a single, "relevant" market, are fully analyzed in Turner, supra note 2; they are also suggested by P. Areeda, Antitrust Analysis, Problems, Text, Cases ¶ 242(c) (2d ed. 1974), and by M. Handler, H. Blake, R. Pitofsky and H. Goldschmid, Trade Regulation, Cases and Materials 283–287 (1975).

(corn flakes) limit power most directly; those within the slightly wider market (dry cereals) limit it significantly; those beyond (other makers of breakfast products) limit it to a lesser degree. All of those variables may be relevant in deciding whether a particular corn flake maker has substantial power over price. Another way would be to select one of the alternative market definitions more or less at random—say, the dry cereal market—but then to take into account in further analysis that some firms within it (other corn flake makers) restrain K Co.'s power more than do other cereal makers and also that some firms outside the market, makers of other breakfast foods, restrain it to some degree.

Either of these approaches seems sensible enough. There are cases, no doubt, which look like examples of each. But if a market situation is particularly complex neither may prove practicable, given the limited capacity of judicial institutions for dealing with economic data. Simplification may be essential if courts are to function at all, attorneys to counsel at all, in the task of identifying firms possessing the degree of power which Section 2 comprehends. That simplification may begin by a decision to select from the alternative markets which are proposed a single, economically meaningful market which will be identified as "the" relevant market.

This course simplifies because it asserts, in essence, that the court, in determining whether K Co. has monopoly power within the market, need assess only data germane to the single market so chosen. As we shall see, the primary structural data which the court will evaluate will be that pertaining to concentration ratios and market shares. The first simplification, the identification of a single relevant market thus sets the stage for later, further simplifications, such as the development of rules of thumb about what degree of concentration within a market signifies monopoly power.

Described in this stark form the process may seem like simplification with abandon, and indeed it is not immune from that charge. In its favor, however, three things may be said. For one, there is a view, if not a theorem, which underlies the approach, which asserts that the more concentrated a market becomes the worse it will perform. If, then, the single market selected truly is "economically meaningful," and not arbitrary or weak in its rational underpinnings, and if the concentration levels marked out as indicative of power are high enough, the procedure, simplified as it may be, should at least identify dominated markets which are likely to be performing poorly. For another, however spare the outline, the application can be rich in subtlety. Choosing the single relevant market from among alternatives may entail a gauging of entry barriers, a measuring of subtle supply and demand interrelationships, a sensitivity to collateral values and interests of various kinds. Thirdly, the demands of administrability and predictability are forceful; they must be attended adequately if there is to be any antitrust enforcement which proceeds upon the premise that like matters ought to be treated alike, or even that the same matter, however unique it may be thought to be, is to be treated in the same way regardless of the particular jurist before whom it is called.

Like boomerangs, these issues are hard to cast off, to be done with. Much that follows reverts to them, at times explicitly, often not. The nature of the inquiry at all events is identified. More empirical information ought to be at hand before a definitive answer is attempted. Simplification would be the more appealing the more confident one became that a single meaningful economic market could in a given instance, or in the generality of them, be identified. A better sense of the power and limits of theoretical knowledge would also be of value. Simplification would be the less appealing the less confident one became that there was a high positive correlation between concentration ratios and performance.

What can be said at this stage can be summarized briefly: Courts in monopolization cases usually begin by defining a single geographic and product market. In most cases the effort is to identify what seems to be, given the practical limitations of available data and the costs of improving it, the one market which is most meaningful economically. But in a few cases the court seems content to choose among alternatives on grounds of smaller convenience, perhaps expecting to balance that casualness by an analysis of power which attends more factors than merely concentration ratios. Even though the precision of analysis which might be achieved if market definition were seen as a process of arraying data in various alternate aggregations is sacrificed in order to simplify, the simplicities which the court is seeking are rarely achieved. With more experience of the cases more trenchant generalizations may be possible.

§ 13. Homogeneous Products

The *Alcoa* case exemplifies the market definition process where a homogeneous, undifferentiated product is involved.[1] Alcoa was charged in 1937 with monopoly in the production of virgin aluminum ingot, a product used as a raw material by fabricators of aluminum products. One unit of virgin ingot is physically identical with that of other units regardless of source; no buyer prefers one source to another; no seller differentiates its virgin ingot from that of other sellers. Alcoa was the only domestic producer of virgin aluminum ingot. It sold most of what it produced, but some was fabricated into end products by Alcoa itself. Alcoa's virgin ingot nevertheless faced some competition. Substantial quantities of so-called "secondary" ingot—ingot made by recycling scrapped aluminum fabrications—was produced and sold by other traders domestically.

---

1. United States v. Aluminum Co. of America, 148 F.2d 416 (2d Cir. 1945).

Proceeding with a structural analysis, the court noted the various ways in which the product market might be defined in order to compute Alcoa's share. If the market were taken to include recycled as well as virgin ingot, but to exclude the ingot Alcoa produced but used itself in its own fabricating operations, Alcoa's share would be about one-third. This was the figure on which the trial court had relied in finding that Alcoa was not a monopolist. If the trial court's approach was adopted insofar as inclusion of recycled aluminum is concerned, but altered by adding to the base the ingot produced and fabricated by Alcoa, the company's share would be about two-thirds. If the trial court's computation was further altered by excluding secondary ingot from the base, Alcoa's share would be about 90%; Alcoa produced that percentage of all virgin ingot sold in the United States.

The Hand opinion accepted the government's contention that 90% fairly characterized the degree of concentration. The reason given for including all ingot produced by Alcoa, not just the portion it sold to other fabricators, was that Alcoa's own fabricating activities caused a *pro tanto* reduction in demand for ingot; Alcoa, by fabricating, displaced non-integrated fabricators who would otherwise have bought Alcoa's production.

If the court's treatment of Alcoa's integrated fabrications seems sound, its handling of the issues concerning secondary aluminum is more questionable. While recognizing that recycled ingot "can, and probably does, set a limit or 'ceiling' beyond which the price of 'virgin' cannot go,"[2] the court excluded this aluminum from the base on the ground that Alcoa had itself originally produced most of the ingot which, after being fabricated and sold, would eventually find its way into reprocessing plants in the form of scrap. A monopolist, the court reasoned, knowing that current production can be reclaimed, will in its own interest make production and pricing decisions not with a view to current market conditions alone but also by taking into account the effect on profits which will be felt in the future by the fact that a part of current production will eventually return as scrap to compete with the monopolist's future production. In effect the court said: Alcoa controls current virgin production; current secondary production was subject to Alcoa's control in the past when Alcoa made its production decisions about virgin then being produced and now being recycled.

A critical appraisal of these aspects of the *Alcoa* decision may deepen understanding of the limits, as well as the strengths, of applied structural analysis. Note that the product excluded from the market, recycled aluminum ingot, was a close substitute for virgin aluminum. Physically, it was substantially identical. There were a few uses for which virgin ingot only could be used, but for most uses

---

2. 148 F.2d at 424.

buyers were indifferent to which they obtained. Consequently, secondary ingot regularly traded at a price close to, but not identical with, that for virgin. Recall that the purpose of defining a market is as an aid in estimating power over price. If one concludes (as did the court), that the amount of secondary ingot available at any time did significantly discipline Alcoa's power over virgin prices, a convincing basis must be found before secondary ingot can be excluded in defining the market. Whether the reason given by the court—that Alcoa had controlled production of the scrap at a prior production stage—is plausible depends upon what one could infer about Alcoa's present market situation from Alcoa's past connection with the scrap. To speak of past "control" by Alcoa over the amount of scrap on the market may have been a misnomer unless Alcoa's past connection with the scrap did in fact give it a power which could have been exercised in such a way as to affect current prices.

The question is whether Alcoa in 1937 is to be charged with controlling the amount of scrap then upon the market merely because Alcoa had taken a production decision at an earlier time which affects the 1937 scrap supply. Control, in this context, implies amenability to rational, self-interested decision-making. Assume that ingot has, on the average, a ten year life cycle and that much of the ingot returning to the market as recycled ingot in 1937 was produced by Alcoa in 1927 and the years immediately before and after. It certainly does not follow that it was feasible for Alcoa during the years 1925 to 1929 to take the 1937 market into its calculations in making decisions about production quantities. And if Alcoa could not have taken future scrap returns into account when it set production levels in the years around 1927, then Alcoa did not have the kind of "control" over the scrap appearing on the market in 1937 which is relevant to judgments about the extent of Alcoa's market power in 1937.

The court should have asked: How long on the average before ingot produced in a given year begins to come back as scrap? What percentage of it eventually returns? In what configuration is the return likely to be spread over future time? How predictable are these matters? What economic or technological variables condition the flow? To what extent can Alcoa at any time even identify these factors, let alone predict how they will in the future enhance or diminish the flow of recycled material? If such questions would have seemed as indeterminate to Alcoa executives as they do to the casual observer, it was unrealistic to impute to Alcoa, whatever its share of current production, the ability to take future scrap flow into account in setting current production targets. And if Alcoa could not take future scrap flow into account in some rational manner, one could not with reason assert that the discipline imposed by that scrap upon Alcoa's market conduct ought to be ignored.

§ 14. Technological Differences

Passing Alcoa's "control" over scrap production, there is an alternative justification sometimes asserted for the court's decision to exclude scrap from the defined market—the fact that virgin ingot and secondary ingot are produced by different technologies. That two otherwise similar products are produced in different ways is clearly significant to market definition in one respect and may be significant in a second respect. First, the extent to which Alcoa's power to raise prices was at any given time disciplined by any specific substitute ingot source would depend not merely upon whether customers would want to turn from Alcoa to the alternative source in response to a price differential, but also upon the extent to which and the rapidity with which the alternative source could be expanded in response to such shifts by customers. Given differences in technology and raw material sources, it cannot be assumed that secondary suppliers and virgin suppliers could expand production at the same rate and for the same costs. Thus, a given amount of competitive production of secondary ingot at any given time may not signify the same limitation on Alcoa's power as would the same amount of competitive virgin production.

Does this observation justify the result the court reached? Intuition may suggest that Alcoa would be less concerned about recyclers than it would be about another virgin producer—that it would view the secondary industry as less capable of rapid expansion than would be a primary competitor. But intuition is not a safe guide in such matters. A competing virgin producer might already be working near capacity; its power over ore sources might be limited. A recycler, on the other hand, might have underused capacity or the ability to add capacity rapidly. The rate at which existing fabrications are scrapped, or the particular kinds of scrapped fabrications it is economically feasible to reclaim, might increase rapidly in response to increasing scrap prices. On the facts before the court, the extent to which secondary aluminum limited Alcoa's power cannot be closely gauged. Absent any evidence about how rapidly secondary sources could have been expanded if Alcoa raised prices, any statement would be entirely speculative; surely, there is no basis for saying secondary aluminum was irrelevant to Alcoa's power—which is what the court in effect asserted when it eliminated secondary aluminum from consideration.

There is another rationale which may justify excluding secondary aluminum from the relevant market. Competition is valued not merely because it disciplines a seller's prices but also because it may spur progressiveness and innovation.[1] Over time, new technological development may reduce production and other costs, thus increasing

---

1. United States v. Aluminum Co. of America, 148 F.2d 416 (2d Cir. 1945).

efficiency and facilitating still lower prices. Theoretical analysis suggests that this pressure to innovate may be felt most strongly between rivals using the same technology. If 100 rival firms make and sell a product capable of being produced in identical form by either of two distinct technologies, the price behavior of sellers practicing each technology will be disciplined by the pricing of all other sellers. But if 99 of the 100 sellers practice one of the two technologies, each of these 99 will also be disciplined in other ways. Efforts by each to increase its own market share will stimulate searches for cost-saving innovations. While it may be assumed that the press of competition will be calling forth reasonably efficient performance throughout the industry, it would require that only one of the 99 sellers be aggressively determined to gain on the others in order to stimulate all to find ways to reduce their costs. But what of the single firm practicing the exclusive technology? If its principals were endowed with a taste for the quiet life, they may have started to relax after having reduced costs to the level where the firm could meet the prices of the other 99, regardless of whether the unique technology afforded opportunities for further efficiencies which would have been uncovered had other competing sellers also been practicing that technology.

Judge Hand considered these possibilities and then restated the view that "possession of unchallenged economic power deadens initiative, discourages thrift and depresses energy; * * * immunity from competition is a narcotic, and rivalry is a stimulant * * * to industrial progress * * *."[2] As he viewed it, even the assumption that competition from recycled aluminum set a price ceiling through which Alcoa could not break would not be a total answer to the contention that Alcoa, monopolizing the virgin technology, possessed excessive power. Because the technological processes for reclaiming aluminum scrap differed significantly from those entailed in producing virgin, the possibility remained that the public suffered from Alcoa's dominant virgin position.[3]

§ 15. Differentiated Products

Aluminum is not without possible substitutes. "Steel, aluminum, magnesium, copper, titanium, high density polyethylene, fiberglass, western pine, bamboo, and dozens of other raw materials are potential substitutes for one another in thousands of fabricated product applications."[1] But possible substitute products such as steel all have different functional characteristics and are produced by different

---

2. 148 F.2d at 427.

3. See also United States v. Grinnell Corp., 384 U.S. 563, 86 S.Ct. 1698, 16 L.Ed.2d 778 (1966) and United States v. Corn Prods. Ref. Co., 234 F. 964 (2nd Cir. 1916) (L. Hand, J.). But cf. United States v. E. I. DuPont De Nemours & Co., 351 U.S. 377, 76 S.Ct. 994, 100 L.Ed. 1264 (1956), discussed in § 16 infra.

1. F. Scherer, Industrial Market Structure and Economic Performance 214 (1972).

technologies. For many uses, for example airplane bodies, other metals cannot be substituted for aluminum. For other uses, buyers of aluminum might be able to make substitutions only after significant alterations in capital equipment and manufacturing methods.

But technological and customary gaps between product markets are not always so wide, even when alternative products differ in material respects. There is a continuum. At one extreme are identical products such as virgin aluminum made by two producers.[2] Next are situations where the products of different manufacturers are physically similar, functionally identical (or substantially so) and made by the same technology, but are differentiated in minor respects, such as style. TV sets and many other consumer hard goods are in this class.[3] Moving further away from homogeneity are situations where competitors' products, as presently manufactured, are not functionally interchangeable, but could be made so by relatively minor changes in manufacturing processes; computer drives, discs, printers and memory equipment, compatible with one manufacturer's equipment, but requiring significant manufacturing modifications to be compatible with that of another, may serve as an example.[4]

Note that there may be a different demand than supply dimension to these problems. Consider, for example, Telex Corporation v. IBM.[5] Many customers already own expensive basic central data processing units of one manufacturer; those customers, when looking for peripheral equipment to be used in association with the basic unit, will be likely to consider only equipment which is already compatible with the basic unit they own; the fact that significant modifications would be needed to make usable by them peripheral equipment now compatible with other manufacturers' basic units may keep such customers from considering such alternatives. However, makers of peripheral equipment may be able to switch fairly easily from making equipment compatible with one manufacturer's central processing units to that compatible with those of other manufacturers; on the supply side there may be considerable potential for movement.

Moving still further along the continuum away from the more homogeneous and toward the more heterogeneous would be situations

---

2. See United States v. Aluminum Co. of America, 148 F.2d 416 (2d Cir. 1945).

3. See Brown Shoe Co. v. United States, 370 U.S. 294, 82 S.Ct. 1502, 8 L.Ed.2d 510 (1962).

4. See Telex Corp. v. IBM Corp., 510 F.2d 894 (10th Cir. 1975); see also Advance Business Sys. & Supply Co. v. SCM Corp., 287 F.Supp. 143 (D.C. Md.1968) (market includes coated paper for all electrostatic process duplicating machines, not paper for one manufacturer's machines); United States v. Charles Pfizer & Co., 246 F. Supp. 464 (S.D.N.Y.1965) (market includes all acids used by beverage manufacturers, not citric acid alone). But cf. Affiliated Music Enterprises, Inc. v. Sesac, Inc., 268 F.2d 13, cert. denied 361 U.S. 831, 80 S.Ct. 82, 4 L.Ed. 2d 74 (1959) (gospel music a market distinct from popular music).

5. 510 F.2d 894 (10th Cir. 1975).

like the virgin aluminum—secondary aluminum contrast; functionally and physically the products are very similar but they are manufactured by distinctly different technologies.[6] Approaching the other end of the continuum are situations where products are made by different technologies and, though functionally interchangeable in some uses, are by and large functionally and physically dissimilar.[7] Finally, the extreme suggested by steel and aluminum is encountered; substitutability is conceivable [8] only in some uses and only after major adjustments.

When the particular problem is near the first end of the spectrum, it is called an issue involving *differentiated* products. For example, are differently styled TV sets, manufactured, advertised and sold under different brand names, to be treated as part of the same product market?[9] Where it moves toward the other end, it is called an issue involving *substitute* products. For example, are excelsior, shredded wood, and shredded paper, which are all usable as package fillers, to be treated as part of the same product market? [10]

Theory about monopolistic competition suggests that if there are a relatively large number of firms selling products which are differentiated only slightly, the long run adjustment may be similar to that which occurs under competition for an undifferentiated product.[11] Unless there are barriers to entry, producers cannot in the long run earn excessive returns; if prices reach the point where firms are earning higher than competitive profits, new entry will be encouraged which will put downward pressure on prices and profits. But if products are differentiated, this adjustment will never be precisely the same as in the classical competitive situation, however open to entry the industry may be. Because of differentiation the producers will not all face exactly the same demand conditions as would competing producers of a homogeneous product. Also, the products, if not being made or marketed by identical technologies, or with the same raw materials, will have cost functions which differ within an indeterminate range.

Nonetheless, the insight is that rivalry among producers of differentiated products will, if there are enough producers and freedom

6. See United States v. Aluminum Co. of America, 148 F.2d 416 (2d Cir. 1945).

7. See Tampa Elec. Co. v. Nashville Coal Co., 365 U.S. 320, 81 S.Ct. 623, 5 L.Ed. 580 (1961). Compare United States v. E. I. DuPont De Nemours & Co., 351 U.S. 377, 76 S.Ct. 994, 100 L. Ed. 1264 (1956).

8. See United States v. Aluminum Co. of America, 148 F.2d 416 (2d Cir. 1945); compare United States v. E. I. DuPont De Nemours & Co., 351 U.S. 377, 76 S.Ct. 994, 100 L.Ed. 1264 (1956).

9. See GTE Sylvania Inc. v. Continental TV, Inc., 537 F.2d 980 (9th Cir. 1976), (en banc).

10. See Virginia Excelsior Mills, Inc. v. FTC, 256 F.2d 538 (4th Cir. 1958).

11. The towering theoretical contribution was E. Chamberlin, The Theory of Monopolistic Competition (1933). See Scherer, supra note 1, at 13–19 (1972).

of entry, tend toward results approaching those that would be achieved under pure competition. This insight supports the inference that differentiated products should usually be treated as part of the same market.[12] One would ask: What is GM's power in the automobile market? What is RCA's power in the TV market? It would not seem appropriate in considering power to limit inquiry only to the particular, differentiated product of one manufacturer, to consider only GM cars or RCA TV sets.

If there is reasonably easy entry into an industry and a significant number of substitutes, the power acquired by any manufacturer through product differentiation can be expected, in most instances, to be small.[13] Often, however, entry is not easy. In many consumer products industries there are only a few manufacturers, each making a differentiated product, and entry appears difficult. The automobile industry is an example; yet even in a situation like this, one would include all manufacturers of the product within the same market—the market for automobiles.[14] One would analyze to see whether, within that total market, one of the firms were exercising monopoly power, or whether two or more firms were acting concertedly to obtain monopoly power.

However, there may be times when a single manufacturer of a differentiated product has been so successful in differentiating his brand from others that it is reasonable to treat the single brand as a market unto itself. If a significant segment of customers regard such a firm's product as so unique that they will not turn to substitutes even upon a substantial price shift, the firm may be said to exercise market power.[15]

§ 16. Substitute Products

Substitute products present intense problems of market definition. Suppose that the contention is made that a firm which manufactures corn flakes has monopoly power. Should the market be limited to corn flakes, to dry cereals of corn, to dry flake cereals, to ce-

12. See, e.g., United States v. Eastman Kodak Co., 226 F.2d 62 (2nd Cir. 1915), appeal dismissed 255 U.S. 578, 41 S.Ct. 321, 65 L.Ed. 795 (1921).

13. But see FTC v. Proctor & Gamble Co., 386 U.S. 568, 87 S.Ct. 1224, 18 L. Ed. 303 (1967).

14. See e.g., Lanzillotti, "The Automobile Industry" in The Structure of American Industry 311-354 (3rd ed. W. Adams 1961). But see Rea v. Ford Motor Co., 355 F.Supp. 842 (W.D.Pa. 1973), vacated 497 F.2d 577, cert. denied 419 U.S. 868, 95 S.Ct. 126, 42 L. Ed.2d 106 (1974).

15. Compare United States v. Klearflax Linen Looms Inc., 63 F.Supp. 32 (D. Minn.1945) and Rea v. Ford Motor Co., 497 F.2d 577 (1974), with H. E. Fletcher Co. v. Rock of Ages Corp., 326 F.2d 13 (2d Cir. 1963). See also Affiliated Music Enterprises, Inc. v. Sesac, Inc., supra note 4; Acme Precision Prods., Inc. v. American Alloys Corp., 484 F.2d 1237 (8th Cir. 1973). Cf. FTC v. Proctor & Gamble Co., 386 U.S. 568, 87 S.Ct. 1224, 18 L.Ed.2d 303 (1967).

reals cooked and dry? Or should it include bread, danish pastry, eggs, bacon, sausage, or any of these, on the ground that if cereal prices increase buyers will switch to other breakfast products which they regard as substitutes?

The teaching of the case law on such issues is not wholly consistent. In *Alcoa*,[1] for example, Judge Hand who excluded secondary aluminum after analysis, excluded steel and other substitute metals virtually without discussion, even though he noted that "substitutes are available for almost all commodities, and to raise the price enough is to evoke them."[2] Similarly, the Supreme Court excluded other media for advertising when defining the market within which to measure the power of a firm selling newspaper advertising.[3] One might contrast the recent *Telex* case,[4] where it was held that all peripheral equipment used in association with central data processing units, not just that compatible with IBM computers, should be considered in defining the market in which to gauge IBM's power as a maker of peripheral equipment.

The decision in *Alcoa* to ignore substitute metals seems warranted when it is remembered that the purpose of market definition is to measure power, and that the issue of power is one of degree.[5] Purchasers of aluminum ingot were not ultimate consumers, but fabricators of aluminum products. They would not have found it feasible to turn to other metals, except in the long run;[6] their fixed investment would preclude any prompt change if aluminum prices were increased. Yet, barriers between even quite distinct products may not always be unyielding. In some situations customers may be able to switch rapidly from one product to a substitute, even though it be used as a raw material in some further commercial process.

DuPont (Cellophane)[7] entailed an attempt to use sophisticated, theoretical concepts to determine whether substitute products should be included in a single product market; it discloses some of the diffi-

---

1. United States v. Aluminum Co. of America, 148 F.2d 416 (2d Cir. 1945).

2. Id. at 426.

3. Times-Picayune Publishing Co. v. United States, 345 U.S. 594, 73 S.Ct. 872, 97 L.Ed. 1277 (1953). See also United States v. Pullman Co., 50 F. Supp. 123 (E.D.Pa.1943), aff'd per curiam 330 U.S. 806, 67 S.Ct. 1078, 91 L. Ed. 1263 (1947) where the court dismissed without serious pause the suggestion that distant substitutes should be considered in defining the market.

4. Telex Corp. v. IBM Corp., 510 F.2d 894 (10th Cir. 1975). Compare Advance Business Systems & Supply Co. v. SCM Corp., 287 F.Supp. 143 (D.C. Md.1968).

5. Compare Tampa Elec. Co. v. Nashville Coal Co., 365 U.S. 320, 81 S.Ct. 623, 5 L.Ed. 580 (1961).

6. The contrary might be argued on the basis of data indicating a high cross-elasticity of demand between aluminum and copper and between aluminum and steel. See M. Peck, Competition in the Aluminum Industry 31–34 (1961).

7. United States v. E. I. DuPont De Nemours & Co., 351 U.S. 377, 76 S.Ct. 994, 100 L.Ed. 1264 (1956).

culties encountered when such concepts are used in litigation. DuPont, which produced 75% of the cellophane sold in this country, was charged with monopolizing trade in that product. In defense the company showed that cellophane shared common properties and was used interchangeably with other flexible wrapping materials such as grease-proof and waxed paper, plain, lacquered, and waxed glassine, aluminum foil, cellulose acetate, pliofilm, saran wrap, polyethylene and sulphite. If the relevant market for measuring power was defined as the flexible packaging material market which included cellophane and all of those substitute products, duPont's share fell to about 20%.

The Court accepted the broader market and the smaller percentage share. It concluded that duPont's power over price was effectively disciplined by competition from other wraps. In reaching this conclusion, the Court relied heavily on evidence that relatively small reductions in the price of cellophane caused relatively large numbers of buyers to switch to cellophane from other wraps. Using the concept of cross-elasticity of demand, an economic concept which theoretically would measure power directly, the Court inferred that such readiness to substitute across product lines indicated the appropriateness of the wide, product-group market.[8]

DuPont has been brutally and convincingly criticized.[9] To understand what the continuing controversy is about one must have a decent grasp of the concepts of elasticity and cross-elasticity. The degree by which the amount of a product purchased will change in response to changes in its price is referred to as the elasticity of the demand for the product.[10] The quantities of a product which consumers will purchase are affected by a number of variables. Of obvious importance is the price of the product; in general, the higher the price, the less will be the total amount purchased. This phenomenon can be illustrated by a demand schedule or demand curve showing the volume which would be purchased at various possible prices

---

8. See to like effect, United States v. Charles Pfizer and Co., 246 F.Supp. 464 (E.D.N.Y.1965) (lactic acid in same market as other citric acids). But see United States v. Corn Prods. Ref. Co., 234 F. 964 (S.D.N.Y.1916) where Judge Hand held that pearl starch was in separate market from brewers grits despite substitutability in making maltos, where the yield of starch was substantially higher than that of grits. Interestingly enough, the concept of cross-elasticity first appeared in the case law in Times-Picayune Publishing Co. v. United States, 345 U.S. 594, 73 S.Ct. 872, 97 L.Ed. 1277 (1953), where it was used to justify the court's conclusion that advertising in other media should not be considered as a close enough substitute for newspaper advertising to be included in the same market.

9. Stocking & Mueller, The Cellophane Case, 45 Am.Econ.Rev. 29 (1955); Turner, Antitrust Policy and the Cellophane Case, 70 Harv.L.Rev. 281 (1956).

10. The textual material which follows is based on conventional theory derivable from any text dealing with cross-elasticity. See, e.g., D. Needham, Economic Analysis and Industrial Structure 19–22 (1969). See also Appendix A.

during some unit of time. A number of factors will have a bearing on demand: the number of consumers in the market area served, their tastes and preferences, the amount of money they have to spend, the range of other goods available to them, and the prices of other goods, particularly complementary products and possible substitute products.

The demand existing for a product at any given time is described by economists not only in terms of its magnitude—how many units of the product would be taken per unit of time at various alternative prices—but also in terms of its "elasticity"—the relationship between the magnitude of changes in quantity purchased per unit of time to the small changes in price with which they are associated. Demand is elastic at any point on a demand schedule at which a small change in price would result in a relatively larger change in total purchases (so that total receipts could be increased by reducing price, or total receipts decreased by increasing price). Conversely, if consumers would respond to a small price change by a change in total purchases which was smaller in percentage than was the price change (so that total receipts would fall upon a price decrease and raise upon a price increase) demand is called inelastic. The degree of elasticity or inelasticity can of course vary. If a small price reduction would result in a very small increase in revenue, demand is slightly elastic; if a small price reduction would yield a very large increase in revenue, demand is highly elastic.

Since one of the factors in addition to its own price which may affect demand for a product is the price of other products, the concept of elasticity can be used to describe with some precision the extent to which small changes in the current price of one product affects demand for another product. Products which are wholly unrelated will show no "cross-elasticity." For example, one might expect the amount which will be spent per day for bubble gum at a given price to be wholly unaffected by a change in the price of atomic reactors; there would be no cross-elasticity of demand between these products. Now consider complementary products, those typically used together. One might expect sales of baseballs, for example, to fall in response to increases in the price of baseball bats. As bat sales fell in response to the price increase, ball sales would also fall, even without a price increase. Cross-elasticity would exist between those products and would be described as negative. By contrast, if products are substitutes for each other they will display positive cross-elasticity. If the price of one stays constant, an increase in the price of the other will generate greater sales of the first as buyers switch to it. Conversely, a decrease in the price of one of two substitutes, while the price of the other stays constant, will result in decreased sales of the constant priced product. For example, if the price falls on orange juice, and grapefruit juice stays constant, less grapefruit juice will be sold as some buyers switch to orange juice.

It may be possible to measure how closely one product substitutes for another by looking at the relationship between the elasticity of demand for the first product and its cross-elasticity with the substitute product. Suppose that at current prices a 2% decrease in the price of peas would lead to an increase in the amount of peas sold of 3%, and also to a compensating decrease in the amount of string beans sold of 3%. One could then say that, at current prices, peas are a perfect substitute for string beans. The full amount of the increase in pea sales would be at the expense of reduced string bean sales. One would not expect to find perfect substitutes in this sense, but if at current prices buyers generally regarded one product as a close substitute for the other, positive cross-elasticity might be very high.

In *duPont (Cellophane)*,[11] the evidence showed that cellophane shared every end use (such as candy wrap, meat wrap, etc.) with several other wraps, and that small reductions in the price of du-Pont's product resulted in large numbers of buyers turning from other wrap materials to cellophane. The majority of the Court saw this as "reasonable interchangeability", even though the products had significantly different physical and functional properties, were manufactured by different technologies, and sold at very different absolute price levels. Moreover, from evidence that duPont's percentage of total wrap sales went up and that of others went down over a substantial period during which duPont had been reducing prices, the Court inferred that a high positive cross-elasticity of demand existed between cellophane and other wraps. The Court felt that if duPont could attract business from others by small price shifts making cellophane relatively less expensive, it would also lose business to others upon any price change which made cellophane relatively more expensive. It was on the basis of these inferences that the Court reasoned that duPont's power over price should be evaluated in reference to the overall "flexible wrap market," of which duPont had only a small share.

The result of this reasoning was to treat duPont as though it were one of several sellers in a market for differentiated products. In such a market, the Court concluded, a seller with 20% does not have sufficient power to be a monopoly. That there were patent and other barriers to entry into cellophane production did not alter the analysis. Entry was easy with respect to several of the substitute products to which buyers could shift. If duPont were to increase prices to excessive levels, buyers would rapidly switch away from cellophane to other wraps. Should those making these substitutes increase prices due to the higher demand, new entry would be attracted.

[11]. United States v. E. I. DuPont De Nemours & Co., 351 U.S. 377, 76 S.Ct. 994, 100 L.Ed. 1264 (1956).

The purpose for market definition in a monopoly case is to see whether the alleged monopolist has power to maintain a price substantially higher than costs (or, by lowering price to competitive levels, to drive others out). Whether a firm can do this obviously turns on whether buyers have alternatives to which they can turn when the seller raises price above the competitive level of cost plus a reasonable return. If cross elasticity is high *when the alleged monopolist is pricing at the competitive level,* so that should it start to increase prices above that level buyers could and would turn in substantial numbers to other sellers, the alleged monopolist is no monopolist at all; even if the other sellers were offering distinctly different substitute products, rather than identical ones, the readiness of buyers to turn to them and the ability of the other sellers to supply the buyers' needs would discipline the alleged monopolist significantly. But the crucial matter is not whether buyers will turn away from the alleged monopolist at some conceivable price, it is whether they will abandon it before it succeeds in pushing its price up to the point where it is earning monopoly returns.[12] If at the current prices where high cross-elasticity is found to exist the alleged monopolist *is already pricing at monopoly levels,* then the fact that it cannot price still higher without rapid loss of sales does not deprive it of monopoly power. Thus, ascertaining that cross-elasticity between substitute products is high at current prices is not, of itself, enough to warrant placing the products in the same product market, as the Court did in *duPont*. One must know more—specifically, whether cross-elasticity is high at prices closely related to cost, or whether the alleged monopolist has a substantial cost advantage which enables it to set prices at supra-competitive levels before the discipline of substitutes sets in.

As a generalization, any monopolist would at prices close to cost find prevailing demand for its monopolized product to be inelastic; because it is a monopolist it will be able to push prices higher with losses in sales that are small relative to the increases in revenue yielded by the price increase. Moreover, a monopolist which wishes to price at the level that yields the maximum current return will always push price up to a level where elasticity of demand for its product becomes evident; it will not stop increasing price until the sales losses that result become large relative to the revenue gained by the higher price. And as prices reach the point where elasticity of demand for the monopolists' product becomes high, the cross-elasticity between that product and any interchangeable substitutes will also become high. The monopolist, having pushed the price up to the point where buyers would abandon the product in volume in response to any further increase, will have reached the point where buyers turn in numbers to substitutes with each further increase.

12. See Turner, supra note 9.

Despite the inadequacy of the cross-elasticity concept when torn loose from an analysis of the relationships between price and cost for the substitute products, courts have persisted in using it—or at least, in explaining the results of analysis in cross-elasticity terms. In some cases the concept serves as a justification for a narrow market definition.[13] In one, the cross-elasticity between championship boxing and other boxing matches was said to be small and this to warrant treating championship matches as a separate market.[14] Factors leading to that conclusion were differences in average revenue for championship and other fights, in rates for television and movie rights, and in admission prices. Similarly, in United States v. Grinnell Corporation,[15] the Court held that substitutes for central station protective services, from alarm bells to guards, did not display high cross-elasticity with central station services due to differences in utility, efficiency, and continuity and therefore were not in the same market. But the fact that the *duPont* concept can point toward a narrow market definition as well as a broad one does not validate the manner in which it has been used.

DuPont, for example, may well have had a substantial cost advantage and been pricing at supra-competitive levels. High cross-elasticity of demand between cellophane and other wraps may only have meant that duPont, being in possession of monopoly power, had increased price to a point where further increases would have caused defections to substitute products.[16] The price at which elasticity was high and positive could well have been a price at which monopoly profits were being earned.

The *duPont* opinion also stressed that movement from other wraps to cellophane as cellophane became relatively cheaper, occurred over a period of years. But during this period the only price changes occurring were reductions in the price of cellophane. If duPont lacked market power, why did other firms suffer this pattern to persist? If duPont was in fact earning excessive profits and other firms were in fact earning only competitive returns, the situation would have been very much like the hypothetical immediately above. Relative reductions in the cellophane price did not cause all buyers to turn to cellophane because cross-elasticity, though high, was not infinite. Though many buyers shifted to cellophane with each relative reduction in price, some buyers continued to prefer other wraps at the

---

13. E.g., Times-Picayune Publishing Co. v. United States, 345 U.S. 594, 73 S.Ct. 872, 97 L.Ed. 1277 (1953).

14. United States v. International Boxing Club of N. Y., Inc., 358 U.S. 242, 79 S.Ct. 245, 3 L.Ed.2d 270 (1959). See also Philadelphia World Hockey Club, Inc. v. Philadelphia Hockey Club, Inc., 351 F.Supp. 462 (E.D.Pa.1972) (relevant market is major league professional hockey).

15. 384 U.S. 563, 86 S.Ct. 1698, 16 L.Ed.2d 778 (1966).

16. See Turner, supra note 9; P. Areeda, Antitrust Analysis, Problem, Text, Cases ¶ 247(e) (2d ed. 1974).

existing relative prices even after each reduction. The threshold at which they too would shift had not as yet been reached.

There is another notable aspect of the treatment of elasticity in *duPont*. The Court dealt only with elasticity of demand. This concept does not take into account constraints affecting suppliers of substitute products which might limit their ability or desire to respond to demand shifts by increasing their production.[17] It cannot be assumed, merely because buyers would *like* to switch in massive numbers from cellophane to other wraps as cellophane prices go up, that sellers will increase the supply of alternative products without also increasing price. Supply also has its elasticity and cross-elasticity among interchangeable products. These may be evaluated much as is elasticity and cross-elasticity of demand, and if one aims for a scientific determination of whether substitute products should be included in a market, one cannot stop at an evaluation of the demand side only.

The appropriate response to the issues posed by substitute products is, perhaps, to rely on the eclectic habits of the lawyer to select from and also to supplement the analytical tools of the economist.[18] Depth analysis of cross-elasticities and their implications may be feasible and appropriate in some cases, yet in others might be too costly relative to what they could be expected to yield. In some cases performance data, particularly data on profits, may be available tending to affirm or deny the existence of power. In some cases the best perspective may be obtained by looking at another reasonably sensitive gauge of what is going on in the marketplace—the perceptions of those who trade in the market. Do buyers and sellers of cellophane think of other wraps as directly competitive and act as though they were directly competitive, or do they think and act as though cellophane was sufficiently differentiated from other wraps so that those buying and selling it constitute a separate market? That, really, is the ultimate question and it might be approached directly as well as through indicators such as the concept of interchangeability.[19] In any event, there is no need for a court to be a captive of *duPont's* artless use of the cross-elasticity concept.[20]

---

17. Though the concept, relevant market, should not be manipulated like an accordion, it is, to be sure, a somewhat evanescent concept. See the discussion in Jones v. Metzger Dairies, Inc., 334 F.2d 919 (5th Cir. 1964).

18. Cf. United States v. Paramount Pictures, 334 U.S. 131, 68 S.Ct. 915, 92 L.Ed. 1260 (1948); H. E. Fletcher Co. v. Rock of Ages Corp., 326 F.2d 13 (2d Cir. 1963); Affiliated Music Enterprises, Inc. v. Sesac, Inc., 268 F.2d 13 (2d Cir.), cert. denied 361 U.S. 83, 80 S.Ct. 32, 4 L.Ed.2d 74 (1959); United States v. United Shoe Mach. Corp., 110 F.Supp. 295, 342 (D.Mass.1953), aff'd per curiam 347 U.S. 521, 74 S.Ct. 699, 98 L.Ed. 910 (1954). Compare Acme Precision Prods. Inc. v. American Alloys Corp., 484 F.2d 1237 (8th Cir. 1973).

19. See the discussion in Handler, Blake, Pitofsky & Goldschmid, Trade Regulation, Cases and Materials 283–86 (1975).

20. See Brown Shoe Co. v. United States, 370 U.S. 294, 325, 82 S.Ct.

§ 17. Diversified Products and Product Clusters

Differentiated products are those which manufacturers, by means of style or other differences, brand marks and names, advertising and the like, have persuaded buyers to think of as distinguishable from competitor's products. Diversification of products is distinctly a different concept. It refers to the extent to which a single manufacturer produces a number of varieties within a product category. Diversification may take either of two forms. In one, the manufacturer diversifies along a line indicated by the developmental possibilities of its own product. The alternative form of diversification occurs when the manufacturer develops clusters of products which differ significantly from each other but which are related because used by the same customers and capable of distribution through the same channels. The first type of diversification would be exemplified by a toothpaste manufacturer which offered fluoride and non-fluoride paste, each in two or three flavors; the second by a toothpaste manufacturer which began to make and distribute tooth brushes and dental floss. The manufacturer of a toothpaste may differentiate its product from that of other manufacturers by advertising about its quality control program, or quoting testimonials from TV stars. At the same time it may diversify by offering a fluoride or non-fluoride paste and several flavors.

Differences among manufacturers in degrees of product diversification can create difficulties in market definition. Suppose, for example, that there was concern about whether one manufacturer dominated the production of family sized cars. Product diversification among auto manufacturers would be a complicating factor. Some family car shoppers will consider sports cars as an alternative, depending upon relative prices. Are sports cars, then, to be considered part of the same market? Station wagons are also considered by many family car buyers as alternatives; arguably these should be included. But station wagons are also alternatives to pick-up trucks and other light work vehicles. As categories are expanded at differing ends of the spectrum, an interlinking chain of products appears. Should they all be grouped as part of the same market, although products at opposite ends of the chain, such as sports cars and work

---

1502, 1523–24, 8 L.Ed.2d 510, 535 (1962) where the Court indicates that the concepts of interchangeability and cross-elasticity of demand or supply need not be taken as determinative in delimiting the relevant line of commerce for Clayton Act purposes. While there may be a degree less rigor in defining markets under Clayton (see § 203 infra) the considerations are, in general, the same, and Clayton cases are used authoritatively in Section 2 proceedings, and conversely. See United States v. Grinnell Corp., 384 U.S. at 572–74, 86 S.Ct. at 1704–05, 16 L.Ed.2d at 787–88. See also Avnet, Inc. v. F. T. C., 511 F.2d 70, 77 (7th Cir. 1975) (Stevens, J.) holding that used and rebuilt components could be excluded from a component market where these units sold from 25 to 50% below new ones and there was no significant interaction in price between new and used components.

vehicles, are rarely viewed by buyers as substitutes? If not, where should the lines be drawn?[1]

The case law gives pragmatic answers to questions such as these. In United States v. United Shoe Machinery Corporation,[2] for example, the defendant manufactured machinery for use in the multiplicity of processes entailed in shoe manufacture. As to machinery for some processes, United had patent protection and relatively little competition. Machines it made for other processes, however, were faced with considerably more competition. Rather than attempting to evaluate United's power with respect to machines for each of the many functions involved, the court aggregated the machines into a single market comprehending machinery for eighteen of the major processes utilized in making shoes. In essence, the court drew upon defendant's conception of its own business (as well as Carl Kaysen's economics)[3] to define the industry in which its power was to be tested, noting that defendant alone covered this full range of products and that, although any shoe manufacturer could obtain an up-to-date plant without a single United machine, any competing processes involved had to meet the rivalry of United in the marketplace.

United States v. Grinnell Corporation,[4] is similar in thrust. The Court treated a cluster of services involving central station alarm systems which were approved by insurance underwriters as a market. So, too, in the bank merger cases the Court has treated the varied cluster of services associated with "commercial banking" as a product market;[5] and in *Brown Shoe*,[6] the Court clustered products manufactured by similar methods and distributed through similar outlets to the exclusion of those which, although manufactured in similar ways, are often distributed separately. A somewhat pragmatic approach is, moreover, essential. The goal is to assess power. At times it will seem sensible to expand the market, to conceptualize more widely than the product cluster achieved by a particular firm's business;[7] at others, disaggregation will be indicated—a breaking down of a particular firm's business and the assignment of segments of it to different markets.[8]

1. See United States v. Grinnell Corp., 384 U.S. 563, 593 n. 8, 86 S.Ct. 1698, 1715 n. 8, 16 L.Ed.2d 778, 799 n. 8 (1966) (Fortas, J., dissenting).

2. 110 F.Supp. 295 (D.Mass.1953), aff'd per curiam 347 U.S. 521, 74 S.Ct. 699, 98 L.Ed. 910 (1954).

3. See generally C. Kaysen, United States v. United Shoe Machinery Corporation (1956) (Professor Kaysen served as "law clerk" to Judge Wyzanski in connection with the case).

4. 384 U.S. 563, 86 S.Ct. 1698, 16 L.Ed. 2d 778 (1966).

5. United States v. Phillipsburg Nat'l Bank & Trust Co., 399 U.S. 350, 90 S. Ct. 2035, 26 L.Ed.2d 658 (1970); United States v. Philadelphia Nat'l Bank, 374 U.S. 321, 83 S.Ct. 1715, 10 L.Ed.2d 915 (1963).

6. Brown Shoe Co. v. United States, 370 U.S. 294, 82 S.Ct. 1502, 8 L.Ed.2d 510 (1962).

7. United States v. Crocker-Anglo Nat'l Bank, 277 F.Supp. 133 (N.D.Cal.1967).

8. American Smelting & Ref. Co. v. Pennzoil United, Inc., 295 F.Supp. 149 (D.Del.1969); United States v. Times

There are various elements to be drawn into service of this pragmatic approach. The major one, of course, is a sense about the utility of the market definition being used for measuring power. The way buyers and sellers tend to view the market tells something about the ambit of competitive forces; so does production and distribution technology. Another pragmatic factor is the availability of data. One can only count things for which there are numbers. Unless exhaustive statistical surveys are to be done the parties must utilize either the data gathered by the census taker, or the business records of firms or trade associations, or both. Markets, then, will tend to be defined the way the Bureau of the Census has defined them, or the way firms have perceived them, despite imperfections. It is more or less inevitable.[9] Remember, also, the market definition only begins the process of gauging power. If the convenient definition seems wider than would be ideal, thus tending to reduce concentration figures, one can adjust by attributing a somewhat higher significance to a given level of concentration, or conversely.[10]

Despite the prevailing, pragmatic tone it is hard to assimilate to the main line of authority the cases occasionally encountered which utilize a product market definition seemingly very narrow. First run movies have been distinguished from other movies,[11] championship boxing matches from other boxing matches,[12] transport products for the use of bus companies from the same products for the use of buyers generally,[13] central station fire and police alarm services from other alarm services,[14] all without much explanation. Usually where this kind of a disaggregation takes place the product which is treated as separate commands a distinctly higher price than others in the broader category to which it belongs. These results might be explained on the ground that there is a substantial group of users for which only the particular product will do, and that if it is not segregat-

---

Mirror Co., 274 F.Supp. 606 (C.D.Cal. 1967), aff'd 390 U.S. 712, 88 S.Ct. 1411, 20 L.Ed.2d 252 (1968); United States v. Provident Nat'l Bank, 259 F.Supp. 373, 262 F.Supp. 397 (E.D.Pa. 1966). Though the banking merger cases cited here and in notes 5 and 7 supra arose under the Bank Merger Act, it is now clear, despite some earlier contrary indications (United States v. Crocker-Anglo Nat'l Bank, 277 F.Supp. 133 (N.D.Cal.1967)), that the difference in statutory language mandates no patently different approach to issues of market definition. See United States v. Third Nat'l Bank of Nashville, 390 U.S. 171, 88 S.Ct. 882, 19 L.Ed.2d 1015 (1968).

9. See F. Scherer, Industrial Market Structure and Economic Performance 52–57 (1970).

10. See §§ 22–24 infra.

11. United States v. Paramount Pictures, Inc., 334 U.S. 131, 68 S.Ct. 915, 92 L.Ed. 1260 (1948).

12. United States v. International Boxing Club of N.Y., Inc., 348 U.S. 236, 75 S.Ct. 259, 99 L.Ed. 290 (1955).

13. United States v. National City Lines, Inc., 186 F.2d 562 (7th Cir. 1951), cert. denied 341 U.S. 916, 71 S.Ct. 735, 95 L.Ed. 1351 (1951).

14. United States v. Grinnell Corp., 384 U.S. 563, 86 S.Ct. 1698, 16 L.Ed.2d 778 (1966).

ed out as a separate market these users will be subject to the seller's power over price, even though other users which can consider alternatives are not.[15] Some decisions, nonetheless, seem to contrast sharply with others. For example, compare the Court's refusal in *duPont (Cellophane)*[16] to treat cellophane as a separate product even though for some users—specifically, manufacturers of cigarettes—only cellophane was a suitable wrap with the Court's holding in *Grinnell* that central station alarm service constitutes a separate market because, for some users, it alone will do.[17] *DuPont* is convincing that the mere fact that demand elasticity is low for one sub-group of buyers does not warrant separate market treatment when demand elasticity (and cross-elasticity with substitutes) is high for buyers generally. How, then, does one explain *Grinnell?*

The resolution of issues like these might be made to turn on whether the high cross-elasticity prevailing generally served to protect from exploitation the sub-group of buyers having a need for the specific product.[18] In *duPont (Cellophane)*, for example, there was no practical way for duPont to charge higher prices on sales to cigarette makers than to other buyers. If it tried to do so, low cost buyers would presumably sell to high cost buyers at a price in between the two that duPont had established. The attempt to discriminate would also be inhibited by the Robinson-Patman Act.[19] Hence, the fact that most buyers would switch to substitutes if prices were raised appreciably protected cigarette makers against high prices even though they would have stayed with cellophane in the face of an appreciable price increase. By contrast, a firm selling a service like that involved in *Grinnell* might well be able to discriminate in price between buyers for which only central station services would do and other buyers. It might, for example, offer the central station service to buyers needing it at a price relatively high in relationship to cost and offer a non-central station protective service to other buyers at a price relatively low in relationship to cost. Buyers of the lower priced service could not resell to buyers needing the central station service and there would not be any Robinson-Patman inhibition.[20] One ought not to claim too much for this analysis as a means of explaining what actually occurred in the decided cases. While it serves to bring several of the cases into a semblance of order it does not explain them all, nor has the Court ever articulated this analysis. Nev-

---

15. See the analysis suggested by M. Handler, H. Blake, R. Pitofsky & H. Goldschmid, Trade Regulation, Cases and Materials 287 (Prob. 5) (1975).

16. United States v. E. I. DuPont De Nemours & Co., 351 U.S. 377, 76 S.Ct. 994, 100 L.Ed. 1264 (1956).

17. United States v. Grinnell Corp., 384 U.S. at 574, 86 S.Ct. at 1706, 16 L.E.2d 788.

18. Handler, Blake, Pitofsky & Goldschmid, supra note 15.

19. See ch. 8 infra.

20. Id.

ertheless the analysis offers a useful perspective which might be of aid both in prediction and in advocacy.

§ 18. The Limits of Economic Theory

DuPont exemplifies one risk involved in the integration of antitrust law and economic theory, that a little scientific knowledge may lead to error. Where knowledge is partial it can perhaps be expanded. But there remains a more profound difficulty. It concerns whether our adjudicatory institutions—the judge, jury, advocacy system, rules of evidence, expert testimony, cross examination, argument and instructions—are appropriate and adequate for processing the materials and making the judgments involved in the kind of analysis which an adequately sophisticated use of economic theory demands.

Consider what would be involved in trying to rectify deficiencies in a case like *duPont* by *adequately* exploring in the courtroom the issue whether at prices closely related to cost there was a high positive cross-elasticity of both demand and supply between cellophane and other wraps, and, if so, what the implications might be in respect of *duPont's* power. Presumably experts called by contending sides would introduce competing theoretical and empirical studies leading to opposite conclusions. Cross examination would disclose inevitable weaknesses of each study and the objective, non-expert judge or juror would emerge rather thoroughly confused. Could a jury adequately resolve such an issue, as a predicate to defining a market, as a predicate to gauging the existence of monopoly power, as a predicate to a finding under Section 2? Could a judge usefully instruct a jury in such a task? Could a court sitting without a jury effectively handle such issues?

Courts have moved a long way in improving techniques for handling complex litigation.[1] Knowledgeable and experienced judges can be specially assigned and they can exercise a broad, effective, managerial control over the litigation. But the question remains whether that control should be aimed at trying to make the trial a more precise instrument of social science inquiry, or whether the aim should be the development of more conventionally judicial norms and techniques of administration. Perhaps it will be possible to develop such norms and, in doing so, to maintain consistency with the strong and steady winds of economic doctrine, so long as judges are wise enough to avoid being led to chase after the wisps carried by each new theoretical breeze.[2]

---

1. See, e.g., Manual for Complex and Multidistrict Litigation (Federal Judicial Center, 1970); Judicial Conference of the United States, Report on Procedure in Antitrust and Other Protracted Cases, 13 F.R.D. 62 (1951); Selected Bibliography, Trial of Protracted Litigation, 21 F.R.D. 533 (1957); Handbook of Recommended Procedures for the Trial of Protracted Cases, 25 F.R.D. 351 (1960).

2. See Bok, Section 7 of the Clayton Act and the Merger of Law and Economics, 74 Harv.L.Rev. 226 (1960); compare Neal, "On Implementing a

Look back to the issue presented in *Alcoa*.³ The concern of the law is with market power and its exercise. Economic theory offers useful concepts, such as that of defining the market in which power is to be measured. But the baseline must remain the statutory concern with monopoly in any line of commerce in any section of the country. The law must therefore be concerned about monopolization in any market, however narrow in terms of product or geography, which is by any means substantially insulated from outside competition.⁴ It is this consideration rather than its somewhat tenuous theoretical exposition, that validates what the court did in *Alcoa*.

Economic theory, sensitively utilized, often suggests that there is no one "right" market, but congeries of interlinked "markets," so that any seller faces competitive impacts of ever reducing significance from other firms ranged further and further away from it. Thus, the party asserting monopoly should have no burden other than that of showing a market which is plausible in the sense that those included within it have a clear and substantial commercial advantage over those who are excluded from it in selling to a designated class of customers. This, after all, is the significant aspect in an evaluation of a firm's market power, and the only purpose for defining a market is to organize available data in a way which facilitates judgment about the extent of that power. Where evidence in the form of elaborate economic studies is offered with a view to expanding or narrowing a market which in itself seems a plausible construct, it should be scrutinized critically with a view to its materiality; complex evidence which would likely afford little help to the trier of fact in deciding the ultimate question whether the firm charged with monopoly has great market power ought to be excluded. Such evidence could confuse or misdirect the inquiry; if it is likely to be of little ultimate help, these negative effects ought not to be tolerated.

If the market definition issue in *duPont*⁵ had been approached in this fashion, the Court would have treated cellophane as an appropriate market. Physically, cellophane was a distinct product which had properties not shared by any other wrap. Users regarded it as different and chose between it and other wraps on the basis of its unique physical characteristics. It was also a product market insu-

Policy of Deconcentration," in Industrial Concentration: The New Learning (Goldschmid, Mann & Weston, eds. 1974).

3. United States v. Aluminum Co. of America, 148 F.2d 416 (2d Cir. 1945).

4. E.g., United States v. Addyston Pipe & Steel Co., 85 F. 271 (6th Cir. 1898), modified and aff'd 175 U.S. 211, 20 S. Ct. 96, 44 L.Ed. 136 (1899); United States v. American Tobacco Co., 221 U.S. 106, 31 S.Ct. 632, 55 L.Ed. 663 (1911); United States v. Yellow Cab Co., 332 U.S. 218, 67 S.Ct. 1560, 91 L. Ed. 2010 (1947); and Lorain Journal Co. v. United States, 342 U.S. 143, 72 S.Ct. 181, 96 L.Ed. 162 (1951).

5. United States v. E. I. DuPont De Nemours & Co., 351 U.S. 377, 76 S.Ct. 994, 100 L.Ed. 1264 (1956).

lated from entry by the makers of other wraps through significant patents and other barriers. Given the concern expressed by the language of the statute, that should have been enough to warrant treating cellophane as a separate market, at least absent the most compelling evidence that in terms of the day to day responses of buyers and sellers, the market for cellophane and other wraps was clearly integrated.

Telex Corporation v. IBM [6] displays some of these problems in blatant form. IBM, dominant for decades in calculating machines, had sold its first central data processing unit ("CPU") in the 1950's and quickly obtained a position of dominance in the computer industry, an industry which it was largely responsible for developing. Its position had been eroding, however, as others entered. By 1972 there were eight or nine "major" firms in the computer industry and over 90 firms in all. IBM's share of aggregate industry revenues was about thirty-five percent. Relatively few firms in the industry made CPU's however, and IBM's share of CPU business was larger. One segment of the industry was the manufacture of peripheral devices for use with CPU's. These included information storage units of various kinds, memory units, and terminal devices such as printers.

In the late 1960's firms which did not make CPU's began making peripheral equipment in volume. When they made a peripheral unit it had to be designed and made to be compatible with some one manufacturer's CPU. The firms, including Telex, making peripherals compatible with IBM CPU's made considerable headway. IBM had started with 100% of the revenues from sales of peripherals compatible with its own CPU's. By 1971 other firms were earning over 15% of the current revenue from some types of peripheral devices. IBM then took a number of steps, including price reductions and changes in pricing methods, which cut into the revenues and profits of Telex and, presumably, others.

Telex brought its action under Section 2 and the District Court held that peripheral equipment compatible with IBM CPU's was the relevant market and that IBM had monopolized this market. The Court of Appeals reversed, holding that peripherals for other CPU's should have been included, first, because makers of peripheral equipment could switch from making equipment for CPU's of one manufacturer to making it for those of another with relative ease and, second, because competition between IBM and other CPU makers affected demand for peripherals as part of a total data processing system.

There are, however, an abundance of analytical difficulties. If, as the court seemed to assume, the market choice was between IBM peripherals and all peripherals, the demand side of the market was pretty well locked in to a single manufacturer's equipment once that manufacturer's CPU was contracted for; there was not, on this side

6. 510 F.2d 894 (10th Cir. 1975).

of the market, a ready interchangeability or high cross-elasticity, as the court seemed to imply. Second, even on the supply side, there could be non-technological constraints against a manufacturer's shifting from equipment compatible with one manufacturer's CPU to that compatible with another. Moreover, the two markets considered are not the only possible ones; there is also the question whether IBM gained power because of its position in reference to CPU's. These and peripherals together can be seen as a single functional system. Some subsidiary functions, like memory, are sometimes fully integrated into a CPU, and sometimes performed by a peripheral; in any event, users are interested in an end result, data processing, and many make purchase decisions from that comprehensive vantage point.

One of the most provocative evidentiary matters was the implication taken by the district court that when IBM decreased prices on peripherals it increased prices on CPU's and expected the net effect on its profits of these off-setting changes to be a wash. On the market definition issue, this strongly suggests that CPU's and peripherals are, on the demand side, part of the same market. If they were separate, one might assume that IBM was already pricing CPU's at a profit maximizing level.[7] If so, it could not respond to peripheral competition by lowering peripheral prices and increasing CPU prices without causing itself further losses of profits because of the CPU price change. But if buyers purchase CPU's and peripherals in a more or less fixed relationship and respond in their purchase decisions to aggregate prices for a full, functioning system, then the crucial demand function would be that for the integrated system. On that assumption IBM might within fairly wide limits shift price relationships among components of the total system without affecting its profits appreciably, so long as it left the aggregate price of the system substantially unchanged.

But that analysis does not foreclose the possibility of there being on the supply side a separate market for peripherals ancillary to the CPU market. It may be that there are barriers to entry into the business of making CPU's which do not affect the business of making peripherals. If so, there may be a potential for having much more competition in the peripheral market than in the CPU market. And if it be assumed that there is in this sense a separate peripheral market, does not evidence that IBM can hold profits constant though it decreases peripheral prices and increases CPU prices to hold ultimate system prices more or less constant compel the conclusion that IBM possesses power in that peripheral market?

---

7. Alternatively, if IBM were practicing limit pricing, its ability to increase CPU prices and lower other prices would be less indicative. The increase might merely bring CPU prices closer to maximizing levels and peripheral prices further from maximizing levels.

If the facts are assumed to fall into that configuration, the ultimate question is whether the antitrust laws should be construed so as to encourage the development of, and to protect the existence of, a more competitive market for the supply of peripherals than will exist for the supply of CPU's, even though, to achieve that goal, it may be necessary to regulate the pricing or other conduct of one or more firms that make both CPU's and peripherals in ways that may seem awkward.[8] That is a significant policy question, but it is not a question that economic analysis is particularly helpful in resolving. One might resolve it on the basis of the general commitment of the antitrust laws to competitive markets and on the basis of the assumption that encouraging competition in peripherals may lead eventually to some erosion of power in respect of CPU's.[9]

§ 19. Local, Regional or National Markets

Geographic market definitions are made for the same purpose as product market definitions. If sellers of a product within a given geographic area can increase price or cut production without a prompt flow of supply into the area from outside of it, those sellers are operating in a separate market from sellers in other areas. The scope of a geographic market may vary with a number of factors. Transportation costs obviously have bearing. Legal restrictions such as city licensing requirements may influence the matter. So may barriers to the free flow of market information, the scope of the available distribution network, the scope of relevant advertising media, and the like.[1] A small retailer may realistically be able to reach customers resident within no more than a few miles of his store location; a larger retail outlet, with wide product variety, an advertising budget, and off-street parking facilities may serve a radius of twenty miles or more; a downtown department store may serve an entire metropolitan area. The three operate in different, increasingly larger, geographic markets. Other sellers—a wholesale distributor, or an automobile manufacturer—may be seen as operating in still wider markets, regional or national in scope.[2]

---

8. Problems associated with regulating pricing conduct are discussed in § 47 infra.

9. The issues are not unlike some of those that might be raised in a Sherman Act case against a utility like AT&T. If there is a "natural monopoly" in the provision of telephonic lines, should the monopolist be permitted to price, or engage in other conduct, which inhibits the development, manufacture and distribution of equipment such as telephones for connection to those lines? A negative answer would not necessarily be required by the conclusion that demand was for a functional telephone system with lines and phones.

1. See Elzinga & Hogarty, The Problem of Geographic Market Delineation in Antimerger Suits, 18 Antitrust Bull. 45 (1973).

2. There are examples in the case law of markets of very varied sizes. *National:* United States v. Grinnell Corp., 384 U.S. 563, 86 S.Ct. 1698, 16 L.Ed.2d 778 (1966); United States v. Aluminum Co. of America, 148 F.2d 416 (2d Cir. 1945); *Regional:* United

The guides to geographic market definition, as with product market definition, should be both administrative feasibility and purposeful in application. The area of effective competition may be any commercially significant geographic area which can reasonably be said to confine the relevant commercial activities. If sellers within the area are making price and output decisions protected from the need to take account of sellers outside the area, there is a distinct market. If sellers within the market must take account of sellers outside it, either because those sellers are mobile and can easily come into the area to sell, or because buyers are mobile and can easily go outside of the area to buy, the market is being defined too narrowly.

The case law on geographic market definition is sparse, but informative. In United States v. Addyston Pipe and Steel Company,[3] the Court defined a multistate market, pointing out that more distant sellers were inhibited from entry by freight costs, which were high relative to price. In United States v. Grinnell Corporation [4] where the product was central station protective services, the Court accepted a national market because the defendant sold in all parts of the country, planned nationally, faced insurance rates computed on a national basis which affected sales, and published national price schedules.

The geographic market should be defined in a realistic way. If a particular region or local area such as a municipality is asserted to constitute a separate geographic market in which the power of a firm is to be evaluated, several questions must be asked. One should begin with practical, commercial realities. Do those in the industry perceive the region as a separate market and customarily treat it as one, in the sense that those outside of it make little or no attempt to sell or promote within it? Are sales actually made within the region by firms outside of it, and conversely? Are prices within the region responsive to changes in conditions of demand and supply elsewhere? Are traders beyond the bounds of the region disadvantaged by transportation costs, or the lack of available storage or distribution facilities? Freight rates, and like factors, may be relevant to these inquiries, but the ultimate question is one of seller and buyer conduct—who are the actual traders who are competitive forces?

Again, the question is one of degree. Seldom will there be blatant divisions between geographic market areas. There will be con-

States v. Columbia Steel Co., 334 U.S. 495, 68 S.Ct. 1107, 92 L.Ed. 1533 (1948); Indiana Farmer's Guide Publishing Co. v. Prairie Farmer Publishing Co., 293 U.S. 268, 55 S.Ct. 182, 79 L.Ed. 356 (1934); *Local:* Lorain Journal Co. v. United States, 342 U.S. 143, 72 S.Ct. 181, 96 L.Ed. 162 (1951); Kansas City Star Co. v. United States, 240 F.2d 643 (8th Cir. 1957).

3. 85 F. 271 (6th Cir. 1898), modified and aff'd 175 U.S. 211, 20 S.Ct. 96, 44 L.Ed. 136 (1899). See also United States v. Columbia Steel Co., 334 U.S. 495, 68 S.Ct. 1107, 92 L.Ed. 1533 (1948).

4. 384 U.S. 563, 86 S.Ct. 1698, 16 L.Ed. 778 (1966).

centrations at population centers. There will be some tendency for customers, whether retail consumers or manufacturers, to shop their own and adjacent centers if the product sought is available there. Retail consumers, in general, will be less likely to range widely in search of better terms of trade than would commercial buyers. In all instances the type of product being sold will be significant. Gum and cigarettes are purchased with little if any shopping; appliances or other major purchases may entail considerable shopping. Whatever geographic bounds are perceived, they will not be solid; some customers may be more or less equidistant from two concentrated areas and, by shopping both, will tend to integrate them. Thus, a given geographic market will be integrated in some degree with other markets nearest to it; these, in turn, will be linked to others. Also, barriers between geographic markets will never be impregnable and may vary considerably in their significance. A freight differential may be high enough to keep distant sellers out of a market at current prices, but not so high that they would not enter if local prices increased slightly.

In defining a geographic market, administrative convenience will also be an important guide to choice. A court will wish to consider data as to any adjacent market which may significantly affect the power of firms in the subject market region. It will not, however, wish to burden the record with data as to geographic areas which are so far distant that, as a practical matter, transactions in them will likely have little effect in the subject market region. Though convenience will generally lead to disaggregation, it may call in some cases for aggregations of regions which, on close analysis, appear to constitute separate markets. The *Grinnell* case exemplifies this phenomenon. Defendant there provided central station protective services in urban areas. Since there were technological and other limits upon the breadth of the area that could be served from each station, the business—like the retail food business—would seem to be one in which any power being exercised as a result of seller concentration would have to be based on concentration in particular local markets. Nevertheless, the Court held that evidence that the defendant controlled 87% of the business nationally warranted a finding of power. A firm with such a large percentage of the business nationally would have as high or higher concentrations in many regional or local markets; it might also, because of its size nationally, have advantages over competitors as a buyer of products or services needed in the business. Yet Grinnell, despite its overall size, might well have had a relatively modest share of the business and faced stiff competition in at least some regions or metropolitan areas. If so, in those markets consumers would have clear alternatives and Grinnell might not be exercising power. Though the Supreme Court apparently felt that administrative convenience warranted analysis of power on the basis of the national data, it ordered that in fashioning a remedy the district court consider each regional or local submarket individually. By doing this, the Court reduced the possibility that the seemingly over-broad market definition would have an adverse impact upon the ultimate outcome of the case.

In United States v. Yellow Cab Company,[5] the defendant was charged with monopolizing sales of cabs to affiliated operating companies which controlled 80% of the cab business in Chicago and higher percentages in three other towns. While there seems little question that a local, metropolitan or, at its widest, a regional market would be an appropriate one within which to evaluate the power of a taxicab operating company as a seller of services, it does not follow that the same market definition would be proper where the issue was the power of a company which manufactures and sells taxicabs. A cab company having monopoly power as a seller in the Chicago metropolitan area, need not at all have monopoly power as a buyer of cabs from firms selling nationally to numerous other buyers in places other than Chicago. Nor, unless there is a local market for sales, would the Chicago market seem an appropriate one in which to gauge the power of a firm making all sales of cabs to buyers in that city. Nevertheless, the Court in *Yellow Cab* held that allegations that a monopoly was obtained over the supply of taxicabs to the Chicago area adequately alleged a violation of Section 2.

§ 20. National or International Markets

Alcoa[1] is the only case which raises significant questions bearing on the choice, in defining a market, between a national and an international market. A discussion of this aspect of *Alcoa* may serve to sharpen some of the issues. The court dealt with the geographic question much as though it presented an issue about the scope of the product market. Alcoa produced all of the virgin ingot produced in this country. The court, however, did not say that Alcoa had 100% of the national market. It added to Alcoa's total production the total amount of imported ingot sold in America, thereby computing Alcoa's share at 90%.

But if ingot from foreign sources was relevant at all, why consider only that portion of foreign production actually reaching America for sale? If the court in *Alcoa* was correct in considering any foreign ingot, there must be compelling reasons not to consider all of it—that is, to redefine the market as an international one. The court thought exclusion of the rest of foreign production to be warranted because of the entry barriers occasioned by tariff and transportation costs. Judge Hand reasoned that Alcoa possessed a competition-free breathing room as wide as the cost differential imposed by the tariff and transportation charges upon foreign producers.

---

5. 332 U.S. 218, 67 S.Ct. 1560, 91 L.Ed. 2010 (1947).

1. United States v. Aluminum Co. of America, 148 F.2d 416 (2d Cir. 1945).

The extent to which Alcoa would be constrained by foreign production would depend upon how responsive this substitute source of supply would be to any price change by Alcoa. True, foreign sellers faced a tariff and transportation cost disadvantage; nonetheless, at present levels of operation they obviously enjoyed offsetting cost advantages, perhaps in respect of labor, perhaps in respect of accessability or purity of ore sources, perhaps in respect of availability of cheap power. Otherwise, they would not be selling in America at all and absorbing the transportation and tariff costs. What must be evaluated, therefore, is whether foreign ingot sources could have been rapidly expanded in response to a price advance in America. Were production facilities in other countries working to capacity already? Did limits to existing shipping capacity (and competitive demand for that capacity in other employments) place a ceiling on the amount of foreign ingot which could have reached this country? And what of political factors? If imports went up significantly, would the tariff rate have followed? If foreign sources were highly elastic, foreign ingot could have responded in volume as soon as Alcoa increased ingot prices above current levels, despite transportation and tariff differentials. The court's conclusion—that foreign sources were not relevant to the extent of Alcoa's power—was therefore not justified without evaluation of whether existing levels of imports might have increased in response to a price increase.

Foreign competition, existing and potential, presents a particularly difficult issue when the problem is to measure the power of a firm in the American market. In the setting like *Alcoa,* inquiry should be phrased in terms of whether the concept of a national market for ingot was a valid theoretical construct within which to gauge Alcoa's power. It was clearly established that aluminum moved to America from abroad. Perhaps there were other indicia that a transnational market would be more relevant. Did Alcoa also ship ingot produced here to foreign countries? Were price levels here and, say, in Western Europe, interlinked and responsive to identical stimuli? Did prices in one country respond promptly to increased demand or increased capacity in another country? America may have been merely a submarket within an integrated international market for aluminum. If so, Alcoa's power might be more accurately gauged by computing Alcoa's share of the aggregate production within that integrated international market than by computing only its share of the national market or submarket. For example, if Alcoa had only 5% of a vast international supply capable of responding to demand and supply shifts across national frontiers, one might get a much more realistic concept of Alcoa's position by focusing upon those facts rather than by ignoring them.

There were, of course, many non-economic reasons for hesitating to appraise a firm's power in terms of an international rather than an American market. Even though in *Alcoa* aluminum seemed to flow readily across oceanic barriers, there would certainly be potential political blocks to transnational responses within the international market. A tariff, itself a barrier, is also a symbol—a reminder that international integration of markets is a partial and sometimes a fragile thing, absent commitments and traditions such as those entailed in a well established common market. Additionally, there are a variety of commercial barriers to international trade which do not affect transactions within one national market; transportation facilities may have to be expanded, for example, to facilitate significant shifts in imports or exports.

§ 21. An Eclectic Approach

The position of any seller can be diagramatically represented within a series of concentric circles, each representing groups of other sellers which affect the subject seller less and less directly. In Alcoa's case, other American virgin producers (if any) would be within the innermost circle; domestic secondary producers might be next, followed by: Canadian virgin producers, foreign virgin producers, and producers of copper, or other substitutes.[1]

The court, however, is compelled to simplify. It cannot explore the world economy in order to decide a single monopoly case. When the court draws a line round a relevant market it is making a critical judgment. In effect it is saying, "this data will be weighed and considered in deciding whether defendant is violating the law; that data will not." That judgment is always in part intuitive. Is there a systematic way to inform the intuition? Consider Judge Hand's intuition in *Alcoa*—to drop from consideration all data less proximate than domestic virgin production. Was this more or less valid than an alternative intuition, say, to press the inquiry far enough to include the circles which would comprehend domestic secondary and imported aluminum ingot, but not so far as to pick up other competitive or potentially competitive metals?

There is no Geiger counter which will identify the regions where data will be significant and the regions which may safely be ignored. Nonetheless, there is a methodology that will be an aid to judgment. The "significance" of data is neither a self-defining nor an irreducible concept. In deciding whether to draw a particular set of data into consideration, the court is mediating between two competing interests, the potential utility of the data to refine the court's ultimate substantive judgment about the extent of the firm's power, and the demands of administrative convenience.[2]

For example, before deciding whether to consider data as to recycled ingot production or data as to steel production the *Alcoa* court

---

1. United States v. Aluminum Co. of America, 148 F.2d 416 (2d Cir. 1945).

2. Cf. Rule 403, Rules of Evidence for United States Courts and Magistrates; McCormick, Evidence § 185 (2d ed. Cleary 1972).

might survey in a preliminary way the kind and quality of data available and then inquire along two distinct lines. First, how complex and extensive are the problems of judicial administration which are likely to be encountered if an effort is made to absorb and analyze the data in question and to relate it to other data in the case? Secondly, what if anything is likely to be gained in terms of reducing the likelihood of substantive error in evaluating power if that effort is made? To deal with data about some entirely different industry, such as steel, might complicate the inquiry immensely. It might be necessary to absorb information about a wholly different technology and industrial structure. Unless there is a convincing, preliminary showing that the substantive advantages would be compellingly high, a balancing test indicates that this complexity should be avoided. To deal with the market for foreign virgin aluminum might also be extraordinarily complex. It would be necessary to determine, not only the extent of historical movements, but the potential for increases in foreign shipments which might be stimulated by Alcoa price increases. This would require information as to total foreign production, the nature and elasticity of the foreign supply and of alternative demands now absorbing that portion of foreign production which is not shipped to America, and the extent to which limits on shipping facilities and other blockages might inhibit additional movement.

In *Alcoa,* however, the provisional showing of the importance of the data had perhaps been made; buyers do purchase the foreign product on a parity with the domestic one. Thus, it might be concluded that this data should have been taken into account. To deal with the domestic secondary aluminum market would perhaps be easier; a different technology is entailed, but the industry may not be exceptionally complex. Furthermore, the close relationship between secondary prices and those for virgin ingot suggests that a full inquiry into the elasticity of secondary and its relationship to virgin would be fruitful. If this approach is accepted, the ultimate determination—does this firm have monopoly power?—will often not turn on the one dimensional measure of the firm's share of a single relevant market. Several submarkets might be comprehended by the widest market deemed to be both relevant and material and data as to these narrower markets would also be relevant. Also, the significance of a particular percentage share of the market will vary with whether the market definition is relatively broad or narrow. From all of the relevant structural data (and from the process of analysis through which the court decided which data were relevant and material) the court would then decide the ultimate issue: does the firm possess such a high degree of market power that it could, if it wished, substantially foreclose competition by reducing price and increasing production, thus driving others from the market? The approach here suggested refines, but is not inconsistent with, the case law. In *Alcoa,* for example, Judge Hand obviously did do the underlying analytical task as well as he could on the evidence presented; his ultimate simplification, that Alcoa had 90% of one discernible market, and therefore was a monopoly, can be seen as a symbolic statement of the ultimate, analytical conclusion. Alcoa had enough power over price to foreclose effective competition.

There are in some of the recent cases a harkening back to earlier simplicities, perhaps to the notion suggested (though not adequately developed) in *Standard Oil*[3] that monopoly power may be identified judicially much as it might be identified by informed participants in the market place, on the basis of a confluence of size, history and conduct.[4] For example, in Woods Exploration and Producing Co. v. Alcoa,[5] the court holds that if actual power to exclude competition is observable from its exercise, there is no need to analyze market shares. It is early, as yet, to assert that the courts are moving away from the economists' techniques to reassert the uses of their own, but that prospect is one which bears watching.[6]

PART C. ESTIMATING A FIRM'S STRENGTH

§ 22. Market Concentration

What has already been said implies that the analysis of power found in the cases is limited, perhaps inevitably so. Once the market has been defined, the modern cases look at the degree of concentration within the market, what an economist would call the single firm concentration ratio, the percentage of the total market held by the alleged monopolist. This percentage, computed in terms of relative production or sales volumes or some other surrogate of total productive activity, is indicative of the defendant's position relative to those firms with which it competes.[1]

---

3. Standard Oil Co. of N.J. v. United States, 221 U.S. 1, 31 S.Ct. 502, 55 L. Ed. 619 (1911).

4. See, e.g., Case-Swayne Co. v. Sunkist Growers Inc., 369 F.2d 449, 454–55 (9th Cir. 1966), rev'd on other grounds 389 U.S. 384, 88 S.Ct. 528, 19 L.Ed.2d 621 (1967); Philadelphia World Hockey Club, Inc. v. Philadelphia Hockey Club, Inc., 361 F.Supp. 462 (E.D.Pa.1972); Twin City Sportservice Inc. v. Charles O. Finley & Co. Inc., 365 F.Supp. 235 (N.D.Cal.1972), reversed, 512 F.2d 1264 (9th Cir. 1975); United States v. IBM, 60 F.R.D. 654, 658 (S.D.N.Y.1973).

5. 438 F.2d 1286, 1304–07 (5th Cir. 1971), cert. denied 404 U.S. 1047, 92 S. Ct. 701, 30 L.Ed.2d 736 (1972).

6. See the discussion in Cooper, Attempts and Monopolization: A Mildly Expansionary Answer to the Prophylactic Riddle of Section Two, 72 Mich.L.Rev. 373, 383–384 (1974).

1. United States v. Grinnell Corp., 384 U.S. 563, 86 S.Ct. 1698, 16 L.Ed.2d 778 (1966); United States v. International Boxing Club, of N.Y., Inc., 348 U.S. 236, 75 S.Ct. 259, 99 L.Ed. 290 (1955); United States v. Aluminum Co. of America, 148 F.2d 416 (2d Cir. 1945); United States v. United Shoe Mach. Corp., 110 F.Supp. 295, 344 (D.Mass.1953), aff'd per curiam 347 U.S. 521, 74 S.Ct. 669, 98 L.Ed. 910 (1954).

Monopoly power can be distinguished from a lesser amount of market power only in degree. Just as market definition can be a complex process, so the ultimate judgment about the extent of a firm's power and whether it should be characterized as a monopoly can be extraordinarily complex. The judicial concentration upon the concentration ratio as the prime criteria is a considerable simplification. As we shall see in Sections immediately following this one there are factors in addition to relative size which are plainly relevant to power and which also should be evaluated. Yet there is no doubt that a firm's share of the relevant market, as defined, has been conceded paramount importance.[2]

The *Alcoa* court reached the ultimate factual inference that Alcoa possessed monopoly power simply by pointing to Alcoa's massive 90% share of the relevant market.[3] It reasoned that a firm holding 90% of its market was, as a practical matter, a single firm industry —a monopoly in fact. It went on to say that two-thirds of a market (the percentage suggested by an alternative market definition) would be a doubtful case, and that one-third of a market (the share resulting when the widest potential market definition was used) would be too small to constitute monopoly.[4] Other courts have made similarly explicit pronouncements; in deciding whether monopoly exists they focus hard upon the percentage share of the one "market" which they have defined as "appropriate" even though that particular definition is only one of several plausible definitions.[5] In *Grinnell*,[6] 87% of a national market (made up by aggregating some services and excluding others) was held to constitute monopoly. In one recent case control of about 60% of a market was held to be monopoly.[7] In two of the earlier cases United States v. U.S. Steel Corporation[8] and United States v. International Harvester Company,[9] the Court found no monopoly power to exist where firms controlled 50% and 64% of their respective markets. *United Shoe Machinery*[10] here, as in market defi-

2. See cases cited in note 1 supra.

3. United States v. Aluminum Co. of America, supra note 1.

4. Id. at 424.

5. E.g., United States v. United Shoe Mach. Corp., supra note 1. See also the other cases cited in note 1 supra.

6. United States v. Grinnell Corp., 384 U.S. 563, 571, 86 S.Ct. 1698, 1704, 16 L.Ed.2d 778, 786 (1966).

7. Amplex of Md., Inc. v. Outboard Marine Corp., 380 F.2d 112 (4th Cir. 1967), cert. denied 389 U.S. 1036, 88 S. Ct. 768, 19 L.Ed.2d 823 (1968). See also Cliff Food Stores, Inc. v. Kroger, Inc., 417 F.2d 203, 207 note 2 (5th Cir. 1969) (something more than 50% essential).

8. 251 U.S. 417, 40 S.Ct. 293, 64 L.Ed. 343 (1920).

9. 274 U.S. 693, 47 S.Ct. 748, 71 L.Ed. 1302 (1927). See also United States v. Eastman Kodak Co., 226 F. 62 (W.D. N.Y.1915), appeal dismissed 255 U.S. 578, 41 S.Ct. 321, 65 L.Ed. 795 (1921) (75 to 80% constitutes monopoly); United States v. E. I. DuPont De Nemours & Co. 351 U.S. 377, 76 S.Ct. 994, 100 L.Ed. 1264 (1956) (20% does not constitute monopoly; an implication that 75% would).

10. United States v. United Shoe Mach. Corp., supra note 1 at 343.

nition, is most sensitive to the intricacies. Judge Wyzanski's opinion gave considerable weight to a finding that defendant had an overwhelming market share (75% or more) but, as we shall see, relied on other factors also and took no position upon whether that share, alone, would warrant an inference of power; the court also said that less than 50% of a defined market did not prima facie indicate monopoly, thus implying that by proving through other facts that a firm with that share had power over price, a violation could be proved.

The passion of most courts for concrete, specific norms in the area is understandable enough. It would be a boon if there were available a self-executing, two dimensional structural test for monopoly power—if the need were simply to define the market and compute defendants share to see if it exceeds a critical threshold. It would be a boon, at least were it accurate; and there is the rub. Unless we are ready to accept the risk of many "false positives" (if we put the critical percentage too low) or many "false negatives" (if we put it too high) we cannot have such a simple test for power. The first difficulty with a rigid analysis like the 30-60-90 rule of *Alcoa* is that it makes too much of the single market definition ultimately selected as appropriate; it obscures the fact that a number of circumstances, few of which can be precisely gauged, must affect the ultimate question of power. The second difficulty with the self-executing rule approach is that, even assuming that in every case the market were "correctly" defined, the significance of any given percentage on the question of power would vary with other structural factors—the height of entry barriers, the point in any monopolistic price rise at which potential competition from outside the market would become actual, for example. The most insightful thing the Court has ever said on this topic is that "[t]he relative effect of percentage command of a market varies with the setting in which that factor is placed." [11] Indeed, data suggested by alternative market definitions may be relevant, as well as other factors. Also, there may be conduct or performance evidence which will be suggestive of the existence or non-existence of substantial market power.

Focus in the cases upon precise ways of measuring the degree of domination and on finding thresholds which permit clear answers, tends to obscure the more important problem of clearly articulating at a general level what is meant by monopoly. Monopoly has been defined as sufficient power over price to exclude competitors, but we know that there are never any absolutes. No firm can ignore others entirely in setting price; at some point customers will find ways to turn elsewhere and other sellers will find ways to meet the customers' needs. Monopoly, then, obviously does not mean absolute power over price or to exclude competitors. Nor are the references to fixing

---

11. United States v. Columbia Steel Co., 334 U.S. 495, 528, 68 S.Ct. 1107, 1124, 92 L.Ed. 1533, 1554 (1948).

prices and to exclusion of competitors intended to imply two separate standards. As the Court said in *duPont (Cellophane)*, "price and competition are so internally intertwined" [12] that the usual formulation is merely a convenient way to suggest a single test—whether a firm has sufficient power to raise prices, and whether it could, by lowering prices, exclude competitors from the market.

The ultimate test ought to be whether a firm has a *substantial* degree of power to exclude competitors by reducing price,[13] and still be profitable. Substantiality is a matter not for precise measurement, but for informed judgment. A norm of self-executing precision is no more warranted, nor more needed, here than in other areas of the law where such general standards govern. A variety of factors may be appropriate for consideration in making the judgment, and guidance can be given and obtained as the courts identify these and exemplify their use. In the sections which follow some of these will be considered.

§ 23. Entry Barriers

When it is recognized that structural analysis is aimed not at discovering some objectively valid single market and measuring a firm's share, but at gauging the extent of a firm's power to foreclose competitors by reducing price, attention is drawn to facts other than single firm concentration percentages. "The relative effect of percentage command of a market varies with the setting in which that factor is placed." [1] Therefore, in an analysis of market power, structural features in addition to market share must be considered.

Entry barriers and barriers to expansion are particularly crucial; no structural analysis is complete without considering these factors which may affect the significance of determinations about the degree of concentration.[2] If the industry is one in which existing firms could rapidly expand production and in which outsiders could rapidly enter if prices were pushed significantly above competitive levels, even a share as large as 90% of a plausibly defined market or submarket may not confer massive power. By contrast, even a firm with substantially less than 50%, because of a significant natural advantage (like prime ore sources) or a comparable patent advantage, might be operating at substantially lower costs than other firms and be the only firm capable of expanding output without significantly in-

---

12. United States v. E. I. DuPont De Nemours & Co., supra note 9.

13. Turner, Antitrust Policy and the Cellophane Case, 70 Harv.L.Rev. 281, 302 (1956).

1. United States v. Columbia Steel Co., 334 U.S. 495, 528, 68 S.Ct. 1107, 1124, 92 L.Ed. 1533, 1544 (1948).

2. See United States v. United Shoe Mach. Corp., 110 F.Supp. 295 (D. Mass.1953), aff'd per curiam 347 U.S. 521, 74 S.Ct. 669, 98 L.Ed. 910 (1954) for an example of a judicial analysis of entry barriers.

creasing its per unit cost. If other firms are already making no more than a competitive return, they would not be able to counter a price cut without significant loss. The firm below 50% would possess the power to drive all others out of the market at any time it elected to do so. Despite statements in some of the cases about 60% being a borderline, such a firm, having massive market power—being able to control access to the market—ought to be called a monopolist. A firm does not cease to be a monopolist when it permits others to share its market by sufferance.

Conceding the importance of entry barriers, how does a court or a lawyer determine whether they are present? What is known about the nature of entry barriers?[3]

Scale economies can be an important barrier. Suppose that there are three firms in an industry, the smallest with 20% of output, and that the most efficient scale for operation in the industry is so large, relative to total industry output, that no firm can operate at the lowest possible per unit cost without producing an amount equal to 20% or more of current total industry production. Entry will be greatly inhibited. Any firm considering entry would not expect the existing firms to suffer such a large diversion. Drastic price and other responses could be expected. Few would-be entrants would be eager to take on the battle of ousting others from such a large share of the market. Entry at a smaller scale might be possible, of course, but only by a firm ready to accept a cost disadvantage such that it would be able to sell profitably only if the existing firms priced high enough above their (lower) costs to allow the new firm to continue operating. There are industries where barriers of magnitudes comparable to these enhance significantly the power attributable to any given market share.[4] In such a market an entrant would be at best a fringe firm operating at the sufferance of the existing firm or firms. Entry barriers may also result from ownership of scarce resources, from vertical integration, from patent research and development policies and from the level and type of promotion expenditures,[5] and from various resource acquisition and product marketing policies.

3. See generally, J. Bain, Barriers to New Competition (1956); F. Scherer, Industrial Market Structure and Economic Performance, 216–20, 226–33, 275–77 (1970).

4. Bain lists minimum plant scale for tractors as 10–15% of national capacity, that for typewriters as 10–30%, that for auto component production and car assembly as 5–10%. Bain, supra note 3, at 72, 84. Another study shows household refrigerators and freezers as 14.1%. Scherer, Beckenstein, Kaufer, & Murphy, The Economics of Multi-Plant Operation: An International Comparison Study, ch. 3 (1975). Consideration of products having regional markets could be expected to increase the number of industries in which scale barriers are significant. For a detailed study illustrating many of the problems see, for example, McGee, Economics of Scale in Auto Body Production, 16 J. Law & Econ. 239 (1973).

5. See generally, Scherer, supra note 3, at 230–31.

United Shoe Machinery is instructive about the significance of entry barriers. The evidence showed a large market share but the court did not predicate a finding of power on this fact alone; it identified numerous barriers to entry, which, conjunctively, indicated that United's market share gave it massive power. These barriers included: an accumulation of patents which in their multiplicity and complexity would deter an entrant from seeking ways to breach United's defense against competitive technology;[6] a pricing policy which kept returns low on the simplest of the company's machines (those most likely to attract would-be competitors to enter) and high on more complex machines;[7] a static or declining aggregate industry demand (which tended to make the industry unattractive to new investment),[8] and various marketing practices (such as a "lease only" policy which also encouraged a firm which leased one United machine to lease other machines from it).[9] The court concluded that these factors greatly reduced the opportunities for rivals to attract business from United.[10]

This was significant doctrinal movement. Judge Wyzanski drew upon Judge Hand's opinion in *Alcoa*,[11] but refined the analysis. There was frank recognition that defining the market is not an act of discovery, but an act of judgment. There was also recognition that no share of any market accords power (at least beyond the very short run) except to the extent that the market is insulated from rapid and easy entry by firms beyond its borders. The dynamics of market power were delineated.

§ 24. Other Structural Features

In gauging power, other structural features, in addition to concentration ratios and entry barriers, may be important in particular settings. One circumstance which may be relevant is the manner in which the shares of the non-dominant firms are distributed. A firm having 60% of a market may have greater single firm power if the remaining 40% is held by 20 firms, each with about 5%, than if it is held by 5 firms each with about 20%.[1] If one or more firms among the five had an ambition to grow and a taste for competition, they

---

6. United States v. United Shoe Mach. Corp., 110 F.Supp. 295, 332–33 (D. Mass.1953), aff'd per curiam, 347 U.S. 521, 74 S.Ct. 669, 98 L.Ed. 910 (1954).

7. Id. at 325–29.

8. Id. at 301.

9. Id. at 314–25.

10. Id. See also Philadelphia World Hockey Club, Inc. v. Philadelphia Hockey Club, Inc., 351 F.Supp. 462 (E.D. Pa.1972) holding that a reserve clause in league player contracts was exclusionary. Compare United States v. Standard Oil Co. of Cal., 362 F.Supp. 1331 (N.D.Cal.1972), aff'd mem., 412 U.S. 924, 93 S.Ct. 2750, 37 L.Ed. 152 (1973).

11. United States v. Aluminum Co. of America, 148 F.2d 416 (2d Cir. 1945).

1. On the other hand, the joint exercise of power through direct or indirect collusion might be easier in the market of fewer sellers. See § 117 infra.

might discipline the dominant firm significantly. Another factor which might have significance is the degree to which industry products are homogeneous.[2] For example, successful product differentiation might make a large firm's market share more significant than it would be if other firms were producing an identical product. If other firms tried to increase their shares by lowering price, their chances of success would be greater in a market for a homogeneous product where price would be of predominant importance and cross-elasticity between suppliers within the industry very high.

Another factor is the long run condition of the industry. If it is expanding, a given share will have less significance than if it is contracting. Justice Wyzanski took note of this in *United Shoe Machinery*.[3]

§ 25. Conduct Analysis

A theoretical assumption of neo-classical economic theory is that a firm will seek to maximize its profits, though some of the later literature supposes that large firms where ownership and management are separated may aim at maximizing other values, such as sales or gross revenues.[1] The particular kinds of conduct such a goal will dictate may vary depending upon the extent of a firm's market power. The firm conscious of its market power will recognize its ability to affect price by its output decisions and can be expected to seek an optimum price-output level. Even if it is a sales or revenue maximizer, rather than a profit maximizer, the firm may aim for an "acceptable" or a "target" profit, and manipulate price and output to achieve the highest possible sales at a price which produces the acceptable return. A firm operating within a market structure where it possesses or can gain power will be aware of its own potency and potential; in striving to maximize profits (or other related values) it will act in ways aimed at preserving and enhancing its endowment of market power. By contrast, a firm in a competitive market will take price as given. Its decisions about output will reflect only its costs and its expectation about how market price may vary.

Given these assumptions about the difference between the way in which a powerful firm will act and that in which a powerless firm will act, a theoretical basis is established for looking directly at con-

---

2. F. Scherer, Industrial Market Structure and Economic Performance 186–192 (1970).

3. United States v. United Shoe Mach. Corp., 110 F.Supp. 295 (D.Mass.1953), aff'd per curiam 347 U.S. 521, 74 S.Ct. 669, 98 L.Ed. 910 (1954).

1. The traditional price theory models assume rational profit maximization. More recent literature, taking account of empirical findings, suggests that the economic goal perceived by the managers of a firm may be different —for example, to maximize sales, so long as this can be done at some acceptable profit level, or to achieve a satisfactory revenue flow. See F. Scherer, Industrial Market Structure and Economic Performance 27–36 and the literature there cited.

duct in seeking to decide whether a firm has market power. If a firm acts as though it possesses market power, the trier of fact may infer that it possesses such power.

A few illustrations will suffice. Suppose a firm is found to set its price on the basis of a decision about the profit which it concludes that it needs, taking account of considerations like its need for capital sources for expansion or replacement of capital equipment, its need for adequate dividends to assure a stable market for its stock, and other factors, perhaps including the possibility that a return above a certain level may stimulate entry. Such pricing conduct, which has been identified, for example, in the steel industry,[2] indicates a consciousness of substantial power. Alternatively, a firm may by some conduct of its own explicitly identify those which it regards as its competitors[3] or may do things to inhibit entry—say, threatening to stop selling to its customers, or to stop buying from its suppliers, if they buy from or sell to a would be entrant;[4] such a strategy would be rational only for a firm with substantial power.

It is argued against a conduct approach to the assessment of power that conduct and its purposes and effects are inherently ambiguous, that predatory conduct is rare and that, for example, the line between a pricing or (spending) policy aimed at driving (or keeping) out competitors, and competitive pricing or spending, is often well-nigh impossible to draw.[5] The unstated premise, of course, is that structural evidence is less ambiguous. But we have seen the indeterminacies that abound in the application of structural analysis; these are intrinsic and, let us recall, are emphasized because the judicial system, particularly the jury system, which can handle issues of conduct and even motive with some degree of comfort, is ill-equipped to deal skillfully with structural analysis. Moreover, the active issue is not whether conduct analysis should be substituted for structural analysis, but whether the two approaches should be used conjunctively.

Courts have intuitively recognized that conduct can be an indication of power. In the early cases, the courts relied almost entirely on

---

2. See, e.g., Adelman, Steel Administered Prices and Inflation, 75 Q.J. of Econ. 16 (1961).

3. Compare United States v. E. I. Du Pont De Nemours & Co., 351 U.S. 377, 418, 76 S.Ct. 994, 1019, 100 L.Ed. 1264, 1293 (1956) (Warren, C. J. dissenting).

4. See §§ 83–86 infra.

5. See, e.g., Koller, The Myth of Predatory Pricing—an Empirical Study, 4 Antitrust L. & Econ.Rev. 105 (1971); Telser, Cutthroat Competition and the Long Purse, 9 J.L. & Econ. 259 (1966).

Predatory pricing and spending may be quite rare and is difficult to prove, though as Areeda and Turner have established, administrable standards can be worked out for identifying it. Areeda & Turner, Predatory Pricing and Related Practices Under Section 2 of the Sherman Act, 88 Harv.L.Rev. 697 (1975). The point being made here is in any event much broader. If a firm develops any pricing strategy, other than selling at the market price, it has indicated a conciousness of some degree of power; and there are countless other ways a firm may act which signify in a similar manner.

conduct for evidence of power;[6] a defendant was deemed to have power over market price, or power to exclude competitors, when such power was overtly used. In United States v. Addyston Pipe and Steel Co.,[7] for example, the Court gave great weight to market price increases as a manifestation of power. Exclusion of competitors was read as signifying power in the oil[8] and tobacco[9] trust cases of 1911.

Alcoa[10] is another important example of the use of conduct analysis as a basis for making a judgment about power. The court noted that early in its development and growth the firm had entered into contracts tending to restrict market access. In contracting for water power, it required suppliers to agree not to supply other aluminum producers; it also entered into foreign cartels. These and other aspects of Alcoa's conduct, while insufficient of themselves to confirm the conclusion that the firm possessed monopoly power, were consistent with that conclusion. Its market conduct was far different from that of a firm in a competitive market. Similarly, in the shoe machinery case,[11] the court in passing upon whether the defendant possessed market power drew conduct into the analysis. It focused particularly on exclusionary practices with respect to leasing, patent accumulation, and price discrimination. All of these Judge Wyzanski saw as indicative that the company possessed substantial power.

An interesting recent example of the use of conduct as evidence of power appears in Denver Petroleum Corp. v. Shell Oil Co.[12] Plaintiff offered evidence of an oil company's imposition of large location differentials in pricing in an effort to show exclusionary practices. While refusing to characterize the differentials as exclusionary, the court stated that a firm without power would not have been able to enforce them due to competitive choices open to customers. Thus, the differentials served as evidence of the existence of monopoly power.[13]

§ 26. Performance Analysis—In General

If monopoly power exists and is exercised, a deficient market performance (increased prices and profits, as well as other aberra-

---

6. See § 10, supra.

7. 175 U.S. 211, 237, 20 S.Ct. 96, 105–106, 44 L.Ed. 136, 146 (1899).

8. Standard Oil Co. of N. J. v. United States, 221 U.S. 1, 31 S.Ct. 502, 55 L.Ed. 619 (1911).

9. United States v. American Tobacco Co., 221 U.S. 106, 31 S.Ct. 632, 55 L.Ed. 663 (1911).

10. United States v. Aluminum Co. of America, 148 F.2d 416 (2d Cir. 1945).

11. United States v. United Shoe Mach. Corp., 110 F.Supp. 295 (D.Mass.1953), aff'd per curiam 347 U.S. 521, 74 S.Ct. 669, 98 L.Ed. 910 (1954).

12. 306 F.Supp. 289, 296–297 (D.Colo. 1969).

13. Compare United States v. Grinnell Corp., 384 U.S. 563, 86 S.Ct. 1698, 16 L.Ed. 778 (1966); United States v. Klearflax Linen Looms, Inc., 63 F.Supp. 32 (D.Minn.1945).

tions) can be expected to result.[1] That is an important reason for social concern about the existence of monopoly power. But the results of such power (in addition to being a reason why power should be dissipated) might serve also as a subsidiary method for determining whether power exists. If a market performs like a monopoly market, it can be inferred that it is a monopoly market.

While this approach may be of some value, it has some grave difficulties. Performance analysis entails developing theoretical norms and empirical information about such matters as complex cost-price interactions, demand-price and demand-inventory interactions, progressiveness, relationships between capacity and output, and the character and level of selling expenditures. The analyst must develop a model of the way the subject firm would perform in these and other particulars if, on the one hand, it had a high degree of market power or, on the other, it did not. The actual performance of the firm must then be compared with the theoretical models and a conclusion reached about the extent of the firm's power. In the present state of the economic art, and given the limits of adjudication as a source of objective and subtle truth about economic relationships, this is not a highly reliable process; indeterminacies and unverifiable judgments will abound.

Those who have pressed for the adoption of performance criteria as the primary or exclusive way of determining whether markets are workably competitive [2] are for these reasons unconvincing. It is fortunate that courts have responded so little to their call But where a market is being analyzed in some depth, as it must be in a monopoly case—we have seen, surely, that simple, self-executing, structural criteria cannot be depended upon—[3] a review of salient aspects of performance may not add greatly to the burden and may help considerably to inform the judgment. Kaysen's analysis of the shoe machinery industry can serve usefully as a model.[4] The process of gauging power is a judgment, not a measurement; structural analysis is never precise and often leaves important questions at least somewhat doubtful. If performance data appears to signify, it should not be arbitrarily excluded.

1. J. Bain, Price Theory 197–207 (1952); Bain, Workable Competition in Oligopoly: Theoretical Considerations and Some Empirical Evidence, 40 Am.Econ.Rev. 35, 37–38 (1950).

2. E.g., A. Kaplan, Big Enterprise in a Competitive System ch. 2 (1954). Compare Mason, The Current Status of the Monopoly Problem in the United States, 62 Harv.L.Rev. 1265 (1949).

3. § 21 supra.

4. C. Kaysen, United States v. United Shoe Machinery Corporation, particularly the discussion at 16–20 (1956). See also Stocking, Economic Tests of Monopoly and the Concept of the Relevant Market, 2 Antitrust Bull. 479, 485–86 (1957); Adelman, Effective Competition and the Antitrust Laws, 61 Harv.L.Rev. 1289 (1948).

§ 27. Profits

Profit evidence has in several cases been introduced and evaluated on the issue of power. *Alcoa*,[1] once again, should be noted. The company there showed that it had over a substantial period failed to earn supra-competitive profits and asserted that this constituted performance evidence that it lacked monopoly power. If it were a monopolist, Alcoa contended, it would have earned a monopolist's profit, not merely a reasonable profit such as a firm facing substantial competition can expect to earn. The court was not persuaded. It noted that monopoly was asserted only as to part of Alcoa's business, but that the profit evidence had not been segregated so as to show specifically the results for that crucial portion, ingot production. It may have been that profits were high here, but that Alcoa, facing competition, did poorly in the fabricating business—thus earning only a modest overall return.

This kind of an objection can be generalized. The profit evidence offered in *Alcoa* and usually offered on the issue of market power is bookkeeping profit—the pre-tax profit available for dividends or reinvestment. This sum is then contrasted with "average" profits of some kind, usually those for manufacturing industries. The theoretical question, however, is whether the firm, due to market power, can earn excess profits—that is, a higher return than the minimum which would be needed to attract the necessary investment into the industry. The data offered is often hard to read as bearing directly on this issue and courts have been skeptical about relying on it.[2]

In the first place, profit will not vary only with power. It will vary, for example, with risk. Unless the industry in question happens to be an average risk industry, a normal profit would be higher or lower than the average profit of all industries. Even if conditions in the industry are more or less average, its profits are not likely to be average; there is to be expected some random variation around any norm that may be established. High profit will also be associated with good performance where good performance has yielded significant innovation; others may enter in time and drive profit down again, but they cannot do so immediately. Additionally, a firm's bookkeeping profit is not necessarily a fair statement of its economic profit. Book profit may be overstated or understated because of the

---

1. United States v. Aluminum Co. of America, 148 F.2d 416 (2d Cir. 1945).

2. E.g., "Years of profit do not establish monopoly power over prices. They establish this: duPont was an efficient business company. Monopoly cases do not rest on such insubstantial evidence to support complete power over price." United States v. E. I. DuPont De Nemours & Co. 118 F. Supp. 41, 208 (D.Del.1953) (Leahy, J.), aff'd on other grounds 351 U.S. 377, 76 S.Ct. 994, 100 L.Ed. 1264 (1956). See also the reciprocal hesitancy to accept low profits as evidence of lack of power in United States v. Aluminum Co. of America, 148 F.2d 416 (2d Cir. 1945).

conventions used to value inventory and to value and depreciate capital equipment, or because of the impacts of any one of several other bookkeeping conventions.[3] For all of these reasons, even if Alcoa's bookkeeping profit were allocated by plausible techniques to the firm's ingot operations, one might hesitate to infer that its earnings were "normal" in the economic sense.

The court in *Alcoa* had other objections to the use of profit evidence. The opinion points out that failure to exploit power by exacting excessive profits is no defense to a charge of monopoly. Since the meaning of this observation is not entirely clear, it may be useful to assume that "economic profits" can be segregated out, and that a "normal" level for that industry can and has been determined, and to consider, on those assumptions, the inferences about performance that might be warranted.

Profit evidence could confirm the existence of market power. If a firm earns substantially higher than normal profits over a prolonged period, that performance would warrant an inference that the firm (either alone, if no other firm in the market has similar profits, or conjunctively with others, if others in the market have similar profits) possesses substantial market power. Indeed, there is no better evidence of power, if we assume that we have adequately measured the firm's profits, accurately judged what profit is "normal" given the risks of the industry, and witnessed results over a sufficiently long period so that factors like a new innovation or a recent demand surge cannot explain the phenomenon. In a competitive market, entry will in the long run be stimulated so long as a new entrant at efficient scale could obtain returns at least equal to per unit costs of production, including a profit equivalent to that which could be achieved by investment elsewhere, adjusted for any difference in risk. In such a market, the tendency will therefore be for sufficient resources to be introduced to push production up to the point where prices fall to the level of average costs; excessive profits will tend to be squeezed out.

But as Judge Hand stated, even the prolonged absence of excessive profits would not necessarily signal a lack of market power. A firm could be a monopolist, though earning no more than a competitive return; it might be using or wasting its power in ways which distort other aspects of performance. A monopolist may pay excessive salaries or wages, or otherwise function inefficiently. It might be trying to price close to normal profits, just a little above that level, to discourage efforts to enter from outside the industry, and may be missing its target, hitting a profit level a bit lower than necessary for that purpose, as the matter is retrospectively evaluated. Or it may be a "good" monopolist, deliberately pricing at competitve levels

---

3. See, e.g., Brozen, "Significance of Profit Data for Antitrust Policy" in Public Policy Toward Mergers 110, 116–120 (J. Weston & S. Peltzman eds. 1969).

even though possessing power to exceed them. Before inferring a lack of power from performance, one ought to evaluate performance far more comprehensively than merely to look at profits.

The Supreme Court's response to profit evidence in *duPont (Cellophane)*[4] is also of interest. Evidence suggested that the defendant was earning excessive profits, though this was subject to many of the same doubts as was the normal profit evidence in *Alcoa*. It will be recalled that the Court approached the issue of power by asking whether various substitute flexible wraps limited duPont's ability to control the price for cellophane. In holding that they did, the Court felt no need to explain why duPont nevertheless earned what was arguably an excessive profit. Convincing evidence of excessive profits over a long period might strongly tend to support an inference of power. But large returns for a short period may signify no more than that demand has increased and new investment has not yet caught up.[5]

§ 28. Responsiveness of Price

Excessive profits is not the only performance deficiency which is theoretically associated with monopoly power. Pricing in a market dominated by a single firm may tend to be rigid and unresponsive to changes in supply and demand. This is not an inevitable development, and the reasons for it are not immediately apparent; however, the tendency is strong enough so that this aspect of performance should be evaluated in making judgments about power.

To understand why a monopolist's prices will tend to be rigid, it is necessary to recall what classical theory teaches about pricing in a monopolized industry. Note first that in any industry the demand curve for the industry as a whole will slope downward; at any given time, buyers as a whole will buy fewer products if prices are relatively high than if any are relatively low. In a competitive industry, the individual firm will perceive this fact as irrelevant to its own price making. Its individual demand curve, unlike the industry curve, will be horizontal at the current price. It can sell all it has at this price, need not take less and cannot get more, for if it tried, buyers would turn elsewhere. By contrast, the individual firm demand curve of a monopolist will replicate the downward slope of the industry curve. In effect, the firm is the industry. It will be aware of its power to charge more by making and selling less or to sell more by charging less. It is this fact which enables the monopolist to set a profit maximizing price for itself which is higher than the price which would

---

4. United States v. E. I. DuPont De Nemours & Co., 351 U.S. 377, 76 S.Ct. 994, 100 L.Ed. 1264 (1956).

5. Compare United States v. General Elec. Co., 82 F.Supp. 753 (D.N.J.1949), holding that profit evidence can be considered on the issue of whether monopoly power is present.

prevail, other things being equal, if the structure of the industry were competitive.[1]

Given these circumstances, any monopolist which accounted for *all* of the output of its industry and which was confident that no other firm could enter its market, would have the same incentive as firms in a competitive market to alter price upward and downward as demand and supply conditions changed. If the goal is to maximize returns, price would have to be changed from time to time in both types of industries to respond to changes in prevailing conditions.

But in actual markets, the "monopolist" will rarely if ever control all output. Monopoly is sufficient power to exercise substantial control over price and output. There will almost always be others in or at the edge of the market, perhaps a few firms each with fairly sizable outputs, perhaps a fairly large number of small firms. In the aggregate, the output of these other firms could well be as high as 30% of total industry production.[2] So long as the dominant firm had power, acting alone, to drive them out by lowering price, it would be a monopolist under the governing legal definition.[3]

The existence of these other firms in the industry will affect the pricing policies of the monopolist. Not wanting to encourage them to try to expand their output and challenge its dominance, it will tend to seek out a price which is acceptable to it and also sufficiently acceptable to smaller rivals so that they will not become restive. Once such a price is attained it will have considerable inertial force; the dominant firm will be disinclined to change it in response to relatively small fluctuations in demand and supply conditions.

Also, entry barriers are rarely so high that the monopolist will feel totally safe from the risk of new entry. For this reason it may be disinclined to adopt a policy of maximizing short run profits. The tendency will be to adopt a price above the level where competitive returns are gained, but not so high as to encourage significant new entry.[4] This strategy will also tend toward price rigidity.

Finally, a firm with monopoly power is, in a sense, freed of the implacable pressure of the market. A firm in a competitive industry must maximize profits if it is to survive at all because the maximum profit it is capable of earning is no more than a reasonable return on its investment. A firm with monopoly power faces no such plight. It can, if it wishes, elect an alternative pricing strategy; it can seek to maximize sales, to maximize cash flow, or to achieve the best possible image as a good corporate citizen.[5] Any pricing strategy alternative

1. F. Scherer, Industrial Market Structure and Economic Performance, 11–19 (1970). See Appendix A.

2. See, e.g. United States v. Aluminum Co. of America, 148 F.2d 416 (2d Cir. 1945).

3. See § 7, supra.

4. Scherer, supra note 1, at 216–30.

5. Id. at 27–36.

to profit maximization is likely to invite more stable prices and fewer changes as demand and supply conditions alter.

The case law indicates that inferences about structure and power may be drawn from evidence about pricing. The Court has stated, for example, that "an artificial price level not related to the supply and demand of a given product may be evidence from which * * * agreement or understanding or some concerted action of sellers operating to restrain commerce may be inferred."[6] American Tobacco Co. v. United States,[7] also inferred that pricing conduct not responsive to underlying conditions was indicative of monopoly power.[8] In *Pfizer*,[9] evidence about price was used in an interesting way in an effort to show power. In the drug industry there had been a history of price reductions as new broad spectrum drugs were introduced. However, the prices of these drugs remained substantially identical and unchanged for about a decade, despite the introduction of tetracycline, which rapidly became the most important single broad spectrum product. During this period of identical, inflexible prices, demand for tetracycline first increased rapidly and then declined, production costs substantially and steadily declined, and market shares among producers varied significantly. The trial court had instructed that the jury could infer conspiracy to maintain prices and to monopolize from the failure of price to respond to demand and supply conditions, and from the excessive profits which resulted. On appeal, the court stated that if the government had tried the case on the theory of a general course of conduct by defendants, this instruction "might well have been apposite."[10] However, because the government had framed the indictment and bill of particulars more narrowly, the introduction of price and profit evidence was prejudicial error.

§ 29. Price Discrimination

In the economic sense, price discrimination is the sale of products to different buyers at prices which do not have the same ratios as do the costs of supplying the products.[1] If the cost of selling one unit to A is 10 and the price is 15, while the cost of selling one unit to B is 8 and the price is 11, or 13, there has been discrimination. Similarly,

---

6. Cement Mfrs. Protective Ass'n v. United States, 268 U.S. 588, 606, 45 S.Ct. 586, 592, 69 L.Ed. 1104, 1112, (1926).

7. 328 U.S. 781, 66 S.Ct. 1125, 90 L.Ed. 1575 (1946).

8. The inference of joint monopoly was there supported by evidence that defendants earned "tremendous profits" by increasing their prices during a period of declining costs and maintaining the increase despite a period of falling demand.

9. United States v. Charles Pfizer & Co., Inc., 426 F.2d 32 (2d Cir. 1970) aff'd per curiam by an equally divided court, 404 U.S. 548, 92 S.Ct. 731, 30 L.Ed.2d 721 (1972).

10. Id. at 39.

1. See, e.g., W. Bowman, Patents and Antitrust Law 100–116 (1973). In Chapter 8 the price discrimination law is discussed; discrimination within the meaning of that law is a very different concept from discrimination in the economic sense.

if the cost of selling to two customers is the same and the price is different, there has been discrimination.

A firm will not discriminate unless it has market power. In a competitive market, a firm cannot sell above the competitive price and has no reason to sell below it; all its sales will cluster at its costs (including a reasonable return). Differences in price between one group or category of sales and another will be reflective of differences in associated costs. For a firm with power, however, this is not necessarily so. We can assume that if it must set a single price to all that the price will be at the profit maximizing level. To lower price further would mean more sales, but the added (the "marginal") revenue would be less than the added cost of making and supplying the additional product. The additional sales add to revenue, even at the lowered price, since but for the reduction, these sales would not be made at all. But these sales can only be made if the price is reduced to all, including those who would buy at the higher price. The net increase in revenue will thus be less than the revenue yielded by the additional sales. But if discrimination is possible, price can be reduced to pick up new customers, thus adding to total revenue, without reducing price to all customers. The total contribution to revenue of the new sales will thus be higher. A firm with power may thus have a motive to discriminate. Of course to successfully do so it will have to be able to segregate its customers into separate categories for price purposes and keep those in the low price category from reselling to those in the higher price category at some intermediate price.[2]

If price discrimination persists in a market over a long period, the inference can be drawn that the firm practicing it possesses substantial market power.[3] Though no court has yet flatly held that an inference of monopoly power may be based in part on such evidence, the court in *United Shoe Machinery*[4] was obviously influenced to some degree by evidence of discrimination, upon which it commented at length.

§ 30. Limitations of Performance Analysis

It has been insisted that care is essential in drawing inferences about the existence of monopoly from performance evidence. These concerns are not the only ones. Even assuming that a performance

---

2. See §§ 47–48 and § 186 infra.

3. Posner, Oligopoly and the Antitrust Laws: A Suggested Approach, 21 Stan.L.Rev. 1562 (1969). The analysis warrants one caveat: the power may not always be that of the seller; conceivably, discrimination initiated by a powerful buyer or buyers could persist over a substantial period of time.

4. United States v. United Shoe Mach. Corp., 110 F.Supp. 295, 325–29, (D. Mass.1953), aff'd per curiam 347 U.S. 521, 74 S.Ct. 669, 98 L.Ed. 910 (1954). Compare LaPeyre v. FTC, 366 F.2d 117 (5th Cir. 1966).

consistent with monopoly is convincingly shown, that evidence alone will not be selective as between the degree of market power which the law calls monopoly and lesser, though still substantial, degrees of power. All or most of the performance characteristics associated with monopoly will also be found in an oligopolistic industry if the firms in the industry are successfully charging supra-competitive prices through either collusive or interdependent conduct. Performance evidence by itself can do no more than show the existence of some pathological condition in an industry. Structural evidence or conduct evidence (or a combination of the two) will always be needed to facilitate a judgment about whether the competitive ills of the industry are due to monopoly or some other defect.

The conclusion, then, is that performance data ought not to be overvalued, but neither should it be ignored when power is being evaluated. Structural data is also problematical. Those who challenge the use of performance data, like those who argue against analyzing conduct, never fully face up to that. Power is hard to assess with precision however one goes about it. In that context, any approach which may in some cases, even if not all, help to refine the judgment, to provide a greater assurance about the conclusion being reached, ought to be explored sympathetically.

§ 31. The Absolute Size of a Firm

Among the non-economic concerns about monopoly are those related to excessive, private financial and political power.[1] These may be associated with a firm's size. Regardless of whether it alone dominates any single market, a firm which is large in absolute terms may influence political processes to an undesirable degree, may have excessive impacts on the setting of national or regional economic goals, and may through an elaborate bureaucracy attain a degree of influence on the lives of numerous individuals which is inappropriate for a non-governmental agency whose policies are not subject to direct political constraint.

Often the courts have stated that size alone is not an antitrust offense.[2] Yet, it is never clear in cases using such language that the court does not mean, merely, that some exclusionary conduct must be shown in addition to size; there exists no flat holding that great absolute size combined with exclusionary conduct does not violate Section 2. Moreover, in *Alcoa*[3] the court stated that size, wholly irrespective of economic distortions attributable to market power, must be considered in applying Section 2. After addressing itself to the economic reasons for forbidding monopoly, the court said "there are

---

1. See § 5 supra.

2. See, e.g., United States v. United States Steel Corp., 251 U.S. 417, 40 S. Ct. 293, 64 L.Ed. 343 (1920); United Banana Co. v. United Fruit Co., 245 F.Supp. 161 (D.Conn.1965).

3. United States v. Aluminum Co. of America, 148 F.2d 416 (2d Cir. 1945).

others, based upon the belief that great industrial consolidations are inherently undesirable, regardless of their economic results * * *. Senator Sherman himself * * * showed that among the purposes * * * was a desire to put an end to great aggegations of capital because of the helplessness of the individual before them * * *. [I]t has been constantly assumed that one of [the statutory] purposes was to perpetuate and preserve, for its own sake and in spite of possible cost, an organization of industry in small units * * *." [4] The court was not at this point discussing abusive conduct or market power. The statement focuses directly on size; it asserts that a massive firm creates concern in the absence of other evidence.

Expressions of this kind are consistent with the legislative history of the Sherman Act [5] and responsive to a widely felt democratic concern. Still, the issue of absolute size is extraordinarily hard to deal with in an antitrust case. If one antitrust goal is organization of the economy in small units for social or political reasons and regardless of market power, what norms are to be invoked and utilized to determine when an excessive size has been reached? For example, how was Judge Hand able to conclude in *Alcoa,* given this concern, that one-third of an industry would not be too large, that two-thirds would be a borderline case and that 90% would be clearly too large? Why is the critical line not far lower, so that even one-third or less of a massive, capital-intensive industry is clearly "too large", socially or politically? Surely, if there were five aluminum companies each with 20% of the market that would not be an "organization of industry in small units," such as Judge Hand says Congress was seeking.

Often, as in *Alcoa,* judicial expressions about the values of smallness serve as buttressing arguments, as something additional brought forth to allay lingering doubt after completion of an economic analysis which already points in the same direction. Judges are entitled to reassure themselves and the rest of us, but care should be exercised that the Sherman Act does not become an ink blot into which each judge is invited to project his own political and social fantasies. Non-economic criteria are no doubt at work in some Sherman Act cases.[6] But where this is so, just as where economic criteria are invoked, the court ought at least to attempt to develop neutral principles—discernable, debatable, restateable rules predicated upon stated value premises, which may be articulated and refined through the processes of adjudication. Until this is done—and thus far it has not been—it must be concluded that size alone, without a showing of the

---

4. Id. at 428–29.

5. See the terse and pointed summary in W. Letwin, Law and Economic Policy in America 85–95 (1965) or the full, detailed treatment in H. Thorelli, The Federal Antitrust Policy 180–229 (1955).

6. This is particularly so where the antitrust claim is based on conduct which is allegedly unfair or coercive, as is often the case where dealers challenge conduct of suppliers. See generally Chapter 5, infra.

power to dominate a defined market, is not an antitrust offense even when exclusionary acts are also shown. At an operational level Section 2 is concerned not with size or perceived social values related to size, but with foreclosure of competition. If a firm has sufficient power over price to foreclose competitors, it is a monopolist, no matter how small it may be in absolute terms. If it lacks that power, it is not a monopolist, no matter how large it may be in absolute terms. Massive absolute size, or its absence, can, at most, have influence as a marginal reason for concluding that a firm is or is not a monopolist where the analysis of market power leaves that question somewhat in doubt.[7]

§ 32. Other Non-Economic Factors

A useful discussion of monopoly power must engage deeply with economic concepts; however, it ought not to confine itself to these. One of the non-economic indicators to which the law can turn is the perceptions of others trading in the same or related markets, of customers, suppliers, competitors, or potential competitors. There are several reasons for turning to these perceptions as evidence which will aid in deciding whether a firm ought to be labeled a monopolist. For one thing, the negative effects of excessive market power manifest themselves in terms of the psychology of others in the market place. For example, if competitors view a firm as possessing substantial power, they will not challenge it. Additionally, observations about the issue of power by those who are involved on an on-going basis and over a substantial period can be accurate and highly discriminating. The characterization, "monopoly power," is a conclusion based on myriad facts, some blatant, some more difficult to elucidate. Human perception is a subtle instrument; what we sometimes call intuition can be an informed summation of a wide variety of complex data, and can take account in its own fashion of far more variables than any highly analytical evaluation. For these reasons the conclusionary judgment of those who are informed and involved ought clearly to be useful to the objective body, the court, jury or agency, which must in the end decide.[1] Naturally, those who deal with a firm may have biases one way or the other, but the trier of fact need not be the victim of these biases any more than of any bias any witness may possess.

Another relevant non-economic factor is the conduct by which a defendant firm attained to its present position. Since the offense of monopolization does not turn on power alone but on power ob-

---

7. We must recognize, nonetheless, that large absolute size is a factor which may sway a judge or jury in a close case. Given Congressional concerns about size, it is hard to argue that it is wrong to be tougher on large firms than on smaller ones in those vague areas where it is a close call whether conduct violates the antitrust laws.

1. Accord, United States v. Griffith, 334 U.S. 100, 68 S.Ct. 941, 92 L.Ed. 1236 (1948).

tained through specified kinds of conduct—it is necessary in a monopoly case to explore how power was acquired.[2] Conduct of varying degrees of blameworthiness will suffice to establish the conduct element of the offense, assuming sufficient power is shown.[3] Where the issue whether monopoly power is possessed could be decided either way, it is appropriate, given the broad objectives of the statute, to try to minimize the risks of cumulative error by looking at conduct issues and power issues conjunctively. If a firm's conduct would tend to be injurious to competition whether or not it possesses monopoly power, a court should be less hesitant about calling the firm a monopolist than if the conduct would be wholesome in a competitive market and harmful only in a monopolized one; if the defendant acted in an obviously predatory manner, a court should be less hesitant about calling it a monopolist than if its conduct invites no sanction. If a court is wrong in its ultimate conclusion that a blatantly predatory defendant possesses monopoly power, the negative social consequence of that decision will be much smaller than if it wrongly labels as a monopolist a firm which actually lacks monopoly power and which, though competing aggressively, has not acted in predatory ways.[4]

Another inquiry of a non-economic nature is whether socially useful remedies seem feasible. If it appears that the functioning of the economy could be improved by characterizing defendant as a monopolist, a court should be less hesitant to take that step than if effective remediation seemed unlikely.[5] Finally, we should perhaps be more reluctant to characterize a defendant as a monopolist if the intervening interests of third parties would clearly be adversely affected.[6] The decision, in short, is one that needs to be made with a degree of practical wisdom. The factors suggested here may have a bearing whenever a case falls within that intermediate area, often wide indeed, where the degree of power is not clearly discernible.

Surely a court could approach the issues in this holistic manner. Though there might be some hesitancy to instruct a jury in terms like these, there is no compelling reason not to do so. If juries are to be trusted to unravel the complexities of economic issues there ought to be no concern about inviting them to do so in a more integrative and humanistic context and manner than that which a more rigorous step by step and issue by issue analysis presupposes. If juries have anything of unique value to contribute in matters like this it is probably a sound, holistic judgment.

2. See §§ 33–39 infra.

3. See §§ 33–39 infra.

4. See § 36 infra.

5. See Markham, An Alternative Approach to the Concept of Workable Competition, 40 Am.Econ.Rev. 349, 361 (1950).

6. Compare United States v. E. I. DuPont De Nemours & Co., 353 U.S. 586, 77 S.Ct. 872, 1 L.Ed.2d 1057 (1957).

PART D. CONDUCT TESTS FOR MONOPOLIZATION

§ 33. Introduction

Proof of the existence of monopoly power alone does not prove the offense of monopolization. If monopoly power is "thrust upon" a firm—if, for example, power arises solely from the fact that the market is small and will support only one firm of efficient scale, or solely from the possession of a lawful patent or franchise, *and* if the firm does not engage in market conduct which has the purpose or effect of protecting, enhancing or extending its power—then the firm, despite its monopoly power, is not in violation of Section 2; it is a lawful monopoly.[1] A party charging the offense of monopolization must prove both the existence of monopoly power and either that the power was acquired or has been used in ways which go beyond normal, honestly industrial business conduct.[2]

The conduct element in the offense of monopolization is difficult to pin down. Its precise nature, and, indeed, whether the law has developed to the point where there ought no longer to be any requirement beyond the existence of monopoly power, are matters subject to debate,[3] as are questions about which party ought to have the burden of proving whatever conduct must be proved to show a violation.[4] The sections which follow first discuss issues pertaining to conduct by which power is acquired and then discuss issues about the way power is used.

§ 34. The Deliberateness Test

The tendency has been to deal with the conduct issue in monopolization cases through the use of suggestive phrases. Monopoly power "thrust upon" the defendant does not violate the act;[1] monopoly

---

1. United States v. Grinnell Corp., 384 U.S. 563, 86 S.Ct. 1698, 16 L.Ed.2d 778 (1966); United States v. Reading Co., 253 U.S. 26, 40 S.Ct. 425, 64 L.Ed. 760 (1920); United States v. Aluminum Co. of America, 148 F.2d 416 (2d Cir. 1945); Union Leader Corp. v. Newspapers of New England Inc., 180 F.Supp. 125 (D.Mass.1959), aff'd as modified, 284 F.2d 582 (1st Cir. 1960); United States v. United Shoe Mach. Corp., 110 F. Supp. 295 (D.Mass.1953), aff'd per curiam 347 U.S. 521, 74 S.Ct. 669, 98 L.Ed. 910 (1966).

2. United States v. Aluminum Co. of America, 148 F.2d 416, 429–30, (2d Cir. 1945).

3. Compare, e.g., Handler, Some Unresolved Problems of Antitrust, 62 Colum.L.Rev. 930 (1962), with Levi and Director, Law and the Future: Trade Regulation, 51 Nw.U.L.Rev. 281 (1956). See also Turner, The Scope of Antitrust and Other Economic Regulatory Policies, 82 Harv.L.Rev. 1207, 1212–1225 (1969); Williamson, Dominant Firms and the Monopoly Problem: Market Failure Considerations, 85 Harv.L.Rev. 1512 (1972).

4. Compare Judge Wyzanski's district court opinion in United States v. Grinnell Corp., 236 F.Supp. 244 (D.R. I.1964) with the Supreme Court opinion affirming the district court at 384 U.S. 563, 86 S.Ct. 1698, 16 L.Ed.2d 778 (1966).

1. United States v. Aluminum Co. of America, 148 F.2d 416, 429 (2d Cir. 1945).

power acquired through an "element of deliberateness" does violate it.[2] Monopoly resulting solely from "superior skill, foresight and industry" does not;[3] monopoly obtained through conduct "not honestly industrial" does.[4] These verbal weather vanes are useful to some extent, but to understand more fully what the cases have to teach one must examine the leading ones more fully; the popular formulations must be considered in their factual settings. In the end, one may return to suggestive phrases like those quoted above as being the most precise formulations available, but with a fuller understanding of what these phrases do and do not imply.

The leading cases concerning the kinds of conduct which render the acquisition of monopoly power unlawful are *Alcoa*[5] and *United Shoe Machinery*.[6] *Alcoa* is the path breaking decision. Defendant showed a record of growth and expansion over many years. Its conduct must be considered in two distinct time periods. During the late 1800's and early 1900's Alcoa had obtained a patent monopoly and then extended that monopoly deliberately by purchasing an important process patent at the time when its product patent was about to expire. It had also entered into a cartel which assigned territories and excluded foreign competitors. Also, when it acquired power sites it exacted from suppliers covenants not to sell similar locations to other aluminum manufacturers. After 1912, the district court found no conduct so extreme as participation in a cartel, or placing restrictions on suppliers, nor even an aggressive policy to acquire exclusionary patents. The company did, however, continue to expand. It anticipated and in various ways encouraged growth in demand for its product. It acquired bauxite mines and power sources well in advance of current needs and was ready to meet promptly all demands of the market as they arose.

In holding Alcoa in violation, the court did not rely directly upon the pre-1912 conduct. There had been an antitrust case brought by the government against Alcoa arising out of that conduct which had terminated in 1912 by a consent decree enjoining Alcoa from continuing certain earlier practices.[7] Rather, the court said on the basis of its post-1912 conduct that Alcoa had monopolized because it had been

2. Report of the Attorney General's National Committee to Study the Antitrust Laws 43 (1955).

3. United States v. United Shoe Mach. Corp., 110 F.Supp. 295, 341 (D.Mass. 1953), aff'd per curiam 347 U.S. 521, 74 S.Ct. 669, 98 L.Ed. 910 (1954).

4. United States v. Aluminum Co. of America, 148 F.2d 416, 431 (2d Cir. 1945).

5. United States v. Aluminum Co. of America, 148 F.2d 416 (2d Cir. 1945).

6. United States v. United Shoe Mach. Corp., 110 F.Supp. 295 (D.Mass.1953), aff'd per curiam, 347 U.S. 521, 74 S. Ct. 669, 98 L.Ed. 910 (1954).

7. The court did not squarely consider whether that decree foreclosed reliance on pre-decree conduct; it avoided that issue and purported, in its conclusion regarding conduct, to rely primarily on the less aggressive post 1912 conduct. United States v. Aluminum Co. of America, 148 F.2d 416, 422–23 (2d Cir. 1945).

something more than a "passive beneficiary" of monopoly power; it had "achieved" monopoly, rather than having monopoly "thrust upon it." [8] Though under no compulsion to do so, it kept doubling and redoubling its capacity before others could enter the field. It proceeded "progressively to embrace each new opportunity as it opened, and to face every newcomer with new capacity already geared into a great organization." [9] As the court saw it, "exclusion" is not limited to "maneuvers not honestly industrial," or "activated solely by a desire to prevent competition." [10] "Exclusion," includes any course of action which is deliberate, in the sense that the firm has a choice whether or not to follow it, and which has the effect of excluding others.

From all of this one can formulate a rule: a firm monopolizes when it achieves or maintains monopoly power by a course of deliberate market conduct which has the tendency to keep other firms which might have done so from entering or expanding. This formulation, here called the deliberateness test, reduces the conduct element in the offense of monopolization to a minimum. If a firm possesses monopoly power rarely will it be impossible, given the benefit of hindsight, to point to some course of conduct which it deliberately embarked upon and which facilitated achievement of monopoly. Alcoa, for example, might have avoided monopoly by not expanding as demand grew; other firms would presumably have entered, seeing the opportunity to meet a demand which was outstripping the available supply.

This is thorny law. To require that a firm to avoid violation, must fail to expand in response to opportunities for profitable growth is to insist upon rather perverse market conduct. Whether any firm can be expected to follow the rubric which *Alcoa* lays down, how it would proceed if it tried to do so, and whether, if it did, the consuming public would benefit in any way, remain perplexing questions.

The deliberateness test also is imprecise. In literal terms, it seems to cover even the few cases of monopoly power which, in purport, it would except. For example, since he conceded a "thrust upon" defense, Judge Hand may be presumed to have intended to except from illegality a monopoly growing solely out of a valid patent. He may also be presumed to have intended that a thin market monopoly—say a single plant of efficient scale which meets an industry's entire demand—would not constitute an unlawful monopoly. Yet, neither of these monopolists can be said to have had monopoly "thrust upon" them. Both, rather, set out deliberately on a course of conduct, made decisions and judgments which could have been made differently, and thereby "achieved" monopoly rather than becoming

---

8. Id. at 429.

9. Id. at 431.

10. Id.

"passive beneficiaries" of it. The patent monopolist, for example, could have decided not to obtain a patent; or could dedicate the patent to the public; or could issue licenses to allow others to make the product. The single plant monopolist could have built its plant with half or one-third of its present capacity, or could operate it only three days per week, or otherwise could have failed to meet the full needs of the market. Such conduct would, of course, be unnatural; it would run contrary to the normal human motives and responses to the market situations described. But in this respect it would not clearly be different from the course of conduct which the Alcoa court implied would have been needed for that firm to avoid liability.

The Supreme Court gave its own commitment to the deliberateness test, or something very much like it, in *Grinnell*. There, it said that monopoly power offends Section 2 only when there is shown a "willful acquisition or maintenance of that power as distinguished from growth or development as a consequence of a superior product, business acumen, or historic accident."[11] The phrase, business acumen, is of course a rather open one. But the context of the opinion, including the Court's leaving open the possibility that once power is established the burden will shift to defendant to show that it was obtained in benign ways, all suggest that the Court was accepting, in its essence, the Alcoa view.

This Alcoa test nonetheless seems flawed in that it fails to deal realistically with the human element in the market situation. It comes very close to stating that any possession of monopoly power violates the act, but it does not quite say this and leaves unclear what, in addition to power, must be shown. It does not provide the firm which wishes to obey the law with rational guides to conduct, nor does it leave open the opportunity for a market response which is both rationally self-regarding and lawful. For example, assume that Alcoa at some point sees that demand for its product is about to increase, and also sees a chance to meet that demand profitably by building a new plant. Alcoa would not be able to predict with confidence whether it would violate the law if it did so. Neither would it in such a situation have any economically rational course open to it other than to build the plant. Let us then examine alternative ways in which courts have dealt with the conduct issue in Section 2 cases.

§ 35. Exclusionary Conduct—The Classic Test

In *United Shoe Machinery*,[1] a gifted judge sought to unravel the strands of doctrine concerning the conduct element in the offense of monopolization. Judge Wyzanski formulated three tests; the first, or "classic" test, was based on the early cases; and the other two,

11. United States v. Grinnell Corp., 384 U.S. 563, 570–71, 86 S.Ct. 1698, 1704, 16 L.Ed.2d 778, 786 (1966).

1. United States v. United Shoe Mach. Corp., 110 F.Supp. 295 (D.Mass.1953), aff'd per curiam 347 U.S. 521, 74 S.Ct. 669, 98 L.Ed. 910 (1954).

discussed in the next two Sections, were based on alternative readings of *Alcoa* and other modern cases.

By the classic test Judge Wyzanski meant the test suggested by the early Section 2 cases like *Standard Oil*[2] and *American Tobacco*.[3] He expressed the test in terms of restraints of trade. If a firm acquires or maintains monopoly power by means which constitute restraints of trade in violation of Section 1 of the Sherman Act, it is also guilty of violating Section 2. As to the accuracy of this formulation, so far as it goes, there can be no question. The opinions in *Standard Oil* and *American Tobacco* make vividly clear that acquisition of monopoly power by action among competitors which violates Section 1 also offends under Section 2; it is in this sense that the two Sections are directly complementary. But since Section 1 applies only to action by two or more firms, there may be a limited number of examples of single firm monopoly where, quite independently of the power obtained, the steps taken to acquire it will have themselves violated Section 1. The most obvious example is where two or more competitors merge into a single firm, which, after the merger, constitutes a monopoly. Such a merger is concerted action by two or more firms and would clearly violate Section 1 as an unreasonable restraint on competition.[4] Since monopoly power was attained by this means, Section 2 would also be violated.[5] Other examples also suggest themselves; if a firm, in return for some concession from another, agrees either to withdraw from or not to enter a market, leaving the second firm in possession of monopoly power, the agreement not to compete would undoubtedly violate Section 1 and the resulting monopoly would thus violate Section 2. Again, if a firm were to obtain or preserve monopoly power at one level of distribution by entering into agreements with its suppliers or customers not to deal with others, such agreements would violate Section 1[6] and the consequent power would violate Section 2.

In saying that the classic test covered only monopoly obtained by unlawful restraints, Judge Wyzanski was reading *Standard Oil* and *American Tobacco* too narrowly. In the first of those cases Mr. Justice White explicitly stated that Section 2 was intended to complement Section 1 by picking up conduct which escaped the ban of Section 1, yet resulted in the feared condition of monopoly.[7] According-

2. Standard Oil Co. of N.J. v. United States, 221 U.S. 1, 31 S.Ct. 502, 55 L.Ed. 619 (1911). See the discussion in § 10 supra.

3. United States v. American Tobacco Co., 221 U.S. 106, 31 S.Ct. 632, 55 L.Ed. 663 (1911). See the discussion in § 10 supra.

4. See Chapter 7 infra, particularly §§ 194, 202 and 204.

5. See Northern Sec. Co. v. United States, 193 U.S. 197, 24 S.Ct. 436, 48 L.Ed. 679 (1904), Standard Oil Co. of N.J. v. United States, 221 U.S. 1, 60–62, 31 S.Ct. 502, 516, 55 L.Ed. 619, 645–46 (1911).

6. See §§ 163–69 infra.

7. Standard Oil Co. of N.J. v. United States, 221 U.S. 1, 60, 31 S.Ct. 502, 576, 55 L.Ed. 619, 645 (1911).

ly, it is clear even under the classic test that some kinds of single firm conduct resulting in monopoly can violate Section 2. Single firm conduct which meets this classic test is conduct of a "predatory" character.[8] Thus, if a firm obtains or holds monopoly power by driving competitors out through threatening or engaging in tortious conduct such as destroying property, that firm violates Section 2.[9] Nor is a tort needed for single firm conduct to violate the classic test announced by Mr. Justice White. A firm violates Section 2 if it gains or holds monopoly power through conduct which is not a normal, industrial response to market opportunities, but is primarily aimed at limiting the opportunities of competitors, so as to drive them out of the market.[10] An example would be cutting prices to abnormally and unprofitably low levels in places where local competition is encountered.[11]

§ 36. The Modern Test of Exclusionary Conduct

Judge Wyzanski's second formulation of the conduct test took into account later cases. There had long been intimations that power obtained by means less reprehensible than predatory practices could violate the act. As early as United States v. Eastman Kodak,[1] the conduct element of the offense was found to have been satisfied by evidence of practices such as acquisition of competing firms, the closing of their plants, and acquisition of control of imported photographic paper. This view was reinforced on occasion.[2] And, as we have seen, Judge Hand in *Alcoa* held that Section 2 was violated where a firm obtained monopoly through deliberate growth to anticipate demand.[3] In framing the modern conduct test Judge Wyzanski sought to take account of these developments, yet to construe *Alcoa* in a manner which simultaneously rendered it more consonant with earlier precedent and less vague as a guide to business conduct than the deliberateness test fashioned by Judge Hand. The formulation Judge Wyzanski came up with states that Section 2 is violated where a firm obtains or holds monopoly power by conduct which is either predatory (in the sense described in the first formulation) or which

---

8. See, e.g., Porto Rican American Tobacco Co. v. American Tobacco Co., 30 F.2d 234, 236 (2d Cir.), cert. denied 279 U.S. 858, 49 S.Ct. 353, 73 L.Ed. 999 (1929). The difficulties presented by the predatory concept are canvassed and a functional definition of predatory pricing is developed in Areeda & Turner, Predatory Pricing and Related Practices Under Section 2 of the Sherman Act, 88 Harv.L.Rev. 697 (1975).

9. See United States v. American Tobacco Co., 221 U.S. 106, 31 S.Ct. 632, 55 L.Ed. 663 (1911).

10. Id.

11. See the discussion in Areeda & Turner, supra note 8.

1. United States v. Eastman Kodak, 226 F. 62 (2nd Cir. 1915), appeal dismissed 255 U.S. 578, 41 S.Ct. 321, 65 L.Ed. 795 (1921).

2. See, e.g., United States v. Pullman Co., 50 F.Supp. 123 (E.D.Pa.1943).

3. United States v. Aluminum Co. of America, 148 F.2d 416 (2d Cir. 1945). See § 34 supra.

is "exclusionary" in purpose and effect. This formulation, by treating exclusionary conduct as an element in monopolization, would cover actions such as those engaged in by United Shoe which at the time the actions were taken could be identified as tending to increase entry barriers. One example would be United's "lease only" policy, by which it marketed machines used in the shoe manufacturing process only through long term leases and refused to sell them. Others would be the specific provisions of the leases, which included a minimum term of ten years, clauses which gave lessees an economic incentive to use all of their United machines fully before using any machines manufactured by others, and clauses which gave lessees an incentive to replace any machine being turned in before the end of a term with another United machine. The leasing program as a whole tended to tie shoe manufacturers to United as a supplier over prolonged periods and to reduce the likelihood that competing manufacturers could break in. It also reduced the likelihood of the development of a secondhand market which would reduce United's power; used machines would always go back to United at the end of a lease term.

Another example of exclusionary conduct would be the provision by United of maintenance service with the machines it leased without separate or additional charge. Since users had no choice but to pay for maintenance as a part of the cost of the lease, they would not consider going to any firm other than United for such service. This inhibited the development of a separate, competitive market for service and maintenance, and also tended to reduce the diffusion of technological information about the machines, which, had it occurred, might have stimulated or eased entry at the manufacturing level.

The exclusionary conduct test is not overbroad, as is the more general language of *Alcoa*. If conduct is to be an element in the offense of monopolization the rule about conduct ought to have certain characteristics. First, it should discriminate between conduct which is harmful in some economic sense, and conduct which is not; second, it ought to discriminate between alternative courses of action in the marketplace in a manner which would be meaningful to an actor there, so that those whose conduct the law would shape can be guided by it in meaningful ways; third, it should not ban conduct which is no more than the normal, rational response of a business manager seeking to maximize profits, sales or revenues. The exclusionary conduct test, if carefully construed, can meet these criteria. We need only read the phrase, "exclusionary conduct" as referring to conduct which tends to exclude not merely by utilizing existing market opportunities, so that they are not thereafter available to be pursued by others, but in the special sense of tending to raise barriers to entry, thus foreclosing in the future even such potential competitors as might have been alert enough to grasp an opportunity before the defendant firm had done so.

Unlike the broader *Alcoa* statement, this second Wyzanski formulation focuses only on conduct which the firm could, at the time it acted, identify as anticompetitive—as tending to increase entry barriers and thus reducing the likelihood of competitive entry or expansion. A firm not yet possessing monopoly power would not know in advance that such conduct was necessarily unlawful, however carefully it might appraise the situation. But it would be capable of knowing, through a degree of care and analysis, two important things which it could not always know about conduct subject to sanction under the broader *Alcoa* formulation. First, it would be able to distinguish conduct which increased entry barriers from conduct which did not, and thus would be able to identify rational, alternative ways of exploiting its market situation so as to maximize its profits. Also, it would know that if it elected to use the conduct which did tend to raise entry barriers it would do so at its peril—should monopoly result, it would be in violation of the Act. In short, an exclusionary conduct test stressing the erection of entry barriers would provide the tools for logical prediction and would never oblige a trader to act in economically irrational ways in order to avoid violation.

This reading of the modern cases is also more consistent with the early cases than is Judge Hand's more sweeping formulation. It was, after all, in *Standard Oil* that the concept of barriers to entry was first introduced into antitrust jurisprudence.[4] It is an appropriate mission of legal thought, then, to draw these elements together, to integrate them in a restatement that harmonizes the cases, old and new, and in an intellectually satisfactory manner, and which meets the salient social needs which should inform a rule of law in this area. One can achieve such a harmonious restatement by saying that conduct which tends to erect barriers to the entry or expansion of other firms is exclusionary, and supplies the conduct element in the offense of monopolization.

§ 37. The Prima Facie Approach

If the exclusionary conduct test of *United Shoe Machinery*[1] seeks to enhance the law's rationality by giving *Alcoa*[2] a restricted reading, the third Wyzanski formulation would achieve rationality while giving Judge Hand's opinion the broadest possible reading. Literally *Alcoa* states (1) that if a firm has monopoly power, and can be shown to have itself taken the steps, however benign, by which that power was attained, the firm has monopolized; and (2) that a firm has not monopolized if it attains monopoly power as a passive benefi-

---

4. Standard Oil Co. of N.J. v. United States, 221 U.S. 1, 71–77, 31 S.Ct. 502, 520–23, 55 L.Ed. 619, 649–52 (1911).

1. United States v. United Shoe Mach. Corp., 110 F.Supp. 295 (D.Mass.1953), aff'd per curiam 347 U.S. 521, 74 S.Ct. 669, 98 L.Ed. 910 (1954). See § 36 supra.

2. United States v. Aluminum Co. of America, 148 F.2d 416 (2d Cir. 1945). See §§ 34, 36 and 37 supra.

ciary of market conditions. The third formulation restates these propositions in this way: if it is proved that a firm has monopoly power, a prima facie case of monopolization has been established; but the firm may rebut that case by carrying the burden of proving that its power is attributable solely to a cause which the law does not wish to discourage, such as a patent or other exclusive franchise granted by the state, a natural advantage such as initial entry into a market which will support only a single firm operating at efficient scale, superior skill or industry, or low profit margins resulting from the consistent maintenance of low and nondiscriminatory prices.[3]

The court in *United Shoe Machinery* did not feel it was necessary to choose between the prima facie test and the exclusionary conduct test. United Shoe Machinery not only possessed power which it failed to show was attributable solely to innocent causes, but also was shown to have engaged in leasing practices which increased entry barriers. Hence, it had violated under either the prima facie approach or the exclusionary conduct test. Indeed, United Shoe Machinery may well have been vulnerable even under the classic test; after all, its original formation by the merger of independent firms arguably constituted a restraint of trade in violation of Section 1.[4] The court did not pass specifically on this question, however, presumably because the original formation of the company's predecessor had been unsuccessfully challenged by the government years earlier,[5] giving rise to a res judicata question if that conduct were now to be relied upon.[6]

§ 38. Choosing Among Conduct Tests

It is settled that the law now extends beyond the classic formulation and at least as far as the exclusionary conduct test set forth in *United Shoe Machinery*.[1] That still leaves three rules to choose from: the exclusionary conduct test, the prima facie approach, and the deliberateness test of *Alcoa*.[2]

The exclusionary conduct test is attractive. By focusing on conduct which is identifiably harmful, in that it tends to raise entry barriers, it meets an important policy desideratum. Encompassing only conduct for which a rational businessman will be able to find alternatives, it does not strain against the realities of the market place.

3. United States v. United Shoe Mach. Corp., 110 F.Supp. 295, 342 (D.Mass. 1953), aff'd per curiam 347 U.S. 521, 74 S.Ct. 669, 98 L.Ed. 910 (1954).

4. See Northern Sec. Co. of N.J. v. United States, 193 U.S. 197, 24 S.Ct. 436, 48 L.Ed. 679 (1904); see also § 35 supra.

5. United States v. United Shoe Mach. Co. of New Jersey, 247 U.S. 32, 38 S.Ct. 473, 62 L.Ed. 968 (1918).

6. See United States v. United Shoe Mach., 110 F.Supp. 295, 344 (D.Mass. 1953), aff'd per curiam 347 U.S. 521, 74 S.Ct. 669, 98 L.Ed. 910 (1954).

1. United States v. United Shoe Mach., 110 F.Supp. 295 (D.Mass.1953), aff'd per curiam 347 U.S. 521, 74 S.Ct. 669, 98 L.Ed. 910 (1954). See § 36 supra.

2. United States v. Aluminum Co. of America, 148 F.2d 416 (2d Cir. 1945). See §§ 36 and 37 supra.

These are strong reasons for accepting the exclusionary conduct test. Completeness requires, however, the marshaling of the arguments against this formulation and in favor of one of the broader ones.

Precedent must be considered, of course. The most forceful one which can be cited against the exclusionary conduct rule is the holding in *Alcoa* itself. Though Judge Wyzanski purported to take *Alcoa* into account in fashioning the exclusionary conduct rule, there is little in the Hand decision indicating that the conduct upon which the case turned was exclusionary in the sense in which Judge Wyzanski used that term. In *Alcoa* there was nothing comparable to the lease-only policy; so far as appears, there was after 1912 only a policy of expansion to meet increasing demand. Also, there is dicta in *duPont (Cellophane)*[3] which tends to support the Hand formulation. Nonetheless, the precedents do not all favor the deliberateness test. In *Grinnell*[4] the Court may have backed away somewhat from the Hand view, and there are a number of cases where accused monopolists were found not to have violated the conduct standards which are explicable only upon the assumption that Judge Wyzanski's exclusionary conduct test must be met before a Section 2 offense is found.[5]

There are policy arguments too, which can be called upon in favor of a diminished conduct test for monopoly; these should be set against those, stressed above, which support the exclusionary conduct formulation.

Assuming, arguendo, that the law does cast a wider net than Judge Wyzanski's exclusionary conduct rule, is there any basis for choice between the third Wyzanski formulation, here referred to as the prima facie approach, and the formulation set forth by Judge Hand in *Alcoa*? The Hand formulation—that power obtained by deliberate conduct violates the law while power passively received does not—fails to clearly identify the differences between guilty and innocent conduct. As a practical matter this formulation comes very close to saying mere possession of monopoly power violates the law, for no firm is ever likely to be the passive beneficiary of monopoly. The conduct element thus becomes a fiction and the law is changed sub rosa. Only if one concludes that the law should condemn all monopolies should this formulation have appeal.

The prima facie approach does not hide what it is about; it states that the possession of monopoly power is, prima facie, offensive. But it recognizes that there are certain situations, such as pat-

---

3. United States v. E. I. DuPont De Nemours & Co., 351 U.S. 377, 391, 76 S.Ct. 994, 1005, 100 L.Ed. 1264, 1278 (1956).

4. 384 U.S. 563, 86 S.Ct. 1698, 16 L.Ed. 778 (1966).

5. E.g., Clark Marine Corp. v. Cargill, Inc., 226 F.Supp. 103 (E.D.La.1964), aff'd per curiam 345 F.2d 79 (5th Cir. 1965), cert. denied 382 U.S. 1011, 86 S. Ct. 620, 15 L.Ed.2d 526 (1966); Hughes Tool Co. v. Cole, 113 F.Supp. 519 (W.D.Okl.1953), aff'd, 215 F.2d 924 (10th Cir. 1954), cert. denied 348 U.S. 927, 75 S.Ct. 339, 99 L.Ed. 726 (1955).

ents or utility franchises, where monopoly is encouraged or created by law, and that there are certain situations, such as the thin local market, where monopoly is inevitable. Once it is established that defendant is a monopolist it places on defendant the burden of proving that it falls within one of these exempt classes. While some vagueness remains (particularly in that part of the formulation which attempts most explicitly to respond to the *Alcoa* statement that liability can be avoided by showing that the defendant took no action to obtain monopoly) this way of putting the matter seems more satisfactory than the Hand statement. If one concludes that monopoly in and of itself is bad and should be outlawed except where expressly sanctioned or inevitable, the prima facie approach of *United Shoe Machinery* rather than the deliberateness test of *Alcoa* would be preferable.

The argument for condemning monopoly power independently of bad conduct is trenchant.[6] Monopoly results in excessive prices and profits and an allocation of fewer resources to the monopolized industry than under competition. The existence of monopoly power has these effects regardless of how that power was obtained or is held. The unilateral, rational, profit-oriented decisions by a monopolist about price and output will have these pernicious consequences. For policy reasons which have been considered above the government may encourage or permit monopoly in special situations, but these could be made exceptions to the general prohibition, as they would be under the third formulation in *United Shoe*.

The counter-argument which, thus far, seems to have prevailed, is rooted in concepts about the nature and purpose of antitrust. It has become increasingly common in the scholarly literature to talk of antitrust as an aspect of national economic policy and, having emphasized its policy components, to assume that antitrust is one of the variables which, like interest rates, can be manipulated as need is perceived to meet politically ascendant goals.[7] Policy at this level concerns itself little with human conduct in business settings, with motives, or with whether conduct is good or bad in terms of some set of shared mores. Rather, it concerns itself almost solely with structure and performance and seeks to identify the most efficient and powerful public interventions which might be utilized to achieve identified economic goals. From such a vantage point, the case is strong for condemning monopoly except where inevitable or encouraged by different policies to which antitrust must give way.

But there is an alternative way of looking at antitrust which is more intimately related to its populist roots. Antitrust is national public policy not only in the sense that it expresses a political commitment of an incumbent administration. Antitrust is also a set of

6. The argument in this paragraph is suggested by P. Areeda, Antitrust Analysis, Problems, Text, Cases, ¶ 206 (2d ed. 1974).

7. See Sullivan, Politics, Planning and Trade Regulation: A Glance Toward an Emerging Utopia, 16 UCLA L.Rev. 1 (1968).

norms, quite judgmental in character, about how human beings in the market place should act. Certainly the evils at which the act was aimed, primarily excessive prices and excessive private power, were seen by those who sponsored the act as stemming, not from inevitable responses to market structure, but from wrongful conduct.[8] Thus, Section 1 aims expressly at conduct—contract, combination or conspiracy. Section 2 does not in terms condemn the status of monopoly, but only the act of monopolizing, or attempting or conspiring to do so. From this perspective it is alien to the purposes of the statute to criminally condemn the monopolist on the basis of his status and without inquiry as to whether he achieved that status on the one hand by conduct, such as erecting entry barriers, which could be identified and perceived as anticompetitive, or on the other hand by conduct, such as foreseeing and responding in efficient ways to market opportunities, which would be difficult to identify beforehand as wrong and which, in general, should be socially encouraged.

Indeed, there may be something intrinsically unfair (as well as socially counterproductive) in a policy which encourages traders to compete as effectively as possible and then imposes criminal sanctions upon any who are so successful as to win the field to themselves.

§ 39. Intent to Exclude as a Surrogate for Conduct

The discussion has proceeded throughout on the assumption that some degree of anticompetitive conduct, in addition to power, is essential to establish monopolization. There is an exception to this general proposition which should not pass unnoticed. Power to exclude competitors also violates Section 2 if it is "coupled with the purpose or intent to exercise that power."[1] Circumstances in which intent can be inferred other than from conduct which is itself exclusionary will no doubt be rare. As in much of antitrust, the relationship between intent and conduct is intimate: thought enlivens the deed; it can also be inferred from the deed. Still, whenever an exclusionary intent can be shown even without exclusionary conduct, the intent will suffice. If the intent is linked to the power, the violation has occurred though no anticompetitive act has yet been committed.

---

8. See Letwin, Congress and the Sherman Antitrust Law: 1887–1890, 23 U. Chi.L.Rev. 221 (1956); H. Thorelli, The Federal Antitrust Policy 180–85, 226–29 (1955).

1. United States v. Griffith, 334 U.S. 100, 107, 68 S.Ct. 941, 945, 92 L.Ed. 1236, 1243 (1948). In context, the Court's reference to an intent to exercise power may be taken to mean an intent to act in exclusionary ways. See also American Tobacco Co. v. United States, 328 U.S. 781, 66 S.Ct. 1125, 90 L.Ed. 1575 (1946).

PART E. EXAMPLES OF CONDUCT WHICH MAY CONSTITUTE MONOPOLIZATION

§ 40. Introduction

In Part B a generalization was developed that monopolization occurs when monopoly power is obtained through unlawful restraints of trade, through predatory practices aimed at controlling or excluding competitors, or (in what seems the preferable way to put the matter) through practices which are exclusionary in the sense that they can be identified as tending to raise barriers to entry or expansion by other firms. In the course of discussion, some examples of conduct transgressing this standard were identified. Here, the aim is to discuss in summary form various types of conduct which have been, or which rationally could be, held to offend the Section 2 conduct standard.[1]

§ 41. Horizontal Merger

A merger between two or more firms each of which is a major competitive factor in a relevant market eliminates competition between them and is thus a restraint of trade in violation of Section 1.[1] Where the result of the merger is monopoly, Section 2 is also violated.[2] In a sense this is to say that monopoly power attained through the fusion of two or more firms is always unlawful, whereas monopoly power attained through the internal growth of a single firm is unlawful only if the power was obtained in exclusionary ways. The justification for this distinction is that monopoly is always undesirable and the social goal is always to forbid it when that can be done in ways that are administratively feasible and which will not discourage desired economic conduct. Acquisition of monopoly power by internal growth, as we have seen, could not always be treated as unlawful except at the expense of penalizing some of the kinds of market conduct that public policy ought to encourage. For this reason, monopoly attained without the use of exclusionary practices of a kind which a rational business person could avoid does not violate the law.[3] But a monopoly created by merger is attained by clearly avoid-

---

1. For a useful checklist of various types of conduct which may constitute "monopolizing," together with case citations exemplifying each type, see Cooper, Attempts and Monopolization: A Mildly Expansionary Answer to the Prophylactic Riddle of Section Two, 72 Mich.L.Rev. 373, 445–448 (1974).

1. United States v. First Nat'l Bank and Trust Co. of Lexington, 376 U.S. 665, 84 S.Ct. 1033, 12 L.Ed.2d 1 (1964). See §§ 194, 204 infra.

2. United States v. Southern Pac. Co., 259 U.S. 214, 42 S.Ct. 496, 66 L.Ed. 907 (1922); United States v. Reading Co., 253 U.S. 26, 40 S.Ct. 425, 64 L.Ed. 760 (1920); United States v. Union Pac. R.R., 226 U.S. 61, 33 S.Ct. 53, 57 L.Ed. 124 (1912); Northern Sec. Co. v. United States, 193 U.S. 197, 24 S.Ct. 436, 48 L.Ed. 679 (1904).

3. See §§ 34, 36 and 38 supra. See also P. Areeda, Antitrust Analysis, Problems, Text, Cases ¶ 206c (2d ed. 1974).

able conduct, and there is no convincing social reason to encourage a merger which leads to such power.[4]

Parity of reasoning insists that Section 2 would be violated if a firm were formed by a merger which sufficiently stifled competition to violate Section 1 and if thereafter the power of the resulting firm were to continue to grow (even by means not themselves exclusionary) until it became a monopoly. Such a firm would possess monopoly power and that power would have been attained in part through a merger in restraint of trade.

The same reasoning would also seem to govern if monopoly power were ultimately acquired by a firm formed by a merger which, though not violating Section 1, did violate the lower threshold imposed by Section 7 of the Clayton Act.[5] In this instance the merger, though not violating Section 1, would still be an avoidable, anticompetitive conduct. But Section 7 casts a wide net. For example, a merger of two firms aggregating less than ten percent or so of a market might violate that section.[6] If the merger went unchallenged and the firm later grew by unobjectionable conduct into a monopoly, it would be anomalous to say that Section 2 was violated. Perhaps the answer is to insist on a qualification, that the monopoly be related not only historically, but proximately and causally with the unlawful merger.

§ 42. Concerted Action Resulting in Joint Monopolization

A monopolist need not be a single firm; two or more firms acting jointly may together exercise sufficient power to constitute a monopoly. For example, picture three firms, none of which individually possesses monopoly power but all of which, if they merge into a single firm, would possess such power. As noted above, a merger between such firms would be a restraint of trade and an act of monopolization violating Section 2.[1] But the firms may succeed without merger in unifying their conduct so as to exercise together the monopoly power which they would possess if they were combined into unified ownership and control through merger. If they coordinate

---

4. The only plausible contrary argument occurs where a market is so thin it will support only one firm of efficient scale and two or more firms have entered. In this situation it can be argued that inevitably one alone will survive and that the efficient course is to allow differences to be composed through merger rather than forcing a competitive struggle to the death, with too great a loss to all, even the victor, and consequent social loss. Compare Union Leader Corp. v. Newspapers of New England, Inc., 180 F. Supp. 125 (D.Mass.1959), aff'd in part and rev'd in part 284 F.2d 582 (1st Cir. 1960), cert. denied 365 U.S. 833, 81 S.Ct. 747, 5 L.Ed.2d 744 (1961).

5. The application to mergers of Sherman Section 1 and Section 7 of the Clayton Act is treated in detail in Chapter 7, infra.

6. See § 204 infra.

1. See § 41 supra.

their conduct to a degree sufficient to achieve monopoly power, that concerted action will have substantially the same pernicious effects as would a merger. It differs from a merger only in that so long as the firms remain in separate ownership and control, their concert may be less complete or less permanent than it would be had they merged.

Because concerted action which results in two or more firms jointly exercising monopoly power inevitably restrains competition between them, such action, like a merger which leads to monopoly, is both a restraint of trade violating Section 1 and the act of monopolization which violates Section 2.[2]

There are various things which firms that together dominate an industry can do to jointly exercise monopoly power. Pricing concertedly, rather than competitively, is the most obvious; also, dividing territories and otherwise acting as classic cartels. The nature of the evidence which will warrant a conclusion that action is being taken concertedly so that firms are jointly exercising monopoly power raises questions substantially identical to those which arise in determining what kinds of concerted conduct constitute "contract, combination or conspiracy" within the meaning of Section 1. For this reason, a full discussion of what constitutes concerted action will be deferred until Section 1 is considered.[3]

It will be noted, also, that if two firms combine to achieve joint monopolization they may also be charged with the separate and distinct offense of conspiracy to monopolize.[4] The elements of that offense are, of course, distinct. The violation can occur even though monopoly power is not successfully attained (and thus joint monopolization has not occurred).[5] And it may just be that firms which do gain monopoly power through concerted action are guilty of joint monopolization, though, because of lack of sufficiently precise conspiratorial intent, they cannot be said to have conspired to monopolize.

§ 43. Predatory Practices

Predatory business conduct can be defined as conduct which has the purpose and effect of advancing the actor's competitive position, not by improving the actor's market performance, but by threatening to injure or injuring actual or potential competitors, so as to drive or keep them out of the market, or force them to compete less effectively. The earliest cases labeled predatory conduct as a violation of Sec-

---

2. United States v. Paramount Pictures, Inc., 334 U.S. 131, 68 S.Ct. 915, 92 L.Ed. 1260 (1948); American Tobacco Co. v. United States, 328 U.S. 781, 66 S.Ct. 1125, 90 L.Ed. 1575 (1946); Swift & Co. v. United States, 196 U.S. 375, 25 S.Ct. 276, 49 L.Ed. 518 (1905).

3. See Chapter 3, Part J., infra.

4. See § 49 infra.

5. Id.

tion 2[1] when it was used to gain or hold monopoly power; the predatory monopolist became a figure in the national demonology.[2]

There has been much talk about predatory behavior, but few efforts to analyze it.[3] Businessmen and judges think they know it when they see it.[4] Economists tend to doubt that it occurs, at least very often, because it is likely to cost the firm using it more than can be gained from it.[5] One of the most interesting contributions to scholarship is the recent Areeda and Turner article [6] which draws out of the aridities of cost-price relationships a functional, objective standard for predatory pricing and related behavior. The article assumes that, however rarely, firms do at times try to drive others out by unremunerative behavior. It thus sees a need to police this kind of behavior but regards the judicial formulations of the legal standard, which speak in terms of intent,[7] as unduly vague, particularly since under the present test, the threat of treble damage litigation may inhibit aggressive but not truly predatory competitive conduct. The

1. E.g., Standard Oil Co. of N.J. v. United States, 221 U.S. 1, 31 S.Ct. 502, 55 L.Ed. 619 (1911); United States v. American Tobacco Co., 221 U.S. 106, 31 S.Ct. 632, 55 L.Ed. 663 (1911).

2. See Cassidy & Brown, Exclusionary Tactics in American Business Competition: An Historical Analysis, 8 UCLA L.Rev. 88 (1961); United States v. International Fur Workers Union, 100 F.2d 541, 546–47 (2d Cir. 1938), cert. denied 306 U.S. 653, 59 S. Ct. 642, 83 L.Ed. 1051 (1939).

3. Of the few, one of the most useful is by a British scholar and member of the British Monopolies Commission, Yamey, Predatory Price Cutting: Notes and Comments, 15 J. Law & Econ. 129 (1972). Most of the analytical discussion has emphasized the fairly obvious fact that predatory conduct, such as local price cutting to drive out a competitor, is not without cost to the perpetrator and is a sensible strategy only if the estimated additional returns, discounted by uncertainties, are high enough to cover the estimated costs. See, e.g., Telser, Cutthroat Competition and the Long Purse, 9 J. Law & Econ. 259 (1966); see also, McGee, Predatory Price Cutting: The Standard Oil (N.J.) Case, 1 J. Law & Econ. 137 (1958) which on the historical evidence, doubts the previously (and judicially) accepted conclusion that predation was used to establish the oil trust. The most recent contribution to the literature is an interesting and useful one which proposes usable, objective standards by which courts could identify predatory pricing or comparable predatory acts. Areeda & Turner, Predatory Pricing and Related Practices under Section 2 of the Sherman Act, 88 Harv.L.Rev. 697 (1975). See also Scherer, Predatory Pricing and the Sherman Act: A Comment, Areeda and Turner, Scherer on Predatory Pricing, and Scherer, Some Last Words on Predatory Pricing, 89 Harv.L.Rev. 869–903 (1976), an internecine debate among scholars whose basic views about the utility of economic analysis in antitrust are quite similar.

4. E.g., Patterson v. United States, 222 F. 599, 613 (6th Cir.), cert. denied 238 U.S. 635, 35 S.Ct. 939, 59 L.Ed. 1499 (1915); MacIntyre & Volhard, Predatory Pricing Legislation—Is it Necessary?, 14 B.C.Ind. & Com.L.Rev. 1 (1972).

5. E.g., Telser, supra note 3; G. Stigler, The Organization of Industry 113–18 (1968).

6. Areeda & Turner, Predatory Pricing and Related Practices under Section 2 of the Sherman Act, 88 Harv.L.Rev. 697 (1975).

7. E.g., Moore v. Mead's Fine Bread Co., 348 U.S. 115, 75 S.Ct. 148, 99 L. Ed. 145 (1955).

solution proposed is to define as predatory pricing those policies which yield returns below average or marginal cost, whichever is lowest.

As a way to get at predatoriness the analysis is a distinct contribution. As *the* way, it has deficiencies. As the authors define it (and as logically they must, given their purposes)[1] the concept of average cost includes a "normal" return on investment. Once that is recognized the apparent precision of the test vanishes. A board with legislative authority and its own staff of economists and accountants might come to a plausible judgment about a normal return for any given industry. It does not at all follow that such a judgment could be reached through a jury trial, or even a trial to the court without a jury. It is not just that opportunities for obfuscation would be unending. It is also that inquiry into the issue in an advocatory context would lead to deeply felt and tenaciously held, yet conflicting, views, each espoused by an earnest expert and supported by regression studies—views which a judge or jury would often have grave difficulty in choosing between. Areeda and Turner concede administrative difficulties in determining a reasonable, non-monopoly price to be too great to permit of a rule against monopoly pricing by a manufacturer, but they under-scrutinize the comparably difficult problems of identifying a normal return on investment in arriving at a concept of average cost.

If we are going to rely on judges and jurors to discover predatory business conduct we cannot deprive them of all traces of the juices in the situation. A firm which seeks to drive out or exclude rivals by selling at unremunerative prices will leave human traces; the very concept is one of a human animus bent, if you please, upon a course of conduct socially disapproved. If there is one task that judges and juries, informed through the adversary system, may really be good at, it is identifying the pernicious in human affairs. To contend that the conventional formulation, which looks, in a sense, for evil, ought to be amended to one which looks solely to an effect validated by economic studies is to assume too much about the precision of applied economics and to assume too little about the value of more humanistic modes of inquiry.

The conviction which informs this section is that predatory conduct, though seldom obvious and usually difficult to identify with certainty, does indeed occur. The fact that predatory activity is costly to the predator and that there is only an uncertain prospect of adequate supra-competitive returns after others are excluded surely must reduce the frequency of predatory forays. It hardly follows that they never occur or can be safely ignored. Man's capacity for destructive conduct has never been totally inhibited merely because he stands himself in the target area along with his would-be victim. The best course, moreover, is to leave the avenues of inquiry as open as may be. Objective data, such as that stressed by Areeda and

Turner, could then be used either to attack or defend, but so also could any other evidence indicative of predatory intent.

Purpose and intent are always difficult to deal with, particularly so in connection with complex business conduct. But the antitrust laws need not disregard the pernicious. There is a difference between competing aggressively and effectively and competing in a predatory way and that difference has to do as much with the human animus which infuses a firm's activities as it does with the objective character of its acts.

The aggressive competitor, while earning a reasonable profit, may cut costs by vigilant management and efficient innovation, and may reduce prices as costs go down to the discomfort of particular competitors who are forced back on their mettle. But such conduct does not run askance of competitive values; it is to encourage such conduct, and resulting public benefits like greater efficiency and lower costs, that the law seeks to maintain competition. By contrast, the predator seeks not to win the field by greater efficiency, better services, or lower prices reflective of cost savings or modest profits. The predatory firm tries to inhibit others in ways independent of the predator's own ability to perform effectively in the market. Its price reduction [8] or predatory expenditure [9] is calculated to impose losses on other firms, not to garner gains for itself; indeed, the predation is likely to involve present losses to the predator, or at all events to foreclose profits which could currently be earned, detriments which are accepted by the predator as the cost of freeing itself for the future from the competition it now faces.[10]

The contrast here drawn is achieved by painting in general language two extremes, the vigorous, efficient competitor and the blatant predator. In actual markets motives may be mixed and practices ambiguous. A price below average cost may be set for promotional purposes, or because it is the best price that can be obtained.[11] It may be difficult to differentiate the transaction which has a significant predatory thrust from that which represents the honestly industrial effort of a competitor to deal with the market forces confronting it. Direct evidence of predatory intent will usually be difficult to uncover.

Yet, there are hallmarks. Predatory conduct will usually display two identifying characteristics. First, there will be something odd, something jarring or unnatural seeming about it. It will not strike

---

8. E.g., Moore v. Mead's Fine Bread Co., supra note 7; Lloyd A. Fry Roofing Co. v. FTC, 371 F.2d 277 (7th Cir. 1966).

9. E.g., United States v. Eastman Kodak Co., 226 F. 62, 73 (2nd Cir. 1915), appeal dismissed 255 U.S. 578, 41 S.Ct. 321, 65 L.Ed. 795 (1921).

10. See the full discussion in Cooper, Attempts and Monopolization: A Mildly Expansionary Answer to the Prophylactic Riddle of Section Two, 72 Mich.L.Rev. 373, 435–40 (1974).

11. Id. at 445–450.

the informed observer as normal business conduct, as honestly industrial. Second, it will be aimed at a target, at an identifiable competitor or potential competitor, or an identifiable group of them. The first of these characteristics, that the conduct be abnormal, seems the vaguer of the two, but it is no less precise than many standards in the law, and no less precise than the seemingly more objective standard based on prices which cover average cost, including a normal return on investment. One approach to applying it would be humanistic in character. It would look to the mores of the marketplace itself. It would ask questions like, what would the consensus among well-intentioned businessmen knowledgeable about the particular industry be about the kinds of conduct which constitute "fair" or "normal" or "honestly industrial" practices in competitive rivalry? While any such consensus may be dynamic rather than fixed, changing with industrial conditions, it would often be sufficiently crystalized to be both discernible and useful. Another approach would be more scientific; it would be to develop a theoretical conception of the competitive process in that industry and to ask whether the conduct in question were an integral part of that dynamic, or whether it would tend to distort the competitive engine like sand in its gears.

The second characteristic of conduct called predatory—that it have an identifiable target—is a characteristic that flows out of its basic goal, to win not by being more efficient and effective, but by causing rivals to suffer greater losses than they can tolerate. This is the crucial characteristic of predatory conduct; unless there is an apparent victim, we need make no further inquiry about whether particular conduct is predatory. The "victim," of course, may not be a specifically identifiable firm; it may be a class of competitors or even potential competitors.

Types of predatory practices from the myths and realities of monopolization are numerous. At one extreme are blatantly tortious threats to or attacks upon person or property.[12] If physical harm were threatened to customers in order to induce them not to deal with a competitor, or if a competitor were told its warehouse would be burned if it persisted in selling in a particular territory, these actions would obviously be predatory. We have already alluded to the predatory practice which receives the most discussion in the case law and literature, predatory or discriminatory price cutting—that is, cutting prices in those markets where competition is being encountered to unreasonably low or unprofitable levels in order to exclude others from those markets.[13] The following practices have also been

---

12. E.g., United States v. International Fur Workers Union, 100 F.2d 541, 546–47 (2d Cir. 1938), cert. denied 306 U.S. 653, 59 S.Ct. 642, 83 L.Ed. 1051 (1939).

13. In addition to cases cited in notes 8 and 9 supra, see, e.g., United States v. Grinnell Corp., 384 U.S. 563, 86 S.Ct. 1698, 16 L.Ed.2d 778 (1966); United States v. American Tobacco Co., 221

held to be predatory: the action of a newspaper publisher in forcing advertisers to boycott a radio station before it would sell advertising space to them,[14] the repeated expenditure of excessive sums for advertising upon the introduction of a series of new bread products,[15] the selective payment of excessive prices for supplies,[16] the obtaining of a controlling interest in a potential competitor in order to vote the stock to exclude the competitor from the monopolized market,[17] sales by a vertically integrated firm at an excessively high price, so that buyers who compete with its own operations at the next vertical level will not be able to do so efficiently.[18]

When one moves away from the tortious toward incidents in the exercise of pricing, advertising, or purchasing policy, the line between "normal" or "honestly industrial" competitive effort and predatory practice aimed at excluding or controlling competitors is increasingly difficult to draw. Perhaps the characteristic feature of such a predatory thrust is that the predator is acting in a way which will not maximize present or foreseeable future profits unless it drives or keeps others out or forces them to tread softly. Thus, the predator may price substantially below the profit maximizing (or loss minimizing) price; or it may expend an amount on advertising which exceeds the sum which would maximize current and reasonably foreseeable returns; or as a vertically integrated producer, the predator may charge firms with which it competes at the next level a higher price than the price which would maximize its returns as a producer. Such conduct makes sense if, but only if, it is seen as a means of driving out or controlling competitors. The losses currently being suffered or the profits currently being foregone by the predator are accepted in the expectation that they will be more than made up at a later date by monopoly profits which can be obtained after the competitive threat from other firms is ended. This kind of activity is to be differentiated, of course, from "salvage operations" aimed at reducing losses or from promotional activities.[19]

U.S. 106, 31 S.Ct. 632, 55 L.Ed. 663 (1911); Ovitron Corp. v. General Motors, 295 F.Supp. 373 (S.D.N.Y.1969); United States v. N.Y. Great Atl. & Pac. Tea Co., 67 F.Supp. 626 (E.D.Ill. 1946), aff'd 173 F.2d 79 (7th Cir. 1949). See text accompanying notes 8–10 supra.

14. Lorain Journal Co. v. United States, 342 U.S. 143, 72 S.Ct. 181, 96 L.Ed. 162 (1951).

15. Bailey's Bakery, Ltd. v. Continental Baking Co., 235 F.Supp. 705 (D. Hawaii 1964), cert. denied 393 U.S. 1086, 89 S.Ct. 874, 22 L.Ed.2d 570 (1969).

16. Peto v. Howell, 101 F.2d 353 (7th Cir. 1938).

17. Pennsylvania Sugar Ref. Co. v. American Sugar Ref. Co., 166 F. 254 (2d Cir. 1908).

18. United States v. Aluminum Co. of America, 148 F.2d 416, 436–38 (2d Cir. 1945).

19. See P. Areeda, Antitrust Analysis, Problems, Text, Cases ¶¶ 605–06 (2d ed. 1974); Areeda & Turner, supra note 6.

§ 44. Conduct Increasing Entry Barriers

If predatory conduct is extreme anticompetitive behavior, an examination of conduct which has the effect of raising entry barriers draws attention to market events which will often be quite subtle. This type of exclusionary conduct may not be black-hearted at all; subjectively, the firm engaging in it may be quite benign. It is of concern because of its effect of eventually altering the structure of the market in a way which inhibits competition.

The leasing policy described in *United Shoe Machinery* [1] is the best example in the case law of conduct which tends to raise entry barriers. During the pre-1912 period Alcoa [2] also engaged in entry-inhibiting conduct, such as entering into contracts with owners of power sources which precluded their dealing with other aluminum producers. There are also cases indicating that a firm, such as a movie theatre chain with monopoly power in some local markets, may not deal with suppliers on a chain-wide basis, because that would tend to give it leverage in its competitive markets on the basis of its power in its monopoly markets.[3]

There are a variety of other practices analyzed in the literature which in some industry settings tend to raise entry barriers and which therefore might be included under the exclusionary practices test. For example, a program of purchasing all patents in a particular field of technology might thoroughly blockade the technology or seem to do so.[4] Similarly, a program of buying up all available sources of a scarce resource such as ore, regardless of need,[5] or entering into requirements contracts or other exclusive arrangements with essential suppliers or customers,[6] could all tend to make entry difficult. Practices concerned with research, advertising and product innovations can also raise significant entry barriers by raising the share of the market needed to operate at maximum efficient scale, by raising absolute costs of entry, or by tending to foreclose competitors from needed resources or outlets.[7] One cannot generalize about these practices. They can be evaluated only in a specific industrial context and when enough is known to have some sense about their function in the dynamics of rivalry in the industry.

1. United States v. United Shoe Mach. Corp., 110 F.Supp. 295 (D.Mass.1953), aff'd per curiam 347 U.S. 521, 74 S.Ct. 669, 98 L.Ed. 910 (1954).

2. United States v. Aluminum Co. of America, 148 F.2d 416 (2d Cir. 1945).

3. United States v. Griffith, 334 U.S. 100, 68 S.Ct. 941, 92 L.Ed. 1236 (1948); see also, United States v. Crescent Amusement Co., 323 U.S. 173, 65 S.Ct. 254, 89 L.Ed. 160 (1944).

4. See §§ 178–79 infra.

5. Compare Continental Ore Co. v. Union Carbide & Carbon Corp., 370 U.S. 690, 82 S.Ct. 1404, 8 L.Ed.2d 777 (1962).

6. See §§ 163–68 infra.

7. See §§ 105, 107, 178 and 179 infra.

§ 45. Invasion of a Thin Market

If a market is so thin that it will support only one firm, any effort to enter could be characterized as a deliberate effort to attain a monopoly. This characterization would be absurd, of course, if applied to the first entrant; its only choice is to "monopolize" or not enter. The ways in which conduct should be characterized become less obvious if there is an attempted entry after the first entrant has secured the field.

Union Leader Corp. v. Newspapers of New England, Inc.,[1] holds that the mere act of entry by the second firm is no more an act of monopolization than was entry by the first. True, if the second entry is successful the first firm must be driven out, but that does not convert honestly industrial, competitive effort into monopolization. The dynamics of the situation, however, often will lead to a more rigorous scrutiny of the business practices of either or both of the contending firms than would be warranted if success by one did not mean the demise of the other. Thus, the court in *Union Leader* moved beyond traditional tests of monopolization by positing a "fairness" standard.[2] Although it employed this standard to evaluate the behavior of the two competing newspapers it did not sufficiently convey the implications of this norm.

The law ought to insist that when a competitive struggle occurs in a market which will support only one firm each must comport itself in a way calculated to assure not merely that the survivor is the most aggressive or the one with the most will, but that it is the firm which makes the better appeal strictly on the competitive merits. Honestly industrial efforts by either firm to appeal through efficiencies, through product or service improvements, or by pricing at reasonable levels should not violate the standard. By contrast, predatory tactics such as pricing below costs, overtly misleading tactics or misdirection, or any tactics calculated to induce buyers to prefer the firm on transient or competitively irrelevant grounds, would be suspect. This elaboration does little to make more specific the court's vague reference to fairness as a guide, but it does stress the principle that the battle ought to be fought out strictly on the competitive merits and provides a guide for evaluating conduct asserted to be deficient under the fairness standard.

§ 46. Wrongful Exercise of Lawfully Attained Power

Thus far discussion has been limited to conduct by which monopoly power is obtained, maintained or extended. There are other acts of monopolization, those concerning the manner in which monopoly power is used. Picture a firm having monopoly power that was law-

---

1. 284 F.2d 582 (1st Cir. 1960), cert. denied 365 U.S. 833, 81 S.Ct. 747, 5 L. Ed.2d 744 (1961).

2. Id. at 586.

§ 47. Pricing Policies

a. *In General*

We have considered predatory pricing (along with other predatory activity) which may be used either to gain or hold monopoly power.[1] Are there other pricing practices by the established monopolist which are legally sensitive? Does a monopolist which obtained power lawfully violate Section 2 (become guilty of monopolization) if it exploits its power by pricing at any of the supra-competitive levels which it might rationally choose? Little in the case law bears on this question and little in the literature deals with it directly.[2] The problem is nonetheless important theoretically and some aspects of it (particularly those discussed below under the subheading, "limit pricing") are of potential practical interest. Perhaps what is said here, though tentative and exploratory, will encourage further analysis.

b. *Profit maximizing pricing*

Classical economic literature assumes that the monopolist will price at the level which maximizes its present return, thus establishing a higher price and a lower output than competitive conditions would yield.[3] It is, as will be seen, a somewhat unrealistic assumption that the monopolist is determined to get all it can now, unmindful of the consequence of that policy on its own longer range interests. Accepting this assumption, does such short-run, profit maximizing conduct constitute monopolization which violates Section 2?

The argument for construing Section 2 as forbidding the monopolist to charge "monopoly prices" would be based in part on authority and in part on policy. The case law[4] and legislative history[5] both emphasize the dread of excessive prices, and the Act is unquestionably aimed at forestalling prices above competitive levels and resulting distortions in the allocation of resources. Construing the Act to forbid pricing above competitive levels thus has a surface appeal. But the considerations which weigh against it are forceful; indeed, overwhelming.

---

1. See § 43 supra.

2. See, however, the brief discussion of limit pricing in Areeda & Turner, Predatory Pricing and Related Practices Under Section 2 of the Sherman Act, 88 Harv.L.Rev. 697, 705–09 (1975).

3. E.g., R. Posner, Antitrust, Cases, Economic Notes and Other Materials 5–14 (1974). See Appendix A.

4. E.g., Standard Oil Co. of N.J. v. United States, 221 U.S. 1, 31 S.Ct. 502, 55 L.Ed. 619 (1911).

5. See, e.g., Letwin, Congress and the Sherman Antitrust Law: 1887–1890, 23 U.Chi.L.Rev. 221 (1956).

First, authority: the cases emphasize that monopolization consists of the exercise of monopoly power in ways which tend to exclude competitors.[6] Profit maximizing prices tend the other way. Such pricing may not always attract entry; if entry barriers are sufficiently high it cannot. However, such pricing will do more to attract competitive entry than would any other pricing policy a monopolist might adopt.

Consider the patent monopolist, for example. If it were to price at a level yielding no more than a reasonable return on investment, no firm would have any particular incentive to challenge its position. But if it were to price at a profit maximizing level, a level substantially above the competitive return, other firms might be encouraged to challenge it. They might succeed in "inventing around" the patented technology so as to be able to enter the market with an acceptable substitute for the monopolized product. In short, monopoly prices can trigger self-corrective processes.[7] If entry barriers are low, these processes will tend to erode monopoly power as new entry is attracted. Even when entry barriers are high, profit maximizing prices will tend to provide the maximum incentive to outsiders to try to cut down the barriers or climb over them.

Another argument against forbidding the monopolist to set a profit maximizing price is humanistic in character. The dynamic of the market calls for rational, self-interested conduct. It is from success that human gratification is obtained in the business setting. Career expectations are based upon it; day to day activities beat to its pulse. It would be distorting, unwieldy and productive of significant strain and inefficiency to impose a legal standard which ran directly counter to these strong forces at work in the situation. But note that dysfunction would not be unavoidably involved. If the legal requirement were stated as one that profits be no more than reasonable, the human activity in the firm might be organized around an effort to maximize sales, and prices might then be cut to the level which would assure that costs plus a reasonable return were attained.

Note also that a rule against short-run profit maximizing monopoly prices would be difficult to administer judicially.[8] Just as it would be difficult to determine predatory pricing by objective tests, so it would be difficult to determine objectively what would be a reasonable non-monopoly price for the purpose of forbidding monopoly pricing.[9] To do so, moreover, would require an enormous resource commitment, even if it were a feasible task to bring off. Courts

---

6. See cases cited in § 36 supra.

7. F. Scherer, Industrial Market Structure and Economic Performance ch. 8 (1970).

8. See Areeda & Turner, supra note 2.

9. See § 43 supra. If non-objective indications were taken into account in the effort to identify profit maximizing pricing these difficulties would be reduced. See the text relevant to footnotes 17–19 infra.

would be asked to act like public utility commissions, policing the business decisions of every patent monopolist, every firm dominating a thin market, and every holder of a scarce resource to see that prices did not yield more than a reasonable return on investment.[10]

The reasonable price standard is intrinsically vague and difficult. The most efficient way to show that prices are higher than competitive levels would presumably be to show that profits are higher than necessary to attract investment. But the reasonable return on investment will vary from industry to industry depending on risk, the extent of innovation, secular trends of demand, and other factors. Courts do rely on profit evidence at times and make judgments about the reasonableness of profits as a subsidiary test of the existence of market power.[11] But if reasonable prices, as indicated by reasonable profits, were accepted as a conduct standard for the firm lawfully possessing monopoly power, an added difficulty would be presented. Any determination made today about what price is reasonable would not hold for tomorrow, when demand or supply conditions might change. Consequently, effective enforcement of the rule would require a continuous scrutiny which it is not feasible for courts to undertake.[12]

In the case of the patent monopolist there is yet another objection to forbidding a profit maximizing price. The patent system is intended to attract investment research and resultant innovation by offering a legal monopoly to the successful inventor.[13] To deprive the patent holder of the fruits of his monopoly would be inconsistent with the policy of the patent laws.

In summary, no single consideration clearly forecloses a construction of Section 2 which would forbid the monopolist to set profit maximizing prices. But the objections to such a construction are numerous and forceful and, in the aggregate, demand the conclusion that the law ought not to be so interpreted.

c. *Limit Pricing*

In the prior subsection it was concluded that the short run profit maximizing prices which classical theory pictures the monopolist as setting should not violate Section 2. Let us consider whether any critical consideration changes when we alter our factual assumptions to make them more realistic. Modern theoretical and empirical studies indicate that the dominant firm will recognize that entry barriers, however high, are never impregnable; the higher the firm's return, the more likely that others will attempt to enter. Given this recognition, the monopolist may set price not at the level which would maxi-

---

10. Compare United States v. Trenton Potteries Co., 273 U.S. 392, 47 S.Ct. 377, 71 L.Ed. 700 (1927).

11. See § 27 supra.

12. See United States v. Trenton Potteries Co., 273 U.S. 392, 47 S.Ct. 377, 71 L.Ed. 700 (1927).

13. See §§ 176–77 infra.

mize profits during the immediate period but at some lower level high enough to yield more than competitive returns, but not high enough to encourage entry.[14] This practice, sometimes called "limit pricing," can be viewed as an effort by the monopolist to maximize profits in the long run by sacrificing the highest return now.

But this kind of pricing differs greatly from short run maximizing. It entails judgments about the dynamic of the market in the future. Therefore, the price which the monopolist will set is not determinate, even if all cost functions are known and some normal profit rate is known or assumed. In short run maximizing, once the cost and demand conditions are known, the price is a matter of computation; with the same information, any rational manager will choose the same price as any other. Not so in limit pricing. We are in an area of judgment where all relevant data about what may or may not happen in the future cannot be known. For this reason and because different persons may discount the future at quite different rates, informed, rational managerial judgments may differ widely about the appropriate price for the monopolist.

There is evidence that monopolistic (and oligopolistic) firms do exercise price restraint in an effort not only to discourage entry, but also to reduce the likelihood of buyers switching to substitute products in the long run.[15] The particular price which any given monopolist sets, therefore, will depend in part upon the firm's assessment of its own vulnerability, of the height of the entry barriers which protect it, and of the potential of customers to switch over an extended time to substitutes. It will also depend on the extent to which the firm discounts the risk of possible future reductions in its earnings as entry is encountered or substitutions begin. And it will depend, finally, upon the firm's posture in dealing with the myriad imponderables and uncertainties which are involved in a dynamic economy. Should it try to keep prices down in order to maintain all possible trade connections as it moves toward an uncertain future? At the other extreme, should it conclude that, given vast uncertainty, it ought to seek to maximize now? Or should it take a stance somewhere in between these positions?

There are two points to be emphasized here. First, limit pricing by a monopolist will have different effects than would pricing for present profit maximization. Short run maximizing will tend to encourage entry; limit pricing will not, or will to a much lesser extent. Second, if we assume limit pricing can be identified (a matter discussed below), a rule forbidding limit pricing would not present the administrative difficulties which would be encountered by a rule which forbade pricing to maximize profit. Given these circum-

14. Scherer, supra note 7, at 219–31; J. Bain, Industrial Organization 269–76 (2d ed. 1968).

15. J. Bain, Barriers to New Competition 190–201 (1956); Scherer, supra note 7, at 231–33.

stances, it is appropriate to inquire whether limit pricing by a monopolist which attained its power lawfully should be construed to violate Section 2.

The basic argument for treating limit pricing as a violation is straightforward enough. Such pricing, unlike short run maximizing, has the explicit purpose and likely effect of inhibiting entry; it thereby extends and preserves the monopoly and partakes of that characteristic which imbues all other kinds of conduct which are treated as monopolizing. Though a monopoly may be lawful in its inception, a deliberate effort by the monopolist to frustrate the market forces which in the ordinary course of business could be expected to erode its power runs counter to the statutory tenets. It is exclusionary conduct in the strictest sense, not different in any important respect from conduct which raises entry barriers.

Such a construction of Section 2 would not be an anomalous standard for a firm subject to it. The mandate not to set prices with a view to protecting power from erosion would be as clear and precise as many legal norms and would leave the firm free to price in alternative and entirely rational ways. Thus, a monopolist could price to maximize its current or short run return, as classical theory long supposed all monopolists to do, or could price to maximize sales, which would tend to bring prices down near competitive levels, or could aim specifically for a price comparable to that which competitive conditions would yield by reducing price to the point where the increased revenue from increased sales offset the increased production costs of the additional product sold.

True, if the monopolist, faced with the need to avoid limit pricing, chose the first of these alternatives and priced to maximize its return, the public would indeed pay higher prices and distortion of resource allocation would be more extreme than if limit pricing were tolerated. This fact is not necessarily fatal to the proposed construction. The monopolist which practices limit pricing does not vary from the profit maximizing price to a degree calculated to be beneficial to the public, but precisely to that degree which the monopolist judges will be more beneficial to itself, and hence more harmful to the public, than profit maximizing in the short run would be. The monopolist does not give up all supra-competitive profits, but only those which it has calculated will purchase for it an increased tenure in its monopoly status. Conceivably the public would discount the future at a different rate than has the monopolist, or would make different judgments about how low prices must go to protect against entry. But surely the monopolist's judgment that its limit price policy will maximize its long run returns is a good first approximation of what pricing policy will do the maximum harm to the public.

The last objection which might be raised to a rule labelling limit pricing by a monopolist as monopolization is that such pricing would be difficult to identify.[16] While it may seem anomalous, given the stress placed earlier on the difficulties in accepting an objective test of predatory pricing as determinative,[17] and in discriminating between profit maximizing and competitive pricing on the basis of cost-price relationships,[18] this objection to a rule against limit pricing may nevertheless be rejected. It is precisely because limit pricing is an inexact and indefinite theoretical concept that adjudicatory processes may be competent to identify it. We are talking here less about objective manifestations than about the attitudes of those managing the firm which enliven and enspirit pricing decisions. If the firm makes deliberate efforts to evaluate and balance the imponderables that are entailed in pricing to discourage entry, yet to earn as high a return as can be earned consistently with that goal, traces discernible to discovery processes, and within the ken of judges and jurors, may well be left. There have been several empirical studies of important industries in which economists have found convincing evidence of limit pricing of kinds which ought to carry conviction to the lay mind.[19] With the wide range of discovery powers available in a litigation context, it may not prove to be exceedingly difficult to identify limit pricing when and where it occurs.

d. *Discriminatory Pricing*

The monopolist may have both the power and the incentive to discriminate in price.[20] We have seen that long continued discrimination may help to identify monopoly, for only a firm with substantial power has an incentive to discriminate.[21] Through a variety of devices, the monopolist may be able to segregate buyers into different classes and charge prices to some which constitute a greater percentage of cost than the prices charged to others.[22] The monopolist may do this openly—for example, by offering relatively low prices to the young, the old, students, government employees, or other similar classes, or by selling essentially the same product under two different brand names, or in regular and luxury models. It may also discriminate secretly, as in offering to large buyers discounts greater than the cost savings which result from quantity sales.[23] The purpose for

---

16. This is the view taken by Areeda & Turner, supra note 2, at 707.

17. See § 43 supra.

18. See Subsection b supra.

19. Scherer, supra note 15.

20. Scherer, supra note 7, at 253–57. See also ch. 8 infra which discusses the distinct prohibitions of the price discrimination law.

21. See § 29 supra.

22. See § 29 supra, §§ 156, 159 and 186 infra and ch. 8 infra.

23. This might occur if some but not all buyers to whom the monopolist sold had countervailing power. The monopolist might, for example, sell to buyers in several competitive industries and also to buyers in an oligopolistic industry; if buyers in the latter industry used the product in large amounts they might have the incentive and resources to produce themselves at the monopolist's level in order to avoid monopoly prices. This

a discrimination may also vary. The monopolist may discriminate in order to maximize profits, in response to countervailing power on the buyers' side of the market, or in predatory fashion to resist competitive forays by other firms.

Here again, neither the case law nor the analysis in the legal literature is comprehensive about whether a lawful monopolist may discriminate. We have already seen that a monopolist which engages in price cutting for predatory purposes violates Section 2.[24] That proposition covers all cases of discrimination which can fairly be characterized as predatory, but only those. The solution for other cases should be as responsive as is feasible to antitrust values. As a preliminary generalization, price discrimination by a monopolist should be held to violate Section 2 where its purpose or likely effect is to inhibit competition or the achievement of values associated with competition, and should be held lawful when its purpose or likely effect is to encourage competition or aid in the achievement of competitive values.[25] As examples will disclose, such a norm will seldom be easy to apply.

Suppose the discrimination consists in a seller, however powerful itself, granting a lower price to a large buyer which as a buyer possesses market power of its own. The net effect may be positive or neutral in terms of competition. If the powerful buyer faces competitive conditions in its resale market, it will pass on to the next level the savings it achieves by obtaining discriminatory price concessions.[26] For example, a company that manufactures cans could conceivably exact discriminatorily low prices from a tin or aluminum plate manufacturer, yet be forced on resale to price at competitive levels because of the competition of other can companies, bottle companies, or makers of other containers. The net effect would be the partial erosion of the excessive profits which would have been earned at the tin or aluminum plate level, but for the competition. On the other hand, a powerful buyer facing a powerful seller—for example, a dominant automobile manufacturer facing a dominant aluminum company—might obtain discriminatory concessions which, because it also holds a strong position as a seller, it is not forced to pass on.[27] In the first case the effect of the discrimination may be beneficial. Though it may give the preferred buyer some advantage over some of its competitors there is enough resale competiton at the buyers' level so that the price preference is not converted at that level to monopoly profit. The price reduction shows up eventually at the consumer level in lower prices and increased production. In the second example the social

would give the monopolist a motive to sell to them for less.

24. See § 43 supra.

25. See Scherer, supra note 7, at 253–57.

26. Id.

27. Id.

effect seems neutral; all one can say is that the discrimination shifts a monopoly profit from one deep pocket, that of the powerful seller, into another, that of the powerful buyer. In neither case is there a socially significant basis for treating the discrimination as an act of monopolization.

Much discrimination arises not from buyer market power, but from efforts by a powerful seller to maximize its returns. A monopolist faces a downward sloping demand curve;[28] at any given level, if it lowers its price, it will be able to sell more. To simplify, assume that a monopolist that cannot discriminate is choosing between a price of $10 at which it can sell 100 units and a price of $8 at which it can sell 200 units. Which of these it will select will depend on whether the cost of producing the additional 100 units is higher than the $600 which the sale of those additional units adds to total revenue. However, if the monopolist could divide buyers into two classes, with those who will pay $10 per unit falling into one class and those who will pay only $8 a unit falling into the other, it would have another choice open to it—to sell to the first class at $10 and to the second class at $8. The revenue yielded by the sale of 200 units would then be higher than if the monopolist could not discriminate and had to reduce the price to $8 for all in order to sell 200 units.[29]

It may be profitable for a monopolist to discriminate in such a manner if it is capable of doing so. Whether the public interest is advanced or injured by such a discrimination can be a factually complex inquiry and, in the end, a matter of judgment. In some instances the monopolist, if forbidden to discriminate, may find it more profitable to sell the lower number of units at the higher price. In these situations, the salient effect of the discrimination would be to enable the monopolist to gain a higher return at the expense of a part of the consuming public.[30] In other instances, however, the monopolist may find it more profitable to sell the higher number of units at the lower price even if it must reduce the price to all. In these cases, allowing discrimination would have the beneficial effect of putting more of the monopolist's product into the hands of those that want it. Proof that a particular discrimination fell into the first category would seem a sufficient basis for holding that such discrimination by a firm with monopoly power violated Section 2.

Even where the discrimination results in increased output and sales, it may injure competition in other ways. Scherer concludes that although unsystematic discrimination (such as secret price concessions) may aid competition by eroding rigid, supra-competitive

---

28. Posner, supra note 3.

29. W. Bowman, Patent and Antitrust Law 100–116 (1973).

30. See United States v. United Shoe Mach. Corp., 110 F.Supp. 295, 325–29 (D.Mass.1953), aff'd per curiam 347 U.S. 521, 74 S.Ct. 669, 98 L.Ed. 910 (1954). See also Scherer, supra note 7, at 258–262.

prices, systematic discriminations in which the favored and unfavored groups are clearly identified and consistently treated in discriminatory fashion will almost always tend to injure competition.[31] Systematic discrimination may help to entrench the seller by creating strong ties with favored buyers, or it may reduce the threat of competitive entry by favoring buyers most likely to attract or be attracted to alternative suppliers.[32]

Discrimination, at least within the meaning of the usual economic definitions, is also practiced by a seller which, though selling any one product at the same price, establishes different relationships between cost and price on different products in its line. In *United Shoe Machinery*[33] Judge Wyzanski implied that the defendant protected its monopoly by selling types of machines over which its monopoly was clear at relatively higher percentages of cost than those represented by prices on types of machines for which substitutes were available. That analysis is a difficult one. Such pricing, as Scherer suggests,[34] may shade over into the predatory, but it could also be nothing other than establishment of a profit maximizing price on all items—monopoly prices on monopolized items and competitive prices on competitive ones. The fact that the court defined an aggregate shoe machinery market should not obscure the fact that the various machines were not all substitutes for one another, nor were they used necessarily in complementary ways, so that there would be a single operative demand function; rather, they were sold in various submarkets some of which were far more competitive than others.[35]

The recent decision in Telex Corporation v. International Business Machines Corporation[36] presents a related but interestingly different question. The court held that, assuming IBM to have monopoly power, it was not monopolization for it to reduce the prices on peripheral equipment for which it was facing increasing competition, thus undercutting the prices of peripheral competitors, while increasing the price on central data processing units ("CPUs") with which the

---

31. Scherer, supra note 7, at 272.

32. The Robinson-Patman Act, an adjunct to the basic antitrust laws, establishes standards independent of, and only partially consistent with, the antitrust laws for determining the legality of price discriminations. These are separately dealt with in Chapter 8 infra.

33. United States v. United Shoe Mach. Corp., 110 F.Supp. 295, 325–29 (D. Mass.1953), aff'd per curiam 347 U.S. 521, 74 S.Ct. 669, 98 L.Ed. 910 (1954).

34. Scherer, supra note 7, at 253–57.

35. There is also case law condemning discriminatory pricing in other contexts which would lend some support to the contention that discriminatory pricing by a monopolist violates Section 2. See LaPeyre v. FTC, 366 F.2d 117 (5th Cir. 1966); Peelers Co. v. Wendt, 260 F.Supp. 193 (D.Wash. 1966); Laitram Corp. v. King Crab, Inc., 244 F.Supp. 9, amended 245 F. Supp. 1019 (D.Alaska 1965). But see Bela Seating Co. v. Poloron Prods., Inc., 438 F.2d 733 (7th Cir.), cert. denied 403 U.S. 922, 91 S.Ct. 2228, 29 L. Ed.2d 701 (1971); La Salle St. Press, Inc. v. McCormick & Henderson Inc., 445 F.2d 84 (7th Cir. 1971).

36. 510 F.2d 894 (10th Cir. 1975).

peripherals would be used, and on which it did not face increased competition. The case differs from *United Shoe Machinery* in that in *IBM* there were indications of a single demand function for CPUs and peripherals, so that IBM could shift cost-price relationships among these items so long as it did not substantially change the total cost to a consumer of a CPU and associated peripherals.[37] Assuming that to be the fact, IBM, if free to price peripherals to yield a relatively low profit, while pricing CPUs to yield a relatively high profit, would be able to effectively exclude from competition any firm capable of entering the peripheral equipment market but not capable of making CPUs. If IBM were denied the power to discriminate, it could undercut peripheral equipment competitors only if it were willing also to reduce CPU prices to yield the same lower return. If unwilling to do that it would be forced to abide the development of peripheral competition. Since either price reduction on CPUs or the development of new competition in the peripheral equipment segment would be desirable it seems appropriate to label the discrimination exclusionary.

In summary, there are some situations in which discrimination by a monopolist appears to injure competition significantly, others where it does not. To make a judgment, given a particular factual setting, one must ask in essence, what the monopolist would do if it were denied the option to discriminate; next, one must contrast the social consequence of that course of conduct with the social consequence of the discrimination. If, as in the IBM example, the analysis suggests that forbidding discrimination will yield a socially preferable response, the discrimination ought to be characterized as exclusionary conduct. Otherwise it should not.

§ 48. Customer Selection

The notion that one possessing a scarce resource must exploit it in ways which entail no arbitrary or invidious distinctions among customers is an ancient one. It is at the root of common law concepts which define the duties of the innkeeper, the public house, and the business affected with a public interest. A well developed rule about the exercise of lawfully attained monopoly power reflects the same conception.[1] A firm which holds a lawful monopoly by virtue of ownership of a unique resource is guilty of monopolization if it exploits that resource in ways which exclude or disadvantage customers arbitrarily or invidiously. For the purpose of assuring reasonable access, this rule treats scarce resource or natural advantage monopolies the way regulatory law treats a public utility.

---

37. See the discussion in § 18 supra.

1. E.g., United States v. Terminal R.R. Ass'n, 224 U.S. 383, 32 S.Ct. 507, 56 L.Ed. 810 (1912); Associated Press v. United States, 326 U.S. 1, 65 S.Ct. 1416, 89 L.Ed. 2013 (1945); Otter Tail Power Co. v. United States, 410 U.S. 366, 93 S.Ct. 1022, 35 L.Ed.2d 359 (1973).

The landmark case is *Terminal Railroad*.[2] There, a corporation jointly owned by several railroads had lawfully acquired ownership and control over facilities which constituted the only feasible terminal for rail traffic coming to the city from the west. The court held that the company was obligated to provide access to non-proprietor railroads upon reasonable terms which did not discriminate between proprietors and others. A number of other cases are of similar import.[3]

This "public utility" approach to duties under the antitrust laws presents its own special anomalies. Note, first, that the two major restraints imposed upon a regulated public utility are a duty to provide reasonable service and nondiscriminatory access, and a duty to charge no higher than reasonable prices. By electing to constrict the unregulated lawful monopolist to a substantially identical requirement as to customer access, does the case law suggest the appropriateness of following the analogy more fully and treating scarce resource monopolies as though they were public utilities with respect to prices and the affirmative duty to serve? Can it be argued that the *Terminal* case called for utility-type regulation of rates by holding that the access defendants were to provide to outsiders must be on reasonable as well as non-discriminatory terms?

We have, above, pursued various objections to imposing a reasonable price requirement on monopolies.[4] Since the same embarrassments are not entailed in an order to provide non-discriminatory access, the *Terminal* case can surely be distinguished on its facts if it is cited in support of a reasonable rate requirement. Nor does the requirement in the opinion of access on reasonable and non-discriminatory terms[5] seem equivalent to a requirement that rates be reasonable, in the sense of being free of any element of monopoly profits. The concept of reasonableness presumably has implications as to the

---

2. United States v. Terminal R.R. Ass'n, 224 U.S. 383, 32 S.Ct. 507, 56 L.Ed. 810 (1912).

3. In addition to the cases cited in note 1 supra, see Silver v. New York Stock Exch., 373 U.S. 341, 83 S.Ct. 1246, 10 L.Ed.2d 389 (1963); American Medical Ass'n v. United States, 317 U.S. 519, 63 S.Ct. 326, 82 L.Ed. 434 (1943); Gamco, Inc. v. Providence Fruit & Produce Bldg., Inc., 194 F.2d 484 (1st Cir. 1952), cert. denied 344 U.S. 817, 73 S.Ct. 11, 97 L.Ed. 636 (1952); United States v. Southwestern Greyhound Lines, Inc., 1953 CCH Trade Cas. ¶ 67,470 (N.D.Okl.1953); compare, E.A. McQuade Tours, Inc. v. Consolidated Air Tour Manual Comm., 467 F.2d 178 (5th Cir. 1972), cert. denied 409 U.S. 1109, 93 S.Ct. 912, 34 L. Ed.2d 640 (1973); Marjorie Webster Jr. College, Inc. v. Middle States Ass'n of Colleges and Secondary Schools, Inc., 432 F.2d 650 (D.C.Cir.), cert. denied 400 U.S. 965, 91 S.Ct. 367, 27 L.Ed.2d 384 (1970). There are also cases more extreme, surely, than any implication to be found in Terminal Railroad, that imply that any monopolist must act fairly in customer selection and distribution. See, e.g., Poster Exch., Inc. v. National Screen Serv. Corp., 431 F.2d 334 (5th Cir. 1970), cert. denied 401 U.S. 912, 91 S.Ct. 880, 27 L.Ed.2d 811 (1971).

4. See § 47, supra.

5. 224 U.S. at 411, 32 S.Ct. at 516, 56 L.Ed. at 820 (1912).

scope of the service which is to be offered. For example, the defendant presumably could not favor proprietors against others by refusing minor modifications in switching service to meet the needs of an outsider which did not happen to be duplicated by any proprietor. The case perhaps requires that prices be reasonable in the sense that the monopolist not covertly discriminate by setting prices so high that only proprietors (who as owners would receive rebates in the form of profits) could use the facility; but it would strain the opinion to read its requirement of reasonableness as having a broader implication upon price.

Whether the *Terminal* case and others like it can be used as authority for a duty of scarce resource monopolists to offer a reasonable range of services to all customers is a more difficult issue. The duty to provide reasonable services could also be read, as we have tended to read it above, as applying only so far as necessary to protect against discrimination. On this reading additional service not presently available would have to be offered only where the refusal to provide it is, in effect, a failure to meet needs of outsiders which are substantially similar to, and as easy to meet with available resources as, the needs of insiders which are being met. A wider reading is also conceivable, which would compel the monopolist to extend his services to meet all reasonable needs of those who wish to be served in the product or service market which the monopolist dominates. Extension of the present law to this degree would present none of the difficulties which would be encountered if the law were extended to compel prices which yielded no more than competitive returns.

Otter Tail Power Company v. United States,[6] is instructive on this point. Otter Tail was an integrated power company which produced, transferred over its own lines (i.e., "wheeled"), and sold electric power at retail in Minnesota and the Dakotas. As a producer of power and the only firm with subdistribution lines in its market area, it had a natural monopoly. As a vertically integrated company it had capacity to sell power wholesale to municipalities which operated their own power distribution companies or to wheel to municipalities power which the Bureau of Reclamation was ready to sell to them. In any given city the business of retailing power, which entailed ownership of the local distribution lines, was also a natural monopoly. Thus if Otter Tail agreed to "wheel" or to wholesale power to a city, the company was agreeing in effect to replace itself as the sole power retailer in that local market. Despite this, the Court held that Otter Tail could not lawfully refuse to wholesale or wheel power where

---

6. 410 U.S. 366, 93 S.Ct. 1022, 35 L.Ed. 2d 359 (1973). For a critical view of *Otter Tail* and a pessimistic attitude about whether antitrust can deal with market problems of the kinds discussed in this section, see Hale and Hale, The Otter Tail Power Case: Regulation by Commission or Antitrust Laws, 1973 S.Ct.Rev. 99.

doing so would not inhibit its ability to continue serving other customers. Holding a natural monopoly of the distribution system at the wholesale level, the company had to provide service to any retailer which wanted service, even to one bent on replacing the company.

The result should not be surprising, given the holding in *Terminal Railroad*. The rationale there is broad enough to raise grave doubt whether the vertically integrated owner of a unique resource which sells to some buyers at the next level may decline service to those of the entrants or would-be entrants at the next level which the monopolist thinks pose the greatest competitive threat to its operations there.[7] At least in those instances where the monopolist relies on outside investment for some of the operations at the next adjacent level it must suffer competition to develop there. Problems of administration are manageable. The monopolist, selling as it does to some buyers, has made a market indicative of the terms on which it might be obliged to sell to others.

Whether a monopolist which has always exploited its monopoly at one level by performing all of the vertically related functions itself must also supply intruders at downstream levels which now want to compete with it there calls, perhaps, for a different answer, at least in those instances where the source of monopoly power is not a public utility franchise. Take, for example, a firm owning the only source of an ore. If it has always produced ingot and fabricated it, the fact that competition at the fabrication level is conceivable may not be enough of an incentive to encourage a public intervention ordering the monopolist to sell ingot to buyers wanting it.[8] For reasons to be reemphasized shortly, ultimate consumers would not benefit in any direct and immediate way by fabrication competition; and there would be a large administrative burden imposed on courts which, without an existing market as a guide, would have to determine whether the prices charged on sales of ingot were low enough to allow buyers to compete in fabrication on even terms with the monopolist. A regulated utility, by contrast, might be ordered to facilitate new entry competitive with its own operations at a vertically adjacent level even though it had in the past filled that market by itself.[9] The

---

7. Compare, also, Associated Press v. United States, 326 U.S. 1, 32, 65 S.Ct. 1416, 89 L.Ed. 2013 (1945); Poster Exch. Inc. v. National Screen Serv. Corp., 431 F.2d 334 (5th Cir. 1970), cert. denied 401 U.S. 912, 91 S.Ct. 880, 27 L.Ed.2d 811 (1971); United States v. Klearflax Linen Looms, Inc., 63 F. Supp. 32 (D.Minn.1945). On a related problem, see the discussion in Austin, Real Estate Boards and Multiple Listing Systems As Restraints of Trade, 70 Colum.L.Rev. 1325 (1970).

8. Compare Bushie v. Stenocord Corp., 460 F.2d 116 (9th Cir. 1972); Industrial Bldg. Materials, Inc. v. Interchemical Corp., 437 F.2d 1336 (9th Cir. 1970). See generally P. Areeda, Antitrust Analysis, Problems, Text, Cases ¶ 218 (2d ed. 1974) and cases there cited.

9. Compare TV Signal Co. v. A.T.& T., 462 F.2d 1256 (8th Cir. 1972); Radio Hanover, Inc. v. United Utils., Inc., 273 F.Supp. 709 (M.D.Pa.1967); Den-

regulatory mechanisms for determining appropriate prices for sales to would-be competitors are already at hand.

Since the "public utility approach" to the duties of a lawful monopolist does not (as a matter of antitrust law) limit the monopolist from charging profit maximizing prices, a rule requiring the monopolist to sell to competitors at the next level would not foreclose the monopolist from its full monopoly profit which (except to the extent precluded by rate regulation there) could be earned at the vertical level it continues to dominate. If only the first level is a natural (or other lawful) monopoly, the monopolist can earn its full monopoly return by setting a profit maximizing price at that level. Competitors at the next level will be forced by competition to set a price yielding only a reasonable return over costs. That "reasonable" price, based as it is upon costs which are increased by the monopolist at the earlier level, will be essentially the same price as that which the monopolist would have set at that level, had it integrated forward alone and attempted to set a profit maximizing price for its production at both levels.[10] Because of this, the rule tending to preclude firms with power at one level from using that power to gain power at another vertical level is sometimes criticized as irrelevant.[11]

But competition is valued for many reasons, only one of which is that it yields a competitive price and the related resource allocation. Encouraging competition at one vertical level even though another is monopolized yields all of the benefits of competition which are not associated with resource allocation and may eventually even yield some or all of those. Additional firms at the non-monopoly level means not only price competition at that level but also competition in innovation. It also increases the number of firms involved and interested in the technology and may provide a base for entry at the blockaded level as firms at the competitive level grow weary of paying monopoly prices and decide to integrate back to the monopoly level.

If (as in *Otter Tail*) each vertical level constitutes a natural monopoly, the ultimate price will again be no higher if the monopolist at the earlier level is forced to make room for an alternative monopolist at the next level. Assuming each monopolist to be devoted to his own interest, the monopoly profit will be shared between the two but their interest will be in acting interdependently to set the ultimate price to consumers which will yield the highest joint return, and then to bargain, in effect, only about the way the profit from this price is shared;[12] only if they are blind to their joint interest is it likely that

---

ver Petrol. Corp. v. Shell Oil Co., 306 F.Supp. 289 (D.Colo.1969).

10. Cf. F. Scherer, Industrial Market Structure and Economic Performance 241–48 (1970).

11. See, e.g., R. Posner, Antitrust, Cases, Economic Notes and Other Materials 704–708 (1974).

12. Scherer, supra note 10, at 241–42.

the ultimate price paid by consumers will be higher or lower than the price which would maximize the return of a single, integrated monopolist. But where (as in *Otter Tail*) the newly entering monopolist at the level closest to the consumer is a municipality or a cooperative, it may be assumed that it will use such power as it possesses vis-a-vis the monopolist at the earlier stage to bargain the price it pays down to a minimum and that its resale price will be set so as to yield only a reasonable return on its own activities.

Where only one level is a monopoly, since the monopolist cannot increase his monopoly return by expanding to the next level, the incentives to integrate are not so high as might first be supposed; but there are some incentives. Forward integration may produce real cost saving efficiencies, in which case it should be encouraged. By contrast, it may serve to protect the monopolized level from later entry by uncontrolled firms who first enter at the competitive level. Also, as Areeda suggests,[13] the monopolist may be regulated as a public utility at its monopolized level, but not at the next level, and may hope if it succeeds in monopolizing the next level, to gain its full monopoly return there despite utility commission control of the price at which, as a utility, it transfers to itself.[14] When (as in *Otter Tail*) both levels are natural monopolies, the monopolist at the first level also has an immediate interest in controlling the second level, even though it cannot increase the profit maximizing price to the ultimate consumer. If the monopolist dominating the first level faces a different monopolist at the second level, it must bargain with that monopolist about how the total monopoly profit is to be divided.[15] But if it succeeds itself to occupy the second level as well as the first it gains the entire monopoly profit, just as it would if the second level were competitive.

Another question which emerges upon analysis of the lawful monopoly cases concerns the conditions which call the "public utility" rule about access into play. In examples of its application, there is a vertical link between the holder of the scarce resource monopoly and the level of production or distribution which the monopolist supplies. The consequence of discrimination in the providing of service is or may be the extension of power at one level of distribution to another; it is a special case of leverage, or of abuse of monopoly power.[16] In the *Terminal* case, for example, the terminal company was owned by railroads which used its services; these competed with other railroads to whom terminal services were denied. The owners of the monopoly at the terminal level could be seen as using their power at that distribution level to extend their domination and control at another level

---

13. Areeda, supra note 8.

14. This, of course, is a hope which the regulating commission can frustrate if it is aware of what is occurring.

15. Scherer, supra note 12.

16. See § 47 supra and §§ 150–62 infra.

where they do encounter competition—in the provision of railroad services. In *Otter Tail, Gamco,* and *Associated Press,* similar factors were involved. Indeed, the court in *Gamco* expressed itself in terms which would limit application of the rule to these kinds of situations. It said that defendants, fruit wholesalers who jointly owned a warehouse from which they excluded a competing wholesaler, were "exploiting [their] natural advantages against competitors." [17]

Now suppose that a firm with a natural advantage monopoly, but without a vertical link to the customer level, were to discriminate. For example, suppose the terminal railroad company engaged only in providing terminal services and that it provided facilities to some railroads coming from the west, but refused them to others; or suppose that Otter Tail operated only as a wholesaler, but sold only to municipalities and refused to sell to private retailers. Would such practices constitute monopolization, the unlawful exercise of monopoly power? Though there is little case law on this point, *Grand Caillou Packing Company* [18] may suggest that it would.[19] As a matter of policy, to require the monopolist in these situations to treat all like firms in the same way—to have, one might say, a rational and relevant basis for any distinctions it may make—is to protect vertically related and adjacent markets from being distorted because of arbitrary decisions by the monopolist.

Finally, let us consider the elements that go into characterizing a position as one of natural advantage which should not be exploited in ways which are disadvantageous to competitors. A firm is clearly in that position when its monopoly arises, literally, from a natural advantage (in the sense that it owns a resource which cannot be duplicated because of geologic or other such factors). The *Terminal* case approaches, if it does not exemplify, this situation. In *Gamco,* by contrast, the resource was merely a building capable of being duplicated. The reason it was unique was that an associated market had developed by custom which gave those in the building an advantage. It may also be that there were scale problems, that there were too few excluded wholesalers to make a competing market economically feasible.

We can generalize by saying that if a group of competitors, acting in concert, operate a common facility and if due to natural advantage, custom, or restrictions of scale, it is not feasible for excluded competitors to duplicate the facility, the competitors who operate the facility must give access to the excluded competitors on reasonable, non-discriminatory terms. This restatement also explains cases like

---

17. Gamco, Inc. v. Providence Fruit & Produce Bldg., Inc., 194 F.2d 484, 488 (1st Cir. 1952), cert. denied 344 U.S. 817, 73 S.Ct. 11, 97 L.Ed. 636 (1952).

18. 65 F.T.C. 799 (1964), enforced in part sub nom., La Peyre v. FTC, 366 F.2d 117 (5th Cir. 1966).

19. See also Areeda, supra note 8, at ¶¶ 217–218 and cases there cited.

Associated Press, though it is not entirely clear in that case that a competing organization could not have been put together by nonmembers.[20]

There must, however, be a limiting case for this rationale. Suppose a group of firms gets together to perform some function in common—say, to develop a new product with a brand name and trademark under which each of them will manufacture and sell, and that they assess themselves on some agreed basis to cover common costs, including national advertising of the brand.[21] There is a degree of investment risk in this enterprise. The advertising campaign adds to costs and may or may not be commercially successful. If the effort proves so successful that participation in it becomes important to any firm wishing to compete successfully in the industry, the natural advantage cases suggest that outsiders must be admitted on reasonable terms. But should this rule apply to all outsiders? A firm in existence at the time of the organization of the joint effort and which was never given the option to enter has a strong claim to participate; yet even this firm is getting a "free ride" in the sense that it did not make the investment at a time when risk was involved. Similarly, a new entrant may have a strong claim. But what about an existing firm which could have participated at the time of organization, but declined to do so? To allow it to enter after success is achieved is to allow it to share in that success without having put up any stake. The answer to these problems, perhaps, is to allow any firm to have access where the need for access to compete successfully is shown, but to allow the original investors an adequate return upon their earlier investment, predicated upon the risk elements which it involved.

PART F. CONSPIRACIES AND ATTEMPTS TO MONOPOLIZE

§ 49. Conspiracies to Monopolize

It is a separate offense under Section 2 for two or more persons to conspire to monopolize. The elements of the offense derive from the law of criminal conspiracy: (1) proof of a concerted action deliberately entered into with the specific intent to accomplish the unlawful result of achieving a monopoly; (2) the commission of at least one overt act in furtherance of the conspiracy. It need not be shown that monopoly power has been attained, nor that if the conspirators continued their course unmolested they would have attained it, but

---

20. Compare Worthen Bank & Trust Co. v. National Bankamericard Inc., 485 F.2d 119 (8th Cir. 1973), cert. denied 415 U.S. 918, 94 S.Ct. 1417, 39 L.Ed.2d 473 (1974).

21. See the analysis suggested by Areeda, supra note 8 at ¶¶ 383 and 385 and by M. Handler, H. Blake, R. Pitofsky and H. Goldschmid, Trade Regulation, Cases and Materials, Prob. 13, p. 523 and Prob. 14, p. 541 (1975).

only that obtaining such power is the purpose which motivates the conspiracy.[1]

Because questions about the quantum and kind of evidence of concerted activity from which conspiracy may be inferred must be fully treated later in connection with Section 1 of the Sherman Act, treatment of these questions will be deferred.[2] For now, it need only be noted that there is a substantial area of potential overlap between the offenses of conspiracy to restrain trade, conspiracy to monopolize, joint monopolization and attempt to monopolize. Though in 1911 Justice White emphasized the interrelationships between Sections 1 and 2,[3] these were rather ignored thereafter until they were again re-emphasized in American Tobacco Co. v. United States.[4] In any event, it is now clear that concerted conduct such as price fixing might offend the law (1) as a conspiracy to restrain trade, and (2) if an intent to monopolize could also be shown, as a conspiracy to monopolize, and (3) if the joint achievement of monopoly power is closely approached, also as an attempt to monopolize, or (4) if joint monopoly power is actually attained, as monopolization.[5]

Beyond proving the conspiracy, the critical fact to be established under a count for conspiracy to monopolize is the specific intent to monopolize. Though a specific intent to achieve the goal of monopoly power must be shown, direct evidence of subjective state of mind is not essential; the intent can be inferred from conduct. Normally, proof of the conspiracy and of its intent or purpose will tend to merge. For example, if firms with substantial shares of a market act concertedly to exclude competitors, to divide the market between them, or to fix prices, it may be inferred that they intend to monopolize.[6] The ways in which evidence about conduct may relate to intent and the uses of structural evidence in this process are ad-

1. United States v. Consolidated Laundries Corp., 291 F.2d 563, 572–73 (2d Cir. 1961); Kansas City Star Co. v. United States, 240 F.2d 643 (8th Cir. 1957), cert. denied 354 U.S. 923, 77 S.Ct. 1381, 1 L.Ed.2d 1438 (1957). See also Lorain Journal Co. v. United States, 342 U.S. 143, 72 S.Ct. 181, 96 L.Ed. 162 (1951); United States v. Griffith, 334 U.S. 100, 68 S.Ct. 941, 92 L.Ed. 1236 (1948); United States v. Yellow Cab Co., 332 U.S. 218, 67 S.Ct. 1560, 91 L.Ed. 2010 (1947); American Tobacco Co. v. United States, 328 U.S. 781, 66 S.Ct. 1125, 90 L.Ed. 1575 (1946); United States v. Socony-Vacuum Oil Co., Inc., 310 U.S. 150, 60 S.Ct. 811, 84 L.Ed. 1129 (1940); United States v. Winslow, 227 U.S. 202, 33 S.Ct. 253, 57 L.Ed. 481 (1913); Swift & Co. v. U.S., 196 U.S. 375, 25 S.Ct. 276, 49 L.Ed. 518 (1905). But cf. Hudson Valley Asbestos Corp. v. Tougher Heating & Plumbing Co., Inc., 510 F.2d 1140 (2d Cir. 1975), cert. denied 421 U.S. 1011, 95 S.Ct. 2416, 44 L.Ed.2d 679 (1975), holding that the absence of any likelihood of success is some evidence that no intent to monopolize existed.

2. See §§ 108–112, infra.

3. Standard Oil Co. of N.J. v. United States, 221 U.S. 1, 49–62, 31 S.Ct. 502, 511–16, 55 L.Ed. 619, 641–46 (1911).

4. 328 U.S. 781, 66 S.Ct. 1125, 90 L.Ed. 1575 (1946).

5. See M. Handler, Cases and Materials on Trade Regulation 639–40 (4th Ed. 1967).

6. American Tobacco Co. v. United States, 328 U.S. 781, 66 S.Ct. 1125, 90 L.Ed. 1515 (1946).

dressed more fully in the sections which deal with the attempts to monopolize; what is said there about evidence of intent is also pertinent here.[7]

§ 50. Attempts to Monopolize

The initial, authoritative statement about the content of the ban in Section 2 against attempts to monopolize was that of Justice Holmes in Swift and Co. v. United States:

> "Where acts are not sufficient in themselves to produce a result which the law seeks to prevent—for instance, the monopoly—but require further acts in addition to the mere forces of nature to bring that result to pass, an intent to bring it to pass is necessary in order to produce a dangerous probability that it will happen. * * * But when that intent and the consequent dangerous probability exist, this statute, like many others, and like the common law in some cases, directs itself against that dangerous probability as well as against the completed result. * * *
>
> * * * Not every act that may be done with intent to produce an unlawful result is unlawful, or constitutes an attempt. It is a question of proximity and degree. The distinction between mere preparation and attempt is well known in the criminal law. * * * The same distinction is recognized in cases like the present."[1]

There has derived from *Swift* the customary statement that attempt to monopolize is an offense separate and distinct from monopolization or conspiracy to monopolize, and that there are two elements that must be proved to show the offense: a specific intent to monopolize and a dangerous probability of success.[2] Yet, the scope of the offense remains unclear, in part because it is usually charged conjunctively with monopolization, conspiracy to monopolize, or conspiracy in restraint of trade, and in the course of adjudication analytical focus is placed elsewhere, and in part because of conflicting attitudes about policy and the uses of economic concepts in antitrust adjudication. As we examine these matters in greater detail we shall refer frequently to an article by Professor Cooper, the most thorough effort to date to analyze these problems.[3]

---

7. See § 51 infra.

1. 196 U.S. 375, 396, 402, 25 S.Ct. 276, 279, 281, 49 L.Ed. 518, 524, 527 (1905).

2. E.g., Walker Process Equip., Inc. v. Food Mach. and Chemical Corp., 382 U.S. 172, 86 S.Ct. 347, 15 L.Ed.2d 247 (1965); Lorain Journal Co. v. United States, 342 U.S. 143, 72 S.Ct. 181, 96 L.Ed. 162 (1951); United States v. Columbia Steel Co., 334 U.S. 495, 68 S.Ct. 1107, 92 L.Ed. 1533 (1948); American Tobacco Co. v. United States, 328 U.S. 781, 66 S.Ct. 1125, 90 L.Ed. 1575 (1946).

3. Cooper, Attempts and Monopolization: A Mildly Expansionary Answer to the Prophylatic Riddle of Section Two, 72 Mich.L.Rev. 373 (1974). See also Turner, Antitrust Policy and the Cellophane Case, 70 Harv.L.Rev. 281 (1956).

§ 51. Evidence of Intent

a. Intent

The anomalies of intent doctrine present themselves when one seeks to probe the elements of the offense of attempting to monopolize. The Supreme Court has indicated that the intent which must be shown to warrant a finding of attempt is not merely an intent to do acts which can be objectively analyzed as tending toward monopoly, but a specific intent to destroy competition or achieve monopoly.[1] The most specific statement to this effect appears in Times Picayune Publishing Co. v. United States, where the Court said that while monopolization "demands only a general intent to do the act, 'for no monopolist monopolizes unconscious of what he is doing,' a specific intent to destroy competition or build a monopoly is essential"[2] before one can be found guilty of an attempt to monopolize.

Though a subjective intent to injure the competitive process is prerequisite, subjective evidence about state of mind is not; evil intent is seldom broadcast and may be inferred from various evidentiary sources. As in the case of conspiracies to monopolize, the most important evidence will be defendant's conduct.[3] When this is recognized, the difficulty of delineating the scope of the offense begins to appear. When conduct becomes a proxy for intent, the attempt offense becomes a means of controlling single firm conduct which threatens competition, a function which in its potential scope is fully as wide as is the concept restraint of trade. Moreover, evidence about industry structure and the way it developed may bear upon the significance of conduct, and may be essential background before particular conduct can be assessed and understood.[4] Thus, an intent to destroy competition or achieve monopoly might reasonably be inferred if a firm, large or small, were using blatantly predatory practices rational only if their current costs would be more than repaid by supra-competitive profits later. But when a firm is already powerful,

---

1. Times-Picayune Publishing Co. v. United States, 345 U.S. 594, 73 S.Ct. 872, 97 L.Ed. 1277 (1953); Lorain Journal Co. v. United States, 342 U.S. 143, 72 S.Ct. 181, 96 L.Ed. 162 (1951); United States v. Columbia Steel Co., 334 U.S. 495, 68 S.Ct. 1107, 92 L.Ed. 1533 (1948). See the cases collected in Cooper, Attempts and Monopolization: A Mildly Expansionary Answer to the Prophylactic Riddle of Section Two, 72 Mich.L.Rev. 373 nn. 60, 61, 63, 64 (1974).

2. 345 U.S. 594, 626, 73 S.Ct. 872, 890, 97 L.Ed. 1277, 1300 (1953).

3. Independent Iron Works, Inc. v. United States Steel Corp., 322 F.2d 656, 667 (9th Cir.), cert. denied 375 U.S. 922, 84 S.Ct. 267, 11 L.Ed.2d 165 (1963); United States v. American Oil Co., 249 F.Supp. 799 (D.N.J.1966); and other cases cited in Cooper, supra note 1, at 397 n. 80.

4. E.g., Cape Cod Food Prods., Inc. v. National Cranberry Ass'n., 119 F.Supp. 900, 908 (D.Mass.1954); Turner, Antitrust Policy and the Cellophane Case, 70 Harv.L.Rev. 281, 305 (1956); Cooper, supra note 1, at 400–03. See also Hudson Valley Asbestos Corp. v. Tougher Heating & Plumbing Co., Inc., 510 F.2d 1140 (2d Cir. 1975), cert. denied 421 U.S. 1011, 95 S.Ct. 2416, 44 L.Ed.2d 679 (structure would make effort to monopolize futile, and thus negatives implication of intent).

less aggressive tactics, so long as they plainly tend to erect barriers to entry, may sufficiently suggest an intent to win the competitive struggle by bringing it to an end.

It is thus clear enough that the requisite intent can be inferred from conduct such as predatory price cutting or coercive refusals to deal.[5] It also seems clear that an intent to monopolize could not be inferred merely from conduct consistent with efficient competitive responses, such as merely expanding to meet new opportunities. Even though such conduct would, on the most sweeping view of the law,[6] suffice for the offense of monopolization if monopoly power were in fact achieved, such conduct does not warrant an inference of specific intent to monopolize. More difficult to evaluate is conduct in the vast middle range—conduct which, though not predatory or coercive, nevertheless could be identified at the time engaged in as being exclusionary in the sense that it would tend to increase entry barriers.[7] This kind of conduct is typified by the use of policies such as the "lease only" policy in *United Shoe Machinery,* a policy which tied customers to a single supplier and inhibited the development of competition.[8]

Conduct tending to raise entry barriers can be recognized as conduct which facilitates the achievement of monopoly. But unless the requirement of a specific intent to monopolize is to be attenuated markedly, one cannot say that every act which raises entry barriers expresses an intent to monopolize. Suppose a leading firm in a hard goods industry introduces a new model every year and that this strategy seems, on careful analysis, to increase entry barriers by increasing the minimum efficient scale; or suppose a firm makes technological improvements which increase minimum efficient plant size. Either course may be in response to the stimuli of the market situation, without any design to dominate. Thus a wide, indeterminate area exists where intent to monopolize might or might not be inferred from conduct which, objectively analyzed, is anticompetitive. In such situations the trier of fact, informed of the governing legal standard, must be permitted to draw inferences from all of the evidence, including, most importantly, such structural evidence as may help to show the potential impact of the conduct.

Of course, if contrary to the analysis proposed above entry barrier generating conduct always gave rise to an irrebuttable presumption of intent to monopolize, that offense would become a versatile and effective weapon against single firm conduct which significantly restrains trade. For example, firms in oligopolistic markets which en-

5. E.g., Porto Rican American Tobacco Co. v. American Tobacco Co., 30 F.2d 234 (2d Cir.), cert. denied 279 U.S. 858, 49 S.Ct. 353, 73 L.Ed. 999 (1929).

6. See § 34 supra.

7. See § 36 supra.

8. United States v. United Shoe Mach. Corp., 110 F.Supp. 295 (D.Mass.1953), aff'd per curiam 347 U.S. 521, 74 S.Ct. 669, 98 L.Ed. 910 (1954). See § 36 supra.

gage in excessive advertising, aimed primarily at product differentiation,[9] or which utilize strategies such as annual model changes irrespective of significant technological advances (which serve primarily to increase the minimum efficient scale),[10] could then be challenged under Section 2. But unless the *Swift* rule is to be ignored and the statutory concept pressed beyond the content it implies, a more fully developed case of specific intent will usually be needed.

b. *Dangerous Probability*

The *Swift* language is less than precise, also, in what it says about the probability of the actual achievement of monopoly. Is proof of inherent probability that monopoly will soon result an element of the offense? If so, proof of an attempt requires proof not only of exclusionary practices which are blatant enough to warrant the inference of monopolistic intent, but also proof that substantial market power is already possessed.[11] However, the *Swift* language plainly leaves open a less rigorous test. On the teaching of that case it ought to be enough to show that the means used, if not abated, are likely to move the defendant progressively closer to monopoly, even though the distance which remains to be traveled and the length of time it may take to cover it are both incalculably large. *Swift* did not hold or state that probability of monopoly in any degree had to be proved as a separate element, let alone that a high risk of successful monopolization had to be shown. A rereading of the first of the paragraphs quoted above in Section 50 will show that Justice Holmes merely identifies the dangerous probability of monopoly as the *rationale* which underlies the legal requirement that there be a specific intent to monopolize before an attempt is found. In Holmes' view the probability that competition will be stifled derives from the evil intent of the actor who is seeking to bring about that end. Nor does the second quoted paragraph suggest anything different or inconsistent; Holmes merely states his recognition that there is a difference in the criminal law between preparing to commit a specific crime, as in buying a gun intent on homicide, and attempting to commit it, as in taking aim and firing. The first step is not an attempt; but the second one may be—even if there really is no dangerous probability because the gun is defective and was bound to misfire. Holmes says nothing about where that line between preparation and attempt falls and certainly does not propose that aiming and firing the defective gun would not constitute an attempted homicide. Holmes was doing no more than proposing the common law of attempts as a guide, and

9. See F. Scherer, Industrial Market Structure and Economic Performance 96–97, 341–45 (1970).

10. It is argued in Snell, Annual Style Changes in the Automobile Industry as an Unfair Method of Competition, 80 Yale L.J. 567 (1969) that style changes in the automobile industry have this effect. But see Selander, Is Annual Style Change in the Automobile Industry an Unfair Method of Competition? A Rebuttal, 82 Yale L.J. 691 (1973).

11. E.g., Bowen v. New York News, Inc., 1973-1 Trade Cas. ¶ 74,590 (S.D.

that guide, surely, does not insist that the criminal actor be within range of success, but only that he have externalized his unlawful animus in a deliberate effort to bring it to actuality. Once he has done that, the law steps in on the ground that by deliberately trying to commit the crime, the actor has shown a serious risk that if not deterred he may persist in his efforts until he succeeds.

Though later cases [12] do suggest that probability of success is a separate element, they do so only by way of dicta and only on the unfounded assumption that *Swift* is authority for that proposition. Surely there is no policy reason for erecting a more rigorous requirment of probability than the *Swift* opinion established. If the intent element were unduly eroded by taking any conduct which heightens entry barriers as indicative, then a limiting of the attempt offense by a separate requirement of near success might well be warranted. But the best way to confine the attempt offense within appropriate bounds is to confine it within the limits of the common law concepts which it utilizes.

Neither is there reason to hesitate to condemn conduct short of close probability of success on the ground that such a rule would unduly discourage effective, though aggressive, competitive conduct. By requiring (under the intent test) that the conduct be of a kind plainly threatening competitive conditions, the rule already filters out any serious risk that desirable conduct will be inhibited. Conduct which constitutes an attempt is predatory, coercive, or calculated to heighten entry barriers; there is nothing which should make us hesitate to condemn it if the evidence leaves no doubt that the conduct has been properly characterized.[13]

N.Y.1973); Southeastern Hose, Inc. v. Imperial Eastman Corp., 1973–1 Trade Cas. ¶ 74,479 (N.D.Ga.1973); TV Signal Co. v. AT&T Co., 462 F.2d 1256, 1261 (8th Cir. 1972), Panotex Pipeline Co. v. Phillips Petroleum Co., 457 F.2d 1279, 1288 (5th Cir.), cert. denied 409 U.S. 845, 93 S.Ct. 48, 34 L.Ed.2d 86 (1972); cases cited in Cooper, supra note 1, at 384–86 nn. 34–37. As Cooper points out, there is no basis for concluding that the Supreme Court approved this view when, in American Tobacco Co. v. United States, 328 U.S. 781, 785, 66 S.Ct. 1125, 1127, 90 L.Ed. 1575, 1581 (1946), it quoted the trial court's charge which arguably took the position that dangerous probability is a separate and distinct element of the offense.

12. See, e.g., Kearney & Trecker Corp. v. Giddings & Lewis, Inc., 452 F.2d 579, 578 (7th Cir. 1971), cert. denied 405 U.S. 1066, 92 S.Ct. 1500, 31 L.Ed. 2d 796 (1972); Lessig v. Tidewater Oil Co., 327 F.2d 459 (9th Cir.), cert. denied 377 U.S. 993, 84 S.Ct. 1920, 12 L. Ed.2d 1046 (1964); Dobbins v. Kawasaki Motors Corp., 362 F.Supp. 54 (D. Or.1973); Huron Valley Publishing Co. v. Booth Newspapers, Inc., 336 F. Supp. 659, 662 (E.D.Mich.1972).

13. See Note, Attempt to Monopolize Under the Sherman Act: Defendant's Market Power as a Requisite to a Prima Facie Case, 73 Colum.L.Rev. 1451 (1973).

§ 52. Evidence of the Market

Closely related to the question whether reasonable probability of eventual monopoly is an element to be proved to show the offense of attempt is the question whether the plaintiff must show the relevant market which the defendant is attempting to dominate. Professor Turner has argued that a definition of the relevant market ought not to be necessary in an attempt or conspiracy case. If defendant is trying "to drive someone out of the market by foul means rather than fair, there is ample warrant for not resorting to any refined analysis" about whether defendant would still face competition from substitutes.[1] Even unqualifiedly stated, this view, adopted in Lessig v. Tidewater Oil Company,[2] though rejected elsewhere,[3] has a certain appeal. Yet, the most satisfactory resolution is not an unqualified one. Rather, it recognizes the complexity of the problem and the relevance of structural data in limited situations.

There are anomalies in the very concept of an attempt to monopolize.[4] Monopolization, though in a sense a course of conduct and a product of volition, is, more precisely, a status, along with the dynamic elements which are associated with attaining to or maintaining that status.[5] A firm acts in a deliberate way to become a monopolist; but its self-definition of its goals may not be power, but market success. This being so, the concept of attempt to monopolize must deal with intent of a very ephemeral kind. Though we say we infer the intent from the conduct we are saying more fully, more accurately, that the conduct, though not resulting in full-blown monopoly, is a sufficient threat to competition to warrant intervention. If the conduct is blatantly a threat to competition, there is no need to be overnice about the degree of power the actor has already attained. On the other hand, conduct may be ambiguous unless examined in its structural setting. It may be honestly industrial, when engaged in by the firm without power, yet exclusionary where engaged in by the firm at or near monopoly levels of power.

---

1. Turner, Antitrust Policy and the Cellophane Case, 70 Harv.L.Rev. 281, 305 (1956).

2. 327 F.2d 459 (9th Cir. 1964), cert. denied 377 U.S. 993, 84 S.Ct. 1920, 12 L.Ed.2d 1046 (1964); see also Twin City Sportservice Inc. v. Charles O. Finley & Co., Inc., 512 F.2d 1264 (9th Cir. 1975).

3. E.g., Hiland Dairy Inc. v. Kroeger Co., 402 F.2d 968 (8th Cir. 1968), cert. denied 395 U.S. 961, 89 S.Ct. 2096, 23 L.Ed.2d 748 (1969); Agrashell, Inc. v. Hammons Prods. Co., 479 F.2d 269 (8th Cir.), cert. denied 414 U.S. 1032, 94 S.Ct. 461, 38 L.Ed.2d 323 (1973); Bendix Corp. v. Balax, Inc., 471 F.2d 149 (7th Cir. 1972), cert. denied 414 U.S. 819, 94 S.Ct. 43, 38 L.Ed.2d 51 (1973).

4. See Cooper, Attempts and Monopolization: A Mildly Expansionary Answer to the Prophylactic Riddle of Section Two, 72 Mich.L.Rev. 373 (1974).

5. See Walker Process Equip., Inc. v. Food Mach. & Chem. Corp., 382 U.S. 172, 86 S.Ct. 347, 15 L.Ed.2d 247 (1965).

In Walker Process Equipment, Incorporated v. Food Machinery and Chemical Corporation,[6] the Supreme Court, in an elaborate dictum, used language which runs counter to the *Lessig* holding. The Court reinstated a counterclaim alleging that defendant had monopolized and had attempted to monopolize by fraudulently obtaining a patent. The Court said that fraud on the patent office would meet the conduct element in a monopolization or attempt case, but added:

> "To establish monopolization or attempt to monopolize a part of trade or commerce under § 2 of the Sherman Act, it would then be necessary to appraise the exclusionary power of the illegal patent claim in terms of the relevant market for the product involved. Without a definition of that market there is no way to measure Food Machinery's ability to lessen or destroy competition."[7]

This dictum is unfortunate and yet may be construed as applying only where monopolization is being alleged, either alone or in conjunction with an attempt, and not to a case in which only an attempt or a conspiracy is being asserted. Structural evidence may be needed in an attempt or a conspiracy case in order to provide a basis for inferring an intent to monopolize from the defendant's conduct, but evidence of a more summary kind than a full-blown market definition may be sufficient for this purpose. If it is shown that defendant has any significant degree of market power and a purpose to exclude, this should be sufficient to warrant the conclusion of danger. The concept of market definition, like other concepts borrowed from economics, should be an analytical tool, drawn upon to the extent it is useful in characterizing conduct in the categories identified by the law. Even in monopolization cases we should not permit this or any other instrumental concept of theoretical economics to become a sacred cow.

It might be answered that unless the market is always rigorously defined the law of attempt to monopolize will be expanded to make every business tort or unfair trade practice a violation of Section 2. But that concern is excessive. Any potential for growth in the law which might be activated by the *Lessig* holding would obviously take the form of selecting out those single-firm practices which were plainly exclusionary—which were, in essence, single-firm restraints of trade. The prohibition would be aimed not at broadly conceived unfair or tortious conduct, but at conduct plainly having the purpose or effect of creating or increasing barriers to entry so as to exclude competitors.

---

6. 382 U.S. 172, 86 S.Ct. 347, 15 L.Ed.2d 247 (1965).

7. Id. at 177, 86 S.Ct. at 350, 15 L.Ed. 2d at 251.

PART G. REMEDIES FOR MONOPOLIZATION

§ 53. Introduction

The end result of a successful monopoly case brought by the government ought to be the end of a monopoly; yet it was a long time before that could be said even as the statement of an ideal and even now it is not an easy thing to point to significant remedial successes in Section 2 proceedings. A little history will suggest some of the problems. In 1911 the holding company through which Standard Oil exercised control over the oil industry was dissolved,[1] but the underlying operating companies were not fashioned into viable competitive units with separate ownership. The decree merely required that the holding company convey interests in all of its holdings pro rata to its stockholders. Since the operating companies tended themselves to be regional monopolies the net effect was "that the decree broke up a national monopoly into a series of regional monopolies under common control."[2] The *Alcoa* case, brought in 1937, ended with final judgments in 1950 which ordered divestiture of Alcoa's holdings in the Canadian subsidiary, but no dissolution of the American firm.[3] The initial 1953 decree in *United Shoe Machinery* granted no structural relief.[4] In 1966 the government sought further relief, the Supreme Court in 1968 reversed the trial court's holding that further relief was not needed,[5] and in 1969 a plan of dissolution worked out by consent was eventually ordered.[6] It required the divestiture of assets reducing defendant's market share to one third.

Why do remedies present such problems? It is not that legal doctrine is inadequate, nor is it that useful theoretical knowledge is lacking. The sections which follow will likely yield a different conviction—that where major structural problems are involved antitrust policy is as yet hesitant, if not ill-formed, and that the diffident elements in the policy are exaggerated by enforcement through a judicial system.

1. Standard Oil Co. of N.J. v. United States, 221 U.S. 1, 31 S.Ct. 502, 55 L. Ed. 619 (1911).

2. R. Posner, Antitrust Cases, Economic Notes, and Other Materials 365 (1974); S. Whitney, Antitrust Policies —American Experience in Twenty Industries 103–11 (1958).

3. United States v. Aluminum Co. of America, 91 F.Supp. 333 (S.D.N.Y. 1950). A consent decree supplementing the judgment was entered a few years later, 1954 CCH Trade Cas. ¶ 67,745 (S.D.N.Y.1954), seventeen years after the original litigation began.

See the discussion in Posner, supra note 2, at 830.

4. United States v. United Shoe Mach. Corp., 110 F.Supp. 295 (D.Mass.1953), aff'd per curiam 347 U.S. 521, 74 S.Ct. 669, 98 L.Ed. 910 (1954).

5. United States v. United Shoe Mach. Corp., 391 U.S. 244, 88 S.Ct. 1496, 20 L.Ed.2d 562 (1968).

6. United States v. United Shoe Mach. Corp., 1969 CCH Trade Cas. ¶ 72,688 (D.Mass.1969). See the discussion in Posner, supra note 2, at 844.

§ 54. The Law of Remedies

By now it should be obvious that to remedy monopoly power one must understand the dynamics of the market which creates and maintains that power. Monopoly inevitably has a structural ingredient; no firm acting alone in a competitive market can possess monopoly power. Concentration will be part of the picture, as will barriers to entry and other structural features. In addition, there will in all likelihood be conduct elements, actions taken by the powerful firm to protect its power against erosion.

Once understanding is gained about the ways in which structure and conduct interrelate to sustain power, ways in which the public might intervene to frustrate the continuance of this power can be thoughtfully designed. These are likely to seek to change conduct, but they are also likely to seek to alter structure. In any event, the critical factor is the way that structure and conduct relate to each other. The question addressed in this section is whether legal doctrine about remedies is adequate to support a remedial program sufficiently responsive to the need.

Legal doctrine about remedies in monopoly cases is inextricably linked to substantive law. Since the latter began by focusing upon the predatory use of power, the former focused first upon conduct and ways of controlling it. *Standard Oil*[1] is classic. The Court granted a remedy which included an injunction and a divestiture order—a remedy which dealt both with conduct and structure. The defendants were found guilty in that case because of predatory practices and the injunction was aimed squarely at forbidding predatory conduct, conduct thought to be not honestly industrial. The order that the defendants divest themselves of ownership and control of subsidiary units focused only upon units which they had utilized to engage in predatory practices; its purpose was to neutralize the aggregation of power through which such conduct was carried out.[2] Neither the conduct nor the structural remedy was imposed because the Court saw them as necessary to terminate defendant's power. Both were ordered because the Court saw them as necessary to ameliorate defendant's conduct.

Today, by contrast, there is far greater substantive interest in structure because of its relationship to the maintenance of power. Structural remedies are likely to be seen as appropriate for the same reason; even conduct remedies are considered primarily as possible ways to reduce power.[3] But courts did not move immediately from

---

1. Standard Oil Co. of N.J. v. United States, 221 U.S. 1, 31 S.Ct. 502, 55 L. Ed. 619 (1911).

2. Id. at 78, 31 S.Ct. at 523, 55 L.Ed. at 652. The remedial aspects of the cases brought during the early merger movements are discussed in Hale, Trust Dissolution: "Atomizing" Business Units of Monopolistic Size, 40 Colum.L.Rev. 615 (1940).

3. United States v. United Shoe Mach. Corp., 391 U.S. 244, 252, 88 S.Ct. 1496, 1501, 20 L.Ed.2d 562, 568 (1968).

the focus on conduct to a focus on power. There was an intermediate step, through which there was developed what is sometimes called the "fruits" doctrine. In a series of cases dealing with the motion picture industry,[4] the courts, on finding that monopoly power was being exercised at the exhibitor level by a conspiracy which entailed vertical links between exhibitors and producers, ordered defendants to divest themselves of various holdings partly on the ground that divestiture was necessary to deprive them of the fruits of their prior offense. The fruits doctrine was an extension of the law; it asserted that a structural remedy, divestiture, was appropriate even though not needed to effectively deal with defendant's future conduct. Divestiture was warranted where defendant had acquired something he would not have acquired had competitive conditions been maintained.

This development had its culmination when courts, as in *Alcoa*[5] and *United Shoe Machinery*[6] began to see the possession of monopoly power as itself a serious public concern and to regard any conduct through which power was attained or held as wrongful. In *Alcoa* the court of appeals holding that defendant had monopolized was entered in 1945. A hearing on remedy was not reached until 1949.[7] In the five wartime years after the closing of the record in the case on the merits, the government had acquired large aluminum production facilities.[8] Wartime legislation[9] required that these be disposed of in ways that tended to promote competition. Thus, changes had occured which tended toward the reduction of Alcoa's power. The court of appeals had emphasized that "[d]issolution is not a penalty, but a remedy. If the industry will not need it for its protection it will be a disservice to break up an aggregation which has for so long demonstrated its efficiency."[10] This language had a dual significance. First, it rejected the penal implications of the fruits doctrine; second, it implied that where dissolution was needed to dissipate monopoly power it should be ordered.

At the level of stating the law, the district court in *Alcoa* responded appropriately. It reviewed the development of remedial doctrine in a thorough and scholarly way. Quoting Schine Theatres v.

---

4. Schine Chain Theatres v. United States, 334 U.S. 110, 68 S.Ct. 947, 92 L.Ed. 1245 (1948); United States v. Paramount Pictures, 334 U.S. 131, 68 S.Ct. 915, 92 L.Ed. 1260 (1948); United States v. Crescent Amusement Co., 323 U.S. 173, 65 S.Ct. 254, 89 L.Ed. 160 (1944).

5. United States v. Aluminum Co. of America, 148 F.2d 416 (2d Cir. 1945).

6. United States v. United Shoe Mach. Corp., 110 F.Supp. 295 (D.Mass.1953), aff'd per curiam 347 U.S. 521, 74 S.Ct. 669, 98 L.Ed. 910 (1954).

7. United States v. Aluminum Co. of America, 91 F.Supp. 333 (S.D.N.Y. 1950).

8. Id. at 402–03.

9. 58 Stat. 765 et seq., 50 U.S.C.A. § 1611 et seq.

10. United States v. Aluminum Co. of America, 148 F.2d 416, 446 (2d Cir. 1945).

United States, it summarized the historical development by saying that divestiture or dissolution served several functions: "(1) It puts an end to the combination or conspiracy when that is itself the violation. (2) It deprives the antitrust defendants of the benefits of their conspiracy. (3) It is designed to break up or render impotent the monopoly power which violates the Act." [11] It emphasized the last function, as had the court of appeals, saying that the propriety of dissolution or divestiture depended, ultimately, upon "the position of the defendant in the market." [12]

Since that time there has been one significant additional doctrinal development: the Supreme Court's flat-out announcement in *United Shoe Machinery* that when monopolization has been adjudicated it is the duty of the court to fashion a remedy which will bring monopoly power to an end.[13] In sum, law at the doctrinal level is at once flexible and comprehensive. If there have been deficiencies in the law's response to monopoly they do not lie here.

§ 55. Institutional Limitations to Effective Remedies

Having remarked that it possessed all the power needed to break up and render impotent defendant's monopoly power, the district court in *Alcoa*[1] concluded, upon a cautious and conservative evaluation of the evidence, that dissolution was not called for. Since the close of the record, Reynolds, a fabricator, had entered ingot production with the aid of a government loan; also, the government, which during the war had built and leased to Alcoa additional plants, had, upon termination of the leases, sold these to Reynolds and Kaiser, another new entrant. Though Alcoa still had 87% of total sales of domestically produced virgin ingot (to 15% for Reynolds and 3% for Kaiser) the court concluded that Alcoa no longer controlled scrap and, therefore, that secondary aluminum now had to be included in the market. On this basis, Alcoa had 46.8%, Reynolds 22% and Kaiser 15% of the relevant market; furthermore, Alcoa's share was falling while that of Reynolds and Kaiser was increasing. The court concluded that divestiture should not be ordered (1) because Alcoa was no longer a monopolist, (2) because a viable aluminum industry was necessary for national security and divestiture might weaken it, (3) because one of Alcoa's plants was old and more costly to operate than Reynolds' or Kaiser's, thus creating doubt whether an independent company using this plant could survive, (4) because it would be difficult to find management for a dissolved Alcoa, and (5) because

---

11. United States v. Aluminum Co. of America, 91 F.Supp. 333, 344 (S.D.N.Y.1950).

12. Id.

13. United States v. United Shoe Mach. Corp., 391 U.S. 244, 250–252, 88 S.Ct. 1496, 1500–1501, 20 L.Ed.2d 562, 567–568 (1968).

1. United States v. Aluminum Co. of America, 91 F.Supp. 333 (S.D.N.Y. 1950).

dissolution would impede Alcoa's research which was in the public interest.

All five reasons the court gave for denying structural relief were doubtful and some of them were plainly irrelevant under the law which the court itself had announced. If the purpose of a remedy is to break up aggregations of power, how could it matter that this particular aggregation was doing useful research? An analytically more forceful opinion could no doubt have been written in support of a divestiture order than against one. Why, then, did the court act as it did?

The answer is that there was significant doubt in the mind of the court about several questions which are crucial to the entire enterprise of ending monopoly through adjudication. What basis did the court have for concluding that it could have structured the industry anew in ways which would have yielded better performance than the existing structure? The argument that Alcoa still possessed substantial power was better perhaps than the contrary argument, but it was not overbearing. Surely a judge, with little guidance other than broad statements of economic theory, will hesitate before entering upon the unaccustomed judicial business of disrupting myriad existing relationships in an effort to make over the structure of an entire industry.

A similar caution is found in the district court opinions in *United Shoe Machinery*.[2] After finding that the defendant had attained and held monopoly power through a series of practices which tended to make entry more difficult, the court refused to order dissolution. The government proposed to dissolve United into three separate manufacturing companies; the court regarded this as unrealistic because United conducted all machine operations in one plant.[3] However, the remedy first granted, though limited to an injunction, was different in concept from the conduct remedies of an earlier day. The court in its opinion on violation had sought to identify the dynamics through which United's practices impeded entry and found these primarily in United's lease only policy and in the restrictive lease terms. Its injunction therefore required United to offer to sell as well as lease, required a reasonable relationship between sale and lease prices, and required repairs to be offered separately. It also required United to get out of certain ancillary fields and to license its patents on a reasonable basis. The court hoped that these conduct measures, because directed at structure, would gradually erode United's power.

This initial remedy opinion did not end the matter. The original decree stated that the court retained jurisdiction to allow either party

2. United States v. United Shoe Mach. Corp., 110 F.Supp. 295 (D.Mass.1953); petition for modification denied, 266 F.Supp. 328 (D.Mass.1967), rev'd, 391 U.S. 244, 88 S.Ct. 1496, 20 L.Ed.2d 562 (1968).

3. United States v. United Shoe Mach. Corp., 110 F.Supp. 295, 348 (D.Mass. 1953).

after the passage of ten years to petition for modification in light of the effects of the decree. Years later cross-petitions were filed, United seeking to have the decree terminated as no longer needed and the government seeking to have dissolution ordered on the ground the original decree had failed to dissolve United's power. The district court, which found that United's power was slowly eroding, concluded that the decree was working successfully, and denied both petitions.[4] On the government's appeal, the Supreme Court reversed and ordered the district court to decree dissolution.[5]

Perhaps the best hope is that, hereafter, courts facing structural remedy issues will get more help than they have customarily received from the Department of Justice. As Judge Wyzanski implied in *United Shoe Machinery,* the government is sometimes extremely casual about remedy. The attention of the trial attorney is invariably on "winning"; if the government prevails on the merits, its attorney may call insistently for dissolution much as an overly ardent district attorney might cry out for capital punishment. But dissolution is not a self-defining remedy. To restructure an industry sensibly one must deeply understand it and the interrelationships of its various parts. It is ironic that in *United Shoe Machinery,* a case which took more than a decade to dispose of, the government's case on the remedial issues should have consisted of rather casual proposals for divestiture.

The ideal presentation in a monopoly case would be one in which remedial proposal arose organically out of the theory of the case. The government, through the staff work of its economists and lawyers together (and utilizing discovery as extensively as necessary) would develop a dynamic conception of the industry in question, a conception which would both identify the loci of excessive power, the media through which that power was obtained or maintained, and the means through which excessive power could be terminated. The remedy would be neither an afterthought, nor a reward allowed to the trial attorney for winning the lawsuit, but a public policy goal integral to the entire proceeding. Until the government proceeds thus, courts are not powerless. Where more assistance is needed in fashioning a remedy than the government has provided, the court could commission its own deeper study. It might suffice to retain an expert and ask him to prepare and put into evidence a factual basis for remedial recommendations.[6] If indicated, the court might, upon a finding of monopolization, put the corporation into a receivership and direct the receiver to administer the corporation so as to preserve it while preparing a plan of dissolution.[7] The receiver could utilize

---

4. United States v. United Shoe Mach. Corp., 266 F.Supp. 328 (D.Mass.1967).

5. United States v. United Shoe Mach. Corp., 391 U.S. 244, 88 S.Ct. 1496, 20 L.Ed.2d 562 (1968).

6. See Anno. 95 ALR2d 390.

7. In United States v. Hartford-Empire Co., 46 F.Supp. 541 (N.D.Ohio 1942), rev'd in part 323 U.S. 386, 65 S.Ct. 373, 89 L.Ed. 322 (1945) the district

such expert assistance as was needed in preparing a plan which would then be submitted for judicial approval.

§ 56. Enforcement Problems of Conduct Decrees

The history of *United Shoe Machinery*[1] suggests another contrast between a decree of dissolution or divestiture and a decree which establishes standards of conduct. Once executed, the former leaves nothing for further judicial supervision. The latter necessitates both the policing of defendant's activities over the years and, if the purpose is to erode power, continuing measurement of the effect of the decree on competitive conditions in the industry. If the conduct decree is specific enough, as was the "no lease only policy" mandate in the *United Shoe Machinery* decree, policing defendant's conduct may not be unduly burdensome. There are likely to be customers or competitors having an interest in decree enforcement who can be counted on to complain to the Department of Justice if violations occur; investigating and proving violations in a contempt proceeding, if necessary, will not be exceedingly difficult.

There are other kinds of conduct decrees which present more onerous problems. *Terminal Railroad*[2] exemplifies one such difficulty. Where the theory of the action is essentially regulatory, requiring a natural monopoly to provide reasonable access to all, the decree will necessarily be phrased in general language which is likely to invite dispute about the way it applies to ongoing situations in the industry. Similarly, if the decree is aimed at inhibiting practices which give rise to entry barriers and if it requires that lines be drawn between permissible and impermissible practices, supervisory problems may arise. For example, if the defendant has blockaded patented technology and is ordered (as was United Shoe Machinery Co.) to license its patents to all applicants at reasonable royalties, someone is going to have to decide, from time to time, whether established royalty rates meet the demands of the decree.[3] There are numerous practices which it might be desirable to inhibit in particular settings, but which can only be described in general language. Discriminatory pricing, for example, is seldom obvious; to identify it requires an analysis of costs and an assignment of costs to different transactions. Thus a decree forbidding discrimination could present significant policing problems. If a decree dealing with ongoing con-

court appointed receivers to take over management in order to keep open the possibility of dissolution; the Supreme Court held this to be unnecessary on the record before it.

1. United States v. United Shoe Mach. Corp., 110 F.Supp. 295 (D.Mass.1953), aff'd per curiam 347 U.S. 521, 74 S.Ct. 669, 98 L.Ed. 910 (1954); petition for modification denied, 266 F.Supp. 328 (D.Mass.1967), rev'd 391 U.S. 244, 88 S.Ct. 1496, 20 L.Ed.2d 562 (1968).

2. United States v. Terminal R.R. Ass'n of St. Louis, 224 U.S. 383, 32 S. Ct. 507, 56 L.Ed. 810 (1912).

3. See the analysis in Posner, A Statistical Study of Antitrust Enforcement, 13 J.Law & Econ. 365 (1970), particularly at 389.

duct were to incorporate even vaguer, more judgmental concepts, the problems would be more severe. Imagine the problems that would be presented in a case in which the court concluded that unreasonably high advertising expenditures by defendant tended to raise entry barriers, and sought by an injunction to moderate defendant's conduct in this respect.

Even where the conduct which expands or protects power can be easily described and violations easily identified, effective antitrust enforcement requires that the effects of a conduct decree be evaluated from time to time. If the methods chosen to reduce power do not achieve that goal with reasonable dispatch, more drastic measures will be needed.[4] For all of these reasons, if conduct decrees are to be effective, substantial time and energy of the enforcement agency and the courts will have to be devoted to this ongoing activity. This tends both to reemphasize the difficulties of engaging in economic regulation through a judicial system and to invite a greater reliance upon structural remedies. Though they are more drastic, their effects are likely to be more determinate. They are also far easier for courts to administer and, in the end, may be easier for the affected firm to deal with. The structural remedy brings the matter to an end and allows all concerned to get on with the business of the marketplace.

§ 57. Criminal Sanctions

Every violation of the antitrust laws is a crime punishable by imprisonment for up to one year and a fine the maximum amount of which was recently increased from $50,000 to $1 millon, if the defendant is a corporation, or $100,000 if a natural person.[1] However, the criminal sanction has been infrequently used;[2] fines have been modest and imprisonment rare. A system of sanctions which removed from the defendants any monopolistic gains would no doubt be an effective deterrent,[3] but criminal sanctions fall far short of this ideal.

Although criminal proceedings are rarely brought in monopoly cases, there seem to be two kinds of situations where the government is inclined to seek criminal sanctions. First, where aggressively predatory conduct is evident, criminal sanctions may be sought for punitive reasons.[4] Second, the government may evoke the criminal remedy where it cannot conceive of any more appropriate remedial response.

4. United States v. United Shoe Mach. Corp., 391 U.S. 244, 88 S.Ct. 1496, 20 L.Ed.2d 562 (1968).

1. Antitrust Procedures and Penalties Act, Pub.L. No. 93–528, 88 Stat. 1706, 93rd Cong., 2d Sess. (1974).

2. See Posner, A Statistical Study of Antitrust Enforcement, 13 J.Law & Econ. 365, 392 (1970).

3. R. Posner, Economic Analysis of Law 360–372 (1973).

4. E.g., United States v. American Tobacco Co., 221 U.S. 106, 31 S.Ct. 632, 55 L.Ed. 663 (1911).

The tobacco case brought during the 1940's [5] and the major movie industry case of that period [6] are instances where criminal sanctions may have been sought because the enforcement agency could not conceive of any more appropriate response. Both cases involved allegations of joint monopolization inferred largely from apparently interdependent conduct on the part of major firms in an industry and without strong evidence of collusion. Since the firms were already independent in form, a dissolution order would not avail, and interdependent conduct, (say, in pricing) would be difficult to deal with by means of a conduct decree. In this circumstance the criminal case serves to declare the law, to impose some financial and social sanction on the violators, and to encourage them to seek out ways of acting independently and not interdependently in the future.

§ 58. Private Remedies

While private actions alleging monopolization have not been numerous there have been some important Section 2 cases brought by private plaintiffs.[1] Issues respecting private enforcement, many of which arise irrespective of the substantive violation alleged, will be dealt with generally in Chapter 9.

Remedial issues in private actions for monopoly can be exceedingly complex and when settlements are reached, grave questions may be raised about whether the remedy advances the public interest or only that of the parties to the suit. For example, a Section 2 complaint brought by Bell and Howell Company against Eastman Kodak Company was recently settled by a consent decree which required the defendant to give early disclosure and licensing opportunity to the plaintiff with respect to technological innovations of specified kinds, and required the plaintiff to keep the data confidential.[2] It does not greatly strain the imagination to see this decree as functioning in effect as a technological cartel between the two firms. Indeed, the agreement spelled out in the decree is not at all unlike the "technological merger" reached, without litigation, by agreement between IBM and Sperry Rand Corporation and which on the suit of another competitor was found to violate Section 1.[3]

---

5. American Tobacco Co. v. United States, 328 U.S. 781, 66 S.Ct. 1125, 90 L.Ed. 1575 (1946).

6. United States v. Paramount Pictures, Inc., 334 U.S. 131, 68 S.Ct. 915, 92 L.Ed. 1260 (1948).

1. E.g., Telex Corp. v. IBM Corp., 510 F.2d 894 (10th Cir. 1975); TWA v. Hughes Tool Co., 409 U.S. 363, 93 S.Ct. 647, 34 L.Ed.2d 577 (1973); Hano-

ver Shoe, Inc. v. United Shoe Mach. Corp., 392 U.S. 481, 88 S.Ct. 2224, 20 L.Ed.2d 1231 (1968).

2. Bell & Howell Co. v. Eastman Kodak Co. (N.D.Ill. July 8, 1974), 674 ATRR A–9 (July 30, 1974).

3. Honeywell, Inc. v. Sperry Rand Corp., 1974 CCH Trade Cas. ¶ 74,874 (D.Minn. Oct. 19, 1973).

Chapter 3

HORIZONTAL RESTRAINTS OF TRADE

Table of Sections

Part		Sections
A.	Cartels and Interdependent Conduct	59–62
B.	Development of the Rule of Reason and the Per Se Doctrine	63–67
C.	The Current Construction of Section 1 of the Sherman Act	68–72
D.	"Naked" Price Restraints	73–78
E.	Horizontal Market Division	79–82
F.	Boycotts	83–92
G.	Data Dissemination	93–97
H.	Standardization Programs	98–100
I.	Miscellaneous Joint Activities	101–107
J.	Contract, Combination and Conspiracy	108–114

PART A. CARTELS AND INTERDEPENDENT CONDUCT

Sec.
59. Introduction.
60. Restraints of Trade at Common Law.
61. The Nature of a Cartel.
62. Interdependent Conduct.

PART B. DEVELOPMENT OF THE RULE OF REASON AND THE *PER SE* DOCTRINE

63. Introduction.
64. The Early Cases.
65. The Classic Rule of Reason.
66. The Scope of the Rule of Reason.
67. The *Per Se* Doctrine.

PART C. THE CURRENT CONSTRUCTION OF SECTION 1 OF THE SHERMAN ACT

68. Rule of Reason Analysis Today.
69. The Place of Market Power in Rule of Reason Analysis.
70. Power, Purpose, and Effect in *Per Se* Analysis.
71. The Relationship of Purpose and Effect in Section 1 Analysis.
72. The Relationship of the *Per Se* Doctrine to the Rule of Reason.

PART D. "NAKED" PRICE RESTRAINTS

Sec.
73. Introduction.
74. Purpose and Effect as Guides to Characterization.
75. Possible Benefits from Price Restraints.
76. Naked Restraints Distinguished from Arrangements to Make or Improve a Market.
77. Naked Price Restraints Distinguished from Restrictions Resulting from Partial Integration.
78. Agreements Establishing Maximum Prices.

PART E. HORIZONTAL MARKET DIVISION

79. History of the Rule—The Cases Before Topco.
80. The Topco Case.
81. The Implications of Topco—Issues of Characterization.
82. Market Division and Price Fixing Compared.

PART F. BOYCOTTS

83. The Characteristics of a Boycott.
84. History and Development of the *Per Se* Rule Against Boycotts.
85. The Justification for a *Per Se* Approach.
86. Purpose and Effect as Guides to Characterization.
87. Explicit Boycotts Used to Police Industry Self-Regulation.
88. Industry Self-Regulation by Conduct Tending to have the Effects of a Boycott.
89. The Application of Boycott Doctrine to Cases of Partial Integration.
90. *Per Se* Doctrine and Concerted Refusals to Deal Other Than Classic Boycotts.
91. Exclusive Franchises Distinguished from Boycotts.
92. Application of Boycott Doctrine to Cases Where Political, Religious, Social or Other Non-Commercial Purposes are Involved.

PART G. DATA DISSEMINATION

93. Introduction.
94. Economic Effects of Disseminating Prices.
95. The Early Cases.
96. The Container Case and Structural Analysis as a Guide to Legality of Price Information Programs.
97. Dissemination of Non-Price Data, Commentary and Recommendations for Action.

PART H. STANDARDIZATION PROGRAMS

98. Product Standardization.
99. Standardization of Trade Terms Other Than Price.
100. Standardization of Hours, Facilities and Other Elements of Competitive Style.

PART I. MISCELLANEOUS JOINT ACTIVITIES

Sec.
101. Concerted Decision Making.
102. Joint Negotiation with Suppliers, Customers, or Unions.
103. Horizontal Agreements (Other Than Boycotts) Not to Deal.
104. Joint Agencies for Buying or Selling.
105. Joint Research.
106. Joint Activities in Making a Market.
107. Joint Arrangements Concerning Advertising.

PART J. CONTRACT, COMBINATION AND CONSPIRACY

108. Introduction.
109. The Classic Conspiracy.
110. "Conscious Parallelism" as Evidence of a Classic Conspiracy.
111. The Strengths and Deficiencies of the Classical Concept of Contract, Combination and Conspiracy.
112. Performance Evidence as "Plus Factor" Evidence of Conspiracy When Conscious Parallelism has been Shown.
113. Remedies in Cases of Classic Conspiracy.
114. Intra-Enterprise Conspiracy.

PART A. CARTELS AND INTERDEPENDENT CONDUCT

§ 59. Introduction

Chapter 2 dealt with the law governing the ways in which a single firm may gain and exercise monopoly power. This chapter begins a consideration of the methods by which two or more separate firms may act concertedly to obtain and exercise power and the law which governs these activities. The focus is on what are called loose knit combinations, arrangements involving concerted action by firms which coordinate their activities, but which remain under separate ownership and control. A later chapter [1] will deal with an intermediate situation in which two or more firms, which originally were separate, gain power by combining through merger into one economic unit under unified ownership and control.

Just as problems of single firm power call uniquely for a consideration of Section 2 of the Sherman Act, and merger problems for a consideration of Section 7 of the Clayton Act, so the loose knit combinations which are the subject of this chapter are governed particularly by Section 1 of the Sherman Act, which forbids "contracts, combinations * * * or conspiracies in restraint of trade." [2] Chief Justice Hughes described the Sherman Act as "a charter of freedom" which possesses "generality and adaptability comparable to that

---

1. See Chapter 7 infra.   2. 26 Stat. 209, 15 U.S.C.A. § 1.

found to be desirable in constitutional provisions." [3] These words have a pointed application to Section 1 of the Act which is, if anything, more spacious in sweep and open to development and change than is Section 2.

There have been two basic approaches in the application of Section 1. The first is known as the rule of reason, the second as the *per se* doctrine. The rule of reason calls for a broad inquiry into the nature, purpose and effect of any challenged arrangement before a decision is made about its legality. The *per se* doctrine labels as illegal any practice to which it applies, regardless of the reasons for the practice and without extended inquiry as to its effects. While these two approaches purport to stand in harmonious relationship, one applying to some kinds of loose knit arrangements and the other to the rest, they signify quite distinct attitudes toward the appropriate role of courts in the regulation of economic conduct. Over time, the area of application of the *per se* doctrine has tended to expand and that of the rule of reason to contract. In addition, the range of considerations which can be introduced in the course of a determination of reasonableness has, with a few exceptions, remained narrow.

Insights from economic theory have played a role in these developments, but not an exclusive, or perhaps even a dominant one. Courts in interpreting the statutory phrase, "restraint of trade," have considerably narrowed the range of inquiry by recognizing one value as dominant, by conceding importance to only one other, and by relegating all the rest to distinctly subsidiary, even trivial roles. The dominant value is the maintenance of competitive industrial activity in all areas to which the Act applies. Commitment to this value is reflected in the development of both the rule of reason and the *per se* doctrine. The other value to which courts have attached importance is that of economic efficiency, primarily as achieved through integration.

There is no basic conflict between competition and efficiency. In a competitive economy, signals which are given through ongoing changes in price relationships are major sign posts which point the way toward efficiency in production, distribution and resource allocation.[4] Competitive pressures will themselves be spurs toward the most efficient organization of resources. If, for example, efficiency in production, distribution, research or any other function could at any time be improved by increasing the present scale of plants or firms operating at any horizontal level, competition would stimulate expansion to the scale which would be the most efficient.

3. Appalachian Coals, Inc. v. United States, 288 U.S. 344, 359–60, 53 S.Ct. 471, 474, 77 L.Ed. 825, 829 (1933).

4. See C. Kaysen & D. Turner, Antitrust Policy 11 et seq. (1959). As to whether allocative efficiency can actually be attained through competition, given the fact that competition cannot prevail in all markets, see the discussion of "second best" problems, § 1 supra.

After all units in the market were organized at efficient scale, so long as there remained a large enough number of independent firms to assure meaningful competition, there would be no clash between the goals of competition and efficiency. Indeed, the two goals would relate as ends and means, competitive structure and conduct being means which should yield efficient organization of plants and firms and the ultimate end of efficient performance.

The manner in which courts have taken direct account of the goal of efficiency under Section 1 is by drawing distinctions which turn upon the degree of integration which is attained by a particular combination among competitors. The more closely woven the combination—the higher the degree of integration achieved in management, production, distribution, and research—the greater will be the potential for real efficiencies to be yielded. A merger of two firms into one and the integration of all their functions would be the archetypical close knit combination, creating potential for cost saving efficiencies in all functions. The less closely woven the combination, the lower the degree of integration achieved and the lower will be the potential for such efficiencies. The archetype of such a loose knit combination would be the "cartel," an arrangement through which two or more firms negotiate concerted decisions about price, output, or territory, yet continue to independently control all other aspects of their operations. Between these extremes are various intermediate arrangements, where many functions are kept separate, but some (perhaps research, sales or the development and advertisement of a common brand name or trademark) are integrated.

In light of the efficiency interest, one would expect under Section 1 that arrangements which may reduce competition, but which show little integration and thus little potential for increasing efficiency, would be treated more severely than are arrangements which, though they may reduce competition, may also increase efficiency. That expectation is fulfilled. This chapter will deal first with combinations which involve a minimum degree of integration. As we shall see, these are likely to be subject to the *per se* doctrine and to be treated very severely. By contrast, loose knit combinations which entail some degree of integration are likely to be evaluated under the rule of reason.

Of course, one can imagine situations in which the values of competition and efficiency collide. Suppose that a new technology which promises substantial savings in production costs is developed in a competitive industry, but that use of the new technology requires plants far larger than the present ones, so large that the entire output of the industry could be produced by two or three plants. While the problem may never be presented so starkly, there are points at which conflicts occur between the goals of an efficient industry and a competitive one. We must be alert to see how these conflicts tend to be resolved.[5]

§ 60. Restraints of Trade at Common Law

A survey of common law heritage will yield little to suggest that the nubs of concern about which the law was woven at earlier stages of industrial development are the ones which draw attention and energy today. It is even less likely to yield any principle still imbued with commanding appeal; too much has changed for the law to have been constant.

But even a brief overview of the past [1] will be indicative of something of more general import. There is an industrial, economic, social and political history, as well as a legal one, and all these histories are inexorably interlinked. Public policy about matters so comprehensive as industrial structure and conduct, even when expressed predominantly through judge made law, will be in dynamic relationship with processes of development and change in the way goods and services are produced in the society and in social and political attitudes about these and related activities. What is valued will seldom be long settled. There will usually be contention about important issues. Any given social consensus will have elements of instability. To these the law in its season and in its fashion will respond.[2]

The point, of course, is that policy about industrial structure and conduct must be placed in its historical context in order to be fully understood.[3] In our English common law heritage no single cohesive policy is discernible; instead we find a line of development which displays vast change over time. Knowing this will give us a richer understanding of the institutions we witness today. We will be better prepared to intuit, perhaps, that in a country with traditions as complex as ours any policy as general as that embodied in the antitrust laws will be under pressure from a variety of loosely related and sometimes antagonistic influences. We will be less likely to suppose that any single mode of analysis (be it drawn from economics or elsewhere) or any one line of judicial decisions embodies an ultimate wisdom. Seeing matters in an enhanced perspective we may discover the basis for a greater ease, a greater responsibility and effectiveness, in the roles we as lawyers, scholars or judges have to play in the development of doctrine.

---

5. See, e.g., § 204(h) infra.

1. In this section two excellent histories are drawn upon: W. Letwin, Law and Economic Policy in America, The Evolution of the Sherman Act (1965); H. Thorelli, The Federal Antitrust Policy (1954).

2. One can also see the dynamic developments in the American antitrust history if one has an eye for them. See Hofstadter, "What Happened to the Antitrust Movement" in the Business Establishment, 113 (E. Cheit, ed. 1964); see also, Thorelli, supra note 1.

3. See Sullivan, Book Review 75 Colum. L.Rev. 1214 (1975).

The law has its own ways of dealing with conflict and not the least important of these is to seek to emphasize, through the development, application and elaboration of principles of some generality, a sense of order and of continuity with the past and with the future. Let us look then, however fleetingly, at the common law past. Until perhaps the seventeenth century, the industrial structure in England was energized and integrated by institutions and attitudes markedly different from those which prevailed in the nineteenth and twentieth centuries. The roles which individuals played in productive processes were primarily related, as was much else in their lives, to status, and were governed in part by custom and in part by the regulations of municipalities and guilds.[4] There was little if any sense of social, economic or geographic mobility or of power or potential to alter existing modes through private arrangements.[5]

It is in this context that one must see the *Dyer's Case,* with which a course in antitrust used to begin.[6] There, the plaintiff brought an action alleging that defendant, a dyer, had violated the obligation of a bond by which he had undertaken not to carry on his trade in a designated town for a period of six months. The court sustained the defendant's demurrer on the ground that an undertaking by an individual not to carry on his trade was void. The vehemence of the court, which proposed "per Dieu, if the plaintiff were here, he should go to prison until he paid a fine to the King," seems not to reflect concern for the improvident dyer, much less a concern about the effect on the market for dyer's services consequent upon the withdrawal of this part of the supply. It was the simple presumption of the contracting parties which called forth the judicial ire. They sought to alter the economic status of the dyer by their private arrangement, a mode of assigning tasks and status which must have seemed quite unsettling.

One must therefore avoid the temptation to find in this case, or other decisions from this period,[7] an ancient commitment to competition as a process for regulating industrial and commercial activity. One also ought to eschew the equally facile (if quite opposite) assertion that the *Dyer* court's invalidation of a contractual arrangement bespoke hostility to a free market. The more balanced response is to acknowledge that the context of trade early in the fifteenth century differed so markedly from that in which there could arise modern issues about the relationship between freedom of contract and restraint

---

4. See National Industrial Conference Board, Mergers and the Law 4–25 (1929).

5. See Maine, Ancient Law (5th ed. 1888).

6. Anonymous—"Dyer's Case," Y.B. 2 Hen. V, f. 5, pl. 26 (1414).

7. E.g., Anonymous—"The Schoolmaster Case," Y.B. 11 Henry IV, f. 47, pl. 21 (1410). (Schoolmaster, having no freehold or inheritance in his schoolmastership, has no cause of action against another schoolmaster offering competition.)

of trade as to render those cases inapposite upon these more recent topics. What the *Dyer's Case* dramatically displays is how different things were then.

As social and economic arrangements altered and developed over the centuries so also did the law. English society in general and English industry in particular began to manifest a greater complexity, of which an increasing flexibility was a pronounced part.[8] Economic forces developing in the society began to bristle at the restrictions imposed by the guilds; they also bridled at privileges granted by the Crown in its efforts to raise revenue—privileges sometimes given in the form of royal patents purporting to exclude all but the patentee from engaging in a specified business within the realm.

Perhaps the earliest judicial manifestation of this force is found in the *Merchant Tailor's Case*,[9] decided at the end of the sixteenth century. It involved a successful challenge to a by-law passed in 1571 by the London Tailor's Guild. The by-law required every merchant who belonged to the guild and who sent cloth out to be finished to have at least half of the work done by fellow members. Since cloth-workers claimed competences which overlapped those of tailors, the case had elements of a jurisdictional dispute between guilds, each contending for dominance in controlling an important trade. Despite a dearth of helpful authority, Lord Coke, who appeared for the defendant against the eminent Thomas Moore, prevailed upon the argument that it would be unreasonable and thus contrary to law to allow a guild to require merchants to give business only to its members without any commensurate requirement on members to do the work or to complete it in a satisfactory way and at reasonable prices.[10]

The forces which favored taming the regal economic authority and that of the guilds found alliance with those supporting Parliament in its competition with the Crown for political power. These groups, along with a developing middle class which had interests as consumers, were giving voice by the end of the seventeenth century to an essentially new political expression, a claim for greater industrial freedom. The *Case of Monopolies*,[11] decided at the beginning of the seventeenth century, reflects a conjunction of these forces and marks even more clearly than did the *Merchant Tailor's Case* a change of direction in the common law.

Queen Elizabeth had conferred on Darcy, a court favorite, a patent granting a monopoly of the manufacture and importation of playing cards. Allen, ignoring the royal grant, made and sold playing

8. See G. Unwin, Industrial Organization in the 16th and 17th Centuries (1904).

9. Davenant v. Hurdis (The "Merchant Tailor's Case"), 72 Eng.Rep. 769 (K.B. 1599).

10. See Letwin, supra note 1 at 23–27.

11. Darcy v. Allen ("The Case of Monopolies"), 77 Eng.Rep. 1260 (K.B. 1602).

cards in London, and was sued by Darcy. Supported by the Mayor and Aldermen of London, who regarded the asserted power of the Crown to grant monopolies as a threat to all the trades and a challenge to the privileges of the city, Allen defended with vigor. The Court of King's Bench held the patent void. They said it prejudiced the public good by raising prices and lowering the quality of playing cards and by depriving workmen of a livelihood. This case, then, is the first common law expression of a social interest in protecting trade against entry restraints, an interest which was related in part to a conception that competitive processes are advantageous to consumers, and in part to the notion that those who would enter a trade or business have an interest which the society should protect. In the society the notion that one who wanted to engage in a business ought to have unrestricted access had been gaining increasing ascendency, but to the law it was a new one, quite out of place with those which had prevailed at the time of the *Dyer's Case*.

Letwin, who provides a far richer treatment of these cases than that attempted here, stresses that the *Merchant Tailor's Case* was not a dispute "between freedom-loving tradesmen and a tyrannical guild as much as a conflict between two guilds for control of an industry," and that in the *Case of Monopolies* Allen was not "a solitary champion bravely contesting the monopoly of a powerful courtier," but a stalking horse for the Mayor and Aldermen of London who were jealously guarding their own power.[12]

Later in the seventeenth century developments began which resulted ultimately in the substantial reduction of the power of the guilds. Of particular interest is Hobbs v. Young.[13] It was there alleged that defendant exercised the trade of clothworker though he lacked training as an apprentice in that craft. The defense was that defendant, an export merchant, did not do the work himself but put it out and only to qualified journeyman. The court overruled this defense. It held that the merchant, not the workman employed by him, was the one exercising the trade. Far from supporting the control of the guild, the decision when placed on that ground established the basis for a journeyman in a trade, acting as an entrepreneur, to hire untrained workers. The guild's control over the entry of labor and the basis for guild protection of the skilled worker against the unskilled was significantly undercut. Workers could now move about and employers, so long as they were themselves guild qualified, could hire whom they wanted. Moreover, it was also becoming established that the power of the guilds was limited to the chartered towns, that even an unqualified employer could set up trade elsewhere and hire whom he would.[14]

12. Letwin, supra note 1, at 30–31.

13. Hobbs v. Young, 87 Eng.Rep. 206 (K.B.1690).

14. E.g., King v. Turnith, 86 Eng.Rep. 704 (K.B.1665); Company of Horners v. Barlow, 87 Eng.Rep. 103 (K.B. 1686); Cudden v. Estwick, 87 Eng.

The forces underlying these decisions were riding a crest; entrepreneurial energies were increasingly regarded as modes of expression entitled to protection. This and an ancillary interest in protecting competition because of the benefits it was thought to yield to consumers eventually led to legal rules calculated more actively to foster competition.

In Mitchell v. Reynolds,[15] the right of an individual to dispose of his freedom to exercise his trade in a particular place was confirmed, subject to conditions intended to protect against unreasonable restraints. This position, nearly one hundred and eighty degrees away from that expressed in the *Dyer's Case,* seems to have been reached theoretically, through sequential stages. One's business skill or—as the matter might be put today—the good will associated with particular modes of expressing it, took on the character of property; the concept of freedom of contract could then be invoked to protect the disposition of it. However, the protection afforded was far from absolute. The notion of a public interest in the economic results of competitive processes, as well as a sense that adverse social consequence might come from private transactions in which a craftsman improvidently gave up his means of earning a living, combined to dictate limits. A covenant not to practice trade was thus held valid only when the journeyman gave up a previously exercised right of practicing the trade at a particular place and did so on a valid consideration.

The precise contours of this rule against contracts which unreasonably restrained trade are somewhat obscured by controversy,[16] but the complexes around which debate developed—and around which it continues to swirl[17]—are prominent enough. A general restraint, unlimited as to time or place, remained unlawful; in all likelihood a restraint would be classed as naked and invalid except when associated with some socially useful commercial transaction such as a contract of employment, the formation of a partnership, or the sale of a business in a particular place. Indeed, even in these circumstances the scope of the restraint might be tested to determine whether it was reasonably necessary to facilitate the underlying commercial purpose.[18]

During this same period, a different but associated common law development, also protective of freedom of trade, grew out of the ancient law concerning conspiracy. It has sometimes been stressed that the essence of common law conspiracy was a commitment by the

Rep. 881 (K.B.1703); Company of Musicians of London v. Green, 88 Eng. Rep. 152 (K.B.1724).

15. 24 Eng.Rep. 347 (Ch.1711).

16. See, e.g., W. Sanderson, Restraint of Trade in English Law (1926).

17. See, e.g., Blake, Employee Agreements Not to Compete, 73 Harv.L.Rev. 625 (1960).

18. See, W. Sanderson, Restraint of Trade in English Law (1926); W. Letwin, Law and Economic Policy in America, The Evolution of the Sherman Act, 39–46 (1965).

members of the combination to interfere with the property or the affairs of another. As applied to the protection of competition, the doctrine rendered attempts by any group of traders to preclude or inhibit the competitive activity of others subject to criminal and civil sanctions.[19] The rule against unreasonable restraints, which was sanctioned only by non-enforcement, thus had a sturdy assistance. The conspiracy doctrine was first applied to interfere with efforts by laborers to organize.[20] Later it was applied more or less evenhandedly to concerted efforts by manufacturers or merchants to hold wages down,[21] or to limit supply or increase prices.[22] In the price fixing conspiracy cases, the element of interference with outsiders was, of course, weak; these early cartels apparently did not seek to force any course of dealing upon outsiders, or did not necessarily do so, but merely agreed among themselves to trade only with those who would meet their terms.

But the process of growth and change in common law development did not end at this point, at least in England. Laissez faire theory eventually gained such ascendancy that the courts backed away from the notion that an agreement among traders not to sell except at specified prices or to divide territories was unlawful. Where no element of coercion was involved, these transactions were by the second half of the nineteenth century generally held lawful.[23] This ultimate expression of trust in the efficacy of freedom of contract to protect the public was reflected also in the increasing scope which was being given to the area within which a craftsman or trader could himself agree not to practice his trade.

By the time the Sherman Act was passed in this country, the English were relying very largely on the market; the principal area in which the long history of judicial intervention seemed to have left its initial mark uneffaced was in the expression of the view that the public interest would be adversely affected by governmental

---

19. The Poulterer's Case, 77 Eng.Rep. 813 (K.B.1611); Queen v. Daniell, 87 Eng.Rep. 856 (Q.B.1704); see also Northern Securities Co. v. United States, 193 U.S. 197, 24 S.Ct. 436, 48 L.Ed.2d 679, 400–411 (1904) (Holmes, J., dissenting opinion).

20. See National Industrial Conference Board, Mergers and the Law 11–14 (1929) which reviews many of the cases cited in text in greater detail.

21. Hilton v. Eckersley, 119 Eng.Rep. 781 (Q.B.1855); Commonwealth v. Carlisle, Brightley's Pa.Rep. 36 (N.P. 1821).

22. Anonymous, 88 Eng.Rep. 1297 (K. B.1699); King v. Norris, 96 Eng.Rep. 1189 (K.B.1758); Cousins v. Smith, 33 Eng.Rep. 397 (Ch.1807); King v. De Berenger, 105 Eng.Rep. 536 (K.B.1814). See generally, Allen, Criminal Conspiracies in Restraint of Trade at Common Law, 23 Harv.L.Rev. 531 (1910).

23. E.g., Mogul S.S. Co. v. McGregor Gow & Co. [1892] A.C. 25 (1891); Hearn v. Griffin, 2 Chitty 407 (1815); Wickens v. Evans, 148 Eng.Rep. 1201 (Ex.1829); Jones v. North, L.R., 19 Eq. 426 (1875); Collins v. Locke [1878–9] A.C. 674 (P.C.1879); Urmston v. Whitelegg, 7 T.L.R. 295 (C.A.1891). Att'y General v. Adelaide S.S. Co., [1913] A.C. 781 (P.C.).

grants of exclusive prerogatives. It is perhaps of interest that the accommodation reached in England at that time was consonant with the views then generally prevailing among economists. As most of them saw the matter, the main threats to consumer interests came not from private arrangements—if firms acting together set prices too high, others attracted by the profits would enter—but from government interventions such as tariffs, which protected positions of private power from the threat of entry from outside.

During the nineteenth century, however, the American common law, by then an independent system, was having its own quite different development. For one thing, the doctrine of restraint of trade embodied in Mitchell v. Reynolds seems to have been given a more rigorous application in some American jurisdictions than it ever had in England.[24] For another, most American decisions treated agreements fixing prices or dividing territories among producers as contrary to public policy;[25] very few American cases hewed to the line that ultimately prevailed in England which discriminated between contracts limiting competition between the contracting parties and those which either suppressed the competitive efforts of outsiders or monopolized the bulk of the supply in a market.[26]

This in a very general way was the status of American law when the Sherman Act was passed. Doctrinal links to the distant past were vague and indirect. But for a century or so there had been a discernible commitment, however general in its expression and multifaceted in its policy bases, to the encouragement of competition. Little was fixed, much was open to development, and there were forces favoring total laissez faire which were as extreme, if not in the end as forceful, as any favoring the regulation of conduct which restricted competition.

§ 61. The Nature of a Cartel

To discuss Section 1 of the Sherman Act is to deal with the law's response to the cartel and to various modes of concerted conduct among competitors which, if not amounting to full blown cartels, nevertheless have some of their effects. Before discussing the law, one should understand the kinds of conduct in which cartels engage and the kinds of industrial structures in which cartels are likely to exist.

---

24. E.g., Wright v. Ryder, 36 Cal. 342 (1969); Alger v. Thacher, 36 Mass. (19 Pick.) 51 (1837); Duffy v. Shockey, 11 Ind. 70 (1858); Hubbard v. Miller, 27 Mich. 15 (1873).

25. E.g., Stanton v. Allen, 5 Denio 434 (N.Y.1848); Sayre v. Louisville Assn., 62 Ky. 143 (1863); Morris Run Coal Co. v. Barclay Coal Co., 68 Pa. 173 (1871); Gibbs v. Smith, 115 Mass. 592 (1874); Craft v. McConoughy, 79 Ill. 346 (1875); Santa Clara Lumber Co. v. Hayes, 76 Cal. 387 (1888).

26. E.g., Ontario Salt Co. v. Merchants' Salt Co., 18 Grant Ch. (U.C.) 540 (1871); Skrainka v. Scharringhausen, 8 Mo.App. 522 (1880); Dolph v. Troy Laundry Co., 28 F. 553 (1886); Central Shade Roller Co. v. Cushman, 143 Mass. 353 (1887); Leslie v. Lorillard, 110 N.Y. 519 (1888); Herriman v. Menzies, 115 Cal. 16 (1896).

It is also important to identify the effects associated with cartels and their impact on the public.

We have seen that in a competitive market, each firm will take costs and prices as given and will set output at a level maximizing returns at the given prices. A monopolist, by contrast, since its output is the output of the industry, will recognize that the higher its output, the lower will be the price it can charge; it will therefore adjust output and price to maximize its return. In consequence, output for the industry will be lower and prices and profits higher than if the industry had functioned competitively.[1] Now consider an industry where there are a substantial, though not an exceedingly large number of firms. Such an industry might function competitively, but if the firms in the industry could work together and agree upon a cooperative policy as to price and output, they would be able to set price and total industry output much as would a monopolist. As a result, industry output would be lower, prices would be higher, and there would then be a higher industry-wide profit for them to share.

Although the cartel solution may seem attractive to the producer at first blush, there are pressures wholly apart from the law which work strongly against it.[2] Information must be gathered and dispersed. Mechanisms must be developed and utilized for the concerted making of complex business decisions and these decisions must be executed through all of the independent firms. If the number of firms in the industry is too large, these necessities may prove too complex to be workable—especially when, as a result of legal restraints, participants must not only be willing to deliberately break the law, but must be capable of successfully handling all of the organizational problems in secret. Thus if the structure of an industry is really competitive—if there are a very large number of firms all relatively small with reference to industry output—cartelization will be exceedingly difficult, if not impossible. On the other hand, as the number of firms in the industry decreases and the relative importance of each firm increases—i.e., as the structure of the industry approaches oligopoly—cartelization tends to become increasingly feasible.

Yet even where the total number of firms is relatively small, there may be strong pressures against cartelization. Obtaining agreement upon the profit maximizing price may itself present difficulties. In the case of the monopoly only one firm is involved; the profit maximizing price for the firm is by definition the same as for the industry. In a cartel situation, even if there are only, say, eight firms in the industry, each firm will have its own cost structure. If these differ significantly, the profit maximizing price for the industry

---

1. P. Areeda, Antitrust Analysis, Problems, Text, Cases ch. 2–B (2d ed. 1974); R. Posner, Antitrust, Cases, Economic Notes and Other Materials 5–13 (1974). See Appendix A.

2. Hay & Kelley, An Empirical Survey of Price Fixing Conspiracies, 17 J. Law & Econ. 13 (1974); McGee, Cartels: Organization and Functions, 27 U.Chi.L.Rev. 191 (1960).

may be significantly higher than that for some firms and significantly lower than that for others.

Moreover, the cartel must do more than set a price. Associated with the agreed price will be the total amount of product which it will be possible for the industry to sell at that price. Since the aggregate of the amounts which each firm would produce and sell if it were acting competitively will be higher than the total which will clear the market at the cartel price, some mechanism will be needed to restrict and divide the output among the participating firms. Agreement on output will be difficult to reach since each firm will be eager to maximize its own returns. Each, indeed, would desire to maximize its own individual profits by electing to make and sell more at the cartel price than it would have elected to sell at a lower and truly competitive price. But instead of the increased output which the higher price appears to invite from each individual firm, an industry-wide output must be maintained which is lower than that which would be produced at a competitive price.

The cartel might agree only on price and let each firm vie for all sales it could make at this price. Total sales will necessarily be lower than at a competing price and the cartel could rely upon the experience of each firm to teach it what portion of that output it can expect to attain. Alternatively, a formula for dividing the restricted output among the participating firms may be agreed upon. If total industry output is to be, say, 70% of industry capacity, each firm may be assigned an output limited to 70% of capacity. Output may also be allocated indirectly by allocating particular customers or particular territories to each participating firm.

Regardless of how the price is set or the output restricted there will usually be a strong temptation for individual participants to cheat. An individual firm will typically be aware that if it could successfully reduce its price while all other firms maintained the agreed upon price, it would be able to substantially expand its sales and its profits. The worst situation for each individual firm would be the competitive one, where profits are kept to the minimum. For the individual firm, the cartel price and its share of industry output at that price would be an improvement; but the ideal situation for each individual firm would be for all other firms to collude on price, while it alone competes. Individual firms will be aware of this and to the extent that they do cheat (or attempt to do so), there will be a tendency for the cartel to break down.

§ 62. Interdependent Conduct

The preceding section discussed concerted conduct to cartelize an industry, noting both that effective cartelization is feasible only where market structure at least approaches a loose-knit oligopoly and that there will exist pressures toward both cartelization and competition in such a structure. Picture now a tight oligopoly—an industry of three firms, one having 40% of the market and the others having 30% each. Assume that the product they make is homogeneous and that their cost structures are substantially identical. It will be obvious to each firm that price competition in the industry would be adverse to its interest, that its rivals will take its price into account in setting theirs, and that its profits and those of its rivals would all be maximized if the industry price were to settle at a price approximately that which each would set for itself if it were a monopolist. When firms are so few, and when the advantages of cooperation and the precise course which cooperation ought ideally to take are both so evident, it is to be anticipated that each of the firms will see as its own profit maximizing price the non-competitive price which maximizes for the industry. Each firm may set and adhere to an industry maximizing price even if the firms reach no explicit accord on any course of conduct. Conduct of this kind is called interdependent conduct.

While interdependent conduct is unlikely unless both the advantages of cooperation and the particular course it can most advantageously take are evident, interdependence might nevertheless develop in oligopolies which are less tightly structured than that supposed above. In an industry of, say, eight or nine large firms and a few smaller ones, an industry maximizing price might be achieved through a series of experimental price moves. As each discovers the ways in which others respond to its moves, the group as a whole will be moving toward the industry maximizing solution—for, assuming that cost structures do not differ drastically and that each firm realizes that if it prices competitively others will follow, the industry maximizing price and quantity will approximate what will maximize for each individual firm. Nor when these conditions exist, is groping the only way in which interdependence can be achieved. The structure of the market may be such as to invite or facilitate a pattern of price leadership by a single firm, known by industry convention or custom to be the price leader. The leader may be the dominant firm, or the low cost firm, or any firm which other industry members regard as sufficiently deft at judging developing market conditions to be allowed to take the price initiatives which others will follow. When demand or supply conditions change so long as one firm consistently takes the lead in seeking to identify and establish the price which will maximize industry profits and so long as other firms are generally satisfied with the judgments made by the price leader, there will be no need for overt collusion or for a grouping process to establish a pattern of supra-competitive pricing.

Just as there are pressures which work against cartelization, there will be pressures against interdependence. Where cost structures differ or where individual firms see or think that they see the opportunity to price independently and competitively while others in the industry retain an interdependent stance, interdependence, like overt collusion, will tend to break down. Also, interdependence will tend to break down unless the special conditions which facilitate it—in particular, the clear and evident value to all of a particular cooperative course—are sustained.

It is the fact that interdependent pricing can be sustained only in limited structural conditions that makes the phenomenon of interdependence particularly important in understanding the application of Section 1 to those concerted arrangements which, unlike cartel arrangements, do not deal directly with price, output, customers or territories. If a pattern of interdependent conduct is to be established or maintained, various collateral agreements may be needed to support the pattern. For example, continued interdependent pricing in a given industry may depend on an agreement to exchange information about product prices, or interdependence may be feasible only if products are sufficiently standardized, leading to an agreement limiting variations in product. The structure of the industry and the possible relationship to a system of interdependent pricing must therefore be considered whenever an issue is presented about the purpose or effect of agreements between competitors other than those which directly and obviously bear upon price, output, territories and customers.

Interdependence is also relevant, of course, to issues under Section 1 about what constitutes a contract, combination or conspiracy, and about the kinds of evidence from which concerted conduct may be inferred.[1] The concept of interdependence, then, like the concept of the cartel, is basic to an understanding of Section 1.

PART B. DEVELOPMENT OF THE RULE OF REASON AND THE *PER SE* DOCTRINE

§ 63. Introduction

In enacting Section 1, Congress condemned in broad language concerted conduct which restrains trade. With such guidance as might be found in the common law cases, it left to the courts the scope and meaning of this mandate. The very breadth of the condemnation unavoidably gives rise to an ambiguity. Congress could not have meant literally to ban every contract which in any sense restrains trade. Virtually every contract does this to some extent. If a buyer closes a deal with a seller, the contract binds both to a particular course and by so doing limits or restrains the commercial opportunities of other sellers who would like to make the sale and of other buyers who might have sought the goods. Some mode of confining the generality of the language of Section 1 is therefore necessary.

---

1. See § 110 infra.

In the years since 1890, a number of competing views have been put forward about the meaning of Section 1. At one extreme is the literalist position championed by the first Mr. Justice Harlan. He insisted to the end that Congress intended "no distinction * * * between restraints of such commerce as were undue or unreasonable and restraints that were due or reasonable. With full knowledge of the then condition of the country and of its business, Congress determined to meet, and did meet, the situation by an absolute, statutory prohibition of 'every contract, combination * * * or conspiracy, in restraint of trade.' "[1] At the other extreme is the view that was accepted early on by Mr. Justice White,[2] but, as we shall see, was later modified profoundly.[3] This view asserts that even significant restraints on competition do not violate the Act if it can be shown that in the particular context in which they are used they tend toward the achievement of other social goals which counterbalance or outweigh the injury to competition. Over the years the predominant judicial position has been in a range between these poles. Restated, the governing law has been that the Sherman Act bans all concerted arrangements which are adopted for the purpose of reducing competition, or which, regardless of purpose, have a significant tendency to reduce competition, but that arrangements which are adopted for and tend to achieve other purposes do not fall within the condemnation of the Act merely because of some incidental and inconsequential restraining effect on competition. This general position, however, has been reached, not directly, but through two subsidiary rules, the rule of reason and the *per se* doctrine, which, taken together, tend to condemn arrangements which have the purpose or effect of significantly restraining competition and to validate those which do not.

It should be emphasized, moreover, that the proposition stated above is one that has prevailed generally, but not exclusively. Under the rule of reason there has been at certain times and in certain types of situations a tendency by courts to validate even some conduct which significantly inhibits competition in support of competing social values.

Before examining the application of the rule of reason and the *per se* doctrine in various contexts,[4] a brief history of their development will be helpful. It will become clear, no doubt, that the author reads the record as demonstrating the soundness as a matter of law of what seems sound as a matter of policy, an interpretation which identifies the maintenance of competition as the overriding value

---

1. Standard Oil Co. of N. J. v. United States, 221 U.S. 1, 89, 31 S.Ct. 502, 527, 55 L.Ed. 619, 656–657 (1911).

2. United States v. Trans-Missouri Freight Ass'n, 166 U.S. 290, 343, 17 S.Ct. 540, 560, 41 L.Ed. 1007, 1028 (1897) (dissenting opinion).

3. Standard Oil Co. of N.J. v. United States, 221 U.S. 1, 31 S.Ct. 502, 55 L. Ed. 619 (1911).

4. See §§ 68–107 infra.

which gives meaning to Section 1, and which makes little if any room for a judge to measure the values of competition against other alternative social values.

§ 64. The Early Cases

The first cases in which the scope of Section 1 was considered by the Supreme Court were United States v. Trans-Missouri Freight Association,[1] and United States v. Joint Traffic Association.[2] *Trans-Missouri* involved a cartel created by the eighteen railroads which provided service west of the Mississippi. The participants formed an association and delegated to one of its committees, on which participants were represented, the power to work out and promulgate a freight rate structure which would be charged by all of the roads. Market shares were not allocated. Participants were left free to engage in rivalry for available business and all means were open other than rate competition. *Joint Traffic* involved a similar cartel among lines serving between Chicago and the east coast.

As an industry, railroading displays structural characteristics which facilitate cartelization. The number of firms in any competitive segment will not be unduly large and cost structures will tend to be similar. Indeed, pressures toward cartelization are particularly strong because of the peculiar characteristics of the cost structure. Each of the competing roads in these cases had an enormous fixed capital investment in right of way and rolling stock. The variable costs of carrying any given volume of business were small, relative to fixed costs. Because of this, if demand fell at all, or if total capacity was too large in times of normal or high demand, the roads, when faced with reductions in or competitive diversion of traffic, would be tempted to reduce rates to the point where variable costs were covered and some contribution was being made toward fixed costs, even though fixed costs were not fully covered. Unless these pressures for prices to fall below total costs were controlled, the economic health of the industry would be seriously threatened.

Cartelization was one way of controlling downward pressures on price. The railroads contended that it was these special circumstances to which their cartels responded, that such an arrangement was essential to the health of the industry and other industries dependent on it, and that the rates set were reasonable. The Department of Justice, however, rejected any temptation to analyze the economics of the industry and flatly contended in each case that the arrangement was a "restraint of trade" in the sense that it significantly limited the commercial freedom of the members and that it therefore violated the Act.

1. 166 U.S. 290, 17 S.Ct. 540, 41 L.Ed. 1007 (1897).
2. 171 U.S. 505, 19 S.Ct. 25, 43 L.Ed. 259 (1898).

Trans-Missouri was the first of the two cases to reach the Court. Defendants argued that Section 1 could not be applied literally without invalidating innumerable reasonable commercial arrangements, and that Congress must have intended application only to restraints which had been held unlawful at common law. They contended, further, that given the nature of the railroad industry, rate arrangements between railroads did not fail that test, at least where the rates established had not been shown to be unreasonable. The Court, in a terse opinion by Justice Peckham, said it was unnecessary to consider whether arrangements such as this one would be invalid at common law, since Congress in Section 1 had condemned "every" restraint of trade without exception.

In *Joint Traffic* the Court was urged to reconsider this conclusion. Defendants pressed that, under the *Trans-Missouri* rationale, illegality would attend transactions like the following: an organization of workmen to affect hours or rate of pay, the formation of a corporation or partnership by two or more persons or firms engaged in the same business, or the appointment of the same selling agent by two or more producers. Defendants also contended that given the nature of the railroad business cartelization was essential to avoid monopoly. Because of high fixed costs and relatively small variable costs, unless rates were fixed cutthroat competition would force rates down until there was only one survivor. Rates would then be raised to excessive levels. The Court persisted in holding that the rate agreement among competitors was unlawful, saying that "[A]n agreement of the nature of this one, which directly and effectively stifles competition, must be regarded under the statute as one in restraint of trade. * * *"[3] The Court stressed that the effect of competition to reduce rates was direct and immediate, while the fancied danger of ultimate monopoly and rate increases was speculative and, in any event, dependent upon the manner in which the defendants conducted their business in the course of competition. It implied, in short, that the railroads might act interdependently to keep rates from falling to levels which did not cover costs.

The Court might have added that if in the public interest there were really a need for a floor to be established under rates in the industry, there was available an alternative to cartelization—rate regulation by a government agency.[4] Cartelization, while no doubt capable of protecting railroads against cutthroat competition, entailed an inevitable pressure to establish rates not at the minimum reasonable level which would yield a fair return, but at an unreasonably high level yielding supra competitive returns.

---

3. Id. at 577, 19 S.Ct. at 35, 43 L.Ed. at 290.

4. The Interstate Commerce Act, which had been passed in 1887, did not authorize the Commission to regulate rates and, as the Court read it, did not exempt the railroads from Section 1 of the Sherman Act.

Though standing upon its holding in *Trans-Missouri,* the Court in *Joint Traffic* backed away from the sweeping statement of the rule which had been articulated in the prior case. First, it distinguished between arrangements which "directly" and "immediately" reduce competition, as would a rate agreement among competitors, and arrangements which had only indirect or incidental effects. Second, in response to defendants' hypothetical parade of horribles, it stated that some arrangements which had an impact on competition, such as "the sale of a good will of a business with an accompanying agreement not to engage in a similar business," were not restraints of trade at all.[5] The Court thus insisted that arrangements which purposefully and explicitly stifled competition between independently operated firms in the same market are unlawful. It did not matter whether the concertedly imposed terms were reasonable. It did not avail that a plausible claim could be made that due to peculiarities of the particular market, concerted arrangements would better serve the real interests of the public than would a competitive struggle. The Court flatly rejected the contrary view, expressed in the *Trans-Missouri* dissenting opinion of Justice White, that even price fixing arrangements were valid if the prices agreed on were reasonable. In contrast with its insistence upon illegality for all arrangements stifling competition, the Court recognized that there might be arrangements such as a limited covenant by the seller of a business not to compete with his buyer, which, being reasonable and not entailing substitution of concerted market management for competition, ought not to fall under the strictures of the Act.

In marking out these differing yet complementary lines of analysis, Justice Peckham provided in *Joint Traffic* a rich jurisprudence which courts since 1898 have been developing and elaborating. The case teaches that the Act establishes the standard of competition, and no other, wherever it applies, and that this standard may not be set aside upon the ground that an alternative mode of operating the market would be more beneficial to the public. Since competition is the standard, arrangements like price fixing, which directly and significantly restrict competition, are invalid without further inquiry. There may be other arrangements which, upon analysis, may appear not to have significant impact on competition; arrangements which are in this sense reasonable are not restraints of trade which the Act outlaws.

Here, then, is an embryonic statement of the *per se* doctrine. It invalidates without further inquiry arrangements which directly stifle competition. Here also, in embryo, is one way of expressing what has come to be known as the rule of reason: where an arrangement does not obviously stifle competition, but may adversely affect

5. 171 U.S. at 568, 19 S.Ct. at 31, 43 L. Ed. at 287.

it, analysis of the arrangement must be pursued to gauge its purpose and effect. Here also, quite matured, is the unifying rationale for both of these branches of Section 1—that the section wherever it applies mandates competition as the rule of trade. Though there have been shifts at times, including a persistent, sub rosa notion that in some conceivable circumstances certain concerted arrangements may be "reasonable" and hence lawful even though they do significantly restrict competition, the principles derived from *Joint Traffic* come reasonably close to an acceptable current statement of the meaning and purpose of Section 1.

Justice Peckham's opinions did leave unanswered questions. They outlined no systematic ways in which concerted arrangements which violate the Act were to be distinguished from those which do not. United States v. Addyston Pipe and Steel Co.,[6] in which the Court more or less perfunctorily reaffirmed the position it had taken in *Trans-Missouri,* is of particular interest, because in that case the circuit court opinion by Judge (later Chief Justice) Taft grapples with the need for an analytical system.[7] The case involved cartelization of the iron pipe trade. An arrangement between six leading producers accounting for 65% of national capacity had divided the country into territories, fixed prices for each territory, and divided business among members. Unlike the railroad cartels, which had been set up before the Sherman Act, the pipe cartel was a secret arrangement. A major device through which it operated was a system of collusive submission of supposedly competitive bids. Despite the embarrassment of clandestine activities, the defendants asserted what were becoming the standard cartel defenses—that the purpose of the arrangement was avoidance of ruinous price competition which had already resulted in numerous bankruptcies and that the prices established by the system were reasonable.

Judge Taft rejected the reasonable price defense on the facts. Perceptive about business conduct, he noted that the defendants had established what economists today would call an entry-discouraging price; it was above competitive levels, thus depriving consumers of the benefit of competition, yet not so high as to encourage distant producers to invade the market. For these reasons, it was beyond a range which was reasonable.[8] In effect, Judge Taft was asserting that the price yielded by competition provides the only objective test of what is reasonable and that any higher price achieved by stifling competition is necessarily unreasonable. But the opinion put forth more than this factual analysis. Relying on common law precedents, the judge stated specifically that the reasonableness of prices is not a defense to a charge of cartelization. "Where the sole object of both

---

6. 175 U.S. 211, 20 S.Ct. 96, 44 L.Ed. 136 (1899).

7. 85 F. 271 (6th Cir. 1898).

8. Id. at 292–93.

parties in making the contract * * * is merely to restrain competition, and enhance or maintain prices, it would seem that there was nothing to justify or excuse the restraint * * *."[9] The opinion, which was rendered after *Trans-Missouri* and before *Joint Traffic*, is therefore another precusor of the *per se* rule, so far as price fixing is concerned.

Judge Taft, unlike Justice Peckham in the earlier *Trans-Missouri* and like Justice Peckham in the later *Joint Traffic* case, found need to explain that there was room under the Act for some legitimate arrangements which affected trade. In his elaboration of the doctrine of ancillary restraints—a tour de force which imposed order on the disarray of common law precedents—he achieved what no earlier opinion had done. He spelled out a rational and useful way of distinguishing between lawful and unlawful restraints. As Judge Taft summarized the matter, all restraints on competition are unlawful except those: (1) which are "merely ancillary to the main purpose of a lawful contract" (such as the agreement of the seller of a business not to compete with the buyer, a buyer of a business not to compete with the seller's retained business, or a partner, employee or agent not to compete with the firm); (2) which are "necessary to protect" the promisee in the enjoyment of the fruits of the contract; and (3) which do not contain any restraint that "exceeds the necessity presented." The Supreme Court, in a brief opinion by Justice Peckham, affirmed the *Addyston Pipe* holding in 1899, but without discussing the ancillary doctrine, to which a favorable reference had been made in *Joint Traffic*.

These early cases, then, mark competition as the standard against which all market conduct is to be measured.[10] Similar views were expressed in the earliest cases dealing with merger, which we shall examine in a later chapter.[11] The implication of the foundation cases is that conduct at odds with competition violates the Act. The only analysis called for is one aimed at determining the purpose of the arrangement and its effect on competition; if competitive restraint is blatant, this process is perfunctory. Let us now pursue the development, first of the rule of reason, and then of the *per se* doctrine.

§ 65. The Classic Rule of Reason

The *Standard Oil* decision, an antitrust classic, was rendered in 1911, a year after Justice White became Chief Justice.[1] The new Chief Justice, who had dissented in *Trans-Missouri*, was obviously in-

---

9. Id. at 282–83.

10. Bork, The Rule of Reason and the Per Se Concept: Price Fixing and Market Division, 74 Yale L.J. 775 (1965) and 75 Yale L.J. 73 (1966).

11. See Chapter 7 infra.

1. Standard Oil Co. of N.J. v. United States, 221 U.S. 1, 31 S.Ct. 502, 55 L. Ed. 619 (1911).

terested in contributing to the developing Sherman Act jurisprudence, particularly in emphasizing the scope of the judicial role and the range of judicial discretion in the interpretation of the statute. He therefore took the opportunity in *Standard Oil* to announce what has come to be known as the "rule of reason," a new and more general rubric under which the legality of concerted arrangements was to be evaluated. In aid of understanding it is necessary, before summarizing what the Chief Justice said in *Standard Oil*, to set forth more fully the position he had taken in the earlier cases.

The Justice White who had spoken through the *Trans-Missouri* dissent would have validated price fixing cartels among railroads on the grounds that price fixing was needed to avoid ruinous rate wars and that the prices fixed were reasonable. He had favored a rule under which a restraint on competition could be justified by a showing (1) that in a particular instance, a concerted determination of prices or other terms of trade was more in the public interest than a determination resulting from the automatic and objective forces of competition; and (2) that the particular terms which were concertedly (rather than competitively) fixed were in fact reasonable.

This early position had clashed head-on with the majority view expressed by Justice Peckham. Because of this and because in stating his earlier view Justice White had asserted that Congress had intended to invalidate only unreasonable restraints, White's majority opinion in *Standard Oil*, which also made "reasonableness" the fulcrum, is sometimes asserted to have backed away from the holdings in *Trans-Missouri* and *Joint Traffic*. It is argued, in effect, that under the newly announced rule of reason as under the old and rejected one, even direct and purposeful restraints on competition could be validated in appropriate circumstances. It must be conceded that there is some acceptance of this view to be found in one or two of the cases which followed *Standard Oil*, particularly *Appalachian Coals*[2] and *Chicago Board of Trade*.[3] But *Standard Oil* itself, despite confusion arising from White's use of language similar to that used earlier when he was expressing quite different views, does not run counter to *Joint Traffic* or *Trans-Missouri*. *Standard Oil* announces a rigorous rule of reason, a rule which is quite in keeping with the earlier cases. It makes competition the rule of trade which cannot be put aside, however reasonable doing so may seem in particular instances. And, as we shall see, the decisions which followed *Standard Oil* are predominantly true to that line.[4] A close look at the actual holding and language of *Standard Oil* will clarify this assertion.

2. Appalachian Coals, Inc. v. United States, 288 U.S. 344, 53 S.Ct. 471, 77 L. Ed. 825 (1933).

3. Board of Trade of City of Chicago v. United States, 246 U.S. 231, 38 S.Ct. 242, 62 L.Ed. 683 (1918).

4. See §§ 68–107 infra.

The case did not involve a cartel, but a close knit combination of thirty-seven oil corporations which were brought under common management and control through a holding company. The combination had been built through partnerships, mergers and other combinations, as well as through internal growth of the existing organization. The case was more like one in which merger or consolidation was being used as a path to power than one in which firms were operating separately but collusively. But the combination had elements which gave it some of the commercial flavor of the worst of clandestine cartels, or so the Court found. Defendants had engaged in industrial espionage and had threatened to engage in predatory local price cutting in order to induce recalcitrants to join in; once the combination was put together, it had used its great power as a buyer to exact discriminatory price concessions from railroads. It was this pattern of conduct by defendants which was challenged and which the Court found violated both Sections 1 and 2 of the Act.

Respecting Section 1, the Chief Justice in a rather prolix opinion made several significant observations. The term "restraint of trade" was said to take its "rudimentary meaning" from the common law, but the statute did not limit the Court to any narrow common law conception. Of particular relevance to an interpretation of the statute were the ends against which the common law was directed—the existence of power to fix prices or limit production, and the danger that quality will deteriorate when the spur of competition is withdrawn. The common law saw all of these dangers as flowing from any "undue limitation on competitive conditions" and for this reason rendered illegal "all contracts or acts which were unreasonably restrictive of competitive conditions." The Sherman Act issued out of this tradition of pre-existing law. So construed, Section 1 was an "all-embracing enumeration to make sure that no form of contract or combination" by which undue restraint was achieved "could escape condemnation." It reached all "undue restraints" on competition whether imposed by methods new or old.[5]

The soft word in all of this is "undue." The function of "reason" in the rule is to discriminate between restraints which have that offensive quality and those which do not. Reason signifies analysis; the Court invokes "the standard of reason" in resolving the only factual issue open for analysis, which is the question whether a particular practice restricts competition to a degree which could be called "undue." There is no suggestion that a saving grace might be judicially conferred upon an arrangement which does significantly restrict competition on the ground that in the particular instance the public is better off.

5. 221 U.S. 1, 58–60, 31 S.Ct. 502, 515, 55 L.Ed. 619, 644–45.

Indeed, express statements in *Standard Oil* about the way the Act had been applied in earlier cases contradicts any assumption that those cases are rejected. *Trans-Missouri* and *Joint Traffic,* it will be remembered, emphasized the sweep of the prohibition of Section 1. Though failing to state a rationale other than the direct-indirect dichotomy for discriminating between arrangements which were forbidden and those, such as ancillary restraints, which in particular circumstances might not be invalid, the majority had flatly rejected the view then espoused by White, that even price fixing agreements could be valid under some circumstances. The Chief Justice in his *Standard Oil* opinion noted that the earlier opinions had failed to announce the concept of undue restraint and the test of reasonableness which was now being put forth; but, he stated, those cases had been correctly decided. The agreements in those cases, he said, called for the fixing of rates among competitors. Thus, their nature, character and "necessary effect" was irreconcilable with competition and gave rise to "a conclusive presumption which brought them within the statute." Such agreements by themselves and irrespective of any predatory, abusive, or unfair practices brought about the injury to competition which the statute forbids. This being so, "resort to reason was not permissible in order to allow that to be done which the statute prohibited." It does not avail that reasonable arguments are put forth to show that in the particular instance, the public would be better served. The Court stated that where the necessary effect of particular contracts is undue restraint on competition, "they could not be taken out of that category by indulging in general reasoning as to the expediency or nonexpediency of having made the contracts or the wisdom or want of wisdom of the statute which prohibited their being made." [6]

Standard Oil thus accepts and reiterates the embryonic *per se* rule, as well as expressing in complete form a rule of reason. It also reinforces the crucial teaching of the earlier cases. When it appears, either on the face of the matter or after analysis, that competition is interfered with to any significant degree, the law has been violated. As the Attorney General's Committee put it, the standard of reasonableness announced in *Standard Oil*:

> * * * permits the courts to decide whether conduct is significantly and unreasonably anticompetitive in character or effect; it makes obsolete once prevalent arguments, such as, whether monopoly arrangements would be socially preferable to competition in a particular industry. * * * [7]

---

6. Id. at 65, 31 S.Ct. at 517–18, 55 L.Ed. at 647.

7. Report of the Attorney General's National Committee to Study the Antitrust Laws 11 (1955).

§ 66. The Scope of the Rule of Reason

The reading of *Standard Oil* and the limits of the rule of reason set forth above is consonant with the facts and language of the decision, maintains a relationship of easy continuity with earlier holdings, and is reflective of such light as legislative history throws upon congressional intent. Beyond this, it is a reading which permits a court in interpreting the statute to perform essentially a judicial function rather than an administrative or legislative one. When maintenance of competition is identified as the statutory goal and the statute is said to invalidate all arrangements which restrict competition to an unreasonable degree, a court in applying the statute faces fairly conventional problems of analysis and inference; they perhaps differ from other judicial issues in complexity and with respect to the manageability of much industrial data, but they do not demand judicial participation in any non-traditional function. Contrast the task of a court if it were permitted or required under the Act not only to judge whether a particular arrangement adversely affected competition but also, if it did, to decide whether in the particular circumstance the public interest was advanced or injured thereby. Such choices are not traditionally judicial, but legislative in nature.

Despite forceful reasons for confining the rule of reason to the limited office of analyzing the extent to which competition may be injured by a particular restraint, the history of adjudication under Section 1 is marked by repeated efforts to broaden the rule. Time and again, litigants have argued expressly or sub rosa that a particular arrangement is reasonable in the sense that it advances the public interest even though it substitutes some concerted regulation of economic affairs for the objective forces of competition. While there are no cases that have openly and unqualifiedly accepted or frankly articulated the view that this kind of "reasonableness" may validate an arrangement detrimental to competition, there are a few opinions, including two by the Supreme Court, which gave considerable credence to it. While both of these cases can be read (and in later decisions have been read) in ways consistent with the narrower and traditional conception of the rule of reason, they nevertheless represent a discontinuity in the history of the rule's development which ought not to pass unnoticed. They also represent an alternative model for the rule of reason which persists in its appeal and to which courts from time to time are tempted to resort.

The first of these provocative decisions is Board of Trade of the City of Chicago v. United States.[1] The Board, an organization of grain warehousemen, brokers and others in the grain trade, operated the nation's leading organized market for grain trading. It had rules which governed sales of grain already located in Chicago for immedi-

---

1. 246 U.S. 231, 38 S.Ct. 242, 62 L.Ed. 683 (1918).

ate delivery ("spot sales"), contracts of sale obliging the seller to acquire grain for delivery at some future date ("futures"), and sales of grain already in transit to Chicago for delivery on arrival ("to arrive sales"). Spot and future sales were made on the exchange floor during regular hours each day. Spot sales were also made at "call" sessions which immediately followed the regular sessions. Traders who were members of the exchange were also free to deal with each other when the exchange was not in session and a few firms did a substantial business by telephone or wire during nighttime hours. In 1906 the Board adopted its "call" rule which forbade exchange members to purchase or offer to purchase any "to arrive" grain during the hours between the close of the call session on any day and the opening of business on the next day at any price other than the closing bid price at the last call session. The Board argued that the purpose and effect of the rule was salutary. It limited hours of trading, reduced the market power of the few warehousemen who gained an advantage by trading at night, and rendered the daytime market more perfect. The government's challenge to the rule as a violation of Section 1 was rejected by the Court in an opinion by Mr. Justice Brandeis.

Analysis of *Board of Trade* must differentiate between what Justice Brandeis said in the opinion and what the case holds. The opinion contains a statement of the rule of reason which has become classic, routinely quoted in jury instructions:

> [T]he legality of an agreement or regulation cannot be determined by so simple a test, as whether it restrains competition. Every agreement concerning trade, every regulation of trade, restrains. To bind, to restrain, is of their very essence. The true test of legality is whether the restraint imposed is such as merely regulates and perhaps thereby promotes competition or whether it is such as may suppress or even destroy competition. To determine that question the court must ordinarily consider the facts peculiar to the business * * * ; its condition before and after the restraint was imposed; the nature of the restraint and its effect, actual and probable. The history of the restraint, the evil believed to exist, the reason for adopting the particular remedy, the purpose or end sought to be attained, are all relevant facts. This is not because good intention will save an achieved objectionable regulation or the reverse; but because knowledge of intent may help the court to interpret facts and to predict consequences.[2]

This statement of the rule elaborates upon that of *Standard Oil*, yet is not unfaithful to the spirit of the earlier case. The Brandeis language starts with the truism that every contract restrains trade in

---

2. 246 U.S. at 238, 38 S.Ct. at 244, 62 L.Ed. at 687.

the sense that a trader binds himself to one course and necessarily cuts off alternatives. It then paraphrases *Standard Oil,* saying that whether a restraint violates the Act depends entirely upon "whether it is such as may suppress or even destroy competition." If so, then it is unreasonable and thus unlawful. The elaboration which alone goes beyond what was said in *Standard Oil* is the catalog of business facts which the Court sets forth as being relevant to reasonableness and these, surely, are the kinds of facts which, in cases where injury to competition is not clear on the face of the matter, would throw light upon whether or not a particular arrangement tends to suppress or destroy competition. Hence, there is nothing troublesome in Brandeis' oft quoted statement of the rule of reason. Indeed, the effort to point to types of facts which might help in determining whether a particular arrangement tends to suppress competition is a distinct and useful advance.

Though most of the Brandeis language is consistent with earlier cases, the *Board of Trade* holding is harder to square with what had gone before. The arrangement was a concerted one which, subject to commercial sanctions, fixed the price which was to prevail on transactions during non-market hours. Buyers were not free during those hours to offer more, nor to pay less, than the price set by the closing bid on the organized market. It can be argued, perhaps plausibly, that the arrangement was one which tended to fix trading hours, rather than prices, and that this was its real purpose and effect. Indeed, if one goes beyond the record, it may be inferred that the wish to control hours of trading stemmed from the wish to stamp out "rate busting" on brokerage fees. The exchange also controlled these by regulations covering transactions which took place on the floor, but could not control them in off-market overnight transactions.[3] But even assuming benign ends and not interference with any competitive forces affecting brokerage fees, the observation that it is hours rather than rates which are fixed does not significantly alter the dilemma. A concerted arrangement which deprives individual traders of freedom of choice as to their hours of trade cannot be said not to restrain competition.

There are various possible ways to rationalize the *Board of Trade* result. It is possible, if only with some forcing of the facts, to read the case as being consistent with the classical rule. This reading would emphasize the linguistic consistency and would dismiss the analytical aspects of the case which appear to be inconsistent with the classic rule by contending that they add up, really, to nothing more than the conclusion that any adverse impact of the arrangements upon competition was *de minimus.* If it moves beyond *Standard Oil* at all, one might suggest, it is only by making more explicit

---

3. R. Posner, Antitrust, Cases, Economic Notes and Other Materials 192 (1974).

what was in *Standard Oil* an unstated premise, that courts in applying the rule look to the significance of things. It is the process of competition with which the Act is concerned, and a practice will not fall under its ban unless it displays an adverse impact on that process which is more than trivial.

However, a more candid assessment is that the case does differ markedly from *Standard Oil*. Though it does not go so far as to convert the rule of reason into that for which Chief Justice White had first pressed in his *Trans-Missouri* dissent, it does indicate that arrangements which suppress competition can be lawful so long as there is an adequate justification. On this reading, the Court is seen as having justified the result in these terms: A restraint which fixes prices overnight (or which fixes trading hours) is a fairly modest restraint, so long as there remains a reasonable opportunity during daytime hours for competitive forces to freely make a market. Such a restraint, being relatively inconsequential, is not "unreasonable" if there are countervailing social gains which it aids in achieving. Here, there are several countervailing advantages. First, it serves the convenience of members and conduces to social betterment by limiting hours of trade and increasing hours of rest and leisure. Second, the restraint reduces the economic powers of that small group of warehousemen who conduct their business at night and who, by that method, are able to keep a large part of the "to arrive" business to themselves. Third, it tends to make a more perfect competitive market during regular trading hours by channelling all transactions into these hours.

One can challenge this analysis on its own terms. The competitive harm of the arrangement is overly minimized by the opinion. In fact, choice of trading hours by a merchant can be a significant element of his competitive style, just as can other aspects of his way of doing business. If, as has been suggested, the choice of non-market trading hours is really a choice to undercut market-fixed brokerage rates, the point is more obvious. Further, the opinion makes too much of the asserted benefits of the restriction. Surely there is serious question whether enforced early closing is a social advantage. Why should traders, buyers and sellers both, not be free to choose business hours unrestrained? The night traders can hardly be said to be exercising market power merely because there are only a few of them, any more than can the cigar store which has stayed open an hour longer than its competitors; others are free to compete during the extra hours if they choose. Finally, the suggestion that the day market is rendered more perfect seems a weak one, for there is already a fully developed exchange with many buyers and sellers and myriad daily transactions. Surely this level of activity is sufficient for a wide enough dispersal of information about prices, quantities and other relevant factors to assure a competitive market.

But the real point is not whether the Court in this case has weighed these issues rightly, but whether it should be weighing them at all. *Trans-Missouri, Joint Traffic* and *Standard Oil* all seem to insist on a negative answer and to suggest that once it is determined that competition is significantly restrained, inquiry is ended. Thus, this more candid reading of the Brandeis opinion leaves a sense of disquiet. To hold as it did, the Court must have felt competent to judge the significance of a restraint by taking account of all that could rationally be said about the social advantages of permitting it. While it may be that there would be restraints so blatant and severe as to be beyond redemption, the test proposed by the case is not merely whether competition is adversely affected in some way that exceeds a threshold. It is whether the arrangement has purposes and effects other than restricting competition and, if so, whether these are such as to validate the arrangement when weighed against the competitive injury.

Nor is *Board of Trade* the only such case decided during the middle years of the rule of reason. Appalachian Coals, Inc. v. United States,[4] is, if anything, more difficult to square with the classic construction of Section 1. In the late 1920's and early 1930's excess capacity was chronic in bituminous coal mining. Bankruptcy was common, industry earnings were low, nonexistent or negative, and the threat posed by substitute fuels was increasing. Faced with these conditions, 137 producers accounting for 12% of production nationally and between 54% and 75% of the regional production (depending on how the market was defined) joined to organize the defendant, Appalachian, which, as their exclusive selling agent, was to sell their coal at "the best prices attainable and, if all cannot be sold, to apportion orders upon a stated basis * * *."[5] The government challenged the arrangement on the ground that it eliminated competition among the members of the group and gave the selling agency power to substantially affect or control market prices.

The Supreme Court found the arrangement reasonable in light of the "deplorable economic conditions in the industry." The opinion by Chief Justice Hughes stated that in the application of the standard of reasonableness "[r]ealities must dominate the judgment. The mere fact that parties to an agreement eliminate competition among themselves is not enough to condemn it."[6] While implying that if either purpose or effect was to fix market prices, the arrangement would be illegal, the Court accepted defendants' statements that their *intent* was not to do this and felt unable to predict that a common sales agency

4. 288 U.S. 344, 53 S.Ct. 471, 77 L.Ed. 825 (1933).

5. Id. at 358, 53 S.Ct. at 473, 77 L.Ed. at 828.

6. Id. at 360, 53 S.Ct. at 474, 77 L.Ed. at 830.

for these producers, which had only 12% of the market nationally, would have the effect of fixing prices.

Appalachian, like *Board of Trade,* can be kneaded into a consistency with the early cases. The usual argument is straightforward enough. The classic rule of reason tests an arrangement by its impact on competition. The *Appalachian* arrangement was as yet prospective. The evidence, while inviting some conjecture, failed to sustain adverse inferences, at least to the degree of certitude which warranted judicial intervention. Suspicion there might be, but the government had not shown a purpose to stifle competition nor yet an adequate basis for prediction that this would be the effect. A better argument, however, for placing *Appalachian* within the mainstream would focus upon the distinction between a selling agency and a cartel. A cartel typically fixes price and may allocate output. It is a "naked" restraint in that it entails no integration of productive or distributive functions; it cannot add to efficiency. The *Appalachian* selling agency, however, involved some integration benefits, or so at least the Court assumed; rephrasing defendants' contentions it found that the agency provided potential for "better methods of distribution, intensive advertising and research, to achieve economies in marketing * * *."[7] Where such efficiencies may be involved, as clearly they were not in cases like *Trans-Missouri,* a higher burden might reasonably be placed upon the government to prove competitive injury. But both of these views of *Appalachian* unhappily leave out of account the tonality of the Hughes opinion.

The Chief Justice, surely, suggests a conviction that at least some degree of restraint upon competition is permissible under the Act. Restraints are appropriate not merely when ancillary to an integration which generates efficiencies, but also when the purpose is to eliminate those "destructive practices" which are associated with competitive excesses. The Court here is responsive to expressions of fear about ruinous competition very much like those which fell upon deaf ears in the early cartel cases. Among the competitive practices which the selling agency was intended to eliminate were downward pressures on the market resulting from "distress coal" ("surplus" coal of a size or grade in excess of "demand" for that size or grade, which was produced as a by-product when coal of a different size or grade was produced on order), and "pyramiding" of coal (which occurs when several agents all authorized to sell the same lot of coal "bid" against each other to make a sale, thus causing a single supply of coal to "compete against itself.") It was also hoped that the selling agency would serve as a countervailing force to deal with "organized buying agencies, and large consumers" which "constitute unfavorable forces." The opinion lists these and other like factors as illus-

---

7. Id. at 359, 53 S.Ct. at 473, 77 L.Ed. at 829.

trative of the competitive problems which, given the industry's state of stress, it was appropriate for producers to try to remedy concertedly. As the governing general standard, the Court said:

> "The restrictions the act imposes are not mechanical or artificial. Its general phrases, interpreted to attain its fundamental objects, set up the essential standard of reasonableness. They call for vigilance in the detection and frustration of all efforts unduly to restrain the free course of interstate commerce, but they do not seek to establish a mere delusive liberty either by making impossible the normal and fair expansion of that commerce or the adoption of reasonable measures to protect it from injurious and destructive practices to promote competition upon a sound basis." [8]

By setting up the purpose of protecting competition from "destructive practices" and promoting it "upon a sound basis" as possible justifications for an arrangement by which competitors could, through a partial integration, "eliminate competition among themselves," the opinion sounds a note which had not been heard since the White dissent in the *Trans-Missouri*.

The last thing to be said of *Appalachian Coal* is perhaps the most significant, for it may remind us that antitrust is no more insulated from the deeper currents of American social, political and economic life than is any other aspect of public law. The relationship between competition and phenomena like depression and inflation are complex, but in times of crisis the nation may invest heavily in a policy which takes strong positions upon matters which at a theoretical level are but dimly understood. So it was in the early New Deal years. National policy, as expressed in the industrial recovery legislation which was eventually held unconstitutional, identified competitive excess as a cause of depression and encouraged cartelization as a means toward fuller employment of national resources. Posner has suggested that "[f]aith in the policy of competition was deeply shaken", and that "this more than anything may explain the outcome in the *Appalachian Coals* case." [9] That, perhaps, assumes too direct a relationship between changes in national attitudes and judicial conduct. Yet, though the New Deal legislation had no direct application to the arrangement challenged in the coal case, one may speculate that the Hughes Court may have participated to some degree in the national mood.

If, as asserted in this chapter, the prevailing theme is that the rule of reason allows inquiry only into the single issue of whether an arrangement significantly decreases competition, *Board of Trade* and *Appalachian Coals* are at all events discordant cases. Read for

---

8. Id. at 360, 53 S.Ct. at 474, 77 L.Ed. at 829.

9. Posner, supra note 3, at 75.

all they are worth, and in any litigation there is always someone ready to do just that, they suggest the appropriateness of a wide inquiry, one which invites a balance to be struck by the court between alternative social goals without more explicit guidance than the concept of the public interest. Except in cases where Congress has expressly or impliedly pointed in other legislation to a relevant goal other than competition, courts should refuse to validate any private arrangement restricting competition on the basis of a claim that the arrangement advances other social ends.

§ 67. The *Per Se* Doctrine

We have seen how the rule of reason grew from the early cases. But recall now what was termed an embryonic *per se* doctrine in the holding of *Joint Traffic,* the statement that arrangements like price fixing, which have a "direct and immediate effect * * * upon interstate commerce" are invalid,[1] and the statement in *Standard Oil* that the fixing of rates among competitors is in "nature, character and necessary effect" adverse to competition and, therefore, subject to a "conclusive presumption" of invalidity.[2]

During its development in the early cases, the *per se* doctrine both complemented and competed with the rule of reason. After *Joint Traffic,* the next *per se* case of importance was United States v. Trenton Potteries Co.[3] There corporations engaged in manufacturing vitreous pottery and, having in the aggregate about 82% of that market, had formed a cartel which fixed prices and limited sales to specified jobbers. Defendants were convicted in a criminal case. The court of appeals reversed, holding incorrect an instruction to the jury that if they found price fixing they should not consider whether or not the prices fixed were reasonable. The Supreme Court reinstated the verdict. In an opinion by Mr. Justice Stone, it ruled that the trial court had been right, saying:

> "The aim and result of every price fixing agreement, if effective, is the elimination of one form of competition. * * * The reasonable price fixed today may through economic or business changes become the unreasonable price of tomorrow. Once established, it may be maintained unchanged because of the absence of competition secured by the agreement * * * Agreements which create such potential power may well be held to be in themselves unreasonable or unlawful restraints, without necessity of minute inquiry whether a particular price is reasonable or unreasonable * * *.[4]

---

1. 171 U.S. 505, 568, 19 S.Ct. 25, 31, 43 L.Ed. 259, 287 (1897).

2. 221 U.S. 1, 65, 31 S.Ct. 502, 517–18, 55 L.Ed. 619, 647 (1911).

3. 273 U.S. 392, 47 S.Ct. 377, 71 L.Ed. 700 (1927).

4. Id. at 397, 47 S.Ct. at 379, 71 L.Ed. at 705.

The opinion thus puts squarely to rest one of the recurrent defenses asserted by cartels, that they were doing scant harm because they fixed only reasonable prices. It contributes to the earlier suggestions that price fixing is so unfailingly at odds with competition that legality is wanting wherever it is found. But the Stone opinion does not cinch that proposition down unyieldingly. At least two questions are left open.

First, the Court asserts that competition is eliminated by every "effective" price fixing agreement and marks out the harm resulting from the persistence of prices once fixed by agreements which "create such potential power" as may be needed to maintain a price in the face of business and economic change. In sum, the opinion addresses itself only to price fixing by groups with market power—groups which, like the pottery makers who had 82% of the national market, will possess, once they have combined, sufficient power to impose a supra-competitive price. The opinion says nothing about the legality of a price fixing agreement where such power is lacking or has not been proven. It thus leaves open the question whether the government can win its case merely by showing the agreement or must also carry on with the vexing business of proving from structural or other evidence that the defendants, once combined, possess substantial market power. Secondly, the Court was not faced in the case with any contention that, given the particulars of this industry, price fixing was more conducive to social well being than competition. The only defense to price fixing with which *Trenton Potteries* was concerned was that the prices fixed were reasonable. Thus the case is not a holding that prices may not be agreed upon in cases where the danger of social injury is diminished or erased by other considerations.

As to the first of these points, it should be remembered that *Appalachian Coals*,[5] decided after *Trenton Potteries*, validated a joint sales agency in part upon the ground that it could not be predicted that the agency would have power to affect prices. *Appalachian*, then, intimates that the prosecution in a price fixing case must prove either actual effects on market price, or at least such market power in the combination as would warrant the inference that the combination is capable through the agreement of affecting market price. The earlier cases also pointed this way. In *Addyston Pipe*[6] for example, market prices had actually been increased by the combination. And in *Trenton Potteries*, though actual market effects were not established, the Court viewed the combination as possessing power to control price in a "substantial part of an industry."[7] But as we shall see

---

5. 228 U.S. 344, 53 S.Ct. 471, 77 L.Ed. 825 (1933); see § 66 supra.

6. 85 F. 271 (6th Cir. 1898), modified and aff'd 175 U.S. 211, 20 S.Ct. 96, 44 L.Ed. 136 (1899); see § 65 supra.

7. 273 U.S. at 396, 37 S.Ct. at 379, 71 L.Ed. at 705 (quoting trial court instructions).

later in this section, *Appalachian* and cases preceding it were not the last word.

The second question which *Trenton Potteries* does not flatly answer, i.e., whether alternative social gains may be metered off against harm to competition, is in essence the same as that which we pursued through the caprices of development which gave content to the rule of reason. If even under the rule of reason—an analytical approach relatively hospitable to wide ranging inquiry—the test is whether competition is adversely affected and proof is not admissible that a particular restraint is a means for attaining other social goals, then surely proof of matters extrinsic to competition must also be rejected with respect to price fixing which is "conclusively presumed" to damage competition. But if the rule of reason is read to invite a balancing of the goal of competition against other social interests, then perhaps such a balancing may also be appropriate with respect to price fixing, even though this restraint is plainly inimical to competition. Indeed, if such balancing is presented under the rule of reason, when that is applicable, but not under the *per se* doctrine when it applies, the assignment of a particular issue to be treated under one form of analysis rather than the other takes on unexpected implications. The two approaches, on this assumption, would become not alternative modes for implementing the same statutory standard, but embodiments of alternative standards. This leads to a recognition that the relationship between the rule of reason and the *per se* concept may embody complications about which we can as yet be only dimly aware.

Both of the issues which *Trenton Potteries* left open were closed thirteen years later in United States v. Socony-Vacuum Oil Co.,[8] a classic opinion which stands in the same relation to the *per se* doctrine as does *Standard Oil* to the rule of reason. Oil refining was a depressed industry during the depression years. Major oil refiners were fully integrated to the retail level; they had ample production, storage and distribution capacity. Thus, they could respond to changes in demand by increasing or decreasing their inventories, the amount of gas they produced or the amount they held, as well as by increasing and decreasing price. But there were also independent refiners which were not integrated, had limited storage capacity, and often had on their hands so-called "distressed" gasoline which they were obliged to offer on the current "spot" market for immediate delivery to retailers. Since prices throughout the industry were affected by prices on the spot market, the majors, in order to inhibit rapid price fluctuations, entered upon a concerted program of bidding for and buying distressed gas, which they were capable of storing whenever that was necessary to hold spot prices to a level which they re-

---

8. 310 U.S. 150, 60 S.Ct. 811, 84 L.Ed. 1129 (1940).

garded as consistent with overall levels of supply and demand. It was this concerted program which was challenged in *Socony-Vacuum* and found by the Court to violate Section 1.

The first thing to note is that the Court labeled as a price fixing agreement defendants' concerted program for entering into the market as buyers in order to affect the prices arrived at by buyers and sellers meeting in the market place. This is an interesting example of characterization to which we shall have occasion to return. Viewing the matter in this light, the Court rejected the predictable defenses which the majors interposed. First, the Court reiterated the position taken in *Trenton Potteries* that reasonableness of prices is no defense, even if, as defendants asserted, the resulting prices were no higher than those which a healthy competitive market would yield. Second, the Court went beyond *Trenton Potteries* to hold that an arrangement fixing prices could not be justified on the ground that it was designed to diminish competitive evils. Any contrary implication in *Appalachian* was placed in shade and left to be reconciled either as having no application to a naked cartel which entailed no integration, or as having no application to a price fixing agreement—a species of restraint which can be analyzed in summary fashion and need not be analyzed under the full-blown rule of reason. Using the now classic phrase, "*per se*," for the first time, the Court said:

> Congress * * * has not permitted the age-old cry of ruinous competition and competitive evils to be a defense to price-fixing conspiracies. It has no more allowed genuine or fancied competitive abuses as a legal justification for such schemes than it has the good intentions of the members of the combination * * *. Under the Sherman Act a combination formed for the purpose and with the effect of raising, depressing, fixing, pegging, or stabilizing the price of a commodity in interstate commerce is illegal per se.[9]

Finally, the *Socony-Vacuum* opinion flatly stated in an elaborate dictum that a price fixing agreement violated Section 1 regardless of whether the conspirators possessed power to affect prices or had any effect on the price prevailing in the market.

> [We do] not mean that both a purpose and a power to fix prices are necessary for establishment of a conspiracy under § 1 of the Sherman Act. That would be true if power or ability to commit an offense was necessary in order to convict a person of conspiring to commit it. But * * * conspiracies under the Sherman Act are not dependent on any overt act other than the act of conspiring * * *. In view of these considerations a conspiracy to fix prices vi-

---

9. Id. at 221–23, 60 S.Ct. at 843–44, 84 L.Ed. at 1167–68.

olates § 1 of the Act though * * * it is not established that the conspirators had the means available for accomplishment of their objective * * *.[10]

By putting aside the issue whether prices were reasonable, in the sense of being equivalent to those competition would yield, and in particular by putting aside the question whether defendants possessed or had acquired through the concerted agreement sufficient market power to impose prices higher than competition would yield, the Court vastly simplified cartel litigation. If power had to be proved, virtually all of the structural and behavioral evidence which is canvassed in a monopoly case could be brought to bear. True, the government's burden might be simplified—for example, by holding that a prima facie case of power could be made out by showing that defendants in the aggregate controlled a substantial percentage of the production of a specified product in a particular geographic area (say 60% of vitreous pottery in the north Atlantic states). But defendant could seek to overcome the presumption by evidence that the single product was part of a larger product market or that ease of shipping called for a national market. A court would in the end be forced to delve nearly as fully into the power issue as in a monopoly case.

PART C. THE CURRENT CONSTRUCTION OF SECTION 1 OF THE SHERMAN ACT

§ 68. Rule of Reason Analysis Today

The rule of reason has been applied in many cases since *Chicago Board of Trade* and *Appalachian*. While the attitude reflected in those two aberrant Supreme Court cases has been influential in a few other decisions,[1] the trend in the development of rule of reason analysis since the 1930's has been toward a more austere position embodied in the earliest conception. Courts are loath to accept a ministerial discretion to decide when a trader has purchased the right to restrict competition by proffering other social gains. As we discuss particular problem areas in later sections, we shall see the kinds of situations in which the rigor of the classic view tends to weaken.[2] But it is fair to say that the dominant modern conception of the rule is infused with that exquisite simplicity drawn from the past which identifies impact on competition as the sole variable to be measured in applying the rule. Flexibility in the attainment of the statutory objective is provided, but not flexibility for the courts to choose what kind of economy we are to have. In

---

10. Id. at 224 n.59, 60 S.Ct. at 845 n.59, 84 L.Ed. at 1168–69 n.59.

1. E.g., United States v. New York Coffee & Sugar Exch., 263 U.S. 611, 44 S.Ct. 225, 68 L.Ed. 475 (1924); Cargill v. Board of Trade, 164 F.2d 820 (7th Cir. 1947), cert. denied, 333 U.S. 880, 68 S.Ct. 912, 92 L.Ed. 1155 (1948). Cf. United States v. Columbia Pictures Corp., 189 F.Supp. 153 (S.D.N.Y.1960).

2. See §§ 92, 101–107 infra.

sum, this tradition reads the rule of reason as condemning every contract, combination or conspiracy which in purpose or likely effect will *significantly* restrict competition. The rule of reason is a standard which calls on courts to judge shades and graduations of competitive impact, a difficult enough inquiry. But the rule does not call on a court to judge whether a restraint of this or that precise degree is justified by its complementary tendency toward some transcendent good.

Even classically conceived, the rule of reason leaves a good deal open to inquiry; analysis is necessary to determine whether a particular practice will restrain or aid competition, or if it has tendencies in both directions, what the net effect is likely to be. The rule is also rich in implication about the type of analysis needed to answer questions like these. The fact situation of *Chicago Board of Trade*[3] may be taken as an example and the Brandeis exposition taken as a text which describes the operations to be performed before the ultimate question about reasonableness can be answered.

To apply the rule, one must first identify specifically the practice involved. In the illustrative case it was the banning of any transactions which altered the last price upon "to arrive" grain after the close of call until 9:30 a.m. the next business day; prices for any overnight transaction were fixed by the last call session transaction. Next, the analyst should scan the evidence to determine the purpose of the restraint. The purposes claimed by the proponents here were: serving the convenience of exchange members as to hours, breaking up the market power of night dealers, protecting ignorant sellers who may be exploited by night dealers, and perfecting the daytime market by channelling all transactions through it. There may of course be other purposes for which no subjective evidence is available. If so, they will be suggested by the next step in the analysis, identifying the likely effects of the practice. Note that the purposes asserted by those responsible for the practice are all sufficiently related to it that each may be seen as a possible or likely effect flowing from it. And all of these purposes and likely or possible effects are either beneficial to competition, like improving the day market, or, like convenience of members, are at least neutral.

But there may be other effects which analysis can identify; these must be identified by picturing the dynamic of competitive interaction in the industry and thinking about the ways in which the challenged practice will alter it. Here, night operation is plainly discouraged, thus depriving buyers and sellers willing to deal at night, or whose convenience is served by being able to do so, of the opportunity to make a market during nighttime hours (or at least limiting

---

3. 246 U.S. 231, 38 S.Ct. 242, 62 L.Ed. 683 (1918); see discussion in § 66 supra.

that opportunity). The restriction may also impede significant movement of market prices during nighttime hours as commodity prices are highly sensitive to conditions of demand and supply and may move rapidly in relatively short periods.

The final question is whether, on balance, the restriction imposed substantially impedes competition. Where, as here, there seem to be legitimate purposes and where effects are both adverse and beneficial, the calculus of decision entails discrimination applied to rather finely shaded gradients. Let us state outright that if lawyers and judges have scanty qualifications for performing this function, economists have no better ones. With respect to any given practice applied in any given market situation, theory and empirical study may be able to suggest and perhaps validate various effects as either helpful or harmful to competition or both. But neither theoretical nor empirical material can devise a single yardstick against which to measure them; this matter must be referred to the arts rather than the sciences of judgment. Having identified purposes and effects one looks at length at each of them. Looking upon them openly and honestly one must call forth his best and most purposeful intuition. One must know and say what he can about each and come to some sense about the weight of each and where the balance lies; one can do no more.

So proceeding in *Board of Trade,* Justice Brandeis concluded that the restraint was on balance reasonable. That conclusion may not be the highest wisdom. Surely none of the benefits is overwhelming. Convenience of members should perhaps weigh lightly when it is purchased at the cost of inconvenience to others. The market power of night traders may be illusory, taking account that all traders are free to trade at night if that be their disposition. There is no evidentiary basis for supposing sellers are not knowledgeable, or in need of protection, or even that overnight prices tend to be lower than prior day closing prices, as this justification must presuppose. In any event, seller protection could be achieved in much less restrictive ways—for example, by providing to night sellers information about daytime markets and prices. And the need to force night transactions into the daytime market in order to perfect the latter is not demonstrated and on its face is suspect; it has the ring of a rationalization, not of a reason for the restriction.

Further, while the harms to competition, at least those apparent on the record, are hardly crippling, they are not below the threshold of notice. A night market may be a substantial convenience to sellers who use it as well as to night buying members of the exchange, and may dry up if night prices are tied to the last day price. Even should this not occur, the restriction on price movement at night is not a matter of indifference either to those trading at night or, perhaps, to the broader economy. The contention that the restraint, on balance, substantially impedes competition, rather than encouraging or regulating it in neutral ways, seems then to be a strong one. However, these questions have been pursued less with a will to criticize the *Board of Trade* result than to illustrate the analytical approach which the rule of reason invites, an approach which must attend with rigor first to the nature, then to the purposes and likely effects (both harmful and beneficial) of any restraint before a balance is struck.[4]

It should be emphasized that the analysis here undertaken presupposes a rule of reason limited to the classic concern of impact on competition. If in any instance a court, responding to the more sweeping implication of *Appalachian,* or *Board of Trade* itself, accords to the rule a broader office by demonstrating a readiness to weigh other social gains against competitive harms, the analysis would be broadened by identifying also any social benefits (and perhaps any offsetting social harms) not related to competition which were attained through the restraint, and by seeking in the process of decision to place these as well as any positive and negative competitive effects upon the scales. Suppose, for example, that merchants in a shopping center or in the shopping area of a town were to agree that retail stores would not be open before 9 a.m. or after 6 p.m. on weekdays and would remain closed one full day each week.[5] Particularly if most of the stores were small, family-owned units, or if employees of any large or chain stores were unorganized, it might be argued that this arrangement advanced the non-competitive social goal of limiting working hours, a general policy goal expressly validated by wage and hour and other social legislation. If the rule of reason were commodious enough to admit alternative social justifications for competitive injury, these considerations would have to be dealt with. The added difficulties this would present are apparent, especially if non-competitive adverse effects would have to be admitted as well as non-competitive benefits.

§ 69. The Place of Market Power in Rule of Reason Analysis

The issue of power is inescapably present in any inquiry about impact on competition. Consider again the issue of store closing hours. Suppose we were to conclude that a 6 p.m. closing rule imposed by a retail trade board which exacted the adherence of 95% of the retail merchants in a metropolitan area unreasonably restrained competition. It does not follow that we would on that account insist that a 6 p.m. closing agreement between the merchants on a single shopping block in a large city is also unreasonable. In the first in-

---

4. See the analysis suggested in P. Areeda, Antitrust Analysis, Problems, Text, Cases ¶ 349, and in the series of problems in ¶¶ 350–355 (2d ed. 1974).

5. Compare Meat Cutters Local 189 v. Jewel Tea Co., 381 U.S. 676, 85 S.Ct. 1596, 14 L.Ed.2d 640 (1965); FTC Advisory Opinion Digest No. 44, CCH Trade Reg.Rep. ¶ 17,529 (May 11, 1966); FTC Advisory Opinion Digest No. 110, CCH Trade Reg.Rep. ¶ 17,825 (Jan. 24, 1967).

stance the restrictive arrangement is market-wide; it affects the variety of alternatives that the process of competition would ordinarily yield. By diminishing competitive opportunities for sellers and subjecting buyers to a monolithic concerted judgment, it alters what a competitive economy would offer in terms of shopping convenience in a way which might be deemed significant. In the second instance, by contrast, consumers are affected only trivially. Anyone seeking the longer shopping hours which a free market affords need only walk a city block. In the first instance the group imposing the restriction, acting concertedly, has market power. In the second, it does not.

The *Board of Trade* opinion, in surveying effect, seeks to make a virtue of the fact that "members were left free to purchase at any price throughout the day from either members or non-members, grain 'to arrive' at any other market." [1] One may contend that the Court inferred that the Board lacked market power and, indeed, that this inference was crucial to the holding of reasonableness. But these implications of diminished power seem, in context, no more than a palliative; the essence of the opinion is that the restriction imposed was not unreasonable, even assuming that defendants possessed sufficient power so that the restriction had discernable impact in the market place. Indeed, as the analysis invited by Areeda suggests, the beneficial effects which the Court attributed to the restriction—as an instance, reducing the market power of warehousemen dealing in "to arrive" grain—are themselves contingent upon the Board's possessing market power.[2]

When we look to other rule of reason cases we find that in some the Court in analyzing advantages and disadvantages of a restriction attempts to gauge market power, but that in many cases, perhaps in most, it does not. Are there ways in which the cases can be organized which will give them a degree of consonance? In developing standards with an administrable degree of generality about the pertinence of power in rule of reason analysis it is well to distinguish at least two types of situations. In one, of which *Board of Trade* is an example, the significant purposes of the arrangement which its sponsors assert as justifications for it are capable of being achieved only to the extent that those acting in concert do possess market power. In the other, the stated purposes can be achieved irrespective of the possession of market power, and it is only collateral effects, adverse to competition, which turn upon whether or not market power is present.

In the first type of situation it seems fair enough to presume the possession of power, to spare the party asserting that the arrangement is illegal the necessity of proving power through complex struc-

---

1. 246 U.S. at 239, 38 S.Ct. at 244, 62 L.Ed. at 688 (1918).

2. Suggested by P. Areeda, Antitrust Analysis, Problems, Text, Cases ¶ 348 (2d ed. 1974).

tural evidence and to withhold from the defendants the opportunity to prove lack of power in their effort to validate the arrangement. If what defendants say they derive from the arrangement can be had only if they possess power, it is not unfair to assess the arrangement on the presumption that they do. Defendants must suppose that they have power. If they are right, by assuming power we accurately assess both the advantages to be attained from the arrangement and its disadvantages. If they are wrong and actually lack power, the court does defendants no injury of consequence even if it enjoins the arrangement. Though because of the lack of power, the arrangement could not actually have done the harm attributed to it, neither could its sponsors have gained from it the advantages they were seeking.

In the second type of situation, where good could come of the arrangement irrespective of power, and harm only if power is present, a different analysis must prevail. To assume power without proof might deprive both the sponsors of the arrangement and the public of a benefit, where there existed no risk of offsetting harm. Imagine, for example, an agreement among a group of hardware manufacturers to standardize sizes of nuts and bolts. Such an arrangement might serve the convenience of the manufacturers and the public, as well as serving the ends of competition, by facilitating both interchangeability of parts and price comparisons. There may be potential harm in the arrangement, however. Product standardization might facilitate cartelization, by facilitating a price list, by making costs more consistent and by making "cheating" by cartel members easier to detect. For the same reasons it might facilitate interdependent pricing. But these potential harms, particularly the latter one, are of consequence only if the industry is so structured as to be susceptible to cartelization or interdependent pricing and only if the participating manufacturers have, in the aggregate, some significant degree of power. If the structure were highly competitive and the participating manufacturers represented but a small percentage of aggregate volume, the danger of harm from the arrangement would be exceedingly small. Assessing such an arrangement under the rule of reason, therefore, logically requires some assessment of power.

The cases yield reasonably well to this key. Where a court in applying the rule of reason proceeds to discuss purpose and effect without discussion of power, analysis usually suggests that both the gains and the pains attributable to the arrangement presuppose possession of power. *Board of Trade* is itself an example.[3] By contrast, where a court proceeds in a rule of reason case to analyze the question of power, we can usually ascertain that sponsors of the arrangement have made some plausible claim of benefit which is not dependent upon the assumption that they possess market power.[4]

3. See 246 U.S. 231, 38 S.Ct. 242, 62 L. 2d. 683 (1918).

4. E.g., United States v. Container Corp. of America, 393 U.S. 333, 89 S.Ct.

Nevertheless, even when advantage may adhere in the arrangement independently of power and harm only if power exists, courts in rule of reason cases seldom proceed to engage in the meticulous analysis of power that is associated with monopolization cases. The issue is not whether defendants possess monopoly power, but whether they possess a substantial degree of market power. On this issue, a truncated or threshold analysis will suffice. For example, if defendants possess substantial shares of the market for a well differentiated product such as cellophane, we would assume significant power without scrupulous inquiry into cross-elasticity of substitute products. Courts are understandably loath to move into the intricacies and imponderables of thoroughgoing analysis of power and tend to avoid doing so where the need is not insistent.

§ 70. Power, Purpose, and Effect in *Per Se* Analysis

The diminishing concern for power and enhancement of interest in purpose and effect appeared as a strong tendency in rule of reason analysis. This tendency is even stronger in the *per se* area, and reaches its zenith in *Socony-Vacuum*.[1] It now is settled that in price fixing cases no question whatsoever is to be asked about the defendants' power if their purpose is to fix prices or if their conduct, should it achieve its goal, will be to affect market price. The rationale for ignoring power in those rule of reason cases where neither benefits nor harms will ensue unless power is present can be used only in part to justify ignoring power in *per se* cases. Where defendants frankly intend to fix prices and contend that in the particular context their doing so serves a public interest, the gains which they postulate are fully as dependant upon their having sufficient power to fix prices as are the harms which we associate with their conduct. In these instances it is defensible to proceed without analysis upon the assumption that the requisite power is present. If in fact it is, analysis conforms to the reality; if in fact power is lacking defendants have lost nothing they were potent enough to attain.[2]

But that rationale may or may not suffice when the law condemns not because of a purpose to fix prices but on the conclusion that price fixing will be the effect of the conduct, even though it is used to attain other and different ends. Here, the logic of the rationale for the rule of reason would require that one look not just at the price fixing effect but also at the special purpose of the arrange-

---

510, 21 L.Ed.2d 526 (1969); Virginia Excelsior Mills, Inc. v. FTC, 256 F.2d 538 (4th Cir. 1958); Blue Bell Co. v. Frontier Ref. Co., 213 F.2d 354 (10th Cir. 1954); United States v. Columbia Pictures Corp., 189 F.Supp. 153 (S.D. N.Y.1960); United States v. American Smelting and Ref. Co., 182 F.Supp. 834 (S.D.N.Y.1960).

1. United States v. Socony-Vacuum Oil Co., 310 U.S. 150, 60 S.Ct. 811, 84 L.Ed. 1129 (1940); see § 67 supra.

2. See § 69 supra.

ments; if the beneficial purpose could be achieved only by firms possessing power, one could fairly assume power just as was done in the comparable rule of reason cases. But if the purpose were a beneficial one which could be attained without power, then failure to analyze power is to risk forestalling some beneficial end even though, in actuality, no harm is present. The total blotting out of power issues in *per se* cases thus cannot be justified by the rationale which warrants only a partial eclipse of those issues in rule of reason cases.

But there is a more sweeping position which does warrant ignoring power in *per se* cases. It is suggested in United States v. Northern Pacific Ry. in the following way:

> [T]here are certain agreements or practices which because of their pernicious effect on competition and lack of any redeeming virtue are conclusively presumed to be unreasonable and therefore illegal without elaborate inquiry as to the precise harm they have caused or the business excuse for their use. This principle of *per se* unreasonableness not only makes the type of restraints which are proscribed by the Sherman Act more certain to the benefit of everyone concerned, but it also avoids the necessity for an incredibly complicated and prolonged economic investigation into the entire history of the industry involved, as well as related industries, in an effort to determine at large whether a particular restraint has been unreasonable—an inquiry so often fruitless when undertaken. * * *[3]

We thus possess in the *per se* doctrine a well developed concept, an anolog to the rule of reason—perhaps, more aptly, a special case of it—which brings analysis to an end once the following two matters have been established: first, that the practice if effective is likely in the great generality of cases to cause substantial injury to competition, and second, that an inquiry into whether the practice will in this instance be injurious to competition would be complex, time consuming, costly and, in the end, uncertain. When both of these propositions derived from *Northern Pacific* accurately characterize a particular trade practice, the principle of judicial efficiency warrants that the practice be banned out of hand.

There also are other gains, incrementally related to judicial efficiency, which derive from the selected use of the *per se* concept. One of these concerns the problem referred to by Chief Justice Stone in *Trenton Potteries*,[4] that a concerted arrangement which is reasonable today may be unreasonable tomorrow, when economic conditions have changed. The *per se* doctrine frees the judicial system of any need for continuous supervision of arrangements within its ban. An-

---

[3] 356 U.S. 1, 5, 78 S.Ct. 514, 518, 2 L. Ed.2d 545, 549–50 (1958).

[4] United States v. Trenton Potteries Co., 273 U.S. 392, 47 S.Ct. 377, 71 L.Ed. 700 (1927); see § 67 supra.

other value of the *per se* doctrine is that it converts the private bar from an instrument tuned very largely to the goal of avoidance to one which presses for enforcement. When the lawyer as counselor advises a client that the validity of a practice depends upon a nice judgment as to reasonableness, the client is unlikely to desist; he will, indeed, enlist the lawyer in efforts to marshal the evidence supporting reasonableness and to tinker with the practice in ways which may have only cosmetic effects. But when a lawyer tells a client that a particular practice is a crime and that to engage in it is to risk jail, the client is likely to be deterred.[5]

As we shall see, the *per se* doctrine is applied to other offenses besides price fixing.[6] Whether all of those to which it has been applied meet the standards suggested by *Northern Pacific* as a basis for the doctrine is a matter into which we must yet inquire, as is the related question whether the doctrine has remained a unitary one, showing the same characteristics in the myriad settings in which it has been invoked.

§ 71. The Relationship of Purpose and Effect in Section 1 Analysis

In our discussion thus far of both the rule of reason and the *per se* doctrine, we have placed the concept of power to one side and analyzed its relationship to purpose and effect, sometimes treating these last two concepts much as if they were one. It bears emphasis that they are not. Purpose and effect are disjunctively linked in antitrust analysis, both under the rule of reason and in the application of the *per se* doctrine. If the purpose or (assuming a very different and innocent purpose) if the predictable effect of conduct is to fix prices (or to achieve anything else held *per se* unlawful) the conduct runs afoul of the *per se* rule. Similarly, if either the purpose or effect of a practice evaluated under the rule of reason is sufficiently adverse to competition to outweigh any benefits, the conduct is deemed unreasonable.

There is an implacable logic in condemning conduct on the basis of ill effects, regardless of benign purposes. It is, in the end, effects —impacts upon the competitive process—which are of social consequence. In situations where market structure is accurately understood and market conduct is accurately perceived, it should be possible, often, to predict effects with similar accuracy, irrespective of what effects the conduct is intended to produce. When competitive processes are or will be stifled by particular conduct, it is small comfort that those engaging in it have other ends in view.

Correlatively, when the purpose for conduct is itself anticompetitive, there is reason for condemning it on that ground, without metic-

---

5. See the analysis suggested by P. Areeda, Antitrust Analysis, Problems, Text, Cases ¶ 319 (2d ed. 1974).

6. See, e.g., §§ 79–92 infra.

ulous inquiry into whether the market structure will facilitate the achievement of the condemned ends. The fullness of information about structure which is needed for confident prediction about effects is not always at hand; often, relevant information can be gathered only at great costs to the parties and the judicial process, and even then leaves ultimate questions cloaked in uncertainty. Purpose, however, can stand as a surrogate for effects. The actors in the marketplace will often be themselves the best judges of what they are capable of achieving and if they are aiming at wrongful ends we may logically treat their purposes as a guide to what they will accomplish. For this reason alone, it is wise policy to inhibit those who try to do wrong, without waiting to determine whether or not they are likely to succeed.

Nor should we hesitate to recognize that inquiry into purpose is uniquely fitting for a judicial system, though purpose may be the last factor about which an economist would ask when analyzing market conduct. Lawyers, judges and juries deal more competently and surely with issues about human motivation than with issues which depend upon modeling an industry structure and theoretically predicting the consequences of perturbations set up by conduct of particular kinds. It is at the moment rather in fashion among some academicians to disdain somewhat the lawyer's usual arts in antitrust analysis and to insist upon the primacy of an ostensibly rigorous and elegant economic analysis.[1] But it is a system of adjudication, not one of scientific inquiry, through which antitrust policy is enforced. Those who press for an excessive emphasis upon a structural analysis and for a diminished inquiry about purpose, ignore the special worth of the judicial institution to which antitrust administration is linked. They also assume, perhaps somewhat arrogantly at times, that problems will yield to structural analysis more readily than many do. In all but extreme situations, much is indeterminate no matter how thoroughly structural issues are probed. It is essential to examine conduct, certainly, and in doing this a wide range of human motivation must be dealt with. For dealing with problems in this genre the law, in its conventional modes, is at least as apt a tool as is theoretical economics, which must sacrifice richness of content to rigor.

§ 72. The Relationship of the *Per Se* Doctrine to the Rule of Reason

The strands can now be gathered to take account of the interrelationship between the rule of reason and *per se* analysis, a matter at which we have already glanced obliquely.[1] The historic policy of Section 1 is unmitigated opposition to all significant inhibitions upon competitive processes. The rule of reason is the comprehensive medium through which that policy is articulated; any concerted action

---

1. See generally R. Posner, Antitrust Cases, Economic Notes and Other Materials (1974).

1. See § 68 supra.

which in purpose or effect would significantly hamper competition violates Section 1. Significance is judged by balancing any tendencies in the arrangement to enhance competition against any tendencies to injure competition. If the latter tendencies predominate, the arrangement is an unreasonable restraint and violates the Act.

When the rule of reason is understood in this way, the *per se* doctrine is precisely a special case of rule of reason analysis. Where experience teaches that a particular practice is of a kind which blatantly restricts competition, we then know without further analysis how the balance will come out; we are spared the need for elaboration. Price fixing, for example, is a naked restraint of competition. Even if in some particular manifestation its negative impacts may be muted, it is hard to conceive that there would be any consequent enhancement of competition in some other respect or, if there were, that the enhancement would be so great as to render the restraint insignificant.

When the rule of reason is understood in this historic way, it will not be a matter of such enormous consequence whether or not a particular kind of restraint is classed as falling within the *per se* doctrine. If there were no *per se* doctrine, the law would invalidate virtually every price fixing arrangement under the rule of reason and, in the overwhelming majority of instances, would do so with dispatch, since the purpose or effect to restrain price competition is self-evident and serious. Since the rule of reason admits of no such defense, a court would hear no evidence that the prices fixed were reasonable or that in the particular setting an administered market would be more consonant with the public interest than a competitive one. Only if the sponsors of the arrangement offered to prove that the arrangement in some way benefited competition would it be necessary to go beyond identifying the conduct as price fixing. If they did, the court would first consider whether the competitive benefit proposed was so great as possibly to overbear the harm of price fixing. Only in the rare situation (indeed, it is hard to imagine one) where the asserted benefit had this quality would it be necessary to put the parties to the matter to proof. Since the *per se* rule is by definition limited in its application to arrangements like price fixing, which are notoriously hostile to competition, opening up *per se* cases to examination under the historic rule of reason analysis would not be likely to alter results except in the rarest of cases, nor would it be likely to alter the processes of proof in any significant respect.

But we have seen that the rule of reason has not always and inevitably been contained within the historic limits; it has displayed an elastic quality and, at times, courts have asked whether the adverse effects on competition which have been shown to be associated with a particular arrangement are offset by other public benefits attributable to it. When this wider reading of the rule is thought to govern, whether a particular kind of concerted arrangement is to be evaluated under the rule or the *per se* doctrine may be a decision fraught with significance. Assigning a particular kind of arrangement to the *per se* category ends all inquiry about its validity. This will have little or no substantive consequence and only modest procedural consequence if the alternative assignment to the rule of reason does not open up the possibility of justifications which measure unrelated public benefits against competitive injury. But if the rule is so copious that such justifications are permitted, the assignment to the rule may permit the successful interposition of defenses which would be foreclosed were the *per se* doctrine to apply.

Ambiguity about the content of the rule of reason thus exacerbates issues about the scope of the *per se* doctrine. In later sections we shall see that at times the *per se* doctrine has been expanded beyond the limits which inhere in the logic of its rationale.[2] One of the reasons for this has been judicial concern about being mired in an analytical swamp when rule of reason analysis is held to apply. But by strictly confining analysis under that rule to historic limits, the swamp can be pumped reasonably dry. There is no need to cut off cogent evidence and argument dealing with the net balance of competitive effects in order to forestall evidence about benefits having no relationship to the maintenance of competition. If the rule of reason is confined to its historic limits, much of the pressure to expand the *per se* doctrine will abate.

PART D. "NAKED" PRICE RESTRAINTS

§ 73. Introduction

We have seen how the *per se* doctrine developed with respect to price fixing and have taken note that the *per se* approach has been utilized in the treatment of other types of restraints, though as yet we have not identified them. In this part we shall discuss more fully the way in which the doctrine is applied with respect to price fixing and to the other horizontal restraints to which it has principally been applied, division of markets and group boycotts. We shall discover that the doctrine is neither unitary nor monolithic. Even with respect to price fixing, its application is not cut-and-dried. A particular practice may be ambiguous, or may have an "aura" about it; questions arise as to characterization. These questions can usefully be treated in two categories. First, where an arrangement between competitors (which does not entail any significant degree of integration of their activities) does not directly or explicitly fix the prices which they will charge, but nevertheless may have an effect on their prices, how do the courts decide whether to characterize the arrange-

---

2. See §§ 89 and 90 infra.

ment as a price restraint, and thus *per se* unlawful, or to characterize it in other terms, which will invoke the rule of reason? Second, where an arrangement between competitors which directly or indirectly affects prices entails a significant degree of integration between the parties to it, how do the courts decide whether to characterize the arrangement as a price restraint, and *per se* unlawful, or, alternatively, as a merger, joint venture, or other joint arrangement which must be more fully analyzed before legality can be determined? Problems of a nearly identical nature are presented with respect to market division. With respect to boycotts there are issues of characterization which are less easily assimilated under well structured headings.

§ 74. Purpose and Effect as Guides to Characterization

Since *Socony-Vacuum* it has been settled law, vigorously applied, that price fixing among competitors is a *per se* violation of Section 1.[1] That rule does not apply only to arrangements which amount to flat-out price fixing cartels. The antitrust laws concern substance, not form, in the preservation of competition. Hence, the *per se* rule against price fixing applies to any arrangement among competitors which, in purpose or effect, directly or indirectly inhibits price competition. Such arrangements, often called "naked restraints" on price, cannot be justified.

---

1. See e.g., Hartford-Empire Co. v. United States, 323 U.S. 386, 65 S.Ct. 373, 89 L.Ed. 322 (1945); United States v. Paramount Pictures, Inc., 334 U.S. 131, 68 S.Ct. 915, 92 L.Ed. 1260 (1948); United States v. McKesson and Robbins, Inc., 351 U.S. 305, 76 S.Ct. 937, 100 L.Ed. 1209 (1956); Goldfarb v. Virginia State Bar, 421 U.S. 773, 95 S.Ct. 2004, 44 L.Ed.2d 572 (1975); California Retail Grocers & Merchants Ass'n v. United States, 139 F.2d 978 (9th Cir. 1943), cert. denied 322 U.S. 729, 64 S.Ct. 945, 88 L.Ed. 1564–65 (1944); Food and Grocery Bureau v. United States, 139 F.2d 973 (9th Cir. 1943); Pennsylvania Water & Power Co. v. Consol. Gas, Elec. Light & Power Co., 184 F.2d 552 (4th Cir.) cert. denied 340 U.S. 906, 71 S.Ct. 282, 95 L.Ed. 655 (1950); Consol. Gas, Elec. Light & Power Co. v. Pennsylvania Water & Power Co., 194 F.2d 89 (3d Cir.), cert. denied 343 U.S. 963, 72 S.Ct. 1056, 96 L.Ed. 1360 (1952); Las Vegas Merchant Plumbers Ass'n v. United States, 210 F.2d 732 (9th Cir.), cert. denied 348 U.S. 817, 75 S.Ct. 29, 99 L.Ed. 645 (1954); Plymouth Dealers Ass'n v. United States, 279 F.2d 128 (9th Cir. 1960); Northern California Pharmaceutical Ass'n v. United States, 306 F.2d 379 (9th Cir.), cert. denied 371 U.S. 862, 83 S.Ct. 119, 9 L.Ed.2d 99 (1962); United States v. United Liquors Corp., 149 F.Supp. 609 (W.D.Tenn.1956), aff'd per curiam 352 U.S. 991, 77 S.Ct. 557, 1 L.Ed.2d 540 (1957); United States v. Utah Pharmaceutical Ass'n, 201 F.Supp. 29 (D.Utah), aff'd per curiam 371 U.S. 24, 83 S.Ct. 119, 9 L.Ed.2d 96 (1962); United States v. Olympia Provision & Baking Co., 282 F.Supp. 819 (S.D.N.Y. 1968), aff'd sub nom. Amalgamated Meat Cutters Local 627 v. United States, 393 U.S. 480, 89 S.Ct. 708, 21 L.Ed.2d 688 (1969). See also the deliberate dicta in International Salt Co. v. United States, 332 U.S. 392, 396, 68 S.Ct. 12, 15, 92 L.Ed. 20, 26 (1947); United States v. Columbia Steel Co., 334 U.S. 495, 522–23, 68 S.Ct. 1107, 1121–22, 92 L.Ed. 1533, 1551 (1948); Northern Pacific Ry. v. United States, 356 U.S. 1, 5, 78 S.Ct. 514, 518, 2 L.Ed.2d 545, 549–50 (1958); United States v. Sealy, Inc., 388 U.S. 350, 355, 87 S.Ct. 1847, 1851, 18 L.Ed.2d 1238, 1243 (1967).

The most obvious naked price restraint is flat-out price fixing. The classic cartel which fixes prices is unquestionably unlawful.[2] Covert arrangements and arrangements which fix the price by a formula are, quite obviously, to be treated as harshly as the less sophisticated cartels of an earlier era.[3] We know from *Socony-Vacuum* [4] itself that the *per se* rule reaches beyond the explicit cartel. There, an agreement to buy gasoline of small competitors in order to hold prices up was treated as a naked restraint and held *per se* invalid. We also know that every arrangement among competitors which has some conceivable impact on price is not *per se* unlawful. *Chicago Board of Trade* [5] is enough to remind us of that. There is a line, then, between arrangements which directly or indirectly restrain price competition and those which, in the language of *Chicago Board of Trade,* merely incidentally affect it. The task now is to determine how courts assign specific cases to one side of that line or the other.

Socony-Vacuum contains the touchstone. Where the combination has been formed "for the purpose or with the effect" of concertedly affecting in any manner the price of a commodity, the combination is illegal.[6] The defendants in that case could not concertedly fix prices by agreement; there was a massive quantity of oil offered by others not parties to the agreement which they did not control. Defendants might indeed have had difficulty in having the impact on price which they sought by the method which they used. Buying what competitors produce to keep it off the market is certainly a mode of price manipulation that might prove cripplingly expensive over the long pull. But the defendants could and did intervene as purchasers with the purpose of affecting the market price by taking "distressed" oil off the market, and with a view to reselling it at times and in quantities when it would have a less depressing effect on price. In the Court's view, the defendants concertedly tampered with "the central nervous system" of the market.[7]

Purpose and effect, we must note, are not concepts which apply themselves. Once an arrangement has been characterized as price fixing, the *per se* doctrine relieves a court of the need to analyze and compare possible benefits and harms. But except in the case of an

2. United States v. Addyston Pipe & Steel Co., 85 F. 271 (6th Cir. 1898), modified and aff'd 175 U.S. 211, 20 S. Ct. 96, 44 L.Ed. 136 (1899); United States v. Trenton Potteries Co., 273 U.S. 392, 47 S.Ct. 377, 71 L.Ed. 700 (1927).

3. See, e. g., Price Fixing and Bid Rigging in the Electric Manufacturing Industry, Parts 27 and 28, Hearings on Adm. Prices, Subcommittee on Antitrust and Monopoly, Committee on the Judiciary, U.S. Senate, 87th Cong. 1st Sess. (1961).

4. 310 U.S. 150, 60 S.Ct. 811, 84 L.Ed. 1129 (1940); see § 67 supra.

5. 246 U.S. 231, 38 S.Ct. 242, 62 L.Ed. 683 (1918); see § 66 supra.

6. 310 U.S. at 223, 60 S.Ct. at 844, 84 L.Ed. at 1168.

7. Id. at 224 n. 59, 60 S.Ct. at 845 n. 59, 84 L.Ed. at 1168–69 n. 59.

unvarnished price fixing agreement, the court is not relieved of the obligation to analyze the facts; it must array and evaluate the evidence in making the preliminary inquiry whether the purpose of the defendants, or the effect of their conduct, is that of "raising, depressing, fixing, pegging, or stabilizing" price.[8]

Moreover, that formulation from *Socony-Vacuum* does not say it all. There is another element which must be present besides a purpose to affect or an actual effect: the effect threatened or achieved must be the result of some inhibition of competitive forces, some substitution of administration by one or more traders for the impersonal forces of the market. Remember, if a market as one finds it is less than fully competitive, a private agreement might make it more competitive and have an impact on price in that way. The Act is not intended to make unlawful arrangements which affect price by improving competition. Suppose, for example, that the purpose and effect of a particular arrangement is to make a better market through the establishment of an organized exchange where all buyers and sellers operate, by standardizing the products to facilitate price comparisons, or by exchanging information in ways facilitating competition. These kinds of practices would affect price, but on our assumptions they would do so by making it more competitive; therefore, they ought not to be treated as *per se* invalid.[9] It is these kinds of arrangements, among others, which a court might describe as having only an "incidental" effect on price. The phrasing is loose, but by now the meaning should be growing clear. If competition is improved by an arrangement, we do not characterize it as a price fixing arrangement merely because it affects price.

Still another purpose and effect, differing from that aimed at raising, lowering, pegging or stabilizing prices, would be that of integrating some of the activities of two or more producers so as to achieve economies of scale, thereby improving economic performance. Such arrangements may also have effects on price competition, but the integration which is achieved has independent significance which may be great and the effect on competition may be slight. Such an effect, if plainly overbalanced by integration advantages, could also be called "incidental."

There are numerous cases in which a purpose or effect to dampen price competition has been found and which serve to exemplify the analysis that supports characterizing an arrangement as a price re-

---

8. Id. at 223, 60 S.Ct. at 844, 84 L.Ed. at 1168.

9. E.g., Cargill, Inc. v. Board of Trade, 164 F.2d 820 (7th Cir. 1947), cert. denied 333 U.S. 880, 68 S.Ct. 912, 92 L. Ed. 1155 (1948); Belz v. Board of Trade, 164 F.2d 824 (7th Cir. 1947), cert. denied 333 U.S. 881, 68 S.Ct. 913, 92 L.Ed. 1156 (1948); Structural Laminates, Inc. v. Douglas Fir Plywood Ass'n., 261 F.Supp. 154 (D.Or.1966), aff'd 399 F.2d 155 (9th Cir. 1968), cert. denied 393 U.S. 1024, 89 S.Ct. 636, 21 L.Ed.2d 569 (1969).

straint. In Nationwide Trailer Rental System, Inc. v. United States,[10] the Court affirmed, per curiam, a holding that the circulation among association members of a lease form containing a rate schedule setting forth "overtime charges" on rented equipment constituted a price restraint. The evidence showed that the schedule was used only as a "guide," that members did not agree to abide by it, and did in fact deviate from it. Though there was little or no evidence of a discernible effect on prices, the court concluded that the schedule must have been circulated for some purpose, and the apparent one was to suggest price levels for overtime charges, even if not to fix them rigidly. Plymouth Dealers' Association v. United States was similar.[11] Here the dealers' association circulated a "suggested price" list which was higher than the manufacturer's suggested resale prices. Though dealers in no sense committed themselves to follow it and in fact did not, evidence showed that many, when negotiating with customers, pointed to these suggested prices as the list prices from which dickering had to begin. The court held that a purpose to influence and an effect upon market price were sufficiently established. In United States v. Jantzen Inc.,[12] defendants were enjoined from agreeing as to the time when each would individually set its price; the effect of the arrangement was, on its facts, to foreclose price changes at other times. In United States v. United Liquors Corp.,[13] an agreement as to the percentage of functional discounts and as to the way customers would be classified in determining whether they were entitled to a discount was held to be a price restraint, even though there was no agreement as to base prices from which individual competitors would compute the discounts. In United States v. Gasoline Retailers Association,[14] an agreement not to advertise price except by a sign on the pump was seen as one which limited price competition in purpose and effect.[15]

The unifying characteristics displayed by all these cases are threefold. First, the practices examined are related to the market in such a way that if they have any effect at all they will have an effect on price formation. Second, they lack any significant degree of integration of functions among the competitors. Third, the arrangements are not ones which help to make or improve a market by facilitating trading, or exchanging information, or standardizing product,

10. 355 U.S. 10, 78 S.Ct. 11, 2 L.Ed.2d 20 (1957), aff'g 156 F.Supp. 800 (D. Kan.). See also Goldfarb v. Virginia State Bar, 421 U.S. 773, 95 S.Ct. 2004, 44 L.Ed.2d 572 (1975).

11. 279 F.2d 128 (9th Cir. 1960).

12. 1966 CCH Trade Cas. ¶ 71,887 (D. Or.1966).

13. 149 F.Supp. 609 (W.D.Tenn.1956), aff'd per curiam 352 U.S. 991, 77 S. Ct. 557, 1 L.Ed.2d 540 (1957).

14. 285 F.2d 688 (7th Cir. 1961).

15. See also National Macaroni Mfrs. Ass'n v. FTC, 345 F.2d 421 (7th Cir. 1965) (agreement fixing the amount of wheat in macaroni intended to reduce demand for wheat and thus to affect price).

or the like, and which thus may aid competition. Since price formation is affected if there is any consequence at all, and since there is no improvement in the market and no integration, it is entirely fair and functionally accurate to treat arrangments like these as naked restraints.[16]

If an arrangement falls short of explicit price fixing, a court determines whether it affects price by looking at it in context and noting its relationship to the pricing process. For example, an agreement between retailers not to advertise price surely tends to reduce price consciousness and price shopping by buyers. One must conclude that it directly or indirectly affects price. The same would be true with an agreement to buy up depressed supplies and hold them off the market, or to use the same base from which discounts may be granted. Concluding that there is a direct or indirect price effect, one tests to see whether the agreement is a "naked" restraint and hence *per se* unlawful by looking for possible competitive benefits. If it is claimed that the arrangement serves to make or improve a competitive market, or that it yields integration efficiencies, an analysis of the kind set forth in Section 76 or 77 is appropriate.

A shorthand method which may help to identify a restraint affecting price as naked is to examine the arguments which are being pressed in justification of the practice. Certain asserted justifications are hallmarks of the naked restraint. If the arrangement is naked, any benefits to the public which can logically be asserted to derive from it will, when closely examined, come down to a contention that, for some reason or other, concerted decision making rather than competition is in this instance socially preferable. *Socony-Vacuum* is illustrative.[17] Concerted action to support prices was said to be needed because of the depressed condition of the economy and the unsettling and disruptive impact of rapid fluctuations in price when distressed oil was dumped on the market. Acceptance of such an argument is flatly foreclosed by the policy of the statute; where the statute applies, Congress has chosen competition and not concerted action as the mode by which trade is to be regulated. Any contention that this judgment should be laid aside in particular instances must be addressed to Congress and not to the courts. This type of justification contrasts markedly with a contention, like that in *Chicago Board of Trade*,[18] that competition is itself improved by the arrangement because it helps to make a more perfect market, or with a contention that economic performance is improved by the arrangement in that it entails integration which enhances economies of scale.

16. E.g., Las Vegas Merchant Plumbers Ass'n v. United States, 210 F.2d 732 (9th Cir.), cert. denied 348 U.S. 817, 75 S.Ct. 29, 99 L.Ed. 645 (1954). See generally cases cited in note 1 supra.

17. 310 U.S. 150, 60 S.Ct. 811, 84 L.Ed. 1129 (1940).

18. 246 U.S. 231, 38 S.Ct. 242, 62 L.Ed. 683 (1918).

The only other arguments which can rationally be made in favor of a naked restraint are that the arrangement is beneficial to the parties and that its negative impact on competition is so slight that the law ought not to trouble itself about it. The first of these is to be rejected out of hand; the law does not accept damage to competition as the cost of allowing a group of traders to gain their own ends. The second, the demurrer argument, is deceptive. To discriminate between those arrangements which do and those which do not threaten significant harm would be a troublesome task, and a rule requiring this would be very costly to judicial resources.

§ 75. Possible Benefits from Price Restraints

In American law, the cartel is unlawful; no justification will be heard for it. However, the anti-cartel laws of Western Europe, the British Restrictive Trade Practices Act, and the competition law of the Common Market are not so single-minded. Under all of these, competition is seen as only one of the ways that trade can be managed in the interest of the public, albeit the principal one; all of them leave room for the validation of price fixing and other cartel arrangements under certain conditions. Is the American law too narrowly focused?

The justifications which might be made for price fixing and to which American law closes its eyes have been elaborated upon in a number of places.[1] The cardinal justification is the claim heard in *Appalachian Coals*[2] and in *Socony-Vacuum*[3] that when economic conditions in an industry are depressed, price fixing is necessary to avoid socially harmful competitive excesses such as "price wars" or "cutthroat competition". The argument possesses additional sophistication and appeal when, as in *Joint Traffic*,[4] the industry is one where fixed costs are high relative to variable costs. If demand falls or capacity is excessive, firms may reduce prices to the point where they will barely exceed variable costs—a course which, in the end, will be ruinous, since all firms will be incurring substantial losses. This contention usually predicts that if price fixing is not resorted to, the end result will be the bankruptcy and withdrawal of all firms save one, which will attain monopoly profits. The most subtle variant, perhaps, is that which sees the role of the cartel as being to facilitate an orderly withdrawal of the excess capacity in the industry which is the root cause of the ruinous price competition.

In its less sophisticated forms, the argument is perhaps sufficiently answered by noting that if prices tend to become excessively low, that fact is an indication of excess capacity. Social satisfaction

---

1. E.g., A. Phillips, Market Structure, Organization and Performance (1962).

2. 288 U.S. 344, 53 S.Ct. 471, 77 L.Ed. 825 (1933); see § 66 supra.

3. 310 U.S. 150, 60 S.Ct. 811, 84 L.Ed. 1129 (1940); see § 67 supra.

4. 171 U.S. 505, 19 S.Ct. 25, 43 L.Ed. 259 (1898); see § 64 supra.

would be enhanced if capital which could be used elsewhere were withdrawn and put into socially preferred employments; capital which is too specialized and which is tied to this industry must be devalued, left idle or scrapped. Competition is a mechanism for achieving precisely these results. It tends to weed out first the least efficient, so that in the end the most efficient combinations of resources consistent with an appropriate allocation of resources to the industry will remain. If in an industry which is capital intensive, like railroads, competition proves unduly costly, the answer should not be price fixing, which will not focus on the public interest, but should be some form of public ownership or regulation. Cartelization will not yield a proper allocation of resources to the industry; it may delay unduly the withdrawal of resources. And, if it is in the end successful it will result in too small an allocation of resources to the industry and in excessive profits. The contention about orderly withdrawal of resources has some appeal, but the private cartel, unlike a public intervention of some kind, is not likely to be able to reach agreement upon such a plan even if one is attempted. Even if it does reach agreement, the terms will be responsive to economic muscle, not necessarily to relative efficiency.

Other benefits assertedly attainable through cartelization and price fixing are similarly subject to question. It is sometimes contended that cartels cannot maintain prices significantly above competitive levels because of competition from other products and potential entry, that the most that they can do is to stabilize price movements so that long range price trends are carried out smoothly, a socially desirable result. But analysis suggests a different conclusion. If there are significant entry barriers, cartelization can result in higher prices, higher profits and lower commitment of resources to the industry than competition would achieve. If there are no entry barriers at all—if the industry is rigorously competitive—cartelization will not even be attempted. In the median area, cartelization may fail or may itself be unstable, but to the extent it succeeds its success will cause misallocation.

It is also sometimes claimed that firms at a competitive level need to cartelize to deal with economically more powerful firms which buy from them or sell to them. But if there is excess market power at any level, the public is not likely to be benefited by allowing those at other levels of the chain to act concertedly. The result will likely be a battle or a concord between the giants about how the spoils from excess market power are to be shared; it would be better for the public that those segments displaying a competitive structure be maintained that way, and that ways be found to reduce power at the other level.

§ 76. Naked Restraints Distinguished from Arrangements to Make or Improve a Market

Although justifications for naked restraints which dampen price competition are rejected *per se,* arrangements which may have the purpose or effect of making or improving a market are not *per se* unlawful, even though they may affect price. An arrangement such as this must be analyzed under the rule of reason to determine whether its net effect is harmful or beneficial to competition. Let us here attempt to make the line between the *per se* doctrine and the rule of reason more precise by discussing that class of cases where a purpose and effect to make or improve a market will forestall the courts from characterizing the arrangement as a naked price restraint.

If the predominant purpose and effect of the arrangement may be to facilitate trading in an organized market where information about demand, supply and prices is disbursed freely and rapidly and a large number of buyers and sellers interact, it is not *per se* unlawful. Such an arrangement no doubt affects price, but it may do so only by improving competition. A fuller inquiry is needed before legality can be judged. The germinal case is *Chicago Board of Trade.*[1] There, the arrangement tended to channel all transactions into the organized daytime market by requiring the few members who traded at night to do so at the prices established on the exchange during the day. We may differ with the Court about the balance between the negative and positive effects of this arrangement, but it is difficult to refute the conclusion that an arrangement aimed at perfecting a market *might* do more good than harm to competition and, therefore, ought not to be forbidden without analysis. An arrangement which may have the purpose and effect of enhancing competition should not be treated as illegal merely because it will affect price formation. More competition can be expected to affect prices, just as will less competition. One must examine the arrangement. Is the assertion that it tends to make a market a sham or a rationalization? Is the real purpose and effect to diminish price competition? If so, analysis can pull back the cloak and expose the naked restraint. Assuming an honest purpose to improve competition, in what manner and to what degree is competition improved? And what harms, if any, are to be measured off against the gains achieved?

The numerous cases dealing with regulation of tobacco auction warehouses are excellent examples of this genre. All involve regulations respecting an organized auction market. Typically, the regulations assign times for sale and have the stated purpose of scheduling auctions in various places sequentially, so that buyers can conveniently attend all auctions. Inevitably, these regulations have an effect on competition and, specifically, affect price formation; yet ar-

---

1. 246 U.S. 231, 38 S.Ct. 242, 62 L.Ed. 683 (1918); see § 66 supra.

guably these regulations aid in perfecting the market. Consequently, the courts have rejected *per se* treatment and have utilized rule of reason analysis.[2]

A similar response occurs in other cases dealing with other types of arrangements which, arguably, help to make or improve an organized, competitive market. Cases involving bid depositories for the building trades are examples.[3] Here too the cases share a consistent quality. Though the challenged arrangement can be said to affect price, it is part of a system of regulation such as may be found on an organized exchange which, depending upon the particulars of the arrangement and the market structure, may facilitate the smooth and effective working of an organized market. Where this condition presents itself, the *per se* doctrine is set aside and a more elaborate analysis pursued—an analysis under the rule of reason which will sometimes end with a conclusion of legality and sometimes not.[4]

§ 77. Naked Price Restraints Distinguished from Restrictions Resulting from Partial Integration

An arrangement involving a partial integration of functions, which may achieve significant economies of scale among competitors, also may escape *per se* treatment, even though it eliminates price competition between the firms that participate in it. To qualify for the application of the rule of reason, the arrangement must have the following two characteristics: first, the elimination of price competition between the participating firms must result directly from the partial integration of their functions; second, this elimination of price competition must not appear to significantly reduce market-wide competition. When these two conditions are met, the arrangement is not characterized as a price restraint and its legality is determined only after a full analysis to determine the extent of any reduction in competition and the extent to which integration benefits may be obtained. When these propositions are understood, cases which other-

---

2. Rogers v. Douglas Tobacco Board of Trade, 244 F.2d 471 (5th Cir. 1957) and 266 F.2d 636 (5th Cir.), cert. denied 361 U.S. 833, 80 S.Ct. 85, 4 L.Ed. 2d 75 (1959); Asheville Tobacco Board of Trade v. FTC, 263 F.2d 502 (4th Cir. 1959) and 294 F.2d 619 (4th Cir. 1961); Roberts v. Fuquay-Varina Tobacco Board of Trade, Inc., 332 F.2d 521 (4th Cir. 1964) and 405 F.2d 283 (4th Cir. 1968) (en banc); Winn Ave. Warehouse, Inc. v. Winchester Tobacco Warehouse Co., 339 F.2d 277 (6th Cir. 1964); Danville Tobacco Ass'n v. Bryant-Buckner Associates, Inc., 333 F.2d 202 (4th Cir. 1964) and 372 F.2d 634 (4th Cir.), cert. denied 387 U.S. 907, 87 S.Ct. 1688, 18 L.Ed.2d 624 (1967).

3. E.g., Mechanical Contractors Bid Depository v. Christiansen, 352 F.2d 817 (10th Cir. 1965), cert. denied 384 U.S. 918, 86 S.Ct. 1365, 16 L.Ed.2d 439 (1966); United States v. New Orleans Ins. Exch., 148 F.Supp. 915 (E.D.La.), aff'd per curiam 355 U.S. 22, 78 S.Ct. 96, 2 L.Ed.2d 66 (1957); United States v. Ins. Board, 144 F.Supp. 684 (N.D. Ohio 1956).

4. Compare Chicago Board of Trade, v. United States, 246 U.S. 231, 38 S.Ct. 242, 62 L.Ed. 683 (1918), with United States v. New Orleans Ins. Exch., 148 F.Supp. 915 (E.D.La.), aff'd per curiam 355 U.S. 22, 78 S.Ct. 96, 2 L.Ed. 2d 66 (1957).

wise seem inconsistent with those applying the *per se* doctrine fall comfortably into a consistent pattern.

The arrangements dealt with in this section involve only a partial integration, not a complete integration such as might occur when two firms merge. Nevertheless, the rationale for the partial integration rule can best be illustrated by an example involving merger. Picture an industry with fifty-one competing firms, forty-nine of which have two percent each of the market, and two of which have one percent each. If the two last firms were to merge, price competition between them would be ended totally; but that would not justify the conclusion that a reduction of price competiton was the purpose of the arrangement, nor, in the sense in which the word "effect" is used in characterizing under the *per se* rule, would it warrant the inference that ending price competition was the effect. The arrangement has other manifest consequences. The operations of the two small firms may now be integrated. That integration may enable them to research, produce, or distribute more economically; they may now be large enough to take advantage of scale economies which were not accessible to them before. And market-wide competition may not be adversely affected; the difference between fifty-one firms and fifty may be insignificant. Indeed, the arrangement may improve competition, in that the ability of the two small firms (which were high cost producers not operating at the most efficient economic scale) to put downward pressure on price may have been small or nonexistent, while that of the combined firms (now of the most efficient size) may be substantial.

As we shall later see,[1] because of its integration effects, a horizontal merger is not treated as a naked restraint which, having ended price competition between the merging units, is *per se* unlawful.[2] The treatment of a partial integration is similar. A partial integration may be one which integrates sales, purchases, research activities or other functions, but which leaves other functions, such as manufacturing, to be carried on independently by the participating firms. Thus, although competing sellers violate the *per se* rule in agreeing on prices at which they will sell, the legality of a joint selling agency established by competing sellers will be analyzed under the rule of reason.[3] Similarly, a buying cooperative organized by competing sellers may be evaluated under the rule of reason even though when no

---

1. See §§ 202–204 infra.

2. Such a merger may be held unlawful because it violates the rule of reason, or because it violates the stringent antimerger provisions of Section 7 of the Clayton Act. But it is not held unlawful *per se* as an arrangement which in purpose and effect amounts to price fixing.

3. Compare Appalachian Coals, Inc. v. United States, 288 U.S. 344, 53 S.Ct. 471, 77 L.Ed. 825 (1933) and United States v. Columbia Pictures Corp. 189 F.Supp. 153 (S.D.N.Y.1960), with Virginia Excelsior Mills, Inc. v. FTC, 256 F.2d 538 (4th Cir. 1958). See also, United States v. Morgan, 118 F.Supp. 621 (S.D.N.Y.1953); Interborough News Co. v. Curtis Publishing Co., 225 F.2d 289 (2d Cir. 1955).

integration occurs, concerted action by buyers to affect price is *per se* unlawful.[4] Again, though agreements limiting price advertising fall within the *per se* rule, the legality of agrements to engage jointly in advertisements, including advertisements about price, may be determined on the basis of reasonableness.[5] In each instance, the distinction is between a naked restraint and a restraint which is a necessary consequence of some degree of integration of distribution functions. A joint selling or buying agent does not merely set joint prices for firms which previously competed as to price; it also performs in an integrated manner functions which the firms had previously performed independently. A joint advertisement is also an integrated promotional activity; it may enable sellers to reach a wider public or to reach their public more cheaply or effectively than they could by acting alone.

We should underscore the two conditions which must be met before a partial integration reducing price competition escapes *per se* treatment. The first is that the price restraint must arise inevitably from the integration. Thus, a selling agent which sells a homogeneous product for two producers necessarily reduces price competition between them. If the integration is to be permitted at all, the consequent reduction in price competition must also be tolerated. These kinds of situations should be distinguished from situations where the partial integration could be accomplished without the price restraint, except for the fact that firms participating in the integration insisted upon the price restraint as a condition to integrating. United States v. Sealy, Inc.,[6] is an example of the latter type of case. There, bedding manufacturers established a joint subsidiary which developed mattress specifications and adopted a trade name and trademark which were nationally advertised. The subsidiary licensed the parent manufacturers to manufacture and sell mattresses meeting these specifications under the Sealy brand and mark, but fixed the prices at which these were to be sold. Because the licensee-manufacturers owned and organized Sealy, the Court quite properly treated the arrangement as a horizontal restraint, one in which the manufacturers had themselves agreed on price. It held the price restraint unlawful *per se,* refusing to view the integration of non-sales functions as a warrant for justifying the price restraint. This was entirely justified. The integration was one involving the development of specifications, trade

---

4. Compare Associated Greeting Card Distribs., 50 FTC 631 (1954), with American Tobacco Co. v. United States, 328 U.S. 781, 66 S.Ct. 1125, 90 L.Ed. 1575 (1946). See also, Parmelee Transportation Co. v. Keeshin, 186 F. Supp. 533 (N.D.Ill.1960), aff'd, 292 F. 2d 794 (7th Cir.), cert. denied 368 U.S. 944, 82 S.Ct. 376, 7 L.Ed.2d 340 (1961); Instant Delivery Corp. v. City Stores Co., 284 F.Supp. 941 (E.D.Pa.1968).

Arkansas Brokerage Co. v. Dunn & Powell, 173 Fed. 899 (8th Cir. 1909).

5. See Report of the Select Committee on Small Businesses of the House of Representatives, H.R.Rep.No. 699, 88th Cong., 1st Sess. (1963).

6. 388 U.S. 350, 87 S.Ct. 1847, 18 L.Ed. 2d 1238 (1967).

symbols and an advertising program. That program could have been carried out while leaving the participating manufacturers free to compete as to price for mattresses meeting the specifications and bearing the mark and name.

Pressing the distinction further, suppose that competing manufacturers are considering an agreement to integrate their research activities. Each of them will have royalty-free access to technology about any new product produced by the jointly run laboratory. Such an agreement and the integrated activity it envisages can be carried out without any direct price restraint. Each participant when it manufactures and sells any new product resulting from the research can set its price independently of the others, just as if the product had arisen from its own independent research. Suppose, however, that the participants, or some of them, are not willing to join in the integration without a collateral agreement setting forth a method for establishing a price on any new product, and that such a collateral agreement is worked out. Since the price restraint is not a necessary consequence of the partial integration, it is not saved from *per se* invalidity because it is factually associated with, or ancillary to, a partial integration.

The second condition to be met before a partial integration which ends price competition escapes the *per se* ban is one which requires the court to look at structure at least in a truncated way. If the arrangement appears likely to dampen price competition market-wide by ending price competition between participants, it will be *per se* unlawful despite the integration. To tell whether it is likely to affect the market significantly, the court must evaluate power. If the market is concentrated, if for example there are five sellers, each with 20%, a joint selling arrangement between two of them would reduce price competition to a significant degree. *Per se* treatment would be warranted without reference to any integration advantages.[7]

Note what has happened to the *per se* doctrine in this course of analysis. Thus far, we have talked of it as if it snapped like a trap to illegalize conduct of a kind subject to it, without any analysis at all. Actually, it cannot be either so simple or so precise. In cases other than an unvarnished price conspiracy, there inevitably is a degree of analysis involved in the process of characterization, in deciding whether to call an arrangement price fixing, for example. That analysis is similar to a rule of reason analysis in truncated form. Here, for example, it entails some judgment about market concentration. We are met once again with questions of degree. How large must the market shares of participating firms be in order to warrant the conclusion that price competition is significantly affected? How is the market to be defined for answering this question? In general,

---

7. United States v. Paramount Pictures, Inc., 334 U.S. 131, 68 S.Ct. 915, 92 L.Ed. 1260 (1948). See also cases cited in note 3 supra.

the cases do not insist on any elaborate market definition. For example, they usually take the defendant's products as a market and seldom look to substitutes. The aggregate shares of the participating firms need not be exceedingly high—certainly they need not even begin to approach monopoly. If in the aggregate the shares are large enough so that an end to price competition between the participants will be noticed, then market-wide competition is affected.

Suppose that a joint arrangement displays both conditions specified and discussed above and so avoids the *per se* ban. The result is not automatic legality, but application of the rule of reason. We shall not at this point pursue the analysis under the rule of reason. That matter will be pursued when we discuss the application of the rule of reason to various kinds of arrangements, including joint buying or selling cooperatives, and the like.[8] The point to be made here is that automatic application of the *per se* doctrine comes to an end at the point where significant, otherwise unattainable integration benefits begin. At this point we are no longer dealing with a naked restraint between competitors, the kind of restraint to which the *per se* rule is limited by the logic of its own rationale. We must thus inquire further to see whether market-wide price competition is significantly affected and, if not, balance all of the relevant interests under the rule of reason.

§ 78. Agreements Establishing Maximum Prices

Although there are two Supreme Court cases which talk about fixing maximum prices, neither entailed horizontal arrangements, strictly speaking. One, the newspaper deliveries case,[1] was a matter of a publisher at one level fixing resale prices at the next. The other, *Kiefer-Stewart*,[2] also involved vertical control of resale prices; but it had a strong horizontal element in that two distillers agreed as to the maximum resale prices they would permit their distributors to charge. Because of their vertical aspects, these decisions might be distinguished on their facts from an uncomplicated compact between two competing producers of the same product that they would charge no less than a specified price. But it is generally accepted, because of the breadth of the price fixing condemnation in *Socony-Vacuum*, which spoke of "depressing" as well as "raising, * * * fixing, pegging, or stabilizing" [3] prices, and because of what the Court more specifically said about maximum price agreements in *Kiefer-Stewart*, that such an agreement is *per se* unlawful. Indeed, in *Kiefer-Stewart*

---

8. See § 104 infra.

1. Albrecht v. The Herald Co., 390 U.S. 145, 88 S.Ct. 869, 19 L.Ed.2d 998 (1968).

2. Kiefer-Stewart Co. v. Joseph E. Seagram & Sons, Inc., 340 U.S. 211, 71 S.Ct. 259, 95 L.Ed. 219 (1951).

3. 310 U.S. 150, 223, 60 S.Ct. 811, 844, 84 L.Ed. 1129, 1168 (1940); see § 67 supra.

the Court emphasized the horizontal element to the point of ignoring the vertical one and spoke directly to this issue:

> [A]greement[s] among competitors to fix maximum resale prices of their products * * * no less than those to fix minimum prices, cripple the freedom of traders and thereby restrain their ability to sell in accordance with their own judgment. We reaffirm what we said in * * * [*Socony-Vacuum*. Such a combination] is illegal *per se*.[4]

Such a resolution of the maximum price fixing question is faithful not only to the rhetoric but also to the populist spirit which shows through the more analytical trappings of *Socony-Vacuum,* a spirit discernably favorable to the protection of all opportunities for independent decision making by small firms. For many, the conclusion which outlaws concerted efforts to hold prices down somehow fails to be completely satisfying. In part this may be on account of a lingering doubt that consumers will really be better off by dint of a policy which would scotch conspiratorial efforts, even those which, on rare occasions, are aimed at keeping prices down. May not traders, organized horizontally, at times conspire to advance the interests of those to whom they sell, or at least may not such customers at times be direct, if unintended, beneficiaries, of cartel policies? In part doubt comes, perhaps, because after decades of inflation and abortive efforts by government to bring it under control by fiscal and monetary policy, it seems a bit perverse for government to use the antitrust laws against any private effort to do, in part, what government has singularly failed to accomplish.

If we start by supposing that producers fixing maximum prices are not acting from undiluted altruism, we must find a self-interested explanation for their conduct. Areeda's analysis suggests several.[5] The most likely is that sellers (in an oligopolistic industry) fear entry if prices go higher and are conspiring to prevent this. More speculative, perhaps, are the suggestions that the agreement may be aimed at stifling changes in product which would demand higher prices, or that it may be a minimum price agreement in disguise. Another possibility is that producers are seeking to allocate a short supply on some basis other than price and feel that collective action is needed to facilitate that goal.

If any of the first three purposes is operative, the threat to the public interest can hardly be ignored. Successful functioning of the price system in the long run requires that prices in an industry be free to rise in response to forces like increased demand, as well as to fall in response to opposed forces. Price increases and resulting high profits for traders already in an industry toward which demand

---

4. 340 U.S. 211, 213, 71 S.Ct. 259, 260, 95 L.Ed. 219, 223 (1951).

5. See P. Areeda, Antitrust Analysis, Problems, Text, Cases ¶ 317 (2d ed. 1974).

is shifting is the basic economic signal that investment in that industry is too low relative to other industries and that resources should be shifted to it. Persistent inflation does not alter any of this in principle or in operation, so long as the rate of increase does not become so severe as to become runaway inflation, which distorts all market signals. In an inflationary economy, industries can still expand and contract. If prices go up in industry A at a rate relatively faster than that for the economy as a whole and in industry B they go down, remain stable, or even rise, but at a slower rate than for the economy as a whole, the signal is that resources should move from B to A.

Agreement aimed at inhibiting product changes could also stifle competition seriously by ending one element of competition and by reinforcing tendencies toward price leadership. The remaining possibility, that producer rationing is taking place in a time of shortage, seems least to threaten consumer interests, but this explanation is likely to seem most like a rationalization and least like a reason for concerted action. In a temporary period of short supply, any single producer which felt that the fair thing to do (and the thing which would maintain for him maximum goodwill among his customers) was to hold prices firm and ration output could take that course unilaterally. Indeed, the goodwill gained would be increased if other producers pushed prices up. If the shortage condition is not a temporary one, the rationing explanation loses credence entirely. On those facts, a concerted limitation on price increases would be totally out of harmony with producer interests. Nor would a long run need for rationing as a basis for concerted price restriction be worthy of approval even if it were worthy of belief. The need for long run rationing implies the need for new investment in the industry. This will only be stimulated if prices are free to realistically and accurately reflect the relationships of supply and demand in one industry relative to others.

The policy which insists on individual decisions about price thus has at its source more than a preference for the independence of the small businessman (though that is surely there) and more than a preference for the lower prices which such a policy will usually yield to consumers (though that too is strongly present). Also at work is the theoretical conviction that the most general function of the competitive process, the allocation and reallocation of resources in a rational yet automatic manner, can be carried out only if independence by each trader is scrupulously required. Created out of the confluence of these parallel strivings, the policy has a breadth which makes it as forbidding to maximum price arrangements as to the more common ones which forestall price decreases.

PART E. HORIZONTAL MARKET DIVISION

§ 79. History of the Rule—The Cases Before Topco

Though courts and commentators have been announcing for a generation that market division among competitors is a *per se* violation, the precise meaning and scope of that proposition remained surprisingly indeterminate until the recent decision in United States v. Topco Associates.[1] Doubt about the rule did not arise from obvious or mechanistic reasons; forms of market division can vary to an almost capricious degree. Collision with competitors can be avoided by agreements which parcel out exclusive territories, exclusive customers, or exclusive products, but all of this has long been assimilated and the law has displayed no tendency to draw overly fine distinctions between such alternative ways of dividing markets. Nor do variations between open agreements and hidden ones, such as the "phases of the moon" conspiracy in the electrical industry, complicate the problem.[2] Whether we call such devices imaginative or crude, once they have been found out they do nothing to drape over the fact that firms which might have given each other the competitive nudge have instead agreed to permit to each other an abundant elbowroom. What has lacked complete illumination over the years is not the categories of arrangements to which the rule about market division should be applied, but whether circumstances like lack of power or some alternative competitive or business justification would cause a court to withhold application of the rule and to characterize the transaction in terms which evoke the rule of reason.

The earliest case which is sometimes cited as showing that market division is *per se* unlawful, *Addyston Pipe & Steel*,[3] does not lack ambiguity. There, the Court condemned an arrangement by which defendants divided territories and allocated the business among themselves. But the evidence suggested that defendants possessed considerable market power and the Court explicitly found harmful effects, including supra-competitive prices, as a "direct and immediate result of the combination."[4] This, then, is no flat holding that market division is always wrong. The most prominent and frequently cited case after *Addyston* is Timken Roller Bearing Co. v. United States.[5] Timken and other companies partially in common ownership had allocated territories throughout a worldwide market. The Court found this to be unlawful, but in a context where power and effects were

---

1. 405 U.S. 596, 92 S.Ct. 1126, 31 L.Ed. 2d 515 (1972).

2. See the materials collected in Handler, Blake, Pitofsky & Goldschmid, Trade Regulation, Cases and Materials 290–94 (1975) and in particular excerpts from deposition of J. V. McQuire at 292.

3. 85 F. 271 (6th Cir. 1898), modified and aff'd 175 U.S. 211, 20 S.Ct. 96, 44 L.Ed. 136 (1899); see § 64 supra.

4. 175 U.S. 211, 240–41, 20 S.Ct. 96, 107, 44 L.Ed. 136, 147 (1899).

5. 341 U.S. 593, 71 S.Ct. 971, 95 L.Ed. 1199 (1951).

evident and where, in addition, it was shown that defendants cooperated to protect each other's assigned markets from outside competition and also engaged in price fixing. Indeed, in holding the territorial division unlawful the Court labeled it as part of "an aggregation of trade restraints." [6]

The next major development was United States v. Sealy, Inc.[7] The government challenged an agreement whereby several mattress manufacturers formed a joint subsidiary which acquired the Sealy trade name and mark, and advertised these nationally. The subsidiary licensed the parent manufacturers, each in an exclusive territory, to make and sell mattresses under the Sealy label. The trial court found price fixing as well as territorial division, and held the former to violate the Act but the latter to be legal. On apppeal, the Supreme Court held the division of markets to be illegal also. It rejected the contention, accepted below, that protected territories were incidents of a lawful program of trademark licensing. It characterized them as *per se* unlawful, but did so specifically because they were part of "an aggregation of trade restraints" which included price fixing.[8]

Sealy did foreclose one argument often advanced as a justification for market division. The Sealy manufacturers argued that they were small regional firms facing a few large firms which formed a tight national bedding business oligopoly, and that combining as they had enabled them to enter and to present themselves as aggressive new competitors in that compacted national market. The decision, of course, did not forbid combining to exploit the name and mark; what it forbade was the territorial protection. But the claim pressed for allowing territorial division was that without it each participant would hesitate to advertise the brand and promote it adequately for fear that others would hold back, seeking to take a free ride on its promotion. The argument is based, in its essentials, on Justice Taft's ancillary concept.[9] It presents the enabling of small firms to enter a national market as the independent lawful purpose, and territorial restraint as necessary to facilitate that purpose, much as a limited covenant not to compete is needed to facilitate the sale of a business. The flaw in this argument is that the territorial restraint is not "reasonably necessary" to facilitate the main purpose; there are less restrictive and more efficient ways than territorial blockades against competition to assure that participants share equitably in promotion expenses. If they agree to stay out of each other's markets, the

---

6. Id. at 598, 71 S.Ct. at 974, 95 L.Ed. at 1206.

7. 388 U.S. 350, 87 S.Ct. 1847, 18 L.Ed. 2d 1238 (1967).

8. The Court did not use the phrase "*per se* unlawful", but said that under these circumstances territorial division was unlawful "without the necessity for an inquiry in each particular case as to their business or economic justification, their impact in the marketplace, or their reasonableness." 388 U.S. at 357–58, 87 S.Ct. at 1853, 18 L.Ed.2d at 1244.

9. See § 64 supra.

"free ride" problem, if it is a real one at all, may still exist. The Maryland manufacturer may still rely on advertising by the Virginia, Washington, Delaware and Pennsylvania manufacturers, for example. But if participants must agree to advertise on some predetermined basis, no participant can avoid its responsibility. Still, *Sealy* cannot be read as calling unqualifiedly for a *per se* approach to market division, for the Court emphasized the factual linkage between territorial and price restraints.[10]

After *Sealy* came Burke v. Ford,[11] where the Court, explicitly finding an effect on commerce, reversed a holding below which had refused to outlaw a statewide market division by liquor wholesalers on the ground that commerce was not affected. Here, the focus was on the commerce issue; the case advances knowledge about territorial restrictions only to the extent of a dictum that horizontal market divisions "almost invariably reduce competition,"[12] an observation which would support *per se* treatment, at least if there were insufficient countervailing gains in cases where competition was not adversely affected, and if it were difficult to discriminate in any given instance between a case which hurt competition and one which did not.

Beyond these cases, which presented market division in situations where power or effect were shown or where market division was linked to price fixing, or both, the Supreme Court jurisprudence about horizontal market division was limited to dicta. Yet these were numerous and consistent; the Court had stated repeatedly that these arrangements were unlawful *per se*.[13] There were, moreover, lower court decisions holding market divisions to be unlawful even though not linked to price fixing or any other aggregate of restraints, and without any showing of market power or effect. In United States v. Consolidated Laundries Corp.,[14] for example, the court applied the *per se* rule to a horizontal agreement allocating customers, stating that nothing save the fact of customer allocation need be proved.[15] Of course, there were also numerous lower court cases in-

10. 388 U.S. at 355–57, 87 S.Ct. at 1852, 18 L.Ed.2d at 1243–44.

11. 389 U.S. 320, 88 S.Ct. 443, 19 L.Ed. 2d 554 (1967).

12. Id. at 321, 88 S.Ct. at 444, 19 L.Ed. 2d at 556.

13. United States v. Arnold Schwinn & Co., 388 U.S. 365, 375, 87 S.Ct. 1856, 1863, 18 L.Ed.2d 1249, 1258 (1967); White Motor Co. v. United States, 372 U.S. 253, 263, 83 S.Ct. 696, 702, 9 L. Ed.2d 738, 746 (1963).

14. 291 F.2d 563 (2d Cir. 1961).

15. See also Gray Line, Inc. v. Gray Line Sightseeing Companies Assoc., 246 F.Supp. 495 (N.D.Cal.1965); United States v. American Linen Supply Co., 141 F.Supp. 105, 115 (N.D.Ill. 1956); United States v. Bayer Co., 135 F.Supp. 65 (S.D.N.Y.1955); United States v. Imperial Chemical Indus. Ltd., 100 F.Supp. 504 (S.D.N.Y.1951); United States v. General Dyestuff Corp., 57 F.Supp. 642 (S.D.N.Y.1944); Johnson v. Joseph Schlitz Brewery Co., 33 F.Supp. 176, 181 (E.D.Tenn. 1940), aff'd per curiam, 123 F.2d 1016 (6th Cir. 1941).

validating market division, *per se*, where it was ancilliary to price fixing.[16]

On the other hand, there were numerous decisions declining *per se* treatment where some mode of market division was achieved in the course of a partial integration,[17] or in the course of an arrangement which might have had the purpose or effect of making or improving a market.[18] There was also dictum in *Sealy* that an arrangement among a number of small grocers dividing territory incident to the use of a common name and common advertising might be held lawful.[19]

§ 80. The Topco Case

The facts in *Topco*[1] were similar to those in *Sealy*,[2] but without price fixing or other restraints and with a fairly forceful argument available for possible benefits to competition arising from possible integration efficiencies. Indeed, the case presented a situation very close to the hypothetical about small grocers entering into a joint venture upon which decision was reserved in *Sealy*. Defendants in *Topco* were operators of independent supermarket chains. Their stores competed with other grocery stores, including those of the large national and regional chains. Those large chains sold nationally advertised products and also utilized so called "house brands" which they had packed for them with their own trade names and marks. None of the independent operators was large enough, alone, to have a house brand, so they all formed a subsidiary which adopted the Topco brand and mark. This subsidiary purchased products bearing this brand label from packers, much as the large chain grocers did, and distributed these name brand products to the participating independents. The arrangement also included provisions to protect the

---

16. Las Vegas Merchant Plumbers Ass'n v. United States, 210 F.2d 732, 741, 748–49 (9th Cir.), cert. denied 348 U.S. 817, 75 S.Ct. 29, 99 L.Ed. 645 (1954); Pennsylvania Water & Power Co. v. Consol. Gas. Elec. Light and Power Co., 184 F.2d 552, 558 (4th Cir.), cert. denied 340 U.S. 906, 71 S.Ct. 282, 95 L.Ed. 655 (1950); United States v. Pennsylvania Refuse Removal Ass'n., 242 F.Supp. 794 (E.D.Pa.1965), aff'd on other grounds 357 F.2d 806 (3d Cir.), cert. denied 384 U.S. 961, 86 S. Ct. 1588, 16 L.Ed.2d 674 (1966); United States v. American Smelting & Ref. Co., 182 F.Supp. 834 (S.D.N.Y.1960).

17. United States v. National Football League, 196 F.Supp. 445 (E.D.Pa. 1961); United States v. Pan American World Airways, Inc., 193 F.Supp. 18 (S.D.N.Y.1961), rev'd on other grounds 371 U.S. 296, 83 S.Ct. 476, 9 L.Ed.2d 325 (1963); United States v. Columbia Pictures Corp., 189 F.Supp. 153 (S.D. N.Y.1960); United States v. E. I. Du Pont De Nemours & Co., 118 F.Supp. 41 (D.Del.1953), aff'd on other grounds 351 U.S. 377, 76 S.Ct. 994, 100 L.Ed. 1264 (1956); United States v. Morgan, 118 F.Supp. 621, 689–91, 731, 733–39 (S.D.N.Y.1953).

18. See cases cited in § 77, note 2 supra.

19. 388 U.S. at 357, 87 S.Ct. at 1852, 18 L.Ed.2d at 1244.

1. United States v. Topco Associates, 405 U.S. 596, 92 S.Ct. 1126, 31 L.Ed.2d 515 (1972).

2. 388 U.S. 350, 87 S.Ct. 1847, 18 L.Ed. 2d 1238 (1967). See the discussion in § 79 in text accompanying note 7.

territories of the participating independents from one another. Refusing to apply the *per se* rule, the district court analyzed the restraint under the rule of reason and found it valid. On review the Supreme Court reversed.

As in *Sealy*, the Court had no difficulty characterizing the arrangement as a horizontal one even though, in form, the territorial restrictions were imposed by the subsidiary, a wholesaler, upon its parent-customers to which it sold. The significant thing about the case is the conclusion the Supreme Court reached in the face of the findings below. The trial court had found that defendants lacked significant power, that the arrangement did not significantly reduce competition between them and did not significantly reduce competition in the market. It also found that defendants could not compete effectively with the large chains without private label merchandise, that the joint action was necessary to attain private label merchandise because defendants individually were not big enough to establish such labels, and that the territorial restrictions were reasonably related to the joint arrangement, since each defendant would be loath to use a so-called private label which other retailers in the same area could share. On this basis the trial court adopted the conclusionary finding that any restriction upon competition between the defendants which resulted from the arrangement was more than compensated for by the competition which the arrangement stimulated by creating an opportunity for the independents to challenge the large chains. The territorial restriction, being essential to the arrangement, was therefore reasonable and valid. The Supreme Court flatly rejected this analysis, not because it questioned the findings or inferences, but because, as it ruled, the *per se* doctrine should have been applied to invalidate the territorial restriction. As the majority put it, courts are ill-equipped to measure whether a restriction on competition in one sector is overbalanced by an increase in competition in another. The congressional policy is to invalidate arrangements which restrict competition, as territorial restraints surely do. If such arrangements are to be upheld though they stifle competition in one area when they are thought to enhance competition elsewhere, Congress must make that decision.

There is, therefore, no longer doubt. A *per se* rule applies to market division arrangements regardless of whether they are linked to price fixing or other restraints, and apparently without need for a specific showing of significant power or discernible competitive effects. The rule also applies, at least in some instances, even though the restriction is associated with a significant integration involving economies of scale. And it applies, at least in some instances, even though it enhances competition by facilitating competitive entry in some market other than that in which the restriction works. As a result of *Topco*, any possibility that the *per se* rule about market division would prove to be softer and more yielding in application than the *per se* rule about price fixing has been ended.

Nevertheless, do not surmise that the rule against market division will in the end prove more rigorous than that against price fixing, that it will be blind to distinctions like a purpose and effect to establish or improve an organized market, or a purpose and effect to achieve integration yielding an economy of scale. We shall see that the rationale for a *per se* rule against naked market division is comparable in strength to the *per se* rule about price restraints.[3] We shall also see that in cases before *Topco* the courts avoided the *per se* rule by avoiding a characterization of market division in instances where either the making of a market or the achievement of substantial integration was entailed, just as a characterization of price fixing is avoided in situations where price restraints aid in making a market or are a direct result of integration.[4] *Topco,* on its own facts, rejected a relationship to integration as a basis for withholding the characterization of market division. But it did not do so in a situation where, had the restraint entailed price rather than territory, the integration characteristics would not have been sufficient to avoid application of the *per se* doctrine. Despite assertions about integration and a new and vigorous challenge to the big chains, no one would argue that if the *Topco* conspirators had fixed prices their conduct ought to be legal. The case, then, holds no more than that market division is not to be treated less harshly than price fixing; it does not imply that the former is to be treated more harshly than the latter.

There are numerous cases opting for application of the rule of reason where diminishment of price competition results from integration, as where a single selling agent sets prices for two or more competitors. But in all of those, the reduction of price competition arises as an essential incident of the integration itself, just as price competition inevitably ends where two firms merge into a single one. There is no case which holds that an integration of non-selling functions (for example, manufacturing, research, or trademark and specification development), which leaves selling functions to continue to be carried out by the separate, competing firms, will serve to justify a restraint on price competition between the firms which continue to sell as independent units. Indeed, insofar as there is any authority it is the implication of *Sealy* on this point. Because price restraints as well as territorial ones were there involved, because the Court implicitly approved the holding below that these were *per se* invalid, and because the Court treated the associated price restraints as a reason for its holding that the territorial resraints were unlawful, *Sealy* persuasively suggests that price restraints, in a context where only non-selling functions are integrated, are to be treated as naked ones. Those who utilize them, when continuing as separate sellers, are not

---

3. See § 82 infra. 4. See § 81 infra.

to be heard to argue that the price restraint was an essential inducement for the participating firms to integrate their non-selling functions. *Topco* treats territorial restrictions associated with but not resulting inevitably from an integration in precisely the same way. On the one hand, there is no case holding or suggesting that a price restraint, unlike a territorial restraint, would avoid *per se* treatment in a situation like *Topco,* and there is no basis in *Topco* for concluding that price fixing will be treated less harshly than market division. On the other hand, there is nothing in *Topco* to suggest that if territorial exclusivity arises as an inevitable consequence of a partial integration the integration becomes for that reason unlawful. The territorial restraint in *Topco* did not issue out of the integration as an effect, but was an explicit arrangement which defendants sought to justify by asserting that they would not integrate without it.

§ 81. The Implications of Topco—Issues of Characterization

The market division rule presents issues of characterization like those involved in price fixing. A flat-out agreement between competitors to divide territories, customers, or products presents no difficulty in characterization. But with arrangements having only a tendency to segregate markets, issues of characterization must be resolved. As with price fixing, the basic guide is purpose and effect; if division of markets is the goal of the arrangement or its overriding effect, it should be characterized as market division even though it achieves that consequence quite indirectly. Moreover (and once again as with price fixing), even a significant tendency to affect the market which sellers serve may be tolerated where an arrangement is aimed at establishing or improving an organized market. Here, as in price cases, rule of reason analysis is utilized. Finally, there are issues concerning partial integration which are analogous to those in price fixing cases. Where a tendency toward market division arises as a necessary consequence of an integration, and when market-wide competition is not reduced, rule of reason analysis may be utilized.

The basic guide, purpose and effect, must discriminate between a naked division of markets and a division consequent upon some arrangement aimed at other ends. Picture, for example, two gasoline refiners. One has refining capacity in the east and retail outlets in both the east and west; the other also has nationwide retail outlets, but refining capacity only in the west. If these firms agree that the one with capacity in the east will supply the other in that area and the one with capacity in the west will supply the other in the west, a likely consequence will be that neither will, as a refiner, invade the territory now occupied by the other. Market division is a clear tendency of the arrangement. But market division is not its inevitable consequence, and the arrangement has other implications and effects as well: each participant gets a satisfactory source of supply for its distant outlets, thus becoming, perhaps, a more effective competitor at the retail level. *Topco* suggests that if this kind of arrangement were accompanied by a commitment by each that it would not enter the other's territory as a refiner, that commitment would be *per se* invalid, despite any contention that the commitment was needed in order to facilitate the basic arrangement. But absent such a commitment, express or implied, the fact that the arrangement will reduce the individual incentive of each participant to enter the territory of the other and thus will tend to keep the markets separate will not warrant its being characterized as a division of markets and *per se* unlawful. Why? Because that tendency is not the only thing of consequence which is involved; there are other independently significant consequences to which the market dividing tendency is related and which may be of much greater consequence, both in terms of the purpose for the arrangement and its effect. This being so, a court should not characterize the arrangement as a division of markets. It should evaluate the affirmative and the negative consequences of the arrangement under the rule of reason before passing upon its legality under Section 1.[1]

The purpose and effect analysis also discriminates between a market division which is *per se* unlawful and the formation of a joint subsidiary to engage in a new business that either of the parents might have considered alone. Suppose company A operates in territory X (or makes product X) while company B operates in territory Y (or makes product Y), and that they jointly form company C to operate in territory Z (or make product Z). Such an arrangement should not be condemned *per se* as market division; we should apply the rule of reason.[2] *Topco* is entirely consistent with this conclusion. If the Topco Company were formed and were to sell to the participating retailers without any commitment by them to respect each other's territories, any resulting tendency for each of them to stay out of the territory of the other, arising merely from the fact of the joint undertaking, would not warrant the arrangement being characterized as a division of territories. It was the fact of an explicit commitment that called for the *per se* rule in *Topco*.

---

1. See Blue Bell Co. v. Frontier Refining Co., 213 F.2d 354 (10th Cir. 1954).

2. United States v. Penn-Olin Chemical Co., 378 U.S. 158, 84 S.Ct. 1710, 12 L. Ed.2d 775 (1964). United States v. Pan American World Airways, Inc., 193 F.Supp. 18 (S.D.N.Y.1961), rev'd on other grounds 371 U.S. 296, 83 S. Ct. 476, 9 L.Ed.2d 325 (1963) went further. It held, in substance, that if an explicit agreement by companies A and B to stay out of territory Z were needed to induce the joint investment, even that commitment, being ancillary to the joint venture, was not a naked division of territory and was also to be analyzed under the rule of reason. *Topco* is entirely inconsistent with what the district court did in *Pan Am*. In *Topco* there was an explicit commitment to respect territories which the district court found was needed to induce the parties to join the venture. The Supreme Court in *Topco* flatly holds that such a restriction cannot be justified on the ground that it is ancillary to some other, independently valid arrangement.

Let us now turn from these basic considerations to the only situation where, despite *Topco,* it would still seem that arrangements which could be viewed as explicit market division may still be held valid. Market division, when used to create or improve an organized market, should be dealt with just as is a price restraint used for that purpose. Indeed, the illustrative cases are highly interchangeable. Arrangements which tend to channel transactions within an organized market can often both be said to affect price formation (thus raising the question whether they should be characterized as price restraints) and to segregate some transactions from others, either in terms of time, products, or locations (thus raising the question whether they should be characterized as market divisions).

Chicago Board of Trade,[3] the germinal case, displays this duality. There, members trading in grain "to arrive" between the close of the market on one day and its opening on the next were required to trade at the last price bid at or before the closing of the market. The argument that this constitutes a concerted arrangement fixing a formula for determining the price is straightforward enough. But it could also be seen as dividing markets by channelling all or substantially all "to arrive" trading into the organized daytime exchange and away from the unorganized nighttime market. This alternative characterization should be rejected for the same reason that the price fixing characterization fails. Since the purpose of the arrangement is to improve an organized market, plainly an appropriate medium for the unbridled expression of competitive forces, it ought not to be invalidated out of hand; its varied impacts should be fully analyzed to determine whether, on balance, they help or hurt competition.

The tobacco warehouse cases are also relevant. They too can be seen either as instances where price effects are concertedly achieved or as examples of situations where market division is accomplished; yet, both these characterizations are rejected and the practices are analyzed under the rule of reason because they may serve to establish or improve organized markets.[4] In these cases, an association allocates the total available selling time for the highly perishable tobacco crop among local warehouses where auctions are conducted. The purpose and effect which may validate these allocations is that because of the allocation all interested buyers will be able to attend all auctions without conflicts in time. This may improve each market by bringing more buyers to it. Courts have refused to apply the *per se* rule even though there is a clear temporal division of markets. Rule of reason analysis permits a balance to be struck between negative and positive effects.

---

3. 246 U.S. 231, 38 S.Ct. 242, 62 L.Ed. 683 (1918). See § 66 supra.

4. See cases cited in § 76, note 2 supra.

Although the tobacco warehouse cases preceded *Topco,* that decision ought not to be read as mandating a change in result. No more in *Topco* than in any other market division case where a *per se* approach is used, was there a claim that the restraint served to make the market in which it applied more competitive; in *Topco* the only claim was that by restricting competition among themselves the participants armed themselves to compete better with others. Where the function of a regulation is to channel the forces of supply and demand into an area where they may freely and fully operate, it may serve to improve the functioning of competition. Where a plausible claim is made that this is the purpose and effect of a regulation, *per se* treatment is not appropriate. Whether competition is in fact improved or whether the dominant effect is really to divide markets and inhibit competition can be judged under the rule of reason.

Finally we have the situation where market division arises in connection with an integration. Although a few lower court cases decided before *Topco* held that an explicit division of markets was not *per se* unlawful when it served to aid a significant integration to which it was ancillary, we must now doubt the authority of these decisions. United States v. National Football League [5] is typical of these pre-*Topco* cases. There, a league rule forbade authorization for the televising of a game into the territory in which the game was being played. While the court recognized this as a "clear case of allocating marketing territories among competitors" for television rights, it viewed the arrangement as ancillary to the integration of the teams into a league and saw it as reasonable because it strengthened the weak teams, which would have found their receipts reduced if games were televised locally, and thus helped the league to survive. *Topco,* however, held that the *per se* rule applied to an explicit division of markets even when ancillary to an integration, and even when the trial court found that the division was reasonably necessary to the successful carrying through of the integration.

Topco does not, however, make the existence of an integration irrelevant. Rather, we must now assume that the relationship between integration and market division will be essentially the same as that between integration and price restraint. We know of no case holding that upon a partial integration firms which in some aspects continue to operate separately may undertake to end price competition in those separate aspects. Partial integration shields from the *per se* rule against price fixing only such dampening of price competition as has necessarily arisen as a consequence of the integration. Thus, where sales functions are integrated, the consequences will be evaluated under the rule of reason, any benefits of the integration being set off against the reduction in price competition. But if, say,

---

5. 116 F.Supp. 319 (E.D.Pa.1953). See also United States v. Pan American World Airways, Inc., 193 F.Supp. 18 (S.D.N.Y.1961), rev'd on other grounds, 371 U.S. 296, 83 S.Ct. 476, 9 L.Ed.2d 325 (1963).

research and advertising activities were integrated, but selling continued to be conducted independently, price fixing could not be validated by the partial integration.

A similar approach should govern where market division is related to an integration. Suppose, for example, that two or three firms with large research budgets had each been doing part of their research in a highly specialized area of interest to all of them. Suppose further that they were each disappointed by results and felt that more effective research would require an effort of substantially larger scale. If the firms merged this aspect of their work into a joint subsidiary, an undoubted consequence would be that the participating firms would individually stay out of the research area entered by the subsidiary. A division of markets would have arisen as a consequence of the integration. Whether that hypothetical was to be treated under purpose and effect analysis, or was to be analogized to the partial integration cases which result in reduction of price competition, the result would be the same. Unless the three firms had such large market shares that it could be stated even on a truncated analysis that market competition would be adversely affected, *per se* treatment would not be appropriate; the legality of the arrangement should be determined by more fully analyzing its benefits and harms under the rule of reason.[6] On the other hand, if the firms entered into an ancillary agreement dividing selling markets by territory or product, that agreement, since not a necessary result of the integrated research, would be *per se* unlawful.

It must be underscored that where there is a clear and strong tendency toward market division, courts will not drop the *per se* approach and use the rule of reason immediately on learning that the arrangement involves a partial integration. As in instances where price competition is dampened by integration, there is another prerequisite to rule of reason treatment—namely, that the arrangement not appear to affect market-wide competition. If the participants in the integration appear on preliminary analysis to have so much market power that market competition will be substantially affected by the tendency toward market division, the *per se* doctrine will be applied even though that tendency arises out of an integration.

Let us contrast two cases which, together, are illustrative of the way the courts proceed. In United States v. American Smelting and Refining Co.,[7] the *per se* rule was applied despite a claim of integration benefits; in United States v. Columbia Pictures Corp.,[8] on facts that were superficially similar, the rule of reason was applied. In *American Smelting and Refining,* two of the nations largest lead miners, one with a sales organization only in the west and the other with a national sales organization, entered into an arrangement whereby

---

6. See United States v. Penn-Olin Chemical Co., 378 U.S. 158, 84 S.Ct. 1710, 12 L.Ed.2d 775 (1964).

7. 182 F.Supp. 834 (S.D.N.Y.1960).

8. 189 F.Supp. 153 (S.D.N.Y.1960).

the latter firm would act in the east as sales agent for the former. The agent was obliged to sell at prices at least as favorable as those charged for its own lead and, in case demand was not sufficient to clear the market at the prices charged, to allocate sales on a reasonable basis. Although there was obviously some integration effect, the court wasted little energy before labeling the arrangement an unlawful division of territories and thus *per se* unlawful. This course seems justified, despite the integration, because of the salience of the power of the two firms. It is hard to suppose that this joint arrangement was the only way the western firm could gain access to eastern markets, and of all conceivable ways it might have achieved this, none could threaten competition as much as this one.

In *Columbia Pictures,* by contrast, massive power was not manifest. There, one of the major film producers, through a subsidiary, marketed films including its own old features to television stations. When the government challenged an arrangement whereby another producer appointed the subsidiary as its agent to market old films, the court rejected the *per se* approach taken in *American Smelting and Refining* and analyzed legality under the rule of reason. The degree of integration achieved here was not significantly greater than that achieved by the lead companies. But in the TV programming case, the agent and the two producers, even in combination, were only minor factors in the marketing of television program material; nor did it appear so obvious that there were less restrictive ways in which the second producer could have sold its films for television.

§ 82. Market Division and Price Fixing Compared

Whether the *per se* doctrine as applied to market division should have equal, greater or lesser rigor than when it is applied to price fixing might be made to turn upon whether the market impacts of the two types of restraints would be likely to vary in severity. We allowed the propriety of *per se* treatment for a naked price restraint upon conviction that price fixing in most manifestations would be injurious, that any gains ever to be attained from it would likely be modest, and that it would be difficult in particular cases to confidently predict that gains were present or that they outweighed the harm attributable to the practice. Can the same arguments be made for *per se* treatment of naked market division? For purposes of the present inquiry we assume a division of markets by a cartel with each participant left free to price as it chooses and we must compare this with a price fixing cartel which does not divide markets.

Note first that even where prices are rigidly fixed, the members of a cartel will still be able to compete with each other with respect to product quality unless a homogeneous product is involved. Indeed, even if the product is homogeneous there will be room for rivalry in such matters as promptness in filling orders and the provision of ancillary services. An effective division of markets, by contrast, might substantially wash out all opportunity for rivalry. Let us look closely at the possibilities.

If each seller has its own geographic territory, none will encounter any other seller there. The severity of the restraint on competition will depend on the extent to which the territories reserved constitute separate geographic markets—competition will be effectively ended except to the extent that the buyers are mobile enough to shop in distant markets. Buyer mobility may at times be possible; a cartel member, though staying out of another's territory, may attract customers to cross over to its own. But this will be unlikely except in the case of products which are of high enough value to warrant investment of considerable time and cost in shopping and which can be cheaply transported. On the other hand, if the assigned territories are too small to constitute separate geographic markets, if the "excusive territories" of two or more sellers are really all within a single integrated geographic market for the product involved, buyers may scarcely notice the separation; they will tend to shop each "territory" within the market and, if price fixing is not taking place, will receive the substantial benefit of competition. For example, except on rather strained assumptions an agreement between two department stores that the territory of one would be the north side of Main Street and the territory of the other would be the south side would, as a practical matter, have no adverse effect on competition at all.

Analysis of an agreement dividing markets by product would yield similar insights. If product X is reserved to seller A, product Y to seller B, and product Z to seller C, the extent to which competition is stifled will depend upon whether the markets for products X, Y and Z are separate or integrated—if you will, upon cross-elasticity of demand. If sellers who want one of these products cannot substitute another, the effect of the division will be to foreclose competition entirely. If, however, most buyers will be indifferent to whether they obtain one or another of the products—that is to say, if all of the products are really part of one fully integrated product market—competition will be scarcely affected at all.

Division of markets by customer exemplifies the most extreme case. If such a division is successful, each buyer, unknown to it, is assigned to one seller which alone will sell to it. The division is monolithically complete and all competition is ended.

Detriments from market division depend, we discern, upon the extent to which self-contained markets insulated one from another are attained. What an antitrust analyst may be pleased to call a market will rarely have wholly secure frontiers; it may be subject to considerable outside competitive pressure. And what a particular trader may be pleased to call his exclusive territory or product may be more a figment of his ambition than a reality. But if these observations highlight the factors which reduce the consequence of market dividing agreements, they do not place in shadow the significance of the insight with which we began: to the extent that by agreement sellers do successfully entrench themselves each in a separate market, the damage to competition is likely to be even more devastating than that consequent upon price fixing.

It is tempting to mark a contrast here, to assert that price fixing is no confluence of shades, gradations and degrees, that sellers have either fixed prices or they haven't, and that the flame of price competition is either snuffed out or glows unshaded. Were that true, the case for treating market division like price fixing would be weakened; the distinction justifying *per se* treatment for price restraints but not for market division would be that a scheme for price fixing always promises or achieves its full measure of harm, whereas a scheme of market division may, in either purpose or effect, merely incline away from competition rather than stamping it out and may, indeed, affect competition greatly, moderately, or scarcely at all, depending upon the delicate balance of factors which can be weighed only by full-blown inquiry.

But the distinction is insubstantial; price fixing agreements subject to the *per se* ban actually affect price competition in varying degrees. In part, this is because cartel members will always be tempted to cheat and such agreements may be adhered to fully, partially or scarcely at all. In part it is because we characterize as price fixing many agreements, such as those relating to price advertising or the use of suggested price lists, which merely reduce, without eliminating, price competition. With respect to effect, if not purpose, variation is also due in part to differences in the degree of market power possessed by parties to the agreement. On the issue of harm we must in the end say of market division what we said of price fixing —the practice is fraught with potential for serious damage to competition. Traders will be unlikely to engage in it unless they suppose themselves to possess sufficient power to have discernible market impact. Therefore, in most manifestations of the practice, significant harm is to be expected. Finally, inquiry of comprehensive scope would be needed to evaluate in any particular case the extent to which harm actually occurred.

That balance of the forces of harm was thought to warrant *per se* treatment for price fixing only after inquiry showed that potential benefits were small, infrequent and difficult to identify with certainty. Are similar observations about the benefits of market division warranted, or does the analogy we have been exploring break down at this juncture?

We are still talking, of course, about naked market division, not a division which can be said to make a market or to facilitate an integration of functions, such as *Topco* displayed. To catalog possible benefits from a naked market division is easy enough. Territorial (or product) division may facilitate the effort of each producer to attain the maximum efficient scale for production, distribution or both. Any form of market division may relieve participants of pressure to utilize socially wasteful promotional techniques like excessive advertising. Any form of market division will protect each participant from the danger that others will compete "unfairly," for example, by coming in from afar to "steal" a customer after the nearest dealer has expended time and money promoting the product in the customer's area, or even demonstrating the product to the customer. Are these truly "benefits" which can be attained consistently with the competitive ideal? If so, how consequential are they, and how easy will it be to mark their presence or absence in particular cases?

Efficiency through scale economies is altogether a worthy goal. But in the present context our conviction about this cannot be unmixed with other reactions, most notably that any claim by a cartel that its program of territorial or product assignments is connected to the achievement of scale efficiencies will be specious. Try for a moment to summon up the picture of a benign director of a state owned enterprise, deeply schooled and rich in experience, deploying plants across the landscape in a manner so gracefully proportional that each is nicely fitted to a geographic market of a size which assures efficiency in high degree. One knows immediately that this image is utterly fanciful; it could be adhered to only by one quite insensible both to the limits of practical knowledge about how maximum efficiency is to be attained and to the vitality and disorder displayed by the industrial establishment which exists in reality at any given time, a disorder and disarray partly frozen into the bricks and mortar which stand as monuments to a sequence of earlier judgments and decisions about plant size, for example. No, the hypothetical director would know too little about relationships between plant or territorial size and efficiency (and would know that he knew too little) and would be too thoroughly constricted by the status quo to permit himself to indulge in the kind of dream we have made for him; he would count himself lucky if he had the opportunity to design a single plant in a single region which approached his best, informed judgment about appropriate plant size and service territory. How much more preposterous, then, is the picture of a group of competing traders, each possessed of its own real plant built to the scale that seemed appropriate to a single, profit-oriented management at some earlier date, sitting down together with intent and prospect of dividing markets in ways which will maximize scale efficiencies. Like the director we envisaged above, they would know too little for such a task and would be allowed even less leeway by the status quo, since the cartel would hardly mandate new plant investment by even a single participant. Unlike the director they would have no overriding motive to seek maximum efficiency on an industry-wide basis since cartel members would speak not for the public interest but for their own.

The unreality of an efficiency claim made by a cartel to justify market division could, of course, be exposed by evidence of cartel deliberations if this were available. Absent the most exquisite window dressing, one would not likely find any sophisticated effort to analyze problems of scale or to link these to territorial or product assignment. Moreover, if scale efficiency were really the goal of a cartel, it could readily pursue that goal by far less restrictive programs than dividing markets—for example, by publicizing to members available information about ideal scale.

Another rejoinder invited by the efficiency rationale for market division is to celebrate the relationship between competitive processes and scale efficiency. One function of competition is to stimulate dynamic elements in industrial activity. The beckoning of opportunity for investment in a more efficient plant becomes the more insistent, the goading of obsolescence is the more starkly felt, precisely because in a competitive industry the devil may take the hindmost. In a competitive industry, the aggregate of individual firm decisions about product specialization, plant size, territory to be served and related questions is an ever churning medley, a disorderly chase after the ever receding goal of efficiency. Competitive conditions, then, can activate for an industry as a whole a self-correcting trend toward scale efficiency, as each individual decision maker takes account of currently available information and as successful decisions are rewarded and reinforced with greater than average profits, while unsuccessful ones are penalized. Under competition, scale efficiency is not achieved industry-wide and for all units at a single juncture, it is approached through small corrections made by individual firms over time. The assertion that concerted decisions dividing markets can improve upon the deployment achieved by competition is not only unconvincing for the reasons earlier examined; when it stands undraped, this rationale is seen to be quite at odds with preservation of the competitive processes, the social goal at which the statute is aimed.

Other claims which might be made on behalf of naked market division are also remarkably artificial if not downright sophistical. It would be difficult indeed to find the market dividing agreement that was actually conceived out of a lofty ambition to protect the public from the costs and blandishments of excessive advertising, or which could be demonstrated to have materially affected advertising levels. Reduction in advertising costs, if it *were* the aim of an organization of competitors, could be achieved more effectively and with far smaller impact on competition by an agreement dealing directly with advertising levels. The rationale based upon the vision of the distant trader swooping in to reap where he had not sown also possesses a mythical quality. The problem as seen by any individual trader is likely to be marginal, and cartels would hardly be organized to deal with it; if this were indeed the objective of an organization, more pointed and less restrictive arrangements—for example, "pass over" arrangements to compensate the local seller for its promotional expenses—could be resorted to. And looked at starkly, the claim that the distant seller who "steals" a local sale is acting unfairly is, like the claim that cartelization leads to more efficient deployment of resources, directly at odds with the competitive ideology that underpins the Sherman Act.

Any seller has a locational advantage over more distant sellers in dealing with nearby customers. But competitive pressures from other sellers are like a series of concentric circles; those sellers which are closest constitute the most severe restraint on a local seller's market power, those at a greater distance being able to challenge only if the local seller is inefficient or miscalculates the profit level which would induce distant sellers to make forays into the local market. If a local seller's balance of price, quality and service is at a level which does permit a distant seller to absorb the costs associated with selling from a distance and still make a more attractive offering, it is a sure sign that local prices are too high or quality or service deficient. The threat of potential competition from a distance is, in short, one of the significant protections afforded to consumers by the competitive process, an important spur to efficiency, and a check upon excessive prices and profits. To clothe in moral overtones the local seller's appeal to be freed of that constraint and permitted the luxury of a quiet life does not alter the essential character of that appeal.

Any appeal for naked market division based on claims of attendant benefits, however pretentiously presented, can earn at best a modest regard. Like those made for price fixing, these claims have a whimsical quality, and when we look hard at them we find that to give them credit we must deny it to the competitive ideal. There is nothing here to call into question the soundness of applying the *per se* doctrine when competitors enter into an arrangement which, in purpose or effect, would divide markets among them.

PART F. BOYCOTTS

§ 83. The Characteristics of a Boycott

When a court strings together a list of *per se* offenses it is likely to include the group boycott, or as it is sometimes called, the concerted refusal to deal. We have seen already that in the employment of the *per se* concept large categorizations often blur significant distinctions. So it is here. Indeed, there is more confusion about the scope and operation of the *per se* rule against group boycotts than in reference to any other aspect of the *per se* doctrine.

Let us be clear about the type of market conduct which we are discussing. In a conventional boycott, traders at one level (let us say wholesalers) seek to protect themselves from competition from non-group members who are competing or who are seeking to compete at that level. They do this by taking concerted action aimed at depriving the excluded wholesalers of some trade relationship which they would need to compete effectively at the wholesale level. Thus, the boycotting wholesalers may concertedly ask manufacturers not to sell to the excluded wholesalers and expressly or impliedly threaten that if the manufacturers do sell to the excluded wholesalers, the boycotting wholesalers will withhold patronage. Alternatively, the boycotting wholesalers may concertedly ask retailers not to buy from the excluded wholesalers, expressly or impliedly threatening that if the retailers do not comply the boycotting wholesalers will stop selling to them.

In some cases those whom the boycotting wholesalers wish to exclude from the wholesale level are themselves manufacturers or retailers seeking to integrate vertically to the wholesale level. In these instances the boycotting firms act directly against the firms they wish to exclude by threatening to stop buying from them as manufacturers, or selling to them as customers, unless they stay out of wholesaling.

In some instances, where it is necessary to their business that firms at the boycotting level deal with each other in order to carry on their trade (for example, as in the case of brokers), the boycott may be effectuated by action at the one level only; thus, a group such as brokers may seek to protect themselves from competition from a non-group member by concertedly ceasing to deal with the non-group members. But usually, the boycott spans two levels and is accomplished through an element of coercion.

The boycotting group members, in effect, say to their suppliers or to their customers, "If you don't stop dealing with non-group members, we will stop dealing with you." If continued trade with group members is more important to a supplier or customer than is trading with non-group members, this threat will be effective. And if all suppliers or customers reached in this manner are, in the aggregate, of significant commercial importance to the non-group members, the boycott will be successful and the victims of the boycott will have been foreclosed from competing with the perpetrators of the boycott.

In some situations the boycotting group does not coerce any supplier or customer not to deal with non-group members by threatening themselves to withhold patronage. Rather, they succeed without such a threat in inducing one or more suppliers or customers to stop dealing with the boycott victim or victims. This might be done in some wrongful way, such as by using fraudulant records to convince a supplier that a non-group member is a bad credit risk. Or it might be done simply by urging the customer or supplier to take the desired course, by saying for example that group members would appreciate it. It does not matter how the end is achieved, if one or more firms is deprived of suppliers or customers (or other essential trade relationships) by concerted action among other firms aimed at keeping the victim firms from competing, the arrangement, is in purpose and effect a boycott.

Because firms perpetrating a boycott usually force suppliers or customers to stop dealing with boycott victims by concertedly threatening not to deal with the suppliers or customers unless they comply, and because in a few cases (such as the broker case supposed above) the boycott is effectuated by a concerted refusal by a group of competitors at one level to deal with another would-be competitor at that same level, the rule against boycotts is often referred to as a rule against concerted refusals to deal. That phrasing is common and, in typical applications, may be more descriptive than the cryptic and emotionally charged term, boycott.

But the term boycott has its own advantage; the phrase "concerted refusal to deal" is too imprecise to be very useful as a legal category. In one way it is too narrow; it doesn't cover all conduct which has the elements of a boycott. Suppose, for example, that manufacturers A, B and C persuade Miner, the sole source of an essential raw material, not to deal with manufacturer D by falsely telling Miner that D has acted in fraudulent ways. The crucial elements of a boycott are present. Firms at one level, manufacturing, have cut out a competitor by persuading a supplier not to deal with the competitor. But we cannot accurately describe the case as a concerted refusal to deal. A, B and C neither refused to deal with Miner, nor threaten to do so.[1] In another respect the phrase "concerted refusal to deal" is too broad. Literally, it covers arrangements which are very different from boycotts and which should be analyzed quite differently. Suppose, for example, that a group of professional football teams agreed not to hire any player found to have gambled on games. This is a concerted refusal to deal. But, whatever the purposes and effects may be thought to be, it is a concerted arrangement

---

1. Also note that the concept, boycott, as we use it here does not *necessarily* involve concert of several traders at the level from which the victim is excluded. A boycott always involves concerted action of some kind; otherwise it would not be vulnerable under Section 1. But it is conceivable that only a single firm at the blockaded level may succeed in coercing or inducing suppliers or customers (or, for that matter, one important supplier or customer) from dealing with one or more would-be competitors of the perpetrator. Such an arrangement would display all essential elements of a boycott. See, as an example of a boycott allegedly perpetrated by a single firm at the blockaded level, Klor's, Inc. v. Broadway-Hale Stores, Inc., 359 U.S. 207, 79 S.Ct. 705, 3 L.Ed.2d 741 (1959).

very different from the typical boycott. It does not constitute concerted action by competing firms at one level to exclude other would-be competitors. It ought, then, not to be analyzed under a generic rule which deals with concerted efforts by traders at a given level to insulate themselves from other competition.

In sum, boycott law deals with concerted efforts by traders at one level to keep others out or inhibit their competitive efforts at that level by making it more difficult for them to find what traders at that level need, usually suppliers or customers but sometimes access to transactions with other traders at the same level. When concerted conduct entails these elements, the boycott rule may have application. The rule should not be used in reference to concerted refusals which are not intended to drive out competitors or to keep them out, but to achieve some other goal. Concerted refusals of the latter kind will be considered separately.[2]

§ 84. History and Development of the *Per Se* Rule Against Boycotts

The Supreme Court in Montague & Co. v. Lowry,[1] early held that an association through which dealer members exacted commitments from manufacturer members not to sell to non-member dealers violated the Act. The case is seldom cited today because it was decided before the main lines of the rule of reason and *per se* doctrine had taken shape. Yet it marks out the direction of later development. The arrangement by which dealers induced manufacturers to exclude other dealers was pregnant with coercion; the potential for inhibiting competition by closing competing dealers off from supplies was large and there was no basis for any pretense that competition was being aided in any way. The Court in the *Lowry* case recognized all this and by summarily adjudicating invalidity plainly foreshadowed *per se* treatment for boycotts.

The elements involved in *Lowry* reappeared in Eastern States Retail Lumber Dealers' Association v. United States,[2] a case often cited as basic in the development of the boycott rule. A group of lumber retailers engaged in concerted action through the circulation of a blacklist to induce retailers not to deal with any wholesaler who also sold at retail. The Court viewed the circulation of the names of offending wholesalers, followed by non-dealing, as tantamount to an agreement not to deal with the listed wholesalers. It said that, although "[a] retail dealer has the unquestioned right to stop dealing with a wholesaler for reasons sufficient to himself," when a retailer "goes beyond his personal right, and, conspiring and combining with others of like purpose, seeks to obstruct the free course of interstate trade and commerce and to unduly suppress competition by placing

---

2. See §§ 87–92 infra.

1. 193 U.S. 38, 24 S.Ct. 307, 48 L.Ed. 608 (1904).

2. 234 U.S. 600, 34 S.Ct. 951, 58 L.Ed. 1490 (1914).

obnoxious wholesale dealers under the coercive influence [of the concerted action] * * * such action brings him and those acting with him within the condemnation of the act * * *."³

Significantly, the Court did not explore the market shares or power of the defendant retailers; it predicated its judgment of illegality on the concerted action with a purpose to coerce wholesalers from entering the retail market. Of course, unless the participating retailers, acting concertedly, did have a degree of monopoly power, their action would be merely futile; thus one may infer that they probably did. A wholesaler faced with the risk of losing all or most of its retail buyers can hardly remain indifferent. True, the wholesaler *might* have been able to integrate to the retail level at the same scale as its wholesale operations and retail its entire supply, or it might find other retail customers who were not part of the boycott. But these steps would not be without frictions and costs, and might not be feasible without substantial loss. Given these inferences, one might say that *Eastern States* does not flatly hold that a boycott violates Section 1 without regard to competitive injury; the likelihood of such injury can be inferred. Nevertheless, the Court's silence on the matter leaves the case at least consistent with the possibility that injury to competition need not be shown in proving the violation.

Posner invites attention to the fact that in *Eastern States* a participating retail dealer might stop dealing with a wholesaler who competed at the retail level not with him but with others.⁴ That retailers would stop buying from wholesalers which offended other retailers but not themselves is suggestive of the degree to which retailers experienced a sense of interdependence. It may also suggest that retailers as buyers had sufficient alternatives that the cost to them of withholding patronage from a wholesaler which challenged other retailers was not particularly high. Or, perhaps, the point is best made by stressing the interplay of interdependence and alternative opportunities. Retailers acted as they did because the sense of interdependence which they shared was high enough to induce them to do so, given whatever costs they may have experienced in turning from a manufacturer with which they would otherwise have dealt. This sense of interdependence is, of course, another basis for implying that retailers, acting together, possessed market power.

Posner also stresses that the arrangement did not entail any coercion of retailers which did not participate.⁵ Coercion may at times be the principle for organizing the group which is to carry out and benefit concertedly from the boycott by reducing the competition its members face. But coercion will not often be expressed in that

---

3. Id. at 614, 34 S.Ct. at 955, 58 L.Ed. at 1500.

4. R. Posner, Antitrust, Cases, Economic Notes and Other Materials 530 (1974).

5. Id. at 531.

direction. What usually brings boycotters together is what brings cartel members together—namely, recognition that if they act concertedly to make their market less competitive, all may benefit. In essence, the boycott serves as an entry barrier; it keeps or forces other firms out. So doing, it may serve to support a preexisting pattern of collusively or interdependently established prices, or may set the stage for the development of cartelization or interdependence.

Another decision of interest, also often cited as supporting the *per se* approach to boycotts, is Fashion Originators' Guild of America v. FTC.[6] The Guild was an organization of firms which designed and manufactured women's dresses and the textiles used in making them, and which relied heavily upon the fashionable appeal of their original designs and prints. Basically, they agreed not to sell to retailers which stocked garments copied by other manufacturers from designs of Guild members. To carry out this purpose, they set up an elaborate system for uncovering violators and enforcing the boycott through trial and appellate procedures conducted by the Guild; in addition they developed a number of ancillary restraints, including prohibition of retail sales by members and the regulation of dates when reductions from regular prices might be offered.

The Court concluded that Guild members, which controlled 38% of all women's garment wholesaling and 60% of the wholesaling of all high priced garments, held a "commanding position" in the business; it found that the arrangement violated the Sherman Act, in that "it narrows the outlets to which garment and textile manufacturers can sell and the sources from which retailers can buy" and in that it "subjects all retailers and manufacturers who decline to comply with the Guild's program to an organized boycott." The Court also stressed that the combination was "an extra-governmental agency, which prescribes rules for the regulation * * * of interstate commerce, and provides extrajudicial tribunals for determination and punishment of violators," thus " 'trench[ing] upon the power of the national legislature * * *.' "[7]

The Court was unimpressed with the contention that concerted action was reasonable because necessary to protect members from "style piracy." It noted that the "original creations" of members were neither copyrighted nor patented, but left unresolved defendant's claim that the copying was tortious—a claim which, if plausible at the time made, is not today. Tortious or not, the Court viewed copying as "one type of manufacture and sale which competed with Guild members" and characterized the purpose of the Guild as being to end this type of competition. The Court concluded that:

> The purpose and object of this combination, its potential power, its tendency to monopoly, the coercion it could and

6. 312 U.S. 457, 61 S.Ct. 703, 85 L.Ed. 949 (1941).

7. Id. at 465, 61 S.Ct. at 707, 85 L.Ed. at 953.

did practice * * * all brought it within the policy of the prohibition declared by the Sherman and Clayton Acts.[8]

Because this purpose was itself unlawful, it was not error for the Commission to exclude evidence on the reasonableness of the methods pursued.

Fashion Originators, then, is a *per se* case only in the sense of holding that firms with a substantial market share may not engage in a boycott aimed at depriving would-be competitors of retail outlets. Though there was no express finding of power and though the existence of power is not conclusively inferable from the facts found, there is on the facts a basis for concluding that defendants more likely than not had sufficient power to make the boycott successful—at least that the risk of success was significant. Conceivably, retail stores would conclude that they could obtain sufficient dress stocks from the "style pirates" and other makers not supporting the Guild boycott and would refuse to be coerced from dealing with "style pirates"; but it seems unlikely that most retailers would react this way. The participating manufacturers represented too large a percentage of total supply, and especially of the supply of fine dresses; retailers, particularly those which featured fine dresses, would not likely anticipate sufficiently rapid entry or expansion of production by non-Guild members to meet all their needs. Of course the power of the Guild came from its horizontal organization. It was able to confront each individual retailer with a credible threat that a substantial part of the industry would drop the retailer because each retailer alone represented a small part of the total business and, thus, could be cut out without great cost to the manufacturers. But if retailers organized also and responded in a monolithic way, the potency of the manufacturers would be much diminished. The latter could credibly threaten to refuse to sell to any one retailer, but not to refuse to sell to all retailers, or even to a large percentage of them.

The next decision in the development of doctrine respecting boycotts is Klor's Inc. v. Broadway-Hale Stores, Inc.[9] Plaintiff, an appliance retailer, alleged that a competing retailer conspired with leading appliance manufacturers to boycott plaintiff. Defendants were granted summary judgment on affidavits showing that there were hundreds of other appliance retailers in the trade area. The district court and the court of appeals both concluded that there was no violation of the Act absent any effect on price, quantity or quality of the goods offered to the public. Where there was no market-wide impact on competition, there was no public injury, despite the alleged injury to plaintiff, a single competitor. The Supreme Court reversed, stating that some classes of restraints were by their nature and character "unduly restrictive, and hence forbidden." As to these "Congress

---

8. Id. at 467–68, 61 S.Ct. at 708, 85 L. Ed. at 954.

9. 359 U.S. 207, 79 S.Ct. 705, 3 L.Ed.2d 741 (1959).

had determined its own criteria of public harm and it was not for the courts to decide whether in an individual case injury had actually occurred." Citing *Eastern States, Fashion Originators* and other cases the Court went on to state that "[g]roup boycotts, or concerted refusals * * * to deal * * * have long been held to be in the forbidden category." [10]

Note that in *Klor's* not only was there but a single competitor excluded, but also that only one of the defendants was engaged in the level being blockaded. In prior boycott cases discussed, we assumed that the power to induce suppliers or customers not to deal with the boycott victims was attained by aggregating several firms at the level being protected from entry into a block large enough so that customers or suppliers could not ignore their request not to deal with firms being excluded. Here, a single retailer (on the uncontested affidavits, just one of many in the market) had induced several manufacturers to exclude a competing retailer. Here, then, there is no basis for inferring power; in that sense the ruling amounts to a full, *per se* treatment of boycotting as a means of excluding competitors. Note also that the record left open the question of how the single retailer achieved the boycott and how it induced manufacturers to cooperate—whether, for example, by threatening not to buy if the manufacturer sold to the competitor, or by falsely (or truthfully) telling them that the excluded firm was a bad credit risk, or merely by means of a polite request. In this sense, too, there is a new *per se* dimension. It has become irrelevant, apparently, how suppliers or customers are induced to cease dealing with the firms which the boycott perpetrators want to exclude. Yet, as Areeda suggests, *Klor's* does not constitute an adjudication that a concerted refusal by manufacturers to sell to a would-be buyer is *per se* unlawful in the sense that no justification for such conduct could ever be availing.[11]

Areeda, emphasizing that defendants in *Klor's* offered no justification for their action—taking the position that they could exclude a firm with impunity if market-wide competition was not adversely affected—asks whether *Klor's* leaves open the question whether justification could be stated for a conventional boycott.[12] Suppose, for example, that several TV retailers demanded that manufacturers exclude a single competitor upon the ground, convincingly established, that the unwanted dealer engaged in false advertising, "bait and switch" tactics, and other conduct injurious to the public and tending to give retailers generally a bad name. As an explicit holding, *Klor's* does not speak to this issue because no such defense was presented. But surely the broad language of the case could be con-

10. Id. at 211–12, 79 S.Ct. at 709, 3 L. Ed.2d at 744.

11. This analysis is suggested by P. Areeda, Antitrust Analysis, Problems, Text, Cases ¶ 377 (2d ed. 1974).

12. Id. at ¶ 380.

strued to imply that whenever one or more traders at one level induce traders at another to exclude a would-be competitor at the first level, Section 1 is violated. This and related questions will be discussed more fully below.[13]

The case of highest interest in the development of the *per se* doctrine for boycotts is Silver v. New York Stock Exchange,[14] which exemplifies a boycott by a group of firms at one level to foreclose that level to a non-group member achieved by themselves refusing to deal with the non-group member. The case involves broker-dealers in non-listed securities. The function which they perform for their customers is to make a market by engaging with other broker-dealers in buying or selling for themselves and for their customers. Thus, any firm with which other broker-dealers will not deal is foreclosed from competing for business; it simply cannot serve its customers, for the essence of the service it wishes to offer is to have access to the market made up by all broker-dealers so as to execute orders to purchase or sell. In *Silver,* broker-dealers, acting under the direction of the exchange, refused to authorize private line connections between their offices and that of plaintiff Silver, connections which were needed to enable plaintiff to transact business. Despite the lack of any evidence that exclusion of plaintiff would injure competition market-wide, the Court held that, unless the action by the exchange was exempt from the antitrust laws, it violated Section 1 *per se*. While it concluded that the SEC Act of 1934,[15] which charged the exchange with self-regulatory duties, did convey a limited antitrust exemption, the Court held this exemption to extend no further than necessary to make the 1934 Act work. It concluded that the exchange had exceeded this limit because it had given plaintiff no notice or hearing on the charges against him.

Concerning the scope of the *per se* rule against boycotts, it is significant that the Court saw "no occasion for us to pass upon the sufficiency of the reasons" which the exchange claimed to justify its action before concluding that, but for the possible exemption, the boycott was a *per se* violation.[16] Arguably, then, the Court here answers the question left open by *Klor's* about justification for a conventional boycott. It may be that plaintiff was being excluded because he was a cheater or a thief. The Court says, in effect, that it doesn't matter what the reason is, unless we assume that some hearing standard might also be critical to legality even where there is no statutory regulatory power. By saying there was "no reason" to look at the asserted justification for the boycott before determining whether it would constitute a *per se* violation, the Court implied that nothing, absent a partial or complete statutory exemption, could justify a conventional boycott. If *Silver* is read this way, it goes the full distance;

13. See §§ 87–90 infra.

14. 373 U.S. 341, 83 S.Ct. 1246, 10 L. Ed.2d 389 (1963).

15. 48 Stat. 881, 15 U.S.C.A. § 78(b).

16. 373 U.S. at 365, 83 S.Ct. at 1261, 10 L.Ed.2d at 404–05.

it establishes an unqualified *per se* rule for a conventional boycott in which one or more traders seek to exclude a competitor by refusing themselves to trade with the competitor or by inducing others to refuse to do so.[17]

The last decision to be noted in this historical development is United States v. General Motors Corp.,[18] where the Court reaffirmed the *per se* approach and announced market exclusion as the rationale for that approach. There, a group of retail automobile dealers took action to induce GM to stop sales to discount outlets which competed with the retailers. The Court labeled the effort a "classic conspiracy" amounting to a group boycott. It stated that it did not intend "to construe the Sherman Act to prohibit conspiracies to fix prices at which competitors may sell, but to allow conspiracies or combinations to put competitors out of business entirely." [19]

§ 85. The Justification for a *Per Se* Approach

Seeing the flow of the cases discussed in Section 84, we cannot doubt that there is in some sense a *per se* rule with reference to boycotts. We shall hereafter explore the scope and limits of that rule, but first we must question whether a *per se* approach is at all justified. We said elsewhere that a *per se* approach is justified when it applies to conduct which in most instances will be harmful to competition, which in few if any will help competition (and then probably not greatly) and which is of such a nature that it will be difficult in individual cases to identify benefits with certainty or, if they are identified, to measure their magnitude relative to harm.

Let us first picture an explicit boycott in classical form. Firms A, B and C, which manufacture widgets, want to barricade entry. They tell firm D, the only operating mine in their region for an ore essential to widget manufacture, that if D sells to any firm other than A, B and C they will stop dealing with it. Firm E which makes widgets elsewhere, is considering building a plant in the region and

---

17. There are, however, a few cases which decline to treat even explicit boycotts as *per se* unlawful where the boycott is ancillary to a partial integration. E. g., McCann v. N. Y. Stock Exch., 107 F.2d 908 (2d Cir. 1939). See § 89 infra.

18. 384 U.S. 127, 86 S.Ct. 1321, 16 L.Ed.2d 415 (1966).

19. Id. at 148, 86 S.Ct. at 1332, 16 L.Ed.2d at 428. This case, together with *Klor's* and *Silver* also make manifest that competition is not valued solely to advance consumer interests. In none of these cases is there a basis for supposing that market-wide competition is affected in ways injurious to consumers. In *Klor's*, *Silver* and *GM* competition is being protected against concerted restraint in order to protect the access of individual traders to the market-place, free of coercion or restraint. Compare United States v. A. Schrader's Sons, Inc., 252 U.S. 85, 99–100, 40 S.Ct. 251, 253, 64 L.Ed. 471, 475 (1920); Northern Pacific Ry. Co. v. United States, 356 U.S. 1, 4–5, 78 S.Ct. 514, 517–518, 2 L.Ed.2d 545, 549 (1958); Brown Shoe Co. v. United States, 370 U.S. 294, 344, 82 S.Ct. 1502, 1534, 8 L.Ed.2d 510, 547 (1962); Simpson v. Union Oil Co., 377 U.S. 13, 21, 84 S.Ct. 1051, 1057, 12 L.Ed.2d 98, 104 (1964).

asks D whether it will supply ore. D, concerned by the threat, refuses. There seems to be no question that the boycott injures competition at least in some degree. Firms A, B and C appear to possess market power as sellers which entry by E would erode. They also have sufficient power as buyers to successfully dictate to D his course of market conduct and they use that power to exclude E's entry. On the face of the matter, nothing is to be said in favor of the boycott and it ought clearly to be unlawful.

Suppose, however, we change the facts to reduce the implications of power. Let us say that in the region there are many other widget makers besides A, B and C, that there also are numerous other buyers of D's ore for other uses, and that D could as easily find alternative buyers if A, B, and C stopped buying D's ore. Now assume that A, B and C ask D not to sell to E and that D consents simply because the mine is already working at capacity so that D could supply no others without diverting ore from a current buyer. D's response to the request is a measure not of D's concern, but of its indifference. Let us suppose, further, that E, on hearing that D will not sell, finds several sellers elsewhere which will absorb the transportation cost to meet D's price in the region, or finds others ready to start mining as yet untapped sources in the region to meet E's needs, and that E goes ahead with the plant. On these facts, the boycott does no harm to competition; no entry barrier is raised. But there still remains nothing to be said in favor of the boycott. The purpose of those who perpetrate it is to injure competition and we need hardly accept the social cost (and risk of error) entailed in allowing them to prove that they have failed in their attempt. It is socially costless to forbid the boycott even though the prohibition is overbroad in the sense of covering some boycotts which fail to do the harm they were intended to do. Moreover, we have in our hypothetical assumed away a good many factual difficulties. It will not only be costly to examine the issues of power in actual markets, doing so will also be fraught with risks of error. Thus, if we permit the defense that competition is not injured, we not only measurably increase the cost of enforcing the ban on boycotts which do injure competition, but may permit some boycotts which do in fact accomplish harm to slip through the net.

So far, the classic boycott appears to meet the tests which support *per se* treatment, but there is another element to be introduced. Suppose that instead of three widget makers in the region there are twenty, of which E is one, and that E had been actively trying to induce widget makers to form a cartel which will fix prices. A, B and C, on hearing of this fact, decide to drive E out in order to protect competitive conditions in the industry. Or suppose that E, to cut costs, deliberately makes his widgets with brittle cores which cannot be easily detected by consumers, but which are liable to shatter when used, and that A, B and C, regarding this method of competition as unfair to themselves as well as to consumers, decide to induce D not to sell to E until E starts using flexible cores like other widget makers.

The first of these hypotheticals may seem farfetched, but the second is less so. They serve, in any event, to make the point. To outlaw a boycott without analysis of effect may not be socially costless if the perpetrators of the boycott assert a justification for their conduct which, if proved, would establish a benefit to competition. In our first and concededly unlikely hypothetical, permitting the boycott might do exceedingly little harm to competition, since the loss of one out of twenty sellers may not be competitively significant; yet not permitting it may leave the industry in danger of cartelization. In our second hypothetical, harm to competition may be small and a substantial benefit done by standardizing product in a way that not only protects consumers from fraud but also enables them to make more accurate judgments about price and other relative merits of competing offerings.

If a *per se* approach is warranted, then, it is not because a boycott can never aid competition, nor because the cases where social advantages are present are few and difficult to identify, for though they may be few, they will also tend to be manifest. The justification for a *per se* approach must stand on the footing that a boycott always tends to do some competitive harm and, even when it also provides an offsetting benefit, that benefit could also be achieved without the boycott, in which case the net social advantage would be higher. As an instance, the efforts of firm E to cartelize which are supposed in the hypothetical above could be brought to a stop without driving E out of the market; public or private action could be threatened or taken against it under the antitrust laws. The problem of the widget with the brittle core could be dealt with in one of several less restrictive ways, such as the development of industry standards, industry inspections with seals of approval, and publicity.

To picture industry standards aimed at giving the public a consensus view about widgets is to move into an area where it might be asserted that conduct not amounting to an explicit boycott has the purpose and effect of a boycott, and should thus be classified as a boycott. Lack of a seal of approval for E's widget might, for example, induce customers not to deal with E and thus drive the firm out or force it to change its style of competition. If the courts were to classify every arrangement which could cause suppliers or customers not to deal with a firm as a boycott (and thus *per se* unlawful) the dilemma of an overbroad *per se* rule would not have been avoided; many of the "less restrictive alternatives" to the explicit boycott, intended to allow for a balancing where significant benefits to competition are apparent, would themselves be called boycotts and thus be illegal. As will be displayed more fully in later sections, it is precisely in the process of characterization that flexibility is introduced in boycott analysis, despite the *per se* doctrine. That flexibility adheres in purpose and effect analysis which is used to decide whether particular actions tending to exclude some competitors should be labeled boycotts. For the moment let us simply leave it at this: a *per se* rule banning all *explicit* boycotts seems warranted, since these boycotts always threaten competitive injury, seldom promise any benefit to competition and never promise a benefit which cannot be achieved in less restrictive ways; [1] other concerted conduct which tends to have the effect of a boycott, in that it tends to induce suppliers or customers not to deal with a competitor of the group who engages in the conduct, should, by contrast, be characterized as a boycott (and held *per se* unlawful) only when that conduct has no alternative purpose or effect which may benefit competition, or where the competitive harm consequent upon the arrangement clearly outweighs any beneficial effects.

§ 86. Purpose and Effect as Guides to Characterization

Fashion Originators is the model boycott case, as it raises no serious questions of characterization. As the Court put it, Guild members "admit that to destroy * * * competition [of copiers] they have in combination purposely boycotted and declined to sell their products to retailers * * * [who sell] garments copied * * * from designs put out by Guild members." [1] But concerted conduct putting pressure on customers or suppliers to cut out one or more competitors may be less explicit and less obvious. Then the court will analyze purpose and effect as an aid to characterization.

Eastern States [2] is suggestive of the approach. There, the association of retail lumber dealers urged members to report to the association the names of any wholesalers known to sell at retail; the association investigated such reports and if it concluded that a wholesaler made retail sales as a general practice, it placed the wholesaler's name on a list which was circulated regularly among retail members. To get off the list, a wholesaler had to give assurance to the association that he was no longer selling at retail. There was no express agreement by members not to deal with listed wholesalers. On proof of these things, a finder of facts might plausibly infer that there was an agreement among members not to buy from competing wholesalers, that the concert of action in reporting, investigating and circulat-

---

1. An "explicit boycott", as the term is used here, means one in which the perpetrators agree not to deal with the victims or request (or demand that) others not deal with the victims. To be contrasted with explicit boycotts are situations where firms at one level take joint action (such as developing product standards and/or seals of approval) which may have the foreseeable but indirect effect of inducing others not to deal with one or more of the competitors of the firms which took the joint action.

1. 312 U.S. 457, 461, 61 S.Ct. 703, 705, 85 L.Ed. 949, 951 (1941).

2. 234 U.S. 600, 34 S.Ct. 951, 58 L.Ed. 1490 (1914).

ing names is rationally explicable only as a forerunner to concerted action by withholding custom. There is little reason to suppose that any member has an interest in individually cutting off any wholesaler, at least unless the individual member is a large enough factor to have by itself a significant impact on the wholesaler's business. *Eastern States* can be read as holding no more than this, as merely concluding that the evidence, and inferences from it, established the existence of an explicit boycott.

But the case need not be read so narrowly. Fairly construed, the teaching of the case goes beyond inviting an inference of an agreement to concertedly refuse to deal. The opinion by Mr. Justice Day assumes that "there is no agreement among the retailers to refrain from dealing with listed wholesalers," thus recognizing that the only concert of action is to gather and circulate the information and that members are left free to decide individually whether or not to deal with any listed wholesaler. But the Court saw in the program a purpose and an effect to induce members to refrain from dealing with offending wholesalers, a purpose and effect substantially identical to those of a classic, express boycott. The Court said that one would be "blind indeed who does not see the purpose in the * * * circulation of this report to put the ban upon wholesaler dealers whose names appear in the list of unfair dealers * * *."³ It also emphasized that "[t]his record abounds in instances where * * * the hoped-for effect * * * [was] realized,"⁴ and an offending wholesaler's trade directly and appreciably reduced. In any event, since withdrawal of trade from listed wholesalers was the effect to be expected from the program, members were fairly charged with conspiring to reach that end. "[T]he conspiracy to accomplish that which was the natural consequence of such action may be readily inferred."⁵ Roundly stated, *Eastern States* establishes that the boycott rule applies not only to an agreement by a group of traders at level B not to deal with suppliers at A or customers at C who either compete themselves at level B or trade with non-group members competing there, but also to any concerted action which has the same purpose or will have the same effect as an explicit boycott. Whether the arrangement is by explicit agreement not to deal in order to coerce a firm at a different level to cut out a competitor, or whether the firm or firms at the other level are coerced or persuaded in some other manner, when the purpose and effect of concerted action is to stamp out competition faced by the perpetrator of the action by influencing one or more firms at a prior or subsequent level to withhold supplies or patronage, the boycott rule is invoked.

3. Id. at 608–09, 34 S.Ct. at 953, 58 L. Ed. at 1498.

4. Id. at 612, 34 S.Ct. at 954, 58 L.Ed. at 1499.

5. Id.

Radiant Burners Inc. v. Peoples Gas Light & Coke Co.,[6] is another interesting example of purpose and effect analysis; the device there used was more complex than circulation of information and the similarity in purpose and effect to a classic boycott was less obvious. The allegations were in substance that the American Gas Association operated testing laboratories for gas appliances and gave its "seal of approval" to appliances found to be safe; that gas utilities relied on the association's ratings and would not supply gas for appliances not approved, which, as a result, were effectively excluded from the market; that plaintiff's gas burner was when judged by objective standards safer than burners approved by the association, and that defendant manufacturers, competitors of plaintiff, had influenced the association and caused it to withhold approval of plaintiff's gas burner by using tests not based on objective standards, thereby making it impossible for plaintiff to compete with them. The district court had granted defendant's motion to dismiss and the court of appeals had affirmed. Hence, the question for the Supreme Court was whether the complaint, assuming its truth, stated a cause of action. The Supreme Court reversed, citing *Klor's*,[7] and stating that, as alleged, the conspiracy "falls within" the *per se* rule. When we draw the analogy to the classic boycott, the "supplier" is, of course, the rating agency; it supplies not raw materials, but an even more essential ingredient, a "seal of approval" without which the product cannot be sold. And the perpetrators of the "boycott" are competing manufacturers which seek to protect themselves from competition by concertedly inducing the agency not to supply to plaintiff the approval which is essential to successful entry.

But there was not here an explicit boycott and although the conduct challenged tended toward boycott effects, it also would have other effects which might be beneficial. The use of a seal of approval might protect customers from unsafe merchandise and might enable them to make more rational judgments in evaluating competing offerings with respect to price and other trade terms. For these reasons the allegation that defendants intended to drive out the competitor by the use of "non-objective" standards seems crucial.[8] Protecting the prosperity of the industry generally by protecting the public from harm through the development of reasonable, objective safety standards might be the goal and the major effect of a seal of approval program. Thus, proof of the allegations that the standards used were

---

6. 364 U.S. 656, 81 S.Ct. 365, 5 L.Ed.2d 358 (1961). See also Structural Laminates, Inc. v. Douglas Fir Plywood Ass'n, 261 F.Supp. 154 (D.Or.1966), aff'd 399 F.2d 155 (9th Cir. 1968), cert. denied 393 U.S. 1024, 89 S.Ct. 636, 21 L.Ed.2d 569 (1969); United States v. Johns-Manville Corp., 259 F.Supp. 440 (E.D.Pa.1966).

7. 359 U.S. 207, 79 S.Ct. 705, 3 L.Ed.2d 741 (1959). See § 84 supra.

8. Compare United States v. Johns-Manville Corp., 259 F.Supp. 440 (E.D. Pa.1966), where industry standards were found "scientifically justified."

not objective and had been adopted under the aegis of competing manufacturers in order to protect themselves from additional competition would, at trial, be an essential part of plaintiff's case.

It bears emphasis that concerted conduct (other than an explicit boycott) having the effect of cutting off the trade of some firm or group does not fall under the boycott rule unless in purpose and effect it is conformable to a classic, naked boycott. By contrast, an explicit boycott may be *per se* unlawful even if it has purposes and effects other than driving out the competitor;[9] a justification for this distinction is that any other purposes could be achieved by less restrictive means. But where means less restrictive than an explicit boycott *are* being used, and where purposes and effects additional to inhibiting a competitor are plausibly asserted to exist, courts cannot avoid the obligation to balance these asserted benefits against the harm. For example, if reasonable, objective safety standards are adopted by an industry association acting as a rating agency, that action ought not to be characterized as a boycott and *per se* unlawful, any more than would a reasonable agreement about product standardization. To be sure, either product standardization or safety testing might have adverse effects on competition. Saying that neither is a boycott is not to say that either is necessarily lawful. The point is that the particular beneficial and harmful effects of either must be analyzed; they ought not to be swept under the boycott *per se* rule.

Similarly, it does not follow from *Eastern States* that the boycott rule is violated any time traders circulate information (or concertedly take other action) which causes suppliers or customers to withhold business from firms competing with those traders. Wholesalers, for example, may concertedly gather and circulate credit information about customers or information about the quality of product or promptness of deliveries of suppliers. There may or may not be bases for challenging programs of these kinds under the rule of reason, but they should not be labeled as boycotts. The core of the boycott concept is a concerted effort to inhibit competitors of the firm or firms instigating the action. Retailers were cut out by manufacturers in *Fashion Originators* not because they were poor pay firms but because they purchased from copiers competing at the manufacturer level whom Guild members wanted to drive out. Wholesalers were cut out by retailers in *Eastern States* not because they supplied poor

---

9. See § 85 supra. The bald proposition that all explicit boycotts are *per se* unlawful is undercut by some of the cases. E. g., McCann v. New York Stock Exch., 107 F.2d 908 (2d Cir. 1939). Most of the cases which seem inconsistent involve a significant degree of integration which may warrant sanctioning some legitimate organizational goals, even through an explicit boycott. Whether cases like *McCann* survive the commitment made in Silver v. N. Y. Stock Exchange, 373 U.S. 341, 83 S.Ct. 1246, 10 L.Ed.2d 389 (1963) to a flat out *per se* rule for explicit boycotts is a matter of some doubt. See § 89 infra.

quality goods, but because they entered into retailing and offered competition to association members.

Cement Manufacturers Protective Association v. United States,[10] typifies the kind of case where a party may try to invoke the boycott rule, but where purpose and effect analysis shows that it ought not to apply. There, the manufacturers' association circulated credit information about contractors. Though this led to some contractors not being supplied, the arrangement could not be treated as a boycott in purpose and effect because it did not constitute an effort by the manufacturers to barricade themselves from competition at their own level. The association also circulated information about so-called specific job contracts between contractors and manufacturers. Under prevailing trade practice, a contractor could obtain from manufacturers a free option fixing the price of concrete for a specific job at the time for bidding on that job. Some of the contractors would get several of these options from several manufacturers and then, if cement prices rose, would pretend to exercise the option for the job with each of the manufacturers, thereby obtaining large quantities of extra cement below the current market price. Circulation of information by the association protected manufacturers from having to supply under an option except in accordance with the terms of the option—namely, if the cement was to be used on the specific job as to which the option had been given. Now, the circulation both of credit information and of information about options obviously had market effects; and in analyzing the trade association's activities under the rule of reason, one might conclude that there was significant harm to competition. But neither information program entailed efforts to stifle competition at the manufacturer level by depriving firms seeking to compete at that level of necessary resources. The *per se* rule concerning boycotts therefore did not apply.

§ 87. Explicit Boycotts Used to Police Industry Self-Regulation

There is a common element in *Radiant Burners*[1] and *Fashion Originators*[2] which is also encountered in many other cases where the boycott rule is invoked: the concerted program challenged as a boycott is defended as a reasonable program of industry self-regulation. The patterns which cases of this kind display serve as an effective test for the utility of boycott doctrine in striking down arrangements which are likely to harm competition while sparing those which do not. The initial question is whether enforcement of a program of industry regulation by means of a classic, conventional boycott will always violate the Act regardless of the reasonableness of the ends

---

10. 268 U.S. 588, 45 S.Ct. 586, 69 L.Ed. 1104 (1925).

2. 312 U.S. 457, 61 S.Ct. 703, 85 L.Ed. 949 (1941).

1. 364 U.S. 656, 81 S.Ct. 365, 5 L.Ed.2d 358 (1961).

which the program seeks to achieve. Suppose, for example, that an association of candy manufacturers adopted reasonable purity standards which discouraged the use of certain preservatives which many responsible doctors thought harmful to health. Suppose, further, that association members, fearful that publicity about health hazards would hurt the industry generally, tried to stamp out the use of these preservatives by refusing to sell to candy wholesalers which marketed candy made by non-complying manufacturers. In Section 86 we showed that a *per se* rule against such an explicit boycott is warranted on policy grounds. Now let us examine the cases.

Though there are distinctions which could be drawn, a fair reading of *Fashion Originators* suggests that even for so laudable an end as that here supposed, the manufacturers could not lawfully police their industry by using an explicit boycott as a sanction. The Court in that case assumed style piracy to be tortious, yet it held an explicit boycott unlawful. On the other hand, the opinion neither holds nor implies that the manufacturers were powerless to use self-help to cope with piracy. The case therefore leaves open the question whether reasonable concerted action aimed at preventing piracy—for example, a program of publicizing the names of pirate firms or joint advertising extolling the virtues of original designs—would have been unlawful. If such conduct would be lawful, the fatal defect in the program actually used must have been its form, that of an explicit boycott.

Fashion Originators is perhaps not conclusive even on the point that industry self-regulation through an explicit boycott is always unlawful. A court might distinguish that case from one where industry interests seem clearly to coincide with interests in consumer protection, such as the hypothetical boycott against food manufacturers using preservatives which threaten health. Even the frequent language labeling boycotts as *per se* violations would not unduly embarrass such a conclusion, since a court could plausibly conclude that if a primary purpose and effect of concerted action is protection of public safety, the action ought not be characterized as a boycott. But *Fashion Originators* does not invite or encourage such a distinction and to make it would be to lean into the gusty winds of Mr. Justice Black's opinion.[3]

Moreover, the Court's more recent decision in Silver v. New York Stock Exchange,[4] implies rejection of the boycott as a permissible device for industry policing regardless of whether the substantive goals being sought by the industry are reasonable, except in situations where congressional enactment authorizes such self-regulation.

---

3. See generally Turner, Consumer Protection by Private Joint Action, 1967 CCH Antitrust Symposium 36; Turner, Cooperation Among Competitors, 61 Nw.L.Rev. 865 (1967).

4. 373 U.S. 341, 83 S.Ct. 1246, 10 L.Ed. 2d 389 (1963).

In *Silver,* broker-dealers who were members of the exchange, upon directions from the exchange, denied to Silver private wire connections which were needed by Silver to facilitate his trading in non-listed securities. The defense to the charge of boycott was that the exchange acted under its statutory duty to regulate the trading activities of members. The Court held that the Securities Exchange Act of 1934 provides for self-regulation, but exempts from otherwise applicable antitrust norms "only if necessary to make the Securities Exchange Act work, and even then only to the minimum extent necessary." [5]

We shall discuss other aspects of *Silver* hereafter.[6] The point here is that, having discerned only a limited exemption, the Court had first to consider whether the boycott would be legal under the Sherman Act; only if it would otherwise be unlawful would a question be presented whether antitrust exemption was necessary to the working of the statutory scheme of self-regulation. In dealing with the issue whether the boycott would be an antitrust violation, absent any exemption, the Court did two things which are pertinent here. First, it labeled as not relevant the reasons disclosed by the exchange for the action it took;[7] second, it stated that the boycott, if not exempt under the SEC Act, would be a "a *per se* violation of Section 1." [8] The Court in adjudicating the *per se* violation expressly stated that it need not consider the self-regulatory reasons for the SEC Act which were summarized and discussed by the district court [9] and by the court of appeals.[10] Presumably, absent a congressional enactment giving antitrust exemption, no self-regulatory reason, however much it might be in the public interest, would warrant a specific boycott.[11]

§ 88. Industry Self-Regulation by Conduct Tending To have the Effects of a Boycott

In instances where concerted action other than an explicit boycott is taken with a view to policing industry self-regulation, and where the action taken makes it hard for affected firms to compete by tending to induce suppliers or customers not to deal with them, validity cannot be summarily determined.[1] A substantial number of

5. Id. at 357, 83 S.Ct. at 1257, 10 L.Ed. 2d at 400.

6. See § 88 infra.

7. 373 U.S. at 365–66, 83 S.Ct. at 1261–62, 10 L.Ed.2d at 404–05. Compare Denver Rockets v. All-Pro Management, Inc., 325 F.Supp. 1049 (C.D.Cal. 1971) (rule forbidding recruiting of high school students invalid).

8. Id. at 347, 83 S.Ct. at 1252, 10 L.Ed. 2d at 394.

9. 196 F.Supp. 209, 216–17, 225–27 (S. D.N.Y.1961).

10. 302 F.2d 714, 716 (2d Cir. 1962).

11. See also FTC Advisory Opinion Digest No. 128, CCH Trade Reg.Rep. ¶ 17,950 (May 23, 1967) (explicit boycott of door to door salesmen found to have used deceptive practices unlawful, but publication of adverse information valid).

1. See Florists' Nat'l Tel. Delivery Network v. Florists' Tel. Delivery Ass'n,

factors must be considered as a preliminary to determining whether to characterize the arrangement as a boycott. Indeed, the scope of the analysis is so spacious that it matters little whether the inquiry is described as one aimed at determining whether a *per se* rule governs or as one in which the rule of reason is being applied, so that a judicial conclusion that "this is a boycott and the *per se* rule governs" is very much the same as saying, "considering everything, this joint action is unreasonable."[2]

First it is necessary to consider whether the asserted self-policing program could be just a cover adopted in an effort to exclude competitors by inducing suppliers or customers not to trade with them while hiding from the impact of the boycott rule. Picture, for example, a city-wide association of automobile dealers, many members of which would like to exclude a particular used car dealer who aggressively cuts prices. Suppose the association, in order covertly to drive that dealer out, developed and advertised a "seal of approval," assertedly granted to "dealers of integrity who stand behind their product," and then granted the seal to all dealers but the price cutter. Upon proof of the anticompetitive animus, the excluded dealer would surely be entitled to invoke the *per se* rule. Given the sham, the seal of approval program must be treated like a naked boycott. It has the effects of a boycott, the purpose which underlies it is to attain only those effects and it appears to have no effects other than these anticompetitive ones. But note that an analysis of the evidence preceded characterization; only after evaluating relevant evidence and concluding that a sham program is involved do we say, "This program is *per se* unlawful." [3]

Next is the question whether, in the language of *Radiant Burner*,[4] the standards used to police the industry are "objective." Consider this situation. Manufacturers of fire alarm equipment, through an association, grant a "seal of approval" to alarm boxes

---

1967 CCH Trade Cas. ¶ 71,965 (7th Cir.); Comment, Trade Association Exclusionary Practices: An Affirmative Role for the Rule of Reason, 66 Colum.L.Rev. 1486 (1966).

2. Compare Union Circulation Co. v. FTC, 241 F.2d 652 (2d Cir. 1957) (Court declines *per se* characterization but upholds conclusion of illegality).

3. See Goldfarb v. Virginia State Bar, 421 U.S. 773, 95 S.Ct. 2004, 44 L.Ed.2d 572 (1975) (ethical sanction for lawyers selling their services for less than association's suggested minimum fees); United States v. National Funeral Directors Ass'n, 1968 CCH Trade Cases ¶ 72,529 (E.D.Wis.1968)

(expulsion of members who do price advertising); cf. United States v. Gasoline Retailers Ass'n., 285 F.2d 688 (7th Cir. 1961); United States v. Utah Pharmaceutical Ass'n., 201 F.Supp. 29 (D.Utah), aff'd per curiam 371 U.S. 24, 83 S.Ct. 119, 9 L.Ed.2d 96 (1962). Compare FTC Advisory Opinion Digest No. 64 (June 22, 1966), 1966 CCH Trade Reg. Rep. ¶ 17,580 with FTC Advisory Opinion Digest No. 119 (April 6, 1967) ("arbitrary or discriminatory expulsion" from membership because of alleged failure to abide by code violates act).

4. 364 U.S. 656, 81 S.Ct. 365, 5 L.Ed.2d 358 (1961). See also the cases cited in § 86, note 6 supra.

which the association's "standards committee" find to be "reliable." The industry is not very progressive and relies primarily on mechanical rather than chemical or electronic devices. Engineer representatives of member firms, who sit on the standards committee, completed their formal educations no less than twenty-five years ago and learned the methodologies of the industry no less than twenty years ago. The committee has never formally adopted any set of reliability standards, but has reviewed new products in a thorough way and rejected only those which have been found to have "bugs" of discernible kinds. All new products submitted have been mechanical. Then a maverick firm develops a novel alarm system based on electronic principles. The standards committee fails to understand the new system adequately, decides it is odd and "hardly to be trusted" and declines a seal of approval.

On these facts, the boycott rule should apply. The standards used are vague, judgmental and imprecise; they surely do not meet the objectivity which *Radiant Burner* indicates to be necessary. A self-policing program with a seal of approval intended to influence customers has an inevitable tendency to function like a boycott—to persuade customers to avoid non-approved industry members, thus making it harder for them to compete. Once it is concluded that the program is not an objective one, no further evaluation of benefits to competition which are supposed to flow from the program is appropriate. The potential for harm is so great and the potential for offsetting benefits so small when the program is not objectively run, that the courts will decline to weigh and measure the harms and benefits and will treat the program precisely as they do an explicit boycott.

Not only must standards be objective, they must also be reasonable. Suppose, for example, that the committee set forth standards of mechanical reliability with admirable clarity and precision and that these had been adopted in good faith. These standards, by excluding alarm systems based on electronic or chemical principles might nevertheless be demonstrably inadequate to select between reliable and unreliable systems. Assume that a new entrant were to develop an alarm system that, properly understood and evaluated by engineers competent in both the old and the new technology, would be found to be as reliable as the mechanical systems presently in existence, but because the industry committee's standards are geared to the old technology, it did not pass them and does not earn a seal. On these facts the industry standards are unreasonable. On proof of unreasonableness, a court should label the program a boycott and declare it *per se* unlawful; any other course would create too great a risk of competitive injury.

Some questions less amenable to systematic resolution must also be answered before a court can determine whether to call a self-policing arrangement a boycott. These questions concern the substance of the industry program, the goals and values it is tuned to advance. A contrast between the program in *Fashion Originators*[5] and a product safety program such as that in *Radiant Burners* will be illustrative. One dimension to be measured is the extent to which customer or supplier interests coalesce with the industry interests which the program advances. Style piracy, the "evil" identified by the Guild, was of interest primarily to industry members. Consumer interests would be adversely affected, perhaps, if copied designs were being passed off as originals, but there is no suggestion that they were and the industry program, which hit at all copiers, was not selective in this respect. If any consumer interests were directly advanced by the program, it was those of customers who paid for unique originals only to find their gowns to be the subject of mass produced copies. And even this consumer interest would be discounted by the market, so long as copying continued. Buyers would know of the possibility of copying and would buy originals only if, given the price, they were content to risk the flattery of cheaper imitations. Another factor is the discreteness and specificity of the industry objective, the extent to which it is amenable to clear, objective explication. It is conceivable to develop reasonably objective standards about product reliability, perhaps, but the line between an "original" style and one which is already in the public domain may be quite intuitive and difficult to validate objectively. Moreover, even conceding originality to a particular style, the line between "copying" it and "being influenced" by it will be a dim and difficult one to mark out objectively. This analysis suggests that the real underlying interest served by a program aimed at style piracy is not that of the consumer, but that of the producer in not having demand reduced by consumer responses to the risk of copying.[6]

Another relevant factor is whether the industry's claim that the goal is socially useful is either blatantly true, as is product safety, or is socially validated in some way, for example by legislation. Style piracy, it was argued in *Fashion Originators*, is tortious; but the Court avoided passing on this and contented itself to note that the designs were not protected by copyright or patent, an observation which, today, seems enough to negative any claim of common law protection.[7] The point to be pressed here is that if the program were aimed at stopping dealers from handling products which did violate

---

5. 312 U.S. 457, 61 S.Ct. 703, 85 L.Ed. 949 (1941).

6. American Medical Ass'n v. United States, 317 U.S. 519, 63 S.Ct. 326, 87 L.Ed. 434 (1943), also exemplifies the situation where a so-called self-policing system really deals with little more than a matter of competitive style between producers. The association, an organization of doctors, tried to induce hospitals not to deal with doctors who engaged in programs of prepaid medicine. The effort was characterized as a boycott.

7. Sears, Roebuck & Co. v. Stiffel Co., 376 U.S. 225, 84 S.Ct. 784, 11 L.Ed.2d

a copyright or a patent, its claim to advance socially appropriate interests would have been greater. One would then at least concede that the industry interest sought to be advanced was one which had a community sanction.

Finally, we come to the matter of enforcement procedures, a matter which the Court in *Fashion Originators* and the Court in *Silver*[8] examined from quite different vantage points. The Court in the style piracy case expressed strong reluctance to cede judicial power to the rather elaborate tribunals of the industry's "private government" which adjudicated the issues raised by a demand to apply the boycott sanction. The *Silver* Court, by contrast, commiserated with the boycott victim who was pounced upon without opportunity to refute the charges against him. Lest we make too much of the apparent double-bind, let us remark straight off that in *Silver* the Court discerned a legislative mandate in the Securities Exchange Act of 1934 obliging it, in effect, to concede to the exchange some degree of power to act as a private government. The message of *Fashion Originators* is that any elaborate private machinery for the trial of those charged with violating privately established norms and holding power to impose severe economic sanctions is to be viewed distrustfully. The message of *Silver* is that where Congress has authorized the development of private standards and the imposition of private sanctions (and inferentially, perhaps, in any situation where it is concluded that private standards and private sanctions are warranted) those sanctions may be imposed only after a fair proceeding. *Silver* surely does not imply that in situations where Congress has not authorized self-regulation, all that is needed to validate a program having boycott effects is procedural fairness. Rather it implies that where a self-regulatory program is otherwise valid, either because sanctioned by Congress or because considering all other factors it is justifiable, it must then meet also the final hurdle of procedural fairness.

What constitutes procedural fairness under the *Silver* requirement? The case itself suggests the answer to that question in footnotes 33 and 34, which gather together judicial and scholarly authority and summarize the Court's policy regarding the scope of the requirement of notice and hearing which is applicable to bodies engaged in private governance, such as unions, clubs and other private associations. The requirement is constitutional in its generality; its precise content will vary with the context. One to be disciplined must be given such notice and opportunity to be heard as will appear fair to a critical lawyer, considering the nature of the issues, the evidence, the sanctions, and the extent to which the interests of the group imposing the sanction appear to conflict with those of the victim. Com-

---

661 (1964); Compco Corp. v. Day-Bright Lighting, Inc., 376 U.S. 234, 84 S.Ct. 779, 11 L.Ed.2d 669 (1964).

8. 373 U.S. 341, 83 S.Ct. 1246, 10 L.Ed. 2d 389 (1963).

pare, for example, the case of a private practitioner being expelled from a hospital by a committee of other private practitioners on a charge that, as a participant in a prepaid group practice, he does not meet his personal responsibilities to his patients, with that of a star basketball player being expelled from league play by a committee of league representatives for gambling on games. No doubt the interests of the affected individuals are equally intense, but several other elements differ. The doctors have a competitive interest which clearly conflicts with that of their colleague; flat out, he is a competitor. Members of the league committee, whether made up of representatives of owners or players, will have no such conflict with the interests of the player charged with gambling; the league is more clearly a joint venture and the presence of a star on the roster of any team tends to benefit all who have an interest in the financial solvency and success of teams in the league.[9]

The factor analysis suggested above may invite the comment that the boycott rule is a "soft" *per se* rule. Explicit price fixing and market division are *per se* unlawful and no justification can be made. When the courts deal with arrangements which are not explicit, unless there is an integration the only question is whether the dominant purpose or effect is that of price fixing or market division; if so, the *per se* rule applies. In the case of boycotts, though we conclude (albeit on the basis of a somewhat inconclusive case law) that no explicit agreement to boycott is valid, once we get away from the explicit arrangement we let down the bars and consider myriad factors. Action which has the purpose and effect of driving a competitor out of the market can be validated if it is done to sanction an industry self-regulatory scheme which meets the subsidiary standards elaborated upon above.

Thus, we have uncovered a discernible lack of consistency in the application of *per se* doctrine. So be it; it is not the last we shall observe. The value of the *per se* approach is not lost because numerous factors must be evaluated before an arrangement having boycott tendencies but not entailing an explicit boycott can be characterized. A claim that a program advances the interests of industry self-regulation is, in a sense, a claim that the rule of reason should apply because the program, though perhaps having some negative effects, also tends in discernible ways to benefit competition. The factor analysis made in the process of characterization puts the claim that there is enough of value in the program to warrant a careful balancing of harms and benefits to a preliminary test. If the self-regulatory program merely deals with matters of competitive style, if it is not suffi-

---

9. Compare American Medical Ass'n v. United States, 130 F.2d 233 (D.C.Cir. 1942), aff'd 317 U.S. 519, 63 S.Ct. 326, 87 L.Ed. 434 (1943), with Molinas v. National Basketball Ass'n, 190 F. Supp. 241 (S.D.N.Y.1961); Deesen v. Professional Golfers Ass'n of America, 358 F.2d 165 (9th Cir.), cert. denied 385 U.S. 846, 87 S.Ct. 72, 17 L.Ed.2d 76 (1966).

ciently objective, or if it fails to assure the fair application of its norms, this diminishes any prospect that upon full analysis it will be shown to yield greater benefits than harm. Full analysis of harms and benefits under the rule of reason is only warranted if upon the factor analysis the claim of significant benefits appears to be a credible one. If a self-regulatory program does pass this test, it could of course still be held invalid after full analysis under the rule of reason.[10] However, this eventuality will prove so unlikely in practice that we can fairly describe any industry self-regulatory scheme which is not characterized as a boycott as being presumptively lawful.

§ 89. The Application of Boycott Doctrine to Cases of Partial Integration

Just as a joint venture or other arrangement yielding integration efficiencies may include an ancillary agreement fixing prices or dividing markets, or may tend toward those results without such an agreement, arrangements which integrate activities of two or more firms may entail or tend toward the effects of a boycott. Authority and policy both suggest that joint venturers may not explicitly agree to a boycott aimed at excluding a competitor any more than they could explicitly agree to fix prices or divide markets. The case most supportive of this conclusion is Associated Press v. United States.[1] The venture there, which included the publishers of more than 1200 newspapers throughout the country, gathered news and distributed it to subscribers to its service. There was a boycott explicitly spelled out in its bylaws. Member newspapers acting concertedly caused the venture not to deal with their non-member competitors; they also agreed that none of them would act as a "wholesaler" of news or sell to a non-member. In holding this arrangement invalid, the Court stated the "[t]he Sherman Act was specifically intended to prohibit independent businesses from becoming 'associates' in a common plan which is bound to reduce their competitors' opportunity to buy or sell * * *."[2]

The Court in finding a violation also stressed that the association, though not a monopoly, was large enough so that loss of access both to it and to all of its individual members as news sources was bound to put a competitive burden on non-members. For this reason the case is sometimes read as being an extension of the doctrine of

---

10. E.g., Washington State Bowling Proprietors Ass'n v. Pacific Lanes, Inc., 356 F.2d 371 (9th Cir.), cert. denied 384 U.S. 963, 86 S.Ct. 1590, 16 L.Ed.2d 674 (1966); Mechanical Contractors Bid Depository v. Palmer-Christiansen, 352 F.2d 817 (10th Cir. 1965), cert. denied 384 U.S. 916, 86 S.Ct. 1365, 16 L.Ed.2d 439 (1966).

1. 326 U.S. 1, 65 S.Ct 1416, 89 L.Ed. 2013 (1945). Compare United States v. Topco Associates, Inc., 405 U.S. 596, 92 S.Ct. 1126, 31 L.Ed.2d 515 (1972) holding that joint venture integrations cannot justify an explicit division of territories. See also §§ 77, 81 and 83.

2. Id. at 15, 65 S.Ct. at 1422, 89 L.Ed. at 2027.

Terminal Railroad,[3] a case which Mr. Justice Douglas cited in his concurring opinion as implying that a venture which possesses an asset which is so uniquely valuable as to be a prerequisite to successful competitive access will be obligated to provide access to that asset in the same manner as though it were a public utility. But *Associated Press* seems too simple to be treated as an elaboration upon the doctrine of *Terminal Railroad,* and the simpler reading leaves the case better linked with adjacent strands of doctrine than does the more complex one. Consider *Terminal Railroad.* Unless its rule is confined to ventures which had power at the very outset, it is a hard teaching indeed; it would require any highly successful joint venture to treat all competitors in the same way as it treats the venturers which initially took the risks. Delimiting the scope of *Terminal Railroad,* then, is a sensitive task and one who sets about it must strive not only for consistency with other Section 1 cases, but must also seek consistency with the law of Section 2, in particular with that aspect of it which finds no offense even in the possession of monopoly power, so long as it has been gained by skill, foresight and industry. It is therefore less unsettling to let *Associated Press* stand, as it seems comfortably to do, for the proposition that even joint ventures may not as a condition of their venture explicitly agree to exclude all others.[4]

This is also a resolute reading of the case and it implies considerable coherence. It rejects the suggestion that an explicit boycott ought to be permissible where necessary to induce competitors to enter into a joint venture and when rule of reason analysis suggests that the gains may outweigh the costs. So doing, it brings the rule respecting boycotts by joint ventures into line with that respecting price fixing or market division by joint ventures. But more than that, the reading of *Associated Press* here proposed takes a stand about the interplay of *per se* concepts and the rule of reason which accords with developments even in less closely related areas. If one asserts, in support of its reasonableness, that a joint venture affords a significant potential for scale efficiencies not otherwise available, one is also asserting that the call of the venture to its participants is the rather insistent call of a potentially large increase in profits. It can then be argued that if the venturers really regard the venture as yielding significant efficiencies, they ought to be ready to proceed

---

3. United States v. Terminal Railroad Ass'n., 224 U.S. 383, 32 S.Ct. 507, 56 L.Ed. 810 (1912); see § 48 supra.

4. There is considerable case law consistent with this view. E.g., Blalock v. Ladies Professional Golf Ass'n., 359 F.Supp. 1260 (N.D.Ga.1973); Denver Rockets v. All-Pro Management, Inc., 325 F.Supp. 1049 (C.D.Cal.1971). Though there are cases which may be hard to square with it, such as American Brands, Inc. v. National Ass'n. of Broadcasters, 308 F.Supp. 1166 (D.D.C.1969), which denied a preliminary injunction against an association rule restricting cigarette advertising, most of these were decided before United States v. Topco Associates, 405 U.S. 596, 92 S.Ct. 1126, 31 L.Ed.2d 515 (1972). See § 80 supra.

without the added inducement of a license to boycott non-members.[5] But even though an explicit boycott in association with a joint venture is a response excessive of reasonable need, the boycott-like effects which a joint venture may have even absent an explicit boycott are by their nature among the minimum social costs which must be borne if the venture is to go forward. The policy question, then, is whether the benefit of the venture is worth these costs. We are then approaching that region where the rule of reason should be ascendant.

Suppose, for example, that newspapers had customarily bought and sold news from each other, each paper covering its area and marketing any story of wider interest which its reporters obtained, and that fifty newspapers spread across the country formed an association to which each member reported its stories and from which each obtained the stories of the others. Absent an explicit boycott, *Associated Press* would not govern, and given the limited size of the association, and the obvious possibility for others to compete without access (either in the old manner or by forming competing associations), *Terminal Railroad* would not apply. Yet it is an exceedingly likely effect that members will stop or substantially reduce news sales to or news purchases from non-members. Or assume that a group of real estate brokers, through an association, exchanges listings and agrees to share commissions where one broker obtains a listing and another finds a buyer; this arrangement will reduce the incentives of members to provide listings to or to obtain them from non-members.

In both hypotheticals the venture has as a likely consequence a withdrawal of trading opportunities from non-member competitors which may be useful to those competitors in their efforts to compete. If the venture is presently or potentially so powerful that loss of access will greatly reduce the competitive effectiveness of non-member firms, and if firms which want to enter are not permitted to do so on reasonable terms, elaborate analysis is not needed to support the conclusion that any gains in efficiency are outweighed by the anticompetitive effect; indeed, it may be suspected that the stifling effect on non-members may have been a purpose for the venture. A court

---

5. Molinas v. National Basketball Ass'n., 190 F.Supp. 241 (S.D.N.Y.1961) is not inconsistent. Plaintiff Molinas, a star player, was suspended by the league for placing bets on league games. The court dismissed his antitrust action saying that "a disciplinary rule invoked against gambling seems about as reasonable a rule as could be imagined." The case does not conflict with boycott doctrine for the *per se* rule applies only to classic boycotts and here no such boycott took place. A classic boycott is an effort by a group of traders to exclude or inhibit a competitor trying to enter or compete in their market either by themselves not dealing with the competitor or by coercing or inducing one or more suppliers or customers not to deal with him. The concerted action in Molinas was by teams in the league and was aimed not at stifling competing teams but at disciplining a player. Though concerted action was involved and an antitrust issue perhaps presented, the *per se* rule had no application. Every concerted refusal to deal is not a classic boycott. See § 90 infra.

should characterize such an arrangement as a boycott and *per se* unlawful. But that way of speaking about the matter should not disguise that a balancing of harms and benefits has taken place; where the weight on one side of the scale manifestly exceeds that on the other, application of the rule of reason (whether in open or disguised form) need not be a complex matter.[6]

§ 90. *Per Se* Doctrine and Concerted Refusals to Deal Other Than Classic Boycotts

While the boycott concept is infinitely expandable, the *per se* doctrine ought not to be. By one frequently encountered use of the term, any concerted refusal to deal is labeled a boycott. If the term boycott is used in this way then all boycotts are not *per se* unlawful, for many concerted refusals to deal lack the distinguishing characteristics which invite application of the *per se* doctrine; one cannot say of them that they always or almost always do substantial harm to competition, that they seldom benefit it, and then only slightly, and that the cases showing a net benefit are hard to identify. As noted earlier, one can say these things about a concerted refusal aimed at depriving competitors of some needed resource, and thus making it harder for them to compete. It is this kind of exclusionary practice, which is in this book called a classic or explicit boycott, to which the *per se* doctrine properly applies. Failure to attend to the distinction between classic boycotts (and arrangements tending toward the same effect) and other concerted refusals to deal often leads to confusion. Some concerted refusals other than classic boycotts may be harmful to competition; others may not. If it be incorrectly assumed that all concerted refusals are comprehended by the *per se* doctrine, which ought only to be applied to classic boycotts, considerable stress is felt. Though many non-boycott concerted refusal cases seem to be *sui generis*, some fall into recurrent patterns. We shall discuss the principal ones here.

Some years after the *Eastern States*[1] decision there were two motion picture cases involving concerted refusals to deal which rather clearly threatened injury to competition, and which were held unlawful. They are often called boycott decisions, though the facts did not involve any effort to inhibit entry. They are therefore not cases of classic boycott and speaking about them as though they were adds to confusion. In Paramount Famous Lasky Corp. v. United States,[2] film

---

6. See also Hopkins v. United States, 171 U.S. 578, 19 S.Ct. 40, 43 L.Ed. 290 (1898); Anderson v. United States, 171 U.S. 604, 19 S.Ct. 50, 43 L.Ed. 300 (1898); Danville Tobacco Ass'n v. Bryant-Buckner Associates, Inc., 333 F.2d 202 (4th Cir. 1964); Gamco, Inc. v. Providence Fruit & Product Bldg., Inc., 194 F.2d 484 (1st Cir.), cert. denied 344 U.S. 817, 73 S.Ct. 11, 97 L. Ed. 636 (1952); United States v. Southwestern Greyhound Lines, Inc., 1953 CCH Trade Cas. ¶ 67,470 (N.D. Okl.).

1. 234 U.S. 600, 34 S.Ct. 951, 58 L.Ed. 1490 (1914). See § 84 supra.

2. 282 U.S. 30, 51 S.Ct. 42, 75 L.Ed. 145 (1930).

distributors concertedly agreed that in their dealings with exhibitors they would use a standard contract form which required arbitration of disputes and further agreed that none of them would deal with any exhibitor which thereafter refused to comply with the arbitration provision. The Court labeled the arrangement as "necessarily and directly" tending to destroy competition. In United States v. First National Pictures Inc.,[3] distributors agreed to use standard form contracts which required security against default to be given by exhibitors and further agreed not to deal either with exhibitors who declined to provide the security or with any new owner which, on taking over an existing theatre, refused to assume and comply with any outstanding contract with the old owner. Again, invalidity was adjudicated with only summary discussion.

There are very different reasons for social disapproval of a classic boycott like that in *Eastern States* than for disapproval of conduct like that in *Famous Lasky* or *First National*. The classic boycott is a method by which traders at one level try to impede entry at that level; it is a way of creating or protecting (or attempting to create or protect) market power. If it is successful the power attained might be exploited through supra-competitive prices or in alternative ways. The conduct in the movie cases, however, is not a method by which traders keep competitors out. It is a method by which competitors may be able to exact for themselves better trade terms by acting concertedly than they could obtain if they competed with each other. Such conduct is cartelization, a way of obtaining and exercising market power by concertedly exacting terms like those which a monopolist might exact. Members of a cartel may seek a trade advantage other than higher prices which would not be available if competition flourished and which, like higher prices, would yield supra-competitive profits either by reducing costs, credit losses, or the like. They are not coercing anyone, at least in the usual sense of that word; they are merely (though concertedly) saying "we will deal with you only on the following trade terms."

Arrangements like those in *Famous Lasky* and *First National* are more like price fixing agreements than they are like classic boycotts. Indeed, if a concerted agreement, say, to include a security deposit in all contracts is a "boycott" because it excludes all buyers who won't agree to it, then by parity of reasoning every price fixing agreement would be a boycott also. The use of the single concept, boycott, to cover agreements so varied in nature can only add to confusion. But there is an even more important reason for not referring to an agreement which concertedly sets non-price terms of trade as a boycott, to which the *per se* doctrine applies. Such agreements may not be as consistently adverse to competition as either price fixing agreements or classic boycotts. In some

---

3. 282 U.S. 44, 51 S.Ct. 45, 75 L.Ed. 151 (1930).

situations—for example if there are large numbers of small sellers and buyers—an agreement fixing collateral terms, like an agreement standardizing product, might tend to increase price competition by reducing confusing variations between the offerings of competing sellers. In other situations concerted decisions about the terms on which competitors will trade may advance other social objectives and be competitively neutral.[4] Though courts should look at all such arrangements critically, a *per se* response may be too severe.

A determination not to call such arrangements "boycotts" does no great violence to judicial usage. Though the casebooks and commentators tend to group *Famous Lasky* and *First National Pictures* with boycott cases, the Court did not use the term boycott in either case. We would, therefore, classify these kinds of agreements with other examples of loose-knit concerted action, such as product standarization agreements, which are generally analyzed under the rule of reason. However, this does not imply that an elaborate analysis will be needed for all such cases. In some of them, such as *Famous Lasky*, the harms which the arrangement does will be so obvious and its potential for benefits so weak that a summary response will be warranted.

Hawaiian Oke[5] typifies another kind of concerted refusal which has purposes and effects very different from a classic boycott. Two distillers, both of which used the same Hawaii distributor, were each dissatisfied by the distributor's performance. Because scale requirements made it easier to attract a desirable replacement if the replacement distributor were offered both distillers' products, the two distillers agreed that they would both drop the old distributor and offer their products to a new distributor. The Ninth Circuit properly held

---

4. See, e.g., Ruddy Brook Clothes, Inc. v. British & Foreign Marine Ins. Co., 195 F.2d 86, 89 (7th Cir.), cert. denied 344 U.S. 816, 73 S.Ct. 10, 97 L.Ed. 635 (1952). Cf. Levin v. Doctors Hosp., 354 F.2d 515 (D.C.Cir. 1965); United States v. Mortgage Conference, 1948 CCH Trade Cas. ¶62,273 (S.D.N.Y.); I.P.C. Distributors v. Moving Picture Mach. Operators Local 110, 132 F. Supp. 294 (N.D.Ill.1955). A recent case of interest which insists on caution in applying the boycott label is Worthen Bank & Trust Co. v. National BankAmericard, Inc., 485 F.2d 119, 125 (8th Cir. 1973), cert. denied 415 U.S. 918, 94 S.Ct. 1417, 39 L.Ed.2d 473 (1974).

5. Joseph E. Seagram & Sons, Inc. v. Hawaiian Oke & Liquors, Ltd., 416 F. 2d 71 (9th Cir. 1969), cert. denied 396 U.S. 1062, 90 S.Ct. 752, 24 L.Ed.2d 755 (1970). See also Instant Delivery Corp. v. City Stores Co., 284 F.Supp. 941 (E.D.Pa.1968); Interborough News Co. v. Curtis Publishing Co., 225 F.2d 289 (2d Cir. 1955). An interesting contrast with all of these cases is found in DeFilippo v. Ford Motor Co., 516 F.2d 1313 (10th Cir. 1975). There, a dealer whose store had been burned out was assured by the manufacturer of a new dealership on especially favorable terms; however, the manufacturer withdrew the assurance on complaints from competing dealers. The court held, quite correctly, that this was not a classic boycott, but was on very doubtful ground in implying, as it did, that the concerted conduct of the competing dealers was clearly lawful. It would have been more appropriate to remand the case for evaluation under the rule of reason.

that the *per se* rule against boycotts had no application. The distillers were not trying to cut any competitor out of the market by denying it a customer or a source of supply. For that reason, the boycott *per se* rule was inoperative. Moreover, the distillers were not even trying to coerce the market conduct of the terminated distributor. If they were, their conduct might have been unlawful for reasons independent of boycott doctrine. However, they were merely ceasing to deal with a firm they thought inadequate. The fact that the two distillers acted concertedly might raise questions under the rule of reason, but it does not render their conduct *per se* unlawful.

Molinas, discussed in Section 89 supra, exemplifies a concerted refusal without boycott effects in a joint venture setting.[6] Concerted refusal could also occur, without group boycott effects, in connection with an industry self-policing program. For example, an agreement by competitors not to use a deleterious ingredient can be fairly characterized as a concerted refusal to buy from suppliers of the ingredient. But this case, like *Molinas,* lacks utterly the purpose or effect which, as the Court stressed in *GM,*[7] validates the *per se* approach, a purpose and effect to "put *competitors* out of business * * *."

It is not excess of rigor that insists that cases like those here discussed should be perceived and dealt with under the rule of reason and not draped over with boycott doctrine. Systematic analysis is needed not only to avoid the surface confusions which inevitably follow when one fails to speak precisely about complex matters, but to avoid distorted results. No harm is done, one might say, by calling *Famous Lasky* a boycott case; but surely grave risks are accepted when an analysis fails to distinguish between concertedly setting trade terms, which may aid or hurt competition, and concertedly barricading entry, which can only be harmful. If we either speak of the *per se* rule as applying to concerted refusals to deal, or call all concerted refusals boycotts, we shall also get arrangements like that in *Molinas* tangled in the net. If the *per se* rule respecting boycotts is to become coherent, we must recognize that it applies only where competitors engage together to inhibit others with whom they compete by depriving those others of elements needed in the competitive context. This is not to say that other concerted refusals may not be illegal; many will be, some of them plainly so. It is only to insist that we look at the others, each for what it is, and do not suppose that as some distant relative of the classic boycott it must be cursed with the same baleful characteristics.

6. See also Deesen v. Professional Golfer's Ass'n., 358 F.2d 165 (9th Cir.), cert. denied 385 U.S. 846, 87 S.Ct. 72, 17 L.Ed.2d 76 (1966), and United States v. U.S. Trading Ass'n., 1960 CCH Trade Cas. ¶69,761 (S.D.Ohio 1960), which are comparable.

7. United States v. General Motors Corp., 384 U.S. 127, 86 S.Ct. 1321, 16 L.Ed.2d 415 (1966).

§ 91. Exclusive Franchises Distinguished from Boycotts

Cases like *Klor's*[1] demonstrate the seamless nature of the fabric of interrelationships with which antitrust must deal; it forces on our attention here issues which, under our organizational structure, it would be more pleasing to defer. Let us then glance at them, leaving until later, and an accumulation of other material, a fuller treatment.

The classic boycott as defined in this book usually entails action by two or more firms at the level being protected from competition. For example, in *Eastern States*[2] there were several retailers trying to protect their level. But concerted action at the protected level is not necessary to a boycott. In *Klor's*, for example, the business which was protected against competition was appliance retailing. Yet there was only one retailer involved, which had allegedly induced several manufacturers to refuse to supply plaintiff, a competing retailer. *Klor's* is nevertheless treated as alleging a classic boycott, a *per se* violation. The crucial element is an effort to exclude or cause disadvantage to one or more competitors by cutting them off from trade relationships which are necessary to any firm trying to compete. The classic boycott, as we have defined it, also usually entails an effort to induce two or more suppliers or customers not to deal with firms being excluded from the protected level. In *Fashion Originators*,[3] for example, all retailers were urged not to deal with style pirates. But again, this plurality is not a necessary ingredient. In *Radiant Burners*,[4] for example, the only "supplier" urged not to deal with plaintiff was the association which supplied a seal of approval. Nonetheless, the conduct alleged—an effort by competitors to force plaintiff out of the market by depriving it of something it needed to compete—was conformable to the concept of a classic boycott which we have developed.

Now suppose that plurality is lacking at each of these levels and that a retailer, such as the defendant in *Klor's*, seeks to protect itself from competition by inducing a single supplier, a manufacturer of TVs, to sell only to it. *Klor's* in a pointed dictum tells us that the holding in that case does not reach such an arrangement, usually called an exclusive distributorship. A single firm, hoping to attain competitive advantage, apparently can induce at least one supplier to deal only with it without falling under the shadow of the *per se* rule concerning boycotts. The distinction does not turn upon the lack of enough concerted action to constitute a contract, combination or conspiracy. The agreement between the manufacturer and the dealer supplies that. The distinction can be rationalized, broadly, by reference to the fact that if a buyer ties up only one supplier, firms seek-

---

1. 359 U.S. 207, 79 S.Ct. 705, 3 L.Ed.2d 741 (1959). See § 84 supra.
2. 234 U.S. 600, 34 S.Ct. 951, 58 L.Ed. 1490 (1914). See § 84 supra.
3. 312 U.S. 457, 61 S.Ct. 703, 85 L.Ed. 949 (1941). See § 84 supra.
4. 364 U.S. 656, 81 S.Ct. 365, 5 L.Ed.2d 358 (1961). See § 86 supra.

ing to compete with the buyer will still have access to suppliers of other competing goods. Indeed, the Supreme Court has implied by way of dicta that the legality of such an exclusive franchise, or exclusive dealership as it is sometimes called, depends upon availability of substitutes.[5]

An exclusive franchise is, of course, a vertical restraint; a buyer imposes on the seller a restriction on the seller's market conduct. It can be best analyzed and understood in relation to similar restraints where a firm at one horizontal level imposes restrictions upon firms at other horizontal levels from which the first firm buys or to which it sells. Here, then, we shall leave the matter, having noted only that the boycott rule does not apply; other problems will be addressed more fully hereafter.[6]

§ 92. Application of Boycott Doctrine to Cases Where Political, Religious, Social or Other Non-Commercial Purposes are Involved

One can hardly pick up a newspaper without finding a reference to a consumer boycott, a refusal to deal by a group of consumers which is typically aimed at essentially non-commercial ends. If the Catholic Bishops of America vote to support the United Farm Workers boycott of non-union grapes, is this a "labor boycott" covered by statutory exemptions from the Sherman Act, a constitutionally sanctioned expression of religious belief, or conduct subject to the Sherman Act? And if the latter, is it *per se* unlawful? Or suppose that a political or religious group concertedly determines not to buy books which express a particular political or religious point of view;[1] or that a racial group determines concertedly to withhold patronage from firms it believes to discriminate against its members in services or employment.[2]

None of these fact situations display the crucial element which has warranted application of a *per se* rule to boycotts; none of them is a classic boycott, as that term is properly used in antitrust analysis, for none of them constitute efforts by a firm or firms at one level to drive out competitors by either directly denying or persuading or coercing suppliers or customers to deny relationships the competi-

---

5. United States v. Arnold, Schwinn & Co., 388 U.S. 365, 87 S.Ct. 1856, 18 L. Ed.2d 1249 (1967). See also Cherokee Laboratories, Inc. v. Rotary Drilling Services, Inc., 383 F.2d 97 (5th Cir. 1967), cert. denied 390 U.S. 904, 88 S. Ct. 816, 19 L.Ed.2d 870 (1968); United States v. Chicago Tribune—New York News Syndicate, Inc., 309 F.Supp. 1301 (S.D.N.Y. 1970).

6. See §§ 147–149 infra.

1. Konecky v. Jewish Press, 288 F. 179 (8th Cir. 1923); Council of Defense v. International Magazine Co., 267 F. 390 (8th Cir. 1920). These and related issues are discussed in Coons, Non-Commercial Purpose as a Sherman Act Defense, 56 Nw.U.L.Rev. 705 (1962).

2. Baker v. F. & F. Inv., 420 F.2d 1191 (7th Cir.), cert. denied 400 U.S. 821, 91 S.Ct. 42, 27 L.Ed.2d 49 (1970); United States v. Mortgage Conference, 1948–49 CCH Trade Cas. ¶ 62,273 (S.D. N.Y.1948).

tors need in the competitive struggle. The church group, political group, or racial group which initiates a consumer boycott is not a group of publishers, sellers, or farmers seeking to blockade entry.

Let us now look at activity of a kind often related to a consumer boycott, efforts by persons with a commercial interest to stimulate consumer action. First, suppose farm workers coerce or induce consumers (or, for that matter, others, such as restaurants or food stores) not to buy non-union grapes. Still, the crucial element to invoke the *per se* rule is lacking. The workers obviously have a commercial interest, but it is not that of competitors of the grape growers whose trade is being reduced. The same is true where firms in an industry concertedly refuse to hire employees because of their political views.[3] None of these arrangements possesses the core characteristic which identifies the classic, commercial boycott—an effort to cut off a competitor by disrupting his trade connections.

It is not proposed here that any one or more of the arrangements referred to is lawful under the Sherman Act, or that no other body of law renders such concerted action unlawful. All of these private actions may have severe economic impacts on firms which are the objects of them. These sanctions may also be imposed under standards which may be vague in the extreme (what is an obscene or an irreligious book or periodical, for example?) and may be implemented without any opportunity for the victim to defend himself, either as to the appropriateness of the standard or as to whether he is in compliance with it. Additionally, some of the activities above supposed are of a kind which may invite constitutional protection, while others are not; some of them are for purposes which may have statutory or other governmental sanction, while others are not. Thus we are not here reaching conclusions about the legality of any of them; we are merely insisting that the *per se* rule applicable to classic commercial boycotts has nothing to do with the matter.

However, the relevance of *per se* theory can come strongly to the fore where consumer action for non-commercial motives is involved, if the initiative to stimulate that action is taken by competitors. Above, we supposed that union workers urged consumers not to buy non-union grapes. Now suppose the non-commercial appeal to consumers not to deal with a particular firm or class of firms is made not by a church, a political organization or a union (which has a derivative commercial interest) but by a competitor. For example, a publisher which features books lacking any overt sexual interest urges church members not to buy books of a rival publisher because some of that publisher's books treat sexual topics too explicitly. Or suppose that an industry self-policing program is informed not by product safety or similar objectives, but by matters concerning politi-

---

3. Young v. Motion Picture Ass'n., 299 F.2d 119 (D.C.Cir.), cert. denied 370 U.S 922, 82 S.Ct. 1565, 8 L.Ed.2d 504 (1962), but see, I.P.C. Distributors v.

cal, religious or moral attitudes. On these assumptions the conduct does, in terms, fall under the *per se* ban applicable to a classic commercial boycott. A trader, seeking to stave off competition, has tried to induce customers not to deal with its competitors. Thus, these hypotheticals raise very sharply the question whether the presence of non-commercial goals on the part of the suppliers or customers who are induced to withdraw renders the *per se* rule inapplicable.

There appears to be no case which deals with this issue in pure form. The case most closely in point is Hughes Tool Co. v. Motion Picture Association,[4] where the producer challenged an industry association which denied a seal of approval to the producer's movie because of advertisements for the movie which the association judged to be indecent. No explicit boycott was involved; association members neither agreed not to deal with Hughes, nor urged exhibitors not to book, nor consumers not to see the picture. Thus, an issue of characterization was presented about whether the association's action should be called a commercial boycott. But boycott effects comparable to, if not so severe as, those in *Radiant Burner*[5] were surely entailed. Hence, on the authority of *Radiant Burner* the conduct should be characterized as an unlawful boycott unless the goals of the policing program were reasonable, the standards objective, and the procedures fair. The court, stressing defendants' "proper purpose" to assure wholesome output by the industry, held the arrangement valid.

Suppose, however, there were an explicit boycott and that as a sanction against firms making films found obscene, other movie makers threatened exhibitors that if they showed the obscene films the other makers would stop supplying them. A court could surely preserve the core of *per se* analysis, and still distinguish *Hughes*. The contention would be that although "proper" (non-commercial) motives can validate a non-explicit boycott they should not be used to validate an explicit one, for the reason that the boycott action in the latter cases is more restrictive in impact than need be to achieve the proper purpose. *American Medical Association*[6] perhaps lends authority to this suggestion. There, while holding invalid an explicit boycott to attack prepaid medical plans at least arguably for non-commercial motives, the court stated that the Association could lawfully take action, like publicizing its views about the dangers of prepaid plans, which would have boycott-like effects.

Yet the distinction between the express and the less direct boycott for non-commercial purposes has a haphazard look about it; if

---

Moving Picture Mach. Operators Local 110, 132 F.Supp. 294 (N.D.Ill.1955).

4. 66 F.Supp. 1006 (S.D.N.Y.1946).

5. 364 U.S. 656, 81 S.Ct. 365, 5 L.Ed.2d 358 (1961). See § 86 supra.

6. 317 U.S. 519, 63 S.Ct. 326, 87 L.Ed. 434 (1943). See § 88 supra. Compare Marjorie Webster Jr. College, Inc. v. Middle States Ass'n of Colleges, 432 F.2d 650 (D.C.Cir.), cert. denied 400 U.S. 965 (1970).

per se analysis meets the case of the explicit boycott, then purpose and effect analysis is indicated to determine how action tending toward similar results should be classified. When in order to pursue comparable purposes, action is taken which tends to the same results as would an explicit boycott, such an analysis, moreover, would suggest that the conduct be characterized as a boycott. It thus suggests that *Hughes* was wrong. To make the point, let us suppose a contrasting case, that producers "policed" the movie industry output to see whether it was excessively dull, or technically shoddy, and denied a "seal of approval" to producers of deficient pictures. Such a self-policing program would surely fall under the ban of *Radiant Burners* and *Fashion Originators;* it would be unable to survive, as appearing to benefit competition, under an analysis like that suggested above.[7] Denial of a seal of approval to a movie because it or its ads are "indecent," "obscene," or "immoral," would seem to suffer the same deficiency. Only if the involvement of non-commercial purposes yields some degree of mitigation of the standards which apply generally to boycotts can the *Hughes* decision be sound. And if non-commercial purposes do serve to mitigate the social goal of protecting competition, there is no obvious reason why mitigation would not occur as well where the boycott is explicit as where it is achieved in purpose and effect.

The court in the *Hughes* case did see something unique in the moral and non-commercial purpose of the association program which made the purpose "proper" and beyond the reach of Section 1 of the Sherman Act. But that conclusion is hard to accept. It may fairly be implied that the association did, in fact, have commercial purposes in mind. It was policing the moral quality of the industry's product precisely because it was concerned that if it did not do so, direct consumer action by church groups would lay even rougher hands upon it. Furthermore, the suggestion that non-commercial, moral, or religious purposes ought to exempt members of an industry which take boycott action—i.e., action calculated to drive out an offending competitor—would substitute an unruly and murky doctrine tuned to no discernible set of values for a disciplined concept focused finely on competition as a goal. Absent a clear, contrary demand from the constitution or a statute, the case against a judicial venture into that quagmire is strong.

Under the boycott rule, then, cases involving non-commercial motives should be treated much as other cases. A consumer refusal to deal or other refusals which are not aimed at inhibiting competitive entry or action at the level occupied by those concertedly responsible for the refusal should not be classified as a classic commercial boycott, amenable to the Section 1 *per se* rule. Such refusals may have competitive consequences which raise Section 1 issues; if they do,

---

7. See §§ 87–88 supra.

and they are not specifically exempt (for example, under the labor exemption or the agricultural cooperative exemption) they should be analyzed under the rule of reason. But all refusals to deal initiated by traders at a given horizontal level and aimed at impeding other traders at that level should be analyzed in conventional boycott terms, except to the extent that explicit alternative constitutional or statutory policies otherwise demand.

PART G. DATA DISSEMINATION

§ 93. Introduction

In Part C we suggested some of the myriad ways in which competitors may relate, remarking in the process on the relevance of market structure to the style and intensiveness of competitive conduct and the extent to which overtly cooperative or interdependent tendencies were likely to display themselves; we traced the development of the rule of reason and the *per se* doctrine, noting the ways in which these two strands relate to each other and stressing the tension which exists about whether non-competitive values may be attended to in rule of reason analysis. In parts D through F, we turned our full attention to the *per se* concept and measured its scope in each of the loose-knit horizontal relationships to which it has applied. Just as the *per se* doctrine had undivided attention in those parts, so does the rule of reason in this and the several parts which follow. We shall examine the rule in its application to a large number of recurrent kinds of horizontal relationships among competitors. In the process we shall not only display the operation in varied settings of the analytical model developed in Section 68, but shall also develop a sense for what matters are settled. Too often antitrust writing gives the impression that the rule of reason is an unending analytical process in which nothing is ever settled beyond the fate of the parties in particular cases. But antitrust is law and cases are not without precedential value, even in the realm of the rule of reason. It is time we took note that many issues are recurrent and have been settled in a satisfactory as well as in an authoritative way. Doing this will be an aid to antitrust enforcement; by celebrating what is clear about the law, we will make the law more potent in the marketplace.

There is, of course, considerable surface variety in the kinds of arrangements which are challenged under the rule, and the kinds of harms and benefits asserted to derive from them. Beneath the tangled connections seen at a glance there are skeletal similarities which can be discerned only upon some probing. But the probing repays the effort. These similarities permit us to group the ways in which concert of action may injure competition and the ways in which it may aid competition. Injury takes place by either (1) the concerted creation of entry barriers (which create, perfect or enhance market power), (2) the concerted exercise of market power (through tempering competitive effort with respect to price, quality or output), (3) the concerted rationalization of an oligopolistic market so as to facilitate cartelization or interdependence (for example by standardizing product or terms of trade, or exchanging information on price, output and the like), or (4) the concerted substitution of administered decision making processes for competitive ones (for example, through common research activity). Benefit can take place only if concerted action (1) achieves integration efficiencies, (2) makes or perfects a market, or (3) rationalizes a competitive market so as to facilitate competitive functioning (for example, by standardizing product, terms of trade, or the like).

All other claims of injury turn out on analysis to be includable within these or to vanish; all other claims of benefit turn out upon analysis to be includable within these or to be not claims that competition will be benefited but either (and at best) claims that the concerted action will achieve better than would competition some goal which we associate with competition itself (such as efficiency, innovation or an allocation of resources in ways which maximize social satisfaction) or (and at worst) claims that some social goal which has little or nothing to do with competition (such as a claim that public morals will be advanced) will be better attained by concerted action. Pursuant to the classic rule of reason, the latter of these claims —an assertion of goals which are normally achieved by police power interventions rather than through the paternalistic largess of competitive industry—is not to be weighed as offsetting any injury to competition. To weigh social benefits extraneous to the competitive process as benefits which might be purchased at the expense of competitive injury would be a clear distortion of traditional Sherman Act jurisprudence. Even the former claim, that a particular restraint advances the performance goals of the competitive process, would not be admissible under a rigorously classical formulation of the rule of reason. Though courts may admit such performance considerations in some degree, they must be examined very critically.

§ 94. Economic Effects of Disseminating Prices

The dissemination of information about prices and other industry statistics has been a major activity of trade associations and other trade groups for seventy years or more. Programs may be local, regional or nationwide and can vary enormously in detail from annual summaries of aggregate data openly and widely published to day-to-day rundowns on specific quotations or transactions between identified buyers and sellers reported only to competitors and not to their customers or others. The competitive effect of one of these programs will vary depending upon how firms respond to the data.

This in its turn will vary with industry structure and with the kinds of data circulated. The effect of such programs on competition depends, therefore, on an interplay of structural and conduct elements.

Let us contrast two examples. In one, the industry is made up of about twenty producers all in one geographic region. Forty years ago there was a cartel; it was abandoned after a short time because of extensive cheating and fear of government prosecution. Twenty-five years ago, after a period of lively price competition, three of the largest firms merged and a tendency for the resulting firm to lead and others to follow in making price changes thereafter developed. At the invitation of the merged firm, the industry members formed an association and through it started circulating each day completed copies of all order forms on orders taken during the day. Since this reporting program was instituted there have been no price changes except those initiated by the largest firm as price leader. In the contrasting example, there are 3,000 relatively small sellers in the nation grouped in three geographic regions and there are several thousand buyers throughout the country. Prices offered by sellers in any one region tend to be the same, though sometimes there are time "lags" of two to four weeks during which a price change initiated by one seller spreads like a slow wave to other sellers. Variations between regions are small and there is an observable tendency for changes in one region to be responded to in the others, though often the interregional time lag may be a month or more. A trade association is formed with numerous members in each region who report their prices weekly. Since the program has been in effect, the frequency of price fluctuations and their relationship to supply and demand factors has not seemed to change, but there has been a discernible tendency for price changes initiated within any one region to be responded to more quickly, both in that region and in other regions; as a result, average prices in any one region have tended to vary less from average prices in any other region than had previously been the experience.

In the first hypothetical, the statistical program might be characterized as a covert price fixing agreement. It does not strain credulity to infer from the facts given that sellers have communicated to each other that all will follow the leader's prices, and that reporting is, in essence, a policing mechanism to make cheating difficult. Whether it is viewed in this way or not, a balancing of harms and benefits should lead to the conclusion that the arrangement is unreasonable. Historically, the industry has shown tendencies toward cartelization and interdependent conduct, as well as tendencies toward rivalry. Since the merger of the largest firm, there has either been collusion between the resulting firm and other firms, or the tendencies in the industry toward interdependent action have been dominant. If the price reporting program is not being used to police compliance with an express cartel (and it may be), it plainly serves to facilitate the tendency toward interdependent pricing; all firms must know that they can share in supra-competitive profits by following the leader, and the fact that they must report (and therefore that any effort to increase volume by lowering price will be discerned and responded to) will chill any motivation to act independently. The program is redolent with competitive harm, whether seen as a prop for conspiratorial price fixing, or as a facilitator of interdependent pricing. It is *per se* unlawful, or unlawful under the rule of reason. In the second hypothetical, by contrast, neither the structure nor the history invites the inference of cartelization or interdependence. The industry, before price reporting, appears to be working competitively, though absence of the rapid diffusion of information results in some lag in price changes within regions and, more clearly, leaves the markets represented by the three regions imperfectly linked. The consequence of price reporting seems to be to make each regional market work more competitively and to facilitate the more complete integration of the three regions into a single national market.

Mark this point. The wide and rapid dissemination of price and related information is one of the prerequisites for a competitive market. If most of the other prerequisites (most importantly a large number of buyers and sellers, none with a substantial market share, and a non-differentiated product) are present, the tendencies toward competitive behavior can be expected to be strong; adding the prerequisite of widespread information can be expected to make the market work more competitively. But if the structure strongly invites collusive or interdependent conduct, the addition of better information will not stimulate competition; it will tend to facilitate collusion or interdependence. In *every* case, better information facilitates more rational self-interested conduct by the firm acting on the information. But in some structures rational, self-interested conduct will be competitive and in others it will be interdependent or collusive. Thus, an analysis of industry structure will be critical to a prediction of the rational response.

§ 95. The Early Cases

Even before the *per se* illegality of price fixing was settled, the Supreme Court in *American Column & Lumber* invalidated the program of a trade association in the hardwood industry which called for the daily reporting, subject to audit, of sales, purchases, production and inventory, and the immediate reporting of any changes in prices.[1] In a setting in which expert analysis of industry conditions stressing dangers of overproduction were circulated to members by the association and members were exhorted to think of the good of the industry, the Court found the program unlawful. In reaching its conclusion, the Court made little of the fact that associa-

---

1. American Column & Lumber Co. v. United States, 257 U.S. 377, 42 S.Ct. 114, 66 L.Ed. 284 (1921).

tion members represented 33% of industry production. While there was some evidence of actual price increases which the Court thought might be attributable to the program, the Court conceded that other factors could have caused these. Rather, the Court stressed the detailed nature of the information given, the opening of books to audit, the analysis of the data which was passed on to all members, and the climate of missionary zeal about the advantages of the program to all industry members. Largely on these grounds, the Court concluded that the purpose and effect were to restrict production and "to encourage members to unite in pressing for higher and higher prices * * *." The lack of a "definite agreement as to production and prices" was supplied by the "disposition of men 'to follow their most intelligent competitors * * *.' "[2]

A purpose and effect analysis which emphasizes the particulars of the program has also led courts to uphold price reporting arrangements. Where there is no commitment to comply with published prices, where individual transactions are not identified, where information goes to buyers as well as sellers, and where no audit procedure, common analysis or suspicious exhortation is associated with price reporting, a purpose and effect analysis focused only on program details will tend to validate the program.[3] This analysis as applied in *Maple Flooring* is perhaps open to criticism even accepting its basic vantage point, in that two of the program particulars—the circulation of average production costs data and of a book showing freight rates from selected cities in the producing area to other parts of the country—are together indicative of an unlawful intent. Computation and circulation of an "average" cost, which will necessarily be arbitrary in the accounting conventions upon which it is based and which may be based on data arbitrarily selected, will have little or no interest to a firm engaged in individual decision making; but such information may be ripe with the implication that prices should be set sufficiently above these costs to enable even marginal firms to profit. Similarly, the freight book, since rates are computed from selected cities rather than from actual plant locations, can be seen as inviting or facilitating the use by all of a basing point pricing system.

The greater limitation in the analysis utilized in all of these early price reporting cases is, however, a limitation shared equally by cases, on the one hand, like *American Column & Lumber,* which held a reporting system invalid, and on the other, like *Maple Flooring,* which held reporting systems to be lawful. The criterion they used,

2. Id. at 407, 399, 42 S.Ct. at 119, 117, 66 L.Ed. at 294, 290. See also, United States v. American Linseed Oil Co., 262 U.S. 371, 43 S.Ct. 607, 67 L.Ed. 1035 (1923).

3. Maple Flooring Mfrs. Ass'n. v. United States, 268 U.S. 563, 45 S.Ct. 578, 69 L.Ed. 1093 (1925); Cement Mfrs. Protective Ass'n v. United States, 268 U.S. 588, 45 S.Ct. 586, 69 L.Ed. 1104 (1925); and Tag Mfrs. Institute v. FTC, 174 F.2d 452 (1st Cir. 1949) all exemplify this.

focusing as it did on program details, screened out information about market structure which profoundly affects the impact of any price reporting program. In evaluating purpose and effect, it is necessary to attend to the specifics of particular price reporting programs, and to look to related conduct for any indication of collusive purpose. But this approach to price reporting is not of itself sufficient. It tends to be unrelievedly mechanistic; it leads to the drawing up of checklists by association counsel and the placid assumption that a lawful and harmless program can be fashioned so long as dangerous elements on the checklist are scrupulously avoided. Even worse, it ignores the powerful insight drawn from economics that industry structure as well as program detail ought to be consulted in making judgments about purpose and effect. The next section proposes the conclusion that the law has now caught up with that insight and passed beyond the limits of the narrower analysis used by the cases discussed here.

§ 96. The Container Case and Structural Analysis as a Guide to Legality of Price Information Programs

Few cases of the last decade have greater potential significance for antitrust development than United States v. Container Corp. of America.[1] Yet it is a troublesome case, because the Court, while utilizing a somewhat groundbreaking method of analysis, reaches conclusions which are vulnerable to criticism from the perspective of that same analysis. Defendants, 18 of 51 firms in the southeastern states which manufactured corrugated containers for use by industry, and accounting for about 90% of container production in that region, participated in an arrangement whereby each could upon request obtain from any other participant information as to the most recent price charged or quoted by it. The industry was one in which entry was relatively easy; the cost of renting and fitting up an efficient plant were modest and an investment of about $50,000 to $75,000 could put a new firm in business. Products which varied in dimension, weight, color and other particulars were made to buyers' specifications from among standardized variations and those of different sellers were substantially identical. Buyers were highly price conscious and would typically obtain more than one bid before placing an order; buyers also tended to shift rapidly from one source of supply to another, so that a major customer of a given seller in any one year might do relatively little business with that seller in another year. Elasticity of demand was low, however, because container costs were a small part of buyers' total production costs and because buyer needs were fixed by their own production levels. And, in general, though the composition of the orders of a particular seller tended to change significantly over time, shares of total production tended to be more

---

1. 393 U.S. 333, 89 S.Ct. 510, 21 L.Ed.2d 526 (1969). See also Morton Salt Co. v. United States, 235 F.2d 573 (10th Cir. 1956).

constant. The industry in the region had grown during an eight year period from 30 firms with 49 plants to 51 firms with 98 plants. Although total sales had doubled as a result of increased demand, the growth in capacity had outstripped growth in demand and some excess capacity had prevailed throughout the period. Prices, moreover, had trended downward. Defendants had other sources of price information including buyers which, on seeking a bid, would sometimes state what had been quoted elsewhere; thus, participants in the arrangement did not call upon each other for price information very frequently. When a participant did ask a competitor what it was currently quoting on containers of a given specification, it usually responded by bidding the same price, but sometimes would bid lower.

Mr. Justice Douglas wrote for the majority. The opinion concludes that "[t]he exchange * * * seemed to have the effect of keeping prices within a fairly narrow ambit * * * The result * * * was to stabilize prices though at a downward level."[2] The Court stressed the fact that capacity was increased by rapid new entry at a faster rate than the growth in demand, and despite an already excessive capacity; it also emphasized the observation that knowledge of a competitor's price usually meant matching it, not undercutting it. In essence, the Court engaged in a theoretical, albeit truncated, structural analysis, saying:

> Price information exchanged in some markets may have no effect on a truly competitive price. But the corrugated container industry is dominated by relatively few sellers. The product is fungible and the competition for sales is price. The demand is inelastic, as buyers place orders only for immediate, short-run needs. The exchange of price data tends toward price uniformity. For a lower price does not mean a larger share of the available business but a sharing of the existing business at a lower return. Stabilizing prices as well as raising them is within the ban of § 1 of the Sherman Act. As we said in United States v. Socony-Vacuum Oil Co., * * * "in terms of market operation stabilization is but one form of manipulation." The inferences are irresistible that the exchange of price information has had an anticompetitive effect in the industry, chilling the vigor of price competition.[3]

Container invites criticism, since an examination of the details of the arrangement tends to suggest a limited, if any, adverse impact. The arrangement involved no agreement by participants not to change a quotation after reporting it, as in *Sugar Institute*.[4] Thus,

---

2. 393 U.S. at 336, 89 S.Ct. at 511, 21 L.Ed.2d at 529–30.

3. Id. at 337, 89 S.Ct. at 512, 21 L.Ed. 2d at 530.

4. Sugar Institute, Inc. v. United States, 297 U.S. 553, 56 S.Ct. 629, 80 L.Ed. 859 (1936).

the agreement was much less likely to inhibit either single-shot or general price reductions by a firm which had reported. Also, the fact that reports were made only on request and that requests were infrequent might be seen to reduce harmful potential, though it may be that knowledge among buyers that sellers could check directly with each other the accuracy of information circulated by buyers would tend to lead buyers to report accurately on other quotes received, thus reducing the need for frequent contacts among sellers. Conduct evidence, then, falls short of showing a violation. Hence, if illegality is to be found, it can only be predicated on a structural analysis.

On available structural evidence the conclusion of the majority is doubtful. Evidence of power, of a structure facilitating cartelization or interdependence, was no more than borderline. Although the 18 defendants had 90% and the largest four of them 45% of the southeast market (if, indeed, that was a separate geographical market, as all seemed to assume)—itself, a moderate degree of concentration—the cross-elasticity of demand among the products of different producers (which was displayed by the rapid changes in suppliers by customers), the great ease of entry, and the existing over-capacity, all must have limited severely the potential of defendants to hold prices at supra-competitive levels. The performance evidence was even more ambivalent. No effort was made by the government to prove high profits or by defendants to prove reasonableness. Prices had been falling though costs were rising, an indication not of the maintenance of market power, but of its erosion. But capacity was increasing faster than demand, an indication that entrants foresaw availability of supra-competitive profits, though also an indication that if power existed, needed corrections were taking place.

If the power issue remains doubtful, there was little if any evidence of a wrongful purpose or of anticompetitive effects. While there was an implication that defendants saw the arrangement as tending toward greater uniformity of price between sellers, that uniformity, absent power evidence, could signify competitive responses as well as noncompetitive ones. Where price information is readily available, rational rivals selling the same product in the same market will be expected to sell at the same price; that they do is simply not selective, one way or the other, between competition and collusion. Nor is there independent effect evidence other than that sellers tended, in part because of the arrangement, to offer the same prices— something they would do in a smoothly functioning market whether it was functioning competitively or collusively.

In narrow terms, the case thus leaves the law in doubt. If one projects from this case alone, then except for the most flagrantly competitive market showing no indications of concentration, it is hard to picture a market where an attorney would confidently predict that an exchange of price information is valid. Apparently any discernible suggestion from the evidence that the defendants, collectively, may possess power is enough evidence to warrant a holding that a price information program is unlawful. On the other hand, the Court in other areas [5] has tended of late to demand a more forceful and rigorous showing that structural evidence is indicative of non-competitive functioning before concluding that competition is threatened. This new posture will, perhaps, play over into an evaluation of structure for the purpose of drawing inferences about purpose and effect of price information programs. However, the overriding significance of the *Container* case is that the Court (both the majority and the dissenters) approaches the question of the legality of market conduct which falls under the rule of reason by taking explicit cognizance of the structural conditions which exist in the industry, and seeks to evaluate the effect of the conduct in light of its relationship to that structure. This approach, one of potentially great power in rationalizing antitrust, may have occurred beneath the surface in some earlier rule of reason decisions; [6] but in *Container* it was for the first time frankly adopted and validated.

The values of this development are numerous. Analysis of the interaction of structure and conduct, however difficult it may be and however likely to generate doubts and disagreements at borderlines like that which *Container* itself exemplified, is the most promising and rational approach available for making judgments about competitive effect where conduct falls under the rule of reason. Furthermore, this way of dealing with rule of reason issues tends to achieve a better integration, a more cohesive relationship, among all aspects of antitrust. Monopoly [7] and merger law [8] focus centrally on structure, the latter on perturbations of structure and their likely effects, and only peripherally on conduct. The analysis which informs these areas of law is, if you will, a structural analysis. *Per se* analysis, though it places greater emphasis on conduct, is also an analysis which draws upon the relationship between structure and conduct; both must be brought to bear to distinguish from other practices those which will almost surely do harm and seldom yield any competitive benefit. In *Container,* the arch is completed. Structure and conduct are simultaneously analyzed in predicting the consequence of conduct assigned to the rule of reason.[9]

5. E.g., United States v. General Dynamics Corp., 415 U.S. 486, 94 S.Ct. 1186, 39 L.Ed.2d 530 (1974).

6. Virginia Excelsior Mills, Inc. v. FTC, 256 F.2d 538 (4th Cir. 1958); United States v. Columbia Pictures Corp., 189 F.Supp. 153 (S.D.N.Y.1960); United States v. American Smelting & Ref. Co., 182 F.Supp. 834 (S.D.N.Y.1960).

7. See Chapter 2 supra.

8. See Chapter 7 infra.

9. At least one court has treated the requirements of the Robinson-Patman Act as one of the structural factors to be taken into account in evaluating the legality of a price information exchange. See Wall Products Co. v. National Gypsum Co., 326 F.Supp. 295 (N.D.Cal.1971), which allowed exchange of price quotations when needed to verify buyer reports of competi-

§ 97. Dissemination of Non-Price Data, Commentary and Recommendations for Action

Several of the cases discussed earlier entailed circulation of non-price data and comments on trade conditions as well as circulation of price information.[1] In general, the analytical approaches sketched in the last two sections are appropriate in evaluating circulation of non-price information and commentaries on industry conditions. This point can be emphasized by recalling what was said in Section 96 about average cost data and about freight books. There are, however, a few points about non-price data which remain to be stressed.

First, data as to production figures is substantially as sensitive as data about prices. It can be used to police production quotas imposed by a cartel or, in an oligopolistic structure, can facilitate interdependent action in reducing output; these dangers are heightened when the product is undifferentiated and when output by particular firms is disclosed.[2]

Economic analysis and forecasts circulated by a trade group among industry members can present problems of some subtlety. At an extreme the matter is clear enough. Exhortation to industry members, such as that displayed in the hardwood case,[3] is an overt call to common action which cannot be muted by any claim of a right to free discourse on matters of general interest. At the other end of the spectrum would be, say, an article by an economist appearing in a trade association publication and dealing in a temperate, professional manner with national economic trends; the interest in free discussion and exchange of views is too great and the possible connection with concerted or interdependent action too remote to warrant any intervention. The *Container*[4] case and *Morton Salt*[5] perhaps suggest that the borderline is reached where commentary and analysis became pregnant with the suggestion that by taking discernible common action supra-competitive profits can be achieved.[6]

---

tors' prices before making a sale at a discriminatively low price in order to meet the equally low price of a competitor.

1. See generally the cases cited in § 95 supra.

2. See Hartford-Empire Co. v. United States, 323 U.S. 386, 406–07, 65 S.Ct. 373, 384, 89 L.Ed. 322, 358–59 (1945); United States v. United Fruit Co., 1958 CCH Trade Cas. ¶ 68,941 (E.D. La.).

3. American Column & Lumber Co. v. United States, 257 U.S. 377, 42 S.Ct. 114, 66 L.Ed. 284 (1921).

4. 393 U.S. 333, 89 S.Ct. 510, 21 L.Ed.2d 526 (1969).

5. Morton Salt Co. v. United States, 235 F.2d 573 (10th Cir. 1956).

6. Compare Verified China Ass'n, 49 FTC 1571 (1953). Virginia St. Bd. of Pharmacy v. Virginia Citizens Consumer Council, 96 S.Ct. 1817 (1976), while protecting commercial speech, is not adverse.

PART H. STANDARDIZATION PROGRAMS

§ 98. Product Standardization

Programs for standardization or simplification of product, often carried on by trade associations, have not received extensive attention. The few relevant cases tend to emphasize the potential of such programs to stimulate price competition by facilitating price comparison by buyers and thus support such programs as presumptively lawful.[1] In *Tag Institute*,[2] as an example, the court was disinclined to view critically a standardization program which facilitated price reporting among association members; despite the oligopolistic structure of the industry, it saw these activities (which included making price information available to buyers) as tending to make buyers and sellers more price sensitive.[3]

A few courts, however, have been ready to view the effects of standardization less charitably, especially where a standardization program is pursued in conjunction with other action which may tend to stifle competition. In Milk & Ice Cream Can Institute v. FTC,[4] the defendant had issued a freight book, engaged in price reporting, discouraged the sale of "seconds" and pressed for standardization. Price uniformity increased and the court attributed this to defendant's activities. It inferred from the standardization program, which surely facilitates uniformity of price, as well as from the other activities, that the purpose was injurious to competition. Similarly, in Bond Crown & Cork Co. v. FTC,[5] the court said that a standardization program "innocent enough by itself" is not innocent when it is part of a program to standardize trade discounts and differentials and to publicize prices, and is associated with industry-wide patent accuracy agreements which fix minimum prices.

National Macaroni Manufacturers Association v. FTC[6] is perhaps unique in predicating liability almost solely upon the standardi-

---

1. See C. Kaysen & D. Turner, Antitrust Policy 151–52 (1959).

2. Tag Mfrs. Institute v. FTC, 174 F.2d 452 (1st Cir. 1949).

3. See also Structural Laminates, Inc. v. Douglas Fir Plywood Ass'n, 261 F. Supp. 154 (D.Ore.1966), aff'd 399 F.2d 155 (9th Cir. 1968), cert. denied 393 U.S. 1024, 89 S.Ct. 636, 21 L.Ed.2d 569 (1969); Roofire Alarm Co. v. Underwriter's Laboratories, Inc., 188 F. Supp. 753 (E.D.Tenn.1959), aff'd mem. 284 F.2d 360 (6th Cir. 1960); United States v. National Malleable & Steel Castings Co., 1957 CCH Trade Cas. ¶ 68,890 (N.D.Ohio), aff'd mem. 358 U.S. 38, 79 S.Ct. 39, 3 L.Ed.2d 44 (1958). But see C-O-Two Fire Equip. Co. v. United States, 197 F.2d 489 (9th Cir. 1952) holding a product standardization program illegal because it facilitated non-competitive pricing. See generally E. Rockefeller, Antitrust Questions and Answers 47–48 (1974).

4. 152 F.2d 478 (7th Cir. 1946).

5. 176 F.2d 974 (4th Cir. 1949); see also Ft. Howard Paper Co. v. FTC, 156 F.2d 899 (7th Cir.), cert. denied 329 U.S. 795, 67 S.Ct. 481, 91 L.Ed. 680 (1946).

6. 345 F.2d 421 (7th Cir. 1965). See also C-O-Two Fire Equip. Co. v. United States, 197 F.2d 489 (9th Cir. 1952).

zation program. There, a disastrous growing season had driven up the price of durum wheat and manufacturers of macaroni had agreed to a standardized reduction of about fifty percent in the use of this flour in their products. All the aspects of the recipe were not standardized; it was anticipated that less expensive wheats than durum would be utilized in its stead. The court viewed this concerted activity, which directly tended to reduce the market for durum wheat and to depress its price and which manifestly had that purpose, as tantamount to price fixing and it held the program unlawful.

In most of the cases discussed in this section, as well as in many of those involving the dissemination of information, there is a tendency toward truncated analysis; courts focus on program particulars and act as though the only choices open to them are either to analogize the program to price fixing, or to the limitation of production, in which case it would be treated as illegal, or to validate the program as harmless. Particulars of standardization programs can be important, of course, and ripe with significance. If "standardization" really means suppression of low cost models, the clear implication may be that standardization is in the service of blocking tendencies toward, or outlets for, price competition. But the *Container* case [7] is a reminder that once the problem is outside the area of naked restraints, a high level of ambiguity may prevail even where program particulars in themselves imply no evil. A full-blown rule of reason analysis requires more than a lyrical survey of program particulars in search of covert price fixing. Such an analysis must take account of structural factors and must search out an understanding of the interplay which is occurring between structure and conduct. Standardization no more needs to be adopted with a specific purpose to fix prices in order to injure competition than does price reporting.

The key to a solid analysis is recognition of the implications of one profoundly powerful fact. Product standardization, like the exchange of price information, will tend to facilitate rational conduct with respect to prices. Thus, if the structure of the industry is one that invites competition, standardization will enhance that tendency. But just as standardization may facilitate more rational pricing in a competitive industry, it may also facilitate more rational pricing in an oligopolistic industry. But in an oligopolistic industry, rational pricing may be non-competitive pricing of the kind the law seeks to inhibit. If there are tendencies in an industry toward cartelization or toward interdependent pricing, standardization may enhance these tendencies.

Suppose, for example, that there are seven sellers of a product used by manufacturers as a raw material, that significant entry bar-

---

7. United States v. Container Corp. of America, 393 U.S. 333, 89 S.Ct. 510, 21 L.Ed.2d 526 (1969); see § 96 supra.

riers exist, that products are differentiated, and that each manufacturer has his own way of putting together components and combinations and aggregating these additions to reach the price for a finished unit. Price leadership would be difficult in such an industry. Moreover, a seller capable of being confused by variations and hard pressed to gather and keep in mind all aspects of each competitor's prices at all times might well be misled into granting a reduction by a buyer who asserts that he has received a better offer elsewhere. The very irrationality of seller responses, the outgrowth of this confusion, may be the source of such limited price competition as the industry displays. But let the product now be standardized so that each seller can keep better track of the other sellers' offerings and the potential for price leadership and interdependent pricing is strongly enhanced. A truncated analysis which uses the categories of the *per se* concept as the analogs for decision under the rule of reason would likely validate standardization in such a setting.[8] But a fuller evaluation of likely effects, taking account of industry structure, would perceive dangers great enough to outweigh the conceivable benefits of standardization.[9]

§ 99. Standardization of Trade Terms Other Than Price

In *Famous Lasky* and *First National Pictures*,[1] the Court summarily labeled unlawful agreements by movie producers fixing non-price terms on which they would deal with exhibitors. In earlier discussion we rejected the suggestion that these "standardization" cases can be assimilated under boycott doctrine and showed that an agreement concertedly fixing non-price terms of sale is more closely analogous to a price fixing agreement than to a boycott.[2] It is tempting, then, to draw the price analogy, to cite the two early cases and to assert that all such agreements, like the price fixing agreements they resemble, are *per se* unlawful. That course must be rejected, however; analysis shows that an agreement fixing non-price trade terms may either help or hurt competition, depending upon industry structure.

The effects of an agreement standardizing non-price terms will vary much as will an agreement standardizing product. By such standardization the variety of offerings open to buyers and opportunities for competitive differentiation open to sellers will inevitably be reduced, as they are when product is standardized. This of itself is a

---

8. Compare Tag Mfrs. Institute v. FTC, 174 F.2d 452 (1st Cir. 1949).

9. There is another way in which product standardization may be beneficial; it may facilitate greater efficiencies in production, reduce inventory costs, and the like. To the extent these gains can be achieved without offsetting injury to competition, the public is the gainer.

1. Paramount Famous Lasky Corp. v. United States, 282 U.S. 30, 51 S.Ct. 42, 75 L.Ed. 145 (1930); United States v. First Nat'l Pictures, Inc., 282 U.S. 44, 51 S.Ct. 45, 75 L.Ed. 151 (1930).

2. See § 90 supra.

competitive deprivation not to be ignored. But standardization of non-price terms, like standardization of product, will have other effects. It will in a sense serve to channel all transactions into a single, better integrated market; buyers will more easily be able to compare their alternative opportunities as to the unstandardized terms, most notably price, and sellers will more likely be aware of competitive offerings. The situation, then, is not unlike the agreement in *Chicago Board of Trade,* where the exchange rule had the cost of reducing competitive opportunities of buyers and sellers by inhibiting night trading, but had the benefit of channelling all transactions through the daytime market.[3]

Because integration into a single market will tend to facilitate more rational pricing, the effect on competition resulting from standardization of non-price terms will vary with industry structure and the extent to which the market is already highly developed. If the market is oligopolistic, rational pricing may be interdependent pricing or even cartel pricing, and facilitating that will hurt competition. If there is not an oligopolistic structure and no tendency toward interdependent pricing, whether the integration will offer sufficient benefit to competition to outweigh the reduction in seller freedom and buyer alternatives will depend on whether a high degree of price competition existed before the standardization. If there are a large number of buyers and sellers, there may have existed extensive price competition for all the variant offerings which were available before standardization. On that assumption, there will be little if any social gain from standardization; the harm consequent upon reduced seller freedom and buyer alternatives would dominate. If, however, there were few sellers of some variants before integration then integration might strengthen competitive tendencies, perhaps greatly, surely a benefit substantially outweighing any harm from reduced product options. At least in this kind of a situation the implication of *Famous Lasky* and *First National Pictures* that standardization of non-price terms is *per se* illegal ought to give way.

Where industry members do not expressly agree on non-price trade terms but take action tending toward standardization of such terms, the problem is one level removed. Take as an example competition among banks for saving deposits. Suppose an association of savings banks or savings and loan institutions which engaged in this business were to circulate standardized contract forms, or were to purchase products such as kitchenware, which it offered to members at cost to be used by them as "premiums" to be given to those who open new accounts.[4] The subjective purpose of the first activity

---

3. Board of Trade of City of Chicago v. United States, 246 U.S. 231, 38 S.Ct. 242, 62 L.Ed. 683 (1918). See § 68 supra.

4. Many trade associations publish and distribute standardized forms. See, e. g., W. Parker & F. Adams, The A.I.A. Standardized Forms and the Law. Cf. § 102 infra.

might be to achieve integration efficiencies in the review of contract forms for compliance with complex state or federal regulatory provisions; it is not likely that the association would perceive it as a way of reducing competition. And the subjective purpose for the second activity would surely be integration efficiencies as well as the stimulation of promotional activities calculated to help industry members as a whole by increasing aggregate industry business. Yet each of these activities might tend to squeeze out some of the few elements of non-price competition and competitive differentiation to be found in the industry. If it were concluded, on the basis of a structural analysis, that the industry was highly competitive as to price, those negative effects might be regarded as insufficiently weighty in light of the innocent purposes and socially useful tendencies or effects. But if price uniformity in the industry were attributed to oligopolistic interdependence and price leadership, any existing non-price competition might be valued highly.[5] In that event, anything tending to standardize the non-price contract terms would be regarded as significantly harmful.

§ 100. Standardization of Hours, Facilities and Other Elements of Competitive Style

Suppose that competing butchers agree not to open before 9 a.m. or to close later than 6 p.m., that competing gas stations agree that none of them will offer trading stamps, or that competing TV sales and service outlets agree to maintain only a grade B, not a grade A, parts inventory. In each instance assume that the number of competitors participating is a sufficiently high share of a discernible market so that potential consequences cannot be dismissed as trivial. There is not a great deal of case law about such arrangements and that which is available is not entirely consistent. *Chicago Board of Trade*[1] suggests a rule of reason approach, at least to agreements standardizing trading hours. Yet, in Jewel Tea Co. v. Associated Food Retailers,[2] the Seventh Circuit held on rather sketchy analysis that a horizontal agreement among competitors as to hours of trade was unlawful, perhaps *per se* unlawful.

A sound rule calls for an appraisal of competitive benefits from any such arrangement, but also recognizes that jointness can aid competition only if it entails some degree of integration which yields efficiency or tends toward perfecting a market. Any claim of public

---

5. Compare Staff Research Associates, Inc. v. Tribune Co., 346 F.2d 372 (7th Cir. 1965).

1. 246 U.S. 231, 38 S.Ct. 242, 62 L.Ed. 613 (1918); see § 66 infra.

2. 331 F.2d 547 (7th Cir. 1964), rev'd on other grounds sub nom. Meat Cutters Local 189 v. Jewel Tea Co., 381 U.S. 676, 85 S.Ct. 1596, 14 L.Ed.2d 640 (1965). See also FTC Advisory Opinion Digest No. 110 (1967), 16 C.F.R. § 15.110 (association may poll members as to preferred business hours).

benefit which points in a direction other than one of these two must, under the Sherman Act, be discounted in advance. It is not senseless to assert that shorter store hours, fixed by horizontal agreement, are good for employees and make for a more stable and placid society in which the commerce of life is kept in proper relation to the rest of living. It is rather that to do so is to lose sight of the fundamental intention of the Act. If the social benefits of shorter hours of employment are worth a reduction of competitive opportunities, a court cannot make that judgment, only a competent legislative authority can do so.

We need pursue the store hour hypothetical no further. It entails no integration at all, hence no efficiency. What little might be said about it as a market making mechanism has already been anticipated in the earlier discussion of *Chicago Board of Trade*.[3] Let us look, however, at the trading stamp hypothetical and consider the elements with which a full analysis of the problem must reckon.[4] If public interests other than enhancement of competition are to be scrupulously excluded, only two plausible claims may be made in favor of this joint action. First, by eliminating trading stamps, transactions are standardized in a way which makes consumers more price conscious and thus facilitates price comparison shopping. The market for gasoline is thereby more fully integrated, as the tendency of stamps to be a basis for product differentiation is eliminated. Second, elimination of stamps ends a "tying" effect which stamps have, a tendency to bring a buyer who has accumulated some green stamps back where these stamps are available even though a slight price advantage may be available elsewhere. Other claims of advantage for this joint program might also be small, but these would begin to move away from relationship to competitive concerns. For instance, the claim that stamps are a wasteful competitive device, or the claim that consumers are deceived by stamps in that they are led to think that they are getting something for nothing, have at best tangential connections with the statutory interest in maintaining competition.

When a court has decided what harms and benefits flow from joint action, it has taken the basic analytical step, but its work is not yet finished. To decide whether the market improving features of the stamp agreement overshadow the potential harm, a court must do more than identify the direction of forces emanating from the agreement. It must also sense their intensities and come to a judgment about which are the stronger. When one considers the effect on particular consumers, the tying aspect of the use of stamps appears not

---

3. See §§ 66–69 supra.

4. Much of the analysis here is suggested by P. Areeda, Antitrust Analysis, Problems, Text, Cases ¶ 352 (2d ed. 1974). The most relevant decision is United States v. Gasoline Retailers Ass'n, 285 F.2d 688 (7th Cir. 1961), which condemned an agreement not to give stamps when found in association with an agreement not to advertise price.

to be a trivial harm. The grocery purchaser completing the last book needed to acquire a desk lamp may be considerably less sensitive to a slight price advantage elsewhere than would either the buyer not collecting stamps or the buyer who collects them haphazardly from all sellers and without a particular premium in mind. But the very existence of uncommitted purchasers—of buyers who save no stamps or all stamps, or save indifferently—will in the aggregate significantly diminish the negative effect of the agreement. Here, as in any comparable problem, it is the effect on marginal sales which is most significant. So long as the price consciousness of a substantial percentage of all consumers is not dulled by stamps, the use of stamps cannot provide sellers with any significant quantum of market power. The gain to competition from the joint action is then rather limited. The harm, that sellers and buyers both are denied a competitive alternative which obviously has a substantial appeal to a large body of consumers, is, by contrast, of some consequence. Furthermore, if the use of stamps is really adverse to the interests of consumers, it will be in the competitive interest of one or more sellers to stop using stamps and to capitalize on that by advertising the fact and either selling at a reduced price without stamps or giving buyers an option—either to take stamps and pay for them or to take the merchandise only and pay for it alone. In short, unless the market is rigged, either by concerted agreement to use stamps or by excessive concentration and interdependent action, the market when left alone ought to adjust to consumer interests with responses at least as fine as those which the industry could concertedly agree upon.

An analysis which counts in favor of agreements fixing nonprice trade terms only such good as they may do for competition and no other kind of benefit at all, may seem to be functionally equivalent to a *per se* rule. Yet it does not follow that a *per se* standard should be adopted. Doctrinal consistency, if nothing more, calls upon courts to remain as open here as they would be with respect to product standardization to the possibility, albeit remote, that situations will occur where common action to root out some competitive variant will serve to improve a market as yet too poorly integrated to perform adequately. But it is not at all excessive to observe that when the offense asserted is common action to homogenize competitive style, courts are, and ought to be, both undisposed to accept justifications which recount the ways in which competition has proved socially wasteful, and skeptical of rarified theoretical arguments about benefits to market competition.

But arrangements like those here pictured may be encountered where the number of competitors involved is so patently an inconsequential share of any identifiable market that risks to market competition are *de minimus*. In these instances (at least if proponents of the arrangement creditably assert that it affords some social benefit which does not depend for its achievement on the assumption that they possess market power) a court ought not to be too zealous to strike it down. The private ordering of complex affairs is itself a social value; where to discern a possible competitive harm would be to indulge in a quibble, a court ought not to inhibit this mode of expression.

PART I. MISCELLANEOUS JOINT ACTIVITIES

§ 101. Concerted Decision Making

We are discussing here not programs involving statistics on price or production, or standardizing other trade terms, but matters further away from the central nervous system of competition. Trade associations often serve as a media through which competitors discuss common problems and sometimes perform for members the function of providing expert advice or information. Suppose the issue is how large an inventory is needed; members may share their experience and judgment in discussions, or the association may hire consultants who work out and report on industry control standards and methods which have applicability for industry members as a whole.[1] Alternatively, suppose the question is the level of credit which ought to be provided in general, or to particular accounts. An association might be the catalyst for discussions where information might be exchanged, advice given, or joint decisions made. Or the association itself might circulate information about credit, give credit ratings to particular firms, or give advice as to appropriate credit standards.[2]

All of these activities pose some threat to competition. The competitive process can itself be the spur to good decision making about inventory levels and credit extension as well as to decisions about product variations, markets to be served, and price. If different decisions about such matters are made by competitors, the market will test them; it will reward those which are right and penalize those which are wrong. The risks of the marketplace will be both a spur to management to watch what it is doing and a medium for selecting those who are most capable of sound decision making for advancement within a firm. The joint activities alluded to above, and others like them, tend to inhibit competition in these areas.

Explicit joint decisions end competition as to all matters comprehended by the joint decision and would obviously be more restrictive than the circulation of advice or information. Nevertheless, the exchange of explicit advice—for example, that inventory should always be at least X% of annual volume, or that credit should not be extended to a specified firm, or to any firm with a rating of C or less—al-

---

1. Compare Verified China Ass'n, 49 FTC 1571 (1953).

2. See e.g., Swift & Co. v. United States, 196 U.S. 375, 25 S.Ct. 276, 49 L.Ed. 518 (1905); Majestic Theatre Co. v. United Artists Corp., 43 F.2d 991 (2d Cir. 1930). See G. Lamb & S. Kittelle, Trade Association Law and Practice ch. 7 (1956).

though it leaves each firm free to make its own decisions, perhaps approaches in purpose and effect the making of joint decisions. The exchange of unprocessed information is at the other extreme. There is a necessarily joint decision about what information to gather and circulate and this itself may be suggestive in its implications; but firms maintain maximum freedom to interpret the information and to act upon it. There may also be benefits to competition in these joint activities; scale economies may be achieved. For example, it may be too costly for any single firm to gather the range of careful credit information which, if gathered collectively, can be made available to all at modest cost to any single firm. Concerted action may also make feasible more extensive study and evaluation of questions relating to inventory control or credit. Finally, concerted decision making, by bringing many heads to the task, or making it feasible to hire better executive talent, may be more expert than individual decision making by each firm. In all of these situations, even the last, some integration efficiencies may be attained.

Any tendency to injure competition arising from common action of the kinds here considered will be more or less potent depending on the degree of market power of the cooperating firms. For example, if a joint decision about credit is adopted by all firms in an industry, this will entirely freeze out any competitive experimentation and will monolithically foreclose any firm denied credit; but if only ten or twenty percent of the firms in the industry participate, there may be ample room for alternative responses.

Cases where explicit decisions are jointly taken have been disposed of with dispatch. In all of these, any claim of integration benefits is vulnerable to the rejoinder that substantially the full benefit would be obtained in a less restrictive way if the resources jointly engaged to yield decisions had been used instead to yield advice. For this reason courts tend to engage in only a truncated analysis before concluding that the program is unreasonably restrictive.[3] It is not that a *per se* rule has been developed, but that the situation is recurrent, the analysis under the rule of reason fairly obvious, and the *stare decisis* effects of earlier cases fairly strong. One might say that if all that has been integrated is the decision making process, joint decision making is presumptively unreasonable; if in a particular case it is not, its proponents had better be prepared to explain why and to do so explicitly.

At the other extreme are cases where information is circulated without constraint about how it is to be used; one may fairly label

---

3. E.g., Harwell v. Growth Programs, Inc., 459 F.2d 461 (5th Cir.), cert. denied 409 U.S. 876, 93 S.Ct. 126, 34 L.Ed.2d 129 (1972); Vandervelde v. Put & Call Brokers & Dealers Ass'n, 344 F.Supp. 118 (S.D.N.Y.1972); United States v. New Orleans Chapter, Associated General Contractors of America, Inc., 41 F.R.D. 33 (E.D.La.1966), aff'd mem. 396 U.S. 115, 90 S.Ct. 398, 24 L.Ed.2d 308 (1969).

this type of activity presumptively reasonable. Though more uniform decisions may be the result, it is not a consequence due to the foreclosing of options, but to individual choices being made in such a way that random, non-rational variations are minimized by the possession of more complete data by all decision makers. If such a joint program is challenged, it must be either on the ground that it is, in purpose and effect, a program of joint decisions masquerading as an information program or on the ground that concentration is sufficiently high that the data exchange facilitates interdependent decision making. The latter contention would seem strained if the subject of the information exchange was one which, like credit, is only distantly related to price formation. But if the subject matter relates to price more directly, a claim of surreptitiousness might be more plausible. For example, if demand changes, it may take time for firms to adjust output. In the interim, inventory levels could be varied in an effort to keep prices stable. Thus, information about inventory levels could be given with the purpose and effect of encouraging the building up of inventories to avoid a price decrease, or the reduction of inventories to avoid a price increase.

The intermediate area—that is, when information and advice are circulated, but decisions are not taken jointly—is less easy to generalize about than either mere circulation of data or full-fledged joint decision making. One can say that a less restrictive alternative is available, the circulation of the raw data, but one cannot confidently assert that this alternative will gain substantially all the efficiencies that concerted analysis of the data could achieve. The tendency is for proponents to analogize to information distribution and for opponents to analogize to joint decision making and for courts to react, at least in part, in terms of whether it is a tightly structured or a loosely structured industry which is being aided. Assume, for example, that a trade association in a concentrated industry were to advise inventory levels of a specified percentage of sales. Even if the purposes were innocent, the danger would be that if the advice were widely followed, the tendency would be to achieve production quotas for the future which were predicated on sales success in the past. In a loosely structured industry where firms would have a much lower appreciation of their ability to affect price by their own output decisions, the risk would be far less.[4]

With respect to credit advice, the critical distinctions turn less on concentration levels than on the percentage of the industry participating in the program. If the coverage is substantial both in terms of percentage of firms participating and percentage of those who follow the advice, a firm with an unacceptable rating may face a monolithic market which has decided it is not to survive. On the other hand, if a relatively small percentage of all potential sellers receives

---

4. Compare FTC Advisory Opinion No. 359 (1973).

or acts on the advice, the consequence on those adversely affected by the decision will be substantially less.

Joint activity—informational, advisory, or decision making—of the kinds here analyzed might occur with respect to any of the myriad choices firms must make, not just with respect to inventory or credit issues here used as examples.[5] While potential harms and benefits will vary with the particulars of the activity, the analytical approach here suggested will be appropriate in any instance, from a joint decision on cost accounting systems [6] to a joint decision about whether or not to deal with a particular supplier.[7]

§ 102. Joint Negotiation with Suppliers, Customers, or Unions

There is an increasing tendency for competitors to combine for negotiation. Industry-wide or regional negotiation of collective agreements on wages, hours and conditions of employment is common; the problems it can present under Section 1 are only those peripheral to the labor exemption to the antitrust laws.[1] More recent developments include the formation of dealers' organizations which process the complaints of franchisees against franchisors, and attempts more generally by retailer or dealer organizations to represent the interests of their members in negotiations with suppliers. Formal or informal efforts by small suppliers to deal collectively with relatively large buyers also occasionally occur.

The case law which bears directly on these problems is spotty. It is clear enough that if buyers at any level (say, retail dealers) concertedly persuade a supplier (say, a manufacturer) to exclude a competing dealer because they object to the excluded dealer's competitive style, a *per se* offense has occurred.[2] It also seems clear enough, in the absence of any claim of integration efficiencies of the kind which

---

5. See, for example, the problems respecting joint insurance investigations and ratings raised by Handler, Blake, Pitofsky & Goldschmid, Trade Regulation, Cases and Materials Prob. 13 (1975).

6. Cf. cases cited in § 98 supra.

7. See, e.g., Instant Delivery Corp. v. City Stores, Co., 284 F.Supp. 941 (E. D.Pa.1968).

1. See Meat Cutters Local 189 v. Jewel Tea Co., 381 U.S. 676, 85 S.Ct. 1596, 14 L.Ed.2d 640 (1965); Prepmore Apparel, Inc. v. Amalgamated Clothing Workers of America, 431 F.2d 1004 (5th Cir. 1970), cert. dismissed 404 U. S. 801, 92 S.Ct. 21, 30 L.Ed.2d 32 (1971). See § 237, infra. The reference in text to industry-wide negotiations should be taken to include various formal and informal, open and covert forms of cooperation. For example, firms in an oligopolistic industry all dealing with the same industrial union may bargain as a unit, may bargain independently, or, though meeting and negotiating separately, may agree or act interdependently on bargaining positions to be taken.

2. United States v. General Motors Corp., 384 U.S. 127, 86 S.Ct. 1321, 16 L.Ed.2d 415 (1966). Compare the Court of Appeals decision in Jewel Tea, 331 F.2d 547 (7th Cir. 1964); Kennedy v. Long Island R. Co., 319 F.2d 366 (2d Cir.), cert. denied 375 U.S. 830, 84 S.Ct. 75, 11 L.Ed.2d 61 (1963); Six-Carrier Mutual Aid Pact, 29 C.A. B. 168 (1959). Klor's Inc. v. Broadway-Hale Stores, 359 U.S. 207, 79 S. Ct. 705, 3 L.Ed.2d 741 (1959).

might be obtained where two or more competitors agree to hire a joint sales or service agent, that if dealers negotiated concertedly with manufacturer over the price charged by the manufacturer on sales to the dealers, the dealers would be violating the *per se* rule against concerted action by competitors affecting price.[3] But there are a great many matters of concern to dealers which, though of competitive significance, do not fall analytically under any *per se* rule. Suppose, for example, the dealers are muffler retailers operating under a franchise and the issues are the extent to which they may handle parts other than mufflers, the size of the inventory they must maintain, and the amount of local advertising the franchisor will do. The case law gives little aid about how far joint negotiation may go; indeed, even despite the clarity of *per se* analysis, the case law may invite a vague hope that dealers can concertedly negotiate with the manufacturer about price, or at least that dealers, through an association, could gather and present data the thrust of which was that the manufacturer's prices were too high and dealers' profits too low.

How ought the law to respond to dealers seeking jointly to bargain with a manufacturer on price? The usual argument made for allowing such collective bargaining is that if the manufacturer is large enough to possess market power, dealers should be permitted to combine in order to aggregate countervailing power.[4] Accepting the premise that the manufacturer has power, it does not follow that the public interest will be served by allowing dealers to negotiate collectively. The manufacturer with power will be able to extract the full advantage of that power in the price charged to dealers if the dealer level is competitive. The manufacturer can rely on competition among dealers to assure that dealers' prices are reduced to the level where profits are no more than a fair return and dealers' (and hence the manufacturer's) sales are the highest which can be attained. Thus, the manufacturer with power will set its own price to dealers at the level maximizing its own profits. The price to the public, the

---

3. Cf. Mandeville Island Farms, Inc. v. American Crystal Sugar Co., 334 U.S. 219, 68 S.Ct. 996, 92 L.Ed. 1328 (1948); United States v. Socony-Vacuum Oil Co., 310 U.S. 150, 60 S.Ct. 811, 84 L. Ed. 1129 (1940). See also National Macaroni Mfrs. Ass'n. v. FTC, 345 F. 2d 421 (7th Cir. 1965), holding illegal an agreement among buyers limiting the amount they would purchase. As to the analysis where a joint buying agency achieves integration efficiencies, see § 77 supra and § 104 infra; as to that where other joint services, such as delivery, are achieved, see text accompanying note 9 § 103, infra.

4. Compare United States v. Women's Sportswear Mfrs. Ass'n., 336 U.S. 460, 69 S.Ct. 714, 93 L.Ed. 805 (1949), holding violative of § 1 joint negotiation and agreement between sportswear manufacturers and an association of contract stitchers and, in substance, rejecting a countervailing power argument, with Appalachian Coals Inc. v. United States, 288 U.S. 344, 53 S.Ct. 471, 77 L.Ed. 825 (1933), which indicates that joint action to deal with "powerful buyers" is a valid purpose. See also Webster County Memorial Hosp., Inc. v. United Mine Workers of Am. Welfare & Retirement Fund of 1950, 536 F.2d 419 (D.C.Cir. 1976) (concerted action to negotiate with hospital on behalf of fund beneficiaries is reasonable).

profit maximizing price given the market power involved, will be the manufacturer's price plus a sum just sufficient to cover the costs of an efficient dealer, plus a fair dealer return.

If dealers combine so as to gain power of their own, the manufacturer may be forced to lower its price to them. However, there is no basis for supposing that the lower price to dealers will result in a lower price to customers of the dealers. It will be in the dealers' interest to continue the profit maximizing price to consumers. If they are able to do so, presumably they will; the only effect of their combining will have been to reduce the price they pay, to reduce the manufacturer's profit, and to increase the dealers' profit. The public will still pay excessive prices, but the profit will be split differently. Dealers will pass on all or part of the benefits of lower manufacturer prices to their customers only if they are forced to do so by competition. For example, if dealers handling the product of one manufacturer combine to attain countervailing power against that manufacturer, but, as sellers, face vigorous competition from retailers of other, substitute products, they may be forced to pass on to buyers in the form of lower prices the benefits of reduced manufacturer prices.

Upon analysis, then, the claim that victims of power can protect themselves through countervailing power is not an overwhelming one, since countervailing power may do nothing to reduce the distortion in resource allocation consequent upon the power already existing.[5] Moreover, allowing countervailing power to develop could worsen the situation, at least marginally. This point can be illustrated by supposing first that dealers, in order to fight the manufacturer's power, merge into a single firm. Note first that if the merger were not permitted and if supra-competitive profits were being obtained at the manufacturer level, entry at that level might be stimulated, perhaps, even by a dealer integrating backwards. If, however, the merger takes place and supra-competitive profits are thereafter shared at both levels, the call at either for the new entry necessary to correct the basic problem will be less clear. Moreover, if after the merger entry did develop at the manufacturer level, and that level were to become competitive, the result would merely be that the full benefit of the market power would be attained at the now concentrated dealer level. Entry there would now be needed also to create conditions where consumers would get the benefit of competitive prices. Overall, then, allowing a dealer merger might not merely fail to reduce the effects on consumers of manufacturer market power, but could make it more difficult for corrective responses to occur. Joint negotiation at the dealer level is, of course, not so formidable a barrier to erosion of manufacturer power as would be a more complete and permanent in-

---

5. See F. Scherer, Industrial Market Structure and Economic Performance 241–251 (1970).

tegration of dealers through merger. But it would have the same tendency to cloud the signal that market power exists at the manufacturer level and would tend toward the other adverse effects of merger.

It is sometimes argued that because market power can only be exercised once down any vertical distribution chain, we ought not to be too concerned about whether the dealer level is competitive if the manufacturer level is not.[6] But any such analysis must assume a static and unchanging condition in the marketplace. When it is realized that market power may be enhanced or eroded over time, it must also be recognized that a structure concentrated at two levels may be more difficult to rectify through market developments than a structure concentrated at only one level.

Is there anything to be said for concerted bargaining where no firm on either side can be said to have great power, but where the concert occurs on both sides of the table to yield substantially equal power? Assume for a moment that the insurance industry is competitive at all levels and that an association of agents sits down with an association of companies to bargain out a standard contract dealing with agent responsibilities and commissions. Or assume that an association of travel agents does the same with a hotel association or airline association.[7] These practices might be defended on the ground that it serves to make a market, that drawing all of the forces of supply and demand into a single medium will assure competitive terms. The difficulty with the argument is that supply and demand are not really being set off against each other in a market where what suppliers will accept is determined by unrestrained competition among suppliers, given the demand, and what buyers will pay is determined by unrestrained competition among buyers, given the supply. They are being set off against each other only in the aggregate. A monolithic judgment is made on the demand side and another on the supply side. The self-corrective influence of a truly competitive market is sacrificed.

Another argument which might be made in favor of joint negotiations is that scale efficiencies are achieved, that better talent and information is available to the group than to individual members. There may be something of substance to this claim in certain situations; matters of countervailing power aside, if real bargaining is taking place one has greater confidence in the process if those on each side of the table are adequately informed and well represented.

---

6. Cf. Bork, The Rule of Reason and the Per Se Concept: Price Fixing and Market Division, 74 Yale L.J. 775 (1965).

7. Numerous associations publish standardized contract forms. See, e. g., W. Parker and F. Adams, the A.I.A. Standardized Contract Forms and the Law. The extent to which these are formally or informally "negotiated" no doubt varies. Cf. § 99 supra.

But given the dangers of additional concentration and the small likelihood that a desire to be able to afford better information and representation, rather than ability to wield countervailing market power, will ever appear to be the real reason for combining, one ought to view this claim with great skepticism. Potential efficiencies in loose-knit aggregations may be worth purchasing where we are dealing with matters like credit reporting. But when the activity we are being asked to approve is joint negotiating over price, we are too close to the central nervous system of the market to affirm the joint activity without a profound and convincing showing of benefits which offset the risks.[8]

§ 103. Horizontal Agreements (Other Than Boycotts) Not to Deal

In Section 84 and those immediately following, we defined a classical group boycott as a concerted effort—often, though not always, by a concerted refusal to deal—to induce suppliers or customers to withhold their trade from a competitor of the concerted group in order to make it difficult or impossible for the competitor to compete. Perhaps the most explicit judicial statement limiting the definition of boycott in this manner is to be found in Potter's Photographic Applications Co. v. Ealing Corp.[1] Concerted refusals to deal may also be used for other purposes which injure competition in quite different ways. In this section these alternative concerted refusals are considered.

Suppose that a large holiday tour operator based in New York were to go bankrupt, that in the bankruptcy proceeding its goodwill and assets were acquired by a conglomerate which intended to recapitalize the enterprise and carry on the business under the old, widely advertised trade name, but that Florida hotels, acting through a trade association, notified the new operator that they would honor no bookings from it unless it paid the defunct corporation's discharged debts in full.[2]

The case law is perplexingly inconsistent about whether non-boycott concerted refusals to deal are *per se* unlawful and, if not, about the factors which are crucial to judgments about legality. Many opinions treat these refusals as though they were classical boycotts,

---

8. See, e. g., Jones Knitting Corp v. Morgan, 361 F.2d 451 (3d Cir. 1966). Confident judgments about many of the issues discussed in this section is rendered difficult by the dearth of empirical information about joint bargaining. For one informative study of relations between automobile dealers and manufacturers and negotiation of dealer grievances, see S. Macauly, Law and the Balance of Power (1966).

1. 292 F.Supp. 92 (E.D.N.Y.1968).

2. Compare Majorca Hotels threaten to turn away Britons because of Horizon debts, The Times (London), Feb. 7, 1974, p. 1 c. 1; Hunt v. Crumboch, 325 U.S. 821, 65 S.Ct. 1545, 89 L.Ed. 1954 (1945); McQuade Tours Inc. v. Consol. Air Tour Manual Committee, 467 F.2d 178 (5th Cir.), cert. denied 409 U.S. 1109, 93 S.Ct. 912, 34 L.Ed.2d 690 (1972); United States v. Nationwide Trailer Rental System, Inc., 156 F.Supp. 800 (D.Kan.1957).

even referring to them as boycotts.[3] Others, while not explicitly analogizing to boycotts, state or imply that any concerted refusal to deal is unlawful.[4] On the other hand, a number of opinions assert that concerted refusals become illegal only when informed by a purpose to restrain competition or when yielding that effect.[5] The course of wisdom, really, is to recognize that the unadorned concept, concerted refusal to deal, is too mechanistic—too lacking in any specific and intrinsic relationship to competition—to provide a satisfactory basis for any definitive rule. Concerted refusals occur in a wide variety of contexts and for varied purposes, sometimes threatening little if any competitive injury,[6] sometimes ripe with dangerous potential.[7] In analyzing them, we ought to develop some subcategories which are predicated upon purpose and effect.

The extremes are always easiest. If, as in *Hawaiian Oke*,[8] a manufacturer wants for ordinary business reasons to drop one dealer or delivery agent or other service firm and replace it with another, but scale economies at the dealer or agent level preclude it from engaging a new firm unless other manufacturers do also, to develop a concert no wider than reasonably necessary to facilitate such a change ought not to be suspect.[9] If, by contrast, the purpose of the concerted refusal is to tame the competitive conduct of traders at the next vertical level—for example, to oblige dealers to maintain suggested prices, or stay in assigned territories—that purpose and effect, being of its nature blatantly anticompetitive,[10] ought sufficiently to mark the refusal as anticompetitive. It is not that concerted refusals to deal are unlawful; it is that concerted refusals are unlawful when they are used to achieve anticompetitive purposes—purposes which would,

---

3. See, e. g., United States v. Nationwide Trailer Rental System, Inc., 156 F.Supp. 800 (D.Kan.1957).

4. E. g., Standard Oil Co. (Cal.) v. Moore, 251 F.2d 188 (9th Cir. 1957), cert. denied 356 U.S. 975, 78 S.Ct. 1139, 2 L.Ed.2d 1148 (1958); Cowen v. New York Stock Exch., 256 F.Supp. 462 (N.D.N.Y.1966), aff'd 371 F.2d 661 (2d Cir. 1967); United States v. Southern Wholesale Grocer's Ass'n, 207 F. 434 (N.D.Ala.1913).

5. Joseph E. Seagram & Sons, Inc. v. Hawaiian Oke & Liquors, Ltd., 416 F. 2d 71 (9th Cir. 1969), cert denied 396 U.S. 1062, 90 S.Ct. 752, 24 L.Ed.2d 755 (1970); GAF Corp. v. Circle Floor Co., 329 F.Supp. 823 (S.D.N.Y1971), aff'd 463 F.2d 752 (2d Cir. 1972); Denver Rockets v. All-Pro Management, Inc., 325 F.Supp. 1049 (C.D.Cal.1971).

6. Joseph E. Seagram & Sons, Inc. v. Hawaiian Oke & Liquors, Ltd., 416 F. 2d 71 (9th Cir. 1969), cert. denied 396 U.S. 1062, 90 S.Ct. 752, 24 L.Ed.2d 755 (1970).

7. E.g., Paramount Famous Lasky Corp. v. United States, 282 U.S. 30, 51 S.Ct. 42, 75 L.Ed. 145 (1930).

8. 416 F.2d 71 (9th Cir. 1969), cert. denied 396 U.S. 1062, 90 S.Ct. 752, 24 L. Ed.2d 755 (1970).

9. See also Interborough News Co. v. Curtis Publishing Co., 225 F.2d 289 (2d Cir. 1955); Instant Delivery Corp. v. City Stores Co., 284 F.Supp. 941 (E.D.Pa.1968); Parmelee Transportation Co. v. Keeshin, 186 F.Supp. 533 (N.D.Ill.1960), aff'd 292 F.2d 794 (9th Cir.), cert. denied 368 U.S. 944, 82 S. Ct. 376, 7 L.Ed.2d 340 (1961).

10. United States v. Arnold, Schwinn & Co., 388 U.S. 365, 87 S.Ct. 1856, 18 L. Ed.2d 1249 (1967).

in point of fact, be unlawful even if achieved by a single manufacturer through agreement with its dealers and without any horizontal agreement.[11]

Where concerted refusals to deal are intended to enforce concerted bargaining demands, as in the tour agency hypothetical, a court might make legality turn upon whether or not the underlying concerted bargaining would be legal.[12] Indeed, any time that concerted bargaining is undertaken, a concerted refusal to deal may implicitly be the sanction if agreement is not reached. While such a formulation may be sufficient, it ought not to obscure the difference to be discerned between an effort by a Florida hotel association to negotiate the terms of a standard contract with an association of tour operators and a decision taken by the same hotel operators to cut out a single tour operator unless it pays debts for which it has no legal responsibility. Though this way of marking the distinction may seem unduly fuzzy, the latter conduct displays a coercive character which the former lacks. If we try to specify what makes it so, we come upon the lack of any pretense in the hypothetical involving the bankrupt tour operator that the market power of the hotel association is only countervailing. Because it is not, the hypothetical is an example of power being gained by concert and then being targeted on a single, less powerful trader, which must give in or be excluded from the market. We allude here to differences in the quality of life in the marketplace which industrial organization economics aids us little to understand. The law, therefore, falls back on its own resources, its own conceptions about differences between negotiation and coercion.[13]

Concerted refusals not amounting to a boycott will be lawful or not depending on purpose or effect. If the purpose is one which itself is plainly anticompetitive, the concerted refusal will be held invalid without nice inquiry as to power and effect. If the purpose is a plainly lawful one, the concerted action will be lawful unless analysis shows that, regardless of purpose, anticompetitive effects are threatened. If the purpose is one which may threaten competition if achieved by a group with power, but which will not threaten competition if achieved by a group without power, a structural analysis will be necessary. But it may be a truncated one. For example, if some oil companies combined to withhold sales of gasoline in an effort to coerce legislative change in national energy policy, the degree of power obviously being exercised and the seriousness of the injury to commerce would warrant holding the arrangement unlawful.[14] Similarly,

11. See §§ 163–169 infra.

12. See § 102 supra.

13. Compare Landon v. Twentieth Century-Fox Film Corp., 384 F.Supp. 450 (S.D.N.Y.1974). It should be emphasized that one of the reasons the law seeks to protect competition is to assure individual traders access to the market and freedom to make trading decisions without coercion or undue restraint.

14. In Chapter 9 the extent to which concerted activity seeking governmen-

if a group of anesthesiologists concertedly withheld services to induce legislative action regarding malpractice insurance rates, though the impact on interstate commerce would be less,[15] the degree of market power being concertedly exercised would be similar; therefore, this conduct also would seem to be injurious in its effect on the market.[16]

§ 104. Joint Agencies for Buying or Selling

Section 77 showed that the appointment by competitors of a joint agent to buy or sell may be characterized as price fixing and thus *per se* unlawful. If the agent, by setting a single price for all and allocating orders, will terminate price competition among participants and if, on a preliminary structural analysis, it appears that the participating firms possess market power, no further inquiry need be made.[1] Such cases demonstrate the way in which *per se* analysis shades into rule of reason analysis; a structural analysis, however truncated, must take place to determine purpose and effect before a decision is made to apply or withhold the price fixing characterization. In any event, it is clear that some joint arrangements to sell or buy will not be summarily held to be unlawful, either because common prices are not intended or because summary analysis does not suggest a degree of market power which clearly demands that integration benefits be forbidden because price competition will be reduced. Joint agency cases such as these must be analyzed under the rule of reason, fully blown.[2]

If a homogeneous product is involved and common prices are intended, the effect of the arrangement turns largely on the degree of market power present. If power there be in the agent, the price can be raised and production allocated; the agency, though seeming to be responding unilaterally to the market, will in fact be performing the functions of a cartel for its members. Hence, even if power is not manifest on truncated analysis, if a more detailed inquiry were to show the existence of significant power, it would plainly invite the conclusion that the arrangement is an unreasonable restraint. Even if there are real and demonstrable integration efficiencies, these should not be purchased at the expense of reduced price competition; and surely no array of justifications focusing on "competitive evils"

---

tal action is exempt from the antitrust laws is discussed.

15. Chapter 9 also discusses the extent to which commerce must be affected for the antitrust laws to operate.

16. But cf. American Brands, Inc. v. National Ass'n of Broadcasters, 308 F.Supp. 1166 (D.D.C.1969).

1. Virginia Excelsior Mills, Inc. v. FTC, 256 F.2d 538 (4th Cir. 1958); United States v. American Smelting & Ref. Co., 182 F.Supp. 834 (S.D.N.Y. 1960).

2. See, e.g., Appalachian Coals, Inc. v. United States, 288 U.S. 344, 53 S.Ct. 471, 77 L.Ed. 825 (1933); United States v. Columbia Pictures Corp., 189 F.Supp. 153 (S.D.N.Y.1960); Webster County Memorial Hosp., Inc. v. United Mine Workers of Am. Welfare & Retirement Fund of 1950, 536 F.2d 419 (D.C.Cir. 1976).

which are being brought under control should be taken seriously as counterweights to reduced price competition.[3] Neither, if significant power over price is being exercised, should a "countervailing power" argument be admissible.[4] By contrast, if a detailed analysis confirms the truncated one and the conclusion is that the common agency lacks power, to forbid the joint activity would be to foreclose the opportunity for efficiencies without producing any social gains.[5]

Because the quality of decision will be in degree with the quality of the evaluation of the existence of market power, the analytical tools fashioned in the analysis of monopoly issues must be sharpened and put to work. The truncated structural analysis which permits some selling agency arrangements to be labeled price fixing and *per se* unlawful will only suffice when implications of power are overwhelming. Elsewhere, courts should proceed with care and should evaluate the alternative ways of perceiving product and geographic markets, noting concentration levels, probing for entry barriers, sensing, if you will, the dynamic of the varied forces which on the one hand goad members of the industry toward rivalry and on the other beckon them to accord. If the proposed selling or buying agency would materially increase concentration and if as a result the balance of forces would shift significantly away from rivalry and toward accord, the arrangement should be rejected as unreasonable. Just as surely, if competition could be expected to continue unabated, or even to improve, the rule of reason will mandate that the market's manner of striving for efficiency not be choked off. It is not enough that structural features be described, they must be interpreted so that the dynamic can be understood.[6]

Suppose, for example, that the proposal is to form a common buying agency to purchase raw materials for twenty firms of about equal size representing 10% of the capacity for the production of a homogeneous product sold to consumers. If the firms, which presently average .5% of capacity each, are typical in size of other firms in the industry, if entry barriers exist, and if firms in this industry are the sole users of some of the raw materials to be purchased, the case for forbidding the change in structure is overwhelming. The aggregation of buying power is obviously substantial; the agency will represent about one-tenth of the demand from all sources for the products it is buying. Even though real efficiencies are attained by means of this larger buying unit, a reasoned judgment would shrink

---

3. But cf. Appalachian Coals, Inc. v. United States, 288 U.S. 344, 53 S.Ct. 471, 77 L.Ed. 825 (1933).

4. See § 102 supra.

5. Compare United States v. Columbia Pictures Corp., 189 F.Supp. 153 (S.D. N.Y.1960).

6. A court might take as suggestive authority cases indicating whether, given the degree of concentration and the market shares involved, a merger between the firms involved would be unlawful. See generally Chapter 7, infra.

from seeing them gained at such a cost in concentration.[7] Moreover, if the product, though homogenized, is one which has not yet been (but is capable of being) differentiated by brand name through advertising, the cooperation started for buying purposes might be extended to the development of a common brand name and mark, and an advertising campaign. The cooperating firms, representing 10% of a consumer goods market, might learn to exercise power as sellers as well as buyers. We need only think of the way bleach, flour, sugar, salt and aspirin are marketed to recognize that homogeneity is not proof against product differentiation for consumer goods.

Now suppose that the twenty firms, each with .5% of capacity, are fringe firms in an industry where the largest firm has 31% of capacity and four others have, respectively, 22, 15, 12 and 10%. Suppose further that these larger firms, due to real efficiencies of scale, are able to buy raw materials for significantly less than the fringe firms. And suppose, finally, that there are no significant barriers to entry, and that sellers of the raw materials used in the industry have numerous other buyers for their products so that the industry, as a whole, takes only about 10% of the output of these sellers. It is sometimes argued that whenever substantial concentration exists in a market, competition can be improved by facilitating consolidation of smaller firms so that they achieve a size which permits them to compete as equals with larger ones,[8] a position we shall examine more fully in discussing mergers.[9] We need not go that far in order to conclude that on facts like those supposed, the joint buying agency is not only reasonable, but salutory. The participants gain little if any power, but achieve efficiencies which are well-nigh essential to their survival as a competitive force.

We have been engaged in structural analysis. If *Appalachian Coals* contains anything of direct interest today about the legality of sales and purchase agencies, it is the suggestion that in rule of reason analysis, as in dealing with monopoly questions, a performance analysis may serve to deepen judgment. The usual way to dispose of *Appalachian Coals* today is to say that the Court concluded that the agency would lack power and that given the structural statistics this conclusion is doubtful at best, so that in that sense the case was probably wrong or of doubtful authority; but that if lack of power be assumed, the conclusion that the agency was lawful was a proper one. To say this is to preserve doctrinal purity by burying the real tensions which radiate from that decision.

The bituminous industry was made up of many small producers. There were over 7000 firms mining coal, none accounting for more

---

7. United States v. American Smelting & Ref. Co., 182 F.Supp 834 (S.D.N.Y. 1960). F.Supp. 867, 932 (S.D.N.Y.1965); E. Singer, Antitrust Economics 125–31 (1968).

8. See discussion in United States v. Manufacturers Hanover Trust Co., 240

9. See § 204 infra.

than 3%, and the 200 largest aggregating less than 50% of output. Exit and entry were frequent and, respectively, painful and easy.[10] As a sales agent, Appalachian would represent 137 miners which produced about 12% of all output and 75% of output from the Appalachian region. It must be recognized that a significant increase in concentration was proposed, particularly in light of the fact that producers in other regions saw this as a test case and might follow suit.[11] One can no doubt argue that price competition will remain lively among five or six aggregations of 10 or 12 percent of capacity each and a vast array of small producers representing the remaining 40% or so of national capacity, but that kind of argument is not what moved Justice Hughes to his conclusion. His opinion is replete with the conviction that the industry, as organized in small units, was performing badly. Over-expansion and excessive capacity were rampant,[12] and industry reaction was not rational contraction but prolonged periods of selling below fully allocated cost and other wasteful practices.[13] The Chief Justice obviously felt these things and was ill-disposed to frustrate an effort to alter the structure in ways which industry members contended would improve performance. A higher degree of concentration may not be a reliable prescription for better performance; but that, surely, is what moved the Court. If we are to learn from the case we ought to come to terms with the view of the Chief Justice and of those economists who would propose a theoretical rationale for the strong connection [14] he intuitively drew between competitive structure and poor performance.

Let us immediately concede that an industry composed of many small producers does not necessarily yield performance of the quality for which we value competition. The ideal requires other features also and these were missing in coal. Vertically adjacent sectors should also be competitively organized, information about price, output and other relevant matters should be freely available to buyers and sellers, there should be no frictions inhibiting market adjustments, such as a work force incapable or unwilling to move to other employments. But it is necessary to go beyond saying this, to go beyond that optimistic affirmation of change which infuses the Hughes opinion, if we are to draw from performance analysis any rational help in resolving rule of reason issues. In theorizing about how a market works, we must draw primarily on structural data. The possible ways of using performance data wisely in rule of reason cases

10. Hamilton & Wright, The Case of Bituminous Coal 41–49, 62–66 (1926).

11. Appalachian Coals, Inc. v. United States, 288 U.S. 344, 364–65, 53 S.Ct. 471, 475–76, 77 L.Ed. 825, 832 (1933).

12. Hamilton & Wright, supra note 10, at 263.

13. 288 U.S. at 364–65, 53 S.Ct. at 475–76, 77 L.Ed. at 832.

14. See A. Phillips, Market Structure, Organization and Performance 119–37 (1962).

are limited. The most obvious is to check performance data for consistency with hypotheses developed on the basis of structure. Suppose, for example, that a group of firms had been operating a joint selling agent, that there were two plausible ways the geographic market might be defined, and that use of one resulted in a high concentration ratio while use of the other did not. If an examination of performance established that the selling agent was allocating orders at levels below actual production by member firms, or that profits of member firms were high, we would conclude that the narrow definition was accurate and that power was present. If, however, the agent sold all that members produced and if profits of members were low, we would conclude that the wider market definition was the proper one, and that no significant power had been attained.

Appalachian Coals implies the possibility of a different but related use for performance data. Let us assume for a moment that performance may in some situations be improved by altering structure in a way which increases concentration. This might be the case where fringe firms, combining through a sales agent, gain economies which enable them to compete more aggressively, thus reducing market power of leading firms. Or it might be the case, and it may have been in bituminous coal, if numerous though small sellers fail to obtain decent market information and if larger selling organizations, by obtaining good information promptly, would improve performance. Whenever a situation like this is claimed to be present it becomes useful to evaluate the performance being yielded by the market before the selling agency begins to operate. If that performance is demonstrably poor and if the proposed change in structure, such as the use of a selling agency, holds promise of improving it, the case under the rule of reason for permitting the change in structure is enhanced.

A caveat is now in order. Whenever an industry performs badly under its existing structure, an analysis like that presented above, intemperately used, could become a rationale for allowing nearly any change. The hopeful contention would be that no change could make performance worse and any change might improve things. This, to be blunt about it, is about what the Hughes analysis in *Appalachian Coals* comes down to. We propose here no such unreasoned optimism. The proponent of an increase in concentration as a means for improving performance ought to be armed with theory about why performance is poor under the present structure and how the proposed changes will improve matters. To carry the day, that theory should be intrinsically plausible, consonant with the main body of theoretical knowledge, and consistent with all the facts available about the relevant markets. We cannot expect to improve performance by increasing concentration to levels where substantial market power is created, and the presumption ought always to be against any increase in concentration which begins to approach levels where discernible power is likely to be attained. The essence of this position can be conveyed by asserting that a joint sales agent, operating on behalf of a substantial number of sellers in an industry of many small sellers, could function very much like an organized exchange; so long as there remained a substantial, competing supply, and the agent sold all the product produced and offered by its principals rather than manipulating price and allocating sales, it would not hurt competition and could improve it by facilitating the flow of information and helping to integrate demand and supply in a single market.

We have looked at ramifications of structural and performance analysis, pointing out some of the ways in which a judgment might be made about whether competition would be adversely affected. We have thus far assumed without much discussion that the consolidation into a sales agency will yield real efficiencies, but that itself may be a doubtful matter. The proponents may really be seeking to establish the agency not to gain efficiencies but to gain market power. If the presence or absence of power can be confidently affirmed on the basis of a structural analysis (or such an analysis supplemented by a performance analysis), it will be unnecessary to examine critically the efficiency claims. If power is not obtained, the entrepreneurial judgment about efficiency ought to be respected. If power is attained, proof of associated efficiencies should not validate it. Unfortunately, problems of power may remain screened in ambiguities which neither structural or performance analysis can easily penetrate. If the court remains in doubt about whether power is present, it would seem appropriate to scan critically the efficiency claims. If defendants can convincingly demonstrate significant cost savings and if it appears doubtful that power is present in a degree which would distort competition, the appropriate judgment would seem to be to allow the joint activity to go forward, to choose the demonstrated good at the risk of the uncertain harm. But if the evidence about efficiency leaves as much doubt as did that about the effect on price competition, the reasonable judgment would be to decline to accept the risk —which, if it eventuated, would be a serious one—in the service of an equally problematical gain. If both the harm (reduced price competition) and the gain (integration efficiency) were certain, the harm would outweigh the benefit and the proposed joint arrangement would be held unlawful. No different result is warranted if instead of being equally certain, the harm and the benefit are equally in doubt.

Somewhat different considerations surface when a common agent or resale outlet, say a liquor distributor, sells differentiated products of competing manufacturers. These arrangements, very common in retailing and even among wholesalers in many industries, are assumed to be competitively harmless, indeed preferable to exclusive distributorships which may make it more difficult for a new manufacturer to enter. Thus, they go unchallenged. This common wisdom is probably right in most instances, but not always. At the retail level, scale economies for many kinds of products demand this kind of an arrangement; we could not have a separate grocer for each brand of cereal or a separate liquor store for each brand of scotch. Also, retail outlets serve to make a market where consumers can compare the offerings of various manufacturers. While joint distributor efficiencies in wholesaling are less obvious, they too are no doubt real, and there is at least something to the notion that the potential for obtaining part of the effort of a multiline distributor makes it easier to enter than it would be if exclusive distribution had to be attracted. But there is, in the wholesale case at least, something to be said on the other side. Use of common distributors may result in two manufacturers sharing, on a basis assigned by their common distributor, rather than competing for many of the promotional advantages which an aggressive distributor seeks, such as preferred display space at retail outlets, and the like. And if two manufacturers have an identical dealership structure, each using the same dealer in every region, there may be tendencies for their relative market shares to become more rigid. If the manufacturers involved represent a significant part of the market as a whole, obviously there is cause for concern. The point to be made is that the rule of reason does apply and, even though joint distributor arrangements are presumptively valid for differentiated products, in particular cases analysis may show that dangers are significant. In such cases if scale efficiencies proved to be small, or if less restrictive ways of attaining them are apparent, a conclusion of invalidity would be indicated.

§ 105. Joint Research

When two or more competing firms combine to conduct or support research, there are several potential benefits which are cognizable under the rule of reason. First, scale economies may be achieved which make it feasible to carry out projects beyond the reach of any of the participating firms acting alone. A number of factors combine to enhance the likelihood of such a gain from joint activity of this kind. No firm will be motivated to do research unless the present discounted value of anticipated profits or savings from new products or techniques are higher than the costs which must be incurred. Uncertainty will tend to increase the discount; and potential profits or savings, as well as being functions of other factors, will tend to vary with the relative size of the firm in relation to its market. Thus, the maximum research investment which would make sense for a firm with a modest share of its product market may, in absolute terms, be fairly small. Moreover, research and development inputs, particularly the more sophisticated ones, tend to be indivisible below a fairly large absolute size. It is not that one cannot employ half a chemist; perhaps one can. But it may well be that the minimum level for efficient functioning requires a team of chemists and some fairly elaborate and expensive laboratory equipment. Because of these conditions, joint activity may be the only way to make adequate research accessible to small firms in an industry. And this may not merely mean facilitating their entry into a new and collateral activity; adequate research may be essential to enable the small firms to stay in the industry at all. In short, doing research may be competitively essential in industries with sophisticated technology and the scale essential for such research may be a crucial entry barrier which can be hurdled, at least partially, by joint research activity.

Second, wasteful duplication may be avoided by joint research. That research is unlike most production and distribution functions in this respect can be quickly demonstrated. Assume that it takes $10,000 of time and materials to produce a widget. Now contrast the situation where two firms each produce a widget with that where two firms combine and share the cost of producing one. The aggregate value of what is produced where two firms each bear the cost and produce alone is sure to be higher than what is produced by the two firms acting jointly. Two widgets may or may not be worth twice as much (or more) than one widget; but two will surely be worth something more than one. But suppose we were considering a research function: contrast the situation where two firms each expend $10,000, the cost of time and material to produce the *idea* or *concept* of a widget with that where the two firms combine and share the $10,000 cost of producing that idea. Here, what is produced by the firms acting separately for twice the expenditure has no value greater than that which they jointly produced for half the aggregate expenditure each.

Third, joint research may often be carried out in ways that facilitate a wider distribution of technology than would result from research conducted by a single firm. For example, if research were carried out by a trade association, its output would normally be accessible to all members on a nondiscriminatory and reasonable basis, and association membership will normally be open to all industry members. Even if joint research is carried on under less comprehensive auspices, such as a joint venture of ten or twelve firms, there will be at least ten or twelve firms that share in the resulting technology.

Because of these possible advantages of joint research and because research is itself something of a sacred cow (in that it often seems to be assumed that we cannot have too much of it) joint research is sometimes talked about as though it presented no competitive problems. In United States v. Line Material Co.,[1] the Court sounded this note when it said that there could be no objection to joint research either on the ground of its scale or thoroughness. Analysis suggests, however, that joint research may injure competition as well as help it. The most salient fact is that competition can

---

[1]. 333 U.S. 287, 310, 68 S.Ct. 550, 562, 92 L.Ed. 701, 713 (1948).

be a spur to efficiency in research as to efficiency in other functions; jointness may substitute a large, lazy research program for several individual programs at least some of which are spare and imaginative. In discussing benefits, we noted the possibility of wasteful duplication where research efforts compete. But competing research activities need not be races toward the same end; they may pursue different lines of inquiry in different ways and go off in different directions.

Secondly, joint activity may reduce total research investment to a level below that which would be sustained if joint programs were inhibited. In part this reduction will reflect avoidance of duplication; but in part it will also reflect joint decision making about the proper level of research investment. As the threat of being outstripped is reduced, so will be the incentive to invest in research; even if firms continue to strive to some extent with individual projects as well as joint ones, a different and perhaps socially less valuable resource allocation will result from any joint decision about the level of research than would result from independent ones. In part this will reflect the tendency, indicated above, for firms in making judgments about the level of research expenditure to give considerable present value to the potential for exclusivity, which is lost in a joint program. If the participating firms would be capable of, and motivated toward, individual research were their joint activity precluded, then the change in the aggregate level of research represents a distortion in resource allocation from the competitive ideal.

Thirdly, though (as suggested among possible benefits) joint research may tend to a wider dispersal of technology, the actual dispersal pattern could in particular instances be harmful to competition. Suppose that five substantial firms in a twenty firm industry were to join in research at a scale which the remaining firms could not attain. If other firms are not permitted to join the group and if research output is confined to the group, the participating firms might by combining attain a decisive advantage over the firms excluded.[2] The significance of the beneficial tendencies and of the harmful tendencies of joint research will vary with the setting and, particularly, with the market power of participant firms—with, if you will, the industry structure.[3] If the joint researchers are a small part of a large market, negative effects may be trivial and substantially outweighed by benefits. By contrast, if the joint researchers represent all or most of the firms in a market, the dangers loom larger; at a minimum, there is thrust forward the question whether scale economies in research are real and, if so, whether attaining them requires so large a unit—whether there are not less restrictive ways to attain the benefits claimed for the joint program.

---

2. Compare Associated Press v. United States, 326 U.S. 1, 65 S.Ct. 1416, 89 L.Ed. 2013 (1945).

3. See Turner, Patents, Antitrust and Innovation, 28 U.Pitt.L.Rev. 151 (1966).

The last of the potential harms is a special case. It occurs only in research, increasingly common in this age of ecological concern, aimed at finding ways to control undesirable side effects of an industry's activities. Examples would be auto industry research on reducing exhaust poisons or airline industry research aimed at noise reduction.[4] The unique aspect of research of this kind is that the economic self-interest of the industry considered as an interdependent whole is injured if the research is successful; though one firm may gain on others if it achieves a technological breakthrough which others do not accomplish, the industry as a whole can only suffer from this success. Because of these unique circumstances, the reasons for which are set out below, joint research may facilitate an interdependent effort to keep research investment low and to avoid success.

When research is directed at finding ways to inhibit harmful side effects, successful results will tend to shift costs of the industry activities from the public at large to the industry's customers. Thus, if an emission control device is added to a car engine, the car buyer must pay for it; but the payment buys nothing that improves the car's performance, but something likely to injure performance, making the car less efficient and more costly to operate. The car buyer is paying for something which is as much in the interest of his neighbors as himself, whether or not they too drive cars. Before the device was invented, part of the "cost" of driving the car was, in the form of air pollution, "externalized,"—that is, shifted to the public at large. The device, by reducing pollution at the expense of car buyers, "internalizes" this cost, puts it upon car drivers, like the cost of tires or fuel.

Increased costs, other things being equal, will reduce sales. The smog device will from the vantage point of a car buyer leave other things largely unchanged. The device, or, rather, the fact that every car has one, helps the public at large, but the device on any one driver's car does little to improve that driver's overall welfare and on balance, probably injures it. The ideal state for the single car buyer would be for all other cars to be equipped with smog devices, but not his own. In consequence, car sales will be lower—and industry profits lower—if research on smog devices is successful and these devices are added to cars. Why then, should firms in the industry research these problems at all, either individually or jointly? Bluntly, such research takes place only when the industry is under pressure from the public at large, exercised largely through government, to do something to internalize the cost. If that pressure were to abate, industry self-interest would dictate that the research abate also.

Posner argues that given a single consumer's interest in not himself having a smog device, but in seeing others have them, the individu-

---

4. See United States v. Automobile Mfrs. Ass'n., 307 F.Supp. 617 (D.C. Cal.1969), aff'd per curiam sub nom. City of New York v. United States, 397 U.S. 248, 90 S.Ct. 1105, 25 L.Ed.2d 280 (1970).

al manufacturer will see it as advantageous to be the last to install these devices. He infers that joint research will thus reduce foot-dragging and speed up research output.[5] But it seems just as likely that the single firm will find advantage in winning the research race, so long as the spur of public concern and public regulation is applied. Without that spur, no research will be done in any event. With it, if the research is not joint, a single firm which got out in front of the rest of the industry might attain patent rights of value or might obtain an increased share of the car market by being the first firm to attain to the smog control standard mandated by public regulation. Such rights might be valuable enough to put the successful firm in a better position than it was in originally; patent royalties or an increased market share might offset losses resulting from reduced industry sales consequent on the price increase. In any event, the individual firm will be far better off if it is collecting the royalties than if it is paying them. Though it is plainly in the interest of the industry as a whole that the problem not be solved, it is also in the interest of each firm that if the problem is going to be solved at all, it be in the vanguard.

Moreover, even if Posner is right in inferring that without joint research little will be done, he is surely wrong in assuming that the joint research will generate effective research. Given the basic incentives and constraints, it seems clear, at least if the industry is oligopolistic and sufficiently tightly structured to permit of interdependent responses, that joint research is dangerous indeed to the public. When they meet governmental pressure to control externalities, firms in such an industry will face a dilemma and will be pulled in two directions. Each will realize that no research success will be a satisfactory solution for it, and may be the optimum solution. Each will realize that research success by it alone will be a satisfactory solution for it and perhaps optimal. Each will realize also that research success if shared among it and other firms will be a not very satisfactory solution for it; it will reduce profits of all. Each will realize, finally, that success by another firm alone, a success from which it is excluded, will be the worst result for it; it would then face not only a less profitable market overall, but the risk of losing part of its share and the need to pay out substantial patent royalties. In this situation the temptation to act concertedly or interdependently to foreclose or delay research success will be substantial. But interdependent action will be to some extent inhibited; each firm will feel exposed to danger if it slows down its own research, and thus runs the risk of a success from which it is excluded. Firms are likely to push forward if the tendencies toward individual action predominate, but to collectively drag their feet if solid assurance that no firm is "cheating" by rac-

---

5. R. Posner, Antitrust Cases, Economic Notes and Other Materials 319–20 (1974).

ing ahead on its own can be obtained. Therefore, if firms research alone, and without overt collusion, there is a strong likelihood that each, doubtful of the other's restraint, will race to achieve its own success. On the other hand, if joint research is permitted, the industry will be supplied with a medium through which concerted decisions can be made, through which each may be able to obtain reasonable assurance that it is not being outdistanced, and through which each may be able to police what others are doing. A low level of investment and delay in achieving results then becomes the more likely, probably the most likely solution.

Given that the public may be harmed by joint research in some instances, a rule of *per se* legality for such activity would be inappropriate. If joint research programs are challenged under Section 1, courts must evaluate harms and benefits under the rule of reason, taking account of the implications of industry structure.

§ 106. Joint Activities in Making a Market

There are few ways in which joint action among competitors can improve competition. One is by integrating production, distribution, research or other functions to attain significant efficiencies. Another is by rationalizing a market which is competitive in major structural aspects but which is performing poorly because of clogs on information flows or as a result of other frictions. The third is to achieve a wider integration of market transactions, to bring more transactions into a single market. This "market making" type of integration may be achieved indirectly; it may result from joint action in any of several ways. Thus, joint action which reduces entry barriers (e.g., by making patents widely available or by providing cheaper transportation between regions or the like) will have the effect of increasing the extent of integration. Better market integration may also be achieved by standardizing product, or warranties, or other non-price terms, or standardizing ancillary services and facilities, so that buyers will be able to more easily compare alternative offerings on the basis of price. If the market is basically competitive, any such action will tend to improve competition by indirectly enhancing the degree of integration. Greater market integration may also be brought about directly and explicitly by establishing an organized exchange, a bid depository, or a system of auctions. It is to these direct efforts that we now turn. As in other situations where a claim of benefit is made, analysis is required to detect its presence and evaluate its force. Walls which channel the flow of supply and demand in a particular direction preclude their flowing into other channels or flooding over the plain; whether this yields socially adverse or beneficial results can be determined only after analysis.

It has long been clear both that it is no offense to establish an organized exchange or market where no purpose or effect to restrain trade are discernible,[1] and that, where such a purpose or effect is discerned, the fact that it is achieved through the formation or operation of an organized market is no defense.[2] Making a market is neither a suspect nor an exempt activity; like other commercial activity it can be helpful or harmful to competition depending on the commercial setting and the particulars of all relevant conduct and must be judged accordingly. Thus, if a market is established or used as a device for price fixing, or for excluding competitors, that conduct is plainly unlawful.[3]

When activities of a market, an exchange, a depository or an auction warehouse are challenged under the Sherman Act, the appropriate analytical response is to recognize that the function of the market is to facilitate commerce, to provide a medium in which sellers and buyers can meet. Without question, the market can be regulated to establish reasonable trading hours and the like. Also, *Chicago Board of Trade* [4] teaches that a limited restraint on trading activity outside of the market may not be objectionable, so long as it helps to perfect the market by channelling more transactions into it, and so long as there are sufficient outside trading opportunities so that drawing some of those that exist into the market will not deprive traders who stay outside of a reasonable number of trading options. A court must obviously evaluate critically any restraint which cuts off or penalizes outside trading; if the market would without it have sufficient transactions for competitive prices to govern, market rules which including this type of restraint would be more restrictive than necessary to achieve the advantages available from the market and thus would be invalid.[5] Nor is it only the impact of market activities on sales which take place on the market to which the law is sensitive.

1. United States v. New York Coffee & Sugar Exch., 263 U.S. 611, 44 S.Ct. 225, 68 L.Ed. 475 (1924).

2. United States v. Tarpon Springs Sponge Exch., 142 F.2d 125 (5th Cir. 1944); United States v. New England Fish Exch., 258 F. 732 (D.Mass.1919).

3. Silver v. New York Stock Exch., 373 U.S. 341, 83 S.Ct. 1246, 10 L.Ed.2d 389 (1963); see also Maryland & Virginia Milk Producers Ass'n v. United States, 362 U.S. 458, 80 S.Ct. 847, 4 L.Ed.2d 880 (1960); Allen Bradley Co. v. Local Union No. 3, IBEW, 325 U.S. 797, 65 S.Ct. 1533, 89 L.Ed. 1939 (1945); Georgia v. Pennsylvania R. Co., 324 U.S. 439, 65 S.Ct. 716, 89 L.Ed. 1051 (1945); United States v. Borden Co., 308 U.S. 188, 60 S.Ct. 182, 84 L.Ed. 181 (1939); United States v. Pacific & Arctic R. & Navigation Co., 228 U.S. 87, 33 S.Ct. 443, 57 L.Ed. 742 (1913); Gulf Coast Shrimpers & Oystermans Ass'n v. United States, 236 F.2d 658 (5th Cir.), cert. denied 352 U.S. 927, 77 S.Ct. 225, 1 L.Ed.2d 162 (1956).

4. 246 U.S. 231, 38 S.Ct. 242, 62 L.Ed. 683 (1918); see § 66 supra.

5. Christiansen v. Mechanical Contractors Bid Depository, 230 F.Supp. 186 (D.Utah 1964), aff'd 352 F.2d 817 (10th Cir. 1965), cert. denied 384 U.S. 918, 86 S.Ct. 1365, 16 L.Ed.2d 439 (1966). But cf. United States v. Morgan, 118 F.Supp. 621, 689 (S.D.N.Y. 1953) holding, in reliance upon *Chicago Board of Trade*, that syndicated underwriting of new securities issues did not violate the rule of reason, even though the potential for competition in underwriting was greatly reduced.

The market may also enhance or reduce competition in secondary functions, like brokerage, and the reasonableness of any regulations affecting these activities must also be evaluated.[6] It now seems clear enough that a rule of a market which purports to fix the brokerage commission on market transactions is *per se* invalid [7] unless there is a statutory exemption which authorizes such regulation of rates.[8]

The bid depository and the tobacco warehouse cases suggest the scope of permissible regulation of primary transactions in the market. Bid depositories are set up, typically by or at the instigation of subcontractors' trade associations, as facilities for receiving, opening, tabulating, and passing on to general contractors the bids of various subcontractors on subparts of public and private contracts upon which general contractors will be bidding.[9] In a well reasoned opinion, the district court in Christiansen v. Mechanical Contractors Bid Depository [10] held invalid a number of depository rules. One, aimed at precluding general contractors from "shopping" for lower offers after bids were in, would have precluded any general contractor using the depository from using any bid other than those received by the depository. Another required each bidder to bid for all the work in his subtrade or none of it; for example, a bid for only part of the plumbing work on a job would not be accepted. Both of these rules, like that in *Chicago Board of Trade* which discouraged night trading, might be defended on the ground that they serve to perfect the market by drawing all transactions into it so that all demand will square off against all supply. But the court recognized the potential for harm inherent in such rules and found this to outweigh any benefit.

If the firms in a market display any tendencies toward concerted action or interdependence, as do those for some of the subtrades, restraints like those in *Christiansen* may facilitate those tendencies, much as did the circulation of price information in the *Container* case.[11] Suppose, for example, that a convention has been developing among electrical subcontractors that overhead runs about twenty-five

---

6. Silver v. New York Stock Exch., 373 U.S. 341, 83 S.Ct. 1246, 10 L.Ed.2d 389 (1963); Thill Securities Corp. v. New York Stock Exch., 433 F.2d 264 (7th Cir. 1970), cert. denied 401 U.S. 994, 91 S.Ct. 1232, 28 L.Ed.2d 532 (1971); Kaplan v. Lehman Bros., 371 F.2d 409 (7th Cir.), cert. denied 389 U.S. 954, 88 S.Ct. 320, 19 L.Ed.2d 365 (1967).

7. United States v. Sugar Institute, Inc., 15 F.Supp. 817 (S.D.N.Y.1934), aff'd and modified on other grounds 297 U.S. 553, 56 S.Ct. 629, 80 L.Ed. 859 (1936).

8. Kaplan v. Lehman Bros., 371 F.2d 409 (7th Cir.), cert. denied 389 U.S. 954, 88 S.Ct. 320, 19 L.Ed.2d 365 (1967).

9. See generally, Schueller, Bid Depositories, 58 Mich.L.Rev. 497 (1960); Comment, Bid Depository Operation: An Invitation to Boycott?, 114 U.Pa. L.Rev. 231 (1965).

10. 230 F.Supp. 186 (D.Utah 1964), aff'd 352 F.2d 817 (10th Cir. 1965), cert. denied 384 U.S. 918, 86 S.Ct. 1365, 16 L.Ed.2d 439 (1966).

11. United States v. Container Corp. of America, 393 U.S. 333, 89 S.Ct. 510, 21 L.Ed.2d 526 (1969); see § 96 supra.

percent of direct costs for labor and material and that to get a "fair" profit of about ten percent over all costs it is necessary to bid from 37 to 40 percent over direct costs. If all transactions are run through the depository, the tendencies of all firms to act on this perception and so preserve the profit margin of the industry as a whole will be reinforced; the depository system will inhibit the conflicting tendency to "break rules," to "cheat," to "cut corners," which would be encouraged by general contractor bid-shopping. It is dissimilarities of these kinds to which a court must be sensitive when evaluating restrictions which are defended on the ground that they serve to make a market. When the market can be established without the restrictions, permitting the restrictions may serve only to funnel into the market (and into the range of influence of any non-competitive tendencies operative there) maverick transactions which had initially developed outside of the market precisely because they carry out a competitive urge which could be most forcefully expressed outside of the market's constraints.[12]

The tobacco warehouse cases, which are cited elsewhere, pose a slightly different issue.[13] Where two or more markets have been established which perform identical or complementary functions, to what extent may they lawfully agree to stay out of each other's way, to restrict their operations to different times or territories? An arrangement like this could be helpful or harmful to competition, depending on its purpose and effect. It might be a cartel among market operators, a program to share the business of providing market facilities so as to keep the price for such facilities up. It might be aimed at, or have the effect of, limiting competition among brokers. It might be a concerted effort by sellers to limit competition for their product, or of buyers to facilitate concerted or interdependent activity by keeping the volume of business being done at any time at levels which are "orderly." It might be none of these things, but rather a reasonable program for assuring that all interested buyers get an opportunity to participate at every sale.

Structural analysis will be useful in providing a basis for evaluating purpose and effect. But to analyze market making activities fully, it is essential to consider the possibility of an express or implied antitrust exemption. Congress has regulated various marketing activities extensively and, in some instances, has authorized self-regulation of various functions. *Silver* stresses that antitrust exemptions are not to be lightly implied.[14] It insists that a statute which authorizes a private organization such as an exchange to regulate private activities grants no immunity wider than the narrowest one which is

---

12. Compare United States v. Bakersfield Associated Plumbing Contractors, 1958 CCH Trade Cas. ¶ 69,087, modified, 1959 CCH Trade Cas. ¶ 69,266 (S.D.Cal.).

13. See cases cited in § 76, note 2 supra.

14. 373 U.S. 341, 83 S.Ct. 1246, 10 L. Ed.2d 389 (1963).

essential to permit the self-regulatory activity which Congress authorized. The limits of the proposition have, however, already been exceeded. In Gordon v. New York Stock Exchange,[15] the Court upheld an exchange rule fixing minimum commission rates on brokerage. It implied an antitrust exemption on several grounds. By conferring power on the SEC to supervise any exchange rule fixing rates and to supersede any such rule if it chose, the Securities and Exchange Act expresses a congressional decision to validate such rate regulation. Moreover, the SEC had actually exercised its supervisory powers (which, indeed, culminated in an SEC regulation effective May 1, 1975 forbidding the exchange to fix rates thereafter). Legislative history pointed in the same direction and the Court concluded, all things considered, that the exemption had to be implied to facilitate a sensible reading of what Congress had done in establishing the regulatory scheme.[16]

§ 107. Joint Arrangements Concerning Advertising

(a) The Economic Effects of Advertising By a Single Firm

The competitive effects of advertising, whether unilateral or joint, are complex. Consider advertising by a single firm. It provides information which is essential if any market is to function well —who the sellers are, where they can be found, what they have to offer and at what price. Informational advertising of this kind—the newspaper ad or the hand-out which displays the supermarket's wares is perhaps typical—provides information needed by buyers fast and efficiently. But much advertising exceeds this necessity. It aims to hammer home a brand name, or to create a consumer need where none existed; it often seeks to manipulate taste and desire, sometimes subtly, more often by linking a product with a gross appeal to sexual appetite, the need for love and security, the need to feel successful, or fears of various kinds.

Where markets are oligopolistic, advertising may raise entry barriers because heavy advertising expenditures increase the capital needed for entry.[1] Even when these can be scaled, such advertising

---

15. 422 U.S. 659, 95 S.Ct. 2598, 45 L. Ed.2d 463 (1975).

16. See also United States v. National Ass'n of Securities Dealers, Inc., 422 U.S. 694, 95 S.Ct. 2427, 45 L.Ed.2d 486 (1975), where the Court on far more tenuous grounds implied under the Investment Act of 1940 an exemption for restrictive agreements maintaining resale prices and suppressing the development of a secondary market in mutual fund shares. Although the SEC's statutory power to regulate was not patently clear, and although the SEC had never put itself forth to exercise any such power, the Court concluded five to four that unless an exemption were implied defendants might fall under conflicting commands from the SEC and an antitrust court. See § 239 infra.

1. There is considerable controversy about whether, the extent to which, and the manner in which advertising may dampen competition. By and large, the Chicago school economists insist that advertising cannot constitute an entry barrier, while Harvard School analysts, taking a more dynamic view of market interactions

may give established firms a distinct advantage over new entrants. A long continued advertising program may solidify brand loyalty so that a new producer may have to expend substantially more to make the same impact.² Furthermore, in oligopolistic industries advertising may serve as an outlet for the impulse for rivalry, thus helping to preserve interdependent pricing; firms, hoping to improve their share of the market, may prefer to attempt this through advertising, which does not threaten supra-competitive prices beneficial to all in the industry.

Informational advertising takes demand as given. Non-informational advertising assumes that the demand curve of the firm can be shifted, either by increasing the demand for the firm's product at the expense of demand for that of rivals or by increasing demand for the industry's product as a whole. To the extent that it is assumed that the expenditure for products of the class in question—say cigarettes —will be fixed in the aggregate, advertising is aimed at obtaining for the advertiser a larger share. Note, too, that a plan aimed at increasing the firm's share by advertising will in a sense serve to disaggregate rather than to widen the integration of the market. A plea for brand X is a plea to see it differently from brand Y, to regard it as a unique product for which there is no close substitute, as having, if you will, its own, separate market. Of course, defensive advertising—"our brand is as good as theirs"—will have an aggregating, a market integrating effect. So too, advertising aimed at increasing total sales of the industry, if the "industry" is narrowly conceived, will tend to disintegrate markets and build barriers between them. For example, consider an ad by a commercial bank, or an association of such banks, stressing the convenience of placing savings deposits where a checking account is kept. By such an ad the bank hopes to draw savings business from its own checking account customers who presently use a savings bank or savings and loan association. The purpose of such advertising is to draw business across the borders of what, from a broader prospective, might be seen as submarkets of a larger integrated market for savings deposits. If when the program begins consumers see savings banks and commercial banks as competitive alternatives—if, in short, the markets are well integrated—the aim will be to lead them to see "savings accounts at

and recognizing the existence of related imperfections, such as those in capital markets, conclude that advertising can make entry harder. Compare Brozen, "Entry Barriers: Advertising and Product Differentiation" in Industrial Concentration: The New Learning 115 (Goldschmid, Mann & Weston, eds. 1974) with Mann, "Advertising, Concentration, and Profitability," at page 137 of the same volume. See also Comanor & Wilson, Advertising, Market Structure and Performance, 49 Rev. of Econ. & Stat. 423 (1967).

2. FTC v. Procter & Gamble Co., 386 U.S. 568, 87 S.Ct. 1224, 18 L.Ed.2d 303 (1967). Here too, the empirical assumptions are speculative; witness the extent to which advertisers in many consumer goods industries emphasize the new, including the new brand name.

commercial banks" as a separate product from "savings accounts at savings banks," just as brand X advertising is aimed at leading consumers to see brand X as a different product from brand Y. On the other hand, if saving and loan associations have previously established consumer acceptance for their separate products, the market is already disaggregated in ways beneficial to savings banks, and the aim may be to integrate the market again so that the commercial banks can participate in it.

We must conclude overall that to the extent non-informational advertising succeeds, it often disaggregates markets—it reduces cross-elasticity of demand between products—and by doing so has the effect of increasing concentration. There may be 50 firms making bleach, but only one making brand X. To the extent consumers are led through advertising to a distinct preference for brand X over other, substantially identical bleaches, to that extent is brand X disengaged from the bleach market and established in a separate market which it alone occupies. Moreover, non-informational advertising may generate responding advertising of equal power by brands Y and Z; this may have further disaggregating effects, although wholly defensive advertising, as we have noticed above, can have the opposite effect of leading consumers to think of A's product as competing with B's.

It is sometimes argued that advertising, by increasing demand, reduces the price of the product. Advertising—even non-informational advertising—can increase demand, either at the expense of direct competitors or others. If scale economies are achieved at higher production levels or per unit profits are reduced at higher levels of sales, or both, a firm which attains a higher demand by advertising may be able to sell for less per unit. But, as noted above, advertising may generate comparable advertising levels by competitors, and the result as between existing firms may be a stalemate which merely increases the costs of all. Such a result will raise entry barriers, but it may not increase demand, nor permit price reduction. Moreover, even when advertising does increase demand it does not automatically result in price reduction; prices can be reduced only where scale economies are achieved or per unit profits reduced as a consequence of higher output. And even then, the efficiency gains may not be passed on.

If advertising by the individual firm—which, at one level, can provide useful information—can, at another, disaggregate markets and raise entry barriers, what is to be said about arrangements among competitors either to engage in joint advertising programs or, expressly or interdependently, to raise or to lower individual advertising budgets? Let us first consider joint advertising programs, then turn to agreements respecting individual levels.

(b) Joint Advertising

To some extent, the potentials of joint advertising parallel those of joint research. In pure informational ads, greater efficiency may be attained through joint effort; for example, independently owned food markets in different areas of a city might join in a city-wide newspaper ad and attain greater coverage at lower price than by individually using handbills. So long as price competition was not adversely affected, such a program would be helpful to competition. Also, joint advertising, combined perhaps with a joint trade name, may be a way for small firms to overcome the entry barrier resulting from the large advertising budgets of large firms; so long as avoidable ancillary restraints are not adopted, such a program would help competition.[3] But obviously joint programs could also be harmful. Suppose that numerous small firms making a consumer product offer effective price competition to the four or five large firms in the industry which advertise a brand name. These small firms, the industry's competitive fringe, may be a far more important limitation on the power of the large brand name advertisers than would one more large firm. If the small firms adopt a common brand name and combine to advertise it, they may end by acting much as would one more large firm; they may join an existing cartel or, what seems the greater danger, the existing pattern of interdependent pricing.

While the possible effects of joint advertising will vary with industry structure, the potential dangers seem, in general, to be less profound than with other joint programs. Also, there is a particular difficulty in evaluating the effects of joint advertising which is not present in other joint programs—the purpose and effects of joint advertising depend on the content of the ads. In a structural setting where informational ads or ads aimed at integrating markets would be beneficial, disintegrating ads might be harmful. Yet it is hardly feasible for a court to police conduct in terms of ad content. Because of these factors, joint advertising has been little questioned under the antitrust laws.

(c) Agreements between Competitors about Individual Firm Advertising

Agreements between competing firms about the quantity and content of their individual ads may vary considerably in purpose and effect. An agreement limiting volume, if it were to impose a low enough ceiling, could preclude all but informational ads. No agreement limiting expenditures would likely occur, however, except in an oligopolistic industry; and it would likely be aimed at cutting off wasteful excesses of brand advertising when these have resulted in stalemate on market shares and higher costs for all. By reducing

---

3. Compare United States v. Sealy, Inc., 388 U.S. 350, 87 S.Ct. 1847, 18 L.Ed.2d 1238 (1967) with United States v. Topco Associates, 405 U.S. 596, 92 S.Ct. 1126, 31 L.Ed.2d 515 (1972).

wasteful expenditures, such an agreement might improve resource allocation and reduce prices, though all of the cost savings might go to profits. Also, such an agreement, even though it did not bring expenditures down to the level supporting only informational ads, would surely tend, in however small a degree, to reduce entry barriers. Unless some special circumstances made such an arrangement harmful in unique ways, it ought, on balance, to be lawful.

Ad content agreements, by contrast, would do nothing to aid competition (unless the content limit outlawed all but informational ads, an unlikely situation) and could seriously injure it by limiting competitive options and styles. When such restrictions are discovered they are usually in aid of industry self-regulation of some kind —for example, the extensive ad review program of the cigarette companies intended to outlaw explicit appeals to youth, or the movie industry program aimed at obscenity. Relevant analytical responses have already been suggested.[4]

PART J. CONTRACT, COMBINATION AND CONSPIRACY

§ 108. Introduction

While Section 2 of the Sherman Act deals primarily with single firm power and conduct, Section 1 can be violated only by two separate entities acting in concert, by a "contract, combination or conspiracy" in restraint of trade. Prior sections imply the requisite element of jointness by referring to "concerted" action; now it is time to discuss the extent to which such concert needs to be shown and the ways in which it may be shown. Our interest will extend beyond Section 1. Section 2 may also, although it need not, entail concerted action, first because it forbids conspiracies to monopolize and second because monopolization, the principal Section 2 offense, may be committed not only by one firm but by two or more acting together. We shall begin by considering the statutory terms found in Section 1. Then we shall discuss the law concerning proof of conspiracy by indirect evidence. Finally we shall explore the question whether interdependent conduct may fall within the ambit of the statutory concepts.

§ 109. The Classic Conspiracy

When courts talk about concerted action among competitors they are talking in terms of conduct. The statutory phrase, "contract, combination or conspiracy," conjures up the classic image of robber barons gathering clandestinely to carve up a market. The statute, classically conceived, aims at bad conduct, at conspirators who deliberately decide on evil, who eschew competition, who plan and execute action to stifle market forces and who, conscious of their own wrongdoing, take precaution to hide their conduct or disguise it.

4. See §§ 87 and 88 supra.

Other things are notable about this vision in addition to its conduct orientation. First, it presents a single concept about common action, not three separate ones: "contract * * * combination or conspiracy" becomes an alliterative compound noun, roughly translated to mean "concerted action." There is little need to grapple with issues about the meanings of the particular words of the statute nor to mark nice distinctions among them. Second, the classical concept of concerted action is a horizontal one; it deals with the way competitors relate to each other, not with the way firms relate to their customers or suppliers. Much of what courts say about the meaning of contract, combination or conspiracy in horizontal cases may have bearing in vertical cases, but surely not all; the concept of concerted action goes through a subtle alteration where it reaches not across a single level of distribution, but up and down between two or more such levels. Third, since the core of the classic offense is mutual assent, a mutual commitment to an anticompetitive course, in proving the offense there is no need to show that the course agreed upon had been successfully carried out or that an injury to competition has actually been accomplished. Fourth, since the concept presupposes covert action, we must not expect direct evidence of the offense to be easily accessible; inference from circumstances will often have to do. Only in those few cases (under the rule of reason rather than the *per se* doctrine) where a telling doubt is presented about whether the purpose of the concerted action renders it illegal, could we expect those engaging in the concerted action to do so openly.

We shall consider hereafter whether this classic concept of concerted action is an adequate one, given the purposes of the Act, the structural conditions extant in American industry and the conduct patterns which those structural conditions tend to foster. We shall later consider also whether the statute, its history, and the case law permit wider and different meanings to be derived from the statute, meanings which might usefully supplement this classic one. About these deferred questions there are prominent points in doubt. About what we say more immediately there is little doubt. Section 1 *is* squarely aimed at the classic horizontal conspiracy, engaged in for a purpose which violates the *per se* doctrine or the rule of reason. An examination of the case law will make this clear and will indicate the kind of circumstantial proof which is appropriate.

The early Section 1 cases involved classic conspiracies; the evidence in each showed an express agreement among competitors to engage in a common course of conduct. *Addyston Pipe and Steel*[1] and *Trenton Potteries*[2] exemplify express agreement on the model of the

1. United States v. Addyston Pipe & Steel Co., 85 F. 271 (6th Cir. 1898), modified and aff'd 175 U.S. 211, 20 S.Ct. 96, 44 L.Ed. 136 (1899). See § 64 supra.

2. United States v. Trenton Potteries Co., 273 U.S. 392, 47 S.Ct. 377, 71 L.Ed. 700 (1927). See § 67 supra.

classic cartel. *American Column and Lumber*[3] involved express agreement for common conduct in exchanging price and related data, conduct which, given the balance of its harms and benefits, was unreasonable because of its strong tendency to inhibit price competition and discourage production increases so as to hold market prices up. *Socony-Vacuum*[4] involved express agreement to enter the market and buy from identified "dancing partners," conduct aimed at bolstering market price and therefore characterized as price fixing. A court may in these cases take inferences from indirect evidence in reaching the conclusion that the conspirators entered into an express agreement to follow a given course.[5] And where the course agreed upon is not explicitly to fix prices or divide territories, there may also be, as there was in *Socony-Vacuum*, inference involved in the conclusion that the purpose and effect of what was expressly agreed upon is tantamount to price fixing or market division or that the purpose and effect (though not capable of being assimilated under one of the *per se* violations) is nevertheless unreasonable.[6] Inference, be it understood, may be involved in one or more of several steps in the analysis, in deciding that an agreement took place, in concluding that the agreement which did take place should be characterized in a way which offends a *per se* rule, or in concluding that the agreement is, on balance, unreasonable. But the bottom layer of the analysis is always the finding that concerted action did occur, that conspirators in one way or another dealt with each other, came to terms on a course of conduct to be concertedly followed.

Now two closely related questions emerge. First, given the need for agreement, must it be expressed (as consistently it was in the early cases) or may it be inferred from conduct, as is a contract when a seller says "The horse is yours for $50" and the buyer puts a halter on the horse and walks away? Second, given the need for agreement (whether express or implied), from what kinds of evidence may its presence be inferred? The Court has not discriminated sharply between these questions and much of what has been said about indirect evidence can be read as applying to one of these questions and not the other, or as applying indifferently to both.

That the prerequisite agreement may exist despite the fact that the parties to it have never spelled it out in terms but have each inferred commitment from the others on the basis of conduct is perhaps clear enough as a matter of general principle. It is ancient learning that contractual assent can be inferred from conduct. Surely there is

3. American Column & Lumber Co. v. United States, 257 U.S. 377, 42 S.Ct. 114, 66 L.Ed. 284 (1921). See § 95 supra.

4. United States v. Socony-Vacuum Oil Co., 310 U.S. 150, 60 S.Ct. 811, 84 L. Ed. 1129 (1940). See § 67 supra.

5. United States v. Trenton Potteries Co., 273 U.S. 392, 47 S.Ct. 377, 71 L. Ed. 700 (1927).

6. American Column & Lumber Co. v. United States, 257 U.S. 377, 42 S.Ct. 114, 66 L.Ed. 284 (1921).

no call here, given the motives for clandestine activity, to insist on undertakings more fully expressed than those which in ordinary contractual concourse would end with the participants bound to each other. In any event, much of the language in the cases, though capable of being construed to bear only on the question whether indirect evidence of conspiracy is sufficient, can also be taken to assert that parties may violate Section 1 when each can infer agreement from the conduct of the other, and without any more explicit or specific accord.[7] *Paramount*, in particular, reads well on this point. It states that "it is not necessary to find an express agreement * * * It is enough that a concert of action is contemplated and * * * conformed to * * *."[8] And there is at least one lengthy and persuasive dictum from a court noted both for its experience and its conservatism on antitrust issues which could mean nothing less than that conduct from which the conspirators would infer a forbidden accord is sufficient to constitute the accord which is forbidden.[9]

The other branch of the question is more explicitly settled. Whatever need be shown, be it an express agreement or only an implied one, it may be shown by evidence from which its existence can be inferred. This is the teaching not only of *Eastern States, Interstate Circuit, American Tobacco,* and *Paramount*,[10] but of numerous additional cases.[11] Some of these cases, as we shall later see, may bear more radical interpretations which tell us that in some markets conduct which falls short of consensual accord may violate Section 1; but all of them contain, if nothing more far reaching, at least the assertion that consensual accord can be inferred from circumstantial evidence.[12]

7. Eastern States Retail Lumber Dealers' Ass'n. v. United States, 234 U.S. 600, 34 S.Ct. 951, 58 L.Ed. 1490 (1914); Interstate Circuit, Inc. v. United States, 306 U.S. 208, 59 S.Ct. 467, 83 L.Ed. 610 (1939); American Tobacco Co. v. United States, 328 U.S. 781, 66 S.Ct. 1125, 90 L.Ed. 1575 (1946); United States v. Paramount Pictures, Inc., 334 U.S. 131, 68 S.Ct. 915, 92 L.Ed. 1260 (1948).

8. United States v. Paramount Pictures, Inc., 334 U.S. 131, 142, 68 S.Ct. 915, 921, 92 L.Ed. 1260, 1284 (1948).

9. Esco Corp. v. United States, 340 F. 2d 1000, 1007 (9th Cir. 1965).

10. Cases cited in note 7 supra.

11. E.g., United States v. Masonite Corp., 316 U.S. 265, 62 S.Ct. 1070, 86 L.Ed. 1461 (1942); United States v. United States Gypsum Co., 333 U.S. 364, 68 S.Ct. 525, 92 L.Ed. 746 (1948); FTC v. Cement Institute, 333 U.S. 683, 68 S.Ct. 793, 92 L.Ed. 1010 (1948); Norfolk Monument Co. v. Woodlawn Memorial Gardens, Inc., 394 U.S. 700, 89 S.Ct. 1391, 22 L.Ed.2d 658 (1969); Triangle Conduit & Cable Co. v. FTC, 168 F.2d 175 (7th Cir. 1948), aff'd by an equally divided court sub nom. Clayton Mark & Co. v. FTC, 336 U.S. 956, 69 S.Ct. 888, 93 L.Ed. 1110 (1949); Milgram v. Loew's Inc., 192 F.2d 579 (3d Cir. 1951), cert. denied 343 U.S. 929, 72 S.Ct. 762, 96 L.Ed. 1339 (1952); C-O Two Fire Equip. Co. v. United States, 197 F.2d 489 (9th Cir.), cert. denied 344 U.S. 892, 73 S.Ct. 211, 97 L.Ed. 690 (1952); Morton Salt Co. v. United States, 235 F.2d 573 (10th Cir. 1956).

12. See also Brett v. First Federal Savings & Loan Ass'n, 461 F.2d 1155 (5th Cir. 1972); Industrial Bldg. Materials, Inc. v. Interchemical Corp., 437 F.2d 1336 (9th Cir. 1970).

All considered, there is a wide range of possible ways to show conspiracy; anything logically indicative will likely be admissible and will warrant a jury making the damning inference. Thus, evidence of meetings [13] or correspondence or memoranda [14] or opportunities for communication may be admissible as foundation evidence of concerted agreement and, given such a foundation, acts of one or more conspirators consistent with the alleged conspiracy may be admitted against all.[15] For example, evidence that a series of meetings among competitors occurred shortly before each change of price in the industry is enough to warrant the inference that price changes were agreed upon.[16] Alternatively, evidence of the entire course of dealings by major firms in an industry, including various acts that seem explicable only on the assumption of concerted goals, may be used to establish a conspiracy.[17]

§ 110. "Conscious Parallelism" as Evidence of a Classic Conspiracy

If circumstantial evidence may be used to show concerted action, should evidence that several competitors acted in the same way, each with knowledge of what the others were doing, suffice to show that they had expressly or impliedly agreed upon the course of conduct followed? It depends. If a newsboy hawks "Extra"! and several passers stop to buy, one cannot infer from their common action that they were acting concertedly in the manner of a group carrying out a shared plan to buy papers. No more is the world of the living a conspiracy to breathe. A classic conspiracy has occurred only when common action has been taken in furtherance of some common design, only if the actors have become a group and have reached an accord about how they will act. One can infer accord from common action only if it occurs in a setting which bespeaks accord.

In *Interstate Circuit*,[1] the leading case on conscious parallelism, a movie theatre chain sent to eight distributors identical letters which disclosed the names of all other addressees; each letter demanded that the distributor refuse to supply first run films to exhibitors who either refused to meet a schedule of minimum prices set out in the letter, or who showed first run films as parts of "double feature" pro-

---

13. E.g., Continental Baking Co. v. United States, 281 F.2d 137 (6th Cir. 1960).

14. E.g., Schine Chain Theatres, Inc. v. United States, 334 U.S. 110, 68 S.Ct. 947, 92 L.Ed. 1245 (1948).

15. E.g., Beatrice Food Co. v. United States, 312 F.2d 29 (8th Cir.), cert. denied 373 U.S. 904, 83 S.Ct. 1289, 10 L.Ed.2d 199 (1963); Continental Baking Co. v. United States, 281 F.2d 137 (6th Cir. 1960); United States v. Johns-Manville Corp., 231 F.Supp. 690 (E.D. Pa.1963).

16. See Continental Baking Co. v. United States, 281 F.2d 137 (6th Cir. 1960).

17. United States v. Singer Mfg. Co., 374 U.S. 174, 83 S.Ct. 1773, 10 L.Ed.2d 823 (1963), on remand 231 F.Supp. 240 (S.D.N.Y.1964).

1. Interstate Circuit, Inc. v. United States, 306 U.S. 208, 59 S.Ct. 467, 83 L.Ed. 610 (1939).

grams. On evidence that all distributors had offices in the same city, that all were contacted by an agent of the chain, that each would gain if all accepted the proposal but lose if it alone accepted, and that all finally responded to the proposal with identical and fairly complex counteroffers, the district court found that the distributors acted in concert. The Supreme Court affirmed, stressing the additional fact that defendants introduced no witness to deny the conspiracy. The Court noted that direct evidence of conspiracy is not essential and, indeed, that where the conspiracy would, if proved, be plainly unlawful, the availability of such evidence is the exception rather than the rule. The Court stated that the circumstantial evidence not only warranted but virtually demanded a finding of conspiracy. It said:

> "It taxes credulity * * * that the several distributors would * * * have accepted * * * and put into operation with substantial unanimity such far reaching changes in their business methods without some understanding that all were to join * * * ." [2]

American Tobacco [3] also entailed complex conduct which was difficult to envisage as having occurred without accord. The charge was conspiracy in violation of Section 1 and joint monopolization and conspiracy to monopolize in violation of Section 2. During the depression, low priced cigarettes, the so-called "ten cent brands," started to make gains on the high priced (fifteen cent) brands of the "big three" producers. The latter companies, which did not use and had not previously bid for cheap tobacco and which seldom bid against each other even for tobacco of the quality which they all did use, all began to bid when cheap tobacco was offered at an auction. In consequence, the price of cheap tobacco rose sharply. Contemporaneously, the big three cut prices on their own brands. Later, after the market share of the cheap brands fell, prices on the major brands were again increased. On this evidence a jury convicted the defendants of conspiracy in restraint of trade and of conspiracy to monopolize; the trial court's charge made agreement among the defendants an "essential element" and "independent ingredient" of each offense. The court of appeals affirmed [4] as did the Supreme Court, which had granted certiorari solely on the question whether actual exclusion of competitors was necessary to establish monopolization. Although the adequacy of the evidence of concert was not an issue reviewed by the Supreme Court, in an extensive dictum it expressed the view that the common course of conduct was sufficient to warrant the finding of "a unity of purpose or a common design." [5] In *Paramount* [6] findings

---

2. Id. at 223, 59 S.Ct. at 473, 83 L.Ed. at 618.

3. American Tobacco Co. v. United States, 328 U.S. 781, 66 S.Ct. 1125, 90 L.Ed. 1575 (1946).

4. 147 F.2d 93 (6th Cir. 1944).

5. 328 U.S. at 810, 66 S.Ct. at 1139, 90 L.Ed. at 1594.

of conspiracy were predicated on evidence that five vertically integrated companies which made, distributed and exhibited movies, specified the same minimum admission prices in licenses, used the same clearances between first and second run theatres and the same "block booking" practices, and imposed substantially identical terms, with reference to a variety of complex matters, on non-integrated exhibitors with which they dealt. The Court saw this evidence as sufficient to warrant the conclusion that concert of action was both contemplated and executed by the five.

This line of cases beginning with *Interstate* is sometimes said to have established a doctrine of "conscious parallelism," under which evidence that two or more firms have acted in the same way, each aware of the other's doings, will warrant a finding of conspiracy under Section 1. But in each of the cases there was something additional, a "plus factor" as the Ninth Circuit has called it.[7] Each was marked by one or more of the following: a proposal for joint action, a complex yet identical set of responses, direct communication or an opportunity for it, a failure to deny agreement, a set of circumstances which made each participant aware that it was in its interest to participate if all did, but adverse to its interest to participate if others did not. As Mr. Justice Clark said for the Court in Theatre Enterprises, Inc. v. Paramount Film Distributing Corp., "'conscious parallelism' has not yet read conspiracy out of the Sherman Act entirely." [8]

The attorney who relies on evidence of consciously parallel conduct in order to establish a classic conspiracy bears more than the burden of convincing a jury that the parties did indeed reach an accord, either expressed or implied. He bears first a preliminary burden. If he is to reach a jury at all, he must present sufficient evidence in addition to mere parallel conduct to warrant an inference that participants have reached accord. There is, in short, the central question whether, as a matter of law, the evidence is enough to support a conclusion that the participants have become a group acting together, rather than individual competitors who happen at the moment to be doing the same thing. Concerted action can be found only if the evidence as a whole warrants the conclusion that defendants have together chosen to act in a certain way, that they have, in one way or another, communicated, and given assurances, one to another.

Talk about "plus factors" should not lead to a mechanistic response; the question is whether all of the evidence warrants an inference of common, rather than individual, conduct. The current state

---

6. United States v. Paramount Pictures, Inc., 334 U.S. 131, 68 S.Ct. 915, 92 L.Ed. 1260 (1948).

7. C-O Two Fire Equip. Co. v. United States, 197 F.2d 489 (9th Cir.), cert. denied 344 U.S. 892, 73 S.Ct. 211, 97 L.Ed. 690 (1952).

8. 346 U.S. 537, 541, 74 S.Ct. 257, 260, 98 L.Ed. 273, 279 (1954).

of the law can perhaps be best summarized by contrasting two cases; in one the evidence was sufficient to warrant the inference in the other it was not. In the *C-O Two* [9] case, four competing manufacturers of fire extinguishers had regularly communicated with each other, had engaged in a meticulous program of product standardization, raised prices at time of an industry surplus, made identical bids on public contracts,[10] used substantially identical licensing agreements with distributors (agreements which included resale price fixing provisions) and carefully policed these arrangements. On this evidence a finding of conspiracy was warranted. But in Pevely Dairy Co. v. United States,[11] when the trial court found conspiracy on evidence that two dairy companies charged identical prices, each promptly following any price change initiated by the other, the court of appeals reversed. In *Pevely*, the product was identical due to natural causes and health requirements applicable to processing. Defendants also had substantially identical cost structures because each paid the same government-controlled price for raw milk and the same wages which resulted from bargaining with the same union. In this context, the court concluded, identity of prices was well-nigh inevitable, and as consistent with the assumption that defendants had not reached a consensual accord as with the conclusion that they had.[12]

The distinction between *C-O Two* and *Pevely* marks the value and the limits of conscious parallelism as evidence of a classic conspiracy. In *C-O Two*, as in *Interstate*,[13] *Paramount*[14] and *American Tobacco*,[15] plaintiffs showed more than the unadorned fact of a common price in a common business setting. In the long run, one must always expect price identity where the product is identical whether or not costs are the same, whether or not there is consensual accord, and whether or not the price set is at a competitive level or higher. No firm can continue to charge more for such a product than another seller and retain a share of the market. In *C-O Two* some of the additional facts—deliberate standardization of product down to the point where the sole distinction was the label, precisely identical bids,

---

9. C-O Two Fire Equip. Co. v. United States, 197 F.2d 489 (9th Cir.), cert. denied 344 U.S. 892, 73 S.Ct. 211, 97 L.Ed. 690 (1952).

10. Identical bids on public contracts provide a useful source of information for trust-busters. See Identical Bidding in Public Procurement, Tenth Report of the Attorney General under Executive Order No. 19036 (1971).

11. 178 F.2d 363 (8th Cir. 1949), cert. denied 339 U.S. 942, 70 S.Ct. 794, 94 L.Ed. 1358 (1950).

12. See also Independent Iron Works, Inc. v. United States Steel Corp., 322 F.2d 656 (9th Cir.), cert. denied 375 U.S. 922, 84 S.Ct. 267, 11 L.Ed.2d 165 (1963).

13. 306 U.S. 208, 59 S.Ct. 467, 83 L.Ed. 610 (1939).

14. 334 U.S. 131, 68 S.Ct. 915, 92 L.Ed. 1260 (1948).

15. 328 U.S. 781, 66 S.Ct. 1125, 90 L.Ed. 1575 (1946). See also United States v. General Motors Corp., 369 F.Supp. 1306 (E.D.Mich.1974), where parallel pricing and practices on fleet sales were not enough to convict auto manufacturers in a criminal conspiracy case.

and a delivered price system, might to a reasonable person have seemed more consistent with the assumption that participants had reached an accord, had expressly or impliedly made commitments to each other, than that they had not. In *Pevely* none of the facts additional to common prices, such as that critical costs and regulatory requirements were identical, had that quality.[16]

Milgram v. Loew's, Inc.,[17] also contrasts nicely with *Pevely*. In *Milgram* the common practice was a refusal by each of eight motion picture distributors to grant first run films to plaintiff, a new and attractive drive-in theatre, even though plaintiff was ready to pay a higher rental rate than that paid by existing first run houses. As the court saw it, "[e]ach distributor has thus acted in apparent contradiction to its own self-interest," which "strengthens considerably the inference of conspiracy * * *."[18] So holding, *Milgram* reduced to a thin edge the plus factor needed in addition to common conduct. If the court had been presented with evidence and a theoretical explanation about why refusing a good offer would advance self-interest if part of a conspiracy, though not advancing it otherwise, the case would have gone no further than *Interstate*. But no such evidence or explanation was offered, and the conclusion of conspiracy is made to stand on the narrow proposition that conduct inconsistent with apparent self-interest may be deemed conspiratorial.

It bears emphasis that when a plaintiff firm does show common action plus an appropriate "plus factor" which may rationally indicate that defendants have expressly or impliedly committed themselves to a common course of action, it merely earns its way to the jury. Defendant, of course, has its turn also both in the witness box and at the closing argument on the evidence. Since the substantive law of conspiracy requires some consciousness of commitment to a common scheme,[19] defendants may show facts which support innocent explanations for common conduct.[20] Thus, defendants may show such things as common costs or other reasons besides conspiracy to explain common action. Also, defendants can obtain direct testimony that decisions were made unilaterally and not in consultation with competitors. Indeed, according to one court, a defendant may even take conclusionary evidence from alleged conspirators that they made no "agreement," and had no "understanding." [21]

---

16. See also Independent Iron Works, Inc. v. United States Steel, 322 F.2d 656 (9th Cir.), cert. denied 375 U.S. 922, 84 S.Ct. 267, 11 L.Ed.2d 165 (1963).

17. 192 F.2d 579 (3d Cir. 1951), cert. denied 343 U.S. 929, 72 S.Ct. 762, 96 L. Ed. 1339.

18. 192 F.2d at 583.

19. E.g., Esco Corp. v. United States, 340 F.2d 1000 (9th Cir. 1965).

20. E.g., Continental Baking Co. v. United States, 281 F.2d 137 (6th Cir. 1960).

21. United States v. Standard Oil Co., 316 F.2d 884 (7th Cir. 1963). See also First Nat'l Bank of Arizona v. Cities Services Co., 391 U.S. 253, 88 S.Ct. 1575, 20 L.Ed.2d 569 (1968).

§ 111. The Strengths and Deficiencies of the Classical Concept of Contract, Combination and Conspiracy

We have sketched above the "bad actor" theory of contract, combination and conspiracy, which predicates a violation of Section 1 upon avoidable concerted conduct. It is a concept which has power to draw us, being rooted in the historic, populist tradition of the Act. It is also manageable; courts and juries are used to conduct standards, to deciding whether arrangements are consensual or not, to deciding whether or not defendants, having a range of choices open to them, have elected for their own gain to strike out on a forbidden course which adversely affects the public. This approach integrates nicely with the criminal character of the statute and with the criminal sanctions of fine and imprisonment, as well as with the accustomed civil remedy of injunctive relief to disband the concerted arrangement and protect against its reemergence. Counting against the classic concept of concerted action is the bluntness of its cutting edge. Where the market situation is complex enough to require fairly elaborate coordination to achieve common action, it distinguishes nicely between competitive conduct and instances of express or implied agreement. In such markets if accord is achieved there will be more than common action; there will also be other traces, the "plus factors" which courts are skilled at identifying.[1] But when express or implied agreement occurs in a market situation of simpler contours, conspirators, if they are careful, may leave no evidence sufficient to reach a jury. Suppose, for example, that in *Pevely*[2] the presidents of the two milk companies had met a year or two ago and agreed that they would set prices pursuant to some satisfactory formula, let us say at some specified percentage above variable costs. A clear violation would have occurred, but unless one of the two participants admitted his crime, there would under the case law be no "plus factor" which would take the case to a jury.

Then again, if identical but supra-competitive prices were achieved by interdependent but non-collusive conduct, as might be the case in an oligopolistic market where the product is homogeneous and costs similar, the concept of the classic conspiracy would make no response at all to mitigate the public harm. Indeed, oligopolistic interdependence may lead to supra-competitive prices in a wide variety of oligopolistic market structures without collusion, without any express or implied commitment by any firm to follow the common scheme. It may result from rational decisions by each trader acting alone, which sees that it serves its own interest best by pricing so as to maximize industry return, leaving rivalry over market shares to other areas, such as packaging, advertising, or other matters of competitive style.

---

1. See § 110, note 7 supra and accompanying text.

2. Pevely Dairy Co. v. United States, 178 F.2d 363 (8th Cir. 1949), cert. denied 339 U.S. 942, 70 S.Ct. 794, 94 L.Ed. 1358 (1950).

In terms of the economic damage done, there may be little difference between collusive and non-collusive cooperation, though the first is possessed of a negative moral quality which does not infuse the latter. Collusion entails people who get together and agree to rig a market. Interdependence entails managers each of whom individually assesses the data available and does what is rational to advance the interests of his own firm. The classical conspiracy doctrine in traditional form, which challenges the first problem squarely, is utterly irrelevant to the second; against this it stands silent.[3]

§ 112. Performance Evidence as "Plus Factor" Evidence of Conspiracy When Conscious Parallelism has been Shown

Could a court treat evidence of conscious parallelism plus evidence of poor performance as sufficient to establish a case of classic conspiracy, as one commentator has suggested?[1] There would be a logical looseness in any factual presumption that conscious parallelism plus bad performance signify conspiracy, but it might be contended that the difficulties attending antitrust enforcement, particularly in oligopolistic industries, should tip the scale in favor of any decision upon any evidentiary, procedural or other collateral issues which will facilitate vigorous enforcement.[2] In boldest form the argument would be that convincing evidence of supra-competitive profits and other elements of noncompetitive performance is sufficient to establish that parallel prices are due either to conspiracy or to non-collusive interdependence and that (the consequent harm to the public being the same whichever the cause) we ought not to be fussy about the distinction. However attractively reliable this position may seem at first blush, it must be rejected at least in this form. First, if the case is a criminal one, and the information or indictment spells out a classic conspiracy, it is more than a nicety to decide whether defendants are guilty or not. The charge of engagement in a classic conspiracy is a charge of reprehensible conduct and conviction brings the punishment and opprobrium associated with that characterization.

---

3. There are other ways, of course, in which the classic doctrine might be modified so as to bring Section 1 to bear on interdependent, non-collusive pricing. We shall look at these in the next Chapter.

1. See Posner, Oligopoly and the Antitrust Laws: A Suggested Approach, 21 Stan.L.Rev. 1562 (1969). This article, an extremely interesting one, rejects the "Harvard School" theoretical approach which envisages the possibility of noncollusive interdependence. Instead, it embraces the "Chicago school" theoretical approach, which assumes that even in tightly structured oligopolistic markets conduct will be either independent or overtly collusive. On this basis the author infers that if noncompetitive performance is shown, collusion is proved; interdependence is ruled out as a possible explanation.

2. Compare Hanover Shoe, Inc. v. United Shoe Mach. Corp., 392 U.S. 481, 88 S.Ct. 2224, 20 L.Ed.2d 1231 (1968); Perma Life Mufflers, Inc. v. International Parts Corp., 392 U.S. 134, 88 S. Ct. 1981, 20 L.Ed.2d 982 (1968); Leh v. General Petroleum Corp., 382 U.S. 54, 86 S.Ct. 203, 15 L.Ed.2d 134 (1965); Minnesota Mining and Mfg. Co. v. New Jersey Wood Finishing Co., 381 U.S. 311, 85 S.Ct. 1473, 14 L.Ed.2d 405 (1965).

Conviction of that crime ought not to be imposed on the innocent because, given the market structure, self-regarding but independent decisions have led to objectionable economic results. Second, whether the case were criminal or civil, a finding that a classic conspiracy occurred would ill serve the end of rectifying the problem if, in fact, the poor performance is rooted in oligopolistic structure and interdependent pricing. Neither a criminal sanction nor an injunction against conspiracy would deal with the real problem or move the market toward competitive performance.[3]

There are, however, softer forms of the enforcement-oriented position which may generate less resistance. One modification would be to exclude the performance evidence in criminal cases where the interest in having the government turn square corners and prove no less than precisely what it has alleged is highest. The other modification would be to characterize performance evidence, together with foundation evidence about structure and evidence of parallel pricing, as sufficient to make out a *prima facie* case, shifting to the defendants the burden of coming forth either with evidence to rebut the showing of poor performance or with evidence to show that the poor performance is due not to conspiracy but to interdependence.

Suppose, for example, that a civil action for conspiratorial price fixing is brought against the five firms which share the market in an oligopolistic industry and that the government's evidence establishes uniform prices at supra-competitive levels, excessive profits and other indications of poor performance. If a conspiracy has taken place and defendants are enjoined, the ends of justice will have been served. But suppose that no conspiracy has occurred, that one of the defendants, the largest of the five, engages in "target return" pricing aimed at a net profit on investment of about twenty percent, that the other four firms regularly follow the prices of this "leader," and that each firm limits its efforts at rivalry to advertising and style changes because each knows that if it were to compete on price the others would follow and all would be losers. Evidence to prove the actual condition will be available to the defendants, and the *prima facie* case rule may smoke it out. If a series of price conspiracy cases were brought in tightly structured oligopolistic industries marked by price leadership and poor economic performance, and if the courts accepted the *prima facie* approach here outlined, the result to be expected would be a series of injunctions in the industries where dominant firms could not successfully rebut the inference of conspiracy, and an accumulation of extensive data about the actual nature of oligopolistic pricing in those industries where collusion did not take place— data which could be of infinite value to Congress, to the Federal Trade Commission and to the courts in the development of law and policy with respect to such industries.

3. See § 113 infra.

§ 113. Remedies in Cases of Classic Conspiracy

To violate Section 1 is a crime. Many of the cases brought by the government which were discussed in the prior section were criminal proceedings.[1] Although jail sentences for corporate executives have been given in extreme cases, the usual sanction is a fine; until recently the maximum was $50,000 for each offense, but now it is $100,000 for an individual or $1 million for a corporation.[2] Where the government brings a civil action for equitable relief, the remedy is cut to the measure of the offense. The classically conceived offense being concerted conduct, such as an agreement fixing price, the remedy is to enjoin its continuance.[3] These remedies have the same limitations as does the related substantive law. A criminal sanction or an injunction may be adequate to deal with discernible, wrongful, concerted conduct. Neither is adequate, however, to handle the problems of oligopolistic interdependence.

§ 114. Intra-Enterprise Conspiracy

A "contract, combination and conspiracy" requires two or more actors. Can the requisite plurality be satisfied by any two legal persons even though they are integrated economically—say, a corporation and its officers who are carrying on its business, or the board members of a corporation voting on its course of conduct, or two interrelated corporations, a parent and its subsidiary, or two corporations owned by the same stockholders? Or does concerted action in the Sherman Act sense require at least two separate economic units, what an economist would call two "firms"? The cases, commentary and settled practices are in disarray. There are cases which hold or imply that a corporation cannot conspire with its own directors, officers or employees by whom its purposes must be formed and through whom it must act if it is to form any purpose or take any action at all.[1] Commentary generally supports this position.[2] While normal

---

1. See § 112 supra.

2. See Antitrust Procedures and Penalties Act, 88 Stat. 1706, 15 U.S.C.A. § 16 (1974). For a survey of remedial responses, see Posner, A Statistical Study of Antitrust Enforcement, 13 J. Law & Econ. 365 at 391 (Table 19) (1970). For a description of one price fixing conspiracy of recent years which resulted in jail sentences for several corporate executives, see J. Fuller, The Gentlemen Conspirators: The Story of the Price Fixers in the Electrical Conspiracy (1962).

3. E.g., United States v. National Ass'n of Real Estate Boards, 339 U.S. 485, 70 S.Ct. 711, 94 L.Ed. 1007 (1950).

1. E.g., Nelson Radio & Supply Co. v. Motorola, Inc., 200 F.2d 911, 913 (5th Cir. 1952), cert. denied 345 U.S 925, 73 S.Ct. 783, 97 L.Ed. 1356 (1953); Marion County Co-Op Ass'n v. Carnation Co., 114 F.Supp. 58 (W.D.Ark.1953). See also Gordon v. Illinois Bell Tel. Co., 330 F.2d 103 (7th Cir.), cert. denied 379 U.S. 909, 85 S.Ct. 197, 13 L. Ed.2d 182 (1964); Goldlawr, Inc. v. Shubert, 276 F.2d 614 (3d Cir. 1960). But see White Bear Theatre Corp. v. State Theatre Corp., 129 F.2d 600 (8th Cir. 1942); Patterson v. United States, 222 F. 599, 618 (1915), cert. denied 238 U.S. 635, 35 S.Ct. 939, 59 L.Ed. 1499 (1915).

2. E.g., Report of the Attorney General's National Committee to Study the Antitrust Laws, 30–36 (1955).

commercial practice and much antitrust counselling presuppose that a corporation acting alone need not concern itself with Section 1, enforcement officials are inevitably and understandably drawn by conspiracy theory in their efforts to strike down single firm conduct which is harmful to competition, but fails to cross the threshold of monopolization or attempt to monopolize. United States v. Lorain Journal Co.,[3] is an example. The government, challenging single firm conduct, charged attempt to monopolize by the firm and conspiracy to restrain trade by the firm and its officers; the Court, holding for the government on the Section 2 ground, declined to pass on the alternative one. While the settled understanding of the bar, widely supported by the commentators, will not easily be upset, the prudent will take note that the directly relevant case law is sharply split and that the enforcement-oriented position draws strength from the long settled doctrine that where a corporation commits a substantive crime, the officers and directors who caused it to act are guilty of criminal conspiracy.[4]

Yet it is the potential which this conspiracy concept holds for the development of a rational enforcement policy which, if anything, will ultimately attract the courts.[5] If conduct of a single corporation which restrains trade were to violate Section 1, a forceful weapon would be available to the government with which to challenge conduct which in oligopolistic industries creates or reinforces entry barriers. Excessive advertising in the cereal[6], drug[7], or detergent industries[8], annual style changes in the auto industry[9] and other such practices could be reached as soon as they threatened to inhibit competition; there would be no need to wait until a "dangerous probability" of monopoly had been reached, the requirement under Section 2 "attempt" doctrine.[10] Nor would a single firm restraint of trade rule be overbroad. It would in no way threaten single firm activity—setting a price, deciding what markets it would deal in, or the like—which did not threaten competitive conditions. But the law does not forbid single firm restraints of trade. Hence, when a single firm restraint

3. 92 F.Supp. 794 (N.D.Ohio 1950), aff'd 342 U.S. 143, 72 S.Ct. 181, 96 L.Ed. 162 (1951).

4. E.g., Egan v. United States, 137 F. 2d 369 (8th Cir.), cert. denied 320 U.S. 788, 64 S.Ct. 195, 88 L.Ed. 474 (1943); Minninsohn v. United States, 101 F.2d 477 (3d Cir. 1939); Barron v. United States, 5 F.2d 799 (1st Cir. 1925).

5. Compare Hanover Shoe, Inc. v. United Shoe Mach. Corp., 392 U.S. 481, 88 S.Ct. 2224, 20 L.Ed.2d 1231 (1968).

6. Compare In re Kellogg Co., FTC File No. 7110004, ATRR No. 547 (Jan. 24, 1972).

7. See Steele, Monopoly and Competition in the Ethical Drug Market, 5 J. Law & Econ. 131 (1962).

8. Cf. FTC v. Procter & Gamble Co., 386 U.S. 568, 87 S.Ct. 1224, 18 L.Ed.2d 303 (1967).

9. See F. Scherer, Industrial Market Structure and Economic Performance 338–40 (1970).

10. See § 122 infra.

is perceived there is often a scramble to identify a co-conspirator, regardless of how closely linked the additional conspirator may be to the first firm's corporate family.

When the cases move from the corporation and its officers or employees to the corporation and its "outside" agents—its lawyers, accountants, advertising agency or consultants—conflict about the result falls away. Though they have not marked out with great precision the line between the insider and the outsider, nor articulated in any elaborate way the policy which the distinction must be made to serve, the cases repeatedly tell us that the outside agent is separate enough from the corporation to conspire with it.[11] The line may be a very practical one. The courts' reason for hesitating to treat a corporation's own officers as conspirators with it rests on the fact that the corporation can act through them alone. The exemption, then, need not extend beyond the immediate corporate family.

Of course, there still must be a restraint of trade, conduct which inhibits competition; decision making upon the ordinary business conduct of a single firm, conduct which does not raise entry barriers or otherwise threaten competition, does not become a violation of Section 1 merely because an outside agent has participated in the decision making. But if there are two separate entities, a firm and its outside agent—say, its advertising agency—and together they plan and execute a program for the single firm which does restrain trade —for example, by raising entry barriers to the market in which the firm functions—that restraint of trade, being the product of concerted action, violates the Act.[12]

A related but distinguishable question is whether affiliated corporations conspire together when they act in a common course. First, note how sweepingly the cases speak; we shall try to draw the lines which a wise and plausible use of them would dictate. In United States v. Yellow Cab Co.,[13] the Court held that where the owner of a cab manufacturer acquired several large cab companies throughout the country, cab purchase contracts between the manufacturer and the operating companies, if they unreasonably foreclosed the manufacturer's competitors from the potential market for the sale of cabs, would violate Section 1. It said flatly that "a conspiracy among those who are affiliated or integrated under common ownership" may violate the Act just as well as may "a conspiracy among those who are otherwise independent."[14] The same view is taken in several

11. E.g., Poller v. Columbia Broadcasting System, Inc., 368 U.S. 464, 82 S.Ct. 486, 7 L.Ed.2d 458 (1962); Brehm v. Goebel Brewing Co., 1953 CCH Trade Cas. ¶ 67,431 (W.D.Mich.); Arthur v. Kraft-Phenix Cheese Corp., 26 F.Supp. 824 (D.Md.1937).

12. Compare Albrecht v. The Herald Co., 390 U.S. 145, 88 S.Ct. 869, 19 L. Ed.2d 998 (1968).

13. 332 U.S. 218, 67 S.Ct. 1560, 91 L.Ed. 2010 (1947).

14. Id. at 227, 67 S.Ct. at 1565, 91 L. Ed. at 2018.

other decisions.[15] In *Timken,* the language was that "common ownership or control of the contracting corporations does not liberate them from the impact of the antitrust laws." [16] Yet, an attitude more hostile to treating separate, affiliated corporations as conspirators was expressed in Sunkist Growers, Inc. v. Winckler & Smith Citrus Prods. Co.[17]

There are points to be made about the appropriate construction and use of these cases. The first is that made already with respect to outside agents. An enterprise need not be carried on through two or more corporations; it is, as the Court has said, a matter of convenience of the enterprise. Therefore, no basis for exemption from the language of the statute is presented comparable to that which protects a corporation acting through its own officers and employees. But there is a second proposition, tangential to this, which is needed for a full understanding: the fact that there are two corporations involved does not mean that there are two enterprises involved; if there are not, we ought not to judge the legality of the action by looking at its effects upon some wholly theoretical competitive relationship between the integrated corporations. A determination whether or not two or more integrated corporations should be viewed as a single firm should turn upon a variety of factors relevant to the statutory purposes, including the scope of the common ownership and management and the history of the integration of the two firms.

Picture, at one end of the spectrum, a family business which operates one retail store in each of three or four adjacent communities. All of the stores are managed as a unit by one individual, the founder of the business who sets policy, does all the buying, decides on all the advertising, sets prices, and hires and fires all employees other than family members. The fact that each store is operated by a separate corporation should not convert a family business into a cartel which is guilty of several *per se* violations of the Sherman Act; and assuming the complete integration in operation which is pictured here, whether or not violations have occurred should not turn on whether the corporations are all owned by the same stockholders in precisely the same percentages, or even whether they are all owned entirely by

---

15. Kiefer-Steward Co. v. Joseph E. Seagram & Sons, Inc., 340 U.S. 211, 71 S.Ct. 259, 95 L.Ed. 219 (1951); Timkin Roller Bearing Co. v. United States, 341 U.S. 593, 71 S.Ct. 971, 95 L.Ed. 1199 (1951). See also Perma Life Mufflers, Inc. v. International Parts Corp., 392 U.S. 134, 88 S.Ct. 1981, 20 L.Ed.2d 982 (1968) (opinion of Mr. Justice Black); United States v. General Motors Corp., 121 F.2d 376 (7th Cir.), cert. denied 314 U.S. 618, 62 S.Ct. 105, 86 L.Ed. 497 (1941).

16. Timken Roller Bearing Co. v. United States, 341 U.S. at 598, 71 S.Ct. at 975, 95 L.Ed. at 1206. See also Schine Chain Theatres, Inc. v. United States, 334 U.S. 110, 68 S.Ct. 947, 92 L.Ed. 1245 (1948); United States v. New York Great Atl. & Pac. Tea Co., 173 F.2d 79 (7th Cir. 1949).

17. 370 U.S. 19, 28–29, 82 S.Ct. 1130, 1135–36, 8 L.Ed.2d 305, 311–12 (1962). See also Deterjet Corp. v. United Aircraft Corp., 211 F.Supp. 348, 353–54 (D.Del.1962).

the same family or other small group. If there is, as a practical matter, an integrated ownership and management, this small business is a single firm. And a single firm cannot compete with itself. Hence it cannot restrain price competition with itself, or divide markets with itself, or act as a common purchasing agent for itself or otherwise restrain competition with itself, regardless of how many separate corporations the single firm may, for reasons unrelated to the act, be divided into.[18]

To change the perspective, picture a parent corporation and its wholly owned subsidiary (or two corporations wholly owned by the same parent or stockholder group) which operate, respectively, a newspaper and a radio station in the same city. If the radio station, which has no local competitors, were to deny advertising to a local business because the latter advertised in a rival newspaper, the integration between the two corporations, however close in terms of ownership or management or both, would not protect them from a charge of conspiracy to restrain trade. Since there are two corporations there is the needed duality for concerted action. And the concerted action here involved is not merely carrying on the business of a single integrated firm, it is action which is aimed at restraining trade by utilizing such market power as is possessed by the firm because of its radio station in order to erect a competitive barrier in front of a competitor of the firm's newspaper.[19]

The Attorney General's Committee sought to sum up this distinction by saying that where two related corporations conspire, no violation occurs if they "restrain no trade other than that of the parent and its subsidiaries * * *."[20] The phrasing is artless but the point for which it gropes is plainly valid. We have in these cases two related questions. Is there a conspiracy? Is trade unreasonably restrained? We need at least two legal persons for a conspiracy and they may be related units. Also, we need at least two firms for trade to be restrained. They may be competitors acting together, or one may be the victim of exclusionary conduct of the other; indeed, one might be a customer or supplier of the other which, by virtue of the restraint, is foreclosed from competing freely at its level. Courts need not take the same test of plurality for both aspects of the problem. It is perfectly defensible when Congress has sought to cast a wide net to catch restraints of trade to conclude that any two legal persons can conspire.[21] But competition is another thing entirely.

18. Compare United States v. Arkansas Fuel Oil Corp., 1960 CCH Trade Cas. ¶ 69,619 (N.D.Okla.1960) with Distillers Corp. v. Seagrams, Ltd., 50 FTC 738 (1954).

19. Compare Lorain Journal Co. v. United States, 342 U.S. 143, 72 S.Ct. 181, 96 L.Ed. 162 (1951).

20. Report of Attorney General's National Committee to Study the Antitrust Laws 34 (1955).

21. See United States v. Standard Oil Co., 316 F.2d 884 (7th Cir. 1963).

Competition is restrained only if either two or more competitors act concertedly, or one competitor erects barriers against competitive activity by another, or uses power at one level to restrict competition at another. To have two competitors acting concertedly two separate firms, not just persons, are needed. Thus "concerted action" by two "legal persons" which is limited solely to the internal management of a single firm does not restrain competition; but "concerted action" by two "legal persons" which erects barriers to entry by another separate firm, a competitor or potential competitor, can be a restraint of trade.

At some point a diminished level of business integration between two related corporations will warrant a conclusion that they are two firms even though there are some elements of common ownership and control. This line is a highly practical one. At what point, in effect, does it begin to be sensible to say, "These two corporations could be competing with each other and really ought to be doing so; they are not so thoroughly integrated that they should be characterized as a single firm"? Among the factors to be considered are the extent of the integration of ownership, whether the two corporations have separate managerial staffs, the extent of the identity of the business they conduct, the extent to which significant efficiencies would be sacrificed if they were required to act as two firms, their history, whether they functioned as separate firms before being partially integrated, and, finally, the extent to which they may, acting as one, wield market power which they would not possess if viewed as separate firms. *Timken* is illustrative.[22] The Court refused to treat the two corporations in partially common ownership as a single firm. Each of the firms had a history of independent existence. Each was a significant competitor in a world market. The two had participated in dividing world markets between themselves and others before they were partially integrated in ownership, and the integration which took place was in a context of market division. To say that the two corporations had become part of a single firm which could not compete with itself would have been to ignore substance for form. They remained not only two legal persons which could conspire, but two firms which by acting concertedly on prices and market division, restrained competition between themselves.

Finally, we should note that there has been some suggestion that separate divisions of a single corporation may conspire together.[23] So far as effect on competition is concerned, the issues are not differ-

---

22. See cases cited in notes 11 and 12 supra.

23. See Kiefer-Stewart Co. v. Joseph E. Seagram & Sons, Inc., 340 U.S. 211, 71 S.Ct. 259, 95 L.Ed. 219 (1951). Compare Hawaiian Oke & Liquors, Ltd. v. Joseph E. Seagram & Sons, Inc., 272 F.Supp. 915 (D.Haw.1967), rev'd on other grounds 416 F.2d 71 (9th Cir. 1969), cert. denied 396 U.S. 1062, 90 S. Ct. 752, 24 L.Ed.2d 755 (1970) with Alpha Distrib. Co. v. Jack Daniel's Distillery, 207 F.Supp. 136 (N.D.Cal.1961), aff'd 304 F.2d 451 (9th Cir. 1962).

ent from those pertaining to a corporation and its employees or a parent and its subsidiary. Clearly a single firm can take action which restrains competition; just as clearly trade is not restrained when a single firm sets its own prices or decides on its territory, or the like. But when we have two divisions of one corporation instead of two corporations, it is hard to see that there are present the two legal persons needed for a conspiracy. It seems a confused answer to merely assert that the law regards substance, not form, without some theoretical basis for choosing which position on a matter of this kind is the substantive and which the formal one. The ultimate answer, perhaps, is that if we are really ready to make single firm conduct which restrains competition a violation of Section 1 we do not need a conspiracy between divisions to achieve that end; we can point to the corporation and the officers through whom it acted.

Chapter 4

ANTITRUST AND OLIGOPOLISTIC MARKETS

Table of Sections

Part	Sections
A. The Oligopoly Problem	115–117
B. Planning a Public Response to Oligopoly	118–120
C. Legal Theories for Dealing with Oligopoly	121–127
D. Legislative Proposals	128–129

PART A. THE OLIGOPOLY PROBLEM

Sec.
115. Introduction.
116. The Pervasiveness of Oligopoly.
117. Structure, Conduct and Performance in Oligopolistic Markets.

PART B. PLANNING A PUBLIC RESPONSE TO OLIGOPOLY

118. Avoidance of Extreme Responses.
119. Planning Antitrust Enforcement in Oligopolistic Industries.
120. Factors for Analysis in Studies of Oligopolistic Industries.

PART C. LEGAL THEORIES FOR DEALING WITH OLIGOPOLY

121. Unsettled Issues.
122. Challenging Non-Collusive, Interdependent Pricing as a Violation of Section 1.
123. Oligopolistic Structure and Poor Performance as Evidence of Classic Conspiracy.
124. Oligopolistic Interdependence as Joint Monopolizing in Violation of Section 2.
125. The Federal Trade Commission, Section 5 of the FTC Act, and Non-Collusive Interdependence.
126. Merger in Oligopolistic Markets.
127. The Relationship Between Legal Theory and Policy Perceptions Which Warrant Legal Intervention.

PART D. LEGISLATIVE PROPOSALS

128. The "Concentrated Industries" Legislation.
129. Other Legislative Approaches to Oligopoly.

PART A. THE OLIGOPOLY PROBLEM

§ 115. Introduction

Chapter 2 dealt with single-firm market power, Chapter 3 with consensual relationships between two or more firms at the same horizontal level which yielded such power. In the latter chapter we began to approach a matter which those who fashion economic theory and those who fashion antitrust law have yet to bring to order—the problem of power in markets of few sellers. There is the pervasive issue whether significant degrees of market power are being exercised without discernible conspiracy in oligopolistic markets such as those which characterize much of American manufacturing industry. Interrelated theoretical and empirical questions are presented in determining whether this is occurring and, if so, how it is occurring and in which specific markets. For the law and the lawyer there are the questions: What is to be done, given what is known? What can be learned? What does intuition suggest?

In addressing these questions, the tension which exists between antitrust as a system of law, possessed of normative qualities and generality associated with law, and antitrust as a set of policies for regulating the economy, possessed of the tentativeness, flexibility and discretionary elements associated with economic planning, becomes very much exacerbated. Though this book has put forth a legal approach rather than an economic planning approach to antitrust, that posture may have to be moderated to a degree if antitrust is to deal effectively with oligopoly. There is so much that is distinctive about each market, so little that can be built into doctrine; so much that can be assimilated in a set of attitudes (in what is best termed an approach) that planning of a sort is all that is possible. In this chapter, then, antitrust law, as we have understood it thus far, is reduced to a subsidiary role. We begin by surveying the oligopoly problems, then we outline a way of developing policy for particular oligopolistic markets. Thereafter we examine the law to see whether it will allow for the intervention which in those markets seem indicated.

§ 116. The Pervasiveness of Oligopoly

An industry is oligopolistic when so large a share of its total output is in the hands of so few relatively large firms that a change in the output of any one of these firms will discernably affect the market price. It is not essential that there be no small firms which, individually, cannot affect market price. There can be a vast number of them; so long as there are two or more large firms, each of which is conscious of its individual power to affect price, oligopoly prevails. The profound effect of oligopolistic structure is consciousness of interdependence. Each of the few large firms will be aware that the amount which it can sell at any given price will depend on the prices set by its large rivals and that the amount they can sell will in turn be affected by the price which it sets.[1]

What number of firms, controlling what percentage of a market, is sufficiently concentrated to be labeled an oligopoly is not a matter for precise calculation. To characterize a market as oligopolistic is rather to claim to exercise an experienced judgment. Most economists who have studied oligopoly visualize a continuum moving from the most highly concentrated markets where three or four firms control 100% of output, to the least concentrated which might still stimulate some awareness of interdependence, say a market in which nine or ten firms control something like one-third of the output, the balance being in the hands of a large number of small firms. The extent of awareness of interdependence will vary not only with the number of large firms and extent of concentration among them, but also with the number of firms which produce the remainder of the output. This has led to systems of classification such as the Kaysen-Turner system which labels as Type I Oligopolies markets in which the first 8 firms make at least 50% of output and the first 20 firms make at least 75%, and labels as Type II Oligopolies those in which the first 8 make $33\frac{1}{3}\%$ and the first 20 make 75%.[2] Even this approach is deceptively precise. The extent of awareness of interdependence will vary also with other structural features such as demand elasticity (the more responsive buyers are to small price changes, the more aware sellers will be of the extent to which their sales can be influenced by price changes by rivals) similarity of cost structures (the greater the degree of uniformity, the greater will be the awareness of sellers of their common interests), and product differentiation (the more successful sellers have been in differentiating their products the less will be their awareness of interdependence). Thus, awareness of interdependence, the essence of oligopoly, will vary with all factors which actually change the extent to which the level of one seller's sales is dependent upon another seller's price and with factors which tend to either inhibit or facilitate awareness of that actuality.

One cannot assume that all national or regional markets falling within the same rough classification of concentration will perform in similar ways, or that markets outside of any given category will be in

---

1. See generally J. Bain, Industrial Organization Chs. 8–10 (1959); F. Scherer, Industrial Market Structure and Economic Performance Chs. 8–11 (1970).

2. C. Kaysen & D. Turner, Antitrust Policy ch. 2 (1959). Note that in considering the extent of oligopoly four firm, eight firm or other multi-firm concentration ratios are computed. The statement is, in essence, that four firms (or some other number) have, say, 80 percent of a specified market. The statement is analogous to that made when a single firm concentration ratio is given to indicate the share of a market held by any one firm.

their functioning free of characteristics displayed by markets within the classification. Nevertheless, a classification system enables us to count and, when the Kaysen-Turner study was done, of the 191 industries included in the 1954 statistics on manufacturing of the Bureau of the Census, of those for which there were national markets 58 were Type I Oligopolies, 46 Type II Oligopolies, and only 43 were unconcentrated. This and other studies have confirmed the widespread observation that large and important segments of American industry, particularly manufacturing industries with national markets, are marked by oligopoly.[3] Among those which reflection is likely to bring to the popular mind are automobiles, steel, cigarettes, detergents and gasoline; the studies tend to verify these unmethodical observations. The Bureau of the Census study cited above indicates, for example, that in 1963 the percentage of shipments accounted for by the four largest firms and the eight largest firms in selected industries was as follows:

Industry	4 firm % Shipments	8 firm % Shipments
Passenger cars	99	100
Locomotives and parts	97	99
Primary aluminium	96	100
Flat glass	94	99
Steam engines & turbines	93	98
Electric lamps	92	96
Cathode ray picture tubes	91	95
Chewing gum	90	97
Cigarettes	80	100
Primary copper	78	98
Household laundry equipment	78	95
Typewriters	76	99
Soap and detergents	72	80
Tires and tubes	70	89

These industries, at least, must be taken in a quite unqualified sense to be highly concentrated.

§ 117. Structure, Conduct and Performance in Oligopolistic Markets

a. Structure

The question for public policy is not how concentrated markets appear to be but how they function and whether their performance can be improved. Economic theory draws direct relationships between structure, conduct and performance in both atomistic and monopolistic markets. Given an atomistic structure, conduct is highly determinate, as, within tolerable limits, is the consequent perform-

---

3. See, e.g., Concentration Ratios in Manufacturing Industry, 1963, a report prepared by the Bureau of the Census for the Senate Subcommittee on Antitrust and Monopoly (1967); J. Bain, Barriers to New Competition (1956); Scherer, supra note 1, ch. 3.

ance. Given monopoly, though sophisticated analysis may show that conduct and performance are not determinate (that the seller may, for example, price to limit entry rather than to maximize in the short run) the kinds of choices to be made and the factors likely to influence them can at least be foreseen. What occurs is, strictly speaking, understandable. But neither theoretical, empirical nor impressionistic knowledge about oligopolistic markets has as yet resolved basic doubts and dilemmas and there is a precious little which, to speak strictly, we can claim adequately to understand. Public policy seems under the sway of economics; and economics has limited things to offer. There is a need for a multifaceted scholarship. Modern sociologists, for example, whose studies of crime and of the family have fed into legal analysis, ought to be encouraged to work more rigorously on issues of structure, power, motivation and value orientations in business organizations.

An initial doubt concerns the determinants of oligopolistic structure. Among economists, there are those who suggest that efficiency is the principal one, that firm size is related primarily, or even solely, to scale economies and the reason why only few firms occupy many markets is that in those markets the share of the total market represented by a firm of minimum efficient size is very large.[1] One cannot disprove this contention with scientific accuracy. But neither can the claim be established empirically or with any convincing theoretical statement. The position is essentially tautological. Firms are defined as profit maximizers. From this two inferences are drawn: first, that firms already in a market will produce in ways that minimize costs and will price so as to maximize current profits, given the constraints of existing and potential competition; and, second, that firms outside of the market will be watching these activities closely and will hasten to enter if prices are pushed above the level which yields a normal profit or if costs which could be avoided are incurred. On those assumptions (which are put forth without empirical validation as though they were self-evidently derivable from something inalterable in the nature of man) it is inferred that whatever is going on in the market at any time must be what would minimize costs. Thus, the present scale must be the most efficient or some other firm would enter at a smaller (or larger) more efficient one.

Other economists, whose observations have a greater appeal to the pragmatic, lay mind, see the matter differently. They are per-

1. See, e.g., R. Bork, Separate Statement, Antitrust Task Force Report (1968), which argues that except in the case of recent mergers or growth through predatory practices, the existing sizes of firms must be taken to be the efficient ones. See, more generally, the papers, commentary and bibliography appearing in ch. 2, "Economies of Scale as a Determinant," in Industrial Concentration: The New Learning (Goldschmid, Mann & Weston, eds. 1974). Emphasis on scale economies as a major determinant of oligopolistic structure is a characteristic of the Chicago school of industrial organization economics. Harvard school theorists are less likely to accord scale economies a predominant role.

suaded that the size of leading firms probably outstrips the needs of scale efficiency in most compacted markets. This view becomes the more persuasive to the non-economist when the concept of scale efficiency is given a content which accords with socially acceptable performance objectives. Identifiable efficiencies of production and of those aspects of distribution related to the physical handling of the product concern plant size, not firm size. These efficiencies, at least, tend to be achieved fully at outputs far lower than prevailing leading firm outputs in oligopolistic markets. For example, estimates suggest that an efficient automobile plant, or an efficient cigarette plant would have to supply no more than 5% of the market, whereas leading firm market shares in these industries are vastly larger.[2] While there may also be some real efficiencies associated with firm size, these are more tenuous, considerably harder to validate.

In any event, Bork and some of the Chicago school people aside, most economists are concerned that there are other barriers to entry besides scale efficiencies and predatory conduct which may persist over long periods and lead to firm sizes substantially in excess of efficiency needs.[3] There is, moreover, powerful impressionistic evidence in most compacted industries that minimum efficient scale is far lower than the existing size of leading firms. In most of these industries there are some firms much smaller than the leaders which have been successful over long periods of time. If these firms were inefficient they could not have survived, unless we assume that the large firms are holding the umbrella of market power over them by keeping prices up where even the inefficient can survive. And if this is occurring, it is itself an indication of excessive compaction and obviously poor industry performance.

None of this proclaims that real efficiencies of scale do not rule out atomistic competition in many industries. One of Dorfman's estimates is that a typewriter factory at minimum efficient scale would produce 10% of national output. Ten firms, the maximum efficient number, would hardly be an atomistic industry, but there is scarcely room to doubt that such a structure would facilitate more rivalry than does the present one in which four firms account for 76% of shipments.[4]

A plausible explanation for present firm size in most oligopolistic industries has to do not with efficiencies in production and distribution of goods but with "efficiencies" which are reflective of market imperfections and which are better characterized as entry barriers

---

2. R. Dorfman, The Price System 97 (1964).

3. J. Bain, Barriers to New Competition (1956) is the classic theoretical contribution to what this text refers to as the Harvard school of industrial organization economics.

4. Concentration of Value of Shipments in Selected Manufacturing Industries, 1963, Concentration Ratios in Manufacturing Industries, 1963, a report prepared by the Bureau of the Census for the Senate Subcommittee on Antitrust and Monopoly (1967).

than as efficiencies. Imperfections in capital markets tend to give large firms an advantage quite out of relationship with any real efficiency. And in buying supplies large firms may be able to get lower prices not because of intrinsic efficiency, but because of market power; they will thus operate at lower costs and appear from bookkeeping figures to be operating more efficiently. Profits based on efficiency should not be attributed to power, but neither should those based on power be attributed to efficiency, which is as great a risk.

In the case of consumer goods, size facilitates mass merchandising techniques which give a distinct advantage over smaller rivals. Dorfman points out that the custom of branding and advertising consumer products is barely seventy years old.[5] Yet, the process of incessantly hammering away at the consumer with a brand name and a simple message, often an appeal to anxiety, pride, or some other basic human emotion and having little if anything to do with product characteristics, has become an important if not the predominant way consumer goods are marketed in America. The retail consumer tends less and less to look to the retailer for guidance or advice and tends more and more to assume "that any firm large enough to advertise expensively cannot afford to put out products that are noticeably inferior * * * ."[6]

To thrive in such a market requires massive sales which will support the massive advertising. Advertising practices become an entry barrier because they drive the minimum scale up to the level where sales revenue will afford repeated access to national media.[7] Also, distribution methods which reinforce the effects of advertising may be utilized. In some instances, say automobiles, exclusive outlets are used; in others, say TV sets, outlets share with only one or two other brands, and these are usually lower or higher priced lines. Even when the chosen outlet is a mass merchandiser—take as an instance cereals or household detergents—the manufacturer's strategy is to achieve good shelf space, end-bin display space, and other preferred selling positions. Whichever the mode of distribution, what the manufacturer needs to succeed can be attained and kept only if sales volume is high. A substantial market share, therefore, becomes the key to successful distribution not because of intrinsic physical or engineering efficiencies, but because mass marketing has taken institutional forms which increase the minimum scale and thus serve as entry barriers, precluding access to a firm which does not have high sales volume.

5. Dorfman, supra note 2.

6. Id.

7. See, FTC v. Procter & Gamble Co., 386 U.S. 568, 87 S.Ct. 1224, 18 L.Ed.2d 303 (1967). Concerning the debate about advertising as an entry barrier (Chicago School economists tend to say it cannot be, others to say it can), see, for example, the papers, comments and bibliography appearing in Ch. 3, "Advertising As An Impediment to Competition," in Goldschmid, Mann & Weston, eds., supra note 1.

These marketing considerations apply primarily to consumer goods industries, but other entry barriers not relating intrinsically to efficiency can often be identified in an industry where high concentration has persisted over time. Style changes may increase minimum scale in the auto industry;[8] research patterns may have that effect for ethical drugs.[9] In still other industries sales mechanisms (such as a lease only policy), tying arrangements, or patterns of vertical relationships which foreclose access to customers or suppliers may reduce access to the industry. To be sure, the theoretical economist seeking a model yielding determinate results will find it a convenience to associate oligopolistic structure solely with scale efficiencies; but the many discordant voices which describe a less orderly market place in which structure is affected by numerous other factors have about them more of the ring of reality.

In the end, anyone making policy decisions will have to concede a degree of doubt. We do not know for sure the extent to which oligopolistic concentration is a function of real efficiencies of scale. But given what we do know, it seems a reasonable judgment that in many instances concentration could be reduced without necessarily reducing efficiency to any significant degree.

b. Conduct

A conclusion that present concentration levels are not dictated by scale economies does not imply a conclusion that performance in oligopolistic industries would be better if concentration were reduced. Performance depends upon firm conduct; so before anyone starts prescribing structural changes to improve performance he had better have some clear and convincing notions about the way oligopolistic structure effects conduct. He had, at any rate, if he purports to be changing structure to improve economic performance. If his policy goals are different—say, a wider dispersion of economic (or political) power—the effect of oligopolistic structure on these desiderata would have to be independently analyzed.

The difficulties in understanding the relationships between structure and conduct in oligopolistic markets are immense. We do not possess a powerful theoretical basis for predicting behavior from structure. But it is wrong to say we lack any theoretical basis for describing what happens, especially in light of recent work which dramatizes the potential for understanding the ways in which traders

---

8. F. Scherer, Industrial Market Structure and Economic Performance 338–40 (1970); see also Snell, Annual Style Changes in the Automobile Industry as an Unfair Method of Competition, 80 Yale L.J. 567 (1969), and Selander, Is Annual Style Change in the Automobile Industry an Unfair Method of Competition? A Rebuttal, 82 Yale L.J. 691 (1973).

9. See Costello, The Tetracycline Conspiracy: Structure, Conduct and Performance in the Drug Industry, 1 Antitrust Law & Econ. Rev. 13 (Summer 1968). See, generally, Bain, supra note 3, 1956.

act, given oligopoly.[10] We also have empirical information of considerable value, as well as informed impressionistic reflections from those dealing with oligopolists. Let us look at the problem in greater detail with reference to the most important aspect of market conduct, the setting of price.

In order to determine its best price, an oligopolist (let us call it firm A) must form some expectation about the prices its rivals will set, knowing that each of them will in turn set its price only after developing its expectation about what its rivals, including A, will do.[11] A perplexing *renvoi* is presented. Although as the rigorous microeconomic theorists can readily persuade you, it is difficult to determine how oligopolists would achieve interdependent prices if each was initially to seek its own profit maximizing price and they were thereafter to match each other's price moves, the problem they face and our theoretical one are both vastly simplified if we make one assumption—that each oligopolist will be aware, just as we are, that returns to each of them will be better if they recognize their interrelatedness straightaway and approach the problem as one of pricing at levels calculated to maximize not individual returns, but the return to the group.[12] Theoretical studies suggest that this often occurs, that many oligopolistic markets tend to perform more like monopolies than like competitive markets, that firms do work out some kind of a mechanism (leave for the moment whether it is cartelization or something else) for pricing in ways which maximize not individual returns, but returns to the industry.[13]

Oligopolists will be less focused on their own demand and cost curves than on what rivals are doing and are likely to do, as well as on preserving or improving their respective shares of the market. They *know* they are part of a group; *they* perceive, just as one looking from the outside so readily does, (1) that if any barriers exist (or can be erected) which will slow entry appreciably, for them to engage in aggressive price competition would depress the profits of all

---

10. See generally, W. Baumol, Business Behavior, Value and Growth (rev. ed. 1967) and sources cited in note 13 infra.

11. P. Asch, Economic Theory and the Antitrust Dilemma 50 (1970).

12. Id. at 75–89.

13. E.g., K. Boulding, Economic Analysis 582ff (1948); Stigler, A Theory of Oligopoly, 72 J.Pol.Econ. 44 (1964); Markham, The Nature and Significance of Price Leadership, 41 Am. Econ.Rev. 891 (1951); Stigler, The Kinky Oligopoly Demand Curve and Rigid Prices, 55 J.Pol.Econ. 432 (1947); W. Fellner, Competition Among the Few chs. 1 & 7 (1949); A. Phillips, Market Structure, Organization and Performance chs. 2 & 3 (1962); K. Boulding, A Reconstruction of Economics (1950); W. Baumol, Business Behavior, Value and Growth (1959). For general discussion, see J. Bain, Industrial Organization 112–123, 273–87, 315–20 (1959); F. Scherer, Industrial Market Structure and Economic Performance (1970). See also the papers, comments and bibliography appearing in ch. 4, "The Concentration and Profits Issue," in Industrial Concentration: The New Learning (Goldschmid, Mann & Weston, eds. 1974).

without necessarily allowing any firm to increase its market share; and (2) that a strategy of maintaining prices at industry-maximizing levels and expressing their rivalry for shares by other means—advertising or product strategies, for example—will be to the benefit of all. This much we know with a high level of confidence. Let no talk about the complexities of the problem, the limits of available theory, or the indeterminancy of oligopolistic pricing becloud it.

What we do not know with any precision is how the oligopolists in any given structural setting, being aware of their interdependence, will respond. We know they will see the advantages of cooperative action and that they will also feel the pressures of intra-group rivalry. Whether they will cooperate in price setting and, if so, through what mechanism and with what degree of stability and success is not theoretically predictable from structural characteristics. Still we can identify factors which make successful cooperation more or less likely and we may be able to judge whether successful cooperation is operating from performance data for particular industries. Moreover, by observing the visible conduct of individual firms we may be able to make telling judgments about the mechanisms through which cooperation is accomplished in many industries, if it is being achieved at all.

Classic conspiracy is one of the ways in which oligopolists may cooperate. Full blown price conspiracies in oligopolistic industries do come to light now and again.[14] We may fairly assume that others exist which are amenable to attack if they can be discovered. Chicago school economists tend to assume that this, if anything, is the real problem in oligopoly—the risk that cartels are formed.[15] Yet, Harvard school theory, most importantly, the work of Bain[16] suggests (and impressionistic evidence tends to confirm) that non-competitive pricing also occurs through price leadership mechanisms or, at times, through a pattern variously referred to by names such as "tacit collusion," "informal collusion," or "spontaneous collusion"—that is, interdependent, group-oriented conduct which differs from classic conspiracy in its lack of explicit, communicated assent or commitment.

Price leadership, which can be observed easily enough in industries such as steel where the product is undifferentiated, involves a

14. J. Fuller, The Gentlemen Conspirators: The Story of the Price Fixers in the Electric Industry (1962); Smith, "The Incredible Electric Conspiracy," Fortune April & May, 1961.

15. See Stigler, A Theory of Oligopoly, supra, note 13; Posner, Oligopoly and the Antitrust Laws: A Suggested Approach, 21 Stan.L.Rev. 1562 (1969); see also Hay & Kelley, An Empirical Survey of Price Fixing Conspiracies, 17 J.Law & Econ. 12 (1974) which seeks empirically (and theoretically) to identify the characteristics of oligopolistic markets (e.g., high concentration, product homogeneity, higher inelastic demand, and a cohesive industry social structure) which predispose toward cartelization.

16. See J. Bain, Industrial Organization 122–23, 273–87, 315–20 (1959); Turner, The Definition of Agreement Under the Sherman Act: Conscious Parallelism and Refusals to Deal, 75 Harv. L.Rev. 655 (1962).

process through which industry members "speak" to each other through price moves, the activities of the price leader being pivotal.[17] It can take various forms including, as Scherer and Ash summarize them: dominant firm leadership, low-cost firm leadership, and barometric leadership—that is, leadership by a firm which, over time, has been accepted by others as the best judge of developing market conditions.[18] Leadership can be rigid, with the leader always acting first and being followed precisely and promptly. It can also be far looser than that with leads sometimes coming from a firm other than the established leader or with leads tending to be exploratory, sometimes being immediately followed, sometimes rejected and then rescinded, and sometimes followed after a delay or modified rather than followed precisely.

Non-collusive interdependent pricing—cooperation based on a shared perception of common advantage but without either agreement or a pattern of leadership—is harder to see and it is therefore harder to be sure that it exists. Yet there are tightly structured industries, particularly those with differentiated products like automobiles or detergents, which do not seem to act competitively, where price leadership does not seem to be occurring, and where no evidence of classic conspiracy appears. Dorfman gives the example of auto pricing in the 1957 model year. Ford announced prices first, about 3% lower than those Chevrolet announced later. Ford then immediately increased its prices; though it was contending vigorously for the largest share of the market, it felt it could not risk doing so on a price basis. As most economists picture the process, after some experience with quantity-price adjustments, the oligopolists are all likely to recognize that the price policies of their rivals are not fixed, but respond to their own price changes. The rivals will also realize that price competition is harmful to all and may experiment with different price-quantity relationships, as well as with policies for rivalry through advertising or model changes, or the like, discarding the ones that seem ineffectual, groping always toward the monopoly result.[19]

Remember that we are talking about tendencies, not about blueprints which we can expect to be followed with precision. Scherer has emphasized that just as there are temptations to cheat in a cartel, the oligopolist will also see the opportunity to maximize his position by selling at least a part of his output below the interdependently established price, so long as others do not similarly "cheat."[20] This

17. E.g., K. Boulding, Economic Analysis (1948); Markham, The Nature and Significance of Price Leadership, 41 Am.Econ.Rev. 891 (1951).

18. Scherer, supra note 13, at 164–70, 172–73, 216–19. P. Asch, Economic Theory and the Antitrust Dilemma 82–88 (1970).

19. Scherer, supra note 13, at 173–74; Asch, supra note 18, at 87. See also R. Caves, American Industry, Structure, Conduct, Performance 45 (2d ed. 1967).

20. Scherer, supra note 13, at 238.

kind of erosion will be greatest—or, stated more generally, the pressures against successful interdependent price solutions will be strongest—when conditions facing the rival oligopolists are most disparate.[21] If all firms use the same technology, buy in the same markets, and sell through similar dealers or other organizations, they will tend to be acutely aware of their interdependence and will have very similar demand and cost functions which will make it much more likely that they will have similar views about what price is the best for the group and for themselves. But as these similarities tend to erode, mutual awareness may also; and as cost and demand functions become disparate, "agreement" on price becomes much more difficult.

Of course, concepts about what price is best may not be precisely the same even though cost conditions and other factors are highly similar. Management of one firm may see pricing to maximize current return as the best strategy, while management of another may favor pricing above the competitive level but below the maximizing price, in the hope of discouraging entry, and there may be different perceptions among different managements about how high it is possible to go without unduly encouraging entry. But if the factors recounted above differ materially, the perception of the best price is almost bound to differ, even assuming quite consistent pricing philosophies.

We should recall also that the dynamic of a market may involve price leadership or non-collusive interdependence in pricing and, in addition, actual agreement upon subsidiary matters which has the purpose and effect of reinforcing interdependent tendencies and reducing the risks that these may dissolve or be frustrated. As Asch has put it, "[f]irms may eliminate or neutralize some problems of mutual interdependence by adopting a collusive framework."[22] Agreement upon the use of a delivered pricing system, while the level of prices were being established from time to time by leadership, would be an example of this,[23] as might programs for the exchange of price information[24] or for product standardization.[25]

Theoretical writing is rich with suggestions about the factors which will act as determinants of the degree to which the industry will succeed in avoiding the dangers of price rivalry. In addition to factors affecting the costs of supplies and raw materials, of produc-

---

21. See, e. g., A. Phillips, Market Structure, Organization and Performance 32–41 (1962). The theory, as outlined above, is supported by many empirical and impressionistic studies. M. Peck, Competition in the Aluminum Industry, 1945–1958 (1961); R. Cassady, Price Making and Price Behavior in the Petroleum Industry (1954); A. Kaplan, J. Dirlam & R. Lanzillotti, Pricing in Big Business: A Case Approach (1958).

22. Asch, supra note 18, at 89. See also Peck, supra note 21.

23. See Turner, The Definition of Agreement Under the Sherman Act, 75 Harv.L.Rev. 655 (1962).

24. See § 96 supra.

25. See § 98 supra.

tion and of distribution, there are others worth noting. In general, the larger the number of firms in the industry, the greater will be the difficulty in achieving solidarity and avoiding price rivalry. Whatever the degree of concentration, if there is a formal cartel, even if kept *sub rosa* to avoid detection, tendencies to price rivalry will be easier to keep in check than if there is not; absent a cartel, trade association activities, circulating price information, standardizing product or trade terms, and generally facilitating communication and a sense of group-relatedness may have the same tendency. Though relationships are complex, the distribution of shares within a group of any given size will have significance. For example, if one firm has 40% and five firms share the balance more or less equally, there will be a "natural" leader and price rivalry will probably be less likely than if there were six firms of about equal size.[26]

c. Performance

When we turn to performance materials, the conclusion that price competition is weak and profits high in oligopolistic industries —that there is a tendency for these industries to perform more like monopolies than competitive markets—is reinforced.[27] Of course we cannot be certain about what is happening in these industries. Accounting measures of profit, the only data available with which to contrast performance of firms in oligopolistic markets with those in other markets, correspond only loosely with the economic concept of profit which is relevant to an assessment of performance.[28] Conceivably we are wrong at least some of the time when we conclude that a tightly structured market is experiencing higher than normal profits. Also, we cannot know with certainty to what the profits are attributable. Non-competitive market conduct is what the theoretical materials and impressionistic evidence suggest, but correlations between higher than average profits and higher than average concentration are never perfect; there may be other variables, such as absolute firm size, amount of advertising or amount of research, which are related to profitability and to concentration in the same way, and one or more of these could conceivably be the causes of supra-competitive profits in concentrated markets.[29] Yet, when we consider the theo-

26. See Phillips, supra note 13; Hay & Kelley, supra note 15.

27. E.g., Bain, Relation of Profit Rate to Industry Concentration, American Manufacturing 1936–1940, 65 Q.J.Econ. 293 (1951); Collins & Preston, Concentration and Price-Cost Margins in Food Manufacturing Industries, 14 J. Industrial Econ. 266 (1966); Fuchs, Integration, Concentration and Profits in Manufacturing Industries, 75 Q.J. Econ. 278 (1961); Mann, Seller Concentration, Barriers to Entry and Rates of Return in Thirty Industries, 1950–1960, 48 Rev.Econ. and Stat. 296 (1966). See generally the papers, comments and bibliography appearing in ch. 4, "The Concentration and Profits Issue," in Industrial Concentration: The New Learning (Goldschmid, Mann & Weston, eds. 1974).

28. E.g., Bain, The Profit Rate as a Measure of Monopoly Power, 55 Q.J. Econ. 271 (1941).

29. See, Brozen, "Significance of Profit Data for Antitrust Policy," and Peltzman, "Profit Data and Public Policy,"

retical and empirical evidence about structure and the apparent validation in performance studies, the case that oligopolistic markets are a source of social concern becomes, as a practical matter, overwhelming.

There are performance deficiencies associated with oligopoly. Because oligopolists must avoid price rivalry, prices in tightly structured markets tend to be artificially stable, to lack the kind of response to changes in costs or demand which a well functioning market would achieve quickly and automatically. A long run increase or decrease in demand calls for a price change. Firms in a competitive industry will make the change promptly; they are virtually compelled to do so. A monopolist will also make it, once the nature of the demand change is clear. Even firms engaged in a collusive cartel can be expected to do so; they will likely discuss the new conditions and try to agree on a new price. But if firms are cooperating interdependently and without meetings and discussions they may be timid about responding to changed conditions. If demand has increased, each firm will fear that if it increases its price others may hang back, taking advantage of a chance to increase market share; if demand has fallen, each will fear that if it reduces price—even to the level which it regards as ideal for the industry as a whole under the new conditions—others may construe the reduction as a competitive foray and respond accordingly, or may disagree as to the new ideal price and make moves which will result in shattering industry-oriented pricing discipline.[30]

Firms in an industry engaged in interdependent pricing will tend to respond to demand changes by increases or reductions in inventory lapse in time between order placement and delivery, or even by allocative rationing should demand increase sharply. Responses of these kinds, being explicable only on the assumption of an industry-wide aversion to price rivalry, may serve as performance indicia of interdependent pricing.[31] Additionally, the outlets for rivalry alternative to price which oligopolists select tend to be wasteful of resources. Excessive sums are put into things like advertising and style changes in consumer goods industries and into "customer relations" (expense account entertaining, etc.) in producer goods industries. It is not, moreover, the resource allocation aspects of performance which alone concern us. We can see, impressionistically, the kinds of advertising and the kinds of innovation which are so frequently stimulated by the strategies for rivalry in these markets. We have some theoretical bases, in most cases, for associating these strategies with market structure, and we can surely make the social judgment that this kind of performance is not satisfactory.

in Public Policy Toward Mergers 110, 128 (Weston & Peltzman, eds. 1968).

30. Scherer, supra note 13, at 170–73.

31. Scherer, supra note 13, at 149–57, 237–38.

PART B. PLANNING A PUBLIC RESPONSE TO OLIGOPOLY

§ 118. Avoidance of Extreme Responses

There is something about the oligopoly problem, perhaps a frustration with what Baumol has called the "remarkable failure" of modern theory to explain pricing and related decisions in tightly structured markets,[1] which calls forth extremes. There may be those who would make oligopoly the whipping boy for every social and economic ill, those who, armed with righteous conviction, seem ready to break up firms in any industry in which concentration ratios exceed whatever limit they have concluded constitutes the danger point.[2] But these impatient souls are not alone upon the field. At the other fringe are the naysayers who are profoundly convinced that we know nothing untoward about oligopoly which warrants our taking the slightest notice of it, that we can expect to learn nothing in the present state of economic science that would warrant intervention, and that anything we may think we know from any other source must be discounted as sheer prejudice and suspicion.[3] In between are varying shades of opinion which are sometimes made to seem more action-oriented than they are, such as the demand in the Stigler Task Force for a policy of "strict and unremitting scrutiny." [4]

Zealots for reform can be a nuisance and can raise a distracting clamour, but they are not the threat to sound social action that the naysayers can become. Any reasonably stable society is less likely to be goaded into excessive action than it is to find in the words of those it is pleased to call wise a justification for taking its ease. We shall therefore address ourselves directly to the position of those who preach quiescence and hope that moderation in what is said will amply refute those who stand at the other extreme.

The position which must be addressed is typified by an article of Professor Brozen entitled *"Significance of Profit Data for Antitrust*

---

1. W. Baumol, Business Behavior, Value and Growth 13 (rev. ed. 1967).

2. It is difficult to find extremes of such populist fervor in the literature, though Machlup, Oligopoly and the Free Society, 1 Antitrust Law & Econ. Rev. 11 (July–August 1967) might be thought to be within the genre. For the views by more balanced exponents of deconcentration programs, see Blake, "Legislative Proposals for Industrial Deconcentration," and the commentaries by Senator Hart and Dean Neal on that and related papers in Industrial Concentration: The New Learning 340–60, 400–03, 408–09 (Goldschmid, Mann & Weston, eds. 1974).

3. E.g., Demsetz, "Two Systems of Belief About Monopoly" in Goldschmid, Mann & Weston, eds., supra note 2, at 164.

4. Recommendation 6 in Report of the Task Force on Productivity and Competition, reprinted at 2 Antitrust Law & Econ.Rev. 13, 15 (Spring 1969).

Policy."[5] The burden of the argument is that profit data are useless to one seeking to make policy for the maintenance of competition. First the inadequacies of accounting rates of return as indicators of economic profits is noted. It is stressed that if monopoly or oligopoly thwart competition, inefficient firms may continue, so that waste rather than profits will be high in the industry. It is also argued that profits may be high in an industry because luck is high, or because of temporary disequilibrium, which is taken as the preferred explanation. These observations are, of course, all true; profit data alone will never be sufficient to tell us what is going on in an industry. But it hardly follows that data on industry profits are useless. It is rather that they must be used with judgment and discretion to supplement other modes of analysis.

However, Professor Brozen does not stop upon making the case that profit data are not reliable for judging what goes on in a particular industry. He next proceeds to use the asserted unreliability of profit data as a basis for rejecting out of hand the persuasive force of the numerous studies which have found a positive correlation between industry profits and degree of concentration.[6] Having thus disposed to his satisfaction of all empirical support for the view that competition does not thrive with oligopoly, he still does not bring his case to a graceful end, but proceeds with the empirical data he has at hand to attack the theoretical case for concluding that oligopoly and competition are not compatible. The attack is founded on data indicating that in a list of 39 industries the correlation between profits and concentration tended to decrease over time, a statistical manifestation which Professor Brozen views as giving support to the hypothesis that positive relationships between profits and concentration are "a manifestation of disequilibrium rather than of oligopoly conspiracy or partial monopoly."[7] This he sees[8] as giving support to the Demsetz conclusion that "the asserted relationship between market concentration and competition cannot be derived from existing theoretical considerations and * * * is based largely on an incorrect understanding of the concept of competition or rivalry."[9]

Like many of its kind, this contribution contains valuable aspects. It serves as a reminder of the limits of what we can know with confidence from empirical sources about the relationship between concentration and market power, and presents a thoughtful alternative hypothesis which could explain relationships usually as-

---

5. In Public Policy Toward Mergers 110 (Weston & Peltzman, eds. 1968). See also Demsetz, "Two Systems of Belief About Monopoly," supra note 3; Demsetz, Why Regulate Utilities, 11 J. of Law & Econ. 55 (1968).

6. Brozen, "Significance of Profit Data for Antitrust Policy", in Public Policy Toward Mergers 115–20 (Weston & Petzman, eds. 1968).

7. Id. at 119.

8. Id. at 119–20.

9. Demsetz, Why Regulate Utilities, supra, note 5, at 55.

signed to a casual connection between these two variables. Unfortunately, its energy is harnessed to drag policy back not only from such exploratory and tentative uses as the Department of Justice, the FTC, and the courts have made of profit data as subsidiary tests of power, but even from the widely shared theoretical, empirical and impressionistic conclusion that oligopolistic markets do present problems with which public policy should come to terms. Part of this is said directly, but part is suggested by innuendo and implication—through devices like making a joke of the Department's uses of profit data. The effect is not unlike that attained by the gratuitous supposition of Professor Bork, appearing in the same volume, that "competitive results are likely to be achieved whenever there are more than two or three firms" at the same horizontal level.[10]

Efforts like these have a common flaw. They assume an identity between social science and public policy, between economics and antitrust. They assume that there are only two ways to know anything, theoretically or empirically, and that action is unthinkable unless certainty of knowledge is possessed.

But none of these assumptions is true.

Public policy has always been more an art than a science and law has always been as closely akin to the humanities, which proceed inclusively and embrace the ineffable, as to any branch of inquiry which proceeds by methodical exclusion and insists upon systematic resolutions. Those who must make and administer public policy in all its manifestations are fully aware that they must often act without fully knowing, that the business of their lives involves bridging data gaps, drawing upon impressions and bringing off the fine finesse.

It is not as scientists, nor with the zeal of the annointed, that we of the law ought to approach issues about proper responses to oligopoly. What is needed is practical wisdom—good judgment, if you will—a kind of sense which, if not common, is not exceedingly rare in the affairs of men. We ought of course to draw on theoretical and empirical knowledge, but the issues to be identified and resolved are public ones, not academic or scientific ones, and we ought not to close off impressionistic and intuitive wellsprings nor pass upon questions about whether public action should be taken as though the question were whether we were ready to commit ourselves to an analytical position in a scholarly journal. The approach ought to be first to ascertain what we do know, what we are reasonably sure about and what we think most likely. Next we ought to identify the interests which are affected and consider the extent to which these make claim for public intervention. Finally, we must make judgments about whether it is possible to improve matters, whether it is possible to take le-

---

10. Bork, "Vertical Integration and the Competitive Process," in Public Policy Toward Mergers 139, 147 (Weston & Peltzman, eds. 1968).

§ 119. Planning Antitrust Enforcement in Oligopolistic Industries

gal action which, in the end, is likely to be salutary. Only then can decisions be made about what ought to be done.

There is basis for a social concensus that tightly structural oligopolistic industries perform badly: that prices tend to be too high and output too low; that rivalry tends to take forms which we should not hesitate to characterize as socially unwholesome;[1] that overcapacity tends to persist; that prices are not adequately responsive to changes in cost or demand; that price discrimination is widely prevalent. We know all of this well enough in general to conclude that this is a condition which is sufficiently widespread in American industry to be a source of real concern. When we observe many industries in which high industry-wide profits persist over time, the inference is powerful that output is artificially restricted and that entry barriers exist. Neither disequilibrium, innovation, or efficiency seem adequately to explain such phenomena. When these conditions correlate highly with high concentration, a social judgment that lack of competition is a cause of the poor performance is justified.[2]

We can also identify the victims. In part they are those lacking market power which must deal with firms that have it—other traders, suppliers and customers. They are also employees, no doubt, unorganized clerical workers, perhaps, or unskilled casual workers. But some traders and employees as classes may often be reasonably well protected against exploitation by the possession of countervailing power of their own.[3] The supplier to an oligopolist may itself be an oligopolist, as may the customer; consider, for example, aluminum and cans. Even distributors and dealers may be powerful, or may act concertedly with others, although franchisees as a class may often be weak relative to the oligopolists with which they deal. Much labor, of course, is organized and one would be rash to suggest that auto workers or steel workers, for example, are exploited.

The main victim of oligopoly power is the consumer. When in the market place buying for personal consumption, the consumer is an unorganized and largely powerless unit which must take what the market presents. Concentrations of countervailing power elsewhere in the market are unlikely to alleviate this disadvantage. This situation suggests a classic role for government: to take action to help a class which, as a practical matter, can do little for itself. This help might be in the form of intervention in the market place in order, through structural or conduct remedies, to make oligopolistic indus-

---

1. For example, wasteful style changes, excessive and exploitive advertising, or research devoted to ends which would stand low on any credible list of social priorities. See F. Scherer, Industrial Market Structure and Economic Performance 341–45 (1970).

2. See Report of the White House Task Force on Antitrust Policy pt. II (1968), reprinted in 2 Antitrust Law & Econ.Rev. 11–76 (Winter, 1968–69).

3. J. Galbraith, American Capitalism (rev. ed. 1956).

tries perform better—to reduce prices and increase output, to achieve a finer articulation between price and changes in costs and demand, and to achieve a socially preferable deployment of resources.[4]

But though we have sufficient knowledge about the adverse effects of oligopoly generally, we need to know much more to plan an enforcement program. We must define the system more narrowly. Because there is little if anything that we can do about oligopoly on a macroeconomic basis by tax policy, or spending, or manipulating the money supply, we must look at particular markets and see what is going on in them and design intervention programs on no more than a market-wide basis. There are two points being made here, and though the first is more obvious, the second is equally important. First, we must learn all we can about specific markets and come to understand them. Second, we must *then* determine whether there is a way in which we can usefully intervene; we can usefully fashion a remedy only *after* we have developed a confident sense of the dynamic of the particular market.

But just as clearly, we should precisely design the remedy as soon as we do understand the dynamic of the market, and *before* we get beyond study and evaluation and into enforcement. A major problem with antitrust enforcement today is that the remedy is an afterthought, something to be worked out at the end to signify who won. If we are to develop a socially useful enforcement program to deal with oligopoly, we must have a very clear conception about what is going on in particular markets and what might be done to improve matters before we proceed to challenge the status quo. Anything less would be wasteful at best, and potentially abortive or harmful.

For many industries the sources for such knowledge are already available. Industrial organization economists have done exceedingly useful studies of many industries.[5] Of course there are problems in processing this material—some of it is marred for present purposes by one or the other of the two flaws addressed in the prior section.[6] And even the most balanced academic inquiry may not be aimed at developing a comprehensive picture of a particular industry but at

4. See, e.g., Shepherd, Conglomerate Mergers in Perspective, 2 Antitrust Law & Econ.Rev. 15, 20 (Fall 1968); Smith, Antitrust and the Monopoly Problem, 2 Antitrust Law & Econ. Rev. 19, 20 (Summer 1969).

5. E.g., D. Wallace, Market Control in the Aluminum Industry (1937); J. Bain, The Economics of the Pacific Coast Petroleum Industry (1944, 1945, 1947); J. Markham, Competition in the Rayon Industry (1952); C. Kaysen, United States v. United Shoe Machinery Corporation (1956); W. Nicholls, Price Policies in the Cigarette Industry, A Study of "Concerted Action" and its Social Control, 1911–50 (1951); J. McKie, Tin Cans and Tin Plate (1959); M. Adelman, A&P—A Study in Price Cost Behavior and Public Policy (1959); M. Peck, Competition in the Aluminum Industry 1945–58 (1961); J. McCarthy, The American Copper Industry, 1947–55 (1964); L. White, The Automobile Industry Since 1945 (1971).

6. § 118 supra.

some narrower goal, perhaps at exploring or refining some analytical technique or process.

What is needed is not a model of the industry worked out with mathematical refinement, but a full and informed conception of the industry as a dynamic system, a conception which incorporates all that can sensibly be taken as known for purposes of making policy, a conception which is sufficiently integrated to explain whether market power is possessed and, if so, by whom and in what manner it is being attained, protected, enhanced and exercised. Development of such a conception requires full access to the theoretical and empirical knowledge of economics and to the skills of economic inquiry and analysis. While this conception is not something that can be attained by the lawyer as such unaided, it also cannot be reached by the economist acting in conventionally professional ways. The need is for one who combines the skills and information of the industrial relations economist with the skills, temper and interests of a planner of public action. There are already some industry studies which reflect these qualities, though they are rare. Useful examples might include Comanor's studies of the ethical drug industry.[7] More studies with this orientation should be encouraged, as should the training of those capable of producing them.

Proceeding in this way, beginning not necessarily in the industry where the worst structural conditions exist, but in that for which the best information is available, or in which the most helpful policy-economists are already at work, we could expect to develop a series of industry studies each ending with an appraisal of the potential for, and recommendations about, remedial action. These recommendations would derive from an understanding of the dynamic of the industry and would take into account both the potential harms and the potential benefits of each remedial change considered.

The conclusion about an industry might be that there is insufficient indication of bad performance to warrant action. It might be that performance was weak, but inevitably so, and that any attempted cure would only make matters worse, from the point of view of the public. This might well be the conclusion, for example, in industries where real and significant scale economies could be realized only by firms large enough to make a sizable share of the total industry demand at relevant prices.[8] It might well be concluded that it would not be sensible to gain competition if, as a result, costs became much greater and prices even higher than they had been when monopoly profits were being earned. On the other hand, conditions might be

---

7. Comanor, Research and Competitive Product Differentiation in the Pharmaceutical Industry, 31 Economica 372 (1964).

8. See Sherman & Tollison, Public Policy Toward Oligopoly: Dissolution and Scale Economies, 4 Antitrust Law & Econ.Rev. 77 (Summer 1971); Esposito, Noel & Esposito, Dissolution and Scale Economies, 5 Antitrust L. & Econ.Rev. 103 (Fall 1971).

found to be bad, but reasonably capable of being improved by specifically identified remedies. In that instance initiation of legal or legislative action would be considered. Throughout, the standard of judgment ought not to be that of the scientist, but that of one knowledgeable about and responsible for important public affairs.

Remedies considered and evaluated where intervention seems indicated could of course run the gamut and might in some instances be thought of as appropriate for sequential application as needed. For example, it might appear that minor conduct remedies would have a significant beneficial effect. If so, it would presumably be recommended that these be tried before more drastic structural ones. It might also appear in some instances that a direct performance remedy is called for—for example, a direction that a firm or firms in an industry reduce prices until profits fall below a specified level.[9]

Thus far we have talked about analyzing the industry and planning the remedy without making mention of the agency under whose aegis this activity is occurring and without talking about the legal theory of the action. Taking the second point first, the major flaw in antitrust policy planning as practiced today is that it is law-bound. This is perhaps understandable while planning is largely in the hands of lawyers, but is nonetheless unfortunate. There is a tendency to think in terms of the way the law is developing to find the interesting implication and press it by analogy. If oligopoly is to be dealt with successfully this must be changed. Activity must be result oriented—and that does not mean aimed at winning cases, but rather aimed at selecting and achieving remedial interventions which are the goals of action from the beginning. Those concerned with oligopoly must first decide, industry by industry and with some precision, what they expect to achieve.[10]

Now a word about the appropriate agency for planning. The conviction of this author is that there is not a single one, but that contributions can be made by several. Obviously the FTC, if properly funded and administered so as to fulfill its promise, could make enormous contributions as both a planning and enforcement agency. In the latter area, indeed, it has unique advantages because of its statutory power to shape the substantive law. Surely, if it proceeded in a methodical and balanced way, the courts would be receptive to its factual and policy conclusions. But there is also a role for the Antitrust Division and opportunistically it may prove to be the major one.

9. Compare the recommendation and order in British Monopolies Commission, A Report on the Supply of Chloride Zesoxide and Diazepam (13 Feb. 1973) (H.M. S. O. London, 1973).

10. The potential for antitrust planning which would include a cost-benefit analysis has been suggested. Asch, Antitrust and the Policymaking Problem: The Law-Economics Dichotomy, 5 Antitrust Law & Econ.Rev. 45 (Spring 1972). Another planning proposal by contrast is a brief for making Chicago School economics the measure of the antitrust laws. See Posner, A Program for the Antitrust Division, 38 U.Chi.L.Rev. 500 (1970).

Its leaner bureaucracy, though making outreach to the community of academic economists less a matter of easy routine, may make that outreach more effective when it occurs. Impact distances will be shorter, impacts more direct. And the Division, being a part of the executive branch, is under a more direct political control, a factor of importance in seeking approval of any novel and far-reaching enforcement program.

Finally, there is an obvious role for Congress, both through its oversight functions and as a law making body. In committee, Congress, by requiring that the FTC and the Department both explain what they are about, can stimulate both of those agencies. If Congress does not react adversely, it also serves to give the enforcement program additional political approval, to perhaps assuage to some degree judicial concern about making new law without Congressional intervention. Congress, in committee, can also participate in the planning process, can develop data, opinions and views about particular industries which may in the end be the basis for Commission or Department action.[11] Congress might also play a legislative role, the nature of which will be deferred until later in the chapter.[12]

§ 120. Factors for Analysis in Studies of Oligopolistic Industries

It is not feasible to draft a blueprint for an industry study; the essence of the need is a focus on the uniqueness of the particular situation. Nevertheless, a few suggestions at a high level of generalization may be indicative. First, an industry must be chosen. One might begin with any of the 57 industries with eight firm concentration ratios of 50% or more, which are identified in Chapter II, Table 1, of Kaysen and Turner, Antitrust Policy, or the 41 industries with eight-firm ratios of 75% identified in the Statistical Appendix, S.A., Table 1, of that book; or a regional industry with high concentration might be selected. Alternatively, observed or suspected poor performance, or restrictive, concerted conduct might suggest an industry for critical study. General economic importance of the industry and availability of data might well be factors relevant to the choice.

Next, one must proceed with an inquiry into structure, conduct and performance and their interrelationships. The "industry" should be an economic "market" with product and geographic configurations based on cross-elasticities and differing cost functions; yet a sense should be developed about the extent of any restraint imposed on the conduct of those within the market by those outside of it and about the extent to which there may exist submarkets sheltered to a degree from pressure from the rest of the market, or, if not sheltered submarkets, indications of complementary "specializations" suggestive of

---

11. An example would be the drug industry hearings. See e.g., Hearings on Administrated Prices in the Drug Industry Before the Senate Subcommittee on Antitrust and Monopoly, 86th Cong., 32nd Sess. (1961).

12. See §§ 128–129 infra.

collusive or interdependent policies of "live and let live."[1] Take the ethical drug industry as an example. The national market for all prescription drugs seems an appropriate construct for considering overall competitive influences. But possible influences from over-the-counter firms which are outside that market should be considered, and attention should also be directed both to the submarkets of particular therapeutic groups and the sub-groups of research-oriented and non-research-oriented firms.

Concentration should be measured within each market, submarket, or area of specialization. It is important to get a picture not only of gross ratios, but of deployment of firms by size in the market as a whole and within each sub-group. The way power is distributed in the market, or in any sub-market, may be important. A sense about the history of the market is important here. Where has it come from? Where does it seem to be going? Has it been shaped by dynamic technological development, a dynamic firm, a dynamic personality? What energizes it today?

Factors restricting entry, slowing it down, or deterring lateral movement from one subsector of the market to another must be identified and understood. The nature of demand for the industry's product must be understood: whether it is volatile or stable; whether in the long run it is increasing or decreasing; its elasticity. Other structural questions which ought to be raised include: is there a trade association or other formal organization? If so, how does it function? Is there some less structured way of organizing cooperative activity among firms—a pricing system, price leadership, information systems? If so, how do these function? To what extent do firms in the industry or any subsector have what Phillips has called similar "value systems," that is, similarity of products, types of customers, marketing channels, technology, and cost and revenue functions generally?[2] The greater the similarity, the greater the likelihood of accord, collusive or interdependent, on what price would maximize return for the industry. Trade association publications disclose a great deal about these and other important matters. Discussion with knowledgeable people engaged in the industry can be very informative, even in informal settings like an academic inquiry, once the investigator has refined his conceptions sufficiently to ask questions which may test or refine factual hypotheses.

1. The study plan described in text is that which the author has used to organize seminars aimed at "antitrust planning" for a particular industry. An inquiry by an agency with subpoena power could, of course, generate data not available to students or other researchers. There is now available a thorough and useful "checklist" of ways markets may be defective which will repay attention. Markovits, The Causes and Policy Significance of Pareto Resource Misallocation—A Checklist for Microeconomic Policy Analysis, etc., 1975 Wis.L.Rev. 950 (1975).

2. A. Phillips, Market Structure, Organization and Performance 32 (1962).

Moving beyond structural factors to performance, attention should be focused upon what by now is the obvious: industry profits and their trend over time, cost-price relationships, capacity-output relationships, discrimination and its persistence, selling expenditures, progressiveness, efficiency.[3] To the extent feasible these should be separately appraised for each significant subsector of the "market" and relationships that suggest themselves between structural features and performance should be noted.

The next descriptive stage deals with conduct. This must be assessed and its relationship to structure and performance considered. Given the structure, to what extent is conduct determinate, and to what extent do firms have conduct choices to make—for example, about whether to price to maximize current return, to price to discourage entry, or to price with other objectives in view? Is it possible to work out a single "rational" course of conduct, or a "rational range" within which choice is likely to be confined? Is there a distinct "rational" course for the larger firms and a different one for smaller firms? For different submarkets? What have various firms actually done? What have their pricing strategies appear to have been? Product research strategies? Advertising strategies? How have these related to structure, to each other and to the strategies of other firms? To what extent is there rivalry in the industry, and what forms does it take? Outside of a context where discovery powers are available, data as to many of these matters may be difficult to obtain, though trade associations may be sources for some of it.

There follows an integrating process, an effort to work data, more vague factual conceptions and intuitions into a concept of the industry as a functioning system. For the particular industry, given all that we know (or hypothesize) about it, how, as specifically as the matter can be stated, do structure, conduct and performance interact? To the extent that hypotheses are questionable or conceptions vague at this stage, do there remain information sources which could be pursued to enhance the dynamic view, to render it more complete, more refined or more accurate?

Now the crucial value questions are asked and detailed. From the vantage point of the public interest, how well or poorly does the industry function? Let us praise it: what are the good things it does for us? Let us look harshly at it: where and how does it fail us? The process of understanding and evaluating the industry should be conducted in as unhurried a fashion as circumstances permit. Much revision of preliminary conceptions is likely to occur here.

3. See E. Mason, The Current Status of the Monopoly Problem in the United States, 62 Harv.L.Rev. 1280 (1949).

Finally, the action questions are asked, the ones toward which the entire process has been directed. In 1950, Jesse W. Markham stated:

> An industry may be judged workably competitive when, after the structural characteristics of its market and the dynamic forms that shape them have been thoroughly examined, there is no clearly indicated change that can be effected through public policy measures that would result in greater social gains than social losses.[4]

The goal here is not in defining a concept of workable competition, but in developing a sound guide to public action in dealing with oligopolistic markets; nonetheless, and general as it may be, twenty-five years has not yielded an improvement upon Markham's statement as a prescription for policy. Upon understanding how the market works we must consider whether there is any intervention which the public might make—an order directed to conduct, a structural order, or a behavior order—which would likely result in a net improvement in industry performance. At this stage, alternative remedies, or sequential ones may, of course, be considered. It is necessary to evaluate each in the context of the dynamic conception of the industry, to see how each remedy considered may alter the functioning of the industry, to trace through, so far as feasible, the sequence of perturbations. There may, of course, be negative consequences as well as desired ones from any intervention considered.

If it is concluded that there is a "clearly indicated change" which would yield more gains then pains, then, and only then, should consideration be given to the question whether existing law provides a basis for the indicated intervention, or whether new legislation is needed. To what these might be we shall next turn our attention.

PART C. LEGAL THEORIES FOR DEALING WITH OLIGOPOLY

§ 121. Unsettled Issues

How do we now treat oligopoly under the Sherman Act? What is settled about the response of the law to the "oligopoly problem"? Most obviously, the law forbids oligopolists to fix the industry maximizing price by means of express agreement, through classic conspiracy.[1] The statute also forbids oligopolists to agree on collateral matters which in purpose or effect facilitate non-competitive pricing.[2] Nor may they act together in ways which raise entry barriers.[3] It is

---

4. Markham, An Alternative Approach to the Concept of Workable Competition, 40 Am.Econ.Rev. 361 (1950).

1. See §§ 73–78 supra.

2. See §§ 98–102 supra.

3. See §§ 98–107 supra.

also very clear that markets tending toward high concentration may not be made more concentrated through merger, a point we shall develop in a later section.[4]

No more is settled than that.

"[A] gap in the law remains. While [merger law] provides strong protection against the growth of new concentration of market power * * *, existing law is inadequate to cope with old ones."[5]

Yet there is a sense abroad that the law is at the brink, that new links may soon be marked out by decision or legislation. This sense of expectation is nurtured by increasing judicial use of structural analysis [6] and increasing readiness by courts to attend to the possible implications of performance data.[7] Let us look then at the possible directions for movement in the law.

§ 122. Challenging Non-Collusive, Interdependent Pricing as a Violation of Section 1

With advances in our understanding of the nature of the competitive dynamic and the conditions which can frustrate it, may we not find sufficient meaning in the phrase, "contract, combination or conspiracy," to apply it to non-collusive, interdependent pricing? [1] If so, a legal weapon would be available to challenge non-competitive pricing in oligopolistic industries without the need of showing that the concerted pricing was achieved by conspiracy. Let us first consider whether such a reading of the act is conceivable, given the current state of the law and of economic theory; thereafter we shall evaluate whether such a development would be a desirable one.

The most compelling argument for reading Section 1 as forbidding interdependent pricing at supra-competitive levels is founded on

---

4. See § 204 infra.

5. Report of the White House Task Force on Antitrust Policy pt. II (1968) reprinted in 2 Antitrust Law & Econ. Rev. 11–76 (Winter, 1968–69); C. Kaysen & D. Turner, Antitrust Policy 44, 110–111 (1959); Stigler, The Case Against Big Business, Fortune (May, 1952).

6. Brodley, Oligopoly Power Under the Sherman & Clayton Acts from (G.M.) Economic Theory to Legal Policy, 19 Stan.L.Rev. 285 (1967).

7. United States v. E. I. Du Pont De Nemours & Co., 353 U.S. 586, 77 S.Ct. 872, 1 L.Ed.2d 1057 (1957); United States v. E. I. Du Pont De Nemours & Co., 351 U.S. 377, 76 S.Ct. 994, 100 L.Ed. 1264 (1956); American Tobacco Co. v. United States, 328 U.S. 781, 66 S.Ct. 1125, 90 L.Ed. 1575 (1946); Sugar Institute, Inc. v. United States, 297 U.S. 553, 56 S.Ct. 629, 80 L.Ed. 859 (1936); United States v. Aluminum Co. of America, 148 F.2d 416 (2d Cir. 1945).

1. See generally, Turner, The Definition of Agreement Under the Sherman Act: Conscious Parallelism and Refusals to Deal, 75 Harv.L.Rev. 655 (1962); Rahl, Conspiracy and the Antitrust Laws, 44 Ill.L.Rev. 743 (1950); Markovits, Oligopolistic Pricing Suits, the Sherman Act and Public Welfare (Part I), 26 Stan.L.Rev. 493 (1974); Schwartz, New Approaches to the Control of Oligopoly, 109 U.Pa.L.Rev. 31 (1960).

two propositions: first, that the act displays a "dread of enhancement of prices" which led Congress "by the 1st section [to forbid] all means of monopolizing trade, that is, unduly restraining it by means of every contract, combination, etc.," of whatever nature [2] and second, that in oligopolistic markets, pricing based on price leadership or other means aimed at maximizing group returns can as effectively link rival firms into groups or combinations which restrain trade and enhance prices as could any classic conspiracy. In "small group markets," to adopt Phillips' phrase, interdependence is rife. What one firm does in the automobile, steel, detergent, or antibiotic industry inevitably affects other firms. Although each firm may retain a rough set of options in pricing and output, its demand and cost conditions are so strongly affected by the pricing and output decisions of the others that it must take their actions into account and, rationally, will identify and respond to the common interest of the group.[3] If one accepts the ancient faith concerning the purpose of the Sherman Act, and if one accepts the near unanimous view of modern economics about what occurs in oligopolistic markets, the pressures for reading Section 1 as reaching fully developed examples of interdependent pricing are strong.

When we recanvass the case law from this vantage point we come upon little that is discouraging. In Section 110 we stressed that *Interstate Circuit*,[4] in striking down parallel action by movie distributors in imposing similar restrictions on exhibitors, was accommodating to circumstantial evidence; the case held that a complex course of consciously parallel conduct, in circumstances of strong interdependence, so forcefully implied a conspiracy as to leave no other "persuasive explanation." Yet, Mr. Justice Stone did not leave it quite there. Speaking for the Court, he went on to add:

> "[W]e think that in the circumstances of this case * * * agreement [of the distributors among themselves] for the imposition of the restrictions * * * was not a prerequisite to an unlawful conspiracy. It is enough that, knowing that concerted action was contemplated and invited, the distributors gave their adherence to the scheme and participated in it * * * ."[5]

The elements which, in that more constricted setting, would substitute for "agreement" in showing a Section 1 violation are not far removed from what occurs when a price leader in an oligopolistic mar-

2. Standard Oil Co. of New Jersey v. United States, 221 U.S. 1, 58, 61, 31 S.Ct. 502 515, 516, 55 L.Ed. 619, 644, 645 (1911).

3. A. Phillips, Market Structure, Organization and Performance chs. 2 & 3 (1962); Asch, Collusive Oligopoly: An Antitrust Quandary, 2 Antitrust Law and Econ.Rev. 53 (Spring 1969).

4. Interstate Circuit, Inc. v. United States, 306 U.S. 208, 59 S.Ct. 467, 83 L.Ed. 610 (1939).

5. Id. at 226, 59 S.Ct. at 474, 83 L.Ed. at 620.

ket announces a supra-competitive price. *Interstate*, then, is charged with a special meaning about the kinds of relationships which can be viewed as concerted. Surely when a price leader announces a price, it contemplates concerted action in the sense of adherence to that price by others; the leader could not maintain the price if others went to a lower, competitive, level. And surely others, upon accepting the leader's price by announcing it as their own, are aware that it was "contemplated" or "invited," and that they are giving "their adherence" to it; all involved are "participating in the scheme" with as much knowledge about its nature and the expectations of others as the Court in *Interstate* asserted would be sufficient. Thus to label the steel or auto industry a conspiracy, a court need only borrow the light of the *Interstate* dictum.

Dictum in United States v. Paramount [6] is germinal in the same way; it gives a further warrant to the assertion that when firms act conjunctively to set supra-competitive prices they are in conspiracy. The tobacco case of the depression years, by a dictum of its own, makes much the same point:

> "The essential combination or conspiracy in violation of the Sherman Act may be found in a course of dealings or other circumstances as well as in any exchange of words * * *." [7]

The hallmarks of concerted action are "planned common course of action, understanding, agreement, combination, or conspiracy," [8] surely a phrase which can comfortably be applied to interdependent pricing. There are also several cases which give strong support to the conclusion that interdependent though non-collusive decisions to follow a basing point system (which facilitates price leadership) violate Section 5 of the FTC Act [9] and, implicitly, Section 1 of the Sherman Act. One of these cases, indeed, indicates that the Commission under Section 5 can characterize as unlawful any conduct having a dangerous tendency to hinder competition, [10] a power ample enough to warrant condemnation of price leadership or other interdependent pricing practices.

---

6. 334 U.S. 131, 142, 68 S.Ct. 915, 922, 92 L.Ed. 1260, 1285 (1948).

7. American Tobacco Co. v. United States, 328 U.S. 781, 809–10, 66 S.Ct. 1125, 1139, 90 L.Ed. 1575, 1594 (1946).

8. FTC v. National Lead Co., 352 U.S. 419, 423, 77 S.Ct. 502, 506, 1 L.Ed.2d 438, 442 (1957); FTC v. Cement Institute, 333 U.S. 683, 689, 68 S.Ct. 793, 797, 92 L.Ed. 1010, 1028 (1948); Triangle Conduit & Cable Co., Inc. v. FTC, 168 F.2d 175, 178 (7th Cir. 1948).

9. See FTC v. Cement Institute, 333 U.S. 683, 68 S.Ct. 793, 92 L.Ed. 1010 (1948); Triangle Conduit & Cable Co. v. FTC, 168 F.2d 175 (7th Cir. 1948), aff'd sub nom. by an equally divided Court, Clayton Mark & Co. v. FTC, 336 U.S. 956, 69 S.Ct. 888, 93 L.Ed. 1110 (1949).

10. FTC v. National Lead Co., 352 U.S. 419, 77 S.Ct. 502, 1 L.Ed.2d 438 (1949).

Nor does the dictum in *Theatre Enterprises*,[11] that conscious parallelism does not alone establish conspiracy under the Sherman Act, embarrass the analysis. The Court in that case was dealing with a fact situation where there was common conduct but little if any indication of interdependence; even so, the Court saw the case as presenting a jury issue under Section 1. We ought not to let the Court's aphorism, which points up a small truth, draw us away from what could be a larger one.

§ 123. Oligopolistic Structure and Poor Performance as Evidence of Classic Conspiracy

The construction of Section 1 discussed in the prior section assumes that oligopolistic structure tends to generate group-oriented market conduct even without conspiracy and that when such conduct is observed, necessary remedies, including structural ones, are appropriate. The legal analysis considered in this section, as well as the economic analysis which underlies it, differ materially. They are informed by a pervasive skepticism about the ubiquity of non-collusive interdependence. Indeed, this analysis, which has been championed by some commentators,[1] assumes that firms in tightly structured markets will elect one of two courses, competition or collusion, and that when they collude, however skillful they may be in covering their tracks, they will leave a record of poor industry performance behind them. When poor performance is found in association with high concentration the existence of a classic conspiracy is inferred. While the emphasis is thus upon oligopolistic structure and supra-competitive profits or other manifestations of poor performance, conduct indications—for example a pattern of price leadership—could also be expected to present themselves. These are read as reinforcing the implication that the firms participating in the group-oriented pricing have conspired so to do.

If this approach to oligopoly gauges the matter correctly, all problems of substantive doctrine and remedy vanish; we are left only with an issue of evidence. The substantive law is simply that conspiracy to fix prices is unlawful; there is no need to develop doctrine about whether a group interrelating less intensively, in the manner perceived by interdependence theory, would violate the act. Since interdependence sans conspiracy is not admitted to exist, the legal question which worried us in the last two sections never arises at all.

---

11. Theatre Enterprises, Inc. v. Paramount Film Distrib. Corp., 346 U.S. 537, 541, 74 S.Ct 257, 260, 98 L.Ed. 273, 279 (1954).

1. See generally, Posner, Oligopoly and the Antitrust Laws: A Suggested Approach, 21 Stan.L.Rev. 1562 (1969). Compare Stigler, A Theory of Oligopoly, 72 J.Pol.Econ. 44 (1964). The economic analysis underlying the view of oligopoly taken as a basis for the legal argument here outlined is a Chicago school analysis. The contrasting economic analysis underlying the legal argument summarized in § 122 is based on Harvard School conceptions which credit the notion that oligopolistic firms may function interdependently without collusion.

The remedy is also a simple one. The violation is agreement; agreement can be enjoined.

Case law supports the obvious part of this theory amply enough; price fixing conspiracies are indeed unlawful.[2] The novel legal question is whether one can get to a jury without evidence other than performance data from which conspiracy could be inferred. There are decisions to the effect that where a foundation case of conspiracy and evidence of consciously parallel prices have been introduced to prove a conspiracy, the plaintiff may also show as a "plus factor" that the defendants have been earning supra-competitive profits.[3] The logic is that if defendants were in fact exercising market power through a successful conspiracy, their prices would exceed the competitive norm, whereas if prices were parallel because, lacking market power, all had to take the competitive market price as given, no excessive profits could be earned. And one need not limit the search to profits; in an oligopolistic industry a number of performance characteristics might be evaluated to determine whether firms were performing reasonably competitively or in some concerted manner.[4] Among these would be long continued excess capacity, long continued price discrimination and nonresponsiveness of prices following reductions in cost.

It is, of course, a considerable step to move from the cases which use profit evidence as an ancillary support for the inference of a conspiracy independently indicated by other evidence to the presumption that poor performance in an oligopolistic market shows conspiracy. The coincidence of oligopoly and poor performance, while a basis for selecting an industry for study to determine whether there are pathologies and, if so, what they are, is, without more, a weak basis for inferring conspiracy. Even if one doubts that non-collusive interdependence is likely to occur, even in very favorable conditions for it, one can hardly say, in the present state of knowledge, that such phenomena simply do not exist. Posner, who tries to make this case, is simply not convincing.[5] The theoretical, empirical and impressionistic reasons for concluding that market power can be maintained and exploited in oligopolistic markets by price leadership and other interdependent decision-making are far too formidable.[6] That being so, the most that one can infer from the mere coincidence of tight struc-

2. See §§ 73–78 supra.

3. See § 110 supra.

4. See Posner, supra note 1.

5. The Posner view is criticized in Markovits, Oligopolistic Pricing Suits, the Sherman Act, and Economic Welfare, Part II, Injurious Oligopolistic Pricing Sequences: Their Description, Interpretation, and Legality Under the Sherman Act, 26 Stan.L.Rev. 717 (1974). See also Posner, A Reply To Professor Markovits, 28 Stan.L.Rev. 903 (1976).

6. See Adams, The "Rule of Reason": Workable Competition or Workable Monopoly? 63 Yale L.J. 348 (1954); F. Scherer, Industrial Market Structure and Economic Performance 164–73 (1970).

ture and poor performance is that coordination is being achieved either by collusion or without it. The most prominent exponent of the use of performance tests as subsidiary tests of power warns that "no one familiar with statistical and other material pertaining to the business performance of firms and industries would deny the extreme difficulty of constructing from this [performance] material a water-tight case for or against particular firms in particular industries."[7] With data about industry characteristics in addition to concentration ratios one might sharpen the judgment, at least to some degree. For example if industry products are heterogeneous or there are factors which would inhibit the quick and easy public flow of price information one would think non-collusive interdependence less likely as an explanation for poor performance than one would if products were homogeneous and public information sources about transactions highly developed. There might be situations where the inhibitions to non-collusive interdependence seemed so extensive that one could conclude, with a reasonable degree of confidence, that the hypothesis of collusion as the course of poor performance would seem far more likely.

There is also the difficulty that evaluations of performance data are difficult. Any conclusion about whether profit levels are reasonable will be less than scientific; it must be highly impressionistic. Those about other elements of performance, if they are to be undertaken, become increasingly so. Judgments about the level or quality of innovation, for example, may be exceedingly difficult to make with any confidence. Also judgments about matters like the level of advertising outlays and the character of these expenditures, must grow largely out of an ethical sense about what industry ideally ought to be doing, not out of statistical models of what a competitive market would do. These difficulties plague any effort to use performance data and explain why performance analysis is relegated to the subsidiary role in antitrust. The objections gain importance when the proposal under consideration is to act on performance data alone, or in conjunction only with concentration data.

Even so, we need not give up the more modest notion that a searching inquiry into performance will be useful in discovering those oligopolistic industries where intervention under the antitrust laws is called for. If we do not go so far as Machlup, who believes that profits are the best index of non-competitive conditions,[8] we may nevertheless assent to Stocking's restrained view that, lacking better resources, economists may be forced to rely on profit data in associa-

7. Mason, The Current Status of the Monopoly Problem in the United States, 62 Harv.L.Rev. 1280, 1282 (1949). See also § 118 supra, notes 25–26 and accompanying text.

8. F. Machlup, The Political Economy of Monopoly, Business, Labor and Government Policies (1952).

§ 124. Oligopolistic Interdependence as Joint Monopolizing in Violation of Section 2

The decision in *American Tobacco*[1] contains a relevant holding and a relevant comment which may provide a different legal tool for prying open oligopolistic markets. The holding was that the three leading cigarette manufacturers (which in the aggregate had a share of cigarette production exceeding monopoly proportions, though none alone had a sufficient market share to be considered a monopolist) could by engaging jointly in activities which tended to raise prices and inhibit competitors be collectively guilty of monopolizing in violation of Section 2. The comment is that the joint nature of their activities could be inferred "from the evidence of the action taken in concert"[2], language which in context rather clearly pointed to consciously parallel practices. If we read this aspect of the case for all it is worth, then interdependent conduct may provide a basis for challenging any group of oligopolists which together have a commanding share of their market; we need only show that they have acted interdependently in exclusionary ways, not that they have conspired to exclude.[3] Indeed, language in the case could be construed as stating that the act of combining through interdependent actions provides the essential conduct element for the Section 2 offense, and therefore that the mere possession by the group of monopoly power (or its "exercise" not to exclude competitors, but merely to set a price) violates the act.

But one ought not to overread the case. The record actually showed, in addition to supra-competitive pricing, joint activities in buying and, in particular, in bidding on low-priced tobaccos for the purpose of forcing up the costs of competing manufacturers which marketed cheaper "10¢ brands." Also, the evidence of concertedness entailed far more than non-collusive, interdependent conduct; from the instantaneousness with which the price leader's upward and unexpected price moves were followed (in the face of testimony that the decision to follow was based on projections about effects of price on advertising revenues) and from the complexity of the bidding, buying, and selling activities which were all carried out in a coordinated

---

9. G. Stocking, Workable Competition and Antitrust Policy 280 (1961). See also E. Mason's "Preface" to C. Kaysen & D. Turner, Antitrust Policy (1959).

1. American Tobacco Co. v. United States, 328 U.S. 781, 66 S.Ct. 1125, 90 L.Ed. 1575 (1946).

2. Id. at 809, 66 S.Ct. at 1139, 90 L.Ed. at 1594.

3. See Rostow, The New Sherman Act: A Positive Instrument of Progress, 14 U.Chi.L.Rev. 567 (1974); see also Turner, The Definition of Agreement Under the Sherman Act: Conscious Parallelism and Refusals to Deal, 75 Harv.L.Rev. 655 (1962).

way, the jury had ample basis to infer the existence of a classic conspiracy.[4]

Yet, one should not underread *American Tobacco* either. In oligopolistic markets, as in monopolistic ones, power to attain excess profits can be maintained in the long run only if entry is effectively impeded. In oligopolistic markets which are not performing competitively, we should expect to find entry barriers and these may be created or reinforced by the conduct of the oligopolists. In some industries product policies, like the annual model change in the auto industry, may constitute an entry barrier.[5] In others, as perhaps in detergents, advertising policies may constitute an entry barrier.[6] In some, as in the ethical drug industry, research policies may inhibit entry.[7] If practices which maintain power in the hands of the few are carried out in coordinated, interdependent ways, courts ought to be reasonably responsive to the contention (similar to that developed about interdependence as a violation of Section 1 [8]) that non-collusive integration taints the activities with enough "jointness" to warrant treating the oligopolists as a single unit in deciding whether they have monopolized their industry.

This approach to the oligopoly problem under the rubric of Section 2 would have a selectivity and a relevance to policy concerns in an area where knowledge is limited which approaches based on Section 1 might lack. For example, a holding that demonstrable examples of interdependent pricing violate Section 1 would apply very broadly. Picture, for example, oligopolists that had little protection against entry and that earned a small increment above competitive returns due to a steady growth in demand which, because of scale economies, had not yet reached the proportion calling for additional entry. Under either of the Section 1 theories, pricing in this industry might violate the law. Yet, there would be scant point in the public intervening to seek a correction which the market itself was in the process of making. But the Section 2 theory could identify for intervention only industries where coordinated practices had the effect of sustaining power, industries which could not be expected to

---

4. The contrary argument is made in R. Posner, Antitrust, Cases, Economic Notes and Other Materials 107–10 (1975).

5. See F. Scherer, Industrial Market Structure and Economic Performance 338–40 (1970). Compare Note, Annual Style Changes in the Automobile Industry as an Unfair Method of Competition, 80 Yale L.J. 567 (1971), with Areeda & Turner, Predatory Pricing and Related Practices Under Section 2 of the Sherman Act, 88 Harv.L.Rev. 697, 732 (1975).

6. See the papers, comments and bibliography appearing in ch. 3 "Advertising as an Impediment to Competition" in Industrial Concentration: The New Learning (Goldschmid, Mann & Weston, eds. 1974).

7. Comanor, Research and Competitive Product Differentiation in the Pharmaceutical Industry, 31 Economica 372 (1964).

8. See § 123 supra.

promptly right themselves and in which public intervention ought to be socially useful.

This brings us, by the long way around, to the question of remedies in cases of joint monopoly. *American Tobacco* was a criminal case. At times (and in that case, one suspects) criminal action may be brought because the Department, having no conception of what remedy would be economically sensible, is content to leave the convicted defendants to find out for themselves how to embark upon a righteous path. But where oligopolists are challenged under Section 2 for interdependently engaging in exclusionary conduct, far more useful remedies may be apparent.[9] A remedy aimed at inhibiting each participant firm from entry restricting conduct, on the lines of the remedy first used in *United Shoe*,[10] would be appropriate. A remedy aimed at breaking up the unlawful combination by seeking to stimulate independent action by its constituent parts would also be appropriate. If need be, the court might go further and break up the constituent units themselves by a dissolution decree.

Note that the dilemma is not the same as that presented regarding conduct remedies for interdependent pricing under Section 1. It may be impossible to enjoin a firm from pricing in a rational way, but it is not impossible to enjoin it from annual model changes or to specify maxima for advertising or research. Although one might conclude that oligopoly when attacked under Section 1 is less amenable to moderate, or non-drastic remedies then when challenged under Section 2, if interdependence is the settled manner of the industry and if individual firms substantially exceed in size the minimum efficient scale, the more drastic remedy of dissolution of individual firms would seem defensible.

Taken one at a time constituent oligopoly firms are not monopolists. It is not merely that they lack some magic minimum market share; it is that none alone possesses market power. No one of them could by reducing price exclude the others, for they too are earning the industry's supra-competitive returns and could match any reduction. It may therefore seem anomalous and perhaps unnecessary to break them up into smaller units. But interdependence may be a pervasive condition and, even though particular patterns which inhibit entry may be checked, firms in the industry may be able, acting interdependently, to price at supra-competitive levels for a long time to come. Given the nature of the problem, any remedy deemed reasona-

9. Cf. In re Kellog Co., FTC File No. 7110004, January 24, 1972, 547 ATTR A-3. See The FTC's Deconcentration Case Against the Breakfast Cereal Industry: A New "Ballgame" in Antitrust?, 4 Antitrust Law & Econ. Rev. 57 (Summer 1971); Kirkpatrick & Brown, The Cereal Case: Opening Shot in FTC War on "Structural" Shared-Monopoly or Attack on "Marketing" Irregularities?, 5 Antitrust Law & Econ. Rev. 89 (Fall 1971).

10. United States v. United Shoe Mach. Corp., 110 F.Supp. 295 (D.Mass.1953), aff'd per curiam 347 U.S. 521, 74 S.Ct. 699, 98 L.Ed. 910 (1954).

bly necessary and expedient to rectify it ought to be held to be appropriate.[11]

§ 125. The Federal Trade Commission, Section 5 of the FTC Act, and Non-Collusive Interdependence

The authority of the Commission to proceed under Section 5 of the FTC Act against "unfair methods of competition" comprehends not only action against misleading advertising or trade practices, but also practices which may adversely affect competition. Thus the FTC can condemn under Section 5 practices which violate the Sherman Act or the Clayton Act,[1] and beyond this, may condemn under that section conduct which has purposes or effects similar to practices which violate either of those acts, or practices which have incipient tendencies to violate either of those acts.[2]

The theoretical and empirical basis for concluding that interdependent pricing can yield essentially the same non-competitive performance in oligopolistic markets as does collusive pricing is ample to place interdependent pricing practices, such as price leadership, within the reach of the Commission under Section 5. In a given industry, a finding of interdependent pricing could be predicated on structural evidence, evidence of the history of price moves, performance evidence [3] and, if available, evidence about the subjective factors which were taken into account in particular pricing decisions. Moreover, where analysis of the industry indicated that the major aspects of interdependent conduct which inhibited competition were not pricing practices, but practices raising entry barriers, these could appropriately be challenged. The recent cereal industry complaint, which focuses on promotional expenditures, is one example.[4] Style changes in the auto industry might be another.[5]

---

11. Id. Cf. Zenith Radio Corp. v. Hazeltine Research, Inc., 395 U.S. 100, 130–31, 89 S.Ct. 1562, 1580, 23 L.Ed.2d 129, 152 (1969).

1. FTC v. Motion Picture Advertising Serv. Co., 344 U.S. 392, 73 S.Ct. 361, 97 L.Ed. 426 (1953); FTC v. Cement Institute, 333 U.S. 683, 68 S.Ct. 793, 92 L.Ed. 1010 (1948); Fashion Originators Guild v. FTC, 312 U.S. 457, 61 S.Ct. 703, 85 L.Ed. 949 (1941); Grand Union Co. v. FTC, 300 F.2d 92 (2d Cir. 1962); Triangle Conduit & Cable Co., Inc. v. FTC, 168 F.2d 175 (7th Cir. 1948).

2. FTC v. Brown Shoe Co., 384 U.S. 316, 86 S.Ct. 1501, 16 L.Ed.2d 587 (1966); Atlantic Refining Co. v. FTC, 381 U.S. 357, 85 S.Ct. 1498, 14 L.Ed.2d 443 (1965); FTC v. Beech-Nut Packing Co., 257 U.S. 441, 42 S.Ct. 150, 66 L.Ed. 307 (1922); American Cyanamid Co. v. FTC, 363 F.2d 757 (6th Cir. 1966).

3. Such as evidence showing supra-competitive profits, a failure of prices to respond to changes in cost or demand, long continued excess capacity or long continued price discrimination.

4. See Wilson, The FTC's Deconcentration Case Against the Breakfast Cereal Industry: A New "Ballgame" in Antitrust?, 4 Antitrust Law & Econ. Rev. 57 (Summer 1971); Kirkpatrick & Brown, The Cereal Case: Opening Shot in FTC War on "Structural" Shared-Monopoly or Attack on "Marketing" Irregularities? 5 Antitrust Law & Econ. Rev. 89 (Fall 1971).

5. See the authorities cited at note 5, § 124 supra.

Those who would challenge FTC power to deal with oligopolistic interdependence might not deny its well established power to denominate substantive violations, but might assert limits on the Commission's remedial arm. The Act authorizes the Commission to issue "cease and desist" orders and the position may be taken that affirmative relief may not be ordered, at least not dissolution or divestiture. Of course, much of what the Commission might wish to accomplish to deal with lack of competition in oligopolistic markets—for example, a reduction in promotional expenditures—could be accomplished through conventional negative orders. The remedies used to deal with basing point pricing systems are, of course, examples.[6] Matters which seem to call for an affirmative mandate can also be dealt with, regardless of the earnestness with which the negative phrasing of the Act is put forward as a bar. By using conditional language there is virtually nothing which the FTC could not achieve through orders negative in form. But there seems no need for cuteness or evasions. The FTC remedial powers are concededly very broad.[7] The Court in another context has held that the power to issue remedial orders granted by "cease and desist" language in an administrative statute is as broad as is reasonably needed to achieve the goals of the Act.[8] The Commission has already issued broad affirmative orders, including in a monopoly case an order for divestiture,[9] and been upheld.[10]

§ 126. Merger in Oligopolistic Markets

The most familiar legal weapon for dealing with oligopoly is preventive in nature. Under Section 1 of the Sherman Act or Section 7 of Clayton proceedings may be brought by the Department of Justice or the FTC to enjoin mergers, joint ventures or other consolidations which intensify concentration in oligopolistic markets,[1] or which, as part of a trend toward concentration, threaten to convert a workably competitive market into an oligopoly.[2] In this chapter we merely

6. E.g., FTC v. Cement Institute, 333 U.S. 683, 68 S.Ct. 793, 92 L.Ed. 1010 (1948). See § 122, note 9 supra.

7. E.g., Jacob Siegel Co. v. FTC, 327 U.S. 608, 612–13, 66 S.Ct. 758, 760, 90 L.Ed. 888, 892 (1946).

8. Pan Am World Airways, Inc. v. United States, 371 U.S. 296, 312, 83 S. Ct. 476, 486, 9 L.Ed.2d 325, 336–37 (1963).

9. L. G. Balfour Co. v. FTC, 442 F.2d 1 (7th Cir. 1971).

10. See generally, Atlantic Refining Co. v. FTC, 381 U.S. 357, 85 S.Ct. 1498, 14 L.Ed.2d 443 (1965); National Lead Co. v. FTC, 352 U.S. 419, 77 S.Ct. 502, 1 L.Ed.2d 438 (1957); American Cyanamid Co. v. FTC, 363 F.2d 757 (6th Cir. 1966); Ekco Products Co. v. FTC, 347 F.2d 745 (7th Cir. 1965).

1. E.g., United States v. Philadelphia Nat'l. Bank, 374 U.S. 321, 83 S.Ct. 1715, 10 L.Ed.2d 915 (1963); United States v. First Nat'l Bank & Trust Co. of Lexington, 376 U.S. 665, 84 S. Ct. 1033, 12 L.Ed.2d 1 (1964).

2. E.g., Brown Shoe Co. v. United States, 370 U.S. 294, 82 S.Ct. 1502, 8 L.Ed.2d 510 (1962); United States v. Von's Grocery Co., 384 U.S. 270, 86 S. Ct. 1478, 16 L.Ed.2d 555 (1966).

take note of the relevance of merger law; it is treated comprehensively in Chapter 6.[3]

§ 127. The Relationship Between Legal Theory and Policy Perceptions Which Warrant Legal Intervention

A word is due about the relationship between the perceptions about an industry which are taken to warrant intervention and the legal theory invoked to support the intervention. If one is talking about law and its enforcement, the presupposition is that action is taken against a party not only when the party is in violation of law, but also because that is so. In the antitrust area in recent years, there has been discernable distinction between the economic basis upon which the Antitrust Division decides that an action is called for and the legal basis upon which it asserts that it ought to prevail. The Division, having satisfied itself on the basis of a complex structural, performance and conduct evaluation that a given action or activity ought to be stopped, seeks on much more summary grounds to satisfy the court that the action or activity is unlawful.

The effect of this drift is to convert antitrust from law to something else. It should be a system where norms are not only generalized, but publicly stated and subject to refinement and change through adjudication, and where parties to a proceeding are permitted to participate in the process in which the facts and inferences relevant under governing norms are found and drawn.

But if a different and more sophisticated set of norms are used in deciding what industries ought to be challenged than those proposed to the court as governing its decision, much of value in what a system of law provides is lost. The agency, in refining its norms, in developing a factual basis and in drawing inferences, will be wholly insulated from the parties. What may be the real decisions will be made without party participation. The presentation in the court becomes something of a charade, where the norms which the Division presses on the court are far more sweeping than those it manipulates by itself.

Because of the complexities of the problem and the courts' tendency to prefer simplified rules which relieve them of the burdens of complexity and uncertainty, there is danger of this kind of development when law is made about oligopoly. Of the legal theories spelled out above, two seem straightforward in the sense that they identify as part of the governing legal rule the factors which constitute the real basis for concluding that intervention is needed. This is plainly so for the Section 2 theory, which predicates illegality on firms having jointly (interdependently) engaged in exclusionary activity. It also seems true of the theory that interdependent pricing constitutes a "combination" in violation of Section 1. Only in the theory that evi-

---

3. See Chapter 6 infra.

dence of interdependence and high profits warrants an inference of classic conspiracy is there any evasion, any tendency for the real basis and the legal theory for the action to drift apart.

PART D. LEGISLATIVE PROPOSALS

§ 128. The "Concentrated Industries" Legislation

The most far-reaching proposal for new legislation to cope with oligopoly is that of the White House Task Force on Antitrust Policy, a group of academic economists and lawyers appointed by President Johnson. They drafted and recommended adoption of a "Concentrated Industries Act" which would mandate the restructuring of a number of highly concentrated markets.[1] The group, chaired by Dean Neal of the University of Chicago Law School, strongly reflected a "Harvard School" rather than a "Chicago School" orientation. But they carried to a startling extreme the two hallmarks of what we have called the Harvard approach, its commitment to a structural theory of oligopoly and its concern with simplifying through rules which will not call too heavily upon judicial discretion in making judgments about economic policy.

The task force thought the evidence that harm flows from oligopoly overwhelming. Though the harms were not specified in great detail it was a conventional wisdom which informed the attitude displayed. The members concluded that a tight structure conditions conduct to yield high prices (and allocative inefficiency), high profits and, possibly, other harms like a slower than optimum rate of innovation and reduced incentive to reduce costs. To deal with this problem the task force chose a highly pragmatic approach. They felt that if courts were going to be used to rectify the oligopoly problem the need was for a set of specific criteria, more or less self-executing, which would identify industries which did not work well, and a clear set of guides for remedial decrees. The legislation they drafted has drawn attention to the potential for legislative change in this area and since its publication there have been other significant proposals for new legislation. We shall here review and discuss its major features.

The "Concentrated Industries" legislation aims explicitly at the goal of restructuring industries to reduce concentration. The standards it sets forth are entirely structural, extremely explicit connotations of high concentration. The Attorney General would be directed to identify industries having sales of $500 million or more and in which four or fewer firms have held 70% or more of the market for seven of the last ten or four of the last five years. He would be authorized to proceed against all "oligopoly firms," defined as firms

---

1. Appendix A, Report of the White House Task Force on Antitrust Policy (1968), reprinted in 2 Antitrust Law & Econ.Rev. 11–76 (Winter 1968–69).

with market shares of 15% or more, in those industries, and after a one year grace period (during which firms could take self-determined remedial action) to press for remedies aimed at reducing the share of each firm to less than 12% (and, thus, the four firm concentration ratio to less than 48%), provided that this could be achieved without reducing any firm to a size (or creating any new firm of a size) smaller than the minimum efficient size necessary for survival in the industry.

Judicial proceedings are contemplated and a wide range of remedial devices would be available to achieve the statutory end. These would include orders requiring modification of contractual relationships and methods of distribution, the granting of patent or other licenses, the divestiture of assets, or anything else which would be appropriate given the findings and the purposes of the act. But the *goal* of the remedial program is a specific and narrow one: to reduce concentration to permissible levels. To facilitate administration a "Special Antitrust Court" would be established composed of judges assigned by the Chief Justice.

The contrast between this approach to the oligopoly problem and the broader, more eclectic and analytical approach proposed in the Part B of this Chapter is manifest.[2] The proposed Act would make concentration (which is concededly one important aspect of structure) the sole indicium of whether a public intervention is needed and would make reduction of concentration the sole goal of remedial orders. The extensive awareness which has been developed about other structural qualities and about direct indicia of performance are not brought into service either in identifying industries subject to the act or in planning means of rectifying them. These and conduct issues as well are ignored.

One might blunt this criticism by asserting that the legislation should not be thought of as a model for use in identifying industries which ought to be restructured, but only as a legal means of restructuring those which are independently selected by the Antitrust Division from among all industries meeting the statutory criteria on the basis either of an additional and more sophisticated structural analysis. But this reading of the legislation gives rise to new objections.

This view of the proposed statute would embrace and gives a fresh sanction to a development in antitrust enforcement which raises grave concern about how well democratic institutions function under our method of regulating markets. It would presuppose two levels of decision making. The most important of these would be the initial one within the Antitrust Division where the "real" decision was to be made. On the basis of an ex parte evaluation of non-statutory criteria, never disclosed or reviewed by any court, the agency would decide which industries need to be restructured. If the industry "lost"

---

2. See §§ 118–20 supra.

at that stage (on the basis of whatever "evidence" the agency had gathered and whatever "analysis" it utilized, in a proceeding which, perhaps, the industry had not even heard about), the case would move on to the second level, the proceeding before the antitrust court where, with all the forms of due process, the parties would be heard only on the more perfunctory structural issues specified by the statute.

To some extent, this kind of a process has gone on in merger cases.[3] A wide prosecutorial discretion has been exercised in selecting on economic grounds the cases to be prosecuted.[4] But the government's posture in the courtroom has been to press for results on the basis of simplified structural criteria and, until recently at least, the Court has gone along.[5] But the process ought not to be amplified and institutionalized in the manner it would be if this proposed legislation were supported on the ground that the Division could exercise discretion to choose which of the covered industries should be challenged under the law, utilizing its own, non-statutory criteria.

The straightforward rationale for the White House Task Force proposal must then be that a highly concentrated structure (such as that in industries covered by the act) invites non-competitive conduct which yields poor performance, and that sufficient loosening of such a structure will rectify the ills. There is nothing wrong with that proposition as a generalization, but it is a very broad generalization. The act, on the basis of this alone, calls for highly specific and drastic remedial responses in a wide range of particular industries. So doing, it may reach industries which are not appropriate targets and may fail to reach others which are. It is simply not sufficiently selective, not nearly so selective as it is possible to be when the whole range of structural indicia and performance and conduct indicia are all consulted.

Among the industries which would be affected by the proposed act may well be a number which are already workably competitive in the Markham sense, that is, there is nothing discernible to be done which would improve matters.[6] Some may perform competitively; there may be sufficient price rivalry because of potential entry to keep prices and profits reasonable, in the economic sense. Reducing concentration in an industry like that would be pointless at best. It could also be harmful, for it might reduce firms below their efficient scale. In other covered industries conditions may be workably competitive in the sense that, although performance is not ideal, it is

---

3. See §§ 201 & 204 infra.

4. See the discussion in the appendix to Sullivan, Politics, Planning and Trade Regulation: A Glance Toward an Emerging Utopia, 16 UCLA Law Rev. 1, 31–35 (1968).

5. See the sections cited in note 3 supra.

6. See Markham, An Alternative Approach to the Concept of Workable Competition, 40 Am.Econ.Rev. 349, 361 (1950).

about as good as we can reasonably hope to make it. Here too, intervention would be pointless and potentially harmful. Despite empirical and theoretical support for the generalization upon which the statute is based, even a market where four firms have between them 80 or 90 percent is not necessarily non-competitive. Theory tells us all too little about what we can expect from an oligopolistic structure.

If the statute risks overinclusion, it risks also the opposite deficiency. Among industries not reached by the statute might be many in which patterns of price leadership and other interdependent conduct could be identified, in which performance is poor, and in which a thoughtfully worked out remedy could significantly improve functioning. The act, by focusing enforcement attention on industries identified by its threshold tests (and by implying a narrow construction limiting the reach of prior law) would immeasurably reduce the likelihood of successful public intervention in any such industry. Nor would this be but a peripheral loss, for the concentration ratio which triggers the act is exceedingly high.

The goal of this approach is, of course, simplification. Courts hate to get into the mire of elaborate economic analysis in big structural cases; they regularly seek for simplifying norms. But the potential costs of so greatly narrowing the range of inquiry is incalculable.[7] The problem lies not merely in the fact that a standard tied to intense concentration may not select out all those industries which perform badly and may select out several which perform well. It is also that without a deeper study of particular industries there is no adequate basis for fashioning a remedy which will deal in a pointed way with the performance deficiencies of the industry. The proposed statute thus makes reduction of concentration the single remedial goal, a course which it is hoped will stimulate better performance. But if entry barriers are high, conduct barriers reinforce these and interdependent pricing have in fact been operative in the industry, reducing concentration below the still high threshold stated in the remedial provisions of the act may have little tendency to rectify the performance inadequacies.

There is also an anomalous relationship between violation and remedy. If the four leading firms in an industry exceed 75%, they must be cut back to less than 12% per firm (less than 48% for the four); yet, no action is called for at all in industries where the four leading firms, though well above 48%, do not reach the critical 75%. Indeed, an industry where the largest firm held 36% and the next three 13% each would not be disturbed. But if any one of them held one percent more, remedial measures would be engaged to reduce all of them to less than 12%. This procrustean standard might constitute

---

7. Compare Dean Neal's defense of the approach the proposal takes. Neal, "On Implementing a Policy of Deconcentration," in Industrial Concentration: The New Learning, 377, 379 (Goldschmid, Mann & Weston eds., 1974).

a highly disturbing disincentive which would inhibit efficient market responses by large firms in industries where market shares were approaching the critical stage. Leading firms would know that increased success would be devastating; the problem would be uniquely disturbing because no firm could be sure how it should act to avoid the disaster. Even by cutting back its own output it might not save itself if others of the leading four expanded or if total industry sales fell.

For all of the reasons here indicated, this heroic kind of oligopoly legislation ought not to be enacted.

§ 129. Other Legislative Approaches to Oligopoly

Senator Hart's "Industrial Reorganization" bill is the most recent proposal for a wide-ranging legislative response to oligopoly.[1] Predicated upon the populist view that the pervasive oligopolistic structure places too much power in too few hands, which is bad for social and political, as well as economic reasons, this proposal would make it unlawful for any corporation or corporations to possess monopoly power in any line of commerce in any section of the country. There is no definition of monopoly power. Presumably that developed under Section 2 of Sherman would govern. However, there would no longer be need to show exclusionary conduct and, by reference to the possession of such power by one or more corporations, the bill emphasizes the concept of joint monopolization. Moreover, the act changes current law by establishing a rebuttable presumption of monopoly power on a showing that there has not been substantial price competition between two or more corporations for three consecutive years out of the last five, or if four or fewer corporations account for fifty percent or more of sales. As originally introduced, the bill would also establish a presumption of power if a corporation had an average rate of return on net worth after taxes in excess of 15 percent over five consecutive years out of the last seven. If monopoly power were established, by one of the presumptions or through other evidence (such as that which might now be used in a Section 2 case), the bill specifies divestiture as the remedy, unless the power is attributable solely to valid patents or would result in loss of substantial economies. The bill would be enforced by an Industrial Reorganization Commission before an Industrial Reorganization Court.

This proposal avoids the great pitfalls of the proposal of the White House Task Force. It accords to limited structural data no more than a presumptive role. Presumably, even a single firm with more than 50% of a market could rebut the presumption with other

---

1. S.3831, 92nd Cong. 2d Sess. (1972), reintroduced as S.1167, 93rd Cong., 1st Sess. (1973), reintroduced with minor modifications as S.1959, 94th Cong., 1st Sess. (1975), co-sponsored by Senators Mansfield, Abourezk, Domenici, Haskell, Kennedy, McGovern, Moss and Nelson. (See 719 ATRR p. A-23 (June 23, 1975).)

structural evidence—that entry barriers and barriers to expansion were low, that there was substantial inter-industry competition, that significant potential entrants and countervailing powerful sellers or buyers affected pricing conduct, or the like. Also, the low threshold of the presumption reduces a risk that firms possessing power will be missed, and in any event power could be shown, were it extant, even although that low structural threshold had not as yet been crossed. The Hart bill also shows a degree of selectivity in designating as defenses that power is based on patents or that deconcentration would substantially reduce efficiency.

Yet, some of the deficiencies of the White House Task Force proposal remain present here. There is an implicit assumption that things are simpler than they are, that competitive ills in oligopolistic markets are easily identified, and that when they are found deconcentration almost always makes things better. As the discussion in Part A of this Chapter shows,[2] the matter is more complex than that. Deeper studies of particular industries and highly particularized remedial reactions are called for.

The Hart bill in its administrative provisions has, indeed, interesting proposals for study. The Commission would be authorized to do industry investigations and specifically directed to do so in several industries.[3]

When ideas in an area proliferate we may focus overmuch on the most recent of them and leave inadequately attended the early, germinal ones. The first comprehensive legislative proposal for dealing with oligopoly was that of Kaysen and Turner. Building on the work of Mason, Bain and others, they proposed a new statute which would contain a general norm, making it unlawful to possess unreasonable market power, a concept defined as the ability of a firm or group of firms, whether or not acting pursuant to agreement or conspiracy, to restrict output or determine prices without losing a substantial share of the market or substantial profits.[4] Standing alone that approach to oligopoly would be very different from that expressed in the Concentrated Industries legislation offered by the Neal Committee and from the Hart approach. It would aim at power—the ultimate condition giving rise to social concern—and would seek to score a hit whenever and however excessive power was shown to exist.

The Kaysen-Turner proposal, however, also was attracted to the potential for simplification through structural evidence. It went on to specify a conclusive presumption that unreasonable market

---

2. See §§ 115–20 supra.

3. The "industries" designated are: chemicals and drugs; electrical machinery and equipment; electronic computing and communication equipment; energy; iron and steel; motor vehicles; and non-ferrous metals.

4. See C. Kaysen and D. Turner, Antitrust Policy 265–72 (1959).

power was exercised where one firm had 50% or four or fewer had 80% of a market for five years or more.

The conclusive presumption Kaysen and Turner proposed suffers from the same deficiencies as those assigned above to the Neal Committee proposal, or to some of them. But the general, normative standard of the Kaysen-Turner proposal is not thus flawed. It might be made the basis of legislation without the conclusive presumption. Indeed, a presumption, expressed in simplified, structural terms might also be considered, so long as it were rebuttable, as in the Hart bill. For example, it might be provided that a prima facie case of unreasonable market power was made out by a showing of a specified degree of concentration persisting over time. Or an additional, performance criterion might be added before the (rebuttable) inference were authorized—say, that the average profit rate in the industry exceeding some stated norm during a specified period. Linking structural and performance concepts in fashioning the presumption would reduce the risk that the presumption might comprehend a firm or group of firms not in fact exercising power. The fact that only a presumption was entailed and that the basic norm was a general one would leave room for those challenged to show through more comprehensive evidence or sophisticated analysis that they did not possess unreasonable degrees of power. Particularizing such requirements would not be easy, as experience with the development of merger guidelines has shown,[5] but neither would it be beyond the reach of effort and judgment.

This survey discusses only statutory proposals having broad and general application. As recent legislative proposals concerning the oil industry show,[6] oligopoly legislation could also be directed toward the problems in a single industry. This, indeed, may ultimately be the manner in which oligopoly will be dealt with, if it is to be effectively dealt with at all. There are grave, if not insurmountable, difficulties with proceeding under existing law. There are strong, if not immovable, resistances to new legislation addressing the problems in a comprehensive and general way. Of course, the prospects for specific legislation dealing with even one industry, let alone a series of such statutes, is hardly sanguine. Yet, the chance of these kinds of public responses may be higher than that of the other kinds of responses discussed in this chapter. If comprehensive studies were completed which would persuade a balanced judgment of the need for public intervention in particular industries, a balance of political forces might at times coalesce which would yield measured and responsible legislation.

---

5. See § 204 infra.

6. The bill, first introduced by Senator Nelson in 1974 (S. 3318) would require restructuring of vertically integrated oil companies. See 658 ATRR A-11 (1974).

Chapter 5

ARRANGEMENTS BETWEEN SUPPLIERS AND CUSTOMERS IN RESTRAINT OF TRADE

Table of Sections

Part	Sections
A. Resale Price Maintenance	131–141
B. Territorial, Customer and Location Restrictions in the Distribution Process	142–149
C. Tying Arrangements and Related Arrangements Involving the Leverage Concept	150–162
D. Exclusive Dealing, Requirements Contracts and Related Arrangements	163–171
E. "Reasonable" Vertical Restrictions	172–175

Sec.
130. Introduction.

PART A. RESALE PRICE MAINTENANCE

131. *Per Se* Illegality of Resale Price Maintenance.
132. History of "Fair Trade", An Alternative to Retail Competition.
133. Basic Market Effects of Resale Price Maintenance.
134. Manufacturer Motives for Resale Price Maintenance and Their Relationship to Competitive Effect.
135. Justification for the *Per Se* Rule.
136. Price Effect on the Ultimate Consumer.
137. Agency, Consignment and Related Arrangements for Controlling Resale Price.
138. Maximum Resale Prices.
139. Refusal to Deal as a Means of Restricting Resale Prices (or Imposing Other Vertical Restraints).
140. The Scope of Liability in Vertical Restraint Cases.
141. Suggested Resale Prices and Vertical "Tampering" with the Price System.

PART B. TERRITORIAL, CUSTOMER AND LOCATION RESTRICTIONS IN THE DISTRIBUTION PROCESS

142. The Varieties of Franchise Arrangements in the Distribution of Goods and Services and the Nature of the Impulses Which Lead to Restrictive Arrangements.
143. Territorial and Customer Restrictions.
144. Characterization Issues Under the *Schwinn* Rule.
145. The Justification for *Per Se* Treatment of Vertical Territorial and Customer Resale Restraints.

Pt. A   SUPPLIER—CUSTOMER ARRANGEMENTS   375

Sec.
146. Consignment and Related Arrangements to Achieve Territorial Separation.
147. Exclusive Franchise Arrangements.
148. Terminating One Dealer at the Request of Another.
149. Exclusive Franchises and the Dominant Manufacturer.

PART C. TYING ARRANGEMENTS AND RELATED ARRANGEMENTS INVOLVING THE LEVERAGE CONCEPT

150. Introduction.
151. Section 3 of the Clayton Act and the Threshold Test of Competitive Effect.
152. The Development of the Basic Rule Respecting Tying.
153. The Relationship Between Clayton and Sherman Act Standards.
154. The Patent Misuse Doctrine and the Tying Concept.
155. The Need for Two Distinct Commodities or Services.
156. Purposes and Effects of Tying.
157. "Package" Pricing.
158. "Full Line" Requirements.
159. Block Booking of Movies and the Licensing of Libraries of Music.
160. Package Licensing of Patents, Grant Back Provisions, and Royalties Which Extend Beyond the Period of the Patent.
161. Promotional Techniques Used by Manufacturers with Dealers.
162. Devices Used by Merchants to Maintain Continuity of Relationships with Consumers.

PART D. EXCLUSIVE DEALING, REQUIREMENTS CONTRACTS AND RELATED ARRANGEMENTS

163. Introduction.
164. The Development of the Law.
165. Competitive Effects of Requirements and Exclusive Dealing Arrangements.
166. Duration of the Contract Term.
167. Agency Arrangements and Exclusivity.
168. Problems of Characterization Under Section 3.
169. Integrating the Law Respecting Requirements Contracts with That Governing Similar Vertical Arrangements.
170. The Nature and Effect of Reciprocal Dealing.
171. Reciprocity Arrangements as *Per Se* Violations.

PART E. "REASONABLE" VERTICAL RESTRICTIONS

172. Introduction.
173. Restrictions to Control the Quality of Goods and Services Sold Under a Trademark License.
174. Requirements about "Competitive Style" in "Franchise" Arrangements Which Do Not Entail Carrying on Business Under the Name and Mark of the Franchisor.
175. Sales "For Professional Application" and the Like.

§ 130. Introduction

Economists quarrel about whether vertical restraints, those imposed as part of a relationship between firms performing functions at successive stages in the production and distribution of a product, can affect market competition in ways adverse to the public.[1] It is argued in this chapter that they can. Though competition does not go on between buyers and sellers, arrangements between them may affect competition at the horizontal level in the market occupied by either or both. It is the potential for such effects which concerns us. But however one may come down in that ongoing theoretical debate, the position that vertical restraints should never violate the antitrust laws can gain no credence in the face of obtrusive congressional enactments to the contrary. The antitrust laws do not deal solely with problems of allocative efficiency. In passing the Sherman and Clayton acts Congress was also concerned to protect the freedom of individual traders to make for themselves, free of compulsion or coercion, decisions about the markets they would enter, the prices they would charge and, in general, how they would compete.[2]

The variety and complexity of vertical relations should be emphasized at the outset. If some firms mine ore, others produce ingot, others fabricate aluminum products, and others distribute these to outlets where they are sold to consumers, they are all vertically related. But where one stage of production begins and another leaves off is not fixed; activity could be organized in ways which involve greater or lesser degrees of integration. All of the myriad functions which occur between the mining of ore and the delivery of aluminum furniture to the home of a buyer could be performed by one firm or by ten (or any other number) relating in a vertical flow. Indeed, there exists such variety in degrees of vertical integration that for most industries it is hard to describe what is typical.

Polar concepts can be marked out easily enough. If firms at successive stages relate solely as buyer and seller, treating each sale as a separate transaction, and if each also deals in the same way with competitors of the other, we would say their functions are totally unintegrated; each relies entirely on a series of market transactions to link its own activities with activities at the production stage occupied by the other. By contrast, if firms at different production or distribution stages are integrated into a single unit, for example by merger, their productive activities may be linked to each other by internal

---

1. In general, Harvard school theorists recognize ways in which restrictions imposed by a seller on buyers for the seller's own purposes may adversely affect competition; by contrast, Chicago school theorists regard such restraints as efficiency-producing, unless the buyers are the real instigators of the restraint, in which case the arrangement is necessarily a horizontal cartel.

2. See, e. g., Kiefer-Stewart Co. v. Jos. E. Seagram & Sons, Inc., 340 U.S. 211, 213, 71 S.Ct. 259, 260, 95 L.Ed. 219, 223 (1951); United States v. A. Schrader's Son, Inc., 252 U.S. 85, 100, 40 S.Ct. 251, 253, 64 L.Ed. 471, 475 (1920).

management decisions.³ Between these extremes are a variety of ways in which the activities of firms at successive stages may be linked in varying degrees of commercial intimacy. It is with these intermediate arrangements and their impacts that this chapter deals. Some vertical arrangements are of concern because they may have an adverse impact at a level upstream or downstream from the point at which a restraint is imposed. For example, a seller may obtain agreements from buyers, such as commitments to resell only at a specified price, which restrict competition at the buyers' level.⁴ But other vertical restrictions may affect competition at the horizontal level of the firm imposing the restriction. Thus, if a seller forbids its buyers to deal with any competitor of the seller, competing firms at the seller's level may feel the pinch. Similarly, if a buyer induces a seller not to sell to any competitor of the buyer, those competitors may be inhibited from competing effectively by the lack of needed supplies. In the sections which follow restraints in each category will be identified more precisely and analyzed.

PART A. RESALE PRICE MAINTENANCE

§ 131. *Per Se* Illegality of Resale Price Maintenance

Unless there is some basis for an antitrust exemption,¹ an agreement between a seller and its buyer fixing the price at which the buyer may resell the product is a *per se* violation of Section 1 of the Sherman Act.² Such an agreement, which courts have viewed as an unreasonable restraint on alienation, forecloses price competition among buyers on the resale of the product. The seller has no interest sufficient to warrant such a restraint; neither the seller's general good will as a maker or vendor nor its interest as the holder of a trademark or a patent on the item sold outweighs the public interest in assuring that buyers remain free to resell at prices dictated by their individual responses to the competitive conditions which they face in the resale market.³ This is the settled law.

Until recently there was federal legislation which granted an exemption from the Sherman Act for certain arrangements by which sellers restricted resale prices, so long as those arrangements were

---

3. In Chapter 7, we shall consider mergers between firms at successive stages and then analyze in some detail the determinants of the degree to which successive functions are performed within a single firm.

4. These kinds of arrangements will be discussed in Part B.

1. See § 132 infra.

2. Albrecht v. The Herald Co., 390 U.S. 145, 88 S.Ct. 869, 19 L.Ed.2d 998 (1961); Dr. Miles Medical Co. v. John D. Park & Sons Co., 220 U.S. 373, 31 S.Ct. 376, 55 L.Ed. 502 (1911).

3. See, e.g., Bauer & Cie v. O'Donnell, 229 U.S. 1, 33 S.Ct. 616, 57 L.Ed. 1041 (1931); Straus v. Victor Talking Mach. Co., 243 U.S. 490, 37 S.Ct. 412, 61 L.Ed. 866 (1917).

authorized under state law.[4] The federal exemption has been withdrawn [5] and the Sherman Act *per se* rule now applies in full force to agreements by which a seller restricts resale prices of the buyer.

§ 132. History of "Fair Trade," An Alternative to Retail Competition

State fair trade laws authorizing manufacturers to specify resale prices for their products were first enacted in the early 1930's at the behest of retail trade associations, which were often dominated by small retailers facing competition from more efficient chain and self-service supermarkets. Though differing in small details, these statutes followed a consistent pattern.[1] Agreements were authorized between a seller and buyer of commodities bearing the brand, mark or name of the seller and which were in free and open competition with like commodities produced by others. These agreements fixed the price at which the buyer would resell and obliged the buyer to impose a similar restriction if he resold other than for consumption. Once a seller had entered into such a contract with even a single buyer in the state, it became unlawful for any person to knowingly and willfully sell the commodities at a price lower than that specified in the so-called "fair trade agreement." This "non-signer clause" enabled the seller to enforce its fair trade prices by injunction against any reseller in the state.

Fair trade laws, including the non-signer clause, were valid under the Federal Constitution [2] and under the constitutions of some but not all states.[3] However, resale price maintenance is a *per se* violation of Section 1 [4] and, under normal constitutional concepts, it was not to be supposed that the courts would hold that state law could legalize these arrangements where interstate commerce was involved and the federal statute was applicable. A federal exemption was also needed. For many years a federal exemption was available. The first federal enactment, the Miller-Tydings Amendment to the Sherman Act,[5] purported to except from the coverage of Section 1 of Sherman agreements prescribing minimum resale prices which were sanctioned by state law; however, ambiguities in the statute lead the Court to hold that it did not validate enforcement against non-signers.[6] Re-

---

4. See § 132 infra.
5. See 15 U.S.C.A. § 1, as amended by Act of December 12, 1975, Public Law 94–145, CCH Trade Reg.Rep. ¶ 25,125 (1976).

1. See 2 CCH Trade Reg.Rep. ¶¶ 6000–6390.
2. Old Dearborn Distrib. Co. v. Seagram-Distillers Corp., 299 U.S. 183, 57 S.Ct. 139, 81 L.Ed. 109 (1936).
3. See 2 CCH Trade Reg.Rep. ¶ 6041 for a listing of state decisions on constitutionality. Many states have held non-signer clauses invalid; some have held fair trade statutes unconstitutional in their entirety.

4. See § 131 supra.
5. Act of August 17, 1937, ch. 690, 50 Stat. 693, 15 U.S.C.A. § 1.
6. Schwegmann Bros. v. Calvert Distillers Corp., 341 U.S. 384, 71 S.Ct. 745, 95 L.Ed. 1035 (1951).

sponding to a vigorous campaign carried out primarily by retail trade groups Congress passed the McGuire Act,[7] which made clear that resale price maintenance agreements sanctioned by state law could, without violating the antitrust laws, be enforced against non-signers, could provide for stipulated as well as minimum prices, and could oblige the buyer to impose like restrictions on resale other than for consumption. The federal exemption thus became as broad as state statutes might generally provide.[8]

Fair trade has always been a politically contentious issue. Though opponents sometimes made headway in state legislatures it was generally assumed that retailers were strong enough in Congress to head off any threat of withdrawal of the federal exemption. In 1975 that received wisdom was proved false. A period of severe inflation and a political climate warmly responsive to proposals to strengthen antitrust led to the repeal of the fair trade exemption. Now, all resale price maintenance agreements within the reach of federal law are unlawful under Section 1 of the Sherman Act.[9]

§ 133. Basic Market Effects of Resale Price Maintenance

When the manufacturer fixes the resale price, price competition is ended among retailers of the manufacturer's product. The effect on overall market competition will vary with a number of factors. If the particular manufacturer has a small share of the product market and there are numerous other brands for which prices are set competitively, the total effect on market competition may be small. The resale price established by the manufacturer for the controlled brand cannot rise significantly above the competitive level or sales may fall off rapidly. By contrast, if the manufacturer is a monopolist, all resale price competition in the product market will be ended when it controls the resale price.

Even when there are competing brands of the product, resale price competition may be significantly reduced. If the price-controlled brand is effectively differentiated, so that substantial numbers of buyers prefer it even at a higher price, resale price maintenance will deprive those buyers of the benefits of intra-brand competition among retailers. Furthermore, even if a particular brand faces competition from other brands, resale prices may also be fixed on those brands. Thus, if all or most manufacturers maintain resale prices, such price rivalry as occurs may be that between five or six manufacturers, not that between twenty or thirty dealers in a given resale market area. More particular assessment of competitive effects, es-

---

7. Act of July 14, 1952, ch. 745, 66 Stat. 632, 15 U.S.C.A. § 45(a).

8. See Hudson Distributors, Inc. v. Upjohn Co., 377 U.S. 386, 84 S.Ct. 1273, 12 L.Ed.2d 394 (1964) which interpreted the act and upheld its validity.

9. See 15 U.S.C.A. § 1, as amended by Act of December 12, 1975, Public Law 94–145, CCH Trade Reg.Rep. ¶ 25,125 (1976).

pecially an evaluation of whether the resulting resale prices will on the average be higher when price maintenance is utilized, requires consideration of manufacturer motives for using the program.

§ 134. Manufacturer Motives for Resale Price Maintenance and Their Relationship to Competitive Effect

a. Manufacturer Interest in Resale Competition [1]

It would appear to be in the interest of the manufacturer that the resale market be competitive. Given whatever price the manufacturer establishes on sales to dealers, the manufacturer's return will increase as the volume of retail sales (and corresponding purchases from the manufacturer by dealers) increases, and retail sales will increase as the retail price falls to the competitive level.

These relationships can be more easily understood if they are contrasted with those which would prevail if manufacturers were integrated forward to the resale level. Conventional theory teaches that the integrated manufacturer selling at retail would set the price which would maximize its returns. It would also seek to reduce the costs of performing the retail function to the lowest possible level, so that it would get to keep as profit the maximum portion of the price paid. For example, assume that a manufacturer's costs, not including retailing, aggregate $90 per unit of product, that the cost to it of the retail function would be $30 per unit, and that the profit maximizing retail price would be $180, yielding a per unit profit of $60. If the manufacturer concluded that efficient, unintegrated retailers could perform the retailing function at a lower cost—say, for $25 per unit including a reasonable return on their investment—the manufacturer could increase its own return by *not* performing the retail function and selling the product to all retailers ready to handle it at $155. Competition would then force the retail price down to $180 (the $155 a retailer pays for the product plus $25 needed to cover retailing cost and a competitive return to the retailer). This is the profit maximizing level previously set by the manufacturer, so it will lose no sales. But the return to the manufacturer will now be $65 per unit ($155, less $90, the cost of pre-retail functions) instead of $60.

In short, unless a manufacturer could itself retail at lower cost then others can, in which case the profit maximizing strategy is to integrate forward, a manufacturer can maximize its own return by stimulating competition at the resale level. It can harness resale competition (1) to reduce the resale price to the level which yields the profit maximizing volume for the manufacturer, and (2) to reduce the cost to the manufacturer of getting the retail function performed. On this analysis it would make no sense for the manufacturer

---

1. See B. Yamey, The Economics of Resale Price Maintenance (1954); Telser, Why Should Manufacturers Want Fair Trade?, 3 J.Law & Econ. 86 (1960); Bowman, The Prerequisites and Effects of Resale Price Maintenance, 22 U.Chi.L.Rev. 825 (1955).

through fair trade to fix the resale price at a higher level, yielding supra-competitive returns to retailers, because doing so would reduce total sales and thus reduce the manufacturer's return.

Why, then, do manufacturers set resale prices? There are a number of possible answers, each with its own implications.

b. *Manufacturer Control of Intra-brand Competition*

Chicago school analysts sometimes argue that because manufacturers have an interest in seeing that distribution is not clogged at the dealer level, the public can, when no dealer cartel appears, rely on manufacturer judgment to see that the prices set at the dealer level will assure no more than reasonable returns there. This position assumes that if the impetus for the resale price fixing program comes from a manufacturer acting without collusion, the resale prices set by the manufacturer will not result in output restrictions at the dealer level. We are talking, remember, about a program which in its typical manifestation fixes only the price below which a dealer may not sell; though this price tends to become a prevailing price, the program leaves dealers free to exceed the maintained price. Some dealers who at additional costs achieve for themselves sheltered situations—for example, TV dealers who provide home demonstrations and who often find themselves negotiating with a householder who has a new color set in the house surrounded by a group of eager and excited children—do go higher. To assume, then, that resale price maintenance will not lead to higher prices than competition among dealers would yield is to assume that cost conditions among all dealers are substantially the same and that the manufacturer, with more precision than the marketplace, can identify the selling price which will just cover the dealers' costs and yield a reasonable return.

But variations in cost structures are almost inevitable in any industry of numerous firms; retailing is no exception. Certainly the cost and revenue functions of the neighborhood store, the outlet in a local shopping center, in a regional center, or in the urban department store will differ markedly. If these outlets are left to price for themselves, there will tend to be price variations too. To the extent consumers value the convenience and service of the local market, that outlet will be able to price at a level covering its higher costs, even though higher volume, more efficient outlets charge less. Any single price the manufacturer may set will inevitably distort those fine variations which the market can make and will tend to hold the more efficient outlets, which would price at the lowest level, to a price at or near that which will be charged by the least efficient. The latter will no longer have to justify in added convenience the additional price they charge.

To vault from the recognition that the manufacturer would tax its own long range interests were it to set a minimum resale price which restricted output at the dealer level to the conviction that the manufacturer, better than the market, had grasped and penetrated the myriad data and come up with precisely that figure which—even though expressed as a minimum price, not a maximum one—would assure the highest output at the dealer level, is to engage in the most fanciful non-sequitur. Business firms frequently make decisions that are adverse to their own best interest; there is no economic law against it. The only economic law of relevance is that which says that *if* competitive conditions are maintained, the market will tend to select out for favor those firms which make the best decisions. If the retail level is competitive and if prices there are left alone to be established competitively, theory tells us that the price ultimately reached will be that which maximizes output at that level and thus maximizes manufacturer revenues. There is no theoretical reason whatsoever for assuming that the same, or in some undefined sense, a better result will be reached if the manufacturer replaces the market in deciding what the retail price will be. Indeed, theory points the other way. A maintained price will tend to be set once and thereafter reviewed and changed only occasionally. Even if it were assumed that it were initially set at the ideal level for maintaining maximum deployment of resources to the sector, it could not be as sensitive to changed conditions as a competitive price would be.

c. *Manufacturer Decisions Concerning Scale and Related Efficiencies at the Dealer Level*

A closely related argument attributes manufacturer established prices to efforts by the manufacturer to facilitate scale efficiencies and efficient promotion at the dealer level by protecting dealers from price cutters who might swoop in from afar to undercut the local dealer's volume, thus making it difficult or impossible for the local dealer to maintain the minimum efficient volume, or to promote locally in an efficient manner. As the argument goes, the manufacturer, *a priori,* must be doing *something* which is in its own interest. Since nothing else suggests itself, it is inferred that the manufacturer must be stimulating greater efficiency among retailers by making better decisions than retailers in the market can make about how the product should be marketed, and then maintaining a price which will cover the associated costs. The theoretical position is as weak as that just examined; indeed, there is an extravagant arrogance on behalf of manufacturers to claim for them that, despite their lack of involvement and experience at the resale level, they can better identify the optimum price, scale and level of promotion at that level, even though acting without the information which would be yielded by a competitive distribution system, than could dealers, involved and experienced there and possessed of that market information. Furthermore, strong impressionistic reasons intimate that resale price maintenance has nothing to do with achieving efficiency. The system is rarely used in industries like the auto industry, where the efficiency argument might have at least a surface plausibility—where there might be real concern about the "free ride" merchant, for example. It is far more likely to be used in the sale of products like brand name medicinals, where little or no promotion expense is incurred at the retail level. Appliance manufacturers, perhaps a median case between autos and brand name bottled goods, formerly used these programs to some degree, but by and large gave them up even before the McGuire Act was repealed.

Nor does the asserted interest of the manufacturer in keeping dealers from diverting to intra-brand competition energy which could better go into inter-brand competition seem a plausible one. A dealer faced with competitive pressure can be expected to reduce price, improve service, promote more aggressively and take other vigorous action—in short to compete itself. All of these actions will be as effective against inter-brand competition as they will against intra-brand competition; and they will be as effective if bestirred by intra-brand competitors as if done in response to inter-brand competitors.

d. *Retailer Cartelization*

In opposition to the manufacturer interest in keeping retail prices low through competition, it will be in the interest of retailers to have manufacturers set resale prices *if those prices can be set at higher levels than retailer competition would yield*. If this is done, retailers, in effect, gain membership in a cartel, one in which the manufacturer acts as a central body to enforce compliance with cartel prices. We may theorize, therefore, that the motivation for resale price fixing often—perhaps usually or even almost always—comes from retailers. The fact that strong support for "fair trade" laws always comes from trade associations of retailers reinforces this inference. However, there remain complications to be explained.

First, the "cartel" will be attractive to retailers only if the manufacturer can and does set supra-competitive resale prices. The manufacturer can do this—i.e., has the power to do it—only if either the brand of the manufacturer is sufficiently differentiated so that it can be sold in volume on the resale market at prices yielding a supra-competitive return, or if enough other manufacturers are doing the same thing so that their products as a group can be sold at higher than competitive prices. If one manufacturer with a small percentage of a competitive market, and without effective brand differentiation, were unilaterally to increase the resale price above competitive levels, it (and those dealers handling its product) would lose sales to other brands; the maintenance program would be of no advantage to the manufacturer and of little advantage to the retailers. Accordingly, we must assume that where resale price maintenance is used at the behest of dealers, either the single manufacturer using it has a brand with market power at the resale level or a plurality of manufacturers which together have such power are all in some way fixing resale prices.

There remains the question why the manufacturer or manufacturers, possessing market power, give in to retailer blandishments. Their own interest is seemingly different—to set resale prices at competitive levels or to let retailer competition set them there. The answer may be in the existence of countervailing power in retailers to influence the brand choices of consumers; this factor may generate in the manufacturer a hope that by setting supra-competitive resale prices it may gain special favor among retailers (if other manufacturers do not set resale prices), or it may instill a fear in the manufacturer that it may be treated harshly by retailers (if other manufacturers set resale prices and it does not do so).

e. Cultivating a Prestige Image

The manufacturer may be making and selling more than a physical product; it may be marketing a concept, a mystique of some sort. Consider perfume as an example. The cost of the physical product and container (plus shipping and customs costs) will likely be a relatively small part of the price to the customer. The manufacturer, through extensive and expensive advertising, has stimulated a demand for the product which makes it profitable to sell in relatively small quantities at a relatively high price. Where such a marketing strategy prevails, the manufacturer may conclude that availability of the product at a reduced price will not increase sales and thus its revenues. Part of what buyers are paying for is the sense that they are getting something expensive, in the ad man's term, something exclusive. Indeed, one of the explicit appeals presented may be that the product is "outrageously expensive." A manufacturer utilizing this strategy may see resale price fixing as an aid.[2]

Note that in this instance, as in others which follow, the manufacturer is not (or, at least, is not necessarily) facilitating dealer efforts to obtain supra-competitive returns. The manufacturer will set the price to the dealer and the resale price charged by the dealer. The spread between these, which is determined by the manufacturer, may yield no more than a competitive return to an efficient retailer.

f. Facilitating Point of Sale Promotion

The manufacturer may be convinced that promotional expenditures are needed and that some or all of these will be more efficient if made at the dealer level. It may also conclude that if it outlaws price competition by fixing resale prices and establishes a price which, absent dealer promotion, would yield a supra-competitive return to the dealer, it may be able to channel competitive striving by dealers into promotional expenditures. Such a manufacturer may rely on competitive experimentation by dealers to find the most effective promotional devices, confident (so long as the resale market is

---

2. See R. Posner, Antitrust Cases, Economic Notes and Other Materials 234–37.

Pt. A   RESALE PRICE MAINTENANCE   385

organized competitively) that dealers will increase promotional expenditures in order to increase their respective shares of the business until the point where supra-competitive returns are no longer being earned. Alternatively, such a manufacturer may designate the promotional service which the dealer is to perform.

g. Manufacturer Cartelization

The final motivation sometimes suggested for resale price fixing takes us full circle to cartelization once again, but here in the manufacturers' own interest. If there is a cartel among manufacturers (or if manufacturers are pricing interdependently), individual manufacturers will at times be motivated to "cheat"—to make some sales at less than the agreed upon price in order to increase output. Cheating enables the manufacturer to increase sales in either (or both) of two ways. First, by lowering the cost to its dealer the cheating manufacturer enables the dealer to lower its resale price, thus increasing its volume and, in turn, its orders from the manufacturer. Second, by lowering its price, the cheating manufacturer may be able to attract some customers away from other manufacturers.

A system of resale price maintenance, if used by all manufacturers in the cartel, will tend to foreclose the first of these ways in which a cartel member can increase sales by cheating. If prices are maintained at the next level, buyers there, although glad to receive any price reduction which may come their way, may not be willing to take a larger quantity even at a lower price because if they must resell at the same fixed price, they might experience difficulty in moving the larger quantity. All incentives to dealers to increase orders will not be gone, however. Dealers may spend some of the increased mark-up in increased promotion and boost sales that way. Or dealers may themselves successfully cheat by lowering prices. Nevertheless, resale price maintenance may in some markets afford some significant degree of aid to members of a manufacturer cartel in policing each other to avoid cheating.

§ 135. Justification for the *Per Se* Rule

The *per se* rule against resale price maintenance must be justified on the grounds that these arrangements are often the means for establishing dealer cartels or aiding manufacturer cartels; that if such arrangements are held lawful when used for a manufacturer's own individual ends, many dealer cartels (and some manufacturer cartels) will go undetected because it will be easy to camouflage them; that most self-interested goals which individual manufacturers may seek to achieve through resale price maintenance could be reached in other ways; that the social losses which result from precluding manufacturers from pursuing in this fashion those individual goals which cannot be achieved at all or achieved as well in other ways will be trivial; and that there is a significant non-economic interest in facilitating dealer independence. We have already seen that dealer cartelization may often be at the bottom of price maintenance and that manufacturer cartelization may sometimes be.[1] It is also evident that when either occurs its presence may not be blatant; seeking to pierce the veil may be a difficult and uncertain business.

It is perhaps less evident that the costs of outlawing resale price maintenance are small in instances where it is not being used to cartelize; but this case, too, can be made with some force. In the first place, in most instances where cartelization is not being accomplished or facilitated, the manufacturer ought to be able to substantially achieve its objective by less restrictive means. Take the manufacturer of perfume or scotch whiskey, which has advertised, in effect, that its product must be good because it costs so much. The promise implicit in those ads can be kept inviolate without controlling resale prices simply by setting the price to dealers at an appropriately high level. If one dealer is more efficient than others, it may be able to shave its resale price slightly and price somewhat below other dealers, but these marginal differences will hardly impeach the image which the manufacturer has established. The manufacturer can maintain the image while it and the public gain such advantages as efficiency in resale may provide. Point of sale promotion can also be encouraged without price fixing. The manufacturer can specify what it wants done and insist that it be done as a condition of continued sales to the dealer. The dealer will then have to price at a level high enough to cover its costs, but if it succeeds through efficiency in performing any of its functions (including those mandated by the manufacturer) more cheaply than other dealers, it will be able to reduce its price and increase its market share. The concern about the dealer which doesn't promote and then sells for less is illusory; the manufacturer is insisting that *all* dealers promote and can police this requirement more easily than it can police the resale price the dealer might alternatively have used.

In addition, manufacturer assertions about what they wish to achieve through resale price maintenance may themselves be inconsistent with the competitive ideal even when they do not entail cartelization. Manufacturer justifications have one common characteristic —they presuppose that an administered decision, a centralized decision made by the manufacturer and which governs all dealers, will in some sense be better than decisions made by dealers in the competitive marketplace. This assertion, in any of its manifestations, is open to challenge from several vantage points. Consider again the manufacturer marketing the product which has a prestige image. Pass over for the moment the question whether there is any social interest at all in facilitating this mode of marketing, at least when it reaches the distorted extreme where one might plausibly conclude, as

---

1. See § 134 (d) and (g) supra.

the manufacturer has evidently done, that a lower price makes the product less desirable. What is challenged here is the assumption that the manufacturer has either a special interest or a special wisdom which warrant its reserving to itself the decision about the way the precise resale price is to be incorporated into the overall marketing strategy. The interest of the manufacturer is hardly overwhelming. The manufacturer has not integrated to the resale level; it relies on sales by myriad retailers, each with its own capital investment. True, manufacturer fortunes are linked to the success dealers have in selling its product, but the dealers' fortunes are also at stake and it is not obvious why the manufacturer's interest is so great as to warrant abandonment of the usual *per se* approach to price fixing.

§ 136. Price Effect on the Ultimate Consumer

Discussion thus far has converged on relationships within the resale market. It may have been assumed that reduced competition there would mean higher prices for the ultimate consumer. Where all levels were previously workably competitive and price maintenance arises out of cartelization at the retailer level, the usual results from the creation of market power will indeed follow—increased consumer prices. Higher consumer prices would also result from manufacturer cartelization; thus, resale price maintenance intended to bolster such a cartel has an adverse impact on consumers.

But where the manufacturer sets the resale price for its own independent ends, the ultimate consequence on price is not so readily predictable. In any case where each manufacturer and all dealers are acting independently, such inter-brand competition as the market affords will limit the manufacturer's discretion in pricing; this would occur whatever the manufacturer's purposes may be, just as inter-brand competition would limit dealer power over price if no resale program were in effect.

Also, if the manufacturer's purpose is to maintain a prestige image, we cannot assume that dealers, given discretion, would set lower prices than those chosen by the manufacturer. The manufacturer, if not allowed to control resale price, will presumably price to dealers at a level equal to the resale price the manufacturer would like to see prevail, less the manufacturer's estimate of average dealer costs and return. If no dealers tend to be noticeably more efficient than others, this wholesale price will probably result in the manufacturer's desired retail price widely prevailing. Indeed, even if there are marked differences in efficiency among dealers, the low cost dealer may find it in its interest, given the nature of the demand which the manufacturer has created, to price at that level also. Comparably, in the instances where the manufacturer would set the price to encourage point of sale promotion, the manufacturer may succeed in encouraging that promotion without setting the resale price; then, dealer price discretion, given dealer promotion costs, may lead to prices at or near the same levels.

In short, taking fetters off the dealers means merely that dealers will set prices in response to competitive conditions at their level. We may expect in most instances that these prices will be less rigid than manufacturer-set prices and that dealers will be quicker to identify and react to changes in demand and cost conditions in their own market than would the manufacturer. We may also expect that there will be some variation among dealer prices, resulting from differences in efficiency or differences in the mixture of amenity, convenience and service which different dealers will offer with the same product. For example, the product may be available at a local store (offering easy access and delivery) at one price, and at a lower price in a larger department store in an urban center. Where manufacturer established prices are not performing a cartelizing function, we cannot say with certainty that prices will on the average be lower if set by dealers than if set by the manufacturer, but we can say that competition leaves room for a variety of dealer responses and for a degree of experimentation which will not likely be associated with prices established centrally by the manufacturer.

§ 137. Agency, Consignment and Related Arrangements for Controlling Resale Price

In the *G.E.* case,[1] decided in 1926, the Court held that the *Dr. Miles*[2] rule, which outlawed resale price maintenance, did not apply a system of distribution whereby the manufacturer, retaining title in itself, consigned light bulbs to independent merchants and specified the price at which the bulbs could be sold. In Simpson v. Union Oil Co.,[3] almost forty years later, the Court backed away from the *G.E.* position and refused to apply the *G.E.* precedent to facts which were at most superficially distinguishable. Union supplied gasoline to gas station operators under consignment contracts which, like the *G.E.* contracts, made the consignee responsible for stock losses other than those caused by catastrophe, and which authorized the consignor to establish the resale price. The Court said that although "an owner of an article may send it to a dealer who may in turn undertake to sell it only at a price determined by the owner," nevertheless a " 'consignment device' * * * used to cover a vast * * * distribution system, fixing prices through many retail outlets" is illegal. The *per se* rule against price fixing is not to be avoided merely by a "clever

---

1. United States v. General Elec. Co., 272 U.S. 476, 47 S.Ct. 192, 71 L.Ed. 362 (1926).

2. Dr. Miles Medical Co. v. John D. Park & Sons Co., 220 U.S. 373, 31 S. Ct. 376, 55 L.Ed. 502 (1911). See § 131 supra.

3. 377 U.S. 13, 84 S.Ct. 1051, 12 L.Ed.2d 98 (1964).

manipulation of words" covering a "coercive * * * device * * * for administering prices on a vast scale." [4]

The *Simpson* majority did not purport to overrule *G.E.*; indeed, the opinion implies that *G.E.* differs because the product there was patented.[5] But candidly analyzed, *Simpson* leaves standing nothing of the earlier holding. *G.E.* had involved two quite distinct issues: whether a license to manufacture under a patent may excuse horizontal price fixing between the patentee and the licensee, and whether a seller may, by consignment, set the price at which its goods are sold at the next vertical level.[6] The existence of a patent was the Court's basis for validating the horizontal restraint, but the *G.E.* Court did not consider the patent relevant, let alone critical, to its decision on the vertical issue. Resale control upon a true consignment was held valid; the rule against resale price fixing was limited to cases where the goods had been alienated. Nor is there any other substantial factual distinction between *G.E.* and *Simpson*. In both there were numerous consignee-firms at the next level. In both the manufacturer bore some but not all of the risks of loss at the next level and, indeed, the risks assumed were essentially the same.

Must we conclude that a manufacturer itself may never sell at the next level, and thus establish the price there, unless it integrates forward to that level? Probably not. The Court in *Simpson* stressed the comprehensive coverage, the market-wide characteristic of the arrangement, and also stressed that the consignment agents displayed many of the indicia of independent businessmen and bore as entrepreneurs many of the risks of operating at their level. If either or both of these elements are missing, the *Simpson* rule may not apply. For example, a firm which at the dealer's option sells its products or consigns them might be permitted to establish price on the consigned merchandise; this approach would eliminate the element of coercion which so troubled the *Simpson* court.[7] Also, a single transaction—say the consignment of a carload of merchandise—would not display the elements which led to the *Simpson* result and, presumably, would not be governed by that case.

If a manufacturer does integrate forward (if it undertakes the capital investment and the payroll and other expenses, as well as the inventory risks) to resell through its own outlet, *Simpson* has no application. Regardless of how vast its distribution network may be, a manufacturer which is not dealing with "independent businessmen," which does not "lace" independent dealers into an arrangement in which they must shoulder the burdens of independence but are de-

---

4. Id. at 21–22, 84 S.Ct. at 1057, 12 L. Ed.2d at 105.

5. Id. at 22–24, 84 S.Ct. at 1057–58, 12 L.Ed.2d at 105–06.

6. See also United States v. Masonite Corp., 316 U.S. 265, 279, 62 S.Ct. 1070, 1078, 86 L.Ed. 1461, 1475–76 (1942).

7. 377 U.S. at 24, 84 S.Ct. at 1058, 12 L.Ed. at 106.

prived of key decision making power, has nothing to fear from that case. Indeed, the *Simpson* rule is one of substance which rejects purely formal distinctions. Thus, a manufacturer which, as a practical matter, can be said to be selling through employees subject generally to its control does not fall subject to the *Dr. Miles* prohibition even if it has labeled its employees as "independent agents." [8]

It is interesting to note a distinction between *Dr. Miles* and *Simpson* which may in the end also have doctrinal implications, though precisely what they may prove to be is less than entirely obvious. In the early case the Court recognized that although the manufacturer was the apparent author of the price maintenance program, the real beneficiaries of it may well have been the dealers, i.e., that a dealer cartel may have been involved. In *Simpson* the Court accepted without qualification the populist conception that the firm at the earlier production stage was large and powerful and that it was coercing dealers which would obviously have preferred to be free to set retail prices themselves. It may of course be that *Simpson* was the expression of a manufacturer and not a dealer cartel; but that hardly follows from the fact that there was one refiner and many dealers, or that the refiner was large and operated regionally and the dealers were small and operated locally. These facts are just as consistent with the existence of a dealer cartel. The ideal solution would be to upset manufacture efforts to set prices at the next level through the consignment mechanism when that mechanism is being used either in the service of dealer cartelization or manufacturer cartelization or interdependence, and to uphold the use of the practice where neither is involved.[9] The difficulties of accurate characterization and the relative lightness of the social interest in using the device serve, perhaps, to explain judicial cynicism about it.

§ 138. Maximum Resale Prices

In Kiefer-Stewart Co. v. Seagram & Sons [1] the Court held it a *per se* wrong for two distributors, acting out of concern that market instability might be excessive when governmental price controls were lifted, to agree to set maximum resale prices for distributors. Because the horizontal element may warrant this result, the case does not stand as a flat holding that the imposition by a single manufacturer of maximum resale prices is banned *per se*. However, the language of the Court strongly implies that the rule respecting resale price fixing has full application whether the prices fixed are maxima, minima, or pegged. Moreover, anything left open in that decision

8. See Loren Specialty Mfg. Co. v. Clark Mfg. Co., 241 F.Supp. 493 (N.D. Ill.1965), aff'd 360 F.2d 913 (7th Cir.), cert. denied 385 U.S. 957, 87 S.Ct. 392, 17 L.Ed.2d 303 (1966).

9. Compare United States v. Arnold, Schwinn & Co., 388 U.S. 365, 87 S.Ct. 1856, 18 L.Ed.2d 1249 (1967).

1. 340 U.S. 211, 71 S.Ct. 259, 95 L.Ed. 219 (1951). See discussion in § 78 supra.

seems to have been closed in Albrecht v. The Herald Co.[2] There, a newspaper publisher violated Section 1 when it disciplined a distributor which ceased to adhere to the maximum resale prices set by the publisher; the Court expressly refused to read *Kiefer-Stewart* as applying only to horizontal agreements.[3]

Justice Harlan has urged that the setting of maximum resale prices could not injure competition, but reflects a manufacturer judgment that competition at the next vertical level is not sufficiently intensive to keep prices down to competitive levels. "Price ceilings * * * drive prices toward the level that would be set by intense competition, and they cannot go below this level unless the manufacturer * * * and the customer * * * have both miscalculated."[4] But competition at the dealer level can be injured in any of several ways. First, the manufacturer in its effort, however benign, to replicate a competitive price, may succeed in lowering prices, and so doing, may also succeed in discouraging the entry at the retail level which would have occurred had the manufacturer not interfered. Indeed, when it has set the maximum price, the manufacturer may be deterred from initiatives it might otherwise have taken to encourage new entry, to go out and look for new dealers which would make the resale market more competitive. These consequences can be harmful because the price set by the manufacturer may not be as low as would be a true competitive price; moreover, the manufacturer as a price administrator can hardly be as sensitive as would be a competitive market to the need for adjustment and change. Finally, the manufacturer, in setting a maximum price, may succeed in exploiting the dealer; it may set a price below that which free competitive processes would yield, and so deprive the dealer of a reasonable return. This need not involve miscalculation, as Justice Harlan supposed. If the investment already made by the dealer in plant or equipment is sufficiently specialized, it may not be possible for the dealer to use it elsewhere; the dealer may by earlier decisions be locked into a situation where it cannot effectively resist such exploitation over the short or medium run. It is in this situation, rather than where, as in *Simpson*, minimum prices are set, that the risks of exploiting dealers seem highest.

§ 139. Refusal to Deal as a Means of Restricting Resale Prices (or Imposing Other Vertical Restraints)

A buyer and a seller can conspire, contract or form a combination—i. e., can engage in that concert of action which is needed for a Section 1 offense.[1] The classic vertical arrangement violating Section 1 is, as in *Dr. Miles,* in the form a contract, an arrangement in

---

2. 390 U.S. 145, 88 S.Ct. 869, 19 L.Ed.2d 998 (1968).

3. Id. at 152 n. 8, 88 S.Ct. at 873 n. 8, 19 L.Ed.2d at 1003 n.8.

4. Id. at 159, 88 S.Ct. at 876–77, 19 L.Ed.2d at 1007.

1. 26 Stat. 209, 15 U.S.C.A. § 1.

which the distributor specifically agrees in return for sales to it by the manufacturer that the distributor will sell at prices established by the manufacturer. But suppose the restraint is imposed less explicitly—for example, the manufacturer, while exacting no promise from any distributor, announces to all that it will stop supplying any distributor that sells below a price suggested by the manufacturer. That arrangement, surely, would be essentially the same in purpose and effect as one in which a prior commitment had been exacted. If we were to apply the mode of analysis utilized in respect of horizontal restraints, we would conclude that there existed a contract, combination or conspiracy restraining resale prices.[2] Indeed, so long as more than one distributor is involved, the arrangement would seem itself to constitute a horizontal conspiracy among dealers on the strength of the analysis in *Interstate Circuit*.[3]

But in vertical cases the courts have in part rejected the analytical media used so effectively to identify concerted action in the horizontal realm. In seeking out concerted action between firms at different distribution stages, there is perceived a novel value in allowing a seller to choose for itself the firms with which it will deal. The Court in *Colgate* held that so long as that choice is exercised unilaterally—that is, by the seller alone, and not by the seller in concert either with other sellers or other buyers—it should not be characterized as conspiratorial even where it is being systematically exercised in a manner which in purpose and effect imposes a resale price maintenance program.[4] As the Court put the matter, "[i]n the absence of any purpose to create or maintain a monopoly, the act does not restrict the long recognized right of trader or manufacturer engaged in an entirely private business, freely to exercise his own independent discretion as to parties with whom he will deal; and, of course, he may announce in advance the circumstances under which he will refuse to sell." [5]

There is an anomaly here, a tension with the rest of the law. When resale price maintenance is imposed by explicit contract, legality does not turn upon whether the manufacturer decided upon that course unilaterally and offered terms to distributors or dealers on a take it or leave it basis. Such an arrangement being a "contract" and restraining trade, violates the Act just as much as it would if the impetus came from a group of dealers or from another manufacturer. The decision by the manufacturer is unlawful even if unilaterally made; it restrains trade, and a concert of firms is involved in its im-

---

2. See, e.g., Esco Corp. v. United States, 340 F.2d 1000, 1007 (9th Cir. 1965). See also § 109 supra.

3. "[K]nowing that concerted action was contemplated and invited, the distributors gave their adherence to the scheme and participated in it." 306 U.S. 208, 226, 59 S.Ct. 467, 474, 83 L. Ed. 610, 620 (1939).

4. United States v. Colgate & Co., 250 U.S. 300, 39 S.Ct. 465, 63 L.Ed. 992 (1919).

5. Id. at 307, 39 S.Ct. at 468, 63 L.Ed. at 997.

plementation. Although there is no greater degree of "concertedness" involved when the price maintenance policy is executed by contract than when it is executed by announcement in advance and termination of dealers which do not comply, the former is held a "contract, combination and conspiracy" and the latter is not.

There is also here an overreaching, an extension of the notion of commercial freedom beyond where the internal logic of the concept would take it. To say that a manufacturer is free to select its customers does not require that it be free to exercise its power to do so in ways that achieve forbidden ends. If a manufacturer refused to trade except with dealers which cheat their customers in accordance with a system promulgated by the manufacturer, we would scarcely hesitate to charge the manufacturer with cheating or conspiring with dealers to do so; we would have little concern for the manufacturer's freedom to select customers and announce its policy in advance. Nor would the law be likely to ignore the manufacturer's default if it announced that it would only sell to dealers which formed and operated a dealer cartel which regularly got together and established the retail price. There is no better reason to protect the manufacturer's right of customer selection when that right is used with the purpose and effect of establishing a program of resale price maintenance; by the settled law, that program is unlawful, just as are cheating and cartelization.

Because of the tension between *Colgate* and the main body of the law, the *Colgate* doctrine, as it has come to be called, has not remained untarnished. While seeking to preserve the smallest quantum of its essence—or at least while refusing expressly to overrule it—the Court has repeatedly drawn distinctions which have limited and contained the implication of the original holding.[6] The cases now come down to this, that if a manufacturer seeks to achieve resale price maintenance or any other unlawful vertical restraint through the exercise of its right to refuse to deal and a prior announcement of policy, the manufacturer's conduct remains lawful only so long as no step in addition to announcement of policy and withdrawal of trade from violators is taken by the manufacturer. If a manufacturer sets up a policing mechanism to discover violators, if it reinstates violators upon declarations of their intent to comply in the future, the *Colgate* defense is gone.[7] If a manufacturer has a two-tier system of dis-

---

6. E.g., United States v. A. Schrader's Son, Inc., 252 U.S. 85, 40 S.Ct. 251, 64 L.Ed. 471 (1920); Frey & Son, Inc. v. Cudahy Packing Co., 256 U.S. 208, 41 S.Ct. 451, 65 L.Ed. 892 (1921); FTC v. Beech-Nut Packing Co., 257 U.S. 441, 42 S.Ct. 150, 66 L.Ed. 307 (1922); United States v. Bausch & Lomb Optical Co., 321 U.S. 707, 64 S.Ct. 805, 88 L.Ed. 1024 (1944); United States v. Parke, Davis & Co., 362 U.S. 29, 80 S.Ct. 503, 4 L.Ed.2d 505 (1960); Simpson v. Union Oil Co. of Cal., 377 U.S. 13, 84 S.Ct. 1051, 12 L.Ed.2d 98 (1964); United States v. Arnold, Schwinn & Co., 388 U.S. 365, 87 S.Ct. 1856, 18 L.Ed.2d 1249 (1967); Albrecht v. The Herald Co., 390 U.S. 145, 88 S.Ct. 869, 19 L.Ed.2d 998 (1968).

7. FTC v. Beech-Nut Packing Co., note 6 supra.

tribution it cannot draw its wholesalers into a program of policing the prices of retailers.[8] Also, if a manufacturer goes into competition with its retailer or engages associates to do so for the purpose of forcing the retailer to reduce its price to that suggested, the *Colgate* defense ceases to avail.[9] So too, if the manufacturer receives reports from retailers about the pricing policies of others and implies to them that it will take appropriate action, it will have done "something more" then merely to announce its policy and then refuse to deal.[10] Similarly, a refiner which responds to a violation of its resale price policy not only by withholding gasoline, but also by cancelling the station operator's lease, has exceeded its *Colgate* rights.[11]

Like the *Colgate* doctrine itself, the cases drawing these laborious distinctions between their own facts and those of *Colgate* are infused with anomaly; many of them require nothing which in any realistic sense can be said to enhance the degree of concert involved in the price maintenance; yet, because of some added fact which is logically unrelated to whether or not an agreement is being reached, they hold that the manufacturer has exceeded the scope of the *Colgate* defense. As one court has put it, "[t]he Supreme Court has left a narrow channel through which a manufacturer may pass even though the facts would have to be of such Doric simplicity as to be somewhat rare in this day of complex business enterprise."[12] Indeed, one may wonder whether *Colgate* is not now more than outmoded, whether its shade has not at last been quietly dispatched. The signal for this may be United States v. Arnold, Schwinn and Co.[13] where the Court found enough of the stuff of conspiracy when the manufacturer "gave dealers to understand" its expectations about how they were to act at the resale level and the dealers complied. Or the end of *Colgate* may be found in *Albrecht* [14] where the Court emphasized that the seller at the earlier level and those at the next level which cooperated with it became a "combination," if not conspirators.

This section must end, then, with a pragmatic recognition. *Colgate* issues usually arise in litigation prompted by the termination of a franchise. The dealer will allege that it was terminated because it sold below suggested retail prices or failed to comply with some other allegedly unlawful vertical restriction. The manufacturer will defend

---

8. United States v. Parke, Davis & Co., note 6 supra.

9. Albrecht v. The Herald Co., note 6 supra.

10. Girardi v. Gates Rubber Co. Sales Div., Inc., 325 F.2d 196 (9th Cir. 1963); cf. United States v. GM Corp., 384 U.S. 127, 86 S.Ct. 1321, 16 L.Ed.2d 415 (1966); but see Klein v. American Luggage Works, Inc., 323 F.2d 787 (3d Cir. 1963).

11. Lessig v. Tidewater Oil Co., 327 F.2d 459 (9th Cir.), cert. denied 377 U.S 993, 84 S.Ct. 1920, 12 L.Ed.2d 1046 (1964); Broussard v. Socony Mobil Oil Co., 350 F.2d 346 (5th Cir. 1965).

12. George W. Warner & Co. v. Black & Decker Mfg. Co., 277 F.2d 787, 790 (2d Cir. 1960).

13. See note 6 supra.

14. See note 6 supra.

that its reason for discharging the dealer was entirely different—failure to exploit the product well, or credit deficiencies, for example—and will contend, as a back-up position, that if it did seek to control what went on in the resale market it did so not by contract but by "merely exercising its *Colgate* rights." *Colgate,* in fine, may often suggest itself to a defendant as a small sheet to windward, but it is quite useless as a planning device or as a basis for counselling. No firm may with any confidence plan to execute a program for maintaining resale prices through policy announcement and exercise of its right to refuse to deal. A major concern of the courts in dealing with vertical restraints, a concern which displays itself time and again, is to assure dealers a reasonable degree of independence and, in particular, to protect them from coercion. Because any full, methodical exercise of the *Colgate* right inevitably intrudes too far in the direction of restricting the retailer or even coercing the retailer to follow the manufacturer's policies, in the current climate of opinion it can for this reason alone be expected to fail.

Thus far, the discussion has presupposed *Colgate* issues arising in the course of an effort to achieve resale price maintenance. It should be emphasized that these issues can be presented when a manufacturer tries to impose some other restriction vertically, such as a restriction on resale territories, or an exclusive dealing or full line requirement. If the manufacturer gives dealers to understand a policy and enforces this policy by refusing to deal with those who do not comply, and if imposition of the policy by explicit contract would violate the law, then the manufacturer's program is in jeopardy. Any indications of involvement of any party other than the manufacturer and any aggressive or ardent involvement even by the manufacturer alone in carrying out the policy will cast the *Colgate* defense into shadow.

§ 140. The Scope of Liability in Vertical Restraint Cases

The wide net which has been cast in finding the plurality of actors which make out a combination or conspiracy in some of the vertical cases gives rise to potentially vexing issues about the ambit of liability.[1] *Perma Life,*[2] for example, implies that the members of the combination and conspiracy include all dealers who did not resist the restriction imposed by the manufacturer. This may be fair enough when the restriction amounts to a dealer cartel, but it does not amount to that in all cases. To hold every participating dealer liable however adverse to their own interests they may have seen the policy, however coercive the manufacturer's insistence that they abide

---

1. See An Interview with the Honorable Donald F. Turner, 37 Antitrust L. J. 290, 300–01 (1968); Pitofsky & Dam, Is the Colgate Doctrine Dead? 37 Antitrust L.J. 772, 781, 784 (1968); Levi, The Parke, Davis-Colgate Doctrine: The Ban on Resale Price Maintenance, 1960 Sup.Ct.Rev. 258.

2. Perma Life Mufflers, Inc. v. International Parts Corp., 392 U.S. 134, 88 S.Ct. 1981, 20 L.Ed.2d 982 (1968).

by it, and however passive their involvement, is enforcement with abandon.³ In governmental enforcement proceedings, discretion may be used in choosing defendants, but it is not clear that treble damage claimants will always be discreet. For example, a franchisee which at some point resists the resale price or territory restrictions imposed by the franchisor may bring its action against the franchisor and some or all other franchisees, including, perhaps, several which had been as fully distressed by the program as had the plaintiff, though they had not as yet resisted so vigorously.

A private plaintiff bringing a jury action must have a sense for the intuitive response to its claim and this will serve to screen out many unfortunate defendants in private actions of these kinds. Typically, these actions are brought either against the manufacturer alone or the manufacturer and one or two competing dealers which were allegedly implicated directly in the action taken by the manufacturer against the plaintiff. But the law ought to be as fine grained as the situations with which it must deal; it may need to learn ways to include a person or firm for the purpose of establishing the concertedness of conduct essential to a Section 1 violation, yet to exclude that person or firm in assigning liability. For example, the word "combination" in the statutory phrase has never been given definitive meaning distinct from "contract" or "conspiracy"; when a different meaning has been suggested the word has usually been taken to signify a firm made up of previously independent units.⁴ In the vertical context, the term "combination" could be taken to suggest the unified distribution structure made up of the manufacturer and its dealers, each doing the manufacturer's bidding in respect to resale prices or territories. Liability could then be made to turn not on membership in the combination, but on responsibility for it. Thus the manufacturer, necessarily an active agent, would be liable. But dealer liability would depend upon some showing of consensual involvement beyond mere acquiescence. Under this approach, a dealer which engaged in policing activities would be liable, as of course would one which had at the outset urged the manufacturer to impose the resale restrictions.

Another possible basis for confining liability would be to respond generously to dealer claims of business coercion. A person who established that he participated in a criminal conspiracy under conditions of physical duress would not share criminal liability. The same

---

3. See § 134 supra. Albrecht v. The Herald Co., 390 U.S. 145, 88 S.Ct. 869, 19 L.Ed.2d 998 (1968) would include in the combination or conspiracy any new dealer which replaced the terminated one, or even an agency engaged by the manufacturer to solicit customers away from a non-complying dealer.

4. See, e.g., Turner, The Definition of Agreement Under the Sherman Act: Conscious Parallelism and Refusals to Deal, 75 Harv.L.Rev. 655 (1962); Baker, Combinations and Conspiracies—Is There A Difference?, 14 Antitrust Bull. 71 (1969).

ought to be true for economic duress. It would be straining the concept of coercion to apply it to a dealer which passively acquiesces in resale restrictions presented on take it or leave it terms, especially since acquiescing dealers may benefit from the dampening of competition. Nevertheless, in order to tune the law more finely to the policy goals which we would have it express, that degree of strain on the concept may be warranted, at least in those instances when it seems clear that the primary impetus for the arrangement comes from the manufacturer, not from dealers.

§ 141. Suggested Resale Prices and Vertical "Tampering" with the Price System

Correlative concepts may develop divergent and independent meanings. While horizontal action tantamount in purpose and effect to price fixing has been characterized as price fixing and held to be *per se* unlawful,[1] this approach has not been applied to vertical contexts. The most obvious example is the widely used practice of manufacturers announcing "suggested" retail prices for their products. So long as nothing more is done, the practice is uniformly regarded as lawful; indeed, unless it is to be frankly overruled, *Colgate* demands at least this. But universal acceptance of the position does not make it consistent with that taken about horizontal restraints. *Socony-Vacuum*[2] instructs that any effort to "tamper" with the free working of the price system is *per se* unlawful. When horizontal restraint is in contemplation these dicta are scrupulously respected. Surely a "suggested" price program which is horizontal in inception and application would violate the law. Yet suggested resale prices are countenanced although the manufacturer can have only one purpose—to affect the price at which dealers resell. Though dealers may or may not universally follow them, surely suggested prices "tend" either to "stabilize" price at the level selected by the manufacturer or to establish that level as the base price from which discounts are computed. If the law as to vertical restraints were wholly consistent with that as to horizontal restraints, suggested resale prices would be *per se* unlawful.[3]

Other examples of vertical "price tampering" have also been treated with generosity. For example, a soft ice cream franchisor which operated some retail outlets did not violate the *per se* rule in supplying to its franchisees information about the prices it charged in its own stores, or in advertising nationally that specialties bearing its trademark were available at a specified price.[4] Similarly, it was

---

1. See Ch. 3, Part B supra.

2. 310 U.S. 150, 60 S.Ct. 811, 84 L.Ed. 1129 (1940). See §§ 67 and 74 supra.

3. See, e.g., Plymouth Dealers Ass'n of N. Cal. v. United States, 279 F.2d 128 (9th Cir. 1960).

4. Engbrecht v. Dairy Queen Co., 203 F.Supp. 714 (D.Kans.1962).

held no violation to print a price on a package sold to retailers.[5] Practices like these have seldom been challenged and when challenged have generally been upheld, though a scrupulous evaluation of purpose would probably show a motive by the manufacturer to stabilize resale price and a scrupulous evaluation of effect would probably show that the hoped for goal was in some measure achieved.[6]

An experienced and respected commentator has argued that the manufacturer's interest in the way his goods are marketed warrants this softening of attitude.[7] If there is anything to this argument, it can hardly apply uniformly to all manufacturers. Where a manufacturer's product becomes but one of a variety of products of many manufacturers in the reseller's inventory, the manufacturer can claim no affinity with the resale process which warrants it to intervene; competition ought adequately to serve the manufacturer's proper interests as well as those of consumers. The argument gains some energy when pressed on behalf of a firm, such as a fast food franchisor, which licenses a trade name and which may sell products to be resold under this trade name. Such a firm must standardize quality, packaging and service characteristics, both to keep from diluting the value of the trade name and to assure a reasonable return for system-wide advertising. Therefore, it has a considerable interest in the resale activities of franchisees and might be given a right to participate with franchisees in price making, at least to the extent of suggesting a price and advertising it. Either of two theories serve to justify this result, while distinguishing cases where no special interest of the seller in the resale processes can be shown. First, that the degree of integration warrants treating the franchisor and franchisees as joint venturers in the retail operation, rather than merely supplier and customer, thus warranting franchisor advertising or suggestions; or second, that the price participation by the franchisor is ancillary to the licensing of the trade name and reasonably necessary to facilitate the main transaction.

It may be objected that these arguments, even when presented only on the behalf of sellers which do have fully developed interests in buyers' resale policies, prove too much. If either the joint venture or the ancillary restraint analogy carried weight at all, it would be logically sufficient to warrant resale price maintenance by any seller passing the required threshold of interest in his buyers' operations, a practice which cannot be validated under settled law.[8] Although this objection is consequential, pragmatically the policy choice now open is not whether to allow sellers with a special interest to set resale

5. Bailey's Bakery, Ltd. v. Continental Baking Co., 235 F.Supp. 705 (D.Haw. 1964).

6. See United States v. Gasoline Retailers Ass'n, Inc., 285 F.2d 688 (7th Cir. 1961) (horizontal agreement limiting price advertising is a *per se* violation).

7. Elman, "Petrified Opinions" and Competitive Realities, 66 Colum.L.Rev. 625 (1966).

8. See §§ 132 and 135 supra.

prices, but whether to limit the right to suggest or advertise resale prices only to such sellers, rather than according it to all.

None of this is intended to suggest that we can in the future expect serious attacks upon suggested resale pricing or related vertical activities. It is rather to insist that we must look elsewhere than to an analysis which convincingly establishes legality for an explanation of why we have not yet seen these programs challenged. Note first that these programs are seldom if ever challenged in private litigation. If any dealers become resistant to the manufacturer's suggestion and the manufacturer seeks to "enforce" the "suggested" prices by refusals to deal or other means, the manufacturer will have crossed the line marked by *Colgate*. And, so long as dealers uniformly are willing to comply or the manufacturer takes no action when they do not, there will simply be no private party with an interest in challenging the program, however much it may be tantamount to vertical price fixing in purpose and effect. Single consumers will have no sufficient interest and barriers to consumer class actions have of late reached astonishing heights.[9] Public litigation could be initiated, of course, but in this area both the Department of Justice and the FTC seem more concerned with protecting the independence of dealers from intrusive manufacturers than with maintaining the pristine integrity of a competitive price system. It is precisely because suggested prices and like programs do not significantly undercut dealer independence, nor coerce dealers into following a course prescribed by others, that any challenge to them is well down on the list of public enforcement priorities.

PART B. TERRITORIAL, CUSTOMER AND LOCATION RESTRICTIONS IN THE DISTRIBUTION PROCESS

§ 142. The Varieties of Franchise Arrangements in the Distribution of Goods and Services and the Nature of the Impulses Which Lead to Restrictive Arrangements

Franchising is an old concept, but distribution systems based on it have been more widely pursued in recent years than ever before. The boom has generated opportunities for small businessmen with modest capital; but with these opportunities have come a number of legal, commercial and social problems.[1] In the resolution of those

---

9. See Eisen v. Carlisle & Jacquelin, 417 U.S. 156, 94 S.Ct. 2140, 40 L.Ed.2d 732 (1974), vacating and remanding 479 F.2d 1005 (2d Cir. 1973); see also, Kline v. Coldwell, Banker & Co., 508 F.2d 226 (9th Cir. 1974).

1. Among the concerns which have received the most attention are that some franchisors have used fraudulent methods in inducing franchisees to invest, have overreached in various ways during the course of the relationship, or have arbitrarily terminated it. See, e.g., Symposium on Franchising, 17 Antitrust Bull. 181 (1972); Restrictions Ancillary to the Protection of Goodwill and Trademarks (Symposium), 36 Antitrust L.J. 49 (1967).

problems which impinge more or less directly upon the competitiveness of market structure and conduct, antitrust has its role to play.

The distinguishing feature of a franchise arrangement is that customers, often the public generally, perceive an identification between the franchisor and franchisee. This quality, however, is one which franchise arrangements may possess in varying degrees. Among the numerous factors which affect the degree of identification —and these vary as widely as do the styles in which a business may present itself to the public—there is one of a categorical nature and, as it happens, of definitional potential. It is the extent to which the franchisor grants to the franchisee rights to use the trademark and trade name of the franchisor. Let us underscore this characteristic by contrasting three arrangements. In the first, a TV manufacturer sells merchandise to a retailer and enters into a "franchise agreement" which states the intent of the parties to deal with each other and the willingness of the seller to meet the buyer's orders at prices from time to time prevailing on specified terms as to credit, delivery and the like, and which states that the franchisor neither authorizes the franchisee to carry on business under the name of the former nor to make any commitment on its behalf. In the second, a bicycle manufacturer sells merchandise to a retail dealer and enters into a "franchise arrangement" which obliges the dealer to maintain a service department adequately equipped and supplied with parts and to maintain in inventory a "representative selection" of the manufacturer's products. The agreement also authorizes the dealer, until directed otherwise, to hold itself out to the public as the manufacturer's "authorized dealer," and to display the manufacturer's brand name and trademark, along with the dealer's own name, in advertising, signs and displays. In the third, a restaurant company which operates some of its own retail units enters into a franchise arrangement in which it authorizes the franchisee to operate a restaurant under the franchisor's name, and using the franchisor's trademark, upon condition that the franchisee's place of business meets architectural and design standards established by the franchisor, and that the business be carried out in accordance with detailed standards established by the franchisor as to hours, style and type of service, menus, food preparation, and all the details of business presentation and merchandising. In the first case, the relationship is essentially that of buyer and seller; though the contract is called a franchise, nothing more is entailed than a continuity of product flow. In the second, though the public may be supposed to recognize the separate commercial character of the manufacturer and the dealer, the retailer operates in some degree under the aura of the manufacturer. In the third case, a large portion of the public is likely to assume that the franchisor operates the outlet and those without this misapprehension will correctly assume that the franchisor controls a great deal about the way business is done there. In the first case, there is nothing that is, strictly speaking, a "franchise." The manufacturer sells merchandise to the dealer; after the dealer buys it, the dealer needs no franchise, no grant of right, to resell it. That right is a basic attribute of title. In the second case the only real franchise conferred is the right given the dealer to hold itself out as an "authorized dealer," thus implying to the public that the manufacturer approves of the way the dealer does business and the service it offers—i.e., that the dealer lives up to the manufacturer's standards. In the third case, the local merchant carries on his entire business under the trademark and trade name of the national firm; the local outlet holds a franchise in the strictest sense—a license granting the right to trade under the mark and name, provided that the licensor's standards for the business are maintained.

Any of these types of franchise may include restrictions of various kinds on the franchisor or the franchisee. We have already mentioned provisions about display and service facilities in the second instance and detailed standards for conduct of the business in the third. There might also be provisions about where the business may be located, what territory it will serve, whether or not and the extent to which either or both parties would deal exclusively with the other, and the like. In this part we will examine territorial, customer and related restrictions imposed on franchisees or other buyers; in the parts which follow we will address other restrictions. The distinctions between different types of franchise arrangements noted in this introduction will have relevance to the problems which will be discussed; to note these distinctions is a first step in understanding the "business stuff" out of which these arrangements arise.[2]

There are of course many other ways in which manufacturer-dealer relationships vary. In some, the manufacturer may offer numerous services to the dealer, such as advice and assistance in site selection, selling and record-keeping methods; in others, the manufacturer may offer no services. In some, the dealer may possess significant market power through customer acceptance of what the dealer has to offer; in others the dealer may be powerless. In some, the dealer may be old, reliable and experienced; in others it may be a neophyte. In some, the dealer may devote all or substantial attention to the manufacturer's line; in others that line may be one of many for the dealer. In some, the dealer may be well financed; in others the dealer may be badly undercapitalized and always on the edge of disaster. In an individual case any or all of these and related variables may suggest themselves as significant in an effort to understand the likely market effect of any particular practice.

2. See Handler, Statement Before the Small Business Administration, 11 Antitrust Bull. 417 (1966).

§ 143. Territorial and Customer Restrictions

The *per se* rule which now governs vertical restrictions imposed by a seller on the territories within which, or the customers to which, the buyer may resell has had an elusive history. These restrictive arrangements were long thought invalid when they were part of an aggregation of trade restraints which included resale price fixing.[1] In 1949, when the Justice Department took the position that all such arrangements were *per se* illegal, few could have been taken by surprise.[2] There followed through the 1950's and early 1960's a series of cases brought by the government to stamp out these restraints.[3] Consistently, these cases ended in consent decrees granting the relief requested; the *per se* position was vindicated without a fight.[4] Nonetheless, the FTC's comparable enforcement program eventually ran into trouble in the courts.[5] And when one of the Justice Department proceedings, that against the White Motor Company, was finally litigated, the outcome left important issues in doubt.

White sold its trucks to distributors, each of which was given an exclusive territory and each of which agreed not to sell except to customers located within the territory, and not to sell to the federal or any state government or political subdivision, accounts which White planned to serve itself. White admitted the restrictions and defended that they were essential to enable it, a small firm, to hold its place in the market. But the restrictions were held invalid *per se* by the district court; it refused to hear evidence in justification. The Supreme Court, facing for the first time the issue of legality of such restraints, reversed. Mr. Justice Douglas, writing for the majority, did not state that these practices were lawful, nor did the opinion indicate that the rule of reason applied. What the Court held was simply this, that absent a factual record and argument, the Court did not know enough about these arrangements and their purposes and effects to decide whether they should be classified as *per se* unlawful or assigned to the rule of reason. The judgment was therefore vacated and the case remanded for trial.[6] On remand, however, this case, like

---

1. United States v. Bausch & Lomb Optical Co., 321 U.S. 707, 64 S.Ct. 805, 88 L.Ed. 1024 (1944).

2. See Rifkind, "Division of Territories," in How to Comply with the Antitrust Laws (Van Cise & Dunn, eds. 1954).

3. See the citations to sixteen consent decrees entered in such cases between 1948 and 1962 in Stewart, Franchise or Protected Territory Distribution, 8 Antitrust Bull. 447, 470 n.51 (1963).

4. Id.

5. In both Sandura Co. v. FTC, 339 F. 2d 847 (6th Cir. 1964) and Snap-On Tools Corp. v. FTC, 321 F.2d 825 (7th Cir. 1963) courts set aside orders entered under Section 5 of the Federal Trade Commission Act which prohibited closed territorial distribution. In Sandura, there was a failing company argument, which had more appeal to the court than to the Commission, but Snap-On entailed a flat-out judicial rejection of the basic Commission position.

6. White Motor Co. v. United States, 372 U.S. 253, 83 S.Ct. 696, 9 L.Ed.2d 738 (1963).

the many before it, was disposed of by a consent decree enjoining continuation of the practice; the case did not yield a record disclosing the "business stuff" the Court felt it needed to decide what rule of law appropriately applied. *White Motor* thus cast in some doubt the prevailing assumption that vertical resale restrictions were *per se* unlawful, but left the question unresolved.

A few years later when the Court did have before it a factual record in a similar case, it promptly rebound what had been briefly loosened by holding that a vertical restraint restricting the territories in which or the customers to which a buyer might resell is illegal *per se*.[7] *Schwinn* involved a bicycle manufacturer which in the early 1950's had been the leading maker with about 25% of the market. In a decade its position deteriorated to about 13% as mass merchandisers like Sears and Montgomery Ward expanded sales under their brand names of bicycles made for them by manufacturers other than Schwinn. In an effort to combat the erosion of its market share, Schwinn set up a complex distribution system. It sold less than half of its bikes to 22 distributors, each of which was instructed to resell only within designated territories and only to retailers franchised by Schwinn. It also consigned a small portion of its bikes to these distributors under similar restrictions. The rest of its bikes, more than half of its product, Schwinn sold and shipped directly to its franchised retailers upon orders taken by the Schwinn distributors, who received a commission on these sales. Retailing was in the hands of 5,000 franchised stores which either bought direct from Schwinn (giving orders to distributors for shipment and billing by Schwinn) or bought from the distributors bikes either owned by them or consigned to them by Schwinn. Each of these dealers was franchised with respect to a designated outlet and agreed not to resell to unfranchised dealers. The district court, after hearing evidence as to purpose and effect (including evidence of Schwinn's view that it needed the restrictions to retain its status in the market) ruled that the territorial restrictions imposed by Schwinn on its distributors with respect to merchandise sold to distributors were unlawful, but that in other respects the program was reasonable and lawful. It therefore enjoined only that territorial restriction. The Supreme Court reversed in part, ordering that the injunction be extended to preclude Schwinn from requiring distributors, once they had purchased the product, from confining their sales to franchised retailers, or from confining the freedom of any retailer, once merchandise was sold to it, as to where and to whom it might resell. The Court, however, drew the same distinction as had the court below between merchandise sold by Schwinn to distributors and merchandise handled by distributors solely as consignees or as sales agents taking orders for Schwinn. As

7. United States v. Arnold, Schwinn & Co., 388 U.S. 365, 87 S.Ct. 1856, 18 L.Ed.2d 1249 (1967).

to the latter transactions Schwinn was left free to restrict the distributors—though not the retailers, once dominion and control over the merchandise passed to them as buyers. As the Court put it, there is a crucial difference "between the situation where the manufacturer parts with title, dominion, or risk with respect to the article, and where he completely retains ownership and risk." [8]

In reaching these conclusions the Court announced the *per se* rule it had declined to announce in *White Motor,* saying:

> "Under the Sherman Act, it is unreasonable without more for a manufacturer to seek to restrict and confine areas or persons with whom an article may be traded after the manufacturer has parted with dominion over it * * *. Such restraints are so obviously destructive of competition that their mere existence is enough. If the manufacturer parts with dominion over his product or transfers risk of loss to another, he may not reserve control over its destiny or the conditions of its resale." [9]

The debate did not end with this pronouncement. There has been considerable resistance to *Schwinn,* although the case has had its champions both on the bench and among commentators.[10] Some commentators have marked out for acidulous treatment the fact that the very same restraints, unlawful as to bikes sold, were held valid when incident to consigned bikes for which the manufacturer reclaimed title, dominion and risk of loss. The difference between the two situations is, of course, the extent of integration. Take a horizontal case as an example. Suppose firms A and B are competitors. If they agree on prices, it would be a *per se* violation. However, we analyze the matter differently if they are integrated; if A merges with B prices will be jointly fixed, but the merger is nonetheless lawful unless an adverse effect on competition is proven. Now consider a vertical case. A, a seller, merges with B, one of its buyers; thereafter the management of A will manage B and determine not only where and to whom B will resell, but also what products and at what prices. Elements are present which would call forth several *per se* rules if A were to impose on B to the same degree without the integration, but merely in the course of making sales to it. But because of the merger, the integration, we test liability not by a *per se* standard, but by whether competition is likely to be injured. The mani-

---

8. Id. at 378–79, 87 S.Ct. at 1865, 18 L.Ed.2d at 1260.

9. Id. at 379, 87 S.Ct. at 1865, 18 L.Ed. at 1260.

10. See Cooper Liquor, Inc. v. Adolph Coors Co., 506 F.2d 934 (5th Cir. 1975) (per Wisdom, J.); Comaner, Vertical Territorial and Customer Restrictions: White Motor and Its Aftermath, 81 Harv.L.Rev. 1419 (1968). See also the dissenting opinions of Judges Kilkenny and Browning in GTE Sylvania Inc. v. Continental T.V., Inc., 537 F.2d 980, 1004, 1018 (9th Cir. 1976) (en banc), cert. granted, U.S.S.Ct.Dkt. No. 76–15 (Oct. 18, 1976). The author is attorney for Continental in this case.)

fest reason is that the restraints arising out of the integration are not naked restraints, they are the concomitants of a new investment and, it may well be, of attained efficiencies. To forbid the integration because of the restraints would certainly remove the restraints, but only at the cost of removing the integration and the social values associated with it. Knowing this cost, the law does not make the integration *per se* illegal, but holds it illegal only if the restraints have a discernible bite.

The above analysis also applies to a system of consignment, which is also an integration by the seller down to the next level, albeit a partial one. There is no buyer now and, although the consignee, which gets its returns through commission, supplies some of the capital at the next level, it is the seller which at that level retains title, dominion and risk with respect to the goods. The intuitive response of the trader in the marketplace would lead him to say in the sale case: "You've taken your price; now, don't start telling me what to do with my merchandise." In the consignment case the dealer would say: "I'll need a commission of twenty percent; how much do you want me to charge for these to cover what you've got tied up in them and where do you want them sold"? Because of the integration —the extension by the consignor of new investment and its risk-taking in the market—there would be a social cost in forbidding the consignee (the owner of the merchandise) from pricing it or controlling the persons to whom and places at which it is sold which, in the sale cases, is simply not present.

The ancient concept of restraints on alienation *is* a convenient one with which to demarcate between the *per se* area and the area in which the rule of reason governs. It is workably precise, surely no small advantage in a realm of the law where much is shrouded in sweepingly vague characterizations. Furthermore, as it discriminates on an economically significant ground—whether the restriction is associated with a partial forward integration or is a naked one—it will tend to screen out for *per se* treatment the instances where there is little or no social advantage in allowing manufacturer interposition at the next level, while assigning for rule of reason treatment cases where hampering manufacturers by discouraging their investment at the next level would entail social costs. It is also consistent with and responsive to the visceral reactions of people in the marketplace about the difference between mine and thine. Indeed it has a Hegelian quality which may reflect deep psychic attitudes about property.[11]

11. See G. Hegel, Philosophy of Rights §§ 44–53 (T. Knox ed. 1953). As Judge Browning stressed in his dissenting opinion in GTE Sylvania Inc. v. Continental T.V., Inc., (note 3 supra), it is not the naked transfer of title that is determinative under *Schwinn*'s alienation rule; the question is whether the position and function of the dealer are, in fact, those of an agent or salesman, on the one hand, or those of an entrepreneur, on the other. The "Hegelian" basis for the *Schwinn* rule was manifested recently by a dealer who stated: "Of course I recognize that the manufacturer continues to have an interest in his merchandise after he sells it to me. He probably

If there is an anomaly in *Schwinn* it is not so much an internal one as a tension between the *Schwinn* position and that of *Simpson*,[12] a resale price fixing case which held that a consignment did not take the transaction out of the ambit of the resale price fixing *per se* rule. *Schwinn* teaches that bona fide consignments are enough to remove resale restraints from the *per se* area; *Simpson* suggests that where a system of consignments is used to cover a network of retailers having other attributes of independent businessmen, it is not.

A consistent approach to the consignment question in both the price and territorial contexts should be developed. The most reasonable response would be to integrate *Schwinn* and *Simpson* by holding that a consignment would take the transaction out of the *per se* area if it involved a significant integration—that is, a significant involvement by the manufacturer at the next stage, in terms of the manufacturer's investment and the risks to which the manufacturer exposes itself—but that a consignment would not take out of the *per se* area a transaction in which the manufacturer's integration to the next level was trivial—a transaction which as a practical matter was tantamount to a sale. For the rest, commentary hostile to *Schwinn* comes either from those who embrace the "horizontalist" view, those who assert that no vertical restriction ought to be of concern, from those who find it somehow incompatible with manufacturers' innate prerogatives that manufacturers cannot tell customers how to deal with merchandise sold to them, or from those who would pick out a different line between lawful and unlawful territorial restraints than that to which *Schwinn* points.[13] Judicial coolness to *Schwinn* is a less focused matter; it shows itself mostly in discussion about the scope of the territorial *per se* rules, a matter to which we now turn.

§ 144. Characterization Issues Under the *Schwinn* Rule

Few antitrust concepts have been subject during the last decade to more debate and disagreement than the scope of the *Schwinn* rule. Even so, there are issues of some importance which, if not settled for all time, are at least clear enough for now. Let us look at particulars to see what one may now say with confidence about the scope of the rule. In the course of that process the underlying principle which guides interpretation of the rule should disclose itself. For one, *Schwinn* does not out-of-hand invalidate a "primary responsibility

---

has the same affection for the merchandise that I have for the money I paid him. And I'll be glad to concede him as much control over my merchandise that used to be his, as he gives me over his money, that used to be mine."

12. Simpson v. Union Oil Co., 377 U.S. 13, 84 S.Ct. 1051, 12 L.Ed.2d 98 (1964); see discussion in § 137 supra.

13. See Adolph Coors Co. v. FTC, 497 F.2d 1178 (10th Cir. 1974), cert. denied 419 U.S. 1105, 95 S.Ct. 775, 42 L.Ed.2d 801 (1975); Robinson, Recent Antitrust Developments, 75 Colum.L.Rev. 243, 270–281 (1975).

clause," whereby a franchisee promises to devote its best efforts to promoting and marketing the product within a designated territory.[1] Under this arrangement the manufacturer, which concededly does have some interest in how effectively franchisees market, exacts from them a direct commitment about the level and intensity of activity to be expected from them. The arrangement gives the manufacturer what it reasonably needs without putting any dealer under wraps; all remain free by making the extra effort and investment to invade the territory of other dealers, so long as they are making effective efforts in the areas for which the manufacturer relies upon them. On the other hand, use of primary responsibility language would not save an arrangement if its purpose and effect were to restrict each dealer to its own resale territory;[2] procrustean enforcement which punished dealers making outward forays even though there was no objective difference between their performance within their home areas and that of more docile dealers would serve to identify a sham arrangement.

Additionally, the *Schwinn* rule does not preclude the licensor of a trademark or name from restricting the places where the licensee is authorized to do business under the mark or name.[3] The license entails no sale of goods, but (quite literally) a franchise, a grant of the right to use in a limited manner an intangible which remains the property of the licensor and in the use of which the licensor obviously retains an interest, indeed, the dominant one. It would be quite otherwise, of course, if the licensor also restricted the place of resale of any products sold by the licensor to the licensee in connection with the franchise; *Schwinn* would apply in full vigor if the licensor told the licensee not to sell merchandise anywhere except in the territory served by the franchised location. Chicken Delight has a right to tell its dealers where they may use its mark and name; but that does not confer on it the right to tell them not to resell chickens they buy from it at other places.

It is equally clear that *Schwinn* forbids restrictions limiting buyers to resales in bulk [4] (or otherwise requiring seller approval of resales) or forbidding a buyer to ship goods for resale to destinations beyond the range of its service facilities. These arrangements not only fall under the literal language of the *Schwinn* proscription, but

---

1. The decree on remand in *Schwinn* authorized the use of such a clause. United States v. Arnold, Schwinn & Co., 291 F.Supp. 564, 565–66 (N.D.Ill. 1968). So do numerous consent decrees which enjoin resale territory restrictions. See, e.g. the decrees cited § 143 note 3 supra.

2. E.g., American Motor Inns, Inc. v. Holiday Inns, Inc., 365 F.Supp. 1073 (D.N.J.1973).

3. See the several opinions in GTE Sylvania Inc. v. Continental T.V., Inc., 537 F.2d 980 (9th Cir., 1976) (en banc) cert. granted, U.S.S.Ct.Dkt. No. 76–15 (Oct. 18, 1976). (The author is attorney for Continental in this case.)

4. United States v. Glaxo Group, Ltd., 302 F.Supp. 1 (D.D.C.1969), 328 F. Supp. 709 (D.D.C.1971), rev'd on other grounds 410 U.S. 52, 93 S.Ct. 861, 35 L.Ed.2d 104 (1973).

they have an apparent purpose or a manifest tendency to inhibit resale competition. Recent cases suggest that so-called "pass through" arrangements, pursuant to which a dealer which sells in another's territory of primary responsibility must pay a commission to the latter, are valid so long as the commission established is reasonably calculated in accordance with plausible cost spreading techniques to do no more than compensate the receiving dealer for promotion expenditures which may have aided the invading dealer to make the sale.[5] A strong contrary argument is available, however. Pass through payments no doubt deter invasions to some degree and there are less restrictive ways, such as the primary responsibility clause itself, or even a direct mandate for specified levels of promotion, by which manufacturer interests can be adequately protected. In any event, it seems reasonable to conclude that pass through arrangements fall under the *Schwinn* ban when in purpose and effect (because of the size of the commission exacted) they tend to limit each dealer to its own territory.[6]

GTE Sylvania, Inc. v. Continental TV, Inc.[7] raised the question whether the *Schwinn per se* rule applied where a TV manufacturer gave dealers to understand that they might resell only from store locations first approved by the manufacturer. The evidence showed that it was not feasible for a dealer to sell to customers more than 20 or 30 miles from a given store location and also showed that the manufacturer's purpose for what it called its "elbow room policy" was to eliminate "same brand" competition among dealers. Justice Clark, sitting as trial judge, gave on this evidence a *per se* instruction. The majority of the court of appeals, sitting en banc, reversed on the ground that Sylvania did not in terms forbid each dealer from selling where others sold (though it limited each to the area of its store it could and did franchise more than one dealer in many metropolitan areas), and that the restraint might have aided interbrand competition, inasmuch as Sylvania, during the period it used the restraint, increased its small market share. The majority found sufficient ambiguity in the *Schwinn* language to allow a distinction on the *Sylvania* facts; it concluded that, since vertical restrictions may at times aid interbrand competition more than they injure intrabrand competition, the distinction should be drawn and the rule of reason applied.[8]

The dissenting Judges in *Sylvania* concluded that the asserted factual distinction between establishing a competition-tight territory

---

5. E.g., Superior Bedding Co. v. Serta Associates, Inc., 353 F.Supp. 1143 (N.D.Ill.1972). See also the decree on remand in United States v. Topco Associates, Inc., 1973 CCH Trade Cas. ¶ 74,391, 74,485 (N.D.Ill.), aff'd mem. 414 U.S. 801, 94 S.Ct. 116, 38 L.Ed.2d 39 (1973).

6. Cf. Reed Brothers Inc. v. Monsanto Co., 525 F.2d 486 (8th Cir. 1975).

7. Supra note 3.

8. The court also relied on law review notes critical of the withdrawn panel decision which had held the restraint illegal. E.g., Note, 88 Harv.L.Rev. 636 (1975).

for the dealer and assigning him a store location will not bear the weight the majority gave to it. The explicit *Schwinn* restriction does not necessarily yield competition-tight compartments any more than does territorial division achieved through store location assignments. The degree to which the territorial restriction in the specific form used in *Schwinn* forecloses intrabrand competition depends on the degree to which the territories assigned are each separate geographic markets in the economic sense. If one retail dealer is assigned Sacramento County and another is assigned San Francisco County, they cannot compete; their exclusive territories are separate retail markets. But if one is assigned one San Francisco or Sacramento neighborhood and the other is assigned another contiguous neighborhood in the same city, they clearly can and will compete to some degree; they will use the same media to advertise, customers will be aware of both and customers residing on one side of the street that separates the territories could be attracted to the other—out of the territory of one and into the territory of the other—to make purchases. Store location restrictions work the same way. If one retail dealer is authorized a store in San Francisco and the other a store in Sacramento they will not compete; but if one is authorized a store in one neighborhood of a city and the other a store in another neighborhood in the same city they may compete. *Schwinn* cannot be made to turn on such trivia as the form of the restriction. Any restriction in the explicit *Schwinn* form will impinge on competition to some degree, serious or slight, depending on particulars. And any degree of impingement achieved through a restriction in that form can be replicated in substance by a location restriction.

The claim that the manufacturer needs store location power to establish scale efficiencies has no greater appeal. In the first place, it does not discriminate between *Sylvania* and *Schwinn*, since the *Schwinn* form of restraints would, if anything, be a better way of restricting the dealer's scale; in the second place, the manufacturer which has not integrated even by consignment to the dealer level has no interest sufficient to warrant the imposition of its monolithic judgment about the most efficient scale for retailing upon the retailers which have made investments there, are experienced there, and are informed (as the manufacturer in a monolithic system could not be) by the responses of the market to their various experiments with scale. Nor does the claim for a distinction between territorial restrictions and location assignments on the ground that vertical restraints may aid interbrand competition more than they injure intrabrand competition have any greater appeal. This is an argument not just against the *Sylvania* result, but against *Schwinn* and the rule against resale price fixing. Rather than suggesting a rational basis for distinguishing *Sylvania* from *Schwinn,* it asserts that *Sylvania, Schwinn* and all the earlier vertical *per se* cases are wrong. It is also an argument which urges the Court to balance the possible beneficial effects of a single brand territorial restraint on interbrand competition against the injury it causes to intrabrand competition, an approach which the Court explicitly declined to adopt in the *Topco* case.⁹

The judicial responses which apply a purpose and effect approach to variegated fact situations seem generally sound. In *Schwinn* itself the Court outlawed not only the explicit territorial restrictions on wholesalers, it also outlawed two other restrictions: one by which distributors (even within their territories) were forbidden to sell except to retailers whom Schwinn had "franchised only as to a designated location or locations," and one by which these franchised retailers were forbidden to resell except at retail or to another franchised retailer. As in the *Sylvania* case, a retailer was theoretically free to sell so long as he could do so from a franchised store location, but as in *Sylvania,* the effect was to confine each retailer to a limited area. The essence of *Schwinn* is to outlaw any resale restraint imposed by the manufacturer which has the purpose or effect of significantly confining the independent judgment of buyers as to where or to whom they will resell. It is thus no exercise of severe logic to hold that the *Schwinn* rule applies where location restrictions, primary responsibility clauses or other devices, are used to attain that end. The alternative response would be to elevate form over substance to a degree affronting reason and would convert the *Schwinn* rule into a trap for the unwary which could be evaded with impunity by clever manipulation.

There is another group of cases which present a *Schwinn* issue somewhat more perplexing. These are the cases in which the resale restraint is plausibly presented by the manufacturer as designed to attain a very different end from the interposition of manufacturer judgment about routine marketing decisions. Suppose, for example, that a manufacturer of dynamite demands that its dealers make no sales to minors—is *Schwinn* violated? One court has held that a cosmetic manufacturer, concerned about protecting consumers from injury and itself from tort liability, could lawfully restrict the resale of preparations which could cause skin damage when not properly used to professional users such as beauty parlors.¹⁰ But two others, one being less than rhapsodic at the necessity, have refused on the authority of *Schwinn* to concede that a beer distributor, marketing an unsterilized product which would spoil if not kept properly refrigerated, could lawfully control resale territories and customers as an aid to quality control.¹¹ On their facts, all three decisions seem right in

9. 405 U.S. 596, 92 S.Ct. 1126, 31 L.Ed. 2d 515 (1972). See discussion in §§ 80–81 supra.

10. Tripoli Co. v. Wella Corp., 425 F.2d 932 (3d Cir.), cert. denied 400 U.S. 831, 91 S.Ct. 62, 27 L.Ed.2d 62 (1970).

11. Cooper Liquor, Inc. v. Adolph Coors Co., 506 F.2d 934 (5th Cir. 1975) (per Wisdom, J.); Adolph Coors Co. v. FTC, 497 F.2d 1178 (10th Cir. 1974), cert. denied 419 U.S. 1105, 95 S.Ct. 775, 42 L.Ed.2d 801 (1975).

result. Both manufacturers asserted legitimate interests which might provide adequate commercial purposes for resale restrictions, even absent any purpose to dampen resale competition. In each case, however, there was at least a derivative effect on resale competition. In the cosmetics case, no less restrictive alternative which would have provided equivalent protection to the public and the manufacturer was apparent; in the beer distribution case, instructions, quality control standards and field inspections would in all likelihood work as well, or nearly so, under a non-restrictive distribution system as they did under the restrictive one; and any slippage would do no devastating damage to the manufacturer or its customers.

The lesson of these cases is that stressed by Judge Wisdom: whatever some of the commentators may be saying about *Schwinn,* there is not the remotest implication that the Supreme Court has backed off from its position there. It has cited the case favorably and has applied it.[12] Cases involving resale restrictions are to be characterized in terms of the principle implicit in *Schwinn* itself. The law protects intrabrand resale competition much as it does interbrand competition. A manufacturer's interest in how effectively its dealers perform can be expressed through the imposition of restrictions or requirements on resellers only up to the point where the manufacturer begins to impinge, significantly, on the freedom of resellers to respond to market forces as they perceive them.

§ 145. The Justification for *Per Se* Treatment of Vertifical Territorial and Customer Resale Restraints

There is no doubt that restricting resale territories or customers tends to inhibit intrabrand competition. The restriction imposed—however denominated—will help to keep dealers from encountering each other. To the extent that separate geographic markets are achieved, intrabrand competition will be ended. The more general significance of this will depend upon how effectively the restricting manufacturer has differentiated its brand—i.e., upon the effectiveness of interbrand competition. In distribution, as in other aspects of the productive process, rivalry between traders tends to keep prices down and to stimulate efforts to reduce costs while increasing quality, service and shopping convenience. Furthermore, since the ability of a trader to offer (or approach) that mixture of high quality, low price, efficient service and attractive, convenient facilities which the public regards as optimal is what maximizes the trader's

---

12. In United States v. Topco Associates, 405 U.S. 596, 92 S.Ct. 1126, 31 L.Ed.2d 515 (1972) the Court again embraced the principle underlying *Schwinn,* that territorial restraints, even when they adversely affect competition in only one brand, are *per se* unlawful, and they cannot be justified on the ground that they aid competition in other aspects. And in Adolph Coors Co. v. FTC, note 11 supra the Court declined the invitation of the Court of Appeals for the Tenth Circuit to grant certiorari and reexamine the *Schwinn* issues.

reward in a competitive distribution market, competition in distribution (as in production) stimulates a response which the public values highly. The Supreme Court has consistently pointed to these goals as basic ones for antitrust policy.[1]

But low prices and optimum allocation are not the only public interests which competition fosters; it also tends toward other important social values: economic stability, fair and rational income distribution, an economic climate in which any person can aspire to independence and growth, dispersion of political and social as well as economic power, and fair and objective decisions dictated by market forces in economic relations between individuals. These values too are relevant to the development of a sound antitrust policy with respect to the distribution sector.[2] Sound public policy thus requires that the decision whether a particular retail trader is to sell in a particular market should be a personal decision based upon a personal readiness to take the risks and suffer the consequences; it should not be an administered decision made for the trader by the home office personnel of a national manufacturer. Any argument against *per se* treatment of territorial or customer resale restraints must then be based on the existence of offsetting advantages which, at least in some instances, may be more beneficial than damaging to competition. Therefore, the arguments which are pressed in favor of these kinds of restrictions should be reviewed and evaluated.[3]

a. *Economies of Scale*

A frequent claim is that territorial restraints are necessary to enable a manufacturer to be sure each dealer achieves an efficient scale of operations; absent restriction, it is asserted, some dealers would invade others' territories and deprive the latter of the minimum volume necessary for efficient operation. Such a result, it is claimed, would injure both interbrand and intrabrand competition by depriving the market of the most efficient competitive units at the dealer level.

This argument breaks down at several points. First, even if we assume that the purpose of a resale restriction were to assure maxi-

---

1. See, e.g., Northern Pac. R.R. v. United States, 356 U.S. 1, 4–5, 78 S.Ct. 514, 517–18, 2 L.Ed.2d 545, 549 (1958).

2. See, e.g., Simpson v. Union Oil Co., 377 U.S. 13, 84 S.Ct. 1051, 12 L.Ed.2d 98 (1964); Brown Shoe Co. v. United States, 370 U.S. 294, 82 S.Ct. 1502, 8 L.Ed.2d 510 (1962).

3. See the catalog of defenses listed and the analysis suggested by the issues posed in P. Areeda, Antitrust Analysis, Problems, Text, Cases ¶ 517 (2d ed. 1974); see also Comparative Note on Exclusive Territorial Distributorship Arrangements in M. Handler, H. Blake, R. Pitofsky and H. Goldschmid, Trade Regulation, Cases and Materials 640–44 (1975). To be set against these defenses, which are reviewed in detail in the text following this note, are the economic and non-economic values associated with preservation of competition. See, e. g., United States v. A. Schrader's Son, Inc., 252 U.S. 85, 40 S.Ct. 251, 64 L. Ed. 471 (1920); Simpson v. Union Oil Co., 377 U.S. 13, 84 S.Ct. 1051, 12 L. Ed.2d 98 (1964).

mum efficiency at the dealer level, to seek efficiency in this way would be inconsistent with competition, not supportive of competition. The argument presupposes an orderly, efficient, retail economy planned and managed by an all-knowing manufacturer which would make all the critical decisions, not just for itself, but also for dealers. This is simply not the kind of economy which the Sherman Act envisages. Absent restraints, some dealers will no doubt seek to invade the territory of others. If an invading dealer is more efficient and more effective than the one it challenges, it is indeed possible that it will drive the latter dealer out of business; but whether the invading dealer is more efficient or not, it is as likely that the result will be a sharing of the market—and probably at a new, higher level of gross sales due to an aggregate increase in promotional expenditures within the territory and competitively generated decreases in price or increases in the level of services, or both. But whether the invading dealer alone survives, or the existing dealer alone survives, or both survive, this kind of contest is precisely what competition is all about. Competition calls not for peace and order, but for vigor and danger to be the rule of trade. It envisages decisions about price, scale and other important matters being made by numerous competing traders, some of whom will judge right and some of whom will judge wrong. It does not call for a monolithic, untested judgment about the appropriate scale for retail operations made by the manufacturer acting as a "manager" of all the units in the economy handling his product, but for a public judgment proved in the marketplace, where the dealer bets his capital that he knows what he is doing and the consumer votes with his purchasing power to tell the dealer whether he is right or wrong.

Secondly, the argument that the restriction assures economies of scale is particularly deficient and, indeed, pernicious, when applied to the commonplace situation in which dealers handling the product in question typically handle more than one manufacturer's line. The dealer's scale of operation in such a situation is not likely to be fixed by the degree of territorial protection offered by one manufacturer; on the contrary, the effect of a territorial restriction is likely to be to induce the dealer in advising those customers who rely on him to favor the product of the protecting manufacturer over those of nonprotecting manufacturers for reasons of self-interest which have nothing to do either with scale efficiencies or with the competitive merits of the product.

Thirdly, the scale economy argument falls down factually in virtually every case where it is proposed. The manufacturer administering the territorial policy does not in fact make judgments about what is the most economical scale for the resale operation and then apply that judgment to its dealers. Such a program would have to be based on a study of scale economies at the retail level. Such a program, moreover, would yield consistent results; one could discern the manufacturer's principle of efficient scale from its territorial allocations. If a trade area of a given size and density were most efficient in one area, it would also be most efficient in others. Significantly, a manufacturer making territorial assignments has yet to present evidence that it studied retail operations in order to determine the most efficient scale, or even developed by intuition norms about scale which it consistently applied. Thus the supposed theoretical merits of the "economies of scale" argument as a justification for territorial resale restrictions never seem to be manifested in the marketplace.

b. *Necessary Promotion, Facilities or Services*

It is sometimes argued, as it was in *White Motor* [4] and *Snap-On Tools,* [5] that a manufacturer must give a dealer territorial protection in order to induce the dealer to provide needed and expensive point-of-sale promotion or display facilities, to provide post-sale services, or the like. It is argued that no dealer will incur these expenses if others are free to invade the market without providing promotional services; accordingly, the argument goes, protection from intrabrand competition is essential. But this argument, like that as to scale economies, falls apart on analysis. It is simply a "managed market" argument in another guise. To the extent that it signifies any real need of the manufacturer, it is one which can be satisfied through far less restrictive means which will not terminate intrabrand competition.

The most comprehensive response to arguments like this is that competition should be the device which determines what the public really needs or wants. Take the claim that display facilities are needed. If the public prefers expensive shopping amenities to lower prices, it will pay the higher prices to have the greater amenities. If this is *really* what the public wants, a dealer which bets its capital that it can sell more by lowering prices and skipping the frills will either find that it makes less return on investment then it could by providing display facilities, or will fail entirely. Other dealers will continue providing showrooms only if it pays them to do so. If sizable numbers of customers use the display facilities of the high-priced dealer to shop and then buy from the low-priced dealer, the high-priced dealer will respond by cutting its display services and its prices.

This is what should happen. If the public generally, or some significant segment of it, would in fact prefer to skip the amenities and pay the lower price, and if some dealer is ready to risk its capital on a judgment that this is so, it would be a grave distortion of the competitive process to allow the manufacturer to impose on all concerned its narrower conception of an orderly market. The manufacturer

---

4. White Motor Co. v. United States, 372 U.S. 253, 83 S.Ct. 696, 9 L.Ed.2d 738 (1963).

5. Snap-On Tools Corp. v. FTC, 321 F. 2d 825 (7th Cir. 1963).

may be right about what is needed in the way of display or services to sell its goods. If it is, attempts by dealers to sell them without these ancillary activities will fail. The market, then, will find out ways to provide display. If a few back street discount houses without displays continue to operate on an order-taking basis, "preying" on the majority of merchants which nevertheless find display facilities in their own self-interest, that trivial circumstances is hardly such a serious inequity as to warrant a significant distortion of the competitive process. The market has never promised precise justice. There are always rewards of sorts for the imitator as well as the innovator, the back street trader, the secondhand dealer, and others. Much of this is what gives zest and color to the urban marketplace, which makes it the stimulating bazaar it is. So long as the market provides equality of opportunity—an unclogged avenue for entry into any one of these media—fine sensibilities about who is earning what need hardly be indulged.

So too with the provision of repair service to customers after sale. When a manufacturer says that merchandise must be sold at a price which will produce a high enough profit to allow for post-sale service and therefore that the dealer must be given territorial protection, the manufacturer is actually giving sanction to a tying arrangement which enables the dealer to carry on an unprofitable or break-even service department with the supra-competitive profits gained on protected sales. This also distorts the allocation of resources which competition would generate. Dealers offering goods to the public should compete with each other in the sale of those goods; those offering repair service to the public (whether the same dealers or others) should compete in the sale of service. If a single seller wishes to offer a "package deal" such as a TV set plus a year's service at a single price, there can be no objection so long as the alternatives of separate purchases are open to buyers. But to say that a manufacturer can provide protected territories in order to enable dealers to gain excess profits on sales, and then subsidize a service department with the excess, is to distort radically the competitive function. Dealers should be encouraged to provide only that investment in each aspect of the business which the public, by its purchases at profit-producing prices, says it really wants.

The contrary view assumes that the manufacturer knows better than the market how dealers ought to be deployed and what services and facilities they should offer in order to maximize output. But this argument, like the comparable one in favor of resale price maintenance, assumes that the manufacturer will always know what is best and that his administered judgment about the ideal deployment of outlets across the nation will be more efficient than the deployment achieved through myriad individual decisions by dealers investing in the distribution process. This assumption undercuts the primary policy commitment which underlies the whole of antitrust, the conviction that market decisions are likely to be more sensitive, flexible and accurate gauges of the way resources should be deployed than any monolithic, administered decision. The contrary view also involves that same display of paternalistic overreaching as does the view that manufacturers should be allowed to set resale prices. Both would accord to the manufacturer, though it is not bearing the risk of forward integration, the prerogative to displace the presumably independent dealer-businessmen who are bearing that risk in the making of crucial business decisions.

Even it it be conceded, arguendo, that there are situations where efficiency calls for the manufacturer to mandate some level of promotion, display or service from all dealers because, if it did not, all dealers would avoid the level which, system-wide, would be ideal, each out of fear that they would be producing external effects upon which other dealers would capitalize, to assume the necessity for manufacturer intervention does not validate territorial or similar restrictions which hamper intrabrand competition. The manufacturer objective, whatever it may specifically be, can be served in ways which are at once more direct and effective and also less restrictive. The manufacturer can expressly require every dealer to provide whatever display, service or other facility, or whatever commitment to local promotional activity the manufacturer regards as needed. All dealers will then be obliged to incur the costs for these, and competition among dealers will keep prices at a level no higher than needed to cover these and other dealer costs. Of course, one dealer may provide the facilities or ancillary devices more efficiently than others and thus be able to price lower, gaining a higher share and return. But that, after all, is what competition is intended to stimulate.

c. *Historical Success*

In *White Motor* and *Schwinn* [6] it was argued with some vigor that the "reasonableness" of territorial restrictions is shown by the fact that while these restrictions were in effect the manufacturer had succeeded in holding or increasing its share of the market in the face of competition from larger, more powerful rivals. One flaw in this argument is that it assumes a direct relationship between size of market share and commercial success. *Sylvania* [7] is a good example. The manufacturer there had a modest percentage of the national market for TV, an enormous volume of business in absolute terms. Without introducing any evidence of its profit levels in this activity,

---

6. See note 4 supra. United States v. Arnold, Schwinn & Co., 388 U.S. 365, 87 S.Ct. 1856, 18 L.Ed.2d 1249 (1967).

7. See United States v. Revlon, Inc., 1975 CCH Trade Cases ¶ 60,202 (S.D. N.Y.1975). But cf. GTE Sylvania, Inc. v. Continental T.V., Inc., 537 F.2d 980 (9th Cir. 1976) (en banc) cert granted, U.S.S.Ct.Dkt. No. 76–15 (Oct. 18, 1976) (The author appears as counsel for Continental in that case.) See also Schild-Kraut, Areas of Primary Responsibility and Other Territorial Restraints in Channels of Distribution Under the Antitrust Laws—A Legal and Economic Analysis, 11 Colum.J. Law & Soc.Prob. 509 (1975).

nor any evidence to show that scale economies in TV manufacturing required a greater volume than it had achieved, it argued that it needed to increase its share to survive in the marketplace. The non sequitur is manifest; there is on the face of the matter no basis for inferring that the firm with 10, 15 or 20 percent of the market is earning greater returns on invested capital than is the firm with 6, 4 or 2 percent. Absent a claim that aggregate volume at these lower levels is below the most efficient scale, data about the percentage of the market held is simply not relevant to the question of whether profits are adequate.

The second defect in the "success" argument is that it identifies the single manufacturer's interest with the public interest; actually, if a given manufacturer could prosper only when there are anticompetitive props insulating its dealers from intrabrand competition, it may well be that the manufacturer's prosperity indicates a less than optimum allocation of resources. If an open, competitive structure would actually result in dealers abandoning the manufacturer's line, or pressing it less effectively, the reason may be that the public really wants more of something else, and that dealers are being "bribed" by territorial protection to promote the line. The only arguable exception to this inference would be a situation in which other entrenched manufacturers had erected a barrier to entry or expansion at the manufacturer level by foreclosing access to dealers at the resale level. If, for example, other manufacturers used restrictive contracts or special inducements to tie up an undue percentage of existing or well-located dealers and if entry at the dealership level was not feasible or easy, it might be thought appropriate to allow a new or failing manufacturer to offer dealers a surcease from intrabrand competition as a means for enticing them to handle its brand. Of course, the socially preferable response to such barriers to entry would be to take action to reduce them. The weak or entering manufacturer would have standing to challenge them.

Moreover, even if it be assumed that getting or keeping a weak brand in the market is clearly a virtue and that antitrust remedies will not break down barriers, it does not follow that an exception should be made here. In the first place, because the facts which would call the exception into play would be extremely rare, refusing to recognize the exception would lead to "wrong" results in few, if any, actual cases. In the second place, a situation calling the exception into play would be hard to identify when it did appear. *Sandura* [8] tends to indicate the difficulties, and it may well be that the *Schwinn* Court took this lesson from the *Sandura* experience. Testimony from dealers, which will inevitably be self-serving, is virtually the only basis for probing the issue whether dealers do in fact

---

8. Sandura Co. v. FTC, 339 F.2d 847 (6th Cir. 1964).

need territorial protection to be encouraged to deal at all. As a result, many cases where protection was not actually needed might be held to fall within the exception on the basis of such dealer evidence. Indeed, if the exception were allowed, it might actually generate the cases to which it applied—dealers who *would* handle the line without territorial protection if the *per se* rule were held to govern might refuse to handle the line, absent territorial protection, if the weak brand exception were available. Based on all of these considerations, the granting of an exception for weak brands seems inappropriate, even assuming the desirability of encouraging new entry or encouraging a weak brand to stay on the market.

The final flaw in the success argument is the lack of logical support for the factual inferences which it insists must be drawn. One can hardly conclude from the fact that a firm has survived, or even prospered, while using a territorial restraint that it "guessed right" about what the market called for, even with respect to its own product. We would normally expect intrabrand competition to work in the same direction as interbrand competition, to stimulate lower resale prices, to push dealer profits down to competitive levels, to increase volume of sales of the brand, and to bestir dealers into the use of innovative marketing techniques in their efforts to compete with each other. Economic theory suggests that any manufacturer which has been following a restrictive resale program might well have done better if it had left its dealers free to compete. Nor do we have in any given fact situation which displays "success" with a particular marketing program, any basis for attributing the success to any specific aspect of the program such as territorial restrictions on dealers. There are far too many variables at work to reach any solid conclusion about what would have happened if competitive forces had remained unencumbered.[9]

d. Dealer Goodwill Through Higher Dealer Profits

It is sometimes argued that a manufacturer "needs" his dealer's goodwill and should be able to "buy" it by giving the dealer territorial protection. This is said to be essential to encourage greater selling effort by dealers and that, by doing so, it is helpful to interbrand competition.[10] This argument, far from being persuasive, actually exposes the anticompetitive nature of the restriction. A manufacturer "needs" a given dealer only in two circumstances—when the dealer has a degree of market power which the manufacturer hopes the dealer will exploit for the manufacturer's profit, or when the dealer is uniquely competent and efficient. In the first case it is patently

---

9. In *Sylvania*, for example, although the manufacturer's share increased in the years after it introduced restrictive distribution policies, at the same time it had also made other changes, such as replacing management, redesigning its product and changing its advertising campaign.

10. See Snap-On Tools v. FTC, supra note 5.

clear that retail competition would be seriously impaired if the manufacturer were permitted to strengthen and reinforce the dealer's market power by granting territorial protection. In the second situation the public gets the full benefit of the dealer's skill and efficiency only if the dealer, free of any artificial constraints, exercises its own judgment about what manufacturer's products to sell and where, and to whom and in what manner. Indeed, one might well conclude that the best way to *blunt* the competitive sharpness of an efficient dealer and to deprive the public of the benefit of dealer efficiency would be to insulate the dealer from competitive forces. A particular dealer, for example, might be an extremely efficient dealer—that may be why it is successful and why a manufacturer may reach out to it and offer it territorial protection as an inducement to take on the manufacturer's line. But such a dealer will be more likely to *remain* efficient if it is left open to competitive challenge from others, not if it is protected against such competition.

Nor does the notion that interbrand competition can be aided by allowing intrabrand competition to be restricted withstand analysis. We may assume, in general, that the more competition a dealer faces, the more vigorous will that dealer be obliged to be; and this holds true whether the competition is interbrand or intrabrand. A dealer worried about losing even those buyers with some pre-commitment to its brand will hustle more earnestly than a dealer free of intrabrand competition and which must worry about losing only those prospective customers who lack a clear preference for the brand. "Effort" is encouraged not by freeing a dealer from important competitive pressures, but by subjecting each dealer to whatever competitive pressure the market generates.

e. *"Established" Dealers Should be Protected From "Irresponsible" Dealers Which "Skim the Cream" Off the Market*

One of the arguments most favored by those who support territorial restrictions has a certain moral or ethical quality. In this argument an invading dealer is made to seem a hostile, yet evasive and shadowy figure which moves into "someone else's territory" with rapier swiftness, quickly culls "the best of the market," and then disappears, having invested nothing, yet reaping a tidy profit where the local dealer had sown. The argument is summed up by saying the invader has "skimmed the cream" off another dealer's market.[11]

The answer presents itself forcefully when one looks beyond the surface of the metaphor in which the argument is usually dressed. As Areeda suggests, "cream," must mean high profit sales—that is, sales which can be made either at higher prices or at lower costs than

11. This argument would be hard to make in support of a location clause, as distinguished from a resale territory restriction, because a location clause does not preclude the outside dealer from entering without investment; it precludes him from entering with investment.

most sales in the market in question.[12] Sales producing "cream," therefore, must be sales made to those buyers with a fixed preference for the particular manufacturer's brand and who therefore will pay more, or who can be sold with less expense, despite the options open to them as a result of interbrand competition. When "cream" is seen for what it is, the argument falls apart in several respects. First, it is extremely weak factually. It is hard to conceive how any new, invading dealer could steal all of these kinds of customers from the established dealer in the area without shading price, or providing better service, convenience or amenity. Would the established dealer be so competitively inert that an outsider could move in quickly and grab all his best, repeat-business customers? Indeed, the means by which an outside dealer can move into an area and "skim the cream" from an established dealer is never explained when the "cream" argument is pressed.

But more important deficiencies than this factual one infect the argument. Upon analysis, the reference to "cream" is reduced to this: if each dealer has territorial protection, there will, in fact, be some "cream" available—some customers will be so committed to almost any widely advertised brand as to be unaffected by interbrand competition. These customers will come to the dealer protected from intrabrand competition and pay his asking price with little or no comparison shopping. As these customers view the market, the protected dealer is a monopolist. Interbrand competition means little or nothing to them; absent intrabrand competition, they can deal only with one seller. However, if another dealer invades the territory, intrabrand competition is provided. Even the presold, brand-committed customers now have more than one option. In this new circumstance, these customers will no longer be ready to pay the seller's asking price without bargaining, or to put up with inadequate service, inconvenience or lack of amenity. After invasion these customers, like those ready to turn to other brands, have more than one seller competing for their trade. In short, once intrabrand competition is introduced, the brand-committed customers who used to be a "cream" on the market, cease to be "cream."

This has been a rather roving review of the endlessly inventive contentions which are made against the imposition of the *Schwinn* rule, or in support of internally illogical limitations upon the scope of its application. Enough has been said to show that none of the broad attacks on *Schwinn* is convincing. To be sure, the *Schwinn* rule, because it applies to all vertical territorial restrictions, not just those that segregate resellers into separate geographic markets, will preclude even those restrictions ("firm A, sell only on the east side of Center Street, firm B, sell only on the west") which will have little adverse competitive effect. But the greatest utility of a *per se* rule is

---

12. See Areeda, supra note 3.

its clarity. If a particular arrangement is *per se* unlawful, the entire bar, counselling on business arrangements, becomes part of the enforcement mechanism. Clients who are told: "It is unlawful, regardless!" are likely to respond. But let a doubt be raised, however narrow, so that lawyers must say: "It is unlawful, *unless* * * *" and the potential for comprehensive enforcement, short of extensive litigation, diminishes enormously. Given the specious or weak nature of the claims on behalf of allowing resale restrictions, the case for a clear prohibition is compelling.

§ 146. Consignment and Related Arrangements to Achieve Territorial Separation

Schwinn confines the *per se* rule against vertical territorial and customer restrictions to transactions where the manufacturer sells the restricted merchandise; if a manufacturer ships goods on consignment or uses a sales agent it may lawfully assign resale territories unless to do so in the particular context would unreasonably restrain competition. The distinction between sales and consignments was greeted with some surprise, coming as it did after *Simpson*, a resale price maintenance case which held that a series of consignments were tantamount to sales.[1] There has been criticism of *Schwinn* on the ground that competitive effect will not likely turn on where the technical concept of title is lodged at a given moment and, therefore, that *per se* liability ought not to be made to turn on this. We have been told, for example, that the present position is a "legal technicality" without basis in "economic analysis" which "obviously leaves a great deal to be desired." [2]

There is, to be sure, a dissonance between *Simpson* and *Schwinn*, but to dismiss as arbitrary the distinction between "controlling the destiny" of one's own goods and controlling that of goods which have been purchased by someone else is to miss something deep about our ways of characterizing the manifold human relationships to which commerce gives rise. In *Schwinn* the traditional "law" element of antitrust becomes in some ways ascendant over the elements deriving from economic policy. Without understanding that, and its implications, we ought not to disdain the distinction.

At the threshold to an understanding of the limits of *Schwinn* is an ancient notion that alienation of chattels ought not to be hampered by restrictions, particularly ones which pass with the goods.[3] (Of old this policy gave way to reasonable ancillary restraints—for example, upon the sale of capital assets, a buyer might bind himself not to use the goods in competition with the seller. However, under this ancil-

1. See discussion in § 137 supra.

2. Warren, Economics of Closed Territory Distribution, 2 Antitrust Law & Econ.Rev. 111, 112 (1968).

3. Chafee, The Music Goes Round and Round: Equitable Servitudes and Chattels, 69 Harv.L.Rev. 1250 (1956).

lary concept these exceptions were limited to the strict necessities of particular kinds of transactions which would be unduly hampered were the narrow exceptions not granted.)

It was that ancient common law doctrine against restraints on alienation which also had been at the base of *Dr. Miles*,[4] and to which the Court instinctively turned in *Schwinn*. Properly it might, not only because as a common law source it was suggestive of legislative intent in the enactment of the Sherman Act [5] but also because the ancient rule, in distinguishing between a "sale" and an "agency" or "consignment"—between the manufacturer which partially integrates forward and assumes additional risks and the one which does not, draws incidentally a distinction which is relevant also in distinguishing between independence and coercion, two values to which the law in this area attends with great interest, whatever their relevance to output restrictions and the economic allocation of goods.

The law cares whether the distributor or dealer is imposed upon by the manufacturer; it seeks to protect him, if it reasonably can, against being given responsibility without power. It is for this reason that the law responds where there is a distributor or dealer, an independent businessman who has made the investment and assumed the risks and ought therefore to have the power to decide where and to whom he will resell and does not respond where the manufacturer retains the risk, and either consigns the merchandise, or holds the merchandise and merely authorizes a commission agent to go out and get orders. If the law by shaping this distinction were to jeopardize rational resource allocation and threaten the creation of situations where output would be restricted, we would face the dilemma of competing values; but it does not. The tendency of the rule is also to preserve competition in the economic sense, certainly not to stifle it.[6]

The difficulty raised by the contrasting tonalities of *Simpson* and *Schwinn* does not undercut the rationale here elucidated, but rather implies differing answers to the inquiry about which dealers are to be treated as independent, about how far the rationale of *Schwinn* is to be carried. The cases, although uttering differing sounds, are rather easily reconciled on their facts. In *Simpson*, the Court saw an evasion, an effort to establish a dealership system in which dealers had all the indications of independence, including substantial risk taking, yet were called consignees, because the refiner retained a legal title. In *Schwinn*, no such position was presented. Distributors acted as distributors and were called distributors with respect to part of the merchandise. As to the part consigned, how-

---

4. Dr. Miles Medical Co. v. John D. Park & Sons Co., 220 U.S. 373, 31 S. Ct. 376, 55 L.Ed. 502 (1911).

5. Compare United States v. Addyston Pipe & Steel Co., 85 F. 271 (6th Cir. 1898), modified and aff'd 175 U.S. 211, 20 S.Ct. 96, 44 L.Ed. 136 (1899).

6. See § 143 supra.

ever, they were consignees and nothing more in a practical as well as a legal sense; investment and risk remained with the manufacturer. For most of the sales not covered by the *per se* rule, those as to which the distributors acted as agents, they never even handled the goods or the money. They merely obtained orders and referred these to the manufacturer, as any commission salesman employed by *Schwinn* would do. Thus, as to consignment sales and the agency arrangement, Schwinn was not blighted with the vice that resulted in the *Simpson* arrangement being recast by the Court.

Where, as in *Schwinn,* a consignment or agency arrangement is real, the validity of territorial and related restrictions is determined under the rule of reason, which has, of course, its own limits. A dominant firm not fully integrated to the distribution level may not utilize consignments or agency arrangements and preclude competition at the next level. This, at least, is implied both by *White Motor* and *Schwinn*.[7] Where, given the market structure, intrabrand competition is the only kind possible, the manufacturer—at least if not fully integrated to the next level and thus having to sell to dealers if not permitted to use consignees or agents—ought to be channeled into the choice which provides such little competition as may be attained. Some economists assert that nothing is gained in resource allocation, that the consumer will pay as much and receive as little whether the dominant manufacturer distributes through a group of competing resellers or itself; when the dominant firm is truly a monopolist they will be right, at least if a static condition is assumed. But even in the case of monopoly, requiring a competitive organization at the dealer level will not hurt resource allocation and will give buyers some sense of choice, perhaps even some real alternatives at the dealer level among various mixes of prices and services, and various competitive styles. Furthermore, when we drop the static assumption and picture developments over time we must recognize that the introduction of a plurality of independent distributorships or dealerships at a level vertically adjacent to the monopolist enhances at least marginally the potential for competitive entry at the monopolist's own level.[8] For one thing, an outside firm considering entry may be able to enter at one level only and sell to the existing dealers in competition with the monopolist; for another, the dealers aware of and victimized by the monopolist's profits and knowing the industry in ways many outsiders would not, may themselves be prime potential entrants, or may be catalysts to encourage others to enter.

§ 147. Exclusive Franchise Arrangements

Often franchise agreements contain a promise by the seller not to sell to any dealer other than the franchisee in a designated territo-

---

7. See also United States v. Bausch & Lomb Optical Co., 321 U.S. 707, 64 S. Ct. 805, 88 L.Ed. 1024 (1944).

8. Compare ch. 7, part D infra, dealing with vertical integration by merger.

ry which the franchisee expects to serve, and a further promise that the seller will not authorize any other dealer which makes sales in the territory to hold itself out as the seller's authorized representative there. These arrangements, variously called exclusive franchise, exclusive selling, sole outlet, or exclusive dealership arrangements, involve a territorial restriction only upon the seller and are often used by sellers to induce buyers to take on a product line and to give it vigorous promotional attention. Frequently, they are used in conjunction with primary responsibility clauses which obligate the dealer to serve the territory effectively.

These arrangements no doubt tend to diminish intrabrand competition to some extent. The only dealer receiving shipments into the area is the authorized one and anyone seeking to compete must, at a minimum, incur the additional cost of shipping from its own location into the area. Also, the would-be competitor loses such advantage as may be derived from presenting itself as the "authorized" dealer. But exclusive dealerships, unlike territorial or location restrictions on dealers, cannot be used to stamp out intrabrand competition entirely. If the authorized dealer sets prices too high, or provides inadequate service, promotes inefficiently or otherwise creates market opportunities, a dealer authorized and receiving shipments elsewhere can ship goods into the exclusive area and sell them there.

Dilemmas abound about the way the law should respond to exclusive dealerships. The Court has stated that judges and juries ought not to be drawn into the business of weighing whether an injury to intrabrand competition is offset by a benefit to interbrand competition.[1] That view suggests that these arrangements should be held *per se* lawful or *per se* unlawful, rather than dealt with under the rule of reason. The harm they do to intrabrand competition cannot be dismissed as *de minimus* and the justification for them must come from their potential to aid interbrand competition. But the case law seems not to support either of these responses. The arrangements have been upheld when the manufacturer is introducing a new product and where significant capital investment must be made or substantial expense incurred by the dealer,[2] or when the seller is a small or weak firm in its market.[3] But in other instances it is not

---

1. United States v. Topco Associates, Inc., 405 U.S. 596, 92 S.Ct. 1126, 31 L.Ed.2d 515 (1972).

2. United States v. Bausch & Lomb Optical Co., 321 U.S. 707, 64 S.Ct. 805, 88 L.Ed. 1024 (1944).

3. Schwing Motor Co. v. Hudson Sales Corp., 138 F.Supp. 899 (D.Md.), aff'd 239 F.2d 176 (4th Cir. 1956), cert. denied 355 U.S. 823, 78 S.Ct. 30, 2 L.Ed. 2d 38 (1957); Packard Motor Car Co. v. Webster Motor Car Co., 100 U.S. App.D.C. 161, 243 F.2d 418 (D.C.Cir.), cert. denied 355 U.S. 822, 78 S.Ct. 29, 2 L.Ed.2d 38 (1957). See Hevermon, Dealer Territorial Security and "Bootlegging" in the Auto Industry, 1962 Wis.L.Rev. 486; Kessler, Automobile Dealer Franchises: Vertical Integration by Contract, 66 Yale L.J. 1135 (1957); B. Pashigian, The Distribution of Automobiles: An Economic Analysis of the Franchise System (1961); Rifkind, "Division of Territo-

entirely clear whether the exclusive is valid *per se* or what will justify it. There is dicta in *Schwinn* which some would read as making exclusive dealerships *per se* lawful except when used by dominant firms, but the language of the case need not be read as granting so sweeping a license.

While holding resale restrictions on buyers to be *per se* unlawful the Court said:

> [A] manufacturer of a product other and equivalent brands of which are readily available in the market may select his customers, and for this purpose he may "franchise" certain dealers to whom, alone, he will sell his goods * * *. If the restraint stops at this point—if nothing more is involved than vertical "confinement" of the manufacturer's own sales of the merchandise to selected dealers, and if competitive products are readily available to others, the restriction, on these facts alone, would not violate the Sherman Act.[4]

This language seems not so pointed as to validate exclusive dealerships generally; rather it seems to express an idea still somewhat at large, less precisely confined than to warrant the confident reading sometimes given it. An alternative reading, at an extreme in the other direction, would take the language as doing no more than restating the *Colgate* doctrine, under which a manufacturer may decide for itself to whom it will sell, but only so long as it acts unilaterally. This construction is fully as satisfying literally and may be more in keeping with the context.

If *Schwinn* does not tell us that exclusives are lawful, how should they be analyzed? One might argue against their general validity that in purpose and in effect they tend in the same direction as territorial restraints imposed on dealers. If a manufacturer limits each dealer to a single territory, intrabrand competition within the territory is foreclosed. If instead the manufacturer agrees to sell only to one dealer in each territory, dealers can invade each other's territories, but not on equal terms. They must either sell from afar or, if they open a location in another territory, they must trans-ship goods from their original location, as the manufacturer will not sell to them elsewhere. The protected dealer receives significant protection against intrabrand competition in its territory. Furthermore, a commitment made by a manufacturer to a dealer not to sell to another is much like a boycott, despite its vertical characteristics. It might therefore be argued that just as vertical forms of price fixing and territorial restrictions are, like their horizontal counterparts, held illegal *per se*, so this device should be outlawed *per se*, as is a horizontal boycott.

ries," in How to Comply with the Antitrust Laws (Van Cise & Dunn, eds. 1954).

4. 388 U.S. at 376, 87 S.Ct. at 1864, 18 L.Ed.2d at 1258.

The *Klor's* case comes to mind as one in which a boycott contained both vertical and horizontal elements and the vertical element, far from saving it, was perceived to make the boycott more pernicious.[5] One must nonetheless admit that concerted action to cut off a single source of supply may not be so serious as concerted action to cut off several or all, either in its impact on the affected dealer or in its impacts on the public. And it should be recalled that in *Klor's* the Court insisted upon placing in the foreground the horizontal characteristics and pointedly stated that the case was not one "of a single trader refusing to deal with another, nor even of a manufacturer and dealer agreeing to an exclusive distributorship."[6] The boycott analogy, then, is less than dispositive either as a matter of analysis or doctrine. Yet today, the broad proposition that non-dominant manufacturers may agree with dealers not to sell to others is a less settled doctrine than it has been. Now that in *Schwinn* territorial restrictions imposed on buyers have been firmly declared illegal and in *Klor's* a dealer's effort to induce several manufacturers to cut off a competing dealer has been outlawed, we have at least the obligation to think through the basis for distinction between those restrictions and the one here under review. There is, surely, a germinal property in *Schwinn,* as there is in any case which presents an answer to an open question. And though the doctrinal base of *Schwinn,* rooted in the concept of restraints on alienation, has thus far given the bent to its growth, there is the possibility that in the future it will be linked more closely with *Topco* and read primarily as a case which protects intrabrand competition. And if there is a current to extend the implication in *Schwinn* and *Topco* that intrabrand competition is to be valued and that contractual commitments which inhibit it are suspect, that current must be moving in a direction which may eventually flood over cases like *Packard,* which sanction exclusives.

Should one therefore conclude that the principle informing the cases which protect exclusives is about to be inundated, or only that it now stands nearer the water's edge? We have seen that the validity assumed for exclusives can be challenged with some force. Is there any defense to the challenge? Although the likelihood of intrabrand competition is markedly reduced by an exclusive, it is not eliminated; the restraint is not complete. To allow the manufacturer to use this system is, in effect, to concede to the manufacturer a legitimate interest in how its goods are handled on resale, while not allowing it to press that interest to an extreme. The distinction between a seller's promise and a buyer's is perhaps a practical, if clumsy, place to draw the line. Moreover, the seller's promise, being less restrictive than the buyer's, can be defended as the less restrictive way of achieving

5. Klor's, Inc. v. Broadway—Hale Stores, 359 U.S. 207, 79 S.Ct. 705, 3 L.Ed.2d 741 (1959). See discussion in § 84 supra.

6. Id. at 212, 79 S.Ct. at 709–10, 3 L.Ed.2d at 745.

manufacturer objectives. In addition, the exclusive franchise differs from the territorial restriction on the buyer in that the latter is often charged with a coercive energy which is likely to be lacking where the only restriction is upon the seller.

Against this accommodation, there are those who have argued that *Schwinn* on the one hand and *Packard* on the other cannot stand together, that the complications of their co-existence are too great. Thus it is proposed that any seller granting an exclusive territory to a buyer would have to be able to impose territorial restraints on other buyers in order to keep its own pledge good and that the territorial restrictions in this context are valid ancillary restraints. What has been said above should demonstrate that the premise of the concern is faulty: it is quite possible to hold that a seller can agree not to sell and deliver to other dealers in a given territory without also authorizing the seller to promise that no dealer receiving the goods elsewhere will transship into the territory. But if it be concluded that a territorial restriction cannot be *per se* invalid if an exclusive dealership is not, then congruence ought to be achieved not by snuffing out *Schwinn*, but by letting its light fall where it may. To hold that a manufacturer could not promise to refrain from selling to others in a territory would no more shake the foundations of the franchise distribution system than did *Schwinn* itself.

§ 148. Terminating One Dealer at the Request of Another

It does not follow from the fact that a manufacturer may, when franchising a dealer, commit itself not to franchise another in a territory defined by the manufacturer, that it may, having earlier franchised two or more dealers, agree at the request of one to terminate the others. It is not merely that the latter promise liquidates palpable interests of existing traders, while the former does not (a difference which is real enough, and which is charged with meaning for the procedural and damage aspects of the law); it is also that the competitive effect of the first promise is less severe than that of the second. The first commitment forecloses potential intrabrand competition only; the second stamps out existing competition at the behest of a firm which is suffering under it.

In the *Packard* case,[1] the court upheld an agreement between a car manufacturer and its most successful Baltimore dealer to terminate others in the area. The case is sometimes read as sanctioning such agreements generally, but *Packard* involved a weak manufacturer seeking to hold out in the face of a deteriorating position and can as well be explained on the basis of the failing company doctrine as it

---

1. Schwing Motor Co. v. Hudson Sales Corp., 138 F.Supp. 899 (D.Md.), aff'd, 239 F.2d 176 (4th Cir. 1956), cert. denied 355 U.S. 823, 78 S.Ct. 30, 2 L. Ed.2d 38 (1957).

can on any more commodious principle.² It would be a glib reading to draw from *Packard* the broad proposition that buyers may freely extract from non-dominant sellers commitments to cut out competing buyers. Suppose firms A and B are two of several firms that make ingot from an ore for which there are three or four sources, and that both A and B happen to be supplied by X, the third largest supplier. Suppose next that A, feeling that it could not successfully compete so long as B remained in the market, were to induce X to stop selling to B, realizing that B might be able to get ore from one of the other sources, but hoping that B would not survive the disruption. Or suppose that a Texaco service station operator rented his facilities from a landowner who rented another site to a competing Shell station, and that the Texaco operator were to persuade the landlord not to renew the Shell operator's lease. We would hardly dismiss either of these arrangements with an easy mind; both would be viewed, conventionally, as efforts by one trader to exclude another.³ They might be challenged as attempts to monopolize under Section 2 or, given the vertical agreement—the exclusive arrangement to which the supplier in each case commits itself—they might be characterized as unreasonable restraints violating Section 1.⁴ Yet there is little to choose between these arrangements and that in *Packard,* if we ignore failing company status as an explanation of that case.

Those who read *Packard* broadly assert that a manufacturer of a brand name product resold by others has an interest in the entire distribution structure. This warrants a manufacturer in setting up a distribution system in which it sells only to one dealer in a territory if it concludes that this method will give it the most efficient and effective market access; one might go as far as to say that, having made the judgment that such a distribution system is preferable, the manufacturer ought to be able to commit itself to it, to restrict itself contractually. But once the manufacturer has exercised a different judgment and a market has been made which is occupied by two or more traders, the manufacturer's action in dropping one customer to please another can no longer claim the sanction due a manufacturer's predetermined marketing program—can no longer be viewed as a planned deployment of resources which, in effect, substitutes for a market deployment. At this stage, if the manufacturer drops the customer it regards as less valuable to satisfy the one it regards as more valuable, it is acting with no different or better sanction than that of any other seller which when threatened by a buyer (or a group of buyers), drops a competitor of the buyer (or group).

At the root of this matter is an intuition which we need to grasp analytically if we are to allow it to play a part in the logic of the law.

---

2. See § 204(g) infra.
3. See Lorain Journal Co. v. United States, 342 U.S. 143, 72 S.Ct. 181, 96 L.Ed. 162 (1951).
4. Cf., Perryton Wholesale, Inc. v. Pioneer Distrib. Co., 353 F.2d 618 (10th Cir. 1965), cert. denied 383 U.S. 945, 86 S.Ct. 1202, 16 L.Ed.2d 208 (1966).

To suggest that there is a relevant distinction between a manufacturer that forecloses potential competition and one that stamps out existing competition is to go part of the way, but this gives no recognition to another conception, perhaps of greater significance. When the manufacturer sets up a dealership structure and binds itself not to add dealers in any existing territory, we truly have a vertical restraint. But when an existing dealer enlists the manufacturer to choke off one of the dealer's competitors, although the "agreement" which enables Section 1 to be invoked is vertical, the restraint thereby achieved is horizontal in its impact; it is an attack by one dealer against another. Of course we can blur this line (as any other) by calling to imagination the case which straddles it. Here, that case would be one in which the system of exclusives, although established by the manufacturer in systematic fashion, owes its origin to the suggestion of a dealer. However that case might be decided, let us in looking at these problems be reminded that it *does* matter who is goring the ox. In *General Motors*,[5] where several dealers concertedly induced the manufacturer to hamper the aggressive selling efforts of a competitor, the Court dismissed out of hand the suggestion that it faced a vertical problem, one that resonated with exclusive franchise arrangements.[6] The Court saw the matter for what it was, a "classic conspiracy" to drive out competition. So in the case posed above we have not so much a vertical arrangement as a classic example of predatory, single firm conduct upon the part of the aggressive dealer to drive out competition.

§ 149. Exclusive Franchises and the Dominant Manufacturer

The cases generally and *Schwinn* in particular imply that a dominant firm may not, by committing itself not to sell to others, grant a dealer in a territory dominance at that later vertical stage. Where a manufacturer is dominant, unless there is resale competition as to its brand, there will be little or no resale competition at all. Of course the dominant manufacturer, in planning and establishing a dealership structure which will maximize its own returns, will not likely act in ways that enable dealers, at their level, to increase prices and restrict output. What the manufacturer will do is try to plan better than would a free market what degree of development at the retail level will stimulate maximum sales at the profit maximizing price. However, the interest of the manufacturer in doing this is a modest one; a competitive market at the dealer level should achieve the manufacturer's goals as well or better. And from the point of view of the public, a competitive market is to be preferred. First, the competitive deployment of resources has a higher warrant for public confidence than does the manufacturer's planned one; by definition, the

---

5. 384 U.S. 127, 86 S.Ct. 1321, 16 L.Ed. 2d 415 (1966).

6. See also Ford Motor Co. v. Webster's Auto Sales, Inc., 361 F.2d 874 (1st Cir. 1966).

market is not mistaken about what deployment best serves the public interest, but the manufacturer may be. Furthermore, absent any forceful economic reason to reject it (and here we have no economic reason at all) a competitive market is to be preferred for reasons of social policy. It leaves more options for individual decision making and assigns less to the discretion of a single powerful firm. In this connection we must recall that the private firm, however powerful, is not called to the same accounts in the exercise of its discretion as is a governmental body. In neither substantive nor procedural terms may we exact from the firm a process that is due. The dominant firm like any other must act through human agents, each with his own worth, his own pretensions, his own sensibility and instinct for what is fine, and his own blunders and prejudices. We can hardly suppose that such an agent will always work with sensitive dispassion to ferret out and do what is best for the firm. The franchise applicant who fits the decision maker's image of what a successful dealer is like in matters of race, culture, style, bearing, and vocabulary will be at an advantage, an advantage which in a competitive dealership structure would go only to the one who had proved his unique worth in the market place.

Additionally, the dominant position of the manufacturer is more likely to be eroded over time if there is a competitive dealership structure than if there is a planned one, with each participant tightly linked (and likely loyal) to the manufacturer. Without competitive dealerships, it is less likely, for example, that a separate second-hand market or repair market will develop which would reduce the manufacturer's power in some degree and, perhaps, form a basis for eventual entry into the manufacturer's own market.[1]

The rationale developed here outreaches the case we have to make. If we have proved anything, it is more than that the dominant firm ought not to be permitted to grant exclusive franchises; the rationale goes at least as far as to suggest that the dominant firm ought not to be permitted to establish a restricted distribution system at all, even through the exercise of its *Colgate* right unilaterally to refuse to deal. If the law has not gone so far as here suggested, surely it is moving in the direction of obligating the dominant manufacturer to justify its distribution policies on some plausible ground.[2] This tendency might well be generalized. For example, a dominant firm which asserted the right under *Colgate* to establish a system of distributors, each spaced so as to face a minimum amount of competition, might at a minimum be charged with the burden of proving

---

1. See United States v. United Shoe Mach. Corp., 110 F.Supp. 295 (D. Mass.1953), aff'd per curiam 347 U.S. 521, 74 S.Ct. 669, 98 L.Ed. 910 (1954).

2. Compare Eastman Kodak Co. v. Southern Photo Materials Co., 273 U. S. 359, 47 S.Ct. 400, 71 L.Ed. 684 (1927); United States v. Klearflax Linen Looms, Inc., 63 F.Supp. 32 (D. Minn.1945); Gamco, Inc. v. Providence Fruit & Produce Bldg., Inc., 194 F.2d 484 (1st Cir.) cert. denied 344 U. S. 817, 73 S.Ct. 11, 97 L.Ed. 636 (1952).

that it had adopted a reasoned and consistent policy and that it had developed and consistently applied rational norms about where dealerships were to be located. Thus the arbitrary exercise of its power through decisions wholly discretionary could be curtailed.[3]

The final issue must be: when is a firm dominant? When must its power to establish exclusives be curtailed? The easiest answer, obviously, would be to say that the rule applies only to the monopolist. But given all we know about the exercise of power in tightly structured markets, it is perhaps wiser to say that any clear and acknowledged leader in any tightly structured market ought to be viewed as dominant for these purposes. Indeed, in a tightly structured oligopolistic market, if all leading firms used restricted distribution systems, that practice might be viewed as the product of noncollusive interdependence, as a quite distinct horizontal issue, if you will, and all firms directed to abandon it.

PART C. TYING ARRANGEMENTS AND RELATED ARRANGEMENTS INVOLVING THE LEVERAGE CONCEPT

§ 150. Introduction

A tie exists when a seller, having a product which buyers want (the "tying product"), refuses to sell it alone and insists that any buyer who wants it must also purchase another product (the "tied product"). The consistent judicial instinct has been that these arrangements have but a single purpose and effect, to extend the seller's power in the market for the tying product into that for the tied product. Hence, courts have repeatedly announced that these arrangements are *per se* unlawful under Section 1 of the Sherman Act, Section 3 of the Clayton Act, or both.[1] As we shall see, neither the conventional assessment of purpose and effect, nor the sweeping assignment of *per se* illegality should be taken quite at face value. In this part we shall trace the major developments in the case law, underscore some of the qualifications about *per se* illegality, and analyze commercial purpose and competitive effects. But before doing this, we must introduce Section 3 of the Clayton Act.

---

3. Schmidt, Antitrust and Distribution Problems in Tight Oligopolies—Case Study of the Automobile Industry, 24 Hast.L.J. 849 (1973).

1. E.g., Motion Picture Patents Co. v. Universal Film Mfg. Co., 243 U.S. 502, 37 S.Ct. 416, 61 L.Ed. 871 (1917); IBM Corp. v. United States, 298 U.S. 131, 56 S.Ct. 701, 80 L.Ed. 1085 (1936); International Salt Co. v. United States, 332 U.S. 392, 68 S.Ct. 12, 92 L.Ed. 20 (1947); Northern Pac. R.R. v. United States, 356 U.S. 1, 78 S.Ct. 514, 2 L.Ed.2d 545 (1958); United States v. Loew's Inc., 371 U.S. 38, 83 S.Ct. 97, 9 L.Ed.2d 11 (1962).

§ 151. Section 3 of the Clayton Act and the Threshold Test of Competitive Effect

The Clayton Act, passed in 1914, was a response to unhappiness over the rule of reason. Like most such legislative responses, it was a child of compromise. Its principal substantive provisions dealt with price discrimination,[1] sales on conditions that the buyer not deal in goods of a competitor,[2] and corporate mergers.[3] What began as absolute or near absolute prohibitions ended as distinctly conditional prohibitions. Section 3, which is typical and which has direct application to tying, made it unlawful for any person in the course of interstate or foreign commerce, to lease or sell any commodity, patented or unpatented, or to contract to do so, for use or consumption within the United States or its territories or possessions, or to fix a price, discount or rebate on any such sale or lease

> * * * on the condition, agreement or understanding that the lessee or purchaser thereof shall not use or deal in the goods, wares, merchandise, machinery, supplies, or other commodities of a competitor or competitors of the lessor or seller, where the effect * * * may be to substantially lessen competition or tend to create a monopoly * * * .[4]

The last phrase, the competitive effect test, recurs in the other Clayton provisions. Clayton substantive offenses (such as tying) would in any event violate Section 1 of Sherman if unreasonably restraining trade. But the "effect may be" and "tend to create" phrases suggest a lower threshold of tolerance for conduct which may restrain, and give the Clayton Act its special significance.

The Act differs from Sherman in several particulars. It avoids the sweeping generality of Section 1 which applies to "any contract, combination or conspiracy" by marking out explicit kinds of arrangements, in the case of Section 3, sales or leases of a commodity or contracts therefore made on the condition that the buyer or lessee not use commodities of the seller's or lessor's competition. And, though it does not go so far as to outlaw all of these arrangements, the Section 3 test does render unlawful any whose "effect *may* be" to substantially lessen competition or to tend to create a monopoly. As the legislative history suggests and as the Court has often held, these words (the emphasis is, of course, added) show an intent to arrest in its incipiency conduct which eventually might develop into a violation of Section 1 or 2 of Sherman.

Behind the enactment of the Clayton Act, not only does one perceive a general congressional dissatisfaction with the softness of the rule of reason, but one can also trace specific sources of congressional

---

1. 38 Stat. 730, 15 U.S.C.A. § 13.

2. Id. at 731, 15 U.S.C.A. § 14.

3. Id. at 731–32, 64 Stat. 1125, 15 U.S.C.A. § 18.

4. See supra note 2.

concern. The merger provisions of Section 7, for example, were responsive to the Court's holding in *U. S. Steel*[5] that the formation of the steel trust did not violate the Sherman Act, regardless of its massive horizontal size. Section 3 can be traced at least in part to Henry v. A. B. Dick Co.,[6] the first tying case which reached the Court. In *Dick*, the plaintiff sold its patented duplicating machine upon condition that the buyer use only ink which plaintiff supplied. The defendant, which had been making and selling ink for use in the machine, was held guilty of contributory infringement of the patent. The Sherman Act provided no defense. Section 3, which was specifically made to apply to sales or leases of commodities "patented or unpatented," was enacted, as the Court later stated, "as if in response to" the *Dick* decision.[7] In any event, it is clear that by enacting Clayton Congress intended to make it easier to establish an antitrust violation. In the section which follows we shall trace the consequence of that development, both in the Court's treatment of tying arrangements under Clayton Section 3 and under Sherman Section 1.

Before proceeding on, however, we should take note of the scope of Section 3. It applies only when a lease or sale is "on the condition * * * that the lessee or purchaser * * * shall not use or deal in the * * * commodities of a competitor * * * of the lessor or seller". There need not be an express condition; otherwise neither a tying arrangement nor a requirements contract, both of which were prime targets of the enactment, would be covered. As the Court has put it, the act applies when the "practical effect" of contract provisions is to prevent use of goods of a competitor, as does either a tying or a requirements contract.[8]

However, some of the language of the Act is quite technical and not given to expansive interpretation. Section 3 applies only in instances where there has been a "sale or a lease" or a contract therefor and when the subject of that transaction is "goods, wares, merchandise, machinery, supplies, or other commodities." It presumably has no application to contracts for the provision of services, like advertising,[9] or to land transactions[10] or the provision of credit.[11] Tying transactions affecting these must be covered, if at all, by Section 1 of Sherman or Section 5 or the FTC Act, not by Section 3. It

---

5. United States v. United States Steel Corp., 251 U.S. 417, 40 S.Ct. 293, 64 L.Ed. 343 (1920).

6. 224 U.S. 1, 32 S.Ct. 364, 56 L.Ed. 645 (1912).

7. Motion Picture Patents Co. v. Universal Film Mfg. Co., 243 U.S. 502, 37 S.Ct. 416, 61 L.Ed. 871 (1917).

8. United Shoe Mach. Corp. v. United States, 258 U.S. 451, 456–57, 42 S.Ct. 363, 365, 66 L.Ed. 708, 716–17 (1922).

9. Times-Picayune Publishing Co. v. United States, 345 U.S. 594, 73 S.Ct. 872, 97 L.Ed. 1277 (1953).

10. Northern Pac. R.R. v. United States, 356 U.S. 1, 78 S.Ct. 514, 2 L. Ed.2d 545 (1958).

11. Fortner Enterprises, Inc. v. United States Steel Corp., 394 U.S. 495, 89 S. Ct. 1252, 22 L.Ed.2d 495 (1969).

is for this reason that Section 1 continues to be important in the tying area and one of the matters about which we must take note is the extent to which the competitive effect test of Clayton Section 3 and the restraint of trade test of Sherman Section 1 have over the years tended to converge.

§ 152. The Development of the Basic Rule Respecting Tying

A black letter statement of the current law on tying would probably assert three propositions: that a tie violates Section 1 whenever the seller possesses any discernible degree of market power in the tying product and the tie effects more than a *de minimus* amount of commerce; that a tie also violates Section 3 when it meets that test, so long as there is a "sale or lease" of a "commodity" or a contract therefore; and that any tie violating Section 1 alone or Sections 1 and 3 also violates Section 5 of the FTC Act. But statements of this kind, useful as they can be at times, are terribly simplistic and for that reason dangerous. Let us first trace the main developments as they occurred over time and then back up to sort out issues relating to whether differences exist in the scope of the statutes and whether subtleties pervade in their application.

We have referred already to *Dick*.[1] There was another pre-Clayton case of some interest, United States v. Winslow,[2] in which the Court found no violation of Sherman even in a tying arrangement imposed by a clearly dominant firm. The first post-Clayton case to reach the Court was Motion Picture Patents Co. v. Universal Film Manufacturing Co.,[3] an infringement case similar to *Dick*. The plaintiff licensed the use of its patented motion picture projector on the condition that it only be used to show films made by plaintiff, a condition imposed by an imprint clearly stamped on each machine. At the time, plaintiff's patented machine was necessary for successful operation of a movie theatre and the restriction, as the Court saw it, extended plaintiff's monopoly from the market for the projector to that for films, in which there would otherwise have been effective competition. Referring to Clayton Section 3, as well as to these competitive harms, the Court expressly overruled *Dick* and held that the patent license restriction purported to extend plaintiff's legal monopoly beyond the congressional grant. Accordingly, the defendant, by using the machine beyond the scope of the license, was not liable for infringement.

Motion Picture Patents was in a technical sense a narrow holding. It went no further than to rule that use in violation of the noticed condition was not infringement; it left open the question whether the restriction could be achieved by exacting a covenant from the user and, despite the Court's reference to Clayton, contained

---

1. See § 151 supra.
2. 227 U.S. 202, 33 S.Ct. 253, 57 L.Ed. 481 (1913).
3. 243 U.S. 502, 37 S.Ct. 416, 61 L.Ed. 871 (1917).

no holding that the attempted tie was a violation of the antitrust laws. A year later, in United States v. United Shoe Machinery Corp.,[4] the government was set back when it attempted to obtain a holding that it was inherently unlawful under Section 1 for a dominant firm to tie leases of some patented machines to the use of others. The Court relied in part on its earlier holding in *Winslow,* but also stated that a manufacturer with a valid patent which leased its machines rather than selling them had an interest in protecting the functioning of the machines, and also had an interest in enhancing their availability on easy terms, both of which might justify some restriction.

Nevertheless, the thrust of *Motion Picture Patents* was strong and its rationale was not long contained. The government, four years later, again brought the United Shoe leases before the Court; this time the Court found them to be unlawful under Section 3.[5] The Court distinguished the prior case on the basis of the difference between the competitive effects clause of Section 3, which outlawed arrangements which "may" adversely effect competition, and the more rigorous Sherman Act requirement that there be a restraint of trade, an established diminishment of competition. It also stressed that the explicit provision that Section 3 applied to patented machines foreclosed the justification which, four years earlier, had been accepted under Section 1. And it based its decision on the proposition that where a manufacturer with substantial power in one market seeks through a tie to extend that power to another market, there is necessarily an adverse competitive effect.

The importance of power in the tying product was further underscored a year later by the decision in FTC v. Sinclair Refining Co.[6] There, the Court upheld a restriction whereby a refiner leased gasoline pumps imprinted with its trademark and name to station operators on condition that they use them only to pump the refiner's brand of gas. The Court stressed the lack of power in the tying product, which was readily available from numerous sources, and the fact that dealers were entirely free to sell another gas at the same location from pumps acquired elsewhere. It also held valid the contention that consumers would be misled and the supplier's goodwill adversely affected if gas refined by others was supplied from its pumps. Though it was applying Section 3, the analysis was an open and wide ranging inquiry into potential harms and benefits; the case thus went far to negate any implication from *Motion Picture Patents* or the more recent *Shoe Machinery* case that a *per se* rule was developing.[7]

4. 247 U.S. 32, 38 S.Ct. 473, 62 L.Ed. 968 (1918).

5. United Shoe Mach. Corp. v. United States, 258 U.S. 451, 42 S.Ct. 363, 66 L.Ed. 708 (1922).

6. 261 U.S. 463, 43 S.Ct. 450, 67 L.Ed. 746 (1923).

7. See also Pick Mfg. Co. v. GMC., 299 U.S. 3, 57 S.Ct. 1, 81 L.Ed. 4 (1936).

In the 1930's however, the Court began to turn sharply toward a *per se* approach. International Business Machines Corp. v. United States,[8] is perhaps the single most significant decision marking this development. Defendant leased its patented computing machine upon condition that it be used only with punch cards made and sold by it. While the Court made no elaborate inquiry into market structure, it did display an interest in whether the defendant had power in the tying product market. It alluded to the patent, noted that the defendant and its only competitors marketed in the same way, and stressed both the quantitative substantiality of the commerce in punch cards covered by the restraint (some $3,000,000 a year) and, indicative of market power, the fact that this amount constituted 81% of the entire punch card market. On this truncated analysis of competitive effect, the Court found sufficient adverse impact to preclude defendant's asserted business justification that improperly made cards could injure the machines and damage defendant's good will. As to this interest of defendant the Court made the obvious comment that a less restrictive alternative would be to publish specifications for cards which would not damage the machines and to restrict the machine to use with cards meeting these specifications.

International Salt Co. v. United States[9] moved further in the same direction; for the first time the Court used *per se* language in a tying case. The decision affirmed a summary judgment that leases of patented salt dispensing machines violated Section 3 and Section 1 in that they obligated the lessee to use the machines only with salt purchased from the lessor. The record showed nothing relevant to power beyond the fact that annual sales of salt for use in the machines aggregated about $500,000. That was enough. In announcing what has come to be known as a test of "quantitative substantiality" the Court said that "it is unreasonable, *per se*, to foreclose competitors from any substantial market", and that the volume of business here affected "cannot be said to be insignificant or insubstantial and the tendency of the arrangement to accomplish monopoly is obvious."[10] Note that the Court utterly lacked any conventional basis for an assumption either that the defendant possessed market power in the tying product or that it had foreclosed any share of the tied market which could significantly affect competition. All the Court found to say about the tying product market was that the defendant held a patent; whether its machine was successfully differentiated or whether it had any appreciable share of its market was undisclosed. We are therefore forced to conclude that power remains a prerequisite for tying liability only if we assume that a firm with a patent

---

8. 298 U.S. 131, 56 S.Ct. 701, 80 L.Ed. 1085 (1936).

9. 332 U.S. 392, 68 S.Ct. 12, 92 L.Ed. 20 (1947).

10. Id. at 396, 68 S.Ct. at 15, 92 L.Ed. at 26.

can be presumed to have power—presumed either conclusively or subject to the burden of establishing otherwise. Weak as was the record on power in the tying product market, it was even weaker on effect in the tied product market. Half a million dollars in sales, even if "quantitatively substantial," cannot be taken without proof as having foreclosed a sufficiently large percentage of the salt market to have achieved a discernable impact on the opportunities of competing sellers of salt. Thus *International Salt,* which applies both Section 1 and Section 3 without drawing any distinction between them, comes exceedingly close to holding that any tying arrangement is unlawful. All that need be shown is that there is a significant dollar volume in tied transactions, at least if the tying product is a patented one.

But the worth of a case is better understood by the way the Court has read it when returning to its problem than by the way it presents itself untouched by subsequent history. The Court has been reinterpreting *International Salt* every few years and not always in identical or obvious ways. It was treated first in Times-Picayune Publishing Co v. United States,[11] a Section 1 case. The Court held that tying violates Sherman only if the defendant has substantial market power in the tying product and a substantial volume of commerce in the tied product is restrained. Section 3 was seen as involving a less exacting test; it was violated by a tie if the seller had power in the tying product *or* if substantial commerce in the tied product was restrained. In explaining away *Salt,* a Section 1 case in which no power was shown, the Court merely pointed to the patents, stating that these "conferred monopolistic, albeit lawful, market control." [12] Of course "monopolistic market control" of the *Salt* defendants was not shown to have derived from the patents; hence this reference must be taken to mean either that the patent is conclusively presumed to grant such control—that if a party exercises his rights under the patent law to obtain protection for an invention he gives up any right he might otherwise have to use it as a tying product—or that a patent is presumed to assure market control in the absence of contrary proof. In any event, the Court in *Times-Picayune* rather flatly held that where neither "patents [n]or copyrights supplied the requisite market control, any equivalent market 'dominance' " must be proved by appropriate data.[13]

Salt was treated in a somewhat different manner in Northern Pacific Ry. v. United States,[14] another Section 1 case. The Court sustained a summary judgment for the government in a case involving "preferred routing" provisions, by which buyers and lessees of land from defendant's large holdings near its right of way committed

11. 345 U.S. 594, 73 S.Ct. 872, 97 L.Ed. 1277 (1953).

12. Id. at 608, 73 S.Ct. at 880, 97 L.Ed. at 1289.

13. Id. at 611, 73 S.Ct. at 882, 97 L.Ed. at 1291.

14. 356 U.S. 1, 78 S.Ct. 514, 2 L.Ed.2d 545 (1958).

themselves to ship on defendant's line when its rates were not less advantageous than those of other carriers. Citing *Salt,* the Court saw the Sherman prohibition on tying as applicable if an appreciable restraint on free competition in the market for the tied product occurs and if that restraint affects a "not insubstantial" amount of commerce in the tied product.[15] The Court brushed aside the notion advanced in *Times-Picayune* that tying product dominance had to be established. It concluded that such power in the tying product as had to be established was shown necessarily when plaintiff proved that defendant had in fact imposed an appreciable restraint on numerous buyers and lessees. This holding thus moved away from the "market dominance" test, but whether the movement was all the way back to the quantitative substantiality test of *Salt* was not made clear. Land, the tying product in *Northern Pacific*, also could be presumed unique, as might a patented product. However, the Court referred not just to the fact that land was involved, but to the strategic location of defendant's land and to the extensiveness of its holdings. These, as well as the fact that defendant had succeeded in inducing numerous land buyers to enter into "this host of tying arrangements" were felt to show "defendant's great power."[16]

The language here quoted may go so far as to imply that if defendant succeeds in tying any "appreciable" amount of commerce, that fact alone shows sufficient power; if so, *Northern Pacific* not only revitalizes the simple "quantitative substantiality" test of *Salt,* but makes clear that the *Salt* test is not dependent on the existence of a patent. Such a reading is invited by a remark in *Northern Pacific* rejecting the view taken in *Times-Picayune* that the *Salt* result turned on the patent as showing dominance. Speaking of *Salt,* the Court in *Northern Pacific* said that the case did not rely upon "the fact that a patent was involved nor did it give the slightest intimation that the outcome would have been different if that had not been the case."[17]

While these swings in the law have been unsettling, they may now have ended. In its two most recent tying decisions, the Court has again shown its readiness to find liability on a showing that some not insubstantial amount of commerce in the tied product is affected and that the tying product is successfully differentiated, whether by patent, copyright or otherwise, so that some significant group of buyers have a preference for it which is strong enough to enable the seller to induce them to buy something else from him in order to get the tying product. This may not be a *per se* rule in the strictest sense. Plaintiff must prove more than the existence of a tie; he must also

---

15. Id. at 6, 78 S.Ct. at 518, 2 L.Ed.2d at 550.

16. Id. at 7–8, 78 S.Ct. at 519, 2 L.Ed. 2d at 551.

17. Id. at 9, 78 S.Ct. at 520, 2 L.Ed.2d at 552.

show that the tying product is successfully differentiated and that the commerce affected by the tie is not *de minimus*. Nevertheless, it is a rule under which liability is triggered upon a showing, in addition to the restraint, of some fairly perfunctory and easily established market facts.

These most recent decisions are United States v. Loew's Inc.[18] and Fortner Enterprises, Inc. v. United States Steel Corp.[19] In *Loew's,* "block booking," whereby copyrighted movies were licensed to TV stations only in packages, so that, for example, to get "Casablanca" a station would also have to take "Nancy Drew, Troubleshooter" and others, was held to violate Section 1. The Court said that power to appreciably restrain competition is "presumed when the tying product is patented or copyrighted" and, when there is no patent or copyright, power can be shown by evidence of "the tying product's desirability to consumers or from uniqueness in its attributes."[20] *Fortner* reversed a summary judgment for the defendant in a case alleging that defendant had, through uniquely beneficial loan terms which were given only in connection with the purchase of its prefabricated houses, used credit as a tying product to sell the houses. The Court held that plaintiff had to be given the opportunity to prove the lender's unique economic advantages. As to the showing which had to be made regarding power in the tying product, the Court said:

> [D]ecisions rejecting the need for proof of truly dominant power over the tying product have all been based on a recognition that because tying arrangements generally serve no legitimate purpose that cannot be achieved in some less restrictive way, the presence of any appreciable restraint on competition provides sufficient reason for invalidating the tie. Such appreciable restraint exists whenever the seller can exert some power over some of the buyers in the market, even if his power is not complete over them * * *. [D]espite the freedom of some or many buyers from the seller's power, other buyers—whether few or many, whether scattered throughout the market or part of some group within the market * * * [could] be forced to accept * * * [a] higher price because of their stronger preferences for the product, and the seller could therefore choose instead to force them to accept a tying arrangement that would prevent free competition for their patronage in the market for the tied product.[21]

18. 371 U.S. 38, 83 S.Ct. 97, 9 L.Ed.2d 11 (1962).

19. 394 U.S. 495, 89 S.Ct. 1252, 22 L. Ed.2d 495 (1969), appeal after remand 452 F.2d 1095 (6th Cir. 1971), cert. denied 406 U.S. 919, 92 S.Ct. 1773, 32 L. Ed.2d 119 (1972).

20. 371 U.S. at 45, 83 S.Ct. at 102, 9 L. Ed.2d at 18.

21. 394 U.S. at 503–04, 89 S.Ct. at 1258–59, 22 L.Ed.2d at 505. One should not pass without noting an analytical absurdity latent in *Fortner*, given its specific facts—the diffi-

In short, tying violates Sherman—and in the case of leases and sales of commodities, violates Clayton—whenever a quantitatively substantial amount of commerce is affected by the tie, and when the tying product is either patented, copyrighted, or in some other way significantly differentiated in the view of some buyers. Moreover, if a substantial number of ties have been imposed, the existence of power may be inferred from that fact alone.

§ 153. The Relationship between Clayton and Sherman Act Standards

The extravagance of growth in the doctrinal development in the tying cases ought to be explored. The development begins with the Court, before Clayton, holding tying no offense even when the tying product is patented and the seller dominant.[1] Next, Congress enacts Section 3. The Court responds to the congressional lead and applies a lower threshold test under Section 3.[2] But then, after vacillating for a while [3] and at one point articulating a fine distinction between the Section 3 and the Section 1 tests,[4] the Court proceeds to reduce the Sherman threshold—as it would now appear—to the Clayton level. One can trace a similar dynamic in the development of merger doctrine under Clayton, Section 7 (as amended).[5] Some effort should

culty in finding a principle which contains the case within rational bounds. If a seller were to sell $10 bills for $5 and to "tie" an item usually sold for $50 at that price, we would presumably say that what the seller really had done was to reduce the price on the second item by $5. It is hard to see why offering below market credit terms is different. On remand, Fortner prevailed. United States Steel Corp. v. Fortner Enterprises Inc., 523 F.2d 961 (6th Cir. 1975). The Supreme Court again granted certiorari and the case is now pending. (Dkt. No. 75–853). One of the anomalies in *Fortner* is made clear by the recent decision in Southern Concrete Co. v. United States Steel Corp., 535 F.2d 313 (5th Cir. 1976). Defendant allegedly used favorable credit terms as a tying product by which it tied the sale of its cement to a manufacturer of ready-mix concrete. The purchaser, by virtue of the favorable terms, was allegedly able to undersell its competitor, the plaintiff, and thus drove plaintiff out of business. The court granted summary judgment for defendant on the ground that tying is a violation which can injure either the seller's competitor (by foreclosing customers) or the buyer (by coercively reducing the buyer's options) and, therefore, that competitors of the buyer have no standing. If a competitively harmful tie has really occurred the buyer will, if anything, be injured, not aided. The serious contention made by plaintiff in the case that it was hurt by the advantageous position conferred on the tied buyer tends to dramatize the observation that when a seller grants favorable credit terms on its products, what it is doing, realistically, is not tying one product to another, but selling one product on attractive terms.

1. E.g., Henry v. A. B. Dick Co., 224 U. S. 1, 32 S.Ct. 364, 56 L.Ed. 645 (1912); United States v. Winslow, 227 U.S. 202, 33 S.Ct. 253, 57 L.Ed. 481 (1913).

2. IBM Corp. v. United States, 298 U.S. 131, 56 S.Ct. 701, 80 L.Ed. 1085 (1936).

3. International Salt Co. v. United States, 332 U.S. 392, 68 S.Ct. 12, 92 L.Ed. 20 (1947); Times-Picayune Publishing Co. v. United States, 345 U.S. 594, 73 S.Ct. 872, 97 L.Ed. 1277 (1953).

4. Times-Picayune, supra note 3.

5. See United States v. Columbia Steel Co., 334 U.S. 495, 68 S.Ct. 1107, 92 L. Ed. 1533 (1948); United States v. Philadelphia Nat'l Bank, 374 U.S. 321,

be made to identify the elements in this relationship between Congress and the Court and to assign to each a distinctive role. Areeda asks us to consider whether Congress by enacting Clayton accorded a recognition to the less rigorous Sherman Act test which would govern where Clayton did not apply and whether the Court, by conforming Sherman to standards developed under Clayton, rendered the later act superfluous.[6] It is in this mode that Mr. Justice Clark's opinion in *Times-Picayune* is written; it strains to make the separate enactments speak against tying with separate degrees of urgency. But this approach seems in the end excessive and somewhat superficial, like taking elaborate precautions against a nonexistent danger. As Areeda's analysis suggests, the generality of Sherman invites doctrinal development as knowledge increases and values ripen. It would be a perversion of Clayton to read it as stifling all growth potential in Sherman, fixing the meaning and intention of that act forever at the level attained in 1914.[7]

Undue formalism, the imposition of a highly elaborate schematic on the relationship between Congress and the Court, is more likely to becloud than to illuminate. In some areas it is obviously appropriate for the Court to take the policy underlying a narrow and specific statute and, as a matter of common law, to generalize it. In another context the fact that Congress has written narrowly on a subject may properly discourage judicial expansiveness. It depends upon the judicial judgment, made after evaluating all sources relevant to the development of doctrine, to determine what is the proper path of the law. In the realm of antitrust, Congress in Clayton as well as Sherman has spoken on crucial issues like competitive effect only in open terms which mandate a continuing process of development. Beyond this, in consistent if subtle ways, Congress has encouraged extension of the law. Save for those pertaining to fair trade, virtually all of the amendments of the antitrust laws from 1890 to date have expressed a congressional purpose to achieve more rigorous enforcement.[8]

§ 154. The Patent Misuse Doctrine and the Tying Concept

Motion Picture Patents held that a patent licensee did not infringe when it violated a license restriction forbidding use of the patented machine with supplies made by others than the patentee.[1] The case also delimits contributory infringement doctrine. A contributo-

---

83 S.Ct. 1715, 10 L.Ed.2d 915 (1963); United States v. First Nat'l Bank & Trust Co. of Lexington, 376 U.S. 665, 84 S.Ct. 1033, 12 L.Ed.2d 1 (1964).

6. See P. Areeda, Antitrust Analysis Problems, Text, Cases ¶ 537 (2d ed. 1974).

7. Id.

8. See, e.g., the discussion of Clayton Act history in D. Martin, Mergers and the Law 20–56 (1959).

1. Motion Picture Patents Co. v. Universal Film Mfg. Co., 243 U.S. 502, 37 S.Ct. 416, 61 L.Ed. 871 (1917). See discussion in § 152 supra.

ry infringement occurs "where one makes and sells one element of a combination covered by a patent with the intention and for the purpose of bringing about its use in [the patented] combination * * *"; one who makes and sells the element to a licensee for this use "is equally liable to the patentee with him who in fact organizes the complete combination."[2] But where, by tying, the patentee seeks to extend the scope of the patent, the seller of the unpatented supplies, like the licensee who violates the tie, has violated no right of the patentee.[3] It is now clear that the *Motion Picture Patents* rule governs whether the patentee tries to achieve the tie by granting a license on the condition that only patentee's non-patented supplies be used, by exacting from the licensee a promise not to use the patented machine with supplies provided by others, or by granting patent licenses only to those who in fact purchase non-patented supplies or ancillary equipment solely from the patentee.[4] Initially, the cases in this line were limited to holding, as did *Motion Picture Patents,* that infringement actions would not lie against defendants using the patented item with unpatented supplies, or that contributory infringement actions would not lie against those supplying unpatented supplies. But in Morton Salt Co. v. G. S. Suppiger Co.,[5] the Court announced the patent misuse doctrine. There, plaintiff, holding a patent on a machine for dispensing salt tablets which was used in canning processes, brought an action against defendant which allegedly made and sold an infringing machine. On affidavits that plaintiff required licensees of its machine to use salt tablets sold by plaintiff, the trial court granted summary judgment to defendant without considering whether the patent was valid or infringed. The court of appeals reversed on the ground that there was no evidence of competitive effect and no showing of a Clayton Act violation. The Supreme Court then reinstated the trial court's judgment, holding that as a matter of patent law and irrespective of whether any antitrust law is violated, an effort to use a patent to restrain trade in a non-patented item is a misuse of the patent and disqualifies the patentee from enforcing the patent even against direct infringers until the misuse has been abated and its effects dissipated. This patent law doctrine, resonating as it does to antitrust values, has been a formidable deterrent to efforts to tie, directly or indirectly. Furthermore, by its application to other anticompetitive practices which make use of patents, the doctrine has helped to integrate patent and antitrust law.

2. Thomson-Houston Elec. Co. v. Ohio Brass Co., 80 F. 712, 721 (6th Cir. 1897) (Taft, J.).

3. Leitch Mfg. Co. v. Barber Co., 302 U.S. 458, 58 S.Ct. 288, 82 L.Ed. 371 (1938); Mercoid Corp. v. Mid-Continent Inv. Co., 320 U.S. 661, 64 S.Ct. 268, 88 L.Ed. 376 (1944).

4. Carbice Corp. of America v. American Patents Dev. Corp., 283 U.S. 27, 51 S.Ct. 334, 75 L.Ed. 819 (1931); Leitch Mfg. Co. v. Barber Co., supra; B.B. Chemical Co. v. Ellis, 314 U.S. 495, 62 S.Ct. 406, 86 L.Ed. 367 (1942).

5. 314 U.S. 488, 62 S.Ct. 402, 86 L.Ed. 363 (1942).

§ 155. The Need for Two Distinct Commodities or Services

One difficulty with the tying concept is its spaciousness; when we start looking we can see ties whenever two or more congruent products or services are sold together. Are the component parts of the auto or the TV tied when the assembled auto or receiver is offered for sale? Are eggs tied to bacon on the breakfast menu? Are vests tied to coats and pants, buttons to shirts, laces to shoes? Almost anything subject to sale or lease can be broken into constituent parts and almost anything can be combined with something else to make for an enlarged and perhaps enhanced offering. The very nature of the tying concept presupposes that there are distinctive and discernible products or services which a buyer ought to be able to obtain alone, if he wishes. In a complex economy of myriad interrelationships, how then do we define the product or service unit?

Integral products and services are identified for tying purposes less by drawing upon economic analysis than by exercising practical judgment. Decisions must take into account the efficiency of various linkages, trade practices and expectations, common understanding, technological feasibility and, perhaps, the reasonableness of obliging a seller to widen buyers' options. Cute cases like the string of hypotheticals listed above are resolved easily enough. The great generality of buyers who seek a left shoe also want a right; it is thus little imposition on buyers for sellers to say they must have it so, and it is an enormous efficiency in the making, packaging and marketing of shoes to treat the pair as the unit. Where nice questions do present themselves, often they are characterized as factual issues to be left in a jury case to that tribunal.[1]

A leading case which exemplifies a practical analysis by the court is United States v. Jerrold Electronics Corp.[2] Defendant provided technologically sophisticated master television antenna systems involving reception, amplification and transmission from distant parts in areas where it was very difficult or impossible to receive signals with ordinary antennas. It offered only its "system," not components and parts, and only under contracts pursuant to which it installed and serviced the system. The court held that the items of equipment making up the system were separate products and that installation and service were separate from these; therefore, the marketing method involved illegal tying. Among facts which showed that "a community antenna system cannot properly be characterized as a single product" were that competitors offered separately various component items of equipment, installation and service; that the number and type of elements combined to form a system varied considerably from one system to another; that prices were determined by ag-

---

1. E.g., Kansas City Star Co. v. United States, 240 F.2d 643 (8th Cir. 1957).

2. 187 F.Supp. 545 (E.D.Pa.1960), aff'd per curiam, 365 U.S. 567, 81 S.Ct. 755, 5 L.Ed.2d 806 (1961).

gregating the elements in the package; and that Jerrold sold some of the items separately to some buyers. Other decisions typifying the pragmatic approach have held that since advertisers did not distinguish between morning and evening newspaper coverage, but merely evaluated the total readership reached, an offering of combined morning and evening coverage was not the tying of two separate products;[3] that since editing, transmission and user interests were separable, a press service's regional wire, general news wire and financial wire were separate services rather than one product, "news";[4] and that stations, linked in a network, were separable so that an advertiser who wanted to sponsor a program in 95 outlets could not be required to choose 130 stations or more.[5] It has been suggested that efficiency considerations should dominate in these cases, that if the seller incurs cost saving in marketing the package he should be permitted to obtain them even despite a desire by a significant number of buyers for separate components.[6] But as we shall see, a seller obliged to offer the components separately can also offer the package; and in doing so he can pass on any savings in the price.[7]

Chicken Delight,[8] a case we shall look at more particularly in considering purposes and effects of ties, presented the question whether a trademark and name, licensed by a franchisor to its franchisees, can be characterized as a tying product when the franchisor grants the license only upon condition that the franchisee buy supplies from it. The court did not follow an FTC decision [9] which held that as a conceptual matter a trademark license could not be considered as separate from the sale of the products or ingredients to which it applied and recognized that a franchisor clearly could license the mark and name for an appropriate compensation, subject to specifications concerning the product and franchisee conduct.

3. Times-Picayune Publishing Co. v. United States, 345 U.S. 594, 73 S.Ct. 872, 97 L.Ed. 1277 (1953).

4. Associated Press v. Taft-Ingalls Corp., 340 F.2d 753 (6th Cir.), cert. denied 382 U.S. 820, 85 S.Ct. 47, 15 L. Ed.2d 66 (1965).

5. American Mfrs. Mut. Ins. Co. v. American Broadcasting-Paramount Theatres, Inc., 221 F.Supp. 848 (S.D. N.Y.1963).

6. See Automatic Radio Mfg. Co. v. Ford Motor Co., 242 F.Supp. 852 (D. Mass.1965).

7. See §§ 156–157 infra.

8. Siegel v. Chicken Delight, Inc., 448 F.2d 43 (2d Cir. 1971), cert. denied 405 U.S. 955, 92 S.Ct. 1172, 31 L.Ed.2d 232 (1972). Accord: Carpa, Inc. v. Ward Foods, Inc., 536 F.2d 39 (5th Cir. 1976). But see Redd v. Shell Oil Co., 524 F. 2d 1054, 1057 (10th Cir. 1975) (holding that precluding buyer from reselling under seller's mark goods manufactured by another does not constitute tying; dicta questions that *Chicken Delight* holding is sound); Ungar v. Dunkin' Donuts of Am., Inc., 531 F.2d 1211, 1215 n. 4 (3d Cir. 1976) (dicta that *Chicken Delight* analysis is "not obvious").

9. Carvel Corp., 68 FTC 128 (1965), CCH Trade Reg.Rep. ¶ 17,298 (1965). See also Ungar v. Dunkin' Donuts, 531 F. 2d 1211, 1215 n. 4 (3d Cir. 1976) and Redd v. Shell Oil Co., 524 F.2d 1054, 1057 (10th Cir. 1975).

§ 156. Purposes and Effects of Tying

The rationale for the tying rule, expressed unqualifiedly by Justice Frankfurter and often repeated, is that a seller may not use power enjoyed in one product market to advance his position in a quite distinct product market on a basis other than the competitive merits of the offering. Tying is said to have no other purpose or effect and thus offends antitrust values in two respects; by foreclosing competitors of the seller from fair access to that part of the market for the tied product which is foreclosed by the tie, and by reducing the range of choice open to buyers of that product.[1] Interestingly enough, none of the conventional judicial comments about tying analyze at any depth the effect of tying on the process of competition. We must therefore begin with the supposition that the hostility to tying embodied in the act and expressed in the cases may have more to do with notions of appropriate competitive behavior (conceptions about fair opportunity or access) and with the polar concepts of coercion and free choice, than it has to do with the efficiency or allocation consequences of competitive structure and process.[2] We shall first consider whether and, if so, to what extent and under what circumstances tying can do injury to the processes of competition. This analysis should also bring to attention any inconsistencies with other goals of competition embodied in Sherman and Clayton which can be attributed to tying. We shall then note and evaluate any benefits which may be attributable to tying; we need not take on faith the judicial assumption that no non-harmful or socially beneficial purposes or goals may be achieved.

Tying can only affect competition if the seller imposing the tie has market power in the tying product. A farmer who refuses to sell his apples unless the buyer also takes his pears can obviously not distort the market, since no buyer will respond unless he happens to want both products in the same proportions in which they are offered and it is convenient to take delivery from a single source. The effect of the tie is to make it much harder for the farmer to sell his fruit, not to foreclose competing sellers of apples or pears from any segment of potential buyers.[3] Even when the sponsor of the tie has power in the tying product, tying can affect competition significantly only when an appreciable share of the market in the tied product is

---

1. Standard Oil Co. of Cal. v. United States, 337 U.S. 293, 69 S.Ct. 1051, 93 L.Ed. 1371 (1949). See discussion in § 164, infra.

2. See, e.g., Northern Pacific Ry. v. United States, 356 U.S. 1, 78 S.Ct. 514, 2 L.Ed.2d 545 (1958); Capital Temporaries, Inc. v. Olsten Corp., 506 F.2d 658 (2d Cir. 1974); Susser v. Carvel Corp., 332 F.2d 505 (2d Cir. 1964), cert. dismissed 381 U.S. 125, 85 S.Ct. 1364, 14 L.Ed.2d 284 (1965); Landon v. Twentieth Century-Fox Film Corp., 384 F.Supp. 450 (S.D.N.Y.1974).

3. See generally, Stigler, United States v. Loew's Inc.: A Note on Block Booking, 1963 S.Ct.Rev. 152; Markovitz, Tie-Ins, Reciprocity and the Leverage Theory, 76 Yale L.J. 1397 (1967), 80 Yale L.J. 195 (1970); P. Areeda, Antitrust Analysis, Problems, Text, Cases ¶¶ 532–33, 540 (2d ed. 1974).

foreclosed. Consider *International Salt*.[4] Suppose that defendant's patent made it the sole maker and seller of salt dispensing machinery for use in canning. Clearly the defendant would then have had power in the tying product. But suppose, also, that the canning industry as a whole utilized less than one-tenth of one percent of all the salt purchased and consumed. Passing the possibility of sub-markets for salt of various grades and kinds, we would have to conclude on a static analysis, that the tie used in *International Salt*, though completely successful in foreclosing the canning industry to other salt sellers, would have only a trivial effect on other salt sellers. Of course there is still a social concern. Just as in monopoly cases we may wish to protect a group of buyers when, for them, there is no close substitute for the monopolized product, even though for others there are substitutes, so here, we might think canners a large enough sub-group to protect because they, if not others, are tied for salt purchases. It is not that the seller can exploit them beyond what his patent facilitates. The monopolist's power to do this is limited, as we shall see. If it charges more than a competitive price for salt it will have to reduce the machine price commensurately. It is simply the overriding conviction that a large group of buyers ought not to be limited to a single seller on a product the seller does not lawfully monopolize.

The greatest effect of tying comes, of course, in those situations where the seller's market power in the tying product is great and uses of it in association with the tied product constitute major parts of the market for the tied product. *Motion Picture Patents* serves as an example.[5] The patentee makes a projector so far superior to others that no movie theatre can be commercially successful without one. The patentee also makes movies, and ties the purchase or rental of his projector to the purchase of his films exclusively. What starts as a patent monopoly of the business of making and selling projectors becomes a monopoly of the business of making and selling movies, because all competing sellers are successfully foreclosed by the tie.

Do any of these ties distort resource allocation, lead to higher prices and profits and lower production of any product? The apple-pear tie obviously does not. On our assumptions, the tie of salt to the salt dispensing machine has no distorting effect on the salt market—the dispensing machine monopolist gains no power there—but given the fact buyers must fill all salt needs from the seller (though no salt quantities are specified), it does enable the machine monopolist to increase its monopoly return; through the tie the monopolist can, in effect, extract a higher price for its monopoly.[6] If, however, the item on which there is a patent or other monopoly (say, hammerheads)

---

4. 332 U.S. 392, 68 S.Ct. 12, 92 L.Ed. 20 (1947). See discussion in § 154 supra.

5. 243 U.S. 502, 37 S.Ct. 416, 61 L.Ed. 871 (1917). See discussion in § 154 supra.

6. Burnstein, The Economics of Tie-In Sales, 42 Rev. of Econ. & Stat. 68 (1960).

were used in fixed proportions with the tied item (say, hammer handles), the tie, though extending the monopoly from heads to handles, would not result in any greater monopoly profit.[7] The monopolist could not increase its return through the tie; it would exact the full measure of its monopoly reward by the price it charged for the patented hammerhead, leaving competition to set the price on handles. To move into the second field earns it nothing over and above a fair return on the additional investment and, though it displaces the prior sellers of handles, it does not increase the aggregate price for hammers, or increase profits, or reduce output.[8]

Some commentators end the analysis here, taking note that (on the supposition of fixed proportions between the related commodities or services) carrying the monopoly over to the tied product does not distort resource allocation. However, the market economy is not static; even on the essential assumption of fixed proportions, there can over time be significant adverse effects. Displacing the competitive handle market with a monopolistic structure will have ongoing implications. Competitive pressure to cut costs or improve products in the handle industry is now reduced; indeed, a potential source for innovation which might erode the power of the hammerhead monopolist has been wiped out. Firms in the competitive handle industry would be knowledgeable about the related head technology and would also be aware that the hammerhead monopolist, by establishing a monopoly price for heads, had effectively reduced demand for handles, a complementary product. This competitive segment is therefore a primary source of potential innovation which would tend to reduce the power of the hammerhead monopolist.[9] These and related dynamic elements are also at work to amplify the adverse effects which occur in cases where, as in the *Motion Picture Patents* situation, the tying and tied products are used in varied proportions. The projection monopolist which takes over film production will also solidify his position by reducing the likelihood that others will successfully invent around his projection patent. More than that, extension of the monopoly to film production will tend to reduce the likelihood of competitive entry for financial reasons, even if an alternative technology is developed. If the projection monopolist were not permitted to monopolize production, a firm with a new projection technology could enter projection alone; but if the monopoly had been extended by the tie to production, the firm seeking to enter projection would either have to enter both fields itself or would have to procure others to en-

---

7. Bowman, Tying Arrangements and the Leverage Problem, 67 Yale L.J. 19 (1957).

8. Bowman, supra note 7, at 21–25; compare Bork, Vertical Integration and the Sherman Act: The Legal History of an Economic Misconception, 22 U.Chi.L.Rev. 157, 197 (1954); Spengler, Vertical Integration and Antitrust Policy, 58 J. of Pol. Econ. 347 (1950). The analysis in text relies heavily on Bowman.

9. See the analysis suggested by Areeda, supra note 3.

ter the production field simultaneously with its entry into projector manufacturing. To take the first course would require additional capital. The would-be entrant may have access to capital sufficient to enter at one stage but not both. Indeed, there may be rising costs of capital as the scale of the capital requirement increases.

Nor is it only capital costs which might make integrated entry much harder than entry into one segment. It is also the whole range of differing entrepreneurial skills and judgments, which would have to be assembled for integrated entry. Because one felt ready to enter the business of manufacturing projectors would not imply readiness to produce films, even assuming capital is available without penalty. It is this sense for how people in the concrete are likely to react which is squeezed out by the analyses of those who assume a near perfect fluidity of talent and resources.

But have we yet plumbed the full depth of concerns? The judicially developed rule about tying may resonate less with concerns about resource allocation than it does with concerns about affording reasonable opportunities for numerous sellers and assuring buyer freedom of choice. If the hammerhead monopolist projects his monopoly into the competitive handle industry, he causes an effect, a substitution of the one for the many, which can appropriately concern us, quite independently of the immediate or long range resource allocation. Other things being substantially equal, we prefer the many to the one, the competitive industry to the monopolized one, for social and political as well as economic reasons. We value opportunity for economic independence; we perceive it as a good, in and of itself, and we sense that political freedom may be related to opportunity for economic decision-making in ways we do not yet fully understand.[10] We cannot go so far as to label tying predatory, certainly not in its impact upon buyers of the tied and tying product, but it does constrict their range of choices. It subjects buyers to economic coercion of a sort.[10a] So doing, it reduces them as free commercial agents. If these harmful effects of tying can be inhibited without social or economic cost, they should be.

This observation leads us to turn the coin over, to reflect about whether tying promises any significant benefits of which society may be deprived by the courts' accustomed hostility to it.[11] Though the

---

10. See United States v. Aluminum Co. of America, 148 F.2d 416, 428–29 (2d Cir. 1945).

10a. See the discussion in Ungar v. Dunkin' Donuts of Am., Inc., 531 F.2d 1211 (3rd Cir. 1976).

11. In this inquiry the principal primary source is Siegel v. Chicken Delight, Inc., 448 F.2d 43 (2d Cir. 1971), cert. denied 405 U.S. 955, 92 S.Ct. 1172, 31 L.Ed.2d 232 (1972). See also the article by Bowman, cited supra note 7; F. Scherer, Industrial Market Structure and Economic Performance, 241–42 (1970); W. Bowman, Patent and Antitrust Law 100–09, 111–16 (1973). For a more technically rigorous treatment covering much the same ground as the Bowman article, see Markovitz, Tie-ins, Reciprocity and the Leverage Theory, 76 Yale L.J. 1397 (1967).

cases are loathe to concede it, tying in some circumstances will enhance efficiency. Take shoes as an extreme example. It obviously costs less to make and distribute shoes in pairs, a left with a right, than singly. In other situations the analysis, though more complex, may yield a similar conclusion—that certain products will reach the consumer at lower prices if we permit one to be tied to another. Though the courts have never recognized an efficiency defense, they have done much the same thing indirectly. Courts do not say that a tie is lawful because of consequent efficiency; they often say it is not a tie at all but the sale of a single product. Most instances where efficiency is achieved through a tie are probably handled in this way, though there is perhaps still room in more complex situations for an affirmative defense of efficiency to be asserted. Some of the package licensing cases—for example where a large group of patents or copyrighted materials are licensed for an inclusive fee—may entail marketing efficiencies of some consequence. Perhaps a showing to this effect ought to be sufficient to validate such arrangements.

Another possibly beneficial purpose for tying is that stressed by Bowman [12] and pressed upon the court in *Chicken Delight*—to force customers to pay for the tying product in proportion to their use of it. As his example Bowman used the *IBM* case.[13] The requirement that users of the patented machine buy cards for use with the machine from the patentee at higher than a competitive price enabled the patentee to set a relatively modest rental on the machine and thus to rent it widely and collect a return from it as cards were sold. Since card use varied directly with use of the machine, IBM could collect more from those who used the machine heavily, and to whom it was of greater worth, than from those who used and valued it less. In *Chicken Delight* the claim was similar. Defendant, a fast food franchisor, licensed its name and mark to franchisees without charge but upon their commitment to buy supplies from the franchisor at a rate above the market.

These arrangements are analogous to a price discrimination. A seller always faces a downward sloping demand curve. Some buyers value the product more highly than others and are ready to pay more for it than would those who value it less. Normally, a seller cannot discriminate; it must select a single price and sell at that price to all. Customers will include many who would have paid more if they had to in order to get the product. A seller discriminates when it succeeds in charging more to those who value the product highly than it charges to those who value it less. When a seller is able to do this, it can achieve a greater return for its product. It brings into the market buyers at the lower end of the demand curve by reducing the price for them only, while maintaining a higher price for those further up

12. See supra note 7.

13. 298 U.S. 131, 56 S.Ct. 701, 80 L.Ed. 1085 (1936).

the demand scale, who will pay more if they have to. In a competitive, integrated market such discrimination would not be possible over any substantial length of time. However, if a seller possesses power and can segregate one segment of its customers from another, it may be able to discriminate successfully. It is essentially this which, as Bowman sees it, IBM had been doing and which Chicken Delight, as it characterized its own purposes, had been doing, each through the use of a tie.

When a tie is used to discriminate, is competition helped or hurt? The answer depends largely upon two variables: first, whether the use of the tying product is extended by the discrimination (which it may or may not be, depending on how the tying seller's cost structure relates to demand); and second, whether the discrimination will have adverse effects on competition among the buyers in the resale market. To simplify, assume that IBM faces two classes of users: those which would use its machines 300 times a year, who would thus need 300 cards and who would be willing to pay $400 a year total for the machine and cards, and those which would use the machines 5000 times a year, who would thus need 5000 cards and who would be ready to pay $5100 in total. Also assume that the first group is larger in number than the second. If IBM can successfully tie, its course is clear. It sets a rental rate of $100 on the machine, ties cards, and sells cards at one dollar each. It thus extracts from every user the maximum it is willing to pay. But if IBM cannot tie so as to discriminate (and if there is no other way to discriminate) the company must make a choice. If it wants to sell to the low demand group at all, it must offer the machines to everyone, including those who would pay much more, at the rental rate of $400 per year (less the cost of 300 cards on the open market). Its other choice is to set the high rental, $5100 per year (less the cost of 5000 cards on the open market), and to deal only with those at the high end of its demand curve. We may assume that it will choose from those options the course which will maximize its return. This choice will depend on the nature of its costs (how much will it save in costs by making only enough machines to meet the high level demand) and the elasticity of its demand curve (in our simplified hypothetical it will depend, more specifically, on the relative number of users in each group).

If IBM would respond to the rule against tying by selling to everyone at the low price, the only conceivably social gain in allowing it to tie and thus discriminate is the rather speculative one that doing so may encourage greater investment in research because the potential rewards now include those to be made by discriminating through a tie, and that this incremental investment in research will be socially preferable to the uses which the capital could otherwise be put. The more palpable effect is that permitting the tie forces some buyers to pay more than they would otherwise have to pay, hardly a benefit to competition. On the other hand, if IBM would respond to the rule against tying by pricing at the high portion of its demand curve there is another, perhaps significant, social advantage in permitting it to tie —doing so facilitates a wider deployment of IBM's technology. Unfortunately, we cannot say whether allowing a tie which is aimed at price discrimination will be helpful in facilitating a wider dispersal of technology. In some cases it will and in some cases it will not; there is no way we can tell what the effect will be in the generality of instances, nor even in a particular one, without an appallingly elaborate inquiry.

Whether the tie which facilitates discrimination will do injury to competition at the next level depends upon the structure of the market at that level. La Peyre v. FTC,[14] where the discrimination was achieved directly rather than through a tie, will illustrate the issues. Peelers Corporation had a patent on the only commercially feasible shrimp peeling machine. It fixed a rental rate for Gulf Coast packers below the labor costs which would be incurred for doing by hand what the peeling a machine would do, and rather rapidly packers on that coast converted from hand peeling to machine. Peelers then began marketing on the Pacific Coast. Its rental rate there was computed in the same way but was higher because Pacific shrimp were smaller and the labor cost of peeling a specified tonnage was higher. Since the packers on east coast competed, the FTC held that the discrimination violated Section 5 and the court affirmed.

After *La Peyre*, it may remain something of a mystery to identify the norm of the law or the ethical insight which led the court and Commission to conclude that West Coast packers were entitled to the same price as their eastern competitors, though their labor savings were larger.[15] Perhaps it is an appropriate generalization that in the marketplace we should all be treated alike, or perhaps the case is a response to the recognition that the power to discriminate is a mark of monopoly power, a power to which the law concedes no greater scope than the patent law requires. In any event the case poses the problem and underscores the fact that differences in prices to differing buyers may but begin a sequence. A judgment about whether discrimination—and hence of a tie used as in *IBM* or *Chicken Delight* to achieve a discrimination—is good or bad for competition must at least scan the likely lines of development. If the buyers paying different prices do not compete with each other—if, for example, they are in different industries, or are ultimate consumers—or if they do compete but the costs involved in the item sold to them at different prices is inconsequential because so small a percentage of their total costs, then the discrimination cannot distort competition at the next level. But if the buyers do compete, and the differing costs are sig-

---

14. 366 F.2d 117 (5th Cir. 1966).

15. See Baxter, Legal Restrictions on Exploitation of the Patent Monopoly: An Economic Analysis, 76 Yale L.J. 267 (1966).

nificant to their competitive positions, then allowing the tie through which discrimination is achieved can distort competition further down the line.[16]

We return now to the issue which prompted this excursion into questions of discrimination: should tying be countenanced where it is used to achieve a price discrimination, on the ground that such a discrimination is or may be harmless or even helpful to competition? The answer we are now prepared to give is that there are many ways in which a discrimination can affect competition and only one—that in some circumstances it may widen the use of a patented product—in which it could be considered helpful. There is no general case for tying in this answer. There is, at best, a case for saying that a court ought to be ready to see whether tying is being used to discriminate and, if so, that it should analyze the effects of the discrimination in the particular instance to see if they are good or bad. However, even if one were to concede all of this, there would remain the question of how burdens of persuasion ought to be shared. The ways in which a tie can do injury are manifold, and include many cases where the purpose of the tie is to discriminate in price. It would thus seem entirely appropriate to treat the proof of a tie, except in the situation of lack of any power in the tying product, as making out a prima facie case of violation of Section 3 or Section 1. If a tie proponent wished to justify on the ground that the tie achieved a harmless or beneficial discrimination, it would then be obliged to come forward with the evidence to establish that the purpose of the tie was to discriminate, that it had no other purpose or effect, and that the discrimination achieved was a benign one which extended the use of the tied product and did no injury to resale competition.

But perhaps, as the court held in *Chicken Delight,* even this is to go too far. Discrimination, a hallmark of the monopolist, should not hold a place of special favor which leads us to bend doctrine to accommodate it. Furthermore, reason and imagination combine to suggest that in any situation where we *might* wish to accommodate discrimination, the discrimination could be achieved (as it was in *La Peyre*) in a direct manner which clearly characterizes itself as a discrimination and which poses no ambiguities about whether it might have alternative or additional purposes and effects. We come once again upon the notion that restrictive arrangement is not reasonable when the beneficial ends which it may gain could be purchased more cheaply by means which yield no restrictive side effects. In *IBM,* for example, the discriminatory aim of the tie—to make those who used the machine most pay most—could be achieved by using a meter on the machine, rather than making card sales a meter. In *Chicken Delight,* the franchisor could have discriminated directly, and without a tie, by setting a charge for the franchise which varied with any one

---

16. See ch. 8, part C infra.

of several factors which would vary directly with the value of the license to the franchise—for example, gross sales, net profits, square footage of premises, value of premises, or the like. If in *IBM, Chicken Delight,* or any like situation, a variation in charge based on intensity or value of use (i. e., a discrimination) would be beneficial and lawful, it could be directly imposed.[17]

There is another more direct way in which a tie can be used to discriminate. Asch suggests the following case. Assume that pens and pencils are complementary goods. A seller has been offering pens at $5 and mechanical pencils at $4. If half of all consumers would be willing to pay $6 for pens, while the other half will pay only $5, the price set on the pens is understandable. Similarly, if half of all consumers would pay only $4 for pencils, though the other half would pay $5, the basis for the $4 price on pencils is also clear. Yet, if substantially all buyers buy both a pen and a pencil, the seller will earn a larger return if it ties pens to pencils and sells the package for $10.[18] The additional return is yielded through a discrimination made possible by the tie. Some buyers, as they view it, are paying $6 for pens and $4 for pencils, while others are paying $5 for each. When the products were sold separately the $5 charge on pens gave the first group pens for $1 less than they would have paid and the $4 charge on pencils gave the second group pencils for $1 less than they would have paid. Stigler observes a similar purpose underlying "block booking"—arrangements requiring theatres or TV stations to take motion pictures in "packages", each containing several features, with a specified price for each such group.[19] The licensing of patents in packages, or the package licensing of copyrighted music is perhaps explicable on similar grounds. The claim that these types of discriminations should be exempt from the ban on tying has nothing to recommend it. They do not significantly extend the use of any technology or copyrighted material; their only significant effect is to enable the seller to charge a higher price and to earn a higher profit.

---

17. There may also be situations where a tie is lawful when it is not being used to discriminate. In FTC v. Sinclair Refining Co., 261 U.S. 463, 43 S. Ct. 450, 67 L.Ed. 746 (1923) and Pick Mfg. Co. v. GM Corp., 299 U.S. 3, 57 S.Ct. 1, 81 L.Ed. 4 (1936), the Court accepted a good will argument comparable to those made and rejected in *IBM* and *Chicken Delight,* but in both of the former cases there was an additional element—the public would likely expect Sinclair gas from a pump labelled "Sinclair" and Chevrolet parts in the repair work at a Chevrolet dealership. It was, perhaps, that element which swayed the Court in those cases, although the interest of the public in getting what it expects could no doubt also be protected without recourse to a tie. Compare General Motors Corp., 34 F. T.C. 58 (1941), where the Commission held that a clause comparable to that upheld in *Pick* violated § 3 of the Clayton Act and § 5 of the F.T.C. Act. See also Susser v. Carvel Corp., supra note 2, and Dehydrating Process Co. v. A. O. Smith Corp., 292 F.2d 653 (1st Cir. 1961), both of which upheld good will defenses.

18. See P. Asch, Economic Theory and the Antitrust Dilemma 347–48 (1970).

19. See Stigler, United States v. Loew's Inc.: A Note on Block Booking, 1963 S.Ct. Rev. at 152–54.

The last defense for tying sees it as a means of erosion of forces hostile to competition. Some economists have proposed that in an oligopolistic market where collusion or interdependence precludes price cutting, a tie may be used as a covert means of price competition; instead of cutting the price on product A, which would or might generate general price cutting and deprive all in the industry of the gains of interdependent or collusive accord, the firm seeking to expand its market share, it is suggested, can offer product A at the regular price but tie in product B at a bargain price.[20] As Asch puts it, "the tied good is akin to a bonus."[21] This suggestion, while imaginative, will not stand analysis, not, at any rate, if it is intended to describe a real tie. If the oligopolist's goal is to covertly cut price and expand its market share, it might offer B as a free good with the primary product A, or it might offer both A and B separately at their regular prices and give buyers an option to take an A-B package at a bargain price.[22] But such a seller would not likely tie B to A, since even at a very low price for B, there would be some buyers who might have purchased A alone at the collusively established price, but who will value B so little that they would be deterred rather than encouraged by the tie. The optional package price will gain for the oligopolist any sales the tie could gain and would not cost it sales as the tie will do; therefore, using a tie as a covert means of price cutting would be irrational. The notion involved here is nonetheless suggestive. It is not only price cuts which are difficult to bring off in situations of oligopolistic interdependence, but also price increases. Oligopoly prices are excessively stable and tend to be inadequately responsive to fluctuations in demand in either direction. Under appropriate conditions of increased demand, an oligopolist perhaps fearful to initiate a price increase not yet sanctioned by the price leader, might utilize a tie not to increase its share, but its price.

In closing, we should note the contention sometimes made that a particular tie is so trivial in character as to be beneath the law's disdain. Practices like selling premiums to children at favorable prices with cereal box tops might be thought to be an example. But even these, upon analysis, may give occasion for pause. Perhaps their function, like that of the trading stamp, is to wed the buyer to the brand, a function which might well be harmful in an oligopolistic market.[23]

§ 157. "Package" Pricing

In *Northern Pacific* the Court defined tying as "an agreement by a party to sell one product but only on condition that the buyer also

---

20. J. Dirlam & A. Kahn, Fair Competition 189 et seq. (1954).

21. Asch, supra note 18 at 360.

22. See § 157 infra.

23. See In re Kellogg Co., FTC File No. 7110004, January 21, 1972, 547 ATRR A-3 (Jan. 25, 1972).

purchase a different (or tied) product" and expressed the view that "where the buyer is free to take either product by itself there is no tying problem even though the seller may also offer the two items as a unit at a single price."[1] That statement might end the matter. The packaged price is hardly one of the more serious conduct problems. Nevertheless, we should briefly examine some of the varied types of package transactions one may encounter in the marketplace and ask whether the *Northern Pacific* dictum adequately deals with them all.

One basis for a package price may be efficiency. If the combined price approaches the aggregate separate prices, and the difference is a fair estimate of cost savings to the seller in marketing the package, there is no social reason for concern. No leverage is being exercised; no tie has taken place. But is it not possible that a package price can be made to serve any of the functions which a tie may serve, that it can be used as a covert tie? Purpose and effect are the keys to analysis here as elsewhere in antitrust. Suppose for example the seller has power in the market for a product A which, if tying were lawful, he would offer for $10, tying in the complementary product, B, at a price of $9. Suppose next that the seller knows that tying is unlawful and he offers product A for $12, product B for $9 and an A-B package for $19. On these assumptions we may infer that the seller has priced B at the market, but priced A substantially higher than its profit-maximizing price, considered alone, in order to channel most sales of A into the package. We could confirm this inference if we found that the bulk of all sales of A were made in the package.[2] Before passing on the legality of such an arrangement, should we analyze competitive effects? We can assert with confidence that they will be substantially the same as those which would have been achieved by the suppressed tie itself. These, as we now know, may vary widely, as can the seller's motive for the tie. It is plausible to say that if we have adequate ground to characterize the arrangement as a covert tie we should treat it as we would an open tie, probing justifications only so far as we would do were it an open

---

1. Northern Pacific Ry. v. United States, 356 U.S. 1, 5–6 n. 4, 78 S.Ct. 514, 518 n. 4, 2 L.Ed.2d 545, 550 n. 4 (1958). See also United States v. Loew's Inc., 371 U.S. 38, 83 S.Ct. 97, 9 L.Ed.2d 11 (1962), where the remedy in a tying case was an injunction which permitted package pricing. In Dunkin' Donuts of America, Inc., 531 F.2d 1211 (3d Cir. 1976), a franchisor offered franchisees the choice either to pay for the franchise directly or as part of a "package deal" with merchandise was guilty of unlawful tying because it utilized a "policy to persuade" franchisees to accept the package. The district court had certified a franchisee class. The court of appeals reversed holding that (whatever the rule may be when suit is brought by a competitor of the seller) when the buyer sues proof of "coercion" to take an otherwise undesired tied product is an essential element of the claim. Therefore, given the large number of buyers a class action would be unmanageable.

2. It is this type of analysis, rather than a "policy to persuade" evaluation, which should be used in package alternative cases like Dunkin' Donuts, supra note 1.

tie. However, it may be necessary to examine motive or consequence in the process of characterizing the arrangement.

There are other examples of the package transaction besides those dictated by efficiency and those which constitute covert ties. The most frequent package transaction pricing is probably the "promotional" package, the widely advertised short period offer of two items at a combined "bargain" price in consumer goods markets. This kind of an offer has the characteristics of promotional pricing generally. Also, as noted earlier, package transaction pricing may constitute an acceptable method of competing, of offering what is in effect a price reduction, in an oligopolistic industry in which direct price competition is foreclosed.[3] When this is evident, such pricing should be encouraged by the law.

§ 158. "Full Line" Requirements

Expressed most generally, the tying rationale would push us to break every transaction down to the smallest components practicable, to insist upon "competition on the merits" separately for each element. Eggs and oranges would have to be available by the unit as well as by the dozen and the haberdasher would have to stand ready to quote on the coat, the vest and the pants, as well as on the suit. As we have seen, we do not push the concept that far, either as a matter of practicality or economics; the tying rule applies only when there are "two products". Yet there are situations where the seller insists on pressing upon the buyer more than the latter would freely take and which, though we cannot identify two products, we treat as analogous to tying. Consider, for example, a chain of theatres that negotiates release dates for the chain as a whole. If some of the theatres are in "closed towns"—if the chain has, with respect to some of them, a substantial degree of market power—we do not permit it to negotiate for the circuit as a unit.[1] We do not ask whether the individual theatres are separate products; we respond to the palpable reality that if one or more confer market power, circuit-wide negotiation involves levering that power from those which do to others which do not. Similarly, because the power associated with one patent or one copyrighted item differs from that associated with another, we do not allow package licensing of patents or block booking of copyrighted films on a mandatory basis.[2]

---

3. J. Dirlam & A. Kahn, Fair Competition 189 et seq. (1954).

1. United States v. Griffith, 334 U.S. 100, 68 S.Ct. 941, 92 L.Ed. 1236 (1948); United States v. Crescent Amusement Co., 323 U.S. 173, 65 S.Ct. 254, 89 L. Ed. 160 (1944).

2. Hazeltine Research, Inc. v. Zenith Radio Corp., 395 U.S. 100, 89 S.Ct. 1562, 23 L.Ed.2d 129 (1969); United States v. Loew's Inc., 371 U.S. 38, 83 S.Ct. 97, 9 L.Ed.2d 11 (1962); United States v. Paramount Pictures, Inc. 334 U.S. 131, 68 S.Ct. 915, 92 L.Ed. 1260 (1948). Compare the sports event season ticket cases, Coniglio v. Highwood Services, Inc., 495 F.2d 1286 (2d Cir. 1974); Laing v. Minnesota Vikings Football Club, Inc., 1973 CCH Trade Cases ¶ 74,601 (D.Minn.), aff'd 493 F.2d

Should we be concerned also about the analogous case in which a manufacturer will "franchise" a dealer only upon the latter's commitment to take and display a "full" or "representative" line of the manufacturer's merchandise?[3] These kinds of arrangements are common in hard good lines and are seldom challenged. It should be noted, nonetheless, that they can have effects very similar to tying and, when they do, ought to be characterized as tying on the basis of a purpose and effect analysis. For example, a manufacturer which has a strong position in the color TV market, say Zenith, may have a much smaller percentage of the market for stereo console sets. Left to its own judgment, a dealer "franchised" by Zenith might wish to stock Zenith television, but stereos made by some other manufacturer. Zenith, if it insists that the dealer carry a full line of its equipment in order to obtain any, may extend its power in the TV market over to the stereo market and foreclose competitors from a significant share of the latter market. The problem will be particularly acute if the principal outlets for stereo consoles are TV show rooms and if all leading TV manufacturers impose a similar restraint. One can picture the market shares in stereo conforming closely to those for TV, although there may exist specialized stereo manufacturers now taking the dregs of the market whose sets are better values and which, it they had better access to show room floor space, would be among the leaders.

There are, of course, justifications urged for allowing the manufacturers to require a dealer to stock a full line. This method of marketing may entail substantial efficiencies for the manufacturer. There is also the general notion that a manufacturer which develops a national reputation, in part through research and advertising, does have a sufficiently strong interest in the way his merchandise is presented to the consumer to warrant the imposition of a wide range of display and service requirements on dealers as a condition for selling to them. These contentions are not without consequence. It would no doubt be an overblown response to treat full line requirements generally as the equivalent of ties—as unlawful whenever the manufacturer had successfully differentiated his product and when, quantitatively, a not insubstantial volume of commerce was involved. Absent a showing of a significant foreclosure of competitors, it is no doubt more constructive to treat the interests of the manufacturer as adequately counterbalancing the dealer's interest in a wider product choice. But where, as in facts like those supposed in the TV hypothetical above, one group of traders is deprived by others of reason-

---

1381 (8th Cir. 1974), Grossman Development Co. v. Detroit Lions, Inc., 1973 CCH Trade Cases ¶ 74,790 (E.D.Mich.), all holding or indicating that it is not unlawful to require season ticket purchasers to take pre-season exhibition games as part of the package.

3. Compare Harley-Davidson Motor Co., 50 F.T.C. 1047, 1056 (1954) with Miller Motors, Inc. v. Ford Motor Co., 252 F.2d 441 (4th Cir. 1958).

able access to a market where they can compete on the merits, there ought to be no hesitation in concluding that Sections 1 and 3 are being violated. Where the manufacturer has power with respect to some of his products but not others, and where he uses the power he has to sell those other products, full line forcing constitutes the exercise of leverage just as clearly as does circuit-wide bargaining, block booking, or package licensing.

Like most tying concepts, this one, too, can get out of hand. Suppose a bicycle distributor has five or six outlets in Northern California, the one in Salinas, a valley market town, being the only such outlet within a radius of forty miles. Is the dealer precluded from negotiating for bicycles for his chain as a whole because Salinas is a "closed town"? Or, pursued further, is any chain, say a twelve unit chain of supermarkets in Southern California, precluded from negotiating for supplies for all its units because, even though no one of them is in a "closed town," such power as the chain possesses as a buyer comes from the aggregation of individual units? Some sensible judgment about potential competitive effects is obviously essential if injury to market competition is the basis for challenging the arrangement.

Another potential basis for challenging the exercise of manufacturer leverage at the dealer level is Section 5 of the Federal Trade Commission Act.[4] Though *Pick*[5] approved a requirement that Chevrolet dealers use only Chevrolet parts in repairing Chevrolets, a similar provision (along with others) was subsequently held unlawful by the FTC.[6] Surely, a requirement so unyielding would today not survive a challenge under Section 5. The good will interests of the manufacturer can be adequately handled by less restrictive alternatives— for example, parts specifications plus, if the manufacturer feels it desirable, a requirement that the customer be given notice if other than G.M. parts are used. But the manufacturer has an interest not only in how well its product is repaired, but also in selling its merchandise, both the basic item (whether a car or a TV or other appliance) and repair parts. Car sales are aided by good repair facilities, or at least it is the trade perception that a buyer will more likely buy a make which can be quickly and successfully repaired by a conveniently located dealer. Additionally, the manufacturer is interested in parts sales, which constitute an important part of its business.

The current response to the interplay of interests such as these may be a franchise which requires the dealer to maintain an adequate display of the manufacturer's merchandise, an adequate repair facility, and an adequate stock of the manufacturer's parts. As yet, no provision of this kind has been struck down. In Miller Motors, Inc. v.

---

4. 38 Stat. 717, 15 U.S.C.A. § 41.

5. Pick Mfg. Co. v. G.M. Corp., 299 U.S. 3, 57 S.Ct. 1, 81 L.Ed. 4 (1936).

6. 34 F.T.C. 58 (1941).

Ford Motor Co.,[7] the court upheld one as reasonable, and in Hammond Ford Inc. v. Ford Motor Co.,[8] the court, regarding the particular provision before it to be ambiguous, refused to pass upon its validity at the motion stage. Cases like *Brown Shoe* and *Atlantic* which seem to expand the FTC's power to make new law under Section 5 reduce confidence about the ultimate legal fate of provisions of those kinds.[9] The Ford dealer is, in his way, as dependent on Ford as is the Texaco dealer on Texaco, and arguably no more able to resist aggressive selling which urges on him an unwanted parts inventory. But, as yet, there are no cases holding against these kinds of provisions. One can only note the doubt and express the expectation that such arrangements will increasingly be challenged when company-dealer litigation, on any subject whatsoever, makes it tactically useful for the dealer to put the legality of franchise clauses in issue.

§ 159. Block Booking of Movies and the Licensing of Libraries of Music

It is black letter law that "a refusal to license one or more copyrights unless another copyright is accepted" is "illegal."[1] There is no need to show power in the work used as the tying product; the protection afforded to it under the copyright laws is a basis for conclusively presuming it to be unique. Indeed, illegality is not solely dependent on the antitrust laws, but derives also by implication from the copyright law. It is in the nature of a misuse of the monopoly granted by Congress to seek to extend it to other works.[2] Application of the principle is not always so clear. Whatever the conception that underlies the copyright law, the marketing of products like movies and popular music is done on a mass basis and is dominated by commercial, not artistic considerations. "Block booking" of movies —the licensing of groups of features in a package to theatres and TV stations—affords efficiencies. Buyers go to the mart not to choose a particular feature film as an artistic work, but to buy supplies much as might a dress merchant placing orders to fill his half empty racks. There are cost savings to the seller in negotiating and selling, in scheduling and making deliveries, if he can dispose, if not of a "full line," then of a package containing several films which will perhaps move as a package from one licensee theatre or TV station to another. It is not that "Gone with the Wind" and "Getting Gertie's Garter" are interchangable; no more are they than are a sensible family sedan and a high performance sports car. It is rather that the com-

---

7. 252 F.2d 441 (4th Cir. 1958).

8. 1966 CCH Trade Cas. ¶ 71,689 (S.D. N.Y.).

9. See discussion in § 161, infra.

1. United States v. Paramount Pictures, Inc., 334 U.S. 131, 159, 68 S.Ct. 915, 930, 92 L.Ed. 1260, 1293 (1948); United States v. Loew's Inc., 371 U.S. 38, 83 S.Ct. 97, 9 L.Ed.2d 11 (1962). See § 158 supra.

2. United States v. Loew's Inc., supra note 1.

mercial buyer will likely need both types of ware, and the seller can save by marketing in a package. For these reasons, courts have not forbidden distributors to offer films in a package, or to grant a lower price on a package than the aggregate of the individual prices of the films which make it up. All the law demands is that the distributor stand ready, in good faith, to license any one or more films on an individual basis, that no licensee be required in order to get one film to take any other.

The difficulty, of course, is that lines become blurred in the marketplace, as the remedy aspects of *Loew's* aptly demonstrate. There, on evidence that defendants had required licensees to accept blocks of films, the district court had entered an injunction which forbade defendants (1) from conditioning the grant of a license of any film upon the licensee's taking a license on any other film or films and (2) from granting any license on two or more films where "the differential between the price * * * for [each] film alone and the price * * * for the same film when * * * licensed with [any] other film has the effect of conditioning the * * * licens[ing] of such film upon the * * * license of one or more other films * * *." [3]

The Supreme Court found this remedy inadequate in several respects and ordered the decree amended. Out of concern that defendants might first offer only to deal in blocks and, despite the risk of contempt, delay or evade if individual quotes were requested, the Court wanted the decree to obligate defendants to quote individual prices as well as a package price when first negotiating a contract. Second, it ordered that the decree specifically forbid any difference between block prices and aggregate individual prices which exceeded legitimate cost savings to the licensor resulting from licensing in a block. Third, the Court ordered an amendment to make clear that although a defendant could "briefly * * * defer licensing * * * to a customer pending the expeditious conclusion of bona fide negotiations already being conducted," [4] defendants could not evade by refusing to make an offer on an individual film on the pretext that it, along with other films, was on offer in a block to some other prospect.

Most of those modifications can be seen as remedial extensions of the basic legal obligation, but the interesting question is the extent to which one licensing copyrighted materials in blocks may vary the charge for the block from the aggregate charges for the units. The district court order in *Loew's* forbade any price difference which "has the effect" of a tie. In considering the Department's assertion that this relief was inadequate, the Court stated that "[d]ifferentials unjustified by cost savings may already be prohibited" by the decree

---

3. Id. at 43, 83 S.Ct. at 101, 9 L.Ed.2d at 17.

4. Id. at 55, 83 S.Ct. at 107, 9 L.Ed.2d at 24.

fashioned below.[5] It nevertheless ordered the decree amended to explicitly forbid any price difference which was not "cost justified." Since the general phrasing first adopted by the district court merely states the general law that a package price having the purpose and effect of a tie is unlawful, the Court's suggestion of equivalence between that standard and the more specific one it substituted suggests that compliance with the cost justification test may be required, as a matter of law, of all package licensors, not just of those which have once been caught tying. Certainly, this is a standard that could be used in counselling. If a licensor complies in good faith with the cost justification test, the risks that it will be proved to have been tying are small. And the converse may also be true, that any package license which fails to comply with this test will be taken to constitute unlawful tying.

The licensing of music libraries like that of ASCAP or Broadcast Music Corporation to radio, TV, theatres, clubs, and halls which use music commercially presents problems even more complex. This is partly because an organization like ASCAP is a horizontal combination; it constitutes a pooling for the purpose of licensing music copyrights held by several proprietors, who compete with each other in other respects and who would presumably compete in granting performance licenses had they not pooled their rights for this purpose.[6] Additionally, the library of an organization like this will be so large that rates, if allocated on a unit basis, will be so small and control by the licensee over the performer so tenuous, that it does not seem commercially feasible for the licensee to request licenses for individual compositions,[7] nor for the licensor to set up facilities to grant and police such licenses. Picture, if you will, the owner of a small club in a suburb of a large city which has "live entertainment" on Saturday nights, usually a rock and roll trio, but sometimes blues or country music performers. It has been operating for three or four years before it is first called upon by the agent of a massive pool of copyrighted music. The agent tells the owner that based on such factors as the size of the club, the business done over the bar, and the frequency of performances, the club falls into the pool's category "D," for which the license rate is $750 per year. In all likelihood the club owner has not the least idea whether the performers who play on Saturday nights use the pool's music, never, occasionally or frequently, and certainly has no basis for requesting a quote on particular units from the library. His realistic choice is either to pay the rate demanded, to take a license on the entire library, of which in the course

---

5. Id. at 54, 83 S.Ct. at 107, 9 L.Ed.2d at 23.

6. See United States v. American Society of Composers, Authors and Publishers, 1940–43 CCH Trade Cas. ¶ 56,104 (S.D.N.Y.1941) (consent decree), decree amended, 1950–51 CCH Trade Cas. ¶ 62,595 (S.D.N.Y.1950), decree amended, 1950 CCH Trade Cas. 69,612 (S.D.N.Y.).

7. See Alden-Rochell, Inc. v. ASCAP, 80 F.Supp. 888, 893 (S.D.N.Y.1948).

of the year performers at the club may use as little as one or two percent, or to refuse to pay at all. And if the owner follows the latter course the club will likely be designated for calls by "shoppers" who will visit it when music is used and, if any pool compositions are played, file a report which will lead to an infringement suit. When the suit comes it has for such an owner an obviously coercive impact.

The issues presented by this kind of block licensing cannot be casually dismissed. One might respond, of course, by saying that so long as the licensor complies with the *Loew's* "cost justification" test the licensee's conundrum is his problem, not the licensor's. But an alternative response is not implausible. Given the business context, the offer made by the pool, because of the power aggregated through the pooling arrangement, may oblige many offerees, as a practical matter, to pay for far more of the pool's music than they want or need. When those conditions prevail it is rather an empty formality to assert that the licensor is not tying because it stands ready, on request, to license any individual unit, even if the licensor is ready to do so at a rate calculated so that the block rate will meet the cost justification criterion.

Indeed, the method of pricing for music pool licenses may itself raise significant questions. A patentee may not price a license in a manner that in purpose or effect extends the scope of the patent.[8] No more may a copyright holder extend the scope of its copyright. Yet, to charge a rate based on such factors as club size, bar sales and the like, is not only a discriminatory method of pricing,[9] it is a method which obviously measures far more than the value contributed to the enterprise by the copyright license. The copyright pool, by dint of its block of rights, levers itself into something like a "partnership" with the club owner. Even if the factors taken into account in the pricing formula are viewed as surrogates which adequately measure the relative contribution of music to the enterprise, they plainly do not measure the contribution of only the pool's music, but that of all music.

Nor does it avail to say that there is no feasible way to price only for what is given. Pool proprietors engage in elaborate counting and sampling techniques with broadcast music for the purpose of computing returns. They also do "shoppings" or "audits" of clubs, even the smallest, which have refused demands that they take a license. Similar devices might be used for the purpose of computing royalties to be paid by small users. In this way, royalty rates could be fixed on the basis of a schedule taking into account frequency of use of music from the library. Other factors like audience size and

---

8. Brulotte v. Thys Co., 379 U.S. 29, 85 S.Ct. 176, 13 L.Ed.2d 99 (1964); Zenith Radio Corp. v. Hazeltine Research, Inc., 395 U.S. 100, 89 S.Ct. 1562, 23 L.Ed.2d 129 (1969).

9. See the discussion of discrimination in § 156 supra.

bar charges could also be taken into account so that there would be one "per use" rate for a large dance hall and another for a small club. The license could provide for an audit for a sample period—say two weeks—to determine the frequency of use. That audit could be done either at a time agreed upon or at a time randomly selected and could control until, upon some significant change in the proprietor's policy regarding music, either the licensor or licensee should conclude that a new audit was appropriate.

§ 160. Package Licensing of Patents, Grant Back Provisions, and Royalties Which Extend Beyond the Period of the Patent

The leverage concept which underlies tying displays itself prominantly in the borderline where patent law and antitrust overlap. The most obvious expression of the concept concerns package licensing; here, the law closely tracks that affecting copyrights which was explored in the prior section. It is a violation, a misuse of the patent, for a patentee to condition the grant of a license of any patent upon the licensee taking a license upon a different and independent patent.[1] As in the case of a copyright, the firm owning the patents may as a matter of commercial convenience negotiate an agreement licensing a package, so long as it comports itself in ways that do not foreclose or inhibit bargaining for a single license. For example, it may not price the package so low relative to individual licenses that it in effect conditions the grant of one license upon the taking of others.[2] As the cases indicate, a pragmatic approach is taken to the question whether a patentee is acting in good faith in response to requests for quotes on less than a package.[3]

There is one respect in which the law regarding patent packages may vary from that governing copyright blocks. In International Manufacturing Company v. Landon,[4] the court distinguished the package licensing cases where a patentee offered only a mandatory package on two patents which disclosed "independent parts of the

---

1. Zenith Radio Corp. v. Hazeltine Research, Inc., 395 U.S. 100, 89 S.Ct. 1562, 23 L.Ed.2d 129 (1969); United States v. Line Material Co., 333 U.S. 287, 68 S.Ct. 550, 92 L.Ed. 701 (1947); Rocform Corp. v. Acitelli-Standard Concrete Wall, Inc., 367 F.2d 678 (6th Cir. 1966); American Security Co. v. Shatterproof Glass Corp., 268 F.2d 769 (3d Cir.), cert. denied 361 U.S. 902, 80 S.Ct. 210, 4 L.Ed.2d 157 (1959); Apex Elec. Mfg. Co. v. Altorfer Bros. Co., 238 F.2d 867 (7th Cir. 1956); Technograph Printed Circuits, Ltd. v. Bendix Aviation Corp., 218 F.Supp. 1 (D.Md. 1963), aff'd on other grounds 327 F.2d 497 (4th Cir. 1964).

2. Zenith Radio Corp. v. Hazeltine Research, Inc., supra note 1; Automatic Radio Mfg. Co. v. Hazeltine Research, Inc., 339 U.S. 827, 70 S.Ct. 894, 94 L. Ed. 1312 (1950); Hazeltine Research, Inc. v. Avco Mfg. Corp., 227 F.2d 137 (7th Cir. 1955); Baker-Cammack Hosiery Mills v. Davis Co., 181 F.2d 550 (4th Cir.), cert. denied 340 U.S. 824, 71 S.Ct. 58, 95 L.Ed. 605 (1950).

3. Compare Baker-Cammack Hosiery Mills v. Davis Co., supra, with United States v. Vehicular Parking, Ltd., 74 F.Supp. 4 (D.Del.1947), aff'd sub nom., Magee-Hale Park-O-Meter Co. v. Vehicular Parking, Ltd., 180 F.2d 897 (3d Cir. 1950).

4. 336 F.2d 723 (9th Cir. 1964), cert. denied 379 U.S. 988, 85 S.Ct. 701, 13 L. Ed.2d 610 (1965).

same product" i.e., where neither patent alone would enable manufacture of the product without violation. The reasoning—that in this context the two patents should themselves be characterized as a single product—is realistic and persuasive. Though no closely comparable situation could arise in copyright law, this "single product" concept might conceivably be widened to validate mandatory package licensing of several parts of a single composition, such as separate chapters of a book which, having initially been serialized, are copyrighted separately.

Quite different leverage issues arise when the patent license contains a "grant back" provision, a covenant by the licensee to assign or license to the patent holder any improvement patents relating to the technology covered by the license. The broad contention that grant backs "necessarily afford to the licensor some rights to the inventions of the licensee, and, to [that] extent * * * may expand the licensor's monopoly," [5] and therefore that these provisions constitute patent misuse and should be *per se* unlawful was rejected five to four in Transparent-Wrap Machine Corp. v. Stokes & Smith Co.[6] As the law stands, grant backs are unlawful only if "employed with the purpose or effect" of monopolizing or restraining trade, a matter to be determined only upon evaluation of evidence about structure, performance and conduct in the market. In one of the *General Electric* cases, the court held that a grant back was unlawful where attached to "basic patents or patents which may be basic," and used in a manner likely to protect the patentee's dominance in the industry.[7] In another the court found grant backs unlawful as part of a policy of funneling to the patentee control of patents held by licensees.[8]

Transparent-Wrap involved two relatively small concerns and no showing of power; the *G.E.* cases are at the other extreme, with the firm having massive power in important markets to which patents were major entry barriers. How are the intermediate cases to be analyzed? What are the ways in which grant backs may tend to lessen competition? First, let us note that Section 3 of Clayton is not involved. The grant back condition does not pertain to a "commodity" but to an intangible, future technology. Legality can therefore be challenged only under Section 1 or 2 of Sherman, or FTC Section 5, not under Section 3. Neither does a grant back provision directly preclude the licensee from dealing in a competitor's technology; how-

---

5. Report of the Attorney General's National Committee to Study the Antitrust Laws 227–28 (1965). Strictly speaking, grant back provisions often present horizontal rather than vertical restraint problems, because the license is granted to a competitor. However, convenience dictates that these issues be dealt with in this chapter with tying and other leverage issues.

6. 329 U.S. 637, 67 S.Ct. 610, 91 L.Ed. 563 (1947).

7. United States v. General Electric Co., 80 F.Supp. 989, 1005–06 (S.D.N.Y. 1948).

8. United States v. General Electric Co., (Lamps), 115 F.Supp. 835 (D.N.J. 1953).

ever, by requiring the licensee to deal with the licensor with respect to any future patent, it may directly or indirectly preclude the licensee from dealing with others. If the challenged provision requires an assignment to the licensor of the improvement patent or requires the grant of an exclusive license, the licensee would have nothing left to grant to others. On the other hand, if it merely requires a non-exclusive license to be given, it would not foreclose dealing with others, but by foreclosing the possibility of an exclusive license to anyone else, it would cut down sharply on what the licensee had to deal with others about.

Considered alone, the competitive effects of a grant back requirement will be conjectural; it will be difficult to predict the likelihood of an improvement being invented by the licensee or to predict significance if one or more is produced. The major guide to evaluation of competitive effect is structure. If the licensor has a substantial share of the relevant market and if the patented technology is a significant entry barrier, a grant back provision which requires assignment or an exclusive license has a tendency which is plainly adverse to competition. The larger the percentage of the industry which has accepted licenses with such grant back provisions, the more marked will that tendency be.

If the grant back calls only for a non-exclusive license, the negative effects are obviously reduced, but they may not vanish and may be significant enough when the structure is tight. In *G.E. (Lamps)* the court, in rejecting the claim that non-exclusivity sufficiently mitigated the harm of the grant back provisions, stressed that the license to be given to G.E. on any improvements made by its licensees would, though non-exclusive, authorize G.E. to grant sub-licenses.[9] The court felt that this arrangement, by permitting G.E. to share with the inventor the sub-license market, would enable G.E. to deprive any licensee of much of the advantage of its invention.

Another lively patent issue concerns post-expiration royalties. If a patentee were to purport to license for a period extending beyond the term of the patent monopoly and to take a royalty at a rate per year which was specifically and evenly assigned over the period (including that portion for which there was no lawful monopoly), one might plausibly assert that the patentee had used its monopoly to require the licensee to buy something other than the patented technology—i.e., post-patent rights which were actually in the public domain. Unfortunately, the marketplace is unlikely to present the issue so sharply. Brulotte v. Thys Co.[10] discloses the obscurities which abound. Respondent, owning various hop picking patents, sold petitioner a machine embodying some of these under a contract which provided that a specified amount would be paid immediately, that pe-

9. Id.

10. 379 U.S. 29, 85 S.Ct. 176, 13 L.Ed.2d 99 (1964).

titioners would be licensed to use the machine in one county only, and that a specified sum per pound of hops harvested with the machine (or a specified minimum amount if the harvest was below a certain tonnage) would be paid each season for the license. The license and the payments were stated to run for a term that exceeded the life of the youngest patent incorporated in the machine. The majority of the Court found an indication that respondent was granting and charging for rights that went beyond the patent term from the fact that the territorial restriction ran beyond the term; it rejected the alternative characterization that the contract was not divisible and that the payments were all attributable to the patent rights which petitioners in fact received. However, as Justice Harlan noted in dissent, the whole transaction could be seen as the equivalent of a conditional sale, a form in which it could lawfully be recast without altering the date or amount of a single payment.

The invitation to recast the transaction in innocent terms could have little appeal if discernible harm to competition were associated with a post-expiration royalty. But even in the flat out case where the licensee has said, in effect, "I won't license you during the term unless you take and pay for a license extending beyond the term," it is hard to see where competitive harm is generated. This form of collecting payment doesn't extend the patent monopoly to any other product, nor does it extend the monopoly in time. Once the patent expires anyone can practice the art; notwithstanding the fact that those who took a license to practice it before expiration are still paying for the rights they then had. The effect on competition is precisely the same whether the post-expiration payments be characterized as applying to the right conferred to share the patent monopoly during the term, or as payment for a right to practice the art after it is in the public domain. If anything in *Brulotte* may have served to dampen competition, it was less the post-expiration payments than the territorial restriction, which also applied after expiration. Such a territorial restriction could conceivably have marginal effects on dissemination of the technology after expiration. In any event, it seems something of a quibble to utilize the leverage concept to restrict the ways in which the return for the invention can be made to flow.

§ 161. Promotional Techniques Used by Manufacturers with Dealers

One of the difficulties with the tying or (more generally) the leverage concept is its breadth. When a buyer places a regular order with a salesman who regularly takes the buyer to a ball game or a night club, the buyer's choice among alternative sellers is probably not made strictly on the competitive merits; the ambience of the sales contract has its effect. We could not police the market sufficiently to eradicate such elements, unless perhaps by more rigorous standards for deductibility of selling expenses; and we probably would not wish to eradicate all of the human amenities that give color and flamboyance to salesmanship even if we could. Yet there are sales strategies which fall easily into analogy with conventional tying concepts. Some of these the FTC has seen fit to challenge under Section 5. Others have been challenged in private treble damage litigation.

FTC v. Brown Shoe Co., Inc.[1] is most provocative. Brown, a shoe manufacturer, offered a "franchise" program to retail dealers under which, in return for commitments from dealers to "concentrate" on Brown's line and to offer no line "conflicting" with Brown's, the manufacturer undertook to supply architectural plans, merchandising records, consulting services of a field representative, and participation in a group insurance program. Without any finding of competitive effect, except that which might be inferred from the quantitative substantiality of Brown's sales, the Commission held the practice unfair and ordered it stopped. The court of appeals thought the "custom of giving free service" to good customers was widespread in the shoe industry and finding this unobjectionable, it reversed. As the Supreme Court saw the matter, the Commission could under the Act "declare it to be an unfair practice for Brown, the second largest manufacturer of shoes in the Nation, to pay a valuable consideration to hundreds of retail shoe purchasers in order to secure a * * * promise from them that they will deal primarily with Brown and will not purchase conflicting lines * * * ."[2]

There was, without doubt, leverage exercised. Indeed, the provision of the ancillary service was expressly "on condition" that the dealer give preference to Brown's shoes over other brands. Viewed most narrowly, then, the case says that the Commission under Section 5 can outlaw an express tie, even though the tying device is the provision without separate charge of some ancillary service, and regardless of any showing of power in the tying product, or any showing about the significance of the foreclosure other than that it was quantitatively large. Yet the implication of the case may be broader. One can hardly doubt that the power of the Commission would suffice even if the tie were not express—if, for example, Brown engaged in the announced practice of supplying ancillary services to shoe stores which featured Brown and which gave it what it regarded as a sufficient share of business, but denied the services to those which did not. Nor can one doubt, unless the case is to be seen as an arbitrary anomaly, that the Commission could predicate a challenge on the provision of other kinds of inducements besides the particular kinds of services

1. 384 U.S. 316, 86 S.Ct. 1501, 16 L.Ed. 2d 587 (1966).

2. Id. at 320, 86 S.Ct. at 1503, 16 L.Ed. 2d at 590–91. Compare FTC v. Sperry and Hutchinson Co., 405 U.S. 233, 92 S.Ct. 898, 31 L.Ed.2d 170 (1972), stating that the Commission may, under the statutory standard of fairness, measure conduct against a wide range of public values which transcend antitrust standards but that, in doing so, it must be sufficiently explicit to facilitate judicial review.

which were the subject of the *Brown Shoe* complaint. And it is just here that the case becomes hard, for it necessarily puts the Commission into the business of policing not competitive effect (which is irrelevant to the holding) but the normalcy or appropriateness of each competitor's chosen blandishments.[3]

Suppose Brown, as an alternative to the services it provided, had an annual convention for dealers in Miami or Hawaii where it flew satisfactory dealers and their families for what was, in substance, an expense-paid five day weekend when the annual "new line" was introduced? Suppose Brown provided satisfactory dealers (but not others) the right to buy at greatly reduced prices its stocks of "old" merchandise after new styles were introduced? Suppose Brown routinely engaged in lavish promotional entertaining of dealers which did not carry "conflicting" lines? As the Commission moves increasingly distant from the process of making its judgments on the basis of an analysis of competitive effect, it approaches nearer to imponderables such as these.

Another group of decisions under Section 5 which lacks a clearly discernible center of gravity are the so-called "TBA" cases.[4] In essence they hold that gasoline refiners cannot encourage dealers to buy a specified brand of tires, batteries and accessories ("TBA") and then collect commissions from the preferred manufacturer. The cases thus predicate an erosion of "competition on the merits" with respect to one group of products on the nature of a continuing relationship between buyer and seller in respect of another group of products. Tying or leverage becomes as much a matter of status as of conduct. *Atlantic* involved evidence that the refiner was paid by Goodyear and that it not only pressed its dealers to buy Goodyear tires, batteries and accessories, but set quotas for each dealer and used coercive tactics such as threatening lease concellations if these quotas were not met. The Court, in upholding the Commission's broad cease and desist order which forbade the continuation of Goodyear's commission scheme, did not stress the coercive conduct; rather, it saw the arrangement as similar to a tie because, given the nature of Atlantic's relationship to its dealers, they were dependent upon its continuing good will. In *Texaco* there was no evidence of overt coercion, but merely vigorous salesmanship by the refiner in order to earn a commission on Goodrich TBA. The Court again affirmed an order directing that no commissions be paid to the refiner for sales to its dealers.

We must underscore how far the tying concept has been extended in these cases. In neither case was the refiner performing the sole

---

3. See Handler, Some Misadventures in Antitrust Policy Making—Nineteenth Annual Review 76 Yale L.J. 92, 93–101 (1966).

4. Atlantic Refining Co. v. FTC, 381 U.S. 357, 85 S.Ct. 1498, 14 L.Ed.2d 433 (1965); Shell Oil Co. v. FTC, 360 F.2d 470 (5th Cir. 1966), cert. denied 385 U.S. 1002, 87 S.Ct. 703, 17 L.Ed.2d 541 (1967); FTC v. Texaco, Inc., 393 U.S. 223, 89 S.Ct. 429, 21 L.Ed.2d 394 (1968).

sales function; the TBA producer had its own sales personnel out making contacts and taking orders. This fact perhaps made it easier to say that what the TBA commission was paid to buy from the refiner was not sales or other services, but the exercise of market power. Yet it is not really that simple, for in both cases the refiner was itself performing some sales functions, in addition to introducing the TBA salesman and giving dealers to understand the refiner's interest and attitude. Also, it seems quite evident that the basis for the Commission's or the Court's objection could not be avoided merely by assigning the entire sales function to the refiner. It is the inherently coercive power which the refiner has over a dealer whose very livelihood depends upon continued good favor of the refiner which the Court saw as warranting the FTC order, even without an showing of overt coercion.

The difficulty with this rationale is to learn how to confine it. In *Atlantic*, Justice Stewart's dissent remarks that the same rationale would preclude the refiner from buying or even manufacturing TBA and selling it to its dealers on its own account. An additional question is whether the rationale is not so broad as to make it unlawful for the refiner to deal with its dealers at all. It is as true when the refiner is selling its own gasoline as when it is selling someone else's TBA, that the dealer, pressed to take a specified amount or to meet a quota, will be mindful that his "supply of gasoline, his lease on his station, and his Texaco identification [are] subject to continuing review." [5] In short, if there is unfairness, or overreaching, or the exercise of leverage, these arise not because the dealer, anxious to get one product, will buy another, but because the refiner is for the dealer a landlord, a source of credit, and a source of trademark identification. It is these aspects of the relationship which give the refiner leverage and that leverage can be exercised in selling gas as well as in selling TBA.

If the FTC cases strain the fibers of analysis, the Supreme Court's holding in Fortner Enterprises, Inc. v. U.S. Steel Corp.[6] rends them apart. Though coercion of buyers was the real policy concern in the TBA cases, it is at least conceivable that foreclosure injuring competing sellers might also have occurred. In *Fortner* the only conceivable rationale was buyer coercion and, horror of horrors, the "coercive" device used by the seller was an excessive generosity in setting credit terms, terms tantamount to a price reduction. Steel, seeking to sell prefabricated houses, granted favorable credit terms to Fortner to finance the acquisition by Fortner of land and housing packages manufactured by Steel; the total loan was $2 million, of which $1.7 million was to be paid to Steel for the housing units Fortner would erect. A term of the loan required Fortner to erect no houses on the land other than Steel's, so long as the loan remained unpaid.

---

5. FTC v. Texaco, Inc., 393 U.S. at 229, 89 S.Ct. at 433, 21 L.Ed.2d at 399.

6. 394 U.S. 495, 89 S.Ct. 1252, 22 L.Ed. 2d 495 (1969).

Alleging that the housing units were defective and more expensive than others available, Fortner sought to develop the land with other products before repaying the loan. When Steel insisted on the loan terms, Fortner sued, alleging that Steel provided credit to it on favorable terms and tied the housing units to the credit extension. The Supreme Court, reviewing a summary judgment for Steel, held that on these allegations a trial was needed to determine whether Steel had sufficient power in the tying product, credit, or other advantages, such as a preferred access to capital, to have successfully tied the housing units by its favorable credit offering.

The absurdity of this result seems manifest. The transaction was tantamount to any credit sale—it is no more a tie than any other in which a seller says, "If you buy my merchandise you may pay me in 90 days." Indeed, if the credit terms were cheap, the advantage given was of no different consequence than would have been a price reduction. It may be that the offering could be challenged on the same grounds as any other price reduction might be—as discriminatory, perhaps, or predatory (if focused only in localities where Steel encountered substantial competition from other housing sellers)—but it is hardly plausible that Steel exercised sufficient market power over money to invoke the leverage concept and no fact alleged suggested the basis for any other offense. Furthermore, even assuming an offense existed, Fortner (the preferred customer) would hardly be an appropriate party plaintiff.[7]

§ 162. Devices Used by Merchants to Maintain Continuity of Relationship with Consumers

The law seldom applies the *Brown Shoe*[1] rationale to transactions with consumers. Yet, if the Commission is going to get into the business of policing practices which tend to tie buyers to one seller and thus reduce the likelihood that each new buy-sell decision will be made on its own competitive merits, there is a fecund field for intervention into the retailer-consumer relationship. Indeed, a major part of the inventive effort of those concerned with reaching the consumer seems to be aimed at relieving competitive pressure on prices by giv-

---

7. The subsequent history of *Fortner* is of interest. On remand, the district court, after a month long jury trial, directed a verdict for Fortner. The court of appeals reversed, holding that the case should have gone to the jury. On retrial, the parties waived jury and the district court found for Fortner. This time the court of appeals affirmed, holding, in substance, that evidence that the loan terms offered by U.S. Steel were unique, that some institutional lenders were precluded by law from offering comparable terms, that other lenders refused to lend on such terms because of the risks, and that many developers accepted the terms even though U.S. Steel's buildings were more expensive than comparable ones, warranted an inference that U.S. Steel had power in the tying product, credit. See United States Steel Corp. v. Fortner Enterprises, Inc., 523 F.2d 961 (6th Cir. 1975). The Supreme Court again granted certiorari and the case is now pending before it. (Dkt.No. 75–853).

1. 384 U.S. 316, 86 S.Ct. 1501, 16 L.Ed. 2d 587 (1966).

ing the consumer incentives, other than price competition, for returning time and again to the same outlet. Supermarkets sell encyclopedias at favorable prices, a new volume reaching the display bins each month. Retail outlets of every description pass out trading stamps.

It is not just that these strategies have overt tying elements, though most of them do; more salient is the fact that all of these devices tend to make the average consumer a less critical shopper for the basic good he is buying—less likely to compare the price and quantity offered by competing markets on, for example, the dozen eggs, the loaf of bread and the can of coffee needed on a given morning. They do this by giving the consumer an incentive, quite independent of competition on the merits, to return habitually to the same outlet. In this respect they do not differ from *Brown Shoe* and, it would seem, could be challenged by the FTC under Section 5.

PART D. EXCLUSIVE DEALING, REQUIREMENTS CONTRACTS AND RELATED ARRANGEMENTS

§ 163. Introduction

An exclusive dealing contract involves a commitment by a buyer to deal only with a particular seller. The related device, a requirements contract, may entail a commitment by a buyer to take all he needs of a given product for a specified period from the seller, or may entail a commitment by a seller to supply all of a buyer's needs, or both. These arrangements tend to foreclose a portion of the market from competitors and to reduce free choice, as do tying arrangements. However, they differ from tying arrangements in that they act less directly and, at least superficially, are less ripe with the implication of power misused. A buyer or seller who commits itself to take or provide all that is needed may do so for any of a thousand reasons; no assumption is invited that it has bargained away freedom to choose in one market in order to gain favor in another. And if the commitment about requirements is bilateral, there is a loose integration achieved. For the duration of the contract, the parties have "planned" a product flow spanning two vertical levels; this relieves each of them from the uncertainties and expense of going repeatedly to the market to purchase or sell in smaller quantities.

Because of these ambiguous qualities, courts have not responded to requirements contracts as harshly as they have to tying arrangements. But it cannot be asserted that they have assigned these devices to the rule of reason; there has been both vacillation and hesitancy, and, if you will, a search for an alternative to the *per se* response which would consume less judicial energy than an elaborate analysis—a search for a method of truncated analysis which will quickly distinguish between arrangements in which negative aspects predominate and those which are on the whole benign. Let us examine the case law development.

§ 164. The Development of the Law

Requirements contracts and other exclusive dealing arrangements were generally upheld both at common law and under the Sherman Act before Clayton was enacted.[1] Although some change in this permissive attitude was invited by Section 3,[2] Congress did not illuminate the extent of the change which it desired either in the language of the statute or in the debates. Here, as in other antitrust areas, Congress merely pointed out a direction and left the Court to travel on its own.

The first Section 3 case to reach the Court, Standard Fashion Co. v. Magrane-Houston Co.,[3] involved exclusive dealing. A pattern manufacturer exacted from its customers (largely department and "notions" stores, which in the aggregate represented two fifths of all pattern retailers nationally) a promise not to handle competitors' patterns. Emphasizing that Clayton was aimed at stopping restraints "in their incipiency," and that foreclosing two fifths of all outlets from competitors could seriously impede the ability of any of them to compete, the Court held the arrangement unlawful. Though Clayton did not outlaw arrangements having "the mere possibility" of injuring competition, it did apply to all "agreements as would, under the circumstances disclosed, probably lessen competition or create an actual tendency to monopoly."[4] The Court found the two-fifths foreclosure substantial enough to exceed this threshold. Except for this effort to discriminate between likely competitive effects and merely possible ones, the analysis is soft and totalistic. The Court reports the facts and expresses its conviction that sufficient harm is threatened without either an exposition of the dynamic consequences of arrangements like the one before it or implications about where the borderlines between legality and illegality may lie.

It was more than a quarter century before the Court faced a comparable question. On this occasion, in the *Standard Stations* case,[5] it delivered three opinions which amply repay study not merely for what they teach about requirements contracts, but for the ways

---

1. See, e.g., Whitwell v. Continental Tobacco Co., 125 F. 454 (8th Cir. 1903); Phillips v. Iola Portland Cement Co., 125 F. 593 (8th Cir. 1903), cert. denied 192 U.S. 606, 24 S.Ct. 850, 48 L.Ed. 585 (1904).

2. See the discussion in Dictograph Prods., Inc. v. FTC, 217 F.2d 821, 826–27 (2d Cir. 1954), cert. denied 349 U.S. 940, 75 S.Ct. 784, 99 L.Ed. 1268 (1955); see also Report of the Attorney General's National Committee to Study the Antitrust Laws, 137–38 (1955).

3. 258 U.S. 346, 42 S.Ct. 360, 66 L.Ed. 653 (1922).

4. Id. at 356–57, 42 S.Ct. at 362, 66 L. Ed. at 658.

5. Standard Oil Co. of Cal. v. United States, 337 U.S. 293, 69 S.Ct. 1051, 93 L.Ed. 1371 (1949).

in which they elucidate or obscure the basic problems of judicial engagement with issues of market conduct, structure and performance. The views expressed by Justice Frankfurter for the majority have become classic, but those stated by Justice Jackson and by Justice Douglas in dissent are equally engaging. It would claim too much to assert that the three opinions present lucid statements which comprehend the spectrum of possible attitudes about the problems, potentials and values which should inform adjudication of economic issues. Nevertheless, the three Justices have given us quite distinct, formidable and suggestive documents.

Standard Oil, a west coast refiner, sold its products in seven western states, an area in which it was the largest seller with about 23% of the market. About 7% of the total sales were made at retail through company-owned gasoline stations. Through its subsidiary, Standard Stations, it had entered into contracts with nearly 6,000 independently owned stations, about 16% of all outlets in the western area; sales to these accounted for about the same quantity as sales through its own stations. The balance of its sales, between 9 and 10% of total sales in the western area, were made to industrial users. Standard's contracts varied in terms, but a common feature was an undertaking by the dealer to buy all his requirements of petroleum products from Standard for a stated period, typically from year to year. Standard's six leading competitors, which absorbed over 42% of total retail sales in the area, also employed exclusive dealing arrangements, and less than 2% of all stations in the area were "split pump" stations where brands of gasoline of more than one refiner were available. The market shares of Standard and others had remained fairly constant over a considerable time. Upon reviewing the earlier Section 3 cases, most of them involving tying, Justice Frankfurter concluded that initially "some sort of showing as to the actual or probable economic consequences of the agreements, if only the inferences to be drawn from the fact of dominant power * * *" [6] was necessary, but that *International Salt,* "at least as to contracts tying the sale of a non-patented to a patented product, rejected the necessity of demonstrating economic consequences once it is established that 'the volume of business affected' is not 'insignificant or insubstantial' and that the effect of the contracts is to 'foreclose competitors from [a] substantial market.'" Since the quantitative substantiality test of *Salt* was clearly met here, the issue became whether "a distinction is to be drawn * * * between requirements contracts and contracts tying the sale of a nonpatented to a patented product * * *." [7]

In resolving this issue, Justice Frankfurter displayed a level of anguish rarely found in the case law. He hefted the argument for making a distinction and found it weighty. Tying arrangements, he felt,

---

6. Id. at 302, 69 S.Ct. at 1056, 93 L.Ed. at 1380.

7. Id. at 304–05, 69 S.Ct. at 1057–58, 93 L.Ed. at 1381.

"serve hardly any purpose beyond the suppression of competition," while requirements contracts "may well be of economic advantage to buyers as well as to sellers, and thus of advantage to the consuming public." They may for the buyer "assure supply, afford protection against rises in price, enable long term planning on the basis of known costs, and obviate the expense and risk of storage in the quantity necessary for a commodity having a fluctuating demand." For the seller they "may make possible the substantial reduction of selling expenses, give protection against price fluctuation, and * * * offer the possibility of a predictable market." [8] Because of these benefits, the harsh treatment accorded to tying arrangements would seem unwarranted for requirements contracts; only if harmful consequences are predictable and only if these outweigh the benefits of the particular arrangement ought illegality to be adjudicated.

But great as were the reasons for differentiating between tying and requirements, the difficulties of responding to these reasons were even more enormous. If the distinctions between tying and requirements contracts were accepted, tests of the economic usefulness and restrictive impact of requirements contracts would be needed. Among these tests would be whether "competition had flourished despite [their] use," the "conformity of the length of their term to the reasonable requirements of the field of commerce," and the status of the defendant, whether it was a "struggling newcomer," or if it had strength, its "degree of market control." Furthermore, application of all such tests would be attended with "serious difficulties." For example, if a firm's position had remained constant during the use of these contracts, as had Standard's, it might be that the share would have fallen but for the use of the device. Indeed, where, as here, others had also used them and their shares too had remained constant, it might be inferred that "their effect has been to enable the established suppliers individually to maintain their own standing and * * * collectively, * * * to prevent a late arrival from wresting away more than an insignificant portion of the market * * *. Moreover, to demand that bare inference be supported by evidence of what would have happened but for the adoption of the [device] * * * or to require firm prediction of an increase of competition" upon abandoning it, would be a "standard of proof if not virtually impossible to meet, at least most ill-suited for ascertainment by the courts." [9] Again, upon abandonment, if it be ordered, a defendant might find other, lawful ways of achieving essentially the same restriction, such as a more complete vertical integration. Because of these difficulties, if Section 3 were interpreted as requiring proof of competitive effect, "its very explicitness would become a means of conferring immunity upon the practices it singles out." [10]

8. Id. at 305–07, 69 S.Ct. at 1058–59, 93 L.Ed. at 1382.

9. Id. at 308–10, 69 S.Ct. at 1059–60, 93 L.Ed. at 1383–84.

10. Id. at 311, 69 S.Ct. at 1060–61, 93 L.Ed. at 1384.

Faced with this frustration and with the conviction that an overbroad prohibition might strike down arrangements which were harmless, but that an overly refined one would outdistance judicial ingenuity, the majority chose the course which would leave the process of decision less burdened. The Court, Justice Frankfurter stated, cannot sit as does the Monopolies Commission under the British Restrictive Practices Act to "determine in each case the ultimate demands of the 'public interest'"; the Clayton Act entails a "specific prohibition of trade practices legislatively determined to be undesirable * * *." Even though the alternative of "buying out independent dealers and making them dependent employees * * * would be a greater detriment to the public interest * * * this is an issue, like choice between greater efficiency and freer competition, that has not been submitted to our decision." [11] For these reasons the Court rejected a rule which would require "some sort of showing as to actual or probable economic consequences." Nevertheless, despite the central place given in the analysis to *International Salt,* it is not clear that the Court went the full distance of transplanting the *Salt* rule of quantitative substantiality from tying to requirements contracts. The opinion simply states:

> We conclude, therefore, that the qualifying clause of § 3 is satisfied by proof that competition has been foreclosed in a substantial share of the line of commerce affected.[12]

If the Court had said "substantial share of the market," one could say with confidence that the test was one of substantiality in percentage terms. If it had said "substantial amount of the line of commerce affected," one could say for sure that quantitative substantiality was the norm. But the juxtaposition of the word "share" with the phrase "line of commerce" leaves the matter in doubt.

We do know, however, that in an opinion which begins by saying that a simplified rule would be unsatisfactory because so lacking in sensitivity and that a rule more sensitive to precise effects would be unsatisfactory because so complex to administer and uncertain in application, the Court ended by choosing a rule which required no showing of competitive effect beyond some showing of the amount (in absolute or relative terms) of commerce affected. The reason for selecting this specific nettle to grasp is not adequately explained. The opinion asserts that Congress made this choice, but this is more a rationalization than a reason. Neither the language nor history of Section 3 speaks with such precision. The opinion also implies, perhaps only by way of answer to the Douglas dissent, that the choice is between a near *per se* approach and a rule so unconfined as to commission the Court to decide, as does the Monopolies Commission,

---

11. Id. at 311–12, 69 S.Ct. at 1061, 93 L.Ed. at 1384–85. It is interesting to note that a more complete downstream integration was seen by the majority as a worse evil.

12. Id. at 314, 69 S.Ct. 1062, 93 L.Ed. at 1386.

whether in a particular instance a competitive or a restrictive market arrangement is in the public interest. Of course, there are stopping points between these extremes—for example, a rule of reason which asks for analysis only on the issue of whether competition is helped or hurt by a given arrangement.

The Frankfurter choice, therefore, must be explained at the level of inference. Given the general posture of the eminent Justice, as well as what he said in *Standard Stations,* we can conclude with confidence that he and (since he spoke for it) the Court felt it inappropriate to assign to the judicial process tasks of economic regulation which entailed wide discrimination and heightened uncertainties. He greatly valued processes and substantive rules which took full account of the limits of judicial competence [13] and his vision here prevailed. It was felt that the Court should not adjudicate questions where value choices are open and where reasonably certain factual bases for decision are not determinate.[14] We can also infer, perhaps with less confidence, that Frankfurter saw the risk of an overbroad rule largely in terms of disaccommodations to commercial freedom, a matter merely of great inconvenience. He spoke of "indirect" benefits to the public deriving from the benefits he saw to buyers and sellers in being able to regulate their affairs as they chose, but he did not seem to identify these with resource allocation or the other social benefits of competitive processes. He may have but dimly grasped or lightly regarded the point that forbidding a requirements contract which does not adversely affect competition may be to deprive the public of the benefits of significant efficiencies.

If Justice Frankfurter found the issues nearly paralyzing, Justice Jackson did not. His dissenting opinion is an eloquent statement of a quite different response to the complexities with which the judicial system must grapple in economic litigation. He read the statute literally. To prevail, the government must show that "the actual or probable effect of the accused arrangement is to substantially lessen competition or tend to create a monopoly." He joined the majority in bemoaning the fact that the act "submits such economic issues" to the Court, because doing so "leaves the law vague as a warning or guide" and because "judicial process is not well adopted to exploring such issues." But though the burden is difficult, it cannot be put down:

> [I]f they must decide, the only possible way for the courts to arrive at a fair determination [of competitive effect] is to hear all relevant evidence * * * and weigh not only

---

13. See Jaffe, The Judicial Universe of Justice Frankfurter, 62 Harv.L.Rev. 357 (1949), especially at 363–72.

14. That theme has often been sounded in later antitrust cases. If Frankfurter's conservative concept of the judicial role has faded in other areas it has often echoed clearly enough in the antitrust area. See, e.g., United States v. Philadelphia Nat'l Bank, 374 U.S. 321, 83 S.Ct. 1715, 10 L.Ed.2d 915 (1963); United States v. Topco Associates, Inc., 405 U.S. 596, 92 S.Ct. 1126, 31 L.Ed.2d 515 (1972).

its inherent probabilities of verity but also compare the experience, disinterestedness and credibility of opposing witnesses. This is a tedious process and not too enlightening, but without it a judicial decree is but a guess in the dark.[15]

This is a counsel which repays attention. What Justice Jackson has to say may be quite profound. Judges are not economists and courts are not laboratories for the exploration of social science problems. Nevertheless, judicial process is capable of being used to resolve policy issues, even very difficult ones. Judges and juries can listen to economic evidence, including the evaluations and comments of economists acting as expert witnesses, and can evaluate not only witness credibility, but the plausibility of opinions as explored through direct and cross-examination. We may permit ourselves some faith that the judgments—partly based on rational analysis, partly impressionistic, partly intuitive—which emerge from such a process are to be preferred to judgments which issue from the application of simplified and mechanistic rules.[16]

The dissent by Justice Douglas is yet another matter, and marks yet another theme which resonates now and again in antitrust litigation. It is a romantic theme, one might say, a remembrance of a populist tradition. Douglas argues that the antitrust laws should engage with "the curse of bigness." A Court of a mind which would permit Standard and other refiners to integrate forward, "to build service station empires of their own," should not close off requirements contracts, an alternative which "at least keeps the independents alive," for as surely as this avenue is closed off the refiners will pursue the other, which "is far worse," which would injure both the independent dealers who would be driven out and the nation:

> Size is allowed to become a menace to existing and putative competitors. Price control is allowed to escape the influences of the competitive market and to gravitate into the hands of the few. But beyond all that there is the effect on the community when independents are swallowed up by the trusts and entrepreneurs become employees of absentee owners. Then there is serious loss of citizenship. Local leadership is diluted. He who was a leader in the village becomes dependent on outsiders for his action and policy. Clerks responsible to a superior in a distant place take the place of resident proprietors beholden to no one. These are the prices which the nation pays * * *.[17]

15. 337 U.S. at 321–22, 69 S.Ct. at 1063, 93 L.Ed. at 1390.

16. This Jacksonian concept has also had its more recent exponents and may, indeed, be finding at last a degree of ascendancy. See, for example, United States v. General Dynamics Corp., 415 U.S. 486, 94 S.Ct. 1186, 39 L.Ed.2d 530 (1974).

17. 337 U.S. at 318–19, 69 S.Ct. at 1066, 93 L.Ed. at 1388–89.

Douglas would thus have the Court act as an agency of social engineers in the broadest sense, ready to strategically identify and select the resolution of any issue about market conduct or structure which will do most to frustrate bigness and to implement the frontier values of independence and self-reliance.

We have, of course, seen all of these themes suggested from time to time and no doubt we shall again sense their presence. It is the particular felicity of *Standard Stations* that it draws them all together and displays them side by side, expressing each of them quite aptly and quite completely. Yet there is one viewpoint missing which cannot lightly be overlooked. It is the structuralist point of view first forcefully expressed in *Alcoa* and which has become more dominant in antitrust analysis with each passing year. We shall, in the section which follows, attempt an analysis of the competitive effect of requirements contracts from that perspective. For the moment let us be content to note that in the one case of importance to follow *Standard Stations,* the analysis draws more fully from the structuralist tradition and is more rigorous, at least in terms of its economics, than anything in *Standard Stations*. The reference is to Justice Clark's opinion for the Court in Tampa Electric Co. v. Nashville Coal Co.[18]

Tampa agreed to buy and Nashville to sell all of Tampa's requirements for coal for a new generator station for a period of twenty years. Tampa had previously built only oil-fired burners and sought continuity of supply and assurances limiting price increases before switching to coal; to obtain the contract, it was ready to give comparable assurances. Quantitatively, the commerce over the period would be high, $128 million, and on this basis the district court and court of appeals had found a violation. But the Court, rejecting "quantitative substantiality" as a touchstone, held flatly that "the dollar volume, by itself, is not the test." It said that the market had to be defined in product and geographic terms and the extent of the foreclosure as a percentage of the market had to be estimated; there is no illegality unless the contract is found to "work a substantial * * * lessening of competition in the relevant market."[19] Justice Clark went on to define the market rigorously. The opinion rejected a market made up of Florida and either part or all of Georgia. While these were areas of consumption recognized as distinct for some purposes (one of them, for example, was identified as an area under the Bituminous Coal Act), they nevertheless could be served by all of the coal producers of the entire multi-state Appalachian coal region. Moreover, the suppliers of coal to Florida, though located in the southern portion of the nine state Appalachian region, were capable of selling elsewhere in the marketing area served by Appalachian producers. Thus, no area smaller than the entire Appalachian region

18. 365 U.S. 320, 81 S.Ct. 623, 5 L.Ed.2d 580 (1961).

19. Id. at 333–34, 81 S.Ct. at 631, 5 L. Ed.2d at 590.

constituted the "relevant market of effective competition." The great "bulk of the overwhelming tonnage marketed from the same producing area as serves Tampa is sold outside of Georgia and Florida, and the producers were 'eager' to sell more coal in those states * * *. [T]he relevant competitive market * * * is of course the area in which respondents and the other 700 producers effectively compete." [20]

When the market was so defined, the foreclosure amounted to less than 1% of the tonnage produced each year. The Court did not label this percentage *de minimus,* but tried to evaluate its impact in light of other structural characteristics. It concluded that given the nature of the market, the small percentage of foreclosure did not actually or potentially cause a substantial reduction of competition nor tend toward monopoly. "There is here neither a seller with a dominant position in the market * * * nor myriad outlets with substantial sales volume, coupled with an industry wide practice of relying on exclusive contracts * * *." [21] Thus there was no suggestion either of coercion or of interdependent action. And though the twenty-year duration might in other settings seem more restrictive than necessary, the needs of a utility for a stable supply at reasonable prices is sufficient in all the circumstances to warrant that length of time.[22]

This opinion, the Court's last word on the matter, is not wholly consistent either with the Frankfurter or the Jackson views expressed in *Standard Stations,* and certainly is out of accord with that of Douglas. It assumes the competence of the Court to undertake fairly sophisticated if somewhat simplified structural analysis and, in this fashion, to reach satisfactory results which validate requirements arrangements which may gain efficiencies without injury to the public, but which screen out those which may substantially lessen competition.

§ 165. Competitive Effects of Requirements and Exclusive Dealing Arrangements

We must read the careful structural evaluation in *Tampa Electric* [1] as meaning more than that a *de minimus* requirements contract is not invalid—as meaning, more, even, than that foreclosures which are substantial in percentage terms are unlawful while those that are insubstantial in these terms are not. Does the case then imply the promise that with the techniques available we can analyze

---

20. Id. at 331–32, 81 S.Ct. at 630, 5 L. Ed.2d at 589.

21. Id. at 334, 81 S.Ct. at 631, 5 L.Ed. 2d at 590.

22. Compare Mytinger & Casselberry, Inc. v. FTC, 301 F.2d 534 (D.C.Cir. 1962); United States v. Chas. Pfizer & Co., 246 F.Supp. 464 (E.D.N.Y.1965); United States v. American Can Co., 87 F.Supp. 18 (N.D.Cal.1949).

1. Tampa Electric Co. v. Nashville Coal Co., 365 U.S 320, 81 S.Ct. 623, 5 L.Ed.2d 580 (1961).

these arrangements and predict their effects with a reasonable degree of confidence? Can such a promise be fulfilled, or is the extension of judicial inquiry which we find in *Tampa Electric* to be viewed only as an expression of a hope that further inquiry may in some instances yield usable data?

Suppose this case: TV manufacturing is a fairly loosely structured oligopolistic industry with four large firms sharing about 70% of the market and ten or twelve firms sharing the balance with some not insignificant foreign competition. About half of the domestic firms, including the majors, make color tubes but the others buy such tubes, in part from their two largest competitors and in part from diversified electronics firms. Assume further that three years ago one of the smaller TV firms entered into a five year bilateral requirements contract for color tubes with one of the diversified tube manufacturers. If another of the small TV manufacturers (Small Co.) were now to enter into such a contract with another of the tube manufacturers (Tube Co.), what would be the competitive effects of this transaction? Let us pursue the analysis of competitive effects some distance to see the kinds of questions that would arise; we then can judge, perhaps, whether it is feasible for courts to handle them.[2]

Clearly, we must consider effects on competition in color TV manufacturing and effects on competition in tube manufacturing. From the first vantage point the contract entails a foreclosure of suppliers which may disadvantage other TV manufacturers which neither make nor have an assured source of supply for color tubes. This may have immediate disruptive effects, great or small, and may have long run effects due to the structural change. The disruptive effects will turn on the characteristics of the supply relationships which previously existed and upon the relationship between Tube Co.'s short run capacity and Small Co.'s requirements. Has Tube Co. been fully supplying Small Co. all along, without a requirements contract? If so there is no disruption worth noting. To the extent that Small Co. buys more from Tube Co. than before, will Tube Co. expand its production to meet Small Co.'s needs, or will it to some extent stop selling to the other unintegrated manufacturers? If it will cut sales to others, how critical will this be to them? If Tube Co. had regularly supplied, say, 10% of the supplies of its largest customer other than Small Co. the potential disruptive effects will be much less than if it had supplied substantially all of the color tubes of another TV manufacturer. And in any event, the effect will turn on whether the rest of the market can respond flexibly. If Tube Co. does not expand output so that Small Co. will now be buying tubes that previously went

---

2. See the thorough analyses which are suggested by P. Areeda, Antitrust Analysis, Problems, Text, Cases ¶ 621 (1st ed. 1967) and by Handler, Blake, Pitofsky & Goldschmid, Trade Regulation, Cases and Materials 922 (Prob. 28) (1975) each of which explores the ramifications of a foreclosure like that here envisaged, but in the context of a vertical merger.

to others, then other tube suppliers will be looking for customers to replace the lost purchases by Small Co.; the TV manufacturers which previously relied on Tube Co. can therefore now turn to those would-be sellers. There may also be other sources which could be tapped—other diversified electronics manufacturers, perhaps, could turn out some color tubes. The extent of disruption will also be seen to vary with the long-run and cyclical state of the industry, whether it is stable, expanding, or contracting.[3]

After likely disruptive effects are identified by such an analysis, it is necessary to evaluate whether they will have a continuing effect on competition, which will occur only if disruption leads either to structural changes (in addition to the requirements contract itself) or to long range changes in conduct. Such reactive structural changes would occur, for example, (1) if disruption were so severe that it caused the failure of one or more TV firms, (2) if it caused other TV firms to seek assured sources either by entering similar contracts, merging with tube makers, or making independent entry into tube manufacturing, or (3) if the disruption resulted in electronic component manufacturers which had not previously manufactured tubes making an entry into the tube market.

On the facts we have supposed, the process of further vertical integration between tube manufacturers and TV manufacturers might well be reinforced; indeed, the contract between Small Co. and Tube Co. can be seen as itself responsive to earlier links both by vertical integration and by requirements contract. But given the general structural situation here supposed, further structural changes such as those above suggested are not likely to result from disruption unless the disruption can be seen by other firms as a consequence of a predatory foreclosure aimed at disciplining market conduct. On our facts, surely, there is no basis for supposing Small Co. to be a predator.[4]

Wholly aside from disruptive effects, there is the basic structural change entailed in the contract itself. By means of the contract, a higher degree of vertical integration is achieved; it is not so high a degree as would result if Small Co. started making tubes itself or if it merged with Tube Co., yet a five year arrangement of this kind is not insignificant. One effect of the structural change may be increased efficiency. There may be cost savings due to a smoother, better integrated flow of tubes into the productive process, or due to reduced costs in buying and selling tubes. Although the existence or non-existence of these savings cannot be determined with certainty, it might

---

3. When the demand for color TV expanded massively in 1964 and 1965 upon the advent of full programming in color by the networks, integrated TV manufacturers which, as tube manufacturers, supplied competing TV manufacturers, apparently provided to competing TV makers a share of expanding tube output commensurate with the buyers' relative share of prior output.

4. See § 43 supra.

be possible to dig more deeply than the assumptions made by some analysts that if such savings were not present management would not have integrated.[5] If management claims that these kinds of savings motivated the contract, the basis for that assertion could be investigated and evaluated and, perhaps, a reasonably confident judgment made about whether economies will be achieved and, if so, how and in what likely degrees. Another effect of the structural change may be reduced competition. Some analysts urge that the foreclosure resulting from the vertical connection cannot affect competition because to the precise extent that Small Co. forecloses its competitors, it reduces the demand on resources alternatively available.[6] On the facts we have chosen, this may be true. If Small Co. by entering into the requirements contract with Tube Co. has reduced by 3% the domestically produced tubes from which the needs of its competitors must be satisfied, it has probably also reduced by 3% the demand upon that remainder. This will often be true, or substantially so, though not always. A firm, as we have noted, may enter a requirements contract to obtain parts it needs in connection with a plan (such as that involved in *Tampa Electric*) to expand its own output. Or a firm, if its motives are predatory, might enter into a requirements contract with a firm making more of a scarce supply than it actually needs in order to cut off market access of others.[7] The crucial thing to understand about foreclosure is that the danger to competition comes not from the fact that after foreclosure there are fewer supplies available; it comes from the fact that, after the foreclosure, the non-integrated TV manufacturers face a more tightly structured tube market. If competition is hurt, it is because the tube market has, by virtue of the contract, become less competitive.

We must begin to assess the effects on competition of that structural change by defining the tube market and determining the extent to which concentration is increased. Do we include foreign tube makers, if any? Do we take into account the tubes made by the large, wholly integrated TV manufacturers which they use themselves, or only the tubes which are available to be purchased by non-integrated TV manufacturers? Do we exclude the tubes already tied up by an earlier requirements contract? Do we consider diversified electronics manufacturers not now making tubes but who may be potential competitors? (Could they enter easily? Do they already command the technology, etc.?) When viewed from such of these varied perspectives as seem relevant (or, if one "market" seems clearly "relevant," when viewed as a phenomenon occurring in that market), does the structural change resulting from the contract actually or po-

---

5. See § 145 supra.

6. Peltzman, "Issues in Vertical Integration," in Public Policy Toward Mergers, 167, 168–69 (Weston & Peltzman, eds. 1969).

7. See § 43, supra. Compare Peltzman supra note 6.

tentially threaten competition? Does it, for example, make collusion or interdependent conduct among the remaining unintegrated tube manufacturers more likely? Or does it reduce the likelihood of entry into tube manufacturing, either (1) because it makes it more difficult for a new entrant to competitively capture the share of the purchases by the unintegrated manufacturers which it will need in order to survive, or (2) because it signals, initiates, or reinforces a trend toward greater vertical integration in the industry which will have that effect, or (3) because the TV manufacturer which participates in the requirements arrangement is itself a potential entrant into tube manufacture which, because of the contract, is not likely to enter during the next five years? Furthermore, if it has been concluded that disruption will lead to additional structural change, either of a kind which will increase or which will decrease competition, the effect of these changes will have to be evaluated too.

These comments and questions are intended to suggest the complexity of any effort to evaluate competitive effects of the requirement contract at one horizontal level, tube manufacturing; a similar analysis is necessary to gauge effects at the other level, where the TV manufacturers compete. From this perspective, the foreclosure is that of a supplier. We must identify and gauge consequences of the disruptive effects on TV manufacturers, consider whether these will stimulate further structural or conduct changes by these manufacturers, and evaluate the effect on competition, if any, of the structural change in the supplier market—a reduction by one of the number of firms selling tubes—or any additional structural changes in that market which may be stimulated by disruption. The problems of defining the market and estimating the consequence will be analytically similar to those discussed above.

We do possess analytical techniques of a certain power. If we gather sufficient information, we can often come to some sense of the dynamic of the market and reach some judgment about how a particular structural change may affect that dynamic. But the telling question remains whether it is a fit occupation for adults in the busy worlds of law, commerce and economic analysis to so dispose their energies. Are either the gains or pains potentially associated with this type of vertical link consequential enough to warrant such a social enormity as the analysis outlined above? If one were truly to come to terms with the dynamic of an industry such as that which we picture and were to prescribe appropriate public intervention to improve performance, is it likely that the abolition of requirements contracts would stand high on the remedial list? A negative intuition here serves sufficiently to impeach any proposal to deal with a practice so narrow and so specific by engaging in an inquiry so sweeping and so general. It is in this sense, really, that structural analysis fails as a technique for dealing with the narrower problems of market conduct to which the law gives rise. It is not that Justice Clark is wrong; we may be able to gauge most accurately the competitive consequences by doing a structural analysis. But doing it is so costly and so painful that it seems cumbersome and excessive to deal in this way with a problem so narrow. Deep and thorough structural analysis is warranted only when the offense charged is one which, if proven, will warrant whatever relief appears to promise better industry performance.

But if we can neither justify a *per se* prohibition—and surely we cannot on economic or other tenable grounds—nor justify a full-blown inquiry, where ought the law to stand when it faces a requirements contract? Let us attempt to fashion a truncated structural analysis which (whatever errors it may, upon occasion, lead us into in those cases which would be difficult to fathom even if we were to undertake a complete analysis) will spare us excesses of litigious effort, yet discriminate between requirements contracts where the risk of social injury is notably high and those where that risk is tolerably small. To do this would in a sense be responsive both to the views of Frankfurter, who called for a rule which was simple to apply, and to the views of Jackson, who insisted that the courts had an obligation to analyze the problem before them, insofar as they could.[8]

The Justice Department *Guidelines* for vertical mergers contain fairly simplified rules for market definition and propose such self-executing tests as that any vertical merger should be challenged if it links a supplying firm with 10% or more of its market with a purchasing firm having 6% or more of its market. This kind of an approach has never been used for requirements contracts, but it could be used to establish standards which, if exceeded, would be treated as presumptive evidence of violation.[9] There are of course grave differences between vertical integration achieved through merger and vertical integration achieved through a requirements contract; we shall touch upon these in the next section. While these differences impinge at least to the degree of precluding the transference in unmodified form of rules for merger to the requirements area, they do not render the merger norms irrelevant as starting points. If one has developed satisfactory guidelines for vertical merger, these, modified primarily to take account of the short duration of many requirements contracts, could serve as models for requirement contract guidelines. The task is one to which the Department of Justice or the FTC might turn.

§ 166. Duration of the Contract Term

There is an aspect of competitive effect upon which we have yet to touch and in connection with which a qualification of the proposition that no simplified rules have been made to pertain to requirements contracts is called for. When vertical integration is achieved

---

8. See § 164 supra.   9. See § 211 infra.

by merger it is in intention achieved permanently. Not so for requirements contracts. Here, expressly or by implication there is a time dimension, a contract term during which the integration achieved prevails and after which it is open to each participant to turn away. This, and the fact that a requirements arrangement entails integration only to the degree of linking at the distribution level two separate production processes (and thus achieves no integration of production, management or other distribution functions), whereas merger can facilitate whatever degree of integration will yield the highest efficiencies, are the most profound differences between these distinct means of attaining vertical integration.

When a requirements contract is under analysis its time dimension provides easy access in any search for less restrictive alternatives. If the goals being sought could be attained in substantial degree by a shorter arrangement, which will entail a less profound foreclosure, accustomed responses suggest that the shorter arrangement be insisted upon. To a degree, courts have pressed this insistence.[1] While there is always something that seems a little mechanical in these responses, they can also be seen as falling within the tradition of the simplifying presumption. Surely, in most situations most beneficial purposes can be attained through arrangements which go on from year to year, renewable, of course, but subject to termination by either party at the end of each year. If this be so, a one year norm is appropriate, so long as it is not so rigidly fixed as to preclude a showing, such as that in *Tampa Electric,* that the special circumstances of a particular case warrant a different treatment. No greater justification is needed for a year as the norm than that a year will be sufficiently long to comprehend one full cycle of seasonal variations in demand and output and that it is convenient to think in terms of the major time unit which we customarily use in analyzing financial and production flows.

What we are here suggesting is that where a requirements contract exceeds a year we might well presume it to be invalid, absent special justification for the longer term. Such a rule would not assure the legality of contracts for a year or less; these would have to be analyzed more fully, at least to the extent of doing a simplified market definition and computing foreclosure percentages.[2] If such a contract appeared to promise no efficiencies or to threaten significant injury despite its short duration, it would be unlawful. Nor would such a rule preclude longer contracts where competition was not significantly threatened and where because of special circumstances a longer term was needed to achieve the benefits sought. To-

---

1. See FTC v. Motion Picture Advertising Serv. Co., 344 U.S. 392, 73 S.Ct. 361, 97 L.Ed. 426 (1953); United States v. American Can Co., 87 F.Supp. 18 (N.D.Cal.1949) (five year contracts invalid; one year contracts acceptable). Compare United States v. Chas. Pfizer & Co., 246 F.Supp. 464 (E.D.N.Y.1965).

2. See § 165 supra. Compare § 211 infra.

gether with a simplified structural evaluation, this approach would invalidate most requirements contracts which have a significant potential for harm and would leave standing most which do not. Furthermore, since the rule would be only a presumption, to the extent that it might prove too coarse or too fine a screen, either the plaintiff or the defendant could press for the corrective of a more thorough analysis.[3]

The kinds of factors which might validate a longer term are various. In *Tampa Electric* the contract was a factor in the choice to build coal rather than oil burning generator facilities, a decision which would have consequence for a period of many years; also, as the Court stressed, the buyer was a utility which was regulated by public authority in the public interest and there was, perhaps, particular reason in this to gratify its desire for stable, predictable prices over a term reasonably commensurate with a generator's useful life. Other factors, such as relevant cyclical patterns which run longer than a year, would also justify longer arrangements when, as in *Tampa Electric,* the threat to competition is small.

§ 167. Agency Arrangements and Exclusivity

The first Section 3 case to reach the Supreme Court presented in one aspect the issue which we have found to recur in one form or another throughout the jurisprudence of vertical restraints—whether a firm at one level can impose restrictions on a firm at the next which could otherwise not be lawfully imposed if it imposes them under an arrangement where the goods are consigned rather than sold, or if the second firm acts as an agent, not an independent contractor. *Standard Fashion*[1] held that a pattern manufacturer having contracts with two fifths of all retail outlets which, in terms, made them its "agents" to sell its patterns and which forbade them to sell patterns made by others violated Section 3. The Court rejected the parties' own characterization of the arrangement as an agency and, on analysis, labeled it a sales contract. But shortly thereafter, in the *Curtis Publishing* case, the Court showed that it did not intend Section 3 to cover arrangements properly characterized as agencies.[2]

---

3. Compare United States v. Pabst Brewing Co., 384 U.S. 546, 86 S.Ct. 1665, 16 L.Ed.2d 765 (1966); United States v. First Nat'l Bank & Trust Co. of Lexington, 376 U.S. 665, 84 S. Ct. 1033, 12 L.Ed.2d 1 (1964); Standard Oil of Cal. v. United States, 337 U.S. 293, 69 S.Ct. 1051, 93 L.Ed. 1371 (1949).

1. Standard Fashion Co. v. Magrane-Houston Co., 258 U.S. 346, 42 S.Ct. 360, 66 L.Ed. 653 (1922). See § 164 supra.

2. In FTC v. Curtis Publishing Co., 260 U.S. 568, 43 S.Ct. 210, 67 L.Ed. 408 (1923), the Court reversed a Commission ruling based on Sections 3 and 5, which struck down a contract forbidding magazine distributors to handle the products of any other publisher. The distributors received magazines from the publisher and committed themselves to devote their full time and attention to the hiring, training and supervision of delivery boys. The publisher supplied the magazines, paid a commission on sales, but retained ti-

The line between *Standard Fashion* and *Curtis,* though drawn very early, may still be assumed to stand. Its existence serves, in a way, as a means of resolving the kind of issue which troubled Justice Douglas in *Standard Stations*.[3] A manufacturer, publisher, or refiner which cannot foreclose its customer from reselling products of others need not invest in distribution outlets of its own, thus driving out the independent; it may integrate less fully by taking some, but not all, of the risks at the next level—to be more precise by taking the product, but not the capital risks. In other words, it can make the otherwise independent retailer or distributor its agent and consign the goods to him.

§ 168. Problems of Characterization Under Section 3

Issues like those which arise under the *Colgate*[1] doctrine in Sherman Section 1 litigation are particularly vexing under Clayton Section 3. In the Sherman cases a pattern of relationships between a manufacturer and a group of dealers can be characterized as a "contract, combination or conspiracy"; action of a concerted nature is all that need be shown.[2] The bedrock requirement of Section 3 is more explicit. There must be a "lease * * * or sale or contract for sale of * * * commodities, * * *" and the "price charged therefore, or discount from, or rebate upon, such price" must be fixed "upon the condition, agreement of understanding" that the lessee or buyer will not deal in the commodities of competitors of the seller or lessor.[3] Some courts have responded to that distinction by refusing to find a Section 3 violation where a seller refuses to sell to a buyer unless the buyer agrees to a condition which, if it were entered into, would violate Section 3. As the court put the matter in Nelson Radio & Supply Co. v. Motorola, the act simply does not cover "a situation where the manufacturer refuses to make a sale or enter into a contract."[4]

tle and risk and took back any unsold copies. In language embracing a conduct orientation which has become somewhat out of fashion, the Court said:
"Effective competition requires that traders have large freedom of action when conducting their own affairs. Success alone does not show reprehensible methods, although it may increase or render insuperable the difficulties which rivals face." Id. at 582, 43 S.Ct. at 213, 67 L.Ed. at 414.

3. See discussion in § 164 supra. See also CBS Business Equip. Corp. v. Underwood Corp., 240 F.Supp. 413 (S.D.N.Y.1964) (if a contract creates a "true agency" there is no Section 3 violation); Preformed Line Products Co. v. Fanner Mfg. Co., 225 F.Supp. 762 (N.D.Ohio 1962), aff'd on other grounds 328 F.2d 265 (6th Cir. 1964). But see FTC v. Motion Picture Advertising Service Co., 344 U.S. 392, 73 S.Ct. 361, 97 L.Ed. 426 (1953), which suggests that *Curtis* applies only to Section 3 cases, not Sherman Act and Section 5 cases.

1. United States v. Colgate & Co., 250 U.S. 300, 39 S.Ct. 465, 63 L.Ed. 992 (1919).

2. See Ch. 3, Part K supra.

3. 38 Stat. 731 (1914), 15 U.S.C.A. § 14.

4. 200 F.2d 911, 915 (5th Cir. 1952), cert. denied 345 U.S. 925, 73 S.Ct. 783, 97 L.Ed. 1356 (1953). See also, Timken Roller Bearing Co. v. FTC, 299 F.2d

It is one thing to assert that absent actual sales or contracts to sell there can be no Section 3 violation,[5] but it is a far different matter to conclude that, even where there *are* sales to some dealers, a refusal to deal with a dealer who handles competitors' goods cannot evidence a violation. The manufacturer is making sales and the question presented is whether those sales are subject to the unlawful condition. That issue is no different than the one presented by the cases decided under Section 1 in the wake of *Colgate*. Perhaps we must conclude, under *Colgate,* that a mere refusal to deal cannot violate Section 3 any more than Section 1. But if the total course of conduct, including the announced policy of the manufacturer and any additional steps which it takes to police the market (such as talking with violators and urging them to get back in line), are enough to warrant the inference that the manufacturer sells and the dealers buy on the tacit "understanding or condition" that they must refrain from dealing with others, a violation of Section 3 seems plainly to be shown (assuming, of course, that adverse competitive effect is proven).[6]

In private litigation a Section 3 case may present complexities which would not be involved if a Section 1 theory were used. In a Section 1 case, if a seller's "refusal to deal" with plaintiff is done in order to implement a "contract, combination or conspiracy" entailing relationships with a group of other dealers and if it causes damage to the excluded dealer, that injury is held to be a proximate result of the concerted arrangement. However, under Section 3 the matter is less clear. Even though the relationships constituting the dealership structure involve sales, and even though the refusal to deal with plaintiff is evidence that those sales are upon the condition which violates Section 3, it is these sales, not the refusal to sell to plaintiff, which constitute the violation; and it is the refusal, not the unlawful sales, which causes plaintiff's injury.[7] A court could overleap this problem, of course. Section 3, like any other statute, can be construed in a manner advancing the policies emanating from it. To say no more than this is enough to show that the section may be read to forbid a refusal to deal except upon terms which would clearly violate it. A court could also confine the problem and hold that the issue of

---

839 (6th Cir.), cert. denied 371 U.S. 861, 83 S.Ct. 118, 9 L.Ed.2d 99 (1962); Leo J. Meyberg Co. v. Eureka Williams Corp., 215 F.2d 100 (9th Cir.), cert. denied 348 U.S. 875, 75 S.Ct. 113, 99 L.Ed. 689 (1954); Hudson Sales Corp. v. Waldrip, 211 F.2d 268 (5th Cir.), cert. denied 348 U.S. 821, 75 S.Ct. 34, 99 L.Ed. 648 (1954); Hunter Douglas Corp. v. Lando Prods., 215 F.2d 372 (9th Cir. 1954).

5. Hunter Douglas Corp. v. Lando Prods., supra note 4 at 376.

6. See Amplex of Maryland, Inc. v. Outboard Marine Corp., 1967 CCH Trade Cas. ¶72,135 (4th Cir.); Osborn v. Sinclair Ref. Co., 286 F.2d 832 (4th Cir. 1960); Dublin Distribs., Inc. v. Edward and John Burke, Ltd., 1953 CCH Trade Cas. ¶67,477 (S.D.N.Y.).

7. See Barber, Refusals to Deal Under the Federal Antitrust Laws, 103 U. Pa.L.Rev. 847, 860 (1955).

causation, though present in a damage action, would not foreclose injunctive relief on behalf of one with whom the seller has refused to deal; the argument here would be that although only the sales constitute a violation, dissipation of the violation and its effects requires no less than that the violator be inhibited from refusing to deal except upon the unlawful condition.

There is another answer which might be made to the assertion that Section 3 does not reach a refusal to deal. It is that the refusal to deal, enforced in this way, violates Section 1 of the Sherman Act, which includes a well formulated way of treating refusals to deal. If anything beyond the "doricly simple" refusal occurs, it treats the dealership structure as a concerted arrangement.[8] The question remains whether the arrangement in question has sufficient competitive effect to violate Section 1, but as we have noted, that statute may absorb the lower standards of competitive injury which have been developed under the Clayton Act.[9] Particularly if the evidence were to show a clear violation of Section 3, plaintiff's only difficulty being that his injury grew out of the refusal to deal with him because of his declining to participate in the violation, a court might be less rigorous in insisting that a discernibly higher threat to competition be made out under a companion count alleging a Sherman violation. In any event, a plaintiff in this posture who is asserting a cause of action under Section 3 ought also to allege a back-up claim under Section 1 of Sherman.

§ 169. Integrating the Law Respecting Requirements Contracts with That Governing Similar Vertical Arrangements

Requirements contracts may or may not threaten substantive injury to competition; the minimum basis for a rational analysis of competitive consequence is a definition of the market and a determination of and inquiry into the pertinence and the degree of foreclosure involved. *Tampa Electric*[1] calls for a fairly rigorous effort to define the market and to understand the dynamics which affect the extent of the impact. It may be that the rigor of *Tampa Electric* has been tempered, that presumptions related to the length of contract term are warranted, or even that a mechanistic definition of the market together with some rough rules about percentages can be given presumptive consequence.[2] Indeed, it may even be that *Standard Stations*[3] remains a better statement of the current law than does *Tampa Electric*. But to the extent that the rigor of *Tampa Electric* reflects the current law, this observation is invited: requirements

---

8. See § 139 supra.

9. See § 151 supra.

1. Tampa Elec. Co. v. Nashville Coal Co., 365 U.S. 320, 81 S.Ct. 623, 5 L.Ed.2d 580 (1961).

2. See §§ 164 and 166 supra.

3. Standard Oil Co. of Cal. v. United States, 337 U.S. 293, 69 S.Ct. 1051, 93 L.Ed. 1371 (1949). See §§ 164–65 supra.

contracts may stand as the only remaining area where the legality of vertical integration is determined by seeking to evaluate competitive effect with any degree of rigor.

Vertical mergers, as we shall see, have not been so rigorously treated.[4] Neither have tying arrangements [5] nor arrangements which in purpose or effect establish continuity of buyer-seller relationships on grounds other than competitive merit,[6] nor yet, reciprocal dealing arrangements.[7] This want of consistency is a reminder that if the law's verities are only partial, so, too, are its miscalculations. There remains, then, at least one area where vertical arrangements which afford a degree of integration can be worked out and where they may be safe from antitrust attack, unless it can be shown in a way at least marginally convincing that competition will be threatened.

§ 170. The Nature and Effect of Reciprocal Dealing

A reciprocal dealing arrangement involves an undertaking by one firm to buy from another on the condition that the second also buy from it. Assume that firm A produces aluminum and that firm B manufactures machines and parts, some of which use aluminum, and some of which are used in aluminum production. The two firms face each other in two markets, that in which A is a seller of aluminum and B a buyer of raw material which it will use in manufacturing operations, and that in which B is a seller of machinery and parts and A a buyer of equipment used in producing aluminum. If A were to tell B that it would buy parts from B if B agreed to buy aluminum from it, and if B were to accept this proposal, a classic reciprocal dealing arrangement would be consummated.

The potential for reciprocal arrangements will vary with a structural feature we have yet to examine, the extent of conglomorate organization. First, picture a national industrial establishment in which each firm operates as a seller in only one market and as a buyer only in markets for products used in its own production and marketing operations. One would not suppose the opportunities for reciprocity to be extensive; single market firms are not likely to find it possible to buy in volume the products of very many of their customers, hence are not often likely to be able to use power as buyers to induce others to buy from them. Moreover, where a single market firm does have opportunity to buy from customers, sellers competing with it in the industry will have the same opportunity; no differential leverage will be available unless one firm is substantially larger than others and thus, as a customer, can "outbid" its competitors

---

4. See Ch. 7 infra. Recent cases, it must be conceded, suggest an increased effort to be rigorously analytical. See, e. g., United States v. General Dynamics Corp., 415 U.S. 486, 94 S.Ct. 1186, 39 L.Ed.2d 530 (1974).

5. See Part C supra.

6. Id.

7. See §§ 170–71 infra.

when it uses buying power as a sales tool. Now picture a national industrial structure in which a hundred firms or more each operate in several different industries; this is called conglomorate organization. If firms typically operate in several unrelated markets—say, firm A as a producer and seller of paper, air transport, glassware and credit, and firm B as a producer and seller of drugs, petroleum products, motion pictures, and whiskey, and other firms have similarly varied activities—the opportunities for reciprocity will increase enormously; firms will frequently find that those whom they face as sellers of one product they will face as buyers of another. Thus, in our example, A as a seller will or may face B as a possible customer in several or all of its functions, and B as a seller of petroleum products will face A as an airline operator. Moreover, conglomorate organization will tend to create differential opportunities for reciprocity, opportunities not shared more or less equally by all competitors. Thus, if one seller of a product is a conglomorate while its competitors are not, the conglomorate may have a distinct advantage in seeking to gain sales through reciprocity. It may have divisions in other industries which buy from several companies, to which it wishes to sell. It can use the buying power of those divisions to achieve sales, a course not open to its competitors which operate only in one industry.

The social concern about reciprocity is markedly similar to that with respect to tying. The ideal is that each market transaction be made on the competitive merits of that particular transaction. If a firm has power in one market as a buyer and exercises that power to gain an advantage as a seller in a different market, the ideal is frustrated. Part of the second market is foreclosed to competing sellers and a buyer in that market, because of its interests as a seller elsewhere, may be deprived of the freedom to decide from whom it prefers to buy. There is, moreover, almost no likelihood that efficiencies will be achieved through reciprocity; the arrangement entails little if any integration efficiencies, consisting as it does of a continuity of buy-sell relationships which, for at least one of the firms, may not be freely chosen because of inherent advantages.

The competitive effect of reciprocity will vary depending upon the extent of the market power being exercised and the extent and significance of the foreclosure, given other structural features and the response to them. Let us first consider power. If power is lacking there is no adverse competitive effect from reciprocity. For example, assume that both wheat farming and bread baking are highly competitive. A, a farmer, is a seller of wheat and B, a baker, is a buyer of wheat; and A, which must provide meals to its farm hands, is a buyer of bread, a product sold by B. It would make little economic sense for either A or B to demand that the other enter into a reciprocal arrangement. Because both markets are competitive both A and B are able to sell all that they can profitably produce at the going market price for their respective products. Neither, as a buyer, has any power to coerce the other to enter into any arrangement which it does not regard as being on the competitive merits. If a reciprocal arrangement is entered into, it will not be to gain or extend market control, but on some basis of convenience or commercial congeniality, and it will not enable either producer to raise its price or to sell more than it otherwise could. If the two producers do enter into a reciprocal relationship, their respective competitors and the public ought to be indifferent.

By contrast, if reciprocity is engaged in by a seller which possesses substantial power as a buyer it may successfully use this power to improve its market positions as a seller. Suppose A is a mining firm and that B is the only refiner within a distance of A's mine to which it is economically feasible to ship the ore. Suppose that B also makes and sells mining equipment. In this situation B can exercise its power as a buyer in either of two ways; it can force A's price for ore down or it can insist on a reciprocal arrangement in which B agrees to buy ore from A and A agrees to buy equipment from B. It thus can, if it chooses, lever its power as a buyer into the market in which it sells, thereby foreclosing A as a customer to competing makers of mining machinery. Additionally, if B exercises its power as a buyer to require A to buy from it, A's freedom of choice as a buyer of equipment is affected. It cannot make choices on the competitive merits of the offerings by B and others. Whether competition as a process will be adversely affected in any significant way by this deprivation of A's free choice will depend largely upon the extent to which A, as a buyer, represents a significant percentage of the market for mining machinery. If A's purchases represent a very small percentage of that market, the competitive impact will be small; if A represents a large percentage of that market, the competitive effect will be more substantial.

The extent of the power of a buyer to use purchases to gain sales is also affected by the differential character of opportunities among competing sellers to exercise reciprocity. If all competing sellers operate in only one industry (or if in several, all in the same ones), the only differential factor which might give one a buyer power not possessed by others would be size. But if the competing firms operate in different industries in addition to the one where they compete as sellers, any one of them might gain power as a buyer which competing sellers could not match. Thus, assuming it is organized as a conglomorate, a firm need not be the largest in the industry where it competes as a seller in order to have power as a buyer not possessed by competitors.

§ 171. Reciprocity Arrangements as *Per Se* Violations

Most examples of actual or potential reciprocity which can be identified seem to threaten foreclosure only of small percentages of any market which might plausibly be defined. Impacts, of course, may be quantitatively significant—a large volume of commerce may be involved—but they seldom seem profound in percentage terms, although in any given case a reciprocity arrangement might, upon analysis, prove to be significant even in these terms. That circumstance, however, has not resulted in a rule of reason approach to reciprocity. Despite the fact that foreclosures are usually small in relative terms, concern about reciprocity was expressed early on, at least by the FTC,[1] and the Justice Department has taken the view, to which the courts may yet become committed, that reciprocity, at least in some of its forms, is *per se* illegal.

A stumbling block to the development of rules for reciprocity is that these arrangements are of potentially infinite variety. Agreement can be express or implicit; terms can be subtle and vague or blatant and precise. Indeed, reciprocity of a sort can occur as unilateral conduct—a seller may buy from a would-be customer in the hope that doing so will create goodwill leading eventually to sales, or buy from a present customer in order to give that customer additional incentives to keep buying from it. For that matter, price, quality and service being equal, it is the most natural thing in the world for a seller to show its gratitude by buying from one of its own customers. Reciprocity in this sense must be as old as trading.

The early FTC decisions focused on what was called coercion, a "threat" by a buyer not to buy from a seller unless the seller bought from it. The rule which developed distinguished between "coercive" reciprocity and "voluntary" reciprocity, the first occurring where one party to the arrangement was reluctant, the second describing arrangements which looked attractive enough to both. That line is hard to draw; where the only element of coercion is a refusal to trade on other terms, any instance of a reciprocal deal is one where both parties preferred the reciprocal deal to any commercially available alternative. True, one can picture situations where both parties are pleased with what the market affords, and those where one is a grumbling recalcitrant. But to discriminate between these, especially in retrospect, is a different matter; and it is hard to see the relevance of any such discrimination to antitrust values. One can also picture situations in which both parties are "free" in the sense of having a wide variety of market alternatives open to them and others where one party faces a customer which it profoundly needs to satisfy; but if this is the discrimination being made, it should be stated in terms of market power, not in terms of coercion. The unsatisfactory nature of the "coercion" rule first applied by the FTC under Section 5 has lead the Department of Justice to press for a rule that any agreement, express or implied, to sell only on reciprocal terms is a *per se* violation under Sherman, Section 1.[2] As yet, no court has

---

1. Waugh Equipment Co., 15 F.T.C. 232 (1931); Mechanical Mfg. Co., 16 F.T.C. 67 (1932); California Packing Corp., 25 F.T.C. 379 (1937).

2. E.g., United States v. General Dynamics Corp., 258 F.Supp. 36 (S.D.N.Y.1966).

ruled upon this position. In *General Dynamics*, the court expressed the view that a reciprocity agreement covering a substantial volume of commerce (the court said $500,000 or more) would be unlawful. But the statement was dictum; the court refused to infer the existence of an agreement from evidence that several customers of the defendant also sold to it. The strong argument for a *per se* response —or, more to the point, for a quantitative substantiality test like that for tying—is that reciprocal agreements do have the potential to damage competition and provide little or nothing of social value, even less than tying arrangements, since reciprocal agreements entail less integration. Given the attitudes expressed by courts in merger cases [3] about the dangers of reciprocity, it would not be unduly bold to predict that, by analogy to tying, a quantitative substantiality test for reciprocity will ultimately emerge.

Nevertheless, the counsel of caution about the need for solid evidence of agreement which was set forth in *General Dynamics* ought to be underscored. Remember, the goal is that each firm be free to buy from any firm it chooses, acting in each transaction on the competitive merits. If the mere fact that a seller purchases from one of its customers was taken to imply a reciprocal arrangement, that freedom could be inhibited by the very rule intended to enchance it. Strictly speaking, the need is not merely to find agreement, but to find a purchase made with a reciprocal motive, a purchase made not because it seemed the best offering on the competitive merits, but made in order to induce the seller to buy, in turn, from the buyer. We ought to have no compunction about inhibiting a firm from buying from a customer if it does so not because it regards the customer's offering as best, but because it sees this transaction as a way to bind the customer to it as a customer. We look for agreement, rather than unilateral action, because when we find a reciprocal agreement we know that motives of reciprocity are at work; if those motives mark themselves clearly enough in other ways, the purpose of the rule is satisfied.

Even when no agreement is present, it may in some cases be possible to identify reciprocity as the motive for a transaction with considerable assurance. For example, a large conglomorate firm might set up a "trade relations" department, having the function of looking over its myriad operations and identifying the firms making products which it purchases and to which it might sell, and of calling these data to the attention of purchasing and sales personnel, the former so that they will place orders, where feasible, with potential customers, and the latter so that when they make sales contacts they can call to the attention of the prospect the sell-buy relationships already existing. If such a pattern appears in the background, and if the firm

---

3. E.g., FTC v. Consolidated Foods Corp., 380 U.S. 592, 85 S.Ct. 1220, 14 L.Ed.2d 95 (1965).

then begins systematically switching its purchases from sellers who could not also be buyers from it to firms which could, we ought not to hesitate to label the purchases as being made from a reciprocal motive. Indeed, we could fairly label the whole operation, including the process of analysis to identify opportunities for reciprocity, as tending to injure competition. It would be entirely appropriate to condemn such conduct under Section 5, despite the lack of any coercive element. On this theory, the FTC, by its voluntary compliance program, has obtained formal assurances from several firms that they will dismantle trade relations departments.[4] Given the commodious concepts of combination or agreement which prevail in vertical cases, an organized trade relations program, leading as it does to a set of interrelationships with numerous buyers and sellers all being enticed to act reciprocally, could plausibly be characterized as a "combination" or "agreement" in restraint of trade.[5]

We shall, in Chapter 7, discuss the relevance of reciprocity to the lawfulness of mergers, particularly those which involve conglomerate expansion,[6] but for the moment we must conclude with the summary observation that reciprocal transactions, when capable of being clearly identified and when entailing a substantial volume of commerce are, if challenged, likely to be held illegal under Sherman Section 1 or Section 5 of the FTC Act.

PART E. "REASONABLE" VERTICAL RESTRICTIONS

§ 172. Introduction

We have already remarked that a firm selling for resale a branded product or the franchisor which licenses a brand name or mark has an interest in the way in which business is carried on with its brand, mark or product at the next and, perhaps, further succeeding vertical levels. Thus far we have emphasized the limits of this interest, the restraints it cannot be taken to justify.[1] In the sections which follow we shall look at some of the "reasonable" vertical restraints, those which are not so central either to the competitive process or to dealer independence as to call for *per se* prohibition. We shall identify major, recurrent examples of restrictions which are valid unless, upon analysis, they are specifically shown because of

---

4. American Radiator and Standard Sanitary Corp., F.T.C. File No. 631,0270; Union Lamp. Corp., F.T.C. File No. 661,0083; GAF Corp., F.T.C. File No. 661,0088; Chase Bog Corp., F.T.C. File No. 681,0090. Compare FTC v. Brown Shoe Co., 384 U.S. 316, 86 S.Ct. 1501, 16 L.Ed.2d 587 (1966).

5. Compare Perma Life Mufflers, Inc. v. International Parts Corp., 392 U.S. 134, 88 S.Ct. 1981, 20 L.Ed.2d 982 (1968); Albrecht v. The Herald Co., 390 U.S. 145, 88 S.Ct. 869, 19 L.Ed.2d 998 (1968); and United States v. Parke, Davis & Co., 362 U.S. 29, 80 S.Ct. 503, 4 L.Ed.2d 505 (1960).

6. See § 209 infra.

1. See part B supra.

their context to have a significant and adverse impact on competition. We shall also examine the analytical approaches which are relevant to dealing with "rule of reason" issues in vertical relationships.

In a sense, we have already identified a number of reasonable vertical restraints. As we discussed each *per se* category we marked out the limits of the rule; so doing, we pointed to arrangements which fell outside of it as well as to ones which fell within. We saw, for example, that a tradename holder could restrict the place at which the name was exploited, though he could not restrict the place at which products were resold. We saw also that although a manufacturer which wanted dealers to have adequate service facilities could not contract to limit price or resale territories to encourage dealers to provide such facilities, it could mandate directly that dealers provide specified services.[2] All of these restraints, not being *per se* invalid, are lawful unless shown in a given case to have been used for unreasonable purposes, or to have unreasonable effects. In what follows, we shall be dealing with these "borderline" restraints and with a broader, residual category of "reasonable" restraints.

§ 173. Restrictions to Control the Quality of Goods and Services Sold Under a Trademark License

One major category of reasonable vertical restraints covers those imposed by a trademark licensor upon licensees which are reasonably necessary to assure uniformity of quality and to protect the validity of the mark. These restraints include reasonable steps to control the activities of each licensee, to assure uniformity of quality so that the mark will continue to identify only the holder's uniform product or service, so that the representation implied from display of the mark that the holder is responsible for quality will be lived up to.[1] Though a licensor may not be free to tie the grant of the license to the purchase of products or ingredients,[2] there are a variety of less restrictive arrangements open to the licensor. These include requirements that the licensee comply with specifications for finished products or ingredients, that the licensee follow production or service procedures spelled out by the licensor, that the licensee produce goods of the same quality as samples identified in the agreement, and that the licensee permit reasonable inspection by the licensor. So long as these arrangements are used for the manifest purpose of protecting the mark and not as a covert way of forcing the licensee to buy from the licensor as a condition of the license,[3] they are open to no objection.

---

2. Id.

1. Comment, Antitrust Problems in Trademark Franchising, 17 Stan.L. Rev. 926 (1965); Comment, Quality Control and the Antitrust Laws in Trademark Licensing, 72 Yale L.J. 1171 (1963).

2. See §§ 155–156 supra.

3. Compare Hobart Bros. Co. v. M. T. Gilliland, Inc., 471 F.2d 894 (5th Cir.), cert. denied 412 U.S. 923, 93 S.Ct. 2736, 37 L.Ed.2d 150 (1973); American Motor Inns, Inc. v. Holiday Inns, Inc., 365 F.Supp. 1073 (D.N.J.1973).

The interest of the licensor in preserving its mark, the interest of the public in finding in fact the uniformity of quality and service which in theory is associated with the mark, and the interest of other licensees which have cooperated in exploiting the mark with the expectation that all licensees would be held to designated quality standards, all warrant the licensor's reasonable policing efforts. These kinds of restraints are the lightest which could be imposed if the mark is to be licensed at all and is to continue to have meaning.[4]

A tougher issue is whether a licensor, when the product is amenable to being described by specifications or sample, can control quality by designating a reasonable number of "approved" sellers which the licensor has inspected.[5] If the licensor uses this device fairly and openly—if it inspects all potential sources wishing to gain market access in a reasonable manner and if it does not take a "cut" or "kickback" on their sales—the restriction would not be materially greater than that resulting from specifications, and would perhaps be more effective and give the licensor greater confidence that standards are being complied with. Yet this device is obviously more susceptible to being perverted into the achievement, in purpose and effect, of a tying arrangement.

§ 174. Requirements about "Competitive Style" in "Franchise" Arrangements Which Do Not Entail Carrying on Business Under the Name and Mark of the Franchisor

Where the manufacturer does not "franchise" the dealer to conduct business under the name and trade mark of the manufacturer, but merely sells to the dealer the manufacturer's own "brand name" products for resale, the interest of the manufacturer in the way the dealer conducts business is obviously less intense. Yet, even here the manufacturer has an interest in seeing that his product is retailed in a way which will yield a high volume of sales. While a manufacturer might rely on competition at the retail level to resolve the myriad issues to be decided, we have seen that many manufacturers with differentiated products wish to "manage" decision-making at the retail level to some degree, to super-impose on the market their own judgments about what mode of retailing will maximize sales and, in consequence, their returns at the manufacturing level. We have also seen strict limits imposed on such efforts by manufacturers: some elements of decision-making by retailers, such as price, territory and customer determination, a manufacturer may not lawfully impose upon.[1] But the law has not with blinding logic denied the manufacturer any privilege to impose conditions on resellers. The manufacturer may still influence many elements of the dealer's competitive

---

4. See, e.g., Engbrecht v. Dairy Queen, 203 F.Supp. 714 (D.Kan.1962); Alligator Corp. v. Robert Bruce, Inc., 176 F.Supp. 377 (E.D.Pa.1959).

5. See Carvel Corp., 68 FTC 128, CCH Trade Reg.Rep. ¶ 17,298 (1965).

1. See parts A and B supra.

style. So long as it avoids *per se* areas it can impose various "quality" conditions on dealers; these will be held unlawful only if in particular circumstances they can be shown to injure competition.

Typical of the kinds of requirements manufacturers may impose on dealers without violating a *per se* rule are ones respecting the character and type of showroom facilities, the amount of advertising done by the dealer, requirements as to signs or displays of the manufacturer's name or products, the provision of service facilities and parts inventories, and the employment of qualified personnel, etc.[2] We have noted before that with respect to territories, a manufacturer may use a "primary responsibility" clause, or perhaps, even a pass through arrangement, and that the rule of reason applies to agreements not to franchise others in a particular territory [3] and to agreements which limit the location or territory in which a dealer is authorized to hold himself out as representing the manufacturer (though agreements restricting where or to whom the dealer may resell the product are *per se* unlawful). A manufacturer may also impose minimum sales quotas which are valid under other applicable law and which do not unreasonably restrain competition.[4]

How is reasonableness evaluated? If any arrangement has substantially the same purpose or effect as an arrangement subject to a *per se* rule or a rule which makes legality turn on whether there is a quantitatively substantial amount of commerce involved, the arrangement will be assimilated under that rule and judged accordingly. For example, a primary responsibility clause or a pass through clause which as a practical matter keeps each retailer out of the territory of others will be *per se* invalid,[5] and a dealer quota requirement which has the purpose and effect of obliging the dealer to take all its requirements from the manufacturer will be analyzed as though it were a requirements contract.[6]

2. See United States v. Arnold, Schwinn & Co., 237 F.Supp. 323 (N.D. Ill.1965), aff'd on other grounds 388 U.S. 365, 87 S.Ct. 1856, 18 L.Ed.2d 1249 (1967).

3. See §§ 144–45 supra. Of course, if there is limited interbrand competition, an intrabrand restraint, even one that would be reasonable in a context of intense interbrand competition, may be unreasonable and therefore unlawful. E. g. Blankenship v. Hearst Corp., 519 F.2d 418, 424–425 (9th Cir. 1975).

4. E.g., Victory Motors of Savannah, Inc. v. Chrysler Motors Corp., 357 F. 2d 429 (5th Cir. 1966); Kotula v. Ford Motor Co., 338 F.2d 732 (8th Cir. 1964), cert. denied, 380 U.S. 979, 85 S. Ct. 1333, 14 L.Ed.2d 273 (1965); Milos v. Ford Motor Co., 317 F.2d 712 (3d Cir.), cert. denied 375 U.S. 896, 84 S. Ct. 172, 11 L.Ed.2d 125 (1963).

5. See §§ 144–45 supra.

6. Compare United States v. Richfield Oil Corp., 99 F.Supp. 280 (S.D.Cal. 1951), aff'd per curiam 343 U.S. 922, 72 S.Ct. 665, 96 L.Ed. 1334 (1952). Cf. Kestenbaum v. Falstaff Brewing Corp., 514 F.2d 690 (5th Cir. 1975) (reasonable for a brewer to increase its price to its distributors when distributors increased their resale prices above the brewer's suggested resale price in order to force distributors to "stay competitive" with other brands).

Aside from this approach, the structural setting in which an arrangement is encountered may result in its having an adverse competitive impact. If the manufacturer holds monopoly power, its scope in treating with dealers is much narrower than that of a manufacturer without power. For example, though manufacturers facing competition may do so, a monopolist may not commit itself to grant a dealer an exclusive outlet; for to do so would be to assure the dealer of a retail monopoly. Similarly, a manufacturer with great power ought to be judged more rigorously if it seeks to limit dealer discretion on matters like store hours, display, advertising, and the like. To allow a powerful manufacturer to dictate these things would be to unduly limit competition at the retail level, since no competing manufacturers would spawn competing dealers using alternative approaches to the retail market. Indeed, even an unilateral refusal to deal may adversely affect competition where the seller has great power.

§ 175. Sales "For Professional Application" and the Like

There is old case law holding that in various situations a manufacturer may preclude buyers from reselling at all.[1] *Schwinn*[2] casts a shadow over all such cases;[3] yet, despite its broad language, *Schwinn* ought not to be read as prohibiting resale restrictions which do not in purpose or effect threaten injury to competition. There may be reasons independent of a desire to limit resale competition which motivate a manufacturer to restrict resales. For example, the product may be dangerous if used by other than an expert. The manufacturer, fearing tort liability and loss of good will, may wish to restrict resales to qualified buyers.

In such instances there will be a collateral impact on resale competition. Hence, restrictions ought not to be permitted for trivial reasons or where less restrictive alternatives, such as label warnings, would reasonably suffice. Nor should specious health or safety concerns be allowed to cloak customer restrictions which are imposed to divide markets. Courts must be alert to forbid evasion of the

---

1. See Note, Restricted Channels of Distribution Under the Sherman Act, 75 Harv.L.Rev. 795, 821–22, 831 (1962). Thus, where equipment is complex and servicing or installation by unauthorized dealers would hurt goodwill, a manufacturer was held to be entitled to impose such a restriction. Green v. Electric Vacuum Cleaner Co., 132 F.2d 312 (6th Cir. 1942), cert. dismissed 319 U.S. 777, 63 S.Ct. 1163, 87 L.Ed. 1723 (1943). Similarly, such a restriction was implied where the product was in short supply and the manufacturer wanted to hold prices down and, in effect, to ration sales, without creating a "black market" for resales at prices higher than the manufacturer's price. Fosburgh v. California & Hawaiian Sugar Ref. Co., 291 F.Supp. 29 (9th Cir. 1923).

2. United States v. Arnold, Schwinn & Co., 388 U.S. 365, 87 S.Ct. 1856, 18 L.Ed.2d 1249 (1967).

3. Compare Adolph Coors Co. v. FTC, 497 F.2d 1178 (10th Cir. 1974) with Tripoli Co. v. Wella Corp., 425 F.2d 932 (3rd Cir.), cert. denied 400 U.S. 831, 91 S.Ct. 62, 27 L.Ed.2d 62 (1970). See the discussion in § 144 supra.

Schwinn rule. But manufacturers acting in good faith ought to be allowed to protect themselves and the public in reasonable ways when real hazards attend the use of a product. Suppose, for example, that a licensing system prevailed governing retail sale of dangerous products, such as guns or explosives. A manufacturer which insisted that dealers not resell except to licensed buyers would not, in purpose or effect, be doing objectionable injury to competition. The same view might be taken of a comparable restriction—say, "no resales of explosives except to persons over 18"—imposed by a manufacturer, even though no state law policy were involved.

Chapter 6

ANTITRUST LAW AND PATENTS

Table of Sections

Part	Sections
A. Introduction	176–177
B. Single-Firm Antitrust Violations and the Patent Laws	178–182
C. Patent Arrangements Constituting Contracts, Combinations and Conspiracies in Restraint of Trade	183–191

PART A. INTRODUCTION

Sec.
176. Allocating Resources Between Present Production and Research and Development.
177. The Major Features of the Patent System and Their Relationship to Antitrust.

PART B. SINGLE-FIRM ANTITRUST VIOLATIONS AND THE PATENT LAWS

178. The Conduct Element in Section 2 Offenses and Its Relation to Policies for the Acquisition of Patents.
179. Circumstances Under Which Patent Acquisitions May Constitute Exclusionary Conduct.
180. The Application of Section 5 of the FTC Act and Section 7 of the Clayton Act to Patent Acquisitions.
181. Patent Enforcement Policy as Exclusionary Conduct.
182. License Restrictions (and Restrictions on Assignees) as Exclusionary Conduct.

PART C. PATENT ARRANGEMENTS CONSTITUTING CONTRACTS, COMBINATIONS AND CONSPIRACIES IN RESTRAINT OF TRADE

183. Introduction.
184. Licenses or Assignments Which Impose Horizontal Restrictions on Territories.
185. Licenses Which Restrict Prices Horizontally.
186. License Provisions Which Impose Horizontal Restrictions Respecting the Fields of Use Within Which the Patent will be Practiced.
187. Customer Restrictions in Licenses.
188. Settlement of Patent Disputes.
189. Grant Back Provisions and Agreements Not to Contest.
190. Vertical Restraints and the Inherency Test.
191. Price, Territorial, Customer and Use Restrictions Imposed by a Patentee Upon Purchasers.

PART A. INTRODUCTION

§ 176. Allocating Resources Between Present Production and Research and Development

For many years Americans have tended to regard all innovation as a good, but recent emphasis on the ecology of life on the planet has caused American pastoralism to gain refreshed potency. Such long-run oscillations in the things we value, as well as myriad judgments and impulses about current needs and future potentials, interact through the numerous media of governmental and private decision making to influence the level and direction of the nation's investment in research and development ("R & D"). National policy is directly implicated in setting the rate and objectives of government sponsored research. Although this accounts for more than half of the total national investment in producing innovations, we cannot attend it here. Rather, this chapter will discuss patents and antitrust, the major means through which public policy affects the level of private R & D investment.

For most private sector activities we rely on the market alone to determine the socially desirable level of investment. We are satisfied for firms to invest in producing a given product up to, but no higher than, the point where they could earn greater profits by investing in other things. However, we take a very different stance about R & D; the patent system presupposes that we cannot rely on the market to determine the socially optimal investment in innovation. The rationale is clear.[1] To invent takes resources—time, energy, money. People will be motivated to invest in innovation, as in other activities, only to the extent that the returns they anticipate are not less than they could anticipate from alternative employments of their resources. The "product" of innovation is, at its essense, an idea, an elusive thing which intrinsically cannot be reduced to possession and, if it is used by the inventor, seldom can be easily protected from being used also by anyone else who can learn and comprehend it. The inventor would see these others as free riders, profiting equally with him from his investment. Hence, investment in innovation would be discouraged. The patent system is designed to give the inventor a property right in those ideas which qualify under the statute for protection. In theory, then, the patent system redresses an imbal-

---

1. See, W. Bowman, Patent and Antitrust Law, Ch. 2 (1973). This book, which contains a detailed and readable analysis of major patent antitrust probems viewed from the vantage point of Chicago school economics is of general interest and value. For an analysis which is theoretically less rigorous, but which is more realistic in that it seeks to take account of more of the realities of the market place, see F. Scherer, Industrial Market Structure and Economic Performance Ch. 15 (1970). See also F. Machlup, An Economic Review of the Patent System, Study No. 15 of the Subcommittee on Patents, Trademarks & Copyrights of the Senate Judiciary Committee, 85th Cong., 2d Sess. (1958).

ance. The inventor, in return for disclosing the invention, is given an exclusive right to it,[2] a right which he may use, convey,[3] license,[4] or even leave dormant as might the owner of some other species of property.[5]

At this juncture correlative concepts must be stressed. Note that once the governmental decision is made to grant the inventor an exclusive property right in his invention, the market as a gauge of the socially optimal level of investment in innovation has been abandoned. The market will still serve to deploy investment between innovation and production, just as it would do were there no patent system. But given the interposition of the patent system, the level of investment in innovation will be higher and that in current production lower, and there is no way to determine *from any market data* whether the altered level is socially preferable to the one that would otherwise have prevailed. There may be a strong political consensus that we ought now to have more innovation and less bread and circuses than we would have without a patent system; but the market does not tell us so.

Neither does the market aid us in deciding how much more innovation we ought to have than the market alone would yield; nor, assuming that those questions are resolved by political judgments, does the market do very much to aid us in designing the particulars of a patent system which will achieve the desired goal. Consider for a moment two hypothetical alternative patent systems. Under the first, the standard for determining whether an idea is patentable is extremely high, so that exceedingly few patents are granted, and when a patent is granted the inventor has rights in his invention for only three years. Even during this period, however, he must grant unrestricted licenses to all who want to use the invention at a royalty rate which may not exceed that determined by a specified formula. Such a system will increase the level of investment in innovation and reduce the level of investment in current production in comparison to the situation which would prevail without a patent system. But now consider a second hypothetical system. The standard for patentability is much lower than in the first and the patent grant is for 50 years. The inventor may license or not as he chooses and may impose in any license such restrictions as he elects in order to control the customers to whom, the prices at which and the uses for which the patented

---

2. Section 154 of the Patent Code of 1952, 66 Stat. 804, 35 U.S.C.A. § 154. See Powell, The Nature of A Patent Right, 17 Colum.L.Rev. 663 (1917).

3. Section 261 of the Patent Code of 1952, 66 Stat. 810, 35 U.S.C.A. § 261.

4. Waterman v. McKenzie, 138 U.S. 252, 11 S.Ct. 334, 34 L.Ed. 923 (1891).

5. Continental Paper Bag Co. v. Eastern Paper Bag Co., 210 U.S. 405, 28 S.Ct. 748, 52 L.Ed. 1122 (1908); Special Equip. Co. v. Coe, 324 U.S. 370, 65 S.Ct. 741, 89 L.Ed. 1006 (1945). See Frost, Legal Incidents of Non-Use of Patented Inventions Reconsidered, 14 Geo.Wash.L.Rev. 273 (1946).

product is sold. This patent system will yield an even higher investment in innovation and an even lower investment in current production. In both cases, the market will allocate resources between innovation and production, but the market can neither be forced nor cajoled into deciding whether the socially preferable allocation is that which prevails with no patent system, with the first system or with the second.

The details of the operative patent system in this nation are determined in part by the particulars of the patent statute and in part by the ways in which antitrust doctrine and patent law are integrated. We turn now to these matters.

§ 177. The Major Features of the Patent System and Their Relationship to Antitrust

In order to "promote the useful arts," patents may be granted, pursuant to Section 101 of the Patent Code, on "any new and useful process, machine, manufacture, or composition of matter, or any new and useful improvement thereof." [1] The inventor must be the first to reduce the invention to practice,[2] and the invention must be nonobvious [3] and have utility.[4] Where these prerequisites are met Section 154 of the Patent Code provides for a grant to an inventor for seventeen years of "the right to exclude others from making, using or selling the invention * * *." [5] The inventor, of course, may admit others to the practice by license, but he need not. In return for this grant the inventor must make a full disclosure of the invention.[6]

Among the preeminent patent law issues is one which has particular relevance to antitrust concerns—what must an applicant show about the creative process or about the novelty of what has been accomplished, in order to qualify for a patent monopoly? The leading case, Graham v. John Deere Company,[7] expresses an attitude more than a principle. The opinion of Justice Clark insists that patents not be granted for conceptions that would be obvious to those skilled in the art. It berates the Patent Office for persistence in granting patents too freely. It stresses that the constitutional basis for a patent is advancement of the useful arts and puts forth that Congress may not, at least under the patent power, grant monopolies

---

1. 66 Stat. 797, 35 U.S.C.A. § 101.

2. Section 102 of the Patent Code of 1952, 66 Stat. 797, 35 U.S.C.A. § 102.

3. Anderson's-Black Rock, Inc. v. Pavement Salvage Co., Inc., 396 U.S. 57, 90 S.Ct. 305, 24 L.Ed.2d 258 (1969); Graham v. John Deere Co, 383 U.S. 1, 86 S.Ct. 684, 15 L.Ed.2d 545 (1966).

4. See Brenner v. Manson, 383 U.S. 519, 86 S.Ct. 1033, 16 L.Ed.2d 69 (1966).

5. 66 Stat. 804, 35 U.S.C.A. § 154.

6. Section 112 of the Patent Code of 1952, 66 Stat. 798, 35 U.S.C.A. § 112.

7. 383 U.S. 1, 86 S.Ct. 684, 15 L.Ed.2d 545 (1966).

except for discoveries which tend toward this end.[8] It recalls Jefferson who is quoted as saying that the line between the patentable and the non-patentable should be between " 'the things which are worth to the public the embarrassment of an exclusive patent, and those which are not.' "[9] In other cases the Court has pressed the same position.[10] But in terms of help in applying the standard, the most that is yielded is an approach to the task of deciding. The Patent Office and, in any case in which the validity of the patent is questioned, the court must comprehend the existing art relevant to the claimed invention, must understand the relationship between that art and the invention, must grasp the problems which the invention was intended to solve, and must attain sufficient familiarity with the level of performance of journeymen in the art so that a judgment is possible about whether journeymen addressing the problem seriously, and drawing on the existing art, could be expected to come up with the claimed invention as a solution.[11]

Let there be no pretense that the patent system is not in potential collision with antitrust; it clearly is.[12] Suppose a firm accumulates enough patents to control a market; does it violate Sherman, section 2? Suppose a patent license purports to restrict the price at which the patented invention may be sold, or the geographic territory or the field of use in which the invention may be practiced; does it violate Section 1? Integration of patent and antitrust law entails a neverending series of adjustments and compromises; often, the choice is about which values are to dominate. Courts sometimes evade responsibility for such choices by saying Congress has made them. A decision giving primacy to patent values (if, for example, a court were to hold that accumulating sufficient patents to become a monopolist did not violate Section 2) might be explained as based upon the demands of the patent statute, without recognition that the antitrust law points the other way.[13] Conversely, a court might read what the antitrust laws imply and ignore the patent statute. Both "easy answers" are unsatisfying.[14]

Choices among these competing laws are inevitable; but there may be ways by which the tension between the two systems can be

---

8. Id. at 5–6, 86 S.Ct. at 687–88, 15 L. Ed.2d at 549–50.

9. Id. at 9, 86 S.Ct. at 689, 15 L.Ed.2d at 552.

10. E.g., Anderson's-Black Rock, Inc. v. Pavement Salvage Co., Inc., 396 U.S. 57, 90 S.Ct. 305, 24 L.Ed.2d 258 (1969).

11. The case which first indicated that the issue of novelty should be approached by considering what one skilled in the art might be expected to achieve was Hotchkiss v. Greenwood, 52 U.S. 248, 11 How. 248, 13 L.Ed. 683 (1851). See the discussion in W. Bowman, Patent and Antitrust Law ch. 3 (1973).

12. Compare Hartford-Empire Co. v. United States, 323 U.S. 386, 452, 65 S. Ct. 373, 404, 89 L.Ed. 322, 382 (1945) (Rutledge, J., dissenting).

13. E.g., Bement & Sons v. National Harrow Co., 186 U.S. 70, 22 S.Ct. 747, 46 L.Ed. 1058 (1902).

14. See the analysis suggested by P. Areeda, Antitrust Analysis, Problems, Text, Cases ¶416 (2d ed. 1974).

eased. One may be able to meter the force of competing patent and antitrust interests and give way to the stronger; or one may be able to discern alternative ways for one or the other of the competing values to be expressed, so that confrontation becomes less direct. Such processes of accommodation may at times necessitate a deeper analysis than that which would be appropriate if either antitrust or patent values were operative alone. For example, if imposition of a particular restraint were arguably supported by patent policy, it might be appropriate to pursue the issue of the extent to which the restraint would affect competition, even though, but for the engagement of patent values, the restraint would be invalid under an antitrust *per se* rule. Yet these kinds of adjustments must be worked out in ways which do not mire the courts in any disproportionate complexity.

During the last few decades courts faced with patent—antitrust conflicts have tended to prefer antitrust law over patent law.[15] This tendency is perhaps a product of the increased use of an analytical approach in the adjudication of economic issues. Available analytical tools are far more sensitive in identifying and validating antitrust dangers than patent benefits. Absent more explicit legislative guidance, courts are likely to respond to competing harms and benefits to the degree in which they can perceive their force.

These comments are by way of introduction, to set the stage for a discussion of the specific issues which are treated in this chapter. The organization of the chapter replicates the organizational structure heretofore used. First we will examine patents and single-firm conduct, and consider the extent to which antitrust concepts limit the rights of the patentee to exploit his legal monopoly. Next, the chapter will discuss horizontal restraints in the exploitation of the patent monopoly, investigating the applicability of both the *per se* concept and the rule of reason to licensing and other restraints. Finally, there will be a brief overview of situations where patents are asserted as a defense to vertical arrangements otherwise violative of the antitrust laws.

PART B. SINGLE-FIRM ANTITRUST VIOLATIONS AND THE PATENT LAWS

§ 178. The Conduct Element in Section 2 Offenses and Its Relation to Policies for the Acquisition of Patents

Chapter 2 stressed the two elements involved in monopolizing—possession of monopoly power and exclusionary conduct deliberately engaged in to obtain, hold, or extend monopoly power. We also saw that the offense of attempting to monopolize entails two elements, a

---

15. See generally, W. Bowman supra note 11.

specific intent to acquire monopoly power and conduct which threatens to achieve that end. Thus, in each of these Sherman Act Section 2 offenses, there is a conduct element which, vague though it may be, has as its core that outreach for power which we have called "exclusionary conduct."

The basic law of Section 2 remains unchanged when it intermeshes with patent law. To establish a violation plaintiff must show either monopoly power plus exclusionary conduct or specific intent to monopolize plus exclusionary conduct.[1] Existence of a patent is much less relevant to the power issues than might at first be supposed. A patent, although creating a legal monopoly of the patented art, does not do away with the need to show possession or intent to acquire that degree of market power called monopoly.[2] The existence of monopoly power cannot be inferred merely from the possession of one or more patents. The protected invention or process may be very narrow. By excluding others from it the patentee may attain very little market power, for there may be numerous other products or processes not covered by the patent which are commercially feasible substitutes.[3] On the other hand, even a single patent may convey sufficient power to constitute a monopoly. If a patent covered a product for which there were no close substitute, the patent would comprehend a whole "product market" and the patentee could, through the patent, exclude all others. So too, if a patent covered a process which was the only commercially feasible one for making products constituting a product market, it would convey monopoly power. Thus, proof that a patent exists does not prove monopoly power; the relevant market and the power of defendant must be proven independently, just as in cases where defendant's power is predicated on other entry barriers.

But existence of one or more patents may well be relevant to the proof of the conduct element in a Section 2 case, whether the charge be monopolizing or attempting to monopolize. If a single patent or a group of patents do comprehend a product market, or if they, along with other barriers, are enough to exclude others, the process of acquiring the patents would constitute exclusionary conduct in fact. Such conduct gives rise, therefore, to that clash to which we have eluded.

In attempting to resolve that clash it is necessary to discuss a variety of practices relating to the acquisition and use of patents. In all instances inquiry will focus on whether the practice partakes of those qualities which supply the conduct element for a Section 2 violation. When it does it will be characterized as "exclusionary." The

1. Walker Process Equip., Inc. v. Food Mach. & Chem. Corp., 382 U.S. 172, 86 S.Ct. 347, 15 L.Ed.2d 247 (1965).

2. Id.

3. United States v. E. I. Du Pont De Nemours & Co., 351 U.S. 377, 76 S.Ct. 994, 100 L.Ed. 1264 (1956).

discussion will ignore the two alternative issues—one or both of which any single firm case under Section 2 must also present—the existence of monopoly power, or the specific intent to achieve it. Our inquiry, in short, is whether conduct which has exclusionary effects in fact will be shielded by the patent law so that it does not constitute exclusionary conduct, within the meaning of that concept as it is used in determining whether Section 2 is violated. When this inquiry is completed, we shall turn to a related one—whether, and the extent to which, Section 7 of the Clayton Act or Section 5 of the FTC Act may provide more rigorous checks on patent acquisition policy.

§ 179. Circumstances Under Which Patent Acquisitions May Constitute Exclusionary Conduct

a. In General

The mere fact that a firm has acquired a patent, whether by application and grant or by assignment from the patentee, does not of itself constitute monopolization, even when the patent conveys monopoly power in the economic sense. The Patent Code authorizes a monopoly of the patented invention; it would diminish the Code unduly to construe it as subject to the implicit limitation that legal monopoly was to be countenanced only in those instances where the patentee would not gain monopoly power in the economic sense.[1] Nor does the acquisition of monopoly power through patents become exclusionary in the Section 2 sense merely because the power is attained through an accumulation of several patents,[2] at least in those situations where the patents are acquired through internal research and invention.[3] It would also be an unwarranted limitation on the Patent Code to read it as permitting (in reference to any particular technology) only one patent to a customer. All of the practices so far discussed—the acquisition of one or more patents by grant or purchase—are, in terms, sanctioned by the Code. To forbid them whenever they tended to create monopoly power would not only reduce the incentives to innovation which the Code creates but would rather blatantly undercut the implicit presuppositions of the patent system. For these reasons, any competing and seemingly conflicting implication in the Sherman Act must give way.

But that wonderful lawyer's word, "mere," so useful in qualifying the general statements immediately above, correctly implies that

---

1. Cf. Automatic Radio Mfg. Co. v. Hazeltine Research, Inc., 339 U.S. 827, 834, 70 S.Ct. 894, 898, 94 L.Ed. 1312, 1319 (1950). See also Section 261 of the Patent Code which recognizes acquisition from the inventor. 66 Stat. 911, 35 U.S.C.A. § 261.

2. Automatic Radio Mfg. Co. v. Hazeltine Research, Inc., 339 U.S. 827, 70 S. Ct. 894, 94 L.Ed. 1312 (1950).

3. Cf. Dollac Corp. v. Margon Corp., 164 F.Supp. 41 (D.N.J.1958), aff'd on other grounds 275 F.2d 202 (3d Cir. 1960); United States v. United Shoe Mach. Corp., 110 F.Supp. 295, 333 (D. Mass.1953), aff'd per curiam 347 U.S. 521, 74 S.Ct. 699, 98 L.Ed. 910 (1954).

the doctrine those statements announce is a limited one. The fact that all patent acquisitions leading to power are not exclusionary does not mean that none are. The acquisition of a patent, like the acquisition of any other species of property, can be characterized as exclusionary—as constituting the conduct element in a single-firm Section 2 offense—under circumstances where it meets the basic test for exclusionary conduct laid down in nonpatent cases.[4] A patent acquisition policy is exclusionary when it is not an "honestly industrial" expression of "superior skill or industry," but represents a deliberate effort to preempt others, in the sense that the defendant could have avoided following the policy without acting in an economically irrational manner, or in a way inconsistent with its own self-interest.

The propositions which apply are general, the same ones applicable to the acquisition of any other scarce resource. If an acquisition of such a resource, whatever it may be, is not essential to a firm's own profitable development but has, as a major purpose or effect, inhibition upon the development of others, it is exclusionary.[5] Consider, for example, a firm with a monopoly on the production of aluminum. The acquisition by this manufacturer of sources of raw material would not of itself be exclusionary, even if part of a long series of acquisitions. But if such a firm were to acquire bauxite mines excessive of its current or reasonably foreseeable needs, if it were to stockpile ore sources, taking them off the market with the purpose or the effect of excluding actual or potential competitors, such conduct would be exclusionary.[6] So in the case of patent acquisitions. At one extreme, there could be no objection if a firm with monopoly power were to invent through its research team (or even if it were to take a patent license from the outside inventor) a new process which increased efficiency.[7] But a different reaction would be warranted if such a firm adopted the policy of outbidding all others and purchasing outright every patent remotely relating to its technology, whether the invention seemed usable by it or not. If in that way it built up an impregnable network of patents, many of which it did not need or

---

4. Walker Process Equip., Inc. v. Food Mach. & Chem. Corp., 382 U.S. 172, 86 S.Ct. 347, 15 L.Ed.2d 247 (1965); United States v. Singer Mfg. Co., 347 U.S. 174, 83 S.Ct. 1773, 10 L.Ed.2d 823 (1963); United States v. United States Gypsum Co., 333 U.S. 364, 68 S.Ct. 525, 92 L.Ed. 746 (1948); Transparent-Wrap Mach. Corp. v. Stokes & Smith Co., 329 U.S. 637, 646–47, 67 S.Ct. 610, 615–16, 91 L.Ed. 563, 570–71 (1947); Kobe, Inc., v. Dempsey Pump Co., 97 F.Supp. 342 (D.Okl.1951), aff'd 198 F.2d 416 (10th Cir. 1952); United States v. General Elec. Co. (Lamps), 82 F.Supp. 753 (D.N.J.1949); United States v. Vehicular Parking, Ltd., 54 F.Supp. 828, 839 (D.Del.1944); United States v. Hartford-Empire Co., 46 F.Supp. 541 (N.D.Ohio, 1942) mod. 323 U.S. 386, 65 S.Ct. 373, 89 L.Ed. 322 (1945); Stewart-Warner Corp. v. Staley, 42 F.Supp. 140, 146 (W.D.Pa.1941). The general tests applicable to determine whether conduct is exclusionary for Section 2 purposes are discussed in Chapter 2, Part D, supra.

5. United States v. Aluminum Co. of America, 148 F.2d 416 (2d Cir. 1945).

6. Id.

7. See cases cited in note 3 supra.

use, and thus effectively foreclosed entry, there would be no hesitation in labeling the conduct exclusionary.[8] Conduct like that would be exclusionary in fact and could be forbidden without mandating economically irrational or self-defeating behavior. Thus, it would meet the basic test, derived from *Alcoa,* for being labeled as exclusionary in the Section 2 sense. Here, antitrust values are obviously and strongly engaged and it is strained, at best, to find any policy emanating from the patent law which suggests that this unique species of property can with impunity be used in blatantly anticompetitive ways.

Although we have hypothesized only at the extremes, the principles are clear enough at an abstract level. That there will be hard cases in the range between the benchmarks does not impeach the principle. A patent acquisition policy which is a rational expression of ordinary, self-regarding business policy should not be labeled exclusionary merely because it results in or contributes to the acquisition of market power. A patent acquisition policy which so far exceeds in outreach the rational expression of a firm's own need, a policy which in intent seems to focus less on gaining access to technology useful to the firm than on discouraging and foreclosing others from technology which they might use to compete, or which in effect is discernibly more hostile to competition than the firm's reasonable needs require, is an exclusionary policy. Many factors may be relevant in making the characterization. The Attorney General's Antitrust Committee Report suggests attention to the nature, number and value of patents acquired, whether the patent would be used by the inventor or the assignee, and whether the acquisition tends to resolve a conflict between patentees as to validity or infringement.[9]

The case law, though slight, is consistent with the analysis here proposed. In *United Shoe Machinery,*[10] the government challenged as exclusionary the accumulation of in excess of 2,000 patents. The bulk of these had been yielded from the firm's research program, but a significant number had been obtained by assignment from others, a course the firm defended as needed to avoid infringement suits and to settle controversies. Although it depended primarily on other exclusionary practices in finding defendant guilty of monopolization, the court also pointed to these practices and remonstrated that any legitimate purpose defendant had for access to outside patents could have been achieved by taking non-exclusive licenses.[11] That case involved taking assignments of patents granted to outsiders as well as patents

---

8. Id. See also United States v. Hartford-Empire Co., 46 F.Supp. 541 (N.D. Ohio 1942), mod. 323 U.S. 386, 65 S.Ct. 373, 89 L.Ed. 322 (1945); United States v. Vehicular Parking, Ltd., 54 F.Supp. 828 (D.Del.1944); Stewart-Warner Corp. v. Staley, 42 F.Supp. 140 (W.D.Pa.1941).

9. Report of the Attorney General's National Committee to Study the Antitrust Laws 227 (1955).

10. 110 F.Supp. 295 (D.Mass.1953), aff'd per curiam 347 U.S. 521, 74 S.Ct. 699, 98 L.Ed. 910 (1954).

11. 110 F.Supp. at 333.

yielded from research supported by the firm. The Attorney General's Report implies that accumulation based entirely on internal research is never exclusionary.[12] There is, to be sure, a strong initial resistance to characterizing a firm's own inventions as exclusionary, regardless of how many there may be. Since the purpose of the patent law is to encourage innovation by protecting inventions, one feels intuitively that the process of invention, application and grant, at least, ought to be safe from antitrust challenge.[13] Yet the logic of the matter may bid for a different response. If one views the relevant process not as inventing and patenting but, more broadly, as making decisions about the level and direction of investment in research and development, the initial abhorrence to the notion that inventing and obtaining patents can violate Section 2 diminishes. A massive R & D program could clearly meet both aspects of the *Alcoa* standard for exclusionary conduct: it could be exclusionary in fact, and it could be more massive (in terms of the size of the resources invested) and broader (in terms of the kinds of research attempted) than reasonably necessary to a firm which is merely acting rationally in its own economic self-interest.

These, it must be conceded, are vague concepts, concepts for which there is no obvious standard of measurement; that, rather than any theoretical difficulty in saying that R & D cannot be exclusionary, is what should make courts hesitate to label internal research as violative of Section 2. But the problem is not one that cannot be grappled with, at least in its extreme manifestations; it is, really, much like the problem we have considered with respect to "excessive" advertising.[14] Research investment involves judgments about what areas for exploration are most fruitful, what the likelihood, time, and expense-over-time of success will be, and judgments about how sharply future successes should be discounted. For any firm there is obviously an exceedingly wide range within which a rational policy might fall. But decisions about research, like other decisions, are made in a context and against a tradition. They are not utterly intuitive and subjective; they are rational actions which are capable of being rationally reviewed. If a decision about the level and scope of a research program were so extreme that the consensus of reasonable people knowledgeable about the industry would see it as whimsical, except for its entry inhibiting qualities, it would be appropriate to label it as exclusionary. The problems of judgment would be not different in kind from those involved in determining, say, whether a program in acquiring ore sources was excessive and unreasonable and thus exclusionary. Moreover, objective confirmation might be found if the program yielded numerous patents not practiced by the inven-

---

12. Report of the Attorney General's National Committee to Study the Antitrust Laws 226 (1955).

13. See Dollac Corp. v. Margon Corp., 164 F.Supp. 41, 62 (D.N.J.1958).

14. See §§ 43–44 supra.

tor, but merely used by it to add to the barricade. Also, subjective indications might be available: direct or indirect expressions of management interest in maintaining the program at a level discouraging to others. If an R & D program clearly has exclusionary characteristics in the sense here discussed, a court should no more hesitate to label it as exclusionary than it would to label as exclusionary a program based on the purchase of inventions.

Indeed, when patent policy is exclusionary the two aspects, invention and purchase, can be expected to go hand in hand, as they did in *United Shoe Machinery*. There will likely be a policy of R & D which, upon analysis against the industry context, appears in purpose or effect to be aimed at discouraging entry either by raising the needed scale for entry, or by blocking access to necessary technology, or both; there will likely be in addition a policy of acquiring patents from others in forms (assignment or exclusive license rather than nonexclusive licenses) which permit exclusion of others, and in quantities calculated to have a wide exclusionary impact.

b. *Fraudulent Patent Acquisition*

The process through which patents are granted entails filing an application with the patent office, specifying and describing the invention sufficiently to disclose it fully, and an examination of and decision upon the application by a patent examiner, who must evaluate whether the technology claimed meets standards of inventiveness, whether it is new and useful, and whether it is adequately disclosed. At times there is a competing application which does or may comprehend the same invention; if so, an "interference" is declared, which gives each claimant an opportunity to challenge the other's claims and to establish his own priority. The application proceeding is investigatory, not adversary in nature. The opportunity for and temptation to engage in frauds, such as the suppression of evidence of a prior practice which might be held to have placed the claimed invention in the public domain, are high, and applicants at times succumb.[15]

It is settled law that fraudulent conduct in obtaining a patent is exclusionary in the Section 2 sense.[16] The integrity of the patent sys-

---

15. Walker Process Equip., Inc. v. Food Mach. & Chem. Corp., 382 U.S. 172, 86 S.Ct. 347, 15 L.Ed.2d 247 (1965); United States v. Singer Mfg. Co., 347 U.S. 174, 83 S.Ct. 1773, 10 L.Ed.2d 823 (1963); Precision Instrument Mfg. Co. v. Automotive Maintenance Mach. Co., 324 U.S. 806, 65 S.Ct. 993, 89 L.Ed. 1381 (1945); American Cyanamid Co. v. FTC, 363 F.2d 757 (6th Cir. 1966); Monsanto Co. v. Rohm & Haas Co., 312 F.Supp. 778 (E.D.Pa.1970), aff'd 456 F.2d 592 (3d Cir. 1972), cert. denied 407 U.S. 934, 92 S.Ct. 2463, 32 L. Ed.2d 817. See the discussion in E. Rockefeller, Antitrust Questions and Answers 359–66 (1974). Cf. Struthers Scientific & Int'l Corp. v. General Foods Corp., 334 F.Supp. 1329 (D.Del. 1971) (fraudulent procurement, without evidence of enforcement, does not give rise to a damage claim).

16. Walker Process Equip. Inc. v. Food Mach. and Chem. Corp., 382 U.S. 172, 86 S.Ct. 347, 15 L.Ed.2d 247 (1965); United States v. Singer Mfg. Co., 347 U.S. 174, 83 S.Ct. 1773, 10 L.Ed.2d 823 (1963).

tem does not require that such conduct be shielded; quite the reverse. Hence, if a firm obtains a monopoly in this manner, it is guilty of monopolizing [17] and, by parity of reasoning, if it intended to do so, and made an attempt which threatened success, it would be guilty of attempted monopolization even if, in the end, it failed to achieve its goal.[18]

Whether any conduct, short of knowingly making false material statements on which the examiner in fact relies, may constitute fraud for these purposes is not entirely clear.[19] Suppose an applicant fails to disclose to the examiner adverse prior art of which he is aware and which he fears the examiner would construe to preclude patentability? Or suppose two parties in an interference proceeding settle, as *Singer*[20] was settled, each in order to avoid the showing against patentability which the other would make if it judged itself the loser on the priority issue? This may be one of those junctures where, given the competing claims of one system, in this instance antitrust,

---

17. Id.

18. See the cases cited in note 15 supra. But see Norton v. Curtiss, 57 C. C.P.A. 1384, 433 F.2d 779, 793 (1970), and Corning Glass Works v. Anchor Hocking Glass Corp., 253 F.Supp. 461 (D.Del.1966), mod. 374 F.2d 473 (3d Cir. 1967) which indicate that in an antitrust action based on fraud in obtaining a patent, the plaintiff must establish that, but for the fraud, no patent would have issued. Courts have dealt with fraudulent acquisitions in two contexts: when a party accused of infringement seeks to defend by attacking patent validity because of fraud, and when fraud in patent procurement is asserted to constitute an antitrust violation. In cases of the first kind, some courts have held that the party attacking validity must show false information given with knowledge of falsity, an intent to deceive, materiality of the false statement in the context of the proceeding, and reliance upon it by the patent office. E.g., Blonder-Tongue Laboratories, Inc. v. University of Illinois Foundation, 422 F.2d 769 (7th Cir. 1970), rev'd on other grounds, 402 U.S. 313, 91 S.Ct. 1434, 28 L.Ed.2d 788 (1971); Waterman-Bic Pen Corp. v. Sheaffer Pen Co., 267 F.Supp. 849 (D. Del.1967); Tractor Supply Co. v. International Harvester Co., 155 USPQ 420 (N.D.Ill.1967). Others, however, have questioned whether a patentee ought to be permitted to enforce a patent when it is shown that deliberate falsehoods were tendered in the application proceeding, regardless of nice judgments about their materiality and whether they were essential to the grant. E.g., Ritter v. Rohm & Haas, 271 F.Supp. 313, 342 (S.D.N.Y. 1967); Diamond Internat'l. Corp. v. Walterhoefer, 289 F.Supp. 550 (D.Md. 1968). In Norton v. Curtiss, and in *Corning Glass Works*, supra, the court accepted the second of these approaches as applicable when the question was patent enforceability but said the first should apply where fraud is made the basis, not of a patent defense, but an affirmative antitrust claim. See also Cataphote Corp. v. De Soto Chemical Coatings, Inc., 450 F.2d 769 (9th Cir. 1971), cert. denied 408 U.S. 929, 92 S.Ct. 2497, 33 L.Ed.2d 341 (1972); Beckman Instruments, Inc. v. Chemtronics, Inc., 439 F.2d 1369 (5th Cir.), cert. denied 400 U.S. 956, 91 S.Ct. 353, 27 L.Ed.2d 264 (1970). This view is also taken in American Bar Association, Antitrust Developments (1975). However that may be in monopolization cases, the logic of the matter insists that an attempt to obtain a patent by fraud ought to be enough for attempt to monopolize when, had the attempt been successful, monopoly power would have been gained.

19. See note 18 supra.

20. United States v. Singer Mfg. Co., 374 U.S. 174, 83 S.Ct. 1773, 10 L.Ed.2d 823 (1963).

the other, in this instance patent law, must be analyzed to a greater depth than would otherwise be usual. As a matter of patent law one might argue that the examiner has a duty to examine for prior art and that this, along with possible judicial determination in a later infringement proceedings, is the protection the law affords against an improper grant, not the intrinsically unreliable method of self-confession by the applicant. But if the patent, alone or with other barriers, would confer monopoly power, it may be no excessive concession to antitrust interests to insist that the would-be monopolist turn exceedingly square corners in attaining its government grant. The choices this would put before a firm in such a posture are difficult, surely, but not more difficult on any count than others placed upon powerful firms under the burden of the *Alcoa* test.[21]

c. *Taking an Exclusive License Where a Non-Exclusive License would Avail for Non-Preemptive Ends*

A decision of germinal potential about the circumstances under which acquisition can be characterized as exclusionary is United States v. Singer Manufacturing Company.[22] Singer had pending a patent application which competed with an application of an Italian competitor. The resulting interference proceeding in the Patent Office was settled: Singer conceded priority to the other firm upon its undertaking that the patent would not be enforced against Singer. Later, when Japanese firms threatened entry into the American market, Singer persuaded the Italian firm to assign the patent to Singer which, it was felt, would be better able to enforce it in American courts against the Japanese firms. Noting that even if the original arrangement did not adequately protect Singer's right to use the invention, a non-exclusive license would have done so, the Court concluded that the purpose for the assignment was to end sales by Japanese firms. Since concerted action by the assignor and assignee was entailed, this conduct was held to violate Section 1. That being so, we cannot doubt that it was also "exclusionary" in the special sense relevant for Section 2 analysis, for even the oldest Section 2 cases treat conduct violating Section 1 as exclusionary for Section 2 purposes.[23] Hence, if Singer possessed sufficient power, such an acquisition would have constituted a monopolization or attempt to monopolize, as well as a violation of Section 1.

Singer, of course, was itself a case where considerable power was probably being exercised, and that may explain the Court's response, which might otherwise seem extreme. But even in the context of

21. See the analysis suggested by P. Areeda, Antitrust Analysis, Problems, Text, Cases ¶ 442 (2d ed. 1974).

22. 374 U.S. 174, 83 S.Ct. 1773, 10 L.Ed. 2d 823 (1963).

23. E.g., Standard Oil Co. (N.J.) v. United States, 221 U.S. 1, 31 S.Ct. 502, 55 L.Ed. 619 (1911). See the discussion in United States v. United Shoe Mach. Corp., 110 F.Supp. 295, 341–43 (D.Mass.1953), aff'd per curiam 347 U.S. 521, 74 S.Ct. 699, 98 L.Ed. 910 (1954).

Section 2 it is hard to develop for *Singer* a rationale which is not extremely broad. If a firm possessing or bidding to obtain power may not acquire a patent where its intent is to exclude, it logically follows that virtually any time a firm takes an assignment or buys an exclusive license it is acting in an exclusionary manner. That, of course, is to push the doctrine further than any court has yet done, further even, than may be taken as the implication of Judge Wyzanski's language in *United Shoe Machinery,* which discriminated sharply between gaining access to prevalent technology in ways that excluded others and in ways that did not.[24]

d. Patent Accumulations Which Are Used to Organize An Entire Industry

The classic situation of exclusionary patent policy is exemplified by *Hartford-Empire*.[25] The defendant firms accumulated patents by internal development and pooled and cross licensed both conflicting, complementary and competing patents. In the end, about 600 patents were brought under concerted control and were used to divide fields between the defendants, to assign territories, and to maintain prices. Utilizing the accumulated patents, defendants regimented an industry. Relying on the program of patent accumulation and pooling the trial court inferred an intent to dominate the industry and adjudicated that Sections 1 and 2 were both violated.

The factual summary and statement of principle above rely upon evocative words which characterize myriad events over a period of years, any one of which—or even any discrete series of which—viewed separately and evaluated in terms of its own purpose and effect would be ambiguous. There is something in the nature of the case which invites these sweeping characterizations.[26] But the case can be read with greater particularity. There is, for example, a considerable difference between pooling complementary or blocking patents (which can only be effectively used if used together) and pooling competing ones. *Hartford-Empire* involved the latter as well as the former. There is, indeed, a distinction worth noting between pooling competing patents in the settlement of genuine disputes about validity, priority and infringement and pooling them when none of these elements is present. The case involved the latter practice, in which the justification for pooling is weakest. There is also a difference between accumulating a great array of patents and then licensing them unrestrictively and pooling and then licensing restrictively to divide markets; the latter was done here. *Hartford-Empire*, then, should not

---

24. United States v. United Shoe Mach. Corp., 110 F.Supp. 295, 333 (D.Mass. 1953), aff'd per curiam 347 U.S. 521, 74 S.Ct. 699, 98 L.Ed. 910 (1954).

25. United States v. Hartford-Empire Co., 46 F.Supp. 541 (N.D.Ohio 1942), mod., 323 U.S. 386, 65 S.Ct. 373, 89 L. Ed. 322 (1945).

26. See P. Areeda, Antitrust Analysis, Problems, Text, Cases ¶¶ 448–449 (2d Ed. 1974); W. Bowman, Patent and Antitrust Law 218–223, 225, 226 (1973).

be read to hold that power alone may be challenged under Section 2 so long as it is predicated upon a vast array of patents. All one can say for sure on the basis of the case is that the courts will at times take a plenary view and will not disdain the values of hindsight in picking out the junctures where the monopolist had choices to make and selected the course leading to power.

The lines which demark the permissible from the unlawful in comprehensive accumulations are difficult to spell out. Despite this, some guides can be discerned. First, it is appropriate in evaluating patent accumulations to take a long view. Though a transaction or series of them may seem innocuous or small in its adverse effects, it may have a different appearance seen as part of a sequence spanning a period of years. Viewed as the product of a dynamic industry history, an existing anticompetitive structure and current inhibitions against entry may appear to be partially attributable to patent policies followed over the years, however much other developments or conduct may have contributed. Second, exclusionary conduct is more easily identified—and thus more likely to be found—where several firms within an industry cooperate in the exploitation of patents. A patent pool may be quite innocuous as a part of a settlement negotiation; but no matter how a pool was formed it may also be in purpose and effect a means of gaining control over a market. In deciding whether accumulations are exclusionary, courts will look at the structure which issues out of the patent arrangements and will consider whether, absent these arrangements, competition would be significantly more intense. If so, the arrangements are properly characterized as exclusionary in the Section 2 sense. Finally, we must advert to the situation in which the accumulations do of themselves confer substantial power over a relevant market. Assume, for example, that an industry consists of five firms each with a patent which gives access to a technology, one of which is essential to participation in the market. If one firm takes assignments of all of these patents, or if a pool is created to bring them under common control, a monopoly has been established just as clearly as if all firms participating in the industry entered into a price and output cartel, or merged. Just as we would say that such a cartel or merger would be exclusionary conduct—nonessential conduct tending to the exclusion of other firms—so we should say that such an accumulation or pool is exclusionary. It is exclusionary in fact and it is avoidable and plainly unnecessary to constructive development and growth.[27] If the patents are pooled in the course of settling a dispute as to priority, validity or infringement, there is, of course, an efficiency argument to be made for allowing the pool—it saves the cost of dispute and its resolution by

---

27. See United States v. Krasnov, 143 F.Supp. 184 (E.D.Pa.1956), aff'd per curiam 355 U.S. 5, 78 S.Ct. 34, 2 L. Ed.2d 21 (1957).

litigation.²⁸ But just as relatively minor efficiencies would not serve to shield a merger to monopoly from the charge of being exclusionary, so these relatively minor efficiencies ought not to avail here.

§ 180. The Application of Section 5 of the FTC Act and Section 7 of the Clayton Act to Patent Acquisitions

Conduct which violates Sections 1 or 2 of Sherman violates Section 5 of the FTC Act.¹ But Section 5 does not leave off at the edge of the Sherman Act; it extends on, under the discretionary guidance of the FTC, to interdict other practices having aspects which may cause unease to a conscience highly sensitive to disturbing tensions in market structure or conduct.² All this considered, one may hazard the judgment that conduct which would be characterized as exclusionary, in the sense relevant to Section 2, may be held to violate Section 5, although due to the absence of sufficient market power to constitute monopoly or threaten success in an effort to obtain it, Section 2 itself has not been violated. This issue is, of course, not peculiar to patents; it could present itself with respect to any conduct having an exclusionary thrust or potential. For example, to inquire whether advertising is excessive enough to be called exclusionary could be to ask whether it violates Section 5.

Section 7 of the Clayton Act is a different matter; it has, at least in potential, a unique relationship to patent acquisition policy, a relationship which would be utterly lacking with respect to exclusionary conduct like excessive advertising. Section 7 forbids one corporation to acquire assets of another where the effect may be to substantially lessen competition or to tend to create a monopoly. The section is of primary concern in evaluating the legality of mergers,³ but it has application here because a patent is "property," ⁴ and hence an

---

28. Compare Standard Oil Co. (Indiana) v. United States, 283 U.S. 163, 51 S.Ct 421, 75 L.Ed. 926 (1931), discussed infra § 188(c).

1. E.g., Atlantic Refining Co. v. FTC, 381 U.S. 357, 369, 85 S.Ct. 1498, 1506, 14 L.Ed.2d 443, 453 (1965); FTC v. Cement Institute, 333 U.S. 683, 693, 68 S.Ct. 793, 800, 92 L.Ed. 1010, 1030 (1948); Times-Picayune Publishing Co. v. United States, 345 U.S. 594, 609, 73 S.Ct. 872, 880–81, 97 L.Ed. 1277, 1290 (1953); FTC v. Motion Picture Advertising Serv. Co., 344 U.S. 392, 394, 73 S.Ct. 361, 363, 97 L.Ed. 426, 430 (1953); Fashion Originators' Guild v. FTC, 312 U.S. 457, 61 S.Ct. 703, 85 L.Ed. 949 (1941).

2. FTC v. Brown Shoe Co., 384 U.S. 316, 320–22, 86 S.Ct. 1501, 1503–05, 16 L.Ed.2d 587, 590–92 (1966); Atlantic Refining Co. v. FTC, 381 U.S. 357, 85 S.Ct. 1498, 14 L.Ed.2d 443 (1965). Cf. FTC v. Sperry & Hutchinson, 405 U.S. 233, 92 S.Ct. 898, 31 L.Ed.2d 170 (1972), which indicates that the FTC, in considering whether conduct is an "unfair method of competition", may implement values which extend beyond the letter and even the spirit of the antitrust laws, but that it must disclose analysis and evaluations sufficiently to facilitate judicial review.

3. See Chapter 7 infra.

4. Dole Valve Co. v. Perfection Bar Equipment, Inc., 311 F.Supp. 459 (N.D.Ill.1970). Cf. United States v. Lever Bros., 216 F.Supp. 887 (S.D.N.Y.1963); Transparent-Wrap Mach. Corp. v. Stokes and Smith Co., 329 U.S. 637, 67 S.Ct. 610, 91 L.Ed. 563 (1947); Wilson v. Rousseau, 45 U.S. (4 How.) 646, 11 L.Ed.1141 (1846).

"asset." Thus, when a patent is assigned by one corporation to another the transaction invokes the statutory test. A patent (and also a trademark, copyright, license, contract right, or other species of intangible property) constitutes an "asset" within the meaning of the section.[5]

No doubt there is a limit to the intangible perceptions that can fairly be called "property" and hence an "asset." Suppose for example a corporation instead of assigning a patent taught another corporation secret "know-how." One court, while declining summary judgment for defendant upon a complaint alleging that such conduct violated Section 7, expressed doubt that "know-how" could constitute as "asset" comprehended by Section 7.[6] An effort to gauge those limits would need to take account of more than merely the customary content of concepts like "property" and "assets" when used as instruments of social policy. The scope of the concept as used in Section 7 ought to be defined with a view of the utility of inclusion or exclusion. Section 7 is unique as a policy resource principally because of the richness and complexity of its analytical development in applying the Clayton Act standard about injury to competition. Section 7 makes the standard, "may be substantially to lessen competition, or to tend to create a monopoly" govern the lawfulness of corporate asset acquisitions.[7] If a bundle of rights or privileges, asserted to be an "asset" within the meaning of Section 7, is so different in nature from corporate acquisitions concededly involving "assets" that the body of Section 7 precedents about competitive effect ceases to be useful, then the incentive to label that bundle an "asset" for Section 7 purposes is greatly reduced.

Whatever the limits of the asset clause in Section 7, they are not transcended by the assignment of a patent. A patent is property in a common sense and the competitive effects of a patent acquisition can be analyzed in ways which do draw upon analysis of competitive effects of acquisition of other intangible assets such as copyrights and trademarks, which facilitate exclusion of others, or even tangible assets such as scarce resources, which have that same thrust. On principle as well as authority we must concede Section 7 a special role in analyzing patent acquisitions. But suppose that the acquiring firm

---

5. Automated Bldg. Components, Inc. v. Trueline Truss Co., 318 F.Supp. 1252 (D.Or.1970); Western Geophysical Co. v. Bolt Associates, 305 F.Supp. 1248 (D.Conn.1969); Smith-Corona Marchant, Inc. v. American Photocopy Equipment Co., 217 F.Supp. 39 (S.D. N.Y.1963). See also United States v. Lever Bros., 216 F.Supp. 887 (S.D.N. Y.1963); United States v. Columbia Pictures Corp., 189 F.Supp. 153 (S.D. N.Y.1960); Farm Journal Inc., 53 F. T.C. 26 (1956). See § 202 infra.

6. United States v. Allied Chem. Corp., 1964 CCH Trade Cas. ¶ 71,193 (S.D.N. Y.). But see United States v. CIBA Corp., 1970 CCH Trade Cas. ¶ 73,269 (S.D.N.Y.), which groups know-how with patents and trademarks as being an "asset" within the meaning of Section 7.

7. See § 202 infra.

takes not an assignment (which is of course a conveyance of the patent) but a license—either an exclusive one which enables it to exclude others, or a non-exclusive one which assures access but no power to exclude. Should either of these transactions be treated as an "asset" acquisition? If the analysis which requires that an assignment of a patent be treated as an acquisition of an asset is correct, then acceptance of an exclusive license should be treated no differently. Conceptually, the licensee has acquired rights in, and hence a "part" of, the asset, the patent; operationally, the taking of an exclusive license places the licensee for purposes of evaluating competitive impact in a position similar, if not virtually identical to, that of an assignee. The exlcusive licensee, like an assignee, need not tolerate intruders on the technology, other than the licensor itself.

With respect to the non-exclusive license, the position is less obvious. Conventional concepts about property might distinguish between an exclusive and a non-exclusive license, though not in ways that seem critical here. But there is a blatant operational distinction which raises grave doubt about calling a non-exclusive license an "asset," within the reach of Section 7—namely that the licensee who holds it does not gain the potential to exclude. Perhaps the fine response would be to treat both an exclusive and a non-exclusive license as being assets, but to take full account of the distinctions between the two in the course of application of the competitive effects clause of Section 7. Taking an exclusive license could obviously have adverse effects while taking a non-exclusive one might not.

It seems, therefore, that Section 7 has a particular impact in cases involving the assignment of a patent from or the grant of an exclusive license by one corporation to another. How do we gauge the competitive effect of such a transaction in a manner consistent with other applications of Section 7? We cannot usefully anticipate here the full range of issues about competitive effect which must be explored in the merger chapter.[8] But we can suggest some of the more salient analytical issues which would need to be raised in passing upon whether the effect of a patent assignment or license "may be substantially to lessen competition or to tend to create a monopoly." First, as in merger cases, a market must be defined.[9] Next, it must be determined whether by means of the patent the acquiring firm is able to foreclose competitors or potential competitors from all or a substantial part of that market or is able to put them at a significant disadvantage in competing in that market.[10] In may also be relevant to determine whether the acquisition of the patent, even if not itself threatening a substantial increase in concentration, reinforces a trend within the market toward greater concentration.[11] The point at which the competitive effect forbidden by Section 7 is reached can

---

8. Chapter 7 infra.

9. See § 203 infra.

10. See § 204 infra.

11. Id.

neither be defined with precision nor mechanically determined. There is no need to show any attained reduction of competition, but only that one is threatened. As to the seriousness of the interference threatened, there is plainly no need to show that power of monopoly proportions may be attained or even remotely approached. But there must be more than a mere possibility of competitive injury; all things considered, it must seem more likely than not that injury to competition will eventuate. And the injury foreseen, though it need not be great, must be of sufficient moment to be worthy of the law's concern.

Drawing together these analytical strands, one sees Section 7's special function. Acquisitions made primarily with the purpose or effect of excluding others will be treated as "exclusionary" under Sherman Section 2;[12] but any acquisition of patented technology motivated by its technological advantages and with an intent to use it cannot readily be so characterized.[13] Just here, Section 7 can have an impact. Even though a patented technology is being acquired primarily with intent to use it, if the patents are taken by assignment or exclusive license—that is, in a form excluding others—and if, given an analysis of the present industrial structure and of the dynamic which affected that structure in the past, it is accurate to say that the acquisition is likely to reduce competition discernibly, then a conventional Section 7 analysis indicates that there has been a violation of that section. Indeed, if the acquiring firm had power enough, if it stood in a position to dominate a market, Section 7 might even be read as inhibiting its attaining by license even non-exclusive access to a new and significant technology. This resolution, by constricting the market for the patent in ways adverse to the inventor, might well be viewed as too great a reduction of the value of the patent to be deemed consistent with the policies of the present law. But arguably, any provision by one corporation to another of access to a patent will violate Section 7 if it has a significant, adverse, competitive potential.

§ 181. Patent Enforcement Policy as Exclusionary Conduct

Courts dealing with whether patent policy is exclusionary sometimes forego the effort to pull out and examine separate elements of policy, like acquisition and enforcement; nor do they always carefully ferret out the distinctions between what the record shows the firm to have done and what, without acting in ways inconsistent with its own interests, it might have done which would have been less exclusionary. Rather, they may react in comprehensive and conclusionary terms to a broad sweep of conduct, assuming to detect in the overall pattern some tendency which, unanalyzed in its detail, is then labeled exclusionary.

12. See § 179 supra.   13. Id.

The *Kobe*[1] case will serve to illustrate what occurs. There, plaintiff sued defendant for infringing patents in the oil pumping industry. The defense was patent misuse[2] and a counterclaim was filed alleging monopolization. Defendant's evidence showed that plaintiff had purchased all patents as they appeared in its technology and routinely took from sellers covenants not to compete, and that plaintiff had sued defendant, a would-be competitor, and told all customers about the suit. On this evidence the trial court found patent misuse and monopolization and awarded damages to defendant based upon the financial impact on it of the infringement suit. In affirming, the court of appeals said:

> "Kobe strenuously contends that * * * to allow recovery * * * resulting from the infringement action would be a denial of free access to the courts. * * * The trial court found that Kobe did not institute the infringement action in bad faith but believed that some of its patents were infringed, and that Kobe intended to secure a judgment which would eliminate defendants as competitors * * *.
>
> "* * * [I]f there was nothing more than the bringing of the infringement action, resulting damages could not be recovered, but * * * [t]he facts * * * support a finding that although Kobe believed some of its patents were infringed, the real purpose of the infringement action and the incidental activities * * * was to further the existing monopoly and to eliminate Dempsey as a competitor. The infringement action and the related activities, of course, in themselves were not unlawful, and standing alone would not be sufficient to sustain a claim * * *, but when considered with the entire monopolistic scheme which preceded them we think, as the trial court did, that they may be considered as having been done to give effect to the unlawful scheme. * * * The result of Kobe's infringement action, its verbal and written statements to the trade, was disastrous to the defendants. There was almost a com-

---

1. Kobe, Inc. v. Dempsey Pump Co., 198 F.2d 416 (10th Cir.), cert. denied 344 U.S. 837, 73 S.Ct. 46, 97 L.Ed. 651 (1952).

2. Patent misuse involves the use of patent rights to control competition in unpatented articles or to achieve other unlawful ends. The Court has frequently indicated that quite independently of antitrust law such conduct violates the patent law. When a patent has been misused the Court will refuse to enforce the patent until the misuse has been abated and its effects dissipated. Thus, an allegation that the patentee has misused the patent may serve as a defense in a patent infringement suit. See Motion Picture Patents Co. v. Universal Film Manufacturing Co., 243 U.S. 502, 37 S.Ct. 416, 61 L.Ed. 871 (1917); Morton Salt Co. v. Suppiger, 314 U.S. 488, 62 S.Ct. 402, 86 L.Ed. 363 (1942); Mercoid Corporation v. Mid Continent Investment Co., 320 U.S. 661, 64 S.Ct. 268, 88 L. Ed. 376 (1944). See also 271(d) of the Patent Code of 1952, 35 U.S.C.A. § 271(d), which may ameliorate the rigor of misuse doctrine, as extended in *Mercoid*.

plete boycott of their products. To hold that there was no liability for damages caused by this conduct, though lawful in itself, would permit a monopolizer to smother every potential competitor with litigation * * *."[3]

The language is broad and moralistic, rather than analytical in tone. It should not be disdained for this, as it provides strong and honest clues about what qualities in patent programs courts can be expected to react to negatively. If a patent program, in all of its aspects and manifestations, seems greedy, overreaching and excessive, if would-be competitors seem cast in the role of victims, we may expect the policy to be vulnerable to antitrust attack.[4] Of course, this is not to say that in counselling or predicting litigation outcomes one can rely on such vague, plenary indications; that is a luxury to be left to the courts.

From the point of view of the lawyer or scholar, there is another question to be asked. Where, as in *Kobe*, the pattern of conduct as a whole has a "feel" about it which leads to the intuition that the patent-holder has been acting too aggressively, will it not often be possible, upon analysis, to make out a plausible case of abuse on quite conventional grounds?[5] A firm possessing patents can act unfairly and in ways tending to be excessively exclusionary in the enforcement of those patents, particularly if it possesses an aggregation of patents which bracket a technology.[6] If a firm possesses monopoly power, such conduct will provide the additional element needed to establish monopolization; if a firm does not possess such power, but by its actions threatens to attain it, such conduct constitutes an attempt to monopolize. But there is a dilemma here. Any action to enforce a patent is in a very explicit sense "exclusionary," both in purpose and, if successful, in effect. How, then, do we identify the point at which such conduct, always exclusionary in this literal sense, has become so intractable as to warrant its being called exclusionary in the sense relevant to the establishment of a Section 2 violation?

3. 198 F.2d at 424–25.

4. See, e.g., Switzer Bros. v. Locklin, 297 F.2d 39 (7th Cir. 1961) cert. denied 369 U.S. 851, 82 S.Ct. 935, 8 L.Ed.2d 9 (1962); Lynch v. Magnavox Co., 94 F.2d 883 (9th Cir. 1938); Zegers, Inc. v. Zegers, 1961 CCH Trade Cases ¶ 70,097 (N.D.Ill.); Jacquard Knitting Mach. Co. v. Ordnance Gauge Co., 108 F.Supp. 59 (E.D.Pa.1952), aff'd 213 F.2d 503 (3d Cir. 1954); United States v. Besser Mfg. Co., 96 F.Supp. 304 (E.D.Mich.1951), aff'd 343 U.S. 444, 72 S.Ct. 838, 96 L.Ed. 1063 (1952). Compare Cole v. Hughes Tool Co., 215 F.2d 924 (10th Cir. 1954), cert. denied 348 U.S. 927, 75 S.Ct. 339, 99 L.Ed. 726 (1955); Microtron Corp. v. Minnesota Mining & Mfg. Co., 269 F. Supp. 22 (D.N.J.1967); Malta Mfg. Co. v. Osten, 215 F.Supp. 115 (E.D.Mich. 1963); Sperry Prods. v. Aluminum Co. of America, 171 F.Supp. 901 (N.D. Ohio 1959); Dollac Corp. v. Margon Corp., 164 F.Supp. 41 (D.N.J.1958); Ronson Patents Corp. v. Sparklets Devices, 112 F.Supp. 676 (E.D.Mo.1953). Compare Minnesota Mining & Mfg. Co. v. Berwick Indus., Inc., 1975–1 CCH Trade Cas. ¶ 60,234 (M.D.Pa.1975).

5. Compare Vitamin Technologists, Inc. v. Wisconsin Alumni Research Foundation, 146 F.2d 941, 942–47 (9th Cir.), cert. denied 325 U.S. 876, 65 S.Ct. 1554, 89 L.Ed. 1994 (1945). See also § 179(d), supra.

6. See cases cited in note 2 supra.

We must again return to basics, to those elements which infuse *any* conduct called exclusionary, when that word is given the special meaning to which we here allude. A patent enforcement program is exclusionary, for Section 2 purposes, when this configuration shows itself: it is exclusionary in fact (as any such program, even if ultimately unsuccessful, will tend to be at least in some degree); there are discernibly less exclusionary alternative courses which could have been adopted in enforcing the patents; and these could have been chosen by the firm without its acting irrationally or in ways adverse to its own economic self-interest. Putting it so, let us underscore that this general standard does not require the patentee to forego enforcement, but only requires that it not devise and execute a program for enforcing its patents which tends to be more exclusionary in its impacts than a rational program, designed by a firm seriously interested in protecting its patent rights, need be.[7]

Compare two hypothetical approaches to enforcement, either of which might be taken by a firm with a strong patent position. First, wherever the firm meets in the market a pertinent challenge from a product which, arguably, violates its patent rights, it brings an enforcement action; second, the firm expends a substantial sum to scrutinize every new product in or adjacent to its technology for possible violations of any of its patents and sues for infringement whenever it thinks it has found one. The first approach is a rational, self-interested enforcement policy; the second is more exclusionary than need be; hence, it is exclusionary in the Section 2 sense.

Indeed, enforcement policy can be excessive even without the development of such a scanning mechanism. To protect itself adequately, no firm need stand always alert with its finger on the litigation button, nor need it sue for infringement every time there comes to its attention any possible violation of any of its patents, without regard to commercial significance, and without sufficient investigation to make a confident judgment about the likely litigation outcome.[8] Nor need a firm which holds patents assert violations of all of them whenever it sues, leaving to the defendant during the tedious processes of discovery the task of sorting out which patents, if any, are serious obstacles to its continued use of the technology which it claims. These are all examples of conduct which can be seen to place higher barriers around the technology than the patentee's legitimate interests warrant. Others might include telling the trade that a given

---

7. By and large the cases are consistent with the doctrinal statement in text. See, e.g., Kobe, Inc. v. Dempsey Pump Co., 198 F.2d 416 (10th Cir.), cert. denied 344 U.S. 837, 73 S.Ct. 46, 97 L.Ed. 651 (1952). Dairy Foods, Inc. v. Dairy Maid Prods. Corp., 297 F.2d 805 (7th Cir. 1961); United States v. Besser Mfg. Co. and other cases cited in note 2 supra.

8. See e.g., Switzer Bros., Inc. v. Locklin, 297 F.2d 39 (7th Cir. 1961), cert. denied 369 U.S. 851, 82 S.Ct. 935, 8 L.Ed.2d 9 (1962). Compare Eversharp Inc. v. Fisher Pen Co., 204 F.Supp. 649, 675 (N.D.Ill.1961); United States v. Besser Mfg. Co., 96 F.Supp. 304 (E.D.Mich.1951), aff'd 343 U.S. 444, 72 S. Ct. 838, 96 L.Ed. 1063 (1952).

firm is an infringer and urging customers not to buy from it, labeling products as being covered by designated patents which are not in fact used in the product, and the like.

§ 182. License Restrictions (and Restrictions on Assignees) as Exclusionary Conduct

By granting a license the patentee shares the monopoly; by imposing license restrictions the competition which might otherwise result can be confined. As we shall see in Part C, some license restrictions are *per se* unlawful under Section 1, while many are lawful unless, in the circumstances, an unreasonable restraint can be shown.[1] Since conduct violating Section 1 is always exclusionary conduct within the meaning relevant for Section 2,[2] any license restriction which violates Section 1 must be characterized as exclusionary. If a patentee were to obtain, protect or exploit monopoly power by such a license restriction, the patentee would be guilty of monopolization; and if the patentee did not possess monopoly power but by use of such a restriction threatened to obtain it, the patentee would be guilty of attempting to monopolize. In this limited sense, all of the materials in Part C are also relevant for a Section 2 analysis.

But the Section 1 test for the legality of license restrictions does not exhaust the question whether a particular restriction is exclusionary for Section 2 purposes. Avoidable conduct which is exclusionary in fact is exclusionary for purposes of applying Section 2 whether or not the conduct also violates Section 1.[3] There is then no doctrinal reason which precludes a patent license restriction from supplying the conduct element for a Section 2 violation even though it passes muster under Section 1. A price restricted license, for example, may not violate Section 1.[4] But such a license would be exclusionary in the sense that it reduced competition. Hence, if it were used by a firm with substantial market power, logic would require that it be labeled an attempt to monopolize or monopolization. Other license restrictions, though not violating Section 1, may also be exclusionary in this sense. The point to remember is that any restriction must be analyzed under Section 2, independently of Section 1, whenever it is used by a firm with substantial power.

1. §§ 183–191 infra.
2. See United States v. United Shoe Mach. Corp., 110 F.Supp. 295, 341–43 (D.Mass.1953), aff'd per curiam 347 U.S. 521, 74 S.Ct. 699, 98 L.Ed. 910 (1954).
3. Id.
4. § 185 infra.

PART C. PATENT ARRANGEMENTS CONSTITUTING CONTRACTS, COMBINATIONS AND CONSPIRACIES IN RESTRAINT OF TRADE

§ 183. Introduction

It is generally thought socially advantageous for a patentee to license a patent rather than to practice it alone, at least if the licenses contain no resale or comparable restrictions.[1] A policy of licensing, especially if numerous licenses are granted, is said to have several beneficial effects. First, the patent, whether for a process or a product, may be exploited more fully, used in all or more of the places where it is cheaper than its near substitutes. If licensees in the same industry as the patentee regard the patented technology as preferable to unpatented alternatives so that, but for the patentee's power to exclude them, they would use that technology, it is socially advantageous that they be accorded through licensing the right to choose the technology they would prefer. If the licensees are in different industries from the patentee, a license may be the only feasible way of extending the new technology to those industries at all; the patentee itself may be quite unready to expand into every field where the patent would be useful. Secondly, by making knowledge of the new technology more diffuse, licensing may heighten competition, either immediately or in the future.[2] If the patent is so valuable in any industry that firms not having the technology it covers would be forced out, licensing is the only way to avoid monopoly and widespread licensing the only way to avoid oligopoly. True, a patentee in such an industry could collect his full monopoly return in royalties, leaving licensees to earn only a fair return. But the situation is dynamic; the existence of two or more participants in the industry will therefore provide to the public some of the advantages of competition even though the patentee is taking a monopoly return through royalties. In striving to outdo each other, the patentee and its licensees may be forced to greater efficiency than the patentee would achieve if it operated alone or through only one or two licensees. Furthermore, there will be several firms, rather than only one or a few, striving to improve the technology—seeking to gain alternative or improvement patents or to attain other innovative efficiencies. Even if the patent is not so important that access to it is essential to participation in the in-

---

1. See generally Baxter, Legal Restrictions on Exploitation of the Patent Monopoly: An Economic Analysis, 76 Yale L.J. 267 (1966); W. Bowman, Patent and Antitrust Law ch. 6 (1973); F. Machlup, An Economic Review of the Patent System, Study No. 15 of the Subcommittee on Patents, Trademarks, & Copyrights of the Senate Judiciary Committee, 85th Cong., 2d Sess. (1958). See also the analysis suggested by M. Handler, H. Blake, R. Pitofsky and H. Goldschmid, Trade Regulation, Cases and Materials 397–98 (1975).

2. See the analysis suggested in P. Areeda, Antitrust Analysis, Problems, Text, Cases ¶ 417 (2d ed. 1974).

dustry, licensing, by making the patented technology more diffuse, may facilitate attempts by licensees to improve upon it, or to "invent around it," so as to be freed of the burden of royalties. Should licensing yield no improvements or alternatives during the life of the patent, the licensing process is nevertheless likely to leave a more competitive structure when the patent expires; licensees will have the know-how to fully exploit the patent and will already be geared up to do so.

But these comments point only to tendencies. It must be conceded—indeed, one should insist—that much is indeterminate and that in any given situation counter tendencies may prevail. For example, a practice of non-licensing might encourage greater effort to "invent around" a useful patent; also, it may do more to encourage challenges to the validity of the patent and, if the patent be invalid, to freeing the mistakenly confined technology. Even the notion that a better base for future competition is created through licensing must be taken with caution, as the base established may be one of firms which have grown used to cooperation, especially if the licenses actually granted contained price or other restrictions. It thus appears that analysis cannot in general or even in particular cases produce firm conclusions about whether or not licensing would be socially preferable. Despite these qualifications most who explore these issues end with the inference that, in general, licensing should be taken as a social advantage.

Yet even that leap of faith does not solve all problems or end the inquiry. To conclude that in general licensing is preferable to non-licensing and that it therefore ought to be encouraged, does not take the matter very far. It is necessary to consider at each relevant juncture for choice whether one policy alternative would tend to encourage licensing more, or discourage it less, than would another—an inquiry which may at times prove rather indeterminate. And supposing that it is concluded that a particular policy will encourage licensing, the next question is whether that policy will have other adverse effects on competition which would offset or even outweigh any encouragement to competition which may be the product of the license-encouraging policy.

What kinds of costs might be associated with license-encouraging policies? As noted earlier, licenses may contain restrictions, horizontal or vertical, which tend to diminish competition. For example, a license may purport to fix the prices or territories of the patentee's licensee-competitors, or may mandate that the licensee fix the resale prices of its buyers. The license may even perpetuate the patentee's control of the technology by obliging the licensee to assign to the patentee any improvement patent. Many of these restrictions raise serious antitrust concerns. The issue is whether the public interest in encouraging licenses is sufficiently strong to warrant rules which allow licenses with restrictions such as these despite the possible negative effects of the restrictions.

But there is yet another important issue. One may insist that to analyze and balance possible harms and benefits to competition is a task calculated to exhaust the analyst; but one may not claim that even this inquiry will exhaust the topic. If the fine judgment is that there is an excess of harm to competition and, therefore, that antitrust interests press for restricting the patentee, one must still know whether quite different policies emanating from the patent law countenance the particular license restrictions independently of their effect upon competition. There may, in short, be a conflict between patent and antitrust and, if so, a need for further analysis to resolve it.[3]

There are temptations to escape these opaque issues by adopting what Areeda has called "easy answers."[4] At one extreme it can be argued that a patent is intended to grant a monopoly reward in order to encourage innovation and that any license restriction, since it enhances the patentee's reward, is an instrument of that social policy and thus should be validated by the patent laws;[5] antitrust policies, no matter how forceful or explicit, should give way. At the other extreme it can be argued that any restriction which, with respect to unpatented technology, would be invalid under the antitrust laws, should be invalid when the technology is patented, unless the patent law explicitly or by irresistible implication grants an antitrust exemption.[6] But neither of these responses performs the work of integration and compromise which is the highest function of analysis when two elements of public policy threaten to collide.[7]

As we proceed we shall see how underlying conflicts have in fact been handled over time. We shall see the extent to which an analysis of likely competitive effects seems pertinent and will reach points where we become convinced that such an analysis, because of the lack both of adequate theory and determinate data, takes on a dream-like quality. We shall also see ways of dealing with the kinds of issues which are alternative to economic analysis, which draw upon an historically informed tradition.

Discussions of these issues usually begin with a consideration of licenses which fix the price at which the licensee will sell the patented

---

3. Buxbaum, Restrictions Inherent in the Patent Monopoly: A Comparative Critique, 113 U.Pa.L.Rev. 633 (1965).

4. P. Areeda, Antitrust Analysis, Problems, Text, Cases ¶ 416 (2d ed. 1974).

5. Compare Bement & Sons v. National Harrow Co., 186 U.S. 70, 22 S.Ct. 747, 46 L.Ed. 1058 (1902).

6. Compare United States v. Line Material Co., 333 U.S. 287, 318–19, 68 S. Ct. 550, 566, 92 L.Ed. 701, 723–24 (1948) (concurring opinion).

7. Much of the case law avoids the difficult issues. The case law is summarized in the American Bar Association Publication, Antitrust Law Developments 346–49 (1975). In this volume an effort is made to explore some of the law's underlying complexities more thoroughly than the case law has yet done and to point up the implications of recent analytical scholarship.

product. The law on that subject is more fully developed than the law which deals with other restrictions. For just that reason this book begins with a discussion of territorial restrictions. The analytical questions are similar to those encountered in connection with price fixing licenses, but because the case law has dealt with these at such a surface level, more open discussion is possible. One mode of analysis, which draws to a degree on concepts about how conflicts of law may be identified and resolved, will be used in connection with territorial restrictions. In a later section dealing with price restrictions, a mode of analysis which relies more heavily on economics will be used. It should be understood that either analytical approach could be used to explore either type of license restriction, and that the techniques are deployed as they are more or less arbitrarily, so as to display both with minimum repetition.

§ 184. Licenses or Assignments Which Impose Horizontal Restrictions on Territories

a. In General

No intersection between patents and antitrust is as under-analyzed in the case law as is the area which concerns territorial restrictions in patent licenses, and in none is the patent bar literature and some of the antitrust literature more self-indulgently oversimplified. One finds cases which assume with little or no discussion that these kinds of restrictions are valid, some, perhaps, in quite benevolent circumstances, but others where substantial adverse impact on market competition is clearly to be suspected.[1] One finds practitioners being informed without qualification (save about vertical restrictions) that "it can be assumed that the imposition of territorial restrictions upon a licensee under either a product or a process patent is valid and enforceable."[2] Such arrangements are said to stand "legislatively approved."[3] The reason for this last and widely held apprehension, which may in the end be held wrong,[4] reposes in the wording of Section 261 of the Patent Code. That section, which deals with the form

---

1. E.g., Industrial Mach. Tool Co. v. Miami Window Corp., 234 F.2d 301 (5th Cir. 1956); Brownell v. Ketcham Wire & Mfg. Co., 211 F.2d 121 (9th Cir. 1954); United States v. Parker-Rust-Proof Co., 61 F.Supp. 805 (E.D. Mich.1945).

2. A. Deller, Deller's Walker on Patents § 649 (2d ed. 1973). See to like effect, Practical Patent Licensing 144 (A. Davis ed. 1970); Report of the Attorney General's National Committee to Study the Antitrust Laws 237 (1955). In the A.B.A. study, Antitrust Laws Developments (1975), the full treatment of territorial restrictions is given in these two sentences: "The Patent Code provides that a patentee may convey exclusive patent rights in 'any specified part of the United States.' However, when used by competitors as part of a larger scheme to divide world markets, territorial restrictions have been condemned." Id. at 349 (footnotes deleted).

3. R. Nordhaus & E. Jurow, Patent-Antitrust Law 67 (2d ed. 1972).

4. See the authorities cited in note 28 infra and the text associated with that footnote.

of patent assignments and frees territorial assignments from the fetters of doctrine about splitting choses in action,[5] has been taken without inquiry as expressing a broad congressional judgment validating territorial restrictions.[6] The subsections which follow first summarize the cases and then present the revisionary analysis.

b. *The Case Law*

If a patent holder assigns the right under the patent to make and sell a patented product or to use a patented process within a specified territory, or licenses these rights only within a specified territory, committing itself that the license will be exclusive, it has by the assignment or license established a protected territory. If it makes other similar grants and, in addition, retains a territory for its own exploitation, it has divided territories horizontally for the practice of the patented art. (A non-exclusive license, even if the license is limited to a territory, need not have these effects since the patentee may, or may authorize others to, practice in the authorized territory).

The cases on horizontal territorial restrictions in patent licenses are few; those which can be found support the conventional view [7] that these restrictions are lawful unless, in particular circumstances, they are structured so as unreasonably to restrain competition. In some cases, courts considering other issues have presupposed the validity of transfers limited by territory or location.[8] There are also decisions which, without discussion or analysis, hold territorial divisions lawful, at least in the sense of predicating other crucial conclusions on the assumption of their legality. One instance is the *Ketcham Wire* case.[9] There, the patent holder in granting a license exacted a promise from the licensee not to export or sell abroad and committed itself not to import into or sell in the United States. In an action charging a violation of Section 1, the Ninth Circuit affirmed a summary judgment for the defendants, saying, as to the restriction on imports, that "exclusive territorial licenses * * * [u]nless they run afoul of the antitrust laws for other reasons * * * are legal." [10] Security Materials v. Mixermobile Company [11] typifies another group of cases. The patent holder had granted a series of exclusive territorial licenses. The action was by one licensee to enjoin another from selling in

5. Baxter, Legal Restrictions on Exploitation of the Patent Monopoly: An Economic Analysis, 76 Yale L.J. 267, 349–351 (1966). The language of Section 261 is set out in the text associated with note 26 infra.

6. Id. And see Buxbaum, Restrictions Inherent in the Patent Monopoly: A Comparative Critique, 113 U.Pa.L.Rev. 633, 658–59 (1965); Gibbons, Domestic Territorial Restrictions in Patent Transactions and the Antitrust Laws, 34 Geo.Wash.L.Rev. 893, 894–96 (1966).

7. Report of the Attorney General's National Committee to Study the Antitrust Laws 237 (1955).

8. E.g., Becton, Dickinson & Co. v. Eisele & Co., 86 F.2d 267 (6th Cir. 1936).

9. Brownell v. Ketcham Wire & Mfg. Co., 211 F.2d 121 (9th Cir. 1954).

10. Id. at 129.

11. 72 F.Supp. 450 (S.D.Cal.1947).

the territory of the plaintiff. The defendant responded that it had purchased the items in question from the patentee itself in a territory not covered by any license and thus that it held the item free of any restraint and could lawfully resell it anywhere. Holding that "part of the patent monopoly consisting of the right to sell and use in the southern California territory belongs exclusively to" the plaintiff, and that the circumstances of sale to defendant, another licensee, did not make defendant an ordinary purchaser who, once having acquired title, could resell anywhere, the court ruled that the patent was infringed.[12]

It has been suggested that there may be a crucial distinction between a *grant* (an assignment or license to exercise the patent only in a designated territory) and the combination of a grant and an answering covenant by the grantee not to exercise it elsewhere. The first, it is argued, is lawful even though the latter is not.[13] The theoretical basis for the proposed distinction is that between achieving the goal by a grant, essentially a permission, and achieving it by imposing a restriction. Yet no court facing the matter squarely is likely to be tempted in this direction, at all events if the promissory undertaking is no broader than to respect the patent in areas where the covenantor does not share the monopoly. It is, after all, a thin promise which gives up nothing the licensee or assignee possesses, if, without it, the patent is enforceable beyond the limits of the license or assignment.

While none of these cases deal analytically with the intricacies of the conflict between antitrust and patent law presented by territorial patent restrictions, all of them tend to support the broad dicta found in the patent bar literature. Let us take up some strands of the law's fabric which these eliptical judicial responses fail to touch even passingly.

c. *An Analytical Framework for Territorial (and Other Horizontal) License Restrictions*

Territorial and all other horizontal limitations on the exercise of patent rights present engaging issues. For example, suppose a patentee grants a license containing a restriction which but for the patent would be a *per se* violation of the antitrust laws and the claim is made that the patent law validates the restriction. The first question is whether the patent law in any sense affirms the restriction; if it does not, there is no patent-antitrust conflict. It is not enough to claim that allowing the restriction would enhance the value of the patent and thus encourage investment in innovation;[14] the patent

---

12. Id. at 456. See also Deering, Milliken & Co. v. Temp-Resisto Corp., 160 F.Supp. 463 (S.D.N.Y.1958).

13. Frost, Restrictions on Fields of Use and Territories, 42 Antitrust L.J. 633, 642 (1973).

14. See § 183 note 4 supra, and accompanying text.

law does not expressly or by implication embrace *every* policy which has this potential. One must, then, find some doctrinal validation by express authority or analogy for inferring that the particular restriction in question has the sanction of the patent law before any collision between patent and antitrust is encountered.

Professor Buxbaum has taught us much about this analytical process.[15] While he underscores the importance of an analysis of the likely competitive consequences of any restriction, he implies that both an historical and a comparative search of patent conceptions is also appropriate in order to determine what means of patent exploitation should be deemed "inherent" in the patent grant, and which excessive of the grant and thus subject to the restraints of antitrust. He implies, moreover, that such a search may indicate a possible distinction between licenses containing horizontal price restrictions and licenses containing horizontal territorial and field of use restrictions.[16] The historical and especially the comparative sources imply that the right to impose the latter types of restrictions may be deemed inherent in the patent grant,[17] although the right to impose the former need not.[18] So far as American experience is concerned, it would be hard to pattern any distinction between price and territorial license restrictions upon a difference in early attitudes. In this country there are indications of as strong an affirmance of the patentee's right to fix prices upon licensing as of power to impose other horizontal restrictions.[19] Thus, any conclusion that the power to restrict prices charged by licensees is not inherent in the grant would presumably have to stand upon a conclusion that price fixing licenses are more harmful than are licenses restricting territory.

However these issues are thought to go, the basic analytical approach which Buxbaum uses is important. If one concluded, independently of the antitrust law, that power to fix the prices charged by the licensee or to divide territories among licensees were no part of the patentee's grant, and if one further concluded under antitrust law that price fixing or territorial division was unlawful, no conflict of law would be presented. If there is no grant under the patent law of power to fix prices, then if a court were to decline to apply the antitrust *per se* rule against price fixing or territorial division to patent licenses, it would have to be not because of patent policy but because patent license restrictions present distinct *antitrust* issues. This leaves open the possibility that one or both of these kinds of license restrictions will be validated under antitrust law. It may be that,

---

15. See generally, Buxbaum, Restrictions Inherent in the Patent Monopoly: A Comparative Critique, 113 U. Pa.L.Rev. 633 (1965).

16. Id.

17. Id.

18. Id.

19. Compare Bement & Sons v. National Harrow Co., 186 U.S. 70, 22 S.Ct. 747, 46 L.Ed. 1058 (1902) with Standard Sanitary Mfg. Co. v. United States, 226 U.S. 20, 33 S.Ct. 9, 57 L.Ed. 107 (1912).

given the fact that they are ancillary to and facilitate licensing, these restraints have (generally or in some instances) beneficial effects on competition which outweigh any negative effects; if so, antitrust policy, without the constraint of deference to patent policy, might best be served by avoiding *per se* responses. But the Buxbaum analysis clarifies matters considerably simply by insisting that the matter not be approached as involving a conflict of patent and antitrust unless a true conflict exists. Thus, if the right to fix the licensee's prices or to restrict the licensee's territory *is* inherent in the patent grant, there may well be a conflict between patent and antitrust law. Antitrust law, either on the strength of a *per se* doctrine or after analysis of a particular transaction, may point to the invalidity of such a restraint. If, as assumed, patent law asserts validity of the restraint, the conflict is palpably presented.

Turning back, now, to territorial restraints, and leaving price restraints for later treatment, let us pursue the analysis. The case law reviewed above is enough, perhaps, to support the inference that in America the right to impose territorial restraints on licenses has long been supposed to be inherently within the patent grant. One might conceivably conclude that antitrust law does not forbid such licenses without analysis of their competitive effects in particular cases. Since licensing, in general, encourages competition, it might be concluded that competition is, on balance, enhanced by allowing territorial restrictions so as to encourage licensing.[20] But given the increasing reluctance of courts to construe the Sherman Act in ways that require the balancing of benefits when a *per se* harm has been done,[21] it is likely that antitrust policy would call for *per se* invalidity. In any event, antitrust policy would presumably be offended by some territorial restrictions on patent licenses; it is hardly plausible that, after analysis, all of them would be found advantageous to competition.[22] Assuming antitrust law to be hostile to the license restriction, the mere existence of a patent law policy in favor of allowing the restriction—that is, the mere finding that the power to impose it is an "inherent" part of the patent grant—does not *resolve* the conflict, does not tell us that antitrust concerns must give way. It merely establishes the existence of the conflict. The reason, of course, is that the opposite and opposing policy—a prohibition against the restriction—is also inherent, not in the patent law, but in the antitrust law.

A conflict between patents and antitrust having been bared, analysis must be pressed further to resolve it. *A priori,* is there a hierarchical order between the two statutes? It is hard to perceive a

20. See § 183 supra, particularly the text accompanying note 2.

21. See, e.g., United States v. Topco Associates, Inc. 405 U.S. 596, 92 S.Ct. 1126, 31 L.Ed.2d 515 (1972); United States v. Philadelphia Nat'l Bank, 374 U.S. 321, 83 S.Ct. 1715, 10 L.Ed.2d 915 (1963).

22. See the analysis suggested by P. Areeda, Antitrust Analysis, Problems, Text, Cases, ¶¶ 410, 417 (2d Ed. 1974).

basis for it. Patent law is older and more settled. But what of that? Antitrust is public law, a social regulation the importance of which is marked by criminal sanctions; patent law, by contrast, is but a branch of private law, of property. None of these observations signify with any strength as to the priority question. If there is no way of ordering these statutes intrinsically, can one meter the conflicting policies specifically expressed by them to see which is the more forceful? Can one judge whether the interest under patent law in allowing territorially restricted licenses is of a higher or lower order than the interest under antitrust law of forbidding territorial divisions? One might infer a diminished importance for the patent policy on the ground that it is possible for a patentee to obtain the full monopoly reward even if deprived of the power to grant territorial licenses; the patentee could, in the alternative, fully exploit the monopoly itself, or having fixed the profit maximizing royalty, could rely on competition among licensees to assure the maximum exploitation which the market would support.[23] But again, the antitrust policy—if we are relying on the *per se* rule—is itself a policy which can be labeled weak, since it applies without any inquiry to determine whether the interests it is aimed at protecting are actually and significantly engaged in any particular situation where the rule applies.

Buxbaum proposes that we therefore take the next step and analyze the particular applications of the policies in the particular settings in which we encounter them.[24] The bounds of this inquiry can be mapped with the use of two contrasting hypotheticals. First, assume that a patentee obtains a basic product or process patent on a revolutionary technology which is so distinct from any conceivable substitute as to create a new industry. Think of something like the electric light, the digital computer, or xerography. The patentee is by the grant an economic monopolist. It decides to exploit the monopoly by granting territorial assignments or exclusive licenses dividing the country into, say, five or six regions, one of which it retains. With that hypothetical contrast this one: Picture a firm in an industry where ten or twenty firms loosely scattered across the country use three or four alternative technologies all in the public domain. Each seller utilizes the advantages of its location and succeeds in making most sales in the area where its delivery cost would be lowest, but there is considerable price competition in peripheral areas and occasionally deep invasions by one seller into the territory of another. One of the firms obtains a patent on a new technology which in some respects marks an improvement on the existing technology but in other respects seems less desirable. For a consideration it assigns the patent to each competitor in a defined territory conformable to the assignee's usual selling area, retaining the patent rights in its own selling area. Thereafter, the patented technology is widely used, the

23. Id. 24. Buxbaum, supra note 15.

public domain technology falls into disuse, and price competition abates.

In the first of these hypotheticals, a lawful monopolist utilized a medium inherently part of the patent grant to exploit the monopoly. Virtue is not attacked, let alone undone. Some of the alternatives, also clearly lawful, such as exploiting the patent as a single producing and selling monopolist or assigning to a single firm would place the public in no better position, but rather distinctly otherwise, since multiple assignments, unlike single firm exploitation, would lay a base for post-patent competition and might stimulate competition even during the term of the patent in efforts to improve the technology. Here, the analysis suggests, the antitrust policy, the *per se* rule against territorial allocations, ought to give way, for the purposes it is intended to serve are not truly engaged; competition is restricted to no greater degree by the assignment than is inherent in the patent grant itself. But the second situation differs entirely. The patentee by the grant has gained no monopoly; it has merely expanded its options somewhat beyond those of others in the field which must draw only from technology in the public domain; patent monopolist though it be, it faces lively competing technologies. As a participant in its industry, whether or not it uses its protected technology, it faces aggressive competition. It then grants a series of territorial assignments of (or territorially exclusive licenses to) the patent which gained it so little real market power and, thereafter, as if by Olympian decree, the marketplace is transformed and competitive striving ceases. What underlying facts can explain this situation? There are several possibilities. The patentee may have suggested to others in the industry that if they all took assignments and switched to the new technology, temptations to engage in price competition would be abated; the others may have agreed. Or some less explicit discussion about the potential for harmony may have occurred; or interdependence on the *Interstate Circuit* [25] model may have precipitated the accord without other discussion once the patentee's intent to impose territorial restrictions become generally known.

If the parties explicitly agreed to cartelize and simply used the patent statute as a rug under which to sweep the signs of their conspiracy, surely important antitrust policies insist that they be brought to account; the patent statute is not seriously encumbered by prohibiting the misuse of a patent as a cosmetic to cover a cartel. Once again, analysis provides a basis for choosing between the seemingly conflicting policies—here, the antitrust statute plainly should prevail. The same point would carry if we assume not an explicit cartel but interdependent conduct to abandon the competitive technology and adopt the restricted one.

25. Interstate Circuit, Inc. v. United States, 306 U.S. 208, 59 S.Ct. 467, 83 L.Ed. 610 (1939).

Does the analytical process end here, with the conclusion that a factual inquiry must be made in each instance to see which policy has the stronger claim to govern? Perhaps not; there are as yet unstated complications. First, the hypotheticals set forth here obscure the potential involvement of policies concerning the nature of courts and adjudication, and the limits of these institutions in sorting out economic issues. Thus far we have contrasted a rather clear economic monopoly arising from a patent with a rather clear use of a patent to hide a cartel. In neither instance was there any empirical or theoretical issue standing between the court and the course of wisdom. The path will not always be so clear. It may be a hard question whether the patent comprehends an economic monopoly; it may be difficult to fathom whether the attraction of the license is the territorial restriction or the new technology. In a word, the issue of whether the patent law interest (or the antitrust law interest) is heavily engaged at all, or the issue of which law is engaged more forcefully may often be expensive to investigate and, in the end, difficult or even impossible to answer with confidence. The very policy reasons which underlie *per se* responses in antitrust cases may be as forcefully present here as anywhere.

Are we not then pushed back once again to the need for a choice between the two statutes at some intrinsic level? That issue can be put off during a preliminary inquiry to see whether one policy or the other clearly dominates as in the hypotheticals above. If one or the other does, that should end the matter. But if preliminary inquiry does not yield an answer, the goal of protecting courts from the search for the unfathomable ought to have an impact. One turns, perhaps, to considerations of policy intensity measured separately for each statute. The justification for the antitrust *per se* rule against territorial restraints signals a fairly strong commitment. The notion is that territorial restraints in the generality of cases are seriously harmful to competition, that the cases where harm is small or nonexistent are few and, in these, there is little penalty imposed on society by the overreach of the doctrine; any benefit which might be achieved by the territorial agreement can be achieved in other ways. The patent interest, by contrast, may be regarded as less vehement since the patentee has alternative ways to gain a full reward.

But before we commit ourselves to the conclusion that the antitrust interest ought therefore to predominate when the preliminary inquiry leaves doubt, we must examine a factor that points to the opposite resolution. Section 261 of the Patent Code provides that "patents, or any interest therein, shall be assignable * * * by an instrument in writing" and that an applicant, patentee or assignee "may in like manner grant and convey an exclusive right * * * to the whole or any specified part of the United States."[26] Whatever

---

26. 66 Stat. 810, 35 U.S.C.A. § 261.

may be the law as to price restricting or field of use restricting licenses, is not this language an explicit congressional statement that territorial restrictions under patents are permissible? Though some courts and many commentators have supposed Section 261 to authorize territorial assignments and licenses and to shield them in some degree from antitrust challenge,[27] recent scholarship has exposed a considerable doubt as to the accuracy of this conclusion.[28] The section is a direct derivative of a statute passed before the Sherman Act which was intended to perform two functions—to specify the formality needed to assign a patent, namely, a writing, and to make clear that rules about splitting choses in action should not be construed to preclude a partial patent assignment. The section can and, it would seem, should be construed as applying only to assignments, not to licenses. Also, in light of its purpose and the fact that it was enacted before the Sherman Act, it cannot be read as a congressional choice in favor of the patent law over conflicting antitrust policies. One can travel with Section 261 far enough to become convinced that the right to give a territorial assignment (and possibly license) is indeed an inherent part of the patent grant; but the section goes no further.

Congress later passed the antitrust laws which speak contrary to this provision. On the face of the matter a conflict of laws is presented; that conflict is not resolved by pointing to the statutory basis for one of the policies any more than it would be by pointing to the statutory basis of the other. But here, it may be urged, unlike any question as to price or field of use restrictions in licenses, the policy emanating from one of the statutes, the patent statute, is explicitly stated, while that emanating from the other, the antitrust statute, is a general, inferential one. Repeals by inference are not favored, thus the more explicitly stated policy should prevail. Possibly. But the issue does not seem one to be resolved on the basis of a general canon of construction; the reason for explicit statutory treatment of this particular patent policy is fortuitous with respect to the opposed policies of the antitrust laws. Consider for a moment the other possible inherent patent rights, such as those which it is claimed countenance price or field of use restrictions. The fact that these inherencies are not expressed in the patent statute may not have been because they were weaker than the inherent power to restrict territories, but because they were stronger and in no need of statutory protection from some seemingly conflicting common law doctrine. It would be strange to handle the territorial inherency differently than others for antitrust purposes because of an unrelated quirk of congressional history.

27. See notes 2, 3 and 4 supra.

28. Baxter, Legal Restrictions on Exploitation of the Patent Monopoly: An Economic Analysis, 76 Yale L.J. 267 (1966); Gibbons, Domestic Territorial Restrictions in Patent Transactions and the Antitrust Laws, 34 Geo. Wash.L.Rev. 893 (1966); Wheeler, A Reexamination of Antitrust Law and Exclusive Territorial Grants by Patentees, 119 U.Pa.L.Rev. 642 (1971).

If this view is accepted the inquiry ends. Section 261 is held to have no bearing. Territorial restrictions are permitted in circumstances where preliminary inquiry shows that the patent confers an economic monopoly and, hence, the granting of restricted licenses imposes no greater tax on competition than would other modes of exploitation, and probably allows for more competition than some. Territorial restrictions are forbidden in all other instances on the ground that they conflict with the antitrust *per se* rule (which has the sanction both of antitrust policy and conceptions about the proper scope of judicial inquiry on economic issues), whereas the interests supported by the patent law are only infringed upon in small degree. On the other hand, if Section 261 is held to perform a special office with respect to antitrust issues, further inquiry must be pressed. First, does the section only apply to assignments or does it include licenses containing territorial restrictions? Literally, it deals only with assignments. Indeed, licenses can unquestionably be granted without the formality of a writing which the section posits. Though the contrary is widely assumed, it is hard to find a basis for construing the section as dealing with licenses at all.[29]

If Section 261 is held to earn preferred antitrust treatment for territorial assignments, or for assignments and for licenses, there remains the need to specify the degree of protection it affords. The most single-minded dedication to the primacy of patent interests would not warrant reading Section 261 as rendering every territorial assignment (or license) free from antitrust challenge. The point can be made with an extreme example. Firm A proposes to its competitors B, C, and D that they allocate territories between them. One of them counsels the use of a patent to shield the transaction from antitrust scrutiny. A patent is found, which none of them owns and which covers a usable technology, though not the most efficient in the industry. Following out the scheme one of them acquires that patent. Territorial assignments are then given to the others, with a territory retained. The four firms thereafter practice this technology and stay in their respective territories. Surely Section 261 does not convert every patent into a license to cartelize. To claim such an office for it would be an affront both to reason and to experience.[30]

Where, then, is the line? Enough has been said to show that even the most generous amplification of Section 261 does not drown

---

29. This leaves open the possibility that a patentee wishing to divide markets could obtain a better antitrust status by using territorial assignments rather than restricted licenses. But the territorial assignment may also have disadvantages not shared by the territorial license. A license can be granted for a limited time and made subject to such lawful restrictions in addition to the territorial restrictions as may be agreed upon. An assignment may contain no limitation on the rights of the assignee inconsistent with the estate granted.

30. Compare United States v. National Lead Co., 63 F.Supp. 513 (S.D.N.Y. 1945), aff'd 332 U.S. 319, 67 S.Ct. 1634, 91 L.Ed. 2077 (1947).

out the antitrust concerns. If two statutes announce conflicting policies they must be reconciled in some reasoned manner. The heaviest burden which Section 261 could conceivably be made to carry is to protect all territorial assignments other than those shown to have been taken primarily to gain access to a territorial division (rather than to gain access to a new and useful technology). The least the section will do, if read to hold off the antitrust laws at all, is to protect the territorial restrictions it covers from the *per se* sanction. If Section 261 is to be read to shield territorial assignments or licenses, it should be read to protect them no further than the point at which analysis of the specific factual context shows a substantial threat to competition. This, as a generalization, seems most sensible.

d. Import and Export Restrictions

An agreement by which the patent holder purports to protect a licensee or assignee from imports being resold in the United States (or in that portion of the United States granted to the licensee or assignee) is in its substantive impact essentially like an exclusive license or assignment; the licensee or assignee is given to assume that neither the patent holder nor any firm authorized by it will sell the product in the area exclusively given over.[31] Logically, arrangements such as this are within the patent grant to the same degree as (but to no greater degree than) are exclusive territorial licenses or assignments. Whether in any particular instance the antitrust laws are violated depends on which branch of the analysis developed in the prior subsection is taken as the most satisfactory. Case law, which generally approves these kinds of arrangements, is much like that about territorially restrictive assignments; it examines little and presupposes much.[32]

Although a few cases go the other way,[33] where a licensee or assignee under a United States patent makes a commitment not to export, the argument that no patent policy protects against unencumbered application of antitrust law seems compelling.[34] American patent law provides no monopoly on the patented device beyond American borders.[35] And surely no policy finding expression in American patent law is served by restricting American export trade in a patented item. If there is a patent law basis for altering the normal ap-

---

31. See, e.g., United States v. L. D. Caulk Co., 126 F.Supp. 693 (D.Del. 1954), wherein an English firm granted defendant exclusive rights in the Western Hemisphere on an invention covered by a United States patent.

32. See United States v. L. D. Caulk Co., 126 F.Supp. 693 (D.Del.1954). See also Osmose Wood Preserving Co. of Canada v. Osmose Wood Preserving Co. of America, 74 F.Supp. 435 (W.D. N.Y.1947).

33. American Optical Co. v. New Jersey Optical Co., 58 F.Supp. 601 (D. Mass.1944); Elliott Co. v. Lagonda Mfg. Co. 205 F. 152 (W.D.Pa.1913), aff'd, 214 F. 578 (3d Cir. 1914).

34. See the convincing analysis in R. Nordhaus & E. Jurow, Patent-Antitrust Law 148–50 (1961).

35. Id.

plication of the antitrust laws, it must therefore be found in a foreign patent law and principles of comity. It follows that an export restriction should gain no sanction at all to the extent that it purports to inhibit exports to countries where the patent holder is protected by no foreign, counterpart patent. If there is a patent monopoly on the technology in any foreign country, the patent holder, not having granted any license under the foreign patent, is free under the foreign law to enforce against the domestic assignee or patentee such rights as the foreign law does grant; the restriction in the domestic license or assignment is to this extent superfluous. And if the restriction in the domestic license or assignment overreaches the protection available under the foreign law by its own unaided force, the antitrust validity of the domestic arrangement is to that extent unaided by the foreign patent.

Suppose, for example, that the American patent grants broader claims than does the foreign patent. An agreement by a licensee of the American patent not to export to the foreign country any products produced under the license would be overbroad; in terms, it would preclude export of items which would not infringe the foreign patent rights. Or suppose that the standards of invention under the foreign law were higher than under American law so that the foreign patent would fail if challenged, though the domestic one would withstand attack. On this assumption also the restriction in the domestic license might dampen export trade beyond the ambit of any foreign patent protection by discouraging an attack on the foreign patent by the would-be exporter.

Some of these subtle restraints, easy enough to identify analytically, might prove trivial in practical consequence; but one cannot be sure that this would be so. One holding a domestic license but not a foreign counterpart license is, perhaps, unlikely to challenge the validity of the foreign patent while continuing to operate under the domestic license; that kind of a disruption of relationship with the patentee may be undesirable in light of domestic relationships. The fact remains, nevertheless, that the firm holding the foreign patent holds by the force of the foreign law all the protection that it is entitled to hold in the foreign market. Therefore, if the domestic agreement has, in fact, any significant effect on the relationship of the parties, that effect can only be to extend the restraint on the domestic licensee or assignee beyond the reach of the foreign law. On this ground such restrictions ought at least to be scrutinized cynically and, to be rigorous about the implications of the analysis, should be held *per se* unlawful.[36]

36. Note, also, that Section 261 applies only to grants of patent rights in all or part "of the United States"; it does not purport to authorize assignments of extra-territorial rights and agreements allocating foreign markets gain no immunity whatsoever by virtue of a domestic patent.

e. *Economic Effects of Patent Territorial Restrictions*

If a patentee uses a patent to establish a territorial cartel covering a product for which there is no close substitute, that arrangement will have substantially the same economic effects as a horizontal division of markets which is not based upon a patent.[37] If territorial division is attempted which does not comprehend the entire product market, its adverse effects will be reduced to the extent those practicing the patent face competition from substitute products; market power, based upon territorial division under the patent, will be diminished.

There is one purpose and effect which may be associated with territorial restrictions which is not likely to be encountered, absent a patent, in any attempt at horizontal territorial cartelization. It is that the territorial restriction may be used by the patentee as a method of discriminating in the price charged for the assignment of the patent, or in the royalty rate charged for a license to use the patent. Let us examine the possibility and evaluate its implications.

Suppose, as in La Peyre v. FTC [38], a particular patent is of greater commercial value if practiced in one geographic market than if practiced in another. Patented farm machinery, for example, might be usable by farmers growing corn and those growing wheat, and have greater value in the corn belt than in the wheat belt. Or, as in *La Peyre,* shrimp canners dealing with small Pacific shrimp may value a shelling machine more than do Gulf Coast competitors shelling the larger variety found there. Obviously, if the patentee can establish two rates, a high one for those to which the machine is most valuable, and a low one to the other users, the return on the patent will be higher than could be attained by any single rate for all users. A territorial restriction in a license might enable the patentee to discriminate in this way.

If a firm with a patent were to discriminate in this manner, its returns would be larger than if it used any single rate for both classes of users. If, absent an opportunity to discriminate, it would have charged a single rate low enough to induce both groups of licensees to take the patent, the effect of the discrimination (and of the territorial restriction supporting it) is to require some users (and eventually consumers) to pay more for the technology. The higher return to the patent holder is, from the vantage point of the public, unnecessary to the stimulation of any socially desired conduct. On the other hand, if we assume that but for the chance to discriminate, the patent holder would have charged a rate high enough to maximize the return from the group of licensees ready to pay more for the license, with the result that those who could economically use the technology only at that lower rate would forego the technology, the effect of the discrimina-

---

37. See § 82 supra, discussing economic effects of a division of territories.

38. 336 F.2d 117 (5th Cir. 1966).

tion (and the territorial restriction supporting it) is not only to enable the patentee to earn higher returns but also to enable some buyers to use the technology who would not have afforded it if discrimination had been forbidden. Thus, allowing the territorial restriction which facilitates the discrimination will in some instances result in a wider dispersion of the technology than would occur if the territorial restriction were not permitted.[39]

From the point of view of social policy, there is much to be said for allowing price discrimination in situations where it can be shown that its effect is a wider dispersion of technology than would be achieved without discrimination; in that instance, the public achieves a net gain. It follows that a case can be made for allowing territorial restrictions in licenses where the purpose and effect is to facilitate such a discrimination. But actual cases of these kinds, where (1) the purpose and effect of a territorial restriction is to facilitate discrimination and (2) the effect of the discrimination is to assure a wider dispersal of the patented technology, may well be quite rare. If a patent holder were to seek to justify a territorial restriction upon these grounds, it ought to carry a distinct burden of proof on both aspects of the claim.

§ 185. Licenses Which Restrict Prices Horizontally

a. *In General*

In the *General Electric* case [1] the Court sanctioned a price restricting license. However, Justice Taft's opinion has not fared well. It has been narrowed in the scope of its application [2] and twice survived direct challenges by an equally divided Court.[3] G.E. held a basic product patent, a process patent, and an improvement product patent. Together these covered "completely the making of the modern electric lights." [4] It licensed Westinghouse to make, use and sell lamps under the patents, Westinghouse agreeing to pay royalties and

---

39. See Areeda, supra note 22, at ¶¶ 430, 432.

1. 272 U.S. 476, 47 S.Ct. 192, 71 L.Ed. 362 (1926).

2. E.g., United States v. Line Material Co., 333 U.S. 287, 68 S.Ct. 550, 92 L.Ed. 701 (1948); Newburgh Moire Co. v. Superior Moire Co., 237 F.2d 283 (3d Cir. 1956); Barber-Colman Co. v. National Tool Co., 136 F.2d 339 (6th Cir. 1943); Tinnerman Products, Inc. v. George K. Garrett Co., 185 F.Supp. 151 (E.D.Pa.1960), aff'd 292 F.2d 137 (2d Cir.), cert. denied, 368 U.S. 833, 82 S.Ct. 58, 7 L.Ed.2d 35 (1961); United States v. Vehicular Parking, Ltd., 54 F.Supp. 828 (D.Del.1944). See Royal Indus. v. St. Regis Paper Co., 420 F.2d 449 (9th Cir. 1969); Ansul Co. v. Uniroyal, Inc., 306 F.Supp. 541 (S.D.N.Y. 1969), aff'd in part, rev'd in part, 448 F.2d 872 (2d Cir. 1971), cert. denied, 404 U.S. 1018, 92 S.Ct. 680, 30 L.Ed.2d 666 (1972).

3. United States v. Line Material Co., 333 U.S. 287, 68 S.Ct. 550, 92 L.Ed. 701 (1948); United States v. Huck Mfg. Co., 227 F.Supp. 791 (E.D.Mich. 1964), aff'd per curiam by an equally divided Court, 382 U.S. 197, 86 S.Ct. 385, 15 L.Ed.2d 268 (1965).

4. United States v. General Elec. Co., 272 U.S. 476, 481, 47 S.Ct. 192, 193, 71 L.Ed. 362, 367 (1926).

to sell only at the prices and on the other terms of sale established by G.E. from time to time for lamps of its own manufacture. The Court, rejecting the government's claim that the license restriction violated the antitrust laws, announced that a patentee could license upon any condition the performance of which was reasonably within the reward to which the patent entitled the licensor. In terms, the Court's formulation reminds one of the test Professor Buxbaum proposes: whether in its broad historical, social and political context the use of the restriction is inherent in the patent monopoly.[5] However, the Court in *G.E.* applied its test narrowly, shunning any historical or comparative inquiry in favor of a rather stunted one. It asked only whether the condition imposed was "normally and reasonably adapted to secure pecuniary reward" to the patentee's monopoly.[6] And the Court's elaboration of these concepts implied that all it really wanted to know was whether a self regarding patentee might want to use the restriction for its own economic ends as a patent monopolist.

The case is unfortunate from many points of view. It is obviously not satisfactory from an analytical perspective like that explored in the last section. The Court looks primarily if not exclusively to the thrust of patent policy; it ignores or deemphasizes antitrust and makes no effort to identify or resolve conflicts between them. In essence, the Court's concept would seem to mandate approval for any patent restriction which a patentee might elect to exploit its monopoly, so long as there is no effort to extend power beyond the patent technology, as for example by using the patent to cartelize the industry.[7] The case is also inadequate from its own analytical perspective. As we shall see, economic analysis indicates that price fixing power is probably never needed to assist the patent monopolist to gain its monopoly return.[8] Putting aside the possibility of enhancing the return through discrimination, the patentee can obtain the full monopoly profit attributable to the patent by estimating (or deciding

---

5. Buxbaum, Restrictions Inherent in the Patent Monopoly: A Comparative Critique, 113 U.Pa.L.Rev. 633 (1965).

6. United States v. General Elec. Co., 272 U.S. 476, 490, 47 S.Ct. 192, 197, 71 L.Ed. 362, 370 (1926).

7. Compare United States v. New Wrinkle, Inc., 342 U.S. 371, 72 S.Ct. 350, 96 L.Ed. 417 (1952). Had the Court in *G.E.* rigorously pursued an inherency test to see whether the patent law sanctioned these licenses, it is not entirely clear where it would have come out. Taking account not only of American but also Western European experience one might conclude that price fixing licenses may not be within the patent grant. But American experience seems to be otherwise. Indeed, the Court in *General Electric* cited an early post-Sherman case, Bement & Sons v. National Harrow Co., 186 U.S. 70, 22 S.Ct. 747, 46 L.Ed. 1058 (1902), which had, in an opinion by Justice Peckham, upheld a price fixing license as a matter of patent law and as free of antitrust taint. But the rest of the analysis, to determine whether the patent interests were paramount to the conflicting antitrust interests, was never even begun.

8. The most cogent criticism appears in Baxter, Legal Restrictions on Exploitation of the Patent Monopoly: An Economic Analysis, 76 Yale L.J. 267 (1966).

upon) the profit maximizing (or desired limit) price, estimating the cost of production (including a reasonable return), subtracting the latter from the former and fixing the difference as its royalty charge. If the patent gives the patentee an economic monopoly (by excluding all others from a widely defined product market), the patentee cannot increase its return by price fixing. If it can increase its return by price fixing it is because the patent does not give it an economic monopoly. In that instance it can gain monopoly returns only by concerted arrangement with competitors to charge a monopoly price; the function of the price fixing license then becomes the function of establishing that cartel price.[9]

Analytically deficient, as it is, it is not surprising that the status of *General Electric* is clouded by the criticism which it has evoked and the stinginess with which it has been construed. Though in some sense the case remains law, one cannot rely on it in counselling; in this respect it is rather like *Colgate*,[10] a rude shelter in a storm. The alacrity with which courts have distinguished *General Electric*[11] and the fact that since 1926 no majority of the Supreme Court has been ready to affirm it serve warning that even narrowly read, the case provides no basis for planning a licensing program. The functional analogy to *Colgate* can be pressed further. The very ambiguity created by *Colgate* has its own uses; it is a precedent transformed and drawn into the service of a new social function.[12] In a similar way, *General Electric*, by its ambiguity—by making it impossible for an attorney to say flatly, "It is unlawful to control the price at which your licensee sells."—makes it harder for attorneys to persuade their clients to avoid serious risks. Because of this the current state of the law may have interesting effects. Let us trace some of the possibilities.

Among firms there will be a continuum as to the intensity of interest in licensing and another continuum as to the intensity of interest in imposing the price restriction. Some firms may not license no matter how permissive the law about price restrictions may be. Others may license and impose the restriction no matter how restrictive the law may be; their preference for licensing and for having the restriction is so high that they will run even a very high risk of legal sanction in an effort to attain it. Other preferences will be in a middle range where the calculus of choice is more finely calibrated. Some firms will not license if there is a slight risk of legal entanglement resulting from a restriction. Others will license, but will judge whether or not to impose the restriction on the basis of an assessment

---

9. Id.

10. United States v. Colgate & Co., 250 U.S. 300, 39 S.Ct. 465, 63 L.Ed. 992 (1919).

11. See cases cited in note 2 supra. See also Cummer-Graham Co. v. Straight Side Basket Corp., 142 F.2d 646 (5th Cir.), cert. denied, 323 U.S. 726, 65 S.Ct. 60, 89 L.Ed. 583 (1944).

12. See § 139 supra.

of the extent of the risk of legal entanglement and its likely consequences. Of these, some will drop the restriction if there is any material risk of facing a sanction for using it. Others will impose the restriction so long as there is any significant chance that doing so will not be challenged or, if challenged, will not be held unlawful. Still others will be spread between these limits.

What, then, is the effect of the uncertainty entailed in the present state of the law about price restricted licenses? It must shift the tipping points in the process of decision making. There is now a significant risk involved in the use of price restrictions in licenses, a higher risk than if *G.E.* were a reliable precedent, but a risk not so great as would flow from a rule of *per se* illegality. Of the firms which would license without restriction if restrictions were clearly unlawful, but would license with restrictions if restrictions were clearly lawful, some (perhaps many) will now shift from using restricted licenses to using unrestricted ones. Uncertainty thus gains the public the advantage of more unrestricted licenses than there would be if the restrictions were clearly lawful. Also, of the firms which would not license at all if restrictions were clearly unlawful, but would license with restrictions if restrictions were clearly lawful, some will now grant restricted licenses. Uncertainty thus gains the public the advantage of a wider dispersion of the technology than would prevail if the restrictions were clearly unlawful. Of course, there are correlative losses. There will now be some firms discouraged from licensing at all which would have licensed with price restrictions if restrictions were clearly lawful and some firms will now use restrictions which would have licensed without them if restrictions were clearly unlawful. There is no theoretical or empirical evidence to suggest whether the net social advantage lies in making price restricted licenses lawful, unlawful, or leaving them in the existing state of uncertainty. Once again we are in an indeterminate area where modes of analysis suggested by economics do no more for us than pose the issues.

One may hazard, nonetheless, the legislative judgment that uncertainty may well yield better results than would clear legality. If restrictions were clearly permissible they would be encountered in many licenses which, under a rules of *per se* illegality, would have been given without them; the public would be paying a high price in the form of these gratuitous restrictions in order to gain the extension of technology through licenses which would not have been granted unless restrictions were permitted. It seems a good guess that rather few of the licenses which would be granted without restriction under a rule making the restriction *per se* unlawful are granted with restrictions under the present uncertain state of the law; most of any price restricted licenses now granted are probably ones which would not have been granted at all if it were settled law that restrictions are prohibited. But about all this we can only guess; and even assuming the accuracy of our guess we must still wonder whether the present state of legal uncertainty is preferable to a rule banning all price restrictions. It is at least possible that most of the firms bold enough to give and take price fixing licenses in face of the present risk are mainly interested in agreeing on price and only secondarily interested in earning royalties or gaining access to a useful technology. If that be so, the public's interests would be enhanced measurably were price fixing licenses made *per se* unlawful.

In sum, there is no solid empirical basis for concluding either that the public interest would be advanced by a rule of clear legality or that it would be advanced by a rule of clear illegality for a simple price fixing license. Yet confusion and uncertainty, despite the argument made above on their behalf, are not ornaments that adorn the law but disturbing elements which have their own costs. Given the numerous indeterminate factors entailed, the wise course would seem to be to follow the law's ancient wisdom. Absent relevant distinctions, like cases should be treated alike. Since the relevance of the distinction between price fixing on the licensing of a patent and price fixing in other contexts cannot be established, price fixing licenses should be dealt with as are other displays of price fixing. *G.E.* should be put to rest.

b. *Licenses Covering a Substantial Part of the Market*

It is tempting, in light of the many indications of doubt about the viability of *General Electric,* to seek the limit of its application, a point delimited in an idiom pertinent to the policy implications either of the antitrust or the patent statute. One which suggests itself is a structural concept—the scope of the market covered by the price fixing arrangement, taking into account the combined shares of licensor and licensees. If a price fixing license, or a series of them, covered a substantial share of the output of a relevant market, it presumptively would threaten competitive injury more than if patentee and licensees together held only a small share. Although in cases such as *Gypsum,*[13] courts in distinguishing *General Electric* have called to attention that the patentee and licensees together accounted for a substantial part of the market, this "industry coverage test" does not really serve to distinguish *General Electric*. One must only recall that *General Electric* and its licensee, Westinghouse, had between them 90% or more of the electric light bulb market. Yet, as *General Electric* is repeatedly distinguished on more trivial grounds, one turns time and again to this concept of market coverage if only for a source of balance. This much can be said: trivial distinctions seem to be accepted more easily when they are linked to a substantive con-

---

13. United States v. United States Gypsum Co., 333 U.S. 364, 68 S.Ct. 525, 92 L.Ed. 746 (1948). See also Newburgh Moire Co. v. Superior Moire Co., 237 F.2d 283 (3d Cir. 1956). Compare United States v. New Wrinkle, Inc., 342 U.S. 371, 72 S.Ct. 350, 96 L.Ed. 417 (1952).

sideration which points toward the result which the trivial distinction accommodates. Thus, a price fixing license is more likely to be challenged and the challenge to it is more likely to be successful when large industry shares are involved then when they are not.

c. Restrictions on the Sale Price of Products Made Under a Process Patent or With a Patented Machine

One of the patents involved in *General Electric* itself covered a process. Nothing in the opinion suggests that the Court's holding applied only to product patents and not the process patent. Despite that fact, and the fact that no principled distinction can be drawn between a product patent and a process patent for these purposes, courts have refused to apply *General Electric* to horizontal price fixing by a patentee upon the products manufactured under a process patent license or manufactured with a patented machine.[14] The law seems to be that holders of such patents may not restrict the licensee's prices on the products produced.[15]

d. Restrictions on the Sale of Products Which Incorporate the Patented Product Along with Other Elements

It also appears that if a license restriction purports to fix the price of a product containing the patented element along with other unpatented ones, any price fixing arrangement loses protection.[16] Here, again, the result cuts back upon *General Electric* significantly. In that case itself some elements of the lamp covered by the price fixing license—for example, snap-in or screw-in devices for making a connection with an electric circuit—were not covered by any patent. But that was not thought to deprive the patentee of the right to price fix. There remains, of course, a margin for interpretation. If the patent dominates the product, perhaps *General Electric* would still be applicable.

e. Licenses Given by A Non-Producing Patentee

There is also case law that a patentee which does not itself manufacture the patented product is not entitled to the benefit of *General Electric*; if it fixes the price at which licensees sell it violates the *per se* antitrust rule.[17] The rationale, that the *General Electric* rule is

---

14. American Equip. Co. v. Tuthill, 69 F.2d 406 (7th Cir. 1934). Cf. Barber-Colman Co. v. National Tool Co., 136 F.2d 339 (6th Cir. 1943).

15. Cummer-Graham Co. v. Straight Side Basket Corp., 142 F.2d 646 (5th Cir.), cert. denied, 323 U.S. 726, 65 S.Ct. 60, 89 L.Ed. 583 (1944). But see Straight Side Basket Corp. v. Webster Basket Co., 82 F.2d 245 (2d Cir. 1936).

16. United States v. General Elec. Co. (Carboy), 80 F.Supp. 989, 1004–1005 (S.D.N.Y.1948). But see General Elec. Co. v. Willey's Carbide Tool Co., 33 F.Supp. 969 (E.D.Mich.1940). Compare United States v. United States Gypsum Co., 333 U.S. 364, 384–85, 68 S.Ct. 525, 536–37, 92 L.Ed. 746, 760–61 (1948).

17. United States v. Vehicular Parking, Ltd., 54 F.Supp. 828 (D.Del.1944). See United States v. American Linen Supply Co., 141 F.Supp. 105 (N.D.Ill. 1956); but see Royal Indus. v. St. Regis Paper Co., 420 F.2d 449 (9th Cir. 1969).

needed to encourage licensing only where the patentee itself manufactures, is persuasive. Yet, one might plausibly contend that the thrust of the original *General Electric* rule, to enable the patentee to maximize returns, presupposes that the patentee may know better than the licensee what selling price will maximize the return on the patent monopoly; this consideration may be involved whether or not the patentee exploits in part by manufacturing itself. Perhaps the best explanation for the non-producing patentee exception to *General Electric* is that the precedent is itself so shaky that courts tend to distinguish it whenever possible.

f. Licenses on Patents of Two or More Patentees

Line Material [18] involved this situation: Following an interference proceeding, a dominant patent on "cut out" devices to protect electric circuits from overload was granted to Southern States and a subservient improvement patent was granted to Line Material. The two firms then gave each other royalty-free cross-licenses on these devices and agreed that Line Material might grant sublicenses under both. Each firm agreed not to sell devices it manufactured which embodied the patent of the other at prices less than those fixed by the patentee. Subsequently, Line Material, after joint meetings with several other manufacturers, granted several licenses under both patents, each license forbidding the licensee to sell any device utilizing Line Material's patent at prices less than those fixed by Line Material. Several licensees had, in bargaining, opposed the price restraint. Yet (because a copy of the proposed license agreement was sent to all prospective licensees following the joint meetings) each licensee knew that the price fixing provision was also contained in the license proposed to its competitors. Four justices voted to hold the licenses violative of Section 1 because, although they saw the case as controlled by *General Electric*, they felt that the case should be overruled. Three justices saw the case as controlled by *General Electric* and felt that on its authority the arrangement should be upheld. Justice Reed, who wrote the opinion of the Court, joined with the three dissenters in refusing to overrule *General Electric,* but with the four who would have overruled it in concluding that this particular arrangement was unlawful. The opinion assumes *General Electric*'s continued validity and holds that it is a violation of Section 1 for "two or more patentees * * * [to] combine their valid patent monopolies * * * through contractual arrangements between themselves and other licensees, for control of the sale price of the patented devices." [19]

The distinction Justice Reed was drawing is clear enough as an abstract matter and would be very persuasive if the two patents were substitutes which competed with each other. Applied in such a situa-

18. United States v. Line Material Co., 333 U.S. 287, 68 S.Ct. 550, 92 L.Ed. 701 (1948).

19. Id. at 305, 68 S.Ct. at 559, 92 L.Ed. at 716.

tion, the principle would be that even though a single patentee may fix prices, nevertheless, holders of two substitute patents may neither agree to do so, nor act jointly to do so. When they do, an additional and significant horizontal restraint is added; price competition is wiped out not only between a patentee and his licensees but also between the licensors as licensors of alternative technologies and between those practicing one patent and those practicing the other. Even if the two patents held by competitors were not competing patents, the Reed position would present no dilemma so long as the two patents did not block each other. One could conclude that, as a generality, price fixing licenses covering two patents in separate hands would impose upon competition more than would a license covering only one patent. But the distinction the opinion presses is arguably tenuous and technical when applied, as it actually was in *Line Material,* to the licensing of a dominant and subservient improvement patent. The latter could not be practiced at all except in conjunction with the former. In this very practical sense they were as one patent, not two.

It can hardly be supposed that Justice Reed failed to see this. Though he did not articulate it in this way, the explanation for his view might well have been the conviction that (even regarding the two patents as functionally equivalent to one) the *General Electric* rule is justified only where the privilege to fix prices may be necessary to encourage licensing coupled with the factual inference that the commercial incentive to cross-license blocking patents will result in licensing even though price fixing is forbidden. Or perhaps though not ready to join in overruling *General Electric,* he saw even a technical distinction as a sufficient basis for limiting its application.

g. *Licenses on Two or More Patents*

Line Material may go even further—far enough to suggest that any price fixing license covering two patents violates Section 1, even if the patents are held by the same patentee. Justice Reed stressed that the power of two patentees were being combined, that one of the patentees was granting licenses covering both patents and, though it was in terms fixing prices only on the exercise of its own improvement patent, it was in fact fixing prices on devices containing both patents, since any device practicing the improvement patent would necessarily involve an exercise also of the dominant patent. In Newburgh Moire Co. v. Superior Moire Co.,[20] price fixing licenses covering two separate patents were granted to two competitors which, with the licensor, accounted for three-fifths of the industry. The court, holding the arrangement invalid, stressed not the extent of industry coverage but that "the patent laws were not intended to empower a patentee to grant a plurality of licenses, each containing provisions fixing the price at which the licensee might sell * * *."[21] No

20. 237 F.2d 283 (3d Cir. 1956).   21. Id. at 293–94.

rationale is suggested for treating a plurality of licenses held by the same patentee differently from a single patent, but it could be argued that, even in the case where there was a single patentee-licensor, combining two patents in this way gives the licensee a greater incentive to seek the license and thus accept the price restriction; and therefore, that the power of one patent monopoly is being levered to achieve price fixing in the exploitation of one or more others.

h. *Cross Licensing and Price Fixing*

In *Line Material* one patentee was given power to grant licenses to use the patent of a competitor as well as its own. Suppose that no sublicensing had been involved, but only a showing that the firms traded price fixing licenses? Would *General Electric* be distinguishable? The Report of the Attorney General's National Committee to Study the Antitrust Laws asserts that cross-licensing is valid unless restrictions are used which would be unlawful in any license or the arrangement contains "some element of illegal horizontal agreement beyond the patent license."[22] Where A licenses its competitor, B, and fixes price in return for a similar license from B, is the extrinsic element of horizontal agreement provided? Leverage is involved here as it is where two patents are licensed together. A is using its power as a patent monopolist to gain not royalties, but access to another patent; B is doing the same. But this leverage analysis does not discriminate between price fixing cross-licenses and others; if accepted it would outlaw any cross-licensing arrangement, a position which is plainly too broad. Thus, if *Line Material* is to be read as forbidding cross-licensing with price fixing clauses, it must be upon some tighter rationale.

Resolution of this doctrinal dilemma may turn on the nature of the relationship between the patents. If they are competitive—so that, as a practical matter, a firm could function successfully in the market with only one of them—a basis for distinguishing *General Electric* is provided. In that case price competition was suppressed between two firms making the same product under the same patented technology. Hence, if price fixing were not allowed, one of those firms, the patent monopolist, might have filled the entire market itself; to the extent that such an alternative was likely, the adverse effect of the price fixing license is minimized. Where, by contrast, patents which otherwise might compete with each other are cross-licensed, a price fixing provision will tend to end price competition between two firms which otherwise would face each other in the marketplace, both selling the same product, each making it with its own technology. In that situation price fixing should plainly be prohibited. The public will be better off even if as a consequence no license

---

22. Report of the Attorney General's National Committee to Study the Antitrust Laws 242 (1955).

is given. Both firms will then stay in the market and compete; neither has the power by virtue of its patent to exclude the other.[23]

If cross-licensed patents, though independent, are not competing, the *General Electric* rule (which would support each of the price fixing licenses, if viewed separately) might be said to cover the cross-licenses. Yet, there is no need to allow price fixing cross-licenses to give both patentees such benefit as the *General Electric* rule still affords, if fixing prices on competing technology is not what they are seeking to achieve. Even under the broad prohibition that no cross licenses with price fixing is ever valid, two patentees could each independently license its own patent (with a price fixing clause). There is no need that the grant of one license be tied to the grant of the other. Hence, even the broadest reading of *Line Material* would not unduly restrict the *General Electric* rule.

i. *Patents Concerning Which There is Little Social Advantage in Encouraging Licensing*

Before deciding that *General Electric* ought to be abandoned entirely, picture this case. The patent is clearly valid. The technology is important and the patent covers a device having many uses which can be made much more cheaply than available substitutes. The patent therefore confers substantial market power. Unless permitted to fix prices charged by licensee-manufacturers for the device, the patentee will grant no licenses. If permitted to price fix, the patentee will license to all applicants. On these facts a rule precluding price fixing might adversely affect the public by depriving it of the benefits of non-price competition on the device, by depriving it of a wider dissemination of the technology, and, perhaps, by precluding an exploitation of the patent as widely as it might be profitably exploited. All aspects of the supposition are necessary to this conclusion, however. If the patent is not clearly valid, there may be a significant social cost in encouraging licensing; a competitor which might otherwise have successfully challenged validity may take a license instead of making the challenge.[24] If the patent does not significantly reduce costs, the social loss in not disseminating the technology and using the patent broadly may be slight. If the patent does not confer substantial power, the price fixing provisions may be a way of attaining power concertedly.[25]

---

23. See generally § 188 infra.

24. The fact that a firm has taken a license does not preclude it from challenging validity of a patent. Lear, Inc. v. Adkins, 395 U.S. 653, 89 S.Ct. 1902, 23 L.Ed.2d 610 (1969). However, the possession of a license may substantially reduce the licensee's incentive to attack the patent, particularly if other firms which are being excluded by the patent might use the technology upon a holding of invalidity.

25. Baxter's analysis (supra note 8) would suggest that, but for power concertedly obtained, price fixing would be ineffectual and superfluous, therefore that the fact of price fixing would warrant an inference of cartelization. But just as a firm with a patent monopoly may want to operate

It does not seem feasible to make a specific inquiry, even of an objective kind, much less a subjective one, in an effort to decide in particular cases what the patentee would hypothetically have done if *General Electric* were not on the books.[26] But if, on the face of the matter, it is clear either that the patentee would license whether or not permitted to fix prices (as might occur, for example, if the patent had no application in the industry where the patentee operated), or that there would be no significant adverse effect on the public were the patentee not to license (as where the patent convincingly appears to have only trivial commercial advantage), then permitting the patentee to fix prices would be gratuitously to allow an unnecessary competitive restriction. If the patent does not offer any significant competitive advantage, the patentee could not, by keeping it to itself, exclude others from the market. True, if the patentee would refuse to license though others were ready to pay royalties, the market for the patent might not be fully exploited. But if the patent had no great competitive significance—if things consumers wanted from the industry could be provided substantially as well and as cheaply without it—the social cost of any under-exploitation would be small. Moreover, if licensees did accept price fixing licenses on a patent of small commercial significance, there would in that fact alone be ground for concluding that the major motivation was not to gain access to the new technology, but to gain access to a price fixing arrangement.[27]

j. Cartelization Through Price Fixing Licenses

United States v. United States Gypsum Company[28] develops what is, in policy terms, the most significant limitation upon the *General Electric* rule. Gypsum had granted substantially identical price fixing licenses to substantially all of the numerous firms in the industry, with the consequence that the prices specified by Gypsum became the prevailing prices industry-wide; sales of unpatented products abated to a substantial extent and to the extent these sales continued, prices were set in differentials referable to the patented products. As the Court put it, "the industry is completely regimented, the production of competitive unpatented products suppressed, a class of distributors squeezed out, and prices on unpatented products stabilized."[29]

itself rather than stay out of the production market entirely and take its profits on licenses, so it may wish to exercise as much control as possible (expand to fill the market to the maximum degree it can) when it finds it necessary, as a means of financing the exploitation or for other reasons, to grant licenses.

26. On the use of objective rather than subjective evidence of hypothetical prospective business decisions, compare United States v. Falstaff Brewing Corp., 410 U.S. 526, 93 S.Ct. 1096, 35 L.Ed.2d 475 (1973).

27. Compare United States v. United States Gypsum Co., 333 U.S. 364, 68 S.Ct. 525, 92 L.Ed. 746 (1948).

28. Id.

29. Id. at 400, 68 S.Ct. at 544, 92 L.Ed. at 769.

Masonite[30] is another case where price fixing licenses were used to cartelize an industry. There, the Court held the arrangement invalid by analogy to *Interstate Circuit*,[31] despite evidence that Masonite imposed the arrangement on the licensees. *New Wrinkle*[32] is to like effect. There a patent holding company was formed by competing industry members, and they then assigned patents to it in settlement of patent litigation between them; the holding company then granted price fixing licenses to over two hundred firms, substantially all members of the industry, under an arrangement which provided for modest royalties and delayed the effectiveness of the price fixing clause until the twelve largest firms in the industry had accepted the arrangement.

There is something perplexing about these cases, a doubt about their scope. Read for their implication, they hold that price fixing licenses are unlawful when from the entire context it appears that either the purpose or the effect of the price fixing licenses is to reduce competition, a conclusion warranted whenever the arrangement serves to fix prices for industry output, with the patentee acting much as might a cartel agent to police and enforce the arrangement. A minimum factual necessity for such a construction would be that sufficient percentage of the industry capacity be drawn into the arrangement so that the "cartel" possesses power to fix prices and that either the patented product itself constitutes a separate market or that output of non-patented substitutes not be so large as to deprive the "cartel" of power. Other factors, found in varying degrees in the cases and strongly or weakly suggestive of anticompetitive purpose or effect, would include: indications of interdependence (like firms hesitating to take licenses without knowledge or assurance that substantial numbers of other firms or that leading or large firms had done so); use of legally weak or commercially insignificant patents; establishment of differentials between non-patented and patented products which take the fixed price on the patented product as a base; and less competitive performance by the industry following the initiation of the arrangement (such as prices less responsive to changes in supply or demand).[33] Pointing the other way would be any evidence suggesting that licensees did not wish to have prices restricted, such as evi-

---

30. United States v. Masonite Corp., 316 U.S. 365, 62 S.Ct. 1070, 86 L.Ed. 1461 (1942).

31. Interstate Circuit, Inc. v. United States, 306 U.S. 208, 59 S.Ct. 467, 83 L.Ed. 610 (1939). See §§ 110, 112 supra.

32. United States v. New Wrinkle, Inc., 342 U.S. 371, 72 S.Ct. 350, 96 L.Ed. 417 (1952).

33. Cf. McCullough v. Kammerer Corp., 166 F.2d 759 (9th Cir.), cert. denied 335 U.S. 813, 69 S.Ct. 30, 93 L.Ed. 368 (1948); National Lockwasher Co. v. Geo. K. Garrett Co., 137 F.2d 255 (3d Cir. 1943). P. Areeda, Antitrust Analysis, Problems, Text, Cases, ¶ 418 (2d ed. 1974); Handler, Blake, Pitofsky and Goldschmid, Trade Regulation, Cases and Materials 394–96 (1975).

dence that one or more of them argued against restriction, or offered higher royalties for an unrestricted license.[34]

Whether this reading of the patent cartel cases, which merely requires evidence that the price fixing licenses have either the purpose or effect of restricting competition, is the correct reading is something of an open question. One can argue from the facts and language of *Gypsum* and *New Wrinkle* that Section 1 is transgressed only when a purpose to cartelize is shown, only when on the evidence the patent license can be characterized as a mere sham with licensees being motivated not to acquire the protected technology but to acquire the price fixing arrangement that goes with it. On this view of the law, a showing that the price fixing license covers a substantial portion of the industry and that its effect is like that of a price cartel would not be enough. *General Electric* itself serves to bolster this purpose-oriented view of the cartel cases, for there, though there was only one license, it was granted to the only significant competitor. But none of the patent cartel cases demand this more permissive reading and, indeed, the fact that in *Masonite* the Court relied upon *Interstate Circuit* suggests that any time firms in an industry participate under a license which effectively sets prices they are in violation.

Moreover, the purpose-oriented reading of these license-cartel cases, which leaves out the possibility of finding a violation on evidence of competitive effect alone, would force forward tough factual issues in every case. In jury cases, the court on proper instructions would have to ask the jury to decide what really motivated the parties to the arrangement, a desire to gain access to useful patented technology, even though price restricted, or a desire to attain a price fixing arrangement, even though a patent license had to be paid for to achieve that goal. It would be an awkward issue to frame, for it is possible that motives will vary from licensee to licensee and that even for any one licensee motives will be mixed. To some licensees or to all or many in some degree, the patent may seem desirable on its own terms; to some of these the license may seem most desirable if not price restricted, but to others the prospect of relief from price competition may also appeal; at the far extreme will be, perhaps, some licensees that regard their own technology as being as good or better than the patented technology and that take licenses only in order to encourage formation of what these licensees perceive as a cartel. Let us be more specific. Assume that no firms fall into the last category (that any which like price fixing but not the technology simply stay out, hoping for a dispensation from price competition attributable to the fact that most others will take licenses) and that most fall into the middle category (that they want the patent and would pay a

---

34. But cf. United States v. Masonite Corp., 316 U.S. 265, 62 S.Ct. 1070, 86 L.Ed. 1461 (1942).

royalty for it, but that many of them like it better because price fixing comes with it). A court will find it extremely difficult to instruct in ways which will enable a jury to deal rationally with a purpose standard on facts such as those.

Putting aside intractability, purpose alone is an inadequate standard. The patent cartel cases, if read to mean that any set of price fixing licenses which has the purpose or the effect of inhibiting price competition in a market is unlawful, will be in better consonance with general legal theory about cartels and with the numerous other cases which have confined *General Electric* narrowly. After all, *G.E.* holds no more than that a price fixing license rolls fair of the antitrust baseline when it is "reasonably within the reward" to which the patentee is entitled.[35] When the effect is to end price competition throughout a substantial part of a definable product and geographic market, the arrangement involves monopolistic extension and cannot be said to be "reasonably" within the patentee's reward.[36] A broad reading of the patent cartel cases, to withdraw the protection of *G.E.* upon any showing of conventional cartelization as the purpose *or* effect of price fixing licenses, is the minimum response which the law in this area ought to make to the insights yielded by economic analysis.[37]

§ 186. License Provisions Which Impose Horizontal Restrictions Respecting the Fields of Use Within Which the Patent will be Practiced

a. In General

A patent may have application in more than one commercial field. License restrictions sometimes confine the licensee by excluding it from some field or fields where the patent might have value. The forms of these restrictions are various. They may be framed as customer restrictions. (For example, a license may authorize one licensee to sell the patented article—or an unpatented article either made with the patented process or containing the patented article as a subpart—only to widget manufacturers and another license may authorize another licensee to sell only to gizmo manufacturers). The license might in form limit the design or style of the product to be manufactured. (For example, a license to one licensee might authorize the manufacture of patented amplifiers in sizes suitable for commercial use and a license to another authorize the making

---

35. United States v. General Electric Co., 272 U.S. 476, 489, 47 S.Ct. 192, 196, 71 L.Ed. 362, 370 (1926).

36. Compare United States v. General Instrument Corp., 87 F.Supp. 157, 193 (D.N.J.1949); United States v. General Electric Co. (Lamps), 82 F.Supp. 753, 891 (D.N.J.1949) (intent need not be shown where effect of pooling or cross-licensing is restrictive). But see Cutter Laboratories v. Lyophile-Cryochem Corp., 179 F.2d 80, 93 (9th Cir. 1949).

37. See Baxter, supra note 8.

of them in sizes suitable only for home use.) The restriction may, in form, limit the type of mechanisms into which the licensee incorporates the patented item (for example, a license authorizing the licensee to make a patented oven but to use it only by incorporating it into gas stoves, and another license authorizing a different licensee to make it but only for incorporation into electric stoves).

All these arrangements enable the patentee to deal separately with licensees which will use the patents in different fields, thus charging to each a price which maximizes the patentee's profit from the exploitation of the patent in that field. In short, field restrictions facilitate price discrimination.[1] In the generality of cases this can be taken to be their purpose. Indeed, field restrictions are closely related in purpose to differential royalty arrangements through which the patentee, though not limiting a license to any field, exacts a royalty on a basis which will reflect the different values of the patent in different applications.

None of this denies that field of use restrictions may have effects in addition to—and, of course, may therefore have purposes other than—discrimination. At worst, a set of field restrictions could be a mechanism around which a group of actual or potential competitors cartelize by dividing fields and avoiding competition.[2] There are, then, a number of variables to deal with—the form of the restriction; whether it falls within the inherent grant of the patent; the way it resonates to antitrust doctrine outside the patent field; the relation of the restriction to discriminatory royalty changes; the purpose and the effect on competition; and, of course, what the case law has to say.

b. Royalty rates which vary from one field of use to another

When field of use restrictions are utilized, discriminatory royalty rates are usually found in association with them. This fact sharply distinguishes these restrictions from price and territorial restrictions. It gives them perhaps a stronger claim to being benign commercial instruments than can be asserted on behalf of either price or territorial restrictions. Sometimes it is possible for the patentee to exact discriminatory royalties without a field restriction. This subsection treats the preliminary question—the competitive effect and legal va-

---

1. See generally, W. Bowman, Patent and Antitrust Law ch. 5 (1973), particularly pp. 100–115. See also Gibbons, Field Restrictions in Patent Transactions: Economic Discrimination and Restraint of Competition, 66 Colum.L.Rev. 423 (1966); P. Areeda, Antitrust Analysis, Problems, Text, Cases ch. 4-C (2d ed. 1974).

2. See United States v. American Linen Supply Co., 141 F.Supp. 105, 112–114 (N.D.Ill.1956); United States v. Associated Patents, Inc., 134 F.Supp. 74 (E.D.Mich.1955), aff'd per curiam sub nom. Mac Inv. Co. v. United States, 350 U.S. 960, 76 S.Ct. 432, 100 L.Ed. 834 (1956). Compare United States v. United States Gypsum Co., 333 U.S. 364, 68 S.Ct. 525, 92 L.Ed. 746 (1948); Hartford-Empire Co. v. United States, 323 U.S. 386, 65 S.Ct. 373, 89 L.Ed. 322 (1945).

lidity of discriminatory royalty provisions when directly imposed. Only if such discriminations are themselves permissible can a claim be made for the validity of field restrictions as instrumental restraints used to achieve discrimination.

Conventional price theory teaches that a patent monopolist, like any other seller, will seek to maximize the difference between total cost and total revenue. If the patentee licenses the patent and establishes a single royalty charge to all licensees, it will seek to set the royalty rate so that the marginal return from additional licenses will be equal to the marginal cost of granting (and policing) them. (Since marginal cost will be relatively very small, this point will be near that at which an increase or decrease in the price for a license would have no effect on total revenue—that is, near the point where, were the royalty increased, the revenue lost from reduced numbers of licenses would just equal the revenue gained from increased payments from those who took licenses.) This price, however, may be based on a demand schedule for licenses which summarizes the demands of individual licensees and potential licensees, each of which value the license quite differently. If the patentee could exploit these differences by charging not one royalty rate for every license, but a higher rate to firms which value the license more and a lower rate to those which value it less, the patentee would be able to earn more. If the reason different licensees value the patent differently has to do with the intensity with which they expect to use the patented device, the patentee may be able to exploit these differences by setting a royalty schedule (applicable to all licensees in all fields) which measures intensity of use. If the reason is that potential licensees in different fields where the patent might be practiced have different demand elasticities, to exploit the situation the patentee might find it necessary to set a different rate for different fields of use.

Is it lawful for a patent holder to charge for a license on a basis that varies the amount paid by the licensee with the utility of the invention to the licensee? Let us consider first a royalty schedule that applies in the same way to all licensees in all fields, but which varies the royalty rate with intensity of use. The old case of Heaton-Peninsular Button Fastener Company v. Eureka Specialty Company [3] suggests that this degree of control over price is inherent in the patent. The firm holding the patent might charge a flat rate for a license to practice the technology. It need not do so. Alternatively, it may charge a specified sum per unit of output or per unit of use, or may use any other measure which gauges the utility of the patent to a particular licensee. In general, the patent holder has as much latitude in pricing its property as does the owner of any other kind of property. An analysis indicating that competitive harm is being done by a particular pricing method may warrant forbidding that

---

3. 65 F. 619 (W.D.Mich.1895).

method.⁴ But merely pricing in a way that meters utility of the patent to the licensee and maximizes the patentee's return is not unlawful.⁵

A royalty rate which discriminates between one field of use and another has essentially the same purpose. Suppose, to simplify, that the patented item, a motion picture projector, can be made in two sizes, one sufficient for commercial use, the other for home movies. One would expect demand elasticities between two such varied fields to differ; the profit maximizing royalty rate for the commercial field may well be higher than that for the home entertainment field. If so, use of any single rate will sacrifice possible returns. If the patent holder elected the high rate to gain all it can from commercial application, it would forego substantially all returns from the home field by pricing its device out of that market; but if it elected a rate low enough to gain maximum returns there, it would be earning less than the maximum possible in the commercial field. So long as some licensees are authorized to practice the invention in each field, the use of such a discriminatory rate involves no collateral restriction and therefore can be analogized to a rate which measures value to the user. A discrimination results, but it is a discrimination which may facilitate wider dispersion of the technology (if forced to choose a single rate, the patentee might find it most profitable to choose the high one). On this kind of an analysis the use of separate royalty schedules for different fields of use ought not to be unlawful.⁶

c. *Field Restrictions Which Facilitate Royalty Rate Differentials with Multiple Licensees in Each Field*

The relationship between field of use restrictions and price discrimination arises because, as a practical matter, a patent holder may not be able successfully to vary the royalty rate from field to field unless it imposes restrictions which inhibit licensees in the low rate field from practicing in the high rate field. Suppose the patented device is a small gear which can greatly increase efficiency of movie projectors, and which is much more valuable in commercial projectors than in the ones made for home use. If the patent holder grants licenses authorizing use in both applications but specifies separate royalty schedules for each, the administrative costs to the licensee of computing royalty costs and to the licensor of auditing to be sure it is being properly paid may be onerous. It is not only that deliberate cheating by licensees becomes relatively easy, it is also that the costs of accuracy become excessive. In situations like that, a patent holder

---

4. See United States v. Paramount Pictures, Inc., 334 U.S. 131, 158–61, 68 S. Ct. 915, 929–31, 92 L.Ed. 1260, 1292–94 (1948).

5. Cf. General Talking Pictures v. Western Elec. Co., 304 U.S. 175, 58 S. Ct. 849, 82 L.Ed. 1273, aff'd on rehearing 305 U.S. 124, 59 S.Ct. 116, 83 L. Ed. 81 (1938).

6. As to discriminatory pricing in the sale of commodities, see Chapter 8 infra.

seeking to utilize differential royalties may adopt field of use restrictions for support. If a licensee is authorized to use the device only in one application, a royalty rate appropriate to that application can be established; no more than the gross, routine investigation that is always needed to protect against infringement will be required to assure that the licensee is not using the technology in unauthorized fields. Other licensees may be authorized at different rates for other fields.

The case law on the legality of field of use restrictions is ambiguous. In *General Talking Pictures* [7] the Supreme Court upheld the validity of a field of use restriction; in its 1950 decision in Automatic Radio Manufacturing Company v. Hazeltine Research, Inc., it avoided the issue.[8] Lower court decisions, though generally upholding validity,[9] do not always do so,[10] and seldom analyze the issues to any depth. Let us then consider how competitive effects might be analyzed.[11]

So long as in each field the patent holder stands ready to license all firms desiring to use the technology, this type of arrangement will not, except in special structural circumstances, be likely to restrict competition to any significant degree. It is conceivable, of course, that a firm operating and licensed in field A will be deterred from

---

7. General Talking Pictures v. Western Elec. Co., 304 U.S. 175, 58 S.Ct. 849, 82 L.Ed. 1273, aff'd on rehearing 305 U.S. 124, 59 S.Ct. 116, 83 L.Ed. 81 (1938). The action was one against a firm which purchased the patented product from a licensee knowing of the restriction and intending to violate it; the holding that the defendant was guilty of infringement necessarily involves a conclusion that the restriction was itself valid.

8. 339 U.S. 827, 70 S.Ct. 894, 94 L.Ed. 1312 (1950). Compare Hartford-Empire Co. v. United States, 323 U.S. 386, 65 S.Ct. 373, 89 L.Ed. 322 (1945) and Ethyl Gasoline Corp. v. United States, 309 U.S. 436, 60 S.Ct. 618, 84 L.Ed. 852 (1940) which the government has argued undercut General Talking Pictures. See Hearings on S.643 Before the Senate Subcommittee on Patents, Trademarks, and Copyrights of the Committee on the Judiciary, 92d Cong., 1st Sess., pt. 2, at 494 (1971).

9. E.g., Benger Labs, Ltd. v. R. K. Laros Co., 209 F.Supp. 639 (E.D.Pa.1962), aff'd per curiam, 317 F.2d 455 (3d Cir.), cert. denied, 375 U.S. 833, 84 S.Ct. 69, 11 L.Ed.2d 64 (1963); Turner Glass Corp. v. Hartford-Empire Co., 173 F.2d 49 (7th Cir. 1949), cert. denied, 338 U.S. 830, 70 S.Ct. 57, 94 L. Ed. 505 (1949); Chemagro Corp. v. Universal Chem. Co., 244 F.Supp. 486 (E.D.Tex.1965); Sperry Prods. Inc. v. Aluminum Co. of America, 171 F. Supp. 901 (N.D.Ohio 1959), aff'd in part, 285 F.2d 911 (6th Cir. 1960), cert. denied, 368 U.S. 890, 82 S.Ct. 142, 7 L. Ed.2d 87 (1961); Westinghouse Elec. Corp. v. Bulldog Elec. Prods. Co., 106 F.Supp. 819 (N.D.W.Va.1952), aff'd 206 F.2d 574 (4th Cir.), cert. denied 346 U.S. 909, 74 S.Ct. 240, 98 L.Ed. 406 (1953).

10. E.g., Baldwin-Lima-Hamilton Corp. v. Tatnall Measuring Systems, Co., 169 F.Supp. 1 (E.D.Pa.1958) aff'd per curiam 268 F.2d 395 (3d Cir.), cert. denied 361 U.S. 894, 80 S.Ct. 190, 4 L. Ed.2d 151 (1959); United States v. Consolidated Car-Healing Co., 1950 CCH Trade Cas. ¶ 62,655 (S.D.N.Y.) Cf. United States v. American Linen Supply Co., 141 F.Supp. 105 (N.D.Ill. 1956).

11. See, generally, the analysis suggested by Areeda supra note 1, ¶¶ 432–435 (2d ed. 1974) and that developed in Bowman supra note 1 and in Gibbons supra note 1.

entering field B, a field it would have entered were it free to acquire the technology for use in that field without giving it up in field A. In special structural circumstances this could be a serious competitive detriment. For example, field B might be a non-competitive field protected by other entry barriers in addition to the patent in question; firms in field A might be among the few potential entrants to field B. Absent the field restriction, the presence of field A firms as potential entrants might motivate firms in field B to price lower so as to deter entry by field A firms; the presence of the field restrictions might give field B firms the assurance they need that field A firms will not enter, thus enabling them to price at supra-competitive levels. This and other hypothetical situations can be supposed in which the inference would be warranted that the field restriction, even though motivated solely to facilitate differential royalties which maximize the return to the patentee, has a serious anticompetitive effect. But absent such special structural circumstances—which, if they exist, ought to be capable of being identified and demonstrated—the use of the field restrictions, when the patentee licenses all applicants within each field, should not be held unlawful.[12]

d. *Field Restrictions Which Preserve One or More Fields for the Patent Holder Exclusively*

Another motive for field restrictions may be to protect the patent holder against use of the patent in the field which it exploits itself. Assuming that the patent holder grants or stands ready to grant multiple licenses to practice the fields it does not exploit, the antitrust arguments against allowing this kind of a restriction are not particularly strong.[13] True, the patent holder maintains for itself an exclusive right which may give it a competitive advantage in its field. But on a static analysis, at least, the effect is little different from that which would result if the patent holder granted multiple licenses, so long as it priced—as we assume it lawfully might—in a manner maximizing its return from each particular field including its own. By multiple licenses it could gain in each field the full monopoly profit adhering in the patent; by exploiting itself, even if it thereby confines the entire field to itself, it can gain no larger return.

Of course, a static analysis may not exhaust the inquiry. By excluding others, the patentee may in its field diminish the likelihood of

---

12. An argument for illegality might be predicated on the broad proposition that the users whose demand is high, especially if constituting a large group, ought to be protected against being discriminated against, just as a large class of users having a different and lower demand cross-elasticity than buyers as a whole will be treated as constituting a separate market for Section 2 purposes in those instances where it is possible to discriminate against the class. Compare United States v. Grinnell Corp., 384 U.S. 563, 86 S.Ct. 1698, 16 L.Ed.2d 778 (1966) (central station alarm services differentiated from other alarm services because for some buyers only these services would do).

13. See the materials cited in note 1 supra. Compare United States v. Birdsboro Steel Foundry & Machine Co., 139 F.Supp. 244 (W.D.Pa.1956).

other innovations over the term of the patent and may facilitate its own dominance even after patent expiration, as a consequence of its long lead time as the sole producer. But these are all advantages the patent holder is plainly entitled to under the patent if it excludes licensees entirely. To allow such exclusivity in one field only does broaden the patentee's options somewhat. If exclusivity within a single field while licensing elsewhere were not permitted, the patentee would have to choose either to license for all fields or not to license at all. If it chose the latter course, the public would be benefited—not as a result of a competitive price immediately, but in light of the dynamic potential. However, the alternative choice—and, *a priori,* we have no basis for supposing it in any instance to be less likely—would intensify the public detriment; it would mean single firm exploitation of the patent in any field where it was exploited and might mean non-exploitation in some fields or even in all save the single field the patentee would itself exploit.

Legality might conceivably be made to turn on an assessment of what the patent holder would do in fact if forced to choose either to license freely in all fields or not to license at all. A license reserving a field would be held lawful only if, were it not permitted, the patent holder would refuse to give any license. But to assign to courts the task of deciding how in an individual case the patent holder, if forced to it, would choose, would burden the courts considerably, would assign them a hypothetical and often speculative or indeterminate question to resolve, and would do so in the service of potential gains which are themselves speculative and indeterminate and in most instances probably rather small. The need, then, is for a rule—a generalization either legitimizing or condemning restraints whereby a patent holder reserves a field to itself while licensing freely in other fields. Given the historic understanding that field restrictions are part of the patent grant, a rule validating such arrangements seems appropriate.

e. *Exclusive Licenses Containing Field of Use Restrictions*

Suppose the patent holder not only reserves a field for itself, but also reserves fields for one or more licensees by granting exclusive licenses to practice the patented technology in specified fields.[14] Or suppose the patent holder, though not contracting to grant field exclusivity, in fact refuses licenses in each field except to a single firm. These arrangements will often involve differential royalty rates and may be defended as examples of field restrictions aimed at price discrimination. But so long as each license restricts to a field, discrimination can be effectively accomplished without limiting the number of licenses in any field; the additional restraint is gratuitous, so far as the accomplishment of discrimination in royalty rates is concerned.

14. See Areeda, supra note 1.

Grants of exclusive fields may also be defended on the ground that the patent holder—concededly permitted to discriminate—cannot obtain the full return in each field unless free to bargain for the best arrangement there, which might require the granting of an exclusive license. But theory teaches that if the monopoly has value in any field, the patent holder can fully exploit that value by fixing a profit maximizing price for that field and licensing to all comers. A single licensee could earn no more in any field than a reasonable return, plus the monopoly profit attributable to the patent; the exclusive licensee, therefore, should be willing to pay for the license up to but no more than the portion of that return attributable to the patent monopoly. The patent holder can extract this same amount by fixing its own profit maximizing royalty for the field and licensing to all comers. The indicated analysis is precisely that which Baxter makes when evaluating price fixing licenses.[15] If the restriction gains the patentee anything that cannot be obtained without the restriction, it can only be market power.

There is, then, no discernible benefit to the patent holder of a kind which ought to be said to be inherent in the patent monopoly which is derived from permitting exclusive licenses containing field restrictions. On the other hand, there are competitive dangers which adhere in such licenses and which are not encountered in other examples of use restrictive licenses. A series of exclusive licenses which limit each licensee to one field may do much more than facilitate the patentee's effort to price discriminate and thus maximize returns; such licenses may also effectively cartelize what otherwise would have been a competitive market where each of the licensees encountered competition from some of the others in whatever field or fields it practiced. One might argue that if cartelization were the purpose or effect of field restricting licenses, it would be possible to demonstrate that. For example, if before the licenses were granted licensees operated with other technology in all fields and, after taking licenses, abandoned all fields except where the patent authorized entry, an inference of cartelization would be warranted; the inference would become well-nigh overwhelming if, in addition, it were shown that the patent was weak and that licensees could have continued to compete profitably without the patent in fields in which they were not licensed.

Despite the possibility of sorting out the cartelization cases from others, there are forceful reasons for invalidating all arrangements where, by exclusive licensing or by unilaterally refusing to grant more than one license, the patent holder divides fields among licensees. Even if discrimination rather than cartelization is the objective, the patent holder has chosen a method of discrimination which maximizes

---

15. Baxter, Legal Restrictions on Exploitation of the Patent Monopoly: An Economic Analysis, 76 Yale L.Rev. 267 (1966).

competitive risks without gaining any consequential additional advantage for itself. There is no sufficient basis for putting judicial machinery to the expense of sorting the one case out from the others and putting the public to the risk that mistakes will at times be made.

§ 187. Customer Restrictions in Licenses

A patent holder may resort to a customer restriction to achieve goals similar to those discussed in early sections. For example, if the patent covered a movie projector, price discrimination might be facilitated by authorizing some licensees to sell only to retailers of home entertainment products and authorizing other licensees to sell to commercial users. So used, the customer restriction performs the function of a horizontal field restriction. Arguably, such an arrangement ought to be analyzed like a field of use restriction where, as in the hypothetical, the purpose and effect are clear. Just as the form of a restriction should not protect it when, in substance, it is unlawful, so the form should not condemn it when, in substance, it is or may be lawful.

Of course, a customer restriction may also be intended not to divide or reserve fields but, though the patent holder is licensing competitors even in its own field, to carve out some customers—such as large or governmental accounts—to whom the patent holder alone may sell. One might defend the latter type of arrangement on grounds similar to those pressed in favor of allowing a patentee to reserve its own field. Suppose, for example, the patented item were usable in association with computers and the patentee reserved to itself sales to the federal and state government and universities, major computer users. The contention would be open that since the patentee can earn no more than its full monopoly return and since it could exclude others entirely, there is no compelling reason to object to the partial exclusion. Indeed, the restriction, even in this form, does no more than facilitate discrimination; the users reserved (which presumably will have to pay higher prices) are in all likelihood those with the highest demands.

Despite the seeming plausibility of these justifications for customer restrictions in a license, there is a case to be made for applying a *per se* prohibition even where the restriction is used to divide fields and thus discriminate or to reserve a customer for the patent holder. The blatant customer restriction is a clumsy and also a provocative device for discriminating or reserving a field. An intent to divide fields to facilitate discrimination can be expressed directly by means of an explicit field restriction. This method will seem less invidious to affected firms. So also, reservation of a field for the patent holder can be accomplished by defining the field reserved in neutral terms which will not generate the kind of resentment which could occur if named customers or a narrow class of customers were singled out to be deprived of competition. Firms marked off from others for seemingly adverse treatment are likely to feel unfairly dealt with though they would not if the discrimination were achieved through some objective mechanism, applied evenhandedly. Furthermore, there are values in the symmetry of the law which would be lost if customer restrictions were not condemned in this context. These kinds of restrictions, wherever else encountered, are *per se* unlawful;[1] to exempt them from that treatment here on the basis of a distinction the force and relevance of which will not be immediately apparent to actors in the marketplace, may be to dilute unduly the authority of the law.

§ 188. Settlement of Patent Disputes

a. *In General*

Patent claims are pregnant with dispute. The issues are varied. Is a claimed invention novel, or already in the public domain? Which of two or more claimants is the inventor? Is a particular patent infringed by a similar but somewhat different technology? Issues such as these can arise at various stages—before a patent is granted (in the course of an interference proceeding before the patent examiner) or after one or more patents has been awarded to one or more of the disputants. They can be settled by any of a variety of devices. During the application stage, priority may be conceded by one party to the other; after a patent has been granted validity may be conceded. In any of these instances the quid pro quo may be a license, or where all or several parties claim patents, a pool may be formed.

Here, as elsewhere, there is a public policy favoring settlement.[1] Dispute resolution through litigation is socially costly. But the interests being adjusted are not wholly private ones. The public is or may be significantly and adversely affected if a settlement results in a technology being monopolized which, but for the settlement, would have become part of the public domain. In assessing settlements under the antitrust laws, the competing public interests in free technology and in settlement of disputes should each be given reasonable scope. The factors which may bear upon the analysis require that consideration be given to the stage of the process at which the dispute is settled, the scope of the issues settled, and the effects which the particular settlement is likely to have, given its industrial setting.

b. *Settlements during Interference Proceedings*

Where competing patent applications are pending, the examiner will declare an interference and each applicant will be heard as to

---

1. See United States v. Topco Associates, Inc., 405 U.S. 596, 92 S.Ct. 1126, 31 L.Ed.2d 515 (1972).

1. See Standard Oil Co. (Indiana) v. United States, 283 U.S. 163, 51 S.Ct. 421, 75 L.Ed. 926 (1931); Apex Elec. Mfg. Co. v. Altorfer, 238 F.2d 867 (7th Cir. 1956); Baker-Cammack Hosiery Mill v. Davis Co., 181 F.2d 550 (4th Cir. 1950), cert. denied 340 U.S. 824, 71 S.Ct. 58, 95 L.Ed. 605 (1950); United States v. Birdsboro Steel Foundry & Mach. Co., 139 F.Supp. 244 (W.D. Pa.1956).

priority and as to the validity of the respective claims. Any firm confronting another in this fashion will see several possible outcomes should the dispute be pursued to the end: it gains priority, its invention is held patentable and broad enough claims are allowed so it can exclude the other firms; the other firm gains priority and a patent and excludes it; it (or the other) gains priority, but no patent issues; it (or the the other) gains priority and only narrow claims are granted which will not exclude the other (or it).[2] The first alternative will obviously be seen as best, the second as worst, the others as in between. But if settlement is introduced as a possibility, new alternatives are presented which in terms of desirability stand at some point bracketed by the alternatives already listed. Thus, a settlement might result in a patent to one firm with it granting a license to the opponent, or conversely. Neither of these is as good as winning it all. But to the contestants either is better than having the technology held exclusively by an opponent or the placement of the technology in the public domain where anyone can use it. In such a contest, given the uncertainties of a litigation outcome, settlement may often occur. The problem for the public is that the settlement, though resulting in a somewhat less restricted technology than if either party prevailed fully, results in a much more restricted technology than if neither gained a patent. In those instances where, but for settlement, no patent would have issued, the public pays a potentially high price for the social gain that some litigation has been avoided.

This backdrop starkly displays the difference between a settlement dealing only with the issues of priority and one which leads to withdrawal of a challenge to patent validity.[3] If only priority were compromised and the challenge to validity went forward with full vigor, no risk to the public would arise from the settlement. But the likelihood of such a settlement at the application stage is small. Even if a firm which must still face a challenge on the ground of validity were willing to grant a license in order to buy peace on the priority issue, a firm which concedes on the issue of priority in return for a license would not be motivated to spend its resources and energy challenging validity. Such a challenge would, if successful, free it of a royalty obligation, but it would also open the technology to all. In most instances where an interference is settled, the party conced-

2. See the analysis of Standard Oil Co. (Indiana) v. United States, 283 U.S. 163, 51 S.Ct. 421, 75 L.Ed. 926 (1931), and of patent settlement issues suggested by McGee, Patent Exploitation: Some Economic and Legal Problems, 9 J. Law & Econ. 135, 150–60 (1966); P. Areeda, Antitrust Analysis, Problems, Text, Cases ¶ 438 (2d ed. 1974); W. Bowman, Patent and Antitrust Law 218–23 (1973); and Report of the Attorney General's National Committee to Study the Antitrust Laws 247 (1955) (comments of L. B. Schwartz).

3. See Standard Oil Co. (Indiana) v. United States, 283 U.S. 163, 51 S.Ct. 421, 75 L.Ed. 926 (1931); compare United States v. Singer Mfg. Co., 374 U.S. 174, 197, 83 S.Ct. 1773, 1785, 10 L.Ed.2d 823, 839 (1963) (White, J. concurring). See also United States v. Union Camp Corp., 1969 CCH Trade Cas. ¶ 72,689, 72,844 (E.D.Va.).

ing priority will have expressly or impliedly agreed to withdraw or, without agreement, would withdraw anyway.[4]

Where, as typically occurs, an interference settlement leads to withdrawal of opposition to validity, either before or after a patent has issued, what are the constraints of Section 1 upon the agreement? If expressly or by implication the parties agree to suppress information adverse to the claim of patentability, the agreement transcends permissible standards and ought to be held to violate Section 1. Such an agreement is plainly unreasonable and strongly tends to the restraint of trade. The most extreme example of suppression would be an overt fraud—presentation to the patent examiner of materials calculated to mislead.[5] But suppression might occur short of an act of fraud. For example, the parties might agree on steps which are intended to reduce the likelihood that the examiner would on his own initiative come upon information adverse to the claim. Concerted action of this kind, which affords no social benefit, should be forbidden under Section 1 because it significantly enhances the possibility that the participating firms will gain a degree of control over the relevant technology which inhibits competition. Patent policy accords no support to a claim that an asserted innovation be shielded from that scrutiny which the Patent Code itself envisages as a means for determining whether protection under the Code has been earned. Indeed, the policy emanating from the Patent Code is in this instance essentially the same as that advanced by the Sherman Act. The integrity of the substantive standards of the patent law and the integrity of the patent procedures both demand that efforts to gain patent protection through suppression of evidence adverse to patentability be inhibited.

If suppression cannot be shown, settlement of an interference (like settlements of a suit challenging validity of a patent already issued) must be treated as lawful even though the likelihood of accurate determination of validity issues is somewhat reduced. The patent application procedure does not rely upon adversary presentations, however helpful they may in fact be, but upon investigation by the patent office to determine whether there is conflicting prior art. It would be extreme to draft as the unwilling champion of the public interest any private party which challenged validity in its own interest —to force it, in effect, to act for the public even though it has

---

4. A competing applicant which accepted a license would not be estopped from challenging validity and even an express agreement not to do so would not foreclose it from challenging validity. Lear, Inc. v. Adkins, 395 U.S. 653, 670–71, 89 S.Ct. 1902, 1911, 23 L. Ed.2d 610, 622–23 (1969). However, the firm settling and accepting a license will have a much diminished incentive to challenge validity.

5. See Walker Process Equip., Inc. v. Food Mach. & Chem. Corp., 382 U.S. 172, 86 S.Ct. 347, 15 L.Ed.2d 247 (1965); American Cyanamid Co. v. FTC, 363 F.2d 757 (6th Cir. 1966); United States v. Union Camp Corp., 1969 CCH Trade Cas. ¶¶ 72,689, 72,844 (E.D.Va.). See § 179(b) supra.

worked out a satisfactory settlement of its own complaint. So long as it does not interfere with the functioning of the established public process, such a party ought to be free to stand aside. True, a contrary implication emerges from the concurring opinion of Justice White in the *Singer* case.[6] The Justice saw it as odd that a challenging party, in return for a concession of its right to practice a technology, could stand aside while a claiming party gained a franchise to exclude others when, had the challenging party persisted, the franchise might not have been granted. But the outcome is not so dangerous as the White opinion suggests—after all, examiners often if not always do discover prior art when their search is not interfered with; and there is opportunity for any affected party to challenge patent validity in later judicial proceedings. Moreover, to respond to the danger under the antitrust laws would require a rule making any settlement entailing withdrawal of a challenge to validity a *per se* violation of Section 1; this would not only be anomalous and extreme as an expression of antitrust policy, but would unduly deter settlements and burden the interference procedures, often, no doubt, in instances where the case against patentability, or the potential contribution of the conceding party to that case, is small.

c. *Patent Pools*

We saw that the creation of a pool may violate Section 2;[7] it may also violate Section 1, even in the context of a settlement. Suppose that two or more competing or potentially competing firms each has a patent or pending application on relevant technology, and that each asserts both invalidity or non-patentability of the claims of each of the others and that the technology used by each of the others infringes its own. In situations like this a settlement may entail pooling of all patents with a license under each being granted to each participant; the pool will thereafter exclude outsiders or license them and divide royalties among pool members in proportions agreed upon. The pool may be implemented through a jointly owned subsidiary to which the patents are assigned, or through an unincorporated association, or through some less formal arrangement whereby one or more pool members grant licenses on their own patents or, as authorized, on all pool patents, accounting to other pool members for royalties.[8]

If access to the patented technology is important to participation in the industry and the cross licenses to pool members or to others contain price, territory or field of use restrictions, it is obvious that the industry may be effectively cartelized and competition signifi-

---

6. United States v. Singer Mfg. Co., 374 U.S. 174, 197, 83 S.Ct. 1773, 1785, 10 L.Ed.2d 823, 839 (1963).

7. See § 179 supra.

8. The classic example in the case law is Standard Oil Co. (Indiana) v. United States, 283 U.S. 163, 51 S.Ct. 421, 75 L.Ed. 926 (1931).

cantly reduced. As *Gypsum* [9] and *Hartford-Empire* [10] both show, any such restriction enforced through a pooling arrangement is violative of Section 1, even though the pool was set up to settle bona fide patent disputes. Settlement could be achieved in less restrictive ways; as components of a settlement the license restrictions are gratuitous and excessive of the needs of the situation. Given developments in other areas, it also seems clear by now that the pool may not flatly exclude non-participants when the technology it controls is significant to the efforts of non-members to enter or compete.[11] Any joint arrangement among competitors which provides a significant advantage which non-participants cannot readily duplicate must be made available to non-member competitors or potential competitors on reasonable, non-discriminatory terms.

The thornier question is whether the establishment of a pool transgresses Section 1, even supposing that unrestricted licenses are granted to all comers. The potential injury to competition is apparent enough. In the first place, if the litigation goes forward, one or more of the patents might be held invalid and one or more of the competing technologies held non-infringing of any patent granted. If so, there would be free access by all actual and potential competitors to at least one technology allowing them to compete. It is not merely that the pool members, the most likely challengers of each others' patents, have by the very act of withdrawing their cross challenges reduced the likelihood that any technology will be opened up; it is also that by aggregating their patents and standing as a unity against all others they have diminished the likelihood of successful challenge from any quarter. The pool, acting concertedly, will likely appear more formidable and may well be a more efficient defender of its patent privileges than would pool members each acting independently. Through the pool, the role of keeping others out is, in effect, specialized and institutionalized.

Beyond this, even if the patents are all assumed to be valid so that each would have survived the challenge of the others, the pool will stamp out competition in the licensing of the relevant technology. If no pool is set up, other competitors or potential competitors have alternative sources from which they might obtain a license granting access to necessary technology; each of these sources, seeking to maximize its own returns, might bid against the others, thus pushing royalty rates down toward zero. As competing purveyors of alterna-

9. United States v. United States Gypsum Co., 333 U.S. 364, 68 S.Ct. 525, 92 L.Ed. 746 (1948).

10. Hartford-Empire Co. v. United States, 323 U.S. 386, 65 S.Ct. 373, 89 L.Ed. 322 (1945).

11. Cf. Associated Press v. United States, 326 U.S. 1, 65 S.Ct. 1416, 89 L. Ed. 2013 (1945); United States v. Terminal Railroad Ass'n., 224 U.S. 383, 32 S.Ct. 507, 56 L.Ed. 810 (1912); Gamco, Inc. v. Providence Fruit & Produce Bldg., Inc., 194 F.2d 484 (1st Cir. 1952), cert. denied 344 U.S. 817, 73 S. Ct. 11, 97 L.Ed. 636 (1952); Honeywell, Inc. v. Sperry Rand Corp., 54 F. R.D. 593 (D.Minn.1973). See the discussion in §§ 89, 90 and 105 supra.

tive technologies, all of these firms, if not acting jointly in the pool, might also have competed in other ways; for example, each would feel a competitive spur to improve its technology by further invention. The pool, by combining these technologies to be marketed as a unit, effectively fixes the price for licenses to any one of them at the level deemed to maximize returns for all. The possibility that competition will reduce royalty rates or yield other benefits is eliminated.

The pool, as will be seen, is a partial integration; in its consequences it is not unlike other partial integrations such as, for example, a joint sales agency.[12] This arrangement, like other joint agencies, may yield efficiencies; indeed, when it arises out of dispute settlement, it presents one advantageous consequence, the saving of the costs of disputation, which will not typically be involved in other partial integrations such as joint sales agencies. In addition, it may yield efficiencies of the kind which other joint agencies usually yield. The myriad tasks involved in marketing the technologies may be carried out more cheaply where several are combined. The negative effects of the patent pool can also be gauged in the manner in which other partial integrations are analyzed. If, in the aggregate, the pool brings under common control a substantial part of a relevant market, the reduction of competition approaches monopoly proportions. By contrast, if the patents controlled by the pool represent a trivial percentage of the relevant market, no significant competitive injury will be done.

A qualification on all this is called for. The comments made here assume that if there were no pool the individual firms would act competitively. Since this may not be the case it may not be true that the result yielded by the pool will always be distinctly worse than would be the result if each firm maintained control of its own technology. For one thing, the interdependence of the several patent holders may be strong and apparent; even without a pool, if two or more patent holders are licensing competing technologies, price leadership or some other pattern of interdependent pricing might well develop to avoid the rigors of full blown price competition. Thus, the supra-competitive pool price, or something close to it, might well be achieved without a pool. Assuming that the firms together control a technology essential to effective participation in the industry, there is still another possibility which might be socially worse than a pool. If no settlement is reached and each patent holder survives the attack of the others and then controls its own patented techology, each, whether acting interdependently or independently, may decide not to license any firm not having its own technology. If a pool is established by firms with this degree of control, they need not then be permitted to exploit their power in whatever manner attracts them. Section 1 of

12. See § 89 supra. See also W. Bowman, Patent and Antitrust Law 200–202 (1973).

the Sherman Act will perform the quite separate office of obliging any joint venture which is permitted, even though it possesses significant power, to exercise that power in relatively benign ways. Authority is convincing that such a venture, if it is to be allowed because of integration efficiencies, would be compelled to grant access to its technology to all competitors on reasonable, non-discriminatory terms.[13] Even assuming that this "public-utility type" antitrust regulation will not hold license rates down to the levels competition would establish if competition in fact occurred, it is not clear that, absent the pool, competition would occur.

The case for disallowing settlement pools is thus not one which approaches *per se* proportions. The case law is in principle consistent with this, although *Standard Oil*[14] seems to the modern eye too permissive in its treatment of the particular pool there involved. That case stands as a flat holding that a pool aggregating several competing patents into a single set of hands for licensing purposes is reasonable and therefore lawful unless the patented technology is so crucial to end product production costs that the pool, by fixing the price of a license, effectively fixes the price of the product. That was a way of putting the matter which, though in one sense accurate, makes the plaintiff's burden of proof more difficult than it ought to be. The real question is whether the pool comprehends a significant enough portion of the technology to have an impact on the price for the technology. If it does, it will necessarily have a derivative effect on end product output and prices. But in the course of analysis one need not even look that far. The public is entitled to the benefits of competition in the licensing of the technology itself, not just in the sale of the end product. The technology constitutes itself a relevant market for these purposes. *Standard Oil* also seems wrong in its analysis of its own particular facts. The Court assumed that through the pool, royalty rates were being fixed for licenses under which a substantial portion of total end product production actually took place; despite this, the Court said there was an insufficient showing of any restriction on the price or quantity of the end product. This was being blind to implication; when producers manipulate the cost of a significant factor for which no substitutes are readily available, end product prices and production are inevitably being manipulated as a consequence.[15]

Standard Oil was decided before either *Socony-Vacuum*,[16] which made price fixing *per se* unlawful, or *Line Material*,[17] which held that

13. See cases cited in note 1 supra.

14. Standard Oil Co. (Indiana) v. United States, 283 U.S. 163, 51 S.Ct. 421, 75 L.Ed. 926 (1931).

15. See McGee, supra note 2, at 150–160.

16. United States v. Socony-Vacuum Oil Co., 310 U.S. 150, 60 S.Ct. 811, 84 L.Ed. 1129 (1940).

17. United States v. Line Material Co., 333 U.S. 287, 68 S.Ct. 550, 92 L.Ed. 701 (1948).

patents gained no exemption from that *per se* prohibition when they were combined. One cannot assert with accuracy that the pool is a naked agreement to fix price on the technology. It is not, any more than would be any other joint venture; it is a partial integration and has the independent social advantage of diminishing conflict and the resources devoted to resolving conflict. It ought to be lawful if it does not comprehend technology significant enough to have adverse impacts on competition in the market.[18] But neither should a court on the strength of *Standard Oil* ignore the effects of a pool and treat pooling as lawful absent a showing of a malicious intent to cartelize.[19] The proper response is to consider both purpose and effect,[20] and the best approach to effect is structural analysis. The integration efficiencies associated with pooling do not warrant a joint venture with power to manipulate market prices. Nor do the dispute settlement advantages; these, at least, could be attained in a less restrictive way —namely, by a settlement of the patent dispute (say, by concessions each to the other of validity) which left each patent holder free to decide independently at what price it would license its own patent.

§ 189. Grant Back Provisions and Agreements Not to Contest

Sometimes a patent holder, in granting a license, requires the licensee to agree to grant to the patent holder an assignment or license on any improvement patent which the licensee may develop. In *Transparent-Wrap*[1] the Court held such an arrangement lawful on the overbroad ground that the patentee's power to license included the right to select the consideration for doing so. In light of the tying cases,[2] one cannot take this rationale seriously; indeed, the result in *Transparent-Wrap,* however rationalized, is difficult to distinguish from those cases.[3] Yet the Court has shown no disposition

---

18. Cf. Apex Elec. Mfg. Co. v. Altorfer, 238 F.2d 867, 873 (7th Cir. 1956); Baker-Cammack Hoisery Mills v. Davis Co., 181 F.2d 550 (4th Cir.), cert. denied 340 U.S. 824, 71 S.Ct. 58, 95 L. Ed. 605 (1950); United States v. Birdsboro Steel Foundry & Mach. Co., 139 F.Supp. 244 (W.D.Pa.1956).

19. See Zenith Radio Corp. v. Hazeltine Research Inc., 395 U.S. 100, 89 S.Ct. 1562, 23 L.Ed.2d 129 (1969); United States v. Krasnov, 143 F.Supp. 184 (E.D.Pa.1956), aff'd per curiam 355 U.S. 5, 78 S.Ct. 34, 2 L.Ed.2d 21 (1957); United States v. Associated Patents, Inc., 134 F.Supp. 74 (E.D. Mich.1955), aff'd per curiam sub nom., Mac Inv. Co. v. United States, 350 U. S. 960, 76 S.Ct. 432, 100 L.Ed. 834 (1956); United States v. Besser Mfg. Co., 96 F.Supp. 304 (E.D.Mich.1951), aff'd 343 U.S. 444, 72 S.Ct. 838, 96 L. Ed. 1063 (1952). But cf. Cutter Laboratories, Inc. v. Lyophile-Cryochem Corp., 179 F.2d 80, 93 (9th Cir. 1949).

20. E.g., United States v. General Instrument Corp., 87 F.Supp. 157 (D.N. J.1949); United States v. General Elec. Co. (Lamps), 82 F.Supp. 753 (D. N.J.1949).

1. Transparent-Wrap Mach. Corp. v. Stokes & Smith Co., 329 U.S. 637, 67 S.Ct. 610, 91 L.Ed. 563 (1947).

2. See §§ 150–162 supra.

3. See the discussion in W. Bowman, Patent and Antitrust Law 228–235 (1973) which approves Transparent-Wrap and is critical of the inconsistent tying cases.

to move away from *Transparent-Wrap* and lower courts grant the holding the full measure of authority.[4]

Of course, the case does not imply that grant backs are always lawful. If in the circumstance of a particular industry one can infer a significant restraint, the arrangement will fall. For example, in *General Electric (Lamps)*[5] the court held that the defendant engaged in exclusionary conduct by licensing a basic patent which dominated the industry only upon terms requiring a grant back license on any improvement, even though any granted back license would be non-exclusive. As that case would imply, in any instance where the patent being licensed is shown to carry substantial market power, a grant back provision is suspect and, surely, one requiring an assignment or an exclusive license ought to be treated as invalid.[6]

§ 190. Vertical Restraints and the Inherency Test

Although the Court early on in Bement & Sons v. National Harrow Company,[1] as well as later in *General Electric*,[2] treated horizontal price fixing—the imposition of a price for sales by a licensee authorized to manufacture and vend in competition with the patentee—as within the patent grant, there are no comparable early authorities which validate vertical price restrictions on patented products. In *Dr. Miles*,[3] which involved a product sold under a trademark and trade name, the Court held that the manufacturer had no power to impose resale prices upon its distributors and dealers. Two years later the same rule was applied to a patented product in Bauer & Cie v. O'Donnell.[4]

Bauer & Cie is a clear holding against any inherent right in the patentee to control resale prices. As the law was then,[5] a patentee

---

4. E.g., Binks Mfg. Co. v. Ransberg Electro-Coating Corp., 281 F.2d 252, 259 (7th Cir. 1960), cert. dismissed 366 U.S. 211, 81 S.Ct. 1091, 6 L.Ed.2d 239 (1961); Blohm & Voss A.G. v. Prudential-Grace Lines, Inc., 346 F.Supp. 1116 (D.Md.1972); Barr Rubber Prods. Co. v. Sun Rubber Co., 277 F.Supp. 484, 506 (S.D.N.Y.1967), aff'd 425 F.2d 1114 (2d Cir. 1970); Old Dominion Box Co. v. Continental Can Co., 273 F.Supp. 550 (S.D.N.Y.1967), aff'd on other grounds 393 F.2d 321 (2d Cir. 1968).

5. United States v. General Elec. Co. (Lamps) 80 F.Supp. 989 (S.D.N.Y.1948). See also United States v. Alcoa, 91 F.Supp. 333, 410 (S.D.N.Y.1950).

6. Compare C. Kaysen & D. Turner, Antitrust Policy 165 (1959).

1. 186 U.S. 70, 22 S.Ct. 747, 46 L.Ed. 1058 (1902).

2. United States v. General Elec. Co., 272 U.S. 476, 47 S.Ct. 192, 71 L.Ed. 362 (1926).

3. Dr. Miles Medical Co. v. John D. Park & Sons, 220 U.S. 373, 31 S.Ct. 376, 55 L.Ed. 502 (1911).

4. 229 U.S. 1, 33 S.Ct. 616, 57 L.Ed. 1041 (1913). See also Jesse Isidor Straus v. Victor Talking Mach. Co., 243 U.S. 490, 37 S.Ct. 412, 61 L.Ed. 866 (1919); Boston Store v. American Graphophone Co., 246 U.S. 8, 38 S.Ct. 257, 62 L.Ed. 551 (1918).

5. See Henry v. A. B. Dick Co., 224 U.S. 1, 32 S.Ct. 364, 56 L.Ed. 645 (1912), which was effectively overruled by Motion Picture Patents Co. v. Universal Film Mfg. Co., 243 U.S. 502, 37 S.Ct. 21, 61 L.Ed. 540 (1917).

could not only fix the price at which the licensee could sell, but could also impose other restrictions. Despite these earlier holdings, and though the patent statute gave the patentee a monopoly over making, using and vending, the Court did not extend the notion of the divisibility of the patentee's monopoly so as to allow maintenance of resale prices. The Court had earlier held [6] that the sole right to vend under the copyright law was exhausted upon the first sale, and when the same issue came up with respect to patents in *Bauer & Cie* the Court extended that principle rather than the seemingly conflicting one embodied in the earlier patent cases. The proposition that resale restrictions on patented articles are to be judged by the general law governing resale restrictions on other articles has prevailed ever since.

§ 191. Price, Territorial, Customer and Use Restrictions Imposed by a Patentee Upon Purchasers

The holder of a patent has no greater power to restrict the terms upon which a buyer of the patented product resells at the next vertical level than does the owner of any other product.[1] The patentee can obtain the full reward of the patent on the first sale; a right to restrict the goods in more remote channels of trade is not a traditional part of the patent grant nor is it needed in order for the patentee fully to enjoy the monopoly of the patent.[2] The holder of the patent may impose resale price, territorial, location or other resale restrictions to the same extent that in comparable circumstances such restrictions could lawfully be imposed were the goods not patented. Thus, under fair trade laws the resale price of a patented product could be established so long as the patented product were in fair and open competition with other like products.[3] Other resale restrictions

---

6. Bobbs-Merrill Co. v. Straus, 210 U.S. 339, 28 S.Ct. 722, 52 L.Ed. 1086 (1908).

1. *Price Restrictions*: United States v. Univis Lens Co., 316 U.S. 241, 62 S.Ct. 1088, 86 L.Ed. 1408 (1942); Ethyl Gasoline Corp. v. United States, 309 U.S. 436, 60 S.Ct. 618, 84 L.Ed. 852 (1940); Boston Store v. American Graphophone Co., 246 U.S. 8, 38 S.Ct. 257, 62 L.Ed. 551 (1918); Jesse Isidor Straus v. Victor Talking Machine Co., 243 U.S. 490, 37 S.Ct. 412, 61 L.Ed. 866 (1917); Bauer & Cie v. O'Donnell, 229 U.S. 1, 33 S.Ct. 616, 57 L.Ed. 1041 (1913). Cf. United States v. Standard Sanitary Mfg. Co., 226 U.S. 20, 49, 33 S.Ct. 9, 15, 57 L.Ed. 107, 117 (1912) (product made under patented process). *Express Territorial Restrictions*: Pfotzer v. Aqua Systems, 162 F.2d 779 (2d Cir. 1947). *Implied Territorial Restrictions*: Keeler v. Standard Folding Bed Co., 157 U.S. 659, 15 S.Ct. 738, 39 L.Ed. 848 (1895); Hobbie v. Jennison, 149 U.S. 355, 13 S.Ct. 879, 37 L.Ed. 766 (1893); Adams v. Burke, 84 U.S. (17 Wall.) 453, 21 L.Ed. 700 (1873); C. A. Norgren Co. v. United States, 154 U.S.P.Q. 214 (D.Colo.1967); Hogue and Berrien County Package Co. v. Wise, 35 U.S.P.Q. 72 (W.D.Mich.1933).

2. See, e.g., Bauer & Cie v. O'Donnell and other cases cited in note 1 supra.

3. See § 132 supra. As the text of that section makes clear the fair trade exemption from the Sherman Act ban on resale price fixing has been repealed. Act of December 12, 1975, Public Law 94–145, CCH Trade Reg.Rep., ¶ 25,125 (1976).

on patented products would be governed by the rules which would apply were the products not patented.[4]

All of this is settled law. It is summarized in the dictum that the "first sale" of a patented article frees it from the protection of the patent monopoly.[5] Since any resale restriction is, by definition, imposed at a point beyond the first sale, the restriction cannot be justified on the basis of the patent. To impose such a restriction may not only violate Section 1 but may constitute patent misuse, foreclosing the enforcement of the patent until the practice is abandoned and its effects vitiated.[6]

Those who challenge the soundness of rules against vertical restrictions in other settings also challenge them here.[7] The conventional "horizontalist" position—that vertical restrictions (not imposed in response to dealer pressures) should be ignored by the law because they do not create market power and can generate efficiencies—has, perhaps, its best claim to support with respect to patents. Here it can at least be claimed that the position of power at the first level, since derived from the patent, is itself quite legitimate. Despite this, "the horizontalist" position has been consistently rejected by the courts.[8]

As Williamson's and Comanor's work demonstrates, the economic analysis which underlies the horizontalist view is, if seemingly rigorous, nonetheless sophistic.[9] Vertical restrictions *can* increase market power. The horizontalists' assumption that if one firm uses a vertical restriction its competitors may do so is not always true. In the first place, the first firm to use the vertical restriction may gain an advantage over its rivals because scale economies may make it impossible to replicate the restrictions achieved by the first firm. In the second place, capital costs associated with entry may be increased by vertical restrictions which, by tying up outlets, compel any firm wishing to enter at one level either to enter itself at the other level or to procure coordinated entry by others there. Thus, any efficiency gains which might be attained through vertical restrictions need not come free, as the horizontalists suppose. There may be social costs

4. See generally, §§ 142–149 supra.

5. E.g., Boston Store v. American Graphophone Co., 246 U.S. 8, 38 S.Ct. 257, 62 L.Ed. 551 (1918).

6. E.g., Boston Store v. American Graphophone Co., 246 U.S. 8, 38 S.Ct. 257, 62 L.Ed. 551 (1918); Strauss v. Victor Talking Mach. Co., 243 U.S. 490, 37 S.Ct. 412, 61 L.Ed. 866 (1917); F. C. Russell Co. v. Consumers Insulation Co., 119 F.Supp. 119 (D.N.J.1954), aff'd on other grounds 226 F.2d 373 (3d Cir. 1955) (maximum price).

7. E.g., W. Bowman, Patent and Antitrust Law 122–139 (1973).

8. See cases cited in note 1 supra.

9. See Williamson, The Vertical Integration of Production: Market Failure Considerations, 61 Am.Econ.Rev. (1971); Comanor, Vertical Territorial and Customer Restrictions: White Motor and its Aftermath, 81 Harv.L. Rev. 1419 (1968).

entailed. Furthermore, the horizontalists are not convincing on the other part of their case—the claim that vertical restrictions always yield efficiency gains. They simply assume that management would not use them unless they did. But micro-analytical theory offers no footing for such an assumption. Management decisions to restrict vertically could be aimed at enhancing market power rather than enhancing efficiency, or could be aimed at maximizing some extrinsic factor like overall size. Or management decisions, though aimed at efficiency, could be wrong, and, because made monolithically, the market evidence of error never or only belatedly yielded. If anything, theory suggests that, absent a particularized basis in a given instance for concluding otherwise, the assumption ought to be that the market organization which disperses decision making power most widely will be the most efficient. This kind of organization, unlike the more monolithic one, provides a basis for testing a variety of possible decisions through experience, for obtaining feedback from the market in small enough and discrete enough packages to facilitate a process of constant adaptation and adjustment.[10]

If one is to opt for a rigid rule, the case for a rule of *per se* illegality is discernibly stronger than that for a rule of *per se* legality. The plausible and operative choice, then, is not between a permissive rule on vertical restrictions which will serve to enhance efficiency and a restrictive rule which inhibits efficiency. It is, rather, a choice between a rule which forbids the vertical restriction because the risks of harm associated with them are higher than the potential benefits associated with them, or a rule which invites a particularlized appraisal of each instance to see whether in that instance vertical restrictions might yield efficiencies without undue cost in the form of enhanced market power.

When one sees the economic issue in that light, one cannot be harsh with the courts for making the choice they have made. The costs associated with opening up the issue to particularized investigation would be large. It is not just that individual cases, when brought, would be time consuming and costly, as surely they would. It is also that many which were brought would be wrongly decided and that many which ought to be brought would not be brought at all. Moreover, without a per se rule, considerable costs would be incurred by firms in attempting to evaluate whether or not they could lawfully impose a particular restraint.

10. See § 145 supra.

Chapter 7

MERGERS

Table of Sections

Part	Sections
A. A Historical Perspective	192–201
B. Horizontal and Market Extension Mergers	202–206
C. Conglomerate Mergers	207–209
D. Vertical Mergers	210–214
E. Remedies	215–216

PART A. HISTORICAL PERSPECTIVE

Sec.
192. Introduction.
193. Early Consolidation Movement and Its Relationship to Pre-Sherman Act Common Law.
194. Earliest Sherman Act Merger Cases and Their Effect on the Merger Movement.
195. The Period from 1904 to 1911.
196. The Rule of Reason—Basic Cases and Beyond.
197. Merger Provisions of the Original Clayton Act.
198. 1930 to 1950.
199. The 1950 Amendment to Section 7.
200. New Clayton Merger Law and the Coalescence of Clayton and Sherman Standards.
201. Impact of Current Merger Policy on Industrial Structure.

PART B. HORIZONTAL AND MARKET EXTENSION MERGERS

202. Statutory Provisions Relevant to Legality of Mergers.
    a. Section 7 of the Clayton Act.
    b. The Sherman Act.
    c. The Bank Merger Act.
203. Market Definition in Merger Cases.
    a. In General.
    b. Product Market.
    c. Geographic Markets.
204. Mergers Between Direct Competitors.
    a. Analyzing Social Consequences.
    b. The *Prima Facie* Case of Violation of Section 7.
    c. The Significance of a Trend Toward Concentration.
    d. Overcoming the *Prima Facie* Case.
    e. Reinforcing the *Prima Facie* Case.
    f. Post-Acquisition Evidence.
    g. The Failing Company Defense.
    h. Efficiency as a Defense or an Additional Basis for Challenging a Merger.

Sec.
205. Market Extension Mergers.
    a. In General.
    b. Competitive Injury Due to Loss of Potential Competition.
    c. Competitive Injury Due to Disparity Between Overall Size of Acquiring Firm and Firms Already in the Market.
    d. Toe-Hold Entry as an Alternative or a Defense.
206. Corporate Joint Ventures and Potential Competition.

PART C. CONGLOMERATE MERGERS

207. Competitive Effects and Other Social Concerns.
208. The Section 7 Enforcement Effort to Date.
209. Possible Bases for Illegality.

PART D. VERTICAL MERGERS

210. Competitive Effects.
211. Substantial Foreclosures in Concentrated Markets.
212. Relevance of a Trend Toward Vertical Integration.
213. Other Bases for Illegality.
214. Efficiency and Other Justifications.

PART E. REMEDIES

215. Preliminary Relief.
216. Final Relief.

PART A. A HISTORICAL PERSPECTIVE

§ 192. Introduction

    Law about merger is law which prohibits certain changes in industrial structure. The concerns which shape it and the analytical concepts which inform it relate directly to those affecting other aspects of antitrust law. Public policy about horizontal consolidation should be consistent with that about cartelization, oligopoly and monopoly. Horizontal merger is, in a sense, an alternative to cartelization, though (involving as it does a fuller integration) it may stem from very different motives and may have effects (including some of social value) which cartelization cannot achieve. To monopoly and oligopoly, horizontal merger may stand as does a means to an end, or, to put aside any implication about motive, as does a cause to a consequence. A merger, or a series of mergers, may increase concentration within a market. Because of the possible consequences of mergers relevant legal issues include: the significance of particular levels of concentration and whether additional empirical data must be analyzed in order to make reliable predictions about competitive effects; the feasibility of developing useful generalizations that will reduce the need for individual analysis; and the extent to which offsetting advantages such as possible efficiencies can and should be evaluated and given weight. Vertical merger is, in turn, analytically related to less complete forms of vertical integration, such as requirements contracts. Analysis of these mergers must dovetail with analyses of those other vertical issues.

Yet, without downplaying the importance of those interconnections, an understanding of merger law (and of antitrust generally) can be enriched by exploring it chronologically, in a way which both emphasizes the relationship between law and industrial structure and identifies the nature of the forces which affect the one and thus influence the other. In merger contexts the relationship between legal doctrine and market structure is so direct, and the forces at work on the law's development so readily discernible, that the history of merger law offers a unique opportunity to explore the dynamic interplay between developing social, economic and political values, the law as a medium for their expression, and the structure of the industrial economy.

This chapter opens, then, with an essentially historical exposition of the growth of the law of merger. Later in the chapter the current status of the law will be examined in detail, and salient analytical issues will be stressed. Although countless disclaimers would be appropriate, a general one will, perhaps, suffice. Despite its ambitions, this historical exploration (limited as it is to the law about merger) is a narrow one. The structure of the economy has undoubtedly been affected by all aspects of antitrust law and administration, not merely merger law. It has been affected more directly by regulatory interventions which tend to inhibit competition, such as those pertaining to transportation, agriculture, banking and labor, than it has by antitrust rules which aim to enhance competition. However, despite its limited scope, an historical examination of merger law can be highly informative about interactions between political and social forces, the law, and the structure of the economy.

§ 193. Early Consolidation Movement and Its Relationship to Pre-Sherman Act Common Law

Merger, the consolidation of previously separate firms into common ownership and control, has had an enormous effect on American industrial structure. The first great merger movement can be taken to have begun in 1879, with the formation of the original Standard Oil Trust, and to have continued until 1892 or 1893.[1] During that

1. D. Martin, Mergers and the Clayton Act 4 et seq. (1959). Any effort to classify merger activity into discrete "movements" is in some sense arbitrary, not only because the statistical data does not segment in patently obvious ways but also because, in addition to the highly specific factors which may motivate any given merger, there is at any given time a variety of general factors which may be supposed to have causal implications, some of which operate for longer periods than others. For example, some scholars regard the first "merger movement" as having begun after 1890 and having run until 1904, the second to cover the period from 1920

brief period several industrial combinations of considerable size were put together.² The relationship between law and industrial structure becomes immediately apparent when the legal and economic conditions then prevailing are recalled.

The nation was in a period of rapid industrialization, characterized by increased availability of capital and great technological change. The latter included the power revolution, which was heralded by steam and which led to a rapid expansion of the transportation system with, in turn, vastly widened potential markets.³ Industrial firms which had previously served limited regions found themselves competing for wider markets. The rigors of this new competition provided a motive for cartelization, and cartelization did widely occur.⁴ But a cartel, it will be remembered, can be a fragile form of organization. Not only was this mode of coordination subject to inherent instabilities,⁵ but in most jurisdictions it was also highly vulnerable to legal attack at common law as a restraint of trade.⁶

The impetus to coordinate was thus frustrated when it turned to cartels as a primary mode of expression; in part this frustration was due to legal intervention through the common law. There is, however, a principle of conservation of the energies available for social or economic change. If the forces pressing in a particular direction are inhibited, they will not cease to exist. They will transform themselves and take different routes. Thus, as cartelization was inhibited, promoters turned to consolidation as an alternative means of attaining relief from competitive vigor and of achieving the greater returns associated with the exercise of market power.⁷ Moreover, consolidation at least potentially promised additional benefits—those associated with greater scale. Indeed, at some periods this was a pro-

to 1929, the third to have started about 1940 and to have continued through the 1960's. E.g., Oppenheim & Weston, Federal Antitrust Laws, Cases and Comments 317–323 (1967). Others, such as Martin, have segregated the activity into a greater number of shorter periods. The classification chosen in particular studies tends to be related to conceptions about causal factors and the periods during which these were operative, as well as to available data as to rates of merger activity. This chapter treats as discrete "movements" the shortest periods for which there is statistical justification and scholarly authority. Thus, the first movement is seen as running from 1879 to 1892 or 1893, the second (perhaps the greatest wave, which did the most to transform the economy) from 1897 to 1904; the third, from 1920 to 1929; the fourth from 1940 to about 1963; with a fifth, essentially a "conglomerate movement," thereafter.

2. See generally J. Markham, Survey of the Evidence and Findings on Merger in Business Concentration and Price Policy 157 (Nat. Bur. for Econ. Res. 1955).

3. See, e.g., W. Letwin, Law and Economic Policy in America 8–9 (1965).

4. There was a significant cartelization movement during the 1880's.

5. McGee, Ocean Freight Rate Conferences and the American Merchant Marine, 27 U.Chi.L.Rev. 191, 197–204 (1960).

6. Mergers and the Law 17–19 (Nat'l. Indus. Conf. Bd. 1929).

7. D. Martin, supra note 1, at 4 et seq.

found impetus to consolidation, quite apart from any hope or expectation of avoiding competition. Furthermore, while the common law treated cartelization harshly, its responses to consolidation was permissive.[8]

In the relatively brief period we are now considering, entrepreneurs who found cartelization either blocked off or inadequate turned with renewed force to consolidation, which first appeared in the form of trusteeships, then holding companies and later (as state corporate laws became facilitating) in the form of mergers.[9] In this manner the first great merger movement began and flourished.

§ 194. Earliest Sherman Act Merger Cases and Their Effect on the Merger Movement

The first merger movement ended shortly after the passage of the Sherman Act. The depression of 1893 was no doubt a factor,[1] as was uncertainty generated by the new antitrust law. The very earliest Sherman Act cases included one involving extensive consolidation in the distillery industry[2] and one involving consolidation in sugar.[3] The distillery merger case involved the acquisition and consolidation of seventy previously independent distilleries aggregating about 75% of national output. The trial court held that Congress had no power under the commerce clause to restrict corporations formed by states or citizens of states in the acquisition, ownership, or disposition of property.[4] The same issue was presented to the Supreme Court in United States v. E. C. Knight Co., the sugar trust case,[5] the first Sherman Act case to reach the Court. The decision in *Knight,* now treated as an oddity and usually ignored in any review of antitrust materials, had a considerable effect on industrial structure and thus is especially significant. It stands as a landmark in the development of the economy, if not in the law's development, and is as indicative as is any single case of the significance of antitrust for the shape and form of American industrial structure.

The *Knight* case involved a challenge to the defendant's acquisition of four Pennsylvania sugar refiners, the last in a series of acquisitions which the record showed brought 98% of the nation's capacity

8. Mergers and the Law, supra note 6, at 19–25.

9. See, e.g., H. Seager & C. Gulick, Jr., Trust and Corporation Problems 55–59 (1929).

1. See D. Martin, Mergers and the Clayton Act (1959).

2. See United States v. Greenhut, 50 F. 469 (1892) and In re Greene, 52 F. 104 (1892).

3. United States v. E. C. Knight Co., 156 U.S. 1, 15 S.Ct. 249, 39 L.Ed. 325 (1895).

4. In re Greene, supra note 2. The view seems in conflict with that expressed by the Supreme Court in United States v. Joint Traffic Ass'n, 171 U.S. 505, 19 S.Ct. 25, 43 L.Ed. 259 (1898), a cartel case.

5. Supra note 3.

for sugar refining under defendant's ownership and control. In a somewhat obscure opinion, the Court held for the defendant. It stated that "the monopoly and restraint denounced by the act are monopoly and restraint of interstate and international trade or commerce, while the conclusion * * * on this record is that the transaction complained of was the creation of a monopoly in * * * manufacture * * *." [6] It went on to say that, although the manufacture of something gives some control over its disposition, the manufacture of the thing does not control commerce in it, and affects it only "incidentally and indirectly. Commerce succeeds to manufacture, and is not a part of it." [7]

Though it is conceivable to read the case as deciding no more than that the complaint was drawn too narrowly because it challenged only the acquisition in Pennsylvania of the stock of Pennsylvania corporations rather than the exercise of monopoly power in interstate commerce in sugar, the thrust of the language is otherwise and the bar and commentators at the time universally construed the case as holding that 98% of the productive capacity of a basic industry could be consolidated by merger without violating the Sherman Act.[8] Indeed, at one point in its opinion the Court restated the view taken in In re Greene that the Sherman Act does not limit corporate power to acquire property of any kind.[9]

It should be stressed, however, that *Knight* cannot fairly be seen as an expression of judicial unresponsiveness to the populist views which might enliven some conceptions of the scope of the antitrust statute. The case presented issues of federalism of contemporary significance, however accustomed we may be today to the ascendancy of federal power in matters of these kinds.[10] This, after all, was a period when, in determining whether a matter fell within the reach of state regulatory power, the Court often proceeded to decide whether the subject was commerce or not;[11] the theory seemed to be that if it was commerce, only Congress could regulate, whereas, if it was not only the states could.[12] Lively political debate arose about the appropriateness of federal intervention in matters closely pertaining to the state's power to regulate corporations.[13]

6. Id. at 10, 15 S.Ct. at 253, 39 L.Ed. at 328.

7. Id. at 12, 15 S.Ct. at 253, 39 L.Ed. at 329. This decision was ultimately expressly overruled by Mandeville Island Farms, Inc. v. American Crystal Sugar Co., 334 U.S. 219, 68 S.Ct. 996 92 L.Ed. 1328 (1948).

8. E.g., Morawetz, The Anti-Trust Act and the Merger Case, 17 Harv.L.Rev. 533 (1904); Adams, Federal Control of Trusts, 18 Pol.Sci.Q. 1 (1903).

9. 156 U.S. 1, 16, 15 S.Ct. 249, 255, 39 L.Ed. 325, 330 (1895).

10. See L. Friedman, A History of American Law ch. VIII (1973).

11. E.g., Railroad Co. v. Huse, 95 U.S. 465, 24 L.Ed. 527 (1877).

12. E.g., Bowman v. Chicago & N.W. Ry. Co. 125 U.S. 465, 8 S.Ct. 689, 31 L.Ed. 700 (1888).

13. H. Seager & C. Gluck, Jr., Trust and Corporation Problems 59 (1929).

Whatever its rationale, the *Knight* decision marked the beginning of an even greater avalanche of horizontal merger activity between 1897 and 1904 than that which had occurred in the decade before passage of the Sherman Act; in basic industry after basic industry, productive capacity quickly came under common ownership and control. Markham's study shows that during this period 257 combinations involving 4,227 plants were achieved in industries as varied as glue making and steel production.[14] This movement, moreover, generated the social concerns and political reactions which later resulted in the enactment of the seemingly more stringent requirements of the Clayton Act.[15] These social concerns, like those which had been expressed through the common law rules pertaining to looser knit arrangements in restraint of trade,[16] focused in part upon the effect that massive industrial aggregations had upon prices consumers ultimately paid and upon business opportunities for those who, but for the aggregations, would have been motivated to enter the market as small producers.[17] But the concerns went beyond these matters of price and industrial opportunity to a concern that large aggregations of capital would exercise undue political power.[18]

§ 195. The Period from 1904 to 1911

The Supreme Court in *Northern Securities*,[1] its next merger case, reached a result dramatically opposite from that in *Knight*. The decision perhaps reflected a new awareness of the relationships between massive consolidations and cartelization, or a new recognition of the intensity of the public concerns and their relationships to the attitudes to which the Sherman Act was responsive. It may also have reflected greater judicial experience with the administration of a national program to control industrial structure, significant changes in Court personnel, and a changing attitude toward the scope of the federal commerce power.

The facts of *Northern Securities* were complex and the transactions involved in it have an aura of the lusty and aggressive promotion that had characterized the 1880's and which, apparently, still displayed itself at times. Morgan and Hill, who acted in concert, controlled the Northern Pacific and Great Northern Railroads; the Union Pacific was controlled by Harriman. All three of these routes to the

14. J. Markham, "Survey of the Evidence and Findings on Merger" in Business Concentration and Price Policy 141, 154–167 (1955); see also R. Nelson, Merger Movements in American Industry, 1895–1956 (1959) which counts 3,238 acquisitions and consolidations between 1895–1905.

15. D. Martin, supra note 1, at 3–19.

16. See W. Letwin, Law and Economic Policy in America 18–52 (1965).

17. Martin, supra note 1, at 3–56.

18. Id.

1. Northern Sec. Co. v. United States, 193 U.S. 197, 24 S.Ct. 436, 48 L.Ed. 679 (1904). See also Loewe v. Lawlor, 208 U.S. 274, 28 S.Ct. 301, 52 L.Ed. 488 (1908).

far west had eastern terminals west of Chicago and were dependent upon the Chicago, Burlington and Quincy for connections to Chicago and the east. Harriman battled with Morgan and Hill for control of the Chicago, Burlington and Quincy, but the latter duo were successful. Harriman then sought to buy sufficient shares to control the Northern Pacific. A compromise was reached whereby the Morgan-Hill and the Harriman interests were all placed in Northern Securities, a jointly owned holding company.[2] The government's antitrust case challenged the lawfulness of the formation of this company.

The litigation was fought with strategic skill by Knox, the Attorney General, and was made a showcase by President Roosevelt to demonstrate his newly acquired ardor as a trust buster.[3] Defendants' characterization of the transaction as a mere acquisition of stock which perhaps had incidental market effects was blown over by the government's factual case, which convincingly showed that the purpose of the stock transactions was to put together a community of ownership interests and control where competition had once prevailed.[4] It was not merely the result of the litigation—a ruling that the formation of the holding company violated the Act—but the basis of the holding which jolted much of the business community which since 1895 had sanguinely assumed the legality of massive consolidations.[5] Justice Harlan wrote an opinion in which three Justices concurred. It rejected the suggestion that the case involved no more than an effort, beyond the constitutional reach of Congress, to control dispositions of stock in a state chartered corporation and stressed that the complaint alleged a combination among stockholders of competing railroads which restrained commerce.[6] It strongly implied, if it did not hold, that the Act would be violated by *any* merger between previously competing firms, however slight the competitive consequences, and regardless of the purpose which motivated the merger. Thus, the opinion stated that the Act "is not limited to restraints of interstate * * * trade or commerce that are unreasonable in their nature, but embraces *all* direct *restraints* imposed by any combination * * *."[7]

Justice Brewer's concurring view[8] was softer. He harkened back to the cartel cases[9] in which he had concurred with the *per se*

---

2. Id. See also, e.g., W. Letwin, Law and Economic Policy in America 184–195 (1965); D. Dewey, Monopoly in Economics and Law, 214–15 (1959); Mergers and the Law 35–39 (Nat'l. Indus. Conf. Bd., 1929).

3. Letwin, supra note 2, at 195–218.

4. Id.

5. Mergers and the Law, supra note 2, at 35.

6. Northern Sec. Co. v. United States, 193 U.S. 197, 334–35, 24 S.Ct. 436, 455–56, 48 L.Ed. 679, 699.

7. Id. at 331, 24 S.Ct. at 454, 48 L.Ed. at 698.

8. Id. at 360, 24 S.Ct. at 466, 48 L.Ed. at 710.

9. Id.

approach of Justice Peckham. He declared that, although those cases had been correctly decided, they should have been decided on the ground that unreasonable restraints violated the law and that that principle, when applied to consolidations, would invalidate this great railroad consolidation, though not all consolidations between previously competing firms.[10] Justice Holmes and White wrote dissents; each was joined by Chief Justice Fuller, who had written the *Knight* opinion. As Holmes saw the matter, the statute was violated only when competitors, by accord, stopped competing (as when they fixed prices) or took action to keep rivals out.[11] In White's view, the particular arrangement before the Court was not unreasonable and was governed by *Knight*.[12]

Despite the vehemence of the dissents and despite the failure of Justice Harlan's opinion to command a majority, the lower courts, the business community and the bar focused on Harlan's view that any arrangement destroying competition between two previously competing corporations violated the law. Accepting this position as the law, the district courts in later cases challenging the oil [13] and the tobacco [14] trusts held these consolidations unlawful simply because they brought together under common ownership previously competing firms.

Without question the decision contributed to a significant decrease in the level of merger activity after 1904.[15] While *Knight* facilitated the great merger movement between 1897 and 1904, *Northern Securities* helped end it. The latter decision, however, should not be thought to have blocked merger activity completely. Members of the corporate bar maintained some hope that legality could be attained by avoiding the holding company form in favor of a new corporation organized to acquire assets of existing companies or into which existing companies were completely merged.[16] Moreover, some support for this view could be found in another of the now ignored early cases, Cincinnati Packet Co. v. Bay,[17] which upheld an asset purchase against a Sherman challenge at least in part upon the ground that any effect on commerce was incidental to the property transaction.

---

10. Id. at 361, 24 S.Ct. at 466–67, 48 L. Ed. at 710.

11. Id. at 403–05, 24 S.Ct. at 469, 48 L.Ed. at 727–28.

12. Id. at 396, 24 S.Ct. at 485, 48 L.Ed. at 724.

13. United States v. Standard Oil Co., 173 F. 177, 183–186 (1909) modified and aff'd 221 U.S. 1, 31 S.Ct. 502, 55 L.Ed. 619 (1911).

14. United States v. American Tobacco Co., 164 F. 700, 702–707 (1908), rev'd 221 U.S. 106, 31 S.Ct. 632, 55 L.Ed 663 (1911).

15. D. Martin, Mergers and The Clayton Act 14–15 (1959).

16. B. Wyman, Control of the Market, A Legal Solution to the Trust Problem 160 (1911).

17. 200 U.S. 179, 26 S.Ct. 208, 50 L.Ed. 428 (1906).

§ 196. The Rule of Reason—Basic Cases and Beyond

The oil[1] and tobacco[2] cases were decided by the Supreme Court in 1911. It is not an undue simplification to say that the rule of reason announced by the majority in those cases established a median position somewhere between the extremes of *Knight*[3] and *Northern Securities*.[4] Though the lower courts had relied in part upon the sweeping rule of the latter case, the Supreme Court was at pains not to do so. *Standard Oil*, which yielded the primary opinion, stressed that only "undue restraints" transcended the Act's limits;[5] both the oil and tobacco consolidations merged a substantial portion of the proprietary interests of a great national industry, and it was this, as well as the calculated way in which the arrangements were carried out—precisely for the purpose of attaining such control—which put them beyond the bounds of the lawful.[6] In addition, the *Standard Oil* opinion asserted that (never mind where, or by what subtle medium of communication) the Act "indicates a consciousness that the freedom of the individual right to contract when not unduly or improperly exercised was the most efficient means for the prevention of monopoly."[7]

But the Court in the oil and tobacco cases also went to the effort, not merely to seal the fate of *Knight,* but to end once and for all the newer and more subtle heresy that the prohibition of the law could be avoided if the consolidation proceeded in a sanitized form, such as by an asset acquisition or a proprietary merger, rather than through a holding company. Although the tobacco consolidation had been achieved primarily through asset and partly through stock acquisitions, and the oil consolidation primarily through a holding company, the Court treated them identically under a general standard which made nothing turn on the particular mechanisms used to attain and exercise control. But lest that point be missed, the Court declared in the oil case that the Act's "all-embracing enumeration" was intended "to make sure that no form of contract or combination * * *" could save an unreasonable restraint.[8]

---

1. Standard Oil Co. v. United States, 221 U.S. 1, 31 S.Ct. 502, 55 L.Ed. 619 (1911).

2. United States v. American Tobacco Co., 221 U.S. 106, 31 S.Ct. 632, 55 L.Ed 663 (1911).

3. United States v. E. C. Knight Co., 156 U.S. 1, 15 S.Ct. 249, 39 L.Ed. 325 (1895).

4. Northern Sec. Co. v. United States, 193 U.S. 197, 24 S.Ct. 436, 48 L.Ed. 679 (1904).

5. 221 U.S. at 60, 31 S.Ct. at 515, 55 L.Ed. at 645.

6. Id. at 76–77, 31 S.Ct. at 521–23, 55 L.Ed. at 651–52.

7. 221 U.S. at 62, 31 S.Ct. at 516, 55 L.Ed. at 646.

8. 221 U.S. at 60, 31 S.Ct. at 515, 55 L.Ed. at 645.

None of this is to imply, however, that these opinions left matters firmly settled; instead, they moved the axis of debate. Some scholars and segments of the bar concluded from these cases that the legality of a merger turned upon whether, on balance, it injured the public or was beneficial or neutral, a decision which could be made only upon completion of exhaustive inquiry into such questions as whether it resulted in price increases or whether operational efficiencies were attained and costs reduced. Others thought the issue to be less particular: was a given merger likely to restrict competition?[9]

That these opinions, which sought to explore in depth relevant issues of fact and policy, presented so vague a contour that each reader could render them in forms to his liking is symptomatic of a problem which has plagued merger law and, for that matter, antitrust law generally. There is something of a mismatch between legal institutions, legal method, the law itself, and the assigned task of regulating industrial structure. At that time it might have been expressed in terms of a conflict between the logic of business facts and the logic of legal principles.[10] Then, the unhappy choice might have been seen as between an exhaustive factual inquiry in every case or a rule triggered by the salient aspects of a merger which common experience suggested would render it problematical.[11] Today, though the problems are likely to be articulated in terms of whether we can distill from economic theory workable generalizations courts can administer,[12] the underlying reality remains unchanged. If issues of industrial structure are to be dealt with as matters of law, there is a felt need for specification at an appropriate level of generality of the limits to which consolidation may be carried. The "appropriate" level of generalization is broad enough to provide an answer for most cases, but narrow enough to provide guidance to those seeking to take law into account when planning their conduct and to provide a standard capable of administration through the ordinary legal institutions.

The task of resolving this dilemma under the rule of reason proved too much for the Court. There were, it is true, cases [13] early in this period which seemed to pay greater heed to the message of *Northern Securities* than to that of *Standard Oil;* but they were railroad cases and, thus, were in a sense under the influence of *Northern Securities* in a way which cases involving industrial consolidations

9. See W. Letwin, Law and Economic Policy In America 265–70 (1965).

10. See J. Clark, The Control of Trusts 81 et seq. (1901).

11. Id.

12. See Bok, Section 7 of the Clayton Act and the Merging of Law and Economics, 74 Harv.L.Rev. 226 (1960).

13. United States v. Union Pac. R.R. Co., 226 U.S. 61, 33 S.Ct. 53, 57 L.Ed. 124 (1912); United States v. Reading Co., 253 U.S. 26, 40 S.Ct. 425, 64 L.Ed. 760 (1920); United States v. Southern Pac. Co., 259 U.S. 214, 42 S.Ct. 496, 66 L.Ed. 907 (1922).

were not. In any event, though the Court in these cases seemed to hold that a consolidation that ended a quantitatively substantial volume of direct competition violated the Act even though the line of commerce affected by the merger had been a small percentage of the combining firms' total business, that proposition was never absorbed into the general law about industrial consolidation, which emerged over the years as an articulation of the rule of reason. Looking over the full range of the Court's decisions in merger cases from 1911 to, say, 1930, one must conclude that the Court failed to undertake the task of deciding (either by developing workable generalizations or by probing particular fact situations) whether structural change brought about by merger violated the law; legality was made to turn not upon structural effects, but upon the pre-merger conduct of the promoters and the post-merger conduct of the consolidated unit.[14]

In that period the Court indicated that, absent predatory conduct, consolidations of a sufficient number of previously competing firms to attain predominant market positions did not violate the law.[15] If a consolidation raised an inference of intent to monopolize, the inference could quickly be dispelled by evidence of the existence of business opportunities or economies in production which were more easily attainable by a firm of large scale.[16] Consequently, the government could confidently challenge a merger only if it could show not only that a substantial share of the business was brought under common control, but also that the promoters displayed a purpose to monopolize, to raise prices, or to exclude others by oppressive tactics.[17]

As we shall see, there was legislative activity during this period; Congress passed the Clayton Act and established the Federal Trade Commission in part to deal with mergers.[18] But actions under these statutes were no more availing than actions under Sherman.[19] It was during this period of legal quiescence from about 1920 to 1929—when illegality turned on how power acquired through merger was used—that the third merger movement occurred.[20] The law, of course, did not "cause" this movement; the energy for it came from other sources. Yet it is interesting to note that this period of frantic merger activity begins in the very year in which the Court decided

14. E. g., United States v. United States Steel Corp., 251 U.S. 417, 40 S.Ct. 293, 64 L.Ed. 343 (1920); cf. United States v. International Harvester Co., 274 U.S. 693, 47 S.Ct. 748, 71 L.Ed. 1302 (1927).

15. Id.

16. Id.

17. See Standard Oil Co. v. United States, supra note 1; United States v. American Tobacco Co., supra note 2.

18. See § 197 infra.

19. Id.

20. See J. Markham, "Survey of the Evidence and Findings on Mergers," in Business Concentration and Price Policy 157 (1955).

the *United States Steel* case,[21] the rule of reason case which best exemplifies a judicial washing of the hands of the structural problem. In any event, the law during this period did little if anything to direct the flow of entrepreneurial responses affecting structure, except, of course, away from cartelization and into merger and, as we shall see, away from stock acquisition and into asset acquisition.[22]

The early history of merger and the law is then a story of groping, vacillation and frustration, as well as an apparently lively interaction between the legal rule seeming at any time to govern and the nature of the structural changes taking place in the economy. One can identify any number of conditioning factors: technological developments significantly affecting the economy, the responses of agrarian interests and small business, fear of change, demagoguery, fear of antitrust as well as actual antitrust enforcement, political disputes. But in the case law one finds something else worth noting—a quality discernibly judicial. *Northern Securities* can serve as an illustration. The case grew out of a battle of titans which resulted in the accord challenged in the litigation;[23] underlying the opinions were the tactical moves of counsel, which themselves make a lively story; beyond these were the series of decisions which led President Roosevelt to take his stand on the trust problem after a period of anguish and indecision and to use this case to educate the public to what he deemed a moderate and responsible view;[24] affecting the Presidential judgement were all of the elements of politics, from demagoguery to disinterested advice. Despite this tempestuous background and although the Justices (as Holmes' opinion implies) were not unaffected by the context, the case displays a special quality one associates with law—a quest for principle, for a way of resolving a particular dispute in a manner that reactivates a past norm and leaves it capable of further service in the future.

§ 197. Merger Provisions of the Original Clayton Act

Public and political debate swirled around *Northern Securities*. Though lively extremes were also evident, the politically dominant view in the years immediately following that case was a mild one. It saw the new forms of business organization as inevitable concomitants of economic progress and identified a need to curb abuses of corporate power, not a need to frustrate corporate growth. This attitude led, for example, to the formation of the Bureau of Corporations, which was to regulate corporate activity by exposing it to public view and the control of public opinion.[1] Legislation amendatory

---

21. Supra note 14.

22. See § 197 infra.

23. See W. Letwin, Law and Economic Policy in America 182–237 (1965).

24. Id. at 195–207.

1. D. Martin, Mergers and the Clayton Act 20–30 (1959); W. Letwin, Law and Economic Policy in America 240–44 (1965).

of the Sherman Act, however, seems not to have been seriously pressed until the Court promulgated the rule of reason in 1911.[2] The oil [3] and tobacco [4] cases, however, stimulated a number of statutory proposals, most aimed at specifying with greater particularity what the law permitted but a few of which went in quite the other direction of turning the matter over to a specialized agency empowered to intervene in particular situations with little statutory guidance. The suggestions for greater particularity included not only substantive positions of various degrees of severity but also various proposed regulatory mechanisms. Some of the latter involved highly particularized sets of norms which would substitute for the general language of Sherman; others involved a particularization which would exemplify but not exhaust Sherman; still others called for pre-clearance of specified corporate actions by an agency or official who could deny permission for any action he deemed to violate Sherman.[5] In any event, during the election campaign of 1912 Taft, Roosevelt and Wilson and their parties, each in their own ways, committed themselves to legislation making the law more rigorous than the Court had left it.[6]

The legislative process after Wilson's election yielded both the Federal Trade Commission Act [7] and the Clayton Act.[8] Section 7 of the latter act addressed holding companies.[9] Its terms forbade, with limited exceptions, any corporation engaged in commerce from acquiring stock in another corporation similarly engaged where the effect might be to substantially lessen competition between them, to restrain commerce in any section of the country, or to tend to create a monopoly.[10] Most of the shades of opinion that had informed the political debate for a decade were reflected in the legislative work, and virtually every phrase of the Section was labored over and altered. Thus the debates and reports do not provide a cohesive view. The Congressional purpose may be stated no more precisely than this: bringing previously competing firms into a community of interest through stock acquisition should be held to violate the law, subject to a test of competitive effect about which Congress cannot now agree and which the Court must work out, under the admonition that by

2. Martin, supra note 1, at 20–56.

3. Standard Oil Co. v. United States, 221 U.S. 1, 31 S.Ct. 502, 55 L.Ed. 619 (1911).

4. United States v. American Tobacco Co., 221 U.S. 106, 31 S.Ct. 632, 55 L. Ed. 663 (1911).

5. Martin, supra note 1, at 20–56; Letwin, supra note 1, at 247–55, 270–78.

6. Martin, supra note 1, at 23–29.

7. Act of September 26, 1914, ch. 311, 38 Stat. 717, 15 U.S.C.A. §§ 41–51.

8. Act of October 15, 1914, ch. 322, 38 Stat. 730, 15 U.S.C.A. §§ 12–27.

9. Martin, supra note 1, at 49–56.

10. The development of the original language of Section 7 is traced in Martin, supra note 1, at 32–43; the language of the Section as passed appears therein at 42 and in P. Areeda, Antitrust Analysis, Problems, Text and Cases 697 (2d ed. 1974).

and large Congress wants a stricter test than the Sherman Act seems to have established.[11] In sum, the legislative effort to specify unlawful structural changes was not noticeably more successful than judicial efforts had previously been.

The Federal Trade Commission gave Section 7 as comprehensive a construction as its language and history would readily tolerate. It did not limit the Section's application to the creation of holding companies, as the legislative history might have been thought to warrant. Rather, it applied the Section to all areas of stock acquisitions having effects the Commission thought forbidden.[12] Though it declined to overturn a merger directly achieved by a straight-out asset acquisition,[13] its orders routinely forbade asset acquisitions consummated after stock had been acquired and, presumptively, in the exercise of power attained by virtue of the stock acquisition.[14] Indeed, the Commission also took the position that asset acquisition, without any related stock acquisition, violated Section 5 of the FTC Act if the acquisition reduced market competition by creating communities of interest among previously competing firms.[15] As to competitive effect, the Commission uniformly required pre-acquisition competition between the acquired and acquiring firms, but it sometimes looked to market structure to judge whether the acquisition would affect market competition,[16] while at other times it merely considered whether the two firms confronted each other as rivals in any market.[17]

The Supreme Court, in one of the quirks of merger history, initially drew an odd line as to the Commission's power to deal with asset acquisitions under Section 7. In an opinion by Justice McReynolds dealing with three companion cases,[18] it held that where a firm, after a complaint by the Commission about a stock acquisition, used its stock position to attain a transfer of assets, the Commission, on finding the stock acquisition unlawful, could require the assets also to be disgorged. But it held that assets acquired before the filing of the Commission's complaint could not be ordered divided, even though the power gained by the unlawful stock acquisition had been used to acquire the assets.

Justice Brandeis wrote a terse and convincing dissent [19], the logic of which ultimately won out. However, the majority eventually re-

11. Martin, supra note 1, at 20–56.

12. Id. at 57–76.

13. Id. at 77–79.

14. Id. at 62–67. See, e.g., FTC v. Swift & Co., 5 F.T.C. 143 (1922), FTC v. Armour & Co., 4 F.T.C. 457 (1922), FTC v. Western Meat Co., 5 F.T.C. 417 (1923), and FTC v. Thatcher Manufacturing Co., 6 F.T.C. 213 (1923), in which the FTC ordered the companies to dispose of assets acquired from a corporation after an acquisition of a controlling stock interest was found to violate Section 7.

15. Martin, supra note 1, at 93–97.

16. See the cases cited and discussed in Martin supra note 1, at 80–89.

17. E.g., FTC v. Armour & Co., supra note 14, at 421–22.

18. FTC v. Western Meat Co., 272 U.S. 554, 47 S.Ct. 175, 71 L.Ed. 405 (1926).

19. Id. at 563–64, 47 S.Ct. 179, 71 L.Ed. 411–12.

solved its dilemma quite differently from Brandeis' suggested approach. In 1934, a five to four majority held that the Commission was powerless under Section 7 to deal with an asset acquisition under any circumstance, whether or not arising out of a stock acquisition and whether or not consummated before or after the Commission's complaint.[20] Thus ended, for most practical purposes, any potential Section 7 ever possessed as a limitation on mergers. Moreover, during the same period the Court put an end to any hope that Section 5 of the FTC Act might be a bulwark against mergers; it held that the Commission lacked power under that section to enter an order requiring a divestiture of acquired assets.[21]

Once again, the relationship between the law and the way entrepreneurial drive is expressed can be clearly seen. As a practical matter, Section 7 of the Clayton Act brought to an end the formation of holding companies as successors to the great trusts, and this is all that one can confidently say that Congress clearly intended. The section also had its impact on mergers, not so much in altering their frequency, but in giving them a new form—the asset acquisition. And certainly the Clayton Act, as construed, tended to facilitate, if not to stimulate, the third great merger movement, that which began in the early 1920's and continued until about 1929.[22]

§ 198. 1930 to 1950

The 1930's represented a quiet period for merger activity. But about 1940, with the war stimulation of the economy, mergers again began to change the industrial structure.[1] However, by 1940 legal quiescence had become the status quo; for this reason and because wartime pressures limited incentives to challenge industrial activity, there were few cases which could be seen as serious efforts to abate the new merger wave.

The leading case of the period, United States v. Columbia Steel Company,[2] reached the Supreme Court in 1948. The government had brought the action under Sherman sections 1 and 2 to enjoin acquisition by Columbia Steel (a wholly owned subsidiary of United States Steel Company, the nation's largest fully integrated steel producer) of Consolidated Steel (an independent which was one of the largest west coast fabricators of steel for building frameworks,

20. Arrow-Hart & Hegeman Electric Co. v. FTC, 291 U.S. 587, 54 S.Ct. 532, 78 L.Ed. 1007 (1934).

21. FTC v. Eastman Kodak Co., 274 U. S. 619, 47 S.Ct. 688, 71 L.Ed. 1238 (1927).

22. See Martin, supra note 1, at 144–47.

1. Litner & Butters, Effect of Mergers on Industrial Concentration, 1940–47, 32 Rev. Econ & Stat. 30 (1950); J. Markham, "Survey of the Evidence and Findings on Mergers" in Business Concentration and Price Policy 141 (1955); R. Nelson, Merger Movements in American Industry, 1895–1956 (1959).

2. 334 U.S. 495, 68 S.Ct. 1107, 92 L.Ed. 1533 (1948).

bridges and welded pipe—called "plates and shapes"). The Government challenged the merger on the dual ground that it would reduce competition between Consolidated and United, insofar as United also fabricated steel plates and shapes, and that it would reduce competition between United, which made rolled steel, a raw material sold to makers of plates and shapes, and other firms making rolled steel, by tying Consolidated to United as its supplier and thus foreclosing sales to Consolidated by United's competitors.

Since the 1930's, the law in monopoly cases and in some of the cases on vertical restraint had attained a degree of sophistication about structural issues and competitive consequences, and the case represented an effort to revitalize Sherman by introducing these conceptions into a merger analysis. It thus became necessary first to define the relevant market and then to evaluate the horizontal and vertical consequences of the merger on the basis of market shares and other structural criteria.

The case has current significance for two reasons. First, the Court responded to the Justice Department's plea and fully entered into an analysis of structural change in order to predict competitive effect; the tone of the majority opinion by Justice Reed is remarkably different from the conduct-oriented merger opinions characteristic of the 1920's. Second, the Court performed its task of structural analysis poorly—indeed, it seemed both to know that it was dealing with manipulations beyond its ken, and to be frustrated by the process. The Court exhibited uncertainty in choosing between defendant's contention for a national market and the government's argument for a market made up of eleven western states; and it found no subsidiary norms to help it decide. In the end, it took the smaller market, which tended to inflate both the concentration figures used in evaluating the horizontal effects and the foreclosure effect pertinent to the vertical issue; but it then minimized the significance of the concentration and foreclosure indicated by those figures.[3]

In terms of result, the Court thus approved entry through merger of the nation's largest steel company into a developing geographic market by absorption of a major firm. It approved an increase in the level of concentration in an already highly concentrated industry, as well as the end of significant actual and potential competition. Justice Douglas stressed these stark circumstances in his dissenting opinion in which three others concurred.[4]

---

3. Compare the analysis suggested by Handler, Blake, Pitofsky & Goldschmid, Trade Regulation, Cases and Materials 283–86 to the effect that in monopoly cases a commonsense definition of the market ought to be selected and entry and related conditions examined to see whether power is being exercised. The Court's view that the significance of concentration and foreclosure percentages varies with the relative breadth or narrowness of the market definition adopted is essentially sound. It is the ultimate conclusion reached in *Columbia Steel* which seems wrong.

4. 334 U.S. at 534–40, 68 S.Ct. at 1127–30, 92 L.Ed. at 1557–61.

§ 199. The 1950 Amendment to Section 7

Just as the first *United States Steel* decision contributed to the initial passage of the Clayton Act, so the 1948 decision [1] gave added impetus to long unsuccessful efforts to amend Section 7 in order to make it effective. In 1950, the Section finally was amended. It was changed, first, to apply to all mergers, whether by acquisition of stock or assets. Second, its statement of requisite competitive effect was broadened to cover any substantial reduction in competition, not just competition between the acquired and acquiring firms, thus extending the Section to vertical mergers which foreclosed competition of the acquired or acquiring firm. As amended, the Act (with certain exceptions) forbids any corporation engaged in commerce to acquire stock or assets of any other such corporation where in any line of commerce in any section of the country the effect may be substantially to lessen competition or to tend to create a monopoly.

The legislative history shows an intent to plug what Congress viewed as a loophole in the original section, the failure to cover asset acquisitions,[2] and the language change served this purpose.[3] The old language had three distinctive normative standards—substantial lessening of competition between the acquired and acquiring firm, restraint of commerce in any section of the country or community, or tendency to monopoly.[4] The new had two—substantial lessening of competition in any line of commerce in any section of the country, or tendency to monopoly in any line of commerce in any section of the country.[5] As to the impact of the new clause concerning competitive effect, the terms of which were altered only slightly, there is as much that is vague in the legislative history of the 1950 act as there was in that of the 1914 statute. But if Congress could not agree on precise norms or standards and again left much to the courts, at least this much came through: Congress was concerned in a very broad and general way about increases in business concentration.[6] It was less a matter of having well formed theories about the changing structure of American industry than of a shared and general feeling of concern, even alarm, about the economic, social and political effects of the changes going on—if you will, about the processes of change themselves and about the reduction in local control of business as operating control of industry generally became more centered in the east. Congress wanted the courts to be tougher than they had been

1. See, as an example, the merger unsuccessfully challenged in United States v. Columbia Steel Co., 334 U.S. 495, 68 S.Ct. 1107, 92 L.Ed. 1533 (1948).

2. See the review of the legislative history in Brown Shoe Co. v. United States, 370 U.S. 294, 312–23, 82 S.Ct. 1502, 1517–1523, 8 L.Ed.2d 510, 528–534 (1962).

3. Celler-Kefauver Act of December 29, 1950, ch. 1184, 64 Stat. 1125, 15 U.S. C.A. § 18.

4. See D. Martin, Mergers and the Clayton Act, 32–43 (1959).

5. Supra note 3.

6. Supra note 2.

since 1911 and not to wait for a showing of power aggressively used, or even for a showing that structural change would inevitably do injury to competitive processes. It wanted the courts to act at the edge of harm in order to choke off those mergers likely alone or as part of a merger movement to cause irreversible injury to the competitive process.

The competitive effects language remains, then, very loose. Even looser, perhaps, were Congressional conceptions about the nature of competition—about whether Congress valued it as an end in itself or as an instrument and, if the latter, what the utimate policy concerns might be.[7] Against this background, the Commission and the courts began a process of working out the law which has been maturing for a quarter of a century. Needless to say, they have had considerable advice from the bar and academia.[8]

§ 200. New Clayton Merger Law and the Coalescence of Clayton and Sherman Standards

The purpose of this section is to complete the brief historical survey attempted in this part. The parts that follow explore in detail the particulars of current law. The emphasis in this section will be on major movements only, upon the ways in which the courts have confronted the task assigned by Congress—the regulation of structural change through merger in a manner conducive to the public interest.

A central issue has been this: Should each case involve an exhaustive exploration of effect, discernible and likely, pursued through an analysis of all relevant structural variables and a probing of purpose, of the animus behind the merger? Or should the Court, mindful of the coalescing limits of judicial method and economic theory, develop more nearly self-executing norms predicated upon major aspects of structure, such as market share? It would overstate the matter to claim that the Court has no more resolved this issue under the new law than it did under the old, or than the Congress did in its most earnest attempts; actually, the Court has come down increasingly on the side of articulating structural norms of fairly wide application. But it has expressed inconsistent views both about whether that is the appropriate course and, assuming it may be, about what structural norms will serve. Consequently, even now one cannot say the matter is properly settled. Let us look briefly at the highlights.

---

7. Id.

8. The literature relevant to merger law is extensive. A good, selective bibliography appears in Handler, Blake, Pitofsky & Goldschmid, Trade Regulation, Cases and Materials 1092–94 (1975); an unselective but more comprehensive one appears at Oppenheim & Weston, Federal Antitrust Laws 315–17 (3d ed. 1968).

Brown Shoe[1] was the first case under the revised Clayton Act to reach the Supreme Court. The Court spoke about the appropriateness of looking at a great range of factors: the market shares resulting from the merger; the degree of concentration in the industry and whether there has been a trend toward increasing concentration; any special significances market shares may have in light of particular industry conditions or because of the particular stature, endowments or trade connections of firm gaining control; the history of the acquired and acquiring firms, including whether they have grown in the past and, if so, whether by merger; whether there are particular competing firms left specially vulnerable because of the merger; and the purposes of those responsible for the merger.[2] However, when one passes beyond the rhetoric of the opinion to the record and to what was done, the conviction grows that the Court acted differently than it spoke; it invalidated a rather slight and unimportant merger in a rather competitive industry on the basis of a modest increase in concentration, if any. In a sense, the decision is the mirror image of that rendered in 1948 in *Columbia Steel*.[3] If the Court there had been permissive about a merger which significantly increased concentration, in *Brown* it was restrictive about a merger which did not.

In later cases the Court backed away somewhat from the language of *Brown Shoe,* which had indicated that all issues were open. *Philadelphia National Bank* recognized the need "[where] it is possible, without doing violence to the congressional objective * * * to simplify the test of illegality * * *."[4] It thus announced not a *per se* rule, but a rule of presumptive illegality for any merger "which produces a firm controlling an undue percentage share of the relevant market, and results in a significant increase in the concentration of firms in that market * * *."[5] While the key words are general, the doctrine focused on market share, held a merger resulting in a 30% share to be unlawful, and allowed for a series of finer articulations as time went on about what percentage would be considered "undue" and what increase would be "significant." Indeed, at the outset the Court gave some clues to the kind of development it envisaged, for it cited economic literature indicating that shares of from 7 to 20 or 25% might be deemed presumptively too great.[6]

---

1. Brown Shoe Co. v. United States, 370 U.S. 294, 82 S.Ct. 1502, 8 L.Ed.2d 510 (1962).

2. Id.

3. United States v. Columbia Steel Co., 334 U.S. 495, 68 S.Ct. 1107, 92 L.Ed. 1533 (1948). See § 198 supra.

4. United States v. Philadelphia Nat'l Bank, 374 U.S. 321, 362, 83 S.Ct. 1715, 1741, 10 L.Ed.2d 915, 944 (1963).

5. 374 U.S. at 363, 83 S.Ct. at 1741, 10 L.Ed.2d at 945.

6. 374 U.S. at 324 n. 2, 83 S.Ct. at 1720, 10 L.Ed.2d at 922. The stunning simplification entailed in this analysis bears emphasis. The Court talks not about four or five firm concentration ratios, or any other measure that gives a shorthand picture of the market; it directs itself only to the matter of the share of the merged firm. Of course, it expresses its recognition

Since 1963 this kind of an approach to merger issues, rather than the open-ended approach invited by *Brown Shoe,* has been generally ascendant.[7] The courts have, at last, begun to work out general norms reflecting structural analysis and the warmly expressed Congressional concerns. The search has been for highly simplified norms. Although theory about the effect of increased concentration leaves a wide number of possible situations in which competition might be improved (or at least in which there is no basis for supposing that competition would be injured) by some possible mergers in oligopolistic industries,[8] the courts have been resistant to efforts to show that particular mergers are helpful or harmless even though they increase concentration significantly.[9]

Nonetheless, the *Brown Shoe* language remains in the background and, at times, results in highly elaborate and seemingly indeterminate analysis.[10] Furthermore, apparent doctrinal solidity can in some instances mask uncertainty and uneven development. In this area the theoretical possibility for merger defendants to overcome the presumption associated with undue market shares by detailed evidence of the kind envisaged by *Brown Shoe,* coexists with the possibility that market shares may be distorted by manipulating market definitions. These and related issues have remained sources of tension.[11]

Before closing this survey another development should be noted. Having moved, as it did in Clayton adjudication, to a rather strict position adverse to mergers which increase market shares in industries which are concentrated or tending toward concentration, the Court in the *Lexington Bank* case [12] brought the Sherman Act standards into closer accord with Clayton than they had previously seemed to be. In an opinion for the Court (concurred in by four other justices), Justice Douglas "confined to its special facts" the decision in *Columbia*

---

that the significance of such share figures will vary in differing settings, but the emphasis is nonetheless worthy of remark.

7. See, e.g., United States v. Third Nat'l Bank in Nashville, 390 U.S. 171, 88 S.Ct. 882, 19 L.Ed.2d 1015 (1968); United States v. Von's Grocery Co., 384 U.S. 270, 86 S.Ct. 1478, 16 L.Ed.2d 555 (1966). But cf. United States v. General Dynamics Corp., 415 U.S. 486, 94 S.Ct. 1186, 39 L.Ed.2d 530 (1974).

8. For example if there were 7 or 8 firms each with eight to twelve percent and a large number of small fringe firms, would competition be hurt or helped by aggregations of the fringe firms to reach 4 or 5 percent each? The relationship between oligopolistic structure on the one hand and market conduct and performance on the other are not so determinate as to allow of theoretical answers to questions like these. See Ch. 4 supra.

9. E.g., United States v. Philadelphia Nat'l Bank, supra note 4.

10. See United States v. General Dynamics Corp., supra note 7.

11. See United States v. Aluminum Co. of America (Rome Cable), 377 U.S. 271, 84 S.Ct. 1283, 12 L.Ed.2d 314 (1964); United States v. Continental Can Co., 378 U.S. 441, 84 S.Ct. 1738, 12 L.Ed.2d 953 (1964).

12. United States v. First Nat'l Bank of Trust Co. of Lexington, 376 U.S. 665, 84 S.Ct. 1033, 12 L.Ed.2d 1 (1964).

Steel,[13] totally ignored the line of cases symbolized by the earlier *United States Steel* decision,[14] and refurbished *Northern Securities*[15] and the railroad cases[16] which had followed shortly after *Standard Oil*[17] and had been ignored since then. The Sherman Act was said to forbid any merger between "major competitive factors in a relevant market" which could cause the "elimination of significant competition between them * * *."[18]

The law had come full circle. Judicial or legislative efforts to work out analytical refinements and workable techniques for digging deeply enough to grasp and understand the market consequence of a particular merger had been largely unavailing. Seeing itself as faced with the necessity of choosing a permissive rule or a forbidding one, the Court had tried each and then each once again as it moved from *Knight* to *Northern Securities,* through *Standard Oil* to *United States Steel,* and finally through *Columbia Steel* to *Lexington Bank.*

There is, perhaps, a certain fitness in all of this. While the Court has not succeeded in working out satisfactory analytical devices, it has tried mightily and, no doubt, will try yet again. And in those periods during which it has relied largely on comprehensive rules, none can suggest that it did not adopt the posture—permissive or prohibitive—most nearly consonant with the national consensus as expressed through the statutory development and the instruments of Congressional oversight.

The nation values incompatible things. One is an economy of abundance. Hence, we are loath to inhibit the attainment of economic efficiency, which may add to our plenty, even when the attainment of efficiency seems to require large industrial units. Another is the freedom to contract with a minimum of governmental interference. Both of these values have pointed toward a permissive posture toward merger. Opposed to both of these has been a commitment to competition as a self-regulatory process, a distrust of large aggregations of economic power, a desire to keep opportunity open for small ventures and, despite protestations otherwise, a zeal to protect individual small firms. By and large we seem to have had at each stage of merger law development if not the policy on merger that we deserved, at least the one with which the politically dominant among us,

13. Supra note 3. See § 198 supra.

14. United States v. United States Steel Corp., 251 U.S. 417, 40 S.Ct. 293, 64 L.Ed. 343 (1920). See § 196 supra.

15. Northern Sec. Co. v. United States, 193 U.S. 197, 24 S.Ct. 436, 48 L.Ed. 679 (1904). See § 195 supra.

16. United States v. Union Pac. R.R. Co., 226 U.S. 61, 33 S.Ct. 53, 57 L.Ed. 124 (1912); United States v. Reading Co., 253 U.S. 26, 40 S.Ct. 425, 64 L.Ed. 760 (1920); United States v. Southern Pac. Co., 259 U.S. 214, 42 S.Ct. 496, 66 L.Ed. 907 (1922). See § 196 supra.

17. Standard Oil Co. v. United States, 221 U.S. 1, 31 S.Ct. 502, 55 L.Ed. 619 (1911).

18. United States v. First Nat'l Bank & Trust Co. of Lexington, supra note 12 at 671–72, 84 S.Ct. at 1037, 12 L.Ed.2d at 6.

in shifting alliances, seem to have been basically content. Yet it has almost always been in some degree a policy of compromise.

§ 201. Impact of Current Merger Policy on Industrial Structure

It was asserted early in this chapter that regulatory interpositions do not end economic manifestations but at most transform them.[1] The current "hard" position on horizontal and vertical merger has in some degree arrested the long standing trend toward consolidation and integration. However, as we shall discover when we look at remedies,[2] the failure of Congress to require prior clearance of mergers, the judicial reluctance to enter preliminary injunctions, and the difficulties often associated with fashioning and executing satisfactory post-merger remedies have loosened the net somewhat, to allow a considerable amount of merger activity which, in strict theory, is probably inappropriate under current normative standards.

In any event, inhibiting the urge to merge has had structural effects which do not all tend in the same direction. Significantly, the strict position came much too late to preclude oligopolization of most mining and manufacturing industries. The discernible effect, then, may be to keep large firms in these industries from concentrating further, and to keep smaller firms within these industries from combining to add a few more large competitors.[3] Despite the possibility of some efficiency losses, a strong consensus view would probably approve the arresting of the trend toward concentration as wholesome, though it would bemoan the lateness of the development. An oligopolistic industry is still preferred to a monopolistic one, a more loosely structured oligopoly to a tighter one; and there is always hope for eventual deconcentration due to entry, technical change and development, or government action to deconcentrate markets where cartelization or interdependence prevails or presents high risks. The second result—keeping smaller firms within an oligopolistic market from combining—is perhaps less easy to justify, at least in instances where it is likely that the larger firms have efficiency advantages. However, there is very little indication that this kind of enforcement has been pushed to extremes.

It must be remembered also that to forbid merger is not to forbid internal growth. When significant efficiencies can be attained at larger scale one or more firms may well reach that scale eventually, even if merger as a means is not permitted, although at the very least there will be delay. Assuming that total demand is insufficient or unlikely to grow enough in the short run to support all or most existing firms at the more efficient larger size, some must be displaced if oth-

1. See § 193 supra.
2. See §§ 215 & 216 infra.
3. See D. Dewey, "The New Learning: One Man's View," in Industrial Concentration: The New Learning 1 (Goldschmid, Mann and Weston, eds. 1974).

ers are to grow. The prospect of a competitive struggle to the death, with ultimate disaster for some and inevitable losses for all, will tend to discourage any firm from making the necessary new investment.

With respect to vertical integration much the same can be said. Some efficiencies are probably lost. To the extent current rules inhibit integrations, like that in *Columbia Steel,* of manufacturing stages in a basic industry, they may aid in the maintenance of lower levels of oligipolistic concentration. To the extent that the current rules primarily affect distribution, it is less clear that avoidance of oligopolistic concentration requires such rigor. Distribution remains, in general, one of the most competitive sectors; it is reasonably clear that some efficiencies can sometimes be gained by vertical integration to this level and it is not at all clear that greater vertical integration through merger would significantly reduce competition. Yet, there is considerable public support for the view that small locally controlled firms ought not to be allowed to pass from the scene. And the case would be hard to make that present policy greatly reduces efficiency; indeed, entry and exit in retailing and in distribution generally being relatively frequent and easy, one might expect substantial efficiencies to be obtained by vertical integration without merger.

Perhaps the major unique structural development during the last two decades has been the substantial increase in conglomorate organization. Numerous firms, some of them giants like ITT, have grown by investing in a series of unrelated industries and functions. Since conglomeration does not lead to increased concentration in any one market as does horizontal merger, or to foreclosure of competitors, as does vertical merger, current merger policy has addressed conglomeration only obliquely.[4] One may infer that present policy, which is quite strict about horizontal and vertical merger, but much less so about conglomorate merger, has tended to encourage conglomeration. Seeking avenues for expansion, entrepreneurs have chosen the one the law has done the least to block. Once again, public policy about structure may have had its principal effect in transforming the kind of structural change which takes place rather than in inhibiting change entirely.

As this chapter unfolds it will become clear that the judicial response to merger has not been constant, even since the enactment of the 1950 amendments to Section 7. The Warren Court tended to resolve doubtful issues against the validity of a merger.[5] Any horizon-

4. See §§ 207–209 infra.

5. See §§ 203–209 infra. See also Handler, Twenty-Fourth Annual Antitrust Review, 72 Colum.L.Rev. 1, 51–63 (1972); Handler, Antitrust: 1969, 55 Cornell L.Rev. 161, 204–08 (1970); Handler, Through the Antitrust Looking Glass, 57 Calif.L.Rev. 182, 204–07 (1969); Handler, Some Misadventures in Antitrust Policy Making, 40 N.Y.U. L.Rev. 823, 837–844 (1965). Professor Handler was one of the most constant critics of the Court's approach to merger issues during the 1960's and early 1970's.

tal merger was likely to be in jeopardy, even when the market was largely unconcentrated and the market share of the merging firm is small.[6] Vertical mergers were also treated severely,[7] and markets were frequently defined not in the way which seemed analytically most rigorous but in the way that heightened any apparent competitive risk.[8] In the last few years the majority of the Burger Court has shown a disposition to be more analytical in handling merger issues.[9] While it would be rash to say that the law has changed in explicit, identifiable ways, it seems reasonably clear that one attacking a merger will be required to develop a theory about how the merger will hurt competition which can survive skeptical scrutiny.

The Court's new analytical rigor needs no defense. Greater rationality in merger litigation is a self-evident value. On the other hand, the adverse judicial attitude toward merger which characterized the Warren years is not likely to pass unlamented. The American economy is highly concentrated.[10] History teaches that merger has been the major instrument through which that concentration has been achieved.[11] We know how extraordinarily hard it is to deconcentrate an already concentrated market through the antitrust laws.[12] Yet we may reasonably hope that through the dynamic of new technology and other changes even highly concentrated markets will become subject to more competition in the future, so long as countervailing tendencies, such as those expressed through merger, are stifled. All of these concerns are reflected in the legislative history of Section 7.[13] There seems little doubt that Congress wanted to stop the long run process of increasing concentration and saw a vigorous attack on merger as a major weapon in the battle. While it will be difficult in many cases to conclude with confidence whether a particular merger does or does not threaten competition, in many of these cases it may well be plausible to conclude that this merger is part of the process of structural change which Congress wanted to stop.

6. See §§ 204–05 infra.

7. See §§ 210–14 infra.

8. See § 203 infra.

9. See §§ 203–05 infra.

10. See §§ 115–17 supra.

11. See §§ 192–200 supra.

12. See Ch. 4 supra.

13. See § 199 infra.

PART B. HORIZONTAL AND MARKET EXTENSION MERGERS

§ 202. Statutory Provisions Relevant to Legality of Mergers

a. Section 7 of the Clayton Act

Much about the law of merger remains to be settled, even about the ways in which Section 7, the principal statutory instrument, applies to horizontal mergers, the merger category raising the most prominent competitive concerns. Indeed, the more the Court attempts to elucidate the less we know for sure. It moved initially from the complex, sometimes sensitive (though also sometimes internally inconsistent) statement, yet somewhat enigmatic judicial action, of *Brown Shoe*,[1] to the gross simplicities of *Von's*,[2] *Continental Can*[3] and *Pabst*.[4] The last three cases symbolize a period when crucial decisions about the legality of mergers were made at the Justice Department; once a case went to court the government couldn't lose.[5] As manifested by its most recent decisions, *General Dynamics*,[6] *Marine Bancorporation*[7] and *Citizens and Southern National Bank*[8] the Court is now moving back again, perhaps to a new and mature merger jurisprudence characterized by a dynamic analysis which draws on

---

1. Brown Shoe Co. v. United States, 370 U.S. 294, 82 S.Ct. 1502, 8 L.Ed.2d 510 (1962).

2. United States v. Von's Grocery Co., 384 U.S. 270, 86 S.Ct. 1478, 16 L.Ed.2d 555 (1966).

3. United States v. Continental Can Co., 378 U.S. 441, 84 S.Ct. 1738, 12 L.Ed.2d 953 (1964).

4. United States v. Pabst Brewing Co., 384 U.S. 546, 86 S.Ct. 1665, 16 L.Ed.2d 765 (1966).

5. From the time of the decision in Brown Shoe Co. v. United States, supra note 1, through the decision in Ford Motor Co. v. United States, 405 U.S. 562, 92 S.Ct. 1142, 31 L.Ed.2d 492 (1972), the United States did not lose any merger case on the merits in the Supreme Court. In addition to the cases cited in notes 1 through 4 supra, and *Ford*, supra, it prevailed in United States v. Philadelphia Nat'l Bank, 374 U.S. 321, 83 S.Ct. 1715, 10 L.Ed.2d 915 (1963); United States v. Aluminum Co. of America (Rome Cable), 377 U.S. 271, 84 S.Ct. 1283, 12 L.Ed.2d 314 (1964); United States v. El Paso Natural Gas Co., 376 U.S. 651, 84 S.Ct. 1044, 12 L.Ed.2d 12 (1964); United States v. Penn-Olin Chem. Co., 378 U.S. 158, 84 S.Ct. 1710, 12 L.Ed.2d 775 (1964). See also FTC v. Consolidated Foods Corp., 380 U.S. 592, 85 S.Ct. 1220, 14 L.Ed.2d 95 (1965); FTC v. Procter & Gamble Co. (Clorox), 386 U.S. 568, 87 S.Ct. 1224, 18 L.Ed.2d 303 (1967) in which the Commission prevailed. Justice Stewart, describing the only consistent thread he could find in § 7 opinions, concluded "the Government always wins." United States v. Von's Grocery Co., supra note 2 at 301, 86 S.Ct. at 1495, 16 L. Ed.2d at 575 (dissenting opinion). Virtually all of these cases involved simplifying standards for market definition, or competitive effect, or both, which eased significantly the prosecutorial burden.

6. United States v. General Dynamics Corp., 415 U.S. 486, 94 S.Ct. 1186, 39 L.Ed. 530 (1974).

7. United States v. Marine Bancorporation, Inc., 418 U.S. 602, 94 S.Ct. 2856, 41 L.Ed.2d 978 (1974).

8. United States v. Citizens & S. Nat'l Bank, 422 U.S. 86, 95 S.Ct. 2099, 45 L.Ed.2d 41 (1975).

structure, conduct and performance to predict the likely consequence of any particular structural change, or perhaps to something less complex, less grandiose, and as yet not fully visible.

It seems inappropriate for the Court to abandon the process of analysis, as it seemed to do for a time. A proper sense of judicial role and a healthy concern for the demands of merger litigation on the judicial system do not call for so drastic a response. On the other hand, certainly a judiciary open to all the theoretical refinements and empirical material the parties can afford to present is not appropriate. A middle ground is needed. Perhaps after its abberrations the law has now reached a balanced intermediate position. The sections which follow attempt to some extent to trace the paths of the law but are more committed to generalization about its present condition. We begin here with a brief overview organized around this question: what are the elements of a Section 7 offense when the complaint alleges an unlawful horizontal merger?

With limited exceptions, Section 7 forbids the acquisition by one corporation in commerce of the stock or assets of another corporation in commerce where the effect may be substantially to lessen competition or the tendency to create a monopoly in any line of commerce in any section of the country. First, the acquiring and acquired firms must be corporations; the Section does not apply to other forms of enterprise. Second, the adverse competitive effect must be shown in a defined product and geographic market. Third, in the case of horizontal mergers, it must be shown that the acquiring and acquired firms actually or potentially compete and that the merger alters structure in a way that threatens competition market-wide to an unacceptable degree. Finally, it must be shown that both firms engage in commerce.[9] Though none of these elements can be ignored,

9. Gulf Oil Corp. v. Copp Paving Co., 419 U.S. 186, 95 S.Ct. 392, 42 L.Ed.2d 378 (1974); United States v. American Bldg. Maintenance Indus., 422 U.S. 271, 95 S.Ct. 2150, 45 L.Ed.2d 177 (1975). There are, of course, other statutory terms which raise constructional issues. There must be an "acquisition;" the subject of the acquisition must be "stock" or "assets." In an earlier section it was shown that the concept, "assets," is a very broad one. See § 180 supra. The concept, "acquisition", is also given a spacious meaning, consistent with the remedial goals of the statute. See, e. g., Nelson v. Pacific Southwest Airlines, 1975–1 CCH Trade Cas. ¶ 60,124 (S.D.Cal.1975); United States v. Columbia Pictures Corp., 189 F. 153 (S.D.N.Y.1960). Of particular interest is United States v. ITT Continental Baking Co., 420 U.S. 223, 95 S.Ct. 926, 43 L.Ed.2d 148 (1975). Affirming the district court, the court of appeals had held that an agreement by which one bakery became the exclusive sales agent of another was an "acquisition" within the meaning of an FTC cease and desist order issued under Section 7. However, that court concluded that the "acquisition" was a single, discrete violation, not a continuing violation, subject to daily penalties under 15 U.S.C.A. §§ 21(l), 45(l). (485 F.2d 16 (10th Cir. 1973)). On the last point, the Supreme Court reversed, ruling that an acquisition in violation of the order subjected ITT to daily penalties. Note also the recent holding that there must be a completed acquisition, that while Section 1 of Sherman may cover an uncompleted merger, Section 7 of Clayton does not. Helix Mining Co. v. Terminal Flour Mills Co., 523 F.2d 1317 (9th Cir. 1975).

the most complex and critical are those which deal with competitive effect—with respect to both market definition and the gauging of competitive effect within the market as defined. These matters will have most of our attention in later sections.

b. *The Sherman Act*

Examination of recent merger cases shows the frequency with which the Justice Department proceeds under both Section 1 of Sherman and Section 7 of Clayton. Why does the Department follow this practice? How do the two sections relate?

Note first the broader coverage of Section 1. It not only applies in the case of those transactions explicitly exempt from Section 7, but it also applies to acquisitions by or of firms other than corporations, and to acquisitions which affect interstate commerce, not just to those in which the acquired and acquiring firms are in commerce. Whenever there is basis for doubt about Section 7's applicability, caution suggests addition of a count under Section 1 to any merger complaint. But caution may fulfill still another function. One would expect the Sherman Act, with its rule of reason, to be a less rigorous test than Section 7 of Clayton, given the Congressional purpose in Clayton to tighten the net. But in the case of a merger between direct competitors, a count under Sherman may serve to simplify the prosecutor's burden. This possibility may lead to the use of Section 1 in many merger cases.

Recall that the general language of Section 1 of Sherman was aimed at corporate consolidations as much as at cartels; the public concern about trusts evoked the statute. And in early decisions, before Clayton was on the statute books, the Court held unlawful horizontal mergers between firms in significant direct competition.[10] In *Lexington Bank*[11] the Court resuscitated that doctrine, flatly holding that a merger activated by no predatory purpose was illegal under Section 1 because significant competition would be eliminated, and for no other reason.

Section 1 ultimately may facilitate a simplified presentation in cases where the merging firms compete directly. We have noted that to prevail under Section 7 the Government must show the "line of commerce" (product market) and "section of the country" (geographic market) in which the competitive effect of the merger is to be measured. In later sections it will be shown that the competitive effects test under Clayton may have spacious ramifications, leaving ample room for defenses. The early Section 1 merger cases, which speak anew through *Lexington Bank,* have, by contrast, a *per se* quality. They seem to teach that if the evidence shows as a practical matter that the acquired and acquiring firms significantly compete, a

---

10. E.g., United States v. Union Pac. R.R. Co., 226 U.S. 61, 33 S.Ct. 53, 57 L.Ed. 124 (1912). See §§ 195, 196.

11. United States v. First Nat'l Bank & Trust Co. of Lexington, 376 U.S. 665, 84 S.Ct. 1033, 12 L.Ed.2d 1 (1964).

matter which can perhaps be established with nontechnical evidence about what and to whom they sell, the violation is shown and the litigation ended.[12]

Of course, it may be that a showing of substantial, direct competition between the acquired and acquiring firms is sufficient under Section 7; all of the recent Section 7 cases where the Court indulged in a more complex analysis involved more tenuous prosecutorial claims, usually concerning the loss of potential competition.[13] But if the Court in its present mood is disposed to demand more under Section 7, it does not have to feel inhibited by the contention outlined above, which would give Section 1 a larger meaning. Reading the early railroad merger cases and *Lexington Bank* for all they are worth still requires the Government to prove that the acquiring and acquired firms did significantly compete. Section 1 could be accommodated to Section 7 simply by saying one cannot determine the significance of competition between two firms without exploring the nature of the structure of the market, the conduct encountered in it, and the performance which they yield to the same degree as these would be explored under Section 7.

In the sections which follow, we shall not stress the differences which might be discerned between Section 1 and Section 7, since in most applications the analytical process will be the same. If there are differences like the one explored here, or in the quantum of evidence of competitive injury needed to establish a violation, they will rarely be crucial and can be left to show themselves when balances are struck between the social harms and benefits a particular merger may be expected to yield.

c. *The Bank Merger Act*

Much recent merger litigation, including cases setting forth generally applicable law, has involved bank mergers. In evaluating these cases, it will be important to note the special structural characteristics of the banking industry, which arise from public regulation, and to recall that bank mergers are subject to special legislation.

Under the Bank Merger Act of 1960[14] no bank merger was lawful unless approved by one of three regulatory agencies, which have contiguous and to a degree overlapping jurisdictions. Mergers involving national banks required approval by the Comptroller of the Currency. The Federal Reserve Board had to approve mergers of state chartered banks which were members of the Federal Reserve System. Mergers of other banks insured by the Federal Deposit Insurance Corporation had to have approval of that corporation. In addition to the needs and convenience of the public in obtaining banking services, the

12. See E. Rockefeller, Antitrust Questions and Answers 169–172 (1974).

13. See § 205(b) infra.

14. 74 Stat. 129 (1960), as amended, 12 U.S.C.A. § 1828.

reviewing agency was required to consider the effect of the merger on competition, and had to obtain and consider a report of the Attorney General about competitive effects.[15] In the *Philadelphia Bank* case,[16] despite the provisions of the 1960 Act and the generally assumed inapplicability of amended Section 7 to bank consolidations, the Court held that bank mergers were also subject to Section 7. Congress then passed the Bank Merger Act of 1966.[17] The new act, in addition to validating bank mergers not challenged by the Justice Department before a specified date, forbids the reviewing banking agency from approving a merger if it would result in monopoly, or is part of an attempt to monopolize. It also forbids approval of a merger which would substantially lessen competition or tend to create a monopoly or restrain trade, unless the anticompetitive effects are clearly outweighed because of the advantage of the merger in meeting the convenience and needs of the community to be served. The Justice Department may, within 30 days after regulatory approval, challenge any approved merger by an action under the antitrust laws. The bringing of such an action stays the effect of the approval unless the court otherwise orders and, because of the way the Supreme Court has read the Act, the district courts have little latitude to lift the stay.

In sum, a bank merger is first subject to agency scrutiny and then may be challenged by the Department of Justice under Section 7 or Section 1. These antitrust statutes apply in the normal manner with the important exceptions that the regulated nature of the industry may be relevant to the competitive effect of the merger,[18] and that the merging banks have a possible affirmative defense not available to firms in other industries—that the anticompetitive effects are "clearly outweighed" in the public interest by the probable effect of the merger in meeting the banking needs and convenience of the public.[19]

In *Third National Bank in Nashville*[20] the Court indicated that it could not review a defense based on noncompetitive advantages without highly specific findings on how aspects of the merger trans-

15. See Note, Federal Regulation of Bank Mergers, 75 Harv.L.Rev. 756 (1962).

16. United States v. Philadelphia Nat'l Bank, supra note 5.

17. 80 Stat. 7, 12 U.S.C.A. § 1828 (1966).

18. United States v. Marine Bancorporation, Inc., supra note 7; United States v. Citizens & S. Nat'l Bank, supra note 8.

19. Bank Merger Act of 1966, supra note 17. The full significance of this affirmative defense has yet to be judicially explored. Banks have won several merger cases in recent years, but always on the ground that a violation of Section 7 or Section 1 has not been established, not on the ground that an otherwise violative merger has been saved because noncompetitive advantages outweigh competitive injuries.

20. United States v. Third Nat'l Bank in Nashville, 390 U.S. 171, 88 S.Ct. 882, 19 L.Ed.2d 1015 (1968).

lated into public benefits and how these benefits compared with specific aspects of the damage to competition caused by the merger. It also indicated that it would have to be shown that the advantages claimed could not be obtained in less restrictive ways. Thus interpreted, the Bank Merger Act demands no less than that the court engage in a sweeping social calculus, an effort to weigh one kind of social harm against quite incomparable advantages—in fine, that the court (ultimately, the Supreme Court) make the crucial value choices. This approach is reminiscent of an aspect of the rule of reason which is gently implicit in some expositions of it,[21] but from which the Court has regularly drawn away.[22] It is not surprising, then, to find indications that the Court will not rush to embrace the opportunity to say whether banking convenience in some particular setting outweighs demonstrated competitive injury.

§ 203. Market Definition in Merger Cases

a. In General

Most of what was said in chapter 2 about the purposes, process and significance of market definition in monopoly cases is pertinent to merger cases as well.[1] In monopoly cases we must know whether a firm's power is overwhelming; to determine this, we must define the market within which its power is to be evaluated. Merger involves structural change and the statutory concern is whether that change adversely affects competition. To evaluate that question one must develop a sense about the competitive dynamic existing before the merger and the ways in which the merger may impinge upon this dynamic. A decently comprehensive view of the structure of the market will be needed. That view begins with the concept of a market as the bounds within which competitive interaction is to be considered.

Although the parallel between market definition in monopoly cases and market definition in merger cases is very close, one must not suppose that no differences may be tolerated. Monopoly, as a status, is conceptually explicit in the law. Though ideally courts in monopoly cases would consider alternative definitions, each of which may expose information bearing on the question of power, courts for reasons of practicality tend to insist on a single correct or best definition and to exclude from consideration any smaller submarket or larger construct involving interindustry competition. Since the question in merger cases is less ultimate—merely whether structural change is likely to affect competition adversely—any of several alter-

---

21. E.g., Chicago Bd. of Trade v. United States, 246 U.S. 231, 38 S.Ct. 242, 62 L.Ed. 683 (1918).

22. United States v. Topco Associates, Inc., 405 U.S. 596, 92 S.Ct. 1126, 31 L. Ed.2d 515 (1972).

1. See Chapter 2, §§ 12–21 supra.

native definitions may be suggestive and the most useful one may be different from that which would govern in an analogous Section 2 case. For example, if the question were whether an aluminum producer were a monopolist, we might define the market to include all aluminum producers and to exclude other firms. But if an aluminum company merged with a steel producer, a market which included steel, aluminum, copper and other metals which compete in various uses and over various time periods might be relevant.

b. Product Market

The Court's treatment of product market issues in merger litigation has been excessively flexible. The decisions do not yet show the earnest yet balanced seriousness that would be appropriate. Nevertheless, the most recent cases invite a hope that the law is now approaching that mature state.

Take as a baseline the 1948 decision in *Columbia Steel,*[2] a Sherman Act case litigated shortly before Section 7 of Clayton was amended, a decision now discredited on its ultimate judgment about competitive effects, but still cited on occasion for its analysis of market scope. The acquired and acquiring firms manufactured structural steel fabrications; though they both had wide product lines there was less than complete overlap and their areas of concentration differed considerably. Without much discussion of the possible competitive significance of these differences, the Court utilized aggregate production figures in analyzing the degree of concentration, thus indicating it assigned both firms to the same product market. Such a response seems not quite articulate enough. One might have hoped for more explanation, for an indication that the impulse behind the particular resolution was an analytical pragmatism which recognized that an assessment of the relationships suggested by a market, including the full line of products made by these two firms, was sufficiently fruitful and attempts to draw finer lines not worth the effort. That attitude governed also in *du Pont (G.M.),*[3] a case decided under the pre-amended Section 7 after the 1950 amendment.

Similar remarks could be made about market definition in *Brown Shoe,* the Court's first decision following the 1950 amendment to Section 7 of the Clayton Act.[4] Chief Justice Warren's opinion alluded in passing to the *du Pont (Cellophane)*[5] concept of inter-

---

2. United States v. Columbia Steel Co., 334 U.S. 495, 68 S.Ct. 1107, 92 L.Ed. 1533 (1948).

3. United States v. E. I. du Pont de Nemours & Co., 353 U.S. 586, 77 S.Ct. 872, 1 L.Ed.2d 1057 (1957) (relevant market held to be fabrics and finishes supplied to automobile industry rather than to all industrial users).

4. Brown Shoe Co. v. United States, 370 U.S. 294, 82 S.Ct. 1502, 8 L.Ed.2d 510 (1962).

5. United States v. E. I. du Pont de Nemours & Co., 351 U.S. 377, 76 S.Ct. 994, 100 L.Ed. 1264 (1956).

changeability and cross-elasticity as determinates of the outer boundaries of a market, but stressed the importance of the "well-defined submarkets" which may exist in any market and appraised the merger in light of its consequences on men's, women's, and children's shoes taken as submarkets.[6] The problem represented an apparent disjuncture between elasticity of supply and demand. A consumer seeking a man's shoe will not regard a woman's or child's shoe as a reasonable substitute; nor, given the accustomed degree of specialization in marketing, is the shoe retailer likely upon modest price shifts to switch back and forth from buying men's to women's or children's shoes. On the other hand, makers of shoes might well be able to shift between men's, women's, and children's sizes and styles in a fairly short period and at modest adjustment expense. Since the substantive issue in merger litigation is merely whether there is some adverse effect on competition, and since, because of demand characteristics, suppliers of one type of shoe would have some advantages over suppliers of other types, the Court chose to define the market narrowly. Yet, tension remains between *du Pont (G.M.), Brown Shoe* and other merger cases, on the one hand, and *du Pont (Cellophane)* and other Sherman Act, Section 2 [7] cases on the other. Indeed, it is even difficult to square these merger cases with the rigorous market definition done by Justice Clark in *Tampa Electric*[8] which involved a vertical integration by requirement contract challenged under Section 3 of Clayton.[9] Quite different examples of how to define the market are thus available. Perhaps a court need not worry unduly about which it takes as a model so long as its responses to data about the market as defined takes account of whether the definition is wide or narrow. For example, in a horizontal merger case a given increase in concentration would signify more or less of a threat to competition depending on whether the definition was wide or narrow.

The Merger Guidelines of the Department of Justice [10] state a general position consistent with *Brown Shoe* and like cases. They treat as a separate market any product or service distinguishable from others as a matter of normal commercial attitudes, even though other products or services would be adequate substitutes for most

6. 370 U.S. at 325–26, 82 S.Ct. at 1523–24, 8 L.Ed.2d at 535–36. The concept of economically significant submarkets is sometimes applied very rigorously. Thus, in determining the extent to which vertical integration in the telephone industry injured competition, a court overruled a finding of a submarket of non-Bell System equipment buyers even though Bell companies are integrated vertically and the Bell manufacturing unit is the only significant supplier of Bell operating companies. I. T. & T. Corp. v. G. T. E. Corp., 518 F.2d 913, 930–932 (9th Cir. 1975).

7. See §§ 12–21 supra.

8. Tampa Electric Co. v. Nashville Coal Co., 365 U.S. 320, 81 S.Ct. 623, 5 L.Ed.2d 580 (1961).

9. See §§ 164–169 supra.

10. Department of Justice Merger Guidelines § 3 (1968).

uses. Reasonable substitutability and high cross-elasticity, then, would not impeach the definition of a particular product market like, for example, cellophane. The justification for this view is pragmatic. If those within the product market have some significant advantage over those outside of it in meeting the demand for the product, they would, except to the extent those within the narrow market limit each other, have a power over price of some significance which suppliers outside of the narrow market could not thwart. Even if the power is not of monopoly proportions, a merger tending to reduce competition within the narrow market could do enough harm to competition to warrant intervention.

Alcoa (Rome),[11] however, gave a clear sign that analytical standards were collapsing. There the Court acted on the exasperatingly irrational proposition that any combination of submarkets could also constitute a relevant product market. By clear implication, if ice cream were a market and chocolate, vanilla and strawberry were separate submarkets, the effect of a merger of ice cream producers could be evaluated in light of the effect on concentration either in the ice cream market, in any one of the submarkets, or in any combination of submarkets such as chocolate and strawberry. The potential for gerrymandering became obvious. If in a given geographic market firm A made 1% of ice cream, but a large percentage of pistachio nut flavor, while firm B made 1% of ice cream, but was the only maker of grapefruit sherbet, the concentration percentages might be made to seem substantial by evaluating the effect on a supposed "pistachio nut-grapefruit" submarket. Also, given the tendency then prevailing to evaluate competitive effects almost entirely on the basis of the merger's impact on concentration ratios, use of specious markets had enormous potential significance.

In *Continental Can*[12] the Court in an equally irrational manner assumed that if two firms make different products which can substitute for each other, then a merger between the firms can be evaluated by aggregating into a market sales of those two products, while excluding other possible substitutes. There, the two primary markets were glass bottles and cans. One might well have treated as relevant an interindustry container market consisting of bottles, cans, plastic bottles and other containers amenable to cross-industry substitution. But the Court aggregated only glass bottles and cans. By the same principle, the acquisition of a coal company by a gas company could be evaluated in a "coal and gas" market which ignores any competition from oil. Such a construct—two or more but less than all of the sub-parts of some larger whole—could conceivably be justified in particular circumstances on the basis of a selective demand by some seg-

11. United States v. Aluminum Co. of America (Rome Cable), 377 U.S. 271, 84 S.Ct. 1283, 12 L.Ed.2d 314 (1964).

12. United States v. Continental Can Co., 378 U.S. 441, 84 S.Ct. 1738, 12 L. Ed.2d 953 (1964).

ment of buyers. For example, brewers might for some reason choose between bottles and cans but not plastic or waxed cardboard cartons. But if special demand characteristics warrant use of some but not all of a group of submarkets as the relevant market, the evidence and analysis should be explicit.[13]

The relationship of these market definition issues to the more general issue of judging competitive effects merits emphasis. In a horizontal merger case, a competitive effects test based largely on market shares which says, in effect, that any merger of direct competitors with significant market shares violates the law, has appeal as a legal rule, for it furthers Congressional objectives, economic and otherwise, while conserving judicial energy and providing predictability, all without being so overinclusive as to do significant harm. Yet, such an approach to merger would be a travesty if the concentration figures which triggered the nearly automatic judicial response had little meaning. Again, the Guidelines are of interest, for they appear to repudiate, if mildly, the Court's excesses. After having sanctioned narrow product markets, they continue:

> On the other hand, the sales of two distinct products to a particular group of purchasers can also appropriately be grouped into a single market where the two products are reasonably interchangeable for that group * * *. [H]owever, it may be necessary also to include * * *

---

13. Compare cases concerning whether a subgroup of buyers having a lower demand elasticity than do buyers generally may be segregated out to form a market in monopolization cases. In United States v. E. I. du Pont de Nemours & Co., supra note 5, the Court refused to establish a "flexible wrap for cigarettes" market, even though only cellophane, du Pont's product, would do for cigarette manufacturers. By contrast, where for "many customers, only central station protection will do," the Court in United States v. Grinnell Corp., 384 U.S. 563, 574, 86 S.Ct. 1698, 1706, 16 L.Ed. 778, 788 (1966) treated central station alarm services as a separate market, even though the evidence did not show that cross-elasticity between these services and other alarm services was low for buyers generally. See also, United States v. International Boxing Club, 348 U.S. 236, 75 S.Ct. 259, 99 L. Ed. 290 (1955). M. Handler, H. Blake, R. Pitofsky & H. Goldschmid, Trade Regulation, Cases and Materials (1975) suggest, in connection with Problem 5, page 287, that segregation is warranted when the seller has the capability of discriminating in price against the sub-segment of buyers (as it arguably did in *Grinnell*, because any firm buying the service cheaply could not resell to any paying more for it) but segregation is not warranted where, because of the possibility of favored buyers reselling to unfavored ones, the existence of a high cross-elasticity of demand for buyers generally serves to protect even those buyers which (like cigarette makers in *du Pont*) have themselves a low cross-elasticity of demand with substitute products. See § 17 supra. A submarket including some but not all of a group of substitute products should be used in a merger case only when an analysis like that used by Handler et al. to justify *Grinnell* and distinguish it from *du Pont* is factually convincing. Compare the opinion in I. T. & T. Corp. v. G. T. E. Corp., supra note 6 at 932–934, where the court rejects a submarket of purchasers of telephone equipment which excludes certain telephone operating companies and excludes other buyers.

one or more other products which are equally interchangeable * * *.[14]

One may wonder about the concept of interchangeability for a group and may wish the last phrase merely said "also interchangeable" rather than "equally interchangeable"; nonetheless it seems clear that the Department rejects any license to gerrymander.

In any event, the judicial frivolities represented by *Alcoa (Rome)* and *Continental Can* may now be behind us. The tone of the Court's merger decisions during the past three terms has been much more analytically rigorous in all aspects, and the cases display a balanced and reasonable approach to issues of market definition. In *General Dynamics*[15] the Court's holding vividly displays the functional character of the market definition process. There, the trial court rejected coal as a product market in favor of a broader energy market. It also passed over another possible distinction—that between deep pit miners and strip surface miners. Though they faced the same demand curve, their supply elasticities were surely different, given the differing natural resources and technologies on which the two types of mining depended. But in the end, product market definition was not crucial for the trial court. Because one of the parties to the merger had so few coal reserves, as the trial court saw the matter, the government had defaulted on its proof of competitive consequence whatever the appropriate definition of the market. The Supreme Court agreed, declaring that no decision had to be made about whether the proper market was the coal market, the energy market, or some submarket of either. Moreover, it stressed that in normal circumstances delineation of a "proper" market is essential, implying, perhaps, that a rational basis is necessary if any submarket or aggregate of submarkets is to be used. Similarly, in *Connecticut National Bank*,[16] where the district court had aggregated commercial and savings banks into a single market, the Court after a fairly rigorous analysis of pertinent considerations reversed and held commercial banking to be distinct and the proper market. It felt that the district court overestimated the extent of overlap between the two types of banks and ignored competition from other credit facilities which would also have been pertinent if the larger interindustry market were used.

Together, these recent cases serve notice that product market definition is neither a technical exercise nor a process of manipulating

---

14. Supra note 10 at § 3(i).

15. United States v. General Dynamics Corp., 415 U.S. 486, 94 S.Ct. 1186, 39 L.Ed.2d 530 (1974). Some recent lower court cases also show a balanced, analytical, yet functionally oriented view of the market definition process in merger cases. See, in particular, United States v. Hughes Tool Co., 1976–2 CCH Trade Cas. ¶ 61,046 (C.D.Cal. 1976); Beatrice Food Co. v. F. T. C., 1976–2 CCH Trade Cas. ¶ 61,036 (7th Cir. 1976).

16. United States v. Connecticut Nat'l Bank, 418 U.S. 656, 94 S.Ct. 2788, 41 L.Ed.2d 1016 (1974).

variables to justify a preconceived result. If it ever was, the rule no longer is that the government always wins. Market definition is a serious, functional activity. The appropriate definition is one which is both manageable for a court and useful as a frame within which to explore the competitive consequences of a particular merger.

c. Geographic Markets

During the late 1960's, when the Court seemed whimsical about product market definition in merger cases, it was also absenting itself and removing the lower courts from significant involvement with geographic market definition. United States v. Pabst Brewing Co.[17] epitomizes this development. The government showed that by virtue of the acquisition of another brewer Pabst became the nation's fifth largest brewer with close to 5% of the national market, and Wisconsin's largest brewer with about 24% of sales in that state. The opinion by Justice Black chided the district court for punctiliousness, declaring that the statute "requires merely that the Government prove the merger has substantial anticompetitive effect somewhere in the United States * * *," and that "Congress did not seem to be troubled about the exact spot where competition might be lessened; it simply intended to outlaw mergers which threatened competition in any or all parts of the country." Geographic market definition was therefore an issue "entirely subsidiary to the crucial question * * * whether a merger may substantially lessen competition anywhere * * *."[18] While that statement is capable of being read more narrowly, it seemed disdainful of concern about market definition. For this reason Justices Douglas and Fortas, though concurring in the *Pabst* result and in part in Justice Black's view of the case, separated themselves from the position quoted above.

In the Merger Guidelines the Department of Justice was not as self-effacing about geographic markets as it was about product markets. The Guidelines read *Pabst* for all it was worth. They say, in substance, that any "commercially significant" section where the product is sold will do, so long as it does not "clearly appear that there is no economic barrier (e. g., significant transportation costs, lack of distribution facilities, customer inconvenience, or established customer preference for existing products) that hinders sales from outside * * *."[19] This is a remarkable inversion of the usual concepts of burden of proof, but it is no more extreme a view than can be found in the language of *Pabst*.

If *Pabst* left matters in a dubious state, *Marine Bancorporation*[20] has clarified them considerably and indicates that the Court is again

---

17. 384 U.S. 546, 86 S.Ct. 1665, 16 L.Ed. 2d 765 (1966).

18. Id. at 549–50, 86 S.Ct. at 1667–68, 16 L.Ed.2d at 769.

19. Supra note 10 at § 3(ii).

20. United States v. Marine Bancorporation, Inc., 418 U.S. 602, 94 S.Ct. 2856, 41 L.Ed.2d 978 (1974).

ready to try to deal with the issue of competitive effect in a reasonably analytical way. In the latter case the Court states flatly that the phrase "section of the country" in Section 7 means relevant geographic market and that the relevant geographic market is one in which the "goods or services at issue are marketed to a significant degree by the acquired firm."[21] Though the last words have a universal ring, the context displays that what the Court demands is a plausible, balanced definition of an area within which discernible buyers and sellers meet. This is shown pointedly by what the Court says about *Pabst*. It rejects the implication of that case that no geographic market need be proven, declaring that *Pabst* "held that the Government had established three relevant markets," and that the "acquiring firm was an actual competitor of the acquired firm in all three * * *."[22] If that is what *Pabst* held on market definition, then its ultimate holding of illegality means no more than that a merger violates Section 7 when it results in competitive harm in more than one market, hardly a proposition to be questioned. Of course, such a reading of *Pabst* puts the language of the case under considerable strain, but perhaps that flaw in *Marine Bancorporation* ought to be forgiven when the purpose is to reestablish tighter standards for analysis in merger cases.

At this juncture we cannot take the confident view that the market definition process is now to be administered with an alertness to analytical nuance, yet an avoidance of excess rigor. To assert that we have reached this point would claim too much on the basis of three recent seasons of judicial output. It would appear, however, that if the new antitrust majority runs risks of error in this realm, it is a new error, one of its own devising. The danger is really one of overreaction to past monstrosities. Merger litigation needs a judicial vantage point from which to view with balanced eye the structural developments in the market and their significance. To paraphrase Ben Jonson, courts ought neither to read the record with a microscope and employ their whole attention upon minute elegance, nor with a telescope, by which they may seem to see with great clearness much that is too remote to be discovered by the rest of mankind. The goal is a definition of the market that brings into focus issues of real concern without amplifying them unduly or obscuring factors which would reduce their significance. Appellate courts should show a degree of deference to any balanced definition adopted by a trial court or the FTC, and should encourage district judges to get on with the matter without straining for an excessive elegance.

21. Id. at 620–21, 94 S.Ct. at 2869, 41 L.Ed.2d at 995.

22. Id. at 521 n. 20, 94 S.Ct. at 2869–70 n. 20, 41 L.Ed.2d at 995 n. 20.

§ 204. Mergers Between Direct Competitors

a. Analyzing Social Consequences

Before discussing more complex problems concerning competitive effects of a merger, let us consider the question least subject to doubt. Assume that we have resolved all issues of market definition and that firms A and B seek to merge. They compete directly in the manufacture of product X. Is the proposed merger socially useful, neutral, or harmful? To answer that question, what else do we need to know?

How simple can we make the matter of competitive effects? Suppose product X is wheat and firms A and B are farmers, representing, respectively .001 and .002 percent of the relevant market. On that supposition, the merger has, as a practical matter, no effect; any consequence traceable to it is beneath notice. At the other extreme, if X is an important ore and A and B its only producers, their merger yields monopoly; it is obviously not to be tolerated. The difficult lines must be drawn when mergers occur in the range between these extremes.[1]

Theory tells us that, in general, oligopolistic markets may perform worse than competitive ones. And if we take a close relationship between cost and prices as a hallmark of good performance, empirical evidence, though it does not demonstrate conclusively an extremely high correlation between concentration increases and decreases in performance quality, does suggest that once certain concentration levels are reached, further increases in concentration correlate with poorer performance.[2] But utility of this knowledge diminishes rapidly when we realize that concentration ratios alone are inadequate statements about the structure of a market. If we take a market with, say, an eight firm concentration ratio of fifty percent as being somewhere near the borderline where the term "oligopoly" is warranted, we must realize that such a market may perform well or poorly depending upon other characteristics; indeed, a market much more highly concentrated may perform well enough and one with lower concentration levels may perform rather badly.

We may infer that correlations between concentration ratios and performance, albeit weak, are explicable on the ground that a tight structure increases the likelihood of collusion or interdependence, or both. We can, perhaps, make finer judgments about the likely effect of any merger by taking into account other variables which theory teaches will affect the likelihood of collusion or interdependence:

---

1. See the analyses suggested by P. Areeda, Antitrust Analysis, Problems, Text, Cases ¶ 638 (2d ed. 1974) and by M. Handler, H. Blake, R. Pitofsky, & H. Goldschmid, Trade Regulation, Cases and Materials (Prob.) 986–87 (1975).

2. See Weiss, "The Concentration-Profits Relationship and Antitrust," in Industrial Concentration: the New Learning 184 (Goldschmid, Mann & Weston, eds. 1974). Compare H. Demsetz, "Two Systems of Belief about Monopoly," id. at 164.

product homogeneity, demand elasticity, cross-elasticities of demand and supply, long-run growth trends, the quality of the industry's information media, consistency of managerial conceptions about the industry, the height of entry barriers, and the like. As these kinds of factors vary, any given increase in concentration levels will take on greater or lesser significance. We might go further and add a more personal element to the judgment, if we learn what we can about the past conduct and attitudes of actors in the industry and, through these, draw conclusions about the current intent of the merging firms and others in the market. As Phillips has stressed, the systems manipulated by industrial organization analysis are not mechanical, but human.[3] Perhaps we can expect things to go along more or less as they have in the past, despite a structural change, except to the extent that the change is motivated by a sense of insecurity or creates such a sense in those controlling other firms. The question for merger law is whether these richer analyses are appropriate, at least to some deeper level than merely identifying a merger as one which increases concentration, or whether the law should forbid, more or less *per se,* any merger which does noticeably increase concentration.

Are there losses in an overly restrictive merger policy, and if so, what are they? Undue strictness may deprive us of socially valuable scale economies, or, more likely, may cause social waste in the achievement of these economies through internal growth. Picture an industry of 100 firms of roughly equal size. Suppose upon the advent of a new technology that significant cost reduction could be accomplished by a firm big enough to supply about 2% of total market demand. If permitted, the firms might pair off; after a series of mergers there would be fifty firms of about equal size, each large enough to gain the efficiencies and together numerous enough, in all likelihood, to perform competitively. If merger were not available, efficient size could be achieved by the growth of some existing firms through internal expansion, but this could only be accomplished after a competitive conflict which would shake half of the existing firms out of the market at considerable social cost.

An unduly restrictive merger policy might impose another social cost, though its general significance is surely open to argument—the cost associated with any reduction in alienability of assets. Firms are, after all, aggregations of assets. An aspect of the American dream has been to go into business, spend prime years "making it," and then to pass the business on to the next generation or to "sell out." Being able to "sell out" is an increasingly important part of the dream. Offspring today are less likely to carry on the family business than they were a generation or two ago; they are now in

3. Phillips, "Competitive Policy for Depository Financial Institutions," in Promoting Competition in Regulated Markets 329, 345 (A. Phillips, ed. 1975).

law, medicine or academia or, if not, are off making pottery or candles. The dream tarnishes, perhaps, if the successfully family business cannot be so readily or successfully sold because merger law inhibits some of the most likely purchasers. Moreover, from the point of view of the acquiring firm the merger may be a good investment, a wise use of capital. A merger may also be an easy way to diversify and enter a new market, to acquire a needed asset, such as a patent or certain kinds of know-how, or the like. In all of these respects a claim can be made for the value of alienability of going concerns.

Besides efficiency and free alienability of assets, there are other non-malevolent motives for merger. Consider such competitively neutral factors as the tax code or the preferences of investors. Acquisition of a "tax loss-carryover" through merger typifies this. The "funny money" merger is a more bizarre example. By trading its own debentures (bearing tax deductible interest) for the stock of the acquired company, the acquiring company may grant to former stockholders of the acquired company an interest flow higher than the dividend flow they give up, but at a cost to itself considerably lower than the dividend flow it gains; through the interest deduction it makes the government participate in the "cost" of the payout. A somewhat different example is the "elastic equity" merger. The stock of the acquiring firm may sell at a higher earnings to price ratio than that of the acquired firm, and if the ratio holds after the acquisition, as it often does, the acquired assets gain in market value upon coming into the new owners' hands. Additionally, a merger may help the acquiring firm gain greater liquidity, or credit, or a commercial status or respectability of a kind valued by those who control it. In sum, the reasons for merger are as varied as the commercial imagination. Today one can no more deny that there are potential social costs in an excessively strict merger policy than one can deny that Congress, in enacting and amending Section 7, was little impressed with claims about the social utility of mergers.

To raise the issue is not to resolve it. It might, of course, be ignored. Or it might be met in any one of various alternative ways. At the other extreme from ignoring the possible costs of forbidding a merger among competitors would be to insist on an analysis which deeply probed the social consequences and then struck a balance. The costs of doing this would be exceedingly high; and many harmful mergers would slip through such a net. Still, there are middle grounds. For example, a merger noticeably increasing concentration might be held unlawful unless the proponents could demonstrate both that significant economies would result from the merger and that after the merger, and any others likely to be proposed in pursuit of the same economies, the structure would still be sufficiently competitive. Let us look now at what the case law indicates about the judicial perception of these matters.

b. *The Prima Facie Case of Violation of Section 7*

Having demonstrated in *Brown Shoe* its ability to perceive the dynamic complexities of a proposed merger, the Court in *Philadephia Bank*[4] with seeming relief announced that its routine approach to a merger of competitors would be simplified through adoption of a rule of a *prima facie* illegality based only on the simplest structural variables. Later cases, particularly *Alcoa (Rome)*,[5] *Continental Can*[6] and *Von's*,[7] led commentators to conclude that the Court's passion for simplification had reached such a level that the *prima facie* case was practically irrebuttable. However, *General Dynamics*[8] and other recent cases[9] demonstrate that this is not true now. The rule of *Philadelphia Bank* has been reinstated as a rule of *prima facie* liability. If a *prima facie* case has been made out, the merger proponents may still rebut it. In this subsection we explore the question: what must be shown to make a *prima facie* case? Using such guidance as post-*General Dynamics* hindsight affords, we first examine the decided cases to see what they reveal about the nature of the *prima facie* case. We then seek to integrate them by relating them to concepts of policy and oligopoly theory. In later subsections we shall consider the kind of inquiry relevant to an attempt to overcome a *prima facie* case of violation.

Philadelphia Bank,[10] *Von's*,[11] *Pabst*[12] and *General Dynamics*[13] all have significance. In *Philadelphia Bank* the merging firms were the second and third largest commercial banks in a market of forty-two competitors. After the merger they would have held about 30 percent of the market, about as much as the largest bank, and thus would have increased the two firm concentration ratio from 45 percent to 60 percent. There had also been a trend in the market toward increasing concentration, much of it (including prior growth of the merging firms) accomplished through merger. The Court concluded that this merger of competitors would produce a firm controlling an "undue" share of the market and would increase concentration "significantly." Because of those two factors it held

---

4. United States v. Philadelphia Nat'l Bank, 374 U.S. 321, 83 S.Ct. 1715, 10 L.Ed.2d 915 (1963).

5. United States v. Aluminum Co. of America (Rome Cable), 377 U.S. 271, 84 S.Ct. 1283, 12 L.Ed.2d 314 (1964).

6. United States v. Continental Can Co., 378 U.S. 441, 84 S.Ct. 1738, 12 L. Ed. 953 (1964).

7. United States v. Von's Grocery Co., 384 U.S. 270, 86 S.Ct. 1478, 16 L.Ed.2d 555 (1966).

8. United States v. General Dynamics Corp., 415 U.S. 486, 94 S.Ct. 1186, 39 L.Ed.2d 530 (1974).

9. E.g., United States v. Marine Bancorporation Inc., 418 U.S. 602, 94 S.Ct. 2856, 41 L.Ed.2d 978 (1974); United States v. Citizens & S. Nat'l Bank, 422 U.S. 86, 95 S.Ct. 2099, 45 L.Ed.2d 41 (1975).

10. Supra note 4.

11. Supra note 7.

12. United States v. Pabst Brewing Co., 384 U.S. 546, 86 S.Ct. 1665, 16 L.Ed.2d 765 (1966).

13. Supra note 8.

that the merger was unlawful "in the absence of evidence clearly showing that the merger is not likely to have * * * anticompetitive effects."[14] The Court thus announced two criteria for a *prima facie* case, a "significant" increase in concentration and a resulting firm with an "undue" market share.[15] The rule draws what might be termed common sense lines, but these can often be obscure. Picture an industry where the three largest firms have 15% each and the fourth and fifth largest have ten and five percent. Suppose that the last two firms merge. Although we know from *Philadelphia Bank* that increasing the two firm ratio from 45 to 60 percent is a significant increase in concentration, would it also be significant to increase the four firm ratio from 55 to 60 percent, although the merger caused no increase in the two firm ratio? We know from *Philadelphia Bank* that a resulting firm with 30 percent of the market is unduly large; what about this one with 15 percent? At least for the purpose of determining whether a *prima facie* case is made out, do we answer these qualitative questions with no data except the market share statistics, or might the significance of the structural changes be made to depend upon other factors? For example, is the past trend toward concentration of which the Court took notice in *Philadelphia Bank* crucial? And assuming that the *prima facie* case is made out by the quantitative data only (or by that and whatever else may be needed to enhance it) what kinds of evidence might the defendant firms bring forth to "clearly show" that there is not sufficient threat to competition to warrant forbidding the merger? Let us look first at when the *prima facie* case is established and then at possible justification evidence.

Not long ago a commentator stated that "[e]xperts generally agree that any consolidation of two healthy competitors with any substantial share of a significant market will be said by the Supreme Court to violate Section 7," and went on to suggest that actual market shares might be much smaller than those in *Philadelphia Bank* and still warrant a finding of illegality.[16] *Brown Shoe* might be cited in support of that view, for the horizontal aspects of that merger seemed modest enough and yet were held a ground for illegality.[17] But literally that case called for perusal of significance against a wide and detailed canvass.[18] The best evidence for this "expert's view," then, may be in such cases as in *Alcoa (Rome),*[19] *Von's Grocery,*[20] and *Pabst.*[21]

14. Supra note 4, at 363, 93 S.Ct. at 1741, 10 L.Ed.2d at 945.

15. Id.

16. E. Rockefeller, Antitrust Questions and Answers 185 (1974).

17. Brown Shoe Co. v. United States, 370 U.S. 294, 82 S.Ct. 1502, 8 L.Ed.2d 510 (1962).

18. Id. The combined share horizontally in *Brown Shoe* was about 5% of retail shoe sales nationally. However, there was also trend evidence the Court thought relevant, and a significant vertical element. Also, though the Court used national statistics it was obviously aware that operative retail markets were local and it was

19. See notes 19, 20, 21 on page 618.

On the basis of a gerrymandered market, *Alcoa (Rome)* entailed a merger between a firm having about 12 percent with a firm having about 5 percent. The implication of the holding, which can be viewed as an application of the *Philadelphia Bank* rule, is that a merger producing a 17 percent market share is *prima facie* unlawful; the holding also implies that an increase in the five firm concentration ratio from about 65 percent to 70 percent is a significant increase within the meaning of *Philadelphia Bank*. Those figures are not overwhelming, but neither do they warrant the claim that in reacting to them the Court has chosen to regard as *per se* unlawful any horizontal merger which is not trivial. A five firm concentration ratio of 70 percent demonstrates, after all, a concentrated industry. Moreover, before the merger the larger of the two firms was of a size which, if approximately replicated by the others in the industry, would allow for an industry of eight or nine firms; after the merger the resulting firm was of a size which, if replicated, would yield an industry of five or six firms. That kind of an increase in concentration cannot be ignored.

But we must be careful. The more we read into specific figures like these the further we may stray from the truth. To be sure, *Alcoa (Rome)* indicates an hostility toward mergers even in circumstances where it would be hard to develop a precise theory that made the concentration figures at issue bristle with significance. But though the Court was talking about horizontal effects in cable markets, Alcoa was more than a fabricator of cable—it was a fully integrated producer, long dominant as a source of ingot. In part, the skepticism that permeated the case may be taken as an expression of attitude about the level of analytical response which is warranted when a massive integrated producer starts expanding horizontally at a level where it happens not to be dominant.

But *Von's* also displays a readiness to react negatively—at least *prima facie*—to horizontal merger where market shares, though noticeable, were hardly high, and it is difficult to explain away this implication.[22] The largest firm in the Los Angeles retail grocery market had 8 percent of sales and the two merging firms, with 4.7 percent and 4.2 percent respectively, were third and sixth. Before the merger the four firm concentration ratio was 24.4 percent and after the merger it would be 28.6 percent. There was also a notice-

reaching to the aggregative effect of a merger which combined retail capacity in more than 100 cities in some of which the combined shares were well above 30%.

19. Supra note 5.

20. Supra note 7.

21. Supra note 12.

22. United States v. Pabst Brewing Co., supra note 12 is another case where the combined national share of the merging firms was modest, less than 6%. But the Court reacted also to much larger shares of smaller regional and statewide "sections of the country."

able increase during the prior decade in levels of concentration as measured by four, eight and twelve firm ratios. But there were, in total, nearly 4,000 firms still in the market, and there was no indication of collusive or interdependent pricing, or that either was threatened. Moreover, entry was relatively easy and the relative shares of leading firms tended to change significantly over fairly short periods, all of which tended to indicate a lively, competitive market. In holding that merger unlawful, the Court stressed that in a decade the total number of independent units in the market had decreased from more than 5,000 to less than 4,000 and that both of the firms merging had been growing rapidly. Though the Court's reliance on the past concentration trend precludes the conclusion that the case is an explicit application of *Philadelphia Bank's* presumptive criteria in a marginal situation, the very minimal basis for finding competitive injury showed the Court's negative response to horizontal mergers even absent discernibly significant indications of harm.[23]

General Dynamics,[24] while having greater importance as an indicator of the potential for rebutting a *prima facie* case, also indicates the relatively modest levels of concentration which will meet the *Philadelphia Bank* test. The government sought to prove a Section 7 violation by showing that in a relevant market coal production was concentrated among a small number of producers and that the acquisition of United Electric by General Dynamics would materially increase the share of the latter firm. After the merger, the two firm concentration ratio in the most comprehensive market considered was 48.6 percent, the four firm ratio was 62.9 percent and the 10 firm ratio was 91.4 percent. The merger increased the two firm ratio from 45 to 48.6 percent and resulted in a firm with 10.9 percent of the market. There was also evidence that concentration had been increasing in recent years. The Court explicitly declared that these data established a *prima facie* case.[25]

A summary is in order to permit us to relate the *prima facie* approach to social policy. The function of the *Philadelphia Bank* test is to simplify, but a court should not simplify at the expense of ignoring its basic purpose. If it has identified a market sufficiently concentrated to pose a significant risk of oligopolistic interdependence or collusion, it should treat any merger between firms in that market as a threat to competition and *prima facie* unlawful, unless effects will

---

23. See Areeda, "Structure-Performance Assumptions in Recent Merger Cases" in Public Policy Toward Mergers (J. Weston & S. Peltzman, eds. 1969).

24. Supra note 8.

25. Id. at 494–97, 94 S.Ct. at 1192–93, 39 L.Ed.2d at 540–41. The court saw the Government's *prima facie* case as roughly comparable to that in *Von's* (4 firm ratio of 24.4%, 8 firm ratio of 40.9%, 12 firm ratio of 48.8%). It indicated that a *prima facie* case was made out on a showing of even small increases of concentration where concentration is already great or has recently increased.

be clearly *de minimis*. Also, if we have identified a market which does not yet seem to threaten interdependence or a special risk of collusion, and face a merger which would increase concentration to a degree presenting such threats, that merger ought to be treated as *prima facie* unlawful. The difficulty is that the concentration ratio and consolidated firm shares are not of themselves sufficient data from which to determine whether danger is presented. Other factors will influence our judgment about the significance of any particular level of concentration.

Given that we are stating only a *prima facie* rule, we can resolve our dilemma by reacting at a low threshold. This, as *Philadelphia Bank* itself suggests, is consistent with the kinds or degrees of concern about concentration which were displayed by Congress. It also will assure that the *prima facie* rule will pick up the great majority of mergers which, if analyzed fully, would appear to threaten competition. It will, of course, pick up additional mergers which, after full analysis, would seem not to threaten injury, but in those instances the merger proponents presumably can demonstrate the factors which diminish the significance of the concentration data.

Adoption of that principle, nevertheless requires a crude line. Industry concentration classifications made by economists are useful as guides. Kaysen and Turner classified as "Type I" oligopolies industries with eight firm ratios of 50% or more and twenty firm ratios of 75% or more and as "Type II" oligopolies those with eight firm ratios of 33% or more and twenty firm ratios of less than 75%.[26] The Merger Guidelines differentiate between highly concentrated markets (four firm ratios of 75% or more) where the government will challenge mergers aggregating to a share of as little as 10% and less highly concentrated ones where the four firm ratio is lower.[27] The Guidelines also indicate that the limits will be reduced if there has been a trend toward concentration.[28] Putting aside the trend issue temporarily, it seems that a reasonable (but low) threshold of concentration at which to trigger the *prima facie* rule of *Philadelphia Bank* would be at about the level of concentration which Kaysen and Turner describe as a "Type I oligopoly." Control of the bulk of industry output by no more than twenty firms represents the most critical part of the standard. If, on any reasonable measure (e.g., production, sales, ore reserves, etc.) it appears that twenty firms or less

26. C. Kaysen & D. Turner, Antitrust Policy 27–37 (1959). See § 116 supra.

27. Department of Justice Merger Guidelines §§ 5 and 6 (1968). The merger guidelines, representing a statement of the enforcement agency's position, have no binding effect on the courts. United States v. Atlantic Richfield, 297 F.Supp. 1061 (S.D.N.Y.1969). However, a court may find them useful or persuasive summary statements of the law, especially where the developing case law is clearly consonant with them. Allis-Chalmers Mfg. Co. v. White Consol. Indus., Inc., 414 F.2d 506 (3rd Cir. 1969) cert. denied 396 U. S. 1009, 90 S.Ct. 567, 24 L.Ed.2d 501 (1970).

28. Id. at § 7.

control 75% or more of the market, the risk of collusion or interdependence commences to be significant and any increase in concentration should be a matter of concern.

It is appropriate, nonetheless, to check also for any skewing of the distribution within those 20 firms. Either collusion or interdependence will require the kinds of initiative or leadership most likely to come from a firm or group of firms with a particularly prominent stake and less likely to develop among twenty firms of substantially equal size. If on any measure eight (or less) of the twenty (or less) control a third of the output, the risks of any non-*de minimis* merger clearly seem high enough to warrant saying, as does the *prima facie* rule, nothing different appearing, that the government has carried its burden of showing probable injury to competition. Given the general congressional concern about concentration and the considerable congressional skepticism about whether we risk significant social loss by strictly inhibiting mergers, a merger in such an industry can fairly be screened out under the *prima facie* rule. The case law is not so explicit as this in identifying the threshold, but the cases are consistent with this proposed approach. *Brown Shoe, Pabst* and *Von's,* for example, all held unlawful mergers that would have led to firms with five to seven percent of the relevant markets where the level of concentration, as measured by appropriate ratios, was at or even somewhat below (in the case of *Von's,* considerably below) that suggested here as a working borderline. *General Dynamics* is also consistent or, as was *Von's,* somewhat more rigorous in screening out possible dangers to competition.

c. *The Significance of a Trend Toward Concentration*

In *Brown Shoe,*[29] *Von's*[30] and *Continental Can,*[31] the Court emphasized the significance of trends toward greater concentration in the industries at issue. Explicating this, the Merger Guidelines declare that a trend is established if in any period of from five to ten years the leading firms (from two to eight in number) have increased their share by seven percent or more.[32] Generalizing from the cases the Guidelines suggest that, given such a trend, any merger in a partially concentrated industry will be subject to challenge if it increases the share of any significant firm by as little as 2%.[33]

Any particular increase in concentration due to a merger gains significance where a clear trend toward increased concentration is discernible. If the case is marginal in terms of invocation of the *prima facie* rule, a trend should be sufficient to bring the merger within that rule. *Von's* and *Brown Shoe* both suggest this, as does *General*

29. Supra note 17.
30. Supra note 7.
31. Supra note 6.
32. Supra note 27 at § 7.
33. Id.

Dynamics. Similarly, if defendants offer evidence to rebut the *prima facie* case, the showing of a merger trend will weigh against that evidence and increase the burden of rebuttal.

All this is rational enough if we recall the nature of the dynamic at issue and if we construe the evidence of a trend in ways germane to the social concern. The evil is a market so concentrated as to facilitate collusion or interdependence. Market structure can be—indeed normally will be—transformed over time, not in one transaction. If a particular transaction can be seen as part of a larger dynamic leading toward a non-competitive structure, it ought to be inhibited. But here, too, excessive reactions must be avoided. Suppose, for example, that the industry consists of one hundred and fifty firms more or less of equal size, that new technology increases efficient scale, and that, discernibly, firms are doubling their size to a new efficient scale which, when the trend has run its course, will leave the industry with about seventy-five firms of more or less comparable size. Since the industry as converted would not be concentrated, the trend is not one to cause distress, and a merger in such an industry ought to be analyzed accordingly.[34]

d. Overcoming the Prima Facie Case

Elaborate proof of probable anticompetitive effects may be dispensed with where concentration and merging firm shares exceed *prima facie* levels. But *Brown Shoe's* statement that statistics about shares "controlled by the industry leaders and the parties" are only the "primary index" still holds; a further examination of the "structure, history and probable future" of the market may be needed to evaluate competitive effects.[35] Accordingly, once the *prima facie* case is established, the proponents of the merger may, as *Philadelphia Bank* itself states, go forward to "clearly show" that the merger is "not likely" to have anticompetitive effects.[36]

What kinds of evidence may overcome the *prima facie* showing? In *General Dynamics* the refutation included a general widening of

---

34. The question whether trend evidence must be limited to other mergers or whether it should comprehend evidence of internal growth of firms ought also to be addressed with reference to the industry's dynamic. In general, if excessive concentration is threatened, any merger which advances that condition ought to be inhibited. But it is possible that there were independent factors at work which stimulated internal growth of large firms. These factors may have worked themselves out (or may be continuing) and a particular merger may or may not be related to them. Thus, a flat response that any merger must be read as associated with any apparent trend toward greater concentration is a little extreme. If, all things considered, the merger does not alone or with other factors pose a threat of excessive concentration, the mere fact that in the recent past concentration has increased due to internal growth ought not to be enough to invalidate the merger.

35. Supra note 17, at 322 n. 38, 82 S.Ct. at 1522 n. 38, 8 L.Ed.2d at 534 n. 38.

36. Supra note 4, at 363, 83 S.Ct. at 1741, 10 L.Ed.2d at 945.

the structural analysis together with an explicit and forceful attack on the significance of the government's *prima facie* data, given the additional structural characteristics shown. Defendants established that coal had been losing ground to other fuels and that utilities were now the major consumers of coal, purchasing almost entirely through long term requirements contracts. They also showed that one of the merging companies had very limited coal reserves, the bulk of which were already committed under such contracts, and little or no opportunity to acquire additional reserves. The trend in coal consumption tended to weaken the significance of past coal market share statistics, if it did not require the use of a wider "energy" market. The status of utilities as buyers and the use of requirements contracts tended to make future ability to compete much more dependent on reserves. Given these facts, the lack of reserves or hope of getting them which plagued one of the merging firms showed that despite its considerable share of past production and sales, this firm would not be an important factor in the market in the future.

The general importance of the case is its reemphasis of the position that market share analysis does not end the inquiry.[37] It also exemplifies the kinds of evidence which might be needed to rebut the *prima facie* case. And there is yet another aspect of interest. The minority disputed the factual conclusions on which the majority relied. In particular, it took issue with the subsidiary fact, accepted by the majority, that the depleted firm, a strip and open pit miner, would not be able to acquire the skills and resources to compete as a deep pit miner. But the majority made clear that on subsidiary factual issues like these (as distinguished from broader issues of characterization such as what constitutes the appropriate market, or ultimate questions such as whether there is a probability of competitive harm) it would defer to trial court findings.

Can we generalize from *General Dynamics* about other kinds of evidence that might rebut a *prima facie* case based on market concentration and undue resulting firm share? Only very cautiously. Theoretically, we can identify general kinds of situations where one would not predict poor performance unless shares were considerably higher

37. Judge Mansfield's dissenting opinion in Stanley Works v. FTC, 469 F. 2d 498 (2d Cir. 1972), is an example of the approach to concentration data suggested by the holding of *General Dynamics*. The majority of the Second Circuit upheld an FTC ruling which struck down a merger largely on the basis of an analysis of degree of concentration. Dissenting, Judge Mansfield asserted that it was necessary to know whether the market definition and concentration data were indicative of actual competitive overlap between the merging firms. If, for example, the market defined were steel fabrication and the firms had markedly different specializations, or if the market defined were national and one of the merging firms made most of its sales in the east and the other in the west, the inference drawn by virtue of the *prima facie* rule would be weakened. It would then be necessary to consider whether significant barriers existed between the apparent sub-markets.

than the *prima facie* threshold. If industry demand were highly elastic, if there were high inter-industry cross-elasticities of demand and supply (e.g., between coal and other fuels or steel and other metals), if industry products were undifferentiated, if maximum efficiency could be achieved at small scale, and if entry were easy, the significance of the *prima facie* evidence would be reduced. Of course, once the *prima facie* case has been made, the merger proponents must come forward with enough to show the lack of a threat to competition. Conservatively speaking, and given the congressional skepticism about the social value of mergers, a successful rebuttal must demonstrate a dynamic conception of the processes of the industry, showing the industry to be competitive and warranting the inference that the proposed structural change will not significantly change these processes. Direct performance evidence about relationships between costs and prices in the industry would also seem relevant; for example, a showing by the government that profits were high would tend to rebut any attack made by the proponents on the government's *prima facie* case.

An enticing issue is whether proponents can ever defend successfully by contending that the merger, though heightening concentration, reduces the likelihood of price leadership or other forms of interdependence. For example, suppose that the largest firm has 28% of the market, that the second has 22%, the next two have 10% each and that the next four have 7%. Suppose further that the two 10% firms or two, three or four of the 7% firms propose to merge, or that both of those changes are independently proposed, and the justification offered is that under the structure of the premerger market, the largest firm sets prices and all others follow, but that if shares were more equally distributed among four or five firms, greater boldness leading to price competition would or might develop.

Neither theoretical analysis nor empirical evidence tells much about the likely effects of small changes in a concentrated structure. We can only speculate on questions such as whether interdependence or collusion is more likely in an industry where 90% is controlled by four or five firms of roughly equal size or in one where 90% control is distributed 35% to one firm and 11% to each of five others. The law might have responded to this uncertainty by saying that the government must show convincingly that the specific structural change proposed is likely to be harmful; but the law has not cut so finely. We know generally that increasing concentration tends to injure competition. We also know that Congress was gravely concerned about further increases in already concentrated markets. There is also a pervasive intuition that intensified concentration threatens competition and that, even if it does not currently make matters worse, it may reduce the likelihood of eventual deconcentration through new entry, erosion of large firm shares, altering of market boundaries through technological change, and the like. Greater doses of concentration in already concentrated markets will therefore not be accepted as a prescription for better performance.[38]

A related issue is quite firmly resolved. Merger proponents have at times contended that even though the merger may cause competitive harm in the market, it will have a greater pro-competitive impact in another market. This issue was presented first in *Philadelphia National Bank*,[39] where the Court refused to consider the contention that a merger, thought to reduce local bank competition, enhanced competition in the national loan market by increasing the loan limits of the resulting bank. Such a position will serve to reduce the judicial burden, but it may in some instances impose a cost on the economy.[40] The problem of choice is the familiar one that is faced in deciding upon *per se* rules. There is not only the cost and uncertainty associated with a rule that required the Court to evaluate and balance every claim of offsetting competitive advantage, there is also the risk of finding offsetting advantages where none exist. And there is the overwhelming difficulty that if a merger does seem to improve competition in one market at the expense of reducing it in another, there is no apparent calculus for determining the net effect for the economy as a whole. Though one may regret that mechanisms are not available for making these kinds of judgments, one who discerns the special nature and limits of judicial competence can hardly be chagrined that the Court has cast this problem back upon Congress where, difficult as it may be, the essentially political decision probably belongs. At all events, the Court has even more recently embraced with even greater vigor the view that under the antitrust laws it cannot contrast possible injury to competition in one market or segment against possible advantage to competition in another.[41]

e. Reinforcing the Prima Facie Case

Just as the *prima facie* case can be rebutted, so it can be reinforced. Indeed, a case of unlawful merger can be made out with the help of additional evidence even if the concentration evidence does

---

38. Ford Motor Co. v. United States, 405 U.S. 562, 92 S.Ct. 1142, 31 L.Ed.2d 492 (1972), although not strictly speaking a vertical case, clearly teaches that claims that increased concentration bring to particular settings benefits to competition will be skeptically received. Where the *prima facie* case is at or near the margin, the opportunity for successful rebuttal will obviously be greater. In that context perhaps a specific analysis proposing that the particular structural change in contemplation will be beneficial, along with evidence of other factors which would mitigate potential future harm (such as a lack of entry barriers), would help merger proponents.

39. Supra note 4.

40. One can hypothesize extreme situations where most persons doing the social calculus would conclude that the gains from improved competition in one area outweigh the harms in the other.

41. United States v. Topco Associates, Inc., 405 U.S. 596, 92 S.Ct. 1126, 31 L. Ed.2d 515 (1972).

not cross the threshold of the *prima facie* rule. We have previously noted the significance of a trend toward concentration. More generally, the most useful guide is theoretical knowledge about the characteristics of an industry which facilitate collusion or interdependence.

Take as an example a factual situation similar to that in United States v. Container Corporation of America.[42] Assume that there are sixty firms making containers, that price information is generally available to sellers from buyers, that interbrand elasticity is very high, but that elasticity for the industry's product is low. One of the two or three largest firms with, say, 6% of the market, proposes to acquire a firm of average size having about 1.5%. The argument against the merger would closely resemble that against the exchange of price information in the actual case. Given the structural characteristics, coordination would be very tempting. Although if it is attempted now it would probably be hard to accomplish, if the structure changes either by increasing noticeably the shares of the largest firms or reducing noticeably the total number of small firms (or both), the prospect for collusion or interdependence will be discernibly enhanced. Thus, absent any convincing counterargument, the merger can plausibly be said to threaten competition.[43]

f. Post-Acquisition Evidence

If any substantial time has elapsed between the consummation of the merger and the time of suit, there will be at least three separate times about which evidence might be taken—the time the merger occurred, the time suit was brought, and the time of trial. In *General Dynamics*,[44] for example, the acquiring firm began buying stock in the acquired firm in 1954 and completed its purchases in 1959. Suit was brought in 1967 and the case went to trial in 1970. Concentration data may change over such a time span and did in that instance. During the period between 1959 and 1970 there was a significant reduction both in concentration ratios and in the combined market share of the acquired and acquiring firm. Although none was offered in *General Dynamics,* there also may be post-merger performance evidence indicating that price leadership patterns may have developed, or that competition may have grown more intense, or that relationships between price and demand may have worsened or improved. If changes of these kinds correlate in time with the merger, if they all point in the same direction, and if they can also be linked to the merger by a plausible theoretical analysis, data and analytical evaluation about them may be useful.

---

42. 393 U.S. 333, 89 S.Ct. 510, 21 L.Ed. 2d 526 (1969). See the discussion of this case in § 96 supra.

43. Compare Brown Shoe Co. v. United States, supra note 17 and United States v. Von's Grocery Co., supra note 7.

44. Supra note 8.

It was settled by *du Pont (G.M.)* [45] that a merger which was unchallenged and apparently lawful when made can later be held unlawful on the basis of post-acquisition evidence bearing either on the purpose or the effect of the merger. There is no applicable statute of limitations; every merger leaves a time bomb ticking in the board room.

The time of suit rule has complex implications. A firm with past unchallenged mergers may hesitate to make a new acquisition for fear that if that were challenged the earlier ones might also be.[46] A firm with an unchallenged merger which later appears to be vulnerable because of post-acquisition developments may also moderate its conduct in other ways, much as might a firm fearful of being labelled a monopolist. This possibility is a mixed blessing. To the extent fear of attack on the merger results in avoidance of collusion or competitive pricing instead of interdependent pricing it is advantageous; but if the management spends its time trying to avoid extensive growth in order to dampen increasing concentration statistics, it may be forced to act in irrational or at least anomalous ways.

Time of suit cases like *du Pont (G.M.)* display the use of evidence of post-merger developments in a challenge to a merger; several cases, however, leave the plain implication that post-merger evidence of lack of competitive injury is to be given scant credit in support of merger validity. *Procter & Gamble (Clorox)* [47] and *Consolidated Foods* [48] both assert that because of the possibility that the acquiring firm may consciously remain on good behavior or avoid concentration increasing growth during the early post-merger years, such evidence is intrinsically unreliable. In *General Dynamics*,[49] however, the majority adopted the view that if the government makes out a *prima facie* case on the basis of time of merger evidence, post-acquisition structural developments are admissible to temper the implications of the government's *prima facie* data. As Justice Stewart put it, evidence about increasing reliance of coal producers on utilities as customers, or about depletion of reserves, is not such evidence as might "reflect a positive decision * * * to deliberately but temporarily refrain from anticompetitive actions

---

45. United States v. E. I. du Pont de Nemours & Co., 353 U.S. 586, 77 S.Ct. 872, 1 L.Ed.2d 1057 (1957). See also United States v. Penn-Olin Chemical Co., 378 U.S. 158, 84 S.Ct. 1710, 12 L.Ed.2d 775 (1964); FTC v. Consolidated Foods Corp., 380 U.S. 592, 85 S.Ct. 1220, 14 L.Ed.2d 95 (1965); United States v. Greater Buffalo Press, Inc., 402 U.S. 549, 91 S.Ct. 1692, 29 L.Ed.2d 170 (1971).

46. The FTC with some frequency and the Justice Department occasionally have made a new merger the occasion for challenging old ones. E.g. Maremount Corp., 3 CCH Trade Reg.Rep. ¶ 18,431 (1968); United States v. Hart, Shaffner & Marx, 5 CCH Trade Reg. Rep. ¶ 45,068 (N.D.Ill.1968).

47. FTC v. Procter & Gamble Co., 386 U.S. 568, 87 S.Ct. 1224, 18 L.Ed.2d 303 (1967).

48. FTC v. Consolidated Foods Corp., 380 U.S. 592, 85 S.Ct. 1220, 14 L.Ed.2d 95 (1965).

49. Supra note 8.

* * *."[50] Post-merger evidence offered in favor of the merger which could logically be explained as merely an effort by the merging firms to minimize the appearance of adverse effects—for example, evidence that price leadership patterns had not developed after the merger—would continue to be excluded or, if admitted, given little weight. But post-merger evidence which is beyond the power of parties to manipulate should be admitted and given its full weight. Thus, *General Dynamics* insists upon a finer analysis of post-merger evidence than the "always a sword, never a shield" view which was implied by prior cases.

Caution about using post-merger evidence to justify a merger is understandable enough, but surely the notion of a possible "good behavior ruse" has its limits. In most instances the theory on which a merger is challenged will relate structural change in the market to the conduct of all firms there and to industry performance. Focusing only on the conduct of the merged unit, rather than competitive interaction more generally and any discernible performance consequences, may be to misplace the attention somewhat. It is possible, of course, that a merger which could facilitate interdependence will be kept from doing so by the merged firm's incentive to compete, out of fear that it is being watched. But that kind of a charade will not likely be kept up for long; if kept up indefinitely it would in any event be a sign that, given another constraint on conduct (fear of legal intervention), the merger did not produce bad competitive results. An unqualified prohibition against post-acquisition evidence supportive of a merger is, then, an overreaction. A trial court ought to be ready to look at such evidence at least in a preliminary way and to consider whether its potential usefulness outweighs any new complexities. If, given its nature, and the time span covered, the risks of fabrication seemed large, that would count against it; the higher the degree of its apparent salience on the ultimate issue of competitive effect, the more ready a court should be to receive it. The trial court should strike a reasonable balance, and on appeal, considerable deference should be accorded to its judgment.

g. *The Failing Company Defense*

The notion in *General Dynamics*[51] that the acquired company was not a significant force because of its low coal reserves and the impossibility of obtaining new ones is suggestive of a more general defense sometimes offered in merger cases—that the acquired company was not a competitive force because it was failing.

Merger as a means of exit for the failing company is a special and uniquely appealing example of the claim that mergers afford a social advantage in that they facilitate alienability of capital assets.

---

50. Id. at 506, 94 S.Ct. at 1198, 39 L. Ed.2d at 547.

51. Supra note 8.

Ease of exit from an industry with a minimum of loss and disruption is one criterion for a well functioning market; those who have entered ought not to be forced to suffer unnecessarily grave losses to get out. For a going concern there may be many possible buyers, but those already in the industry are obviously an important group of possible buyers. Closing this group off would be particularly harsh on a failing firm, which might find it exceedingly difficult to find a buyer outside of the industry.

The failing company defense dates to the decision in *International Shoe*,[52] where acquisition by a competitor of the stock of a firm whose condition necessitated liquidation was held not to violate the pre-amendment version of Section 7. The case was referred to with approval in the legislative history of the amended act but, as Bok pointed out, Congress did not reveal whether it was responding to efficiency interests (like improving management through merger), the interest of creditors, employees, or perhaps stockholders (who might suffer losses avoidable through merger), or the notion that if the acquired firm would have disappeared through failure, but for the merger, it would not have offered competition to the acquiring firm in any event.[53] In *Citizen Publishing*[54] the Court has more recently expressed a most conservative view about the scope of the defense. The proponents must show that the acquired firm was moribund, that all alternative ways to save it were tried or fully explored and clearly found wanting, and that a thorough search for buyers showed the acquiring firm to be the only prospect or, if there are more than one, the one with which merger will be the least threatening to competition. Much of this was, however, no more than dicta, however well considered. In fact, the allegedly failing firm in *Citizen Publishing* was not in dire straits and was never offered on the market except to the acquiring competitor; the failing company argument seemed more a rationalization than a realistic defense.[55]

Though the dissenters would have it otherwise, the majority opinion in *General Dynamics* did not itself involve a failing company defense but something from a different genre. That case did not soften

---

52. International Shoe Co. v. FTC, 280 U.S. 291, 50 S.Ct. 89, 74 L.Ed. 431 (1930).

53. See Bok, Section 7 of the Clayton Act and the Merging of Law and Economics, 74 Harv.L.Rev. 226, 339 (1960).

54. Citizen Publishing Co. v. United States, 394 U.S. 131, 89 S.Ct. 927, 22 L.Ed.2d 148 (1969).

55. Other cases rejecting a failing company defense include: United States v. Third Nat'l Bank in Nashville, 390 U.S. 171, 88 S.Ct. 882, 19 L.Ed.2d 1015 (1968); United States v. Von's Grocery Co., supra note 7; United States v. El Paso Gas Co., 376 U.S. 651, 84 S.Ct. 1044, 12 L.Ed.2d 12 (1964); United States v. Philadelphia Nat'l Bank, supra note 4; United States v. Diebold, 369 U.S. 654, 82 S.Ct. 993, 8 L.Ed.2d 176 (1962). See also Farm Journal Inc., 53 F.T.C. 26 (1956), Dean Foods Co., 70 F.T.C. 1146, 1272–88, 1302–03 (1966). Cf. United States v. Reed Roller Bit Co., 274 F.Supp. 573, 584 (W.D.Okla.1967).

or expand an old defense but widened the gamut of defenses generally. The easy assumptions on which the dissenters worked thus lend no aid in an effort to see whether *General Dynamics* altered in any way the teaching of *Citizen Publishing* about the failing company defense. The new case perhaps exposes the latent fiction of *Citizen Publishing,* that the scope of the failing company concept can be specified with fine precision. Given the greater openness of response which *General Dynamics* generally encourages, we may say, in answer to Bok's inquiry, that Congress having left the matter open, the failing company defense can in any instance serve any one or more of the functions implicit in the dilemma and it is up to trial and reviewing courts, informed by the particulars of the situation *sub judice,* to decide the scope of the defense in every instance. A degree of judicial discretion in this area, where concern must encompass earthy values as well as economic ones, is perhaps a fitting antidote to the confining rigor of structural analysis in merger law, an analysis which, however powerful we may deem it to be, leaves out much that is important with regard to life as it is lived in the market place.

h. *Efficiency as a Defense or an Additional Basis for Challenging a Merger*

It is sometimes claimed that competition is valued because it tends toward efficiency and that efficiency-yielding mergers should therefore be held valid. But the Court has taken cognizance of the broad, populist attitudes reflected in the legislative history. *Brown Shoe*,[56] *Procter & Gamble (Clorox)*[57] and *Philadelphia Bank*[58] all involved efficiency claims of one kind or another and in each the Court displayed indifference or hostility to the notion that cost savings might be achieved through merger.

In *Brown Shoe* the claimed efficiencies were cost savings associated with a vertical aspect of the merger, the addition of direct distribution outlets to the acquiring firm's manufacturing capacity. Though the Court referred to the possibility of countervailing benefits from a merger, the opinion implied that the advantage thus gained over competitors was an adverse factor in the assessment of the merger. In the *Clorox* case the claimed efficiencies were in reducing the cost of brand name promotion through quantity discounts and reducing credit costs in a comparable way. The FTC, though implying that real cost saving efficiencies would count in favor of a merger, had labelled these efficiency claims as deficient; it saw them as tending to increase entry barriers. The majority, in an opinion by Justice Douglas, treated these factors as adverse to the merger without clearly indicating whether efficiencies might ever count on the other side of the scale.

---

56. Supra note 17.

57. Supra note 47.

58. Supra note 4. See also I. T. & T. Corp. v. G. T. E. Corp., 518 F.2d 913, 936 (9th Cir. 1975) which rejects efficiency as a defense.

A more balanced view was taken by Justice Harlan, who concurred in *Clorox*. He saw cost savings as a merger justification, but felt that the burden of convincingly proving the existence of efficiencies and their magnitude was on the merger proponents. He also thought that if cost savings were once established, any claim that they were of a kind which threatened to create entry barriers should be shown by comparably convincing evidence, not by gross and unexplicated claims about general relationships between brand differentiation and entry barriers. Also relevant is Justice Clark's opinion in *Tampa Electric*[59], a case involving a long term requirements contract, an arrangement functionally similar to a vertical merger. In that case efficiency evidence weighed in favor of legality. But even if credit is given to the Clark and Harlan views, pitfalls remain. Assuming the presence of manifest efficiencies stemming from a merger which otherwise threatens competition, we will likely be able to do little more than guess about cost saving magnitudes. And we cannot calculate, but only guess, whether the public is better off (immediately or in the long run) if it attains the efficiency at the expense of the threat to competition. Subsidiary to this is the issue whether the efficiency gains will be passed on in the form of reduced prices or retained in the form of excessive profits or personnel costs (or other offsetting waste).

The Court's most recent responses to these dark things has been to say figuratively, "Tell us not about efficiency; tell Congress if you wish." But that is not necessarily the best response. An alternative, not leading the Court into an unbearably complex or value laden area of judgment, would be to say that where cost saving efficiencies are clear, and arise in a context where market forces will oblige the seller to pass them on to consumers, and where competitive harm is only speculative (as for example where the basis for the challenge to the merger is an increased concentration in some setting near the *prima facie* threshold), the wise course is to risk the possible social harm for the certain benefit. Even if the Court is not ready to weigh the social benefit of efficiencies against the social harm of competitive injury when both seem similarly likely or certain to eventuate, it might nevertheless value a significant and likely social benefit higher than a much more doubtful harm.

§ 205. Market Extension Mergers

a. In General

Suppose the acquired and acquiring firms market the same products, but in different geographic markets; or suppose they operate in the same industry but at different ends of the diversified line of products usually assigned to the industry or operate in different but adja-

---

59. Tampa Electric Co. v. Nashville Coal Co., 365 U.S. 320, 81 S.Ct. 623, 5 L.Ed.2d 580 (1961).

cent product markets which utilize closely related technologies or distribution facilities or both. Such an acquisition, which the Supreme Court has labeled a market extension merger, has affinities not only with horizontal mergers but also with conglomerate mergers. Although to analyze such a merger we must use concepts applicable to conglomeration, a market extension merger has enough in common with purely horizontal mergers to make it pedagogically convenient to consider them at this point. Numerous mergers fall into the market extension category, and they often require an analysis more complex than the *prima facie* test for mergers among direct competitors. Dealing with them therefore illustrates ways in which a merger may alter structure adversely without increasing concentration in any particular product or geographic market.

Here, as in any merger case, analysis begins with market definition and the development of concentration and market share statistics. The precision of the marget definition determines whether a case is to be characterized as a horizontal or market extension problem. For example, if firm A, which sells in New York, adjacent parts of New Jersey and occasionally Pennsylvania, acquires firm B, which sells in Maryland, Delaware and occasionally Pennsylvania, defining a mid-Atlantic regional market made up of those three states will portray them as direct competitors; by contrast, defining a greater New York and a separate Delaware-Maryland market will not. Again, if the acquiring firm sells soaps, detergents, cleaners and waxes, while the acquired firm sells brooms, brushes, mops and waxes, a broadly defined product market will display a merger of competitors while a narrow one will disclose a market extension merger.

In a market extension merger the importance of concentration data is less obvious than in the case of a merger of direct competitors, though their implications are similar. If neither market is significantly concentrated there is no reason to worry about the merger. Only if there is a risk of interdependence, collusion, or other conduct yielding poor performance in at least one of the affected markets need we concern ourselves about the merger. Market extension mergers require an analysis of whether the particular merger enhances the risks already presented by the concentrated condition of one or both of the affected markets. Even though concentration levels are unchanged, such a merger might increase the risks of collusion or interdependence in ways which are conceptually quite simple, and reasonably determinate factually. Thus, courts ought to be able to handle market extension issues reasonably well.

Potential competition and disparity between the overall size of the acquiring firm and those already in the market are the concepts raising competitive concerns. There are, nonetheless, two paths to error. One, which was more of a concern from the mid-1960's to the early 1970's when the Warren Court commonly gave the government its way in merger cases, is to assume that if competition might be hurt under any conceivable theory, nothing more is needed—i.e., that an empirical nexus between the theory and the market place is superfluous. The other path to error, more of concern today given the Burger Court's current intellectual stamp in antitrust matters, is to assume that setting oneself adrift upon the swirls and eddies of subtlety is itself a productive judicial enterprise.

b. *Competitive Injury Due to Loss of Potential Competition*

In general: During the early years of the Sherman Act economists saw potential competition as a force which severely limited the market power of firms, however large their shares. Economists of that age thought that market power was largely the product of government grants and restrictions, such as patents, tariffs, and regulations limiting entry, which protected those in the market from further entry. The received wisdom today is otherwise. Of course, government barriers to entry are still perceived as a source of market power, but not as the only sources. No longer do we view the great reservoir of private capital as capable of flowing into any market where present occupants increase prices above competitive levels.[1]

The conception widely accepted today grants potential competition a narrow and more selective function. In a concentrated market, existing firms will perceive the advantages of coordination and may achieve coordination collusively or interdependently. They are not disciplined by the theoretical possibility that any outside source of capital may enter; entry barriers keep out most such sources. However, there may be some firms which have the skills, technology and resources necessary to scale the entry barriers. These firms are "potential entrants" in a very special sense. Their existence may reduce market power—that is, may inhibit price increases to excessive levels—in either of two ways. First, their perceived existence in the wings, so to speak, may lead the firms already on stage to act differently than otherwise they would have acted. Firms in the market may engage in limit pricing at closer to competitive levels in order to defer entry. They will want to price just below the level that would draw in the potential entrants.[2] If the potential entrants were not

---

1. But see Demsetz, "Two Systems of Belief About Monopoly," in Industrial Concentration: The New Learning 166 (Goldschmid, Mann & Weston eds. 1974), which revises, restates and reasserts the classic view that monopoly is the product of government interference with the marketplace, purporting, in the process, to dispose of all the adverse evidence based on empirical studies of relationships between concentration and profits. At bottom, the theoretical position is that unless government shields it, no firm can earn excessive profits without attracting new entry.

2. See J. Bain, Barriers to New Competition 1–13 (1956). See also United States v. El Paso Natural Gas Co., 376 U.S. 651, 84 S.Ct. 1044, 12 L.Ed.2d 12 (1964); United States v. Penn-Olin Chem. Co., 378 U.S. 158, 84 S.Ct. 1710, 12 L.Ed.2d 775 (1964).

there, firms in the market would be able to raise prices.[3] Second, regardless of whether its presence in the wings affects present conduct in the market, any potential entrant may in the future actually enter, thus reducing concentration and enhancing the possibility of more competitive market performance at that time.[4]

The significance of all this for market extension merger reposes in another abstraction. The most likely entrants into any market are those already in markets related to it by product, geographical, distributional, or vertical affinities. For example, steel makers are less likely to enter the bleach business than detergent makers, chemical companies, or grocery chains. Firms having some nexus with a market more likely will be aware of opportunities there and more capable of conceptualizing and executing means to exploit them successfully. The reasons do not differ from those that make propinquity significant in social relationships. People do the things that occur to them. Things occur to them if the environment they occupy stimulates the thoughts. Thus, when firms in adjacent markets merge, those markets each lose a potential entrant. If such entrants are few, that loss may be competitively significant, due either to the removal of a perceived potential entrant whose presence disciplined present occupants or to the elimination of the possibility of an eventual independent entry.

The potential entrant as a present competitive force: The case law begins with *El Paso*.[5] The government under Section 7 challenged the acquisition by El Paso Natural Gas Company of the stock and assets of Pacific Northwest Pipeline Corporation. El Paso was the only out-of-state firm that supplied natural gas in California; it had 50% of the California market. Pacific Northwest was the only interstate natural gas pipeline of any consequence with a distribution system west of the Rockies. It operated in adjacent states and had enormous natural gas reserves in areas accessible from California. Pacific Northwest also possessed the management and the competitive initiative which suggested its potential for entry into California. Indeed, it had made unsuccessful attempts to enter the California market, attempts to which El Paso had responded vigorously. In one instance El Paso reduced its price by twenty-five percent in order to stave off a threatened Pacific Northwest invasion.

Though Pacific Northwest had not succeeded in entering the California market, the Court viewed the firm as a potent competitive force in California. It had a distinct interest in entering, had tried to do so, and could be expected to try again. It also possessed a unique capacity to enter; there was no other discernible potential entrant

3. See United States v. Falstaff Brewing Corp., 410 U.S. 526, 93 S.Ct. 1096, 35 L.Ed.2d 475 (1973); FTC v. Procter & Gamble Co., 386 U.S. 568, 87 S.Ct. 1224, 18 L.Ed.2d 303 (1967).

4. FTC v. Procter & Gamble Co., supra note 3.

5. United States v. El Paso Natural Gas Co., supra note 2.

with anything like a comparable affinity with the California market. El Paso, moreover, plainly saw Pacific Northwest as a competitive threat requiring it to moderate its own market conduct. The merger, therefore, posed a substantial threat to competitive conditions in California and was held to be unlawful.

The case has classic dimensions. It illustrates forcefully that a potential entrant can affect a market from the wings and to a degree comparable to that which might be produced by a firm already in the market; it also facilitates understanding of the circumstances under which this may occur. Protected by high entry barriers, the California natural gas market was highly concentrated. Pacific Northwest, if not the only firm capable of entry, was one of very few. Altering any of these circumstances would reduce the level of concern about eliminating Pacific Northwest as an independent force in the market. If the market were less concentrated, there would be more competitive stimulation within it and less reason to value a firm in the wings. The Court recently underscored the significance of this factor in *Marine Bancorporation*,[6] where it stated flatly that potential competition becomes a factor only when "there are dominant participants in the target market engaging in interdependent or parallel behavior and with the capacity effectively to determine price and total output of goods or services."[7] Also, if entry barriers had been lower in *El Paso,* there might have been many potential entrants and the loss of any one of them would have been less consequential.

Thus, there are inherent limitations in the notion that a potential competitor may be a current factor in the market; ignoring these limitations will lead to distortion. Merely identifying a firm as a potential competitor does not alone give the firm special status. We have not supposed that there is a *per se* rule even against merging with an actual competitor; much less ought there to be one against merging with a possible or potential entrant.[8] To invoke the prohibition there must be a rational basis for concluding that to sweep this particular potential competitor out of the wings and, as it were,

---

6. United States v. Marine Bancorporation, Inc., 418 U.S. 602, 94 S.Ct. 2856, 41 L.Ed.2d 978 (1974).

7. Id. at 630, 94 S.Ct. at 2874, 41 L.Ed. 2d at 1001.

8. Ford Motor Co. v. United States, 405 U.S. 562, 92 S.Ct. 1142, 31 L.Ed.2d 492 (1972) also exemplifies the potential entrant as a present factor in the market. There were three significant American makers of spark plugs, one integrated with a major car maker, two independent. Ford, the second largest car producer, had shown an interest in the spark plug market. As the Court said, "while [a potential competitor] stays near the edge, it is a deterrent to current competitors * * *. This was Ford uniquely, as both a prime candidate to manufacture and the major customer of the dominant member of the [existing spark plug] oligopoly." Id. at 567, 92 S.Ct. at 1146, 31 L.Ed.2d at 998. In concluding that Ford's acquisition of one of the plug makers would violate Section 7, the Court thus stressed both the degree of concentration in the plug market and the special relationship which made Ford a firm to be feared by those already in the market.

either onto the stage under the control of one of the firms already there, or away from the stage entirely, will have a dampening impact because of the particular relationship between the acquired firm and those already occupying the market.[9]

The potential entrant and future deconcentration: The friction between firms in the market and one or more firms on its edge may be only latent. Present competitors may not have identified a particular firm as a potential threat, nor modified their conduct because of it. Yet if the market is concentrated and investigation shows the likelihood that a particular firm, if denied the option to enter by merger, is likely to enter the market independently, then to allow it to enter by merger is to deprive the market of a new, independent competitor. If El Paso exemplifies a case where a firm in the market was denied a merger with a potential competitor because it represented a present market force, *Procter & Gamble (Clorox)* [10] seems to be one in which a potential entrant was denied access to the market through merger in part because of the chance that, the merger being foreclosed, it might have entered independently.

"Seems to be" is as far as one may comfortably go in characterizing *Clorox*. The Court did not differentiate with any clarity between the utility of a potential competitor based on its present market impact, and its utility because it might actually enter in the future. The relevant product market was household bleach, a solvent which manufacturers sought to differentiate through advertising, although the various brands were chemically the same. The relevant geographic markets consisted of a national market and several regional submarkets. Clorox was the only national seller, and had 50% of the national market. The second firm, which only sold west of the Mississippi, had 16% of sales nationally. The six firm concentration ratio was 80% and the remaining 20% was shared by more than 250 fringe firms, most of which sold in only one region. Regional figures often displayed greater concentration than these national ones.

Procter & Gamble, a large diversified manufacturer of detergents, soaps and other high-turnover household cleaning products

---

9. The Court in United States v. Marine Bancorporation, Inc., supra note 6, indicated that the market deficiencies needed to warrant treating a potential competitor as a present market force could be established through conventional structural evidence; but it impliedly warned that concentration ratios are not likely to be determinative. Other structural factors are obviously important. The case also invites the use of performance evidence either to rebut or reinforce inferences drawn from structure. See also Ford Motor Co. v. United States, supra note 8, where structural factors are also stressed. The recent decision in United States v. Hughes Tool Co., 1976–2 CCH Trade Cas. ¶ 61,046 (C.D.Cal.1976) is also suggestive. There, the court rejected the loss of potential competition as a competitive concern, given what the court regarded as a reasonably competitive structure, a deconcentration trend, increasing overall demand, easy entry, and strong, sophisticated buyers.

10. Supra note 3.

proposed to acquire Clorox. P & G had over 50% of all sales nationally of such household cleaning products; it and two other firms had in total 80% of these sales. P & G was also the nation's largest advertiser. The Supreme Court upheld the FTC's ruling that the merger was unlawful because it would eliminate Proctor & Gamble as a potential competitor. The Court saw liquid bleach as a "natural avenue" for diversification by Procter & Gamble; bleach was complementary to P & G's products, distributed through the same channels, capable of promotion in the P & G fashion and at relatively low cost to P & G because of economies associated with the size and scope of the company's advertising budget. Though neither the FTC nor the Court found that Procter & Gamble was more likely than not to enter independently if it could not enter by merger, the Court labelled Procter & Gamble the single most likely entrant into the highly concentrated bleach market. The loss of that possibility of entry of another competitor to the highly concentrated bleach market was one reason why the FTC entered its order and why the Court affirmed. The case, then, seemed to establish that the Section 7 was violated by entry through merger into a highly concentrated market by a firm which could be labelled the most likely independent entrant, even though there was no finding that the firm in question was more likely than not to enter.

But there have been subsequent developments which undermine such a broad reading of *Procter & Gamble*. In *Falstaff*[11] the Supreme Court gave more focused attention to the notion that a firm which might enter independently at some point ought to be prohibited from merging with a significant existing competitor. The brewing industry was quite concentrated. The national four firm ratio exceeded 60% and had been increasing for over a decade. Falstaff, the fourth largest brewer in the nation, sold everywhere but the Northeast. Of the ten largest brewers, seven sold nationwide. Falstaff was the largest which did not and had closer access to its uncovered territory than did either of the other large, non-national brewers. Attaining national distribution apparently meant that a brewer gained some economies in promotion and acquired a prestige which may have boosted marketing. Also, national distribution meant regional diversity with reference to the seasonal character of labor markets and sales; this tended to flatten out some of the cost and income curves of the business. For these and other reasons Falstaff had shown a well developed interest in becoming a national brewer. However, it chose to achieve this goal not by independent entry into New England, but by seeking to acquire Narragansett, a New England regional brewer with the largest share (20%) of that market.

11. United States v. Falstaff Brewing Corp., supra note 3.

The government based its case on the assertion that Falstaff's independent entry was not only plainly feasible but was highly probable if the merger were forbidden. Secondarily, it contended that if acquisition of a New England brewer were needed to ease the way, Falstaff could have purchased a small brewer to gain a toe-hold in the market and that this would have been competitively preferable to entry by acquisition of the largest independent. The district court found that Falstaff had considered but rejected independent entry and thus ought not to be labelled a potential entrant. The Supreme Court reversed, five to two, and remanded for further findings.[12]

The case yielded four opinions. Justice White's opinion for the Court hints at approval of the government's theory of the case—that if Falstaff in fact would enter independently or by toe-hold acquisition if forbidden to acquire a large firm like Narragansett, the probability of deconcentration from such an alternative course would warrant enjoining the merger. However, this was not the Court's holding, nor did the Court overturn the district court's finding that Falstaff was unlikely to enter independently or by toe-hold acquisition. Justice White (as well as Justice Blackmun and the Chief Justice) showed concern that the district court failed to pursue adequately the other branch of potential competition analysis; the district court had made no findings about whether other firms in the New England market regarded Falstaff as a potential entrant and moderated their conduct because of Falstaff's perceived presence in the wings. It is, perhaps, a question whether a potential entrant which is not a "present competitive force", in the sense explored in the prior subsection, will ever appear to be a sufficiently likely actual future entrant so that its entry by merger will significantly reduce chances for future deconcentration. Hence, the theory the White opinion passively approves may, as a practical matter, be more a make-weight than an independent basis for forbidding a merger. However that may be, this separate, future deconcentration theory was the subject of separate opinions by Justices Marshall and Douglas who dealt in detail with whether the loss of a possible source of future deconcentration should render a merger illegal.

Justice Marshall wrote perceptively about this subject. He noted that the government had not relied on the contention that Falstaff represented a present competitive force due to its perceived presence at the edge of the market. He wanted the Court expressly to sanction the government's distinctly different legal theory and to remand

---

12. On remand the district court held that the government had failed to carry its burden of proving that the entry by merger of Falstaff, "an on-the-fringe potential competitor" in the Northeast, "would probably lead to a substantial lessening of competition." United States v. Falstaff Brewing Corp., 383 F.Supp. 1020, 1028 (D.R.I. 1974). The opinion leaves some doubt whether the court adequately discriminated between the two theories about how loss of a potential competitor can injure competition and some doubt about whether it fully considered the second of these theories.

for a further hearing on that theory. In his view the district court improperly had excluded evidence relevant to that issue. Justice Douglas went further. As he conceived the law, *Procter & Gamble* had established that if the acquiring firm is the most likely independent entrant (or, implicitly, if on other bases there appears to be a clear possibility of independent entry) then any entry by merger (with the possible exception of a toe-hold acquisition) is unlawful; he would not even require, as Marshall would, a showing of probable independent entry. The question for him was merely whether there was a possibility sufficiently high to protect. He concluded that the evidence already in the record necessitated a finding of such a possibility. Thus he would have remanded with directions to enter judgment for the government.

Pondering these opinions, one finds yet another issue latent in the case. To gauge significance, should we not assess the likely competitive effects of independent or toe-hold entry as well as the likelihood of its occurring? Concerning this, Justice Marshall focused only on the district court's utter failure to address the government's future deconcentration theory. Justice Douglas addressed the effect of entry question implicitly, but not from the vantage point of assessing economic injury. He spoke of the congressional concern with concentration generally and of its concern with the diluting of local control of industry. For him, independent entry by Falstaff was preferable simply because such entry, unlike the merger the defendants sought to justify, would have left a strong local competitor intact. This shift in the frame of reference, if not idiosyncratic to Justice Douglas, is one which the Court's majority as now constituted cannot be expected to make.

We are not without clues about how the Court's present majority will respond when presented with the question whether a challenge to merger on the basis of a possible future, independent entry must include an analysis of the likely effects of that independent entry, should it occur. *Marine Bancorporation*[13] resonates with the issue, though in a special way which leaves much open. There, the government challenged a geographic market extension merger between banks on the grounds that the market of the acquired firm was highly concentrated and that the acquiring firm was a potential entrant which might deconcentrate it. We have seen already that the Court found regulatory restraints sufficient to preclude the inference that blocking the challenged merger likely would lead to independent entry. But the Court went further. It said that to succeed under the theory of future deconcentration the government must prove both the capability of independent (or toe-hold) entry and that such an entry is likely to produce deconcentration or other pro-competitive effects.

---

13. Supra note 6.

Significant in all of this was the regulated character of the market; one cannot say whether the same rigorous stand would be taken about a merger in an unregulated market. Thus, the case raises as many questions as it answers. But the new majority may not long be able to avoid deciding the dual issues presented by this branch of potential competition analysis. If a showing that a particular firm is a potential entrant into a concentrated market does not preclude its merger with a significant firm already there, what else must be shown to justify an injunction? Without excessive factual exploration, yet with reasonable confidence, is it possible to make judgments about how much more competition would result from independent entry than from entry by merger? Does one additional entrant offer a greater potential benefit in a highly concentrated market than in a moderately concentrated one? The tighter the oligopoly, the more directly existing firms will feel any significant diversion of trade to the new entrant, and the more likely such firms will be to respond with a sequence of price cuts. But this relationship is only general; much may depend upon whether the independent entrant is price conscious and ready to fight aggressively for its market share, or inclined to slide into the market gently, disturbing the status quo as little as possible.

Cases like *Clorox* suggest that Justice Douglas was right—that if the target market is highly concentrated, it is enough to show that the acquiring firm has attributes that make it the most likely *de novo* entrant. Taking a cue from the *prima facie* approach of *Philadelphia Bank*, one might say this is enough to make the government's case unless the proponents of the merger affirmatively show that despite the special attributes of the acquiring firm the chances of independently entering and/or the net social gains which would be yielded by such entry as against entry by merger is sufficiently small that one cannot logically say that the merger tends substantially to lessen competition. Though *Falstaff* suggests that a finer analysis is needed than *Clorox* itself provided, the more recent case does not foreclose the use of a *prima facie* response such as that envisaged here.

Objective or subjective evidence of potential entry: Regardless of the aspect of potential entry analysis emphasized in a case, a question arises whether the inference about likelihood of entry must be made entirely from objective data about the characteristics of the firms, the nature of market, and prior displays of interest by the firm in making entry, or whether subjective evidence is also admissible. If the theory of the case involves the potential for future deconcentration by actual entry, subjective data would focus on current and past attitudes of the management; these might bear upon its likely attitude in the future. If the theory was that the potential entrant, being perceived as such by others, was a present market force, there might be two sources of subjective evidence, the possible entrant and those already in the market. Attitudes of the potential entrant openly expressed would be relevant as data which might influence the perceptions of those already in the market; unexpressed attitudes of the potential entrant might also have bearing on the theory that its actual attitudes would be displayed indirectly and those in the market would have a sense about them. Subjective evidence about what firms already in the market thought about the outsider might show whether they perceived the potential entrant as a present competitive threat.

There is ample precedent for the use of objective evidence on all of these issues. *El Paso*,[14] exemplifies useful objective facts, including a concentrated market and a single outside firm with both the resources needed for entry and a history of attempted entry. So do *Penn-Olin*,[15] *Procter & Gamble (Clorox)*[16] *and Falstaff*.[17] In *Penn-Olin*, one potential entrant made the product at issue in another geographic market and possessed the general capacity to enter. Another potential entrant had relevant marketing experience and was a purchaser in the target geographic market. In circumstances we shall explore more fully later, the Court thought this evidence to be probative but not conclusive of the likelihood of entry. In *Clorox*, objective evidence included proof that Procter & Gamble had the marketing capacity and resources for *de novo* entry, would gain certain scale efficiencies upon entry, and had a history of entering other, comparable markets. In *Falstaff*, the evidence demonstrated that only three of the ten largest brewers did not sell nationwide and that the alleged potential entrant was the largest of these, that operating nationally yielded efficiencies which would encourage the entry, and that the asserted potential entrant had been expanding and had shown interest in entry into the target market.

Can subjective evidence also play a role? Suppose those controlling the potential entrant testify or establish through internal memoranda that independent entry was considered but rejected: is that evidence admissible? Does it warrant a finding that the firm is not a likely source of future deconcentration? Not a present competitive force? Would testimony from other firms in the market that they never concerned themselves about the alleged potential entrant, or that it did not affect their market conduct at all, prove that it is not a present force? Or suppose the government offers testimony from executives of other firms to the effect that they were aware of the presence of the potential entrant in the wings and that it was taken into account when pricing decisions were made. Should such testimony be heard? None of these questions is idle. They would all be dealt with by a mature legal theory of potential competition. The

14. Supra note 2.

15. United States v. Penn-Olin Chem. Co., supra note 2.

16. Supra note 3.

17. United States v. Falstaff Brewing Corp., supra note 3.

answers which courts give as doctrine evolves will determine whether the potential competition concept is an aspect of structural analysis, an approach to market behavior, or a pragmatic response to a varied set of market problems. One may hope it proves to be the latter primarily.

Justice Marshall addressed these issues in his concurring opinion in *Falstaff*. The opinion stressed the self-serving nature of subjective views and labelled them irrelevant to the issue of the likelihood of actual future entry. But a witness' interest is often a concern in litigation and one which triers of fact can weigh along with the intrinsic credibility of the testimony and the witness' demeanor. A more telling argument against admitting subjective evidence is the fact that the subjective views actually experienced may not be relevant ones. For example, if an executive of a firm bent on entry by merger testifies that he carefully considered independent entry and decided against it, he has given only the merest clue to what his view would be if he knew he was forced to decide between independent entry and no entry at all. To hear him hypothetically on the latter question, moreover, would strain reliability.

If one were to give full credit to the logic of *Consolidated Foods*,[18] which opposes the use of post-acquisition conduct as evidence because such conduct may be tempered by the exigencies of litigation, the solution might be to exclude all subjective evidence on the issue of probable entry. But *General Dynamics* [19] softens the force of the view expressed in Consolidated Foods and in any event there is no logical compulsion to follow it by analogy here. Objective evidence about probability of a particular firm's entry will often, perhaps almost always, leave the matter indeterminate. Whatever the objective facts, they will seldom indicate with such clarity what a rational management would do. The question, of course, is not so ultimate as whether the firm would enter; it is only whether others fear it will (or whether it is likely that it will). Even so, since objective evidence will not often put the matter beyond dispute, admission of subjective views, subject to such limitations and restrictions as the trial judge reasonably deems useful, should be acceptable.

Regulatory (or other) restrictions on entry as a refutation: Both facets of potential competition doctrine presuppose that the potential entrant has special affinities with the market and, by implication, that it can gain access if it decides to. Suppose it cannot, that regulatory restrictions or other barriers exclude not only firms in general but also the "most likely entrant," however great its affini-

---

18. FTC v. Consolidated Foods Corp., 380 U.S. 592, 85 S.Ct. 1220, 14 L.Ed.2d 95 (1965).

19. United States v. General Dynamics Corp., 415 U.S. 486, 94 S.Ct. 1186, 39 L.Ed.2d 530 (1974).

ties for the market. Does the potential competition concept even then foreclose entry by merger?

In *Marine Bancorporation*,[20] the government challenged the acquisition of a medium sized commercial bank with several branches in the Spokane area by a large Seattle-based commercial bank which had branched nearly statewide, but not into Spokane. The contention was that Spokane was a concentrated banking market, that the acquiring bank, the National Bank of Commerce, was a potential *de novo* entrant, and that, if it entered *de novo* or by toe-hold acquisition, it would help to deconcentrate the Spokane market. The Court dealt with an aspect of potential competition left in abeyance in *Falstaff*—what must be shown to warrant characterizing the outside firm as a future source of deconcentration? Specifically, it held that an element of the government's case was proof that means were available to the outside firm to enter independently or by toe-hold acquisition. This element may not be consequential in non-regulated markets, but carrying that burden may be difficult where entry is restricted by regulation. And, logically, there may be insurmountable obstacles in non-regulated markets also.

Suppose, for example, that a market has a four firm concentration ratio of 80%, that there are seven or eight fringe firms, that successful participation in the market requires access to a patented technology, and that an outside firm with affinities for the market can acquire the technology by merging with the second largest firm (which is for sale) but not otherwise. Does not *Marine Bancorporation*, rationally applied, teach that the merger is unobjectionable?

One of the difficulties with the *Marine Bancorporation* opinion is its inaccurate implication that market accessibility through alternative means is a determinate fact. It may not be, either in a regulated market or in other situations. The rule of the case ought therefore to be softened, to be construed as speaking about a relevant concern. One might also bring other relevant concerns to bear in resolving particular cases. One of these is concern about the performance of the regulatory agencies. If independent entry seems unduly inhibited by regulatory agencies, then a judicial decision to allow entry by merger reduces the pressures the regulatory agency might feel to open the market to independent entry. In circumstances such as these the court might decide to deny entry by merger in the expectation that the regulatory agency might thereafter be influenced, in part by the antitrust decision, to allow independent entry. Similarly, even if one rejects the Douglas concern about preserving local control as an independent basis for denying a national brewer's bid to acquire

---

20. Supra note 6. For an interesting opinion applying *Marine Bancorporation* in rejecting a government challenge to a market extension merger, see United States v. The Black and Decker Mfg. Co., 779 ATRR A-3 (D. Md. August 20, 1976).

Narragansett, or that of a statewide bank, itself part of a holding company system, to acquire a Spokane bank, one might nevertheless give scope to these kinds of concerns in the wide interstices between our occasional certainties about questions like whether a firm with affinities for a market will or can enter.

c. Competitive Injury Due to Disparity Between Overall Size of an Acquiring Firm and Firms Already in the Market

In general: We have seen that a market extension merger may injure competition because the lost prospect of independent entry was of value; the cases,[21] and the theory underlying them,[22] also indicate a market extension merger can injure competition because it makes easier a particular entry which would be injurious however achieved.

Ford (Autolite),[23] and *Procter & Gamble (Clorox)*[24] each suggest this theory. Entry by Ford into the three firm spark plug market, whether by acquisition of one of the two independent firms in that market or *de novo*, would have tied Ford's own purchases, one-third or more of the original equipment market, to the Ford owned spark plug firm, just as General Motor's purchases were already tied to the spark plug firm it owned. Also, because of the custom of mechanics to use as replacement plugs the same brand the car bore as original equipment, any entry by Ford would have tied a comparable portion of the replacement market to Ford. With G.M. already integrated into the plug market, the only portion of the market not irrevocably tied would then be that represented in the new and replacement markets by demand for plugs for Chrysler, American Motors and foreign cars. Similarly, entry by Procter & Gamble into the bleach market, whether by acquisition or original entry, might have adverse consequences for that market. The new entrant's advantages would arise out of its power to obtain discounts on advertising and favorable credit terms and also out of its ability to achieve scale economies in advertising. These would be enough to give Procter & Gamble an advantage over other bleach makers.

Though the matter is not vividly apparent, each of these advantages (and particularly those in *Clorox*) has a relationship to the massive absolute size of the entrant relative to the firms on which it intrudes. Furthermore, some of the cases attribute possible competitive injury to such disparities in absolute size. That view has been systematized to a degree and now offers its own subsystem of categories. Putting aside momentarily whether there is truth to be found

21. E.g., Ford Motor Co. v. United States, supra note 8; FTC v. Procter & Gamble, supra note 3.

22. See Edwards, "Conglomerate Bigness as a Source of Power," in Business Concentration and Price Policy 331 (1955).

23. Supra note 8.

24. Supra note 3.

here, let us summarize the theories about how disparities in relative size can hurt competition in a market.[25]

Entrenchment of a dominant firm: Courts have said that size disparity can injure competition by helping to entrench a dominant firm. *Clorox* typifies this situation. The acquired firm clearly dominated the bleach industry. The acquiring firm, Procter & Gamble, had a potential for offering efficiencies in marketing and promotion and had better access to capital markets than existing firms, all of which would tend to discourage others to enter or to challenge the Clorox dominance. In consequence, the possibilities of future deconcentration were reduced, or so both the FTC and the Court concluded. The basis for the factual inference of entrenched dominance in *Clorox* had to do primarily with P & G's advertising budget, but entrenchment presumably could occur for other reasons. The acquiring firm might offer research capacity, management skills, or scale efficiencies other than in advertising and capital accumulation. The acquiring firm might also have a reputation for predatory conduct, or might simply be so big that its presence strikes awe in the imaginations of competitors in the small firm market, causing them to tread softly.

Emergence of a price leader: A concentrated market may perform collusively, interdependently or reasonably competitively. Interdependent conduct may not emerge in the absence of a recognized leader. General experience indicates that such a leader will be a firm with a large share of the market. If a firm which is relatively large in absolute size enters a market by acquiring one of the large firms in that market, its potential for taking on a leadership role will be enhanced.

All of this is exceedingly general and it is also speculative theorizing supported neither by empirical evidence nor by any thorough or refined concept about commercial motivations. Like much populist analysis, it draws more from emotion than reason. But we cannot dismiss it out of hand. Populist concerns were voiced in Congress; judicial response to these concerns is therefore not inappropriate. But the position must at least be modified before it is made the basis of law.

Perhaps it would suit to say this: If a firm proposes to enter by market extension merger a concentrated market occupied by firms which in absolute terms are small relative to it, it is appropriate to inquire whether, given its particular characteristics and those of the market it is entering, its presence will tend to facilitate interdepend-

---

25. In addition to the article by Edwards, supra note 22, the comment by G. Stocking following the article should be consulted. See also the testimony of Willard F. Mueller, Hearings on Economic Concentration Before the Subcomm. on Antitrust and Monopoly of the Senate Comm. on the Judiciary, Pursuant to S.Res. 40, 89th Cong., 1st Sess. pt. 2 at 515 (1965).

ence or to inflict other competitive harm. If it acquires a firm with a large share of the target market, the possibility of price leadership may be significant. For example, if the firm is a price leader or otherwise participates in interdependent pricing in other markets where it operates, its propensities may suggest risks in the new market.

If these kinds of risks are present they should be taken into account in judging the merger. If there are no other bases for concern, this one ought not to preclude the merger unless the potentialities for leadership in the market seem quite clear and the propensities of the acquiring firm to exercise leadership are manifest. However, if there are also other competitive concerns, even a less fully developed disquiet about leadership possibilities might be drawn into the balance. For example, if the case against the merger on potential competition grounds seems marginal, the fact that the acquiring firm was much larger in absolute terms than others in the market might be enough to swing the scale against the merger.

In terrorem effects: While we cannot set vast store in a general analysis of the effects of relative size, we can pursue more specific inquiries into shadowed corners. Picture a high volume consumer-goods market. Now hypothesize this awesome firm: it is vastly larger than those already in the market. It has a reputation in its principal markets as a predator, a reputation based on some well-documented examples of localized price cutting to painfully low levels when regional firms disregarded its national price increases. It has a massive advertising budget and its general advertising program enables it to obtain substantial discounts on advertising for a new product if it adds one to its diversified line. Suppose that demand in a given consumer product market is expanding and that this firm enters that market by acquisition of a large firm. Is it not plausible to infer that its presence will discourage entry by others more than did the presence of the independent it replaces?

To generalize, an absolutely large firm (given the appropriate particular characteristics) may by its presence raise entry barriers. This may be due in part to actual advantages over existing firms—particularly scale economies of one kind or another. But some apparent scale advantages, like advertising or credit advantages, may result from monopsonistic or oligopsonistic power as a buyer.[26] And others, even though real, may have their major utility in extending power through brand differentiation. In part, entry barriers may arise because of conceptions of the large firm as aggressive and as having pockets deep enough to permit it to persist in any predatory foray until it gets its way.

If these kinds of problems arise in merger litigation, they ought to be analyzed in the light of the specific record made about condi-

---

26. A monopsonist is a firm with power as a buyer comparable to that a monopolist has as a seller. An oligopsonist is one of few buyers within a market which may act concertedly or interdependently.

tions in the particular industry. A court ought to be hesitant to find illegality on conceptions of this kind alone unless the objective evidence of industry structure and firm characteristics and subjective evidence of perceptions of existing firms about the entering firm all convincingly show the nature and seriousness of the competitive threat. On the other hand, a less forceful showing of danger that entry barriers may be increased through perceptions about the character of the large entrant may make more convincing a case against merger which seems marginal on potential competition grounds.

While the case law is sparse, what there is of it generally follows the approach outlined here. The majority in *Clorox* weighed *in terrorem* effects much as might a butcher weigh a thumb on the scale. In *Alcoa (Rome)* and *Ford (Autolite) in terrorem* concerns could be seen lurking below the surface. The opinion of then Circuit Judge Burger in *Reynolds Metals*[27] also merits note. Reynolds was the nation's largest producer of aluminum foil, and the FTC found its acquisition of Arrow, which converted foil for decoration of flower pots and foods, to violate Section 7. As in *Ford,* there were both vertical extension and foreclosure issues, as well as the potential of entry and an issue related to disparity of size. In affirming the Commission, the court placed the last of these issues in context:

> "The truer picture of anti-competitive effect emerges from even the most cursory consideration of the post-acquisition competitive postures of the eight previously independent florist foil convertors *vis a vis* one another. Arrow's assimilation into Reynolds' enormous capital structure and resources gave Arrow an immediate advantage over its competitors who were contending for a share of the market * * *. The power of the 'deep pocket' or 'rich parent' for one of the florist foil suppliers in a competitive group where previously no company was very large * * * opened the possibility and power to sell at prices approximating cost or below * * *. [T]he Commission on substantial evidence has additionally [found that] as an apparent consequence of retroactive price reductions for Arrow foil after the acquisition * * * sales of 5 of Arrow's 7 competitors had * * * dropped * * * [while] Arrow's sales [have] * * * increased * * *."[28]

Stressing that each factual situation has "its own atmosphere of economic freedom and viability or lack thereof," [29] the court invited a temperate analysis of these kinds of issues in each factual context where they arise.

---

27. Reynolds Metals Co. v. FTC, 309 F. 2d 223 (D.C.Cir. 1962).

28. Id. at 229–30.

29. Id. at 230.

Atmosphere is, without doubt, elusive stuff out of which to fashion a conclusion about whether a particular merger helps or hurts competition. If one were to challenge a merger solely or primarily on the basis of *in terrorem* effects, a more rigorous analysis should be demanded of the Commission and the court. But given other concerns, a vague and general atmosphere of threatened or possible predatory conduct may be enough.

Opportunity for predatory practices: The *in terrorem* issue focuses on perceptions of other firms in, or potentially in, the market. Objective evidence may be relevant, but only because of what may be inferred from it about these perceptions. Yet there is another way of looking at problems like that presented in *Reynolds*. It is to ask whether the merger enhances the opportunity for and likelihood of predatory conduct.

Though in *Reynolds* the FTC concerned itself with opportunity and conduct, the court of appeals seemed to imply that increased opportunity for predatory action might itself be a sufficient basis for finding a merger unlawful. Unless the record demonstrates enough explicit collateral circumstances to warrant a reliable prediction about the likelihood of predatory conduct, the notion that increased opportunity for such conduct will render a merger unlawful should be rejected. Any deep-pocket firm in any market has an opportunity for predatory conduct, but occasions on which it demonstrably occurs are probably rather rare. If in any situation one can reliably infer that, given the acquiring firm's propensities and the situation existing in the market it proposes to enter, predatory conduct is actually likely, or if one can conclude from post-acquisition evidence that predatory conduct occurred, the merger may properly be forbidden or undone. Unless there is a basis for such a finding, any sense that opportunity for predatory conduct is increased seems an unpersuasive reason for forbidding or undoing a merger.

d. *Toe-Hold Entry as an Alternative or a Defense*

If merger is the only or most convenient way to scale entry barriers, the situation may be such as to invite contrast between two or more potential partners for the acquiring firm. If acquisition of the subject firm seems to pose greater risk of competitive harm than would acquisition of an available smaller firm having the patents or other resources needed to provide a market toe-hold, caution would insist that merger with the larger firm be forbidden. Indeed, one might argue that in antitrust law reasonableness always necessitates that the less restrictive alternative be pursued.[30]

There is, however, another value involved—preserving an open market for capital assets. Unless the proposed merger can plausibly

---

30. In Bendix Corp. v. FTC, 450 F.2d 534 (6th Cir. 1971) the FTC had taken precisely this position; it was, however, reversed by the Court of Appeals on other grounds.

be seen as presenting a competitive problem of sufficient moment to engage the law's concern, to forbid it on the assumption that an even less troublesome alternative might be worked out would be a somewhat quixotic policy. The clear availability of a less problematic toe-hold opportunity may appropriately be given significance in cases where the proposed merger seems at least marginally harmful because of loss of potential competition. But the existence in the market being entered of a smaller firm with which a merger might have been worked out ought not to be allowed to turn any merger with a larger firm into a *per se* violation. Note also that where the concern about the merger proposed is not potential competition but disparities in absolute size, acquiring a smaller firm as an alternative may not meet the problem. If the perceived danger is that the large acquiring firm may become a price leader the risks are undoubtedly reduced by its acquiring a firm with a small market share. But if the risk is that after entry a large firm may act in a predatory way, the fact that it enters with a small vehicle rather than a large one may not be of great consequence.[31]

§ 206. Corporate Joint Ventures and Potential Competition

Potential competition doctrine has obscure and tangled ramifications as well as straightforward ones. Some of the former appear when two corporations jointly enter a market adjacent to their previous markets. A standard manner of proceeding is to establish a joint subsidiary—and that is enough to invoke the provisions of Section 7.

Suppose this situation: x, y and z are products so closely related that sequential extension from one to the other would be a normal course of corporate expansion; regions, p, q and r are adjacent geographic markets so related that expansion from one to another would be a normal development. All product and regional markets are concentrated. Now assume that firm A makes and sells product x in region p and firm C makes and sells product z in region r. Each has been considering expanding into other markets. Eventually they form a joint subsidiary, company B, which makes and sells: (1) product x in region r; or (2) product x in region q, or product y in region r; or (3) product y in region q. Does the formation of company B in any or all instances violate Section 7?

The sweeping contention at one extreme would be that firms A and C might each have entered any one or more of the nearby product and geographic markets and that any joint exploitation by them ends potential competition for these markets and is therefore unlaw-

---

31. Note that the toe-hold concept can also be used defensively. If acquisition is the only or optimum way to enter, and if the firm being acquired is the smallest or in other respects the least threatening firm through which entry could in fact be achieved, those facts might be presented in defense of a merger being challenged on potential competition grounds.

ful. For example, firm A might have made and sold its product x in region q, and then in region r, or skipped over q to move from p to r; it also might have moved from product x to y and then z, or skipped over y from x to z, or done any combination of these things. The possibilities for firm C are the inverse. If firms A and C enter jointly into any one of these markets they may be making a single entry where, had joint entry been forbidden, one might have entered alone, with the other remaining a potential competitor, or entry by both might even have occurred. At the other extreme one might argue that since any new entry is preferable to no entry, the appropriate response is to bless any joint entry by the two firms into any of these adjacent markets without indulging in speculation about the lost prospect of a double entry or of an entry by one alone with the other standing in the wings.

There are intermediate responses, and from the range of these we can perhaps find a better solution. The facts are intended to imply a greater likelihood of independent entry by one of the firms in some markets than in others. For example, it is probably more likely that firm A will move from product x to product y in its own region, p, or from region p to region q in its own product x, than it is that it will move through or over product y to product z or through or over region q to region r, or that it will move both to the next product y, and the next region q. Thus we might be more hesitant about A entering into a joint venture to make its current product x, in the next adjacent region q, or to make the next adjacent product y in its present region p, than we would about a joint venture which involved entry by A and by C jointly into a market, such as the product y/region q market, which is somewhat more remote for each, involving as it does two moves for each, a product change and a region change.

Two things should be emphasized as guides to analysis. First, a court should be slower to inhibit a joint entry into a market, since it adds one competitor to that market, than it would be to inhibit an acquisition by a firm outside of a market of a firm within, which adds no additional competitor (although it may revitalize an incumbent by changing management and resources). Second, by looking at the way the jointly entered market relates to the ones the joint venturers individually exploited, we may be able to make a judgment about the likelihood if joint entry were forbidden either (1) that individual entry would be made by both of the venturers or (2) that individual entry would be made by one of them with the other remaining a viable potential competitor.[1] To sharpen the analysis, assume that A and C

---

1. There is, of course, the implicit assumption that the entry is being made on a scale which adds a viable new competitor, not on so small a scale as to be trivial, nor on so large a scale as to threaten monopolization of the market entered. If a joint entry of the latter kind were made, it would

form B to make and sell y in region q. The possible negative effects are various. A is now less likely to move from product x to y or region p to q, and A certainly will not make both moves, as it otherwise might have done; C is now less likely to move from product z to y or region r to q, and will not do both, as it might have except for the venture. A and C are also less likely now to move all the way to the other's product or geographic market, or both, steps which might have developed at some point but which now would likely be disruptive of the good relations needed for the venture.

How consequential are these negative possibilities? Keep in mind that to avoid them we must sacrifice new entry into a concentrated market. By definition we have made the joint market one which lies on the course of normal development for each of the ventures, but for each it is probably two moves away, and it is far from certain that either would have ever taken even one of those moves, let alone that both of them would have taken both.

To attain a social situation as good in the subject market as the proposed joint venture, entry by at least one of the firms must occur. To attain a situation better than joint entry there must be entry by one and either entry by or significant potential competition from the other. By significant potential competition we mean potential competition which either (1) has a present market impact because the potential entrant is obvious to those in the market and seen by them as a likely entrant and thus a threat, in the face of which they moderate their conduct (a condition which will occur only if there is inadequate real competition in the market and few other potential competitors), or (2) is likely to develop in the future into an actual entry which will deconcentrate the market. The prior section explores the strands that feed this kind of analysis.[2] These must all be engaged here, but in a somewhat different light. Here, there is a considerable weight on the other side of the scale. Unless the likelihood of actual entry by one and significant potential competition from the other is sufficiently high to outweigh the deconcentrating effects of the actual new entry jointly proposed, the present joint entry does not tend to injure competition, but to aid it.

Penn-Olin,[3] which marks the current state of judicial art on this matter, does not insist that the costs and benefits be measured with

presumably violate Section 7 and possibly Sections 1 and 2 of the Sherman Act wholly regardless of how the firms might have acted if joint entry were forbidden. See Pitofsky, Joint Ventures under the Antitrust Laws: Some Reflections on the Significance of Penn-Olin, 82 Harv.L.Rev. 1007 (1969).

2. See § 205 supra.

3. United States v. Penn-Olin Chem. Co., 378 U.S. 158, 84 S.Ct. 1710, 12 L. Ed.2d 775 (1964). See also United States v. Monsanto Co., 1967 CCH Trade Cas. ¶ 72,001 (W.D.Pa.1967) (consent decree requiring American com-

an unpractical precision. It poses two questions and teaches that if both are answered affirmatively, the venture is unlawful. The questions are these: (1) Is it probable that, if the venture were forbidden, one of the firms would enter alone? (2) Is it probable that, if one firm entered, the other would either enter or remain in the wings as a viable potential competitor? Giving appropriate consideration to the gloss of later cases, where potential competition has been extrapolated in other settings,[4] we can fairly construe the last question as asking whether there would be significant potential competition in the sense outlined above.[5]

It must be remembered, of course, that the challenge to joint entry must be predicated not only on the likelihood of independent entry and potential competition but upon the existence of a structure sufficiently concentrated to give significance to the distinction between those two alternatives. If the market is already competitive, two firms, each of which had been planning to enter separately, could at the last minute join forces to make joint entry without threatening competitive injury; the difference between one new entry or two would not be competitively significant in such a market. Indeed, if *Penn-Olin* and later cases are taken at full value, if there were a large number of potential entrants, all as likely and as visible as the joint venturers, a finding that one would have entered and one would have maintained interest would not be enough to establish illegality even if the market were concentrated; the difference between the competitive effect of joint entry and single entry plus potential entry would be too slight to warrant the law's intervention.

pany to drop out of joint venture with foreign competitor).

4. E.g., United States v. El Paso Natural Gas Co., 376 U.S. 651, 84 S.Ct 1044, 12 L.Ed.2d 12 (1964); United States v. Falstaff Brewing Corp., 410 U.S. 526, 93 S.Ct. 1096, 35 L.Ed.2d 475 (1973). See generally § 205 supra, and cases there cited.

5. In *Penn-Olin*, supra note 3, the Court remanded the case for consideration of whether without the venture there would have been independent entry and potential entry. The district court, after hearing evidence on these, including subjective evidence from management, found that neither of the ventures would have entered independently and dismissed the complaint. United States v. Penn-Olin Co., 246 F. Supp. 917 (D.Del.1965). The Supreme Court affirmed per curiam by an equally divided court. 389 U.S. 308, 88 S.Ct. 502, 19 L.Ed.2d 545 (1967).

PART C. CONGLOMERATE MERGERS

§ 207. Competitive Effects and Other Social Concerns

A firm (or group of jointly owned or controlled firms) is a conglomerate if it operates in several unrelated markets—if, for example, it bakes bread, mines copper, and produces motion pictures. A merger is conglomerate if it links two firms each of which operates in a market or markets not horizontally or vertically related to any in which the other functions. During the late 1960's, as entrepreneurial energy was directed away from horizontal and vertical merger and into new avenues, conglomerate business organization took on a new importance and merger became the mechanism through which conglomerate firms, large and small, extended their activities into new markets. This "conglomerate merger movement" reached its height in 1968, when almost 4000 such mergers took place.[1]

There is an affinity between a conglomerate merger and what the courts have called a market extension merger; distinctions between them are matters of degree. For this reason, any merger defined as conglomerate could hurt competition for reasons which we considered and discussed in Part B.[2] Conglomerate merger may generate other harms which we have not considered elsewhere. The most important is an increase in opportunity for reciprocal dealing. Reciprocity requires a structure in which firms meet as seller to buyer in one (or more) markets and as buyer to seller in another (or others). These relationships could result from different vertical links along a single product line. Firm A may manufacture ingot; firm B may fabricate aluminum furniture; firm A may distribute or retail furniture. A, in the last capacity, can refuse to buy from B unless B buys ore from A. Obviously, opportunities for reciprocal arrangements are greatly enhanced if several firms operate in different markets.

Other effects associated with conglomeration relate to increases in overall industrial concentration. It is theorized, for example, that a conglomerate firm will more likely rely on "soft" competition than a firm in a single industry because of a fear that if it utilizes an oppor-

---

1. Federal Trade Commission Bureau of Economics, Current Trends in Merger Activity 1971, Table 6 (1972). See generally the discussions in J. Markham, Conglomerate Enterprise and Public Policy (1973); P. Areeda, Antitrust Policy, Problems, Text Cases 835–37 (2d ed. 1974).

2. See § 205 supra. Indeed, concepts like potential competition and disparity in size, which were considered in connection with market extension mergers, could as readily have been considered here. The choice to treat them as market extension concepts relates more to the fact that the Court, particularly in FTC v. Procter & Gamble (Clorox), 386 U.S. 568, 87 S.Ct. 1224, 18 L.Ed.2d 303 (1967), addressed those issues in connection with a transaction it labelled a market extension merger, rather than to anything intrinsic to market extensions which cannot occur in conglomerate mergers.

tunity to be aggressive in one market, it may suffer reprisals upon encountering its victims in other markets where the victims hold the whip hand.[3] There is also, as conglomeration expands, a danger of dilution of the functioning of capital markets. If a firm which mills wheat looks for capital to build a new plant, its performance as a miller can be evaluated by investors. If the firm also operates in several other unrelated markets, its performance as a miller may be hidden in conglomerate results. In consequence, investors may be enticed to support expansion of the milling operations with new capital which would have been withheld but for the confusions arising out of conglomeration.

Movement toward a structure in which large firms spanning many markets own larger and larger shares of productive assets may also be opposed on social and political grounds. From this vantage point a conglomerate merger adding discernibly to overall concentration—for example, the acquisition of one of the leading firms in any industry by a firm already affiliated with a leading firm or firms in any other industry or industries—might be challenged.

§ 208. The Section 7 Enforcement Effort to Date

Conglomeration was much in the news in the middle to late 1960's and was also the source of some Congressional concern. The head of the Antitrust Division took the position in 1967 that the present law did not reach conglomerate mergers and that new legislation was necessary. The Assistant Attorney General under the Nixon Administration, took a different view; several complaints were filed against conglomerate acquisition, beginning in 1969.[1] Developments to date do not establish conclusively which view of the law is correct. The series of cases initiated in 1969 all challenged acquisitions of leading firms by large conglomerates. Each set forth the novel claim that a merger was illegal because it was part of the current trend of acquisitions of dominant firms in concentrated markets by large companies and thus furthered increasing concentration of control of manufacturing assets. However, all of the cases also made more conventional assertions. They alleged reduction of potential competition and increased opportunity for reciprocity, and in some instances other accustomed harms.[2]

In any event, there have been no definitive rulings about conglomerate mergers which advance the inquiry far beyond *Procter &*

---

3. See Edwards, "Conglomerate Bigness as a Source of Power," in Business Concentration and Price Policy 331 (1955).

1. This history, with relevant citations, is reviewed in M. Handler, H. Blake,

R. Pitofsky & H. Goldschmid, Trade Regulation, Cases and Materials 1075–76 (1975).

2. Id.

*Gamble (Clorox).*³ In *Allis-Chalmers,*⁴ the merger was abandoned after a preliminary injunction issued; in *Ling-Temco-Vought,* major divestitures were ordered in a consent decree.⁵ However, IT&T brought the cases against it to trial. In the most comprehensive "pure conglomerate" opinion to date, IT&T's acquisition of Grinnell was found not to violate Section 7 on the basis of a conservative reading of the law and factual findings adverse to the government.⁶ In the *Hartford Fire*⁷ case a preliminary injunction was denied; in the *Canteen Corporation*⁸ case no violation was found. Finally, in a transaction with an infamous aura,⁹ the three cases were settled, pending appeals to the Supreme Court, by a consent decree which required divestiture of a division of Grinnell, Hamilton Life, and the Canteen Company plus either Hartford Fire, Avis, or Levitt & Sons.¹⁰

That summarizes the government's effort. Certainly no new legal principle has emerged; indeed the decision that yielded the most comprehensive opinion is cautious and not enlightening. Let us proceed, then, to summarize the bases on which a conglomerate merger may be attacked. In so doing, we must draw largely on somewhat earlier cases.

§ 209. Possible Bases for Illegality

a. Size Disparities and Potential Competition

The district court in *IT&T*¹ viewed the "entrenchment" aspect of the *Clorox*² case as applying only when a large firm enters a concentrated market by acquiring the dominant firm there and, because of promotional and marketing efficiencies accessible to the large firm, is

---

3. FTC v. Procter & Gamble Co., 386 U.S. 568, 87 S.Ct. 1224, 18 L.Ed.2d 303 (1967).

4. Allis-Chalmers Mfg. Co. v. White Consol. Indus. Inc., 414 F.2d 506 (3rd Cir. 1969), cert. denied 396 U.S. 1009, 90 S.Ct. 567, 24 L.Ed.2d 501 (1970).

5. United States v. Ling-Temco-Vought, Inc., 315 F.Supp. 1301 (W.D.Pa.1970).

6. United States v. IT&T Corp., (Grinnell) 324 F.Supp. 19 (D.Conn.1970).

7. United States v. IT&T Corp., 306 F. Supp. 766 (D.Conn.1969) (Hartford & Grinnell). In the same opinion a preliminary injunction against the Grinnell acquisition was denied.

8. United States v. IT&T Corp. (Canteen) 1971 CCH Trade Cas. ¶ 73,619 (N.D.Ill.1971).

9. See United States v. IT&T Corp. (Hartford), 349 F.Supp. 22 (D.Conn. 1972), aff'd sub nom. per curiam, Nader v. United States, 410 U.S. 919, 93 S.Ct. 1363, 35 L.Ed.2d 582 (1973).

10. United States v. IT&T Corp. (Canteen), 1971 CCH Trade Cas. ¶ 73,667 (N.D.Ill.1971); United States v. IT&T Corp. (Hartford & Grinnell), note 7 supra, appeal dismissed per stipulation, 404 U.S. 801, 92 S.Ct. 20, 30 L. Ed.2d 34 (1971), consent decrees entered, 1971 CCH Trade Cas. ¶ 73,665 (D.Conn.1971) (Grinnell), 1971 CCH Trade Cas. ¶ 73,666 (D.Conn.1971) (Hartford), 1972 CCH Trade Cas. ¶¶ 74,093 (D.Conn.1971).

1. United States v. IT&T Corp., 324 F. Supp. 19 (D.Conn.1970).

2. FTC v. Procter & Gamble Co., 386 U.S. 568, 87 S.Ct. 1224, 18 L.Ed.2d 303 (1967). See the discussion of entrenchment as a basis for illegality of a market extension merger in § 205, supra.

able to reinforce the dominant position of the acquired firm. But if *Clorox* stands for any principle at all it must be broader than that. The principle must cover entry by a large firm through acquisition of a dominant firm whenever *any* factor associated with the corporate personality of the large firm reduces the likelihood of a challenge to the dominant firm it has acquired. It is the effect of entrenchment, not the particular mechanism, which is central to the *Clorox* analysis.

Acceptance of this view reasonably leads to another. A size disparity between the acquiring firm and those in the acquired firm's market might adversely effect competition even if the acquired firm were not dominant in the market. Entrenchment of a dominant firm is itself but a mechanism, one that represents a type. Even if the acquired firm was not dominant, its acquisition by the larger firm may serve to facilitate interdependence or otherwise damage competition. The new status of the acquired firm may assist it to become a price leader, for example, or may create *in terrorem* effects which hurt competition. If these are the effects, a purely conglomerate merger ought to be just as vulnerable to challenge as a geographic market extension would be. Similar comments are warranted about potential competition: if the circumstances are substantially the same as those which would lead to illegality of a market extension merger due to dampening of potential competition, a conglomerate merger ought likewise to be unlawful.[3]

b. *Reciprocity*

Reciprocity can be challenged directly under Section 1,[4] but a merger may also be challenged as an instrumental step toward reciprocity. It was settled by *Consolidated Foods*[5] that a merger creating a structure conducive to reciprocity can be violative, at least where post-merger evidence shows that reciprocity was actually used or attempted. The district court holding in *General Dynamics*[6] is in accord with this view. *Consolidated Foods* is sometimes construed broadly—in *Allis-Chalmers*[7] and *Ingersoll-Rand*,[8] mergers were enjoined preliminarily because they created a reciprocity potential, and

---

3. See § 205 supra.

4. See § 171 supra.

5. FTC v. Consolidated Foods Corp., 380 U.S. 592, 85 S.Ct. 1220, 14 L.Ed.2d 95 (1965). See also Allis-Chalmers Mfg. Co. v. White Consol. Indus., Inc., 414 F.2d 506 (3rd Cir. 1969), cert. denied, 396 U.S. 1009, 90 S.Ct. 567, 24 L.Ed.2d 501 (1970); United States v. IT&T Corp., 306 F.Supp. 766 (D.Conn. 1969), appeal dismissed per stipulation, 404 U.S. 801, 92 S.Ct. 20, 30 L. Ed.2d 34 (1971); United States v. Northwest Indus. Inc., 301 F.Supp. 1066 (N.D.Ill.1969).

6. United States v. General Dynamics Corp., 415 U.S. 486, 94 S.Ct. 1186, 39 L.Ed.2d 530 (1974).

7. Allis-Chalmers Mfg. Co. v. White Consol. Indus., Inc., supra note 5.

8. United States v. Ingersoll-Rand Co., 320 F.2d 509 (3d Cir. 1963).

without evidence that reciprocity had been used. But *Consolidated Foods* has also been read more narrowly—in *Penick & Ford*[9] and *Northwest Industries*,[10] structural change facilitating reciprocity was held not to be a basis for prohibiting merger where the firms involved had established policies against using reciprocity.

When a merger creates a greater opportunity for some other unlawful conduct, such as tying, courts have not held the merger invalid for that reason alone. The notion that a merger facilitating reciprocity ought to be unlawful is, then, a novel one. Different treatment for a merger facilitating reciprocity than for one facilitating some other offense might be justified on the ground that reciprocity is peculiarly difficult to identify if any subtlety is used. Nevertheless, the adverse effects of a particularly subtle program of reciprocity are not likely to be very serious. Hence, a court should be slow to forbid a merger, especially one which promises real benefits, such as discernible efficiencies, on the sole ground that the merger creates a structure in which reciprocity might more easily occur.

PART D. VERTICAL MERGERS

§ 210. Competitive Effects

Vertical merger issues have commanded considerable attention from the Supreme Court and have stimulated considerable commentary. Despite this, vertical issues do not loom large in any balanced view of the "merger problem" or merger litigation. But this is not to say that vertical merger creates no competitive concern. Let us look at the ways in which it may do so.

When a firm acquires a supplier or customer, the possible effects are similar to those which would be achieved if the firm had integrated backward or forward by *de novo* entry at the vertically adjacent level, or those which might be achieved by looser forms of contractual integration, such as requirements contracts. The purpose and effect of vertical integration, by merger or otherwise, may be cost reduction. Greater efficiency will be achieved by such integration when the transaction costs of buying and selling between the two vertical levels are relatively high and when decisions about the manner and quantities in which outputs at the two sequential levels should be produced tend to be stable, so that the value of a rapid, current flow of market data is relatively low. Vertical integration may also be utilized for other purposes: to avoid being a price victim of an upstream or downstream monopolist; to avoid dependence upon an already vertically integrated competitor either as a supplier (which in times of short supply might prefer itself) or as a customer

---

9. United States v. Penick & Ford, Ltd., 242 F.Supp. 518 (D.N.J.1963).

10. United States v. Northwest Indus. Inc., supra note 5.

(which in times of weak demand might prefer itself), or which might try to drive the dependent firm out by predatory discrimination in prices asked or bid.

Despite these seemingly wholesome purposes, vertical merger, like other forms of vertical integration, can have adverse effects.[1] Let us count the ways.

a. Foreclosure

Just as it can be used defensively to avoid being foreclosed by an already integrated firm, vertical merger can be a device to foreclose other unintegrated competitors—or, whatever its purpose, may have that effect. Though defensive as to those already vertically integrated, any vertical merger can be a threat to any remaining firms which are not integrated. Suppose a manufacturer, firm M, which makes 10% of a product acquires firm D, which distributes 15% of that product. Ten to fifteen percent of the market available to M's competitors may disappear. If other firms are already integrated, the percentage may be much higher; M's 15% of the total sales of the product could be, say, 50% of the sales of that product by unintegrated competitors. Whatever the motive of the integration, its impact in foreclosing customers and potential customers of unintegrated firms may be so severe that some of the unintegrated firms will be driven from the market, thus increasing concentration. This is not inevitable, however, even when a large portion of the previously unintegrated part of the market is linked. The newly integrated firms M and S may have dealt with each other to the same degree before the merger as after, so that unintegrated firms lose no otherwise available cutomers by reason of the merger. Or if firm S after the merger stops buying from others (say X and Y) and starts buying from M, then M will (if it continues to produce at the same volume) stop supplying some of its former customers, which will then look to the other producers (like X and Y who are looking for new customers to replace S's former volume). Unless M keeps all its old customers and *expands* to meet S's needs, competitors of M will suffer only a disruption of relationships, not a market foreclosure.

b. Supply Squeeze

As a vertical merger could be defensive as against a predator, it could also set the stage for predatory conduct. If firm S's competitors must rely on firm M for supplies, M can charge them more than it charges S, thus putting them at a disadvantage in competing with

---

1. See generally, F. Scherer, Industrial Market Structure and Economic Performance 69 et seq. (1971); Holton, "The Role of Competition and Monopoly in Distribution," in Competition, Cartels and Their Regulation 284 (J. Miller, ed. 1962), P. Areeda, Antitrust Analysis, Problems, Text, Cases ¶¶ 604–609, 611 (2d ed. 1974).

S.[2] Indeed, S could also cut prices, making it more difficult for the competitors. This course would not be costless, however. The integrated firm M–S would have to forego present profits to apply the squeeze, a course which would be sensible only if it foresaw future profits arising from a sufficiently great enhancement of its market power to repay the current costs of its predatory conduct. Future profits at such high levels are conceivable, though perhaps not very likely in most settings. M could hope to drive out S's competitors, thus achieving higher concentration at S's level. If that concentration were high enough, monopoly profits might be earned. Short of that, S might, with the new structure, earn supra-competitive returns based on cartelization or interdependence with the few remaining competitors at its level. Achievement of such goals, however, would depend upon entry barriers high enough to keep others out after the new, denser level of concentration had been achieved. A related but different reason for applying the squeeze would be to preserve a cartel or a system of interdependent pricing already established at firm S's level. If S's competitors started to "cheat" by reducing prices, M might squeeze long enough to discipline them.

c. *Need for Integrated Entry*

Besides foreclosure effects and squeeze possibilities, the linking of firms M and S, if it appreciably reduces the unintegrated sector, or forms part of a trend which does so, may reduce the likelihood of independent entry at either level. A firm considering entry at M's level may conclude that to enter at minimum efficient scale, it would need to attract too large a share of the unintegrated portion of the customer market away from existing firms to make success likely; a firm considering entry at S's level may feel it would have to bid away from present customers too large a portion of the unintegrated portion of the supply market. Entry at both levels might still be possible; but now any inhibition on entry at either level will affect both levels. Profits may be high enough at one level to attract entry there, but not high enough at both to attract the larger investment needed for entry at both levels. Moreover, the skills, technology or other resources needed for entry at one level may be readily available, while those needed for entry at the other may not be. Also the minimum efficient scale at one level may be a smaller percentage of total production than at the other level; linking the levels so that entry at both becomes necessary extends the scale barriers at the level at which those barriers are highest to both levels.

d. *Product Differentiation*

The Merger Guidelines stress that not only foreclosures but also product differentiation, a process which inhibits competition, can be

---

2. The legality of discrimination such as that here supposed under the price discrimination law is discussed in Chapter 8 infra.

facilitated by integration.[3] An unintegrated firm, S, as a wholesaler or retailer selling the goods of various manufacturers either at the same time or from time to time, may find it profitable to emphasize similarities between firm M's product and that of other manufacturers; S may compete by stressing the quality of its own delivery or repair service, through displays, or on the basis of price, rather than by hawking what is unique about a given manufacturer's goods. Once linked with firm M, however, S will act differently. It will stress the special value of firm M's product, thus helping to insulate M somewhat from price competition with makers of other, differentiated products.

e. *Countervailing Power Diminished*

If firm M has market power, it may nevertheless shade prices for independent firm S, if the latter is a particularly large buyer, and this may lead to softening of the oligopolistic (or monopolistic) price structure generally.[4] By integrating with S, firm M may be able to soften this basis for instability in the supra-competitive pricing structure.

f. *Ending Potential Competition*

In one of its aspects, a vertical merger is a special case of a market extension merger. For example, firms upstream from a market may be among the most likely entrants into it. If one of them enters by merger it decreases by one the array of potential *de novo* entrants. There may of course be other adjacent firms, those making the same product at the same horizontal level but in different geographic areas, those making a related product which might diversify into the market in question, and those related vertically on the downstream side. The loss of potential competition due to a vertical merger may be relatively inconsequential. Nevertheless, when vertical merger occurs this aspect should be evaluated. If firm M acquires S, then M is removed as a potential *de novo* entrant into S's market and S is removed as a potential *de novo* entrant into M's market. Should either of those markets be highly concentrated, and should the loss of the potential entrant remove a present competitive force or a likely future *de novo* entrant, competition will have been injured.

g. *Analysis of Particular Mergers*

To make any judgment at all about the likely competitive effects of a specific vertical merger, one must know something about particulars. How is the upstream market defined? The downstream market? How concentrated are these markets? What share of each will the newly linked firm hold? What share of each is held by previously integrated firms, and how much remains free? What is the

---

3. Department of Justice Merger Guidelines § 11 (1968).

4. See Scherer, supra note 1 at 242–249.

purpose of the merger? Is it likely to result in exclusive dealing between the acquired and acquiring firms? Does it yield substantial cost savings? What percentage of the previously unintegrated portion of the upstream (or downstream) market does it tie up, and thus actually or potentially foreclose from unintegrated downstream (or upstream) buyers? Is the merger defensive? Is it part of a series of such responses by firms in the industry, or is it likely to initiate a defensive reaction among others? Are there significant entry barriers in either or both of these markets? Does the merger add to these? To the opportunity for predatory conduct? If so, would predation seem a sensible strategy?

The relevance of these questions is apparent and is in any event related to analysis done with respect to other kinds of vertical integration.[5] We shall proceed to discuss some of these issues further in connection with particular merger decisions and problem areas.

§ 211. Substantial Foreclosures in Concentrated Markets

It is time to turn from the mechanisms through which competitive impact is transmitted to the law's ways of generalizing about these myriad particulars. In vertical merger cases, as elsewhere, the law must simplify; it does so in the now familiar way. It starts by defining relevant markets, and then asks what percentage of the unintegrated portions of the upstream and downstream markets are being linked by the merger. "What share of the customer or supply market is being foreclosed?" is the way the inquiry is put. In *Brown Shoe*,[1] the Court labelled this datum as a starting point for analysis. It indicated that the percentage foreclosed would not be determinative of illegality unless it approached monopoly proportions nor determinitive of legality unless it was *de minimis*. Any foreclosure percentage between these bounds called for a broad-gauged inquiry into the particular consequences of the merger in its own particular settings.

But *Brown Shoe* also taught other things, some of which would later return to mute or even contradict that dictum. One of these was the ever present need to work out ways to handle merger cases with which courts could adequately cope. Another was that the Congress which enacted Section 7 cared about things like local control of business, ease of market access for small entrepreneurs, and an environment in which established small firms might prosper or at least survive. In *Brown Shoe* itself there is reference to the possibility

---

5. See § 165 supra.

1. Brown Shoe Co. v. United States, 370 U.S. 294, 82 S.Ct. 1502, 8 L.Ed.2d 510 (1962).

that locally controlled units will come increasingly under national control.[2]

The cases following *Brown Shoe* show a considerable change in the law of vertical merger. *Brown Shoe,* of course, involved horizontal as well as vertical elements and it will be recalled that as to horizontal aspects, merger law was simplified by the announcement in *Philadephia Bank*[3] of a rule creating a rebuttable presumption of illegality on the basis of concentration and share data alone. No such presumption has been announced for vertical mergers. However, a reading of the cases suggests that, operationally, such a presumption exists. There has been, at least in the dominant judicial attitude reflected in the cases, a transposition of the doctrine announced in *Philadelphia Bank* from the horizontal to the vertical realm.

Note this about the Supreme Court vertical merger cases: *Du Pont (G. M.),*[4] decided even before *Brown Shoe,* predicated illegality on a foreclosure of about 20 to 25 percent. *Brown Shoe* itself involved a 5% foreclosure, but other factors were also present, most importantly reinforcement of a trend. In *Ford (Autolite),*[5] the automobile and spark plug markets were highly concentrated and an acquisition which foreclosed 15 percent of the spark plug market was held to be unlawful. As to the vertical case nothing else was shown, though a case based on a market extension analysis was also presented. Furthermore, note this about lower court vertical cases: *Standard Oil (Potash)*[6] predicated illegality on concentration and the linking of 2 percent in the customer market with about 18 percent in the supply market. *Reynolds Metals (Arrow)*[7] predicated illegality on concentration and a 33 percent foreclosure in a (softly defined) downstream market. While none of these cases expressly announces a presumption like that in *Philadelphia Bank,* the tone in every one of them is critical of any vertical merger in any concentrated market which entails substantial foreclosure. Not one displays any appetite for actually *doing* the kind of detailed analysis of competitive effects which *Brown Shoe* talked about doing.

2. Id. at 315–16, 82 S.Ct. at 1518–19, 8 L.Ed.2d at 530. Alacrity to protect existing small competitors is not necessarily inconsistent with insistence that Section 7 is aimed only at forbidding structural change which theatens competitive process. The merger which the act forbids in order to stop greater concentration might have made the market especially uncongenial for some of the existing small firms.

3. United States v. Philadelphia Nat'l Bank, 374 U.S. 321, 83 S.Ct. 1715, 10 L.Ed.2d 915 (1963). See § 204(b) supra.

4. United States v. E. I. Du Pont De Nemours & Co., 353 U.S. 586, 77 S.Ct. 872, 1 L.Ed.2d 1057 (1957).

5. Ford Motor Co. v. United States, 405 U.S. 562, 92 S.Ct. 1142, 31 L.Ed.2d 492 (1972).

6. United States v. Standard Oil Co. (Potash), 253 F.Supp. 196 (D.N.J.1966).

7. Reynolds Metals Co. v. FTC, 309 F.2d 223 (D.C.Cir. 1962).

In point of fact, then, a court no longer needs (if it ever did) to analyze in depth the factual nuances of a merger when the degree of foreclosure proves neither *de minimis* nor overbearingly large. If the market is concentrated and the merger forecloses a portion which in the general context seems substantial, the government's *prima facie* case seems to have been made. This presumptive approach (as well as the response to a vertical integration trend discussed in section 212) simplifies considerably the government's litigation burden. If the share foreclosed is high enough, the prosecutor need not articulate any particular theory about why the merger is injurious; it need only insist that it is. The presumption and trend concepts also reduce significantly the threshold above which a vertical merger is likely to be successfully challenged.

Viewed from the vantage point of neo-classical economic analysis, this approach is no doubt overinclusive in its prohibitions. Despite that conclusion, the rule may be salutory and "right" in the sense of being harmonious with the purpose of Congress, as illuminated by the legislative history, and the continuing attitude of Congress toward industrial structure, manifested with sufficient frequency and clarity to become part of the statutory tradition. The presumptive approach protects competition and conserves judicial energy. It discourages vertical merger generally and invites entrepreneurs to look for other outlets, such as vertical integration by *de novo* entry at adjacent levels, or merger or entry into other markets entirely. At least to a degree, the current approach protects competitors too, perhaps some that would not long survive in a rigorously efficient market structure. But the cases do not make protecting competitors the central mission and, in doing so at all, concede something to the populist pulses that give rhythm to the statute. This degree of judicial populism may help to maintain for Section 7 that consensus of public support which in the long run it needs to remain a viable national policy. If significant efficiencies are indeed to be attained by vertical integration, the firm seeking them can enter *de novo*.[8] If the prohibition against merger is overbroad and if the integration would yield economies, the prohibition unfortunately precludes what may be the most efficient and least disruptive way for firms to achieve those

---

8. While there are cases indicating that if a firm at one level integrates to the next downstream level it may not take action to keep its customers at that level from competing with it (e.g. Roux Distrib. Co. Inc., 55 F.T.C. 1386 (1959); United States v. Revlon, 1964 CCH Trade Cas. ¶ 71,040 (S.D.N. Y.1964); Belliston v. Texaco, Inc., 455 F.2d 175 (10th Cir.), cert. denied 408 U.S. 928, 92 S.Ct. 2494, 33 L.Ed.2d 341 (1972)), it is perfectly clear that vertical integration by independent entry is not itself an offense, unless under all the circumstances it constitutes monopolization or attempt to monopolize. See United States v. Columbia Steel Co., 334 U.S. 495, 524–25, 68 S. Ct. 1107, 1122–23, 92 L.Ed. 1533, 1552–53 (1948). See also Hanson v. Shell Oil Co., 1976–2 CCH Trade Cas. ¶ 61,052 (9th Cir. 1976). See generally Handler, Blake, Pitofsky & Goldschmid, Trade Regulation, Cases and Materials 766–792 (1975).

economies; but it does not foreclose attainment of those economies altogether.

The degree of concentration needed to make a market subject to the presumptive approach seems generally comparable to that needed for the *Philadelphia Bank* presumption. Thus, the level of foreclosure required to invoke the "presumption" is suggested, perhaps, by the cases referred to above.[9] The Justice Department's Merger Guidelines[10] threaten any vertical merger where the upstream firm has 10% or more of its market and the downstream firm has 6% or more. While these shares are lower than the cases to date indicate would suffice, absent other factors such as a trend, an indication of anticompetitive intent, or the erection of higher entry barriers, they are at least suggestive; surely the point at which courts begin to react presumptively is not vastly higher. As a rough guide one might expect presumptive responses to begin at least by the point where a firm with a share of 15% or so of a concentrated market forecloses 10 or 12% or so of customers or sources of supply.

§ 212. Relevance of a Trend Toward Vertical Integration

The existence of a trend toward greater market concentration is an important factor in assessing the legality of a horizontal merger;[1] for similar reasons, a trend toward greater concentration in the upstream or downstream market (or both) will heighten concerns about a vertical merger. We do not worry about vertical merger in unconcentrated markets; no firm will be foreclosed by the merger if there are many other sellers or buyers with which it can deal. But the level of concentration at which vertical merger will begin to worry us will fall if we see the present level as a point on a scale of ever increasing concentration—that much is clear from *Brown Shoe*[2] alone. The more enticing question is whether a trend toward vertical integration, or a trend toward such integration by merger, will alter a court's response to a vertical merger independently of a concentration trend.

Put to one side the instance of an integration trend between two wholly unconcentrated levels of production; that is the limiting case which undergirds basic doctrine, not a situation likely to be encountered. If 100 manufacturers of equal size sell to 1000 distributors of equal size which sell to 100,000 retailers of equal size a trend toward the linkage of 10 distributors and 100 retailers with each manufacturer ought not to concern us unduly. One hundred integrated units is still too many to significantly enhance risks of non-competitive performance. The trend which may yield socially valuable efficiencies

---

9. See cases cited in notes 1, 3, 4, 5, 6 and 7, supra.

10. Department of Justice Merger Guidelines §§ 12–13 (1968).

1. See § 204(c) supra.

2. Brown Shoe Co. v. United States, 370 U.S. 294, 82 S.Ct. 1502, 8 L.Ed.2d 510 (1962).

and threatens no harms ought not to call down the statutory prohibition.

But what of the instance when concentration is high enough so that a merger foreclosing a significant share would be forbidden, yet where a particular merger involves only a rather modest foreclosure, say, two percent or so. Does the existence of a trend toward vertical integration result in forbidding that merger which, absent such a trend, would not be interdicted? *Brown Shoe*[3] suggests that it does. Though that position has been criticized as displaying a confusion between a concentration trend and an integration trend, it is not that easily faulted. Assuming a level of concentration which warrants reaction to foreclosures which exceed some assumed threshold, a merger which does not exceed that threshold logically takes on a new significance if, as part of a sequence of mergers, it will with those other mergers aggregate to a foreclosure exceeding the assumed threshold. For instance, it might be conceded that in a market with an eight firm concentration ratio of 80%, an acquisition by a firm with 10% or more which foreclosed 6% or more of the available customers would warrant concern. If so, a merger by such a firm in such a market ought to generate concern even if it foreclosed only 1 or 2 percent if that acquisition was one of a series by which that firm had foreclosed or threatened to foreclose 6% or more of the market. It might also cause concern if it was part of a sequence by which that firm and others threaten to foreclose a significant percentage of all customers.

The case law is consistent with this view. *Brown Shoe* itself clearly entailed a trend toward vertical integration. Chief Justice Warren referred to a finding of a "definite trend among shoe manufacturers to acquire retail outlets."[4] As to this trend the data were convincing. He also referred to a trend indicating a reduction in the number of plants manufacturing shoes, and to some decrease in the number of firms doing so; but the data—1,077 firms in 1947 and almost 10 percent less in 1954—even if it marked a trend toward reduced numbers of firms, could hardly be labelled as a trend toward anything we would fairly call "concentration." Indeed, the Court took the "trend" into account in assessing the vertical aspects of the merger and invalidated the merger in part because of a vertical foreclosure which, viewed apart from the trend, would seem exceedingly small. Though in doing so the Court labelled the trend as one "toward concentration," the findings and evidence to which the opinion alludes really showed a trend toward integration.[5] The Merger Guidelines also take the view that mergers aggregating toward a level of foreclosure which is of concern ought to be inhibited and, in-

---

3. Id.

4. Id. at 301, 82 S.Ct. at 1510, 8 L.Ed. 2d at 521.

5. Id. at 332–33, 82 S.Ct. at 1527–28, 8 L.Ed.2d at 540.

deed, speak of a "trend toward vertical integration" which may increase entry barriers.[6]

§ 213. Other Bases for Illegality

The relationships between the possible competitive effects suggested in section 210 and the principal bases of illegality summarized in sections 211 and 212 are anything but direct; by and large courts have made significant concentration (or a trend toward it) and significant foreclosure (or a trend toward it) surrogates for a showing of competitive injury. Doing this, as we have noted, leads to over inclusion; mergers which would appear competitively benign if fully understood are caught in the law's trailing web. But the law's blunt statement fails of perfection in the opposite direction as well. If we evaluate vertical mergers largely blind to all concerns except high concentration and substantial foreclosure, we may miss also some threatened competitive injuries which a nicer discrimination would show.

We have seen that the ways in which vertical merger might threaten competition are numerous; the possible ways in which a vertical merger could be illegal will thus not be readily catalogued. In general, we must conclude that an evidentiary showing of threatened significant injury of any one or more of the types reviewed in section 210 would make out a *prima facie* case even if the foreclosure percentages were relatively modest. Also, there may be unique situations were special characteristics of the structure render a merger dangerous despite a lower foreclosure effect than is usually thought to be critical. Examples of other bases for illegality follow.

a. Linking Regulated to Non-regulated Levels

Vertical integration between a firm in a regulated and a firm in a non-regulated sector presents its own uncommon problems which may amplify the significance of any given degree of foreclosure. If a supplier merges with a firm in a market to which entry is restricted, foreclosure problems are intensified. Not only will there be a limited number of possible customers at the level where entry is restricted, but to the extent the foreclosure discourages entry at that level by unintegrated firms, it may inhibit entry entirely. Even if a firm had the resources, skill and will to enter on an integrated basis, the public restriction on entry at the regulated level would have to be surmounted. If, by contrast, the regulated level were unconnected to the supply level, any firm could enter the supply level and bid for customers at the regulated level.

Note, too, that the rationalization that the integration must be efficient or else management would not integrate is even less credible here than usual. Management has in this instance an important

---

6. Department of Justice Merger Guidelines § 14(a) (1968).

non-efficiency goal. By integrating, it may be able to take supra-competitive profits at the supply level, thus evading the regulatory restraint on exploiting its franchise by taking such profits at the regulated level.[1]

b. Facilitating Price Discrimination

Vertical merger between a supplier and customer may facilitate discrimination which, without the merger, arbitrage would have precluded. If in that context the discrimination ought to be subject to challenge, the merger facilitating it might be forbidden as instrumental to the discrimination.

c. Multiple Acquisitions at the Same Level

As Mississippi River Corp. v. FTC[2] exemplifies, there may be a challenge to sequential acquisitions where a firm at one level integrates with two or more suppliers or customers; irrespective of effects normally associated with vertical mergers, these acquisitions have a horizontal aspect in that two or more units at one level are being brought under common ownership and control. This element should, of course, be analyzed as would a horizontal merger between those units.

§ 214. Efficiency and Other Justifications

Judicial language is coldly inhospitable to efficiency claims as justifications for merger.[1] Yet, commentators incline to the view that the attitude is not so hostile as the broad statements seem to imply.[2] Let us hope that this is so. With respect to vertical mergers, where sequential operations can be effectively linked, real efficiency claims are often quite plausible. Since the competitive harms consequent upon vertical merger are often conjectural, especially when analysis is pushed no further than to identify the existence of concentration in one or both markets and a seemingly material percentage foreclosure, a court ought to hesitate to disdain efficiency evidence completely.

---

1. Compare United States v. Yellow Cab Co., 332 U.S. 218, 67 S.Ct. 1560, 91 L.Ed. 2010 (1947). IT&T Corp. v. GT&E Corp., 351 F.Supp. 1153 (D. Haw.1972), rev'd in part 518 F.2d 913 (9th Cir. 1975) (ATRR No. 713), surveys some of these issues. IT&T, a competitor of GTE in the manufacture and sale of electronic and other equipment used by operating telephone companies, brought a private action under Section 7 challenging GTE's acquisitions of operating telephone companies. The district court found for IT&T and ordered structural relief. The Ninth Circuit, however, reversed in part.

2. Mississippi River Corp. v. FTC, 454 F.2d 1083 (8th Cir. 1972).

1. See § 204(h) supra. See also Department of Justice Merger Guidelines § 14 (1968).

2. E.g., M. Handler, R. Blake, R. Pitofsky, H. Goldschmid, Trade Regulation, Cases and Materials 918–22 (1975). An important case which, though it involved vertical integration by a requirements contract rather than a merger, suggests that efficiencies must be weighed in favor of the integration is Tampa Electric Co. v. Nashville Coal Co., 365 U.S. 320, 81 S.Ct. 623, 5 L.Ed.2d 580 (1961).

This much, at least, is in order. If the government's case relies on the conventional numerology—a mere showing that the markets are concentrated (say an eight firm ratio of 80%) and that the supplier or customer share foreclosed is significant (say 6 percent), or, if lower, that there is an integration trend—then, if the defendant convincingly shows significant cost savings based on the integration, the government's *prima facie* case should be held to have been overcome. To win, in the face of clear and significant real efficiencies, the government ought to be forced to prove the competitive injury it fears with greater precision and a higher order of probability. In essence the broad, analytical approach called for in *Brown Shoe*[3] should be refurbished once efficiencies are made to appear. A foreclosure which is neither *de minimis* nor overwhelming may yet be the basis for forbidding a vertical merger even though it yields efficiencies, but in such cases, at least, "the percentage of the market foreclosed * * * cannot itself be decisive * * *. [I]t becomes necessary to undertake an examination of various economic and historical factors in order to determine * * *" legality.[4] If it would overrun efficiencies, the government must carry the burden of proving its case fully, and without the benefit of any presumption tied to the percentage of foreclosure.

Furthermore, though the government may appropriately be taken to have made out a *prima facie* case when it shows concentration and a significant foreclosure, the sponsors of the merger ought to be permitted to show in order to offset the *prima facie* case not just that efficiencies are achieved but, alternatively, that despite the apparent foreclosure, competition is not significantly impaired. For example, the sponsors might show that entry is easy at the foreclosed level, that a firm wishing to enter the foreclosing level could relatively easily enter both, or encourage others to enter the foreclosed level. Or it might be shown that the minimum efficient scale of operations at the foreclosing level is so small that the still unintegrated firms at the foreclosed level would constitute a relatively wide range of customers (or suppliers) for a firm entering at the foreclosing level.

An analysis based on the business compulsions of the system may also be relevant to show the unlikeliness of adverse effects. Suppose the auto industry were disaggregated, with three firms making automotive engines, each with one-third of the market, and twen-

---

3. Brown Shoe Co. v. United States, 370 U.S. 294, 82 S.Ct. 1502, 8 L.Ed.2d 510 (1962). The position the Court stated in *Brown Shoe* was not rigorously applied even in the case itself. The actual decision in *Brown Shoe* treated the achievement of efficiency through vertical integration as a negative factor because it would make the commercial environment less congenial to small enterprises. Obviously, the congressional concern for small business should not be ignored. But it would be an extreme response to forbid a merger on this social and political ground even though the merger yielded real efficiencies and did not threaten competition in the economic sense.

4. Id. at 329, 82 S.Ct. at 1526, 8 L.Ed. 2d at 538.

ty firms assembling automobiles, each having about 5%, and that an auto assembler acquired one of the engine producers. The engine market is highly concentrated and the auto market marginally so. On a Guideline approach, the foreclosure of one-third of supply would be of grave concern.[5] But should we not consider the alternative investments involved and ask whether the buyer realistically could expand from 5% to utilize 33% of engine output if it were disposed to do so, and whether, given its investment in the engine producing facilities, it could conceivably *afford* to withhold supplies from others, or could afford to discriminate, or the like.[6] The Chicago school contention that vertical integration never makes things worse is overbroad; but there may be particular factual situations where the conventional Chicago arguments about the constraints on the anti-competitive use of vertical connections have considerable force.

PART E. REMEDIES

§ 215. Preliminary Relief

The key issue in a merger case may be whether a temporary restraining order and a preliminary injunction will issue under Section 15 of Clayton, which authorizes such temporary and preliminary relief as shall be deemed just.[1] If an order maintaining the status quo is granted, the proponents may abandon merger plans;[2] if it is not, the government has on occasion discontinued suit,[3] or has found itself incapable of attaining wholly satisfactory permanent relief at the end

---

5. Department of Justice Merger Guidelines §§ 12–13 (1968).

6. See generally P. Areeda, Antitrust Policy, Problems, Text, Cases ¶ 609 (2d ed. 1974).

1. 38 Stat. 736, 15 U.S.C.A. § 25. By Section 16 preliminary relief is also authorized in private actions. 38 Stat. 737, 15 U.S.C.A. § 26. See Lewis, Preliminary Injunctions in Government Section 7 Litigation, 17 Antitrust Bull 1 (1972). The Hart-Scott-Rodino Antitrust Improvement Act of 1976, Public Law 97–435 (Sept. 30, 1976) requires certain companies with $100 million or more in sales or assets to give a 30 day pre-merger notification of proposed acquisitions of $15 million in stock or assets or 15% of the voting securities of any company with $10 million or more in sales or assets. This act, passed as a compromise measure, would facilitate pre-merger investigations and greatly enhance the potential for preliminary relief. See Appendix D, infra p. 850.

2. Temporary orders led to abandonment of mergers in, e.g., United States v. Chrysler Corp., 232 F.Supp. 651 (D. N.J.1964); United States v. Allied Chem. Corp., 1964 CCH Trade Cas. ¶ 71,311 (S.D.N.Y.1965); United States v. Ingersoll-Rand Co., 218 F.Supp. 530 (W.D.Pa.1963), aff'd 320 F.2d 509 (3rd Cir. 1963). On other occasions merger plans have been abandoned on the filing of a government suit. This occurred in United States v. Standard Oil Co., 147 ATRR A–19 (S.D.Cal.1964) and United States v. America Corp., 1963 CCH Trade Cas. ¶ 70,923 (S.D. Cal.1963).

3. In United States v. FMC Corp., 218 F.Supp. 817 (N.D.Cal.1963), appeal dismissed 321 F.2d 534 (9th Cir. 1963) application for temporary injunction denied, 84 S.Ct. 4, 11 L.Ed.2d 20 (1963), the government dropped the suit after unsuccessful efforts to obtain temporary relief. See the discussion in E. Rockefeller, Antitrust Questions and Answers 225–37 (1974).

of successful merger litigation because of changes which the merger has brought about.[4]

Preliminary relief is warranted on a showing of reasonable probability that the government (or private plaintiff) will prevail on the merits and that the balance of inconvenience to the proponents if such relief is granted is less than the danger to the public if it is not.[5] If the potential for serious and immediate injury to competition seems slight (as, perhaps in a marginal vertical foreclosure case, or a horizontal acquisition between firms each with relatively modest shares) and if there is a high likelihood that adequate relief will be available on completion of the case even if none is given preliminarily (as, for example, where the acquisition is of a controlling stock interest, but without a plan to unify operations), the usual caution of federal courts on application for preliminary relief will probably and appropriately prevail.[6] Indeed, where immediate competitive injury does not seem a serious threat, a court will at times deny an order which would forbid consummation of the merger but grant instead an order requiring that the two firms continue to be operated as separate businesses so that, should the government prevail, divestiture remains feasible.[7] But courts should not too lightly assume that separate operation orders are adequate to assure that the merger can later be effectively undone and the status quo ante reestablished. Records, trade secrets and other confidential information will almost in-

---

4. See, e.g., Elzinga, The Antimerger Law: Pyrrhic Victories? 12 J.Law & Econ. 43 (1969).

5. See United States v. Northwest Indus. Inc., 301 F.Supp. 1066 (N.D.Ill. 1969); United States v. Atlantic Richfield Co., 297 F.Supp. 1061 (S.D.N.Y. 1969), aff'd sub nom. 401 U.S. 986, 91 S.Ct. 1233, 28 L.Ed.2d 527 (1971); Hamilton Watch Co. v. Benrus Watch Co., 114 F.Supp. 307 (D.Conn.1953), aff'd 206 F.2d 738 (2d Cir. 1953); Allis-Chalmers Mfg. Co. v. White Consol. Indus. Inc., 414 F.2d 506 (3rd Cir. 1969), cert. denied 396 U.S. 1009, 90 S.Ct. 567, 24 L.Ed.2d 501 (1970). When the plaintiff is a private party, problems arise which transcend the question of preliminary relief. One court of appeals has held that in providing for injunctive relief to private litigants under § 16 of Clayton, Congress did not intend to authorize divestiture at the suit of a private party. I. T. & T. v. G. T. E., 518 F.2d 913 (9th Cir. 1975). But cf. N. B. O. Industries Treadway Companies v. Brunswick Corp., 523 F.2d 262 (3d Cir. 1975), cert. granted sub nom. Brunswick Corp. v. Pueblo Bowl-O-Mat, Inc., 44 U.S.L.W. 3741 (1976). Any decision concerning preliminary relief ought to be consistent with the issuing court's conception about the scope of injunctive relief which might be available to the plaintiff if it prevails ultimately.

6. E.g., United States v. G. Heileman Brewing Co., 345 F.Supp. 117 (D. Mich.1972); United States v. Gimbel Bros. Inc., 202 F.Supp. 779 (D.Wis. 1962); United States v. E. I. Du Pont De Nemours & Co., 167 F.Supp. 957 (N.D.Ill.1958); United States v. Crocker-Anglo Nat'l Bank, 223 F.Supp. 849 (N.D.Calif.1963), 263 F.Supp. 125 (N. D.Calif.1966), 277 F.Supp. 133 (N.D. Calif.1967). But cf. United States v. Third Nat'l Bank in Nashville, 1964 CCH Trade Cas. ¶ 71,209 (M.D.Tenn.), 260 F.Supp. 869 (M.D.Tenn.1966), rev'd 390 U.S. 171, 88 S.Ct. 882, 19 L. Ed.2d 1015 (1968).

7. E.g., United States v. Brown Shoe Co., 179 F.Supp. 721 (E.D.Mo.1959), aff'd, 370 U.S. 294, 82 S.Ct. 1502, 8 L. Ed.2d 510 (1962); United States v. General Telephone & Electronics Corp., 156 ATRR A-5 (S.D.N.Y.1964) (stipulation for separate operation).

evitably pass between personnel of the merged businesses. In the case of horizontal mergers, affinities will be established which will tend to reduce competitive striving between the firms: orders may be exchanged; customers moved from one to the other. In the case of vertical mergers, the foreclosure effects may lead to the loss or loosening of old trade connections between the acquired firm and competitors of the acquiring firm which cannot be readily reestablished upon divestiture.

Though the government loses merger cases as well as wins them, it is hard to make a case that it often acts frivolously. Given that fact, and given the strong congressional concern about increasing concentration, the limits of judicial resources, and the grave difficulty often encountered in providing satisfactory final relief where a preliminary injunction against the merger was denied, courts ought to be disposed to enter orders maintaining the status quo whenever the government offers by affidavits a colorable case that the merger transcends legal standards and that adequate ultimate relief would be jeopardized by allowing consummation. It is fair enough to insist in addition that the government have its case in such order that it can go to trial with reasonable promptness, but the merger proponents' claim that they want an immediate trial date should not be allowed to foreclose preliminary relief where the government is disposed to proceed with decent dispatch.[8]

Preliminary relief in private anti-merger litigation often presents quite different questions. Management may try to use Section 7 to beat off a takeover bid; in such a context a court should be particularly cautious to see that the plaintiff has fully established its likelihood of prevailing on the merits before granting preliminary relief. Well reasoned cases support the view that a private plaintiff may have preliminary relief only on a clear showing that it is likely ultimately to prevail and that if such relief is denied it will suffer irreparably and more severely than defendants will suffer if relief is granted.[9] Despite this, district courts located outside of major corporate centers may at times grant preliminary relief out of an undue zeal to protect managements of local corporations from efforts by

---

8. Though the matter was long in doubt, it is now settled that the FTC can also obtain preliminary relief by application to the appropriate court of appeals, which has jurisdiction under the all writs section to enter an order to protect its appellate jurisdiction. FTC v. Dean Foods Co., 384 U.S. 597, 86 S.Ct. 1738, 16 L.Ed.2d 802 (1966). The courts of appeals presumably grant preliminary relief on essentially the same standards as do district courts on application by the Department of Justice. Thus far, the FTC has used this power sparingly.

9. E.g., Hamilton Watch Co. v. Benrus Watch Co., supra note 5; Allis-Chalmers Mfg. Co. v. White Consol. Indus., Inc., supra note 5; C. Leonardt Imp. Co. v. Southdown, Inc., 313 F.Supp. 1146 (C.D.Cal.1970); LunkenHeimer Co. v. Condec Corp., 268 F.Supp. 667 (S.D.N.Y.1967). But cf. Boyertown Burial Casket Co. v. Walco Nat'l Corp., 344 F.Supp. 1357 (D.Pa.1972); Briggs Mfg. Co. v. Crane Co., 185 F. Supp. 177 (D.Mich.1960).

outsiders to win control. True, local control is one of the values that Section 7 was intended to advance, but it ought to do so through the instrumentality of protecting competition. Unless plaintiffs can show convincingly that they have a case that competition will be impaired, the capital markets ought to be permitted to function without precipitate judicial interference.

§ 216. Final Relief

The equitable power of a federal court is as comprehensive as the condition to be rectified requires.[1] If an unlawful merger has not been consummated the court can forbid it;[2] if an unlawful merger has been consummated, the court can order it to be undone.[3] The court can also order any ancillary relief reasonably appropriate to the objective of rectifying the wrong.[4] Despite this, when preliminary orders maintaining the status quo are not obtained, frustration often occurs at the final stage. If the acquired and acquiring firms have been integrated it will be extremely difficult, after the passage of any

---

1. E.g., Ford Motor Co. v. United States, 405 U.S. 562, 92 S.Ct. 1142, 31 L.Ed.2d 492 (1972); United States v. Greater Buffalo Press, Inc., 402 U.S. 549, 91 S.Ct. 1692, 29 L.Ed.2d 170 (1971); United States v. E. I. du Pont de Nemours & Co., 366 U.S. 316, 81 S.Ct. 1243, 6 L.Ed.2d 318, modification denied 366 U.S. 956, 81 S.Ct. 1913, 6 L.Ed.2d 1251 (1961). See generally the critical analysis of the effects of merger litigation in Pfunder, Plaine, & Whittemore, Compliance with Divestiture Orders Under Section 7: An Analysis of the Relief Obtained, 17 Antitrust Bull. 19 (1972).

2. E.g., United States v. Philadelphia Nat'l Bank, 374 U.S. 321, 83 S.Ct. 1715, 10 L.Ed.2d 915 (1963). It is not only the government which can obtain equitable relief against a prospective unlawful acquisition. Zenith Radio Corp. v. Hazeltine Research Inc., 395 U.S. 100, 89 S.Ct. 1562, 23 L.Ed.2d 129 (1969) emphasizes that a private party suing under § 16 of Clayton is entitled to relief against threatened injury. See also United States v. W. T. Grant Co., 345 U.S. 629, 632–633, 73 S.Ct. 894, 897, 97 L.Ed. 1303, 1309 (1953), which suggests that a defendant's post-litigation decision to abandon an unlawful activity or plan may warrant skepticism, and need not be a basis for denying equitable relief.

3. E.g., United States v. First Nat'l Bank and Trust Co. of Lexington, 193 ATRR A-10 (E.D.Ky.1965), on remand after the decision at 376 U.S. 665, 84 S.Ct. 1033, 12 L.Ed.2d 1 (1964). The order required separation of already merged banking operations by the setting up of a separate, competitive, independent bank which should be established to be the substantial equivalent of the bank which had been merged out of existence. See the discussion of such "egg unscrambling" orders in E. Rockefeller, Antitrust Questions and Answers 240–41 (1974). There is, however, an unsettled question whether divestiture of a consummated merger will be ordered at the behest of a private suitor. Compare I. T. & T. v. G. T. E., 518 F.2d 913 (9th Cir. 1975) with N. B. O. Industries Treadway Companies v. Brunswick Corp., 523 F.2d 262 (3d Cir. 1975), cert. granted sub nom. Brunswick Corp. v. Pueblo Bowl-O-Mat, Inc., 44 U.S.L.W. 3741 (1976). Although a court of equity ought not to order divestiture unless satisfied that the objectives underlying the law can only be adequately satisfied by such an order, there seems no legal reason why such an order should be denied where in a private suit the court reaches the conclusion that only divestiture will sucessfully redress the violation.

4. E.g., United States v. Greater Buffalo Press, Inc., supra note 1; United States v. Ford Motor Co, supra note 1.

significant amount of time, to unscramble the omelet. Divestiture, of course can be ordered. The acquiring firm can be directed to set up a separate firm replicating as nearly as possible that which it acquired, to convey to that new firm the tangible and intangible properties, and to provide to it the management and other personnel it needs.[5] But however earnestly the attempt is made, what comes out of it is a new firm with the problems of a new firm and with inevitable affinities with the spawning parent which can be expected to affect both competitive style and the degree of independence.

Even when the acquired and the acquiring unit are maintained as separate operations during litigation, either because of a court order or despite the lack of one, difficulties are often encountered in providing adequate final relief. The capacities of the acquired firm to function independently are sapped; its independent banking connections may be weakened, its potential for access to capital markets is greatly reduced, its integrity as a separate socio-economic system is ended. If the firm was owner-managed before acquisition, as is the prototypical successful family firm which is a happy target for acquisition at a certain stage (say, where the second generation of owner-management, the sons of the founder, are reaching retirement), these problems will be even more salient. Once the family's equity in the firm is liquidated and those who have managed the closely held enterprise have gone into retirement, the prospect for maintaining the business as an independent unit may be irrevocably lost. If the merger was an asset acquisition rather than a stock acquisition, these problems may be exacerbated. The selling firm may be liquidated after the sale and when the merger is ultimately held unlawful, even though the court can order that assets roughly comparable to those unlawfully acquired be disgorged, to reestablish the status quo will be literally impossible.

For all of these reasons, the acquiring firm cannot merely "let go" of what it acquired when the acquisition is held to have been illegal. Even when the acquired firm has maintained a separate existence, if the acquired firm is to survive, it will frequently be necessary to find another sheltering parent to replace the existing one. Even if that mode of relief is accomplished with success, in the sense that the new parent has no horizontal, vertical or market extension relationship to the acquired unit, but only a conglomerate one, the vigorous independence we may take as the statutory ideal is not achieved. Injuries to overall concentration, if not to market concentration, are still done. And often divestiture is not or cannot be accomplished even as well as this. The Department of Justice and the court may in the end settle for a sale of the acquired firm to a new parent which might itself have been challenged if it had proposed a merger in the

---

5. United States v. First Nat'l Bank and Trust Co. of Lexington, supra note 3.

first instance—or which, if it would not have been challenged *de novo*, would at least have been passed over only after some deliberation and concern.[6]

The situation in *Brown Shoe* will serve to illustrate. Kinney Shoe, a retail chain, was a family firm which had enjoyed great success. When Brown Shoe was held after a long litigation to have acquired it illegally and the need to reestablish Kinney independently of Brown was presented, it was manifest that a new parent would have to be found. The original family control, which had combined the needed capital, management and *chutzpah*, was beyond recall. Nor was it reasonable to suppose that new owner-managers with the right mix of cash, acumen in chain shoe retailing, and the appropriate hormonal qualities would magically appear. A large firm which could offer a professional and competent (if less intensively involved) management seemed the only alternative. In the end, a sale to F. W. Woolworth was effected by Brown and approved by the court.[7] Though the transaction did not present the horizontal and vertical concerns involved in the original merger, it did entail some market extension qualities (albeit weak ones) and certainly contributed to the trend toward higher overall concentration through conglomerate organization.[8]

In stock acquisition cases where the acquired unit has been operated independently and where the acquiring firm is widely and publicly held, there is sometimes an effort to solve the divestiture problem by "spinning off" the acquired firm by conveying its stock pro-rata to the stockholders of the acquiring firm. This device may also be brought into service when divestiture occurs following integration of operations with a firm of which the stock or assets had been purchased. Instead of looking for a buyer for the already separately maintained or newly established separate firm, the acquiring firm's stockholders receive it as a dividend, on the assumption that the community of interest between the parent firm and the spun off firm will be ended as market transactions in the stock of each occur.[9] Usually, ancillary orders are entered to insulate against obvious communities of interest. For example, the order may forbid persons to hold office in both companies and may forbid those with significant holdings in the parent firm to participate in the management of the second.

This device, with its manifest shortcomings, may at times be the best of a group of alternatives each of which is in some way deficient. If the market for the stock of both firms is lively, it promises eventual independent operation and for this reason may be preferable to a sale of the subsidiary firm to a new parent. But it has a chance

---

6. See Rockefeller, supra note 3, at 241–43.

7. Id.

8. Id.

9. E.g., A. G. Spalding & Bros., Inc., 56 F.T.C. 1125 (1960) aff'd, 301 F.2d 585 (3rd Cir. 1962).

of succeeding only if there is a competent independent management available for the spun off unit, and only if that unit is adequate in scale and resources to gain access (without parental sponsorship) to credit and capital at rates comparable to those available to firms with which it will be competing. However, if these qualities are really available there is no obvious reason why the parent cannot simply market the stock of the new enterprise through normal underwriting channels.

To summarize, the law of merger is ridden with problems and uncertainties at every stage, including the law that governs the precise end of the proceeding. There has been a good deal of harsh yet fair criticism of the remedial aspects of the performance of both courts and enforcement agencies.[10] One can join in this criticism and focus on what seems to be the signal failing—the infrequency with which preliminary relief is granted—without losing sight of the considerable consequence merger law has had and is having for the structure of the American economy.

10. E.g., Elzinga, Antimerger Law: Pyrrhic Victories? 12 J. Law & Econ. 43 (1969); Pfunder, Plaine & Whittemore, Compliance with Divestiture Orders under Section 7 of the Clayton Act: An Analysis of the Relief Obtained, 17 Antitrust Bull. 19 (1972), Lewis, Preliminary Injunctions in Government Section 7 Litigation, 17 Antitrust Bull. 1 (1972).

Chapter 8

THE PRICE DISCRIMINATION LAW

Table of Sections

Part	Sections
A. Introduction	217–219
B. Horizontal Competitive Effects	220–221
C. Vertical Competitive Effects	222–225
D. Brokerage and Advertising Allowances	226–227
E. Affirmative Defenses	228–229
F. Buyer Liability	230–231

PART A. INTRODUCTION

Sec.
217. Nature of the Legislation.
218. Scope of the Principal Statutory Concepts.
219. Meaning and Significance of Discrimination.

PART B. HORIZONTAL COMPETITIVE EFFECTS

220. Discrimination as an Exclusionary Practice Affecting the Seller's Level.
221. Discrimination Which Diverts Business from Competitors or Threatens Adverse Structural Change.

PART C. VERTICAL COMPETITIVE EFFECTS

222. Social Effects in General.
223. Loss of Business by Disfavored Customers as a *Prima Facie* Case.
224. Substantial Profit Advantage for the Favored Customer as a *Prima Facie* Case.
225. Rebutting a *Prima Facie* Case of Competitive Injury.

PART D. BROKERAGE AND ADVERTISING ALLOWANCES

226. The Brokerage Provision.
227. The Advertising Allowance Provision.

PART E. AFFIRMATIVE DEFENSES

228. Cost Justification.
229. Meeting Competition.

PART F. BUYER LIABILITY

230. Inducing and Receiving Price Discriminations.
231. Inducing and Receiving Brokerage or Advertising Allowances.

PART A. INTRODUCTION

§ 217. Nature of the Legislation

Section 2(a) of the Clayton Act, as amended in 1936 by the Robinson-Patman Act [1] makes it unlawful for any seller engaged in commerce to directly or indirectly discriminate in the price charged purchasers on the sale of commodities of like grade and quality where the effect may be to injure, destroy or prevent competition with any person who grants or knowingly receives a discrimination, or the customer of either. There are related provisions dealing with brokerage [2] and promotional and advertising allowances and services [3] and a provision about buyer liability.[4] There also are statutory defenses.[5] Robinson-Patman also contains a section, not amendatory of Clayton, which makes granting some discriminations a crime.[6] Economic aspects of the price discrimination law are dealt with thoroughly in a book by Edwards; [7] Frederick Rowe's book [8] reviews the decisions of the courts and the FTC more fully than is feasible here.[9] This chapter is a brief introduction to major issues under the law and stresses their relationships with antitrust policy.[10]

Before being amended by Robinson-Patman, Section 2 of Clayton made it unlawful to discriminate in price "where the effect * * *

---

1. Act of June 19, 1936, ch. 592 § 1, 49 Stat. 1526, 15 U.S.C.A. § 13(a) (1973). See §§ 220–25 infra.

2. 15 U.S.C.A. § 13(c) (1973). See § 226 infra.

3. 15 U.S.C.A. §§ 13(d) and 13(e) (1973). See § 227 infra.

4. 15 U.S.C.A. § 13(f) (1973). See §§ 230–31 infra.

5. 15 U.S.C.A. §§ 13(a) and 13(b). See §§ 228–29 infra.

6. The criminal provision is Section 3 of the Robinson-Patman Act of 1936, 15 U.S.C.A. § 13a (1973). This provision should not be confused with Section 1 of Robinson-Patman, 15 U.S.C.A. §§ 13(a) through 13(f), which amends Section 2 of the Clayton Act.

7. C. Edwards, The Price Discrimination Law (1959).

8. F. Rowe, Price Discrimination Under the Robinson-Patman Act (1962).

9. Among the other interesting works from a voluminous literature are Dam, Economics and Law of Price Discrimination: Herein of Three Regulatory Schemes, 31 U. of Chi.L.Rev. 1 (1963); Elman, The Robinson-Patman Act and Antitrust Policy: A Time for Reappraisal, 42 U. of Wash. L.Rev. 1 (1966); Fulda, The Per Se Provisions of the Robinson-Patman Act, 49 Tex.L.Rev. 961 (1971); McGee, Some Economic Issues in Robinson-Patman Law, 30 Law & Contemp. Prob. 530 (1963). Discrimination and its relevance to issues under antitrust concepts deriving from the Sherman Act and other sections of Clayton have been discussed in §§ 29, 47, 156, 159, 186 supra.

10. Technically, those portions of Robinson-Patman which amend Section 2 of the Clayton Act, specifically, 15 U.S.C.A. §§ 13(a)–13(f), are parts of the "antitrust laws" as defined in Section 1 of the Clayton Act, 38 Stat. 730 (1914), 15 U.S.C.A. § 12 (1973). Section 3 (15 U.S.C.A. § 13a) of Robinson-Patman, the criminal provision, is not. Nashville Milk Co. v. Carnation Co., 355 U.S. 373, 78 S.Ct. 352, 2 L.Ed.2d 340 (1958). Nevertheless, the legislative history of Robinson-Patman, which is summarized in Rowe, supra

may be to substantially lessen competition or tend to create a monopoly in any line of commerce * * *." [11] The legislative history of Robinson-Patman is marked by compromise as well as by the confusion that so frequently attends statutory changes considered to be socially or economically significant by contending groups. Some in Congress were seeking a bill which would protect small business—independent retailers and the wholesalers and distributors that supplied them—from the rigors of more efficient, large scale, integrated chains; others wanted the legislation to protect competition as a process, whatever its effect on individual competitors or classes of competitors.[12] As construed, the original Clayton Act provision forbade predatory discriminations—typically, local price cutting by large, nationwide firms—intended to drive smaller local competitors out of the market or to force them to sell out to large consolidations.[13] Whatever the actuality may be, such discriminations have been regarded as one of the techniques by which the great trusts were built.[14] As amended by Robinson-Patman, Section 2 of Clayton covers these and other discriminations. There was some question whether the original act covered discrimination which did injury to competition at the buyer's level.[15] As amended by Robinson-Patman,

note 8, ch. 1, and, as we shall see, many of the judicial interpretations of the Act are vitalized by a concern for protecting small competitors, not competition as a process; in this sense Robinson-Patman is to be likened to the resale price maintenance legislation discussed in § 132 supra and contrasted with the hard core of antitrust doctrine which derives from Sherman and Clayton provisions other than those in Clayton Section 2 and which focuses more purposefully on competitive structure and competitive process. It is this lack of integration between Robinson-Patman and antitrust concepts which is implied in the phrases, such as the references to Robinson-Patman as the "price discrimination law," which in this chapter tend to demarcate Robinson-Patman and antitrust.

11. Clayton Act § 2, Ch. 323, § 2, 38 Stat. 730 (1914). The principal purpose of the section was to eliminate predatory, geographic price cutting. See H.R. Res. No. 627, 63d Cong., 2d Sess. 8–9 (1914); S. Res. No. 698, 63d Cong., 2d Sess. 3–14 (1914); Rowe, supra note 8, at 6.

12. Rowe supra note 8, at 11–23.

13. Compare Porto Rican American Tobacco Co. v. American Tobacco Co., 30 F.2d 234 (2d Cir.), cert. denied, 279 U. S. 858, 49 S.Ct. 353, 73 L.Ed. 999 (1929), with Goodyear Tire & Rubber Co. v. FTC, 101 F.2d 620 (6th Cir.), cert. denied, 308 U.S. 557, 60 S.Ct. 74, 84 L.Ed. 468 (1939). See the survey of enforcement of old Section 2 in McAllister, Sales Policies and Price Discrimination Under the Clayton Act, 41 Yale L.J. 518 (1932).

14. See Rowe, supra note 8, at 11–23.

15. Initially the old Section was held to be violated only upon a showing of injury to competition at the horizontal level of the seller (a so-called "primary line" competitive injury). E.g., National Biscuit Co. v. FTC, 299 F. 733 (2d Cir.), cert. denied, 266 U.S. 613, 45 S.Ct. 95, 69 L.Ed. 468 (1924). Although the Court later read the Section as covering injury to competition among buyers (so-called "secondary line" effects), e.g., George Van Camp & Sons v. American Can Co., 278 U.S. 245, 253, 49 S.Ct. 112, 113, 73 L.Ed. 311, 313 (1929), it was held that price differences based on differences in quantity were not discriminatory. Goodyear Tire & Rubber Co. v. FTC, 101 F.2d 620 (6th Cir.), cert. denied, 308 U.S. 557, 60 S.Ct. 74, 84 L.Ed. 468 (1939). In consequence it became impossible as a practical matter to es-

Pt. A   INTRODUCTION   679

Section 2 of Clayton plainly covers discriminations of this kind.[16] Nevertheless, Robinson-Patman left a great deal unclear. The "competitive effect" language used in other Clayton Sections was abandoned for vaguer language. The enactment thus raised new issues about how courts should decide whether a discrimination does the forbidden injury either at the seller's level or further downstream. Parts B and C of this Chapter are addressed to these questions of competitive effect.

§ 218. Scope of the Principal Statutory Concepts

Robinson-Patman is a technical, yet loosely drafted, statute. In this section some of the basic pre-conditions for violation will be summarily stated.

First, there must be two sales to different customers at different prices; for example, a sale and an offer at different prices will not suffice.[1] Second, the sales must be sales in the technical legal sense; leases, for example, are not covered[2] nor are licenses,[3] consignment arrangements[4] or the like.[5] Third, the statute explicitly gives a defense for price changes in response to "changing conditions affecting the market for or marketability" of the commodities;[6] defendant can prevail by carrying the burden of showing that the sales were not contemporaneous,[7] and that between the first sale and the second

tablish a violation due to secondary line effects, so long as the seller took pains to grant lower prices to large buyers only under a quantity discount plan.

16. E.g., FTC v. Morton Salt Co., 334 U.S. 37, 68 S.Ct. 822, 92 L.Ed. 1196 (1948).

1. Bruce's Juices, Inc. v. American Can Co., 330 U.S. 743, 755, 67 S.Ct. 1015, 1021, 91 L.Ed. 1219, 1228 (1947); Hartley & Parker, Inc. v. Florida Beverage Corp., 307 F.2d 916 (5th Cir. 1962); Package Closure Corp. v. Sealright Co., 141 F.2d 972, 979–80 (2d Cir. 1944); A. J. Goodman & Sons, Inc. v. United Lacquer Mfg. Corp., 81 F.Supp. 890 (D.Mass.1949). Cf. Aluminum Co. of America v. Tandet, 235 F.Supp. 111 (D.Conn.1964) (sale and contract to sell sufficient). But cf. Nachman v. Shell Oil Co., 1944–45 CCH Trade Cas. ¶ 57,361 at 57,762 (D.Md.1945) (charge to jury that confronting a recurrent purchaser with discriminately high price violates the Act).

2. E.g., Export Liquor Sales v. Ammex Warehouse Co., 426 F.2d 251 (6th Cir. 1970), cert. denied, 400 U.S. 1000, 91 S.Ct. 460, 27 L.Ed.2d 451 (1971); Plum Tree, Inc. v. N. K. Winston Corp., 351 F.Supp. 80 (S.D.N.Y.1972).

3. E.g., Record Club of America, Inc. v. Columbia Broadcasting Sys., Inc., 310 F.Supp. 1241 (E.D.Pa.1970); Country Theatre Co. v. Paramount Film Distribution Corp., 146 F.Supp. 933 (E.D.Pa.1956); Kearuth Theatre Corp. v. Paramount Pictures, Inc., 1956 CCH Trade Cas. ¶ 68,674 (S.D.N.Y.).

4. E.g., Students Book Co. v. Washington Law Book Co., 232 F.2d 49 (D.C.Cir.1955), cert. denied, 350 U.S. 988, 76 S.Ct. 474, 100 L.Ed. 854 (1956).

5. Loren Specialty Mfg. Co. v. Clark Mfg. Co., 360 F.2d 913 (7th Cir.), cert. denied, 385 U.S. 957, 87 S.Ct. 392, 17 L.Ed.2d 303 (1966) (agency arrangement); Bichel Optical Labs, Inc. v. Marquette Nat'l Bank, 336 F.Supp. 1368 (D.Minn.1971) (loan).

6. 15 U.S.C.A. § 13(a) (1973).

7. Bruce's Juices, Inc. v. American Can Co., 330 U.S. 743, 67 S.Ct. 1015, 91 L.Ed. 1219 (1947); cf. Atalanta Trading Corp. v. FTC, 258 F.2d 365, 372 (2d Cir. 1958).

there were changes affecting the product or the market which altered the market price of the goods. Fourth, the subject of the sales must be a tangible personal property—commodities, sales of services and intangibles are not covered.[8] Fifth, the commodities must be of like grade and quantity.[9] This standard adverts to the significant objective characteristics of the goods themselves, not to subjective buyer attitudes about them; thus, when physical differences between commodities are trivial they are of like grade and quantity,[10] even though sold under different brand names, trademarks and labels.[11] By contrast, two commodities which are significantly different physically are not of like grade and quality,[12] nor are two products when one is in merchantable condition while the other is defective.[13] Sixth, there must be a difference in price, though it may be either direct or indirect. Though the legislative history teaches that discrimination in price implies not just a difference, but a difference where relationships are such that prices ought to be the same,[14] the Court has indicated that any price difference is a discrimination.[15] An indirect discrimination occurs if the seller sells the same goods at the same price but provides different services, credit terms, return privileges, or delivery.[16]

One can picture efforts to construe this rather technical sounding statute in ways which would aid in integrating it with the main thrust of antitrust. By and large, courts have neither worked to-

---

8. E.g., TV Signal Co. v. American Tel. & Tel. Co., 462 F.2d 1256 (8th Cir. 1972); Baum v. Investors Diversified Services, Inc., 409 F.2d 872 (7th Cir. 1969); General Shale Prods. Corp. v. Struck Constr. Co., 132 F.2d 425 (6th Cir. 1942), cert. denied, 318 U.S. 780, 63 S.Ct. 857, 87 L.Ed. 1148 (1943); Karlinsky v. New York Racing Ass'n, 310 F.Supp. 937 (S.D.N.Y.1970); Record Club of America Inc. v. Columbia Broadcasting Sys., Inc., 310 F.Supp. 1241 (E.D.Pa.1970). Cf. Saturn Airways v. CAB, 483 F.2d 1284 (D.C.Cir. 1973) (non-affinity group, advanced booking, reduced air rates upheld).

9. FTC v. Borden Co., 383 U.S. 637, 86 S.Ct. 1092, 16 L.Ed.2d 153 (1966).

10. Bruce's Juices, Inc. v. American Can Co., 87 F.Supp. 985, 987 (S.D. Fla.1949), aff'd, 187 F.2d 919, 924 (5th Cir.), cert. dismissed, 342 U.S. 875, 72 S.Ct. 165, 96 L.Ed. 657 (1951).

11. FTC v. Borden Co., 383 U.S. 637, 86 S.Ct. 1092, 16 L.Ed.2d 153 (1966); Hartley & Parker, Inc. v. Florida Beverage Corp., 307 F.2d 916, 923 (5th Cir. 1962).

12. Atalanta Trading Corp. v. FTC, 258 F.2d 365 (2d Cir. 1958); Boss Mfg. Co. v. Payne Glove Co., 71 F.2d 768 (8th Cir.) cert. denied, 293 U.S. 590, 55 S. Ct. 104, 79 L.Ed. 684 (1934); Central Ice Cream Co. v. Golden Rod Ice Cream Co., 184 F.Supp. 312 (N.D.Ill. 1960), aff'd, 287 F.2d 265 (7th Cir. 1961). But cf. Moog Indus., Inc. v. FTC, 238 F.2d 43 (8th Cir. 1956), aff'd, 355 U.S. 411, 78 S.Ct. 377, 2 L.Ed.2d 370 (1958). FTC rulings are not entirely consistent on these issues. See F. Rowe, Price Discrimination Under the Robinson-Patman Act 65–69 (1962).

13. Cf. cases cited in note 11 supra.

14. See F. Rowe, Price Discrimination Under the Robinson-Patman Act 93–95 (1962).

15. FTC v. Anheuser-Busch, Inc., 363 U.S. 536, 80 S.Ct. 1267, 4 L.Ed.2d 1385 (1960).

16. E.g., Corn Prods. Ref. Co. v. FTC, 324 U.S. 726, 740, 65 S.Ct 961, 968, 89 L.Ed. 1320, 1333 (1945).

Pt. A INTRODUCTION

wards that end nor been sympathetic to the claim that this law ought to function as part of a cohesive policy about competition. By its detail and explicitness Robinson-Patman may invite interpretive literalism. In any event, many opinions have an acid ring, as though the judicial attitude were, "This being what Congress has done, the marketplace will have to live with the technical quibbles, as well as the rest."

§ 219. Meaning and Significance of Discrimination

By "discrimination" the economist means the sale of the same or similar products to different buyers at prices bearing different ratios to marginal costs. However, the courts have in view a different concept of discrimination when they state that any price difference on two sales of the same commodity is a discrimination within the meaning of Section 2(a) of Robinson-Patman.[1] An economic discrimination may or may not occur where prices on separate sales of the same commodity differ; if the ratio between the marginal cost and the price are the same for both sales no economic discrimination has occurred. Moreover, if price on two sales of the same commodity is the same, but costs differ, an economic discrimination has occurred, even though it is not a discrimination under the Act as the courts have construed it. This book deals with discrimination in discussion of major antitrust issues.[2] This section will reinforce ideas developed in those earlier contexts.

A firm lacking market power has neither the incentive nor the ability to discriminate. A firm with power will be able to increase total revenue if it can sell at relatively higher prices to buyers with relatively inelastic demands and at relatively lower prices to buyers with relatively elastic demands. It can discriminate only if it can deal separately with buyers or groups of buyers with differing elasticities. Firms offering services, such as advertising or fire and burglar warning systems, can often do this directly. Firms selling commodities which brokers could purchase from low elasticity buyers and resell to high elasticity buyers cannot discriminate so easily.

Brokers will engage in this practice and the would-be discriminator will find that its high price to buyers with inelastic demands cannot be maintained. Usually, when discrimination was encountered in earlier chapters it was in connection with some device used by the seller to place the high elasticity and low elasticity buyers in separate markets—tying devices,[3] vertical merger,[4] and territorial or custom-

---

1. See FTC v. Anheuser-Busch, Inc., 363 U.S. 536, 80 S.Ct. 1267, 4 L.Ed.2d 1385 (1960).

2. See §§ 29, 47, 156, 159, 186 supra. For a holding that the Robinson-Patman Act does not cover two sales at the same price, even though an economic discrimination may have been involved, see Caroll v. Protection Maritime Ins. Co., Ltd., 512 F.2d 4 (1st Cir.1975).

3. See Chapter 5, pt. C. supra.

4. See Chapter 7, pt. D. supra.

er restrictions [5] can all be used for this purpose. Pressure upon a seller to discriminate may also come from a buyer with power. Such a buyer may insist on price advantages which the seller gives in to but which it does not make available to other buyers.

Discrimination can be socially harmful. It might be used predatorily by a deep pocket seller if the circumstances were appropriate for a successful predatory foray. Such a seller could, by reducing prices to buyers in areas where competition was encountered, try to drive competitors out or to discipline them against competitive pricing. Discrimination of this kind might injure competition at the seller level.[6] By contrast, discrimination could also do injury to competition at the buyer level if it were a means by which a buyer used power. But discrimination can also be neutral or even beneficial in its impact. Though sustained discrimination signifies the existence of market power, it may be a relatively unobjectionable way for such power to be used. If the seller, foreclosed from discriminating, would charge a relatively high price to all, the product would become less widely accessible than it would be if the seller were permitted to discriminate. Moreover, discrimination may be the way in which firms acting collusively or interdependently in an oligopolistic market begin to "cheat" on other members of the cartel or interdependent group—in short, it may be the way competition begins.[7] To stifle it may be to help to keep the cartel intact or to facilitate interdependent pricing.

To the extent that Robinson-Patman separates out for attack competitively harmful discrimination, it can be a positive instrument which aids antitrust enforcement; to the extent it may reach competitively neutral discriminations, its impingement on market freedom cannot be justified on antitrust grounds but only on other social grounds, if at all; furthermore, by limiting competitive choices, it begins to impinge upon the interests protected by antitrust. To the extent that Robinson-Patman inhibits discriminations which are actually beneficial to competition it collides with antitrust policy. As we shall see, the vigorous criticism so often lodged against the law is that it is not effectively integrated with antitrust and probably does more harm than good to competition. Moreover, it is often asserted that it does this harm without discernibly advancing any other comparably important social goal.[8]

5. See Chapter 5, pt. B. supra.

6. See § 220 infra.

7. See generally, F. Scherer, Industrial Market Structure and Economic Performance 261–62, 267–70, 272, 495 (1970).

8. See, e.g., Bowman, Restraint of Trade By the Supreme Court: The Utah Pie Case, 77 Yale L.J. 70 (1967).

PART B. HORIZONTAL COMPETITIVE EFFECTS

§ 220. Discrimination as an Exclusionary Practice Affecting the Seller's Level

At first glance Robinson-Patman may seem a partial reiteration and reemphasis of the prohibition in Section 2 of the Sherman Act against exclusionary conduct, a singling out of a particular exclusionary technique because of its historical association with the great consolidation movement which occurred at the end of the last century. Viewed in this way the function of Section 2(a) of Clayton, as amended by Robinson-Patman, is to forbid predatory price cutting. It would keep a firm from selling at a low price when it encounters competition and at a high price when it does not if the purpose or effect of that practice were to drive competitors out of the market. It would also forbid other similar exclusionary discriminations. For example, it would cover discrimination aimed at forcing a would-be competitor to join in a consolidation, or at disciplining a firm which started to reduce prices or otherwise compete in ways which might increase its market share at the expense of industry profits.

There is no doubt that the law forbids predatory discriminations of these kinds.[1] The original Section 2 of Clayton forbade deep, local price slashes adopted with predatory intent[2] and the amended Section does also.[3] The predatory character of a cut can be established by direct evidence of the seller's subjective attitude,[4] or by other evidence from which predatory purpose or effect can be inferred.[5] Persistent sales below average cost in a market where competition is encountered are a strong indication of predation.[6] A court may also

---

1. See, e.g., Moore v. Mead's Fine Bread Co., 348 U.S. 115, 117–18, 75 S.Ct. 148, 149–50, 99 L.Ed. 145, 148–49 (1954); Cornwell Quality Tools Co. v. C.T.S. Co., 446 F.2d 825 (9th Cir. 1971), cert. denied, 404 U.S. 1049, 92 S.Ct. 715–16, 30 L.Ed.2d 740 (1972); National Dairy Prods. Corp. v. FTC, 412 F.2d 605, 618–19 (7th Cir. 1969); Maryland Baking Co. v. FTC, 243 F.2d 716, 718 (4th Cir. 1957); E. B. Muller & Co. v. FTC, 142 F.2d 511 (6th Cir. 1944); Foster Mfg. Co., 62 F.T.C. 852 (1963), aff'd in part and rev'd in part, 355 F.2d 47 (1st Cir. 1964), cert. denied, 380 U.S. 906, 85 S.Ct. 887, 13 L.Ed.2d 794 (1965).

2. Porto Rican American Tobacco Co. v. American Tobacco Co., 30 F.2d 234, 237 (2d Cir. 1929). See the discussion in Anheuser-Busch, Inc. v. FTC, 289 F.2d 835, 841–42 (7th Cir. 1961).

3. See the cases cited in note 1 supra. See also Utah Pie Co. v. Continental Baking Co., 386 U.S. 685, 87 S.Ct. 1326, 18 L.Ed.2d 406 (1967). Although the evidence of predation was trivial the *Utah Pie* decision (discussed more fully in the next section) could be explained as one where a jury verdict was upheld, given some evidence that discrimination was predatory in the classic sense. Cf. Lloyd A. Fry Roofing Co. v. FTC, 371 F.2d 277 (7th Cir. 1966); Forster Mfg. Co., v. FTC, 335 F.2d 47 (1st Cir. 1964), cert. denied, 380 U.S. 906, 85 S.Ct. 887, 13 L.Ed.2d 794 (1965).

4. See e.g., Cornwell Quality Tools Co. v. C.T.S. Co., 446 F.2d 825 (9th Cir. 1971), cert. denied, 404 U.S. 1049, 92 S.Ct. 715–16, 30 L.Ed.2d 740 (1972).

5. See e.g., National Dairy Prods. Corp. v. FTC, 412 F.2d 605 (7th Cir. 1969).

6. See FTC v. Anheuser-Busch, Inc., 363 U.S. 536, 80 S.Ct. 1267, 4 L.Ed.2d 1385 (1960). See also F. Rowe, Price Discrimination Under the Robinson-Patman Act § 7.2 (1962).

look at the timing of the cut,[7] its relationship to the injured competitor's strategy or tactics,[8] its relationship to other changes (or to stabilities) in cost, demand or other factors which may affect price.[9]

In forbidding predatory discriminations, Section 2(a) of Clayton serves, therefore, as an analogue to the "monopolization" and attempt to monopolize concepts of Section 2 of Sherman. That section now forbids such discriminations where used by a firm with monopoly power or by a firm which, by use of these along with other devices, threatens to attain such power.[10] The Robinson-Patman provision amplifies Section 2 of Sherman by making such conduct unlawful because of its threat to competitors even when it is used by a firm that neither possesses monopoly power nor is close enough to possessing it to be caught up by the attempt concept.[11]

§ 221. Discrimination Which Diverts Business from Competitors or Threatens Adverse Structural Change

Even if a price discrimination does not involve predatory intent or below cost pricing it can have effects on competition at the seller's level. Where predatory purpose cannot be established, the law is vague concerning the particular effects or tendencies at the seller's level which violate Section 2(a). The FTC was for a substantial period accustomed to hold that any sustained discriminatory reduction which diverted business from competitors to the seller was a violation[1] and indeed, that the diversion could be inferred from the discrimination.[2] One court of appeals upheld this view in part,[3] taking the view that the seller could rebut the "presumption" that diversion occurred and competitive injury resulted by showing that competitors did not lose sales or that their profits had grown, or that entry was easy and, in general, that there was a thriving, competitive market.[4] Though there has been some vacillation in FTC opinions,[5]

---

7. See Rowe, supra note 6.

8. Id.

9. Id.

10. See §§ 47, 50 and 51 supra.

11. See the cases cited in note 1 supra.

1. E.g., Borden Co., 64 F.T.C. 534 (1963), vacated sub nom. Borden Co. v. FTC, 339 F.2d 133 (7th Cir. 1964), rev'd, 383 U.S. 637, 86 S.Ct. 1092, 16 L.Ed.2d 153 (1966); General Natural Gas Corp., FTC Dkt. 7782 (June 30, 1960). See F. Rowe, Price Discrimination Under the Robinson-Patman Act § 7.3 (1962) and cases therein cited.

2. See cases cited in Rowe, supra note 1.

3. Samuel H. Moss, Inc. v. FTC, 148 F.2d 378 (2d Cir.), cert. denied, 326 U.S. 734, 66 S.Ct. 44, 90 L.Ed. 438 (1945), modified, 155 F.2d 1016 (2d Cir. 1946). See also Enterprise Indus., Inc. v. Texas Co., 240 F.2d 457 (2d Cir.), cert. denied, 353 U.S. 965, 77 S.Ct. 1049, 1 L.Ed.2d 914 (1957) which is to the same effect. For a discussion see C. Edwards, The Price Discrimination Law 527 (1959).

4. Compare Anheuser-Busch, Inc. v. FTC, 289 F.2d 835 (7th Cir. 1961) with Samuel H. Moss, Inc. v. FTC, 148 F.2d 378 (2d Cir.), cert. denied, 326 U.S. 734, 66 S.Ct. 44, 90 L.Ed. 438 (1945), modified, 155 F.2d 1016 (2d Cir. 1946).

5. A number of the Commission's decisions seem inconsistent with a strict "diversion" test for a violation. E.g.,

the Commission seems at times still to follow the view that proof of a price discrimination causing diversion makes out a *prima facie* case.[6]

Some courts have announced that more than diversion must be shown to establish a violation but have seldom been very clear about what in addition is needed. *Dean Milk*[7] implies that in addition to diversion there must be a showing either of a significant reduction in the number of sellers or a significant increase in concentration. *Utah Pie*[8] implies that persistent discriminations are enough if they result in a drastically declining price structure. Moore v. Mead's Fine Bread Co.[9] could be read to imply an "aid from other markets" test, although its actual holding dealt with a different matter, the relationship between profits from interstate sales and local price cutting which must be shown to make out jurisdictional limits. The implication of that case is that to show geographic discrimination, it may be necessary to show that the low price in one area was somehow made possible, or "subsidized", by the higher price elsewhere.[10] Other factors are also implicit in many cases. It would seem, for example, that if a seller's market position is strong it will be more likely that a discrimination by it will be held to be unlawful than if its position is weak.[11] In this sense, at least, Section 2(a) of the amended Clayton Act is consistent with attempt to monopolize doctrine.

From an antitrust perspective it would be preferable if illegality required a showing either that the discrimination is predatory or that it initiates structural change which tends to harm competition. If, for example, in a market which was, or bordered upon becoming, oligopolistic, the effect of a discrimination were to threaten to drive out some competitors or to discourage significant potential entry, the discrimination might have adverse effect even though it did

---

Beatrice Foods Co., 76 F.T.C. 719, 800 (1969), aff'd sub nom., Kroger Co. v. FTC, 438 F.2d 1372 (6th Cir.), cert. denied 404 U.S. 871, 92 S.Ct. 59, 30 L. Ed.2d 115 (1971); Lloyd A. Fry Roofing Co., 68 F.T.C. 217, 260 (1965), aff'd 371 F.2d 277 (7th Cir. 1966); Champion Spark Plug Co., 50 F.T.C. 30 (1953).

6. Use of the diversion test may be implicit in the cease and desist orders in Faber Brothers, Inc., FTC Dkt. 8062 (Mar. 16, 1961); Gojer, Inc., FTC Dkt. 7851 (Dec. 1, 1960); Empire Plastic Corp., 55 F.T.C. 103 (1958).

7. Dean Milk Co. v. FTC, 395 F.2d 696 (7th Cir. 1968).

8. Utah Pie Co. v. Continental Baking Co., 386 U.S. 685, 87 S.Ct. 1326, 18 L. Ed.2d 406 (1967).

9. 348 U.S. 115, 119, 75 S.Ct. 148, 150, 99 L.Ed. 145, 149 (1954).

10. At least one court has held that "injury to a competitor" due to discrimination is a violation if, but only if, the low price is supported by higher prices elsewhere. Shore Gas & Oil Co. v. Humble Oil & Ref. Co., 224 F. Supp. 922, 926–27 (D.N.J.1963). The way a party would establish the existence or non-existence of the crucial causal relationship, assuming that the seller was selling at different prices to different buyers and earning profits on its total operations, remains a matter of speculation.

11. See, e.g., Anheuser-Busch, Inc. v. FTC, 289 F.2d 835, 839 (7th Cir. 1961).

not entail sales below cost or otherwise display conventional signs of predation.

Even if the rule were that such a threat to structure had to be shown, one might be concerned, perhaps, that efficiency might be stifled, or that price competition might be discouraged. The existence of discriminatory differentials, if not explicable on the basis of cost differences, would be some assurance that the discrimination had pronounced tactical qualities and was not merely the reflection of a long run competitive strategy to price at a low level in the particular market. But there would remain the danger, perhaps not easily avoided, that such a rule would cut against efforts by oligopolists to surreptitiously reduce cartel-established or interdependent prices, and hence serve to support an anticompetitive pricing structure. There is a shadowy line between forbidding discriminations which threaten structure and forbidding those that reflect more lively price competition. Suppose, for example, that there are in a market six large firms and twenty small ones and that one of the large firms begins a course of discriminatory reductions which the other large firms follow, a course which threatens the profits of the small firms severely. The pre-existing pricing system may have been one of oligopolistic "limit pricing"; the large firms may have been taking monopoly profits and holding a price umbrella over smaller, less efficient firms which remained in the market at the dominant firm's largesse. Is the structure worsened if the small firms, or the least efficient of them, are driven out by the advent of price competition among the large firms? Certainly performance is not worsened, but improved, at least if the price competition does not prove to be a temporary tempest which soon settles once again to stability.

But the case law is highly ambiguous even about whether harmful structural change must be shown when predatory intent has not been established through evidence of price-cost relationships. Some cases besides *Dean Milk* suggest that a threat to structure must be shown when predatory intent is not established. *Anheuser-Busch* [12] indicated that it is lawful for a firm to reduce its prices in one of several regional, oligopolistic markets, so long as it does not act in a predatory or vindictive way; there, the court saw the cuts as part of a general intensification of sales effort—that is, as a lawful attempt to gain a larger market share. Indeed, the Commission itself once took the position that harmful structural impacts need to be shown if a violation is assertedly based on primary line effects.[13] However, the

---

12. Anheuser-Busch, Inc. v. FTC, 289 F.2d 835 (7th Cir. 1961).

13. E.g., Dean Milk Co., 68 F.T.C. 710 (1965) (finding of violation warranted on evidence of discrimination causing losses to competitors which portend either a financial crippling of competitors, a possibility of anticompetitive concentration of business in larger sellers, or significant reduction of number of sellers in the market). The Commission was reversed on the ground that the factor showed only

Supreme Court's decision in *Utah Pie* [14] stands against that view.[15] Utah Pie, the plaintiff, sold frozen pies only in one regional market, where it had at one time over 65% of sales. Three national firms entered that market where there were also a number of smaller firms. Price cutting, usually initiated by one of the national firms, broke out and over a period of years (during which the national firms consistently sold at lower prices than in other regional markets) general price levels went down considerably. There was some evidence from which the jury could have inferred predation: each of the national firms had at one time or other made sales below cost in the heat of the price wars, one of them with some frequency, and one of those firms had also used industrial spies. But all of this was of rather small consequence in the total context. During the four year period, volume increased fourfold, Utah Pie's sales and profits both increased considerably, and it retained its volume lead by a substantial margin. In the end, Utah Pie's share fell to about 45%. It remained the largest firm in the market, its nearest rival being one of the national firms which had less than 30%. The Court, affirming a jury verdict, held that the national firms engaged in unlawful discriminations.

The opinion indicates that the crucial facts which warranted the verdict were (1) differences in price between markets and (2) a general and lasting decline in the local price structure. The opinion does not make legality turn on the fact of sales below cost or on any general assessment of evidence of predatory intent. The essence of it seems to be that a firm operating in two or more markets cannot engage (except perhaps sporadically) in price competition in any one or more of those markets without doing so in all. One can hardly conceive of an approach better calculated to protect oligopolistic price structures against erosion; as soon as any multi-market firm begins to "cheat" on the cartel or to undercut interdependent prices in any market, the other firms there can sue to recover their lost monopoly profits. There is little doubt, on the *Utah Pie* facts, that the plaintiff's profits (and the profits of the national firms and the small firms) were lower, as a consequence of the falling price levels, than they would have been had the large firms refrained from any local reductions; but the healthy profits still being earned in the market strongly suggested that all that happened was that some of the monopoly profits previously being earned in an oligopolistic market had been squeezed out.[16]

sporadic, rather than persistent discrimination. Dean Milk Co. v. FTC, 395 F.2d 696 (7th Cir. 1968).

14. Utah Pie Co. v. Continental Baking Co., 386 U.S. 685, 87 S.Ct. 1326, 18 L. Ed.2d 406 (1967).

15. *Utah Pie* has been forcefully criticized. Among the most trenchant of the comments on the case is Bowman, Restraint of Trade by the Supreme Court. The Utah Pie Case, 77 Yale L.J. 70 (1967).

16. Id.

Over against *Utah Pie*, a case out of harmony with traditional antitrust concerns, must be placed the decision in *Cement Institute*.[17] The latter case condemned the industry-wide use of a multiple basing point pricing system as violative of Clayton Section 2(a). The Court held that sales at delivered prices to distant buyers on which substantial freight was paid by the seller were discriminatorily lower than sales at the same nominal delivered price to nearby firms, where the seller's freight cost was lower. It concluded that seller line competition was injured because the practice facilitated price leadership and the abeyance of price competition. Here, in short, Section 2(a) was brought adeptly into service to challenge a practice which facilitated cartelization or interdependent pricing. The Court had earlier held that delivered pricing systems violated Robinson-Patman on the more tenuous ground that nearby buyers, who were discriminated against, were injured in resale competition.[18] Although the FTC has apparently abandoned the view that the "price" for Robinson-Patman Act purposes is the "mill net return," even when customers are billed on a delivered price basis,[19] there is still an occasional case suggestive of the possibility that delivered prices, even when used noncollusively, can be challenged as discriminatory.[20] Circumstances under which delivered prices may be vulnerable, however, are shrouded in doubt. The best solution, perhaps, is to treat any consistently applied and seemingly rational pricing system as non-discriminatory, and to evaluate legality of pricing systems under the Sherman Act, which is much more sensitive than Robinson-Patman to competitive values.[21]

Viewing the primary line cases as a whole,[22] one cannot do better in seeking to restate the law than to turn to Frederick Rowe's factor analysis, published more than a decade ago. Indicative of injury are such factors as: large market share in seller; aggressive objectives toward weaker rivals; deep and sustained undercutting; sales below cost; demise of rivals. Pointing the other way are such

17. FTC v. Cement Institute, 333 U.S. 683, 68 S.Ct. 793, 92 L.Ed. 1010 (1948).

18. Corn Prods. Ref. Co. v. FTC, 324 U.S. 726, 65 S.Ct. 961, 89 L.Ed. 1320 (1945); FTC v. A. E. Staley Mfg. Co., 324 U.S. 746, 65 S.Ct. 971, 89 L.Ed. 1338 (1945).

19. National Lead Co., 49 F.T.C. 791 (1953), modified sub nom. National Lead Co. v. FTC, 227 F.2d 825 (7th Cir. 1955), original order aff'd, 352 U. S. 419, 77 S.Ct. 502, 1 L.Ed.2d 438 (1957). But cf. Advisory Op. No. 147, 72 F.T.C. 1050 (1967).

20. E.g., Guyott Co. v. Texaco, Inc., 261 F.Supp. 942 (D.Conn.1966); Chicago Spring Prods. Co. v. United States Steel Corp., 254 F.Supp. 83 (N.D.Ill. 1965), aff'd per curiam, 371 F.2d 428 (7th Cir. 1966).

21. See generally §§ 47, 93–100 supra.

22. Among the more recent cases are Continental Baking Co. v. Old Homestead Bread Co., 476 F.2d 97 (10th Cir.), cert. denied, 414 U.S. 975, 94 S. Ct. 290, 38 L.Ed.2d 218 (1973); Gas-A-Car, Inc. v. American Petrofina, Inc., 484 F.2d 1102 (10th Cir. 1973); National Dairy Prods. Corp. v. FTC, 412 F.2d 605, 623 N. 11 (7th Cir. 1969); Lloyd A. Fry Roofing Co. v. FTC, 371 F.2d 277 (7th Cir. 1966); Bergjans Farms Dairy Co. v. Sanitary Milk Prods., 368 F.2d 679 (8th Cir. 1966).

factors as: small market share in seller; growth of competitors in terms of shares, volume or profits; prevalence of comparable price variations by others; inroads by various sellers on customers of others; ease of entry; and other traditional indicia of a vigorous, competitive market.[23] If courts would evaluate factors such as these and find seller line injury only when predatory intent was plainly discernible or damage to the structure of the market was imminent, Robinson-Patman could be a useful adjunct to antitrust, rather than a statute at odds with antitrust.

PART C. VERTICAL COMPETITIVE EFFECTS

§ 222. Social Effects in General

The original Section 2 of the Clayton Act, with the standard Clayton Act test as to competitive effect, was applied principally when injury to competition at the seller level was feared.[1] It also contained an explicit exception for quantity discounts; thus it did not preclude retail chains or other large buyers from obtaining lower prices than smaller competitors whether or not they used market power to gain such price advantages.[2] The Robinson-Patman amendment was, in part, a measure to help small retailers fend off large competitors irrespective of efficiency differences. It brought Section 2 of Clayton into service to challenge some price concessions to large buyers. Again, the difficult question is, which ones?

To the extent that the price discrimination law precludes a buyer from using substantial power to gain price advantages over competitors, it may help to achieve the goals of competition. Compare a firm exercising monopoly power with one exercising monopsony power. The former sets a higher than competitive selling price. In doing so, it takes into account the demand curve of the entire industry of buyers;[3] it also takes into account not just its own individual supply curve, but the supply curve of the industry it represents.[4] Any small firms which are in the same market as the monopolist get the benefit of the spread between the monopolist's price and a competitive price; buyers cannot force these small firms to sell at any lower price. Thus, even if the small competitors are less efficient than is the monopolist they can stay in the market so long as the monopolist's profit maximizing (or entry limiting) price is high enough

---

23. Rowe, supra note 1, at 160–63.

1. See § 220 supra.

2. See F. Rowe, Price Discrimination Under the Robinson-Patman Act at 7, 114–20, and 267 (1962).

3. See §§ 6 and 7 supra.

4. Id. If the firm is in theoretical terms a true monopolist its own supply curve is the industry curve. In law, a firm may be a monopolist though there are other less powerful firms supplying the same market. See §§ 12–32 supra.

to cover the costs incurred by the less efficient small firms. By contrast, a firm with monopsony power sets a lower than competitive purchase price. In doing so, it does not consider that it is setting a price for itself and for small buyers in the same market; it need think only of its own demand curve. Given any assumed supply curve for the selling industry, the monopsonist is able to obtain a lower price than would prevail under competition; and sellers, since they may exact higher prices from any other buyers lacking power, will reach a different adjustment than if they were forced to give the lower price to all. Unlike small firms selling in a monopolist's market, which have the ability to shelter under the monopolist's price, small firms buying in the same market as a monopsonist get no benefit from the monopsonist's low price. Sellers which have buckled under to the monopolist may still insist on prices at higher levels from small, powerless buyers.

But if the law intervenes to effectively preclude such discrimination, that distinction between monopsony and monopoly, that seeming anomaly, is ended. Then, the monopsonist will succeed in exacting from sellers only such reductions as the sellers are willing to give also to other buyers; given the supply curve of the supplying industry, the monopsonist now sets a price for all firms purchasing in its market just as a monopolist sets a price for all firms selling in its market. The monopsonist becomes the mirror image of the monopolist. Its lower purchase prices are available also to competitors; less efficient competitors can stay in and more efficient ones gain supra-competitive returns.

Is it socially beneficial that the monopsonist not be able to force sellers to discriminate in its favor? As a consequence, sellers would tend to be paid prices which were higher and their output would tend to be higher, closer to competitive levels. Though one cannot say that this adjustment improves resource allocations in any ultimate sense, it may nonetheless be seen as preferable simply because it reduces the power of the monopsonist; the range within which the monopsonist is able to alter prices and output is reduced. There may also be a concept of political fairness at work. It may seem more appropriate that buyers, large and small, receive the same price if there is no efficiency reason for the large buyer to obtain a lower one.

But the price discrimination law may not stop where monopsony power ends. What are the standards for evaluating downstream competitive effects, the impacts on "secondary line" competition? How do these and the statutory defenses interact? Does the law, by reason of its broad sweep, prohibit those discriminations that may aid competition, that may, indeed, be fairly characterized as competition in action? Does it inhibit price differences based on efficiency? To these and related questions we now turn.

§ 223. Loss of Business by Disfavored Customers as a *Prima Facie* Case

Most Section 2(a) cases involve secondary line competitive effects. The FTC has used a "diversion" test for identifying injury to competition between the buyer and others: if the buyer which knowingly receives the advantage of a discrimination resells at a lower price than his competitors and, in consequence, the competitors (or one of them) lose substantial business to the favored buyer, a *prima facie* case of injury to competition has been made out. This diversion test was first expressly announced in *Standard Oil* where the Commission found a violation on the basis of the competitive advantage resulting from a discrimination which was used to divert large amounts of business from other retailers.[1] From this the Commission inferred injury to the competitors' ability to continue in business and successfully compete.[2] In *Morton Salt*[3] this position was pressed to an extreme. Even though salt represents a very small portion of a retail grocer's business, the Commission inferred from a substantial discrimination on salt—the only fact directly proved—that because the favored buyer was able to resell at lower prices, it was able to divert business, and thus cause competitive injury. In affirming, the Supreme Court stressed that the discrimination was significant, and that the resale market was characterized by low profit margins and keen competition. The opinion may thus imply that if the amount of the discrimination is small or profits are large an inference of diversion would not be warranted. This implication is even clearer in *Minneapolis-Honeywell*.[4] The court held that quantity discounts on temperature controls sold to manufacturers of oil burners did not violate the Act. It emphasized that the evidence failed to show a direct relationship between the prices for these components and the ultimate price charged by manufacturers for oil burners. Despite these indications from *Morton Salt* and *Minneapolis-Honeywell* that diversion (and hence, competitive injury) are not to be inferred routinely from the mere fact of discrimination, the FTC decisions continue to hold that, subject to rebuttal, secondary line injury is established by

---

1. 41 F.T.C. 263 (1945), aff'd sub nom. Standard Oil Co. v. FTC, 173 F.2d 210 (7th Cir. 1949), order set aside on other grounds, 355 U.S. 396, 78 S.Ct. 369, 2 L.Ed.2d 359 (1958).

2. Id.

3. FTC v. Morton Salt Co., 334 U.S. 37, 68 S.Ct. 822, 92 L.Ed. 1196 (1948).

4. Minneapolis-Honeywell Regulator Co. v. FTC, 191 F.2d 786 (7th Cir. 1951), cert. dismissed, 344 U.S. 206, 73 S.Ct. 245, 97 L.Ed. 245 (1952). See also American Oil Co. v. FTC, 325 F.2d 101 (7th Cir. 1963), cert. denied, 377 U.S. 954, 84 S.Ct. 1631, 12 L.Ed.2d 498 (1964) which held that an inference of adverse effect was unwarranted where discrimination lasted only a short time. Accord: International Film Center Inc. v. Graflex, Inc., 427 F.2d 334 (3d Cir. 1970). FTC decisions in which the commission concluded that inference of injury was not warranted under the *Morton Salt* doctrine include: Frank G. Shattuck Co., 65 F.T.C. 315 (1964); Fred Bronner Corp., 57 F.T.C. 771 (1960).

evidence of discrimination in the sale of homogeneous products where resale markups and profit margins are low.[5]

§ 224. Substantial Profit Advantage for the Favored Customer as a *Prima Facie* Case

In *Corn Products*[1] the FTC and the court of appeals approved the inference of competitive injury where some manufacturers were forced to pay more than some of their competitors for a raw material even though, because of high elasticity of demand, they did not increase resale prices at all and thus suffered no diversion of business. The inference of competitive injury was based on the inference that the higher price meant a lower profit even though business was not lost. The Supreme Court affirmed without considering this question. In *Standard Motor Products*[2] the FTC predicated findings of injury on discrimination plus vigorous resale competition and small profit margins, and the reviewing court affirmed, without evidence of, and without any inference of, a resale price differential or a diversion. As the Court of Appeals for the Seventh Circuit put the matter, it is "not necessary that [the] price advantage be used to lower the resale price and thereby attract business away from non-favored competitors."[3] That court's view, like that of the Eighth Circuit,[4] was that a profit penalty upon the disfavored buyer is all that need be shown, and that this is inferred from the cost difference itself.[5] Though there are some cases which seem to call for more meticulous analysis of the competitive dynamic, and which seem to hold that secondary line injury will not be lightly inferred,[6] there are many cases to the effect that evidence of low profit margins and price-sensitive

---

5. For summaries of the Commission's view in cases sustaining its findings see Kroger Co. v. FTC, 438 F.2d 1372, 1379 (6th Cir.), cert. denied, 404 U.S. 871, 92 S.Ct. 59, 30 L.Ed.2d 115 (1971); Foremost Dairies, Inc. v. FTC, 348 F. 2d 674 (5th Cir. 1965), cert. denied 382 U.S. 959, 86 S.Ct. 435, 15 L.Ed.2d 362 (1965); United Biscuit Co. v. FTC, 350 F.2d 615 (7th Cir. 1965), cert. denied 383 U.S. 926, 86 S.Ct. 930, 15 L. Ed.2d 845 (1966). Cf. Gold Strike Stamp Co. v. Christensen, 436 F.2d 791 (10th Cir. 1970).

1. Corn Prods. Ref. Co. v. FTC, 144 F. 2d 211 (7th Cir. 1944), aff'd, 324 U.S. 726, 65 S.Ct. 961, 89 L.Ed. 1320 (1945).

2. Standard Motor Prods. v. FTC, 265 F.2d 674 (2d Cir.), cert. denied, 361 U. S. 826, 80 S.Ct. 73, 4 L.Ed.2d 69 (1959). For other like cases in the same industry, automotive parts, see the cases collected in F. Rowe, Price Discrimination Under the Robinson-Patman Act 184 n. 49 (1962).

3. E. Edelmann & Co. v. FTC, 239 F.2d 152, 155 (7th Cir. 1956), cert. denied 355 U.S. 941, 78 S.Ct. 426, 2 L.Ed.2d 422 (1958).

4. Moog Industries, Inc. v. FTC, 238 F.2d 43, 50 (8th Cir. 1956), aff'd. 355 U.S. 411, 78 S.Ct. 377, 2 L.Ed.2d 370 (1958).

5. See also Kroger Co. v. FTC, 438 F. 2d 1372 (6th Cir.), cert. denied, 404 U. S. 871, 92 S.Ct. 59, 30 L.Ed.2d 115 (1971); Mississippi Petroleum, Inc. v. Vermont Gas Sys., Inc., 1972 CCH Trade Cas. ¶ 73,843 (S.D.Miss.).

6. Borden Co. v. FTC, 381 F.2d 175, 180 (5th Cir. 1967) (a price difference no greater than the consumer preference for the higher priced advertised brand product over the lower priced unadvertised brand product does not cause injury); Tri-Valley Packing Ass'n v. FTC, 329 F.2d 694, 703–04 (9th Cir. 1964) (availability of the lower price

conditions warrant an inference of injury on a mere showing that buyers were charged different prices.[7] Evidence that the disfavored buyer is failing due in whole or in part to the discrimination would reinforce the inference, no doubt, but seems not to be essential as a basis for the inference.

§ 225. Rebutting a *Prima Facie* Case of Competitive Injury

a. *De Minimis Effect on Total Operations*

Suppose the accused seller shows that buyers of the product use it as a raw material in a manufacturing process, that to each buyer the cost of seller's product is a trivial part of total manufacturing or processing costs, and that considered as a part of buyers' total costs the difference between what the preferred and disadvantaged buyers pay for seller's product is *de minimis*. Does this showing rebut the inference of injury drawn in cases like *Corn Products*[1] and *Standard Motor Products*[2]? *Minneapolis-Honeywell*[3] supports an affirmative answer. There the court held that discounts on temperature control units did not impair resale competition on burners since there was little, if any, relationship between prices for the controls and those for the burners. Factors like manufacturing methods, overhead, distribution costs, service, and advertising all had important bearings on cost and price which rendered the cost difference on controls relatively trivial. Though the case may seem difficult to distinguish from *Morton Salt*,[4] many courts[5], though not all,[6] have given the view it adopts full credence.

from the discriminating seller or from other sellers negates competitive injury); Chapman v. Rudd Paint & Varnish Co., 409 F.2d 635 (9th Cir. 1969) (availability). See also Quaker Oats Co., 66 F.T.C 1131 (1964), where the Commission critically evaluated evidence of competitive effect at the buyer level.

7. E.g., Fowler Mfg. Co. v. Gorlick, 415 F.2d 1248, 1253 (9th Cir. 1969) (lessening of competition inferred from price difference); United Biscuit Co. v. FTC, 350 F.2d 615 (7th Cir. 1965), cert. denied 383 U.S. 926, 86 S.Ct. 930, 15 L.Ed.2d 845 (1966) (evidence of cumulative monthly discount to some buyers sufficient to establish competitive effect); Purolator Prods., Inc. v. FTC, 352 F.2d 874 (7th Cir. 1965), cert. denied 389 U.S. 1045, 88 S.Ct. 758, 19 L.Ed.2d 837 (1968) (inference drawn although favored customer incurred added expenses for additional services); Mueller Co. v. FTC, 323 F.2d 44 (7th Cir. 1963), cert. denied, 377 U.S. 923, 84 S.Ct. 1219, 12 L.Ed.2d 215 (1964) (inference drawn though only small portion of instances business affected).

1. Corn Prods. Ref. Co. v. FTC, 144 F. 2d 211 (7th Cir. 1944), aff'd, 324 U.S. 726, 65 S.Ct. 961, 89 L.Ed. 1320 (1945). See § 224 supra.

2. Standard Motor Prods. Inc. v. FTC, 265 F.2d 674 (2d Cir.), cert. denied, 361 U.S. 826, 80 S.Ct. 73, 4 L.Ed.2d 69 (1959). See § 224 supra.

3. Minneapolis-Honeywell Regulator Co. v. FTC, 191 F.2d 786, 791 (7th Cir. 1951), cert. dismissed, 344 U.S. 206, 73 S.Ct. 245, 97 L.Ed. 245 (1952).

4. FTC v. Morton Salt Co., 334 U.S. 37, 68 S.Ct. 822, 92 L.Ed. 1196 (1948).

5. E.g., American Oil Co. v. FTC, 325 F.2d 101 (7th Cir. 1963), cert. denied, 377 U.S. 954, 84 S.Ct. 1631, 12 L.Ed.2d 498 (1964); cf. Borden Co. v. FTC, 381 F.2d 175, 180 (5th Cir. 1967).

6. E.g., Foremost Dairies, Inc. v. FTC, 348 F.2d 674 (5th Cir. 1965), cert. de-

The issue is not unlike those presented in case law under the rubric of proximate cause. If operations at the downstream level tend to be standardized, so that all competitors tend to experience similar costs for all other aspects of their business, and if profit margins are low so that any cost disadvantage will be experienced as a competitive threat, it seems plausible to follow the reverberations of any discrimination through the system. If, by contrast, the reseller has a wide discretion as to all or many of its other costs, the effect of the discrimination may stand to the ordinary eye as but one of many factors having impact on the competitive contest—one which, by itself, does not have much consequence.

Of course, even where the effect of the discrimination can be traced through, all that has been shown is an impact on the disadvantaged competitors. Unless this disadvantage threatens eventual structural change adverse to competition, it is difficult to perceive a basis for inferring injury to the process of competition. One of the major differences between antitrust and Robinson-Patman is that secondary line cases lack any requirement that injury be shown to competitive structure or process; they rely instead on injury to particular firms in the market. Perhaps we must at this stage accept that Robinson-Patman is tuned in significant degree to the task of protecting individual small competitors irrespective of their significance to the competitive process and without regard to their efficiency. There is warrant in the history of the statute for construing it so [7] and the courts have regularly done so.

b. *Offsetting Additional Costs Incurred by the Favored Buyer*

Suppose that a buyer undertakes to perform functions of advantage to the seller, such as keeping an inventory on hand, and that the seller grants a price concession no greater than sufficient to offset the additional costs of that function. In logic the price difference is not discriminatory; in law it is. Though the price difference cannot cause a lower price, nor a diversion, nor a higher profit, the case law is adverse. *Mueller* serves as an example.[8] The manufacturer gave a lower price to so called limit jobbers. These jobbers, unlike regular jobbers, maintained an inventory and made deliveries. Regular jobbers merely took orders, the manufacturer itself making deliveries. The FTC rejected the contention that the price difference was not unlawful if no greater than necessary to cover the inventory expense of limit jobbers; it said that this method of doing business was itself a

---

nied 382 U.S. 959, 86 S.Ct. 435, 15 L. Ed.2d 362; United Biscuit Co. v. FTC, 350 F.2d 615 (7th Cir. 1965), cert. denied, 383 U.S. 926, 86 S.Ct. 930, 15 L. Ed.2d 845 (1966).

7. See F. Rowe, Price Discrimination Under the Robinson-Patman Act Ch. 1, particularly §§ 1.1, 1.3 and 1.7 (1962).

8. Mueller Co. v. FTC, 323 F.2d 44 (7th Cir. 1963), cert. denied, 377 U.S. 923, 84 S.Ct. 1219, 12 L.Ed.2d 215 (1964). See also Purolator Prods., Inc. v. FTC, 352 F.2d 874 (7th Cir. 1965), cert. denied, 389 U.S. 1045, 88 S.Ct. 758, 19 L.Ed.2d 837 (1968).

competitive advantage to limit jobbers and the price difference a way of preferring the limit jobbers by paying for that advantage! Other courts may yet accept the contrary view, at least upon convincing proof that the lower price to the "favored" buyers no more than offset their added costs.

Some manufacturers sell at lower prices to buyers at a higher level in the distribution chain than to buyers at a lower level. For example, a manufacturer might charge $1.00 to distributors, $1.50 to wholesalers and $2.00 to purchasers lower on the chain which use the product as a raw material in further processing. If each buyer resells only at its own functional level—distributors only to wholesalers, wholesalers only to users, users only after processing—analysis suggests that these "functional discounts" cannot injure resale competition. That is the position the Commission initially took,[9] thereafter doubted [10] and eventually abandoned.[11]

Functional discounts are most likely to be challenged when a buyer at the vertical level receiving a price preference resells to a firm at the next level with which it is integrated. Suppose, for example, that a manufacturer sells to wholesalers at 70 and to retailers at 100. If one of the wholesalers buying at 70 supplies a subsidiary at the retail level, other competing retailers which buy direct at 100 may claim they have been disadvantaged.[12] The actual economic consequence is not determinate merely because the wholesaler and a retailer are integrated. The integrated wholesaler might have performed all of the same functions as other wholesalers, or it might not. The amount of the functional discount might accurately reflect differences in costs incurred by the seller in selling to wholesalers and to retailers, or it might be higher or lower than the cost difference. Such factors ought to signify in deciding whether there is injury to competition between the integrated retailer and the non-integrated retailers which buy from the manufacturer at 100. At one extreme, the "wholesaler" may be merely a corporate name through which orders are placed for one or more retailers which own the wholesaler; actual deliveries may be made to the retailers at their places of business much as they are to retailers buying at 100. There may conceivably be some savings to the manufacturer in billing to the wholesale corporation, but they are probably not large enough to justify the price difference.

9. Doubleday & Co., 52 F.T.C. 169, 209 (1955).

10. General Foods Corp., 52 F.T.C. 798 (1956).

11. Mueller Co., 60 F.T.C. 120, 127 (1962), aff'd sub nom. Mueller Co. v. FTC, 323 F.2d 44 (7th Cir. 1963), cert. denied, 377 U.S. 923, 84 S.Ct. 1219, 12 L.Ed.2d 215 (1964).

12. E.g., Mid-South Distributors v. FTC, 287 F.2d 512 (5th Cir.), cert. denied, 368 U.S. 838, 82 S.Ct. 36, 7 L. Ed.2d 39 (1961); Standard Motor Prods. Inc. v. FTC, 265 F.2d 674 (2d Cir.), cert. denied, 361 U.S. 826, 80 S. Ct. 73, 4 L.Ed.2d 69 (1959).

In these circumstances the lower price to the wholesaler than to retailers competing with the wholesaler's "customers" may be held to injure competition,[13] or the transaction may be recast as one in which the preferred retailers are treated as the real purchasers, the transaction with the wholesaler being characterized as a screen.[14]

Where some of the elements noted above are present, but others are not, applicability of Section 2(a) may be a matter of doubt. Suppose, for example, that an independent wholesaler operates without warehouse or other facilities, taking orders from retailers, placing them with the manufacturer, billing the customer, and bearing the credit risk, but that the manufacturer makes direct deliveries. Or suppose that a firm performing a full line of wholesale functions, including warehousing and reshipping, is cooperatively owned by retailers. In neither instance would the manufacturer's sale to the wholesaler at a price below its price on direct sales to retailers be fairly characterized as a mere cloak to disguise direct sales to retailers.

Note also that some buyers (like the manufacturer-seller itself) may sell to buyers at different horizontal levels. For example, a distributor which buys from the manufacturer and sells mostly to wholesalers which resell to retailers may also sell in competition with wholesalers to retailers. It might then be argued that the distributor's "functional discount" from the first seller, the manufacturer, enabled it to resell to retailers at lower prices than could wholesalers. In such a case, a showing by the first seller that the distributor incurred costs not incurred by wholesalers which offset the price difference ought to be sufficient to rebut any inference of adverse competitive effect. The case law, however, looks the other way.[15]

There is yet another offsetting cost issue of some interest. Suppose firms A and B sell in the same market, and that A has some competitive advantage—a better location, perhaps, or a patented technology—which gives it a cost advantage over B of $1.00 per unit

---

13. See cases cited in note 12 supra.

14. E.g., Monroe Auto Equip. Co. v. FTC, 347 F.2d 401 (7th Cir. 1965), cert. denied, 382 U.S. 1009, 86 S.Ct. 613, 15 L.Ed.2d 525 (1966); National Dairy Products Corp. v. FTC, 395 F.2d 517 (7th Cir.), cert. denied, 393 U.S. 977, 89 S.Ct. 444, 21 L.Ed.2d 438 (1968).

15. Cf. Purolator Prods., Inc. v. FTC, 352 F.2d 874 (7th Cir. 1965), cert. denied, 389 U.S. 1045, 88 S.Ct. 758, 19 L.Ed.2d 837 (1968). There, the FTC had found competitive injury on the ground that lower prices to one buyer than to another cannot be excused because the lower priced buyer performs functions involving additional costs and the court affirmed on the basis of the substantial evidence rule. In Alhambra Motor Parts v. FTC, 309 F.2d 213 (9th Cir. 1962), the court refused to accept the conclusion that a wholesaler was not entitled to the functional discount given other wholesalers merely because it was owned by retailers; the court did not see how the arrangement resulted in injury to other retailers if the integrated wholesaler performed the same function as other wholesalers. However, on remand the FTC reached the same result it had reached originally, although on a somewhat different theory. Alhambra Motor Parts, 68 F.T.C. 1039 (1965).

of output. Now suppose that C, a raw material supplier, selling to both, discriminates in B's favor to a degree which no more than offsets A's cost advantage. An efficiency oriented view of competition would insist that each seller is entitled to its own natural advantages and that it is a distortion of the competitive process to think in terms of handicapping the efficient so as to even things up. If it were assumed that C's costs were the same on sales to A and to B, any economist would define the supposed transaction as a discrimination, whatever he might think about whether the law should be concerned about it.

Yet, there is another attitude which shows itself at times in the law, an egalitarian attitude which pays scant heed to efficiency. For example where a seller treats buyers "equally"—charges all the same prices—the law says no discrimination has occurred even though one buyer may thus be deprived of a locational or other advantage which makes the cost of selling to it lower. One moved by that attitude might say of the above hypothetical that to equalize the position of A and B is to make the competitive struggle a fairer one. Although an early FTC policy statement seemed to adopt the view that price differences sufficient only to even the struggle between firms experiencing different costs in other factors would not be discriminatory,[16] no actual decisions seem to look in that direction. This is an occasion for satisfaction. To adopt the proposition that a pricing program did not discriminate when it merely penalized firms with advantages would be to distort the concept of competition severely.

PART D. BROKERAGE AND ADVERTISING ALLOWANCES

§ 226. The Brokerage Provision

Section 2(c) of Clayton,[1] as amended by Robinson-Patman, makes it unlawful for a buyer to exact price concessions in the form of brokerage commissions to itself or its agents. In terms, it is unlawful for a seller or buyer:

> "to pay or grant, or receive or accept, anything of value as a commission, brokerage, or other compensation, or any allowance or discount in lieu thereof, except for services rendered in connection with the sale or purchase of goods * * * either to the other party to such transaction or to an agent, representative or other intermediary therein where such intermediary is acting in fact for or in behalf, or is subject to

---

16. FTC Policy Statement on Geographic Pricing (1948), 1 CCH Trade Reg.Rep. 5350 (1948). This policy statement is summarized and discussed in Rowe, supra note 7, at 188–89.

1. 15 U.S.C.A. § 13(c) (1973).

the direct or indirect control, of any party to such transaction other than the person by whom such compensation is granted."

The sweeping language of this section covers payments by a seller or by the seller's broker to a buyer, to a purchasing agent or broker owned by or affiliated with a buyer, or to an independent purchasing agent or broker selected by and representing the buyer.[2] So long as the commerce requirement is met all such payments are unlawful, regardless of whether or not any adverse competitive effect occurs.[3] In this respect, Section 2(c) creates a statutory *per se* rule.

The section is sometimes construed exceedingly broadly in yet another respect. Though the statutory language seems to say that the section does not forbid such payment when made to compensate "for services rendered," the cases prior to *Broch* [4] converted the section into a flat prohibition against all such payments.[5] Those cases quite consistently held that only an independent broker retained and controlled by the seller can render real serviecs, and only to these does the statutory exception allude. However, the Supreme Court in *Broch* made a point of not approving that view of the law.[6] Moreover, although some rulings still hew to the line that only payments to brokers wholly independent of the seller can be justified, regardless of the services exception,[7] in the dominant line of cases after *Broch* the Commission itself and many reviewing courts have given a larger and more literal reading to the "for services rendered" exception.[8]

If a transaction is structured in a way which warrants characterizing the payment not as brokerage but as an indirect discrimination, it may be possible to avoid the *per se* rule against brokerage payments to a buyer or its representative. Payment in the form of a rebate of part of the purchase price would, for example, warrant that

2. F. Rowe, Price Discrimination Under the Robinson-Patman Act 350–62 (1962).

3. FTC v. Simplicity Pattern Co., 360 U.S. 55, 65, 79 S.Ct. 1005, 1011–12, 3 L.Ed.2d 1079, 1086 (1959). See also FTC v. Henry Broch & Co., 363 U.S. 166, 170–71, 80 S.Ct. 1158, 161–62, 4 L.Ed.2d 1124, 1128–29 (1960); FTC v. Washington Fish & Oyster Co., 282 F. 2d 595 (9th Cir. 1960).

4. FTC v. Henry Broch & Co., 363 U.S. 166, 80 S.Ct. 1158, 4 L.Ed.2d 1124 (1960).

5. E.g., Quality Bakers of America v. FTC, 114 F.2d 393 (1st Cir. 1940); Great Atlantic & Pac. Tea Co. v. FTC, 106 F.2d 667 (3d Cir. 1939), cert. denied 308 U.S. 625, 60 S.Ct. 380, 84 L. Ed. 521 (1940); Oliver Bros. v. FTC, 102 F.2d 763 (4th Cir. 1939); Biddle Purchasing Co. v. FTC, 96 F.2d 687 (2d Cir. 1938), cert. denied 305 U.S. 634, 59 S.Ct. 101, 83 L.Ed. 407 (1938).

6. FTC v. Henry Broch & Co., 363 U.S. 166, 173–74, 80 S.Ct. 1158, 1162–63, 4 L.Ed.2d 1124, 1130–31 (1960). (The Court upheld a finding of violation but said that "quite a different case" would be presented if the buyer "rendered any service" for the commission).

7. E.g., Norval Co., 1970–73 Transfer Binder, CCH Trade Reg.Rep. ¶ 19.33 (1970) (advisory opinion); Venus Foods, Inc., 57 F.T.C. 1025 (1960).

8. Central Retailer-Owned Grocers, Inc. v. FTC, 319 F.2d 410 (7th Cir. 1963); Thomasville Chair Co. v. FTC, 306 F. 2d 541, 545 (5th Cir. 1962).

characterization.⁹ So characterized, the payment ought to violate the law only if adverse competitive effects result from it.¹⁰ A firm cannot plan on this basis, however. Cases selecting between the alternative ways of viewing a transaction, one of which is *per se* unlawful and one of which is not, are too whimsical to facilitate prediction.

§ 227. The Advertising Allowance Provision

Section 2(d) of Clayton, as amended by Robinson-Patman,¹ applies to payments by a seller to a buyer for the performance of advertising services; Section 2(e), as so amended,² applies to the provision of such services by a seller to a buyer. Where such payments are made or services rendered by a seller, the seller must treat all buyers on "proportionally equal terms."³ Though the concept of "availability" of payments or services on "proportionally equal" terms provides a standard of sorts against which to measure seller conduct, this section also establishes what is, in essence, a *per se* rule. If the payments are made or services rendered on other than proportionally equal terms, there is a violation; no showing of adverse competitive effect is required.⁴ If the Commission shows that promotional offers made available to some customers were not affirmatively called to the attention of competing customers it has made out a *prima facie* case of nonavailability.⁵ Where the seller offers different arrangements to different competing sellers it has the burden of showing that what it offered is "proportionally equal."⁶ The Commission has not been rigid in deciding what constitutes proportional equality but the safest course is to provide to all customers services having a cost (actual or closely approximate) which bears the same relation to the dollar volume or quantity of goods purchased as do the services available to other customers.⁷

The FTC guide for advertising allowances provides a summary of the agency's enforcement policies.⁸ The guide indicates that a seller

---

9. See e.g., General Foods Corp., 52 F.T.C. 798, 814, 828 (1956); New England Confectionery Co., 46 F.T.C. 1041, 1059–60 (1949). Cf. Corn Prods. Ref. Co. v. FTC, 324 U.S. 726, 743–44, 65 S.Ct. 961, 969–70, 89 L.Ed. 1320, 1334–35 (1945).

10. Id. See Rowe, supra note 2, at 106–07.

1. 15 U.S.C.A. § 13(d) (1973).

2. 15 U.S.C.A. § 13(e) (1973).

3. Id. Recently the provision was held to cover payments made as a commercial bribe. Computer Statistics, Inc. v. Blair, 1976–2 CCH Trade Cas. ¶ 61,055 (D.Tex.1976).

4. FTC v. Simplicity Pattern Co., 360 U.S. 55, 79 S.Ct. 1005, 3 L.Ed.2d 1079 (1959).

5. J. Weingarten, Inc., 62 F.T.C. 1521 (1963); Chesnut Farms Chevy Chase Dairy, 53 F.T.C. 1050 (1957).

6. See House of Lords, Inc., 69 F.T.C. 44 (1966); Sunbeam Corp., 56 F.T.C. 1657 (1960).

7. See Sunbeam Corp., 56 F.T.C. 1657 (1960).

8. 1969 Guides for Advertising Allowances and Other Merchandising Payments and Services, 16 C.F.R. § 240.1–.17 (1973). (The Guides, which became effective in 1969, were amended in several respects in 1972.)

which provides or pays for advertising, handbills, window and floor displays, demonstrations or the like must do so under a plan, of which all buyers are notified, and under which all buyers can receive a payment or service proportional to their purchases. For example, a firm selling to retailers might offer a plan for cooperative radio or newspaper advertising; but if, as a practical matter, the plan would be inaccessible to some buyers because they are too small to warrant advertising in those media, the plan would not meet the statutory standards. To comply, the seller would have to amend the plan to offer small customers a feasible alternative, such as cooperative cost sharing on handbills or mailings, on a basis proportionately equal to that on which radio or newspaper advertising was made available.[9]

One of the interesting interpretations of the Section is that in *Fred Meyer, Inc.*[10] which holds, in essence, that a seller which gives promotional assistance to direct buying retailers must also offer it on proportionally equal terms to wholesalers which resell to retailers competing with those that buy direct. Presumably, the wholesalers will have a derivative duty to pass on the allowance to retail customers.

PART E. AFFIRMATIVE DEFENSES

§ 228. Cost Justification

Section 2 of Clayton, as amended by Robinson-Patman, has two important provisos. The first, to be discussed here, appears in Section 2(a) and excepts from the ban on price discrimination "differentials which make only due allowance for differences in cost of manufacture, sale, or delivery resulting from the differing methods or quantities" in which the buyers are supplied.[1] The second, set forth in Section 2(b)[2] and discussed below, excepts discriminations made in good faith to meet competition. The cost justification proviso of Section 2(a) gives the seller an affirmative defense when the seller can prove cost differences of the kinds the proviso describes. If one purchaser has special needs which require special steps in manufacture, that buyer can be charged for these additional costs.[3] The same is true of higher or lower selling or delivery costs.[4] Thus if special dies had to be made for one buyer's orders it would be appropriate to allocate these costs to that buyer; again, if delivery to one buyer were in

---

9. See FTC v. Simplicity Pattern Co., 360 U.S. 55, 79 S.Ct. 1005, 3 L.Ed.2d 1079 (1959).

10. FTC v. Fred Meyer, Inc., 390 U.S. 341, 88 S.Ct. 904, 19 L.Ed.2d 1222 (1968).

1. 15 U.S.C.A. § 13(a) (1973).

2. 15 U.S.C.A. § 13(b) (1973).

3. Thompson Prods., Inc., 55 F.T.C. 1252 (1959); United States Rubber Co., 46 F.T.C. 998 (1950).

4. E.g., American Motors Corp. v. FTC, 384 F.2d 247 (6th Cir. 1967), cert. denied, 390 U.S. 1012, 88 S.Ct. 1260, 20 L.Ed.2d 164 (1968).

carload lots at carload prices and to others in smaller lots at higher prices, charges to the latter might lawfully reflect these differences.

Withal, the proviso has not been particularly useful as a practical matter to sellers seeking to avoid liability. The Commission and the courts have required a fairly precise showing of cost differences and a precise relationship between these differences and the price advantage conceded to the low cost buyer. As a predicate for a cost justification, customers may be grouped into classes and the costs computed for each class. It is not necessary that the cost of each specific buyer, or each transaction, be computed and compared.[5] But the limits to which aggregation of data can be pushed are not very wide. Cost justification classes must be "composed of members of such self sameness as to make the averaging of the cost of dealing with the group a valid and reasonable indicium of the cost of dealing with any specific group member."[6] The justification is most likely to work if a careful cost study is designed and carried out *before* the price differential is established. There is an Advisory Committee Report which may be of some use in designing a study.[7] The study should be done by competent professionals who are directed to compute any measurable cost differences as accurately as reasonably possible. They should avoid groupings which may fail under the *Borden* test. They should avoid excessive averaging. They should avoid devices for measuring central tendency which entail wide deviations. If a rigorous and tight study is done and if the price differences are conformable to this, the likelihood of the justification standing up are high. But a cost study done to justify or rationalize a price difference granted on other bases is not likely to be successful.

It is to be noted that the cost justification, appearing as a proviso to Section 2(a), serves as a defense only to a price discrimination otherwise violative of that section. It does not afford a defense to the granting of a brokerage payment unlawful under 2(c) nor to a discriminatory payment for advertising or promotional services or facilities unlawful under 2(d) or 2(e), nor to the provision by the seller of such services or facilities to one buyer and not others.[8]

---

5. See United States v. Borden Co., 370 U.S. 460, 82 S.Ct. 1309, 8 L.Ed.2d 627 (1962).

6. Id. at 469, 82 S.Ct. at 1314, 8 L. Ed.2d at 634.

7. Advisory Committee to the Federal Trade Commission, Report on Cost Justification (1956). While the Commission has not adopted the guidelines or sanctioned them, they have been cited and given credence by the Court. See United States v. Borden Co., 370 U.S. 460, 469 n. 12, 82 S.Ct. 1309, 1314 n. 12, 8 L.Ed.2d 627, 634 n. 12 (1962).

8. Note also that the statute contains a proviso which authorizes the FTC to override the cost justification by establishing quantity limits for particular commodities or classes of commodities when it finds that "available purchasers in greater quantities are so few as to render differentials on account thereof unjustly discriminatory * * *." 15 U.S.C.A. § 13(b) (1970).

§ 229. Meeting Competition

The first part of Section 2(b)[1] states that when a *prima facie* case of unlawful discrimination has been made out the burden of rebuttal by showing a justification shall be on the party charged.[2] There follows a proviso which states that nothing shall prevent a seller from rebutting the *prima facie* case by showing that "his lower price or the furnishing of services or facilities to any purchaser or purchasers was in good faith to meet an equally low price of a competitor, or the services or facilities furnished by a competitor."[3] This justification differs, then, from the cost justification in that it is available as a defense to the provision of advertising or promotional services or facilities otherwise violative of 2(d) or 2(e);[4] however, the meeting competition proviso presumably would not serve as a defense to a payment for brokerage violative of 2(c),[5] since the proviso refers only to a "price" or the "furnishing of services or facilities."[6]

Standard Oil established that the meeting competition defense, when applicable, is absolute.[7] If the party charged shows that its conduct is covered by the proviso there is no violation. It does not matter that the discrimination may nonetheless injure competition. There are, however, important limitations on the availability of the defense. The question of the legality of the price being met is a matter of some complexity. When primary line injury is charged the seller may not show that it defensively adopted a discriminatory pricing system, such as a basing point system; use of an unlawful pricing system by competitors will not entitle a seller to use it also.[8] On the other hand, in a primary line case a seller which cuts a price to meet a specific offering by a competitor may have the benefit of the proviso even if the competitive price is itself discriminatory and thus unlawful, and, indeed, is known by the firm meeting it to be unlawful.[9] In this kind of a case it is the justifying seller which is the victim of the unlawful price which it is responding to. Its being allowed to respond is, perhaps, the best deterrent to keep the original

---

1. 15 U.S.C.A. § 2(b) (1973).

2. Id.

3. Id.

4. 15 U.S.C.A. § 2(d) and (e) (1973). See § 227 supra.

5. 15 U.S.C.A. § 2(c) (1973).

6. 15 U.S.C.A. § 2(b) (1973).

7. Standard Oil Co. v. FTC, 340 U.S. 231, 251, 71 S.Ct. 240, 250, 95 L.Ed. 239, 251–52 (1951).

8. FTC v. A. E. Staley Mfg. Co., 324 U.S. 746, 753, 756, 65 S.Ct. 971, 974–75, 976, 89 L.Ed. 1338, 1343–44, 1345–46 (1951); FTC v. Standard Oil Co., 335 U.S. 396, 78 S.Ct. 369, 2 L.Ed.2d 359 (1958); Standard Motor Products Inv. v. FTC, 265 F.2d 674, 677 (2d Cir.), cert. denied, 361 U.S. 826, 80 S.Ct. 73, 4 L.Ed.2d 69 (1959); Exquisite Form Brassiere, Inc. v. FTC, 360 F.2d 492, 493 (D.C.Cir. 1965), cert. denied, 384 U.S. 959, 86 S.Ct. 1584, 16 L.Ed.2d 672 (1966). But cf. Callaway Mills Co. v. FTC, 362 F.2d 435, 441 (5th Cir. 1966).

9. Balian Ice Cream Co. v. Arden Farms Co., 231 F.2d 356, 360 (9th Cir. 1955); Dean Milk Co. v. American Processing & Sales Co., 1950–51 CCH Trade Cas. ¶ 62,777 (N.D.Ill.1951).

offending seller from continuing to violate. In secondary line cases the refinements are somewhat different. Although a seller may not meet a competitor's price known to be unlawful, or which it reasonably should know to be unlawful,[10] it should not be obliged to take a legal opinion before reacting to the market. If it meets a price, not knowing whether that price is lawful or not, the availability of the proviso ought not to turn upon its being able to show later that the price it met was lawful, but only upon its having acted in good faith in a situation of competitive necessity.[11]

Good faith bears importantly in another respect. Although normally a seller may only meet and not beat a competitor's price, a firm clearly acting in a defensive manner which inadvertently offers a price somewhat lower than that which it is trying to meet should not lose the benefit of the defense.[12] The defense should be sustained on proof of facts which resulted in a reasonable belief that a price at a particular level was necessary to meet a competitor's price. On the other hand, if the seller acts recklessly, without taking such steps as in the context would be reasonable to verify, the defense ought not to be available.[13] The seller must, of course, avoid verifying with competitors if it is operating in an oligopolistic market in circumstances where a price information exchange would violate Section 1 of the Sherman Act by threatening interdependent prices.[14]

PART F. BUYER LIABILITY

§ 230. Inducing and Receiving Price Discriminations

Section 2(f) of Clayton, as amended by Robinson-Patman, makes it unlawful for a buyer "knowingly to induce or receive a discrimination in price which is prohibited" by Section 2(a).[1] To prove

---

10. See Standard Oil v. Brown, 238 F. 2d 54, 58 (5th Cir. 1956); National Dairy Prods. Corp. v. FTC, 395 F.2d 517, 524 (7th Cir.), cert. denied, 393 U.S. 977, 89 S.Ct. 444, 21 L.Ed.2d 438 (1968); Standard Motor Prods., Inc. v. FTC, 265 F.2d 674 (2d Cir.), cert. denied, 361 U.S. 826, 80 S.Ct. 73, 4 L. Ed.2d 69 (1959).

11. Compare Forster Mfg. Co. v. FTC, 335 F.2d 47, 56 (1st Cir. 1964), cert. denied, 380 U.S. 906, 85 S.Ct. 887, 13 L. Ed.2d 794 (1965).

12. Forster Mfg. Co. v. FTC, 335 F.2d 47 (1st Cir. 1964), cert. denied, 380 U. S. 906, 85 S.Ct. 887, 13 L.Ed.2d 794 (1965) (unrealistic for Commission to insist the buyer obtain "chapter and verse" information before responding);
Callaway Mills Co. v. FTC, 362 F.2d 435 (5th Cir. 1966); Beatrice Foods Co. FTC Dkt. 8663, [1967–1970 Transfer Binder] CCH Trade Reg.Rep. ¶ 19,045 (1969).

13. Viviano Macaroni Co. v. FTC, 411 F.2d 255 (3d Cir. 1969).

14. United States v. Container Corp. of America, 393 U.S. 333, 89 S.Ct. 510, 21 L.Ed.2d 526 (1969). See § 96, supra.

1. 15 U.S.C.A. § 13(f) (1973). For recent cases applying this section see: Mark Plastic Prods., Inc. v. Exxon Corp., 1972–3 CCH Trade Cas. ¶ 74.784 (E.D.Mich.); General Auto Suppliers, Inc. v. FTC, 346 F.2d 311 (7th Cir.), cert. dismissed, 382 U.S. 923 86 S.Ct. 304, 15 L.Ed.2d 239 (1965).

a violation of Section 2(f) a violation by the seller of 2(a) must be established.[2] The party charging a violation does not prevail merely on showing a *prima facie* case of seller violation (either on a primary line or secondary line theory) and that the buyer knew the relevant facts. The charging party prevails only if the buyer also knew that the discrimination was not cost justified or otherwise capable of being defended. In *Automatic Canteen,* the Supreme Court held that there is no violation of 2(f) if the lower price is either within one of the seller's defenses or not known by the buyer not to be.[3] Though the burden of proving facts from which the requisite buyer knowledge could be inferred is placed squarely on the charging party, the Court indicated that the burden could be carried by establishing that the buyer had sufficient trade experience to warrant an inference of such knowledge. For example, having proven the unlawful discrimination granted at the buyer's behest, the party charging a buyer violation may prevail by proving further that the buyer knew that other buyers were paying a higher price and that the others purchased in quantities and received delivery by methods comparable to those on the sales to the preferred buyer, so that no cost justification would be available.[4] Some cases, indeed, have upheld an inference of sufficient buyer knowledge that the price is discriminately low on quite sketchy evidence, such as that seller protested the buyer's price demands, or insistence by the buyer upon the price, despite seller resistance or demand for some concession in addition to normal quantity or other discounts.[5]

The case law is less clear about what kind of evidence will carry the charging party's burden of showing that the buyer knew that the seller could not cost justify; it seems that the burden of proof requires no more than that facts be shown from which it can be inferred that the importuning buyer would, had he considered the matter, have realized that a successful cost justification defense was distinctly unlikely.[6] Obviously the buyer does not win merely by showing that he never did a cost study and thus did not know what the

---

2. Automatic Canteen Co. of America v. FTC, 346 U.S. 61, 73 S.Ct. 1017, 97 L.Ed. 1454 (1953).

3. Id.

4. Compare American Motor Specialties Co., 55 F.T.C. 1430 (1959), aff'd, 278 F. 2d 225, 228 (2d Cir.), cert. denied, 364 U.S. 884, 81 S.Ct. 169, 5 L.Ed.2d 105 (1960); Mid-South Distributors v. FTC, 287 F.2d 512 (5th Cir.), cert. denied, 368 U.S. 838, 82 S.Ct. 36, 7 L. Ed.2d 39 (1961).

5. See Fred Meyer, Inc. v. FTC, 359 F. 2d 351 (9th Cir. 1966), cert. denied, 386 U.S. 908, 87 S.Ct. 851, 17 L.Ed.2d 782 (1967); Giant Food, Inc. v. FTC, 307 F.2d 184 (D.C.Cir. 1962), cert. denied, 372 U.S. 910, 83 S.Ct. 723, 9 L.Ed.2d 718 (1963); American News Co. v. FTC, 300 F.2d 104, 110 (2d Cir.), cert. denied, 371 U.S. 824, 83 S.Ct. 44, 9 L. Ed.2d 64 (1962); R. H. Macy & Co. v. FTC, 326 F.2d 445, 449 (2d Cir. 1964). Although some of these cases involve buyer liability under Section 5 of the FTC Act for inducing seller to grant allowances, the applicable principles seem identical.

6. See Suburban Propane Gas Corp., 73 F.T.C. 1269 (1968).

outcome of one would be. It has also been held that a buyer acting in bad faith may be liable for inducing a discrimination—for example, by misleading the seller about what other sellers are offering—even though the seller—since acting in good faith—can make out a defense on the basis of the "meeting competition" provision.[7] That holding, although not directly relevant on the question of buyer ability to avoid liability because of a claimed lack of cost information, is suggestive of the critical attitude courts may take to the buyer which seeks to hide conduct that violates the spirit of Section 2(f) under a cloak of punctiliousness. Note, also, that the charging party's burden to show buyer knowledge may not relate to the defense of meeting competition or changed conditions.[8]

§ 231. Inducing and Receiving Brokerage or Advertising Allowances

Section 2(c) specifically provides that it is unlawful "to receive or accept" as well as "to pay or grant" brokerage except for services rendered;[1] there is not even any requirement that this be done "knowingly." Hence, the brokerage provisions apply to buyers and sellers with the same rigor.[2] Section 2(d),[3] dealing with payments by sellers to buyers for promotional and other services and facilities, and section 2(e)[4] dealing with the seller's furnishing of such services or facilities to the buyer, are silent as to buyer liability. Section 2(e) describes the offense to which it applies as a "discrimination" and, thus, a construction of 2(f) to cover a knowing inducement and receipt of discriminatorily favorable services of facilities might be a plausible reading of the latter section. By contrast, section 2(d) describes the offense it prohibits simply as a "payment" for the forbidden purpose. Hence, construing 2(f) to create a buyer violation reciprocal to a 2(d) violation by the seller would be more strained.

In *Automatic Canteen*[5] the Court left open the question whether 2(f) applies to the knowing inducement or receipt of a service or facility violative of 2(e) or a payment violative of 2(d). In *Grand*

---

7. See Kroger Co. v. FTC, 438 F.2d 1372 (6th Cir.), cert. denied, 404 U.S. 871, 92 S.Ct. 59, 30 L.Ed.2d 115 (1971).

8. American Motor Specialties Co., 55 F.T.C. 1430, 1446 (1959), aff'd, (without discussion of this point) 278 F.2d 225 2d Cir.), cert. denied, 364 U.S. 884, 81 S.Ct. 169, 5 L.Ed.2d 106 (1960). But cf. Mid-South Distributors v. FTC, 287 F.2d 512, 517 (5th Cir.), cert. denied, 368 U.S. 838, 82 S.Ct. 36, 7 L.Ed.2d 39 (1961). On this point cases like *American Motor Specialties* may be out of harmony with *American Canteen*, supra note 2.

1. 15 U.S.C.A. § 13(c) (1973).

2. E.g., Great Atlantic & Pac. Tea Co. v. FTC, 106 F.2d 667 (3d Cir. 1939), cert. denied, 308 U.S. 625, 60 S.Ct. 380, 84 L.Ed. 521 (1940); see Arden-Mayfair, Inc., 77 F.T.C. 705 (1970); Modern Marketing Serv. Inc., 71 F.T.C. 1676 (1967).

3. 15 U.S.C.A. § 13(d) (1973).

4. 15 U.S.C.A. § 13(e) (1973).

5. Automatic Canteen Co. of America v. FTC, 346 U.S. 61, 73 S.Ct. 1017, 97 L.Ed. 1454 (1953).

Union,[6] the Court of Appeals for the Second Circuit held that a buyer knowingly rendering or receiving payments violating 2(d) could be attacked under Section 5 of the FTC Act. The same analysis would apply to inducing or accepting services or facilities, the grant of which violated 2(e). Hence, under Section 2(f) of Clayton, as amended, supplemented by Section 5 of the FTC Act, there is a complete body of buyer liability law which, though no more consistent with Sherman than are Robinson-Patman provisions applying to sellers, is at least internally coherent.

6. Grand Union Co. v. FTC, 300 F.2d 92 (2d Cir. 1962). See also R. H. Macy & Co. v. FTC, 326 F.2d 445 (2d Cir. 1964).

Chapter 9

COVERAGE, EXEMPTIONS AND PROCEDURE

Table of Sections

Part	Sections
A. Relationship to Trade or Commerce	232–234
B. Exemptions	235–239
C. Governmental Enforcement	240–245
D. Private Enforcement	246–253

PART A. RELATIONSHIP TO TRADE OR COMMERCE

Sec.
232. Introduction.
233. Interstate Commerce.
234. Foreign Commerce.

PART B. EXEMPTIONS

235. Introduction.
236. Agricultural Cooperatives.
237. The Labor Exemption.
238. Governmental Action and Its Solicitation.
239. Regulated Industries.

PART C. GOVERNMENTAL ENFORCEMENT

240. The Antitrust Division of the Department of Justice.
241. The Federal Trade Commission.
242. Antitrust Investigations.
243. Informal Enforcement and Prior Clearance Procedures.
244. Civil Actions.
245. Criminal Proceedings.

PART D. PRIVATE ENFORCEMENT

246. Introduction.
247. Standing, Injury and Causation.
248. Statute of Limitations.
249. Class Actions and *Parens Patriae*.
250. *In Pari Delicto* and Unclean Hands.
251. Damages.
252. Passing On.
253. Attorney's Fees.

PART A. RELATIONSHIP TO TRADE OR COMMERCE

§ 232. Introduction

This chapter, something of a miscellany, deals briefly with several loosely related topics. Though the scope of this volume precludes fuller treatment, its claim to comprehension requires at least a summary. The effort, then, will be to set forth basic concepts about the coverage of the antitrust laws under the commerce clause, about the various areas of commerce and industry which are wholly or partially exempt from these laws, and about matters of practice and procedure which are central to antitrust enforcement.

§ 233. Interstate Commerce

Analytically, the applicability of any one of the antitrust laws raises two distinguishable issues, each of which must be subdivided both as a question of constitutional power and as a question of statutory construction. The initial question is whether the activity constitutes "commerce" within the meaning of the commerce clause and, if so, whether the activity is within the ambit of the relevant statutory language, such as the phrase "trade or commerce" used in the Sherman Act. Assuming that commerce is involved in both of these senses, there is the question whether the activity has sufficient interstate or foreign connections to be "interstate" or "foreign" commerce, constitutionally amenable to congressional control and to be within the ambit of the particular statute asserted to be applicable. Though it was not always so, today virtually any activity of a kind regularly engaged in for financial gain will be characterized as "commerce" in the constitutional sense.[1] Thus, although at one time manufacturing was not commerce,[2] that day is long gone.[3] And if insurance was not commerce before 1944, it clearly has been since.[4] It is the same with service activities[5] and with the learned professions.[6]

---

1. "Trade or commerce" covers any "occupation, employment or business * * * carried on for the purpose of profit or gain." United States v. National Ass'n of Real Estate Bds., 339 U.S. 485, 490–91, 70 S.Ct. 711, 715, 94 L.Ed. 1007, 1013–14 (1950). It includes, for example, the professions (Goldfarb v. Virginia State Bar, 421 U.S. 773, 95 S.Ct. 2004, 44 L.Ed.2d 572 (1975)), furnishing news (Associated Press v. United States, 326 U.S. 1, 65 S.Ct. 1416, 89 L.Ed. 2013 (1945)), sports (Radovich v. National Football League, 352 U.S. 445, 77 S.Ct. 390, 1 L.Ed.2d 724 (1957)), and entertainment enterprises (United States v. Paramount Pictures, Inc., 334 U.S. 131, 68 S.Ct. 915, 92 L.Ed. 1260 (1948)).

2. See United States v. E. C. Knight Co., 156 U.S. 1, 15 S.Ct. 249, 39 L.Ed. 325 (1895).

3. E.g., Mandeville Island Farms, Inc. v. American Crystal Sugar Co., 334 U.S. 219, 68 S Ct. 996, 92 L.Ed. 1328 (1948).

4. United States v. South-Eastern Underwriters Ass'n., 322 U.S. 533, 64 S. Ct. 1162, 88 L.Ed. 1440 (1944). But see the McCarren-Ferguson Act, 15 U.S.C.A. §§ 1011–1015, which confers a partial exemption from the antitrust laws on the insurance industry.

5. E.g., United States v. National Ass'n. of Real Estate Bds., 339 U.S. 485, 70 S.Ct. 711, 94 L.Ed. 1007 (1950)

6. E.g., Goldfarb v. Virginia State Bar, 421 U.S. 773, 95 S.Ct. 2004, 44 L.Ed.2d 572 (1975).

In passing the Sherman Act, Congress stretched substantially as far as the Constitution would permit.[7] Hence, most activities which are "commerce" in the constitutional sense constitute "trade or commerce" within the meaning of the Act.[8] There are exceptions. Of the professional sports, the one timeless game, baseball, remains somehow untouched by the law's movement over time; it was not commerce in the Act's original contemplation and it is not commerce today.[9] Baseball aside, a worldly, practical test is applicable. If there is a dollar to be made, it's trade or commerce. Peradventure, that very practical test serves the statutory objective in a highly functional way: if an activity is "commercial" in the sense implied by that practical test, then absent some specific reason for allocating resources to it on some other basis, competition is likely to be the socially preferable way for the activity to be organized.

But labeling an activity "trade or commerce" does not necessarily bring it under the antitrust laws; there remains a constitutional and a statutory question about the relationship between the commercial activity and interstate commerce or foreign commerce. These issues are more complex. For one thing, the reach of the Sherman Act is wider than that of other antitrust statutes. Also, foreign commerce presents special problems. Here, we shall trace the doctrinal lines concerning interstate commerce. What follows is not highly analytical; the goal is merely to trace the principal strands upon which subtleties must be strung.

a. The Sherman Act

In the Sherman Act, Congress has been taken to have exercised to the fullest its power over commerce.[10] Though it is no doubt a simplistic way to categorize the cases, it is said that there are under the Sherman Act two jurisdictional tests related to the constitutional conception.[11] The first is whether the activity occurs "in" or "in the flow of" interstate commerce. If it does, it is covered; it matters not that its major effects are local, nor how little it may affect the flow

---

7. United States v. South-Eastern Underwriters Ass'n., 322 U.S. 533, 558, 64 S.Ct. 1162, 1176, 88 L.Ed. 1440, 1460 (1944). See also, e.g., Mandeville Island Farms, Inc. v. American Crystal Sugar Co., 334 U.S. 219, 234, 68 S.Ct. 996 1005, 92 L.Ed. 1328, 1339 (1948); United States v. Employing Plasterers Ass'n, 347 U.S. 186, 74 S.Ct. 452, 98 L.Ed. 618 (1954); Burke v. Ford, 389 U.S. 320, 88 S.Ct. 443, 19 L.Ed.2d 554 (1967).

8. See, e.g., cases cited in note 1 supra.

9. Compare Federal Baseball Club v. National League of Professional Baseball Clubs, 259 U.S. 200, 42 S.Ct. 465, 66 L.Ed. 898 (1922), with Flood v. Kuhn, 407 U.S. 258, 92 S.Ct. 2099, 32 L.Ed.2d 728 (1972).

10. Mandeville Island Farms, Inc. v. American Crystal Sugar Co., 334 U.S. 219, 68 S.Ct. 996, 92 L.Ed. 1328 (1948). See also cases cited note 1 supra.

11. Report of the Attorney General's Nat. Comm. to Study the Antitrust Laws 62–64 (1955).

of interstate commerce.¹² The second test applies when the challenged conduct is not "in commerce;" it will nevertheless be subject to the Act if it materially affects interstate commerce.¹³ In deciding these issues, quantitative factors become pertinent. It is necessary not only that there be a logical, causal connection between the activity and the flow of commerce, it is also necessary that the flow of commerce be affected in some substantial way; if the impact is trivial, the Sherman Act does not apply.¹⁴ Thus, the only commercial activities beyond the reach of the Sherman Act are those which are local in the double sense that they are neither within nor have any significant effect on the flow of interstate commerce.

The conventional way of restating the matter will suffice for most purposes, but there are places where the general statements of the kind used here lead to erroneous conclusions unless their import is more particularly understood. It needs emphasis that it is not the quantitative substantiality of the impact on the flow of commerce that is critical under the second test; if a local activity has in a practical sense a significant impact on competition in commerce and if the commerce so affected is substantial in amount, the Act applies to the local activity even though the activity does not reduce the quantity of interstate commerce in any discernible degree, or perhaps even if it does not alter it at all, or, indeed increases it. Goldfarb v. Virginia State Bar will illustrate.¹⁵ There, a bar association minimum fee schedule operated to fix prices for legal services in the examination

12. United States v. Socony-Vacuum Oil Co., 310 U.S. 150, 223–24, 60 S.Ct. 811, 844–46, 84 L.Ed. 1129, 1168–70 (1940); United States v. Richter Concrete Corp., 328 F.Supp. 1061 (S.D. Ohio 1971); Denver Rockets v. All-Pro Management, Inc., 325 F.Supp. 1049 (C.D.Cal.1971). But cf. Sun Valley Disposal Co. v. Silver State Disposal Co., 420 F.2d 341, 343 (9th Cir. 1969); Yellow Cab Co. of Nevada v. Cab Emp. Automotive and Warehousemen, Teamsters Local No. 881, 457 F.2d 1032 (9th Cir. 1972).

13. E.g., Burke v. Ford, 389 U.S. 320, 321–22, 88 S.Ct. 443, 444, 19 L.Ed.2d 554, 555 (1967); United States v. Yellow Cab Co., 332 U.S. 218, 67 S.Ct. 1560, 91 L.Ed. 2010 (1947); United States v. National Ass'n of Real Estate Bds., 339 U.S. 485, 70 S.Ct. 711, 94 L.Ed. 1007 (1950); Goldfarb v. Virginia State Bar, 421 U.S. 773, 95 S.Ct. 2004, 44 L.Ed.2d 572 (1975); Gulf Oil Corp. v. Copp Paving Co., 419 U.S. 186, 195, 95 S.Ct. 392, 398, 42 L.Ed.2d 378, 386 (1974); Hospital Building Co. v. Trustees of Rex Hospital, — U.S. —, 96 S.Ct. 1848, 48 L.Ed.2d 338 (1976). Rasmussen v. American Dairy Ass'n, 472 F.2d 517 (1973), cert. denied 412 U.S. 950, 93 S.Ct. 3014, 37 L.Ed.2d 1003 (1973).

14. E.g., Yellow Cab Co. of Nevada v. Cab Emp. Automotive and Warehousemen, Teamsters Local No. 881, 457 F.2d 1032 (9th Cir. 1972); Ford Wholesale Co. v. Fibreboard Paper Prods. Corp., 344 F.Supp. 1323 (C.D.Cal.1972). Recently the Court emphasized that the substantial-effect-on-commerce test can be met without showing that market price will be affected; allegations that a conspiracy would block a hospital expansion, which would have expanded the purchase of medicine and supplies from out of state, affected revenues from out of state health insurance programs, and the like were sufficient to charge a substantial effect on commerce. Hospital Building Co. v. Trustees of Rex Hospital, supra note 13.

15. 421 U.S. 773, 95 S.Ct. 2004, 44 L.Ed.2d 572 (1975).

of titles. Although that activity, the only one subject to the trade restraint challenged under the Act, was purely local, a significant portion of the purchase money for local home purchases came from out of state and a significant portion of mortgage loans on these transactions were guaranteed by out of state lenders under federal mortgage insurance programs. The Court held that "[g]iven the substantial volume of commerce involved, and the inseparability of this particular legal service from the interstate aspects of real estate transactions, we conclude that interstate commerce has been sufficiently affected." [16] The lack of a showing that home buyers were discouraged by the price fixing was no default in plaintiff's proof, for "[o]therwise, the magnitude of the effect would control," and it does not.[17]

It is interesting to explore this conception with limit-pushing hypotheticals. Suppose A, B and C each manufacture mish-mash in California and sell it in commerce in a substantial volume. Suppose that each of them buys an important raw material, mish, from various California suppliers, and that each buys its other raw material, mash, from a supplier in Oregon. The sales to A, B and C of mish are not in commerce. However, a significant restraint on these sales could affect commerce in mish-mash. Thus, if the California sellers of mish formed a cartel and increased the price of mish, that restraint, having a significant impact on the interstate business of A, B and C, would violate the Act; the increased raw material price, leading to higher overall manufacturing costs, would probably result in an increased price on the finished product and lower sales of that product. But even if demand for mish-mash was highly inelastic and sales fell only trivially, or even if the increased costs were absorbed by A, B and C in reduced profits, commerce would be affected.

Now suppose this: Y, a seller of mash located in Oregon, uses mash as a tying product and insists that A, B and C buy all their mish from him. As a result, A, B and C stop buying their mish in California and buy it from out of state. One might argue that interstate commerce is increased, not reduced; but that is not the critical thing. The restraint is on a sale in commerce of mish and mash and it also affects commerce in mish-mash. The Act clearly applies.[18]

An interesting question concerns the quantum of proof of effects on commerce (or competition in commerce) that is needed when the

16. 421 U.S. at 785, 95 S.Ct. at 2012, 44 L.Ed.2d at 583.

17. 421 U.S. at 785, 95 S.Ct. at 2012, 44 L.Ed.2d at 584.

18. Compare Rasmussen v. American Dairy Ass'n, 472 F.2d 517 (9th Cir.), cert. denied 412 U.S. 950, 93 S.Ct. 3014, 37 L.Ed. 1003 (1973); Allen Ready Mix Concrete Co. v. John A. Denie's Sons Co., 1972 CCH Trade Cas. ¶ 73,955 (D.Tenn.); Radzik v. Chicagoland Recreational Vehicle Dealers Ass'n, 1972 CCH Trade Cas. ¶ 73,836 (N.D.Ill.1971).

activity asserted to violate the law is local in character. To show effects with any extreme of rigor, it may be necessary to present rather elaborate theoretical and empirical evidence of the way the market works and how the local activity reverberates through the system to have its interstate impact. Some courts seem to have demanded proof of this kind.[19] Such a showing may well be an essential part of plaintiff's case on the liability issue where the rule of reason is applicable, but where plaintiff asserts a claim based on a *per se* rule, proof of the nature of the industry sufficiently detailed to warrant analysis of particular effects on commerce would be an extraneous additional element. To require that kind of proof when a *per se* rule is being invoked would be to deprive the *per se* rule of its principal value, avoidance of detailed economic analysis. That disparity has led commentators to pose the question whether there are two standards, one for rule of reason cases and one for *per se* offenses.[20]

Virginia State Bar, which involved a *per se* allegation, may suggest an answer to this dilemma. The opinion by the Chief Justice did not suggest that there were two standards of proof related to the separate analytical approaches to antitrust issues; quite the contrary. But neither is the opinion disdainful of the need to protect courts from being enmeshed in overly elaborate economic analysis. It insists that the question whether commerce is sufficiently affected be evaluated in a wholly practical sense. There, it was enough that attorneys' opinions on the marketability of titles were needed in real estate transactions, and that many of these had interstate financial links. If prices were being fixed on attorneys' title opinions, commerce was in a practical sense being affected. That same simple, intuitive, more or less conclusionary approach would presumably apply in deciding whether interstate commerce was affected even in a case where the theory of antitrust liability was based on the rule of reason. If a fuller economic analysis would be needed on substantive issues, evidence introduced on that issue might illuminate the commerce issue; but the jurisdictional question is not of its nature a complex, economic problem. It is a pragmatic and practical one. At all events *Virginia State Bar* places in shadow those lower court cases which in price fixing or other *per se* cases called for explicit and necessarily elaborate proof of an effect in the flow of commerce.[21]

19. See Rosemound Sand & Gravel Co. v. Lambert Sand & Gravel Co., 469 F.2d 416 (5th Cir. 1972); Marston v. Ann Arbor Property Management Ass'n, 422 F.2d 836 (6th Cir.), cert. denied 399 U.S. 929, 90 S.Ct. 2244, 26 L.Ed.2d 796 (1970); United States v. Starlite Drive-In, Inc., 204 F.2d 419 (7th Cir. 1953); De Voto v. Pacific Fidelity Life Ins. Co., 354 F.Supp. 874 (N.D.Cal.1973).

20. See P. Areeda, Antitrust Analysis ¶ 183 (2d ed. 1974).

21. See also Burke v. Ford, 389 U.S. 320, 88 S.Ct. 443, 19 L.Ed.2d 554 (1967) where the Supreme Court inferred an

b. *The Clayton, Robinson-Patman and FTC Acts*

The Clayton Act in Section 1 contains a broad statutory definition of commerce.[22] The various subsections of Clayton (including the Robinson-Patman amendments) and the FTC Act do not apply to local activities which affect commerce, but only to activities "in commerce" by firms "engaged in commerce." For example, Clayton Section 2(a), as amended by Robinson-Patman, makes it unlawful "for any person engaged in commerce in the course of such commerce" to discriminate in price.[23] Section 2(a) also requires that either of the two purchases be "in commerce."[24] The provisions of 2(c), (d) and (e),[25] though not expressly requiring that one of the purchases be in commerce, are very similar. Consequently, for a Robinson-Patman violation there must be proof that one of the sales which establish the discrimination was an interstate sale.[26] Section 3 of Clayton, dealing with tying arrangements and requirements contracts, also applies only to leases, sales or contracts for the sale of goods by a "person engaged in commerce, in the course of such commerce."[27] Section 7, dealing with mergers, states that "no corporation engaged in commerce shall acquire" stock or assets of "another corporation engaged also in commerce."[28] Section 5 of the FTC Act is similarly phrased; it makes unlawful "unfair methods of competition in commerce. * * *"[29]

These "in commerce" requirements are rigorously applied. There is to be no leakage. In United States v. American Building Maintenance Industries,[30] the Court rejected the contention that the Clayton Act, because enacted to supplement the Sherman Act and to arrest incipient Sherman Act violations, should be construed as broadly as Sherman. It held that Clayton Section 7 has no application to the acquisition by a national building maintenance firm which is engaged in commerce of a local building maintenance service firm which,

---

effect on commerce on the basis of a rather summary, theoretical analysis. There, intrastate territorial divisions by liquor wholesalers were alleged to violate the Act. Since the liquor, though moving in commerce, "came to rest" in wholesaler warehouses, sales by the wholesalers were not "in commerce." The Court held that the effect on commerce could be inferred from the nature of the offense, if the offense were proven. Horizontal territorial divisions reduce competition. Reduction in competition causes prices to rise. Increased prices results in lower sales. Lower sales will mean lower imports from manufacturers outside the state. Q.E.D.

22. 15 U.S.C.A. § 12 (1973).

23. 15 U.S.C.A. § 13(a) (1973).

24. Id.

25. 15 U.S.C.A. § 13(c), (d) and (e) (1973).

26. E.g., Moore v. Mead's Fine Bread Co., 348 U.S. 115, 75 S.Ct. 148, 99 L. Ed. 145 (1954); Food Basket, Inc. v. Albertson's, Inc., 383 F.2d 785 (10th Cir. 1967).

27. 15 U.S.C.A. § 14 (1973).

28. 15 U.S.C.A. § 18 (1973).

29. 15 U.S.C.A. § 45 (1973).

30. 422 U.S. 271, 95 S.Ct. 2150, 45 L. Ed.2d 177 (1975).

prior to the acquisition, was not in commerce. That the Robinson-Patman provisions are similarly confined was established in Gulf Oil Corp. v. Copp Paving Co.[31] And it has long been settled that the FTC Act cannot be invoked to regulate intrastate conduct which affects commerce.[32]

The significance of these distinctions between Sherman coverage and Clayton coverage is muted because to some extent the substantive requirements of Sections 3 and 7 of Clayton have been carried back into Sherman;[33] hence, conduct affecting, but not in, commerce, which offends the substantive standards of Sections 3 or 7 of Clayton may be vulnerable to attack under Section 1 of Sherman.[34] There has been no comparable transposition of Robinson-Patman requirements into the Sherman Act; hence, the manner in which the coverage cases under Clayton Section 2, as amended by Robinson-Patman, hew to the literal language of the trade or commerce provisions has considerable substantive significance. That is just as well. Sections 3 and 7 of Clayton are integral parts of a coherent antitrust policy. It is anomalous that they are subject to different commerce provisions than is the Sherman Act. But given the tension between Robinson-Patman and Sherman, the goal of coherence is best (although imperfectly) served by confining the range of Robinson-Patman as narrowly as the jurisdictional terms permit.

§ 234. Foreign Commerce

a. Subject Matter Jurisdiction

The Sherman Act also applies to activities "in" or "affecting" American foreign trade or commerce [1] under a two-pronged test similar to that outlined above. Transactions in foreign commerce, of course, include both exports and imports.[2] Both activities in foreign

---

31. 419 U.S. 186, 95 S.Ct. 392, 42 L.Ed. 2d 378 (1974).

32. FTC v. Bunte Bros., 312 U.S. 349, 61 S.Ct. 580, 85 L.Ed. 881 (1941).

33. See §§ 153 and 200 supra.

34. See § 233(a) supra.

1. Sections 2 and 3 of the Clayton Act and Section 5 of the FTC Acts also apply to certain transactions in foreign commerce. See 15 U.S.C.A. §§ 12 and 44 (1973). Section 2(a) of Clayton, as amended by Robinson-Patman, and Section 3 of Clayton, covering tying and some other arrangements, only apply in the case of sales for use, consumption or resale in the United States or a place under its jurisdiction. See 15 U.S.C.A §§ 13(a) and 14. The other Robinson-Patman amendments apparently apply also to sales for export. See Baysoy v. Jessop Steel Co., 90 F.Supp. 303 (W.D. Pa.1950). Section 7, which applies to mergers between two corporations engaged in commerce, would presumably apply to a merger between an American and a foreign corporation if either were engaged in either American interstate commerce or American foreign commerce. Another "antitrust" act applicable to foreign commerce is the Wilson Tariff Act, 15 U.S.C.A. §§ 8–11 (1973) which, in effect, applies Sherman Act standards to imports.

2. E.g., United States v. Aluminum Co. of America, 148 F.2d 416, 440–45 (2d Cir. 1945) (imports); Continental Ore Co. v. Union Carbide & Carbon Corp., 370 U.S. 690, 82 S.Ct. 1404, 8 L.Ed.2d 777 (1962) (imports); Zenith Radio Corp. v. Hazeltine Research, Inc., 401 U.S. 321, 91 S.Ct. 795, 28 L.Ed.2d 77 (1971) (exports).

countries and activities in this country which affect America's foreign commerce are covered by Sherman.[3] In short, any contracts, combinations or agreements, even those involving only foreign firms, may violate the Act if they affect competition in or affecting American interstate or foreign commerce. The crucial questions are whether the forbidden results within the United States are accomplished and, where no American firm or conduct in this country is involved, whether the defendants can be brought before a federal court here. As in the case of interstate commerce, it is not necessary to show a reduction in the flow of foreign commerce, but only a violation substantially affecting interstate commerce. As Judge Wyzanski put it in United States v. Minnesota Mining & Manufacturing Co., "Congress has not said you may choke commerce here if you nourish it there."[4]

It is sometimes contended that the antitrust laws are altered substantively as they apply to foreign activities—for example, that the constraints of foreign law and custom may make demands which render reasonable in a foreign setting activities which would be unreasonable within the United States. There is, of course, something to the notion that the setting of an activity can alter its competitive consequence. But courts, quite rightly, have rejected the broad contention that the *per se* rules ought not to apply with full vigor to foreign activities.[5] The reasons for these rules, which make legal consequences more predictable and simplify litigation are, if anything, the more forceful when the setting is shifted to a foreign environment. The only qualification, then, upon the conclusion that *per se* rules apply to foreign as to domestic commerce is the recognition that where

---

3. Continental Ore Co. v. Union Carbide & Carbon Corp., 370 U.S. 690, 82 S.Ct. 1404, 8 L.Ed.2d 777 (1962). See also United States v. Sisal Sales Corp., 274 U.S. 268, 47 S.Ct. 592, 71 L.Ed. 1042 (1927); Thomsen v. Cayser, 243 U.S. 66, 37 S.Ct. 353, 61 L.Ed. 597 (1917); United States v. Pacific & Arctic Ry. & Nav. Co., 228 U.S. 87, 33 S.Ct. 443, 57 L.Ed. 742 (1913); United States v. American Tobacco Co., 221 U.S. 106, 31 S.Ct. 632, 55 L.Ed. 663 (1911); Pacific Seafarers, Inc. v. Pacific Far East Line, Inc., 404 F.2d 804 (D.C.Cir. 1968), cert. denied 393 U.S. 1093, 89 S.Ct. 872, 21 L.Ed.2d 784 (1969); United States v. Aluminum Co. of America, 148 F.2d 416, 440–45 (2d Cir. 1945); United States v. Watchmakers of Switzerland Information Center, Inc., 1963 CCH Trade Cas. ¶ 70,600 (S.D.N.Y.1962), modified, 1965 CCH Trade Cas. ¶ 71,352 (S.D.N.Y.). Restatement (Second), Foreign Relations Law of the United States § 18 (1965). The contrary view, once taken in American Banana Co. v. United Fruit Co., 213 U.S. 347, 29 S.Ct. 511, 53 L.Ed. 826 (1909) is no longer law. The *Alcoa* case is particularly important in showing the scope of the Act. In all other cases cited herein, one or more of the defendants was an American firm and some conduct involved in the violation took place in America. In *Alcoa*, however, the court held the Sherman Act forbade conduct engaged in by foreign firms outside of the territorial limits of America where the conduct was intended to and did affect American imports.

4. 92 F.Supp. 947, 962 (D.Mass.1950).

5. E.g., Timken Roller Bearing Co. v. United States, 341 U.S. 593, 71 S.Ct. 971, 95 L.Ed. 1199 (1951).

only foreign firms and foreign conduct are involved it will be necessary to prove effects in America and an intent to achieve them.[6]

b. *Jurisdiction of the Person or Property*

A factor limiting the scope of the application of the Sherman Act to foreign firms is the need to obtain personal service on the defendant. Venue in an antitrust action against a corporation may be laid in the district where the defendant is an inhabitant or may be found or transacts business;[7] a treble damage action may be brought in the district where the defendant resides or is found or has an agent.[8] An alien defendant may be sued in any district.[9] Assuming venue is proper, service may be made in the district where the corporation is an inhabitant, or is found,[10] or as prescribed by state law, or, in the case of a foreign corporation, in the form acceptable to its own country,[11] a rule which may facilitate service pursuant to a state or foreign "long arm" provision.[12]

Assuming the venue to be proper against all defendants, personal service must still be made. Section 12 of Clayton authorizes a corporation to be served in the district of which "it is an inhabitant, or wherever it may be found."[13] Rule 4(e) and (i) of the Federal Rules of Civil Procedure authorize service in the manner provided by state law or, in the case of a foreign corporation, in a manner acceptable to the foreign state.[14] The application of these provisions to foreign corporations which have business contacts in a district but which have neither a general business office nor a resident agent authorized to receive process in the district is subject to the same constitutional limitations which govern service on nonresident domestic corpora-

---

6. United States v. Minnesota Mining & Mfg. Co., 92 F.Supp. 947 (D.Mass. 1950).

Where, as in the case of foreign oil cartels, the alleged violation may be based in part on acts of a foreign state within its sovereign territory, the "act of state doctrine" may in whole or part serve as a defense. See Hunt v. Mobil Oil Corp., 410 F.Supp. 10 (S.D.N.Y. 1976).

7. 15 U.S.C.A. § 22 (1973).

8. 15 U.S.C.A. § 15 (1973).

9. 28 U.S.C.A. § 1391(d) (1973). It is clear that this provision applies to authorize suit in any district (assuming the defendant can be served) even when there is a narrower, special venue statute governing suits of the kind being brought. See Brunette Mach. Works, Ltd. v. Kockum Industries, Inc., 406 U.S. 706, 92 S.Ct. 1936, 32 L.Ed.2d 428 (1972).

10. 15 U.S.C.A. § 22 (1973).

11. Fed.R.Civ.P. 4(e), (i) (1973).

12. See, e.g., Engine Specialties Inc. v. Bombardier, Ltd., 454 F.2d 527 (1st Cir. 1972); Fisons Ltd. v. United States, 458 F.2d 1241 (7th Cir.), cert. denied 405 U.S. 1041, 92 S.Ct. 1312, 31 L.Ed.2d 581 (1972). Recent cases concerning venue over and service upon foreign corporations are more fully discussed in ABA, Antitrust Law Developments 360–64 (1975).

13. 15 U.S.C.A. § 22 (1973).

14. Fed.R.Civ.P. 4(e), 4(i) (1973).

tions or individuals. Due process permits service on a foreign corporation which has such contacts within the district that the maintenance of the suit does not offend substantial justice.[15]

Brewster has pointed out that the governing concept of fairness may require that a foreign corporation have more intimate contacts with a district before suit there would be appropriate than would be required in the instance of an out-of-state domestic corporation.[16] A domestic corporation is tightly laced into the federal system. Its management ought to be mindful both that the antitrust laws apply to its activities and that if it exceeds a rather low threshold of activity in any district it may be sued there. Management of the foreign corporation may be less informed in each of these respects. But the danger of a foreign entity becoming enmeshed in American law and litigation in ways that are unfair to it is probably decreasing. It is not just that world markets are becoming increasingly integrated, and that the multinational corporation has served as a carrier of business and governmental information across oceanic as well as national lines, it is also that European Common Market "antitrust" and increasingly rigorous national cartel laws have made it even less likely that a foreign firm—at least a western European firm—doing business here will be unaware of the kinds of activities which generate antitrust problems.

PART B. EXEMPTIONS

§ 235. Introduction

America relies only in part upon competition to regulate market structure and conduct. Governmental regulation of entry, prices and other economic decisions by private enterprise also play a major role. The most pervasive category of antitrust exemptions are those affecting the various regulated industries.[1] In part these are exemptions specifically granted by Congress, in part they are court created on the basis of implication from regulatory scheme or on the basis of doctrine emphasizing administrative specialization, such as the primary jurisdiction concept.[2] In so-called natural monopolies regulation may be used in an effort to attain levels of services and prices comparable to those competition might yield if it were feasible. There is no consistent pattern as to the scope of regulation. In a particular industry it may be confined to those aspects which as a practical matter could never be competitive, or may extend far be-

---

15. Hanson v. Denckla, 357 U.S. 235, 78 S.Ct. 1228, 2 L.Ed.2d 1283 (1958); United States v. Scophony Corp., 333 U.S. 795, 68 S.Ct. 855, 92 L.Ed. 1091 (1948). Cf. International Shoe Co. v. Washington, 326 U.S. 310, 66 S.Ct. 154, 90 L.Ed. 95 (1945).

16. K. Brewster, Antitrust and American Business Abroad 55 (1958).

1. See § 239 infra.

2. See § 239(b) infra.

yond into collateral activities which could be organized competitively. In some instances regulation is used where the social case for its need is weak or non-existent. Its use is supported by industry firms which see it as a means for cartelizing the industry and keeping new entrants out.

Once established, regulatory schemes have great staying power. Those set up at one stage of social, economic and political development may carry on long after the conditions or public attitudes which initially warranted them have faded from memory. Aspects of some regulated industry exemptions will be discussed in later sections.

Sometimes the choice to abandon competition is not based on the notion that competition will not work but upon a decision expressed through legislation to transfer economic power (and income) from one group to another or to facilitate greater stability, or because it was thought that other goals which could be achieved through cartelization were in the public interest. Sometimes this is a response to widely felt needs; at others it is a manifestation of political excesses or of blocks of political and economic power.

Section 6 of the Clayton Act [3] and the Capper-Volstead Act [4] both grant in vague terms an exemption to agricultural or horticultural organizations and cooperatives. These exemptions are intended to shift power to the beneficiary groups and, perhaps, to enhance stability.[5] The Fisherman's Cooperative Marketing Act [6] gives a comparable exemption to cooperatives engaged in fishing or processing and marketing of fish.

The limited exemption for labor organizations, in part attributable to express statutory declaration, in part an implication from national labor policy as manifest in labor legislation, is also reflective of the notion that labor cartelization should be encouraged.[7] The Webb-Pomerance Act [8] exemption for acts or agreements in the course of export trade by an association of producers formed solely for the purpose of engaging in export trade is another example of a deliberate congressional effort to encourage cartelization—here, presumably, on the theoretically doubtful assumption that doing so might encourage a higher national investment in the covered activities, thus aiding the nation's balance of payments. The assumption was that since foreign business is often cartelized, American firms

---

3. 15 U.S.C.A. § 17 (1973).

4. 7 U.S.C.A. §§ 291–92 (1964). See also the Cooperative Marketing Act of 1926, 7 U.S.C.A. §§ 451–57 (1964).

5. See Maryland & Va. Milk Producers Ass'n v. United States, 362 U.S. 458, 464–67, 80 S.Ct. 847, 852–54, 4 L.Ed.2d 880, 886–88 (1960) which discusses the basis for this legislation. See also § 236 infra which discusses the agricultural cooperative exemption in greater detail.

6. 7 U.S.C.A. § 291 (1964).

7. See § 237 infra.

8. 15 U.S.C.A. §§ 61–65 (1973).

would have to be permitted or encouraged to cartelize in order to warrant their entry.

Retailing as an economic sector has been accorded special antitrust treatment, which can best be understood when it is recognized that Congress has, at least in part, responded to the notion that small businesses ought to be able to cartelize. Fair trade legislation was in this pattern.[9] Much of Robinson-Patman is best understood as an effort to give to independent retailers through legislation some of the benefits that might be achieved through cartelization.[10] In sum, the legislative attitude about cartelization reflected in the Sherman Act has never been single-mindedly accepted.

The exemption for governmental action, treated at length below,[11] has a related but broader rationale. Its predicate is the conviction that action inconsistent with the antitrust laws which is directly taken by the federal government or by a state in its sovereign capacity represents implicitly a sovereign decision that the role of competition should in the particular instance be displaced. When the governmental action involved is federal, the issue becomes, analytically, whether the legislation authorizing it involves an implied repeal of the antitrust laws. When state action is entailed, more complex questions of federalism are presented.

§ 236. Agricultural Cooperatives

The agricultural cooperative exemption is based on two statutes. By Section 6 of the Clayton Act, the primary function of which was to grant a labor exemption, Congress also stated that:

> "Nothing * * * in the antitrust laws shall * * * forbid the existence and operation of * * * agricultural or horticultural organizations, instituted for * * * mutual help, and not having capital stock or conducted for profit * * * nor shall such organizations, or the members thereof, be held or construed to be illegal combinations or conspiracies in restraint of trade under the antitrust laws."[1]

The limitation of this section to organizations without capital stock and its failure to expressly sanction cooperative marketing activities led to the passage eight years later of the Capper-Volstead Act.[2] Section 1 of that Act authorizes persons engaged in the production of agricultural products to "act together in associations, corporate or otherwise, with or without capital stock" for the purpose of "collectively processing * * *, handling, and marketing products of persons so engaged * * *."[3]

9. See § 132 supra.

10. See Chapter 8 supra.

11. See § 238 infra.

1. 15 U.S.C.A. § 17 (1973).

2. 7 U.S.C.A. §§ 291–92 (1964).

3. 7 U.S.C.A. § 291 (1964).

While the legislative history of these provisions is not radiantly illuminating, it seems clear that Congress thought cartelization among farmers not a particular threat to agricultural prices.[4] When Clayton was passed the attitude seems to have been that it was politically appropriate to treat farmers like laborers. Congress thought that the nation stood in a different relationship to farmers than to industrial capitalists. Cartelization through cooperatives might enable farmers to gain distributional efficiencies and would give them a sense of fellowship as well as media for exchanging information and developing greater control over their economic well-being. Individual farmers being relatively small and thus numerous, it was not supposed that cooperative organization would result in common control over enough production to significantly affect prices; none of the debates express concern that this might occur.

These two statutes together establish what is usually called the "agricultural cooperative exemption" from the antitrust laws. The statutes, however, do not specify organizational form with particularity. The Clayton Act reference is to organizations without capital stock. Capper-Volstead requires only that the association be operated for "the mutual benefit of members" and either that no member be allowed more than one vote because of the amount of his stock or capital, or that the association not pay dividends in excess of 8% per year on stock or capital. The legislative history of both provisions, and the tenor of the opinions construing them, indicate that they apply only to mutual aid organizations organized by agricultural producers.[5] Thus, they clearly cover organizations of agricultural producers in the form of cooperatives (i.e., where members have a single vote and where profits, if any, are distributed on the basis of patronage).[6] Though it is sometimes supposed that corporations with control and distribution of profits proportional to the amount of capital invested could not be covered even though all or substantially

---

4. See the discussion in Maryland & Va. Milk Producers Ass'n v. United States, 362 U.S. 458, 464–67, 80 S.Ct. 847, 852–54, 4 L.Ed.2d 880, 886–88 (1960).

5. Sunkist Growers, Inc. v. Winckler & Smith Citrus Prods. Co., 370 U.S. 19, 82 S.Ct. 1130, 8 L.Ed.2d 305 (1962); Maryland & Va. Milk Producers Ass'n v. United States, 362 U.S. 458, 80 S. Ct. 847, 4 L.Ed.2d 880 (1960); North Texas Producers Ass'n v. Metzger Dairies, Inc., 348 F.2d 189, 194 (5th Cir. 1965), cert. denied 382 U.S. 977, 86 S.Ct. 545, 15 L.Ed.2d 468 (1966).

6. Sunkist Growers, Inc. v. Winckler & Smith Citrus Prods. Co., 370 U.S. 19, 82 S.Ct. 1130, 8 L.Ed.2d 305 (1962), held that Capper-Volstead protected three legally separate agricultural cooperatives which had substantially identical memberships and which were acting together. In a later case, upon a showing that 15% of the members were non-farm corporations or partnerships, the Court held that the exemption was not available. Case-Swayne Co. v. Sunkist Growers, Inc., 389 U.S. 384, 88 S.Ct. 528, 19 L.Ed.2d 621 (1967). The Agricultural Adjustment Act also provides a related, limited immunity. The Secretary of Agriculture is authorized to enter into marketing agreements with producers and processors, and these agreements

all stockholders were farm producers, the statutory language is broad enough to cover organizations of agricultural producers which, technically, are not "cooperatives" and seems explicitly broad enough to cover any membership corporation which appropriately limits dividends.

Assuming the actor to be a cooperative which qualifies for the exemption, many activities of kinds which would otherwise violate the antitrust laws are protected by the agricultural cooperative exemption. Assume, for example, that separate producers of oranges throughout a large orange growing region were to market their own output and were to meet together each season as independent producers to agree upon the price they would accept for oranges of different grades. That conduct, on its face, would be a *per se* violation of the antitrust laws.[7] Suppose, now, that instead of agreeing on price directly the producers organize a cooperative to which they supply their oranges and which sets the price for and sells the oranges; that conduct is exempt. If it were not for the agricultural exemption the legality of the use of such a joint sales agent would depend upon whether the producers represented a significant enough share of the market so that, acting jointly, they might have an effect on price.[8] But the cooperative exemption seems to enable farm producers to market jointly irrespective of the size of the cooperative, or the extent to which it has organized producers within the market.[9]

The most obvious limit on an exempt cooperative's potential for gaining and exploiting market power by organizing producers into a single selling unit is a provision granting the Secretary of Agriculture power to order a cooperative to stop monopolizing or restraining trade if he finds that its activities have resulted in an undue enhancement of agricultural prices.[10] But there are other limits, less apparent on the face of the statute, which, as a practical matter, may be of greater importance. For one, it is settled that a cooperative may not join with persons outside of the cooperative to fix prices, limit production, or otherwise restrain trade.[11] For another, since the exemption applies only to joint activities in processing, handling

---

are immune under the antitrust laws. See 7 U.S.C.A. § 608b (1964).

7. See §§ 73–78 supra.

8. See § 104 supra.

9. See Sunkist Growers, Inc. v. Winckler & Smith Citrus Prods. Co., 370 U.S. 19, 82 S.Ct. 1130, 8 L.Ed.2d 305 (1962).

10. 7 U.S.C.A. § 292 (1973).

11. Maryland & Va. Milk Producers Ass'n v. United States, 362 U.S. 458, 80 S.Ct. 847, 4 L.Ed.2d 880 (1960); United States v. Borden Co., 308 U.S. 188, 60 S.Ct. 182, 84 L.Ed. 181 (1939). It has been held that three legally separate cooperatives constituting a single economic entity can concertedly do things covered by the exemption. Sunkist Growers, Inc. v. Winckler & Smith Citrus Prods. Co., 370 U.S. 19, 82 S.Ct. 1120, 8 L.Ed.2d 305 (1960). Presumably two or more cooperatives representing different members would not be permitted to act concertedly and cloak otherwise unlawful conduct under the exemption.

and marketing agricultural products,[12] it does not authorize exempt organizations to engage in boycotts [13] or other predatory practices.[14]

The most important and unresolved question about agricultural cooperatives is whether they may concertedly reduce output of members through acreage allocation programs or the like. The legislation refers only to processing, handling and marketing and there is legislative history which bears the interpretation that Congress pictured individual producers, taking the market price as given, using cooperatives only to gain efficiencies of scale like those businesses can lawfully gain through the corporate form.[15] Certainly a holding that cooperatives may not directly or indirectly limit output would go far toward reintegrating these agriculture statutes and the basic tenets of antitrust.[16] It might be argued that inasmuch as there is no limit on the size or market share of a single cooperative, mergers between two or more cooperatives are inferentially exempt from scrutiny under Clayton Section 7. While this conclusion is hardly inevitable, enforcement agencies have ignored agricultural cooperative mergers even in the face of a substantial merger movement probably involving many mergers which would be illegal under ordinary standards. The only challenges have been to acquisition by cooperatives of noncooperative competitors.[17]

12. United States v. Borden Co., 308 U.S. 188, 60 S.Ct. 182, 84 L.Ed. 181 (1939); United States v. Dairy Cooperative Ass'n, 49 F.Supp. 475 (D.Or. 1943); United States v. King, 229 F. 275 (D.Mass.1915), 250 F. 908, 910 (D. Mass.1916).

13. Boise Cascade Int'l, Inc. v. Northern Minnesota Pulpwood Prods. Ass'n, 294 F.Supp. 1015 (D.Minn.1968); cf. North Texas Producers Ass'n v. Metzger Dairies Inc., 348 F.2d 189 (5th Cir. 1965), cert. denied 382 U.S. 977, 86 S. Ct. 545, 15 L.Ed.2d 468 (1966); April v. National Cranberry Ass'n, 168 F. Supp. 919 (D.Mass.1958).

14. Otto Milk Co. v. United Dairy Farmers Cooperative Ass'n, 388 F.2d 789 (3d Cir. 1967); Cincinnati Milk Sales Ass'n v. National Farmers' Organization, Inc., 1967 CCH Trade Cas. ¶ 72,092 (S.D.Ohio); Bergjans Farm Dairy Co. v. Sanitary Milk Producers, 241 F.Supp. 476 (E.D.Mo.1965), aff'd 368 F.2d 697 (8th Cir. 1966).

15. See Maryland & Va. Milk Producers Ass'n v. United States, 362 U.S. 458, 464–67, 80 S.Ct. 847, 852–54, 4 L. Ed.2d 880, 886–88 (1960).

16. There are other statutory exemptions which are tangentially relevant. The Cooperative Marketing Act of 1926 authorizes agricultural producers to exchange pricing, production and marketing data. 7 U.S.C.A. § 455 (1964). There is now a Robinson-Patman exemption for payment by cooperatives to their members. 15 U.S.C. A. § 13b (1973), 7 U.S.C.A. § 207(f) (1964). The Agricultural Marketing Agreement Act of 1937 grants exemption for marketing agreements between the Secretary of Agriculture and processors, producers and others engaged in handling agricultural commodities. 7 U.S.C.A. § 608(b) (1964). None of these, however, imply that members of cooperatives may agree to limit their own production or that cooperatives may directly or indirectly impose production quotas on members.

17. See Note, Trust Busting Down on the Farm: Narrowing the Scope of Antitrust Exemptions for Agricultural Co-Operatives, 61 Va.L.Rev. 341 (1975).

§ 237. The Labor Exemption

The labor exemption is also the product of several statutes. Section 6 of the Clayton Act [1] states that labor is not an article of commerce and that the antitrust laws should not forbid labor organizations. Section 20 of that Act [2] limits the power of federal courts to grant injunctions in labor disputes and lists certain labor activities which should not be held to violate any law of the United States. These activities include conventional labor activities such as ceasing to perform work or urging that others cease to patronize or to employ any party to a dispute or urging that others do. The Norris-La Guardia Act,[3] passed in 1932, contains a declaration of policy favoring freedom of employees to organize and further limits the jurisdiction of federal courts to grant injunctions in labor disputes. Because it is so directly related in purpose and effect to Section 20 of Clayton, the practices which Norris-La Guardia protects from injunctions have been taken to be exempt under Section 20 from the antitrust laws. Read together, the two statutes thus grant antitrust exemption to a broad range of conduct of the kind traditionally engaged in by unions.

The National Labor Relations Act,[4] and the Labor Management Relations Act [5] affect antitrust less directly. These acts establish a national policy favoring collective bargaining. They set forth methods and procedures for the determination of bargaining units and the certification of bargaining representatives, and, where employees are represented, impose a duty to bargain collectively about wages, hours and terms and conditions of employment both on the employer and the bargaining representative. These acts also regulate the bargaining process in various particulars and, in addition to mandatory bargaining, forbid various employer practices and labor practices as unfair. They also establish the National Labor Relations Board as an enforcement agency. Although neither act contains any explicit antitrust exemption, there may be conduct which seems to be required or permitted by these acts but forbidden by antitrust; hence, a proper accommodation between labor policy and antitrust policy may require that policies of one act or the other be altered or give way.

The Court's effort to integrate labor and antitrust has a tortured history. The modern era begins with United States v. Hutcheson [6] or, perhaps, with the enforcement program which led to that decision: Thurmond Arnold's determination, as head of the Antitrust Division, that various "unreasonable" restraints imposed by labor (such

---

1. 15 U.S.C.A. § 17 (1973).
2. 29 U.S.C.A. § 52 (1973).
3. 29 U.S.C.A. §§ 101–10, 113–15 (1973).
4. Act of July 5, 1935, ch. 372, 49 Stat. 449.
5. [Taft Hartley] Act of June 23, 1947, ch. 120, 61 Stat. 136 (29 U.S.C.A. § 141 et seq. (1973).)
6. 312 U.S. 219, 61 S.Ct. 463, 85 L.Ed. 788 (1941).

as prevention of the use of cheap materials, more efficient methods or equipment, feather-bedding, price-fixing, and disruption of established collective bargaining relationships) would be challenged under the antitrust laws.[7] *Hutcheson*, one of the cases brought to advance that policy, involved a jurisdictional dispute and union resistance to the installation of new equipment. The union's activity was challenged as a criminal conspiracy under Section 7 of the Sherman Act. The Supreme Court affirmed a dismissal of the complaint holding that, so long as a labor organization does not combine with non-labor groups, all activities of the general kind described in Clayton Section 20 are exempt. The exemption was broad enough to include even secondary picketing and boycotts; the "right and the wrong, the selfish and the unselfish" were not to be distinguished. There was, in essence, a *per se* exemption. If the challenged activity was conventional labor activity by a labor organization alone, that ended the inquiry.

But in *Allen Bradley*,[8] a case decided a few years later, the Court began to work out limits to the exemption. In the interest of obtaining better wages, hours and working conditions, a union induced electrical contractors to agree to use only equipment manufactured by firms having contracts with the union. Although the union was the prime mover, this arrangement, unlike *Hutcheson,* combined the union with employers in a common cause. The Supreme Court rejected the view taken by the Second Circuit that so long as the union was acting solely in its own self-interest and by means sanctioned by Clayton Section 20, the conduct escaped antitrust liability. Rather, the Court adopted another *per se* rule, alternative to that in *Hutcheson:* immunity is lost when a labor group is acting to "aid and abet businessmen" in conduct which, if carried out by businessmen alone, would violate the Act. Given the primacy of the union's interest and initiative, the case seemed to make clear that immunity was not achieved merely because the union, acting for its own ends, was the architect of an employer-union combination; if manufacturers agreed, even though unwillingly and under union pressure, to a scheme of joint action which would violate the law if arranged by the manufacturers alone, then the union, and presumably the manufacturers, were in violation.

So the matter stood until *Pennington*[9] reached the Court in 1965. There, a mine operator challenged as an antitrust violation an agreement negotiated by the United Mine Workers and an association which represented large mine operators. Employers had made substantial wage and other concessions in the agreement and the union

---

7. See C. Summers & H. Wellington, Labor Law; Cases and Materials 195 (1968).

8. Allen Bradley Co. v. Electrical Workers' Local 3, 325 U.S. 797, 65 S.Ct. 1533, 89 L.Ed. 1939 (1945).

9. United Mine Workers v. Pennington, 381 U.S. 657, 85 S.Ct. 1585, 14 L.Ed.2d 626 (1965).

had agreed to abandon its previously vehement opposition to increased mechanization. The union also agreed that it would impose the same wage and other terms of employment on small operators who were not members of the association. The anticipated consequence was that wages would be improved, jobs reduced, and marginal mine operators forced out of the market. A small mining company, allegedly forced out of business by the agreement, charged in a treble damage action that the agreement constituted a conspiracy by the union and large companies in violation of the Sherman Act. Though reversing a verdict for the mine operator on other grounds, the Supreme Court split three ways on the question whether the union's conduct was exempt from antitrust liability. Justice White in an opinion concurred in by Chief Justice Warren and Justice Brennan gave voice to the goal of accommodation which would, where possible, resolve apparent conflicts between antitrust and labor policy in ways which avoided the need to choose one policy over the other. Given what was explicit in the labor law, where a multi-employer bargaining unit was appropriate, a union could lawfully negotiate with a representative of several companies even though this took wages (and skill at negotiating with unions) out of the area in which competition would be effective between the companies.[10] Moreover, these Justices felt that a union, acting independently and not in concert with employers, can determine that all employers will have to meet the rate set in negotiations with the most efficient. A union need not set its wage demands with the problems of marginal producers uppermost in mind; it may take action of the kinds listed in Clayton Section 20 and in Norris-La Guardia to gain its ends even

10. The opinion does not address important issues that lurk in the background. But for the national labor policy, concerted action by employers to negotiate wage rates would involve serious antitrust jeopardy. Such conduct might be characterized as price fixing and held to be unlawful *per se*. Alternatively, if it were concluded that significant scale efficiencies were feasible, it might be tested under the rule of reason; in this event it would nevertheless be unlawful where, as in *Pennington*, the arrangement brought a substantial part of the market under common control and yielded power to affect market price. See §§ 101–07 supra. Since the national labor policy purports to sanction multi-employer bargaining only where the multi-employer unit is the "appropriate" unit, in terms of the goals of national labor policy, it appears that, should a multi-employer unit in any instance be held not to be appropriate, bargaining for that unit would not be exempt conduct. Even more interesting are the unexplored questions whether the national policy of maintaining competition among employers is entitled to weight where a decision is made about whether in any industry a multi-employer unit is appropriate and whether appropriateness of the unit can be considered by the court in an antitrust case or only initially by the Labor Board. See § 239(b), infra.

A related question concerns whether a "mandatory" subject for collective bargaining under the labor law is one on which employers may act concertedly even though no agreement with a union has yet been reached. In Smith v. Pro-Football, Inc., 780 ATRR E–1 (D.D.C. Sept. 8, 1976) the court held that no labor exemption was gained until a union, for its own interest, negotiates an agreement.

though marginal producers are driven out. When it acts alone, all such conduct is exempt.

But Justice White and those who concurred with him were just as clear that when a union agrees with one employer about the wages it will exact from another employer not involved in the negotiation, the union has forfeited its antitrust exemption. Nothing in the national labor policy suggests a sanction for concerted action between a union and one or more employers about the labor market condition which competing employers will be forced to meet. Antitrust policy stands forcefully against such concerted action. There is, then, no conflict between the application of antitrust policy and the demands of labor policy. Consequently, the antitrust prohibition should prevail. That response was seen, indeed, as particularly appropriate where one group of employers was conspiring with the union on a course of conduct designed to eliminate other employers from the market. The opinion analogized what occurred to an agreement between the union and the companies about the price at which coal would be sold, an agreement which, as Justices White, Warren and Brennan saw it, would be clearly illegal.

In another opinion [11] Justice Douglas, with whom Justices Black and Clark concurred, suggested that the labor exemption would be exceeded only if the union and employers agreed upon a particular wage scale to be enforced against all employers, knowing that some could not meet it and with the intent of driving those employers out of business. As they saw it, such a labor-management conspiracy to drive competitors out of the market would both make the conduct illegal under antitrust and de-energize the labor exemption. Justice Douglas came close as a practical matter to the view expressed by Justice White, however, in that he conceded that under the *Interstate Circuit* [12] doctrine evidence that an industry-wide agreement was negotiated which in fact exceeded the ability of some operators to pay would be sufficient evidence to reach a jury on the conspiracy issue. Justice Goldberg, joined by Justices Stewart and Harlan, wrote a single opinion for this case and *Jewel Tea,* next to be discussed; [13] as to *Pennington,* he dissented from the views expressed in the other opinions for reasons which will be elaborated upon below, but concurred in the result.

The most significant thing in *Pennington* was the view developed in the White opinion that the Court does not merely determine whether the specific activities challenged are cataloged in Clayton Section 20 or in Norris-La Guardia and, if so, assume exemption; nor

11. 381 U.S. 657, 672, 85 S.Ct. 1585, 1594, 14 L.Ed.2d 626, 638 (1965).

12. Interstate Circuit Inc. v. United States, 306 U.S. 208, 59 S.Ct. 467, 83 L.Ed. 610 (1939). See §§ 62, 110 supra.

13. Meat Cutters Local 189 v. Jewel Tea Co., 381 U.S. 676, 697, 85 S.Ct. 1607, 14 L.Ed.2d 640, 654 (1965).

does it mechanically conclude, where a labor-management combination is accomplished, that exemption is gone, as *Allen Bradley* might have been read to imply. Two important national economic policies are interacting; the appropriate response is to determine whether there is, on the face of the matter, some conflict and, if so, whether it can be rationally reconciled. Only if it cannot need a choice be made between the conflicting policies; and when choice cannot be avoided the Court must gauge the force of the competing policies as they apply in the particular context so that the weaker may be made to give way to the stronger. This much, it seems, is implicit in Justice White's opinion; though one might quarrel with the way in which labor and antitrust policies were assessed in that case, it is hard to stand in opposition to this way of structuring the problem. Anything else would be unduly simplified and mechanical. Despite the contrary implications, each in a different direction, both of *Hutcheson* and *Allen Bradley,* this is not an area where the Court can hope to fashion simple, workable, self-administering *per se* rules.

Jewel Tea,[14] a companion case, reinforces the notion that the Court must meter conflicting policies. The case grew out of an industry-wide agreement between the meat cutters union and Chicago butchers which restricted store hours from 9:00 a. m. to 6:00 p. m. an agreement which Jewel Tea accepted under threat of a strike. After signing, Jewel Tea sued under Sherman Section 1, alleging that the union and the employers who negotiated the agreement had conspired to prevent Jewel Tea from marketing at such hours as it, as an individual competitor, chose for itself. The district court found that the union's sole motive was to gain desirable working conditions for members and held the arrangement within the labor exemption. The Seventh Circuit reversed and the Supreme Court, on certiorari, split in the same three-three-three pattern that marked *Pennington,* with six Justices voting to hold that Jewel Tea had no cause of action.

The White opinion viewed the collective bargaining agreement as a "combination" between union and employers to affect a matter of competitive concern. The lack of an intent or motive to inhibit competition as to hours did not require a different characterization since that was the clear effect. Hence, under the approach of *Allen Bradley,* mechanically applied, the conduct would be unlawful; since the agreement involved a combination of labor and employers the Clayton/Norris-La Guardia exemption was gone. But even though such a combination existed there could be, as the opinion indicated, an exemption implied by the statutes setting forth the national labor policy. The problem was not a simple one; it involved accommodating labor and antitrust policy. There are subjects, such as wages, hours and working conditions, which are mandatory subjects of

14. Meat Cutters Local 189 v. Jewel Tea Co. 381 U.S. 676, 85 S.Ct. 1596, 14 L.Ed.2d 640 (1965).

collective bargaining. Where a union and employers in a bargaining relationship agree on these, no antitrust violation occurs even though a combination of a labor group and several competing employers is achieved through industry-wide bargaining. But should a union and employers agree on things such as prices, which are not mandatory bargaining subjects, the protection of the implicit exemption derived from the NLRA and Taft-Hartley would be gone. In this instance, hours of operation had been a historic concern of the butchers' union and there were indications that night operations alter the character of the work itself. In that context, hours of operation are sufficiently related to wages, hours and working conditions, to fall within the proper scope of collective bargaining for the multi-employer unit; thus the agreement is exempt.

The opinion by Justice Douglas expressed the view that since the employers could not themselves agree on hours of operation the union, by joining with them, exceeded the *Allen Bradley* rule and lost its exemption. This mechanical response is hardly satisfactory. Employers alone could not agree, for example, on the wages they would pay their employees; yet it is obvious that in a multi-employer unit sanctioned under the labor laws, a union and employers may join in fixing that element and taking it out of the competitive struggle.

Justice Goldberg's opinion, which expressed his view on *Jewel Tea* and *Pennington*, harkened back to the *Hutcheson* case. As Justice Goldberg saw the matter, hours of operation was clearly a matter of working conditions and, that being so, a mandatory subject of collective bargaining. Any agreement between a union and employers on such a subject is exempt from the antitrust laws. So with *Pennington*. Discussion of wage rates naturally involves discussion of the impact of the wage demanded upon the employer's business and this, in turn, inevitably involves discussion of the wages to be exacted from competitors. In the view of Justice Goldberg, to deny the right to consider such matters in bargaining is frustrating to the collective bargaining process.[15]

Though *Pennington* and *Jewel Tea* stood for years unexplained and unelaborated, the Court has more recently given further guid-

---

15. *Pennington*, in indicating the illegality of an agreement between a union and an employer about the terms the union will insist upon in bargaining with others, places in jeopardy common arrangements in addition to explicit agreements about the matter. A common event is for an employer, in signing with a union, to seek and obtain a "most favored nation" clause, providing that if the union later grants more favorable terms to any other employer those terms will apply to the earlier signing employer also. At least in the situation where that clause is entered into between a union and a dominant employer or group of employers, so that all parties will realize that the union will as a practical matter concede no less onerous terms later, that arrangement is no different in effect from an explicit arrangement like that in *Pennington*. Therefore one cannot confidently assume its legality.

ance. Ramsey v. United Mine Workers [16] is another case arising out of the coal agreement. Construing a phrase in Justice White's *Pennington* opinion, the lower courts had held that the jury must be instructed that "clear proof" of an employer-union conspiracy to drive out competing employers had to be shown to warrant a plaintiff's verdict. The majority of the Court disagreed and, in opinion by Justice White, held that a plaintiff suing on a *Pennington* theory need establish his case only by a preponderance of the evidence. Though Justice Douglas' *Pennington* and *Jewel Tea* opinions were even less hospitable to the labor exemption than the White opinions, in this instance Justice Douglas dissented. As Justice Douglas viewed it, bargaining with a multi-employer unit was itself no violation. He would therefore insist on clear proof of the conspiratorial animus before finding an antitrust violation, at least where the alleged conspiracy concerned wage rates alleged to be so high that some employers would be driven out, as distinguished from instances where the union and employers agreed, as in *Jewel Tea,* to standardize some competitive factor other than wages.

In their totality these cases suggest both an analytical stance and an objective: to reconcile labor and antitrust policy where possible and, where not, to weigh claims of each and give way to the stronger. The difficulty of this task was reemphasized most recently in Connell Construction Co. v. Plumbers and Steamfitters Local 100.[17] A union for one of the construction industry sub-trades had successfully used picketing to force a number of general contractors to agree to subcontract work in the trade only to subcontractors which had current collective bargaining agreements with the union. Connell, one of these contractors, wanted to let subcontract work by competitive bidding to any qualified subcontractor and had signed the agreement under the duress of job site picketing which caused its own employees, represented by a different union, to walk off the job. Connell asserted in its suit against the union that the contract it was obliged to sign violated Section 1 of Sherman. Justice Powell, writing for the majority, held that the statutory exemption of Clayton Section 20 was not available because the arrangement involved both labor and non-labor groups and that the "non statutory" exemption which can arise by implication from the NLRA or LMRA was not available for two reasons: first, because the union did not represent or seek to represent Connell's employees; second, because the "construction industry proviso" to Section 8(e) of the NLRA,[18] which authorizes secondary activity of the kind here involved, was, as the syllabus tersely put it, "not intended to authorize subcontracting agreements that are neither within the context of a collective bargaining

16. 401 U.S. 302, 91 S.Ct. 658, 28 L.Ed. 2d 64 (1971).

17. 421 U.S. 616, 95 S.Ct. 1830, 44 L. Ed.2d 418 (1975).

18. 29 U.S.C.A. § 158(e) (1973).

relationship nor limited to a particular job site."[19] Justice Stewart, joined by Justices Douglas, Brennan and Marshall, dissented, first on the ground that secondary activity is subject to detailed and comprehensive regulation under Section 8(b)(4) of the NLRA,[20] and Section 303 of the Labor Management Relations Act,[21] which gives a cause of action for single damages in the event of a violation, and because secondary activity of the kind involved was specifically authorized by Section 8(e).[22]

The most important issue of general, theoretical importance which this case seems to resolve is whether the antitrust exemption implied from the NLRA and LMRA applies whenever an activity, otherwise violative of antitrust, is of a kind which is dealt with in detail by the labor statutes, or only when the activity is in some sense authorized or approved by the labor statutes. There is no question but that the labor statute regulates in considerable detail secondary activity of the genus involved in this case; NLRA Section 8(b)(4) makes that activity an unfair labor practice, except insofar as it is shielded by other provisions. Section 8(e) shields some secondary activity of the general kind involved, but not all. Section 303 of the LMRA gives a cause of action for single damages for 8(b)(4) violations, among others. The majority, held that NLRA Section 8(e) did not protect this particular secondary activity from the prohibition of Section 8(b)(4), and that LMRA Section 303, by giving a single damage cause of action for violations of 8(b)(4), did not imply the absence of a treble damage action under the antitrust laws. Thus, the majority impliedly held that an antitrust exemption does not apply to all activities of a class regulated by labor law but only to activities approved and protected by labor law. Although the minority opinion argued vehemently that even assuming the majority to be right on the more specific statutory issues, the various strands of regulation constituted a sort of "occupation of the field" by the labor statutes to the exclusion of the antitrust laws, the majority assumed almost without discussion that unless a particular practice is affirmatively sanctioned by labor law it is entitled to no exemption. That need not be so. Although the minority's "occupancy" concept seems unduly mechanical, it is surely possible that in some instances there is sufficient importance in allowing unions to push the edges of labor policy, subject only to correction under the labor laws, to warrant holding that any conduct within the ambit of the labor law should be free from antitrust attack whether that conduct is mandated, tolerated or forbidden by labor law. The particular conduct in *Connell* may not be in an area where labor policy demands such deference from

19. 421 U.S. at 617, 95 S.Ct. at 1833, 44 L.Ed.2d at 423.

20. 29 U.S.C.A. § 158(b)(4) (1973).

21. 29 U.S.C.A. § 187 (1973).

22. 29 U.S.C.A. § 158(e) (1973).

antitrust; but that matter is one to be decided after consideration, not blithely assumed.[23]

Note also that whenever a union negotiates with a group of employers in a multi-employer bargaining arrangement it is agreeing with each about the wage rates of the others. Where the multi-employer unit is the appropriate unit for collective bargaining, within the meaning of the NLRA, the union would, of course, have an exemption based on the implication of the NLRA. But if the multi-employer unit should not be held appropriate, *Connell* may imply union and employer liability for jointly agreeing on wages. If the unit is not appropriate, then labor policy may not call for any exemption. And if there is no exemption, antitrust policy has free reign.[24]

§ 238. Governmental Action and Its Solicitation

a. Reconciling the Antitrust Laws and State Law Regulating Economic Affairs

The constitutional primacy of federal over conflicting state law assures that antitrust will dominate whenever there is a head-on conflict between antitrust and state law or policy; state law may prevail only to the extent that Congress is held to have deferred to it. But that way of putting the matter may do as much to obscure as to illuminate important problems. Indeed, the conventional power metaphor which evokes an image of separate sovereigns with separate legal systems engaged in a struggle to settle priorities is not very felicitous. The dynamic between state law and antitrust is better understood as a search for synthesis or adjustment of issues of policy. An antitrust court faced with a defense based on state law will proceed

---

23. The specific statutory issues in the *Connell* case, though of less general importance, are not devoid of interest. Section 8(e), literally construed, would shield the union-employer contract from the prohibition of 8(b)(4) as "an agreement between a labor organization and an employer in the construction industry relating to * * * subcontracting of work to be done at the site of the construction * * *"; and it is not particularly clear that the majority got the better of the argument about the limit upon the meaning of the phrase emanating from its legislative history. Yet the minority also overleaped a significant question. The minority assumed without discussion that if Section 8(e) saved the activity involved from being an unfair labor practice forbidden by Section 8(b)(4), it must also save it from being an antitrust violation. That surely does not follow as a necessity. To say that a particular activity falls barely within the scope of a proviso which thus barely keeps it from being an unfair labor practice is not to make a strong case for protecting the activity from antitrust prohibition because of the activity's importance to labor policy. If, as the majority holds, exemption applies only when there is a greater interest under the labor law in allowing the conduct than there is under the antitrust law in forbidding it, unless there were some positive reason under labor policy for encouraging a practice, any significant antitrust policy against it ought to suffice to make it illegal.

24. See footnote 10 supra. Note that if industry-wide bargaining is not carried on, but employers act concertedly in agreeing on the position each will take in bargaining with the union, there is after *Connell* virtually no room left for employers to claim a labor exemption. The lawfulness of such joint employer activity must therefore be determined under normal antitrust principles.

much as might a court dealing with conflicts within a single system of law; it will seek to identify the major values which are relevant and to assign to each an appropriate scope. This subsection will mark out the parameters by reference to some of the landmark cases. After that, more specific issues will be addressed.

The dominant themes are suggested by two important cases, Schwegmann Brothers v. Calvert Distillers Corp.[1] and Parker v. Brown.[2] The first involved integration of antitrust with state fair trade policy in a situation where Congress had tendered some guidance to the Court. The Miller-Tydings amendment to Section 1 of Sherman exempted from the ban of Sherman contracts specifying minimum resale prices when "contracts or agreements of that description" are lawful under state law.[3] A Louisiana fair trade statute contained a so-called non-signer provision. It not only permitted contracts for the sale of a commodity to provide that the buyer would not resell except at the price specified by the vendor but, in addition, stated that once a seller had entered into such a contract with any buyer, any sale by any other seller in the state at a lower price was unfair competition. The Court noted that the Miller-Tydings Act, though authorizing vertical agreements fixing minimum prices, left intact the Sherman Act prohibitions against vertical agreements pegging prices at specific levels or fixing maxima, and against horizontal price fixing. The Court inferred that Congress did not intend to defer to state power generally, but only to grant a limited immunity from the federal law. Miller-Tydings did not literally authorize state enforcement of non-signer provisions. The Court indicated that the choice whether to construe the Act to do so should be made in a way which modified federal policy no more than necessary to give reasonable elbow room to the state policy Congress intended to accommodate. Given the fact that Congress did not authorize states to validate horizontal price fixing agreements among distributors, the Court concluded that Miller-Tydings should not be read to authorize state law to allow a distributor, by entering into a price fixing agreement with a manufacturer, to impose specified resale prices on its competitors. The case teaches, then, that states do not have power to grant general exemptions from federal antitrust policy merely by adopting legislation which announces cartelization as state policy. A state may afford antitrust exemption only where and to the extent that Congress has indicated its intent to defer to state law.

Parker v. Brown[4] makes a puzzling contrast. A California statute authorized the establishment of agricultural marketing programs restricting competition among growers and maintaining prices.

---

1. 341 U.S. 384, 71 S.Ct. 745, 95 L.Ed. 1035 (1957).

2. 317 U.S. 341, 63 S.Ct. 307, 87 L.Ed. 315 (1943).

3. Act of August 17, 1937, c. 690, 50 Stat. 693.

4. 317 U.S. 341, 63 S.Ct. 307, 87 L.Ed. 315 (1943).

Under the statutory scheme, growers, in the classic manner of an agricultural cartel, would concertedly develop a marketing and price-fixing program and nominate an administrative committee to enforce it. However, the legislation created a state commission to which industry proposals had to be submitted. A program became effective only if the commission, after hearings, found that the program would prevent agricultural waste and would not permit producers to earn unreasonable profits, and then only if approved by a specified percentage of producers in a referendum supervised by the commission. The action to test the state legislation was brought by a raisin grower against state officials charged with administering and enforcing the program. The grower charged that the state scheme was invalid under a federal statute dealing with agricultural marketing agreements, under the commerce clause and (after being adverted to the issue by the Court) under the Sherman Act.

In upholding the California statute the Court, as to the Sherman issue, emphasized two things: first, that Congress, in enacting Sherman, did not intend to invalidate state action regulating economic activity; second, that the state, while retaining power to regulate within the scope of its own constitutional power, could not authorize private persons or corporations to act in ways violative of the antitrust laws. *Parker*, celebrated until recently only for its teaching on the first of those propositions, was often said to create an exemption from the antitrust laws for "state action." We shall explore the present scope of that exemption hereafter. The underlying rationale of *Parker* is somewhat obscure. The Court referred to state sovereignty and the anomaly of making acts by state officers done under legislative direction unlawful. But the anomaly fades when the question is posed more realistically as whether state policy must give way when it conflicts with federal. The Court also remarked on the legislative history of Sherman, which focuses on the evils of business combinations, not governmental regulatory programs. But the Court has always recognized the potential of the Sherman Act to expand to meet new methods for achieving business combinations; one might expect Sherman to reach cartels which successfully marshal state officialdom in the performance of enforcement activities on the ground that cartels such as these are not less threatening than naked cartels to the public interest Sherman aims to protect, but more threatening to that interest. In short, even assuming (as commentators long did on the authority of *Parker*) the validity of programs of economic regulation initiated, implemented and carried out by state government in order to advance a state interest (other than merely to inhibit the enforcement of antitrust policies in sectors where the state legislature thinks cartelization would be better), state legislative action and action by state officials must nevertheless be examined and characterized before it is assumed that it is exempt from Sherman. Action by state officials pursuant to a state statute which substitutes public regulation for private competition may be exempt; but there is no exemption for a state activity which merely seeks to free an industry from the strictures of antitrust law on the basis of a state judgment (conflicting with that made by Congress) that in some sector cartelization is preferable to competition; nor does *Parker* itself disclose whether (or the extent to which) private parties acting under state law are exempt, or, for that matter, whether a particular state statute might be invalid (and thus no defense even for state officials) because of repugnancy to Sherman, even though the statute was not (as was that in *Schwegmann*) so blatantly at odds with Sherman as to be a mere charade.

Indeed, a difficult question of characterization was presented in *Parker* itself. On the face of the matter, the California program invited private action which, if not sanctioned by state law, would plainly violate Sherman. The state statute also set up a state agency to review the private action under legislatively sanctioned standards. But the procedures for industry initiative in developing a program, for selecting the program committee from industry nominees, for holding an industry referendum before a commission approved program became effective, were all indicative of a state policy to sanction cartelization by private groups, subject only to a review as to reasonableness of prices by a commission which, given the nature of its mission, could be expected to have a strong orientation toward industry interests. Considering all of these elements the scheme might well have been characterized as a state effort to exempt private conduct from Sherman, much as did the Louisiana statute considered in *Schwegmann Brothers*. In deciding that, on balance, the action by California officials in enforcing the California program should be characterized as state action regulating prices rather than a state effort to exempt private action from federal law, the Court was influenced by the fact that the state marketing statute was consistent with a federal statute which authorized a federal program of marketing restrictions on agricultural products and which showed that Congress knew that the states had legislation in this field also and did not intend to oust state regulation. That ancillary source of information about the extent to which Congress was ready both to try cartelization as federal agricultural policy and to defer to state movements in that direction may well have been crucial to the Parker v. Brown holding. *Parker* is a decision rooted in a particular legislative context, not a sweeping deference to state granted exemptions from federal antitrust law.

As more recent cases forcefully demonstrate, the state action exemption is not an imperative, nor a rule to be mechanically applied, but an invitation to judgment about the proper relationship of state policy to antitrust in particular factual and statutory settings. While the factors a court should take into account in making that judgment cannot be encapsulated, *Schwegmann* and *Parker* suggest that state displacement of federal policy will be sanctioned only when the state has made a legislative judgment to adopt a cohesive regulatory program alternative to antitrust and only to the extent needed to give that policy the scope which its alternative philosophy requires. Other decisions reinforce these implications. In Sears Roebuck & Co. v. Stiffle Co.,[5] a mass retailer had copied lamps made by a famous manufacturer, the designs for which were not protected by any patent or copyright. The state court enjoined copying on the basis of its common law doctrine against unfair competition. It felt that the copies of Stiffle's widely advertised products might confuse consumers as to source. The Supreme Court reversed. The Court conceded that the state could enforce a policy to protect consumers from deception. But it took note that a comprehensive federal policy called for competition, subject to a few explicit exceptions under patent and to copyright law, none of which obtained here. It felt that the state could adequately implement its goal of protecting consumers without so seriously undercutting the federal competition policy as did the state rule against copying.

Lear, Inc. v. Adkins[6] pushes further in the same direction. It establishes that state policy inconsistent with antitrust gains no precedence over federal law when there are ways in which the state could achieve its objectives which conflict less directly with antitrust. Thus, it makes explicit what was implicit in *Stiffel*. The plaintiff in *Lear,* at a time when it had a patent application pending, granted a license to the defendant under a contract calling for a periodic royalty payment before and after the patent issued. The licensee concluded after a time that the claimed invention was in the public domain and stopped making royalty payments. A patent was later granted and the plaintiff brought suit for pre-issuance and post-issuance royalties. Although the trial court held the patent invalid, the California Supreme Court held that under state contract law the licensee was estopped from challenging validity and obligated to pay. On certiorari, the United States Supreme Court ruled otherwise. It concluded that the federal policy to foster competition required that patent licensees be permitted to challenge patent validity irrespective of contrary state law. It held that federal policy precluded California from enforcing the contract for royalty payments due after the issuance of an invalid patent.[7]

---

5. 376 U.S. 225, 84 S.Ct. 784, 11 L.Ed.2d 661 (1964).

6. 395 U.S. 653, 89 S.Ct. 1902, 23 L.Ed. 2d 610 (1969).

7. The majority left open the question whether the state could enforce the contract to pay royalties during the prepatent period for the benefit of having had the invention disclosed and available for use during that period. Goldfarb v. Virginia State Bar, 421 U.S. 773, 95 S.Ct. 2004, 44 L.Ed.2d 572 (1975) is also significant. The Court emphasized that exemption is gained by state instrumentalities only for conduct required by the state acting as a sovereign.

Though the *Parker* exemption has often been construed more broadly than the comments above suggest is warranted, the era when it was plausible to give *Parker* a broad reading has now been brought to a definitive end. In Goldfarb v. Virginia State Bar,[8] the Court refused to apply the *Parker* doctrine to activities of a state bar association which dampened price competition among lawyers. The opinion made clear that the "so called state action exemption"[9] did not cover any activity that was not required by the state, acting as a sovereign. It implied, moreover, that even if an activity passed that "threshold inquiry"[10] it might fail to obtain exemption on other, unspecified grounds. In Cantor v. The Detroit Edison Company,[11] the Court, in what may prove to be one of the most important antitrust decisions in recent years, has filled in some of the gaps left by *Virginia State Bar*, has set forth an agenda of open issues concerning relations between state law and antitrust, and has suggested the manner in which lower courts should address those open issues.

In *Cantor* a power company's practice of supplying light bulbs to residential purchasers of electric power without additional charge was held not to be exempt from antitrust challenge even though the practice was specified in the company's rate tariff which had been approved by the state utility commission, and even though, under state law, the company could not abandon the practice spelled out in its tariff without obtaining commission approval of an amended tariff. No majority concurred in a single opinion. Justice Stevens wrote a plurality opinion for himself and Justices Brennan, White and Marshall with which Chief Justice Burger concurred in substantial part. Justice Blackmun expressed his concurring views in a separate opinion. Justice Stewart wrote for the three dissenters.

All six Justices voting with the majority agreed that private conduct does not gain antitrust exemption merely because it is required by state law. Five of the majority (all save Justice Blackmun) also agreed about the kind of inquiry that is necessary. The antitrust court must examine the mix of public and private motivation and initiative reflected in the state program. Where (as in the case of a utility filing a tariff which is accepted by the state agency) private participation is significant, the arrangement does not achieve antitrust immunity on the ground that it is authorized, approved, encouraged or participated in by the state. Where, by contrast, the state's participation in a decision is dominant and plainly overbears the private elements, additional issues must be analyzed before it can be determined whether antitrust exemption is appropriate. The mere fact that the state regulates the activity in question does not give rise

---

8. 421 U.S. 773, 95 S.Ct. 2004, 44 L.Ed.2d 572 (1975).

9. 421 U.S. at 788, 95 S.Ct. at 2014, 44 L.Ed.2d at 586.

10. 421 U.S. at 790, 95 S.Ct. at 2015, 44 L.Ed. at 587.

11. —— U.S. ——, 96 S.Ct. 3110, 49 L.Ed.2d 1141 (1976).

to a conflict between state and federal policy. Often it will be possible to insist without logical inconsistency that firms meet state regulatory criteria (where they do not face competition) and also meet antitrust requirements (where they do or may encounter competition). Assuming an active conflict between antitrust and state regulatory law it becomes essential for the court to decide which policy ought to defer to the other and to what degree. The issue is whether to infer a Congressional intent to defer to state policies of the particular kind involved. The analytical process is essentially the same as that of reconciling antitrust policy and federal regulatory policy; [12] there is no basis for assuming that Congress intended to give greater power to preempt antitrust laws to state agencies than to federal agencies.

Finally, there are questions of fairness to be addressed. Where a firm which did not participate in the development of the state policy in good faith does what a sovereign state commands, it may be unfair to hold the firm retrospectively subject to inconsistent antitrust norms, even though, upon analysis, the court concludes that antitrust preempts the inconsistent state command.

These, then, are the main outlines of the law in this area as it exists today. Many particulars remain to be filled in and the "state action exemption" can be expected to be a fertile source of dispute and litigation for some time to come.[13]

b. *State Regulation of Resale Prices: A Model Analysis*

With the repeal of the fair trade exemption to the Sherman Act [14] the implications of *Schwegmann* take on new importance. Suppose that fair traders, having lost at the federal legislative level, seek to recoup by persuading state legislatures to enact laws which impose fair trade schemes? We may take it from *Schwegmann* that (except perhaps with respect to the liquor industry, as to which the states may have especially comprehensive power because of the twenty-first amendment) [15] a state may not confer a Sherman exemption simply by passing a statute which allows manufacturers to specify resale prices and forbids resellers from deviating from these. But suppose a state were to enact a resale price maintenance statute modeled upon the agricultural marketing statute held valid in Parker v. Brown? Would the state by that device be able to avoid the consequences of the recent repeal of the federal fair trade statutes? An antitrust casebook hypothesizes a statute which establishes a state Fair Trade Price Review Board, which reviews fair trade price lists submitted by manufacturers or wholesalers.[16] If the legislation made such resale prices

---

12. See § 239 infra.

13. Even before *Cantor* there was extensive litigation.

14. P.L. 94–145 (Dec. 12, 1975). See § 132 supra.

15. U.S. Const., 21st amend.

16. M. Handler, H. Blake, R. Pitofsky & H. Goldschmid, Trade Regulation, Cases and Materials 583–84 (1975).

binding on all resellers in the state whenever the commission, after a public hearing, found that the prices were fair and reasonable and would not yield unreasonable profits to resellers, would that statute be enforceable on the strength of the *Parker* case? Would it if it replicated the *Parker* statute even more closely by providing also for a referendum among resellers before the designated prices became binding?

This hypothetical churns up the waters of that seemingly quiet pool that stands between the *Schwegmann* shore and the *Parker* shore. The factual analogies to Parker v. Brown are obvious and if that case is to be read literally such a statute would clearly be valid. But after *Cantor* that result is not at all likely. Mediating between state and federal policy requires probing beneath surface manifestations; important factors are thus perceived. In *Parker* there was an independent federal policy, contrasting with the antitrust laws, by which Congress had expressed its approval of programs to regulate agricultural marketing in ways which reduced competition. By that program Congress showed its recognition that the special circumstances of agricultural markets might require special solutions which mitigated the rigors of competition. In our hypothetical situation, Congress has not only failed to take action mitigating competition in the interests of resellers in the distribution chain, it has, in fact, after fully considering the plight of resellers (to which Congress had for many years accorded special relief) decided to withdraw federal sanction for a narrow antitrust exemption.[17] So doing, it embraced the view that the public interest in the lower prices which competition may yield outweighs the claimed need to protect retailers against the rigors of competition. Given that congressional judgment, the argument that the hypothetical statute is governed by *Schwegmann* rather than *Parker* seems compelling.

One might go further, indeed, and emphasize the cosmetic qualities of the hypothetical program supposed above. It would not be unfair, perhaps, to label such legislation as a transparent effort by a state to exempt resellers within its borders from the requirements of Sherman by providing the trappings of a state regulatory program. The validity of this kind of a challenge to state law could be evaluated, perhaps, by closer attention to factual details. Is there some cohesive *regulatory* theory that underlies the state legislation? Or is the only theory that underlies it the notion the cartelization is good? Does the state commission function independently, thoroughly and quasi-judicially? Does it actually apply the regulatory theory which is asserted as justifying the statute? Has it developed plausible and administrable norms about when prices and profits are unreasonable and when they are not? Affirmative answers to questions like these would tend to support a Parker v. Brown characterization; negative

---

17. P.L. 94–145 (Dec. 12, 1975). See § 132 supra.

answers would tend to suggest that the real basis for the state legislation was the policy notion, rejected by Congress, that fair trade is a better way to run markets than is competition. This hypothetical analysis is put forward here not on the supposition that efforts may be made at the state level to revive fair trade, but to suggest one of the ways in which *any* state statute, asserted to confer an antitrust exemption, might be analyzed for consistency with federal policy.

c. *Business Activity by Governmental Agencies*

It is taken for granted that the antitrust laws do not forbid a state from socializing an industry entirely or in substantial part and becoming a monopolist. Neither a county school system, a municipal fire department, nor a state university is threatened by the Sherman Act no matter what share of its market it may gain. It is also clear enough that a municipality may, without offending against the antitrust laws, take the property of a utility within its borders and substitute a state monopoly for a private one.

Could a municipality also take all the grocery stores and then restrict entry? The pervasive notion that a state or local government is not subject to antitrust scrutiny when it owns and operates a means of production and distribution is an untested one. It is probably sound enough as a generalization when applied to governmental ownership of natural monopolies or of facilities, like schools, which have in this country been traditionally socialized and which may relate both to constitutional concepts and to the quality of life in ways that distinguish them from conventional commercial activities. Perhaps that is as far as one need probe at this juncture. But one should at least take note that state entry into conventional commercial fields need not result in state exemption from the antitrust laws in the performance of commercial, market functions.[18]

Sometimes a court can finesse the bald question whether a state can gain exemption for commercial activity which by a private party would violate the antitrust laws. Duke & Co. v. Foerster[19] is an example. The statute had in the accustomed manner granted to a municipal agency all of the power "necessary and convenient" to run a number of publicly owned facilities. The agency was charged with engaging in an unlawful boycott and, in denying exemption, the court held that immunity could not be claimed unless the state legislation required the state agency to act in ways that would be unlawful if not exempt. *Virginia State Bar*[20] also suggests that "state action" within the meaning of Parker v. Brown means action pursuant to a de-

---

18. Compare, Hecht v. Pro-Football, Inc., 444 F.2d 931 (D.C.Cir. 1971). See also Asheville Tobacco Bd. of Trade v. FTC, 263 F.2d 502 (4th Cir. 1959), emphasizing that individual action masquerading as state action gains no exemption.

19. 521 F.2d 1277 (3rd Cir. 1975).

20. Goldfarb v. Virginia State Bar, 421 U.S. 773, 95 S.Ct. 2004, 44 L.Ed.2d 572 (1975). In City of Lafayette v. Louisiana Power & Light Co., 532 F.2d 431,

740 COVERAGE, EXEMPTIONS & PROCEDURE Ch. 9

liberate decision on state policy by its legislative branch, or at least action which partakes more of sovereign qualities than does discretionary action by a board charged with the performance of commercial functions.[21]

d. Private Efforts to Obtain Governmental Interference with a Competitor

Having, as we do, two principles, one which protects some state action even though it threatens competition, another which makes illegal private action having that effect, we inevitably need to work out accommodations in those hazy areas where each may seem applicable. Eastern Railroads Presidents Conference v. Noerr Motor Freight, Inc.,[22] presented the problem in a blatant form. Defendant railroads and their trade association and agents conducted a deceptive publicity campaign to foster laws restricting truckers and injuring their ability to compete with railroads. Plaintiffs, truckers and their association, sought treble damages and an injunction under the Sherman Act. The conduct objected to was concerted and had the purpose and effect forbidden by Sherman. On its own terms Parker v. Brown[23] provided no shield. There was no challenge to state action, only to that of private parties. Yet, in a democracy the process of governance involves not just official action but private efforts to influence official action. Just as some activities by instrumentalities of a state which are of a commercial and non-governmental character might be characterized as market activities and declared to be subject to Sherman, so too some private action may be closely enough related to governmental activity to warrant the exemption which is accorded to governmental or regulatory action by the state itself.

---

434 (5th Cir. 1976), cities were charged with unlawfully using gas and water as tying products to force buyers to purchase electric power, and of similar offenses. The district court dismissed on motion holding that the cities' activities were within the *Parker* exemption. The court of appeals reversed. It held that the trial court should hear the evidence and consider all relevant statutes and their reasonable implications to decide whether the cities' acts were "clearly within the legislative intent." But cf. State of New Mexico v. American Petrofina, 501 F.2d 363 (9th Cir. 1974), a pre-*Virginia State Bar* case looking the other way.

21. See also United Mine Workers v. Pennington, 381 U.S. 657, 671, 85 S.Ct. 1585, 1594, 14 L.Ed.2d 626, 637 (1965) which stated that exemption required state action taken in a deliberative way with full awareness of competitive effects, and Continental Ore Co. v. Union Carbide Corp., 370 U.S. 690, 82 S.Ct. 1404, 8 L.Ed.2d 777 (1962), holding that the state action exemption did not apply to private action authorized, but not required, under Canadian law. On the scope of the state action exemption generally, see Washington Gas Light Co. v. Virginia Elec. & Power Co., 438 F.2d 248 (4th Cir. 1971); George R. Whitten Jr., Inc. v. Paddock Pool Builders, Inc., 424 F.2d 25 (1st Cir.), cert. denied 400 U.S. 850, 91 S.Ct. 54, 27 L.Ed.2d 88 (1970); E. W. Wiggins Airways, Inc. v. Massachusetts Port Authority, 362 F.2d 52 (1st Cir.), cert. denied 385 U.S. 947, 87 S.Ct. 320, 17 L.Ed.2d 226 (1966).

22. 365 U.S. 127, 81 S.Ct. 523, 5 L.Ed.2d 464 (1961).

23. 317 U.S. 341, 63 S.Ct. 307, 87 L.Ed. 315 (1943).

The Court in *Noerr* confronted these issues. It did not reformulate the rule of Brown v. Parker to cover appropriate aspects of private activity; instead it announced what has been taken as a new Sherman Act exception, itself a principle which after a decade and a half remains one of vague contours, the so-called "*Noerr* doctrine." In order to protect the right of private parties to petition government and to protect the governmental interest of a free flow of information and views, the Court held that concerted action consisting solely of activities aimed at influencing public officials did not violate the Sherman Act.[24] But the right to petition is no more a principle of infinite application than is any other, nor is the government's interest in obtaining information necessarily unyielding when it competes with other important public concerns. The *Noerr* doctrine, conceding much to the complexities of political processes in an industrial society, does more than protect the right of an individual citizen to petition government and the interest of the government in hearing the citizen; it creates a right in one firm to combine with other firms to petition and assumes an interest in government to hear the presentation developed to express the concerted interests of firms which exercise that right. Once it is recognized that the Court has moved some distance from constitutional bedrock, the urgency of the interests protected become more open to question.

The findings in *Noerr* showed that the campaign of the railroad interests was built upon what public relations people call the "third party device," falsely attributing to disinterested individuals views and statements which actually come from interested ones. Given the specific facts of *Noerr*, the case for allowing the exemption was strong despite the finding of concerted action and even though one insists that a concerted group of firms have no right to deceive voters and public officials. For one thing, the issues of fact and policy subsumed under the trial court's findings about the deceptive nature of the publicity campaign were themselves highly complex. One might rationally conclude that the rectitude of complex political action of debatable propriety ought not be a triable issue in an antitrust case. Appropriate political action might be unduly chilled if that were allowed to happen. The worthiness of political advertising is a delicate issue which, if it is to be dealt with by adjudication at all, ought to be dealt with in a context where legislative guidance has been provided and where, procedurally, the propriety of the political conduct is the central subject of inquiry. For another thing, the findings in *Noerr* showed that both parties had used similar conduct, a fact which if

---

24. The principle was restated in much the same terms in United Mine Workers v. Pennington, 381 U.S. 657, 85 S.Ct. 1585, 14 L.Ed.2d 626 (1965) a case in which a union and large employers, conspiring to eliminate small coal companies, sought to induce the Secretary of Labor to establish high wage minima for employees of firms supplying coal to TVA. The Court said that such conduct was not itself illegal and could not be considered as part of a broader scheme violative of Sherman.

not strictly relevant, given the other findings, could be expected to dampen any judicial ardor to grant relief. But there may be situations where the improper character of concerted political action is manifest, or where the legislature *has* established standards and these have been transgressed, or even where the concerted political conduct a plaintiff wishes to challenge under the antitrust laws violates legislation governing political activity and has already been adjudicated to do so in a procedure established for that purpose.

At all events, the shield of *Noerr* does cease to provide cover when the reasons related to the first amendment for protecting concerted action grow sufficiently weak. Bribery, for example, ought not to be protected.[25] Neither, as the Court held in *California Motor Transport*,[26] is concerted conduct to press sham claims before a state agency in order to clog its process and deprive a competitor of a reasonable opportunity to have entry applications heard. The latter case may cut back on the *Noerr* doctrine considerably, for deciding whether an administrative or judicial procedure is pursued in good faith or for wrongful purposes may well be as difficult as deciding whether given political activities are useful or misleading. Just where the line ought to fall we shall better know after more experience with the doctrine and with problems of regulating political and related activity. It is enough for now to say that the more clear it is that the conduct defendant seeks to protect is not conduct that there is a social interest in protecting as part of the political process, the less likely it will be that the *Noerr* doctrine will afford protection.

California Motor Transport differed from *Noerr* and from *Pennington* in yet another respect. The latter two cases both involved legislative and executive action and allegedly wrongful political activity seeking to influence it. *California Motor Transport* involved administrative or quasi-judicial action and conduct allegedly constituting an abuse of those processes. That the Court dealt with administrative decision making under the rubric of the *Noerr* doctrine emphasizes the breadth of the doctrine. It has been held to protect the bringing of a lawsuit,[27] but not the provision of false information to

---

25. Rangen, Inc. v. Sterling Nelson & Sons, Inc., 351 F.2d 851 (9th Cir. 1965), cert. denied 383 U.S. 936 86 S.Ct. 1067, 15 L.Ed.2d 853 (1966). Compare Sun Valley Disposal Co. v. Silver State Disposal Co., 42 F.2d 341 (9th Cir. 1969). But see Cow Palace, Ltd. v. Associated Milk Producers, Inc., 390 F.Supp. 696 (D.Colo.1975) which rejects the contention that the exemption does not cover bribery and illegal campaign contributions.

26. California Motor Transport Co. v. Trucking Unlimited, 404 U.S. 508, 92 S.Ct. 609, 30 L.Ed.2d 642 (1972). In *Noerr* itself, the Court indicated that a sham publicity campaign, ostensibly directed toward influencing governmental action, but actually interfering directly with the private market, would not be exempt. (365 U.S. at 144, 81 S.Ct. at 533, 5 L.Ed.2d at 475). For other exceptions to the *Noerr* doctrine see Anno., 17 A.L.R. Fed. 645, 650 (1973).

27. See Bracken's Shopping Center, Inc. v. Ruwe, 273 F.Supp. 606 (S.D. Ill.1967). Compare United States v. Otter Tail Power Co., 331 F.Supp. 54, 62 (D.Minn.1971), aff'd. in part and vacated in part 410 U.S. 366, 93 S.Ct.

an agency authorized to forbid a competitor from marketing a product,[28] or to stop a competitor from doing business.[29] The area of government action in which a *Noerr* defense is least likely to be available is when the government decision the defendants seek to influence is itself a commercial one. The *Paddock Pool* decision [30] provides an example. There an effort to induce a governmental purchasing agent to use specifications which excluded competitors was held entitled to no protection under the *Noerr* doctrine.[31]

§ 239. Regulated Industries

a. Introduction

Issues about the compatibility of regulation and competition pervade every regulated industry. The extent to which antitrust applies, or to which particular kinds of activities (mergers, joint ventures, horizontal or vertical agreements of various kinds) are exempt from antitrust vary with differences in the scope and purposes of regulation, whether there is an express indication in the regulatory statute that exemption is contemplated, whether the regulatory statute mandates that competition be relied upon in part, the history and traditions of particular industries or particular regulatory agencies and other even more idiosyncratic factors. It is important to recognize that there is no single conception which defines the scope of the exemption for a regulated industry. Although one can draw on case law from one industry for guidance as to outcome in another, there are, in a sense, as many sets of exemption doctrines as there are industries subject to state or federal regulation. In each industry the process of accommodating regulatory doctrine to antitrust doctrine is responsive to particulars such as those here referred to and, in some degree no doubt, to the degree of confidence which the court has in the quality of the regulatory performance by the particular regulatory

---

1022, 35 L.Ed.2d 359 (1973). There the district court held *Noerr* applicable only to efforts to influence the legislative and executive branches, and not courts. The Supreme Court, in light of *California Motor Freight*, remanded for consideration of the *Noerr* defense. See also Woods Exploration & Producing Co. v. Aluminum Co. of America, 438 F.2d 1286, 1296–98 (5th Cir. 1971), cert. denied 404 U.S. 1047, 92 S.Ct. 701, 30 L.Ed.2d 736 (1972), which held the *Noerr* doctrine **inapplicable to the filing of false** production forecasts to influence production allocations since no effort was being made to infuence the agency on matters of policy.

28. Israel v. Baxter Laboratories, Inc., 466 F.2d 272 (D.C.Cir. 1972).

29. Harman v. Valley Nat'l Bank, 339 F.2d 564 (9th Cir. 1964).

30. George R. Whitten Jr., Inc. v. Paddock Pool Builders, Inc., 424 F.2d 25 (1st Cir.), cert. denied 400 U.S. 850, 91 S.Ct. 54, 27 L.Ed.2d 88 (1970).

31. Of course, a unilateral effort by a firm to induce one or more purchasers, whether governmental agencies or not, to select the firm's product to the exclusion of competitors' products is not an antitrust violation, as the plaintiff in *Paddock Pool* found out when the case was ultimately considered on the merits. George R. Whitten, Jr., Inc. v. Paddock Pool Builders, Inc., 508 F.2d 547 (1st Cir. 1974).

agency. Industries which gain a measure of exemption from antitrust are numerous. Among them are the natural monopolies like electrical, gas, water and telephonic lines (regulated both at the state and federal level), air, motor and rail carriers, pipelines, ocean shipping and water carriers, banking, stock exchanges, and TV and radio communications.

Where federal or state legislation grants to an administrative agency authority to control entry and regulate rates and services, competition cannot be the organizing force which shapes market structure and conduct. This is the condition in the conventional utility industries, such as water, telephone, gas and electricity.[1] It is also the prevailing mode in rail,[2] air,[3] and much of water[4] and truck[5] transportation, communications,[6] and banking.[7] There are also pronounced regulatory constraints which limit entry and otherwise dampen competition in many professions and occupations[8] and even on the organized exchanges.[9]

Antitrust concepts are not irrelevant to any of these industries, even those in which regulation is most pervasive.[10] The relevant

1. See e.g., Utility Users League v. FPC, 394 F.2d 16 (7th Cir.), cert. denied 393 U.S. 953, 89 S.Ct. 377, 21 L. Ed.2d 365 (1968). In the regulated power and water industries, as in some of the transportation industries (e.g., rail) and some of the communication industries (e.g., telephone), the theory supporting regulation is that the activities are natural monopolies and that regulation is necessary as an alternative to competition. The validity of this theory has often been challenged on both theoretical and empirical grounds. See, e.g., Spann & Erickson, The Economics of Railroading: The Beginning of Cartelization and Regulation, 1 Bell J. 227 (1970); Stigler & Friedland, What Can Regulators Regulate?: The Case of Electricity, 5 J. Law & Econ. 1 (1962).

2. See Keogh v. Chicago & N. W. Ry., 260 U.S. 156, 43 S.Ct. 47, 67 L.Ed. 183 (1922) holding that the statutory rate regulatory scheme for the railroads ousted antitrust action by a private party alleging a conspiracy to fix rates, but suggesting that a government action might not be barred. Later legislation seems specifically to authorize concerted rate making. See 62 Stat. 472, 49 U.S.C.A. § 5b (1959).

3. E.g., United States v. Pan American World Airways, Inc., 371 U.S. 296, 83 S.Ct. 476, 9 L.Ed.2d 325 (1963).

4. E.g., Pacific Seafarers, Inc. v. Pacific Far East Line, Inc., 404 F.2d 804 (D.C.Cir. 1968), cert. denied 393 U.S. 1093, 89 S.Ct. 872, 21 L.Ed.2d 784 (1969).

5. E.g., McLean Trucking Co. v. United States, 321 U.S. 67, 64 S.Ct. 370, 88 L. Ed. 544 (1944).

6. E.g., National Broadcasting Co. v. United States, 319 U.S. 190, 213, 63 S. Ct. 997, 1008, 87 L.Ed. 1344, 1361 (1943). See also United States v. RCA, 358 U.S. 334, 79 S.Ct. 457, 3 L.Ed.2d 354 (1959) holding, in substance, that an agency gains an exclusive jurisdiction ousting the antitrust court entirely, only when there is a pervasive regulatory scheme which would be disrupted by allowing antitrust actions.

7. See § 202(c) supra and United States v. Marine Bancorporation, Inc., 418 U.S. 602, 94 S.Ct. 2856, 41 L.Ed.2d 978 (1974).

8. E.g., Goldfarb v. Virginia State Bar, 421 U.S. 773, 95 S.Ct. 2004, 44 L.Ed.2d 572 (1975).

9. E.g., Silver v. New York Stock Exch., 373 U.S. 341, 83 S.Ct. 1246, 10 L.Ed.2d 389 (1963); Ricci v. Chicago Mercantile Exch., 409 U.S. 289, 93 S.Ct. 573, 34 L.Ed.2d 525 (1973).

10. See cases cited in footnotes 1 through 9. See, in particular, the Court's statement in United States v.

statute may be silent as to whether an antitrust exemption is intended,[11] may explicitly make certain anticompetitive practices illegal,[12] may state that antitrust laws apply,[13] may expressly or implicitly provide for competition as to rates and services to the extent consistent with the public interest.[14] Even a very general statutory standard like "the public interest" may in some industries be properly construed to require that effect on competition be taken into account by the regulatory agency making regulatory decisions.[15] Such a standard may leave room for the direct application of antitrust rules [16] or may cause the regulatory agency or reviewing court to draw on antitrust concepts in formulating regulatory law and policy.[17] Moreover, even though an exemption applies in whole or part to activities of a firm in a regulated market—say, to its activities at one horizontal level, such as the production of power or the provision of telephonic lines—that exemption need not carry over to another market—say, the transportation of power, or the manufacture or sale of equipment to attach to the end of the telephone lines.[18] Also, where power gained through controls on entry at one level might be levered upstream or downstream, antitrust may apply fully to vertical relationships with both customers or suppliers even though a regulatory exemption applies at one of the horizontal levels.[19] Similarly, antitrust may apply to relations between different sectors like railroads and

---

Philadelphia Nat'l Bank, 374 U.S. 321, 372, 83 S.Ct. 1715, 1746, 10 L.Ed.2d 915, 950 (1963), that the "fact that banking is a highly regulated industry * * * makes the play of competition not less important but more so."

11. E.g., Securities Exchange Act of 1934, 15 U.S.C.A. § 78 (1970).

12. E.g., Section 106 of the Bank Holding Company Act Amendments of 1970, 12 U.S.C.A. § 1972 (1969).

13. E.g., Section 313 of the Communications Act, 47 U.S.C.A. § 313 (1962).

14. For explicit expression of a competition policy see, e.g., Section 7(g) of the Natural Gas Act, 15 U.S.C.A. § 717(g) (1963), and section 102(d) Federal Aviation Act, 49 U.S.C.A. § 1302(d) (1963). For a rigorous construction of the latter act see Continental Airlines, Inc. v. CAB, 519 F.2d 944 (D.C.Cir. 1975) (certification of one or more competing carriers mandated where the market yields sufficient traffic to support more than one carrier).

15. See e.g., Gulf States Util. Co. v. FPC, 411 U.S. 747, 93 S.Ct. 1870, 36 L. Ed.2d 635 (1973); Federal Maritime Comm. v. Swedish American Line, 390 U.S. 238, 88 S.Ct. 1005, 19 L.Ed.2d 1071 (1968). See also Otter Tail Power Co. v. United States, 410 U.S. 366, 93 S.Ct. 1022, 35 L.Ed.2d 359 (1973); cf. McLean Trucking Co. v. United States, 321 U.S. 67, 64 S.Ct. 370, 88 L.Ed. 544 (1944). But see FPC v. Texaco, Inc., 417 U.S. 380, 94 S.Ct. 2315, 41 L.Ed.2d 141 (1974), holding that where Congress gave an agency power to regulate rates the agency could not elect to rely on market forces to establish rates.

16. Gulf States Util. Co. v. FPC, 411 U.S. 747, 93 S.Ct. 1870, 36 L.Ed.2d 635 (1973).

17. E.g., Seaboard Air Line R.R. v. United States, 382 U.S. 154, 86 S.Ct. 227, 15 L.Ed.2d 223 (1965). See also United States v. C. A. B., 511 F.2d 1315 (D.C.Cir. 1975).

18. See, e.g., Otter Tail Power Co. v. United States, 410 U.S. 366, 93 S.Ct. 1022, 35 L.Ed.2d 359 (1973).

19. Id. See also Poller v. Columbia Broadcasting System, Inc., 368 U.S 464, 82 S.Ct. 486, 7 L.Ed.2d 458 (1962).

trucks, or radio and television, or banks and savings and loan associations, where lively competition may exist across the sectors even though competition between firms within each sector is dampened by regulation.[20]

The extent to which antitrust enforcement is consistent with the regulatory scheme will obviously vary from industry to industry. If any generalization is warranted, it is that there is an increasing tendency to assume that competition, and hence antitrust norms, ought to apply, except to the extent that these are inconsistent with clear, discernible regulatory objectives expressed or implied in the regulatory statute.[21] Once again, the now familiar theme of accomodation between seemingly disparate goals and policies is the one which infuses the cases.

b. *Primary Jurisdiction*

These varying interrelationships between competition and regulation give rise to intertwined issues of substance, jurisdiction and procedure. There are, in fact, several separate concepts often invoked under the general rubric of primary jurisdiction. There is the underlying substantive question whether antitrust law applies to the activity under consideration, or whether the regulatory intervention exempts the activity from antitrust; there is the related question whether, if antitrust does not apply, the regulatory law mandates (or authorizes) the regulatory agency to require competition; there are legal and factual questions about the legality of particular conduct under antitrust or regulatory norms about competition; there is the issue whether one or more of these questions must be considered by the regulatory agency, subject to appropriate judicial review, before an antitrust court may consider it; and even assuming that it has been established that antitrust continues to apply in pristine or modified form, there is the question whether the agency must nevertheless be permitted to adjudicate and make findings and conclusions on related issues under the regulatory statute before the antitrust court may proceed.

The cases in this area are difficult to reconcile. Three 1973 decisions will illustrate the problems. In Hughes Tool Co. v. TWA,[22] TWA, an airline subject to CAB regulation, sued its former parent corporation, Hughes Tool, alleging that transactions between the parent and the airline during the time the parent controlled the airline

---

20. Cf. Eastern Railroad Presidents' Conference v. Noerr Freight, Inc., 365 U.S. 127, 81 S.Ct. 523, 5 L.Ed.2d 464 (1961).

21. See Baker, The Role of Competition in Regulated Industries, 11 Bos. Col.Ind. & Comm.L.Rev. 571 (1970), which reviews the efforts of the antitrust division, which have met with some success, to press for a greater emphasis on competition in the resolution of regulatory issues.

22. 409 U.S. 263, 93 S.Ct. 647, 34 L.Ed. 2d 577 (1973). See also United States v. Pan American World Airways, Inc., 371 U.S. 296, 83 S.Ct. 476, 9 L.Ed.2d 325 (1963).

violated the antitrust laws to the injury of the airline. The CAB, acting under its statutory authority, had in 1944 and 1950 approved control by Hughes Tool of TWA, subject to a requirement that specified types of transactions between the two companies be submitted for review. Many transactions, including those that were the bases for the antitrust suit, had been submitted and approved over the years. Hughes Tool contended that all of these were therefore immune from antitrust infirmity despite the fact that in many instances the agency seems to have acted *pro forma* and given no mature consideration to whether the arrangements restricted competition or, for that matter, were undesirable from any other perspective relevant to regulatory goals. The Supreme Court accepted this position, holding that the CAB's jurisdiction to allow or disallow the parents " 'control' and to investigate and alter the manner in which that 'control' is exercised leads us to conclude that this phase of CAB jurisdiction * * * pre-empts the antitrust field." [23] In short, the agency not only had first opportunity to consider the issues—and no word in the opinion suggests the extent to which in its consideration of them it was obliged to give weight to concerns about competition—the agency, however it acted, by virtue of its power to act, served to exempt the conduct considered from antitrust scrutiny at any stage.

Ricci v. Chicago Mercantile Exchange,[24] presents an interesting contrast. A broker sued the Mercantile Exchange alleging that it had violated the antitrust laws by transferring plaintiff's membership to another broker. The Supreme Court upheld an order staying the antitrust action until related issues in the dispute were adjudicated before the Commodity and Exchange Commission, stating that it would be up to the antitrust court to decide whether the application of the antitrust laws would be incompatible with the Commodity Exchange Act, but that adjudication before the Commission of facts within its jurisdiction would materially aid the antitrust court in deciding whether the applicability of antitrust standards and remedies was consistent with the statutory scheme.

Even more hospitable to antitrust was the decision in Otter Tail Power Co. v. United States.[25] The government charged that the defendant, an electric utility, violated the antitrust laws by refusing to transport power, which it alone had the facilities to transport, from a supplier willing to sell power to Otter Tail's competitors in Otter

---

23. 409 U.S. at 385, 93 S.Ct. at 660, 34 L.Ed.2d at 592. See also Gordon v. New York Stock Exch., Inc., 422 U.S. 659, 95 S.Ct. 2598, 45 L.Ed.2d 463 (1975), holding that because the SEC possessed and exercised regulatory authority, an exchange rule which established minimum brokerage commissions was impliedly exempt from antitrust, and United States v. National Ass'n of Securities Dealers, Inc., 422 U.S. 694, 95 S.Ct. 2427, 45 L.Ed.2d 486 (1975), implying an exemption on certain mutual fund transactions apparently on the sole ground of an unexercised power in the SEC to regulate.

24. 409 U.S. 289, 93 S.Ct. 573, 34 L.Ed. 2d 525 (1973).

25. 410 U.S. 366, 93 S.Ct. 1022, 35 L. Ed.2d 359 (1973).

Tail's retail service area. Otter Tail contended that the antitrust laws were displaced because the Federal Power Commission had power to order Otter Tail to transport the power but had not done so. The Supreme Court saw no reason to assume exemption, as in *Hughes Tool,* nor to forestall an antitrust decision pending agency guidance, as in *Ricci.* It held that Otter Tail had violated the Sherman Act.

While the three cases do underscore the risks of trying to generalize from cases involving one regulated industry about what will happen in a different regulated industry, they are not irreconcilable. In *Hughes Tool* the Court construed the regulatory statute, first, as forbidding transactions of the kind being challenged in the antitrust action unless the transactions were authorized by the CAB and, second, as making them lawful (and thus exempt from antitrust) if authorized. As to the latter point, it would have been anomalous, surely, to superimpose antitrust norms which could subject parties to the transactions to severe civil and criminal sanctions despite agency approval. If there is room for doubt about *Hughes Tool,* it has to do with whether exemption should have been accorded only upon a clearer showing of a deliberative judgment upon the issues by the CAB. *Otter Tail* was very different. The Court found nothing in the legislation to suggest that a regulatory interest could be served by shielding the utility from the antitrust norm. All that could be said was that the agency might or might not find sufficient independent reason for ordering that the connection be made; there was no implication that the regulatory body might set itself against the conduct which, if applicable, the antitrust law required.

Ricci is intermediate between those cases and exemplifies a traditional application of the primary jurisdiction concept.[26] It was unclear and difficult to determine whether there might be regulatory reasons for treating the Commodity Exchange Act as incompatible with the application of the antitrust norms on which plaintiff relied. If it was incompatible, an ultimate decision like that in *Hughes Tool* would be required; if, on the other hand, there was no regulatory reason to shield defendant from plaintiff's antitrust attack, and if an antitrust violation were proved, an ultimate result like that in *Otter Tail* would be appropriate. The Court felt that the antitrust court would be aided in resolving that question if it had the views of the regulatory agency about what the regulatory scheme required and what regulatory interests were intended to be advanced by those requirements.

Those three cases are not the only models. There is another, an analogue of the *Ricci* case, provided by California v. Federal Power

---

26. See, e.g., Far East Conference v. United States, 342 U.S. 570, 72 S.Ct. 492, 96 L.Ed. 576 (1952). Other cases involving the relation of antitrust and regulatory procedures include: United States v. Borden Co., 308 U.S. 188, 60 S.Ct. 182, 84 L.Ed. 181 (1939); National Broadcasting Co. v. United States,

Commission.²⁷ El Paso Natural Gas Company, which was in the process of acquiring and merging with another pipeline company, applied to the FTC for approval, as was required by the Natural Gas Act.²⁸ The government challenged the merger under the antitrust laws and sought unsuccessfully to persuade the Commission to stay its hearings until the antitrust case was decided. The antitrust court then stayed the antitrust case pending the FTC determination, much in the manner the Court later held proper in *Ricci,* pending disposition of issues before the Commodity Exchange Commission. Here, however, the Supreme Court reversed. Holding that FPC approval under a "public commerce and necessity" standard would not render the merger antitrust-immune, and stressing both that FPC approval might unduly sway an antitrust court (especially since the FPC would purport to consider the bearing of competition policy) and that the merger, once completed, would be complicated to unscramble, the Court said the Commission should have been required to wait, not the court.

Just as *Ricci,* calling for initial agency adjudication followed by antitrust adjudication, can be reconciled with *Hughes Tool,* which cut out the antitrust court entirely, and *Otter Tail* which held that the agency had no relevant role to play, so too *Ricci* can be squared with the holding of California v. FPC. One need only turn back to the initial rationale for the primary jurisdiction concept as expressed by Justice Brandeis, that when an agency has relevant expertise on the issue in dispute which the Court does not share, the Court should stop and harken to the agency.²⁹ The antitrust violation alleged in *Ricci* raised questions of reasonableness which might well be thought to turn on particulars of the industry and the specific regulatory intervention by the agency. Thus the antitrust question could be considerably illuminated by prior agency deliberation. In California v. FPC, by contrast, the alleged violation of Section 7 of Clayton³⁰ which was the basis for the antitrust action was plainly within the special competence of the antitrust court and, given the governing legal standards,³¹ the court was not likely to find assistance in the FPC's deliberations.

319 U.S. 190, 63 S.Ct. 997, 87 L.Ed. 1344 (1943), 15 U.S.C.A. § 717b; Maryland & Va. Milk Producers Ass'n v. United States, 362 U.S. 468, 80 S.Ct. 847, 4 L.Ed.2d 880 (1960); Silver v. New York Stock Exch., 373 U.S. 341, 83 S.Ct. 1246, 10 L.Ed.2d 389 (1963); United States v. National Ass'n of Securities Dealers, 422 U.S. 694, 95 S.Ct. 2427, 45 L.Ed.2d 486 (1975); Gordon v. New York Stock Exch., 422 U.S. 659, 95 S.Ct. 2598, 45 L.Ed.2d 463 (1975).

27. 369 U.S. 482, 82 S.Ct. 901, 8 L.Ed.2d 54 (1962).

28. Natural Gas Act § 7, 15 U.S.C.A. § 717f(c) (1976).

29. See Great Northern Ry. v. Merchants Elevator Co., 259 U.S. 285, 42 S.Ct. 477, 66 L.Ed. 943 (1922).

30. 15 U.S.C.A. § 18 (1973).

31. See §§ 204–205 supra.

c. *The Deregulation Movement*

The temporary nature of any specific set of attitudes towards the maintenance of competition as national economic policy is displayed once again in rapidly changing public attitudes toward industrial regulation. In the New Deal period regulation was widely assumed to make sense not only in the natural monopolies but in many other industries.[32] The system of free competition was popularly regarded as a failure; eyes were being cast in all directions for alternatives, and regulation, a mid-point between free competition and socialization, had many exponents.[33] But in the last decade or so regulation has been under attack by scholars,[34] muckrakers,[35] the Neal[36] and Stiegler[37] Presidential Task Forces and numerous others.[38] A severe inflation at a time of reduced economic growth has led to an increasing political likelihood that at least at the federal level regulatory legislation will be repealed or amended to require greater reliance on competition,[39] or that, even without statutory change, regulators will rely more on competition and do less to stifle it.[40]

---

32. See A. Schlesinger, The Age of Roosevelt: The Coming of the New Deal 87–102 (1959); E. Hawley, The New Deal and the Problem of Monopoly 3–146 (1966).

33. See the discussion in W. Jones, Regulated Industries 55–59 (1976).

34. Opposition to regulation is not new, of course. There is an extensive legal and economic scholarship extending over a substantial period. E.g., Gray, The Passing of the Public Utility Concept, 16 J.Land & Pub.Util.Econ. 8 (1940); W. Hamilton, The Politics of Industry (1957); Adams, The Role of Competition in Regulated Industries, 48 Am.Econ.Rev. 527 (1958); Coase, The Federal Communications Commission, 2 J. of Law and Econ. 1 (1959). A similar legal article is Schwartz, Legal Restriction of Competition in Regulated Industries: An Abdication of Judicial Responsibility, 67 Harv.L. Rev. 456 (1954). For good examples of current economic scholarship see A. Phillips, ed., Promoting Competition in Regulated Markets (1975), which contains a powerful paper by the editor on financial markets and papers by other economists on airline, surface freight, ocean freight, electric power, telecommunications, automobile insurance industries and the stock exchange, the thrust of all of which is that substantially greater reliance on competition in the markets considered would improve performance. Recent legal scholarship includes, Nelson, The Role of Competition in the Regulated Industries, 11 Antitrust Bul. 1 (1966); Turner, Scope of Antitrust and Other Regulatory Policies, 82 Harv.L.Rev. 1207 (1969); Baker, Competition and Regulation: Charles River Bridge Recrossed, 60 Cornell L.Rev. 159 (1975).

35. E.g., R. Fellmeth, The Public Interest and the ICC (1970); M. Green, ed., The Monopoly Makers (1973).

36. Report of the White House Task Force on Antitrust Policy (1968), reprinted in Cong. Rec., vol. 115, p. 1, 91 Cong. 1 sess. pp. 13890–13907 (1969).

37. Report of the Task Force on Productivity and Competition (1969), partially reprinted in Cong. Rec., vol. 115, pt. 12, 91 Cong. 1 sess. pp. 15652–15661 (1969).

38. E.g. Presidents' Advisory Council on Executive Organization, A New Regulatory Framework & Report on Selected Independent Regulatory Agencies (1971); The Report of the Presidents' Commission on Financial Structure and Regulation (1972).

39. See, e.g., the many legislative initiatives of the Ford Administration outlined in Address of Thomas E. Kauper, Assistant Attorney General, Antitrust Division, to the Annual Meeting of the New York State Bar, January 22, 1975, 19 Law Quadrangle Notes 5 (Univ. of Mich. Law School, 1975).

40. The Antitrust Division has also been making appearances in regulato-

The deregulation movement, a regular topic at meetings of those interested either in antitrust or regulation or both, has taken on vitality and is one of today's political subcultures. Like most such movements, it lacks either a comprehensive and widely accepted program or a cohesive theory, and it is strongly resisted, mainly by spokesmen for business corporations, such as air carriers, which are subject to regulation, presumably in the public interest.[41] It is not possible here to assess the political future of this movement. To be noted, however, is the success of the movement in the repeal of fair trade laws,[42] and the risk of ideological reactions instead of tightly analyzed responses to specific policy alternatives.

PART C. GOVERNMENTAL ENFORCEMENT

§ 240. The Antitrust Division of the Department of Justice

The Department of Justice has statutory power to enforce the Sherman Act by civil[1] and criminal proceedings.[2] It shares this power with private parties injured by violations of that act who may bring civil actions for treble damages[3] or equitable remedies.[4] The Department also has power to enforce the Clayton Act by civil proceedings.[5] It shares this power with the Federal Trade Commission[6] as well as with private parties.[7] In addition, the Department intervenes before federal administrative agencies on matters where competitive effect may be an important question.[8]

ry proceedings, pressing for competition-monitoring regulatory policies. See Address of Thomas E. Kauper, supra note 39.

41. The Senate Judiciary Subcomittee on Administrative Practice and Procedure, following a year long hearing and investigation in which industry representatives consistently opposed deregulation policies, has developed a program for a gradual but irrevocable deregulation of the airline industry. Respecting entry, first route restrictions would be lifted and charter rules liberalized, then carriers would be authorized to extend existing routes on a showing that they were fit, willing and able (and without need to show that present services are inadequate), finally complete new entries would be allowed on a similar showing. Rate regulation would be limited to rate ceilings; competition would be permitted to push rates downward. See the Summary of Senate Subcommittee Report, Airline Regulation By The Civil Aeronautics Board, 752 ATRR D-1 (February 24, 1976).

42. P.L. 94–145 (Dec. 12, 1975). See § 132 supra.

1. 15 U.S.C.A. § 4 (1973).

2. 15 U.S.C.A. §§ 1 and 2 (1973).

3. 15 U.S.C.A. § 15 (1973) (Section 4 of Clayton).

4. 15 U.S.C.A. § 26 (1973). (Section 16 of Clayton).

5. 15 U.S.C.A. § 25 (1973). (Section 15 of Clayton).

6. Section 11 of the Clayton Act, 15 U.S.C.A. § 21, provides (with exceptions applicable to certain regulated utilities) for Commission enforcement of Sections 2, 3, 7 and 8 of that Act.

7. 15 U.S.C.A. §§ 15, 26 (1973) (Sections 4 and 16 of Clayton).

8. See § 239 supra.

The Antitrust Division is headed by an assistant attorney general appointed by the President. There are deputy assistants (currently three) with like responsibilities and various staff officials, such as a Director of Planning and a Director of Economic Policy, and a substantial staff of lawyers, economists and supporting personnel. The table of organization is altered from time to time as each new incumbent of the top post establishes arrangements deemed suitable, but the actual operation of the office, which inevitably varies from the concepts expressed in the table of organization, has strong continuities.

The Antitrust Division is a law office, a good one with a strong tradition of high competence that transcends and perhaps inhibits programmatic change. It has a staff of several hundred lawyers and about the same number of non-lawyers. Its budget for the fiscal year 1977 is $23,426,000.[9] Most of the work of the Division is done in Washington where the basic, on-going litigation activities and various specialized functions such as legislative liaison and decree compliance supervision are carried on. There are also field offices, two in the east, one in the south, two in the mid-west, and two in the west, which are engaged primarily in litigation and related activities.

The size of the Division's caseload is suggested by these statistics:[10] In 1962 it initiated 336 and closed 442 investigations, filed 41 and terminated 14 civil actions, filed 32 and terminated 16 criminal cases, and had at year end a total of 180 cases pending. In 1972 it initiated 437 and closed 422 investigations, filed 72 and terminated 44 civil actions, filed 15 and terminated 12 criminal cases, and had at year end 143 pending cases. The number of investigations have not increased much in recent years. Neither have criminal cases. The number of civil actions filed has shown fairly constant growth.

§ 241. The Federal Trade Commission

The Federal Trade Commission, established in 1914, consists of a chairman who serves at the pleasure of the President and four commissioners who are appointed by the President and confirmed by the Senate and serve for staggered seven year terms.[1] The Commission shares with the Antitrust Division of the Department of Justice, as

---

9. Budget of the United States Government-Fiscal Year 1977 (Appendix) 496.

10. Current statistics on the Antitrust Division's caseload are found in Annual Reports of the Attorney General and Annual Hearings Before the Subcommittee of the House Committee on Appropriations. Statistics for the years 1952–1972 are set forth in M. Handler, H. Blake, R. Pitofsky and H. Goldschmid, Trade Regulation, Cases and Materials 156 (1975).

1. See 15 U.S.C.A. §§ 41–51. There is an extensive and critical literature on the Commission. One of the most illuminating is the study, President's Advisory Council on Executive Organization, A New Regulatory Framework: Report on Selected Independent Regulatory Agencies (1971).

well as with injured parties who may sue for treble damages or injunctive relief, power to enforce Sections 2, 3, 7 and 8 of the Clayton Act, the sections dealing respectively with price discrimination, tying arrangements and requirements contracts, mergers and interlocking directors.[2] It also has sole authority to enforce the ban against unfair methods of competition, set forth in Section 5 of the Federal Trade Commission Act;[3] this section covers any conduct which would violate the Sherman Act, as well as conduct which conflicts with the policies of the Sherman Act or is analogous to conduct prohibited by the Clayton Act, though not technically violative of either of those statutes.[4] The Commission also enforces several consumer protection statutes not directly related to antitrust.[5]

The Commission has a larger budget and staff than the Antitrust Division.[6] Its Bureau of Competition is the antitrust enforcement arm, which does investigation, evaluation, litigation, enforces compliance and develops guides. The Bureau of Economics is an advisory staff resource. There are eleven field offices which engage in investigation and litigation under general supervision from Washington.

The Commission proceeds against violations by an administrative complaint which, after hearing, may result in a cease and desist order.[7] It may seek preliminary injunctions against violations of the Federal Trade Commission Act to maintain the status quo until it has filed an administrative complaint and proceeded to adjudicate it.[8] It may bring actions for civil penalties of up to $10,000 for each day violation of any final order continues.[9]

Some of the Commission's enforcement activities give rise to questions of fairness. Questions are raised, for example, when the Commission begins proceedings challenging one firm for a practice widely used in its industry without filing similar complaints against its competitors. The Court has on two occasions declined to limit FTC activity in ways which would guard against selective enforcement.[10] Though particular problems may arise, the general practice of the Commission to approach issues on an industry-wide basis reduces risks that any competitor will be unfairly disadvantaged. Of course, a firm adversely affected by selective enforcement may be in a position to protect itself by bringing a private action for damages or equitable relief against competitors which persist in violations.

2. 15 U.S.C.A. § 21.

3. 15 U.S.C.A. § 45.

4. See §§ 161–62 supra.

5. See e.g., 15 U.S.C.A. §§ 68–70, 1451–61, 1601–65 (1973).

6. The FTC budget for fiscal year 1977 is $52,833,000. Budget of the United States Government—Fiscal Year 1977 (Appendix) 736–37.

7. 15 U.S.C.A. §§ 21(b) and 45(b) (1973).

8. 15 U.S.C.A. § 45.

9. 15 U.S.C.A. § 45(1) (1973).

10. Compare Moog Indus., Inc. v. FTC, 355 U.S. 411, 78 S.Ct. 377, 2 L.Ed.2d

The Antitrust Division and the FTC seem to coordinate their activities with a minimum of friction. The Commission enforces the price discrimination law. Both enforce the antimerger provisions. The Department brings most price fixing cases and, until recently, was the only agency to initiate major structural cases. Recently, the Commission has brought structural cases in oligopolistic industries. Both have brought vertical cases. Where, as in the merger area, both are active, the tendency is for each agency to build up specialization with particular industries upon which the other avoids infringing. There is also an interagency clearance procedure aimed at avoiding duplication.[11]

§ 242. Antitrust Investigations

a. *In General*

Information leading to an investigation by the Antitrust Division or the FTC may come to attention through a complaint by a competitor, customer or supplier, a news story in the business or trade press, a related investigation, an examination of conditions or practices in a concentrated industry, a congressional inquiry, a private suit, or other sources. Both agencies have been attempting in recent years, and with some success, to make planned and deliberate decisions about where resources are directed, to be less reactive to day-to-day stimuli.

b. *Antitrust Division Investigations*

Before the passage of the Hart-Scott-Rodino Antitrust Improvement Act of 1976,[1] the Division often relied on informal inquiries undertaken by Division Field Office attorneys or by the FBI. Usually such informal investigations occur prior to a decision whether to initiate an action. Informal but obviously very serious investigations were also sometimes undertaken after a criminal indictment, for no investigatory subpoena was then available. Considerable information may be obtained informally from officers or employees of customers, suppliers or competitors of a firm under investigation, especially if these are injured by the alleged violation or fancy themselves to be. Information may also come from "neutral" fact witnesses, from former employees of the firm under investigation, and

---

370 (1958), which stressed the breadth of the FTC's discretion as to enforcement, with FTC v. Universal Rundle Corp., 387 U.S. 244, 87 S.Ct. 1622, 18 L.Ed.2d 749 (1967), where the Court, although upholding Commission discretion, warned against proceedings which may destroy one of many competing violators.

11. The present method for dividing responsibility and authority between the Division and the Commission is critically evaluated by a former Commission official in Roll, Dual Enforcement of Antitrust Laws by the Department of Justice and the FTC: The Liaison Procedure, 31 The Bus.Lawy. 2075 (1976).

1. Public Law 94–435 (Sept. 30, 1976). This act greatly expands the power of the Division to use mandatory process to obtain information from people and to discover documents. See Appendix D, infra. Giving false

even from officers and employees of the firm being investigated. The Division can also initiate a formal investigation by a federal grand jury which has subpoena power or can conduct its own formal investigation through the use of the civil investigation demand.[2]

Grand juries are routinely used to gather evidence where criminal action is anticipated. However, the Division normally does not seek to indict except for serious and clear violations. The grand jury can subpoena witnesses and may issue subpoena duces tecum to corporations and to individuals.[3] Usually broad subpoenas duces tecum are first issued, then narrower ones. Finally, after substantial documentation has been obtained from available sources, individuals are brought before the jury to testify as to crucial facts. In this way, the Division not only makes out the basis for an indictment, but completes an elaborate discovery, and organizes and refines its case.

Grand jury proceedings are closed. Only the jurors, the government attorneys and the witness under interrogation are entitled to be present; its results are secret. Though individual witnesses may disclose what they testified if they wish to do so, no one has a right to discover the testimony taken, except to the very limited extent that the Federal Rules of Criminal Procedure give a defendant a right of discovery.[4]

An individual subpoenaed to testify may exercise the privilege against self-incrimination, though a corporation may not.[5] If a witness refuses to testify or is likely to, the United States Attorney, with the approval of the Attorney General, may obtain an order from the court requiring that the testimony be given; thereafter, neither the testimony or information compelled to be provided under the order, or any information directly or indirectly derived therefrom, can be used against the witness in any criminal proceeding.[6]

The civil investigations demand ("C.I.D.") is a discovery method authorized by legislation [7] after the Supreme Court held that grand

---

information may be a criminal offense even in informal investigations. 18 U.S.C.A. § 1001.

2. For a fuller discussion see C. Hills, ed., Antitrust Advisor 489–512 (1971).

3. Rule 17(c) Fed.R.Crim.P.

4. Rules 6 and 16(a)(3) of Fed.R.Crim. P. See In re Biaggi, 478 F.2d 489 (2d Cir. 1973).

5. See e.g., Maricopa By-Products, Inc. v. United States, 1968 CCH Trade Cas. ¶ 72,346 (9th Cir. 1967), cert. denied 392 U.S. 926, 88 S.Ct. 2274, 20 L. Ed.2d 1385 (1968).

6. 18 U.S.C.A. §§ 6001–6003 (1973). This statute allows the government to compel testimony of witnesses invoking the fifth amendment by conferring immunity from use of the compelled testimony and evidence derived from it against the witness. The statute is not unconstitutional on its face. Kastigar v. United States, 406 U.S. 441, 92 S.Ct. 1653, 32 L.Ed.2d 212 (1972).

7. Antitrust Civil Process Act, 15 U.S. C.A. §§ 1311–14 (1973), as amended by the Hart-Scott-Rodino Antitrust Improvement Act of 1976, Public Law 94–435 (Sept. 30, 1976). See Appendix D, infra which describes the 1976 act.

jury investigations could not be used where the Division intended to proceed only in a civil proceeding.[8] The C.I.D. now enables the Division to compel individuals and corporations to testify on interrogatories or depositions and to provide records relevant to a civil antitrust investigation. Demands are used by the Division to determine whether there is sufficient evidence to warrant filing a civil antitrust complaint. Civil investigation demands may be served in hand or by registered mail on any partnerships, corporations, associations or other legal entities, but may not be served on individuals. Like grand jury subpoenas, these demands may be served anywhere in the United States.[9]

c. FTC Investigations

The Commission has extremely broad powers to investigate violations of the acts it enforces. It can require a corporation to file annual or special reports and to answer in writing interrogatories submitted to the corporation.[10] It can obtain by notice documents of any corporation being investigated.[11] It can subpoena witnesses and documents.[12] The governing immunity provisions are the same as those that apply to investigations by the Department of Justice.[13] The FTC or its investigator is obliged by Commission Rules [14] to disclose the purpose and scope of the investigation to any person compelled or requested to furnish information or documents.

§ 243. Informal Enforcement and Prior Clearance Procedures

a. Federal Trade Commission

The Commission's potential for nonadjudicatory enforcement and prior clearance is more extensive and fully developed than that of the Antitrust Division. For one thing, the Commission after conducting appropriate studies, reports, investigations and hearings, may issue trade regulation rules [1] which specify with particularity the Commission's construction of some of the substantive requirements of statutes administered by the Commission. While this power has been used sparingly with respect to antitrust enforcement, it is a signifi-

The amendment give the Division investigatory powers as broad as those now held by the F.T.C. See 779 ATRR AA–1 (August 31, 1976).

8. United States v. Procter & Gamble Co., 356 U.S. 677, 78 S.Ct. 983, 2 L. Ed.2d 1077 (1958).

9. The constitutionality of the statute authorizing civil investigation demands has consistently been upheld. E.g., Petition of Gold Bond Stamp Co., 325 F.2d 1018 (8th Cir. 1964); Hyster Co. v. United States, 338 F.2d 183 (9th Cir. 1964).

10. 15 U.S.C.A. § 46 (1973).

11. 15 U.S.C.A. § 49 (1973).

12. 15 U.S.C.A. § 49 (1973).

13. 18 U.S.C.A. §§ 6001–6003 (1973).

14. 16 C.F.R. § 1.33, 15 U.S.C.A. following § 45 (1973).

1. 16 C.F.R. § 1.12 (1973).

cant one. The rules have the force of law. They may be very broad in scope or may apply to particular products, industries or practices.

The Commission also issues guidelines, statements of its views about the requirements of the laws it administers. For many years these were called Trade Practice Conference Rules;[2] now they are called Industry Guides.[3] They spell out the way a law subject to the Commission's jurisdiction applies to a particular industry. For example, there are several which deal with mergers in particular industries. These guides are issued after a legislative hearing in which the views of industry members, suppliers, customers and members of the public are solicited. Like Trade Practice Rules, they are published in the Federal Register. They thus serve to inform members of the industry of the Commission's view of the law and the factors it will take into account in making decisions.

The Commission also issues advisory opinions on the legality of specific courses of action which a firm requesting the opinion proposes to carry out.[4] Opinions will generally be given upon a specific disclosure of the proposed course of action, unless the course of action has already been initiated, or it or a substantially similar one is already subject to a proceeding, order or decree, or where advice could be given only after extensive investigation. The Commission does not consider itself bound by an advisory opinion, but will not bring enforcement proceedings against a firm which has relied upon an advisory opinion, so long as the firm discontinues the course of conduct upon being notified that the advisory opinion is withdrawn.

The Commission also has informal procedures available when an investigation discloses what the Commission regards as a violation.[5] One of these involves closing the file upon the acceptance of a letter from the firm under investigation which states that the challenged practice has ceased and giving assurance of adequate safeguards against its resumption. The Commission also seeks and accepts consent decrees as a way of disposing of cases without hearing.

b. *The Antitrust Division*

The Antitrust Division does much less in the way of nonadjudicatory enforcement. It has issued only one set of guidelines, the merger guidelines,[6] and these were issued without the kind of consultation or hearing that is involved prior to issuance of FTC industry guides. It gives advisory opinions, of sorts, through its Business Review Procedure.[7] A full and complete disclosure of all relevant facts

2. See, e.g., 16 C.F.R. §§ 2.21–2.32, 15 U.S.C.A. following § 45 (1963).

3. 16 C.F.R. §§ 1.5–1.6, 15 U.S.C.A. following § 45 (1973).

4. 16 C.F.R. §§ 1.1–1.4, 15 U.S.C.A. following § 45 (1973).

5. 16 C.F.R. § 2.21, 15 U.S.C.A. following § 45 (1973).

6. Department of Justice Merger Guidelines (1968). See §§ 202–214 supra.

7. 33 Federal Register 2442 (1968), 2 CCH Trade Reg.Rep. ¶ 8559 § 50.6.

about a proposed course of conduct may be submitted in writing to the Division with a request for disclosure of the Division's present enforcement intentions with reference to the practice disclosed. Relevant documents must also be submitted, along with any additional information requested by the Division. After reviewing the material the Division may state its present enforcement intention or decline to do so. Ordinarily, it will decline to state its civil enforcement intention except with respect to mergers and acquisitions. Even if it states a present intention not to initiate enforcement proceedings, the Division explicitly retains the right to do so at any time in the future if it decides that the public interest so requires. Despite the cautious and limited nature of the policy, the Justice Department has, as yet, never initiated criminal proceedings with respect to conduct covered by an earlier letter indicating intent not to enforce, and where full disclosure was made.

The Division's consent decree practice is, by contrast, a major element in its enforcement program.[8] The Division does not initiate settlement negotiations but is ready to enter into them upon initiation by the other side. The Division may seek to obtain the relief which it would seek at trial, but, inevitably, is more flexible in negotiating a settlement than it is in pressing for relief at the end of successful litigation. The likelihood that substantial compromises may be possible must be evaluated much as it would be in any other litigation context; much depends upon how the risks and likely outcome of the litigation are assessed.

Consent decrees are of enormous value as an enforcement tool. Yet, consent decree procedures are not without problems. The IT & T settlement,[9] made by the Nixon administration during the Watergate period, under a cloud of political interference and marked by conduct by some government and private attorneys which raised serious ethical issues, symbolizes the dangers of political favoritism and influence peddling. The settlement during the 1950's of a major case against AT & T also made under political clouds, is, perhaps, another example of the danger.[10] A matter of even greater day-to-day concern is the possibility that the Department (or the FTC) may make a poor settlement simply because of the ordinary risks and pressures faced by an overburdened litigation staff. The implication of including or excluding a particular provision may not be fully understood or adequately appraised in the light of the industry context. Too sanguine a view may be taken of the potential benefits of some remedial measure, or too bleak a view taken of litigation prospects.

---

8. It has been estimated that more than 80% of all cases are disposed of by consent decrees. C. Hills, ed., Antitrust Advisor 537 (1971).

9. United States v. International Tel. & Tel. Corp., 306 F.Supp. 766 (D.Conn. 1969), appeal dismissed per stipulation, 404 U.S. 801, 92 S.Ct. 20, 30 L. Ed.2d 34 (1971). See § 208 supra.

10. United States v. Western Electric Co., Inc., 1956 CCH Trade Cas. ¶ 68,246 (D.N.J.1956).

The Antitrust Procedures and Penalties Act [11] is a response to concerns such as these. It requires the Department of Justice to file for industry and public consideration and comment a copy of the proposed decree and a public impact statement which analyzes the theory and predicts the effects of the decree. The court entering the decree is then required to hold a hearing on the decree and, after receiving such presentations as may be made about its efficacy, must make findings as to the effects to be expected from the decree and about whether the decree is in the public interest.

There has, as yet, been too little experience under the new Act to assess its consequences.[12] Surely it will not have the dire consequence of drastically reducing consent decrees and diluting Division control of its own cases which opponents predicted. But neither is it likely to ring in a new era of wisdom, awareness and sounder judgment. The only people who are likely to have much to say about pending consent decrees are people with an interest, and they would have made themselves heard at least to some extent even without the new procedure.[13]

§ 244. Civil Actions

a. Size and Complexity

Antitrust litigation is renowned for its scope and complexity. These characteristics are hardly to be denied; they present myriad problems that must be dealt with. But a first step in dealing with them is to recognize that any plausible antitrust claim worth the time and energy of an enforcer to assert will likely be simple in concept. The theory of the case, both on the facts and the law, ought to be capable of being expressed clearly and concisely in relatively few well chosen sentences. The same should be true of the theory of the de-

---

11. Act of December 21, 1974, 15 U.S. C.A. §§ 1, 2, 3, 16, 28 and 29, 47 U.S. C.A. § 401, 49 U.S.C.A. §§ 43–45 (1976).

12. See the discussion in United States v. Associated Milk Producers, Inc., 1975–1 CCH Trade Cas. ¶ 60,326 (W.D. Mo., 1975).

13. Long before the Act was passed the Division began a practice of making proposed decrees public at least 30 days before entry and inviting comments from interested persons which were evaluated before entry. Even in an age of consumerism, the parties most likely to utilize the new procedures to challenge a proposed decree are those who would have done so under the old law by making presentations to the Division during its voluntary 30 day period and by amicus memoranda to the court considering the decree—namely, treble damage suitors interested in gaining the *prima facie* evidence effect that section 5(a) of the Clayton Act accords to decrees in litigated cases, but not to consent decrees.

Despite their inherent limitations, the procedures of the new act constitute a serious effort to deal, at least in part, with one of the anomalies of utilizing litigation as a means of controlling industrial structure and market conduct—namely, that a wide range of persons not parties to the litigation are likely to have interests seriously affected by it. While the problem presents itself in all cases, not just those settled by consent, experience under the new act may be instructive on future efforts to deal with the problem more broadly.

fense. All the rest is elaboration, and the process is not different in its essentials from that entailed in any other case. Materials must be gathered and controlled, working relationships established, strategic and tactical decisions made and implemented. These activities are of the family, litigation, of the genus, complex litigation, and of the species, antitrust. What they have in common with activities characteristic of other examples of the family and certainly the genus is as important to those involved as anything that differentiates antitrust from other litigation.[1] Techniques are available for managing a big case.[2] These must be mastered and used by the attorneys and the court and, in the process, transformed and improved.

b. Intervention

A case brought by the Antitrust Division may affect private interests profoundly. In consequence, private parties often seek to intervene in order to protect their interests, an effort which the government, as well as the defendants, are likely to resist.[3] The standards announced by the Federal Rules are clear enough at the level of generality at which they are pitched.[4] There is a right to intervene when as a practical matter the disposition of the action may impair or impede the intervenor's ability to protect an interest which he claims and which is not adequately represented by an existing party. In circumstances less compelling a court may allow intervention at its discretion if in its judgment the balance of conveniences show that course to be desirable. In Cascade Natural Gas Corp. v. El Paso Natural Gas Co.[5] the Supreme Court gave the provisions about intervention of right an unexpectedly broad reading. The merger of two sup-

---

1. Antitrust litigation before the FTC is also civil litigation, though of a special character in that the Commission is an administrative body with its own procedures, customs and traditional ways of carrying out its tasks. Much of what is said in this section has bearing, direct or by implication, for FTC litigation, though the explicit focus is upon civil actions brought by the Division in the district courts.

2. The literature is copious. See Selected Bibliography: Trial of Protracted Litigation, 21 F.R.D. 533 (1957). See particularly the Manual For Complex Litigation (1973) published by a panel of federal judges.

3. There is an increasing literature on these issues. For contrasting views see Buxbaum, Public Participation in the Enforcement of the Antitrust Laws, 59 Calif.L.Rev. 1113 (1971) and Handler, The Shift from Substance to Procedural Innovations in Antitrust Suits—The Twenty-Third Annual Antitrust Review, 71 Colum.L.Rev. 1, 17–23 (1971). See also C. Sullivan, Enforcement of Government Antitrust Decrees By Private Parties: Third Party Beneficiary Rights and Intervenor Status, 123 U.Pa.L.Rev. 822 (1975) which analyzes the potential for the rise of contract concepts, as well as the procedural concept of intervention, to give non-parties an interest in enforcing government decrees. One of the major developments arising in part out of the debate on this issue was the enactment of the Antitrust Procedures and Penalties Act, 15 U.S. C.A. § 1 et seq., 47 U.S.C.A. § 401, 49 U.S.C.A. §§ 44–46 (1975). See § 243 supra.

4. Fed.R.Civ.P. 24.

5. 386 U.S. 129, 87 S.Ct. 932, 17 L.Ed.2d 814 (1967). See also Utah Public Service Commission v. El Paso Natural Gas Co., 395 U.S. 464, 89 S.Ct. 1860, 23 L.

pliers of natural gas had already been held illegal by the Supreme Court and its mandate had called for divestiture.[6] On remand, a large natural gas user, a distributor which relied on one of the merging firms for supplies, and a state which claimed both an interest in its own behalf as a user and an interest in protecting the welfare of citizens, sought to intervene in the divestiture proceedings, claiming that the Antitrust Division was consenting to inadequate relief which did not comply with the Supreme Court mandate. The district court denied intervention and entered the decree consented to by the government. On appeal, the Supreme Court held that intervention as of right should have been allowed and, announcing that the government could not, by settlement, limit the power of the district court to carry out the mandate, reversed and remanded.

The implications of that decision on the intervention issue are not easily fathomed. Let us assume that the intervenors had, within the meaning of the rule, interests which might as a practical matter be impaired. A difficulty still remains, for they must also establish that no party—here, specifically, the government—is adequately representing those interested.[7] Conceivably the case means that the difference in status between the government (which is charged to represent the public interest) and the intervenors, as affected customers, is enough to disqualify the government as an adequate representative of the interests of the intervenors. But such a reading would imply the rather startling conclusion that the Antitrust Division can never be taken adequately to represent the interests of affected private parties.[8] Neither was there anything particularly special about these intervenors which enhanced their particular interests beyond those of users, competitors, suppliers or other affected firms generally. One must conclude that it was the fact remarked on by the Court that the Division "knuckled under to El Paso"[9] that warranted the conclusion that intervenors' interests were not adequately represented. The Court cared about the result; it did not want the government settling a case it had already won for a weaker remedy than the Court had already held it was entitled to obtain.

Ed.2d 474 (1969), where the Court held, after proceedings on remand leading to another order, that appellant's motion to dismiss the appeal did not deprive the Court of jurisdiction to determine whether its mandate had been complied with, and, on the argument of amicae, that the mandate again was not complied with.

6. United States v. El Paso Natural Gas Co., 376 U.S. 651, 84 S.Ct. 1044, 12 L.Ed.2d 12 (1964).

7. Fed.R.Civ.P. 24(a).

8. That view was rejected in United States v. Western Elec., 1968 CCH Trade Cas. ¶ 72,415 (D.N.J.), aff'd mem. sub nom. Clark Walter & Sons, Inc. v. United States, 392 U.S. 659, 88 S.Ct. 2286, 20 L.Ed.2d 1348 (1968). See the discussion of these and related issues in C. Sullivan, Enforcement of Government Antitrust Decrees By Private Parties: Third Party Beneficiary Rights and Intervenor Status, 123 U.Pa.L.Rev. 822, 873–92 (1975).

9. 386 U.S. at 141, 87 S.Ct. at 940, 17 L.Ed.2d at 822.

The Court's characterization of the Division's posture in the remedy hearing expressed a judgment about the adequacy of the remedy, given the structure and competitive problems of the industry. Such a judgment could only be ventured by a Court already familiar with the merits. It is, therefore, a strange predicate for permission to intervene. The motive to intervene is to establish that the remedy is inadequate. If intervention is likely to be granted only if the Court already knows enough to be persuaded of inadequacy on the motion papers, the "right" will be of limited value. There was also an unbecoming transference in this particular application of the standard. It was because of the Court's own prior connections with the case that it could level the judgment that the Division knuckled under. The intervenors were made to serve as instruments of the Court's own goal, a remedy which it thought adequate. It is not a strained idea that the Supreme Court may exercise novel opportunities to interpose when that may be necessary to assure a just result,[10] but the Court should have labeled what it was doing as an extraordinary interposition. Having, instead, found the claim of a right to intervene a worthy one, it has left the law in that confused state which always results when lower courts infer that on a certain point the Supreme Court could not really have meant what it said or implied.[11]

10. The Court probably could not have interposed even to assure that its own mandate were carried out without holding that the intervenors were entitled to be before it. True, when the government is a party to litigation the Court is not obliged to do what the government has agreed to. If the Solicitor General confesses error, for example, the Court will often make an independent examination of the record before accepting the confession and, indeed, may appoint an amicus to support a judgment for the government. See P. Bator, P. Mishkin, D. Shapiro & H. Wechsler, Hart & Wechsler's The Federal Courts and the Federal System 104–05 (2d ed. 1973) and cases there cited. But the Court has no roving commission to reach out on its own initiative to rectify the wrong every time a district court fails properly to carry out the Court's mandate; it can act on the case only when the case is brought before it by interested parties in the orderly course of litigation. From this perspective the Court's internally inconsistent statement in *Cascade Natural Gas* that, although the Attorney General can settle suits after as well as before they reach the Supreme Court, he "by stipulation or otherwise has no power to circumscribe the power of the courts to see that our mandate is carried out." (386 U.S. at 136) becomes almost unfathomable.

11. See, e.g., United States v. Paramount Pictures, Inc., 333 F.Supp. 1100, 1102 (S.D.N.Y.), aff'd mem. sub nom. Syufy Enterprises v. United States, 404 U.S. 802, 92 S.Ct. 79, 30 L.Ed.2d 37 (1971); United States v. Automobile Mfrs. Ass'n, 307 F.Supp. 617, 619 n. 3 (C.D.Cal.1969), aff'd per curiam sub nom. City of New York v. United States, 397 U.S. 248, 90 S.Ct. 1105, 25 L.Ed.2d 280 (1970). Compare United States v. International Tel. & Tel. Corp., 349 F.Supp. 22 (D.Conn. 1972), aff'd sub nom. Nader v. United States, 410 U.S. 919, 93 S.Ct. 1363, 35 L.Ed.2d 582 (1973) (Nader group, as "private attorney's general," not allowed to intervene, but permitted to present brief as amicus). It is to be noted that the Antitrust Procedures and Penalties Act, 15 U.S.C.A. § 1 et seq., 47 U.S.C.A. § 401, 49 U.S.C.A. §§ 44–46 gives private parties a statutory right of participation where the government proposes to settle an antitrust action by consent decree. See § 243 supra. The availability of this right ought to reduce further the likelihood that a court will grant intervention under Rule 24.

c. Collateral Effects

Section 5(b) of the Clayton Act [12] provides that a civil or criminal proceeding instituted by the United States to prevent, restrain or punish antitrust violators will toll the running of the statute of limitations on any private right of action under the antitrust laws based in whole or in part on any matter complained of in the government proceeding during the pendency of that proceeding and for one year thereafter. Section 5(a) of Clayton [13] provides that in any such proceeding a final judgment or decree to the effect that a defendant has violated the antitrust laws shall be prima facie evidence against such defendant in any later private action. Let us consider these sections in reverse order.

The estoppel consequence of Section 5(a) arises when the government's civil or criminal case goes to judgment after trial,[14] or on a plea of guilty.[15] It does not arise when a consent decree has been entered [16] unless, as occurred in a group of consent decrees entered some years ago, the decree includes a so-called "asphalt clause" in which the defendants agree, in effect, that in any private litigation which follows the decree will be entitled to the collateral effect it would have had if it had not been entered by consent.[17] Neither does

---

A related issue is whether affected nonparties may in some sense enforce a government decree after it has been entered by consent or following litigation. Enforcement might be attempted by petition in the court which entered the decree, seeking to have the defendant held in contempt, or might be in a separate or collateral proceeding (in the same or a different court) alleging rights under the decree on some theory—for example, if the decree had been entered by consent, under a third party beneficiary theory bottomed on contract concepts. By and large, efforts such as these have been ineffectual. E.g., United States v. ASCAP, 341 F.2d 1003, 1008 (2d Cir.), cert. denied 382 U.S. 877, 86 S.Ct. 160, 15 L.Ed.2d 119 (965) (no standing to initiate contempt procedings); Control Data Corp. v. International Business Mach. Corp., 306 F.Supp. 839 (D.Minn.1969), aff'd 430 F.2d 1277 (8th Cir. 1970) (accord and holding that no third party beneficiary claim can be based on decree in government suit). See C. Sullivan, Enforcement of Government Antitrust Decrees by Private Parties: Third Party Beneficiary Rights and Intervenor Status, 123 U.Pa.L.Rev. 822 (1975).

12. 15 U.S.C.A. § 16(b) (1973).

13. 15 U.S.C.A. § 16(a) (1973).

14. E.g., Emich Motors Corp. v. General Motors Corp., 340 U.S. 558, 71 S.Ct. 408, 95 L.Ed. 534 (1951).

15. General Elec. Co. v. City of San Antonio, 334 F.2d 480, 486–87 (5th Cir. 1964); Federated Dept. Stores, Inc. v. Grinnell Corp., 287 F.Supp. 744 (S.D. N.Y.1968).

16. 15 U.S.C.A. § 16(a) (1973). But see Michigan v. Morton Salt Co., 259 F. Supp. 35 (D.Minn.1966), aff'd sub nom. Hardy Salt Co. v. Illinois, 377 F.2d 768 (8th Cir.), cert. denied 389 U.S. 912, 88 S.Ct. 238, 19 L.Ed.2d 260 (1967) (consent decree admissible on finding based on memorandum of court entering decree that consenting defendant's participation in the conspiracy had been adjudicated prior to consent). See generally, Zimmer and C. Sullivan, Consent Decree Settlements by Administrative Agencies in Antitrust and Employment Discrimination: Optimizing Public and Private Interests, 1976 Duke L.Rev. 163 (1976).

17. E.g., United States v. Lake Asphalt & Petroleum Co., 1960 CCH Trade Cas. ¶ 69,835 (D.Mass.); United States

Section 5(a) result in an estoppel when a plea of *nolo contendere* is accepted in a criminal case.[18] Though once in doubt it now seems settled that FTC orders based on findings that the Clayton Act has been violated are entitled to the collateral effect specified by Section 5(a).[19] There is also recent case law holding that even those FTC orders enforcing Section 5 of the FTC Act, concededly not itself an antitrust law,[20] are entitled to collateral effect under Section 5(a) of Clayton when the underlying theory of the FTC findings and order is that one of the antitrust laws was violated.[21]

Clayton Section 5(b), which specifies the tolling effects of government antitrust litigation, presents the same issues about the effect of FTC proceedings. The Supreme Court has held that an FTC complaint alleging a Clayton violation tolls the statute of limitations.[22] There is also case law accumulating to the effect that an FTC proceeding charging a violation of Section 5 of the FTC Act which, in substance, is based on an allegation of violation of one of the antitrust laws, will toll the running of the statute on the alleged underlying antitrust violation.[23] The other issues to which Section 5(b) has

v. Allied Chem. Corp., 1961 CCH Trade Cas. ¶ 69,923 (D.Mass.1960).

18. E.g., Twin Ports Oil Co. v. Pure Oil Co., 26 F.Supp. 366 (D.Minn.1939), aff'd on other grounds 119 F.2d 749 (8th Cir.), cert. denied 314 U.S. 644, 62 S.Ct. 84, 86 L.Ed. 516 (1941); City of Philadelphia v. Westinghouse Elec. Corp., 1961 CCH Trade Cas. ¶ 70,143 (E.D.Pa.).

19. Purex Corp. v. Procter & Gamble Co., 453 F.2d 288 (9th Cir. 1971), cert. denied 405 U.S. 1065, 92 S.Ct. 1499, 31 L.Ed.2d 795 (1972); Farmington Dowel Prods. Co. v. Forster Mfg. Co., 421 F.2d 61 (1st Cir. 1969). Cf. Minnesota Mining & Mfg. Co. v. New Jersey Wood Finishing Co., 381 U.S. 311, 85 S.Ct. 1473, 14 L.Ed.2d 405 (1965) (Section 5(b) tolling provision triggered by FTC proceeding charging a Clayton violation). Earlier cases to the contrary relied in part upon the fact that FTC orders were at one time not "final" until "enforced" upon review by a court of appeals. See e.g., the discussion in Highland Supply Corp. v. Reynolds Metal Co., 245 F.Supp. 510, 514 (E.D.Mo.1965). See also Nashville Milk Co. v. Carnation Co., 355 U.S. 373, 78 S.Ct. 352, 2 L.Ed.2d 340 (1958).

20. Nashville Milk Co. v. Carnation Co., 355 U.S. 373, 78 S.Ct. 352, 2 L.Ed.2d 340 (1958).

21. There is considerable case law the other way. See, e.g., Rader v. Balfour, 1969 CCH Trade Cas. ¶ 72,709 (N.D.Ill.1968); Laitram Corp. v. Deepsouth Packing Co., 279 F.Supp. 883 (E.D.La.1968). Recent cases, however, are consistent with the statement in text. E.g., Lippa's, Inc. v. Lenox, Inc., 305 F.Supp. 182 (D.Vt.1969). Conceivably there also are situations in which, even though the collateral effect of Section 5(a) is not available, an antitrust plaintiff may assert against the defendant a "one way collateral estoppel" based on prior litigation between the defendant and the Antitrust Division or the FTC. Compare United States v. United Air Lines, Inc., 216 F.Supp. 709 (E.D.Wash., D.Nev.1962). The seminal case on one way collateral estoppel is Bernhard v. Bank of America, 19 Cal. 2d 807, 122 P.2d 892 (1942). The most recent significant decision is Blonder-Tongue Laboratories, Inc. v. University of Ill. Foundation, 402 U.S. 313, 91 S.Ct. 1434, 28 L.Ed.2d 788 (1971), holding that a patentee which lost an infringment suit against one alleged infringer on ground of invalidity is estopped from asserting the patent against another alleged infringer.

22. Minnesota Mining & Mfg. Co. v. New Jersey Wood Finishing Co., 381 U.S. 311, 85 S.Ct. 1473, 14 L.Ed.2d 405 (1965).

principally given rise concern how long an action may be said to pend. It is now established that tolling actions can be "tacked"—for example, if the government during the pendency of a criminal action begins a civil action which continues to pend after the criminal action is disposed of.[24] The period of an action's pendency ought to include any period within which any appeal or petition for certiorari might be taken.[25] Finally, it is to be emphasized that the statute is tolled not just against named defendants or co-conspirators, but against all participants in a conspiracy that is the subject of a government proceeding, whether or not named in the government suit.[26] Thus, entry of a consent decree against one of several defendants charged with conspiracy does not end the tolling period as to that defendant; as to all defendants, the statute is tolled only when the action in its entirety is terminated.[27]

There may be important but less formal collateral consequences of the government proceeding. The Publicity in Taking Evidence Act,[28] provides that in a Sherman Act case brought by the Division for equitable relief, deposition proceedings shall be open to the public. Also, as the Court noted in Minnesota Mining & Manufacturing Co. v. New Jersey Wood Finishing Co.,[29] the Division may permit private plaintiffs to obtain whatever benefit they can from the Division's work product; the Division may make pleadings, transcripts, and various documents available to affected parties. Indeed, the Ninth Circuit held in Olympic Refining Co. v. Carter[30] that a treble damage claimant ought to be given access to defendant's interrogatory answers in a case brought by the Division, even though these involved trade secrets and were subject to a protective order; the court ordered disclosure subject to an appropriate order to prevent disclosure beyond the extent necessary for the purposes of the treble damage suitor.

23. Rader v. Balfour, 440 F.2d 469 (7th Cir.), cert. denied sub nom. Alpha Chi Omega v. Rader, 404 U.S. 983, 92 S.Ct. 444, 30 L.Ed.2d 367 (1971). See also Luria Steel and Trading Corp. v. Ogden Corp., 484 F.2d 1016 (3d Cir. 1973); In re Antibiotic Antitrust Actions, 333 F.Supp. 317 (S.D.N.Y.1971).

24. E.g., Michigan v. Morton Salt Co., 259 F.Supp. 35, 51 (D.Minn.1966), aff'd on other grounds sub nom. Hardy Salt Co., v. Illinois, 377 F.2d 768 (8th Cir.), cert. denied 389 U.S. 912, 88 S.Ct. 238, 19 L.Ed.2d 260 (1967). For a fuller collection of cases on this and related issues, see C. Hills, ed., Antitrust Advisor §§ 2.39, 2.44, 12.14, 13.29 (1971).

25. Electric Theater Co. v. Twentieth Century-Fox Film Corp., 113 F.Supp. 937 (W.D.Mo.1953).

26. Zenith Radio Corp. v. Hazeltine Research, Inc., 401 U.S. 321, 91 S.Ct. 795, 28 L.Ed.2d 77 (1971).

27. New Jersey v. Morton Salt Co., 387 F.2d 94 (3d Cir. 1967), cert. denied sub nom. International Salt Co. v. New Jersey, 391 U.S. 967, 88 S.Ct. 2035, 20 L.Ed.2d 880 (1968).

28. 15 U.S.C.A. § 30 (1973).

29. 381 U.S. 311, 85 S.Ct. 1473, 14 L.Ed.2d 405 (1965).

30. 332 F.2d 260 (9th Cir.) cert. denied 379 U.S. 900, 85 S.Ct. 186, 13 L.Ed.2d 175 (1964).

d. Remedial Issues

This book deals with remedies in government civil actions in connection with various specific offenses.[31] One of the unexplored general remedy issues is whether in an equitable proceeding brought by the government a court could order the defendant to disgorge its gains from the violation in ways benefiting those injured by the violation, or whether such an order could be entered by the FTC. It would be no great extension of the ancillary remedy theory to hold that a federal district court could construct such a remedy in a civil action. Federal courts have in cases enforcing federal statutes not only the power but the obligation to construct remedies which will advance the congressional purpose. In SEC v. Texas Gulf Sulphur Co.,[32] the Second Circuit had occasion to emphasize the broad scope of that obligation. The SEC had brought an action under rule 10b-5 against corporate officers, alleging insider trading. The district court had entered an order requiring the officers to pay their profits from the wrongful transactions into a fund established by the court. That order provided that any award against defendants in any private action would be paid out of the fund and that any balance would be disposed of as the court would order in ancillary proceedings upon application of the SEC or any interested party. The court of appeals approved the district court order. It approved the remedial goal, to deprive defendants of their gains in a situation where it was not clear that private actions would do so, yet to protect defendants against double recovery if private actions were brought, and to give the SEC, the defendants and any injured parties an opportunity to work out bases for a *cy pres* remedy similar to the fluid class recovery remedies that have been used in some class actions.[33]

While none of the Supreme Court cases on ancillary remedies have gone so far as *Texas Gulf Sulphur,* there are recent decisions of that Court which strongly support the view of the Second Circuit that general equity powers support an order requiring that profits gained from violation of a federal statute be disgorged in a manner having restitutionary consequences. For example, in Mitchell v. Robert De Mario Jewelry Inc.,[34] the Court, absent specific statutory authority, held that a district court may order reimbursement of wages after an illegal dismissal, and in Porter v. Warner Holding Co.[35] it held that a firm violating price control legislation could be ordered to make restitution. Holdings like these take on larger significance when it is remembered that in J. I. Case Co. v. Borak,[36] the Court re-

31. See §§ 53–58, 113, 215–16 supra.

32. 446 F.2d 1301 (2d Cir.), cert. denied 404 U.S. 1005, 92 S.Ct. 561–63, 30 L. Ed.2d 558 (1971).

33. See § 249 infra.

34. 361 U.S. 288, 80 S.Ct. 332, 4 L.Ed.2d 323 (1960).

35. 328 U.S. 395, 66 S.Ct. 1086, 90 L.Ed. 1332 (1946).

36. 377 U.S. 426, 84 S.Ct. 1555, 12 L. Ed.2d 423 (1964).

cently insisted that district courts have a duty to fashion whatever remedies are needed to effectuate remedial legislation.

A major problem of antitrust enforcement is the inadequacy of present remedies to deter violations, such as price cartels which yield high aggregate returns to the conspirators though they increase cost to individual purchasers by amounts too small to encourage them to sue.[37] The chance that such a violation will be discovered and challenged in an equity proceeding is small and the customary consequence if such a violation is successfully challenged is merely an order that it be stopped. The risk of criminal sanctions successfully being invoked is probably smaller still. The potential deterrent power of private treble damage actions has been greatly reduced by recent class action decisions,[38] so there is considerable force to the notion that it is now essential that the district courts be permitted or even required to work out fluid recovery mechanisms in equity actions brought by the government whenever the violation is one which is unlikely to be successfully and adequately redressed by private damage actions.

e. *Appellate Review*

Prior to 1975 if the United States was the plaintiff in an antitrust proceeding seeking equitable relief, there was, under the Expediting Act of 1903, a right of direct appeal to the Supreme Court.[39] Now, pursuant to the Antitrust Procedures and Penalties Act,[40] that right of direct appeal is virtually eliminated.[41] In almost all cases appeals must now be taken from the district court to the court of appeals.[42] Review by the Supreme Court will now normally be upon petition for certiorari after disposition by the court of appeals.

The change is an important one. The direct appeal was predicated on the notion that antitrust cases (and some others) were particularly important and that expedition was appropriate, especially where

---

37. See R. Posner, Antitrust Cases, Economic Notes and Other Materials 110–14 (1974).

38. See § 249 infra.

39. 15 U.S.C.A. § 28; 49 U.S.C.A. § 44. The act not only provided for direct appeal but also authorized the Attorney General to require that a three judge district court be convened to hear the case; the latter power was rarely used.

40. 88 Stat. 1706, P.L. 93–528, enacted December 21, 1974. 15 U.S.C.A. § 29 (1976).

41. The 1974 act also abolished the right of the Attorney General to require a three judge district court for antitrust cases.

42. The 1974 act in Section 5(b) authorizes a direct appeal to be docketed with the Supreme Court upon certification by the district court judge who heard the case that immediate consideration of the appeal by the Supreme Court is of general public importance in the administration of justice. The Supreme Court may either dispose of the appeal or, in its discretion, deny the direct appeal and remand to the court of appeals. 88 Stat. 1706, P.L. 93–528, Section 5(b), 15 U.S.C.A. § 29(b) (1976).

injunctive relief was being sought.[43] But the consequence of the old system was both to burden the Supreme Court unduly and to foreclose the ripening process that occurs when cases go first to the courts of appeal and to the Supreme Court on certiorari. While it is impossible to predict with any particularity what effects these institutional changes will have, there is litle doubt but that legal development in the antitrust area will be affected to some degree. In the past, the Court's special relationship to antitrust may have given it as an institution a somewhat proprietary attitude at some level of awareness; it may have been the more ready to make policy in the large, to act more like an agency developing economic policy and less like a court applying rules of law than it might have done if it had before it the work product of the courts of appeal. If so, the Court may now distance itself to a greater degree from the antitrust area. As a result, the "law" aspects of antitrust may receive more emphasis and the "policy" aspects less emphasis. Review on certiorari after issues have been explored by one or more of the courts of appeal may facilitate doctrinal development.

§ 245. Criminal Proceedings

Indictment often follows an investigation which shows a serious *per se* violation or one which involves patently predatory conduct. Though a case is begun by indictment there is often a companion civil case seeking equitable remedies. Officers and employees of a corporation having substantial responsibility for an indictable practice will be indicted along with their corporation when the violation is a serious one, like price fixing, and their participation is clear.

The Division frequently accepts *nolo contendere* pleas. It will oppose such a plea, however, unless the defendant acknowledges to the court that the plea is an admission of guilt and subjects the defendant to the same penalties as a guilty plea. It may also oppose a *nolo* plea if the violation was blatant or if conviction would substantially aid private plaintiffs to recover in treble damage actions. Even with a *nolo* plea, a criminal case can aid the private plaintiff. Although access to grand jury evidence is not easily obtained (historically, the jury's proceedings are secret and Rule 6(e) of the Federal Rules of Criminal Procedure forbids disclosure of evidence received by the grand jury except to the attorneys of parties to the proceeding as needed for the performance of their duties, or as "directed by the court preliminarily to or in connection with a judicial proceeding"), in the *Electrical Equipment Cases* the court allowed discovery of testimony in later treble damage cases.[1] A procedure was established which made substantial portions of the transcript available to treble

---

43. See, e.g., Swift & Co. v. Wickman, 382 U.S. 111, 119–20, 86 S.Ct. 258, 263, 15 L.Ed.2d 194, 200–01 (1965).

1. Atlantic City Elec. Co. v. A.B. Chance Co., 313 F.2d 431, 434 (2d Cir. 1963).

damage claimants throughout the country.² Even if access to jury evidence is not obtained there may be other useful documents which can be obtained.³

The scope of discovery available to a defendant in a criminal antitrust case is itself an area of considerable interest, debate and development. Given the nature of the proceeding, the relevance of structural data and other economic material, and the extent to which the case is likely to be based on documentary evidence, the arguments for allowing broad discovery under Rules 16(a) and 16(b) ⁴ are forceful. A recurrent question is whether so-called "de-briefing" memoranda taken by a criminal defendant's counsel from witnesses called before the grand jury can be discovered in a later civil suit. If the witnesses were officers or employees within the "control group" of the corporation, the attorney-client privilege should apply.⁵

PART D. PRIVATE ENFORCEMENT

§ 246. Introduction

Private actions constitute a major part of the antitrust caseload of the federal courts. Section 4 of the Clayton Act provides a treble damage remedy for antitrust violations.¹ Section 16 of that act authorizes private suits for injunctive relief.² Most private actions are treble damage cases, though the number of suits for injunctive relief is increasing.³ Private actions may be brought for virtually any anti-

---

2. The basis of the order was apparent inconsistencies between the witness depositions and grand jury testimony. The trial court, on motion, will review the grand jury testimony and the depositions and release only that part of the grand jury transcript that is relevant. See Illinois v. Harper & Row Publishers, Inc. v. Decker, 1969 CCH Trade Cas. ¶ 72,965 N.D.Ill., rev'd in part sub nom. Harper & Row Publishers, Inc. v. Decker, 423 F.2d 487 (7th Cir. 1970), aff'd by equally divided Court 400 U.S. 348, 91 S.Ct. 479, 27 L.Ed.2d 433 (1971); United States v. Darling Delaware, Inc., 1972 CCH Trade Cas. ¶ 73,818 (S.D.N.Y.1971).

3. For example, the government usually files a sentencing memorandum after the plea and before sentencing and the defendant is entitled to obtain copies of these. See C. Hill, ed., Antitrust Advisor §§ 10, 23 (1971). If defendant has done so, the treble damage plaintiff may be able to discover them, or at least those portions that are not directly based on grand jury proceedings. United States Indus., Inc. v. District Court for Southern Dist. of Cal., Central Division, 345 F. 2d 18 (9th Cir. 1965). But see Hancock Bros. v. Jones, 293 F.Supp. 1229 (N.D.Cal.1968).

4. Fed.R.Crim.P. 16(a), (b).

5. See Continental Oil Co. v. United States, 330 F.2d 347 (9th Cir. 1964). The attorney's "work product" exception may also be applicable. See Duplan Corp. v. Monlinage Ct. Retorderie de Chavanoz, 1972–73 CCH Trade Cas. ¶ 74,748 (4th Cir. 1973).

1. 15 U.S.C.A. § 15 (1973).

2. 15 U.S.C.A. § 26 (1973).

3. Recent examples include: Interphoto Corp. v. Minolta Corp., 417 F.2d 621 (2d Cir. 1969); Telflex Indus. Prods., Inc. v. Brunswick Corp., 410 F.2d 380 (3d Cir. 1969); National Screen Serv. Corp. v. Poster Exch., Inc., 305 F.2d 647 (5th Cir. 1962).

trust offense. There are cases challenging vertical restraints.[4] There are also many important cases brought by competitors and by customers challenging horizontal restraints.[5] Suits by major firms are becoming increasingly common,[6] as are class actions.[7] Damage awards and settlement sums have often been substantial.[8] While the deterrent effect of the treble damage remedy is difficult to assess, there can be little doubt that private actions are a major part of the nation's antitrust enforcement program.

The materials in this part are intended to introduce the reader to some of the more important problems to which private enforcement gives rise. There has been no attempt to be comprehensive nor to deal with strategic or tactical questions.[9] But an attempt has been made to discuss some legal issues which uniquely occur in these cases or which have special significance for them.

§ 247. Standing, Injury and Causation

Section 4 of Clayton says that "any person injured in his business or property" by an antitrust violation shall be entitled to recover damages;[1] Section 16 says that "any person, firm, corporation or association shall be entitled to sue and have injunctive relief * * * against threatened loss or damage" due to such a violation.[2] Neither has been read literally. The scope of each of these provisions has been narrowed through standing requirements invented and elaborated upon by the courts. The judiciary has not been generous in construing Section 4 and the devices courts have developed to limit

---

4. E.g., Simpson v. Union Oil Co., 377 U.S. 13, 84 S.Ct. 1051, 12 L.Ed.2d 98 (1964).

5. Often private action follows upon successful government proceeding, e.g., Hanover Shoe, Inc. v. United Shoe Mach. Corp., 392 U.S. 481, 88 S.Ct. 2224, 20 L.Ed.2d 1231 (1968). But in other instances the private action may be the only action or may precede or run parallel with a government action, e.g. Data Processing Fin. & Gen. Corp. v. International Business Mach. Corp., 430 F.2d 1277 (8th Cir. 1970).

6. E.g., Hughes Tool Co. v. Trans World Airlines, Inc., 409 U.S. 363, 93 S.Ct. 647, 34 L.Ed.2d 577 (1973); International Tel. & Tel. Corp. v. General Tel. & Electronics Corp., 518 F.2d 913 (9th Cir. 1975); Data Processing Fin. & Gen. Corp. v. International Business Mach. Corp., 430 F.2d 1277 (8th Cir. 1970).

7. See § 249 infra.

8. E.g., Hughes Tool Co. v. Trans World Airlines, Inc., 409 U.S. 363, 93 S.Ct. 647, 34 L.Ed.2d 577 (1973) (damage award of $137 million and attorneys' fee award of $7.5 million reversed on grounds not pertaining to the amount of these awards); West Virginia v. Chas. Pfizer & Co., 440 F.2d 1079 (2d Cir.) cert. denied 404 U.S. 871, 92 S.Ct. 81, 30 L.Ed.2d 115 (1971) (settlement fund of $82 million).

9. C. Hills, ed., Antitrust Advisor (1971) contains several chapters with useful, practical advice to the litigator. See particularly the chapters on investigations by J. Hanson and I. Woodland, that on prosecuting private actions by M. Mitchell, and that on defending antitrust actions by A. Hartzwell and J. Barbash, id., chs. 10, 12 and 13.

1. 15 U.S.C.A. § 15 (1973).

2. 15 U.S.C.A. § 26 (1973).

the treble damage remedy granted by that section have been applied also to narrow the availability of equitable relief.

Section 4 provides that a person be compensated for injury "in his business or property." This phrase has not been the subject of artful elaboration. By and large, any injury to financial interests, including those to a consumer which must pay more for a product because of a violation, have been held to be compensable.[3] While there

---

3. A purchase by a business firm for use or consumption in connection with its business, as well as a purchase for resale, gives the buyer a cause of action under § 4 if the buyer must pay a higher price because of an antitrust violation. See Chattanooga Foundry & Pipe Works v. Atlanta, 203 U.S. 390, 27 S.Ct. 65, 51 L.Ed. 241 (1906). The item purchased may be either goods or services. Thomsen v. Cayser, 243 U.S. 66, 88, 37 S.Ct. 353, 360, 61 L.Ed. 597, 607 (1917). Analysis suggests that a non-business consumer who has paid a higher price because of an antitrust violation also has a cause of action under § 4. The municipal utility in *Chattanooga Foundry*, supra, had a cause of action for the excessive cost of pipe it purchased to install in its water system not because it sold water to the public but because its aggregate property was reduced by the violation which increased the price it paid. Justice Holmes noted that Congress referred disjunctively to "business or property" (thus indicating that property meant something other than business). But he laid even greater stress on the fact that the statutory reference to one who is "injured in his . . . property" implies a far broader conception of property than would a phrase like "injury to property." Congress not only wanted to protect "property" as well as and in addition to "business," it chose words which showed that it wanted to protect against injuries to property in a general sense, not just injuries to specific items of property. Thus, as Congress used the terms, a "person whose property is diminished by a payment of money wrongfully induced is injured in his property." (203 U.S. at 396, 27 S.Ct. at 66, 51 L.Ed. at 244). This rationale clearly covers the "property" of an ultimate consumer as well as that of business firm. Courts and commentators seem to have accepted this position without much discussion. E. g. Cleary v. Chalk, 488 F.2d 1315, 1319 n. 17 (D.C. Cir. 1976). The dicta in Hawaii v. Standard Oil Co., 405 U.S. 251, 264, 92 S.Ct. 885, 892, 31 L.Ed.2d 184, 194 (1972) is not to the contrary. There, the Court said that the words "business or property" refer to "commercial interests or enterprises." The Court was not contrasting business with consumer interests, but was contrasting matters of commerce generally with the interest of a state in vindicating injuries to its general economy. In context, the phrase "commercial interests," used by the Court, is broad enough to include any injury to a consumer who, making a purchase in commerce, suffers an injury "in his * * * property." This conclusion is reinforced by other parts of the opinion in *Hawaii*. For one thing, the Court makes clear that a state can recover for any injury affecting property held by it in a proprietary capacity, not just for injuries relating to property held by it in a business capacity. (405 U.S. at 262, 92 S.Ct. at 891, 31 L.Ed.2d at 193). For another, the Court suggests both that "private citizens" can combine their interest in a class action and that, subject to the requirements of Rule 23 of the Federal Rules of Civil Procedure, a state may bring a class action on behalf of "some or all of its consumer citizens." (405 U.S. at 266, 92 S.Ct. at 893, 31 L.Ed.2d at 194). Moreover, in Hanover Shoe, Inc. v. United Shoe Machinery Corp., 392 U.S. 481, 494, 88 S.Ct. 2224, 2232, 20 L.Ed.2d 1231, 1241–42 (1968), the Court discusses the "passing on" of illegal overcharges in terms which presuppose that "ultimate consumers" although having "only a tiny stake in a law suit and little interest in attempting a class action" do have a cause of action, however difficult it may be, as a practical matter, for them to assert that cause of action.

Contract rights are also property (North Texas Producers Ass'n v. Young, 308 F.2d 235, 243 (5th Cir. 1962), cert. de-are cases denying that plans and preparations to enter into a business constitute business or property,[4] better reasoned decisions properly hold that such interests should also be protected if they have materialized sufficiently to constitute an asset of reasonably determinate value which might, for example, be bought and sold or taxed, and which is capable of being appraised.[5] A cause of action for injunctive relief under Section 16 does not require a showing of injury to business or property but imposes a lower threshold requirement—that there be a "threatened loss or damage" to the plaintiff.[6]

There must also be a proximate causal connection between the violation alleged and the injury sustained, a necessity which the lower federal courts have elaborated into a varied set of standing requirements. These have been expressed in numerous ways—that the injury to plaintiff must be direct, not indirect;[7] that the antitrust violation must be the proximate cause of the injury;[8] that the plaintiff must have been within the "target area" that defendant "aimed at" or intended to hit;[9] or that the rationale for the antitrust rule which defendant violated must be intended to protect those in plaintiff's position.[10] The thrust of these statements is best indicated by exam-

nied 372 U.S. 929, 83 S.Ct. 874, 9 L. Ed.2d 733 (1963)) including rights under an employment contract (Radovich v. National Football League, 352 U.S. 445, 77 S.Ct. 390, 1 L.Ed.2d 456 (1957)), although an advantageous relationship not yet ripened into a contractual one (Peller v. International Boxing Club, 227 F.2d 593, 596 (7th Cir. 1955)), or even a contractual relationship which a third party can terminate at any time (VTR, Inc. v. Goodyear Tire & Rubber Co., 303 F. Supp. 773 (S.D.N.Y.1969)) have been held not to constitute property.

4. E.g., Duff v. Kansas City Star Co., 299 F.2d 320, 323 (8th Cir. 1962).

5. E.g., Woods Exploration & Producing Co. v. Aluminum Co. of America, 438 F.2d 1286, 1310 (5th Cir. 1971), cert. denied 404 U.S. 1047, 92 S.Ct. 701, 30 L.Ed.2d 736 (1972); Pennsylvania Sugar Ref. Co. v. American Sugar Ref. Co., 92 C.C.A. 318, 166 F. 254 (2d Cir. 1908).

6. 15 U.S.C.A. § 26 (1973). See Hawaii v. Standard Oil Co., 405 U.S. 251, 260–64, 92 S.Ct. 885, 850–852, 31 L.Ed. 2d 184, 191–94 (1972); Buckley Towers Condominium, Inc. v. Buchwald, 533 F. 2d 934 (5th Cir. 1976); In re Multidistrict Vehicle Air Pollution Cases, 481 F.2d 122, 130 (9th Cir.), cert. denied 414 U.S. 1045, 94 S.Ct. 551, 38 L.Ed.2d 336 (1973); Calnetics Corp. v. Volkswagen of America, Inc., 348 F.Supp. 606 (C.D.Cal.1972), rev. on other grounds, 532 F.2d 674 (9th Cir. 1976), all of which indicate that the Section 16 requirement is lower than the injury requirement of Section 4.

7. E.g., Schaffer v. Universal Rundle Corp., 397 F.2d 893 (5th Cir. 1968); Productive Inventions, Inc. v. Trico Prods. Corp., 224 F.2d 678 (2d Cir. 1955), cert. denied 350 U.S. 936, 76 S. Ct. 301, 100 L.Ed. 818 (1956); Loeb v. Eastman Kodak Co., 106 C.C.A. 142, 183 F. 704, 709 (3d Cir. 1910).

8. E.g., Highland Supply Corp. v. Reynolds Metals Co., 327 F.2d 725, 732 (8th Cir. 1964).

9. E.g., Southern Concrete Co. v. United States Steel Corp., 535 F.2d 313 (5th Cir. 1976); South Carolina Council of Milk Producers, Inc. v. Newton, 360 F.2d 414, 418 (4th Cir.), cert. denied 385 U.S. 934, 87 S.Ct. 295, 17 L.Ed.2d 215 (1966); Karseal Corp. v. Richfield Oil Corp., 221 F.2d 358, 362–64 (9th Cir. 1955).

10. Twentieth Century Fox Film Corp. v. Goldwyn Productions, 328 F.2d 190, 220 (9th Cir.), cert. denied 379 U.S. 880, 85 S.Ct. 143, 13 L.Ed.2d 87 (1964).

ples. If defendant used predatory practices to drive out a competitor, that injured competitor concededly has standing. But, on standing theories of one kind or another, a right to sue might well be denied to that injured competitor's suppliers,[11] landlord,[12] employees[13] and stockholders,[14] however much they may have been injured by the failure of the competitor which was driven from the market, unless under the particular circumstances they could show a more immediate relationship to the violation than is typically associated with any such status.[15] Any injury derivative in nature may not be redressed under Section 4.[16]

Various reasons have been suggested for these nonstatutory standing formulas, among them fear of double recoveries and of debilitating defendants by large aggregate awards, perhaps associated, in some instances, with relatively minor wrongs. Another reason may be associated with the increasing use of *per se* rules. Courts feeling ill-equipped to unravel complex economic analyses have simplified standards of proof of some offenses to the point where the facts which show a violation do not necessarily signify significant harm to competitive structure or process. Simplifications such as these are acceptable when the enforcement agency, being committed to the public interest, can be expected to select cases on the basis of its judgment about the harmful effect or potential of the conduct being challenged. But the private antitrust plaintiff is under no compunctions against suits which challenge practices having effects which are socially trivial; the only constraint on a private suitor is whether the costs of the litigation outweigh its potential benefits to him. The Supreme Court having rejected a test which would have required private plaintiffs to show that the public was injured by the practice

---

11. Volasco Products Co. v. Lloyd A. Fry Roofing Co., 308 F.2d 383, 393–95 (6th Cir. 1962), cert. denied 372 U.S. 907, 83 S.Ct. 721, 9 L.Ed.2d 717 (1963). But see South Carolina Council of Milk Producers Inc. v. Newton, 360 F.2d 414 (4th Cir.), cert. denied 385 U.S. 934, 87 S.Ct. 295, 17 L.Ed.2d 215 (1966); Karseal Corp. v. Richfield Oil Corp., 221 F.2d 358 (9th Cir. 1955).

12. Harrison v. Paramount Pictures, Inc., 115 F.Supp. 312 (E.D.Pa.1953), aff'd per curiam 211 F.2d 405 (3d Cir.), cert. denied 348 U.S. 828, 75 S.Ct. 45, 99 L.Ed. 653 (1954). But see Congress Bldg. Corp. v. Loew's Inc., 246 F.2d 587 (7th Cir. 1957).

13. Reibert v. Atlantic Richfield Co., 471 F.2d 727 (10th Cir.), cert. denied 411 U.S. 938, 93 S.Ct. 1900, 36 L.Ed.2d 399 (1973). Cf. Cordova v. Bache & Co., 321 F.Supp. 600 (S.D.N.Y.1970).

14. Pollack Co. v. Balfour Co., 1973 CCH Trade Cas. ¶ 74,339 (N.D.Ill. 1972); but see Kolb v. Chrysler Corp., 357 F.Supp. 504 (E.D.Wis.1973).

15. See, e.g., Steiner v. 20th Century-Fox Film Corp., 232 F.2d 190 (9th Cir. 1956), where a lessor was accorded standing upon allegations that the lessee was not merely a victim but a participant in the conspiracy.

16. In addition to the cases in notes 11 through 14, see Martens v. Barrett, 245 F.2d 844, 846 (5th Cir. 1957) (creditors of antitrust victim denied standing); Productive Inventions, Inc. v. Trico Prods. Corp., 224 F.2d 678 (2d Cir. 1955), cert. denied 350 U.S. 936, 76 S.Ct. 301, 100 L.Ed. 818 (1956) (patentee which had granted license to victim); Nationwide Auto Appraiser Service, Inc. v. Association of Cas. & Sur. Companies, 382 F.2d 925 (10th

of being challenged,[17] lower federal courts have in a sense used standing requirements as a sort of coarse-grained sieve to limit the number of private suits, on grounds which have a less satisfactory rationale than did the public injury test.[18]

Of course, all of the interests said to be served by the standing requirement could be served by rules or principles more precisely attuned to the policy interest involved. Under traditional tort notions, a court can proceed selectively to assure that the injury a plaintiff seeks to redress by a damage remedy is sufficiently related to the violation alleged.[19] Many of the other problems now dealt with as standing issues could be dealt with under damage rules and instructions.[20] And the potential problem of double recovery can be handled in sophisticated ways as well as gross and blunt ones.[21] It is, then, not at all clear that the Supreme Court will ultimately accept the standing limitations which the courts of appeal and the district courts have invented. In rejecting the public injury test the Court said that a treble damage plaintiff need show no more than that there was a violation and that plaintiff was injured;[22] the Court has also stated in another context that the lower courts should "not add requirements to burden the private litigant beyond what is specifically set forth * * *" in the statutes.[23]

Cir. 1967) (franchisor of victims); Billy Baxter, Inc. v. Coca-Cola Co., 431 F.2d 183, 187 (2d Cir. 1970), cert. denied 401 U.S. 923, 91 S.Ct. 877, 27 L.Ed.2d 826 (1971) (franchisor).

17. Radiant Burners, Inc. v. People's Gas Light & Coke Co., 364 U.S. 656, 81 S.Ct. 365, 5 L.Ed.2d 358 (1961); Klor's Inc. v. Broadway-Hale Stores, 359 U.S. 207, 79 S.Ct. 705, 3 L.Ed.2d 741 (1959).

18. The nostalgia of lower courts for the public injury test is also to be seen in the anomalous holdings by some lower federal courts that, inasmuch as a merger may violate Section 7 although its prospect for hurting the public remains incipient, there should be no private damage action on account of such a merger; e.g., Isidor Weinstein Inv. Co. v. Hearst Corp., 303 F.Supp. 646 (N.D.Cal.1969); Bailey's Bakery, Ltd. v. Continental Baking Co., 235 F.Supp. 705 (D.Haw. 1964), aff'd per curiam 401 F.2d 182 (9th Cir. 1968) cert. denied 393 U.S. 1086, 89 S.Ct. 874, 21 L.Ed.2d 779 (1969). Of course, other courts have rejected that strained view; e.g., Gottesman v. General Motors Corp., 414 F.2d 956 (2d Cir. 1969).

19. See, e.g., Mulvey v. Samuel Goldwyn Productions, 433 F.2d 1073 (9th Cir. 1970), cert. denied 402 U.S. 923, 91 S.Ct. 1377, 28 L.Ed.2d 662 (1971), one of a number of cases in which courts have drawn on conventional tort concepts to deal with multiple causation problems.

20. See § 251 infra.

21. Risks of double recovery can be reduced by devices like joinder and consolidation. There is a need for detailed and explicit scholarship addressing the ways in which alternative devices might be used.

22. Radiant Burners, Inc. v. Peoples Gas Light & Coke Co., 364 U.S. 656, 660, 81 S.Ct. 365, 367, 5 L.Ed.2d 358, 361 (1961).

23. Radovich v. National Football League, 352 U.S. 445, 454, 77 S.Ct. 390, 1 L.Ed.2d 456 (1957). See also Hanover Shoe, Inc. v. United Shoe Mach. Corp., 392 U.S. 481, 88 S.Ct. 2224, 20 L.Ed.2d 1231 (1968). The only Supreme Court dicta which can be cited in support of the target area or similar standing tests is the statement in Hawaii v. Standard Oil Co., 405 U.S. 251, 263, 92 S.Ct. 885, 891, 31 L.Ed. 2d 184, 193 n. 14 (1973) to the effect that "lower courts have been virtually

§ 248. Statute of Limitations

Before 1955 there was no federal statute of limitations for private antitrust actions; the federal courts borrowed state rules.[1] In 1955 Congress amended the Clayton Act to impose a four year limitation period on treble damage actions and actions by the United States to recover for injury to its business or property.[2] The application of the statute to discrete acts which violate the law and which do immediate and obvious injury presents no particular difficulty.[3] But many antitrust violations presuppose a continuing course of conduct, such as a price conspiracy or interdependent pricing; indeed, the violation may even be predicated primarily on defendant's having a certain status—that of a monopolist. In cases such as these the point at which a plaintiff's cause of action accrues and the statute begins to run is not obvious.

Mindful of the remedial and deterrent purposes of the treble damage action, the courts have taken a pragmatic approach which does not start the statute running prior to the time the injured party is likely to be motivated to sue. If the plaintiff has suffered no loss, its cause of action has not accrued even though defendant would be liable should the government bring a civil or criminal action.[4] The private cause of action does not arise until some act is done that injures the plaintiff, and it arises at that point even though there may be further injuries in the future arising from the same wrongful

unanimous in concluding that Congress did not intend the antitrust laws to provide a remedy in damages for all injuries that might conceivably be traced to an antitrust violation." This observation does not commit the Court to all or any part of the judical gloss which shimmers in the standing area.

1. E.g., Chattanooga Foundry & Pipe Works v. Atlanta, 203 U.S. 390, 27 S. Ct. 65, 51 L.Ed. 241 (1906).

2. 15 U.S.C.A. § 15(b). The Clayton Act, though imposing no limitation period, had contained a tolling provision and the 1955 legislation also amended this. 15 U.S.C.A. § 16(b). As to the tolling effects of government proceedings see § 244 supra. The four year limitations statute applies, in terms, only to damage actions under Clayton § 4, not to private actions under § 16 for equitable relief. Nevertheless, it was recently held by the Ninth Circuit that the equitable defense of laches may be available in a suit under § 16 and that the four year statutory period should be used as a guideline in determining whether suit was brought within a reasonable time. I. T. & T. Corp. v. G. T. E. Corp., 518 F.2d 913, 926–929 (9th Cir. 1975).

3. E.g., Pioneer Co., v. Talon, Inc., 462 F.2d 1106 (8th Cir. 1972) (action for refusal to deal allegedly violating antitrust laws accrued when the orders were placed with manufacturer which refused to fill them.) Accord, Southeastern Hose, Inc. v. Imperial-Eastman Corp., 1973 CCH Trade Cas. ¶ 74,479 (D.Ga.). See also Weber v. Consumers Digest, Inc., 440 F.2d 729 (7th Cir. 1971) holding that the statute begins to run on a conspiracy on the date of the last overt act done in perseverance of the conspiracy.

4. E.g., Steiner v. Twentieth Century Fox Film Corp., 232 F.2d 190 (9th Cir. 1956). See also Ansul Co. v. Uniroyal, Inc., 448 F.2d 872, 883–85 (2d Cir. 1971), cert. denied 404 U.S. 1018, 92 S. Ct. 680, 30 L.Ed.2d 666 (1972); Flintkote Co. v. Lysfjord, 246 F.2d 368 (9th Cir.), cert. denied 355 U.S. 835, 78 S. Ct. 54, 2 L.Ed.2d 46 (1957); Twentieth Century Fox Film Corp. v. Brookside Theatre Corp., 194 F.2d 846 (8th Cir.), cert. denied 343 U.S. 942, 72 S.Ct. 1035, 96 L.Ed. 1348 (1952).

conduct.[5] So long as the future injuries can be foreseen and compensation for them computed, the cause of action is entire and has accrued once the wrong has resulted in any discernable harm.

But the conduct constituting the violation may also go on for years. The effects on plaintiff may be insignificant at some periods, significant at others. Suppose plaintiff allowed four years to go by after it had suffered some discernible harm and thus had a cause of action; does defendant have a defense to a later suit for other and perhaps more intensive damage which begins to occur after the four year period? In Zenith Radio Corp. v. Hazeltine Research, Inc.,[6] the Court insisted that the cause of action available to a plaintiff at any given time covers all past damage and such future damages as could then be proved and which would not be speculative. If a plaintiff which has begun to suffer damage allows four years to go by without suit it will be barred as to any damages—past or future—which it might have proved had it brought suit during the four year period. Only if there were elements of future damage which during the four years were too speculative to prove may the plaintiff hold off bringing suit; for these elements the cause of action accrues when the damage has actually been incurred.[7]

The statute of limitations is tolled not only by certain government proceedings,[8] but also by fraudulent concealment of the cause of action.[9] A conspiracy will usually be *sub rosa*, of course. That the defendants acted covertly may, under old and respected authority, be enough to toll the statute.[10] But there are specific indications that plaintiff may have to show something more than that defendants did not make their conduct public—at a minimum, that plaintiff acted in a diligent and self-regarding way but learned nothing during the statutory period which put it on notice of the violation.[11] Some cases seem to require more—that plaintiff prove affirmative acts by de-

---

5. See cases cited in note 4 supra.

6. 401 U.S. 321, 91 S.Ct. 795, 28 L.Ed.2d 77 (1971).

7. Id. See also Poster Exch., Inc. v. National Screen Serv. Corp., 456 F.2d 662 (5th Cir. 1972). A more severe analysis would suggest that the statute should begin to run on each of the elements of damage which was too speculative to be proved during the first four years, as soon as that particular element, although not as yet actually incurred, became capable of being proved without the use of unduly speculative evidence.

8. See § 244 supra.

9. E.g., Westinghouse Elec. Corp. v. Pacific Gas & Elec. Co., 326 F.2d 575 (9th Cir. 1964); Westinghouse Elec. Corp. v. City of Burlington, 117 U.S.App.D.C. 148, 326 F.2d 691 (1964); General Elec. Co. v. City of San Antonio, 334 F.2d 480 (5th Cir. 1964); Atlantic City Elec. Co. v. General Elec. Co., 207 F.Supp. 613 (S.D.N.Y.), aff'd 312 F.2d 236 (2d Cir. 1962), cert. denied 373 U.S. 909, 83 S.Ct. 1298, 10 L.Ed.2d 411 (1963).

10. See, e.g. Bailey v. Glover, 88 U.S. (21 Wall.) 342, 22 L.Ed. 636 (1874). Compare the discussion in Holmberg v. Armbrecht, 327 U.S. 392, 66 S.Ct. 582, 90 L.Ed. 743 (1946).

11. E.g., Laundry Equip. Sales Corp. v. Borg-Warner Corp., 334 F.2d 788 (7th Cir. 1964).

fendant to conceal the facts which constitute the violation.[12] There is in the recent cases scant effort to grapple with theory, but there are rational bases upon which a choice might be made. To deprive a plaintiff of its action even against covert defendants unless the plaintiff can show that diligence on its own part could not have brought the offense to light would achieve two things. First, it would tend to impose costs on those plaintiffs who were not as diligent as they might have been, thus encouraging their greater diligence to uncover wrongs against them. Second, it would tend to grant security to those defendants that succeed in hiding their wrong for four years or more, thus encouraging their greater diligence to disguise their wrongs. The alternative policy would tend to the opposite effects. Absent any basis for deciding which policy would result in the greater deterrence of violations, the law, on the basis of its ethical commitments, ought to reject the policy that rewards the wrong-doer that is sufficiently diligent in keeping his conduct under cover.

§ 249. Class Actions and *Parens Patriae*

a. *Class Actions*

Class actions are governed by Rule 23 of the Federal Rules of Civil Procedure, as revised in 1966.[1] Rule 23(a) requires that the class must be so numerous that joinder is impracticable, that there be common questions of law and fact, that claims of the class representatives typify those of the class, and that the representative parties fairly and adequately represent the interests of the class. Rule 23(b)(1) and (2) authorize actions which, if brought individually, would affect interests of others in specified ways.[2] Rule 23(b)(3), which is of special relevance for antitrust, authorizes class actions when "questions of law or fact common to members of the class predominate" over other questions and when the class action would be "superior" to other possible ways of adjudicating the controversy.[3]

---

12. E.g., Forbes v. Greater Minneapolis Area Bd. of Realtors, 1972–3 CCH Trade Cas. ¶ 74,627 (D.Minn.1973).

1. The rule in its present, revised form became effective July 1, 1966. The original rule, promulgated in 1937, was very different and cases under the rule prior to revision must be used with caution. The original rule differentiated between "true" class actions to enforce joint, common or secondary rights, "hybrid" class actions, where the rights of class members were several but there was a common *res* for which they were competing and "spurious" class actions, which was merely a permissive joinder provision where common questions of law or fact were involved in claims which were several. In all instances the class had to be so numerous as to make it impracticable to bring all members before the court and the named representatives had to adequately represent the class as a whole. As will be seen from the text, the revised rule makes very different distinctions and establishes very different requirements.

2. A very rough analogy may be drawn between 23(b)(1) and hybrid class actions under the old rule, though the hybrid concept and the concepts covered by 23(b)(1) are not identical. 23(b)(2) deals, in essence, with situations where injunctive relief would be warranted.

3. Fed.R.Civ.P. 23(b)(3).

Although this language is clearly broad enough to cover some actions which under the unrevised rule would have been "spurious" class actions, and hence binding only on class members who appeared,[4] the way the rule is now phrased absent class members will be bound by the action unless they request exclusion.

The courts, recognizing the purpose of the rule to save resources by aggregating large numbers of claims into a single efficiently managed law suit, have in many respects construed the rule liberally. Impracticability of joinder, required by 23(e) for all class actions, may be found whenever there is a substantial number of class members.[5] For example, a group of thirty or forty franchisees would, as a practical matter be difficult to join; thus, if other prerequisites were met they would be an appropriate class. Typicality of the claims of the class representative, also a requirement for all types of class actions, requires essentially that there be nothing significant which differentiates the claims of the representatives to a degree which might bring their interests into conflict with those of class members generally.[6] Though common questions of fact and law must be shown for any class action, predominance of these over other questions is a prerequisite only under 23(b)(3). "Predominance" under the rule means predominance in a practical sense; differences that bear only on the computation of damages, for example, will not keep the class action from going forward.[7]

But a punctilious construction of one aspect of the rule, the requirement that the class action be superior to other modes of adjudicating the controversy, has greatly limited the utility of the rule in an area where it might otherwise have had great value for antitrust enforcement—namely, in those situations where the class members are extremely numerous, but claims of individual members are as a practical matter too small to warrant bringing the action.[8] The most

---

4. See note 1 supra.

5. E.g., Research Corp v. Asgrow Seed Co., 425 F.2d 1059 (7th Cir. 1970); Iowa v. Union Asphalt & Roadoils, Inc., 281 F.Supp. 391 (S.D.Iowa 1969); Illinois v. Harper & Row Publishers, Inc., 301 F.Supp. 484 (N.D.Ill.), cert. denied 394 U.S. 944, 89 S.Ct. 1273, 22 L.Ed.2d 478 (1969); Siegel v. Chicken Delight, Inc., 271 F.Supp. 722 (N. D.Cal.1967), order modified 412 F.2d 830 (9th Cir. 1969).

6. Compare Siegel v. Chicken Delight, Inc., 271 F.Supp. 722 (N.D.Cal.1967), order modified 412 F.2d 830 (9th Cir. 1969) and West Virginia v. Chas. Pfizer & Co., 440 F.2d 1079 (2d Cir.) cert. denied 404 U.S. 871, 92 S.Ct. 81, 30 L. Ed.2d 115 (1971), with Chicago v. General Motors Corp., No. 520 ATRR A–1 (N.D.Ill., June 25, 1971).

7. E.g., Green v. Wolf Corp., 406 F.2d 291 (2d Cir. 1968); Berland v. Mack, 48 F.R.D. 121 (S.D.N.Y.1969); Herbst v. Able, 47 F.R.D. 11 (1969), order modified 49 F.R.D. 286 (S.D.N.Y.1970); Siegel v. Chicken Delight, 271 F.Supp. 722 (N.D.Cal.1967), order modified 412 F.2d 830 (9th Cir. 1969).

8. Eisen v. Carlisle & Jacquelin, 479 F. 2d 1005 (2d Cir. 1973), vacated and class action dismissed on other grounds 417 U.S. 156, 94 S.Ct. 2140, 40 L.Ed.2d 732 (1974); Hackett v. General Host Corp., 455 F.2d 618 (3d Cir.), cert. denied 407 U.S. 925, 92 S.Ct.

significant case is Eisen v. Carlisle & Jacquelin.[9] The plaintiff sought damages for himself and as representative of all buyers and sellers of in odd lot transactions on the New York Stock Exchange, alleging that defendants had conspired to monopolize trading in odd lots and had fixed commissions at excessive levels. The district court had initially granted a motion to dismiss, holding that Eisen, whose individual interest was miniscule, could not adequately represent the class, but the court of appeals had reversed and remanded.[10] On remand, the district court concluded that all requirements of the rule were met.[11] The major issue—which under the rule, bears upon whether the class action is superior to other possible modes of litigation—was whether the suit was manageable as a class action. There were about 6 million members of the plaintiff class. About 2 million could be identified from available records. Although in the aggregate damages would run in the neighborhood of $60 million, the damages of individual class members, though varying considerably, would often be miniscule, and typically would be small, averaging about $10 per class member. The problem, then, was whether it would be feasible to give an adequate notice and whether, assuming liability were established, the administrative costs of proving damages would not exceed the amounts which might be recovered.

The district court dealt with both problems in innovative ways. It held that the aggregate damages of all class members could be proved by the class representative. The defendant could then be ordered to pay these damages into a fund. A claim procedure could be worked out to enable individual class members to collect from the fund, but if, as was to be expected, relatively few individual claims were processed, the balance of the fund could be expended in a manner tending to benefit the class generally, as for example by reducing future commission rates. This "fluid recovery," though not satisfying individual claimants in a precise one-to-one manner (and doubly benefitting claimants who did file and collect individual damages and who thereafter continued to trade) would give every individual claimant an opportunity to recover what was due, would advance interests of class members generally, and would serve the deterrent function which the treble damage action is intended to perform. The district court also devised a novel method of notice to meet the minimum requirements of due process, which it held was all that was required by the "best notice practicable" standard which is set forth in the rule. It directed that individual notice be mailed to the 2,000 or so class

2460, 32 L.Ed.2d 812 (1972), Reinsch v. New York Stock Exch., 52 F.R.D. 561 (S.D.N.Y.1971). See also Ungar v. Dunkin' Donuts of Am., Inc., 531 F.2d 1211 (3d Cir. 1976) holding that because "coercion" of each individual buyer must be shown in a tying case, a franchisee class is unmanageable.

9. 479 F.2d 1005 (2d Cir. 1973), vacated and class action dismissed on other grounds 417 U.S. 156, 94 S.Ct. 2140, 40 L.Ed.2d 732 (1974).

10. 391 F.2d 555 (2d Cir. 1968).

11. 52 F.R.D. 253 (S.D.N.Y.1971).

members who had ten or more transactions during the four year damage period covered by the action, that individual notice be mailed to 5,000 others chosen at random from the 2 million readily identifiable class members, that individual notice be sent to various financial institutions, and that all other class members be given notice by publication. Before deciding how the cost of notice should be assigned, the district court conducted a preliminary hearing on the merits, much like that which a court of equity might hold before issuing a preliminary injunction. On the basis of that hearing it concluded that plaintiff was likely to prevail on the merits and ruled that defendants should bear ninety percent of the cost of notice, its expenditures for this purpose to be credited against any recovery.

The innovative trial court decision, applauded in some quarters [12] and condemned in others,[13] did not fair well on appeal. Sitting en banc the Court of Appeals for the Second Circuit held that the fluid recovery concept violated both Rule 23 and due process, that the notice procedure fashioned below did not meet the requirements of the rule, that the preliminary hearing to allocate notice costs was not authorized by the rule, and that the case was unmanageable as a class action.[14] The Supreme Court vacated that decision but dismissed the class action upon closely related grounds.[15] It held that the rule required individual notice to all members of the class who could be identified through reasonable effort, not just to a sample of these, regardless of whether the cost of this notice would make the action impracticable; it also held that the cost of notice had to be borne by the plaintiff.

There is something to be said for the ultimate result in *Eisen*. The decision will tend to reduce federal court congestion by discouraging or foreclosing the possibility for many actions which cannot be brought at all, if they cannot be brought as class actions. The result will also reduce to some extent the number of actions which have specific and discernible financial advantage primarily to the attorneys who bring them. But these gains have been purchased at a high cost. Rule 23 has been sapped of its utility for challenging antitrust violations in which defendants, through monopoly or cartelization, impose higher prices that work serious economic dislocation in the aggregate but do relatively trivial damage to individual purchasers. The consumer class action for damages is simply not feasible any longer.

---

12. E.g., Kohn & Kaplan, The Antitrust Class Suit: A Manageable Instrument for Social Justice, 41 Antitrust L.J. 292 (1972); Note, Managing the Large Class Action: Eisen v. Carlisle & Jacquelin, 87 Harv.L.Rev. 426 (1973).

13. E.g., Handler, The Shift from Substance to Procedural Innovations in Antitrust Suits—The Twenty-Third Annual Antitrust Review, 71 Colum. L.Rev. 1, 5–12 (1971).

14. 479 F.2d 1005 (2d Cir. 1973).

15. 417 U.S. 156, 94 S.Ct. 2140, 40 L.Ed.2d 732 (1974).

There is, of course, the possibility of legislative reform. Despite the court of appeals' contrary conclusion, there is no overriding constitutional inhibition to actions of the kind involved in *Eisen*. Although an in personam judgment ordinarily cannot bind one who has not been served with notice of the action,[16] the class action is a long-established exception.[17] Adequate representation by one or more class members of the interests of absent members may fulfill the due process requirements ordinarily met by notice. Although due process may require that representation by one with similar interests be supplemented by some type of notice to absent members where the interests of the representative and those of all class members are not irreducibly identical, there is no constitutional prerequisite that the supplemental notice be by formal service of process or, indeed, in any other specified way. The minimum constitutional requirement is that the action be fair to all class members, taking into account all of the interests involved, including, surely, both the interest shared by all class members with small claims that a way be found to give them *some* redress, and the interest of the public in developing effective private enforcement media to supplement public enforcement of antitrust and other laws which might be involved in class actions. It is clear enough, therefore, that Congress by appropriate legislation could authorize consumer class actions like that in *Eisen*.

One of the interesting sidelights associated with the rise and fall of the consumer class action was the confusion and emotion displayed about the appropriate role of the lawyer and about the values which should guide a lawyer's conduct. There are within the bar two predominant cultures. The one, well represented on the federal bench (especially at the appellate levels) and in the large law firms likely to be representing antitrust defendants in class actions, constitutes a sort of legal establishment. Its members are likely to have university educations, to have studied law at one of the eight or ten leading law schools, to have come to journeyman status in a firm with a long and solid tradition. The other culture has a maverick quality. Its members will think of themselves primarily as plaintiff's lawyers. They may have experience in tort, products liability and condemnation cases, as well as in securities fraud and antitrust cases. Most of its members will be in small firms. Many of its members may have had the basic entry qualifications for the legal establishment but were less comfortable with the staid life. Others will never have had a chance for an establishment career. These are typified by the night school lawyer who feels that his success was the product of his own energy, ability, aggressiveness and luck (probably in that order). Lawyers

---

16. Pennoyer v. Neff, 95 U.S. 714, 24 L.Ed. 565 (1877).

17. Compare Hansberry v. Lee, 311 U. S. 32, 61 S.Ct. 115, 85 L.Ed. 22 (1932) with Mullane v. Central Hanover Bank & Trust Co., 339 U.S. 306, 70 S. Ct. 652, 94 L.Ed. 865 (1950). See the discussion in Note, Managing The Large Class Action: Eisen v. Carlisle & Jacquelin, 87 Harv.L.Rev. 427 (1973).

drawn from the establishment culture represent corporate America. Plaintiffs' class action lawyers are drawn in substantial numbers, if not predominantly, from the bar's maverick culture.

Some members of the legal establishment seem to be less aware of their own competitiveness and their own drives than are their maverick brothers. Perhaps they share in a tendency many humans have to despise in others the faults they fear most in themselves. At any event, many establishment lawyers claim to see in the aggressive drive of the plaintiffs' class action lawyer an abandonment of the lawyer's traditional commitment to the welfare of his client; they claim to see instead a commitment to self aggrandizement and fees. To make matters worse, the maverick branch of the trial bar has its own similar misconceptions about the establishment branch. Many plaintiffs' antitrust lawyers see the corporate defense lawyer as an arrogant posturer whose main interest is contriving to complicate litigation and achieve delay in order to enhance his own time charge.

In fact, each of these visions is a burlesque which grossly distorts reality. There are in both branches of the bar lawyers of ability, dignity and conscience. There is, also in each—and, one might suppose, most strongly displayed among the most successful practitioners within each branch—a healthy commitment to self-welfare. But all lawyers struggle with the differences between their own interests and those of their clients and there is absolutely no basis, theoretical or empirical, for supposing that establishment lawyers succeed at this any better than the mavericks. Furthermore, no competent lawyer from either group is likely to see his own long range interest as out of harmony with the interests of the clients he customarily represents. Not only a strong professional tradition, but also self-interest, rationally expressed, will tend to assure both that the defendants' lawyers represent the defendants' interests as effectively as possible, and that the lawyers for the plaintiff class represent the interests of the class as effectively as possible.

To some extent at least, a malevolent stereotype of the plaintiffs' class action lawyer has gained currency. It would be unfortunate if simplistic misapprehensions distorted public policy decisions. The practice of law is, of course, an economic activity, a business as well as a profession. Sound policy development begins with a recognition of this. Able lawyers capable of handling complex litigation effectively will not devote themselves to that activity instead of others unless there are commensurate rewards. The corporate sector is adequately represented by able lawyers. Anyone who would seek to motivate lawyers of equal competence to try to enforce regulatory legislation like the antitrust laws, must find ways to reward that activity adequately. The consumer class action, authorized and regulated by appropriate legislation, could be such a medium.

b. Parens Patriae

Although possessed of a very different historical basis,[18] the *parens patriae* now provides an alternative to the class action, a way in which actions could be brought by a state as the representative of its citizens who are being hurt by antitrust and other violations which have a large aggregate impact but an impact on individuals too small to warrant suit.[19] Again, the Supreme Court had discouraged hope that a basis could be found for such actions without legislation.[20] But the considerable legislative interest made the prospect for legislation to facilitate actions of these kinds possible even though there was no prospect for class action legislation.[21]

§ 250. *In Pari Delicto* and Unclean Hands

The four opinions rendered in Perma Life Mufflers Inc. v. International Parts Corp.[1] indicate that the *in pari delicto* defense to a private antitrust action will be available in exceedingly limited circumstances, if at all. Yet, the case does not rule out the possibility that an antitrust defendant may win a law suit by showing plaintiff's involvement in the violation. The principal opinion in *Perma Life* was written by Justice Black and concurred in by a majority of the Court. It states flatly that even if the conduct of plaintiff is as reprehensible as that of defendant, plaintiff should not be summarily barred, and that "the doctrine of *in pari delicto,* with its complex scope, contents, and effects, is not to be recognized as a defense to an antitrust action."[2] But Justice White's concurring opinion[3] asserts that to recover a plaintiff must show that defendant's wrong caused plaintiff's injury and suggests that if plaintiff's responsibility for the violation is equal to or greater than that of the defendant, plaintiff's case on causation may fail. The separate concurring opinion of Justice Fortas[4] is consistent with the White view. Moreover, the majority opinion itself puts to one side the question whether some concept apart from *in pari delicto* might forestall a plaintiff who was equally

---

18. See the discussion in Georgia v. Pennsylvania R. Co., 324 U.S. 439, 65 S.Ct. 716, 89 L.Ed. 1051 (1945).

19. *Parens patriae* suits are specifically authorized by the Hart-Scott-Rodino Antitrust Improvement Act of 1976, Public Law 94–435 (Sept. 30, 1976). See Appendix D, infra.

20. Hawaii v. Standard Oil Co., 405 U.S. 251, 92 S.Ct. 885, 31 L.Ed.2d 184 (1972).

21. Here, unlike the situation prevailing with respect to class action, a compromise led to the passage, over strong opposition, of the Hart-Scott-Rodino Antitrust Improvement Act of 1976, supra n. 19. It authorizes states, subject to certain restrictions, to bring suits for money damages for Sherman Act violations on behalf of all citizens of the state. See Appendix D, infra.

1. 392 U.S. 134, 88 S.Ct. 1981, 20 L.Ed. 2d 982 (1968).

2. Id. at 140, 88 S.Ct. at 1985, 20 L.Ed. 2d at 991.

3. Id. at 142, 88 S.Ct. at 1986, 20 L.Ed. 2d at 992.

4. Id. at 147, 88 S.Ct. at 1989, 20 L.Ed. 2d at 995.

responsible with defendant for the violation, thus leaving open the possibility of a defense in that circumstance.

Perma Life involved a suit by franchisees against the franchisor challenging vertical restraints to which plaintiffs had assented and from which they presumably had benefited. The case probably typifies the situation in which defendant will seek to avoid liability on the ground that plaintiff participated in the wrong. The opinions properly stressed that the public interest in having antitrust violations brought to light and penalized militates against the availability of an *in pari delicto* defense. The question whether defendant is liable to plaintiff, if the latter is injured in the course of the administration of the scheme, ought to turn on two factors: whether the plaintiff was as much the instigator of the scheme as was defendant, and whether the conduct which plaintiff challenges was taken to retaliate against plaintiff for seeking to withdraw from or abandon the scheme. If plaintiff-dealer cartelized the industry by inducing defendant-manufacturer to impose restrictions on plaintiff and all its competing dealers, it would be anomalous to allow plaintiff, thereafter, to recover damages from defendant for having done as bidden.[5] But there is a public as well as a private interest in having the unlawful arrangement challenged. Therefore, if the defendant-manufacturer (or some other dealer) were the author of the scheme, the fact that plaintiff participates for a time ought not to deprive plaintiff of a cause of action when it withdraws, even though plaintiff should have resisted from the outset. Indeed, if it has plainly withdrawn and started to compete, even a firm which was the initial instigator of the unlawful arrangement ought to be granted a cause of action for any damage done to it by other participants if they take retaliatory action because of the withdrawal. The crucial thing is to assure that notions of fairness inter se do not reduce unduly the likelihood of competitive conditions being restored.

Where plaintiff seeks equitable relief, essentially the same principles should govern; the defense of *in pari delicto* should not be available to foreclose otherwise appropriate relief to a firm which has withdrawn from an unlawful arrangement and which either did not instigate the arrangement or, though it did, is being sanctioned by

---

5. See Columbia Nitrogen Corp. v. Royster Co., 451 F.2d 3 (4th Cir. 1971). South-East Coal Co. v. Consolidation Coal Co., 434 F.2d 767, 784 (6th Cir. 1970), cert. denied 402 U.S. 983, 91 S.Ct. 1662, 29 L.Ed.2d 149 (1971). The bulk of the cases since *Perma Life* are disinclined to deny the theoretical possibility of a defense in extreme circumstances, but are rigorous in their perusal of any claim that conditions for the theoretically possible defense have been met in a particular instance. See, e.g., Semke v. Enid Auto Dealers Ass'n, 456 F.2d 1361 (10th Cir. 1972); Premier Elec. Constr. Co. v. Miller Davis Co., 422 F.2d 1132, 1138–39 (7th Cir.), cert. denied 400 U.S. 828, 91 S.Ct. 56, 27 L. Ed.2d 58 (1970); Skouras Theatres Corp. v. RKO Corp., 58 F.R.D 357 (S. D.N.Y.1973); Skil Corp. v. Black & Decker Mfg. Co., 351 F.Supp. 65 (N.D. Ill.1972).

Pt. D   PRIVATE ENFORCEMENT   785

other participants for seeking to withdraw.[6] The related "unclean hands" defense which might deprive a petitioner of equitable relief because of its own quite different though related wrong has even less place in a private antitrust action.[7]

§ 251. Damages

To be entitled to damages in a private antitrust action, plaintiff must prove that defendant's violation caused an injury to plaintiff's business or property and must establish the basis for a reasonable estimate of the amount of money necessary to compensate for the injury.[1] Proof that injury occurred—proof of the fact of damage, as the process is sometimes called—is usually straightforward. There has been no tendency to lighten plaintiff's burden; the preponderance of evidence rule applies in unqualified form. Proof of an overcharge, an exclusion from a market, a termination or a loss of suppliers or customers are illustrative of the kinds of things that serve to meet the burden. Plaintiff's burden of proof as to the amount of damages has, however, been ameliorated considerably.[2] The court or jury is entitled to make a "just and reasonable estimate" of the damages from "relevant data" which may include the "probable and inferential, as well as direct and positive proof."[3]

In an overcharge case, proof of the amount of the overcharge is sufficient; plaintiff may proceed on the theory that the full amount of the overcharge constitutes an injury to its property, if not to its

---

6. Skil Corp. v. Black & Decker Mfg. Co., 351 F.Supp. 65 (N.D.Ill.1972).

7. See Kiefer-Stewart Co. v. Joseph E. Seagram & Sons, Inc., 340 U.S. 211, 71 S.Ct. 259, 95 L.Ed. 219 (1951); Wilshire Oil Co. v. Riffe, 409 F.2d 1277, 1283 (10th Cir. 1969); American Motor Inns, Inc. v. Holiday Inns, Inc., 365 F.Supp. 1073 (D.N.J.1973); Skil Corp. v. Black & Decker Mfg. Co., 351 F.Supp. 65 (N.D.Ill.1972); Purex Corp., Ltd. v. General Foods Corp., 318 F.Supp. 322 (C.D.Cal.1970). But cf. Ancora Corp. v. Stein, 445 F.2d 431, 434 (5th Cir. 1971) (defense available where the suit before the court is alleged by the defendant to be part of an illegal coercive scheme).

In *Perma Life* the Court stressed "the inappropriateness of invoking broad common law barriers to relief where a private suit serves important public purposes." (392 U.S. at 138, 88 S.Ct. at 1984, 20 L.Ed.2d at 990). That policy applies to defenses like estoppel, as well as to *in pari delicto* and unclean hands. Bernstein v. Universal Pictures, Inc., 517 F.2d 976 (2d Cir. 1975).

1. Bigelow v. RKO Radio Pictures, Inc., 327 U.S. 251, 264, 66 S.Ct. 574, 579–80, 90 L.Ed. 652, 660 (1946); Story Parchment Co. v. Paterson Parchment Paper Co., 282 U.S. 555, 51 S.Ct. 248, 75 L.Ed. 544 (1931); Eastman Kodak Co. v. Southern Photo Materials Co., 273 U.S. 359, 47 S.Ct. 400, 71 L.Ed. 684 (1927). See Anno. 16 ALR Fed. 14.

2. See cases cited in note 1 supra. See also Zenith Radio Corp. v. Hazeltine Research, Inc., 395 U.S. 100, 123, 89 S.Ct. 1562, 1576–77, 23 L.Ed.2d 129, 148 (1969); Continental Ore Co. v. Union Carbide & Carbon Corp., 370 U.S. 690, 700, 82 S.Ct. 1404, 1411, 8 L.Ed.2d 777, 784–85 (1962).

3. Flintkote Co. v. Lysfjord, 246 F.2d 368, 392 (9th Cir.), cert. denied 355 U.S. 835, 78 S.Ct. 54, 2 L.Ed.2d 46 (1957). See also Haverhill Gazette Co. v. Union Leader Corp., 333 F.2d 798 (1st Cir.), cert. denied 379 U.S. 931, 85 S.Ct. 329, 13 L.Ed.2d 343 (1964).

business, and need not trace through the net effect of the overcharge on profits.[4] Of course, if the overcharge results from monopoly or conspiracy, plaintiff must provide a basis for estimating the price that would have prevailed in a competitive market, but in doing this plaintiff is given a wide latitude. Proof of the pre-conspiracy,[5] or post-conspiracy price [6] will normally suffice, although evidence showing other relevant differences between conditions prevailing during the conspiracy period and the non-conspiracy base period may warrant the trier of fact in adjusting the base period price upward or downward to decrease or increase the spread. The essential thing is that the plaintiff develop a rational theory about how the amount of the injury can be measured and introduce the data necessary to make the estimate.[7] Expert testimony will normally be helpful,[8] though it is not essential.[9] Defendant, of course, may put on its own alternative case to show the amount of damage, though defendants that are challenging a case on liability grounds are often loath to do that for strategic reasons, and therefore rely upon a challenge to plaintiff's damage evidence and analysis.

Where the damage theory is not an overcharge, but a loss of net profits, plaintiff must prove from his records the profit or loss actually experienced during the damage period and prove, in addition, a basis for estimating what the (higher) profit or (lower) loss would have been but for the violation. A loss of profit approach would be appropriate if the violation caused an increase in costs, a reduction in revenues, an exclusion from a market, or the destruction of a business. Again, the plaintiff has a wide latitude. Profit during the violation period may be compared with that during an earlier [10] or later [11] base period where no violation was reducing profits. Profits experienced by plaintiff during the damage period may be compared

---

4. Chattanooga Foundry & Pipe Works v. Atlanta, 203 U.S. 390, 396, 27 S.Ct. 65, 66, 51 L.Ed. 241, 244 (1906); Thomsen v. Cayser, 243 U.S. 66, 88, 37 S.Ct. 353, 360, 61 L.Ed. 597, 607 (1917). Cf. Siegel v. Chicken Delight Inc., 448 F.2d 43 (9th Cir. 1971), cert. denied 405 U.S. 955, 92 S.Ct. 1172, 31 L.Ed.2d 232 (1972).

5. Cf. American Crystal Sugar Co. v. Mandeville Island Farms, Inc., 195 F.2d 622, 625–26 (9th Cir. 1952).

6. Wall Prods. Co. v. National Gypsum Co., 357 F.Supp. 832 (N.D.Cal.1973).

7. E.g., Joseph E. Seagram & Sons v. Hawaiian Oke & Liquors, Ltd., 416 F.2d 71 (9th Cir. 1969), cert. denied 396 U.S. 1062, 90 S.Ct. 752, 24 L.Ed.2d 755 (1970); Albrecht v. Herald Co., 452 F.2d 124 (8th Cir. 1971), mandamus denied sub nom. Albrecht v. Matthes, 405 U.S. 1063, 92 S.Ct. 1493, 31 L.Ed.2d 810 (1972). See C. Hills ed., Antitrust Advisor §§ 12.35–12.37 (1971).

8. See, e.g., Twentieth Century-Fox Film Corp. v. Goldwyn, 328 F.2d 190, 213 (9th Cir.), cert. denied 379 U.S. 880, 85 S.Ct. 143, 13 L.Ed.2d 87 (1964).

9. See, e.g., Rangen, Inc. v. Sterling Nelson & Sons, 351 F.2d 851, 856 (9th Cir. 1965), cert. denied 383 U.S. 936, 86 S.Ct. 1067, 15 L.Ed.2d 853 (1966).

10. E.g., American Crystal Sugar Co. v. Mandeville Island Farms, Inc., 195 F.2d 622, 625–26 (9th Cir. 1952).

11. See, e.g., Herman Schwabe, Inc. v. United Shoe Mach. Corp., 297 F.2d 906 (2d Cir. 1962).

with those experienced by some other similar firm (perhaps the defendant, in a horizontal case) operating in the same or a similar market free of the constraining impact of the violation.[12] The essential thing is that the available data be used in rational ways which warrant confidence that the damage figure reached is, in fact, a reasonable if imprecise estimate, rather than a speculative guess.[13]

§ 252. Passing On

The "passing on" issue as it is called, presents the most complex problems in antitrust enforcement. Picture a firm that has been the victim of a conspiratorial or monopolistic overcharge. It sues seeking to recover the amount of the overcharge on the basis of conventional damage doctrine.[1] But defendant asserts that the plaintiff was not injured because plaintiff resold the product, adding on its usual mark up, thus passing on any damage resulting from the overcharge to downstream buyers. Or a mirror image of this issue may be presented if the manufacturer which conspired to increase prices is sued not by a firm buying from it, but by a vertically more remote buyer that claims that the overcharge was passed on to it. The patent fact is that an illegal overcharge at, say, the manufacturing level, may have consequences which radiate to vertical levels much further downstream. Moreover, its consequences at any particular level may not be obvious either in direction or magnitude. Monopolist A sells product x in bulk to firms B which package it and resell to firms C which process it to form product xy which they sell to firms D, which use the xy as an ingredient in product xyz which they sell to firms E. The B firms may absorb all, part, or none of A's overcharge by reducing their mark up on the resale of x. It is conceivable, indeed, that some will act one way and some another. If a B firm passes on all or part of the overcharge it paid to its C level customers, its total sales may be reduced substantially, slightly, or hardly at all, depending upon the elasticity of demand; hence, even though it passes on the entire overcharge its profits may fall as a result of lower output. As the impact of the original overcharge moves further downstream it may become more and more diluted, to the point

---

12. E.g., Elyria-Lorain Broadcasting Co. v. Lorain Journal Co., 358 F.2d 790 (6th Cir. 1966).

13. The particular manner in which lost profits are estimated should, of course, be adjusted to the particulars of the injury sustained. In cases involving the destruction of plaintiff's business, an alternative theory would be to estimate the capital value of the business as a going concern and to compare this with the salvage value of the assets. Indeed, damage to good will can be an element even though a business is not wholly destroyed, though when good will and lost profit elements are both estimated care must be used to avoid double recovery. See Hobart Bros. Co. v. Malcolm T. Gilliland, Inc., 471 F.2d 894 (5th Cir.), cert. denied 412 U.S. 923, 93 S.Ct. 2736, 37 L.Ed.2d 150 (1973).

1. E.g., Chattanooga Foundry & Pipe Works v. Atlanta, 203 U.S. 390, 27 S. Ct. 65, 51 L.Ed. 241 (1917). See § 251 supra.

where any effect it may have will be exceedingly difficult to estimate and may be greatly diminished.²

The passing on concept has a considerable history. The earliest cases affirmed the right of the immediate victim of an overcharge to recover against the violator, despite claims that the plaintiff passed the overcharge on. In Chattanooga Foundry and Pipe Works v. Atlanta ³ the city, a public utility engaged in selling and distributing water, had paid overcharges on pipe for its water distribution system. The Court, in an opinion by Justice Holmes, rejected a contention that the city was not injured because the overcharge was built into the rate base upon which the city computed charges for water. As the rather simplistic opinion expressed the matter, the city was injured in its property by being obliged to pay more, even if one might on further analysis conclude that it was ultimately not injured in its business. Later, Justice Holmes returned to this theme and elaborated upon it. In Southern Pacific Co. v. Darnell-Taenzer Lumber Co.⁴, he insisted that the necessary task of the law is simplification of what is inevitably complex, given the myriad interrelationships of a dynamic economy. As he put it, the law seldom goes "beyond the first step." ⁵ It does not hold the defendant liable for all the remote radiations of its wrong because that is too complex a business for a court to undertake with skill and social profit. As a corollary, the law does hold the defendant when "proximately the plaintiff has suffered a loss," ⁶ although the Court when dealing with a regulated industry once looked in quite a different manner upon the problem.⁷ At all events courts have not been reluctant to grant relief to the first purchaser where, given the context, it is reasonable to conclude that the benefit of the award will be passed on, if the overcharge earlier had been.⁸ But in seeming conflict, and despite the clear position stated by the Holmes opinions discussed above, lower federal courts in the "oil jobber" or "middleman" cases were not hesitant to deny re-

---

2. Passing on problems are sometimes couched in terms of standing (See § 247 supra), sometimes in terms of causation (See § 247 supra), sometimes in terms of damage measurement (See § 251 supra). The complexity of the concept and its relevance in various types of situations can, of course, be affected by the theoretical terms in which it is conceived. In this book it is discussed separately to emphasize the importance of deciding with care precisely how the defense should be conceived.

3. 203 U.S 390, 27 S.Ct. 65, 51 L.Ed. 241 (1917).

4. 245 U.S. 531, 38 S.Ct. 186, 62 L.Ed. 451 (1918).

5. Id. at 533, 38 S.Ct. at 186, 62 L.Ed. at 455.

6. Id. at 533–34, 38 S.Ct. at 186, 62 L. Ed. at 455.

7. See Keogh v. Chicago & Northwestern Ry. Co., 260 U.S. 156, 43 S.Ct. 47, 67 L.Ed. 183 (1922) (shipper cannot recover from carrier on proof of conspiratorially established rate).

8. E.g., Public Utility Dist. No. 1 v. General Elec. Co., 230 F.Supp. 744 (W.D.Wash.1964) (first purchaser a regulated public utility). See also Atlantic City Elec. Co. v. General Elec. Co., 226 F.Supp. 59, 61–62 (S.D.N.Y.), appeal denied per curiam 337 F.2d 844 (2d Cir. 1964); Ohio Valley Elec.

covery for an overcharge to a first purchaser when the evidence that the overcharge was passed on was convincing.[9]

With that prelude, let us turn to Hanover Shoe, Inc. v. United Shoe Machinery Corp.[10] The case was a treble damage action by a shoe manufacturer against a manufacturer of machinery used in making shoes. Hanover alleged that United's policy of leasing United's machines and refusing to sell them, a policy already held to constitute monopolization under Section 2, had increased the cost of plaintiff's manufacturing operations; Hanover sought damages measured by the difference in cost to it. United pressed the claim that Hanover was not injured because Hanover passed these costs on to buyers in the form of higher prices for shoes. This defense was rejected by the lower courts and the Supreme Court granted certiorari.

In also rejecting the passing on defense, the Supreme Court relied on the authority of *Chattanooga Foundry* and like cases, but it gave new content to those precedents; it accepted but altered the emphasis of the view earlier announced by Justice Holmes.[11] It spoke of the grave difficulty a defendant would have in showing that a proximate victim of an overcharge was not injured. Even if a buyer prices for resale simply by marking up the purchase price, the higher price at which it must resell may reduce its volume of sales, and hence its profit. The extent to which sales will fall with such an increase depends, of course, on the elasticity of the demand which the reseller faces. Inquiry into all of these matters can be extremely complex. The Court indicated that except perhaps in those special situations where the first purchaser makes its resales on cost plus contracts, where both the fact of the sale and the profit to plaintiff are independent of the fact and amount of defendant's unlawful overcharge, a monopolist or conspirator ought not to be able to avoid responsibility for its offense on the ground that the particular plaintiff motivated to sue had recouped some of its losses by making sales to others.[12] The rule which holds the monopolist or conspirator liable to the first purchaser for the full amount of the overcharge is a workable rule. When the wrongdoer is sued only by the first purchaser the rule works no grave injustice, though it may compensate the plaintiff by more than

---

Corp. v. General Elec. Co., 244 F. Supp. 914, 950 (S.D.N.Y.1965).

9. E.g., Clark Oil Co. v. Phillips Petroleum Co., 148 F.2d 580 (8th Cir.), cert. denied 326 U.S. 734, 66 S.Ct. 42, 90 L. Ed. 437 (1945); Northwestern Oil Co. v. Socony-Vacuum Oil Co., 138 F.2d 967 (7th Cir. 1943), cert. denied 321 U.S. 792, 64 S.Ct. 790, 88 L.Ed. 1081 (1944); Twin Ports Oil Co. v. Pure Oil Co., 119 F.2d 747 (8th Cir.), cert. denied 314 U.S. 644, 62 S.Ct. 84, 86 L. Ed. 516 (1941).

10. 392 U.S. 481, 88 S.Ct. 2224, 20 L. Ed.2d 1231 (1968).

11. Id. at 491–93, 88 S.Ct. at 2230–31, 20 L.Ed.2d at 1241.

12. Id. at 494, 88 S.Ct. at 2232, 20 L. Ed.2d at 1241–42. See, as applications of this principle, Yoder Bros., Inc. v. Calif.-Fla. Plant Corp., 1976–2 CCH Trade Cas. ¶ 61,047 (5th Cir. 1976); Obron v. Union Camp Corp., 477 F.2d 542 (6th Cir. 1973).

his actual loss. In doing that, it merely takes a windfall from the wrongdoer and lodges it with one of the victims.

Second, the Court gave emphasis to an overriding social policy in addition to that of making the legal rules manageable for the courts which must enforce them: the need to make the treble damage remedy an effective deterrent to antitrust violations. The Court stressed that in the context before it, shoe manufacturers which purchased machinery from United were the most likely—perhaps the only likely—plaintiffs; the possibility of a suit by purchasers of shoes to which the overcharge was allegedly passed on seemed extremely remote. Giving voice to a value which has also appeared in other contexts,[13] the Court insisted that in private antitrust litigation all rules subsidiary to those used to determine basic questions of liability should be fashioned in ways which encourage suits by private firms which are victims of a violation.[14] Only thus can the congressional goal that private actions serve the important social function of inhibiting and redressing violations be achieved.

The *Hanover Shoe* principle is, then, a highly pragmatic one. It has two goals in view. One is simplifying the proof of damages and protecting the courts from an unmanageable morass of complexity. The other is easing the course of a likely plaintiff with a significant interest in challenging a violation. Although the Court did not mention it, there is another concern. Defendant must be protected from excessive risk of "double liability trebled,"[15] should the defendant be forced to account to plaintiffs at two or more levels of distribution. Application of *Hanover Shoe* ought, therefore, to give due weight to each of these concerns as well as to any other values which may be salient in a particular setting. As yet, lower courts have not been particularly successful in juggling these values. Cases allowing the passing on defense against a first purchaser where the plaintiff resells on "cost plus" or some arrangement close to that seem consistent enough with the standards laid down by the Court.[16] But some lower courts have read *Hanover Shoe* as denying a cause of action to downstream purchasers prepared to prove that they were injured, unless they can bring themselves within the specific "cost plus" exception spelled out in *Hanover Shoe* as a basis for allowing a defense

---

13. E.g., Perma Life Mufflers, Inc. v. International Parts Corp., 392 U.S. 134, 88 S.Ct. 1981, 20 L.Ed.2d 982 (1968) (*in pari delicto* defense rejected because it would threaten effectiveness of private action as an enforcement mechanism); Minnesota Mining & Mfg. Co. v. New Jersey Wood Finishing Co., 381 U.S. 311, 85 S.Ct. 1473, 14 L.Ed.2d 405 (1965) (doubt about whether FTC proceeding tolls statute of limitations resolved in way maximizing likelihood that treble damage actions will be effective enforcement weapon); Leh v. General Petroleum Corp., 382 U.S. 54, 86 S.Ct. 203, 15 L.Ed.2d 134 (1965).

14. 392 U.S. 481, 494, 88 S.Ct. 2224, 2232, 20 L.Ed.2d 1231, 1241–1242 (1968).

15. See City & County of Denver v. American Oil Co., 53 F.R.D. 620, 631 (D.Colo.1971).

16. E.g., Obron v. Union Camp Corp., 355 F.Supp. 902, 906 (E.D.Mich.1972) aff'd per curiam 477 F.2d 542 (6th Cir. 1973).

against a suit by the first purchaser.[17] This seems a perversion of the *Hanover Shoe* principle. The case is, after all, explicitly result oriented. Where remote purchasers are before the court, the basic policy objectives of *Hanover Shoe* are met by allowing those purchasers an opportunity to prove their case.[18] Potential problems of double recovery can be dealt with by joinder, consolidation and other devices. Those who would read *Hanover Shoe* as foreclosing suit by remote purchasers ought to carry the burden of showing that in the specific instance double recovery will occur if defendant is not protected, and that there is no way less onerous to some of the injured parties by which defendant can be protected.

Another point to be made is that passing on ought not to be treated as a problem of standing, or proximate cause,[19] except perhaps at the most extreme outer reaches of a causal chain.[20] Take the case where a product runs down a chain of distribution, being marked up and resold first by a manufacturer, then by a distributor, then by a wholesaler, then by a retail dealer. If the manufacturer imposes an illegal overcharge, the distributor, wholesaler, retailer and consumer may all suffer, or any one or more of them may. Each of them is plainly within the target area, or the area of intended protection emanating from the rule making the overcharge unlawful. It may be that some of them are not hurt at all, or are hurt only to the extent that the mark up they have imposed and passed on has reduced total sales. Those at one distribution stage may be able to prove a case with greater ease than those at another; those at one stage may be more likely plaintiffs than those at another; on one suit or another means of measuring damages may have to be selected with an eye to reducing risks of double recovery. But to read *Hanover Shoe* or any

---

17. E.g., Mangano v. Am. Radiator & Standard Sanitary Corp., 438 F.2d 1187 (3d Cir. 1971).

18. See, e.g., Illinois v. Ampress Brick Co., Inc., 1976–1 CCH Trade Cas. ¶ 60,939 (7th Cir. 1976); In re Liquid Asphalt Cases, 487 F.2d 191 (9th Cir. 1973), cert. denied sub nom. Standard Oil Co. v. Alaska, 415 U.S. 919, 94 S.Ct. 1419, 39 L.Ed.2d 474 (1974); Armco Steel Corp. v. North Dakota, 376 F.2d 206 (8th Cir. 1967); West Virginia v. Chas. Pfizer & Co., 440 F.2d 1079 (2d Cir.), cert. denied 404 U.S. 871, 92 S.Ct. 81, 30 L.Ed.2d 115 (1971); In re Master Key Litigation, 1973 CCH Trade Cas. ¶ 74,680 (D.Conn.); Boshes v. General Motors Corp., 1973 CCH Trade Cas. ¶ 74,483 (N.D.Ill.); In re Ampicillin Antitrust Litigation, 55 F.R.D. 269 (D.D.C.1972); In re Antibiotic Antitrust Actions, 333 F.Supp. 310 (S.D.N.Y.1971).

19. See Pollock, Standing to Sue, Remoteness of Injury, and the Passing-On Doctrine, 32 Antitrust L.J. 5 (1966).

20. For example, a standing or proximate cause defense would have merit where the plaintiff, purchasing a house from a contractor, alleges that a manufacturer of one element of the utility system which has, since being sold by the manufacturer, passed through several hands and been incorporated at each stage into larger units, has illegally overcharged to the injury of plaintiff. In such a situation the plaintiff's claim is too trivial and remote to warrant burdening the court. Compare Philadelphia Housing Authority v. American Radiator & Standard Sanitary Corp., 50 F.R.D. 13 (E.D.Pa.1970), aff'd per curiam sub nom. Mangano v. American Radiator & Standard Sanitary Corp., 438 F.2d 1187 (3d Cir. 1971).

of the earlier cases as implying that any plaintiff in such a chain can be closed out at the threshold on the ground that it lacks standing is simply too extreme a response.

The approach suggested here calls for a court to work out a balanced response to passing on issues in the particular context before it. This approach leaves some things uncertain which might be clarified by more mechanical rules. But the uncertainties are not matters of economic fact likely to plunge a court into endless bodies of economic and financial data. They are uncertainties of the order that inevitably appear whenever a matter is committed to a discriminating judgment. Certainty and predictability are values in the law, particularly with respect to issues about whether or not a particular course of conduct is lawful. But there are also places in which uncertainty has its uses, and this may well be one of them. A fully satisfactory resolution of a case where liability is conceded or capable of being readily established and where there are several steps in a distribution chain at which an overcharge has probably had an effect might result in the defendant having to pay three times the amount of the overcharge, and would divide that sum among claimants at each level in proportion to the impact upon them.[21] The most efficient way to reach or to approximate that result may be to avoid precisely articulated rules about the passing on issues, to permit courts the leeway to develop solutions which seem sensible and responsive to all of the relevant values in the particular situations before them, and to allow settlement negotiations to take their natural course in a context of some uncertainty.[22]

§ 253. Attorney's Fees

Section 4 of the Clayton Act requires the award to the successful treble damage plaintiff of a reasonable attorney's fee.[1] Because Section 16[2] originally contained no similar provision, a federal court could not award attorney's fees to a successful plaintiff in a suit for injunctive relief until Section 16 was amended to so authorize.[3] Before that amendment, fees could be awarded only if there was a substantial financial benefit to a class which could be regarded, meta-

21. Even this resolution ignores, of course, the possibility that resellers at one or more stages may suffer additional damage as a result of reduced sales.

22. E.g., West Virginia v. Chas. Pfizer & Co., 440 F.2d 1079 (2d Cir.), cert. denied 404 U.S. 871, 92 S.Ct. 81, 30 L.Ed.2d 115 (1971). Cf. In re Gypsum Cases, 386 F.Supp. 959, 962–966 (N.D.Cal.1974).

1. 15 U.S.C.A. § 15 (1973).

2. 15 U.S.C.A. § 26 (1973).

3. In recent years a number of lower federal courts had regarded it as established "that one party may be ordered to pay the legal fees of another who has acted as a 'private attorney general'." Incarcerated Men of Allen County Jail v. Fair, 507 F.2d 281, 284 (6th Cir. 1974) (collecting numerous cases). The Supreme Court, however, has flatly rejected this view. Although the Court has tended to construe statutes liberally in order to

phorically, as a fund produced by the attorney's efforts on behalf of the class.[4]

A fee hearing to fix the fees is held after the main trial. The plaintiff must prove the nature of the legal services rendered and their value. This is often done by affidavits from the successful attorneys stating in some detail the nature of the services, the time spent, and expressing opinions as to the value of the services. Although all of the conventional criteria indicative of the value of legal services are said to govern [5] and though some courts have stressed factors like the amount recovered [6] and the public benefit resulting from the action,[7] courts in several cases have stressed particularly the time spent by counsel.[8] With increasing frequency trial courts have been requiring that detailed attorneys' time diaries be presented

---

facilitate "private attorney general" fee awards (e.g. Bradley v. School Board, 416 U.S. 696, 94 S.Ct. 2006, 40 L.Ed.2d 476 (1974)), the Court recently held that when there is no statutory basis, the Court cannot sanction so far reaching an exception to the general American rule that each party pays its own attorneys' fees. Alyeska Pipeline Co. v. Wilderness Society, 421 U.S. 240, 95 S.Ct. 1612, 44 L.Ed.2d 141 (1975). This result is legislatively overruled in the Hart-Scott-Rodino Antitrust Improvement Act of 1976, Public Law 94-435 (Sept. 30, 1976), which amends Section 16 of Clayton. See Appendix D, infra.

4. See, for example, the second court of appeals opinion in Eisen v. Carlisle & Jacquelin, 479 F.2d 1005, (2d Cir. 1973), vacated and class action dismissed on other grounds 417 U.S. 156, 94 S.Ct. 2140, 40 L.Ed.2d 732 (1974). Compare Sprague v. Ticonic Nat'l Bank, 307 U.S. 161, 164–67, 59 S.Ct. 777, 778–80, 83 L.Ed. 1184, 1185–87 (1939); Mills v. Electric Auto-Lite Co., 396 U.S. 375, 90 S.Ct. 616, 24 L. Ed.2d 593 (1970). Dawson, Lawyers and Involuntary Clients in Public Interest Litigation, 88 Harv.L.Rev. 849 (1975) is a knowledgeable discussion putting recent developments into perspective.

5. Factors often mentioned include time and labor spent, standing of counsel and of opposing counsel, magnitude and complexity of the litigation, scope of responsibility undertaken, the result, rates in the community for comparable work. See, e.g., Farmington Dowel Prods. Co. v. Forster Mfg. Co., 421 F.2d 61 (1st Cir. 1969); Twentieth Century Fox Film Corp. v. Goldwyn, 328 F.2d 190 (9th Cir.), cert. denied 379 U.S. 880, 85 S. Ct. 143, 13 L.Ed.2d 87 (1964); Hanover Shoe, Inc. v. United Shoe Mach. Corp., 245 F.Supp. 258 (M.D.Penn. 1965), vacated on other grounds 377 F.2d 776 (3d Cir. 1967), aff'd in part & rev'd in part on other grounds 392 U. S. 481, 88 S.Ct. 2224, 20 L.Ed.2d 1231 (1968); Bal Theatre Corp. v. Paramount Film Distrib. Corp., 206 F. Supp. 708, 716 (N.D.Cal.1962); Noerr Motor Freight Inc. v. Eastern Railroad Presidents Conference, 166 F. Supp. 163 (E.D.Pa.1958), aff'd 273 F.2d 218 (3d Cir. 1959), rev'd on other grounds 365 U.S. 127, 81 S.Ct. 523, 5 L.Ed.2d 464 (1961); Anno. 21 A.L.R. Fed. 750 (1974).

6. E.g., Union Carbide & Carbon Corp. v. Nisley, 300 F.2d 561, (10th Cir. 1961), cert. dismissed 371 U.S. 801, 83 S.Ct. 13, 9 L.Ed.2d 46 (1962); Union Leader Corp. v. Newspapers of New England, Inc., 218 F.Supp. 490 (D. Mass.1963), set aside on other grounds sub. nom. Haverhill Gazette Co. v. Union Leader Corp., 333 F.2d 798 (1st Cir.), motion to recall mandate denied 333 F.2d 808, cert. denied 379 U.S. 931, 85 S.Ct. 329, 13 L.Ed.2d 343 (1964).

7. E.g., Vanderveld v. Put & Call Brokers & Dealers Ass'n, 344 F.Supp. 157 (S.D.N.Y.1972).

8. E.g., Courtesy Chevrolet, Inc. v. Tennessee Walking Horse Breeders' & Ex-

in evidence, and that the attorneys testify as to their accuracy, subject to cross-examination and interrogation by the court.[8.5]

Some courts have indicated a readiness to segregate out time devoted to parts of plaintiff's case which were not successful or which was unnecessarily spent [9] or, where several attorneys are involved, to discount for duplicative effort.[10] Courts obviously should require that a careful and scrupulous record be made showing the nature of the work done, the attorneys by whom it was done, and the time expended. But practical reasonableness should be used in critically evaluating claims that particular expenditures of time were unnecessary or repetitive. In the first place, time should not be segregated between successful and unsuccessful antitrust counts, with the time devoted to the unsuccessful ones being ignored; if all of the counts arose out of the same industrial setting and the same sequence of market conduct, any reasonable steps taken by the plaintiff's attorneys to process the suit to its ultimate successful conclusion ought to figure in the fee computation.[11] As to whether particular activities were reasonable or repetitive, a similarly pragmatic approach should govern. The test ought to be whether the activity later challenged seemed at the time it was engaged in by an attorney in the midst of the litigation to be a prudent step to advance his client's interests in the litigation. Only if a reasonable, prudent attorney would at the time have identified it as unnecessary or repetitive, ought it to be discounted.

No contingent element is involved in an award based primarily on time expended and a time rate commensurate with the attorney's

---

hibitors' Ass'n, 393 F.2d 75 (9th Cir.), cert. denied 393 U.S. 938, 89 S.Ct. 301, 21 L.Ed.2d 274 (1968); Trans World Airlines, Inc. v. Hughes, 312 F.Supp. 478 (S.D.N.Y.1970), mod. on other grounds 449 F.2d 51 (2d Cir. 1971), rev'd on other grounds 409 U.S. 363, 93 S.Ct. 647, 34 L.Ed.2d 577 (1973); See also Perkins v. Standard Oil Co., 474 F.2d 549 (9th Cir. 1973), cert. denied 412 U.S. 940, 93 S.Ct. 2778, 37 L. Ed.2d 400 (1973), amended on other grounds 487 F.2d 672 (9th Cir. 1973). See Comment, Attorneys' Fees in Individual and Class Action Antitrust Litigation, 60 Calif.L.Rev. 1056 (1972).

8.5 E.g. Lindy Bros. Builders, Inc. v. Am. Radiator & Standard Sanitary Corp., 1976-2 CCH Trade Cas. ¶ 61,039 (3d Cir., July 2, 1976); In re Meade Land & Development Co., 527 F.2d 280 (3d Cir. 1975).

9. E.g., Union Leader Corp. v. Newspapers of New England, Inc., 218 F. Supp. 490 (D.Mass.1963), set aside on other grounds sub nom. Haverhill Gazette Co. v. Union Leader Corp., 333 F.2d 798 (1st Cir.), motion to recall mandate denied 333 F.2d 808, cert. denied 379 U.S. 931, 85 S.Ct. 329, 13 L. Ed.2d 343 (1964); Bergjans Farm Dairy Co. v. Sanitary Milk Producers, 241 F.Supp. 476 (D.Md.1962) aff'd 368 F.2d 679 (8th Cir. 1966).

10. See, e.g., Perkins v. Standard Oil Co., 474 F.2d 549 (9th Cir. 1973), cert. denied 412 U.S. 940, 93 S.Ct. 2778, 37 L.Ed.2d 400, amended on other grounds 487 F.2d 672 (9th Cir. 1973); Vandervelde v. Put & Call Brokers & Dealers Ass'n, 344 F.Supp. 157 (S.D. N.Y.1972); Bowl America, Inc. v. Fair Lanes, Inc., 299 F.Supp. 1080 (D.Md. 1969).

11. See, e.g., Trans World Airlines, Inc. v. Hughes, 312 F.Supp. 478 (S.D.N.Y. 1970), modified on other grounds 449 F.2d 51 (2d Cir. 1971), reversed on other grounds 409 U.S. 363, 93 S.Ct. 647, 34 L.Ed.2d 577 (1973).

skill and experience. In non-class actions, where the attorneys proceeding on a contingent basis can arrange by contract with the client for additional compensation contingent upon success, the conventional time-rate approach to fee setting may be satisfactory, at least if used with discretion and adjusted as needed to reflect other factors, such as the difficulty of the case and the quality of counsel, which may be salient in a particular case. One of the problems with the principle which identifies contingency factors as inappropriate is that courts tend to take results into account to reduce fees below time rates, even though not to increase them above time rates. A court unwilling to award *more than* a conventional compensation for time, despite great success, ought to be ready to award a sum *equal to* conventional compensation for time, even though success is modest or limited, so long as the time spent was not clearly disproportionate to the potential benefits to the plaintiff inherent in the litigation.[12]

In class actions, the attorneys' compensation is of necessity largely upon a contingent basis; however, it is not possible to contract with absent class members for contingent compensation. While the court should award adequate contingent compensation to the attorneys in a successful class action, it would be inappropriate to pass the additional cost of the contingent element on to the defendants. The court ought to compute the "reasonable attorney's fee" to be paid by the defendant under Section 4 just as it would in any treble damage case, taking into account relevant conventional factors. Then, it should award an additional sum to appropriately compensate for the contingency, which should be paid out of the fund recovered for the class.[13] The basis for that additional award is not the provision in Section 4 for attorneys' fees, but the established doctrine of "salvage," on the basis of which fees are awarded out of the fund obtained for the class even on claims to which no attorney's fee statute applies.[14]

In some recent class actions a hostile tone can be detected in judicial discussion of fees. Obviously a court, as well as defendant's attorneys, ought to be alert to ferret out overreaching. But a lack of

---

12. See, e. g., Advance Business Sys. & Supply Co. v. SCM Corp., 415 F.2d 55 (4th Cir. 1969), cert. denied 397 U.S. 920, 90 S.Ct. 928, 25 L.Ed.2d 101 (1970).

13. See Attorneys' Fees in Individual and Class Action Antitrust Litigation, 60 Calif.L.Rev. 1656 (1972) and cases therein cited. See also, In re Gypsum Cases, 386 F.Supp. 959 (M.D.Cal.1974) (where the court completed a thorough and seemingly fair evaluation of the contributions of numerous attorneys to a complex class action), and Merola v. Atlantic Richfield Co., 515 F.2d 165 (3d Cir. 1975) (where the court of appeals insisted that the district court recognize and compensate not only for time, but also take account of the contingent nature of class action litigation and the quality of the work performed in complex litigation). Accord, Lindy Bros. Builders, Inc. v. Am. Radiator & Standard Sanitary Corp., note 8.5 supra.

14. See Mills v. Electric Auto-lite Co., 396 U.S. 375, 90 S.Ct. 616, 24 L.Ed.2d 593 (1970); Bakery & Confectionary Workers Internat'l Union v. Ratner, 118 U.S.App.D.C. 269, 335 F.2d 691 (1964). See Anno., 38 ALR 3d 1384 (1971).

candor or basic integrity on the part of the attorney is not lightly to be assumed, and, given the "two cultures" which exist side by side at the bar, a trial judge may find it necessary at times to avoid converting his own negative attitudes toward class actions into a conclusion that greed prevails where an objective assessment would discover nothing worse than an abundance of zeal and tenacity.

Fees may also be awarded for appellate proceedings.[15] Given the statutory goal, they should be awarded when the appellate work contributes substantially to the plaintiff's success in the litigation. Once it is recognized that Section 4 authorizes such awards, it is difficult to see any convincing theoretical or policy reason for the prevailing view that such awards are discretionary and should not be routinely made.

While Section 4 makes no provision for compensation to attorneys for an unsuccessful plaintiff,[16] a fee may be awarded under corporate law principles in the case of an unsuccessful minority stockholder's derivative action if it can be shown that the suit, though not resulting in a judgment in favor of the corporation, materially benefited the corporation.[17] It has been widely supposed that awards are not appropriate in proceedings where an injunction is obtained, but only in damage actions, since Section 4 of Clayton provides specifically for attorneys fees and Section 16 does not.[18] Recent cases, however, suggest grounds upon which awards might also be made in proceedings where the successful attorney obtains injunctive relief which has significant public advantage.[19]

15. Perkins v. Standard Oil Co., 399 U.S. 222, 90 S.Ct. 1989, 26 L.Ed.2d 534 (1970); Farmington Dowel Prods. Co. v. Forster Mfg. Co., 421 F.2d 61 (1st Cir. 1969); Perkins v. Standard Oil Co., 322 F.Supp. 375 (1971), modified on other grounds 474 F.2d 549 (9th Cir. 1973), cert. denied 412 U.S. 940, 93 S.Ct. 2778, 37 L.Ed.2d 400 (1973), amended on other grounds 487 F.2d 672 (9th Cir. 1973). It would seem that the simplest procedure would be for the appellate court to make the award. See, e.g. Twentieth Century Fox Films Corp. v. Goldwyn Productions, 328 F.2d 190, (9th Cir.), cert. denied 379 U.S. 880, 85 S.Ct. 143, 13 L.Ed.2d 87 (1964).

16. But see Finley v. Music Corp. of America, 66 F.Supp. 569 (S.D.Cal. 1946).

17. Schechtman v. Wolfson, 244 F.2d 537 (2d Cir. 1957); Pergament v. Kaiser-Frazer Corp., 224 F.2d 80 (6th Cir. 1955).

18. E.g., Perryton Wholesale, Inc. v. Pioneer Distributing Co., 353 F.2d 618 (10th Cir. 1965), cert. denied 383 U.S. 945, 86 S.Ct. 1202, 16 L.Ed.2d 208 (1966); Ring v. Spina, 84 F.Supp. 403, 308 (S.D.N.Y.1949), modified 186 F.2d 637 (2d Cir. 1951), cert. denied 341 U.S. 935, 71 S.Ct. 854, 95 L.Ed. 1363 (1951).

19. E.g., Calnetics Corp. v. Volkswagen of America, Inc., 353 F.Supp. 1219 (C.D.Cal.1973); [2d Eisen Court of Appeals decision dictum]; See also H. Friendly, Federal Jurisdiction: A General View 120 (1973—) and the authorities cited in Notes 3 and 4 supra. International Tel. & Tel. Corp. v. General Tel. & Electronics Corp., 351 F.Supp. 1153 (D.Haw.1972), rev'd on other grounds 518 F.2d 913 (9th Cir. 1975).

APPENDIX A

Introduction: Economic theory and modes of economic analysis are used in a number of important antitrust cases and are used, as complementary to other styles of analysis, at various points in this book. What follows in this appendix is not intended as a substitute for that material, nor even as an introduction to it. The purpose of this appendix is a very limited one—to establish theoretically by the use of a simple, static, short run model that a monopolized market will attract less investment, produce lower output, and establish higher prices than would a competitive one, if all things other than the structure of the market were identical. The showing made is the conventional one found briefly set forth in antitrust case books [1] and more fully in other sources.[2] The reader should be aware of all of the factual assumptions which are made, that these are crucial to the demonstration, and that the demonstration may have relevance to the real world only insofar as the assumptions are consistent with reality.[3]

Scarcity, and consumer efforts to maximize satisfaction: Resources are scarce relative to human wants. Scarce resources can be allocated through a system of markets in which prices reflect and respond to decisions by producers and consumers. A consumer (the term is used here to denote an individual, couple, household or other unit in which consumption decisions are made) cannot have all the products the unit wants. Choices must be made. It is assumed theoretically that each consumer will try to maximize satisfaction and will on that basis decide what to forego and what to purchase, given prevailing prices and its resources. In the process of making choices each consumer (having its individual and more or less unique preference patterns) will do some fine tuning at the margin. If a particular consumer (say a family) has, say, $10,000 to spend in a year, a car that sells for $6,000 may be rejected out of hand, a car that sells for $3,000 may be considered and rejected, and a car that sells for $1500 may be purchased. That consumer, however, might not consider an identical second car even if the price per car were $1,200, though it might purchase two of the cars if the price were $800 per car. The same consumer may also reject meat selling at $1.60 per

---

1. E.g., R. Posner, Antitrust, Cases, Economic Notes and Other Materials 12–13 (1974); P. Areeda, Antitrust Analysis, Problems, Text, Cases 12–15 (2d ed. 1974).

2. E.g., Gellhorn, An Introduction to Antitrust Economics 1975 Duke L.J. 1 (1975); Raulett and Curry, Economic Principles: The "Monopoly", "Oligopoly" and "Competitive" Models 1 Antitrust Law and Econ.Rev. 107 (1968).

3. An economist might say that the test of a theory's value is not whether its inevitably simplified assumptions about real world conditions are validated empirically, but whether it is useful in predicting what happens in the real world.

pound, buy a small amount of meat selling at $1.20, and buy meat selling at 90¢ per pound in larger quantities—but not in such large quantities as it would if that meat were selling at 80¢ or 70¢ per pound. In the latter event, the consumer might, for example, buy less fish or eggs and more meat.

Theory assumes that the more a particular consumer possesses of a particular product, the less that consumer will be willing to pay for more of that product; the more it has of a product the lower will be the value to it of a marginally additional quantity of the product. For this reason, consumers in the aggregate will buy more of any particular product if its price is low than they will if its price is high, other things being equal.

Scarcity, and producer efforts to maximize profits: Producers—individual firms—also make decisions. It is assumed theoretically that the objective of each firm's decisions is to maximize its profits. If this be so the firm will seek to produce as efficiently as possible, to use a mix of factors which minimizes the cost of any given output. It will also make decisions about the rate of output (or, if it has the power to affect price, about price and output) which in its judgment will maximize profits.

Demand: Given current consumer preferences (and producer preferences to the extent the product is used as a factor in producing other goods), a schedule of the demand prevailing at any time can be constructed for any product. A demand schedule discloses the number of units of the product which buyers would be willing to purchase in a given period of time at each of the various alternative prices which might prevail. A demand schedule for a product (which depends upon the resources available to and the preferences of all consumers in the market, and which assumes that these factors remain constant for the given period) can be set forth in the form of a graph showing the "demand curve" for the product. Figure 1 shows two possible demand curves D–D^1 and d–d^1. The curve D–D^1 in Figure 1 signifies that at a price of $10 consumers would purchase about 380 units of the product in the given period (say, a week), that at a price of $40 they would purchase about 225 units, and that at a price of $70 they would purchase about 75 units. Given the theoretical assumptions about the way consumers will seek to maximize satisfactions, a demand curve will be expected to slope downward to the right, as do both of those in Figure 1. The quantity demanded of any product will vary inversely with the price.

Though the slope of any demand curve will normally be downward, these curves can vary in a number of respects. The slope may be steep or gradual; steepness may change over the length of the curve. The steepness of the slope shows the relative responsiveness of buyers to small price changes. The less responsive buyers are to small changes in price the steeper the curve will be, and con-

APPENDIX A

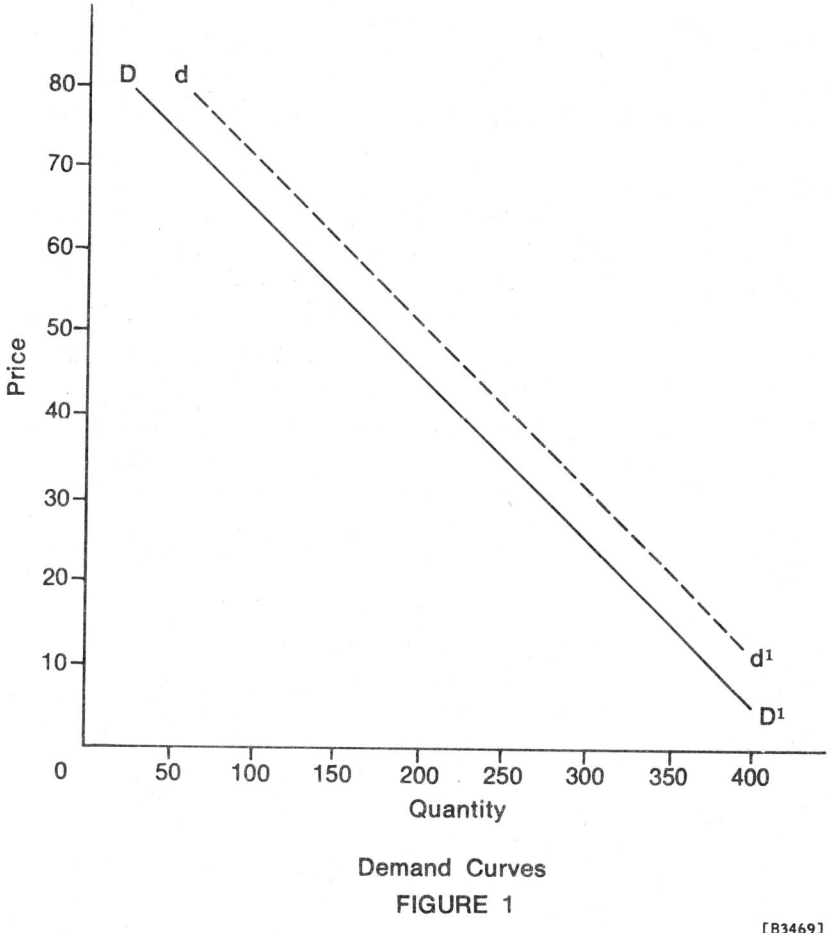

Demand Curves
FIGURE 1

versely. The responsiveness of the amount buyers will purchase to small changes in price is called the elasticity of demand; more precisely, elasticity is the percentage change in quantity divided by the percentage change in price. If at any point on the curve buyers are highly responsive to price changes, then a small decrease in price would increase sales sufficiently to increase total receipts; demand at that point is said to be elastic or to have an elasticity greater than 1. If at any point a small decrease in price would increase sales by such an amount as would leave total receipts unchanged, demand at that point is said to have unitary elasticity. If at any point a small decrease in price would increase total sales by so small an amount that total receipts would decrease demand at that point is said to be inelastic or to have an elasticity of less than 1.[4]

4. Methods of notation are available by which the degree of elasticity can be designated with specificity. See, e.g., G. Stigler, The Theory of Price, App. A. (3d ed. 1966).

Various factors effect the characteristics of the demand for any product. These include consumer tastes and preferences, the number of consumers and the amount of their available income, and other factors. Since these factors can change over time the position of the demand curve can also change. For example, greater consumer incomes or newly discovered uses for a product the demand for which is represented by $D-D^1$ in Figure 1 would tend to shift the entire demand curve to the right to a position such as that indicated by $d-d^1$.

Supply: One can also construct a supply schedule or a supply curve for a particular product which will show the quantity which producers would be willing to sell in a given unit of time at each of various alternative prices. Supply, of course, is a function of various factors such as the state of technology and labor, material and other costs, and a supply schedule assumes that all of these factors remain constant for the given unit of time. Theory suggests that firms will make and sell more of a product at a higher than at a lower price. Assuming this, a supply curve will slope upward to the right. Figure 2 shows two such supply curves.

The supply curve $S-S^1$ in Figure 2 shows that if a price of $20 prevailed during the period, about 100 units would be offered for sale, that at a price of $50 about 250 units would be offered, and that at a price of $70 about 350 units would be offered. The curve $s-s^1$ illustrates a position to which that demand curve might shift if circumstances changed—for example, if costs of suppliers for certain factors used in production were to increase.

Equilibrium price and quantity: Given the supply and demand functions for a product it is possible to determine a price, called the equilibrium price, at which the amount demanded and the amount supplied are equal. If the supply curve and demand curve are superimposed on the same graph the equilibrium price and quantity will be indicated by the point at which the curves intersect. Figure 3 is an example. It discloses that with the supply curve $S-S^1$ and the demand curve and $D-D^1$, the equilibrium price will be $40. At that price sellers will offer and buyers will buy 200 units (the equilibrium quantity).

Economic theory suggests that a market will tend toward equilibrium. If the current price is higher (say, $50 in Figure 3) than the equilibrium price, sellers will be offering more than 200 units and buyers will be buying less than 200 units. Sellers, not able to sell all their units, will start reducing prices in order to sell more. As the price falls new buyers will make purchases and old buyers will buy more. Theory asserts that this process will tend to continue until equilibrium is reached. Similarly, if the current price is below equilibrium (say $30) buyers will be bidding to buy more than sellers are willing to offer. Sellers will increase the price to ration the

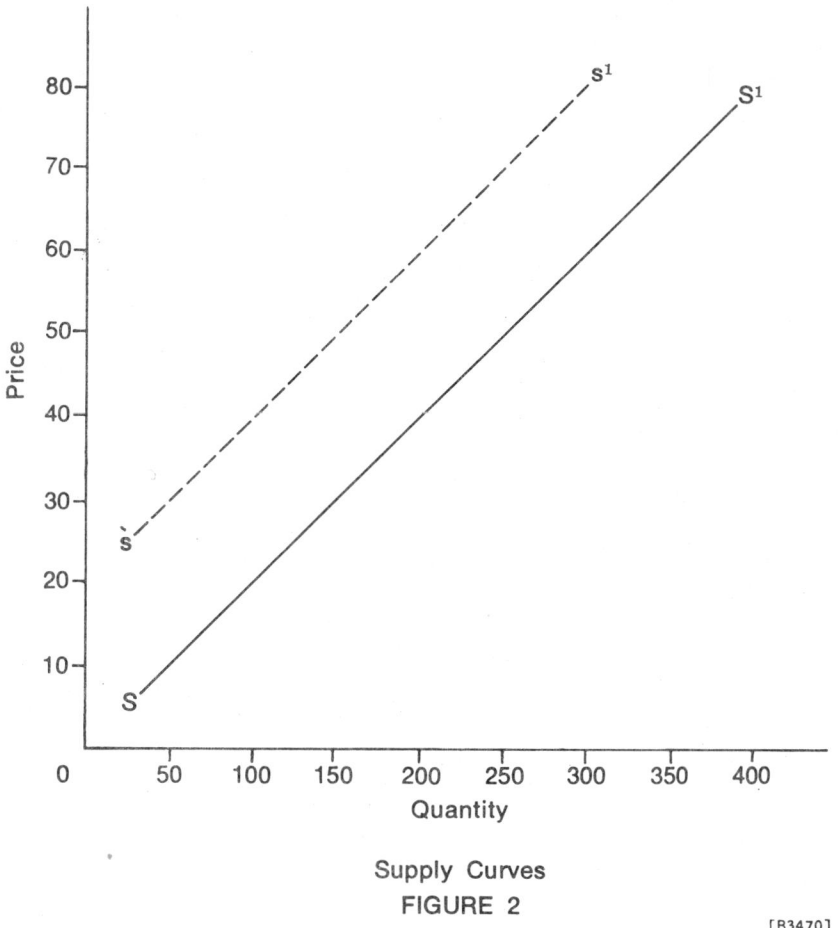

Supply Curves
FIGURE 2

available supply. As they do some buyers will lose interest. Again, the process will tend to continue until equilibrium is achieved.

Note that if the demand for the product signified in Figure 3 were to shift to the right to the position of the curve $d-d^1$ (say, because a new use had been discovered for the product) the original equilibrium price of 40 would no longer clear the market. Assuming that the supply curve has not also changed, a price of about 50 will now be needed for equilibrium. At that price sellers will be willing to sell and buyers will be willing to buy about 250 units.

Marginal costs, marginal revenues and output determination: Theory teaches that a seller (because seeking to maximize its profits) will keep expanding its output so long as each incremental unit of output adds to its total profits. Each incremental unit of output will add to the firm's total costs and, when sold, will add to its total revenues. An incremental unit of output will increase profit so long as the marginal revenue derived from selling that unit is greater than the marginal cost associated with producing (and selling) it. Thus, the profit maximizing firm will keep increasing output so long as the marginal cost of one more unit is less than the marginal revenue yielded by it and will stop increasing output when that ceases to be true.

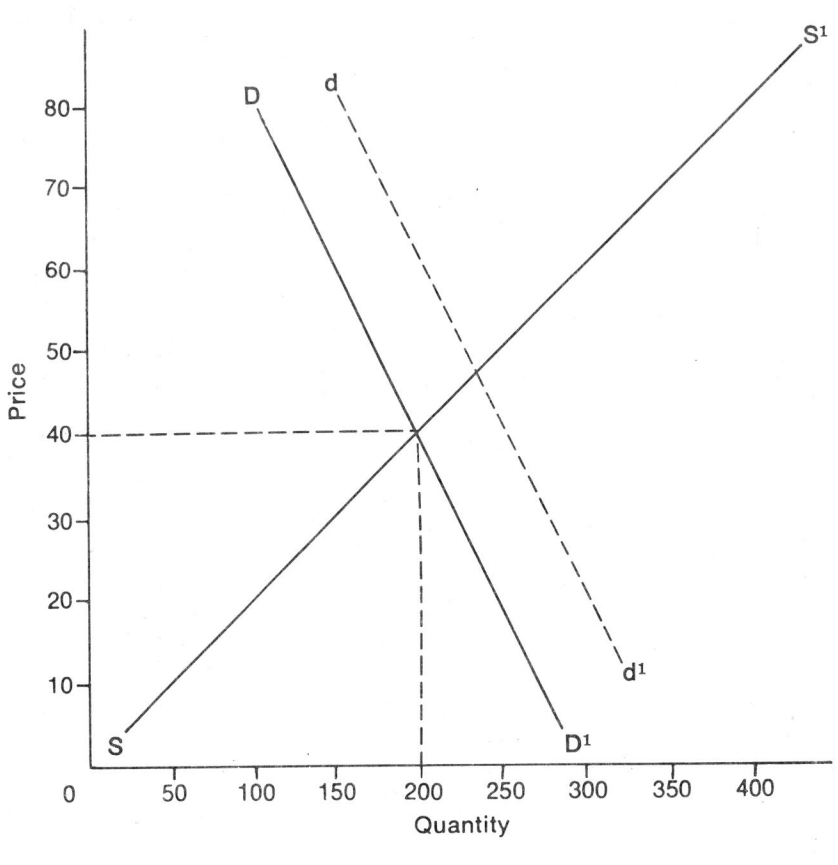

Equilibrium Price and Quantity
FIGURE 3

Assume that there is only one seller of a particular product, a monopolist. What will the marginal revenue curve and the marginal cost curve of such a seller look like? If that seller faces a demand curve like D–D¹ in Figure 4, the marginal revenue for the seller will be signified by the curve D–MR in Figure 4. Assume that the monopolist is making Q^1 units and selling them at p^1 each. Since the demand curve slopes downward to the right the seller in order to sell more units would have to take a lower price. Often (indeed, usually, as theory suggests) a seller will not be able to discriminate by charging a higher price to some buyers than to others. If it tries to do so buyers to which it sells at a discriminatorily lower price will find it profitable to resell at some intermediate price to those buyers from whom the first seller is asking a discriminatorily higher price. Theory suggests that this process of arbitrage will continue, with downward pressure on price, until a single equilibrium price is achieved. If in the example being considered the monopolist is unable to discriminate, then in order to sell more than the Q^1 units (for which it could charge p^1 per unit), the monopolist would have to accept a lower price than p^1 not just for the additional units to be sold, but for the first Q units sold as well. Thus, if the monopolist wants to sell, say Q^2 units, it must sell all units for a price of p^2. Given that characteristic of the demand curve, the marginal revenue curve will necessarily lie below the demand curve and will slope away from it, as does the curve MR on Figure 4. The total contribution of the sale of each additional unit to total revenue will necessarily be less than the price at which that additional unit is sold because in order to sell that additional unit the seller must accept a lower price not just for the additional unit, but for all units sold. The marginal contribution of the additional sale to revenue is not the sale price, but the sale price less the reduction in revenue resulting from the need to accept the lower price for all other units as well.

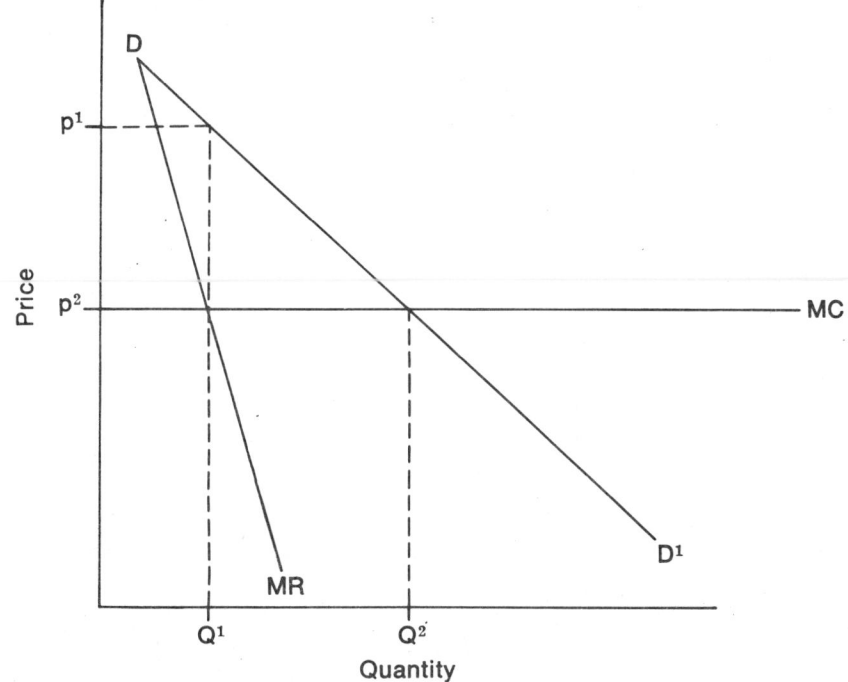

Demand, Marginal Revenue
and Marginal Cost

FIGURE 4

The shape of a firm's marginal cost curve is not so precisely determinate. Let us first consider average cost per unit. Theory suggests that for any given scale of capital investment (let us say, for a plant of any given size) there will be an efficient rate of output or range of such rates at which the average cost per unit of production will be lowest. At any smaller rate of output average cost per unit would be higher and could be reduced if output were increased to a more efficient level. Similarly, at any rate of output greater than the most efficient rate (or range of rates), average cost per unit would be higher. These considerations suggest an average cost curve which first falls as output increases until it reaches a low point. It may stay at that low point over some substantial range of outputs, but eventually it begins to rise as output increases further. Marginal cost is a function of average cost much as marginal revenue is a function of average revenue. When average cost is falling, marginal cost will also be falling and will be below average cost. This is because the marginally additional unit of output not only is produced at a lower per unit cost, but all prior units are also produced at the lower cost. For analytically similar reasons, when average cost begins to increase, marginal cost will also increase and will be above average cost. In light of these relationships, a marginal cost curve may, over its full length be U shaped, first falling, then leveling out, then rising. For purposes of convenience of demonstration we have assumed in Figure 5 a marginal cost curve flat throughout its full length.

Price and output decisions by the firm: Using the concepts introduced above, economists examine the conduct of individual firms and the market in which they operate under various alternative theoretical assumptions about the structure of the market. The principal market structure models used by economists are models of a competitive, a monopolistic, and an oligopolistic market structure. On the basis of the theoretical assumptions of neo-classical economics, the ways firms will act in deciding on price and output are highly determinate under a competitive structure or a monopolistic structure. Firm decisions on price and output are highly indeterminate under an oligopolistic structure. In this appendix, only competitive and monopoly structures are considered.

A market is called perfectly competitive when it fulfills all of these conditions: the total number of sellers is so large, and each of them individually is so small relative to the market as a whole, that no single seller is able to influence price by its individual decision about the quantities it will offer for sale; the product is standardized; there are no barriers to entry or exit; all sellers receive accurate market knowledge without delay.

In a market meeting these theoretical conditions no individual seller would exercise any power over price. Each seller would be aware that it could sell all that it wished to sell at the prevailing market price, and that it could not sell any amount at any higher price.

Individual sellers would be capable of adjusting to the market only by varying the quantity they offered to sell, but not by varying the price they would charge. The demand curve perceived by each seller would be horizontal at the market price. The market price would be given by the point where the down-sloping market-wide (i. e. industry) demand curve and the up-sloping market wide (industry) supply curve intersected.

A market is a monopoly when it fulfills all of these very different conditions: a single firm supplies the entire output for the market and sets the price and determines the quantity produced without direct interference from a government agency; the product has no close substitutes; there are barriers to the entry of other firms.

In a monopoly market the downward-sloping market-wide (industry) demand curve is the demand curve perceived by the monopoly firm. The monopolist can produce whatever quantity it wishes, but the price it may charge varies inversely with the quantity offered.

Price and output in monopoly: Neo-classical theory says that a monopolist, like any other seller, will maximize profits by expanding output to the point where marginal cost and marginal revenue are equal. On that assumption the profit maximizing output for a monopolist with the cost and revenue curves shown in Figure 4 would be about Q^1 units. By extending a line at this output up to the demand curve we see that at this output the monopolist would be able to sell all the units made at a price of about p^1 per unit. This, then, is the profit maximizing or monopoly price.

Price and output in competition: If we now assume an industry identical to that signified in Figure 4 except that it is organized competitively, theory suggests that a significantly different price and output will result. In the monopoly market there was a single seller establishing the total quantity produced and, given the demand, price. In the competitive market there are (by the definitional concepts of the theory) numerous small sellers making the product. Theory teaches that each of these sellers, in order to maximize its profits, will decide upon an output which equates its marginal cost and its marginal revenue, just as did the monopolist. But none of the competitive sellers controls a large enough share of the market for any individual seller to perceive that its decision about output can alter market price. On these theoretical assumptions each seller in the competitive market takes the price as given when it makes its individual decision about the output which will maximize its return. Each individual competitor will thus increase output until the marginal cost of producing the last unit equals the market price which the seller takes as given and at which it can sell all of its output. In short, each individual competitive seller increases output until marginal cost reaches the market price and, in consequence, all the competitive sellers in the aggregate increase industry output until marginal cost reaches demand. This necessarily produces a higher output and lower price than that of the monopolist which increased output only until marginal cost reached marginal revenue which is lower than demand. On Figure 4 a competitive market would thus yield a quantity of Q^2 and a price of p^2, a higher quantity and lower price than monopoly yielded. In consequence, the conversion of a monopolized market to a competitive one results in a transfer of wealth from the producer to the consumers of the industry's products; and, conversely, conversion of a competitive industry to a monopoly will shift wealth in the other direction.

The theoretical difference between the two structures can also be demonstrated by assuming that the market is organized competitively but that the first seller charges a price higher than the competitive price of p^2 which is indicated by Figure 4. The other firms may initially sell at that higher price too. But all firms will then be earning monopoly profits; theory suggests that firms will start to increase output striving to gain more of those monopoly profits. But as output is increased, the equilibrium price will fall, and the tendency will be for the price to go down to clear the market. This process will tend to continue until the market price has fallen to p^2, and output has increased to Q^2, for only at this point will the total revenues of sellers just cover their total costs including a competitive return on investment.

Caution: Note that simplifying theoretical assumptions are made throughout this appendix which limit the verisimilitude of the analysis. For example, a real world "monopolist" would never be totally alone, nor totally safe from entry. Though setting price and output as described above would nevertheless maximize profits in the short run, the real world monopolist would price at some (indeterminate) lower level to discourage entry.

APPENDIX B

Note: In this appendix all statutes included are set forth with amendments through March 1, 1975. The history of some but not all amendments is set forth in notes. There are some deletions which are indicated by ellipses.

SHERMAN ACT [1]

SEC. 1. Every contract, combination in the form of trust or otherwise, or conspiracy, in restraint of trade or commerce among the several States, or with foreign nations, is hereby declared to be illegal. Every person who shall make any contract or engage in any combination or conspiracy hereby declared to be illegal shall be deemed guilty of a felony and, on conviction thereof, shall be punished by fine not exceeding one million dollars if a corporation, or, if any other person, one hundred thousand dollars, or by imprisonment not exceeding three years, or by both said punishments, in the discretion of the court.

SEC. 2. Every person who shall monopolize, or attempt to monopolize, or combine or conspire with any other person or persons, to monopolize any part of the trade or commerce among the several States, or with foreign nations, shall be deemed guilty of a felony, and, on conviction thereof, shall be punished by fine not exceeding one million dollars if a corporation, or, if any other person, one hundred thousand dollars, or by imprisonment not exceeding three years, or by both said punishments, in the discretion of the court.

SEC. 3. Every contract, combination in form of trust or otherwise, or conspiracy, in restraint of trade or commerce in any Territory of the United States or of the District of Columbia, or in restraint of trade or commerce between any such Territory and another, or between any such Territory or Territories and any State or States or the District of Columbia, or with foreign nations, or between the District of Columbia and any State or States or foreign nations, is hereby declared illegal. Every person who shall make any such con-

---

[1]. The Sherman Act is the Act of July 2, 1890, c. 617, 26 Stat. 209, 15 U.S.C.A. §§ 1–7. So called "fair trade" provisos were added to Section 1 of the Act by the Miller-Tydings Act, Act of August 17, 1937, c. 690, 50 Stat. 693 but were repealed by Act of December 2, 1975, Public Law 94–145. The fine for violation of the act was increased from $5,000 to $50,000 by the Act of July 7, 1955, c. 281, 69 Stat. 282 and increased again to $1,000,000 for a corporation and $100,000 for other persons by the Antitrust Procedures And Penalties Act, Public Law 93–528, 88 Stat. 1706, 15 U.S.C.A. § 1 (1976). The latter amendment also made violations of the Sherman Act felonies (previously they were misdemeanors) and increased the maximum term of imprisonment from one year to three years. Section 7 of the Sherman Act which dealt with the same general subject matter as does Section 4 of the Clayton Act, infra, was repealed in 1955 by Act of July 7, 1955, c. 283, 69 Stat. 283.

tract or engage in any such combination or conspiracy, shall be deemed guilty of a felony, and, on conviction thereof, shall be punished by fine not exceeding one million dollars if a corporation, or, if any other person, one hundred thousand dollars, or by imprisonment not exceeding three years, or by both said punishments, in the discretion of the court.

SEC. 4. The several district courts of the United States are invested with jurisdiction to prevent and restrain violations of this act; and it shall be the duty of the several United States attorneys, in their respective districts, under the direction of the Attorney General, to institute proceedings in equity to prevent and restrain such violations. Such proceedings may be by way of petition setting forth the case and praying that such violation shall be enjoined or otherwise prohibited. When the parties complained of shall have been duly notified of such petition the court shall proceed, as soon as may be, to the hearing and determination of the case; and pending such petition and before final decree, the court may at any time make such temporary restraining order or prohibition as shall be deemed just in the premises.

SEC. 5. Whenever it shall appear to the court before which any proceeding under section four of this act may be pending, that the ends of justice require that other parties should be brought before the court, the court may cause them to be summoned, whether they reside in the district in which the court is held or not; and subpoenas to that end may be served in any district by the marshal thereof.

SEC. 6. Any property owned under any contract or by any combination, or pursuant to any conspiracy (and being the subject thereof) mentioned in section one of this act, and being in the course of transportation from one State to another, or to a foreign country, shall be forfeited to the United States, and may be seized and condemned by like proceedings as those provided by law for the forfeiture, seizure, and condemnation of property imported into the United States contrary to law.

SEC. 8. The word "person," or "persons," wherever used in this act shall be deemed to include corporations and associations existing under or authorized by the laws of either the United States, the laws of any of the Territories, the laws of any State, or the laws of any foreign country.

CLAYTON ACT [2]

AN ACT To supplement existing laws against unlawful restraints and monopolies, and for other purposes.

---

[2]. The Clayton Act is the Act of October 15, 1914, c. 322, 38 Stat. 730, 15 U.S.C.A. §§ 12–27. Section 2 of the Clayton Act was amended by the Robinson-Patman Act, Act of June 19, 1936, c. 592, 49 Stat. 1526. Section 3 of the

APPENDIX B

SEC. 1. *Be it enacted by the Senate and House of Representatives of the United States of America in Congress assembled,* That "antitrust laws," as used herein, includes the Act entitled "An Act to protect trade and commerce against unlawful restraints and monopolies," approved July second, eighteen hundred and ninety; sections seventy-three to seventy-seven, inclusive, of an Act entitled "An Act to reduce taxation, to provide revenue for the Government, and for other purposes," of August twenty-seventh, eighteen hundred and ninety-four; an Act entitled "An Act to amend sections seventy-three and seventy-six of the Act of August twenty-seventh, eighteen hundred and ninety-four, entitled 'An Act to reduce taxation, to provide revenue for the Government, and for other purposes,' " approved February twelfth, nineteen hundred and thirteen; and also this Act.

"Commerce," as used herein, means trade or commerce among the several States and with foreign nations, or between the District of Columbia or any Territory of the United States and any State, Territory or foreign nation, or between any insular possessions or other places under the jurisdiction of the United States, or between any such possession or place and any State or Territory of the United States or the District of Columbia or any foreign nation, or within the District of Columbia or any Territory or any insular possession or other place under the jurisdiction of the United States: *Provided,* That nothing in this Act contained shall apply to the Philippine Islands.

The word "person" or "persons" wherever used in this Act shall be deemed to include corporations and associations existing under or authorized by the laws of either the United States, the laws of any of the Territories, the laws of any State, or the laws of any foreign country.

SEC. 2. (a) That it shall be unlawful for any person engaged in commerce, in the course of such commerce, either directly or indirectly, to discriminate in price between different purchasers of commodities of like grade and quality, where either or any of the purchases involved in such discrimination are in commerce, where such commodities are sold for use, consumption, or resale within the United

---

Robinson-Patman Act, which appears as 15 U.S.C.A. § 13a, made price discrimination criminal in certain instances. Sections 4A and 4B were added by the Act of July 7, 1955, c. 283, 69 Stat. 282–283. Section 5 was amended by the Act of December 21, 1974, Pub.L. 93–528 Section 2, 88 Stat. 1706. Section 7 of the Clayton Act was amended by the Celler-Kefauver Act of December 29, 1950, c. 1184, 64 Stat. 1125. Section 9 was repealed by the Act of June 25, 1948, c. 645, 62 Stat. 683. Its substance now appears as 18 U.S.C.A. § 660. Sections 17 through 19 and 21 through 25 were repealed by the Act of June 25, 1948, c. 646, 62 Stat. 869. Rule 65 of the Federal Rules of Civil Procedure now covers, in substance, the provisions of Sections 18 and 19 of the Clayton Act as originally enacted. Title 18 U.S.C.A. §§ 402, 3285 and 3691 now cover, in substance, the provisions of Sections 21 through 25 of the Clayton Act as originally enacted. Note: The text of the Clayton Act in this Appendix does not contain the amendments enacted in the Hart-Scott-Rodino Antitrust Improvement Act of 1976, Public Law 94–435, Sept. 30, 1976. For a summary of these changes, see Appendix D, infra.

States or any Territory thereof or the District of Columbia or any insular possession or other place under the jurisdiction of the United States, and where the effect of such discrimination may be substantially to lessen competition or tend to create a monopoly in any line of commerce, or to injure, destroy, or prevent competition with any person who either grants or knowingly receives the benefit of such discrimination, or with customers of either of them: *Provided*, That nothing herein contained shall prevent differentials which make only due allowance for differences in the cost of manufacture, sale, or delivery resulting from the differing methods or quantities in which such commodities are to such purchasers sold or delivered: *Provided, however*, That the Federal Trade Commission may, after due investigation and hearing to all interested parties, fix and establish quantity limits, and revise the same as it finds necessary, as to particular commodities or classes of commodities, where it finds that available purchasers in greater quantities are so few as to render differentials on account thereof unjustly discriminatory or promotive of monopoly in any line of commerce; and the foregoing shall then not be construed to permit differentials based on differences in quantities greater than those so fixed and established: *And provided further*, That nothing herein contained shall prevent persons engaged in selling goods, wares, or merchandise in commerce from selecting their own customers in bona fide transactions and not in restraint of trade: *And provided further*, That nothing herein contained shall prevent price changes from time to time where in response to changing conditions affecting the market for or the marketability of the goods concerned, such as but not limited to actual or imminent deterioration of perishable goods, obsolescence of seasonal goods, distress sales under court process, or sales in good faith in discontinuance of business in the goods concerned.

(b) Upon proof being made, at any hearing on a complaint under this section, that there has been discrimination in price or services or facilities furnished, the burden of rebutting the prima facie case thus made by showing justification shall be upon the person charged with a violation of this section, and unless justification shall be affirmatively shown, the Commission is authorized to issue an order terminating the discrimination: *Provided, however*, That nothing herein contained shall prevent a seller rebutting the prima facie case thus made by showing that his lower price or the furnishing of services or facilities to any purchaser or purchasers was made in good faith to meet an equally low price of a competitor, or the services or facilities furnished by a competitor.

(c) That it shall be unlawful for any person engaged in commerce in the course of such commerce, to pay or grant, or to receive or accept, anything of value as a commission, brokerage, or other compensation, or any allowance or discount in lieu thereof, except for services rendered in connection with the sale or purchase of goods, wares, or merchandise, either to the other party to such transaction

APPENDIX B

or to an agent, representative, or other intermediary therein where such intermediary is acting in fact for or in behalf, or is subject to the direct or indirect control, of any party to such transaction other than the person by whom such compensation is so granted or paid.

(d) That it shall be unlawful for any person engaged in commerce to pay or contract for the payment of anything of value to or for the benefit of a customer of such person in the course of such commerce as compensation or in consideration for any services or facilities furnished by or through such customer in connection with the processing, handling, sale, or offering for sale of any products or commodities manufactured, sold, or offered for sale by such person, unless such payment or consideration is available on proportionally equal terms to all other customers competing in the distribution of such products or commodities.

(e) That it shall be unlawful for any person to discriminate in favor of one purchaser against another purchaser or purchasers of a commodity bought for resale, with or without processing, by contracting to furnish or furnishing, or by contributing to the furnishing of, any services or facilities connected with the processing, handling, sale, or offering for sale of such commodity so purchased upon terms not accorded to all purchasers on proportionally equal terms.

(f) That it shall be unlawful for any person engaged in commerce, in the course of such commerce, knowingly to induce or receive a discrimination in price which is prohibited by this section.

SEC. 3. That it shall be unlawful for any person engaged in commerce, in the course of such commerce, to lease or make a sale or contract for sale of goods, wares, merchandise, machinery, supplies or other commodities, whether patented or unpatented, for use, consumption or resale within the United States or any Territory thereof or the District of Columbia or any insular possession or other place under the jurisdiction of the United States, or fix a price charged therefor, or discount from or rebate upon, such price, on the condition, agreement or understanding that the lessee or purchaser thereof shall not use or deal in the goods, wares, merchandise, machinery, supplies, or other commodities of a competitor or competitors of the lessor or seller, where the effect of such lease, sale, or contract for sale or such condition, agreement or understanding may be to substantially lessen competition or tend to create a monopoly in any line of commerce.

SEC. 4. That any person who shall be injured in his business or property by reason of anything forbidden in the antitrust laws may sue therefor in any district court of the United States in the district in which the defendant resides or is found or has an agent, without respect to the amount in controversy, and shall recover threefold the damages by him sustained, and the cost of suit, including a reasonable attorney's fee.

SEC. 4A. Whenever the United States is hereafter injured in its business or property by reason of anything forbidden in the antitrust laws it may sue therefor in the United States district court for the district in which the defendant resides or is found or has an agent, without respect to the amount in controversy, and shall recover actual damages by it sustained and the cost of suit.

SEC. 4B. Any action to enforce any cause of action under sections 4 or 4A shall be forever barred unless commenced within four years after the cause of action accrued. No cause of action barred under existing law on the effective date of this section and sections 4A and 5 of this Act shall be revived by said sections.

SEC. 5. (a) A final judgment or decree heretofore or hereafter rendered in any civil or criminal proceeding brought by or on behalf of the United States under the antitrust laws to the effect that a defendant has violated said laws shall be prima facie evidence against such defendant in any action or proceeding brought by any other party against such defendant under said laws or by the United States under section 4A, as to all matters respecting which said judgment or decree would be an estoppel as between the parties thereto: *Provided*, That this section shall not apply to consent judgments or decrees entered before any testimony has been taken or to judgments or decrees entered in actions under section 4A.

(b) Any proposal for a consent judgment submitted by the United States for entry in any civil proceeding brought by or on behalf of the United States under the antitrust laws shall be filed with the district court before which such proceeding is pending and published by the United States in the Federal Register at least 60 days prior to the effective date of such judgment. Any written comments relating to such proposal and any responses by the United States thereto, shall also be filed with such district court and published by the United States in the Federal Register within such sixty-day period. Copies of such proposal and any other materials and documents which the United States considered determinative in formulating such proposal, shall also be made available to the public at the district court and in such other districts as the court may subsequently direct. Simultaneously with the filing of such proposal, unless otherwise instructed by the court, the United States shall file with the district court, publish in the Federal Register, and thereafter furnish to any person upon request, a competitive impact statement which shall recite—

(1) the nature and purpose of the proceeding;

(2) a description of the practices or events giving rise to the alleged violation of the antitrust laws;

(3) an explanation of the proposal for a consent judgment, including an explanation of any unusual circumstances giving rise

to such proposal or any provision contained therein, relief to be obtained thereby, and the anticipated effects on competition of such relief;

(4) the remedies available to potential private plaintiffs damaged by the alleged violation in the event that such proposal for the consent judgment is entered in such proceeding;

(5) a description of the procedures available for modification of such proposal; and

(6) a description and evaluation of alternatives to such proposal actually considered by the United States.

(c) The United States shall also cause to be published, commencing at least 60 days prior to the effective date of the judgment described in subsection (b) of this section, for 7 days over a period of 2 weeks in newspapers of general circulation of the district in which the case has been filed, in the District of Columbia, and in such other districts as the court may direct—

(i) a summary of the terms of the proposal for the consent judgment,

(ii) a summary of the competitive impact statement filed under subsection (b) of this section,

(iii) and a list of the materials and documents under subsection (b) of this section which the United States shall make available for purposes of meaningful public comment, and the place where such materials and documents are available for public inspection.

(d) During the 60-day period as specified in subsection (b) of this section, and such additional time as the United States may request and the court may grant, the United States shall receive and consider any written comments relating to the proposal for the consent judgment submitted under subsection (b) of this section. The Attorney General or his designee shall establish procedures to carry out the provisions of this subsection, but such 60-day time period shall not be shortened except by order of the district court upon a showing that (1) extraordinary circumstances require such shortening and (2) such shortening is not adverse to the public interest. At the close of the period during which such comments may be received, the United States shall file with the district court and cause to be published in the Federal Register a response to such comments.

(e) Before entering any consent judgment proposed by the United States under this section, the court shall determine that the entry of such judgment is in the public interest. For the purpose of such determination, the court may consider—

(1) the competitive impact of such judgment, including termination of alleged violations, provisions for enforcement and modification, duration or relief sought, anticipated effects of

alternative remedies actually considered, and any other considerations bearing upon the adequacy of such judgment;

(2) the impact of entry of such judgment upon the public generally and individuals alleging specific injury from the violations set forth in the complaint including consideration of the public benefit, if any, to be derived from a determination of the issues at trial.

(f) In making its determination under subsection (e) of this section, the court may—

(1) take testimony of Government officials or experts or such other expert witnesses, upon motion of any party or participant or upon its own motion, as the court may deem appropriate;

(2) appoint a special master and such outside consultants or expert witnesses as the court may deem appropriate; and request and obtain the views, evaluations, or advice of any individual, group or agency of government with respect to any aspects of the proposed judgment or the effect of such judgment, in such manner as the court deems appropriate;

(3) authorize full or limited participation in proceedings before the court by interested persons or agencies, including appearance amicus curiae, intervention as a party pursuant to the Federal Rules of Civil Procedure, examination of witnesses or documentary materials, or participation in any other manner and extent which serves the public interest as the court may deem appropriate;

(4) review any comments including any objections filed with the United States under subsection (d) of this section concerning the proposed judgment and the responses of the United States to such comments and objections; and

(5) take such other action in the public interest as the court may deem appropriate.

(g) Not later than 10 days following the date of the filing of any proposal for a consent judgment under subsection (b) of this section, each defendant shall file with the district court a description of any and all written or oral communications by or on behalf of such defendant, including any and all written or oral communications on behalf of such defendant, or other person, with any officer or employee of the United States concerning or relevant to such proposal, except that any such communications made by counsel of record alone with the Attorney General or the employees of the Department of Justice alone shall be excluded from the requirements of this subsection. Prior to the entry of any consent judgment pursuant to the antitrust laws, each defendant shall certify to the district court that the requirements of this subsection have been complied with and that such filing is a true and complete description of such communications known to the defendant or which the defendant reasonably should have known.

(h) Proceedings before the district court under subsections (e) and (f) of this section, and the competitive impact statement filed under subsection (b) of this section, shall not be admissible against any defendant in any action or proceeding brought by any other party against such defendant under the antitrust laws or by the United States under section 4A nor constitute a basis for the introduction of the consent judgment as prima facie evidence against such defendant in any such action or proceeding.

(i) Whenever any civil or criminal proceeding is instituted by the United States to prevent, restrain, or punish violations of any of the antitrust laws, but not including an action under section 4A, the running of the statute of limitations in respect of every private right of action arising under said laws and based in whole or in part on any matter complained of in said proceeding shall be suspended during the pendency thereof and for one year thereafter: *Provided, however,* That whenever the running of the statute of limitations in respect of a cause of action arising under section 4 is suspended hereunder, any action to enforce such cause of action shall be forever barred unless commenced either within the period of suspension or within four years after the cause of action accrued.

SEC. 6. That the labor of a human being is not a commodity or article of commerce. Nothing contained in the antitrust laws shall be construed to forbid the existence and operation of labor, agricultural, or horticultural organizations, instituted for the purposes of mutual help, and not having capital stock or conducted for profit, or to forbid or restrain individual members of such organizations from lawfully carrying out the legitimate objects thereof; nor shall such organizations, or the members thereof, be held or construed to be illegal combinations or conspiracies in restraint of trade, under the antitrust laws.

SEC. 7. That no corporation engaged in commerce shall acquire directly or indirectly, the whole or any part of the stock or other share capital and no corporation subject to the jurisdiction of the Federal Trade Commission shall acquire the whole or any part of the assets of another corporation engaged also in commerce, where in any line of commerce in any section of the country, the effect of such acquisition may be substantially to lessen competition, or to tend to create a monopoly.

No corporation shall acquire, directly or indirectly, the whole or any part of the stock or other share capital and no corporation subject to the jurisdiction of the Federal Trade Commission shall acquire the whole or any part of the assets of one or more corporations engaged in commerce, where in any line of commerce in any section of the country, the effect of such acquisition, of such stocks or assets, or of the use of such stock by the voting or granting of proxies or otherwise, may be substantially to lessen competition, or to tend to create a monopoly.

This section shall not apply to corporations purchasing such stock solely for investment and not using the same by voting or otherwise to bring about, or in attempting to bring about, the substantial lessening of competition. Nor shall anything contained in this section prevent a corporation engaged in commerce from causing the formation of subsidiary corporations for the actual carrying on of their immediate lawful business, or the natural and legitimate branches or extensions thereof, or from owning and holding all or a part of the stock of such subsidiary corporations, when the effect of such formation is not to substantially lessen competition.

Nor shall anything herein contained be construed to prohibit any common carrier subject to the laws to regulate commerce from aiding in the construction of branches or short lines so located as to become feeders to the main line of the company so aiding in such construction or from acquiring or owning all or any part of the stock of such branch lines, nor to prevent any such common carrier from acquiring and owning all or any part of the stock of a branch or short line constructed by an independent company where there is no substantial competition between the company owning the branch line so constructed and the company owning the main line acquiring the property or an interest therein, nor to prevent such common carrier from extending any of its lines through the medium of the acquisition of stock or otherwise of any other common carrier where there is no substantial competition between the company extending its lines and the company whose stock, property, or an interest therein is so acquired.

Nothing contained in this section shall be held to affect or impair any right heretofore legally acquired: *Provided*, That nothing in this section shall be held or construed to authorize or make lawful anything heretofore prohibited or made illegal by the antitrust laws, nor to exempt any person from the penal provisions thereof or the civil remedies therein provided.

Nothing contained in this section shall apply to transactions duly consummated pursuant to authority given by the Civil Aeronautics Board, Federal Communications Commission, Federal Power Commission, Interstate Commerce Commission, the Securities and Exchange Commission in the exercise of its jurisdiction under section 10 of the Public Utility Holding Company Act of 1935, the United States Maritime Commission, or the Secretary of Agriculture under any statutory provision vesting such power in such Commission, Secretary, or Board.

SEC. 8. * * * [This section of the Clayton Act dealing with interlocking directorates of certain banking and other financial corporations and related matters is deleted].

APPENDIX B

SEC. 10. * * * [This section dealing with transactions among common carriers having interlocking directorships and related matters is deleted].

SEC. 11. (a) That authority to enforce compliance with sections 2, 3, 7, and 8 of this Act by the persons respectively subject thereto is hereby vested in the Interstate Commerce Commission where applicable to common carriers subject to the Interstate Commerce Act, as amended; in the Federal Communications Commission where applicable to common carriers engaged in wire or radio communication or radio transmission of energy; in the Civil Aeronautics Board where applicable to air carriers and foreign air carriers subject to the Civil Aeronautics Act of 1938; in the Federal Reserve Board where applicable to banks, banking associations, and trust companies; and in the Federal Trade Commission where applicable to all other character of commerce to be exercised as follows:

(b) Whenever the Commission or Board vested with jurisdiction thereof shall have reason to believe that any person is violating or has violated any of the provisions of sections 2, 3, 7, and 8 of this Act, it shall issue and serve upon such person and the Attorney General a complaint stating its charges in that respect, and containing a notice of hearing upon a day and at a place therein fixed at least thirty days after the service of said complaint. The person so complained of shall have the right to appear at the place and time so fixed and show cause why an order should not be entered by the Commission or Board requiring such person to cease and desist from the violation of the law so charged in said complaint. The Attorney General shall have the right to intervene and appear in said proceeding and any person may make application, and upon good cause shown may be allowed by the Commission or Board, to intervene and appear in said proceeding by counsel or in person. The testimony in any such proceeding shall be reduced to writing and filed in the office of the Commission or Board. If upon such hearing the Commission or Board, as the case may be, shall be of the opinion that any of the provisions of said sections have been or are being violated, it shall make a report in writing, in which it shall state its findings as to the facts, and shall issue and cause to be served on such person an order requiring such person to cease and desist from such violations, and divest itself of the stock, or other share capital, or assets, held or rid itself of the directors chosen contrary to the provisions of sections 7 and 8 of this Act, if any there be, in the manner and within the time fixed by said order. Until the expiration of the time allowed for filing a petition for review, if no such petition has been duly filed within such time, or, if a petition for review has been filed within such time then until the record in the proceeding has been filed in a court of appeals of the United States, as hereinafter provided, the Commission or Board may at any time, upon such notice and in such manner as it shall deem proper, modify or set aside, in whole or in part, any report or any order made or issued by it under this section. After the expiration of the time allowed for filing a petition for review, if no such petition has been duly filed within such time, the Commission or Board may at any time, after notice and opportunity for hearing, reopen and alter, modify, or set aside, in whole or in part, any report or order made or issued by it under this section, whenever in the opinion of the Commission or Board conditions of fact or of law have so changed as to require such action or if the public interest shall so require: *Provided, however*, That the said person may, within sixty days after service upon him or it of said report or order entered after such a reopening, obtain a review thereof in the appropriate court of appeals of the United States, in the manner provided in subsection (c) of this section.

(c) Any person required by such order of the commission or board to cease and desist from any such violation may obtain a review of such order in the court of appeals of the United States for any circuit within which such violation occurred or within which such person resides or carries on business, by filing in the court, within sixty days after the date of the service of such order, a written petition praying that the order of the commission or board be set aside. A copy of such petition shall be forthwith transmitted by the clerk of the court to the commission or board, and thereupon the commission or board shall file in the court the record in the proceeding, as provided in section 2112 of title 28, United States Code. Upon such filing of the petition the court shall have jurisdiction of the proceeding and of the question determined therein concurrently with the commission or board until the filing of the record, and shall have power to make and enter a decree affirming, modifying, or setting aside the order of the commission or board, and enforcing the same to the extent that such order is affirmed, and to issue such writs as are ancillary to its jurisdiction or are necessary in its judgment to prevent injury to the public or to competitors pendente lite. The findings of the commission or board as to the facts, if supported by substantial evidence, shall be conclusive. To the extent that the order of the commission or board is affirmed, the court shall issue its own order commanding obedience to the terms of such order of the commission or board. If either party shall apply to the court for leave to adduce additional evidence, and shall show to the satisfaction of the court that such additional evidence is material and that there were reasonable grounds for the failure to adduce such evidence in the proceeding before the commission or board, the court may order such additional evidence to be taken before the commission or board, and to be adduced upon the hearing in such manner and upon such terms and conditions as to the court may seem proper. The commission or board may modify its findings as to the facts, or make new findings, by reason of the additional evidence so taken, and shall file such modified or new findings, which, if supported by substantial evidence, shall be conclusive, and its recommendation, if any, for the modification or setting aside of its original order, with the return of such additional evidence. The judgment and decree of the court shall be final, except that the same shall be subject to review by the Supreme Court upon certiorari, as provided in section 1254 of title 28 of the United States Code.

(d) Upon the filing of the record with it the jurisdiction of the court of appeals to affirm, enforce, modify, or set aside orders of the commission or board shall be exclusive.

(e) Such proceedings in the court of appeals shall be given precedence over other cases pending therein, and shall be in every way expedited. No order of the commission or board or judgment of the court to enforce the same shall in anywise relieve or absolve any person from any liability under the antitrust laws.

(f) Complaints, orders, and other processes of the commission or board under this section may be served by anyone duly authorized by the commission or board, either (1) by delivering a copy thereof to the person to be served, or to a member of the partnership to be served, or to the president, secretary, or other executive officer or a director of the corporation to be served; or (2) by leaving a copy thereof at the residence or the principal office or place of business of such person; or (3) by mailing by registered or certified mail a copy thereof addressed to such person at his or its residence or principal office or place of business. The verified return by the person so serving said complaint, order, or other process setting forth the manner of said service shall be proof of the same, and the return post office receipt for said complaint, order, or other process mailed by registered or certified mail as aforesaid shall be proof of the service of the same.

(g) Any order issued under subsection (b) shall become final—

(1) upon the expiration of the time allowed for filing a petition for review, if no such petition has been duly filed within such time; but the commission or board may thereafter modify or set aside its order to the extent provided in the last sentence of subsection (b); or

(2) upon the expiration of the time allowed for filing a petition for certiorari, if the order of the commission or board has been affirmed, or the petition for review has been dismissed by the court of appeals, and no petition for certiorari has been duly filed; or

(3) upon the denial of a petition for certiorari, if the order of the commission or board has been affirmed or the petition for review has been dismissed by the court of appeals; or

(4) upon the expiration of thirty days from the date of issuance of the mandate of the Supreme Court, if such Court

directs that the order of the commission or board be affirmed or the petition for review be dismissed.

(h) If the Supreme Court directs that the order of the commission or board be modified or set aside, the order of the commission or board rendered in accordance with the mandate of the Supreme Court shall become final upon the expiration of thirty days from the time it was rendered, unless within such thirty days either party has instituted proceedings to have such order corrected to accord with the mandate, in which event the order of the commission or board shall become final when so corrected.

(i) If the order of the commission or board is modified or set aside by the court of appeals, and if (1) the time allowed for filing a petition for certiorari has expired and no such petition has been duly filed, or (2) the petition for certiorari has been denied, or (3) the decision of the court has been affirmed by the Supreme Court, then the order of the commission or board rendered in accordance with the mandate of the court of appeals shall become final on the expiration of thirty days from the time such order of the commission or board was rendered, unless within such thirty days either party has instituted proceedings to have such order corrected so that it will accord with the mandate, in which event the order of the commission or board shall become final when so corrected.

(j) If the Supreme Court orders a rehearing; or if the case is remanded by the court of appeals to the commission or board for a rehearing, and if (1) the time allowed for filing a petition for certiorari has expired, and no such petition has been duly filed, or (2) the petition for certiorari has been denied, or (3) the decision of the court has been affirmed by the Supreme Court, then the order of the commission or board rendered upon such rehearing shall become final in the same manner as though no prior order of the commission or board had been rendered.

(k) As used in this section the term 'mandate,' in case a mandate has been recalled prior to the expiration of thirty days from the date of issuance thereof, means the final mandate.

(*l*) Any person who violates any order issued by the commission or board under subsection (b) after such order has become final, and while such order is in effect, shall forfeit and pay to the United States a civil penalty of not more than $5,000 for each violation, which shall accrue to the United States and may be recovered in a civil action brought by the United States. Each separate violation of any such order shall be a separate offense, except that in the case of a violation through continuing failure or neglect to obey a final order of the commission or board each day of continuance of such failure or neglect shall be deemed a separate offense.

SEC. 12. That any suit, action, or proceeding under the antitrust laws against a corporation may be brought not only in the judicial

APPENDIX B

district whereof it is an inhabitant, but also in any district wherein it may be found or transacts business; and all process in such cases may be served in the district of which it is an inhabitant, or wherever it may be found.

SEC. 13. That in any suit, action, or proceeding brought by or on behalf of the United States subpoenas for witnesses who are required to attend a court of the United States in any judicial district in any case, civil or criminal, arising under the antitrust laws may run into any other district: *Provided*, That in civil cases no writ of subpoena shall issue for witnesses living out of the district in which the court is held at a greater distance than one hundred miles from the place of holding the same without the permission of the trial court being first had upon proper application and cause shown.

SEC. 14. That whenever a corporation shall violate any of the penal provisions of the antitrust laws, such violation shall be deemed to be also that of the individual directors, officers, or agents of such corporation who shall have authorized, ordered, or done any of the acts constituting in whole or in part such violation, and such violation shall be deemed a misdemeanor, and upon conviction therefor of any such director, officer, or agent he shall be punished by a fine of not exceeding $5,000 or by imprisonment for not exceeding one year, or by both, in the discretion of the court.

SEC. 15. That the several district courts of the United States are hereby invested with jurisdiction to prevent and restrain violations of this Act, and it shall be the duty of the several district attorneys of the United States, in their respective districts, under the direction of the Attorney General, to institute proceedings in equity to prevent and restrain such violations. Such proceedings may be by way of petition setting forth the case and praying that such violation shall be enjoined or otherwise prohibited. When the parties complained of shall have been duly notified of such petition, the court shall proceed, as soon as may be, to the hearing and determination of the case; and pending such petition, and before final decree, the court may at any time make such temporary restraining order or prohibition as shall be deemed just in the premises. Whenever it shall appear to the court before which any such proceeding may be pending that the ends of justice require that other parties should be brought before the court, the court may cause them to be summoned whether they reside in the district in which the court is held or not, and subpoenas to that end may be served in any district by the marshal thereof.

SEC. 16. Any person, firm, corporation, or association shall be entitled to sue for and have injunctive relief, in any court of the United States having jurisdiction over the parties, as against threatened loss or damage by a violation of the antitrust laws, including sections two, three, seven, and eight of this Act, when and under the same conditions and principles as injunctive relief against threatened conduct that will cause loss or damage is granted by courts of equity, under the rules governing such proceedings, and upon the execution of proper bond against damages for an injunction improvidently granted and a showing that the danger of irreparable loss or damage is immediate, a preliminary injunction may issue: *Provided,* That nothing herein contained shall be construed to entitle any person, firm, corporation, or association, except the United States, to bring suit in equity for injunctive relief against any common carrier subject to the provisions of the Act to regulate commerce, approved February fourth, eighteen hundred and eighty-seven, in respect of any matter subject to the regulation, supervision, or other jurisdiction of the Interstate Commerce Commission.

SEC. 20. That no restraining order or injunction shall be granted by any court of the United States, or a judge or the judges thereof, in any case between an employer and employees, or between employers and employees, or between employees, or between persons employed and persons seeking employment, involving, or growing out of, a dispute concerning terms or conditions of employment, unless necessary to prevent irreparable injury to property, or to a property right, of the party making the application, for which injury there is no adequate remedy at law, and such property or property right must be described with particularity in the application, which must be in writing and sworn to by the applicant or by his agent or attorney.

And no such restraining order or injunction shall prohibit any person or persons, whether singly or in concert, from terminating any relation of employment, or from ceasing to perform any work or labor, or from recommending, advising, or persuading others by peaceful means so to do; or from attending at any place where any such person or persons may lawfully be, for the purpose of peacefully obtaining or communicating information, or from peacefully persuading any person to work or to abstain from working; or from ceasing to patronize or to employ any party to such dispute, or from recommending, advising, or persuading others by peaceful and lawful means so to do; or from paying or giving to, or withholding from, any persons engaged in such dispute, any strike benefits or other moneys or things of value; or from peaceably assembling in a lawful manner, and for lawful purposes; or from doing any act or thing which might lawfully be done in the absence of such dispute by any party thereto; nor shall any of the acts specified in this paragraph be considered or held to be violations of any law of the United States.

SEC. 26. If any clause, sentence, paragraph, or part of this Act shall, for any reason, be adjudged " * * * invalid, such judgment shall not affect, impair, or invalidate the remainder thereof * * *."

APPENDIX B

FEDERAL TRADE COMMISSION ACT [3]

AN ACT To create a Federal Trade Commission, to define its powers and duties and for other purposes.

SEC. 1. *Be it created by the Senate and House of Representatives of the United States of America in Congress assembled*, That a commission is hereby created and established, to be known as the Federal Trade Commission (hereinafter referred to as the commission), which shall be composed of five commissioners, who shall be appointed by the President, by and with the advice and consent of the Senate. Not more than three of the commissioners shall be members of the same political party. The first commissioners appointed shall continue in office for terms of three, four, five, six, and seven years, respectively, from the date of the taking effect of this Act, the term of each to be designated by the President, but their successors shall be appointed for terms of seven years, except that any person chosen to fill a vacancy shall be appointed only for the unexpired term of the commissioner whom he shall succeed: *Provided, however*, That upon the expiration of his term of office a Commissioner shall continue to serve until his successor shall have been appointed and shall have qualified. The President shall choose a chairman from the commission's membership. No commissioner shall engage in any other business, vocation, or employment. Any commissioner may be removed by the President for inefficiency, neglect of duty or malfeasance in office. A vacancy in the commission shall not impair the right of the remaining commissioners to exercise all the powers of the commission.

The commission shall have an official seal, which shall be judicially noticed.

SEC. 2. That each commissioner shall receive a salary * * *

SEC. 3. * * *

---

[3] The Federal Trade Commission Act is the Act of September 26, 1914, c. 11, 38 Stat. 717, 15 U.S.C.A. §§ 41–51. Sections 12 through 18 were added by the Wheeler-Lea Act, 52 Stat. 114 (1938). Section 5 was amended by the McQuire Fair Trade Act, Act of July 14, 1952, c. 745, 66 Stat. 631, which made certain so-called fair trade agreements legal. Those amendments were repealed by the Act of December 2, 1975, Public Law 94–145. Substantial amendments were also made in Sections 5 and 10 by the Act of January 4, 1975, Public Law 93–637, Title II, Section 203(c), 88 Stat. 2199. Section 13(b) was amended and 13(c) was added by the Act of November 16, 1973, Public L. 93–153, Title IV, Section 408(f), 87 Stat. 592. Section 16 was amended by the Act of January 4, 1975, Public Law 93–637, Title II, Section 204(a), 88 Stat. 2199. The Act of January 4, 1975, Public Law 93–637 Title II, Sections 202(a), 88 Stat. 2193, 206(a), 88 Stat. 2201, and 207, 88 Stat. 2203, added Sections 19 through 21. Portions of the Act not deemed relevant to antitrust issues have been omitted from this Appendix.

SEC. 4. The words defined in this section shall have the following meaning when found in this Act, to wit:

"Commerce" means commerce among the several States or with foreign nations, or in any Territory of the United States or in the District of Columbia, or between any such Territory and another, or between any such Territory and any State or foreign nation, or between the District of Columbia and any State or Territory or foreign nation.

"Corporation" shall be deemed to include any company, trust, so-called Massachusetts trust, or association, incorporated or unincorporated, which is organized to carry on business for its own profit or that of its members, and has shares of capital or capital stock or certificates of interest, and any company, trust, so-called Massachusetts trust, or association, incorporated or unincorporated, without shares of capital or capital stock or certificates of interest, except partnerships, which is organized to carry on business for its own profit or that of its members.

"Documentary evidence" includes all documents, papers, correspondence, books of account, and financial and corporate records.

"Acts to regulate commerce" means the Act entitled "An Act to regulate commerce," approved February 14, 1887, and all Acts amendatory thereof and supplementary thereto and the Communications Act of 1934 and all Acts amendatory thereof and supplementary thereto.

"Antitrust Acts," means the Act entitled "An Act to protect trade and commerce against unlawful restraints and monopolies," approved July 2, 1890; also sections 73 to 77, inclusive, of an Act entitled "An Act to reduce taxation, to provide revenue for the Government, and for other purposes," approved August 27, 1894; also the Act entitled "An Act to amend sections 73 and 76 of the Act of August 27, 1894, entitled 'An Act to reduce taxation, to provide revenue for the Government, and for other purposes,' " approved February 12, 1913; and also the Act entitled "An Act to supplement existing laws against unlawful restraints and monopolies, and for other purposes," approved October 15, 1914.

SEC. 5. (a)(1) Unfair methods of competition in or affecting commerce, and unfair or deceptive acts or practices in or affecting commerce, are hereby declared unlawful.

(2) The Commission is hereby empowered and directed to prevent persons, partnerships, or corporations, except banks, common carriers subject to the Acts to regulate commerce, air carriers and foreign air carriers subject to the Federal Aviation Act of 1958, and persons, partnerships, or corporations insofar as they are subject to the Packers and Stockyards Act, 1921, as amended, except as provided in section 406(b) of said Act, from using unfair methods of

competition in or affecting commerce and unfair or deceptive acts or practices in or affecting commerce.

(b) Whenever the Commission shall have reason to believe that any such person, partnership, or corporation has been or is using any unfair method of competition or unfair or deceptive act or practice in or affecting commerce, and if it shall appear to the Commission that a proceeding by it in respect thereof would be to the interest of the public, it shall issue and serve upon such person, partnership, or corporation a complaint stating its charges in that respect and containing a notice of a hearing upon a day and at a place therein fixed at least thirty days after the service of said complaint. The person, partnership, or corporation so complained of shall have the right to appear at the place and time so fixed and show cause why an order should not be entered by the Commission requiring such person, partnership, or corporation to cease and desist from the violation of the law so charged in said complaint. Any person, partnership, or corporation may make application, and upon good cause shown may be allowed by the Commission to intervene and appear in said proceeding by counsel or in person. The testimony in any such proceeding shall be reduced to writing and filed in the office of the Commission. If upon such hearing the Commission shall be of the opinion that the method of competition or the act or practice in question is prohibited by this Act, it shall make a report in writing in which it shall state its findings as to the facts and shall issue and cause to be served on such person, partnership, or corporation an order requiring such person, partnership, or corporation to cease and desist from using such method of competition or such act or practice. Until the expiration of the time allowed for filing a petition for review, if no such petition has been duly filed within such time, or, if a petition for review has been filed within such time then until the record in the proceeding has been filed in a court of appeals of the United States, as hereinafter provided, the Commission may at any time, upon such notice and in such manner as it shall deem proper, modify or set aside, in whole or in part, any report or any order made or issued by it under this section. After the expiration of the time allowed for filing a petition for review, if no such petition has been duly filed within such time, the Commission may at any time, after notice and opportunity for hearing, reopen and alter, modify, or set aside, in whole or in part, any report or order made or issued by it under this section, whenever in the opinion of the Commission conditions of fact or of law have so changed as to require such action or if the public interest shall so require: *Provided, however*, That the said person, partnership, or corporation may, within sixty days after service upon him or it of said report or order entered after such a reopening, obtain a review thereof in the appropriate court of appeals of the United States, in the manner provided in subsection (c) of this section.

(c) Any person, partnership, or corporation required by an order of the Commission to cease and desist from using any method of competition or act or practice may obtain a review of such order in the court of appeals of the United States, within any circuit where the method of competition or the act or practice in question was used or where such person, partnership, or corporation resides or carries on business, by filing in the court, within sixty days from the date of the service of such order, a written petition praying that the order of the Commission be set aside. A copy of such petition shall be forthwith transmitted by the clerk of the court to the Commission, and thereupon the Commission shall file in the court the record in the proceeding, as provided in section 2112 of title 28, United States Code. Upon such filing of the petition the court shall have jurisdiction of the proceeding and of the question determined therein concurrently with the Commission until the filing of the record and shall have power to make and enter a decree affirming, modifying, or setting aside the order of the Commission, and enforcing the same to the extent that such order is affirmed and to issue such writs as are ancillary to its jurisdiction or are necessary in its judgment to prevent injury to the public or to competitors pendente lite. The findings of the Commission as to the facts, if supported by evidence, shall be conclusive. To the extent that the order of the Commission is affirmed, the court shall thereupon issue its own order commanding obedience to the terms of such order of the Commission. If either party shall apply to the court for leave to adduce additional evidence, and shall show to the satisfaction of the court that such additional evidence is material and that there were reasonable grounds for the failure to adduce such evidence in the proceeding before the Commission, the court may order such additional evidence to be taken before the Commission and to be adduced upon the hearing in such manner and upon such terms and conditions as to the court may seem proper. The Commission may modify its findings as to the facts, or make new findings, by reason of the additional evidence so taken, and it shall file such modified or new findings, which, if supported by evidence, shall be conclusive, and its recommendation, if any, for the modification or setting aside of its original order, with the return of such additional evidence. The judgment and decree of the court shall be final, except that the same shall be subject to review by the Supreme Court upon certiorari, as provided in section 1254 of Title 28.

(d) Upon the filing of the record with it the jurisdiction of the court of appeals of the United States to affirm, enforce, modify, or set aside orders of the Commission shall be exclusive.

(e) Such proceedings in the court of appeals shall be given precedence over other cases pending therein, and shall be in every way expedited. No order of the Commission or judgment of court to enforce the same shall in anywise relieve or absolve any person, partnership, or corporation from any liability under the Antitrust Acts.

APPENDIX B

(f) Complaints, orders, and other processes of the Commission under this section may be served by anyone duly authorized by the Commission, either (a) by delivering a copy thereof to the person to be served, or to a member of the partnership to be served, or the president, secretary, or other executive officer or a director of the corporation to be served; or (b) by leaving a copy thereof at the residence or the principal office or place of business of such person, partnership, or corporation; or (c) by registering and mailing a copy thereof addressed to such person, partnership, or corporation at his or its residence or principal office or place of business. The verified return by the person so servicing said complaint, order, or other process setting forth the manner of said service shall be proof of the same, and the return post office receipt for said complaint, order, or other process registered and mailed as aforesaid shall be proof of the service of the same.

(g) An order of the Commission to cease and desist shall become final—

(1) Upon the expiration of the time allowed for filing a petition for review, if no such petition has been duly filed within such time; but the Commission may thereafter modify or set aside its order to the extent provided in the last sentence of subsection (b); or

(2) Upon the expiration of the time allowed for filing a petition for certiorari, if the order of the Commission has been affirmed, or the petition for review dismissed by the court of appeals, and no petition for certiorari has been duly filed; or

(3) Upon the denial of a petition for certiorari, if the order of the Commission has been affirmed or the petition for review dismissed by the court of appeals; or

(4) Upon the expiration of thirty days from the date of issuance of the mandate of the Supreme Court, if such Court directs that the order of the Commission be affirmed or the petition for review dismissed.

(h) If the Supreme Court directs that the order of the Commission be modified or set aside, the order of the Commission rendered in accordance with the mandate of the Supreme Court shall become final upon the expiration of thirty days from the time it was rendered, unless within such thirty days either party has instituted proceedings to have such order corrected to accord with the mandate, in which event the order of the Commission shall become final when so corrected.

(i) If the order of the Commission is modified or set aside by the court of appeals, and if (1) the time allowed for filing a petition for certiorari has expired and no such petition has been duly filed, or (2) the petition for certiorari has been denied, or (3) the decision of the court has been affirmed by the Supreme Court, then the order of the Commission rendered in accordance with the mandate of the court of appeals shall become final on the expiration of thirty days from the time such order of the Commission was rendered, unless within such thirty days either party has instituted proceedings to have such order corrected so that it will accord with the mandate, in which event the order of the Commission shall become final when so corrected.

(j) If the Supreme Court orders a rehearing; or if the case is remanded by the court of appeals to the Commission for a rehearing, and if (1) the time allowed for filing a petition for certiorari has expired, and no such petition has been duly filed, or (2) the petition for certiorari has been denied, or (3) the decision of the court has been affirmed by the Supreme Court, then the order of the Commission rendered upon such rehearing shall become final in the same manner as though no prior order of the Commission had been rendered.

(k) As used in this section the term "mandate," in case a mandate has been recalled prior to the expiration of thirty days from the date of issuance thereof, means the final mandate.

(*l*) Any person, partnership, or corporation who violates an order of the Commission after it has become final, and while such order is in effect, shall forfeit and pay to the United States a civil penalty of not more than $10,000 for each violation, which shall accrue to the United States and may be recovered in a civil action brought by the Attorney General of the United States. Each separate violation of such an order shall be a separate offense, except that in the case of a violation through continuing failure to obey or neglect to obey a final order of the Commission, each day of continuance of such failure or neglect shall be deemed a separate offense. In such actions, the United States district courts are empowered to grant mandatory injunctions and such other and further equitable relief as they deem appropriate in the enforcement of such final orders of the Commission.

(m) (1) (A) The Commission may commence a civil action to recover a civil penalty in a district court of the United States against any person, partnership, or corporation which violates any rule under this chapter respecting unfair or deceptive acts or practices (other than an interpretive rule or a rule violation of which the Commission has provided is not an unfair or deceptive act or practice in violation of subsection (a) (1) of this section) with actual knowledge or knowledge fairly implied on the basis of objective circumstances that such act is unfair or deceptive and is prohibited by such rule. In such action, such person, partnership, or corporation shall be liable for a civil penalty of not more than $10,000 for each violation.

(B) If the Commission determines in a proceeding under subsection (b) of this section that any act or practice is unfair or deceptive, and issues a final cease and desist order with respect to such act or practice, then the Commission may commence a civil action to

APPENDIX B

obtain a civil penalty in a district court of the United States against any person, partnership, or corporation which engages in such act or practice—

    (1) after such cease and desist order becomes final (whether or not such person, partnership, or corporation was subject to such cease and desist order), and

    (2) with actual knowledge that such act or practice is unfair or deceptive and is unlawful under subsection (a)(1) of this section.

In such action, such person, partnership, or corporation shall be liable for a civil penalty of not more than $10,000 for each violation.

(C) In the case of a violation through continuing failure to comply with a rule or with subsection (a)(1) of this section, each day of continuance of such failure shall be treated as a separate violation, for purposes of subparagraphs (A) and (B). In determining the amount of such a civil penalty, the court shall take into account the degree of culpability, any history of prior such conduct, ability to pay, effect on ability to continue to do business, and such other matters as justice may require.

(2) If the cease and desist order establishing that the act or practice is unfair or deceptive was not issued against the defendant in a civil penalty action under paragraph (1)(B) the issues of fact in such action against such defendant shall be tried de novo.

(3) The Commission may compromise or settle any action for a civil penalty if such compromise or settlement is accompanied by a public statement of its reasons and is approved by the court.

SEC. 6. That the commission shall also have power—

(a) To gather and compile information concerning, and to investigate from time to time the organization, business, conduct, practices, and management of any person, partnership, or corporation engaged in or whose business affects commerce, excepting banks and common carriers subject to the Act to regulate commerce, and its relation to other corporations and to individuals, associations, and partnerships.

(b) To require, by general or special orders, persons, partnerships, and corporations engaged in or whose business affects commerce, excepting banks, and common carriers subject to the Act to regulate commerce, or any class of them, or any of them, respectively, to file with the commission in such form as the commission may prescribe annual or special, or both annual and special, reports or answers in writing to specific questions, furnishing to the commission such information as it may require as to the organization, business, conduct, practices, management, and relation to other corporations, partnerships, and individuals of the respective persons, partnerships, and corporations filing such reports or answers in writing. Such reports and answers shall be made under oath, or otherwise, as the commission may prescribe, and shall be filed with the commission within such reasonable period as the commission may prescribe, unless additional time be granted in any case by the commission.

(c) Whenever a final decree has been entered against any defendant corporation in any suit brought by the United States to prevent and restrain any violation of the antitrust Acts, to make investigation, upon its own initiative, of the manner in which the decree has been or is being carried out, and upon the application of the Attorney General it shall be its duty to make such investigation. It shall transmit to the Attorney General a report embodying its findings and recommendations as a result of any such investigation, and the report shall be made public in the discretion of the commission.

(d) Upon the direction of the President or either House of Congress to investigate and report the facts relating to any alleged violations of the antitrust Acts by any corporation.

(e) Upon the application of the Attorney General to investigate and make recommendations for the readjustment of the business of any corporation alleged to be violating the antitrust Acts in order that the corporation may thereafter maintain its organization, management, and conduct of business in accordance with law.

(f) To make public from time to time such portions of the information obtained by it hereunder, except trade secrets and names of customers, as it shall deem expedient in the public interest; and to make annual and special reports to the Congress and to submit therewith recommendations for additional legislation; and to provide for the publication of its reports and decisions in such form and manner as may be best adapted for public information and use.

(g) From time to time to classify corporations and (except as provided in section 18(a)(2) of this Act) to make rules and regulations for the purpose of carrying out the provisions of this Act.

(h) To investigate, from time to time, trade conditions in and with foreign countries where associations, combinations, or practices of manufacturers, merchants, or traders, or other conditions, may affect the foreign trade of the United States, and to report to Congress thereon, with such recommendations as it deems advisable.

Provided, That the exception of "banks and common carriers subject to the Act to regulate commerce" from the Commission's powers defined in clauses (a) and (b) of this section, shall not be construed to limit the Commission's authority to gather and compile information, to investigate, or to require reports or answers from, any person, partnership, or corporation to the extent that such action is necessary to the investigation of any person, partnership, or corporation, group of persons, partnerships, or corporations, or industry which is not engaged or is engaged only incidentally in banking or in business as a common carrier subject to the Act to regulate commerce.

SEC. 7. That in any suit in equity brought by or under the direction of the Attorney General as provided in the antitrust Acts, the court may, upon the conclusion of the testimony therein, if it shall be then of opinion that the complainant is entitled to relief, refer said suit to the commission, as a master in chancery, to ascertain and report an appropriate form of decree therein. The commission shall proceed upon such notice to the parties and under such rules of procedure as the court may prescribe, and upon the coming in of such report such exceptions may be filed and such proceedings had in relation thereto as upon the report of a master in other equity causes, but the court may adopt or reject such report, in whole or in part, and enter such decree as the nature of the case may in its judgment require.

SEC. 8. That the several departments and bureaus of the Government when directed by the President shall furnish the commission, upon its request, all records, papers, and information in their possession relating to any corporation subject to any of the provisions of this Act, and shall detail from time to time such officials and employees to the commission as he may direct.

SEC. 9. That for the purposes of this Act the commission, or its duly authorized agent or agents, shall at all reasonable times have access to, for the purpose of examination, and the right to copy any documentary evidence of any person, partnership, or corporation being investigated or proceeded against; and the commission shall have power to require by subpoena the attendance and testimony of witnesses and the production of all such documentary evidence relating to any matter under investigation. Any member of the commission may sign subpoenas, and members and examiners of the commission may administer oaths and affirmations, examine witnesses, and receive evidence.

Such attendance of witnesses, and the production of such documentary evidence, may be required from any place in the United States, at any designated place of hearing. And in case of disobedience to a subpoena the commission may invoke the aid of any court of the United States in requiring the attendance and testimony of witnesses and the production of documentary evidence.

Any of the district courts of the United States within the jurisdiction of which such inquiry is carried on may, in case of contumacy or refusal to obey a subpoena issued to any person, partnership, or corporation issue an order requiring such person, partnership or corporation to appear before the commission, or to produce documentary evidence if so ordered, or to give evidence touching the matter in question; and any failure to obey such order of the court may be punished by such court as a contempt thereof.

Upon the application of the Attorney General of the United States, at the request of the commission, the district courts of the United

States shall have jurisdiction to issue writs of mandamus commanding any person, partnership, or corporation to comply with the provisions of this Act or any order of the commission made in pursuance thereof.

The Commission may order testimony to be taken by deposition in any proceeding or investigation pending under this Act at any stage of such proceeding or investigation. Such depositions may be taken before any person designated by the commission and having power to administer oaths. Such testimony shall be reduced to writing by the person taking the deposition, or under his direction, and shall then be subscribed by the deponent. Any person may be compelled to appear and depose and to produce documentary evidence in the same manner as witnesses may be compelled to appear and testify and produce documentary evidence before the commission as hereinbefore provided.

Witnesses summoned before the Commission shall be paid the same fees and mileage that are paid witnesses in the courts of the United States, and witnesses whose depositions are taken, and the persons taking the same shall severally be entitled to the same fees as are paid for like services in the courts of the United States.

SEC. 10. That any person who shall neglect or refuse to attend and testify, or to answer any lawful inquiry, or to produce documentary evidence, if in his power to do so, in obedience to the subpoena or lawful requirement of the commission, shall be guilty of an offense and upon conviction thereof by a court of competent jurisdiction shall be punished by a fine of not less than $1,000 nor more than $5,000, or by imprisonment for not more than one year, or by both such fine and imprisonment.

Any person who shall willfully make, or cause to be made, any false entry or statement of fact in any report required to be made under this Act, or who shall willfully make, or cause to be made, any false entry in any account, record, or memorandum kept by any person, partnership, or corporation subject to said Act, or who shall willfully neglect or fail to make, or to cause to be made, full, true, and correct entries in such accounts, records, or memoranda of all facts and transactions appertaining to the business of such person, partnership, or corporation or who shall willfully remove out of the jurisdiction of the United States, or willfully mutilate, alter, or by any other means falsify any documentary evidence of such person, partnership, or corporation or who shall willfully refuse to submit to the Commission or to any of its authorized agents, for the purpose of inspection and taking copies, any documentary evidence of such person, partnership, or corporation in his possession or within his control, shall be deemed guilty of an offense against the United States, and shall be subject, upon conviction in any court of the United States of competent jurisdiction, to a fine of not less than $1,000 nor more than $5,000, or to imprisonment for a term of not more than three years, or to both such fine and imprisonment.

If any persons, partnership, or corporation required by this Act to file any annual or special report shall fail so to do within the time fixed by the Commission for filing the same, and such failure shall continue for thirty days after notice of such default, the corporation shall forfeit to the United States the sum of $100 for each and every day of the continuance of such failure, which forfeiture shall be payable into the Treasury of the United States, and shall be recoverable in a civil suit in the name of the United States brought in the case of a corporation or partnership in the district where the corporation or partnership has its principal office or in any district in which it shall do business, and in the case of any person in the district where such person resides or has his principal place of business. It shall be the duty of the various United States attorneys, under the direction of the Attorney General of the United States, to prosecute for the recovery of forfeitures. The costs and expenses of such prosecution shall be paid out of the appropriation for the expenses of the courts of the United States.

Any officer or employee of the commission who shall make public any information obtained by the commission without its authority, unless directed by a court, shall be deemed guilty of a misdemeanor, and, upon conviction thereof, shall be punished by a fine not exceeding $5,000, or by imprisonment not exceeding one year, or by fine and imprisonment, in the discretion of the court.

SEC. 11. Nothing contained in this Act shall be construed to prevent or interfere with the enforcement of the provisions of the antitrust Acts or the Acts to regulate commerce, nor shall anything contained in the Act be construed to alter, modify, or repeal the said antitrust Acts or the Acts to regulate commerce or any part or parts thereof.

SEC. 12. * * *

SEC. 13(a). * * *

(b) Whenever the Commission has reason to believe—

(1) that any person, partnership, or corporation is violating, or is about to violate, any provision of law enforced by the Federal Trade Commission, and

(2) that the enjoining thereof pending the issuance of a complaint by the Commission and until such complaint is dismissed by the Commission or set aside by the court on review, or until the order of the Commission made thereon has become final, would be in the interest of the public—

the Commission by any of its attorneys designated by it for such purpose may bring suit in a district court of the United States to enjoin any such act or practice. Upon a proper showing that, weighing the equities and considering the Commission's likelihood of ultimate success, such action would be in the public interest, and after notice to the defendant, a temporary restraining order or a preliminary injunction may be granted without bond: *Provided, however,* That if a complaint is not filed within such period (not exceeding 20 days) as may be specified by the court after issuance of the temporary restraining order or preliminary injunction, the order or injunction shall be dissolved by the court and be of no further force and effect: *Provided further,* That in proper cases the Commission may seek, and after proper proof, the court may issue, a permanent injunction. Any such suit shall be brought in the district in which such person, partnership, or corporation resides or transacts business.

(c) Whenever it appears to the satisfaction of the court in the case of a newspaper, magazine, periodical, or other publication, published at regular intervals—

(1) that restraining the dissemination of a false advertisement in any particular issue of such publication would delay the delivery of such issue after the regular time therefor, and

(2) that such delay would be due to the method by which the manufacture and distribution of such publication is customarily conducted by the publisher in accordance with sound business practice, and not to any method or device adopted for the evasion of this section or to prevent or delay the issuance of an injunction or restraining order with respect to such false advertisement or any other advertisement,

the court shall exclude such issue from the operation of the restraining order or injunction.

SEC. 14. * * *

SEC. 15. * * *

SEC. 16. (a)(1) Except as otherwise provided in paragraph (2) or (3), if—

(A) before commencing, defending, or intervening in, any civil action involving this chapter (including an action to collect a civil penalty) which the Commission, or the Attorney General on behalf of the Commission, is authorized to commence, defend, or intervene in, the Commission gives written notification and undertakes to consult with the Attorney General with respect to such action; and

(B) the Attorney General fails within 45 days after receipt of such notification to commence, defend, or intervene in, such action;

the Commission may commence, defend, or intervene in, and supervise the litigation of, such action and any appeal of such action in its own name by any of its attorneys designated by it for such purpose.

(2) Except as otherwise provided in paragraph (3), in any civil action—

    (A) under section 13 of this Act (relating to injunctive relief);

    (B) * * *

    (C) to obtain judicial review of a rule prescribed by the Commission, or a cease and desist order issued under section 5 of this Act; or

    (D) under the second paragraph of section 9 of this Act (relating to enforcement of a subpena) and under the fourth paragraph of such section * * *;

the Commission shall have exclusive authority to commence or defend, and supervise the litigation of, such action and any appeal of such action in its own name by any of its attorneys designated by it for such purpose, unless the Commission authorizes the Attorney General to do so. The Commission shall inform the Attorney General of the exercise of such authority and such exercise shall not preclude the Attorney General from intervening on behalf of the United States in such action and any appeal of such action as may be otherwise provided by law.

(3)(A) If the Commission makes a written request to the Attorney General, within the 10-day period which begins on the date of the entry of the judgment in any civil action in which the Commission represented itself pursuant to paragraph (1) or (2), to represent itself through any of its attorneys designated by it for such purpose before the Supreme Court in such action, it may do so, if—

    (i) the Attorney General concurs with such request; or

    (ii) the Attorney General, within the 60-day period which begins on the date of the entry of such judgment—

        (a) refuses to appeal or file a petition for writ of certiorari with respect to such civil action, in which case he shall give written notification to the Commission of the reasons for such refusal within such 60-day period; or

        (b) the Attorney General fails to take any action with respect to the Commission's request.

(B) In any case where the Attorney General represents the Commission before the Supreme Court in any civil action in which the Commission represented itself pursuant to paragraph (1) or (2), the Attorney General may not agree to any settlement, compromise, or dismissal of such action, or confess error in the Supreme Court with respect to such action, unless the Commission concurs.

(C) For purposes of this paragraph (with respect to representation before the Supreme Court), the term "Attorney General" includes the Solicitor General.

(4) If, prior to the expiration of the 45-day period specified in paragraph (1) of this section or a 60-day period specified in paragraph (3), any right of the Commission to commence, defend, or intervene in, any such action or appeal may be extinguished due to any procedural requirement of any court with respect to the time in which any pleadings, notice of appeal, or other acts pertaining to such action or appeal may be taken, the Attorney General shall have one-half of the time required to comply with any such procedural requirement of the court (including any extension of such time granted by the court) for the purpose of commencing, defending, or intervening in the civil action pursuant to paragraph (1) or for the purpose of refusing to appeal or file a petition for writ of certiorari and the written notification or failing to take any action pursuant to paragraph 3(A)(ii).

(5) The provisions of this subsection shall apply notwithstanding chapter 31 of Title 28, or any other provision of law.

(b) Whenever the Commission has reason to believe that any person, partnership, or corporation is liable for a criminal penalty under this chapter, the Commission shall certify the facts to the Attorney General, whose duty it shall be to cause appropriate criminal proceedings to be brought.

SEC. 17. If any provision of this Act, or the application thereof to any person, partnership, corporation, or circumstance, is held invalid, the remainder of the Act and the application of such provision to any other person, partnership, corporation, or circumstance, shall not be affected thereby.

SEC. 18. (a)(1) The Commission may prescribe—

(A) interpretative rules and general statements of policy with respect to unfair or deceptive acts or practices in or affecting commerce (within the meaning of section 5(a)(1) of this Act), and

(B) rules which define with specificity acts or practices which are unfair or deceptive acts or practices in or affecting commerce (within the meaning of section 5(a)(1) of this Act). Rules under this subparagraph may include requirements prescribed for the purpose of preventing such acts or practices.

(2) The Commission shall have no authority under this chapter, other than its authority under this section, to prescribe any rule with respect to unfair or deceptive acts or practices in or affecting commerce (within the meaning of section 5(a)(1) of this Act). The preceding sentence shall not affect any authority of the Commission to prescribe rules (including interpretative rules), and general statements of policy, with respect to unfair methods of competition in or affecting commerce.

(b) When prescribing a rule under subsection (a)(1)(B) of this section, the Commission shall proceed in accordance with section 553 of Title 5 (without regard to any reference in such section to sections 556 and 557 of such title), and shall also (1) publish a notice of proposed rulemaking stating with particularity the reason for the proposed rule; (2) allow interested persons to submit written data, views, and arguments, and make all such submissions publicly available; (3) provide an opportunity for an informal hearing in accordance with subsection (c) of this section; and (4) promulgate, if appropriate, a final rule based on the matter in the rulemaking record (as defined in subsection (e)(1)(B) of this section), together with a statement of basis and purpose.

(c) The Commission shall conduct any informal hearings required by subsection (b)(3) of this section in accordance with the following procedure:

(1) Subject to paragraph (2) of this subsection, an interested person is entitled—

(A) to present his position orally or by documentary submissions (or both), and

(B) if the Commission determines that there are disputed issues of material fact it is necessary to resolve, to present such rebuttal submissions and to conduct (or have conducted under paragraph (2)(B)) such cross-examination of persons as the Commission determines (i) to be appropriate, and (ii) to be required for a full and true disclosure with respect to such issues.

(2) The Commission may prescribe such rules and make such rulings concerning proceedings in such hearings as may tend to avoid unnecessary costs or delay. Such rules or rulings may include (A) imposition of reasonable time limits on each interested person's oral presentations, and (B) requirements that any cross-examination to which a person may be entitled under paragraph (1) be conducted by the Commission on behalf of that person in such manner as the Commission determines (i) to be appropriate, and (ii) to be required for a full and true disclosure with respect to disputed issues of material fact.

(3)(A) Except as provided in subparagraph (B), if a group of persons each of whom under paragraphs (1) and (2) would be entitled to conduct (or have conducted) cross-examination and who are determined by the Commission to have the same or similar interests in the proceeding cannot agree upon a single representative of such interests for purposes of cross-examination, the Commission may make rules and rulings (i) limiting the representation of such interest, for such purposes, and (ii) governing the manner in which such cross-examination shall be limited.

(B) When any person who is a member of a group with respect to which the Commission has made a determination under subparagraph (A) is unable to agree upon group representation with the other members of the group, then such person shall not be denied under the authority of subparagraph (A) the opportunity to conduct (or have conducted) cross-examination as to issues affecting his particular interests if (i) he satisfies the Commission that he has made a reasonable and good faith effort to reach agreement upon group representation with the other members of the group and (ii) the Commission determines that there are substantial and relevant issues which are not adequately presented by the group representative.

(4) A verbatim transcript shall be taken of any oral presentation, and cross-examination, in an informal hearing to which this subsection applies. Such transcript shall be available to the public.

(d)(1) The Commission's statement of basis and purpose to accompany a rule promulgated under subsection (a)(1)(B) of this section shall include (A) a statement as to the prevalence of the acts or practices treated by the rule; (B) a statement as to the manner and context in which such acts or practices are unfair or deceptive; and (C) a statement as to the economic effect of the rule, taking into account the effect on small business and consumers.

(2)(A) The term "Commission" as used in this subsection and subsections (b) and (c) of this section includes any person authorized to act in behalf of the Commission in any part of the rulemaking proceeding.

(B) A substantive amendment to, or repeal of, a rule promulgated under subsection (a)(1)(B) of this section shall be prescribed, and subject to judicial review, in the same manner as a rule prescribed under such subsection. An exemption under subsection (g) of this section shall not be treated as an amendment or repeal of a rule.

(3) When any rule under subsection (a)(1)(B) of this section takes effect a subsequent violation thereof shall constitute an unfair or deceptive act or practice in violation of section 5(a)(1) of this Act, unless the Commission otherwise expressly provides in such rule.

(e)(1)(A) Not later than 60 days after a rule is promulgated under subsection (a)(1)(B) of this section by the Commission, any interested person (including a consumer or consumer organization) may file a petition, in the United States Court of Appeals for the District of Columbia circuit or for the circuit in which such person resides or has his principal place of business, for judicial review of such rule. Copies of the petition shall be forthwith transmitted by the clerk of the court to the Commission or other officer designated by it for that purpose. The provisions of section 2112 of Title 28 shall apply to the filing of the rulemaking record of proceedings on which the

Commission based its rule and to the transfer of proceedings in the courts of appeals.

(B) For purposes of this section, the term "rulemaking record" means the rule, its statement of basis and purpose, the transcript required by subsection (c)(4) of this section, any written submissions, and any other information which the Commission considers relevant to such rule.

(2) If the petitioner or the Commission applies to the court for leave to make additional oral submissions or written presentations and shows to the satisfaction of the court that such submissions and presentations would be material and that there were reasonable grounds for the submissions and failure to make such submissions and presentations in the proceeding before the Commission, the court may order the Commission to provide additional opportunity to make such submissions and presentations. The Commission may modify or set aside its rule or make a new rule by reason of the additional submissions and presentations and shall file such modified or new rule, and the rule's statement of basis of purpose, with the return of such submissions and presentations. The court shall thereafter review such new or modified rule.

(3) Upon the filing of the petition under paragraph (1) of this subsection, the court shall have jurisdiction to review the rule in accordance with chapter 7 of Title 5 and to grant appropriate relief, including interim relief, as provided in such chapter. The court shall hold unlawful and set aside the rule on any ground specified in subparagraphs (A), (B), (C), or (D) of section 706(2) of Title 5 (taking due account of the rule of prejudicial error), or if—

(A) the court finds that the Commission's action is not supported by substantial evidence in the rulemaking record (as defined in paragraph (1)(B) of this subsection) taken as a whole, or

(B) the court finds that—

(i) a Commission determination under subsection (c) of this section that the petitioner is not entitled to conduct cross-examination or make rebuttal submissions, or

(ii) a Commission rule or ruling under subsection (c) of this section limiting the petitioner's cross-examination or rebuttal submissions,

has precluded disclosure of disputed material facts which was necessary for fair determination by the Commission of the rulemaking proceeding taken as a whole.

The term "evidence", as used in this paragraph, means any matter in the rulemaking record.

(4) The judgment of the court affirming or setting aside, in whole or in part, any such rule shall be final, subject to review by the Su-

preme Court of the United States upon certiorari or certification, as provided in section 1254 of Title 28.

(5) (A) Remedies under the preceding paragraphs of this subsection are in addition to and not in lieu of any other remedies provided by law.

(B) The United States Courts of Appeal shall have exclusive jurisdiction of any action to obtain judicial review (other than in an enforcement proceeding) of a rule prescribed under subsection (a)(1)(B) of this section, if any district court of the United States would have had jurisdiction of such action but for this subparagraph. Any such action shall be brought in the United States Court of Appeals for the District of Columbia circuit, or for any circuit which includes a judicial district in which the action could have been brought but for this subparagraph.

(C) A determination, rule, or ruling of the Commission described in paragraph (3)(B)(i) or (ii) may be reviewed only in a proceeding under this subsection and only in accordance with paragraph (3)(B). Section 706(2)(E) of Title 5 shall not apply to any rule promulgated under subsection (a)(1)(B) of this section. The contents and adequacy of any statement required by subsection (b)(4) of this section shall not be subject to judicial review in any respect.

(f) * * *

(g)(1) Any person to whom a rule under subsection (a)(1)(B) of this section applies may petition the Commission for an exemption from such rule.

(2) If, on its own motion or on the basis of a petition under paragraph (1), the Commission finds that the application of a rule prescribed under subsection (a)(1)(B) of this section to any person or class or persons is not necessary to prevent the unfair or deceptive act or practice to which the rule relates, the Commission may exempt such person or class from all or part of such rule. Section 553 of Title 5 shall apply to action under this paragraph.

(3) Neither the pendency of a proceeding under this subsection respecting an exemption from a rule, nor the pendency of judicial proceedings to review the Commission's action or failure to act under this subsection, shall stay the applicability of such rule under subsection (a)(1)(B) of this section.

(h)(1) The Commission may, pursuant to rules prescribed by it, provide compensation for reasonable attorneys fees, expert witness fees, and other costs of participating in a rulemaking proceeding under this section to any person (A) who has, or represents, an interest (i) which would not otherwise be adequately represented in such proceeding, and (ii) representation of which is necessary for a fair determination of the rulemaking proceeding taken as a whole, and (B) who is unable effectively to participate in such proceeding because such person cannot afford to pay costs of making oral presentations, conducting cross-examination, and making rebuttal submissions in such proceeding.

(2) The aggregate amount of compensation paid under this subsection in any fiscal year to all persons who, in rulemaking proceedings in which they receive compensation, are persons who either (A) would be regulated by the proposed rule, or (B) represent persons who would be so regulated, may not exceed 25 percent of the aggregate amount paid as compensation under this subsection to all persons in such fiscal year.

(3) The aggregate amount of compensation paid to all persons in any fiscal year under this subsection may not exceed $1,000,000.

SEC. 19. (a) (1) If any person, partnership, or corporation violates any rule under this chapter respecting unfair or deceptive acts or practices (other than an interpretive rule, or a rule violation of which the Commission has provided is not an unfair or deceptive act or practice in violation of section 5(a) of this Act), then the Commission may commence a civil action against such person, partnership, or corporation for relief under subsection (b) of this section in a United States district court or in any court of competent jurisdiction of a State.

(2) If any person, partnership, or corporation engages in any unfair or deceptive act or practice (within the meaning of section 5(a) of this Act) with respect to which the Commission has issued a final cease and desist order which is applicable to such person, partnership, or corporation, then the Commission may commence a civil action against such person, partnership, or corporation in a United States district court or in any court of competent jurisdiction of a State. If the Commission satisfies the court that the act or practice to which the cease and desist order relates is one which a reasonable man would have known under the circumstances was dishonest or fraudulent, the court may grant relief under subsection (b) of this section.

(b) The court in an action under subsection (a) of this section shall have jurisdiction to grant such relief as the court finds necessary to redress injury to consumers or other persons, partnerships, and corporations resulting from the rule violation or the unfair or deceptive act or practice, as the case may be. Such relief may include, but shall not be limited to, rescission or reformation of contracts, the refund of money or return of property, the payment of damages, and public notification respecting the rule violation or the unfair or deceptive act or practice, as the case may be; except that nothing in this subsection is intended to authorize the imposition of any exemplary or punitive damages.

(c) (1) If (A) a cease and desist order issued under section 5(b) of this Act has become final under section 5(g) of this Act with respect to any person's, partnership's, or corporation's rule violation or unfair or deceptive act or practice, and (B) an action under this section is brought with respect to such person's partnership's, or corporation's rule violation or act or practice, then the findings of the Commission as to the material facts in the proceeding under section 5(b) of this Act with respect to such person's, partnership's, or corporation's rule violation or act or practice, shall be conclusive unless (i) the terms of such cease and desist order expressly provide that the Commission's findings shall not be conclusive, or (ii) the order became final by reason of section 5(g)(1) of this Act, in which case such finding shall be conclusive if supported by evidence.

(2) The court shall cause notice of an action under this section to be given in a manner which is reasonably calculated, under all of the circumstances, to apprise the persons, partnerships, and corporations allegedly injured by the defendant's rule violation or act or practice of the pendency of such action. Such notice may, in the discretion of the court, be given by publication.

(d) No action may be brought by the Commission under this section more than 3 years after the rule violation to which an action under subsection (a)(1) of this section relates, or the unfair or deceptive act or practice to which an action under subsection (a)(2) of this section relates; except that if a cease and desist order with respect to any person's, partnership's, or corporation's rule violation or unfair or deceptive act or practice has become final and such order was issued in a proceeding under section 5(b) of this Act which was commenced not later than 3 years after the rule violation or act or practice occurred, a civil action may be commenced under this section against such person, partnership, or corporation at any time before the expiration of one year after such order becomes final.

(e) Remedies provided in this section are in addition to, and not in lieu of, any other remedy or right of action provided by State or Federal law. Nothing in this section shall be construed to affect any authority of the Commission under any other provision of law.

SEC. 20. There are authorized to be appropriated to carry out the functions, powers, and duties of the Federal Trade Commission * * *.

SEC. 21. This Act may be cited as the "Federal Trade Commission Act."

APPENDIX B

ANTITRUST CIVIL PROCESS ACT [4]

§ 1311. Definitions

For the purposes of this chapter—

(a) The term "antitrust law" includes:

(1) Each provision of law defined as one of the antitrust laws by section [1 of the Clayton Act];

(2) The Federal Trade Commission Act; and

(3) Any statute enacted on and after September 19, 1962 by the Congress which prohibits, or makes available to the United States in any court of the United States any civil remedy with respect to (A) any restraint upon or monopolization of interstate or foreign trade or commerce, or (B) any unfair trade practice in or affecting such commerce;

(b) The term "antitrust order" means any final order, decree, or judgment of any court of the United States, duly entered in any case or proceeding arising under any antitrust law;

(c) The term "antitrust investigation" means any inquiry conducted by any antitrust investigator for the purpose of ascertaining whether any person is or has been engaged in any antitrust violation;

(d) The term "antitrust violation" means any act or omission in violation of any antitrust law or any antitrust order;

(e) The term "antitrust investigator" means any attorney or investigator employed by the Department of Justice who is charged with the duty of enforcing or carrying into effect any antitrust law;

(f) The term "person" means any corporation, association, partnership, or other legal entity not a natural person;

(g) The term "documentary material" includes the original or any copy of any book, record, report, memorandum, paper, communication, tabulation, chart, or other document; and

(h) The term "custodian" means the antitrust document custodian or any deputy custodian designated under section 1313(a) of this title.

§ 1312. Civil investigative demand—Issuance

(a) Whenever the Attorney General, or the Assistant Attorney General in charge of the Antitrust Division of the Department of Justice, has reason to believe that any person under investigation may be in possession, custody, or control of any documentary material rele-

---

4. The Antitrust Civil Process Act was enacted as 76 Stat. 548 (1962). It appears as 15 U.S.C.A. §§ 1311–14. The U.S.C.A. section numbers and headings are used herein. Note: The text of the Antitrust Civil Process Act in this Appendix does not contain the amendments enacted in the Hart-Scott-Rodino Antitrust Improvement Act of 1976, Public Law 94–435, Sept. 30, 1976. For a summary of these changes, see Appendix D, infra.

vant to a civil antitrust investigation, he may, prior to the institution of a civil or criminal proceeding thereon, issue in writing, and cause to be served upon such person, a civil investigative demand requiring such person to produce such material for examination.

(b) Each such demand shall—

(1) state the nature of the conduct constituting the alleged antitrust violation which is under investigation and the provision of law applicable thereto;

(2) describe the class or classes of documentary material to be produced thereunder with such definiteness and certainty as to permit such material to be fairly identified;

(3) prescribe a return date which will provide a reasonable period of time within which the material so demanded may be assembled and made available for inspection and copying or reproduction; and

(4) identify the custodian to whom such material shall be made available.

(c) No such demand shall—

(1) contain any requirement which would be held to be unreasonable if contained in a subpoena duces tecum issued by a court of the United States in aid of a grand jury investigation of such alleged antitrust violation; or

(2) require the production of any documentary evidence which would be privileged from disclosure if demanded by a subpoena duces tecum issued by a court of the United States in aid of a grand jury investigation of such alleged antitrust violation.

(d) Any such demand may be served by any antitrust investigator, or by any United States marshal or deputy marshal, at any place within the territorial jurisdiction of any court of the United States.

(e) Service of any such demand or of any petition filed under section 1314 of this title may be made upon a partnership, corporation, association, or other legal entity by—

(1) delivering a duly executed copy thereof to any partner, executive officer, managing agent, or general agent thereof, or to any agent thereof authorized by appointment or by law to receive service of process on behalf of such partnership, corporation, association, or entity;

(2) delivering a duly executed copy thereof to the principal office or place of business of the partnership, corporation, association, or entity to be served; or

(3) depositing such copy in the United States mails, by registered or certified mail duly addressed to such partnership, corporation, association, or entity at its principal office or place of business.

(f) A verified return by the individual serving any such demand or petition setting forth the manner of such service shall be proof of such service. In the case of service by registered or certified mail, such return shall be accompanied by the return post office receipt of delivery of such demand.

§ 1313. Antitrust document custodian—Designation; deputy custodians

(a) The Assistant Attorney General in charge of the Antitrust Division of the Department of Justice shall designate an antitrust investigator to serve as antitrust document custodian, and such additional antitrust investigators as he shall determine from time to time to be necessary to serve as deputies to such officer.

(b) Any person upon whom any demand issued under section 1312 of this title has been duly served shall make such material available for inspection and copying or reproduction to the custodian designated therein at the principal place of business of such person (or at such other place as such custodian and such person thereafter may agree and prescribe in writing or as the court may direct, pursuant to section 1314(d) of this title) on the return date specified in such demand (or on such later date as such custodian may prescribe in writing). Such person may upon written agreement between such person and the custodian substitute for copies of all or any part of such material originals thereof.

(c) The custodian to whom any documentary material is so delivered shall take physical possession thereof, and shall be responsible for the use made thereof and for the return thereof pursuant to this chapter. The custodian may cause the preparation of such copies of such documentary material as may be required for official use under regulations which shall be promulgated by the Attorney General. While in the possession of the custodian, no material so produced shall be available for examination, without the consent of the person who produced such material, by any individual other than a duly authorized officer, member, or employee of the Department of Justice. Under such reasonable terms and conditions as the Attorney General shall prescribe, documentary material while in the possession of the custodian shall be available for examination by the person who produced such material or any duly authorized representative of such person.

(d) Whenever any attorney has been designated to appear on behalf of the United States before any court or grand jury in any case or proceeding involving any alleged antitrust violation, the custodian may deliver to such attorney such documentary material in the possession of the custodian as such attorney determines to be required for use in the presentation of such case or proceeding on behalf of the United States. Upon the conclusion of any such case or proceeding, such attorney shall return to the custodian any documentary material so withdrawn which has not passed into the control of such court or grand jury through the introduction thereof into the record of such case or proceeding.

(e) Upon the completion of (1) the antitrust investigation for which any documentary material was produced under this chapter, and (2) any case or proceeding arising from such investigation, the custodian shall return to the person who produced such material all such material (other than copies thereof made by the Department of Justice pursuant to subsection (c) of this section) which has not passed into the control of any court or grand jury through the introduction thereof into the record of such case or proceeding.

(f) When any documentary material has been produced by any person under this chapter for use in any antitrust investigation, and no such case or proceeding arising therefrom has been instituted within a reasonable time after completion of the examination and analysis of all evidence assembled in the course of such investigation, such person shall be entitled, upon written demand made upon the Attorney General or upon the Assistant Attorney General in charge of the Antitrust Division, to the return of all documentary material (other than copies thereof made by the Department of Justice pursuant to subsection (c) of this section) so produced by such person.

(g) In the event of the death, disability, or separation from service in the Department of Justice of the custodian of any documentary material produced under any demand issued under this chapter, or the official relief of such custodian from responsibility for the custody and control of such material, the Assistant Attorney General in charge of the Antitrust Division shall promptly (1) designate another antitrust investigator to serve as custodian thereof, and (2) transmit notice in writing to the person who produced such material as to the identity and address of the successor so designated. Any successor so designated shall have with regard to such materials all duties and responsibilities imposed by this chapter upon his predecessor in office with regard thereto, except that he shall not be held responsible for any default or dereliction which occurred before his designation as custodian.

§ 1314. Judicial proceedings—Petition for enforcement; venue

(a) Whenever any person fails to comply with any civil investigative demand duly served upon him under section 1312 of this title or whenever satisfactory copying or reproduction of any such material cannot be done and such person refuses to surrender such material, the Attorney General, through such officers or attorneys as he may designate, may file, in the district court of the United States for any judicial district in which such person resides, is found, or transacts business, and serve upon such person a petition for an order of such court for the enforcement of this chapter, except that if such person transacts business in more than one such district such petition shall be filed in the district in which such person maintains his principal place of business, or in such other district in which such person transacts business as may be agreed upon by the parties to such petition.

(b) Within twenty days after the service of any such demand upon any person, or at any time before the return date specified in the demand, whichever period is shorter, such person may file, in the district court of the United States for the judicial district within which such person resides, is found, or transacts business, and serve upon such custodian a petition for an order of such court modifying or setting aside such demand. The time allowed for compliance with the demand in whole or in part as deemed proper and ordered by the court shall not run during the pendency of such petition in the court. Such petition shall specify each ground upon which the petitioner relies in seeking such relief, and may be based upon any failure of such demand to comply with the provisions of this chapter, or upon any constitutional or other legal right or privilege of such person.

(c) At any time during which any custodian is in custody or control of any documentary material delivered by any person in compliance with any such demand, such person may file, in the district court of the United States for the judicial district within which the office of such custodian is situated, and serve upon such custodian a petition for an order of such court requiring the performance by such custodian of any duty imposed upon him by this chapter.

(d) Whenever any petition is filed in any district court of the United States under this section, such court shall have jurisdiction to hear and determine the matter so presented, and to enter such order or orders as may be required to carry into effect the provisions of this chapter. Any final order so entered shall be subject to appeal pursuant to section 1291 of Title 28. Any disobedience of any final order entered under this section by any court shall be punished as a contempt thereof.

(e) To the extent that such rules may have application and are not inconsistent with the provisions of this chapter, the Federal Rules of Civil Procedure shall apply to any petition under this chapter.

ANTITRUST PROCEDURES AND PENALTIES ACT—EXPEDITING ACT [5]

* * *

SEC. 4. Section 1 of the Act of February 11, 1903 (32 Stat. 823), as amended (15 U.S.C. 28; 49 U.S.C. 44), commonly known as the Expediting Act, is amended to read as follows:

"Section 1. In any civil action brought in any district court of the United States under the Act entitled 'An Act to protect trade and

---

5. The Antitrust Procedures and Penalties Act was enacted as Public Law 93–528, 88 Stat. 1706. (15 U.S.C.A. §§ 1, 2, 3, 16, 28, 29; 47 U.S.C.A. § 401; 49 U.S.C.A. §§ 43–45 (1976)). Sections of that Act which amend the Sherman Act and the Clayton Act are reflected in those acts, as set forth in this Appendix, and are deleted here. Certain other sections are also deleted.

commerce against unlawful restraints and monopolies', approved July 2, 1890, or any other Acts having like purpose that have been or hereafter may be enacted, wherein the United States is plaintiff and equitable relief is sought, the Attorney General may file with the court, prior to the entry of final judgment, a certificate that, in his opinion, the case is of a general public importance. Upon filing of such certificate, it shall be the duty of the judge designated to hear and determine the case, or the chief judge of the district court if no judge has as yet been designated, to assign the case for hearing at the earliest practicable date and to cause the case to be in every way expedited."

SEC. 5. Section 2 of that Act (15 U.S.C. 29; 49 U.S.C. 45) is amended to read as follows:

"(a) Except as otherwise expressly provided by this section, in every civil action brought in any district court of the United States under the Act entitled 'An Act to protect trade and commerce against unlawful restraints and monopolies', approved July 2, 1890, or any other Acts having like purpose that have been or hereafter may be enacted, in which the United States is the complainant and equitable relief is sought, any appeal from a final judgment entered in any such action shall be taken to the court of appeals pursuant to sections 1291 and 2107 of title 28 of the United States Code. Any appeal from an interlocutory order entered in any such action shall be taken to the court of appeals pursuant to sections 1292(a)(1) and 2107 of title 28 of the United States Code but not otherwise. Any judgment entered by the court of appeals in any such action shall be subject to review by the Supreme Court upon a writ of certiorari as provided in section 1254(1) of title 28 of the United States Code.

"(b) An appeal from a final judgment pursuant to subsection (a) shall lie directly to the Supreme Court if, upon application of a party filed within fifteen days of the filing of a notice of appeal, the district judge who adjudicated the case enters an order stating that immediate consideration of the appeal by the Supreme Court is of general public importance in the administration of justice. Such order shall be filed within thirty days after the filing of a notice of appeal. When such an order is filed, the appeal and any cross appeal shall be docketed in the time and manner prescribed by the rules of the Supreme Court. The Supreme Court shall thereupon either (1) dispose of the appeal and any cross appeal in the same manner as any other direct appeal authorized by law, or (2) in its discretion, deny the direct appeal and remand the case to the court of appeals, which shall then have jurisdiction to hear and determine the same as if the appeal and any cross appeal therein had been docketed in the court of appeals in the first instance pursuant to subsection (a)."

APPENDIX C

Cross references of the original sections of the Sherman, Clayton, Federal Trade Commission, and Antitrust Penalties and Procedures Acts to the United States Code Annotated.

THE SHERMAN ACT [1]

Original Section Numbers Sec.	U.S.C.A. Citations
1	15 U.S.C.A. § 1 (1976)
2	15 U.S.C.A. § 2 (1976)
3	15 U.S.C.A. § 3 (1976)
4	15 U.S.C.A. § 4 (1973)
5	15 U.S.C.A. § 5 (1973)
6	15 U.S.C.A. § 6 (1973)
8	15 U.S.C.A. § 7 (1973)

THE CLAYTON ACT [2]

Original Section Numbers Sec.	U.S.C.A. Citations
1	15 U.S.C.A. § 12 (1973)
	29 U.S.C.A. § 53 (1973)
2	15 U.S.C.A. § 13 (1973)
3	15 U.S.C.A. § 14, 13a (1973)
4	15 U.S.C.A. § 15, 13b (1973)
4A	15 U.S.C.A. § 15a (1973)
4B	15 U.S.C.A. § 15b (1973)
5	15 U.S.C.A. § 16 (1976)
6	15 U.S.C.A. § 17 (1973)
7	15 U.S.C.A. § 18 (1973)
8	15 U.S.C.A. § 19 (1973)
10	15 U.S.C.A. § 20 (1973)
11	15 U.S.C.A. § 21 (1973)
12	15 U.S.C.A. § 22 (1973)
13	15 U.S.C.A. § 23 (1973)
14	15 U.S.C.A. § 24 (1973)
15	15 U.S.C.A. § 25 (1973)
16	15 U.S.C.A. § 26 (1973)
20	29 U.S.C.A. § 52 (1973)
26	15 U.S.C.A. § 27 (1973)

1. See n. 1, Appendix B supra, for a summary of the legislative history of the Sherman Act.

2. See n. 2, Appendix B supra, for a summary of the legislative history of the Clayton Act.

APPENDIX C

FEDERAL TRADE COMMISSION ACT [3]

Original Section Numbers Sec.	U.S.C.A. Citations
1	15 U.S.C.A. § 41 (1973)
2	15 U.S.C.A. § 42 (1973)
3	15 U.S.C.A. § 43 (1973)
4	15 U.S.C.A. § 44 (1973)
5	15 U.S.C.A. § 45 (1976)
6	15 U.S.C.A. § 46 (1976)
7	15 U.S.C.A. § 47 (1973)
8	15 U.S.C.A. § 48 (1973)
9	15 U.S.C.A. § 49 (1976)
10	15 U.S.C.A. § 50 (1976)
11	15 U.S.C.A. § 51 (1973)
12	15 U.S.C.A. § 52 (1976)
13	15 U.S.C.A. § 53 (1976)
14	15 U.S.C.A. § 54 (1973)
15	15 U.S.C.A. § 55 (1973)
16	15 U.S.C.A. § 56 (1976)
17	15 U.S.C.A. § 57 (1973)
18	15 U.S.C.A. § 57a (1976)
19	15 U.S.C.A. § 57b (1976)
20	15 U.S.C.A. § 57c (1976)
21 (formerly § 18 short title)	15 U.S.C.A. § 58 (1976)

THE ANTITRUST PROCEDURES AND PENALTIES ACT [4]

Original Section Numbers Sec.	U.S.C.A. Citations
1 (short title)	15 U.S.C.A. § 16 (1976) (see note following section)
2	15 U.S.C.A. § 16(b)–(h) (1976)
3	15 U.S.C.A. § 1 (1976)
	15 U.S.C.A. § 2 (1976)
	15 U.S.C.A. § 3 (1976)
4	15 U.S.C.A. § 28 (1976)
	49 U.S.C.A. § 44 (1976)
5	15 U.S.C.A. § 29 (1976)
	49 U.S.C.A. § 45 (1976)
6(a)	47 U.S.C.A. § 401 (1976)
6(b)	49 U.S.C.A. § 43 (1976)
7 (effective date of amendment)	15 U.S.C.A. § 29 (1976) (see note following section)

3. See n. 3, Appendix B supra, for a summary of the legislative history of the Federal Trade Commission Act.

4. See n. 5, Appendix B supra.

APPENDIX D

The Hart-Scott-Rodino Antitrust Improvement Act of 1976 [1] was signed into law by the President on September 30, 1976. Though it does not change substantive antitrust law, this new law makes significant procedural changes. Salient features are briefly summarized below.

Department of Justice Investigations: Title I of the new law amends the Antitrust Civil Process Act [2] so as to expand the power of the Department of Justice to investigate possible antitrust violations without convening a grand jury or initiating a civil action.

Department investigatory powers are now essentially the same as those possessed by the FTC. Specifically, Section 3 of the Antitrust Civil Process Act, as amended,[3] broadens the Department's power to issue Civil Investigation Demands ("CID's"). Previously, CID's could only be issued to business firms under investigation for a suspected violation. Now they may be issued to any person (natural persons as well as business entities) if the person has information relevant to an investigation or is a suspected violator. Any such person may be required under oath to answer written interrogatories, or to appear and give oral testimony. Persons may also be required to produce documents in their possession, custody or control. The subject matter of investigators for which CID's may be issued is also broadened to include, in addition to suspected antitrust violations, any actively in preparation for a merger, acquisition, joint venture or similar transaction which, if consummated, might result in a violation.

Premerger Notification: Title II of the new law adds a new Section 7A to the Clayton Act [4] which facilitates earlier action by enforcement agencies against mergers. The new section requires disclosure (in accordance with rules to be promulgated by the FTC, with the approval of the Assistant Attorney General) of any plan by any firm (the word "person" is used in the statute to cover non-corporate as well as corporate business associations) to acquire voting securities or assets of another firm, where the following two conditions are met: (1) the acquiring or the acquired firm has assets (or, in the case of a manufacturing corporation, either assets or total net annual sales) of $100 million or more, and the other of the two firms has assets (or, in the case of a manufacturing corporation, either assets or total net annual sales) of $10 million or more; and (2) the acquiring firm acquires 15% or more of the acquired firm's stock or assets, or $15 million in value of its stock or assets. When both these conditions are

---

1. Public Law 94–435, September 30, 1976.
2. 15 U.S.C.A. §§ 1311–1314.
3. 15 U.S.C.A. § 1312, as amended by P.S. 94–435, Sept. 30, 1976.
4. 15 U.S.C.A. § 18A, added by P.L. 94–435, Sept. 30, 1976.

met, the firms must (or, in the case of a tender offer, the acquiring firm alone must) report the planned transaction in accordance with the rules and must then wait thirty to fifty days (or, in the case of a tender offer, fifteen days) before consummating the transaction. During the waiting period either the Department of Justice or the FTC may require that additional information be provided to enable it to evaluate the legality of the merger. The new law also provides for an expedited hearing on application for preliminary injunction if either enforcement agency determines during the waiting period that consummation of the merger would violate the antitrust law.

Parens Patriae Actions by States: Title III of the new law authorizes state attorneys general to sue firms violating the Sherman Act for monetary relief for injury caused by the violation to natural persons residing in their states. This title adds new Sections 4C through 4H to the Clayton Act.[5] Section 4C, which contains the basic authorization for *parens patriae* suits, provides for the award of threefold the total damage sustained, and costs, including a reasonable attorney's fee. The section specifies, however, that the award shall not include any of the following: amounts awarded for the same injury (for example, if one of the state's residents sued individually and recovered); any sums properly allocable to damage to persons who exercise their election (granted by the section) to be excluded from the suit; and any sums properly allocable to damage to any business entity. The section also authorizes an award of a reasonable attorney's fee to the prevailing defendant if the court finds that the state attorney general acted in bad faith, vexaciously, wantonly, or oppressively.

Pursuant to the new Section 4E, monetary awards recovered under Section 4C shall be distributed as the court in its discretion authorizes or may be deemed a civil penalty by the court and paid into the state's general funds, subject in either case to a distribution procedure which affords each injured person a reasonable opportunity to secure his share.

Other provisions do the following: require that the attorney general bringing the action give such notice (by publication, unless the court concludes that publication notice would be constitutionally defective) as the court requires to injured persons whose damage may be an element in the recovery; simplify the method of proof of damages in price fixing violations; limit recovery to damages for injuries occurring after the effective date of the law; direct the Attorney General of the United States to give certain assistance to state attorneys general; and authorize any state to provide by law for the non-applicability of the Sections 4C through 4H of Clayton to its residents.

---

5. 15 U.S.C.A. §§ 15C through 15H, added by P.L. 94–435, Sept. 30, 1976.

Miscellaneous Provisions: The new law also makes two miscellaneous changes in prior law, one pertaining only to the newly authorized *parens partriae* actions, the other, however, being more general. First, the new law adds Section 1407(h) of the Judicial Code [6] which provides that the judicial panel on multidistrict litigation may consolidate and transfer actions brought under Section 4C or Clayton for purposes of trial, as well as for pretrial purposes, under the same standards that govern transfers for pretrial proceedings in other multidistrict litigation. The second and more general miscellaneous changes is an amendment to Section 16 of the Clayton Act.[7] That section, which authorizes private suits for equitable relief against threatened loss or damage from an antitrust violation, did not previously provide for any award of attorneys fees to a successful plaintiff. As amended, the section provides that the court shall award a reasonable attorneys fee to a plaintiff which substantially prevails in the proceeding.

6. 28 U.S.C.A. § 1407(h), added by P.L. 94-435, Sept. 30, 1976.

7. 15 U.S.C.A. § 26, as amended by P.L. 94-435, Sept. 30, 1976.

*

TABLE OF CASES

A

Acme Precision Prods., Inc. v. American Alloys Corp., 51, 58
Adams v. Burke, 572
Addyston Pipe & Steel Co., United States v., 64, 68, 82, 170, 199, 312, 422
Adolph Coors Co. v. FTC, 406, 410, 411, 499
Advanced Business Sys. & Supply Co. v. SCM Corp., 49, 52, 795
Affiliated Music Enterprises, Inc. v. Sesac, Inc., 49, 51, 58
Agrashell, Inc. v. Hammons Prods. Co., 139
A. J. Goodman & Sons, Inc. v. United Lacquer Mfg. Corp., 679
Albrecht v. Herald Co., 210, 325, 377, 391, 393, 394, 396, 495, 786
Albrecht v. Matthes, 786
Alcoa, United States v., 571
Alden-Rochelle, Inc. v. ASCAP, 461
Alger v. Thacher, 161
Alhambra Motor Parts v. FTC, 696
Allen Bradley Co. v. Electrical Workers' Local 3, p. 724
Allen Bradley Co. v. Local Union No. 3, IBEW, 304
Allen Ready Mix Concrete Co. v. John A. Denie's Sons Co., 711
Allied Chem. Corp., United States v., 518, 669, 763
Alligator Corp. v. Robert Bruce, Inc., 497
Allis-Chalmers Mfg. Co. v. White Consol. Indus., Inc., 620, 655, 656, 670, 671
Alpha Chi Omega v. Rader, 765
Alpha Distributors Co. v. Jack Daniels Distillery, 328
Aluminum Co. of America v. Tandet, 679
Aluminum Co. of America, United States v., 20, 30, 33, 39, 44, 47, 49, 50, 52, 64, 67, 70, 72, 74, 75, 79, 82, 84, 87, 90, 94, 95, 99, 101, 102, 113, 114, 141, 143, 144, 355, 448, 509, 595, 600, 608, 616, 714
Alyeska Pipeline Co. v. Wilderness Society, 793
Amalgamated Meat Cutters Local 627 v. United States, 198
America Corp., United States v., 669
American Banana Co. v. United Fruit Co., 714
American Brands, Inc. v. National Ass'n of Broadcasters, 254, 292
American Bldg. Maintenance Indus., United States v., 601, 713
American Can Co., United States v., 479, 485
American Column & Lumber Co. v. United States, 268, 274, 313
American Crystal Sugar Co. v. Mandeville Island Farms, Inc., 786
American Cyanamid Co. v. FTC, 364, 365, 512, 565
American Equip. Co. v. Tuthill, 546
American Linen Supply Co., United States v., 215, 546, 555, 558
American Linseed Oil Co., United States v., 269
American Mfrs. Mut. Ins. Co. v. American Broadcasting-Paramount Theatres, Inc., 444
American Medical Ass'n v. United States, 126, 250, 252
American Motor Inns, Inc. v. Holiday Inns, Inc., 407, 496, 785
American Motors Corp. v. FTC, 700
American Motor Specialties Co., 704, 705
American News Co. v. FTC, 704
American Oil Co. v. FTC, 691, 693
American Oil Co., United States v., 135
American Optical Co. v. New Jersey Optical Co., 538
American Security Co. v. Shatterproof Glass Corp., 463
American Smelting & Ref. Co., United States v., 192, 216, 223, 273, 292, 294
American Society of Composers, Authors and Publishers, United States v., 461
American Tobacco Co. v. United States, 88, 105, 108, 133, 134, 138, 149, 208, 314, 316, 355, 357, 361
American Tobacco Co., United States v., 23, 29, 33, 35, 39, 64, 82, 98, 99, 109, 112, 148, 583, 584, 586, 588, 714

TABLE OF CASES

Ampicillin Antitrust Litigation, In re, 791
Amplex of Maryland, Inc. v. Outboard Marine Corp., 75, 488
Ancora Corp. v. Stein, 785
Anderson v. United States, 256
Anderson's-Black Rock, Inc. v. Pavement Salvage Co., 504, 505
Anheuser-Busch Inc. v. FTC, 683–686
Ansul Co. v. Uniroyal, Inc., 541, 775
Antibiotic Antitrust Actions, In re, 765, 791
Apex Elec. Mfg. Co. v. Altorfer Bros. Co., 463, 563, 570
Appalachian Coals, Inc. v. United States, 153, 172, 179, 207, 286, 292, 293, 295
April v. National Cranberry Ass'n, 722
Arden-Mayfair, Inc., 705
Arkansas Brokerage Co. v. Dunn & Powell, 208
Arkansas Fuel Oil Corp., United States v., 327
Armco Steel Corp. v. North Dakota, 791
Arnold, Schwinn & Co., United States v., 215, 261, 290, 390, 393, 394, 403, 407, 416, 498, 499
Arrow-Hart & Hegeman Electric Co. v. FTC, 590
Arthur v. Kraft-Phenix Cheese Corp., 325
ASCAP, United States v., 763
A. Schrader's Sons, Inc., United States v., 238, 393, 412
Asheville Tobacco Bd. of Trade v. FTC, 206, 739
Associated Greeting Card Distributors, 208
Associated Milk Producers, Inc., United States v., 759
Associated Patents, Inc., United States v., 555, 570
Associated Press v. Taft-Ingalls Corp., 444
Associated Press v. United States, 125, 128, 253, 300, 567, 708
Atalanta Trading Corp. v. FTC, 679, 680
Atlantic City Elec. Co. v. A. B. Chance Co., 768
Atlantic City Elec. Co. v. General Elec. Co., 776, 789
Atlantic Refining Co. v. FTC, 364, 365, 468, 517
Atlantic Richfield Co., United States v., 620, 670
Att'y General v. Adelaide S.S. Co., 160
Automated Bldg. Components, Inc. v. Trueline Truss Co., 518
Automatic Canteen Co. of America v. FTC, 704, 705
Automatic Radio Mfg. Co. v. Ford Motor Co., 444
Automatic Radio Mfg. Co. v. Hazeltine Research Inc., 463, 508, 558
Automobile Mfrs. Ass'n, United States v., 301, 762
Avnet, Inc. v. FTC, 59

B

Bailey v. Glover, 776
Bailey's Bakery, Ltd. v. Continental Baking Co., 113, 398, 773
Baker v. F. & F. Investment, 261
Baker-Cammack Hosiery Mills v. Davis Co., 463, 563, 570
Bakersfield Associated Plumbing Contractors, United States v., 306
Bakery & Confectionary Workers Int'l Union v. Ratner, 795
Baldwin-Lima-Hamilton Corp. v. Tatnall Measuring Systems, Co., 558
Balian Ice Cream Co. v. Arden Farms Co., 702
Bal Theatre Corp. v. Paramount Film Distributors Corp., 793
Barber-Colman Co. v. National Tool Co., 541, 546
Barron v. United States, 324
Barr Rubber Prods. Co. v. Sun Rubber Co., 571
Bauer & Cie v. O'Donnell, 377, 571, 572
Baum v. Investors Diversified Services, Inc., 680
Bausch & Lomb Optical Co., United States v., 393, 402, 423, 424
Bayer Co., United States v., 215
Baysoy v. Jessop Steel Co., 714
B. B. Chemical Co. v. Ellis, 442
Beatrice Foods Co. v. F. T. C., 610, 685
Beatrice Foods Co. v. United States, 315
Beckman Instruments, Inc. v. Chemtronics, Inc., 513
Becton, Dickinson & Co. v. Eisele & Co., 529

Bela Seating Co. v. Poloron Prods. Inc., 124
Bell & Howell Co. v. Eastman Kodak Co., 149
Belliston v. Texaco, Inc., 663
Belz v. Board of Trade, 200
Bement & Sons v. National Harrow Co., 505, 527, 531, 542, 571
Bendix Corp. v. Balax, Inc., 139
Bendix Corp. v. FTC, 648
Benger Labs, Ltd. v. R. K. Laros Co., 558
Bergjans Farm Dairy Co. v. Sanitary Milk Producers, 688, 722, 794
Berland v. Mack, 778
Bernhard v. Bank of America, 764
Bernstein v. Universal Pictures, Inc., 785
Besser Mfg. Co., United States v., 522, 523, 570
Bichel Optical Labs, Inc. v. Marquette Nat'l Bank, 679
Biddle Purchasing Co. v. FTC, 698
Bigelow v. RKO Radio Pictures, Inc., 785
Billy Baxter, Inc. v. Coca-Cola Co., 773
Binks Mfg. Co. v. Ransberg Electro-Coating Corp., 571
Birdsboro Steel Foundry & Machine Co., United States v., 559, 563, 570
Black & Decker Mfg. Co., United States v., 643
Blalock v. Ladies Professional Golf Ass'n, 254
Blankenship v. Hearst Corp., 498
Blohm & Voss A.G. v. Prudential-Grace Lines, Inc., 571
Blonder-Tongue Laboratories, Inc. v. University of Illinois Foundation, 513, 764
Blue Bell Co. v. Frontier Ref. Co., 192, 220
Board of Trade of City of Chicago v. United States, 172, 175, 278
Bobbs-Merrill Co. v. Straus, 572
Boise Cascade Int'l, Inc. v. Northern Minnesota Pulpwood Prods. Ass'n, 722
Bond Crown & Cork Co. v. FTC, 275
Borden Co. v. FTC, 684, 692, 693
Borden Co., United States v., 304, 701, 721, 722, 748
Boshes v. General Motors Corp., 791
Boss Mfg. Co. v. Payne Glove Co., 680
Boston Store v. American Graphophone Co., 571-573
Bowen v. New York News, Inc., 138
Bowl America, Inc. v. Fair Lanes, Inc., 794
Bowman v. Chicago & N. W. Ry. Co., 580
Boyertown Burial Casket Co. v. Walco Nat'l Corp., 671
Bracken's Shopping Center, Inc. v. Ruwe, 742
Bradley v. School Bd., 793
Brehm v. Goebel Brewing Co., 325
Brenner v. Manson, 504
Brett v. First Federal Savings & Loan Ass'n, 314
Briggs Mfg. Co. v. Crane Co., 671
Broussard v. Socony Mobil Oil Co., 394
Brown v. Parker, 741
Brownell v. Ketcham Wire & Mfg. Co., 528, 529
Brown Shoe Co. v. United States, 49, 58, 60, 238, 365, 412, 592, 594, 600, 606, 617, 626, 661, 664, 668
Brown Shoe Co., United States v., 670
Bruce's Juices, Inc. v. American Can Co., 679, 680
Brulotte v. Thys Co., 462, 465
Brunette Mach. Works, Ltd. v. Kockum Indus., Inc., 716
Brunswick Corp. v. Pueblo Bowl-O-Mat, Inc., 670, 672
Buckley Towers Condominium, Inc. v. Buchwald, 771
Burke v. Ford, 215, 709, 710, 712
Bushie v. Stenocord Corp., 128

C

C. A. B., United States v., 745
California v. Federal Power Commission, 748, 749
California Motor Transport Co. v. Trucking Unlimited, 742
California Packing Corp., 493

TABLE OF CASES

California Retail Grocers & Merchants Ass'n v. United States, 198
Callaway Mills Co. v. FTC, 702, 703
Calnetics Corp. v. Volkswagen of America, Inc., 771, 796
C. A. Norgren Co. v. United States, 572
Cantor v. The Detroit Edison Co., 736
Cape Cod Food Prods., Inc. v. National Cranberry Ass'n, 135
Capital Temporaries, Inc. v. Olsten Corp., 445
Carbice Corp. of America v. American Patents Development Corp., 442
Cargill, Inc. v. Board of Trade, 186, 200
Carlisle, Commonwealth v., 160
Caroll v. Protection Maritime Ins. Co., Ltd., 681
Carpa, Inc. v. Ward Foods, Inc., 444
Carvel Corp., 444, 497
Cascade Natural Gas Corp. v. El Paso Natural Gas Co., 760
Case-Swayne Co. v. Sunkist Growers, Inc., 74, 720
Cataphote Corp. v. De Soto Chemical Coatings, Inc., 513
CBS Business Equip. Corp. v. Underwood Corp., 487
Cement Mfrs. Protective Ass'n v. United States, 88, 245, 269
Central Ice Cream Co. v. Golden Rod Ice Cream Co., 680
Central Retailer-Owned Grocers, Inc. v. FTC, 698
Central Shade Roller Co. v. Cushman, 161
Champion Spark Plug Co., 685
Chapman v. Rudd Paint & Varnish Co., 693
Charles Pfizer & Co., United States v., 49, 53, 88, 479, 485
Chattanooga Foundry & Pipe Works v. Atlanta, 771, 775, 786–788
Chemagro Corp. v. Universal Chem. Co., 558
Cherokee Laboratories, Inc. v. Rotary Drilling Services, Inc., 261
Chestnut Farms Chevy Chase Dairy, 699
Chicago v. General Motors Corp., 778
Chicago Bd. of Trade v. United States, 206, 605
Chicago Spring Prods. Co. v. United States Steel Corp., 688
Chicago Tribune—New York News Syndicate, Inc., United States v., 261
Christiansen v. Mechanical Contractors Bid Depository, 304, 305
Chrysler Corp., United States v., 669
CIBA Corp., United States v., 518
Cincinnati Milk Sales Ass'n v. National Farmers' Organization, Inc., 722
Cincinnati Packet Co. v. Bay, 583
Citizen Publishing Co. v. United States, 629
Citizens & S. Nat'l Bank, United States v., 600, 604, 616
City of. See under name of city.
Clark Marine Corp. v. Cargill, Inc., 103
Clark Oil Co. v. Phillips Petroleum Co., 789
Clark Walter & Sons, Inc. v. United States, 761
Clayton Mark & Co. v. FTC, 314, 357
Cleary v. Chalk, 771
C. Leonardt Imp. Co. v. Southdown, Inc., 671
Cliff Food Stores, Inc. v. Kroger, Inc., 75
Cole v. Hughes Tool Co., 522
Colgate & Co., United States v., 392, 487, 543
Collins v. Locke, 160
Columbia Nitrogen Corp. v. Royster Co., 784
Columbia Pictures Corp., United States v., 186, 192, 207, 216, 223, 273, 292, 293, 518, 601
Columbia Steel Co., United States v., 67, 68, 76, 77, 134, 135, 198, 440, 590, 592, 594, 606, 663
Commonwealth v. Carlisle, 160
Company of Horners v. Barlow, 158
Company of Musicians of London v. Green, 159
Compco Corp. v. Day-Bright Lighting, Inc., 251
Computer Statistics, Inc. v. Blair, 699
Congress Bldg. Corp. v. Loew's, Inc., 772
Coniglio v. Highwood Services, Inc., 456
Connecticut Nat'l Bank, United States v., 610
Connell Constr. Co. v. Plumbers and Steamfitters Local 100, 729

Consolidated Car Heating Co., United States v., 558
Consolidated Gas, Elec. Light & Power Co. v. Pennsylvania Water & Power Co., 198
Consolidated Laundries Corp., United States v., 133, 215
Container Corp. of America, United States v., 191, 270, 276, 305, 626, 703
Continental Airlines, Inc. v. CAB, 745
Continental Baking Co. v. Old Homestead Bread Co., 688
Continental Baking Co. v. United States, 315, 319
Continental Can Co., United States v., 595, 600, 608, 616
Continental Oil Co. v. United States, 769
Continental Ore Co. v. Union Carbide & Carbon Corp., 114, 714, 740, 785
Continental Paper Bag Co. v. Eastern Paper Bag Co., 503
Control Data Corp. v. International Business Mach. Corp., 763
Cooper Liquor, Inc. v. Adolph Coors Co., 404, 410
Cordova v. Bache & Co., 772
Corning Glass Works v. Anchor Hocking Glass Corp., 513
Corn Prods. Ref. Co. v. FTC, 680, 688, 692, 693, 699
Corn Prods. Ref. Co., United States v., 48, 53
Cornwell Quality Tools Co. v. C.T.S. Co., 683
C–O–Two Fire Equip. Co. v. United States, 275, 314, 317, 318
Council of Defense v. International Magazine Co., 261
Country Theatre Co. v. Paramount Film Distribution Corp., 679
Courtesy Chevrolet, Inc. v. Tennessee Walking Horse Breeders' & Exhibitors' Ass'n, 793
Cousins v. Smith, 160
Cowen v. New York Stock Exchange, 290
Cow Palace, Ltd. v. Associated Milk Producers, Inc., 742
Craft v. McConoughy, 161
Crescent Amusement Co., United States v., 114, 143, 456
Crocker-Angelo Nat'l Bank, United States v., 60, 61, 670
Cudden v. Estwick, 158
Cummer-Graham Co. v. Straight Side Basket Corp., 543, 546
Cutter Laboratories, Inc. v. Lyophile-Cryochem Corp., 544, 570

D

Dairy Cooperative Ass'n, United States v., 722
Dairy Foods, Inc. v. Dairy Maid Prods. Corp., 523
Daniell, Queen v., 160
Danville Tobacco Ass'n v. Bryant-Buckner Associates, Inc., 206, 256
Darcy v. Allen, 157
Darling Delaware, Inc., United States v., 769
Data Processing Financial & General Corp. v. International Business Mach. Corp., 770
Davenant v. Hurdis, 157
Dean Foods Co., 629
Dean Milk Co., 686
Dean Milk Co. v. American Processing & Sales Co., 702
Dean Milk Co. v. FTC, 685, 687
De Berenger, King v., 160
Deering, Milliken & Co. v. Temp-Resisto Corp., 530
Deesen v. Professional Golfers Ass'n of America, 252, 259
DeFilippo v. Ford Motor Co., 258
Dehydrating Process Co. v. A. O. Smith Corp., 453
Denver, City and County of v. American Oil Co., 790
Denver Petroleum Corp. v. Shell Oil Co., 82, 128
Denver Rockets v. All-Pro Management, Inc., 247, 254, 290, 710
Deterjet Corp. v. United Aircraft Corp., 326
De Voto v. Pacific Fidelity Life Ins. Co., 712
Diamond Int'l Corp. v. Walterhoefer, 513
Dictograph Prods., Inc. v. FTC, 472
Diebold, United States v., 629
Distillers Corp. v. Seagrams, Ltd., 327
Dobbins v. Kawasaki Motors Corp., 138
Dr. Miles Medical Co. v. John D. Park & Sons Co., 377, 388, 422, 571
Dole Valve Co. v. Perfection Bar Equip., Inc., 517

Dollac Corp. v. Margon Corp., 508, 511, 522
Dolph v. Troy Laundry Co., 161
Doubleday & Co., 695
Dublin Distributors, Inc. v. Edward and John Burke, Ltd., 488
Duff v. Kansas City Star Co., 771
Duffy v. Shockey, 161
Duke & Co. v. Foerster, 739
Duplan Corp. v. Monlinage Ct. Retorderie de Chavanoz, 769

E

E. A. McQuade Tours, Inc. v. Consolidated Air Tour Manual Comm., 126
Eastern Railroads Presidents Conference v. Noerr Motor Freight, Inc., 740, 746
Eastern States Retail Lumber Dealers' Ass'n v. United States, 232, 314
Eastman Kodak Co. v. Southern Photo Materials Co., 430, 785
Eastman Kodak Co., United States v., 51, 75, 99, 111
E. B. Muller & Co. v. FTC, 683
E. C. Knight Co., United States v., 579, 584, 708
E. Edelmann & Co. v. FTC, 692
Egan v. United States, 324
E. I. DuPont De Nemours & Co., United States v., 30, 33, 34, 40, 48, 50, 52, 55, 62, 64, 75, 77, 81, 84, 86, 93, 103, 216, 355, 507, 606, 609, 627, 662, 670, 672
Eisen v. Carlisle & Jacquelin, 399, 778–781, 793
Ekco Products Co. v. FTC, 365
Electric Theater Co. v. Twentieth Century-Fox Film Corp., 765
Elliott Co. v. Lagonda Mfg. Co., 538
El Paso Natural Gas Co., United States v., 600, 629, 633, 634, 652, 761
Elyria-Lorain Broadcasting Co. v. Lorain Journal Co., 787
Emich Motors Corp. v. General Motors Corp., 763
Empire Plastic Corp., 685
Employing Plasterers Ass'n, United States v., 709
Engbrecht v. Dairy Queen Co., 397, 497
Engine Specialties Inc. v. Bombardier, Ltd., 716
Enterprise Indus., Inc. v. Texas Co., 684
Esco Corp. v. United States, 314, 319, 392
Ethyl Gasoline Corp. v. United States, 558, 572
Eversharp Inc. v. Fisher Pen Co., 523
E. W. Wiggins Airways, Inc. v. Massachusetts Port Authority, 740
Export Liquor Sales v. Ammex Warehouse Co., 679
Exquisite Form Brassiere, Inc. v. FTC, 702

F

Falstaff Brewing Corp., United States v., 551, 634, 637, 638, 642, 652
Far East Conference v. United States, 748
Farmington Dowel Prods. Co. v. Forster Mfg. Co., 764, 793, 796
Farm Journal Inc., 518, 629
Fashion Originators Guild v. FTC, 234, 364, 517
F. C. Russell Co. v. Consumers Insulation Co., 573
Federal Baseball Club v. National League of Professional Baseball Clubs, 709
Federal Maritime Commission v. Swedish American Line, 745
Federated Dept. Stores, Inc. v. Grinnell Corp., 763
Finley v. Music Corp. of America, 796
First Nat'l Bank & Trust Co. of Lexington, United States v., 106, 365, 441, 486, 595, 596, 602, 672, 673
First Nat'l Bank of Arizona v. Cities Services Co., 319
First Nat'l Pictures Inc., United States v., 257, 277
Fisons, Ltd. v. United States, 716
Flintkote Co. v. Lysfjord, 775, 785
Flood v. Kuhn, 709
Florists' Nat'l Tel. Delivery Network v. Florists' Tel. Delivery Ass'n, 247
FMC Corp., United States v., 669
Food and Grocery Bureau v. United States, 198

TABLE OF CASES

Food Basket, Inc. v. Albertson's, Inc., 713
Forbes v. Greater Minneapolis Area Bd. of Realtors, 777
Ford Motor Co. v. United States, 600, 625, 635, 636, 644, 662, 672
Ford Motor Co. v. Webster's Auto Sales, Inc., 429
Ford Wholesale Co. v. Fibreboard Paper Prods. Corp., 710
Foremost Dairies, Inc. v. FTC, 692, 693
Forster Mfg. Co., v. FTC 683, 703
Ft. Howard Paper Co. v. FTC, 275
Fortner Enterprises, Inc. v. United States Steel Corp., 433, 439, 469
Fosburgh v. California & Hawaiian Sugar Ref. Co., 499
Foster Mfg. Co., 683
Fowler Mfg. Co. v. Gorlick, 693
FPC v. Texaco, Inc., 745
Frank G. Shattuck Co., 691
Fred Bonner Corp., 691
Fred Meyer, Inc. v. FTC, 704
Frey & Son, Inc. v. Cudahy Packing Co., 393
FTC v. A. E. Staley Mfg. Co., 688, 702
FTC v. Anheuser-Busch, Inc., 680, 681, 683
FTC v. Armour & Co., 589
FTC v. Beech-Nut Packing Co., 364, 393
FTC v. Borden Co., 680
FTC v. Brown Shoe Co., 364, 467, 495, 517
FTC v. Bunte Bros., 714
FTC v. Cement Institute, 314, 357, 364, 365, 517, 688
FTC v. Consolidated Foods Corp., 494, 600, 627, 642, 656
FTC v. Curtis Publishing Co., 486
FTC v. Dean Foods Co., 671
FTC v. Eastman Kodak Co., 590
FTC v. Fred Meyer, Inc., 700
FTC v. Henry Broch & Co., 698
FTC v. Morton Salt Co., 679, 691, 693
FTC v. Motion Picture Advertising Service Co., 364, 485, 487, 517
FTC v. National Lead Co., 357
FTC v. Proctor & Gamble Co., 51, 308, 324, 336, 600, 627, 634, 644, 653, 655
FTC v. Simplicity Pattern Co., 698–700
FTC v. Sinclair Ref. Co., 435, 453
FTC v. Sperry & Hutchinson Co., 467, 517
FTC v. Standard Oil Co., 702
FTC v. Swift & Co., 589
FTC v. Texaco, Inc., 468, 469
FTC v. Thatcher Mfg. Co., 589
FTC v. Universal Rundle Corp., 754
FTC v. Washington Fish & Oyster Co., 698
FTC v. Western Meat Co., 589

G

GAF Corp. v. Circle Floor Co., 290
Gamco, Inc. v. Providence Fruit & Produce Bldg., Inc., 126, 131, 256, 430, 567
Gas-A-Car, Inc. v. American Petrofina, Inc., 688
Gasoline Retailers Ass'n, United States v., 201, 248, 280, 398
General Auto Suppliers, Inc. v. FTC, 703
General Dyestuff Corp., United States v., 215
General Dynamics Corp., United States v., 273, 477, 490, 493, 595, 600, 610, 616, 642, 656
General Elec. Co. v. City of San Antonio, 763, 776
General Elec. Co. v. Willey's Carbide Tool Co., 546
General Elec. Co., United States v., 86, 388, 464, 509, 541, 542, 546, 554, 570, 571
General Foods Corp., 695, 699
General Instrument Corp., United States v., 554, 570
General Motors Corp., 453
General Motors Corp., United States v., 238, 259, 285, 318, 326

General Shale Prods. Corp. v. Struck Constr. Co., 680
General Talking Pictures v. Western Elec. Co., 557, 558
General Telephone & Electronics Corp., United States v., 670
George R. Whitten Jr., Inc. v. Paddock Pool Builders, Inc., 740, 743
George Van Camp & Sons v. American Can Co., 678
George W. Warner & Co. v. Black & Decker Mfg. Co., 394
Georgia v. Pennsylvania R. Co., 304, 783
G. Heileman Brewing Co., United States v., 670
Giant Food, Inc. v. FTC, 704
Gibbs v. Smith, 161
Gimbel Bros., Inc., United States v., 670
Girardi v. Gates Rubber Co. Sales Div., Inc., 394
Glaxo Group, Ltd., United States v., 407
GM Corp., United States v., 394
Gold Bond Stamp Co., Petition of, 756
Goldfarb v. Virginia State Bar, 198, 201, 248, 708–710, 735, 736, 739, 744
Goldlawr, Inc. v. Shubert, 323
Gold Strike Stamp Co. v. Christensen, 692
Goodyear Tire & Rubber Co. v. FTC, 678
Gordon v. Illinois Bell Telephone Co., 323
Gordon v. New York Stock Exchange, 307, 747, 749
Gottesman v. General Motors Corp., 773
Graham v. John Deere Co., 504
Grand Union Co. v. FTC, 364, 706
Gray Line, Inc. v. Gray Line Sightseeing Companies Ass'n, 215
Great Atlantic & Pacific Tea Co. v. FTC, 698, 705
Greater Buffalo Press, Inc., United States v., 627, 672
Great Northern Ry. v. Merchants Elevator Co., 749
Green v. Electric Vacuum Cleaner Co., 499
Green v. Wolf Corp., 778
Greene, In re, 579, 580
Greenhut, United States v., 579
Griffith, United States v., 30, 92, 105, 114, 133, 456
Grinnell Corp., United States v., 30, 40, 48, 59–62, 67, 68, 74, 75, 82, 94, 97, 112, 559, 609
Grossman Development Co. v. Detroit Lions, Inc., 457
GTE Sylvania, Inc. v. Continental TV, Inc., 50, 404, 405, 407, 408, 416
Gulf Coast Shrimpers & Oystermans Ass'n v. United States, 304
Gulf Oil Corp. v. Copp Paving Co., 601, 710, 714
Gulf States Utilities Co. v. FPC, 745
Guyott Co. v. Texaco, Inc., 688
Gypsum Cases, In re, 792, 795

H

Hackett v. General Host Corp., 778
Hamilton Watch Co. v. Benrus Watch Co., 670, 671
Hammond Ford Inc. v. Ford Motor Co., 459
Hancock Bros. v. Jones, 769
Hanover Shoe, Inc. v. United Shoe Mach. Corp., 149, 321, 324, 770, 771, 774, 789, 793
Hansberry v. Lee, 781
Hanson v. Denckla, 717
Hanson v. Shell Oil Co., 663
Hardy Salt Co. v. Illinois, 763, 765
Harley-Davidson Motor Co., 458
Harman v. Valley Nat'l Bank, 743
Harper & Row Publishers, Inc. v. Decker, 769
Harrison v. Paramount Pictures, Inc., 772
Hartford-Empire Co. v. United States, 198, 274, 505, 555, 558, 567
Hartford-Empire Co., United States v., 146, 509, 510, 515
Hartley & Parker, Inc. v. Florida Beverage Corp., 679, 680
Hart, Shaffner & Marx, United States v., 627
Harwell v. Growth Programs, Inc., 283

TABLE OF CASES

Haverhill Gazette Co. v. Union Leader Corp., 785, 793, 794
Hawaii v. Standard Oil Co., 771, 774, 783
Hawaiian Oke & Liquors Ltd. v. Joseph E. Seagram & Sons, Inc., 328
Hazeltine Research, Inc. v. Avco Mfg. Corp., 463
Hazeltine Research, Inc. v. Zenith Radio Corp., 456
Hearn v. Griffin, 160
Heaton-Peninsular Button Fastener Co. v. Eureka Specialty Co., 556
Hecht v. Pro-Football, Inc., 739
H. E. Fletcher Co. v. Rock of Ages Corp., 31, 51, 58
Helix Mining Co. v. Terminal Flour Mills Co., 601
Henry v. A. B. Dick Co., 433, 440, 571
Herbst v. Able, 778
Herman Schwabe, Inc. v. United Shoe Mach. Corp., 786
Herriman v. Menzies, 161
Highland Supply Corp. v. Reynolds Metal Co., 764, 772
Hiland Dairy Inc. v. Kroger Co., 139
Hilton v. Eckersley, 160
Hobart Bros. Co. v. Malcolm T. Gilliland, Inc., 496, 787
Hobbie v. Jennison, 572
Hobbs v. Young, 158
Hogue & Berrien County Package Co. v. Wise, 572
Holmberg v. Armbrecht, 776
Honeywell, Inc. v. Sperry Rand Corp., 149, 567
Hopkins v. United States, 256
Hospital Building Co. v. Trustees of Rex Hospital, 710
Hotchkiss v. Greenwood, 505
House of Lords, Inc., 699
Hubbard v. Miller, 161
Huck Mfg. Co., United States v., 541
Hudson Distributors, Inc. v. Upjohn Co., 379
Hudson Sales Corp. v. Waldrip, 488
Hudson Valley Asbestos Corp. v. Tougher Heating & Plumbing Co., 133, 135
Hughes Tool Co. v. Cole, 103
Hughes Tool Co. v. Motion Picture Ass'n, 263
Hughes Tool Co. v. TWA, 746, 770
Hughes Tool Co., United States v., 610, 636
Hunt v. Crumboch, 289
Hunt v. Mobil Oil Corp., 716
Hunter Douglas Corp. v. Lando Prods., 488
Huron Valley Publishing Co. v. Booth Newspapers, Inc., 138
Hutcheson, United States v., 723
Hyster Co. v. United States, 756

I

IBM Corp. v. United States, 431, 440
IBM, United States v., 74
Illinois v. Ampress Brick Co., 791
Illinois v. Harper & Row Publishers, Inc., v. Decker, 769, 778
Imperial Chemical Indus. Ltd., United States v., 215
Incarcerated Men of Allen County Jail v. Fair, 792
Independent Iron Works, Inc. v. United States Steel Corp., 135, 318, 319
Indiana Farmer's Guide Publishing Co. v. Prairie Farmer Publishing Co., 68
Industrial Bldg. Materials, Inc. v. Interchemical Corp., 128, 314
Industrial Mach. Tool Co. v. Miami Window Corp., 528
Ingersoll-Rand Co., United States v., 656, 669
Insurance Board, United States v., 206
Instant Delivery Corp. v. City Stores Co., 208, 258, 285, 290
Interborough News Co. v. Curtis Publishing Co., 207, 258, 290
International Boxing Club of N. Y., Inc., United States v., 57, 61, 74, 609
International Business Machines Corp. v. United States, 436
International Film Center, Inc. v. Graflex, Inc., 691
International Fur Workers Union, United States v., 109, 112

International Harvester Co., United States v., 75, 586
International Mfg. Co. v. Landon, 463
International Salt Co. v. New Jersey, 765
International Salt Co. v. United States, 198, 431, 436, 440
International Shoe Co. v. FTC, 629
International Shoe Co. v. Washington, 717
International Tel. & Tel. Corp. v. General Tel. & Electronics Corp., 770, 796
International Tel. & Tel. Corp., United States v., 758, 762
Interphoto Corp. v. Minolta Corp., 769
Interstate Circuit, Inc. v. United States, 314, 315, 356, 552, 534, 726
Iowa v. Union Asphalt & Roadoils, Inc., 778
I.P.C. Distributors v. Moving Picture Mach. Operators Local 110, pp. 258, 263
Isidor Weinstein Inv. Co. v. Hearst Corp., 773
Israel v. Baxter Laboratories, Inc., 743
IT&T Corp. v. G. T. E. Corp., 607, 609, 630, 667, 670, 672, 775
IT&T Corp., United States v., 655, 656
ITT Continental Baking Co., United States v., 601

J

Jacob Siegel Co. v. FTC, 365
Jacquard Knitting Mach. Co. v. Ordnance Gauge Co., 522
Jantzen Inc., United States v., 201
Jerrold Electronics Corp., United States v., 443
Jesse Isidor Straus v. Victor Talking Mach. Co., 571, 572
Jewel Tea Co. v. Associated Food Retailers, 279, 285
J. I. Case Co. v. Borak, 766
Johns-Manville Corp., United States v., 243, 315
Johnson v. Joseph Schlitz Brewery Co., 215
Joint Traffic Ass'n, United States v., 167, 579
Jones v. Metzger Dairies, Inc., 58
Jones v. North, L. R., 160
Jones Knitting Corp. v. Morgan, 289
Joseph E. Seagram & Sons, Inc. v. Hawaiian Oke & Liquors, Ltd., 258, 290, 786
J. Weingarten, Inc., 699

K

Kansas City Star Co. v. United States, 68, 133, 443
Kaplan v. Lehman Bros., 305
Karlinsky v. New York Racing Ass'n, 680
Karseal Corp. v. Richfield Oil Corp., 772
Kastigar v. United States, 755
Kearney & Trecker Corp. v. Giddings & Lewis, Inc., 138
Kearuth Theatre Corp. v. Paramount Pictures, Inc., 679
Keeler v. Standard Folding Bed Co., 572
Kellogg Co., In re, 324, 363, 454
Kennedy v. Long Island R. Co., 285
Keogh v. Chicago & Northwestern Ry. Co., 744, 788
Kestenbaum v. Falstaff Brewing Corp., 498
Kiefer-Stewart Co. v. Joseph E. Seagram & Sons, Inc., 210, 326, 328, 390, 785
King v. De Berenger, 160
King v. Norris, 160
King v. Turnith, 158
King, United States v., 722
Klearflax Linen Looms, Inc., United States v., 51, 82, 128, 430
Klein v. American Luggage Works, Inc., 394
Kline v. Coldwell, Banker & Co., 399
Klor's Inc. v. Broadway-Hale Stores, Inc., 23, 231, 235, 285, 426, 773
Kobe, Inc. v. Dempsey Pump Co., 509, 521, 523
Kolb v. Chrysler Corp., 772
Konecky v. Jewish Press, 261
Kotula v. Ford Motor Co., 498

TABLE OF CASES

Krasnov, United States v., 516, 570
Kroger Co. v. FTC, 685, 692, 705

L

Lafayette, City of v. Louisiana Power & Light Co., 739
Laing v. Minnesota Vikings Football Club, Inc., 456
Laitram Corp. v. Deepsouth Packing Co., 764
Laitram Corp. v. King Crab, Inc., 124
Lake Asphalt & Petroleum Co., United States v., 763
Landon v. Twentieth Century-Fox Film Corp., 291, 445
LaPeyre v. FTC, 89, 124, 131, 451, 540
La Salle St. Press, Inc. v. McCormick & Henderson Inc., 124
Las Vegas Merchant Plumbers Ass'n v. United States, 198, 202, 216
Laundry Equip. Sales Corp. v. Borg-Warner Corp., 776
L. D. Caulk Co., United States v., 538
Lear, Inc. v. Adkins, 550, 565, 735
Leh v. General Petroleum Corp., 321, 790
Lehigh Valley R. Co., United States v., 37
Leitch Mfg. Co. v. Barber Co., 442
Leo J. Meyberg Co. v. Eureka Williams Corp., 488
Leslie v. Lorillard, 161
Lessig v. Tidewater Oil Co., 138, 139, 394
Lever Bros., United States v., 517, 518
Levine v. Doctors Hospital, 258
L. G. Balfour Co. v. FTC, 365
Lindy Bros. Builders, Inc. v. Am. Radiator & Standard Sanitary Corp., 794, 795
Line Material Co., United States v., 299, 463, 527, 541, 547, 569
Ling-Temco-Vought, Inc., United States v., 655
Lippa's, Inc. v. Lenox, Inc., 764
Liquid Asphalt Cases, In re, 791
Lloyd A. Fry Roofing Co., 685
Lloyd A. Fry Roofing Co. v. FTC, 111, 683, 688
Loeb v. Eastman Kodak Co., 772
Loewe v. Lawlor, 581
Loew's, Inc., United States v., 431, 439, 445, 453, 455, 456, 459
Lorain Journal Co. v. United States, 64, 68, 113, 133–135, 327, 428
Lorain Journal Co., United States v., 324
Loren Specialty Mfg. Co. v. Clark Mfg. Co., 390, 679
LunkenHeimer Co. v. Condec Corp., 671
Luria Steel and Trading Corp. v. Ogden Corp., 765
Lynch v. Magnavox Co., 522

M

McCann v. New York Stock Exchange, 238, 244
McCullough v. Kammerer Corp., 552
Mac Inv. Co. v. United States, 555, 570
McKesson & Robbins, Inc., United States v., 23, 198
McLean Trucking Co. v. United States, 744, 745
McQuade Tours, Inc. v. Consol. Air Tour Manual Committee, 289
Magee-Hale Park-O-Meter Co. v. Vehicular Parking, Ltd., 463
Majestic Theatre Co. v. United Artists Corp., 282
Malta Mfg. Co. v. Osten, 522
Mandeville Island Farms, Inc. v. American Crystal Sugar Co., 286, 580, 708, 709
Mangano v. American Radiator & Standard Sanitary Corp., 791
Manufacturers Hanover Trust Co., United States v., 294
Maple Flooring Mfrs. Ass'n v. United States, 269
Maricopa By-Products, Inc. v. United States, 755
Marine Bancorporation, Inc., United States v., 600, 604, 611, 616, 635, 636, 744
Marion County Co-Op Ass'n v. Carnation Co., 323
Marjorie Webster Jr. College, Inc. v. Middle States Ass'n of Colleges and Secondary Schools, Inc., 126

Mark Plastic Prods., Inc. v. Exxon Corp., 703
Marston v. Ann Arbor Property Management Ass'n, 712
Martens v. Barrett, 772
Maryland & Virginia Milk Producers Ass'n v. United States, 304, 718, 720–722, 749
Maryland Baking Co. v. FTC, 683
Masonite Corp., United States v., 314, 389, 552, 553
Master Key Litigation, In re, 791
Meade Land & Development Co., In re, 794
Meat Cutters Local 189 v. Jewel Tea Co., 189, 279, 285, 726, 727
Mechanical Contractors Bid Depository v. Palmer-Christiansen, 206, 253
Mechanical Mfg. Co., 493
Mercoid Corp. v. Mid-Continent Inv. Co., 442, 521
Merola v. Atlantic Richfield Co., 795
Michigan v. Morton Salt Co., 763, 765
Microtron Corp. v. Minnesota Mining & Mfg. Co., 522
Mid-South Distributors v. FTC, 695, 704, 705
Milgram v. Loew's, Inc., 314, 319
Milk & Ice Cream Can Institute v. FTC, 275
Miller Motors, Inc. v. Ford Motor Co., 458
Mills v. Electric Auto-Lite Co., 793, 795
Milos v. Ford Motor Co., 498
Minneapolis-Honeywell Regulator Co. v. FTC, 691, 693
Minnesota Mining & Mfg. Co. v. Berwick Indus., Inc., 522
Minnesota Mining & Mfg. Co. v. New Jersey Wood Finishing Co., 321, 764, 765, 790
Minnesota Mining & Mfg. Co., United States v., 714, 716
Minninsohn v. United States, 324
Mississippi Petroleum, Inc. v. Vermont Gas Sys., Inc., 692
Mississippi River Corp. v. FTC, 667
Mitchell v. Reynolds, 159, 161
Mitchell v. Robert De Mario Jewelry, Inc., 766
Modern Marketing Serv., Inc., 705
Mogul S.S. Co. v. McGregor Gow & Co., 160
Molinas v. National Basketball Ass'n, 252, 255
Monroe Auto Equip. Co. v. FTC, 696
Monsanto Co. v. Rohm & Hass Co., 512
Monsanto Co., United States v., 651
Montague & Co. v. Lowry, 232
Moog Indus., Inc. v. FTC, 680, 692, 753
Moore v. Mead's Fine Bread Co., 109, 111, 683, 713
Morgan, United States v., 207, 216, 304
Morris Run Coal Co. v. Barclay Coal Co., 161
Mortgage Conference, United States v., 258, 261
Morton Salt Co. v. Suppiger, 442, 521
Morton Salt Co. v. United States, 270, 274, 314
Motion Picture Patents Co. v. Universal Film Mfg. Co., 431, 433, 434, 441, 521, 571
Mueller Co., 695
Mueller Co. v. FTC, 693–695
Mullane v. Central Hanover Bank & Trust Co., 781
Multidistrict Vehicle Air Pollution Cases, In re, 771
Mulvey v. Samuel Goldwyn Productions, 773
Mytinger & Casselberry, Inc. v. FTC, 479

N

Nachman v. Shell Oil Co., 679
Nader v. United States, 655, 762
Nashville Milk Co. v. Carnation Co., 677, 764
National Ass'n of Real Estate Bds., United States v., 323, 708–710
National Ass'n of Securities Dealers, Inc., United States v., 307, 747, 749
National Biscuit Co. v. FTC, 678
National Broadcasting Co. v. United States, 744, 748
National City Lines, Inc., United States v., 61
National Dairy Prods. Corp. v. FTC, 683, 688, 696, 703

TABLE OF CASES 867

National Football League, United States v., 216, 222
National Funeral Directors Ass'n, United States v., 248
National Lead Co., 688
National Lead Co. v. FTC, 365, 688
National Lead Co., United States v., 537
National Lockwasher Co. v. Geo. K. Garrett Co., 552
National Macaroni Mfrs. Ass'n v. FTC, 201, 275, 286
National Malleable & Steel Castings Co., United States v., 275
National Screen Serv. Corp. v. Poster Exchange, Inc., 769
Nationwide Auto Appraiser Service, Inc. v. Association of Cas. & Sur. Companies, 772
Nationwide Trailer Rental System, Inc. v. United States, 201
Nationwide Trailer Rental System, Inc., United States v., 289, 290
N. B. O. Industries Treadway Co. v. Brunswick Corp., 670, 672
Nelson v. Pacific Southwest Airlines, 601
Nelson Radio & Supply Co. v. Motorola, Inc., 323, 487
Newburgh Moire Co. v. Superior Moire Co., 541, 545, 548
New England Confectionery Co., 699
New England Fish Exchange, United States v., 304
New Jersey v. Morton Salt Co., 765
New Orleans Chapter, Associated General Contractors of America, Inc., United States v., 283
New Orleans Ins. Exchange, United States v., 206
New Wrinkle, Inc., United States v., 542, 545, 552
New York, City of v. United States, 301, 762
New York Coffee & Sugar Exchange, United States v., 186, 304
N.Y. Great Atl. & Pac. Tea Co., United States v., 113, 326
Noerr Motor Freight, Inc. v. Eastern Railroad Presidents Conference, 793
Norfolk Monument Co. v. Woodlawn Memorial Gardens, Inc., 314
Norris, King v., 160
Northern California Pharmaceutical Ass'n v. United States, 198
Northern Pacific R. v. United States, 20, 198, 238, 412, 431, 433, 437, 445, 455
Northern Pacific R., United States v., 193
Northern Sec. Co. v. United States, 35, 98, 102, 106, 160, 581, 582, 584, 596
North Texas Producers Ass'n v. Metzger Dairies, Inc., 720, 722
North Texas Producers Ass'n v. Young, 771
Northwestern Oil Co. v. Socony-Vacuum Oil Co., 789
Northwest Indus., Inc., United States v., 656, 657, 670
Norton v. Curtiss, 513

O

Obron v. Union Camp Corp., 789, 790
Ohio Valley Elec. Corp. v. General Elec. Co., 789
Old Dearborn Distributors Co. v. Seagram-Distillers Corp., 378
Old Dominion Box Co. v. Continental Can Co., 571
Oliver Bros. v. FTC, 698
Olympia Provision & Baking Co., United States v., 198
Oylmpic Ref. Co. v. Carter, 765
Ontario Salt Co. v. Merchants' Salt Co., 161
Osborn v. Sinclair Ref. Co., 488
Osmose Wood Preserving Co. of Canada v. Osmose Wood Preserving Co. of America, 538
Otter Tail Power Co. v. United States, 125, 127, 742, 745, 747
Otter Tail Power Co., United States v., 742
Otto Milk Co. v. United Dairy Farmers Cooperative Ass'n, 722
Ovitron Corp. v. General Motors, 113

P

Pabst Brewing Co., United States v., 40, 486, 600, 616, 618
Pacific & Arctic R. & Navigation Co., United States v., 304, 714
Pacific Seafarers, Inc. v. Pacific Far East Line, Inc., 714, 744
Package Closure Corp. v. Sealright Co., 679

TABLE OF CASES

Packard Motor Car Co. v. Webster Motor Car Co., 424
Pan American World Airways, Inc., United States v., 216, 220, 222, 365, 744, 746
Panotex Pipeline Co. v. Phillips Petroleum Co., 138
Paramount Famous Lasky Corp. v. United States, 256, 277, 290
Paramount Pictures, Inc., United States v., 58, 61, 108, 143, 149, 198, 209, 314, 317, 357, 456, 459, 557, 708, 762
Parke, Davis & Co., United States v., 393, 394, 495
Parker v. Brown, 732, 738–740
Parker-Rust-Proof Co., United States v., 528
Parmelee Transportation Co. v. Keeshin, 208, 290
Patterson v. United States, 109, 323
Peelers Co. v. Wendt, 124
Peller v. International Boxing Club, 771
Penick & Ford, Ltd., United States v., 657
Penn-Olin Chemical Co., United States v., 220, 223, 600, 627, 633, 641, 651, 652
Pennoyer v. Neff, 781
Pennsylvania Refuse Removal Ass'n, United States v., 216
Pennsylvania Sugar Ref. Co. v. American Sugar Ref. Co., 113, 771
Pennsylvania Water & Power Co. v. Consolidated Gas, Elec. Light & Power Co., 198, 216
Pergament v. Kaiser-Frazer Corp., 796
Perkins v. Standard Oil Co., 794, 796
Perma Life Mufflers, Inc. v. International Parts Corp., 321, 326, 395, 495, 783, 790
Perryton Wholesale, Inc. v. Pioneer Distributing Co., 428, 796
Peto v. Howell, 113
Pevely Dairy Co. v. United States, 318, 320
Pfotzer v. Aqua Systems, 572
Philadelphia, City of v. Westinghouse Elec. Corp., 764
Philadelphia Housing Authority v. American Radiator & Standard Sanitary Corp., 791
Philadelphia Nat'l Bank, United States v., 20, 60, 365, 440, 476, 532, 594, 595, 600, 604, 616, 629, 662, 672, 744
Philadelphia World Hockey Club, Inc. v. Philadelphia Hockey Club, Inc., 57, 74, 79
Phillips v. Iola Portland Cement Co., 472
Phillipsburg Nat'l Bank & Trust Co., United States v., 60
Pick Mfg. Co. v. GM Corp., 435, 453, 458
Pioneer Co. v. Talon, Inc., 775
Plum Tree, Inc. v. N. K. Winston Corp., 679
Plymouth Dealers Ass'n of Northern Cal. v. United States, 198, 201, 397
Pollack Co. v. Balfour Co., 772
Poller v. Columbia Broadcasting System, Inc., 325, 745
Porter v. Warner Holding Co., 766
Porto Rican American Tobacco Co. v. American Tobacco Co., 99, 136, 678, 683
Poster Exchange, Inc. v. National Screen Serv. Corp., 126, 128, 776
Potters Photographic Applications Co. v. Ealing Corp., 289
Precision Instrument Mfg. Co. v. Automotive Maintenance Mach. Co., 512
Preformed Line Products Co. v. Fanner Mfg. Co., 487
Premier Elec. Constr. Co. v. Miller Davis Co., 784
Prepmore Apparel, Inc. v. Amalgamated Clothing Workers of America, 285
Procter & Gamble Co., United States v., 756
Productive Inventions, Inc. v. Trico Prods. Corp., 772
Provident Nat'l Bank, United States v., 61
Public Utility Dist. No. 1 v. General Elec. Co., 788
Pullman Co., United States v., 52, 99
Purex Corp. v. Procter & Gamble Co., 764
Purex Corp., Ltd. v. General Foods Corp., 785
Purolator Prods., Inc. v. FTC, 693, 694, 696

Q

Quaker Oats Co., 693
Quality Bakers of America v. FTC, 698
Queen v. Daniell, 160

TABLE OF CASES

R

Rader v. Balfour, 764, 765
Radiant Burners, Inc. v. Peoples Gas Light & Coke Co., 243, 773, 774
Radio Hanover, Inc. v. United Utilities, Inc., 128
Radovich v. National Football League, 708, 771, 774
Radzik v. Chicagoland Recreational Vehicle Dealers Ass'n, 711
Railroad Co. v. Huse, 580
Ramsey v. United Mine Workers, 729
Rangen, Inc. v. Sterling Nelson & Sons, Inc., 742, 786
Rasmussen v. American Dairy Ass'n, 710, 711
RCA, United States v., 744
Rea v. Ford Motor Co., 51
Reading Co., United States v., 94, 106, 585, 596
Record Club of America, Inc. v. Columbia Broadcasting Sys., Inc., 679, 680
Redd v. Shell Oil Co., 444
Reed Brothers, Inc. v. Monsanto Co., 408
Reed Roller Bit Co., United States v., 629
Reibert v. Atlantic Richfield Co., 772
Reinsch v. New York Stock Exchange, 779
Research Corp. v. Asgrow Seed Co., 778
Revlon, Inc., United States v., 416, 663
Reynolds Metals Co. v. FTC, 647, 662
R. H. Macy & Co. v. FTC, 704, 706
Ricci v. Chicago Mercantile Exchange, 744, 747
Richfield Oil Corp., United States v., 498
Richter Concrete Corp., United States v., 710
Ring v. Spina, 796
Ritter v. Rohm & Haas, 513
Roberts v. Fuquay-Varina Tobacco Bd. of Trade, Inc., 206
Rocform Corp. v. Acitelli-Standard Concrete Wall, Inc., 463
Rogers v. Douglas Tobacco Bd. of Trade, 206
Ronson Patents Corp. v. Sparklets Devices, 522
Roofire Alarm Co. v. Underwriter's Laboratories, Inc., 275
Rosemound Sand & Gravel Co. v. Lambert Sand & Gravel Co., 712
Roux Distributors Co., 663
Royal Indus. v. St. Regis Paper Co., 541, 546
Ruddy Brook Clothes, Inc. v. British & Foreign Marine Ins. Co., 258

S

Samuel H. Moss, Inc. v. FTC, 684
Sandura Co. v. FTC, 402, 417
Santa Clara Lumber Co. v. Hayes, 161
Saturn Airways v. CAB, 680
Sayre v. Louisville Ass'n, 161
Schaffer v. Universal Rundle Corp., 772
Schechtman v. Wolfson, 796
Schine Chain Theatres, Inc. v. United States, 143, 315, 326
Schwegmann Bros. v. Calvert Distillers Corp., 378, 732
Schwing Motor Co. v. Hudson Sales Corp., 424, 427
Scophony Corp., United States v., 717
Seaboard Air Line R. v. United States, 745
Sealy, Inc., United States v., 198, 208, 310
Sears, Roebuck & Co. v. Stiffel Co., 251, 735
SEC v. Texas Gulf Sulphur Co., 766
Security Materials v. Mixermobile Co., 529
Semke v. Enid Auto Dealers Ass'n, 784
Shell Oil Co. v. FTC, 468
Shore Gas & Oil Co. v. Humble Oil & Ref. Co., 685
Siegel v. Chicken Delight, Inc., 444, 448, 778, 786
Silver v. New York Stock Exchange, 126, 237, 244, 246, 304, 305, 744, 749
Simpson v. Union Oil Co., 238, 388, 393, 406, 412, 770

Singer Mfg. Co., United States v., 315, 509, 512–514, 564, 566
Sisal Sales Corp., United States v., 714
Skil Corp. v. Black & Decker Mfg. Co., 784, 785
Skouras Theatres Corp. v. RKO Corp., 784
Skrainka v. Scharringhausen, 161
Smith v. Pro-Football, Inc., 725
Smith-Corona Marchant, Inc. v. American Photocopy Equipment Co., 518
Snap-On Tools Corp. v. FTC, 402, 414, 418
Socony-Vacuum Oil Co., United States v., 133, 184, 192, 286, 313, 569, 710
South Carolina Council of Milk Producers, Inc. v. Newton, 772
South-East Coal Co. v. Consolidation Coal Co., 784
Southeastern Hose, Inc. v. Imperial Eastman Corp., 138, 775
South-Eastern Underwriters Ass'n, United States v., 709
Southern Concrete Co. v. United States Steel Corp., 440, 772
Southern Pacific Co. v. Darnell-Taenzer Lumber Co., 788
Southern Pacific Co., United States v., 106, 585, 596
Southern Wholesale Grocer's Ass'n, United States v., 290
Southwestern Greyhound Lines, Inc., United States v., 126, 256
Special Equip. Co. v. Coe, 503
Sperry Prods., Inc. v. Aluminum Co. of America, 522, 558
Sprague v. Ticonic Nat'l Bank, 793
Staff Research Associates, Inc. v. Tribune Co., 279
Standard Fashion Co. v. Magrane-Houston Co., 472, 486
Standard Motor Prods., Inc. v. FTC, 692, 693, 695, 702, 703
Standard Oil Co. v. Alaska, 791
Standard Oil Co. v. Brown, 703
Standard Oil Co. v. FTC, 691, 702
Standard Oil Co. v. United States, 584, 586, 588, 596
Standard Oil Co. (Indiana) v. United States, 517, 563, 564, 566, 569
Standard Oil Co. of Cal. v. Moore, 290
Standard Oil Co. of Cal. v. United States, 445, 472, 486, 489
Standard Oil Co. of Cal., United States v., 79
Standard Oil Co. of New Jersey v. United States, 6, 20, 23, 29, 35, 36, 38, 74, 82, 98, 101, 109, 116, 133, 141, 142, 166, 171, 356, 514
Standard Oil Co., United States v., 319, 327, 583, 662, 669
Standard Sanitary Mfg. Co. v. United States, 531
Standard Sanitary Mfg. Co., United States v., 572
Stanley Works v. FTC, 623
Stanton v. Allen, 161
Starlite Drive-In, Inc., United States v., 712
State of New Mexico v. American Petrofina, 740
Steiner v. Twentieth Century Fox Film Corp., 772, 775
Stewart-Warner Corp. v. Staley, 509, 510
Story Parchment Co. v. Paterson Parchment Paper Co., 785
Straight Side Basket Corp. v. Webster Basket Co., 546
Straus v. Victor Talking Mach. Co., 377, 573
Structural Laminates, Inc. v. Douglas Fir Plywood Ass'n, 200, 243, 275
Struthers Scientific & Int'l Corp. v. General Foods Corp., 512
Students Book Co. v. Washington Law Book Co., 679
Suburban Propane Gas Corp., 704
Sugar Institute, Inc. v. United States, 271, 355
Sugar Institute, Inc., United States v., 305
Sunbeam Corp., 699
Sunkist Growers, Inc. v. Winckler & Smith Citrus Prods. Co., 326, 720, 721
Sun Valley Disposal Co. v. Silver State Disposal Co., 710, 742
Superior Bedding Co. v. Serta Associates, Inc., 408
Susser v. Carvel Corp., 445, 453
Swift & Co. v. United States, 108, 133, 134, 282
Swift & Co. v. Wickman, 768
Switzer Bros. v. Locklin, 522, 523
Syufy Enterprises v. United States, 762

T

Tag Mfrs. Institute v. FTC, 269, 275, 277
Tampa Electric Co. v. Nashville Coal Co., 50, 52, 478, 479, 489, 607, 631, 667

TABLE OF CASES

Tarpon Springs Sponge Exchange, United States v., 304
Technograph Printed Circuits, Ltd. v. Bendix Aviation Corp., 463
Telex Corp. v. IBM, 30, 40, 49, 52, 65, 149
Telflex Indus. Prods., Inc. v. Brunswick Corp., 769
Terminal R. Ass'n of St. Louis, United States v., 125, 126, 147, 254, 567
Theatre Enterprises, Inc. v. Paramount Film Distributing Corp., 317, 358
Thill Securities Corp. v. New York Stock Exchange, 305
Third Nat'l Bank in Nashville, United States v., 61, 595, 604, 629, 670
Thomasville Chair Co. v. FTC, 698
Thompson Prods., Inc., 700
Thomsen v. Cayser, 714, 771, 786
Thomson-Houston Elec. Co. v. Ohio Brass Co., 442
Times Mirror Co., United States v., 60
Times-Picayune Publishing Co. v. United States, 52, 53, 57, 135, 433, 437, 440, 444, 517
Timken Roller Bearing Co. v. FTC, 487
Timken Roller Bearing Co. v. United States, 213, 326, 715
Tinnerman Prods., Inc. v. George K. Garrett Co., 541
Topco Associates, Inc., United States v., 213, 216, 253, 254, 310, 408, 411, 424, 476, 532, 563, 605, 625
Tractor Supply Co. v. International Harvester Co., 513
Trans-Missouri Freight Ass'n, United States v., 166, 167
Transparent-Wrap Mach. Corp. v. Stokes & Smith Co., 464, 509, 517, 570
Transworld Airlines, Inc. v. Hughes, 794
Trenton Potteries Co., United States v., 118, 182, 193, 199, 312, 313
Triangle Conduit & Cable Co. v. FTC, 314, 357, 364
Tripoli Co. v. Wella Corp., 410, 499
Tri-Valley Packing Ass'n v. FTC, 692
Turner Glass Corp. v. Hartford-Empire Co., 558
Turnith, King v., 158
T. V. Signal Co. v. AT & T Co., 128, 138, 680
Twentieth Century Fox Film Corp. v. Brookside Theatre Corp., 775
Twentieth Century Fox Film Corp. v. Goldwyn Productions, 772, 786, 793, 796
Twin City Sportservice Inc. v. Charles O. Finley & Co., 30, 40, 74, 139
Twin Ports Oil Co. v. Pure Oil Co., 764, 789
TWA v. Hughes Tool Co., 149

U

Ungar v. Dunkin' Donuts of America, Inc., 444, 448, 455, 779
Union Camp Corp., United States v., 564, 565
Union Carbide & Carbon Corp. v. Nisley, 793
Union Circulation Co. v. FTC, 248
Union Leader Corp. v. Newspapers of New England Inc., 94, 107, 115, 793, 794
Union Pac. R. Co., United States v. 106, 585, 596, 602
United Air Lines, Inc., United States v., 764
United Banana Co. v. United Fruit Co., 90
United Biscuit Co. v. FTC, 692–694
United Fruit Co., United States v., 274
United Liquors Corp., United States v., 198, 201
United Mine Workers v. Pennington, 724, 740, 741
United Shoe Mach. Corp., United States v., 30, 33, 34, 40, 58, 60, 74, 75, 77, 79, 80, 82, 83, 89, 94, 95, 97, 101, 102, 114, 123, 124, 136, 141, 142–148, 348, 363, 430, 433, 435, 508, 514, 515, 524
United States v. Addyston Pipe & Steel Co., 64, 68, 82, 170, 199, 312, 422
United States v. Alcoa, 571
United States v. Allied Chem. Corp., 518, 669, 763
United States v. Aluminum Co. of America, 20, 30, 33, 39, 44, 47, 49, 50, 52, 64, 67, 70, 72, 74, 75, 79, 82, 84, 87, 90, 94, 95, 99, 101, 102, 113, 114, 141, 143, 144, 355, 448, 509, 595, 600, 608, 616, 714
United States v. America Corp., 669
United States v. American Bldg. Maintenance Indus., 601, 713
United States v. American Can Co., 479, 485
United States v. American Linen Supply Co., 215, 546, 555, 558

United States v. American Linseed Oil Co., 269
United States v. American Oil Co., 135
United States v. American Smelting & Ref. Co., 192, 216, 223, 273, 292, 294
United States v. American Society of Composers, Authors and Publishers, 461
United States v. American Tobacco Co., 23, 29, 33, 35, 39, 64, 82, 98, 99, 109, 112, 148, 583, 584, 586, 588, 714
United States v. Arkansas Fuel Oil Corp., 327
United States v. Arnold, Schwinn & Co., 215, 261, 290, 390, 393, 394, 403, 407, 416, 498, 499
United States v. ASCAP, 763
United States v. A. Schrader's Sons, Inc., 238, 393, 412
United States v. Associated Milk Producers, Inc., 759
United States v. Associated Patents, Inc., 555, 570
United States v. Atlantic Richfield Co., 620, 670
United States v. Automobile Mfrs. Ass'n, 301, 762
United States v. Bakersfield Associated Plumbing Contractors, 306
United States v. Bausch & Lomb Optical Co., 393, 402, 423, 424
United States v. Bayer Co., 215
United States v. Besser Mfg. Co., 522, 523, 570
United States v. Birdsboro Steel Foundry & Mach. Co., 559, 563, 570
United States v. Black & Decker Mfg. Co., 643
United States v. Borden Co., 304, 701, 721, 722, 748
United States v. Brown Shoe Co., 670
United States v. C. A. B., 745
United States v. Charles Pfizer & Co., 49, 53, 88, 479, 485
United States v. Chicago Tribune-New York News Syndicate, Inc., 261
United States v. Chrysler Corp., 669
United States v. CIBA Corp., 518
United States v. Citizens & S. Nat'l Bank, 600, 604, 616
United States v. Colgate & Co., 392, 487, 543
United States v. Columbia Pictures Corp., 186, 192, 207, 216, 223, 273, 292, 293, 518, 601
United States v. Columbia Steel Co., 67, 68, 76, 77, 134, 135, 198, 440, 590, 592, 594, 606, 663
United States v. Connecticut Nat'l Bank, 610
United States v. Consolidated Car-Healing Co., 558
United States v. Consolidated Laundries Corp., 133, 215
United States v. Container Corp. of America, 191, 270, 276, 305, 626, 703
United States v. Continental Can Co., 595, 600, 608, 616
United States v. Corn Prods. Ref. Co., 48, 53
United States v. Crescent Amusement Co., 114, 143, 456
United States v. Crocker-Anglo Nat'l Bank, 60, 61, 670
United States v. Dairy Cooperative Ass'n, 722
United States v. Darling Delaware, Inc., 769
United States v. Diebold, 629
United States v. Eastman Kodak Co., 51, 75, 99, 111
United States v. E. C. Knight Co., 579, 584, 708
United States v. E. I. DuPont De Nemours & Co., 30, 33, 34, 40, 48, 50, 52, 55, 62, 64, 75, 77, 81, 84, 86, 93, 103, 216, 355, 507, 606, 609, 627, 662, 670, 672
United States v. El Paso Natural Gas Co., 600, 629, 633, 634, 652, 761
United States v. Employing Plasterers Ass'n, 709
United States v. Falstaff Brewing Corp., 551, 634, 637, 638, 642, 652
United States v. First Nat'l Bank & Trust Co. of Lexington, 106, 365, 441, 486, 595, 596, 602, 672, 673
United States v. First Nat'l Pictures, Inc., 257, 277
United States v. FMC Corp., 669
United States v. Gasoline Retailers Ass'n, 201 248, 280, 398
United States v. General Dyestuff Corp., 215
United States v. General Dynamics Corp., 273, 477, 490, 493, 595, 600, 610, 616, 642, 656
United States v. General Elec. Co., 86, 388, 464, 509, 541, 542, 546, 554, 570, 571
United States v. General Instrument Corp., 554, 570
United States v. General Motors Corp., 238, 259, 285, 318, 326

TABLE OF CASES

United States v. General Telephone & Electronics Corp., 670
United States v. G. Heileman Brewing Co., 670
United States v. Gimbel Bros., Inc., 670
United States v. Glaxo Group, Ltd., 407
United States v. GM Corp., 394
United States v. Greater Buffalo Press, Inc., 627, 672
United States v. Greenhut, 579
United States v. Griffith, 30, 92, 105, 114, 133, 456
United States v. Grinnell Corp., 30, 40, 48, 59–62, 67, 74, 75, 82, 94, 97, 112, 559, 609
United States v. Hartford-Empire Co., 146, 509, 510, 515
United States v. Hart, Shaffner & Marx, 627
United States v. Huck Mfg. Co., 541
United States v. Hughes Tool Co., 610, 636
United States v. Hutcheson, 723
United States v. IBM, 74
United States v. Imperial Chemical Indus., Ltd., 215
United States v. Ingersoll-Rand Co., 656, 669
United States v. Insurance Board, 206
United States v. International Boxing Club of N.Y., Inc., 57, 61, 74, 609
United States v. International Fur Workers Union, 109, 112
United States v. International Harvester Co., 75, 586
United States v. International Tel. & Tel. Co., 758, 762
United States v. IT&T Corp., 655, 656
United States v. ITT Continental Baking Co., 601
United States v. Jantzen, Inc., 201
United States v. Jerrold Electronics Corp., 443
United States v. Johns-Manville Corp., 243, 315
United States v. Joint Traffic Ass'n, 167, 579
United States v. King, 722
United States v. Klearflax Linen Looms, Inc., 51, 82, 128, 430
United States v. Krasnov, 516, 570
United States v. Lake Asphalt & Petroleum Co., 763
United States v. L. D. Caulk Co., 538
United States v. Lehigh Valley R. Co., 37
United States v. Lever Bros., 517, 518
United States v. Line Material Co., 299, 463, 527, 541, 547, 569
United States v. Ling-Temco-Vought, Inc., 655
United States v. Loew's, Inc., 431, 439, 445, 453, 455, 456, 459
United States v. Lorain Journal Co., 324
United States v. McKesson & Robbins, Inc., 23, 198
United States v. Manufacturers Hanover Trust Co., 294
United States v. Marine Bancorporation, Inc., 600, 604, 611, 616, 635, 636, 744
United States v. Masonite Corp., 314, 389, 552, 553
United States v. Minnesota Mining & Mfg. Co., 714, 716
United States v. Monsanto Co., 651
United States v. Morgan, 207, 216, 304
United States v. Mortgage Conference, 258, 261
United States v. National Ass'n of Real Estate Bds., 323, 708–710
United States v. National Ass'n of Securities Dealers, Inc., 307, 747, 749
United States v. National City Lines, Inc., 61
United States v. National Football League, 216, 222
United States v. National Funeral Directors Ass'n, 248
United States v. National Lead Co., 537
United States v. National Malleable & Steel Castings Co., 275
United States v. Nationwide Trailer Rental System, Inc., 289, 290
United States v. New England Fish Exchange, 304
United States v. New Orleans Chapter, Associated General Contractors of America, Inc., 283
United States v. New Orleans Ins. Exchange, 206
United States v. New Wrinkle, Inc., 542, 545, 552
United States v. New York Coffee & Sugar Exchange, 186, 304
United States v. N. Y. Great Atl. & Pac. Tea Co., 113, 326
United States v. Northern Pacific Ry., 193
United States v. Northwest Indus., Inc., 656, 657, 670

United States v. Olympia Provision & Baking Co., 198
United States v. Otter Tail Power Co., 742
United States v. Pabst Brewing Co., 40, 486, 600, 616, 618
United States v. Pacific & Arctic R. & Navigation Co., 304, 714
United States v. Pan American World Airways, Inc., 216, 220, 222, 365, 744, 746
United States v. Paramount Pictures, Inc., 58, 61, 108, 143, 149, 198, 209, 314, 317, 357, 456, 459, 557, 708, 762
United States v. Parke, Davis & Co., 393, 394, 495
United States v. Parker-Rust-Proof Co., 528
United States v. Penick & Ford, Ltd., 657
United States v. Penn-Olin Chem. Co., 220, 223, 600, 627, 633, 641, 651, 652
United States v. Pennsylvania Refuse Removal Ass'n, 216
United States v. Philadelphia Nat'l Bank, 20, 60, 365, 440, 476, 532, 594, 595, 600, 604, 616, 629, 662, 672, 744
United States v. Phillipsburg Nat'l Bank & Trust Co., 60
United States v. Procter & Gamble Co., 756
United States v. Provident Nat'l Bank, 61
United States v. Pullman Co., 52, 99
United States v. RCA, 744
United States v. Reading Co., 94, 106, 585, 596
United States v. Reed Roller Bit Co., 629
United States v. Revlon, Inc., 416, 663
United States v. Richfield Oil Corp., 498
United States v. Richter Concrete Corp., 710
United States v. Scophony Corp., 717
United States v. Sealy, Inc., 198, 208, 310
United States v. Singer Mfg. Co., 315, 509, 512–514, 564, 566
United States v. Sisal Sales Corp., 714
United States v. Socony-Vacuum Oil Co., 133, 184, 192, 286, 313, 569, 710
United States v. South-Eastern Underwriters Ass'n, 709
United States v. Southern Pac. Co., 106, 585, 596
United States v. Southern Wholesale Grocer's Ass'n, 290
United States v. Southwestern Greyhound Lines, Inc., 126, 256
United States v. Standard Oil Co., 79, 319, 327, 583, 662, 669
United States v. Standard Sanitary Mfg. Co., 572
United States v. Starlite Drive-In, Inc., 712
United States v. Sugar Institute, Inc., 305
United States v. Tarpon Springs Sponge Exchange, 304
United States v. Terminal R. Ass'n, 125, 126, 147, 254, 567
United States v. Third Nat'l Bank in Nashville, 61, 595, 604, 629, 670
United States v. Times Mirror Co., 60
United States v. Topco Associates, Inc., 213, 216, 253, 254, 310, 408, 411, 424, 476, 532, 563, 605, 625
United States v. Trans-Missouri Freight Ass'n, 166, 167
United States v. Trenton Potteries Co., 118, 182, 193, 199, 312, 313
United States v. Union Camp Corp., 564, 565
United States v. Union Pac. R. Co., 106, 585, 596, 602
United States v. United Air Lines, Inc., 764
United States v. United Fruit Co., 274
United States v. United Liquors Corp., 198, 201
United States v. United Shoe Mach. Corp., 30, 33, 34, 40, 58, 60, 74, 75, 77, 79, 80, 82, 83, 89, 94, 95, 97, 101 102, 114, 123, 124, 136, 141–148, 348, 363, 430, 435, 508, 514, 515, 524
United States v. United States Gypsum Co., 314, 509, 545, 546, 551, 555, 567
United States v. United States Steel Corp., 33, 39, 75, 90, 433, 586, 596
United States v. United States Trading Ass'n, 259
United States v. Univis Lens Co., 572
United States v. Utah Pharmaceutical Ass'n, 198, 248
United States v. Vehicular Parking, Ltd., 463, 509, 510, 541, 546
United States v. Von's Grocery Co., 365, 595, 600, 616, 626, 629
United States v. Watchmakers of Switzerland Information Center, Inc., 714
United States v. Western Elec. Co., 758
United States v. Winslow, 133, 434, 440

TABLE OF CASES

United States v. Women's Sportswear Mfrs. Ass'n, 286
United States v. W. T. Grant Co., 672
United States v. Yellow Cab Co., 64, 70, 133, 325, 667, 710
United States Gypsum Co., United States v., 314, 509, 545, 546, 551, 555, 567
United States Indus., Inc. v. District Court for Southern Dist. of Cal., Central Div., 769
United States Rubber Co., 700
United States Steel Corp. v. Fortner Enterprises, Inc., 440, 470
United States Steel Corp., United States v., 33, 39, 75, 90, 433, 586, 596
United States Trading Ass'n, United States v., 259
Univis Lens Co., United States v., 572
Urmston v. Whitelegg, 160
Utah Pharmaceutical Ass'n, United States v., 198, 248
Utah Pie Co. v. Continental Baking Co., 683, 685, 687
Utah Public Service Commission v. El Paso Natural Gas, 760
Utility Users League v. FPC, 744

V

Vandervelde v. Put & Call Brokers & Dealers Ass'n, 283, 793, 794
Vehicular Parking, Ltd., United States v., 463, 509, 510, 541, 546
Venus Foods, Inc., 698
Verified China Ass'n, 274, 282
Victory Motors of Savannah, Inc. v. Chrysler Motors Corp., 498
Virginia Excelsior Mills, Inc. v. FTC, 50, 192, 207, 273, 292
Vitamin Technologists, Inc. v. Wisconsin Alumni Research Foundation, 522
Viviano Macaroni Co. v. FTC, 703
Volasco Prods. Co. v. Lloyd A. Fry Roofing Co., 772
Von's Grocery Co., United States v., 365, 595, 600, 616, 626, 629
VTR, Inc. v. Goodyear Tire & Rubber Co., 771

W

Walker Process Equip., Inc. v. Food Mach. & Chemical Corp., 134, 139, 140, 507, 509, 512, 565
Wall Prods. Co. v. National Gypsum Co., 273, 786
Washington Gas Light Co. v. Virginia Elec. & Power Co., 740
Washington State Bowling Proprietors Ass'n v. Pacific Lanes, Inc., 253
Watchmakers of Switzerland Information Center, Inc., United States v., 714
Watermen v. McKenzie, 503
Watermen-Bic Pen Corp. v. Shaeffer Pen Co., 513
Waugh Equipment Co., 493
Weber v. Consumers Digest, Inc., 775
Webster County Memorial Hosp., Inc. v. United Mine Workers of America Welfare & Retirement Fund of 1950, pp. 286, 292
Western Elec. Co., United States v., 758
Western Geophysical Co. v. Bolt Associates, 518
Westinghouse Elec. Corp. v. Bulldog Elec. Prods. Co., 558
Westinghouse Elec. Corp. v. City of Burlington, 776
Westinghouse Elec. Corp. v. Pacific Gas & Elec. Co., 776
West Virginia v. Chas. Pfizer & Co., 770, 778, 791, 792
White Bear Theatre Corp. v. State Theatre Corp., 323
White Motor Co. v. United States, 215, 402, 414
Whitwell v. Continental Tobacco Co., 472
Wickens v. Evans, 160
Wilshire Oil Co. v. Riffe, 785
Wilson v. Rousseau, 517
Winn Ave. Warehouse, Inc. v. Winchester Tobacco Warehouse Co., 206
Winslow, United States v., 133, 434, 440
Women's Sportswear Mfrs. Ass'n, United States v., 286
Woods Exploration & Producing Co. v. Aluminum Co. of America, 74, 743, 771
Worthen Bank & Trust Co. v. National Bank Americard, Inc., 132, 258

Wright v. Ryder, 161
W. T. Grant Co., United States v., 672

Y

Yellow Cab Co. of Nevada v. Cab Emp. Automotive and Warehousemen, Teamsters Local No. 881, p. 710
Yellow Cab Co., United States v., 64, 70, 133, 325, 667, 710
Yoder Bros., Inc. v. Calif.-Fla. Plant Corp., 789
Young v. Motion Picture Ass'n, 262

Z

Zegers, Inc. v. Zegers, 522
Zenith Radio Corp. v. Hazeltine Research, Inc., 364, 462, 463, 570, 672, 714, 765, 776, 785

INDEX

References are to Pages

ADVERTISING
By single firm, economic effects, 307–309.
Competitor agreements, 310, 311.
Joint arrangements, 310.

ADVISORY OPINIONS
Antitrust Division, 757.
Federal Trade Commission, 757.

AGENCY ARRANGEMENTS
Exclusive dealing, restraints, 486, 487.

ALCOA **CASE**
Monopolization, 39, 40, 44–48, 52, 64, 70–74.

ALLOCATIVE EFFICIENCY
Antitrust goal, 2–7.

ANTITRUST CIVIL PROCESS ACT
Text of Act, 842.

ANTITRUST DIVISION
See also Antitrust Enforcement.
Department of Justice, 751, 752.

ANTITRUST ENFORCEMENT
Antitrust Division, Department of Justice, 751, 752.
  Advisory opinions, 757.
  Consent decrees, 758, 759.
  Coordination with FTC, 754.
  Guidelines, 757.
  Informal enforcement, 756, 757.
  Investigations, 754, 755.
  Planning, 350, 351.
Federal Trade Commission, 752–754.
  Advisory opinions, 757.
  Coordination with Antitrust Division, 754.
  Guidelines, 757.
  Informal enforcement, 756, 757.
  Investigations, 756.
  Planning, 350.
  Prior clearance, 756.
Government, 751–759.
  Civil actions, 759–768.
    Appellate review, 767, 768.
    Collateral effects, 763–765.
    Equitable relief, 766.
    Intervention, 760–762.
    Remedial issues, 766, 767.
    Size and complexity, 759, 760.
  Criminal proceedings, 768, 769.
    Access to jury evidence, 768, 769.

ANTITRUST ENFORCEMENT—Cont'd
Government—Cont'd
  Criminal proceedings—Cont'd
    Indictments, 768.
    Nolo contendere pleas, 768.
    Scope of discovery, 769.
  Planning, 347–351.
Investigations, 754–756.
  Antitrust Division, 754, 755.
  FTC, 756.
Private enforcement, 769–796.
  Attorney fees,
    Appeals, 796.
    Contingent fees, 795.
    Fee hearing, 793.
  Causation requirement, 771, 772.
  Class actions, 777–782.
    Consumer actions, 779–781.
    Federal Civil Rule 23, pp. 777–780.
    Fluid recovery concept, 779–780.
  Clayton Act,
    Section 4, treble damages, 769–771, 775.
      Attorney fees, 792–796.
    Section 16, injunctive relief, 769–771.
  Damages, 785–787.
    Burden of proof, 785, 786.
  In pari delicto defense, 783, 784.
  Injury requirement, 771–773.
  Parens patriae, 783.
  Passing on concept, 787–792.
  Standing requirements, 770–774.
  Statute of limitations, 775–777.
    Tolling, 776.
  Treble damages, 769–771, 775.
  Unclean hands, 785.

ANTITRUST EXEMPTIONS
See Exemptions.

ANTITRUST LAWS
See also Clayton Act; Sherman Act.
Eclectic view, 10–13.
Non-economic goals, 11, 12.
Objectives, 20, 21.
Pro-competition policies, 20, 21.
Relation to economics, 1–10.
Secondary sources, 14–17.
Statutory sources, 13, 14.
  See Clayton Act; Sherman Act.

ANTITRUST PROCEDURES AND PENALTIES ACT
Text of Act, 847, 848.

INDEX
References are to Pages

BANKS
Mergers, see Mergers.

BOYCOTTS
Generally, 229–265.
Characteristics, 229–232.
Characterization,
  Purpose and effect analysis, 241–245.
Concerted refusals to deal, non-boycott, 256–259.
Consumer boycotts, 261–265.
Defined, 289.
Elements, 260.
Exclusive franchise, distinguished, 260, 261.
Industry self-regulation,
  Conduct having boycott effect, 247–253, 426.
    Characterization tests, 252, 253.
    Enforcement procedures, 251, 252.
    Improper standards, 248, 249.
    Interest of consumer, 250.
  Enforcement via boycott, 245–247.
Integration agreements,
  Joint ventures to exclude, 253–256.
Joint venture refusals to deal, 253–256.
Non-boycott refusals to deal, 256–259.
Non-commercial purposes, 261–265.
Per se rule against,
  Justification for, 238–241.
  History and development, 232–238.

CARTELS
Deficiencies, 578.
Naked price restraints, 198, 199.
Nature of, 161–163, 167–171, 180.
Possible justifications, 203, 204.
Price fixing licenses, 551–554.
Railroads, 167–169.

CLASS ACTIONS
Generally, 777–782.
Consumer actions, 779–781.
Federal Civil Rule 23, pp. 777–780.
Fluid recovery concept, 779, 780.

CLAYTON ACT
Holding companies, 588–590.
Jurisdiction over "commerce", 713, 714.
Labor exemptions,
  Section 6, p. 723.
  Section 20, pp. 723–729.
Section 2, see Patents; Price Discrimination.
Section 3, violations, 472–475, 487–489.
  Burden of proof, 488, 489.
  Characterization problems, 487–489.
  Elements of, 487, 488.
  Refusals to deal, 487–489.
  Requirements contracts, 472–475.
    Tests, 474.
  Tying arrangements, 431–440.
    Threshold test, 432–434.
Section 4, treble damages, 769–771, 775.
  Attorney fees, 792–796.

CLAYTON ACT—Cont'd
Section 5, pp. 763–765.
Section 6, see Exemptions.
Section 7, see Mergers; Patents.
Section 16, private injunctive relief, 769–771.
Text of Act, 808–822.

COMMERCE
Activities constituting "trade or commerce", 708–712.
Commerce clause, 708.
Effect on, burden of proof, 712.
Foreign commerce, 714–717.
  Jurisdiction of person and property, 716, 717.
  Sherman Act, 714–716.
  Subject matter jurisdiction, 714–716.
Interstate commerce, 708–714.
  Clayton Act, 713, 714.
  FTC Act, 713.
  Robinson-Patman Act, 713, 714.
  Sherman Act, 709–714.

COMMON LAW
Restraints of trade, 155–161.
  Conspiracies, 159.
  Guilds, 157–159.
  Patents, 157, 158.

CONGLOMERATE MERGERS
See Mergers.

CONSENT DECREES
Antitrust Division, 758, 759.
Antitrust Procedures and Penalties Act, 759.

CONSIGNMENTS
Territorial and pricing restraints, 405, 406, 421–423.

CONSPIRACY
Generally, 311–329.
Affiliated corporations, 325–328.
Analysis of conduct, 313–315.
Classic concept, 311–323.
  Elements of, 312, 315.
  Evidence of, 313–322.
    See Evidence, this topic.
  Remedies, 323.
  Strengths and deficiencies, 320, 321.
Evidence of offense, 313–322.
  Conscious parallelism, 315–319.
    Burden of proof, 317–319.
    Plus performance evidence, 321, 322.
  Inferential, 313–319.
  Performance, 321, 322.
  Plus factors, 317–322.
Intra-enterprise, 323–329.
Monopolization, 132–134.
Oligopoly, 358, 359.
Single firm conduct, 323, 324, 328, 329.

CRIMINAL PROCEEDINGS
Access to jury evidence, 768, 769.

INDEX

References are to Pages

CRIMINAL PROCEEDINGS—Cont'd
Indictments, 768.
Nole contendere pleas, 768.
Scope of discovery, 768.

CUSTOMER RESTRICTIONS
See Resale Restrictions.

DATA DISSEMINATION
See Restraints of Trade.

DU PONT **CASE**
Monopolization, 52–58, 62–64, 77, 86.
    Criticism of holding, 53.

ECONOMICS
Limits of economic theory, 63–67.
Relation to antitrust, 1–10.
    Allocative efficiency, 2–7.
    Limitations on utility, 7, 8.

ENFORCEMENT
See Antitrust Enforcement.

EXCLUSIVE DEALING ARRANGEMENTS
See Requirement Contracts.

EXEMPTIONS
Generally, 717–751.
Agricultural cooperatives, 718–722.
    Capper-Volstead Act, 718–720.
    Clayton Act (Section 6), 718–722.
Baseball, 709.
Federal primacy over state, 731–738.
Government action, 719, 731–743.
    See also State laws, this topic.
    Private influence on, 740–743.
Labor, 718, 723–731.
    Clayton Act,
        Section 6, p. 723.
        Section 20, pp. 723–729.
    Labor Management Relations Act, 723, 729, 730.
    Limitations on exemption, 724–731.
    National Labor Relations Act, 723, 728–732.
    Norris-La Guardia Act, 723, 725–727.
Miller-Tydings Act, 732.
Regulated industries, 743–751.
    Deregulation movement, 750, 751.
    Primary jurisdiction, 746–749.
State laws, 731–739.
    Fair trade laws, 737–739.
    Federal primacy over, 731–738.
    Resale prices, 737–739.
    Sherman Act effect, 733–738.
    State business activities, 739, 740.
    Webb-Pomerance Act, 718.

FAIR TRADE LAWS
See also Resale Price Maintenance.
State laws, 737–739.

FEDERAL TRADE COMMISSION
Enforcement functions, see Antitrust Enforcement.

FEDERAL TRADE COMMISSION ACT
See also Antitrust Enforcement.
Mergers, 589, 590.
Text of Act, 823–842.

FRANCHISE ARRANGEMENTS
See also Resale Restrictions.
Generally 399–411, 423–431.
Competitive style requirements, 497–499.
Distinguished from boycott, 260, 261.
Exclusive arrangements, 423–431.
    Dominant manufacturer, 429–431.
    Schwinn rule application, 426, 427.
"Full line" requirements, 457, 458.
Manufacturer services, 466–468.
Terminating dealerships, 427–429.

GOALS OF ANTITRUST LAWS
Allocative efficiency, 2–7.
Eclectic view, 10–13.
Non-economic goals, 11, 12.

HOLDING COMPANIES
Clayton Act (Section 7), 588–590.

HORIZONTAL MERGERS
See Mergers.

INTEGRATION AGREEMENTS
See Boycotts; Restraints of Trade.

INTERSTATE COMMERCE
See Commerce.

INTERVENTION
Antitrust civil actions, 760–762.

JOINT ACTIVITIES
Advertising agreements,
    Joint arrangements, 310.
    Single firm, 307–309.
Market making, 303–307.
    Bid depository, 305, 306.
    Organized exchanges, 303–305, 307.
        Commission rates, 307.
    Structural analysis, 306.

JOINT AGENCIES
For buying or selling, 292–298.

JOINT NEGOTIATIONS
With suppliers, customers, or unions, 285–289.

JOINT RESEARCH
Generally, 298–303.
Advantages, 298–300.
Potential restraint of trade, 299–303.

JOINT VENTURES
Corporate, potential competition, 649–652.
Illegal integration agreements, 253–256.

LABOR
Antitrust exemption, see Labor.

LICENSES
See also Patents.
Quality controls of licensor, 496, 497.

MARKET DIVISIONS
See Restraints of Trade.

INDEX

MARKETS
See also Monopolization.
Conduct, 23, 24, 28, 29.
Joint activities in market making, 303–307.
Market concentration, 74–77.
Performance, 22, 23, 28.
Power,
  Nature of, 30–33.
  Legal inquiry, 33–35.
Relevant market definition, 33, 40–74.
  Differentiated products, 48–51.
  Diversified products, 59–63.
  Eclectic approach, 72–74.
  Geographic markets, 67–70.
    National or international, 70–72.
  Homogeneous products, 44–46.
  National or international markets, 70–72.
  Product clusters, 60–62.
  Purpose in monopoly case, 56.
  Substitute products, 51–58.
    Cross-elasticity, 52–58, 62.
    Elasticity, 52–58.
  Technological differences, 47, 48.
Structure, 24–29.
  Competitive, 25.
  Monopolistic, 25, 26.
  Oligopolistic, 26, 27.

MERGERS
Generally, 575–675.
Bank mergers,
  Bank Merger Act, 603–605.
  Clayton Act (Section 7), 604, 616–621.
  Prima facie case, 616–621.
  Sherman Act (Section 1), 604.
Clayton Act (Section 7),
  Bank mergers, 604, 616–621.
    Bank Merger Act, 603–605.
    Prima facie case, 616–621.
  Conglomerate mergers, 654, 655.
  Current application, 600, 601.
  Early application, 588–590.
  Elements of offense, 601–603.
  Geographic markets, 612.
  Horizontal mergers, 601–604, 612, 616–621.
  Prima facie case, 616–631.
  Joint subsidiaries, 649.
  Market extension mergers, 634.
  1950 Amendment, 592, 593.
  Post-1950 application, 593–596.
    Presumptive illegality test, 594, 595.
    Structural analysis, 594, 595.
  Prima facie case, 616–621.
Clayton Act (Section 15), injunctions, 669.
Concentration ratios and trends, 613, 617–622.
  Merger Guidelines, 620, 621.
  Significance, 621, 622.
  Thresholds, 620, 621.

MERGERS—Cont'd
Conglomerate mergers, 653–657.
  Bases for challenge,
    Reciprocity, 656, 657.
    Size disparities, 655, 656.
  Competitive effects, 653, 654.
  Section 7, enforcement, 654, 655.
Current merger policy, 597–601, 610.
  Effect on industrial structure, 597–599.
    Conglomerations, 598.
    Efficiencies, 597, 598.
Defenses, 622–625.
  Efficiency, 630, 631.
  Failing company, 628–630.
Direct competitors, 613–631.
  See also Market definition; *Prima facie* case, this topic.
  Prima facie case, 616–621.
  Social consequences, 613–615.
Guidelines, Department of Justice, 757.
  Concentration thresholds, 620, 621.
  Geographic markets, 611, 612.
  Product markets, 607–610.
  Vertical mergers, 484, 664.
Historical development, 576–599.
  Clayton Act (Section 7),
    Holding companies, 588–590.
    Mergers, 592–596.
    1950 Amendment, 592, 593.
  Early consolidations, 577–579.
    Standard Oil Trust, 577.
  Early Sherman Act cases, 579–581.
    Effect on merger activity, 580, 581, 583.
    Knight case, 579–581.
    Northern Securities case, 581–583.
  1897–1904, p. 581.
  FTC Act (Section 5), 589, 590.
  1904–1911, pp. 581–583.
  1930–1950, pp. 590, 591.
  Rule of reason, 584–587.
Horizontal mergers, 106, 107, 600–631.
Joint ventures, 649–652.
  Analysis, 650–652.
  Potential competition, 651, 652.
Market definition, 605–612.
  Geographic markets, 611, 612.
    Merger Guidelines, 611, 612.
  Product market, 606–611.
    Competitive effects test, 609.
    Merger Guidelines, 607–610.
    Submarkets, 608.
    Substitute products, 608.
Market extension mergers, 631–649.
  Clayton Act (Section 7) illegality, 634, 637.
  Competitive injury,
    Loss of potential competition, 633–644.
    Size disparities, 644–648.
  Concentration data, 632.
  Deconcentration effects, 636–640.
  Elements of, 631, 632.

INDEX

References are to Pages

MERGERS—Cont'd
Market extension mergers—Cont'd
  Entrant as present market force, 634–640.
    Deconcentration effects, 636–640.
  Injury due to size disparities, 644–648.
    Emergence of price leader, 645, 646.
    Entrenchment of dominant firm, 645.
    In terrorem effects, 646–648.
    Opportunity for predatory practices, 648.
  Loss of potential competition, 633–644.
    Entrant as present market force, 634–640.
    Evidence of potential entry, 640–642.
    Regulatory restrictions, 642–644.
  Market definition, 632.
  Toe-hold entry, 648, 649.
Prima facie case (Section 7), 616–631.
  Bank merger, 616–621.
  Concentration thresholds, 620, 621.
  Criteria, 617–620.
  Efficiency defense, 630, 631.
  Failing company defense, 628–630.
  Post acquisition evidence, 626–628.
  Rebuttal evidence, 622–625.
    Efficiency defense, 630, 631.
    Failing company defense, 628–630.
  Reinforcement evidence, 625, 626.
Remedies, 669–675.
  Ancillary relief, 672.
  Final relief, 672.
    Divestiture, 673.
    Spin-off, 664.
  Preliminary relief, 669–672.
    Injunction, 669.
Sherman Act (Section 1) offenses,
  Bank mergers, 604.
  Early cases, 579–581, 602, 603.
  Elements of offense, 602, 603.
  Merger application, 602.
Social consequences, 613–615.
Tax benefit motive, 615.
Vertical mergers, 657–669.
  Bases for challenge, 661–667.
    Concentration analysis, 662–665.
    Facilitating price discrimination, 667.
    Foreclosures in concentrated markets, 661–665.
    Multiple acquisitions, 667.
  Competitive effects, 657–661.
    Analysis of particular mergers, 660, 661.
    Ending potential competition, 660.
    Foreclosure, 658.
    Need for integrated entry, 659.
    Product differentiation, 659, 660.
    Supply squeeze, 658, 659.
  Concentration analysis, 662–664.
  Degree of foreclosure, 661–664.
  Foreclosures in concentrated markets, 661–665.

MERGERS—Cont'd
Vertical mergers—Cont'd
  Foreclosures in concentrated markets —Cont'd
    Justice Department Guidelines, 484, 664.
  Justifications, 667–669.
  Market definition, 661.
  Presumption of illegality, 662–664.
  Trends toward, relevance, 664–666.

MILLER–TYDINGS ACT
Resale price contracts, 732.

MONOPOLIZATION
  See also Markets; Sherman Act, Section 2, monopolization.
  Generally, 18–149.
Alcoa case, 39, 40, 44–48, 52–58, 64, 70–74, 84, 99–101.
  Conduct analysis, 82.
  Deliberateness test, 94–97.
  Divestiture, 141–144.
  Geographic markets, 70, 71.
  Homogeneous products, 44–48.
  Market concentration, 75, 76.
  Profit evidence, 84–86.
  Size of firm as factor, 90, 91.
  Substitute products, 52–58.
Attempts, 134–140.
  Elements of offense, 134–140.
    Evidence of market, 139, 140.
    Probability of success, 137, 138.
    Specific intent, 135–137.
Burden of proof, 64, 94.
Conduct constituting, 106–132.
  Concerted action, 107, 108.
  Customer selection, 125–132.
  Horizontal merger, 106, 107.
  Invasion of thin market, 115.
  Joint monopolization, 107, 108.
  Predatory actions, 108–113.
  Pricing policies, 116–125.
    Discrimination, 121–125.
    Limit pricing, 118–121.
    Profit maximization, 116–118.
    "Public utility" approach, 125–131.
  Raising entry barriers, 114.
Conduct tests, 94–105.
  Choosing among tests, 102–105.
  Deliberateness test, 94–97.
  Exclusionary conduct, 97–103.
    Classic test, 97–99.
    Modern test, 99–101.
  Intent to exclude, 105.
  Predatory conduct, 97–99.
  Prima facie approach, 101–104.
Conspiracies, 132–134.
Early cases, 35–39.
  American Tobacco, 35, 38, 39.
  Northern Securities, 36.
  Standard Oil, 35–39.
  United States Steel, 39.
Elements of offense, 29, 30.

INDEX

MONOPOLIZATION—Con'td
Intent requisite, 135.
Market power, 30–35.
    See also Markets.
    Concentration, 74–77.
    Defined, 33.
    Nature of, 30–33.
        Legal inquiry, 33–35.
Markets,
    Conduct, 23, 24, 28, 29.
    Performance, 22, 23, 28.
    Relevant market definition, 33, 40–74.
    See also Markets.
    Structure, 24–29.
        Competitive, 25.
        Monopolistic, 25, 26.
        Oligopolistic, 26, 27.
Monopoly power, 19–40.
Prohibition against, 29, 30.
    Sherman Act, Section 2, pp. 29, 30.
Remedies, 141–149.
    Conduct decrees, 147, 148.
    Criminal sanctions, 148, 149.
    Dissolution, 143–146.
    Divestiture, 142–144.
        Functions of, 144.
    Institutional limitations, 144–146.
    Private remedies, 149.
    Structural, 142–146.
Sherman Act, Section 2, pp. 29, 30.
Strength of firm, estimation, 74–93.
    Absolute size, 90–92.
    Conduct analysis, 80–82.
    Entry barriers, 77–79.
    Market concentration, 74–77.
    Performance analysis, 82, 83.
        Limitations, 89, 90.
    Price discrimination, 88, 89.
    Price responsiveness, 86–88.
    Profit evidence, 84–86.
Structural analysis, 39, 40.

OLIGOPOLY
Generally, 330–373.
Actions prohibited, 354, 355.
    Conspiracy elements, 358, 359.
    Interdependence as joint monopolization, 361–363.
    Non-collusive, interdependent pricing, 355–358.
Adverse effects, 347.
Antitrust enforcement planning, 347–351.
    Role of Antitrust Division, 350, 351.
    Role of Congress, 351.
    Role of FTC, 350.
Characteristics, 331, 332.
Classifications, 332, 333.
Concentration-performance correlation, 358–360.
Conduct, 337–342.
    Price setting, 338–341, 343.
        Interdependent pricing, 340, 341, 343.
        Price leadership, 339–341.

OLIGOPOLY—Cont'd
Conspiracy evidence, 358, 359.
Efficiencies of size, 334–338.
Interdependence as joint monopolization, 361–363.
Interdependent pricing, 340, 341, 343.
Legal remedies, 354–367.
    Clayton Act (Section 7), 365.
    FTC Act (Section 5), 364, 365.
    Merger enjoining, 365.
    Sherman Act,
        Section 1, pp. 355–360, 365.
        Section 2, pp. 361–363.
Legislative proposals, 367–373.
    Concentrated industries bill, 367–371.
    Industrial reorganization bill, 371.
    Kaysen-Turner bill, 372, 373.
    Single industry proposals, 373.
    White House Task Force, 367.
Non-collusive, interdependent pricing, 355–358.
Performance, 342, 343.
    Criticism of, 347.
    Deficiencies, 343.
Performance-concentration correlation, 358–360.
Pervasiveness of, 331–333.
Price setting, 338–341, 343.
    Interdependent pricing, 340, 341, 343.
    Price leadership, 339–341, 357.
Profit-concentration correlation, 344.
Public response planning, 344–354.
    Antitrust enforcement, 347–351.
    Factors for analysis, 351–354.
    Profit-concentration correlation, 344–346.
Scale economies, 334–338.
Structure, 333–337.
Types, 332, 333.
Victims, 347.

PATENTS
Generally, 501–574.
Accumulations and pooling, 515–517.
Antitrust relationship, 505, 506.
Application process, 512.
Clayton Act (Section 7) illegality, 518–520.
Common law, 158, 159.
Exclusionary conduct, 507–517.
    FTC Act (Section 5) illegality, **517**.
    Patent enforcement policy, 520–524.
    Section 2, illegality, 507–517, 520–524.
        Fraudulent patent acquisition, 512–514.
        License restrictions, 524.
        Patent accumulations and pooling, 515–517.
        Patent enforcement policy, 520–524.
        Restrictions on assignees, 524.
Fraudulent acquisitions, 512–514.
Grant back provisions, 570, 571.
Licensing, 525–554.
    See also Tying Arrangements.

INDEX

References are to Pages

PATENTS—Cont'd
Licensing—Cont'd
  Beneficial effects, 525, 526.
  Customer restrictions, 562, 563.
    Per se illegality, 562, 563.
  Fields of use restrictions, 554–562.
    Exclusive licenses, 560–562.
    Multiple licensees, 557–559.
    Royalty rate differentials, 557–559.
    Royalty rate discrimination, 555–557.
  Grant back provisions, 570, 571.
  Horizontal price restrictions, 541–554.
    Cartelization, 551–554.
    Cross-licensing, 549, 550.
    Industry practices, 543, 544.
    Non-producing patentee, 546, 547.
    Substantial share of market, 545, 546.
    Two or more patentees, 547, 548.
    Two or more patents, 548, 549.
    Uncertain state of law, 543–545.
  Horizontal territorial restrictions, 528–541.
    Analytical framework, 530–538.
    Case law, 529, 530.
    Code Section 261, pp. 535–538.
    Economic effects, 540, 541.
    Import and export, 538, 539.
  Restrictions, see Tying Arrangements.
Major features, 504–506.
Patent pools, 566–570.
  Negative effects, 568.
  Positive effects, 568.
Prerequisites, 504.
Resale price restrictions, 571, 572.
Restrictions on assignees, 524.
Settlement of disputes, 563–570.
  During interference proceedings, 563–566.
  Patent pools, 566–570.
  Priority disputes, 563–566.
  Validity disputes, 563–566.
Sherman Act (Section 2) illegality, 507–517.
  Burden of proof, 507.
  Elements, 507.
  Exclusionary conduct, 507–517, 520–524.
  Monopoly power, 507.
Vertical restrictions, 571–574.
  Resale price restraints, 571, 572.

PER SE DOCTRINE
See also Restraints of Trade.
Restraints of trade, 153.

PRICE DISCRIMINATION
Generally, 676–706.
Advertising allowances, 699, 700.
Affirmative defenses,
  Cost justification, 700, 701.
  Meeting competition, 702, 703.
Brokerage allowances, 697, 698.

PRICE DISCRIMINATION—Cont'd
Buyer liability, 703–705.
  Inducing and receiving,
    Allowances, 705, 706.
    Price discriminations, 703–705.
Clayton Act (Section 2) offenses,
  Adverse structural change, 685–689.
  Advertising allowances, 699, 700.
  Affirmative defenses,
    Cost justification, 700, 701.
    Meeting competition, 702, 703.
  Broker allowances, 697, 698.
  Buyer liability, 703–705.
  Delivered prices, 688.
  Diversion of business, 684, 685.
  Elements of injury, 688, 689.
  Exclusionary conduct, 683, 684.
  Horizontal competitive effects, 683–689.
  Predatory discrimination, 683, 684.
  Robinson-Patman Act amendment, 677.
  Vertical competitive effects, 689–697.
Factor of market power, 88, 89.
Horizontal competitive effects, 683–689.
  Adverse structural change, 685–689.
  Delivered prices, 688.
  Diversion of business, 684, 685.
  Elements of injury, 688, 689.
  Exclusionary conduct, 683, 684.
  Predatory conduct, 683, 684.
Robinson-Patman Act, 677–684.
  Exclusionary conduct, 683, 684.
  Legislative history, 678.
  Predatory discrimination, 683, 684.
  Scope of Statute, 679, 683.
  Violation pre-conditions, 679, 680.
Secondary line effects, 689–697.
Significance of discrimination, 681–683.
Vertical competitive effects, 689–697.
  Diversion of business, 691.
  Functional discounts, 695.
  Prima facie case, 691–697.
  Quantity discounts, 689, 691.
    Diversion of business, 691.
    Favored customer profits, 692, 693.
    Rebuttal evidence about effects, 693–697, 702, 703.
  Social effects, 689, 690.

PRICING POLICIES
See also Monopolization, Conduct constituting; Resale Price Maintenance; Restraint of Trade.
Dissemination of prices, 266–273, 275.
Interdependent pricing, 164, 165.
Oligopolies, 338–341, 343.
  Interdependent pricing, 340, 341, 343.
  Price leadership, 339–341, 357.

PRIVATE ACTIONS
See Antitrust Enforcement.

PUBLIC UTILITIES
Duty to provide service, 126–131.

RECIPROCITY ARRANGEMENTS
Abuses of power, 492.
Burden of proof, 494.
    Agreement requirement, 494.
    Pattern of conduct, 494, 495.
Coercion rule, 493.
Competitive effects, 491, 492.
Defined, 490.
Nature and effect, 490–492.
Per se illegality, 492–495.
    Agreement requirement, 494.
    Coercion rule, 492.
    Pattern of conduct, 494, 495.

REGULATED INDUSTRIES
Antitrust exemption, see Exemptions.

REQUIREMENT CONTRACTS
Generally, 471–486, 489, 490.
Burden of proof, 474–476.
Clayton Act (Section 3) illegality, 472–475.
    Tests, 474.
Competitive effects, 479–484, 489, 490.
    Structural changes, 480–483, 489.
    TV manufacturers, 480–483.
Defined, 471.
Development of law, 472–479.
    Clayton Act (Section 3) illegality, 472–475.
        Tests, 474.
Duration of term, 484–486.
    Factors validating term, 486.
    Illegality presumption, 485, 486.
Justification, 474, 476.
Proposed guidelines, 484.
Structural analysis, 474–479, 484.
TV manufacturers, 480–483.
Tying arrangements differentiated, 474.

RESALE PRICE MAINTENANCE
See also Resale Restrictions.
Consignment arrangements, 388–390.
Effect on consumer prices, 387, 388.
Fair trade laws,
    Federal exemption, 378, 379.
        McGuire Act, 379.
        Miller-Tydings Amendment, 378.
        Repeal, 377.
    History, 378, 379.
Manufacturer motives, 379–385.
    Cartelization, 385.
    Control of intra-brand competition, 381, 382.
    Cultivating prestige image, 384.
    Efficiencies at dealer level, 382, 383.
    Interest in resale competition, 380, 381.
    Promotional expenditures, 384, 385.
    Retailer cartelization, 383, 384.
    Scale efficiencies, 382.
Market effects, 379.
Maximum resale prices, 390, 391.
Per se illegality, 377, 378.
    Justification for rule, 385–387.

RESALE PRICE MAINTENANCE—Cont'd
Price "tampering", 397–399.
Refusals to deal, manufacturer, 391–395.
Scope of liability, 395–397.
    Defendant selection, 396.
Suggested prices, 397–399.

RESALE PRICES
State regulation, 737–739.
    Miller-Tydings Act, 732.

RESALE RESTRICTIONS
    See also Resale Price Maintenance.
    Generally, 399–431.
Consignments, 405, 406, 421–423.
Franchise arrangements, 399–411, 423–427.
    Exclusive, 423–431.
        Dominant manufacturer, 429–431.
        Schwinn rule application, 426, 427.
    Terminating dealership, 427–429.
Per se treatment, 402–421.
    Justification for, 411–421.
        Dealer goodwill, higher profits, 418, 419.
        Dealer protection, 419–421.
        Economies of scale, 412–414.
        Facilities and service, 414–416.
        Historical success, 416–418.
        Promotion, 414–416.
    Schwinn Rule, 403–411, 416, 420–427.
        Actions prohibited, 410.
        Characterization issues, 406–411.
Types, 400, 401.
See Resale Price Maintenance.

RESTRAINTS OF TRADE
Advertising practices,
    Competitor agreements, 310, 311.
    Joint arrangements, 310.
    Single firm, 307–309.
Agreements not to deal (non-boycott), 289–292.
Boycotts, see Boycotts.
Cartels, 161–163, 167–171, 180.
    Railroads, 167–169.
Common law, 155–161.
    Conspiracies, 159.
    Guilds, 157.
    Patents, 158, 159.
Concerted actions,
    Decision making, 282–285.
        Credit policy, 283, 284.
        Inventory levels, 282, 284.
    Refusals to deal (non-boycott), 289–292.
    Types of injury, 265, 266.
Conspiracy, see Conspiracy.
Data dissemination, 265–275, 282–285.
    Container case, 270.
    Early cases, 268–270.
    Economic effects, 266–268.
    Non-price data, 274, 275.
    Prices, 266–273, 275.
    Structure and conduct analysis, 270–273.

INDEX

RESTRAINTS OF TRADE—Cont'd
Horizontal market division, 213–229.
    Characterization of arrangements, 219–224.
    Integration, effect, 222–224.
    Justification arguments, 227–229.
        Efficiency, 227, 228.
    Per se violation, 213–217, 222–224, 229.
    Price fixing comparison, 224–229.
    Purpose and effect analysis, 219, 220.
    Topco case, 216–224.
        Implications, 219–224.
Horizontal restraints, 150–329.
Interdependent conduct, 163–165.
Joint activities in market making, 303–307.
    Bid depository, 305, 306.
    Organized exchanges, 303–305, 307.
    Structural analysis, 306.
Joint agencies for buying or selling,
    Characterization, 293.
    Joint distributor, 297, 298.
    Performance analysis, 294–297.
    Structural analysis, 293, 294.
Joint negotiations, 285–289.
    Justification, 288, 289.
    Suppliers, unions, customers, 285–289.
Joint research, 298–303.
    Advantages, 298–300.
    Potential abuses, 299–301.
Joint venture refusals to deal, 256–259.
"Naked" price restraints,
    Characterization, purpose and effect, 198–203.
    Distinguished from,
        Arrangements to make or improve market, 205, 206.
        Restrictions resulting from partial integration, 206–210.
    Inhibiting product change, 212.
    Market division comparison, 224–229.
    Maximum price agreements, 210–212.
    Per se violations, 198–202.
    Possible justifications, 202–204.
    Rationing of output, 212.
Non-boycott refusals to deal, 289–292.
Per se doctrine,
    Advantages, 193, 194, 197.
    Development, 166–171, 174, 182–186.
    "Naked" price restraints, 198–202.
    Preferability of doctrine, 193, 194.
    Relationship of purpose and effect, 194, 195.
    Relationship to rule of reason, 195–197.
    Significance of power, purpose, and effect, 192–194.
Refusals to deal, non-boycott, 256–259.
    See also Boycotts.
Resale price maintenance, 374–399.
    See also Resale Price Maintenance.
Rule of reason,
    Application of rule, 187, 188.
    Classic rule, 171–174.

RESTRAINTS OF TRADE—Cont'd
Rule of reason—Cont'd
    Current construction, 186–192.
    Development, 166–174.
    Relationship of purpose and effect, 194, 195.
    Relationship to *per se* doctrine, 195–197.
    Role of market power, 189–192.
    Scope of rule, 175–182.
    Standard Oil case, 171–175.
Standardization programs, 275–282.
    Competitive styles, 279–282.
    Hours, 279, 280.
    Non-price trade terms, 277–279.
    Products, 276, 277.
    Trading stamps, 280, 281.
Vertical restraints,
    See also Requirement Contracts; Resale Price Maintenance; Resale Restrictions; Tying Arrangements.
    Generally, 374–500.
    Reasonable restrictions, 495–500.
        Competitive style arrangements, 497–499.
        Quality controls of licensor, 496, 497.

ROBINSON–PATMAN ACT
See Price Discrimination.

RULE OF REASON
See Restraints of Trade.

SHERMAN ACT
Effect on state laws, 733–738.
Jurisdiction over "commerce", 709–714.
Section 1, restraints of trade,
    See also Restraints of Trade.
    Generally, 98, 102, 152–154.
    Application approaches,
        Per se doctrine, 153.
        Rule of reason, 153.
    Conduct constituting, 152, 166.
    Elements of offense, 311.
    Tying arrangements, 431–440.
Section 2, monopolization, 29, 30, 90–92, 98, 99, 105.
    See also Monopolization.
    Attempts to monopolize, 134–140.
    Conspiracies to monopolize, 132–134.
    Elements of offense, 132.
    Exclusionary conduct test, 97–101.
    Horizontal merger, 107.
    Limit pricing, 118–121.
    Price discrimination, 122.
    Price maximization, 116–118.
    Private remedies, 149.
    Size of firm factor, 90–92.
Text of Act, 807, 808.

***STANDARD OIL* CASE**
Monopolization, 35–39, 74, 101.
Rule of reason, 171–175, 182.

INDEX

STANDING TO SUE
Private actions, 770–774.

STATE ANTITRUST LAWS
Exemptions, 731–739.
  See also Exemptions.
Fair trade laws, 737–739.
Resale prices, 737–739.
  Miller-Tydings Act, 732.
Sherman Act effect, 733–738.

STATUTE OF LIMITATIONS
Private antitrust actions, 775–777.

TERRITORIAL RESTRICTIONS
See Resale Restrictions.

TRADEMARKS
Quality controls of licensor, 496, 497.

TREBLE DAMAGES
See Antitrust Enforcement.

TYING ARRANGEMENTS
  Generally, 432–471.
Block booking of movies, 456, 459–461.
  Efficiencies, 459.
Block licensing, 456, 459–463.
  Movies, 459–461.
  Music libraries, 461–463.
Burden of proof, 438, 439.
Clayton Act (Section 3) illegality, 431–441.
  Legislative history, 432, 433.
  Sherman Act relationship, 440, 441.
  Threshold test, 432–434.
Copyright licensing, 459.
Defined, 431, 454, 455.
Development of basic rule, 434–440.
"Full line" requirements, 456–459.
  Auto dealers, 458, 459.
  FTC Act (Section 5) illegality, 458, 459.
  Franchise arrangements, 457, 458.
  Justifications, 457.

TYING ARRANGEMENTS—Cont'd
Land lease, 437, 438.
Licensing of movies, 459–461.
Licensing of music libraries, 461–463.
Licensing of patents, 463–466.
  Grant back provisions, 464, 465.
  Package licensing, 463, 464.
  Post-expiration royalties, 465, 466.
Market dominance test, 435–440, 445–448.
Movie licensing, 459–461.
"Package" pricing, 454–456.
  Basis for, 455.
  Promotional package, 456.
Patent license restrictions, 433–442, 463–466.
  Contributory infringement, 441, 442.
  Grant back provisions, 464, 465.
  Package licensing, 463, 464.
  Post-expiration royalties, 465, 466.
Per se illegality, 436–440.
Promotional techniques, 466–470.
  Credit terms, 469, 470.
  FTC Act (Section 5) illegality, 467, 468.
  Manufacturer services, 466–468.
  TBA arrangements, 468, 469.
Purposes and effects, 445–454.
  Discrimination uses, 449–454.
  Social and economic benefits, 448–454.
Requirement of integral products, or services, 443, 444.
Requirements contracts differentiated, 474.
Sherman Act (Section 1) illegality, 431–440.
  Clayton Act relationship, 440, 441.
TBA arrangements, 468, 469.
Threshold test, 432–434.
Trademark and name, 444.

VERTICAL MERGERS
See Mergers.

VERTICLE RESTRICTIONS
See Resale Restrictions.